CIM/AIMM: A STORY OF VISION, COMMITMENT AND GRACE

JIM BERTSCHE

FIRST EDITION
Copyright © 1998 by
Jim Bertsche

Library of Congress Catalog Card Number: 98-72866

ISBN 0-7880-1415-3

DEDICATION

To the rural Mennonite founding fathers

of a daring inter-Mennonite venture in

Christian Mission in Central Africa

and

To countless African brothers and sisters

in Christ whose uncluttered faith has

immeasurably enriched the lives of all

CIM/AIMM people who have learned

to know and love them.

ACKNOWLEDGMENTS

As my writing project for the AIMM Board draws to a close, I'm aware of a great sense of indebtedness to many people:

First and above all to my wife, Jenny, with whom I made a joint pilgrimage of service in Africa which has largely colored and shaped my approach to my assignment. Without her tolerance and encouragement, this project would never have been accomplished.

My children Sandra, Linda and Timothy, who shared with us in some of the joys and trauma of our early years in Africa and who emerged from their experiences into adulthood affirming us, their missionary parents, affirming the Christian faith and seeking, each in their own turn, service opportunities in Africa under the sponsorship of the AIMM.

The AIMM Board for entrusting me with the assignment to tell the story of CIM/AIMM across an 85 year span of time.

Loyd and Marie Diller Brown, missionary colleagues of ours, whose early enthusiasm regarding my writing project was reassuring and whose sizeable gift toward the purchase of a personal computer launched me in my undertaking.

An editorial committee comprised, at various times, of Jeanne Zook, Elmer Neufeld, Jim Juhnke, Sara Regier and Earl Roth, whose unswerving support has been a constant source of encouragement.

Mel Loewen from whose earlier research for his book entitled "Three Score" I have freely drawn information.

Levi Keidel who permitted me to quote extensively from some of his published work regarding our mission/church history.

Many others among our fellow CIM/AIMM missionaries who have generously permitted me to draw material from their own writings and personal files.

John and Tina Bohn, Loren and Donna Entz, Peter Falk, Peter Sawatzky, Rick Derksen, Stan Nussbaum, Jonathan Larson, Dennis and Jeanne Rempel who read through segments of the manuscript and provided critique and corrections that were most helpful.

My son-in-law, Rod King, for guiding me into some of the mysteries of our computerized age while, at times, untangling some of the electronic snarls into which I blundered.

My daughter Sandra whose editorial critique has been most useful.

Steve Nolt who upon completion of a doctorate in history at the University of Notre Dame graciously accepted, on short notice, to give generous amounts of personal time to a reading of the manuscript while cleaning up discrepancies and errors in phrasing and punctuation.

And finally, the AIMM staff in Elkhart: Marlene Habegger for her skillful research/secretarial help with the personnel rosters; Cindy Neuenschwander and Rachel Nolt who allowed me frequently to interrupt their work to provide information I needed; Garry Prieb and Leona Schrag whose unflagging interest in the project has spurred me on; and Wade Handrich for his cheerful patience in guiding me through the process of converting diskettes into the printed pages which the reader finds between these covers.

FOREWORD

The history of Congo's precipitous rush toward independence (June 30, 1960) and of the tumultuous post-independence years is full of political intrigue, including involvement of the western powers. Surely to be included in the annals of Congo's independence and post-independence history will be political leaders such as Joseph Kasavubu, Patrice Lumumba, Moise Tshombe, Joseph Désiré Mobutu, and Laurent Kabila.

But there is another history - - another story - - which has had a profound impact upon the Congolese people and will continue to shape the nation even when the impact of the pioneers of political independence has waned. This is the story of the Christian missions, primarily from Europe and North America, which were a part of the colonial era, and the churches which were established as a result of the missionary enterprise.

One relatively small but nevertheless significant part of that missionary movement was the Congo Inland Mission - - later the Africa Inter-Mennonite Mission - - including a half dozen Mennonite groups. Those Mennonite missionary pioneers of the early 1900's had a rather limited understanding of Africa, but they understood clearly and deeply that God's love and grace made most clear in the incarnation - - in the life, teachings, crucifixion, and resurrection of Jesus Christ - - was intended for all people, and that all of us who call ourselves disciples of Christ are called to incarnate that same love and grace in our own lives.

To be sure the lives of those early missionaries and the mission programs they established in Congo were not untainted by the colonial enterprise - - as all of our human endeavors are shaped by our finitude and the times in which we live - - and yet God used and blessed those efforts to establish a thriving Mennonite church community in Congo, and in more recent times also a significant witness in Botswana, Lesotho, Burkina Faso, and Transkei/Republic of South Africa.

That missionary community in Congo - - though often discounted by post-independence critics - - went through the fiery trials of revolutionary violence, including the so-called Congo rebellion of 1964 and 1965. Many Christian missionaries in Congo, along with their African brothers and sisters, laid their lives on the line in faithfulness to Christ during those post-independence years. I personally happened to lead the joint Protestant missionary service in Kinshasa following the 1965 rescue operation in Kisangani, during which a number of missionary lives were lost, and I shall never again acquiesce to the easy modern critique of the missionary enterprise.

I am grateful to James Bertsche for giving a major part of his retirement years to write the story of the Congo Inland Mission (AIMM) focusing especially on the post-independence years in Congo, and also recounting the new beginnings in Botswana, Lesotho, Burkina Faso, and Transkei/South Africa. No one could have done this better than James Bertsche, not only because of his and Jenny's (Mrs. Bertsche's) long years in Congo, as well as his sensitivity to African language and culture and his strong identification with the African church community, but also because of his deep personal commitment to sharing the story of God's providence and grace. I shall never forget walking with Jim through the ruins of the Kandala mission/church center as well as the ashes of their own home where they were held captive during the Congo rebellion and sustained by their African brothers and sisters.

I am also grateful for having had a small part, along with Jim Bertsche, in AIMM explorations in Botswana, Lesotho and Burkina Faso.

May this story of a courageous missionary community, along with their deeply committed African brothers and sisters - - who walk the Jesus way with so much less material security than those of us in North America - - be a continuing challenge to new generations of Christians in both North America and Africa to fulfill their responsibilities for sharing the Christian gospel of God's love and grace in our own times.

Elmer Neufeld, President Emeritus
Bluffton College
July 1998

PREFACE

In the course of its 85 years of existence, CIM/AIMM has published three histories of its work, i.e., <u>Twenty-Five Years in the Congo</u>, by William B. Weaver and Harry E. Bertsche (Chicago: Congo Inland Mission, 1938); <u>Thirty-Five Years in the Congo</u>, by William B. Weaver (Chicago: Congo Inland Mission, 1945); and <u>Three Score</u>, by Melvin J. Loewen. (Elkhart: Bethel Publishing Co., 1972).

This account, then, is a fourth attempt to trace God's hand at work in Africa via the intermediary of an inter-Mennonite organization brought into being shortly after the turn of this century. Whereas the previous three histories had the Belgian Congo as their primary focus, this material briefly reviews that colonial period and then traces the exploding events of the post-independence era in Congo/Zaire as well as CIM/AIMM's expansion of ministry into southern and western Africa.

In my writing I have approached the CIM/AIMM history as a story because it is my conviction that it is precisely that - - a captivating story which merits being told. Furthermore, I have sought to tell the story in terms of the people, both missionaries and Africans, whose lives have been part and parcel of that story. In the telling, there is no fiction. For this reason there are frequent quotations and careful footnoting of sources used.

I have approached my assignment with my own cluster of biases as does any writer who attempts to depict and interpret the events of the past. My bias cluster includes my identity as a white-skinned North American who grew up as a rural Mennonite, the grandson of an immigrant grandfather; my background of service with the CIM/AIMM which has carried across the bulk of my adult life; my sense of a great indebtedness toward Africa, its people and the growing Mennonite community of that continent; my belief that African Christians have much to teach us about faith, prayer and dependence upon God's grace on a daily basis; my conviction that the mandate for Christian Mission is an ongoing one which must be confronted by North American Mennonites of every generation; my persuasion that CIM/AIMM is a unique organization whose work in Africa is not done.

This history is not a treatise on the theology of mission nor a study of missiological principles per se. While these issues will at times clearly surface in these pages, the primary focus is to try to describe what God has done and continues to do in areas of Africa to which CIM/AIMM has been led.

It was not my assignment nor do I feel competent to write a history of the Congo Mennonite Church for African Mennonites. But in the telling of the CIM/AIMM story, it inevitably becomes, in part, a story of the Church as viewed and experienced by its missionaries. The time will come when Africans will write histories of their own Church reflecting their own experience and perspective. It is for this reason that considerable detail is contained both in the text and in the footnoted material. If, at times, the North American reader feels that there is more detail than necessary, it should be remembered that I have had future African Mennonite readers, researchers and writers in mind. Resource material in Africa regarding the emergence of the church is sketchy at best. Rebellions, tribal conflicts, evacuations, inadequate filing equipment, tropical climate and termites have all taken a heavy toll on rural African archives. It is my hope, therefore, that this history (which is to be translated into French) with its supportive documentation will serve as a valuable source of information for African church leaders and writers of the future.

In my writing I have also tried to sketch a broad socio-political background in the various areas where CIM/AIMM has served. While this has added significantly to the bulk of this history, it is my conviction that without such background, it is impossible for the reader to adequately understand the dynamics which have surrounded both missionaries and African Christians and shaped the events of which they frequently were a part. Particularly is this the case in Zaire during the Mobutu regime and in southern Africa during the era of *apartheid*.

There likely are some CIM/AIMM-related folk and MCC Africa "alumni" who will read through most of the following pages because of their acquaintance and/or personal involvement with many of the people, places and events which appear in them. I recognize, however, that others will come to this history for reading of a more selective nature. Some may want to focus largely on one particular geographical area of CIM/AIMM's ministry. Others may come to this history wanting to learn about the life and experiences of specific missionaries and/or African Christians of their acquaintance. Some may look into it in search of stories of faith - - and there are many. Still others may want information on specific organizations or institutions or political leaders. Others may seek details on the experience of missionaries and the African Church amidst the fire of rebellion and tribal conflict. Whatever the reader's interest, a detailed table of contents and index are provided which should make it possible to quickly find what is sought.

Conference affiliations of CIM/AIMM personnel throughout the history are usually not mentioned. As an inter-Mennonite organization from day one, specific conference ties in North America were unimportant once people arrived in Africa. The focus was always on an inter-Mennonite team effort to plant a Mennonite Church in Africa. For historical record, however, the conference affiliation of all CIM/AIMM personnel - - missionaries, home staff and board members alike - - is documented in an addendum to this history.

Then, finally, a word about the names of people, places and organizations. Non-English terms are italicized. African names and terms are followed by parentheses giving help as to pronunciation. Whenever a new organization or institution is introduced into the text, its acronym follows in parenthesis. Thereafter, to conserve space, often just the acronyms are used. The profusion of names and terms and their acronyms is further complicated by the fact that across the time span covered, many of these names have been changed - - and changed again! Given all of the above, it will be easy for readers not well acquainted with CIM/AIMM to become confused. To help keep track of all the terms, a glossary is found in the section of addenda which lists acronyms, the organizations for which they stand as well as any changes which may have occurred over time.

This story takes us into the lives and experiences of a truly improbable mix of the Lord's servants, both missionaries and Africans. It allows us to glimpse something of the vision, disappointments, achievements, heartaches, joys, testing and rewards which were all parts of their experience as they sought to be God's servants in their time and setting.

It is my hope and prayer that this has been done in a manner that is honest, fair, readable and, above all, in a way that clearly reflects what God has seen fit to accomplish through a remarkably hardy inter-Mennonite venture in Christian Mission on the continent of Africa.

Jim Bertsche
July 1998

TABLE OF CONTENTS

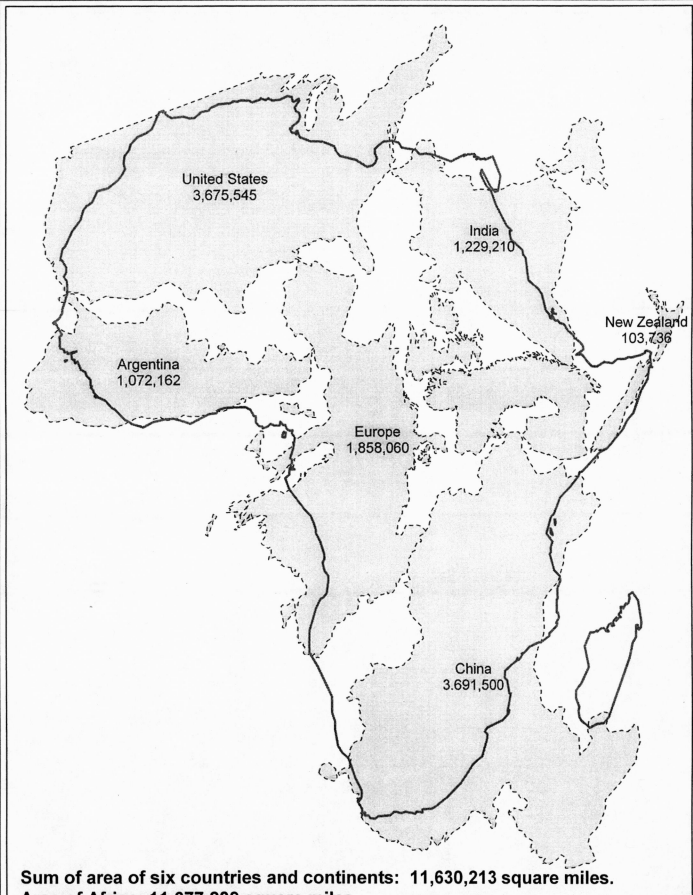

United States
3,675,545

India
1,229,210

New Zealand
103,736

Argentina
1,072,162

Europe
1,858,060

China
3.691,500

Sum of area of six countries and continents: 11,630,213 square miles.
Area of Africa: 11,677,239 square miles.

Sources: Areas from Rand McNally, Webster's New Geographical Dictionary.
Global Mapping International - (719) 531-3599, 5/98

AFRCOMPP

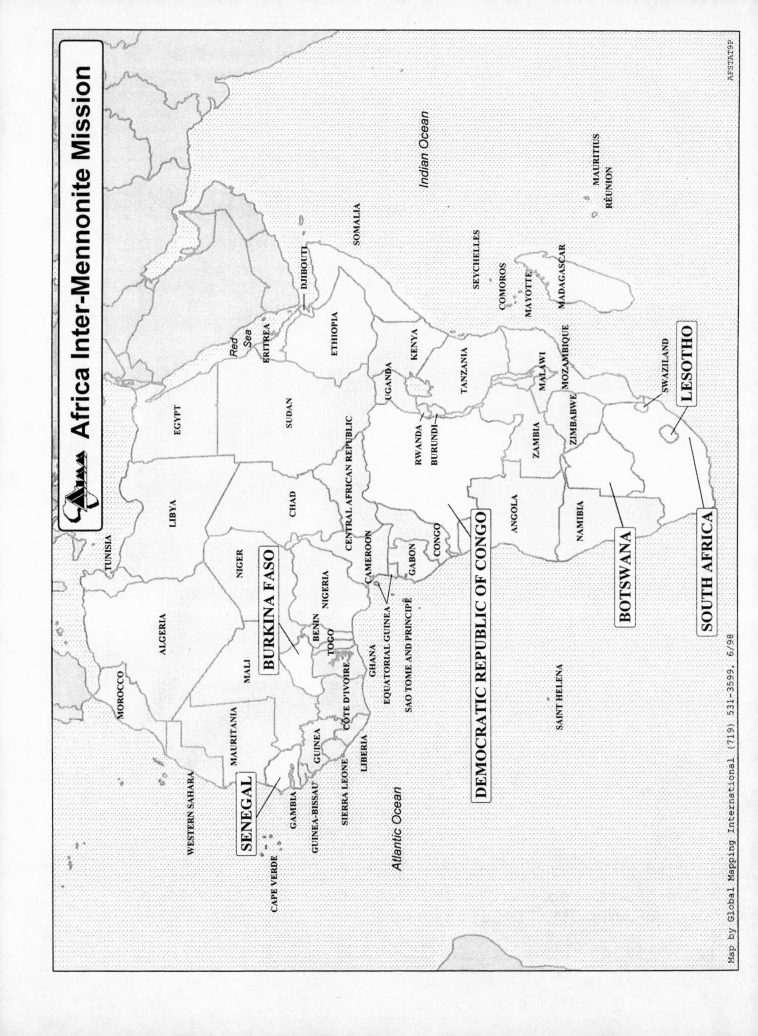

Africa Inter-Mennonite Mission

AFSTAT9P

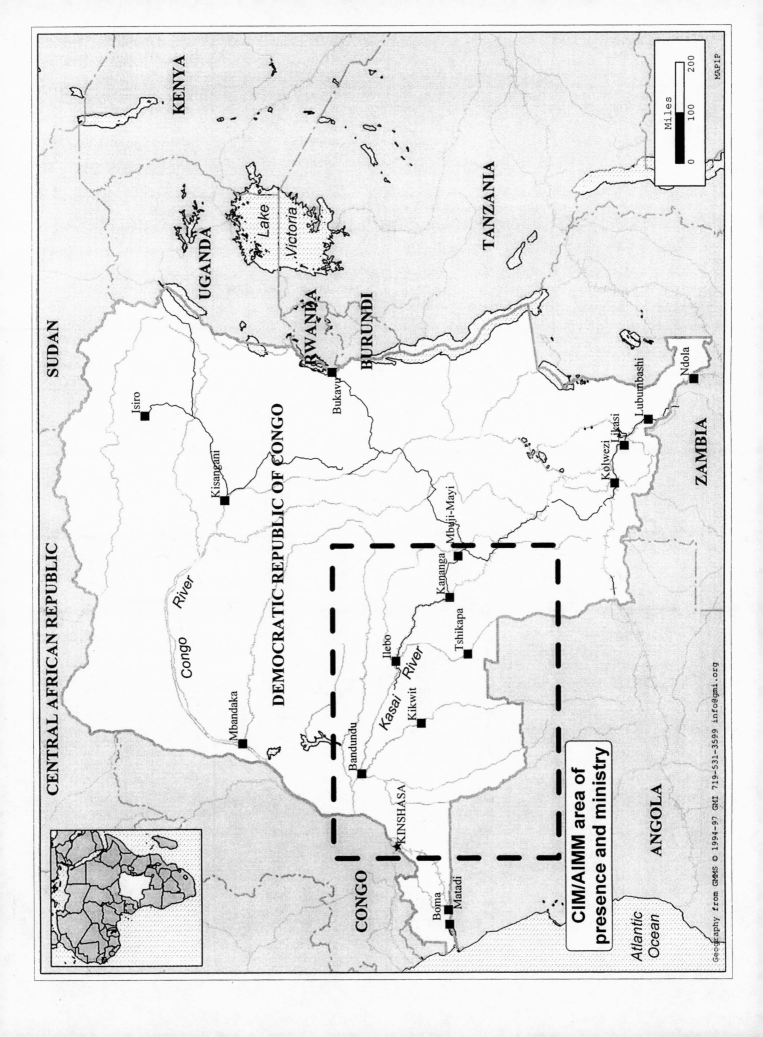

CIM/AIMM area of presence and ministry

SUDAN

KENYA

UGANDA

Lake Victoria

RWANDA

BURUNDI

TANZANIA

CENTRAL AFRICAN REPUBLIC

DEMOCRATIC REPUBLIC OF CONGO

CONGO

ANGOLA

ZAMBIA

Atlantic Ocean

Isiro

Kisangani

Mbandaka

Bandundu

Ilebo

Kikwit

Tshikapa

Kananga

Mbuji-Mayi

Bukavu

Kolwezi

Likasi

Lubumbashi

Ndola

KINSHASA

Boma

Matadi

Congo River

Kasai River

Miles
0   100   200

MAP1P

Geography from GMMS © 1994-97 GMI 719-531-3599 info@gmi.org

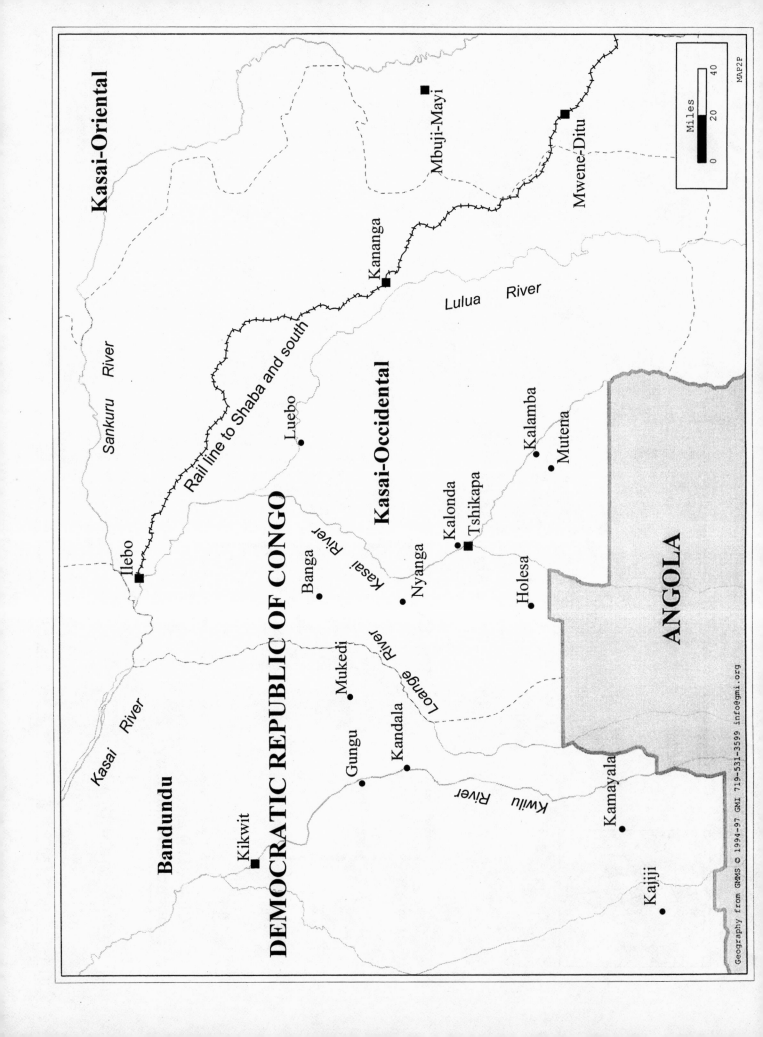

CHAPTER 1   PEOPLE OF DESTINY

a corpse found on its knees

Chitambo village, that May morning in 1873, was stirring to life in the distinctive manner of African villages everywhere. (1) Against the background of crowing cocks, bleating animals and barking dogs, the sound of village folk calling out to each other was to be heard. The smoke of freshly stirred hearth fires hung in the air. The dawning of a new day was once again triggering the daily cycle of activity of a village deep in the African bush as it had from time immemorial.

But for the small encampment of travelers out at the edge of the village, that morning was not like any other that had preceded it. Troubled by the silence which surrounded a simple stick and thatch shelter, African fellow travelers approached in the early light to peer inside. What they discovered struck both fear and sorrow to their hearts. David Livingstone, on his knees beside his camp cot, was dead. It was May 1, 1873.

Born in Blantyre, Scotland, in 1813, Livingstone secured a medical degree in 1838, studied theology for two years and was ordained in 1840 to the Christian ministry. Applying to the London Missionary Society, he was appointed in 1841 to a place called Kuruman in Bechuanaland, Southern Africa, (2) a mission post established by Robert Moffat. Here Livingstone met Moffat's daughter, Mary, whose hand he won in marriage.

It early became evident that Livingstone was driven by two all-consuming commitments. The first was to do all he could to open the vast uncharted interior of Africa to a witness to Christ. The second was to strike whatever blows he could to help defeat the brutal slave trade which at that time was decimating entire tribal groups along both the east and west coasts of the continent.

Relentlessly driven by these commitments, he soon became restless at Kuruman. Equipping himself for travel, he struck out to the northwest and eventually arrived at Lake Ngami, located in present-day Botswana. In the process he became the first white man to cross the Kalahari Desert (1849).

Realizing upon his return that it would be impossible to pursue his dreams and still provide adequately for his family, he sent his wife, Mary, and four children home to Scotland in 1852 and promptly organized a second expedition toward the northwest. Following the Chobe and Zambezi Rivers he crossed the Cuango and via footpaths eventually reached Luanda on the Atlantic coast in Portuguese Angola (1851). He next returned to the Zambezi and followed it southeastward eventually coming out on the east coast of Africa at Quelimane in Portuguese Mozambique (1853-1856). Not only did he become the first European to cross the continent from west to east but, along the way, became the first to view the majestic geological fault into which the river plunges. He named this awesome spectacle Victoria Falls.

Returning to England for rest and time with his family, he came to the attention of the diplomatic and scientific community of his homeland. The result was that in 1858 he was commissioned to be the British Consul for Quelimane and to continue his exploration of eastern and central Africa. Upon his arrival he led an expedition inland tracing and describing among other things the contours of Lake Nyasa (1859-1863).

During a subsequent break in England, he devoted time to writing and lecturing - - sharply highlighting the brutality and inhumanity of the slave trade as he had observed it first hand. In 1866 he made his final departure for Africa, this time commissioned as the British Consul for northern Africa. Having by this time acquired world renown, international curiosity and interest grew as months slipped by with no further word from him. Finally, in 1869, James Gordon Bennett, the publisher of the New York Herald, sent a Welsh-born staff reporter named H. Morton Stanley with instructions "to find Livingstone."

After patient and persistent tracing of the route of Livingstone's fourth exploratory expedition, Stanley at last arrived at a village called Ujiji, on the shores of Lake Tanganyika, on November 10, 1871. The ensuing greeting has become part of the folklore of the English speaking world, i.e. "Dr Livingstone, I presume!"

Noting his poor health and depleted supplies, Stanley attempted to persuade Livingstone to accompany him back to the coast. Failing that, Stanley helped him break camp and traveled with him for several months eventually leaving him in March of 1872 to return to New York. It was just a bit more than a year later that Livingstone breathed his last at Chitambo village.

There then followed an epic story of human loyalty and devotion. His African fellow-travelers decided upon two courses of action. Feeling that in a profound way Livingstone belonged to them and to their land, they cut open his chest, lifted out his heart and buried it there where he had spent his last hours among them. They then preserved his body as best they could, wrapped it in calico and sheets of bark with his journals and instruments and began the long trek back to the east coast. After a journey of some 1,000 miles on foot they arrived at Zanzibar on February 15, 1874. where they entrusted his remains to the care of British officials. Primarily responsible for this herculean accomplishment were three African friends named Jacob Wainwright, Abdullah Susi and James Chuma.

Today Livingstone lies entombed in London under the central aisle of Westminster Abbey. The plaque which marks his tomb carries this inscription: "For thirty years his life was spent in his unwearied effort to evangelize native races, to explore the undiscovered secrets, and abolish the desolating slave trade of Central Africa." (3)

In his youth he had vowed to open central Africa to the light of the Christian Gospel and to deal a major blow to the hated slave trade or to die in the attempt. In the end, Livingstone did both.

Africa's heartland laid bare

News of Livingstone's death spread quickly around the world. Among those who heard the news with much more than passing interest was H. Morton Stanley. Was it his deep personal respect for this dead missionary trail blazer? Was it the challenge of a task still not completed? Was it his own personal desire to find answers to the many questions concerning the immense heartland of Africa which continued to puzzle and tantalize the world's geographers? Was it his intuitive sense that here was an opportunity for possible fame and fortune which comes but once in a lifetime?

Whatever the reasons, Stanley returned to Zanzibar on the east coast of Africa in 1874 and, over time, gathered a group of some 350 men, both black and white, and set off once again into the African interior. By 1875, he had arrived at Lake Victoria in eastern Africa and, eventually, once again at Ujiji where he had first met Livingstone. Doggedly continuing their travel in a westerly direction, they came upon a sizeable stream which flowed on a northerly course. Wondering if, at long last, the headwaters of the legendary Nile River had been found, he and his men camped to equip themselves with boats, rafts and supplies intent on proving or disproving their conjecture.

Encountering both rapids and hostile local populations along the river shores, their progress was at best slow and often painful with considerable loss of life and equipment. It was with growing perplexity that Stanley eventually discovered that the ever larger river began first bearing them to the west and, eventually, to the southwest rather than toward the north as it should have had their destination really been the mouth of the Nile. Ultimately, after 999 days of travel from the date of launching their boats into an unknown stream, they found themselves, in 1877, on the Atlantic coast. By that time two thirds of his original group of 350 men had either died or deserted along the way. But Stanley, his trip journals in hand, was headed for Europe. He had a story to tell.

King Leopold II

Going first to England, Stanley attempted to interest the British political and scientific communities in the account and implications of his travels and discoveries but he found scant attention paid to his reports. Even his widely-read book, Through the Dark Continent, attracted little official notice.

In the meantime, however, there was someone of considerable political stature across the English Channel who was manifesting more than passing interest in Stanley and the tales of his exploratory travel. King Leopold II was a man of imposing physical appearance. A regal posture, an immense spade beard and a large aquiline nose easily set him apart in a group of peers. But the King lived with galling frustration. Possessed of a dream of an expanding empire, he chafed under the harsh limits imposed upon him by the pocket-sized Kingdom of Belgium wedged, as it was, between Holland to the north, Germany to the east, Luxembourg to the southeast and France to the south and southwest. If he was ever to realize his ambition of presiding over an enlarged domain, he obviously needed to seek opportunities beyond his restrictive European borders.

He early let it be known via official couriers that he would welcome the opportunity of meeting Stanley and discussing his recent findings in Africa at length. When it became clear to Stanley that there was no significant British response to the information he had to share, he crossed the Channel for a meeting with the Belgian King. For the population of the African Congo Basin, a historic and fateful series of events was swiftly launched into motion.

Already prior to Stanley's arrival, King Leopold had convened a geographic conference in Brussels which was attended by scientists from ten different countries. Under his astute guiding hand, it was proposed that a series of *stations scientifiques, hospitalières et pacificateurs* (scientific, medical and pacifying stations) be established in Central Africa. This "International Association" was to have national committees in each of the countries from which representatives had come as well as a central commission and an executive committee. As the host convener of the conference, it seemed appropriate that King Leopold become the president of both bodies. (4)

In November of 1878, at a secret meeting held in Brussels, the King convened a select group of Belgian bankers to meet with him and Stanley. Two key steps were taken. First, a "Committee for the Study of the Upper Congo" was established. Second, persuaded by Stanley's firstperson account of the valuable natural resources available in the Congo Basin, finances were put in place to fund what was to become basically a personal venture on the part of the King. Before the close of the year 1878, Stanley was once again bound for Africa, but this time to the west coast where with funding and personnel provided by the newly founded "Committee," he had instructions to retrace his steps up the Congo River. Along the way he was instructed to establish pacts of friendship and subservience in the name of a new, white, overseas King who had decided to impose himself upon them.

an ensuing scramble

By this time, however, the Belgian monarch was not alone in his efforts to stake out claims in the suddenly opened heartland of Africa. By the mid-1880's, a variety of similar expeditions were crisscrossing Central Africa. Their paths were intersecting each other with increasing frequency.

Once again it was the far-sighted King Leopold who took the initiative. Persuading the German government to convene a conference in Berlin to which all parties engaged in African exploration were invited, negotiations were begun in November, 1884, and were concluded in February, 1885. The agreements secured at that Berlin round table could hardly have been more satisfactory for the Belgian monarch. Essentially, the European powers who signed the convention recognized not the country of Belgium but rather the King, himself, as the ruler of the immense Congo basin which today is known as the Democratic Republic of Congo. Conditions imposed for the granting of this largesse were modest enough, i.e. the liberty of access of commerce for all; no taxes on imports; political and religious neutrality throughout the region.

On July 1, 1885, the Congo Basin was officially named "The Congo Free State."

a surge of missionary concern

If there was a concerted effort on the part of European powers to carve out colonial empires in Africa, it is also a fact of history that there was a simultaneous surge of concern within the world Christian community for the populations of the African continent who had yet to hear, for the first time, the name of Jesus. Among Protestant communities in scattered places such as Germany, Britain, Scotland, Sweden, Canada, New Zealand and the United States, Christians began to ask themselves what their responsibility was before the reality of the heartland of an enormous continent which was so dramatically being opened to them in their day.

It is to the enduring credit of the international Christian community of that era that action was taken. In some cases, existing mission boards restated priorities and raised funds and personnel to respond to the door newly opened to them. In other cases, totally new mission organizations were brought into being with a particular focus on Africa.

For our purposes it is of particular interest to note that by January, 1878, the first two pioneers of the Baptist Missionary Society of Britain, Thomas J. Comber and George Grenfell, had arrived at Banana on the mouth of the Congo River. Between 1878 and 1897, twelve different Protestant mission organizations from Britain, Sweden and North America placed pioneer missionary personnel in northwestern, western, south central and southeastern Congo. (5) One of the twelve was the Christian and Missionary Alliance who numbered among their pioneering team a single woman named Mathilda Kohm. Commissioned and sent by what was then known as the Defenseless Mennonite Church in 1896, she became the first Mennonite to set foot in the Congo. (6)

Noting this influx of Protestant missionaries and fearing that they perhaps nurtured political loyalties and dreams for their home countries in that part of the world, King Leopold turned to the Catholic Church hierarchy of his own country offering free land concessions and immediate legal status for any Catholic Orders which would recruit and place missionary personnel in his area.

the Free State: a morass of abusive greed

Even by royal standards, the occupation and exploitation of the resources of the Congo Basin was a costly proposition. To assure return on the funds invested by his partners in the venture launched by the "Committee for the Study of the Upper Congo" - - to say nothing of the personal fortune of the King himself which was at stake - - it was urgent that raw products begin to flow from the Congo to the Antwerp harbor as soon as possible. In the context of the world markets of that day, this basically meant natural rubber and ivory. To secure these lucrative raw resources, the "Committee" turned to the services of "agents" whose instructions were simply to secure these coveted African products in as large a quantity and as quickly as possible. The more they secured and shipped to Belgium, the greater was their personal commission. Just how they would accomplish their task was basically up to them.

To secure anything from the African forests, the agents were obviously dependent upon African labor and skill. Having little comprehension of or interest in this sudden hunger for the congealed sap of the rubber trees and elephant tusks to be found in their forests, the African tribal people were understandably reluctant to cooperate. Driven by dreams of personal fortunes just beyond their finger tips while being accountable to no one in the isolation of the African bush, the agents turned increasingly to brutal, bloody coercion of the vulnerable African populations available to them.

If methods used in the isolation of the African interior were sickening, they were nonetheless productive and this is what counted as viewed from the royal palace in Brussels. In 1893, 233 tons of ivory and 241 tons of raw rubber were off-loaded in Antwerp. By 1906 the traffic had about tripled to 600 tons of ivory and 600 tons of rubber, this with a market value of 47 million Belgian *francs* of which 30 million were destined for King Leopold's personal accounts. It is sadly informative to realize that at this same time, the total Belgian national budget came to only 32 million francs. (7)

But tales had begun to filter out of the isolated reaches of the Congo bush land. Missionaries began to encounter undeniable evidence of the merciless abuse which was rampant. Once confronted by undeniable proof, there was courageous action and protest. There were the American Baptist missionaries Sjoblom, Banks and Murphey who were the first to publicize the rubber-related atrocities. There were missionaries Morrison and Sheppard of the American Southern Presbyterian Mission who, because of their open challenge of the policies of the Company of the Kasai, were brought to trial by Free State authorities - - though eventually acquitted. (8)

It was particularly in England that these increasingly frequent reports from the Congo Free State found a concerned hearing. Since Britain was a co-signer of the Berlin Convention of 1885, it was felt in Protestant Church, government, and philanthropic circles that there were compelling reasons to review the terms of the document.

Fully aware of the swell of international criticism, the Belgian parliament also began to express concern. But such was the power and influence of King Leopold that he was able to deflect proposals of intervention on the part of his own government for nearly a decade.

Desperately needed change, however, would inevitably come. In 1903 the British government instructed Roger Casement, its Consul General in Kinshasa, Congo, to make a thorough study of the situation on the scene. When the finished document arrived in London, it became a powerful force in precipitating action. In effect it "affirmed numerous testimonies and gave troubling precisions regarding the extermination of the populations along the river due to the hell of forced labor." (9) In what may have been an effort by the King to put a more benevolent face on things in the Free State, he signed an "accord" with the Roman Church hierarchy on May 26, 1906, whereby the Catholic faith was to be officially introduced and recognized in the whole of the Congo.

Nevertheless, in August, 1908, the Belgian government invited King Leopold to study with it the manner in which Belgium would annex the Congo Free State. The King was furious and sought to undermine the proposal. However on November 15, 1908, in the absence of the King and in the face of his bitter opposition, the Parliament deputies voted unanimously to take control of the King's infamous domain.

The Congo Free State was renamed "The Belgian Congo" that same year. King Leopold died just 13 months later on December 17, 1909.

the Mennonites arrive

If the first decade of the 20th century was a decisive one in the history of the Belgian people, it was no less so in the history of two small Mennonite groups in the American mid-west known as the Stucky Amish and the Egly Amish. They were named for their founding leaders, Amish bishops Joseph Stucky and Henry Egly, (10) who in the course of their personal Bible study had come to a new understanding and experience of salvation through grace by faith. Preaching with new-found confidence and vigor, both soon acquired small followings amidst the conservative Amish communities of which they were a part. Their combined rural membership clustered in Illinois, Indiana and Ohio, in all probability, did not total more than 3,500 people. But, caught up as they were in the joy of their new experience of God's grace and the excitement of their newly discovered call to discipleship, these rural folk dared to launch a series of new cooperative Mennonite endeavors. Inter-Mennonite institutions which were conceived and put in place in the decades just before and after the turn of the century in central Illinois were The Salem Orphanage Association of Flanagan in 1896, the Meadows Mennonite Home for the Aged in Meadows in 1919, and the Mennonite Hospital of Bloomington in the same year. (11)

Insight into this burst of concern for the broader non-Mennonite society around them is found in a comment of the 1924 Annual Report of the Defenseless Mennonite Church: "Institutional work does not give us salvation, but we do it because we have salvation. We must do all we can to help the poor and the needy." (12) Acting upon this conviction, these Mennonite Christians reached for still broader horizons. In spite of the conservative, rural background of their Amish origins, both groups launched home mission efforts in Chicago, some one hundred miles to their northeast on the shores of Lake Michigan.

It surely would have been understandable if, at that point, they had decided that they had undertaken enough to keep them occupied in the Lord's work for several decades to come, but there was still more. They were hearing of an immense continent halfway around the globe which had suddenly been opened to the outside world. What was their responsibility in the light of this news? Did not Scripture say something about being witnesses even "unto the uttermost part of the earth?" Thus it was that having attempted to respond to the challenge of their Judea and Samaria, they next turned their attention toward Africa.

It is an improbable story. None of those rural Mennonite Christians were well-educated or well-traveled by today's standards. Africa might as well have been situated on the moon as far as any first hand knowledge was concerned. But from their perspective, Scriptural commands were for them both clear and inescapable. It was with this conviction that on March 22, 1911, in the hamlet of Meadows, Illinois, representatives from the Central Conference of Mennonites and the Defenseless Mennonite Church (as the Stucky and Egly Amish were by then known) met and organized a fledgling inter-Mennonite organization known as the United Mennonite Board of Missions. Before that year ran its course, Rev. Lawrence and Rose Haigh, the first missionary couple of this new organization, were already engaged in exploratory travel in the South Kasai region of the Belgian Congo. On January 23, 1912, this new inter-Mennonite Mission was renamed the Congo Inland Mission. (It quickly came to be widely-known as the CIM.) Soon thereafter, the Haighs were joined by Rev. Alvin Stevenson. By year's end, joint recommendations of the trio of pioneers had been made and approval had been given to begin work at two points along the Kasai River - - at Djoko Punda to the north and at Kalamba to the south. An inter-Mennonite effort to bring a witness to the Gospel of Christ among the tribal people of south-central Congo had been launched.

CHAPTER 2   COLONIAL RULE AND CHRISTIAN MISSION

different verse: same tune

As viewed from the government halls of Brussels, the conversion of the Congo Free State into the Belgian Congo undoubtedly represented a humanitarian intervention in Africa. Among philanthropic groups and government figures of surrounding countries who had been following the unfolding story with concern, there was a collective sigh of relief.

To be sure, in the newly established Belgian Congo, some changes were quickly made. The terrorizing, maiming and killing of bush tribes-people for failing to meet high rubber and ivory quotas were immediately stopped. It was also true that the new Belgian administrators, taking the long colonial view of things, were interested in much more than rubber and elephant tusks. Among other things they recognized that for a long term presence, they needed to arrive at a working relationship with the local populations as soon as possible.

The Congo people, however, soon realized that even though they were looking at new faces and dealing with people of a less hostile demeanor, they were still encountering familiar demands. Confronted on every side by enormous projects of construction, road building, exploration and exploitation of rich natural resources, Belgian administrators, like their Free State predecessors, needed a ready supply of inexpensive labor. To assure such help, several methods were used. First, there was the simple expedient of forced recruitment. Although such labor was largely used for public works, required labor also eventually took the form of the cultivation of cash crops according to acreage quotas established village by village. When harvested, the growers were assured of a government market but at fixed prices.

In addition to the above forms of conscripted labor, a poll tax was also added. This had the double value of providing a not insignificant revenue for the colonial administration but also "encouraged" able-bodied men to seek employment with the many commercial enterprises which were rapidly finding their way into the Congo. Many a Congolese man, who had no desire to work for a cash wage, was obliged to do so in order to pay his annual tax and that of his family. Even though much was said of the African's noble share in bettering and developing his own land, for most of them the Belgians simply represented a continuing disruptive and intrusive presence among them.

To the imposed requirement for labor was added the insult of sharply reduced authority of tribal chiefs and elders. The Belgians soon discovered that chiefs who exercised traditional roles of authority in accordance with their tribal traditions and values often resisted them and refused to cooperate with their demands. To overcome this difficulty, the Belgians put in place a system of "medal chiefs," i.e., so-called chiefs who gave promise of being more pliable and cooperative with them. While routine village disputes were still heard and settled by traditional chiefs in keeping with tribal customs, clear limits were placed upon their jurisdiction and power. Any cases beyond their granted authority were heard before a white administrator and this in keeping with Belgian colonial law. "Justice" was dispensed with a firm hand. Incarceration, hard labor and the use of a hippo hide whip became standard procedure for those who ran afoul of the white man's law.

It is not surprising that in the first decade or two of Belgian rule, tribal rebellions were a common occurrence across the Congo Basin. To deal with such manifestations of resistance, the government early organized an armed police force of Congolese called *La Force Publique*. Making sure that units called for action in a given tribal area came from distant unsympathetic tribes, orders given by white officers to open fire were seldom ignored. If opposition persisted after the arrival of this police force, leaders were tracked down and either executed or subjected to exile. During the year 1915 alone, these armed units was used to intervene in 30 different areas where local populations were violently expressing their opposition to the Belgian presence and rule. (1)

discovery of immense natural resources

Even while the "pacification" of the Congo's tribal populations was in process, much Belgian effort was devoted to the probing of the natural resources of their new colony. It soon became evident that great agricultural and mineral potential was present to be tapped. Over the years, such products as palm oil and the precious hardwoods of the immense tropical forests were increasingly harvested and exported. The tropical climate and soil were soon utilized for the cultivation of tea, coffee and nut palm plantations. Products such as manioc flour, ground nuts, cotton, and citrus fruits began to find their way to European markets.

But above all, it was the incredibly rich mineral deposits of the Katanga Province in the southeast and the profusion of diamonds in the south central Kasai area which became the object of concerted exploration. In due time efficient mining operations were established under the direction and control of a multi-national consortium in which Belgian financiers maintained a major holding.

a network of sandy trails and tropical waterways

Given the rapid development of Congo's vast interior, some sort of transport system had to be put in place quickly. Utilizing the immense river system as fully as possible, rail links were added to traverse the stretches where rivers were not navigable. This made for cumbersome, repeated handling of freight. With plenty of strong black arms and backs available, it nonetheless afforded a functional and dependable way of moving increasing tonnage of supplies inland while moving raw products out to the sea.

The immense, rolling, sandy depression that it is, the Congo confronts the road builder with formidable engineering problems and excessive costs if hard surfaced roads are envisioned. The Belgians bypassed this dilemma by the expedient of a highly labor-intensive system. Trails were cut and cleared through the Congo bush; sandy road surfaces were rounded off with a crown; drainage ditches were dug along the edges mile after mile. The basic piece of road equipment was a man with a long handled shovel. On a flat, monthly stipend, someone, somewhere, was responsible for every kilometer of sandy road. These *cantonniers*, as they were called, soon learned that the more promptly they repaired their assigned segments of road after a tropical rain, the less was the labor required overall to keep their stretch of road crowned and their drainage channels clear. With such constant care, it was often possible to travel cross-country at 50 mph.

a solid, growing economy

The Congo *franc*, undergirded by a profusion of natural resources, on the one hand, and linked to the Belgian *franc*, on the other, became a hard currency with posted value on the world's currency exchanges. While salaries paid the growing Congo work force were set by the colonial government at modest levels, so were the prices of basic goods in the stores. Within a closed economy, salaries earned, by and large, represented a living wage. This enabled the heads of households who opted to make at least a partial transition to a cash economy to feed, clothe and adequately care for their dependents.

With passing time, more and more Portuguese, Asiatic and West African commercial people came into the Congo and opened networks of bush stores where the basic commodities needed for simple, rural life were readily available at prices affordable to the village people. It would be only later that better educated Congolese would come to understand how modest the benefits were for them as compared to those realized by the commercial enterprises which took root among them.

the CIM in the 1930's

As the colonial regime in the Congo settled into a stable pattern of operation by the decade of the 1930's, so also had the personnel and program of the Congo Inland Mission. Twenty five years into its history found the CIM with a missionary staff averaging 25 to 30 people divided among four mission stations. There were the two established at the outset in 1912 along the Kasai River. The first was Djoko Punda (pr. djoh-koh

PUH-ndah; named Charlesville during the Belgian era) to the north near the Wissman Falls. The second was Kalamba, (pr. kah-LAH-mbah) well over 100 meandering miles by foot to the south, the home village of the King of the Lulua people. Those two mission posts had been thus situated so as to facilitate access to river transport at Djoko Punda to the north and ministry among the Tshiluba (pr. tshi-LOO-bah) speaking Baluba (pr. bah-LOO-bah) and Lulua (pr. loo-LOO-wah) people who intermingled between these two stations along the east bank of this major river.

To the west two more stations had been added: Nyanga (pr. NYAH-ngah) approximately midway between the Kasai and Loange Rivers in 1921, and Mukedi (pr. moo-KAY-di) to the west of the Loange in 1923 which was also located adjacent to the village of a principal chief. Both new mission outposts were located among a third major tribal group known as the Baphende (pr. bah-PEH-ndi.). The four stations were envisioned as points of departure for ministries of witness and service in an area roughly the size of the state of Illinois. By this time, this region of the Congo had become the sole mission responsibility of the CIM.

Separated from each other by expanses of grasslands and forests, inter-station communication was largely limited to mail sacks carried by African porters. Transport of supplies was accomplished for the most part via a device called a "push-push." It was a two-wheeled affair with a small wooden deck, a long wooden tongue, a sturdy cross piece before and a solid rack behind which permitted four- or five-man teams to pull, steer and push the conveyance across hundreds of kilometers of sandy trails between stations.

Annual conferences were the occasion for both missionary and African delegates to trek across the countryside to one of the four stations for several days of fellowship, Bible study, prayer and decision making. The pattern was for church conferences to convene first, which brought together African delegates with some of their missionary colleagues to transact business for the Church. One of the oft commented highlights of the conferences of that era were the African mass choirs. Organized by Rev. J.P. Barkman, a gifted musician, laboriously hand copied sheet music was distributed to the four stations ahead of time for rehearsal. Upon arrival at conference, the four station sections were combined into a single choir. The renown of those groups of the early days has become part of the lore of the Zaire Mennonite Church.

Following these church conferences, the missionaries then met alone to make plans and decisions for the Mission for the coming year. (2) Given the limited personnel and funds available in the 1930's, missionary business sessions frequently gave rise to spirited debate and competition as each station team sought budgetary support to further the programs and dreams of their respective areas.

Aside from these annual gatherings, missionaries and African colleagues lived and worked in comparative isolation. Ministries and methods strongly resembled each other in the four regions. Typically, each station had a primary school offering education of four or five years; a post-primary Bible School of two or three years for the training of teacher/evangelists; a clinic and maternity; on-the-job training of African carpenters and masons and was the recognized hub of church activity for the entire area. Membership growth, though modest, was steady. (3)

Christian missions and colonial empire

Early on, Belgian administrators recognized that in order to implement their approach to the development of the Congo, they would need an abundant supply of both illiterate unskilled and literate semi-skilled labor. To meet this urgent need, they turned to Christian missions.

As was earlier seen, the first Protestants arrived in the Congo simultaneously with the emissaries of King Leopold II. It was approximately a decade later that the first Catholic missionaries put in their appearance at the personal request of the King. By the time the Belgian Parliament assumed responsibility for the Congo, a significant missionary presence, both Protestant and Catholic, was already on the scene.

A dominant and oft repeated theme heard across the years, not only in Belgian pronouncements but also on the part of the African colonizing powers in general, was that of their opportunity and responsibility to bring the "blessing of civilization" to the "pagan" populations of a "dark continent." Casting thus their colonizing ventures in terms of humanitarian and even sacrificial concern, it was only reasonable that Christian missions be invited to collaborate in this worthy undertaking -- especially since the hoped for Christianizing of the African people was a goal with which few were apt to quarrel. So went the rationale.

It would not be quite fair to dismiss all of this as simple opportunistic rhetoric. There certainly were people in high places in the colonial structure who were sincerely committed to their Catholic faith and who across the years genuinely believed that the planting of the Christian church in Central Africa was an endeavor worthy of their fullest support. It must further be recognized that the lofty view held of the superiority of western civilization and the belief that its transplantation in Africa would automatically result in untold blessing and benefit for the African people reflected assumptions broadly and sincerely held during that time by both colonial agents and missionaries alike.

The fact, however, still remains that the objectives of the Belgian colonial regime required an immense pool of healthy, literate and vocationally trained Africans. To have undertaken the formation of such a labor force with expatriate teachers, technicians and medical personnel recruited and employed by the government itself would have represented formidable cost. The perfect answer was the growing volunteer missionary force at hand.

missionary complicity?

But what about the apparent readiness, if not eagerness, of the Christian missionary force of that era to collaborate with the colonial regimes around them? Were they not guilty of facilitating the building of empires? Did they not, at the very least, allow themselves to be used?

Such persistent criticism has indeed been laid at the door of Christian missions of that era. It needs to be recognized, however, that such critique is easy to voice after the fact. It must simply be acknowledged that pioneering generations of missionaries had no more choice regarding the political realities of their world than we have in ours. If there was to be a witness to the name of Christ on the continent of Africa at the turn of the century, they had no choice but to go under the shadow of a variety of flags hoisted by European powers. If their efforts in evangelism, education and health ministries largely served the purposes of those colonial regimes, it is no less true that their ministry met tremendous human need and resulted in the planting of a large, growing Christian community across sub-Saharan Africa. It should further be noted that though proclaimed under colonial rule, imbedded within the Gospel taught and preached were revolutionary concepts which contributed largely to understandings of self-worth, freedom and justice. The time would come when the affirmation of these truths would powerfully impact Congo's unfolding history.

priest and pastor collide

While Christian Missions were invited to partner with colonial governments, it must be understood that, in the Congo, it was initially the Catholic Missions who were the primary object of that invitation. The sharp suspicions regarding non-Belgian missionary personnel early manifested by King Leopold were not automatically discarded by the Belgians who later supplanted his agents. An instructive reflection of this stance is found in the vocabulary which was long used to distinguish between Belgian and non-Belgian missionaries, i.e. "national missionaries" and "foreign missionaries." While Belgian administrators were usually correct and polite in their dealings with Protestants, it soon became very clear that subsidies, prompt clearance for choice building sites and quick intervention in the event of menace were basically reserved for "national missions."

Coming from a homeland which was overwhelmingly Catholic and where Protestants were a minuscule minority, it is understandable that both Belgian priest and Belgian administrator shared a single dream, that of seeing the Catholic faith assume the same overpowering dominance in their immense colony that it enjoyed at home.

Thus it was that with the help of major subsidies both from the government and various commercial enterprises, Catholic Missions were able to undertake imposing construction projects all across the land. With the capital investments came a steady stream of priests, brothers and sisters of a variety of Catholic orders. Quality schools were started, dispensaries built, a variety of vocational training programs established all of which resulted in a steady flow of baptismal candidates.

In the meantime, while colonial administrators could not deny Protestant missionaries access to the Congo, they did not need to facilitate their work, either, and usually did not. Thus "foreign missions" were reduced to doing what they could with the much more limited funds which could be made available via their supporting constituencies in North America and Europe.

If at the level of colonial administrators Protestant Missions were primarily the object of disinterest and neglect, in the seclusion of the African bush, they more typically were the object of distrust, resentment and, frequently, thinly veiled animosity on the part of Catholic priests. Many of them had to come to the Congo to meet their first flesh-and-blood Protestant and these contacts frequently were not reassuring. Unaccustomed to energetic, confident and, in some cases, combative Protestant pastors, they soon came to view Protestant Missions as a serious threat to their cherished dreams of bringing into being a Congo as Catholic as it was Belgian. Relying heavily on their favored status, they sought to combat the ministry and influence of the Protestants among them with very aggressive methods which, at times, included menace and physical abuse of African villagers.

Given the circumstances and the dynamics of the era, it was unfortunately predictable that heated encounters of all kinds would take place between Protestant pastors and Catholic priests in the isolation of the African bush. These encounters, on occasion, provided high theater for audiences of partisan villagers but did little to enlarge their understandings of Biblical themes of joy, peace, charity and brotherly love!

a powerful triad emerges

With the flow of Congo events, it early became apparent to the African population that there were three major sources of influence and power to be reckoned with: the colonial government, the rapidly growing commercial/industrial community and the Roman Catholic Church. While each had their own specific sphere of activity, they became increasingly interwoven as distinctive strands within a common fabric of colonial reality. The government encouraged major foreign investment particularly in the mining sector. The system of taxation introduced at an early date effectively nudged able bodied men to seek employment. There was a growing array of goods displayed in bush stores which exercised a further leverage upon village folk to make their way into a consumer market.

With regard to Catholic Missions, Africans did not fail to notice that priests and sisters were typically granted a cordial and respectful entry into offices of government and management. The pressure of government influence was early brought to bear upon village chiefs for "volunteers" to build village schools, teacher housing and to register their children in these schools. Major business enterprises demonstrated open-handed generosity in funding major Catholic chaplaincies in a variety of places. By the 1930's, the Congo was in many ways a tidy, self contained pocket in Central Africa, insulated from the outside world and promising much for all three members of the power structure.

the Congo Protestant Council

It was against the background of such unfavorable political realities that Protestant missionaries early sought periodic occasions to meet for purposes of fellowship, worship and discussion of common interests and concerns. As early as 1902 a first such missionary gathering met in Leopoldville, the colonial capital, sponsored by what was then called "the General Conference of Missionaries." There were subsequent meetings every two or three years until 1911 at which time the name was changed to "The Congo Continuation Committee." Missionary gatherings continued under this umbrella until 1924 at which time a constitution was drafted proposing the creation of the Congo Protestant Council, or CPC in its acronym form. Minutes of that meeting already listed the CIM as a participating mission.

A constitution committee met briefly in 1925 to ratify the working draft in hand. In 1928 an office was established in Leopoldville and Dr. Emory Ross, a missionary leader of the Disciples of Christ Mission, was appointed as the first full-time secretary of the newly constituted Council. (4)

If it was the sting and stigma experienced by all Congo Protestants in a largely hostile Belgian environment which provided an early spur for broad-based inter-mission gatherings, it soon became apparent to all that there were many benefits to be derived from membership in a closely knit, well-led consultative Protestant body in that country. Among other things, the CPC soon became a vehicle for speaking to government officials with a single, united voice on a whole spectrum of issues which were important to them all. Under the guidance of a series of gifted missionary statesmen who served as CPC secretaries, it became, in time, a respected and increasingly influential voice both in Leopoldville and in Brussels. (5) It also became the driving force behind the establishment of a series of major inter-mission projects such as the publication of a Protestant quarterly which carried news from across the Congo; and the construction in the capital of a mission guest house and a large Protestant Press on adjacent lots contributed by the British Missionary Society.

But most significant of all was the impact the CPC had upon the emerging concept and shape of the Protestant community of the Congo. Two powerful dynamics were at work. One was the early criticism that Protestants were busily importing a hodgepodge of American and European denominations to the Congo, this in the presence of a single Catholic Church. A second dynamic was the simple need to close ranks, as Protestants, in a largely hostile Belgian setting.

In attempting to respond to these challenges, delegates to CPC meetings early agreed that while at local mission levels denominational identity would be maintained, at a national level the broad Protestant community would be highlighted under the name, "The Church of Christ of Congo". Church membership cards were standardized and it was agreed that members in good standing would be accepted without further formality into the membership and fellowship of Protestant Churches wherever they traveled or moved.

This ecumenical milieu was to have major impact upon the unfolding story of the Mennonite Church in the Congo.

CHAPTER 3   **THE CIM, THE CONGO AND WORLD WAR II**

<u>**World War II, a powerful catalyst**</u>

The little Kingdom of Belgium was an early victim of the German *blitzkrieg* unleashed in 1940. In the Congo, a shocked Belgian community quickly rallied, pledging Congo's rich natural and human resources to the allied effort to defeat the Nazi forces. This commitment had early implications for the Congolese. In a public speech, Congo's Governor General Ryckmans stated that Congo would do its utmost to meet the Allied need for such commodities as gold, wood, tin, diamonds, palm oil, copper, copal and rubber. This was no empty promise for, in striving to meet these needs, rural farmers were forced to work in "compulsory fields" up to a total of 120 days a year. It is a somber historical footnote that the uranium used by Americans to build the atomic bombs dropped on Hiroshima and Nagasaki was mined in the Congo.

The western Allies, however, were in need of more than raw materials. They also needed troops. As the conflict spread to North Africa, many young Congolese men were conscripted, outfitted, trained in the rudiments of combat and shipped northward to join other allied forces in a white man's conflict concerning which they understood little. In the course of the war, these troops were assigned to campaigns in West Africa where Vichy French colonies posed problems for the Allies. Congolese troops also fought in Ethiopia, North Africa and the Middle East.

As the war ground its way to a conclusion, the surviving Congolese troops were returned to their tropical homeland and mustered out of service. Filtering back into their rural home villages, they quickly became the objects of awe and rapt attention around the evening village fires where they described what they had seen and experienced. They explained that they had been drafted and sent to fight because the Belgians' homeland had been overrun by a different European tribe. Once this news had been digested, some expressed their amazement that the seemingly all-powerful Belgians among them were apparently not invincible after all. What was even more astounding to the isolated village folk was the declaration that their fellow clansmen had helped defeat white troops in battle! And stranger still, they heard that there were at least a couple of places in Africa where black people ruled themselves. After repeated rounds of such information shared by their returned clansmen, the inevitable question began to be softly but persistently posed in many Congolese settings: "And what about us?"

But if the seeds of revolutionary new ideas had been sown within Congo, still more dramatic forms of impact were soon to come from outside the country. First, there was the turmoil within Belgium itself. The defeat of the axis powers and the declaration of peace left a large majority of Belgian citizens harboring deep resentment both against their King Leopold III and the political regime which had for years been the vehicle of Catholic interest and influence in Belgian political life. Accused of a hasty capitulation to German forces and, worse yet, of collaboration with the occupying troops, a fire storm of public protest forced the King to vacate his throne. Furthermore, at the occasion of the first post-war elections, the long dominant Catholic Party was defeated. In its place, a new coalition of the Labor and Socialist Parties took power.

Fully aware and critical of the policy of exclusion of Congo Protestant Missions from government subsidies, legislation was promptly passed placing Protestant and Catholic Missions on an equal footing and offering subsidies for Protestant educational and medical work which met government standards. This represented a dramatic shift in Belgian policy and suddenly confronted Congo Protestant Missions with a controversial and far reaching decision.

Standing in the Free Church tradition - - as did a great majority of the Congo Missions - - it was of course predictable that troubling questions would quickly surface among CIM missionaries and Board members. Since such entanglement with government was feared and spurned by their sponsoring churches in the west, how could principle now be compromised in the Congo? Would they not knowingly be submitting to alliances which could easily become strangling nooses? Would they not risk losing the freedom to continue their efforts of evangelism and church planting as they saw best? Allured by the tempting offer of financial help, might they not later discover that they had naively submitted to agreements which would curtail and handicap their ongoing efforts to win the Congolese for Christ?

But no matter how the issue was approached or debated, invariably the CIM, like a large majority of other Congo Protestant Missions, came back to an unavoidable set of facts and conclusions: 1) the colonial government, as the result of an amazing shift in the political winds in Belgium, was placing Protestant Missions on an equal basis with Catholic Missions; 2) as a result, the government was now, for the first time, offering major financial help which would go far to redress the long resented imbalance in resources available to the two branches of Christian mission at work in the Congo; 3) the acceptance of such subsidy would make possible a major expansion of Protestant educational and medical services for the populations among whom they worked; 4) to spurn such help was to literally stand between the local Congolese people of their areas and the sharply improved services which the government was now prepared to make possible for them; 5) the realization that were this offer to be refused, no amount of effort to justify the decision on abstract philosophical or theological grounds would be understood or accepted by the Congolese who would bear the brunt of such a decision.

Before this set of unyielding realities, an overwhelming majority of Congo Protestant Missions made the decision to sign formal agreements with the colonial regime whereby they committed themselves to seek to bring their educational and medical programs to government standards and accept the range of subsidies which would consequently be available to them.

It was in this context that the CIM Board voted its approval in 1948. Official documents were signed in the Congo in 1949.

extended frontiers

The explosion of World War II had a disruptive impact on the CIM in a variety of ways. Mail service became less predictable. International travel for missionary personnel became hazardous if not impossible. But for missionaries on the scene, the decade of the 40's was one of aggressive itineration in the enormous area which had become their responsibility. In spite of the war, there were forward looking projections for the opening of new mission stations and for the broadening of ministries.

In reports to the home office there was frequent reference to itineration by Djoko Punda missionaries toward the northwest among the Bashilele (pr. bah-shi-LAY-lay). A hardy, independent, iron-working and hunting people, they had long been resistant to change whether proposed by government agents or Christian missionaries. After years of discouraging response, the reporting in the 40's carried an optimistic ring. By the close of that decade, the dream of a new CIM station somewhere among these resistant folk was an annual agenda item at missionary conferences. (1)

Furthermore, it was both Djoko Punda and Kalamba missionaries who were making periodic trips to and around Tshikapa (pr. tshi-KAH-pah). Situated at the confluence of the Kasai and Tshikapa Rivers between the two CIM stations, this was the site of the sprawling administrative headquarters of the *Forminière* Diamond Mining Company. Attracted by the opportunity for employment, there were increasing numbers of CIM converts who sought employment with the company and thus lived in the company worker camps. Efforts to minister to them were consistently met by cool indifference by Company officials. Having generously subsidized the installation of its own Catholic chaplaincy in the form of an impressive Catholic mission on a bluff overlooking the two rivers, the officials viewed any Protestant missionary presence as an intrusion which was barely tolerable.

It took a remarkable mix of humility and tenacity on the part of CIM missionaries of the 40's to keep returning to camp officials, hats in hand, to request permission to meet with their own converts among the Company employees. Missionary Elmer Dick tells the poignant story of one time being granted the grudging permission of an official to conduct a communion service for "their Protestant employees" providing it was done completely out of sight of the camp. Thus it is was that under the shade of some mango trees along a busy road he met with a cluster of believers. Amidst the noise and dust of passing truck traffic, bread was broken, hymns sung and prayers offered as they recommitted themselves to one another and the Lord amidst prejudice and ostracism.

Such persistence ultimately carried the day and a new CIM station was eventually established near that center, but not in the decade of the 40's.

It was also in this decade that the Congo missionaries came to grips with a problem that had surrounded their Kalamba station for years. The post had originally been located near and named for Chief Kalamba who at the time was recognized as the King of the Lulua people. In view of his invitation extended to them, they were hopeful that his influence would be a key to establishing an effective witness among his people. With passing years, however, it became clear that while the dominant local clan welcomed the presence and ministry of the Mission, they resented any efforts to reach beyond them to other clans and ethnic groups of the area. After living with the frustration of this impasse for some years, Board permission was given in 1946 to relocate and the process of moving to a new site some 8 miles to the northwest was immediately begun. The relocated mission post was named Mutena (pr. moo-TEH-nah).

a means to an end

But it was, above all else, the CIM decision to apply for educational and medical subsidies that was the landmark event of the 40's. This action sparked an immediate flurry of effort to bring CIM's school system in line with established government standards. A major need was to upgrade teacher training, both missionary and African. For CIM personnel this meant routing educational and medical personnel via Belgium to study French and to take what was then known as the *Cours Colonial*, an intensive five or six week set of lectures, in French, ranging over such topics as Belgian history, the Belgian system of law, Congo history, Belgian colonial philosophy, tropical hygiene and state/church relations in the Congo. To be approved for subsidized educational and medical service, passing these courses was required. In 1947 Miss Lodema Short of Archbold, OH, became the first CIM missionary to take this course. A long series of others were to follow.

In the Congo, an enlarged school system obviously meant a major expansion of the Congolese teaching staff. To meet this challenge, special two-year training programs called, initially, *Ecoles d'Apprentissage Pédagogique* (i.e., Schools of Pedagogical Apprenticeship, or EAPs as they quickly came to be known in their acronym form) were started in 1949 at Mukedi, Djoko Punda and Mutena. Generous Belgian grants were received to construct buildings to house these new schools. (2) Since these schools were designed only to produce teachers for the lower primary grades, there was immediate need to lay plans for an *Ecole de Moniteurs*, i.e., a four-year teacher training school at a secondary level which would produce a teaching corps for the upper grades. This school, too, was opened in due time.

Underlying all of this concentrated effort to qualify for government subsidies was the conviction that a greatly expanded school system could become a powerful ally of evangelism and church planting. Given the total freedom promised to teach Scripture and the Christian faith in every subsidized class room regardless of level, it was foreseen that this would offer a tremendous opportunity to share the life and teachings of Jesus with literally thousands of young Congolese students. This being the case, it was anticipated that at some point during their school days many would respond in personal acts of faith and commitment to Christ as Savior and Lord. It was further envisioned that an expanding network of regional schools in rural areas could, in turn, become church centers where new believers, both students and adults, could be shepherded by teacher/evangelists or resident pastors.

As missionaries with educational qualifications plunged into the development and extension of CIM's school system, parallel efforts were being invested in the Mission's medical services since special government funds were also being offered for such purposes. (3) As the era of the 40's came to a close, projects of maternity hospitals were on the CIM drawing boards for several of its stations. To the usual personnel requests addressed to the home board there now was added the urgent need for qualified missionary teachers, doctors and nurses.

In the midst of these major new developments for the CIM, other events were also taking place which, though less publicized, were nonetheless very significant in their own right: the first draft of a CIM church manual for use by both missionary and African pastors in 1942; a newly opened air link between Miami and Leopoldville in 1944; a CIM missionary recommendation to the home board in 1945 to make a capital investment in the inter-Protestant Press in Leopoldville known initially as LECO, i.e., the Evangelical Bookstore of the Congo (this large combined retail and publishing center would later be renamed CEDI, i.e., *Centre Protestant d'Editions et de Diffusion* in its French form); and the notice in 1946 that Miss Agnes Sprunger's translation of the Old Testament in Giphende had reached the halfway point. (Her translation of the Giphende New Testament had already been published in 1935.) It was most rewarding for the missionaries to note a general growth pattern that was setting in. Between 1940 and 1949 the registration of students in CIM schools had grown from 7,295 to 9,704 and church membership from 5,004 to 8,736 with 3,785 people requesting baptism.

The financial constraints and limited personnel of the 1920's and 30's were now history. A stronger economy and new missionary recruits in the homeland equipped the CIM to move aggressively through new doors which were opening in the Congo. The decade of the 40's came to a close on an upbeat, forward-looking note.

CHAPTER 4   THE FABULOUS FIFTIES

It was summer of 1949. Over 100 Protestant missionaries were taking a six week colonial course in the city of Brussels as was by then required by the Belgian government of all who wanted credentials for working in subsidized mission schools and medical facilities in the Congo.

One topic to which a major block of time was devoted in the daily lectures had to do with the Belgian approach to the rule of its African colony. Over a period of days a wide range of issues were dealt with in detail such as the Belgian philosophy of colonization, principles adopted, methodology employed, attitudes vis-à-vis the African people and their world view and, above all, the rationale for staking out claims to the immense heartland of the African continent. (1)

One morning, as he brought his lecture to a close, a professor acknowledged that the Belgians, as one of the colonizing powers present in Africa, were not without their critics. Then, in a manner which reflected great pride and haughty confidence as to the future, he concluded by quoting a proverb: *"Les chiens aboient; la caravane passe,"* i.e., "The dogs bark; the caravan passes."

full steam ahead

The Belgian lecturer may be forgiven the exaggerated optimism which he reflected that mellow 1949 summer's morning in Brussels since both the colonial government and Christian missions stood on the threshold of a new decade which seemed rich with promise for all concerned. As regarded the Belgian presence in Central Africa, a great deal had indeed already been accomplished. The bloody chapter of the brutal rubber and ivory days of the Congo Free State had been terminated. Some desperately needed humanitarian reforms had been initiated. Earlier revolts against the expanding Belgian presence had been suppressed. The fabulous natural resources of the Congo basin had been probed and were in process of exploitation with the major help of a growing trained African labor force. In the face of great odds, an infra-structure of communication, transport and government services was under steady development. The homeland had been freed of the German tyrants; the world was again at peace and international markets provided a steady and profitable outlet for Congo's raw products.

Nothing reflected this optimism and long range planning any better than the drafting and publication of a document dated 1950 and entitled A Ten Year Plan for the Economic and Social Development of the Belgian Congo. In this statement Pierre Wigny, the newly appointed Minister of Colonies, laid out the Belgian vision for an ongoing presence and endeavor in Central Africa. A document of 72 pages, it provided a thorough review of Belgian vision and concern in the ongoing administration of their immense colony astride the equator. In it were found statements and observations such as these:

"In the Belgian Congo, public authority has charge of more than 10 million natives. They are incapable of assuring for themselves sufficient rapidity in evolution of their methods of production and a progressive rise in their standard of living. They are counting on the Belgians." (2)

"The demographic condition of the white population is good. The time is past when only a few adventurers, to the despair of their families, set out for Africa. Colonial vocations are on the increase. . . . Colonization should be encouraged." (3)

"We do not permit the presence of 'poor whites' who, as a result of the social dumping of indigenous peoples, are obliged to be satisfied with a standard of living incompatible with the dignity of a civilized man.... The white man can justify his presence in the Congo only by his superiority. It is his duty to enrich the Congo economic system by bringing thereto those qualities of which it is devoid. He has traditions, a professional training and capital which the natives lack and which will benefit the country as a whole." (4)

"Hereafter, those only will be admitted to the Congo who will be an asset to the community, ... not those who wish to live at its expense." (5)

"Improvement of the natives' living conditions is the justification of our presence and the moral reward of our efforts. But, let us again repeat, this policy is imperative for economic reasons as well." (6)

"In these tropical lands, clothing is an ornament and satisfies a requirement of decency. That is a primary and adequate justification. Naked men can hardly be civilized." (7) "Money will not be lacking while there is question of saving human life but we must find men. The recruiting of doctors is difficult. We no longer find sufficient colonial vocations among them." (8)

"Public education has just been reorganized. Some people will, perhaps, be surprised to discover that a place has been reserved for the ancient classics in the field of secondary education. Surely the Congolese must have a more practical education. That is true for the masses. But, by establishing 'colleges' for the natives, we wanted to prove that we were not reserving for our children alone the monopoly of a high intellectual training and, as a consequence, of the professions to which it gives entry. . . . Functional agreements have been signed determining the conditions for the collaboration of the Administration with the Belgian and foreign missions and the educational system, and syllabuses have been worked out." (9)

"30 million [francs] for the agricultural programs, 40 million for housing, 20 million for drinking water, 40 million for education, 40 million for training; these are the sums the Public Services will spend directly for the welfare of the native population." (10)

"Belgium must once more prove to the world that it is carrying on its mission of civilization in the heart of Africa with generosity and a sense of greatness." (11)

Underlying the document were two faulty assumptions: 1) that the ongoing Belgian presence and endeavors in the Congo was welcomed by the Congolese, and 2) that given what was considered to be an enlightened colonial philosophy, the Belgians would remain in Congo for an indefinite period of time.

the 50's: a decade of explosive expansion for Christian missions

Among Christian missions, both Catholic and Protestant, poised on the threshold of the 50's there was a tingle of excitement, a sense of high expectation, a perception that a new day of great opportunity had suddenly dawned - - and this with good reason. Behind them were earlier decades of struggle in the face of high odds. There had been the price paid in lives as earlier generations of ill-equipped white skinned pioneers encountered tropical climate, malarial fever, strange foods and the hazards of frontier life. (12) River systems, rolling grasslands and forest trails had been explored and traced on maps; major tribal languages had been analyzed and reduced to writing with a growing list of Scriptures offered to the Africans in their mother tongues; the disruption and constraints of World War II were by now a receding memory; inter-continental travel via air was a welcomed new development; a network of mission posts by now dotted the interior from border to border; a functional system of roads and ferries maintained by the government was in place which greatly facilitated travel. Beyond that, some missions were experimenting with war surplus short-wave radio equipment in an effort to introduce daily communication between isolated bush stations.

It was no longer necessary to devote time and energy to cajoling and persuading village elders and parents to enroll their children in mission schools. By this time it was recognized even in the most isolated areas that the golden key to "progress" for their children was that of literacy. To make the transition from rural village life to job training and employment, a certificate verifying at least primary level education was an increasingly precious document. Consequently, it was no longer a problem of filling the mission classrooms. It was now rather a problem of finding ways of accommodating the ever larger numbers of rural youth who sought an opportunity to study. No longer did missionary nurses need to seek ways of enticing village folk to come to the station dispensaries and maternities to seek help for their illnesses and the deliveries of their babies. Villagers were by this time convinced that there was genuine benefit for them in doing so.

There was, furthermore, the ongoing subtle but highly effective pressure of a colonial regime which placed a premium upon literate, vocationally trained Africans who had been baptized by one of the missions, who had celebrated a Christian marriage and who maintained a monogamous family structure. It had become evident that there were powerful forces at work which were channeling increasing numbers of Congolese, youth and adults alike, into the spheres of influence of Christian missions at work across the land.

There was, however, a darker side to all of this. In the decade of the 50's, there was a growing perception among the Congolese that the western technology and commercialism introduced by white skinned people represented a way of life superior to their own. Since they were "backward" and "uncivilized," they were now in a hurry to catch up and were eager to pursue whatever course of action that would help them to attain the coveted status of a *civilisé*, i.e., a civilized person. A counterpoint to the spirit of this decade was a certain apologetic mood vis-à-vis their own culture. Worse still, there was a growing disenchantment with village life and disdain for manual labor. In the new order of things, it was thought, dirty hands would be the lot of the unlettered and unsophisticated while the educated would make their way into the new world of the class room, commerce and government service.

the 50's and the Protestant perspective

Focusing more specifically on the Protestant missions of the Congo as the decade of the 50's dawned, it was clear that new doors of opportunity were swinging open on every side. At home, there was a remarkable surge of new missionary candidates in the aftermath of World War II. In some cases, youth exposed to overseas need during military service made personal commitments to return at a later date under different sponsorship in a more constructive role. In other cases, young men who had received draft exemptions as theological students during the war were now volunteering for "battle" of a different nature.

But not only were new recruits volunteering in record numbers. New funding was also forthcoming from the homeland churches which made it possible to process, appoint and support a new wave of missionaries to fields which during the 30's and 40's were largely limited to holding operations.

Most significantly of all, the broad Congo Protestant mission community welcomed the 50's with the happy knowledge that a major political and psychological shift was under way which was working in their favor. While there would continue to be encounters between priest and pastor and between Catholic and Protestant African church personnel, there was the reassuring fact that the ground rules had been rewritten. There were now some limits beyond which even the most zealous Flemish priest could no longer go in efforts to curtail the rapid expansion of Protestant witness and service in the land.

the Congo Inland Mission amidst the excitement

All of the events and dynamics traced thus far were very much a part of the context within which the Congo Inland Mission also came to the decade of the 50's. The CIM, too, had written its own pioneering chapters when simple survival in the tropical bush was reason enough for profound gratitude. It, too, had marked its first missionary graves. (13) It, too, had its early history of struggle with inadequate transport, spasmodic communication, unknown tribal languages, strange African world-views and customs. It, too, had felt the harsh pinch of the American economic depression and struggled to keep missionary personnel on the field. (14)

The CIM, too, had felt the sting and frustration of being classified as a "foreign mission" by the pre-war colonial regime and of witnessing the rapid growth of Catholic Missions in its area thanks to financial help which was denied non-Belgian missions. It, too, had agonized over the issue of signing service contracts with the post-war colonial regime. It, too, was being approached by scores of new candidates at home while the supporting churches of this inter-Mennonite venture in Africa were responding with enthusiasm and open-handed generosity. Whenever the field executive committee met, long hours were devoted to themes of program expansion and the launching of new initiatives. Broadened and intensified mission effort was evident on a variety of fronts.

from four to eight

Within its first eleven years in the Congo, the CIM had planted four stations, i.e., Djoko Punda, Kalamba, Nyanga and Mukedi. For 25 years thereafter, these four mission posts had absorbed all of the personnel and financial resources that CIM could muster. While they all wielded a steadily growing impact on the regions around them, the missionary staff remained acutely aware that a number of major ethnic groups and strategic areas of the CIM territory remained without a sustained witness. Much remained to be done. Thus it was that with the prospect of a new wave of missionary personnel and financial undergirding, an early priority was to expand its network of mission stations. Action toward this end was not long in coming.

First, the persistent itineration of the late 40's among the Bashilele people to the northwest of Djoko Punda had finally borne fruit. African chiefs were eager to give land for a new CIM station among them. Some 35 miles to the northwest of Djoko Punda, a rural crossroads on a bluff overlooking an immense valley was chosen. When in 1950 government permission for occupancy was given, Russell and Helen Yoder Schnell were released from Djoko to move to the new site. Taking its name from a local village, the new station was called Banga (pr. BAH-ngah). The CIM dream of many years to establish missionary personnel among the Bashilele people was finally realized.

At Tshikapa, however, CIM efforts to establish a new station were still meeting determined opposition from local Catholic priests and company officials. It was only after months of repeated requests and the intervention of the CPC secretary in Leopoldville that, at long last, 1950 also became the year for the formal installation of a CIM presence in that area. Archie Graber, (15) who had eagerly been awaiting the opportunity, was released from his responsibilities at Djoko to lay out a sixth station on a gently sloping hillside overlooking the Kasai River and the sprawling complex of the *Forminière* Diamond Mining Company. This station was named Kalonda (pr. kah-LOH-ndah) in honor of the local chief who had resolutely maintained his offer of land in the face of all opposition on the part of the local white community. Located at a confluence of the Tshikapa and Kasai Rivers, Tshikapa was not only a growing commercial and population center, it also marked the juncture of several traditional tribal boundaries, i.e., Baphende from the west, Lulua/Baluba from the east and Babindi/Chokwe (pr. bah-BIH-ndi CHO-kway) from the south.

Other dynamics were also at work in the early 50's which offered the CIM still further opportunity for expanded horizons of ministry. To the west of the CIM, in what was then known as the Kwilu/Kwango areas, there was a cluster of independent missions at work. The largest of these was the Unevangelized Tribes Mission (UTM) which had been founded and developed by a remarkable dynamo of a woman named Alma Doering. (16) An early station established by the UTM was Kamayala (pr. kah-mah-YAH-lah), near the Angolan border, in 1929. Evidently like attracted like because among the pioneering personnel recruited and sent by Doering to this distant post were the Miller sisters (17) who were to become legends in their own time. Sometimes without male missionaries on the station, they forged ahead. Bertha was the verbose, energetic people person; Mary was the quiet, perceptive, organizing nurse. Over time they planted a strong church, an extensive primary school system, a clinic and maternity, a shelter for orphans and a leprosarium.

When in the aftermath of World War II the loosely knit UTM was unable to cope with the suddenly increased demands and opportunities of the Congo, inquiries were made of other Protestant Missions of the area as to the possibility of affiliation. Having ties of acquaintance and friendship with several of its missionaries, the Miller sisters early approached the CIM with the request that they, their church and mission program be absorbed into its field and work. By 1953 formalities had been concluded and CIM's range of ministry was extended as far south as the Angolan border on the west side of the Loange River. This opened the door to CIM for ministry among two new major ethnic groups - - the Chokwe and Lunda. (18)

Between Mukedi and Kamayala stations was Kandala (pr. kah-NDAH-lah), another independe begun in 1926 by Rev. Percival and Rosalind Near, a Canadian Baptist couple. With modest financial from their Canadian home church and friends in Toronto, they had faithfully contributed what they the broader Protestant witness of the area. Though this mission endeavor had resulted in a smalle membership and a primary school effort largely confined to the station, Kandala was strategically located as far as the CIM was concerned. Not only did it lie between Mukedi and Kamayala but it also was situated among the Baphende people, a major tribe for which the CIM had long carried a large concern. When amidst the rapidly changing post-war Congo mission scene the Nears also initiated conversation with the CIM relative to the future of their work, there was immediate interest. After several rounds of discussions, final agreement was reached in 1954. (19) Thus, within a period of four years, the CIM expanded its bases of ministry and witness from four to eight stations.

It should also be noted that during this same period the Mennonite Brethren Board of Missions and Services decided to respond to the request of a couple of other small Mission groups of the area and to assume responsibility for some of their work which had been established in the 1920's and 30's. They made a mission station named Kafumba (pr. kah-FUH-mbah) their initial base of operations. Situated near a river port named Kikwit, it had been started in 1921 by pioneers Rev. Aaron and Ernestina Janzen. Having initially served two terms with the CIM, (November 1912 to July 1916 and January 1919 to November 1921) they felt burdened for a large area to the west of Mukedi station where there was no Protestant presence or witness. Unable at that time to secure the formal support of their home conference, they supplemented the help they were given by their home congregation in Mt. Lake, MN, by developing a productive coffee plantation. By the close of World War II, the Janzens had planted a growing church at Kafumba which became the nucleus for a thriving Mennonite Brethren mission endeavor on the western edge of CIM territory.

centralization of training programs

For decades the CIM had, of necessity, maintained small scale teacher and church leadership training programs on each of the four original stations. In their semi-isolation, these programs largely duplicated each other. But the rush of events of the early 50's obliged the missionaries to think and plan in new global, long range terms.

Applying for government educational subsidies made two immediate demands, i.e., 1) a standardized curriculum across the field and 2) a uniform teacher training program for all schools. In keeping with government guidelines, three special EAP programs were started at Mukedi, Djoko Punda and Mutena (cf. ch. 3, p. 15). With these two year programs of orientation to concepts of lesson planning and teaching, graduates were eligible for subsidized salaries as teachers in the first two primary grades. (20) In their era, the schools at the three stations counted a total enrollment of 200 to 225 students from year to year.

Determined, however, that teachers of the lower grades in the rapidly expanding mission school system have grounding in Scripture as well as in class room methodology, CIM created its own two-year Biblical training courses called *Ecoles Evangéliques* in which students were introduced to concepts of evangelism and the teaching of Biblical stories in a manner appropriate for the lower grades. As the two training programs were integrated, it was typically students who had finished the two-year Bible Schools who were admitted into the government sponsored two-year teacher training programs.

These lower level schools were no more than operative, however, when CIM needed to address the looming necessity of training other teachers for the upper four years of primary school. (21) To respond to this need, a single four year *Ecole de Moniteurs*, i.e., "Teachers' School" was established at Nyanga in the fall of 1954 into which bright students from across the growing CIM area were channeled for instruction in pedagogy, methodology, mathematics, French, history and the basics of the Christian faith. For not only were they one day to teach the three "R's" to their young Congolese students but, as Christians, it would often be their opportunity to lead their young charges to faith in Christ, as well. (22)

compassion ministries expanded

Amidst the surge of post-war missionary candidates were also those who offered excellent medical credentials. Arriving the first time in Congo in the spring of 1941, Merle and Dorothy Bowman Schwartz had struggled for years, as the only doctor/nurse couple on the CIM field, to provide at least minimal medical help from station to station, They, therefore, warmly welcomed several new colleagues in the course of the 1950's, i.e., Dr. John and Jeanne Pierson Zook, Dr. Elvina Neufeld Martens, Dr. Jim Diller and Dr. Henry Hildebrand.

Greatly relieved, also, was a corps of veteran missionary nurses who in the isolation of their individual stations had for years been obliged to make medical decisions which far surpassed their formal training. Among them were Kornelia Unrau, Aganetha Friesen, Lois Slagle, Leona Enns Entz and Irma Beitler who arrived on CIM bush stations in the following order: 1926, 1938, 1945 and 1949. The decade of the 50's saw the arrival of a number of new missionary nurses including Lena and Sara Friesen, Eudene King Keidel, Helen Reimer Eidse, Amanda Reimer and Donna Williams.

Thus, provided with both new personnel and Belgian funding, CIM medical services on the various stations were upgraded and soon became hubs for growing networks of bush dispensaries and maternity services in the hands of mission-trained African staff.

concern for both heart and hand

Committed to the goal of planting a self-sustaining church in the Congo, the CIM missionaries frequently discussed the problem of a growing membership comprised largely of rural people who lived out their lives on a subsistence level. In such a setting, was it not part of their mandate to enlighten not only minds and hearts but to also train and equip hands?

To be sure, little clusters of masons, carpenters and woodworkers were to be found at all of the CIM stations. In the course of their on-the-job experience these workers had acquired skills which were usable not only in Mission employ but also in the context of their adjacent villages. These training opportunities, however, were limited to the fortunate few who made up the work crews of each station. What of the increasing numbers of young students, both boys and girls, who were either not gifted for or interested in study beyond primary school but who very much wanted to provide for themselves, their families and their church?

In the decade of the 50's vocational training was added to the rapidly expanding CIM educational system. In a land where good lumber was abundant, training in carpentry became an immediate focus. Also added was a section in masonry and, eventually, cabinet making. The CIM *Ecole Artisinale*, i.e., "Vocational School" enrolled its first students in the spring of 1954 at Mutena under the leadership of Loyd and Marie Diller Brown. Though both staff and location of this school later changed, from this two-year course came many young men who, with their newly acquired skills, found their way into productive and supportive roles in their communities and local church fellowships.

The first *Ecole Ménagère*, i.e., "Home Economics School" was opened late in the decade of the 50's for a few African girls at Djoko Punda under the direction of Miss Irena Liechty. Though the events of 1960 were to abort this effort short of its first full year of life, a direction had been pointed. Training specifically designed for Zairian girls was later revived in another form.

on the ecumenical front

Not only had the CIM entered a new day of inter-station collaboration within its own territory, it was also probing possibilities of broader cooperation with surrounding Missions in projects of common interest and concern. Already in 1952 preliminary discussions had been opened with field personnel of the American Mennonite Brethren Mission (then best known by its acronym AMBM) who by that time were also fielding a growing missionary team as CIM's mission neighbor to the west. Inter-Mennonite from its inception, the CIM field leadership saw no reason why Mennonite missionaries at work as neighbors should not enter into joint projects in Congo which would be mutually beneficial. Confronted, as were both Missions, by the sudden opportunity of subsidy for their educational programs, the task of quickly training qualified teachers was formidable. By pooling missionary teachers from both Missions, a quick start could be made.

To be sure, some uneasiness regarding this proposal was expressed both in Congo and at home. Coming from across the Mennonite spectrum of North America, some of the CIM and AMBM missionaries carried memories of local histories of their home communities where barriers of bias and historical tradition between Mennonite churches stood high and firm. How could a joint project such as this have a happy ending in Congo when it would not even be thinkable at home? But such minority opinion, though firmly stated, was diplomatically deflected. Working agreements were soon spelled out on the field and approved by the Boards at home. Mennonite Brethren teachers and students soon found their way to Nyanga and a joint teacher training program was under way. Not only did it prove to be a success, it turned out to be only the first of a series of projects in which the neighboring Mennonite Missions were to collaborate. (23)

In the fall of that same year, CIM and AMBM opened a second joint venture, that being a missionary children's school at Kajiji (pr. kah-JEE-jee), an AMBM station along the Angolan border which had been acquired from the UTM. With both missions experiencing rapid growth in missionary personnel, the question of children's education was swiftly posed. Once again, a problem that promised to be difficult for each Mission separately found a solution in the launching of a joint effort known as *Ecole Belle Vue*, i.e., "the Beautiful View School," so named for the panorama offered due to its elevation amidst the rugged terrain around it. This school, staffed by a mix of CIM and AMBM missionaries, experienced steady growth in enrollment until it was suspended by the turbulence of political independence in 1960. (24)

The inter-Mennonite nature of the CIM team was to be yet further expanded and enriched in the course of the 1950's by the advent of the Mennonite Central Committee (MCC) sponsored PAX program for young men who filed for alternative service with local draft boards. The first contingent of what was to be a long series of volunteers arrived in Congo in April 1955. (25) They came not only from CIM's supportive network at home but also from a broad spectrum of the North American Mennonite community. To these volunteers were soon added young teachers sponsored under the MCC "Teachers Abroad Program" which quickly came to be known by its acronym TAP.

partnership extended still further

Not only did CIM reach out to fellow Mennonites in this era, it also soon began to take on an international flavor. Among the stations of the UTM founded by Alma Doering was one called Wamba Luadi (pr. WAH-mbah LWAH-di). Also located in an isolated, forested area near the Angolan border, it lay to the southwest of Kikwit and was accessible only via difficult bush roads which were often impassable during the rainy season. A Swiss couple, Max and Ruth Germann Grütter, and a member of the Swiss Landlai Deaconess Order, Miss Berta Mangold, were among those who were deliberating not only the fate of their station but also their own future in Congo amidst the post-war dissolution of their Mission. Well aware that their former UTM station Kamayala had affiliated with the CIM, they initiated dialogue with CIM personnel regarding the possibility of service with this Mennonite Mission. Assured by CIM field leadership that they were both needed and welcome at Kamayala, they applied, were accepted and appointed for service to that station. (26)

There was yet another dimension of CIM's ecumenical stance which came into focus during the 1950's. Already in the 1920's CIM had become a full member of the Congo Protestant Council. Capital investments were made along the way in the establishment and development of a Protestant Guest house in Leopoldville, originally known as the Union Mission House or UMH. It later was known as CAP, the French acronym for *Centre d'Accueil Protestant*, or Protestant Welcome Center. CIM also helped fund the construction of a Protestant Press in the capital originally known as LECO and later renamed CEDI. When in 1953 a series of circumstances left LECO desperately short of staff, CIM responded to an emergency appeal from the LECO Board and appointed Bob and Mabel Busch Bontrager, a first-term educational couple at Djoko Punda, to join the staff there. In 1960 Bob was appointed director and served in that capacity until their departure to pursue graduate studies in the States in 1965. A precedent was set that would see still other CIM personnel assigned to this inter-mission enterprise for administrative roles in later years. (27)

But it was with the large mission neighbor to the east that CIM would across the years knit the greatest variety of cooperative relations. The American Presbyterian Congo Mission (known locally by the acronym APCM) had pioneers on the scene in south central Congo two decades before the arrival of CIM's Lawrence and Rose Haigh in 1912. As a matter of fact, it was aboard a ship bound from the Congo Free State to New York City in 1906 that Alma Doering, returning home from a term of service on the Swedish Baptist field in Congo, met a fellow passenger Dr. William Sheppard. An Afro-American, he had engaged in pioneering exploration for the Presbyterians in the early 1890's. Long hours of mid-ocean conversation ensued during which Dr. Sheppard succeeded in impressing Doering with the need of south central Congo which was without witness to the Gospel. As a result of this encounter, Dr. Sheppard was invited in May 1912 to address the newly formed Congo Inland Mission Board. His presentation played a decisive role in the Board's decision to send its first couple to explore the area so passionately described by Sheppard. Early on, CIM missionaries experienced warm hospitality and much practical help at the hands of the APCM personnel along with encouragement to become their Protestant mission neighbors to the west - - a proposal which soon became reality.

A powerful common denominator for both CIM and APCM was their ministry among the same two ethnic groups, the Tshiluba speaking Lulua and Baluba people. CIM missionaries quickly benefitted from the excellent Tshiluba grammar and dictionary early worked out by the Presbyterian pioneers. There were, further, the school materials and an early translation of the Bible which were of invaluable help. Though standing in two different streams of church history and theology, the Mennonites and Presbyterians shared some broad, solid convictions and goals as regarded their common area of endeavor, e.g., the urgency of evangelism and church planting, early attention to education and humanitarian ministries and the high priority given to the translation, publishing and dissemination of Scripture and Christian literature in the language of the people.

By the mid-50's, two joint endeavors were already in place. There was LIPROKA (*Librairie Protestante du Kasai*), a publishing and distribution center of Tshiluba Christian literature, and a Regional Tshiluba Literature Committee which had the dual roles of screening/approving new Tshiluba manuscripts and of proposing new literature related projects for the large Tshiluba-speaking area shared by the two missions. Other joint projects were to follow in succeeding decades.

a rapidly growing African Church

With the advent of government funds, missionaries at all eight CIM stations aggressively developed networks of regional outposts where evangelistic and educational thrusts were integrated into a single program. Located as centrally as possible to clusters of surrounding villages, teacher housing and classrooms were built with the cooperation of village chiefs and parents. One of the buildings was always large enough to serve as a chapel, as well. Religious instruction was given on a daily basis from first grade onward. Scripture memorization and the study of a simple catechism were also incorporated into the curriculum. In the absence of trained evangelists, the school director or a senior member of the teacher team served as the convener of morning chapels and Sunday services for students, parents and villagers who were all invited to attend. As qualified Africans became available, a full time resident evangelist was assigned to such centers and, in time, pastors as well. Itinerating missionaries spent weekends at such centers for the multiple purposes of checking on teachers, giving exams, interviewing baptismal candidates while providing counsel and encouragement to the outpost teams. Sundays, on such weekends, were days of high activity often starting with an early morning trip to the local stream for the baptism of new believers followed by a lengthy worship service in which delegations of Christians from surrounding villages took part. Later in the day there was a second service during which new members were welcomed into the fellowship of the church. The activities were typically brought to a close with the celebration of communion.

Though often with modest formal training, the Africans have consistently been the primary and most effective evangelists of their own people from the earliest days of CIM history. With a perfect command of their maternal tongues, a firm grasp of tribal lore, proverbs and world-view and their marvelous gift for memorizing Scripture, they share their own faith and experience of grace in terms that are both clearly understandable and convincing. Whereas in the 30's and 40's annual church growth was noted by the hundreds, once launched into the 50's new believers from year to year were literally recorded by the thousands. The long dreamed of integration of educational and evangelism efforts had at last become a reality. (28)

a new generation of shepherds needed

But as great as had been their success, by the decade of the 1950's the scene was swiftly changing around the graying generation of church leaders who had become the pioneers of the Congo Mennonite Church. Their appointments to roles of church ministry had not been due to their modest formal training but rather because of their demonstrated love for the Lord and their innate pastoral gifts. In the semi-isolation of their respective areas among barely literate people, they had been dramatically effective. But a younger, better educated generation was now growing up around them who represented a new mix of needs, questions and potential. Attempting to train a new generation of shepherds for the African Church on a piecemeal basis at different stations could no longer suffice.

Already in 1951 a formal proposal was made by the field evangelism commission that a Bible Institute be established for the entire field and that it already be in session the following year. As it turned out, it took two more years to follow through on this recommendation but the new school (known as the *Institut Biblique*, or the IB in its acronym form) did open its doors in the fall of 1953 under the direction of Waldo and Abbie Claassen Harder. The initial class was made up of older, seasoned pastors and their wives who had already served the Church with distinction. Some following enrollments also included older couples, but gradually each new class was comprised of younger applicants whose lives and devotion to the Lord and their Church spoke well for their declared sense of call to a pastoral vocation. A new building was dedicated in February of 1956 at Kalonda Station. This Bible Institute has seen scores of couples enter, study and return to their rural settings to become shepherds of clusters of village Christians who comprise a large majority of the total membership of the Zaire Church. For years successive graduates of the Kalonda IB, as it has come to be known, have provided the backbone of the Zaire Church's pastoral staff and have wielded major influence for good.

CHAPTER 5   FERMENT IN AGING WINE SKINS

African leaders: roles and status

During the first decades of missionary presence, African leaders emerged who had close ties with their missionary counterparts. With modest formal education, theirs was literally on-the-job training as understudies of the missionary pastors and evangelists with whom they traveled and associated closely. Frequently their relationships became enduring ones of mutual confidence and respect. Typically the first generation of church leaders would refer to their missionary colleagues with terms of respect and affection such as *Muambi*, the Tshiluba term for teacher, or *Ngambi*, the Giphende word for a person of wisdom, or simply *Tata*, the Bantu noun for a literal biological father or one considered to have such importance and status in their lives and experience.

As regarded terminology used by missionaries to denote fellow servants of the church, the tendency emerged early to use French words such as *catéchiste* (i.e., a teacher of Scripture and Christian beliefs), *évangéliste* (a preacher or evangelist), or *Pasteur Assistant* (an assistant pastor). The use of the qualifying term "assistant" was primarily due to Belgian insistence that the term "Pastor" be reserved for those candidates who had achieved the theological studies associated with that term in Europe. There was further, however, the missionary sense through the 30's and 40's that a full fledged pastoral ministry within the Church of Christ was not one to be either lightly sought or accorded. The fact that the imposed probationary status accommodated the resolute Belgian stance on this topic was likely not without significance. In the light of this situation, as the decade of the 50's opened, missionaries were by and large still screening most of the baptismal candidates and officiating at most communion services and weddings - - this primarily on one or another of the eight mission stations.

Annual missionary and African conferences were still scheduled separately, back to back, at the same location. Although missionaries met alone to conduct mission business, some missionaries were always present as delegates to the church conference where, in the manner and mood of that time, they wielded clear influence on decisions made.

As the 1950's dawned, the sense of identity of the African Christians had primarily to do with the CIM and the station where they had been baptized. Thus it was that comments were frequently heard such as *Tuetu tudi bietu bena CIM* or *Esue tudi enya Nyanga*, i.e., "We are CIM people" or "We are Nyanga folk" either of which identified them not only geographically but, more importantly, as CIM Protestants. (1)

Question may well be posed from the perspective of elapsed time as to why yet in the early 50's missionaries and Africans alike could still be comfortable with the restricted roles accorded African pastors and with the lack of a more sharply focused church identity on the part of the African Christians.

In all fairness it needs to be understood that relations between early missionaries and a first generation of African leaders clearly reflected the powerful pressures which were at work in the Congo of that time. As for the question of identity, there was still at that point of Congo mission/church history a deeply shared concern to present as cohesive and broad a Protestant community as possible before the all-pervasive power and influence of Catholic missions and a prejudiced colonial government. To highlight denominational identities was seen not only as counter-productive fragmentation but also as meaningless and confusing for colonial authorities as well as for the Africans themselves.

But all of this was soon to change.

ferment within the status quo

As in all other areas of Congo life and experience in the decade of the 50's, missionary/African and mission/church relations were being submitted to new scrutiny - - however subtle and indirect it was. Teachers of a new generation were now being graduated from the mission schools whose education, command of French and general world awareness surpassed that of the graying generation of church leaders around them. They had a way of asking questions regarding the Christian faith which seemed not to occur to simple village folk. The Bible Institute at Kalonda had already produced its first graduates. As they returned to their home areas to take up their pastoral duties, was it to be, they discreetly wondered, with the same restrictions on their roles as before their departure for study? And what about Mission matters? Had the time not come for Africans to be invited to and consulted in missionary gatherings just as missionaries were invited to and consulted in church conferences? Here and there an occasional introspective voice could be heard: "Who are we really? Are we just simply *Bena CIM* (i.e., CIM people) or *Bena Kilisto*?" (i.e., the people of Christ).

There were, furthermore, questions of a different kind also being whispered here and there in CIM area. Up and down the Kasai River, where Lulua and Baluba folk had lived together for decades, there was word of a secret association being formed which brought together Lulua youth and elders for heated discussions regarding their future amidst a growing and often better educated population of their Baluba cousins.

No longer were the Congolese living in the isolation of the pre-war days. Little transistor radios had made their way into the most remote corners of the land. Not only were they tuned to the Leopoldville station. It was discovered soon enough that with equal ease they could also capture French programs coming from a variety of other sources outside the Congo. It was a rare rural area which did not have one or two former Congolese soldiers who had fought with Allied troops and who were ready to add their explanations and interpretations to what was being heard on the little pocket radios. And there were the persistent rumors brought by those who visited the urban centers that in some places Congolese were quietly meeting to envision the unthinkable: an independent Congo freed of Belgian presence and authority.

But in spite of these muted signals, the CIM missionary personnel was immersed in, preoccupied with and excited by a literal explosion of Mission projects. Missionary staff was growing dramatically. Church membership was angling sharply upward on the statistical graphs prepared annually for the home board. New chapels in permanent materials were rising across the CIM landscape as local clusters of believers enthusiastically gathered building materials from the valleys and forests around them. New projects of witness and ministry so long dreamed of were finally becoming reality. So many good things were happening that it was difficult to focus much attention on the possibility of an uncertain future.

enter a visionary trio

Providentially, there were three key individuals who emerged on the CIM scene early in the decade of the 50's who were to greatly influence the course of CIM mission/church events to follow. Already in 1949 veteran church planter and longtime Nyanga missionary, Frank J. Enns, had been appointed as a Board representative on the field. In North America Rev. C.E. Rediger, who had served the CIM with devotion for 14 years (1936-1950) as executive secretary/treasurer, was in 1951 replaced by Harvey A. Driver who was initially named "corresponding secretary-treasurer." In 1954, Albert Neuenschwander, an insurance executive from Ft. Wayne, IN, concluded a 20 year stint as the CIM Board Chairman and was replaced by Dr. Milo A. Rediger.

In the course of the 1950's, these three men were to jell into a leadership team of remarkable wisdom and vision. Frank and Agnes Neufeld Enns from Inman, KS, first arrived in the Congo in 1926. They were assigned to Nyanga Station which had been officially opened only three years earlier. "Uncle Frank," as he came to be affectionately known and respected by his fellow missionaries, was the only person in CIM history privileged to start his missionary career at a new station, find a young church in its infancy and spend his entire missionary career (2) in one place. There have been other CIM missionaries who have served as many or more years but who, in the process, were reassigned once or more to different locations thus breaking the continuity and cumulative knowledge of and impact on a single area which Enns achieved. His grasp of CIM history, his insight into the African world-view, his sense of the pulse of African church life and his lifelong openness to new ideas and methods qualified him in a unique manner for his critical role as the Board representative in Congo in the 1950's.

H.A. Driver of Wauseon, OH, brought a broad mix of training and experience to his new role of leadership. Trained in education and anthropology with experience as a public school teacher and administrator, he came to the CIM office as a continuing partner in a thriving turkey growing, processing and distributing business of the area. Well-read, well-traveled and energetic, he merged his business acumen with a deep commitment to his church and the Biblical mandate for Christian mission.

Milo Rediger joined the trio of leadership as a Christian educator with a heart for Christian mission. The academic dean of Taylor University of Upland, IN, he was respected both for his scholarship and for his compassionate interest in the world around him. His role with the Mission was to have an impact not only on the CIM of the 50's but on the student body at Taylor as well. An informative glimpse of the perspective he brought to his new role as CIM Board chairman is found in an article dated 1952 in which he outlined what he considered to be a "Trinity of Central Themes": one central historical fact, the resurrection; one central doctrine, redemption and one practical result, salvation. In a concluding summary he wrote: "It is true that the revelation of God and the teachings of Jesus challenge the intellect and call for deep thought as well as a careful organization of knowledge, but we must never forget that, first of all, Jesus Christ came into the world to redeem mankind, to seek and to save that which was lost. He is a teacher, a miracle-worker, a healer, yes even a King - -but above all, He is the Savior. Let us arrange our system of doctrine with the idea of redemption at the center, else we shall miss the main point of the whole truth." (3)

As for Harve Driver, the straightforward and unambiguous style which was to characterize his leadership was early in evidence. In April of 1951 in his first reporting to the CIM Board as the newly appointed secretary, he said: "I have been surprised at the large number of young people both from the affiliated Mennonite bodies and other groups that are inquiring about the possibilities of service and offering themselves. Our young people are challenged by the stirring events of our day and are doing something about it. I hope you brethren ponder that significant statement." (4)

Driver made his first trip to Africa in 1952. It is not without significance that he sought out Orie Miller of MCC renown to be his traveling companion. He also prevailed on Dr. C.B. Bowman, a surgeon and brother of missionary Dorothy Bowman Schwartz, to join them while carrying an 8 millimeter movie camera. Bowman exposed extensive footage of film and upon his return put together a travelogue which was entitled "Along African Paths" which Driver put to considerable use. As regards Miller's participation in the travel, having seen the opportunities and challenges of the Congo first hand, within three years this area became the destination of a growing contingent of MCC-sponsored voluntary service personnel assigned to work under the administrative cover of the CIM.

In the course of his first travel in Africa, Driver sent back periodic updates on his experiences and perceptions. These afford an interesting Driver perspective. For instance: "Leopoldville has all the appearances of a rip-roaring frontier city. Buildings going up, streets being paved, traffic lights installed, policemen everywhere, cafés and bars plentiful. . . . There is a beautiful post office, a large bank building and a telegraph and telephone complex about half finished that reminds one of the Pentagon in Washington. The new white section is being planned very carefully and the buildings now there and those planned indicate that some day Leopoldville will also be one of the most beautiful cities of the world. Along with all of this so-called progress there are the usual gambling, vice and treachery. Prices are high and many opportunities for the traveler or newcomer to be 'taken in.' Why all this activity and interest in the once dark continent? It's the incentive of the centuries. Gold, wealth, material advancement, the resources and wealth of nobody knows how rich Congo and Equatorial Africa are being discovered and new surprises every day. Disease and unhealthful conditions are largely conquered. In fact, I met a Swede last night who told me he actually came here for his health. It is strange how our health is so closely related to our economic successes and failures." (5)

Written later from Nyanga Station there was the following: "One is impressed with the almost desperate eagerness of the faces of these people, their craving for knowledge, facts, learning and then expectancy of something great about to happen to them as they receive this that they are craving for. One is also deeply moved as the missionary faces these expectant people in the church, in the school room, at the dispensary and out in the path or from his veranda, at the overwhelming challenge and his deep desire to break through the superficial expectancy of the native, to the true spiritual soul need he has. Missionary work to a pagan people is not easy. It is not even humanly possible to do. A missionary must depend on the supernatural and definite divine guidance. Could YOU be a missionary with these demands?" (6)

Having observed the African scene first hand, Driver's letters to the missionary staff began to contain such pithy comments as: "Join and lead the revolution that is coming; do not allow yourselves to be overrun by it. - Our problems are many and varied. Let us be sure that we are under His wings. - These are stirring days there. I almost envy you who are in the middle of it. - Keep your goals clearly in view and your eyes on the Lord." (7)

Board chairman, Milo Rediger, made his first trip to Africa in the summer of 1954. He went as member of a study group that toured several sub-Saharan countries and the Middle East under the leadership of Dr. Emory Ross, then the executive secretary of the Africa Committee of the National Council of Churches. His personal itinerary included some time in the Congo. In his reporting to the CIM Board, he centered his comments around five basic observations: 1) Time is running out ". . . at least for certain kinds of missionary activities. . . . We need to face the fact that we're going to have to build the framework of our future in Africa through our educational work, our medical work and other applied aspects of Christianity. We must strengthen these social frameworks within which we carry on a primarily evangelistic task . . . . We need to think of these aspects of our work not just as arms of it - - they are the work." 2) The missionary must expect to give his work to others. "We must discover and train and counsel and trust African leaders for the church, for the schools and for other responsibilities. . . . We must always be working toward the establishment of a church, of a society that is deeply and definitely Christian and that will continue to grow if the missionary does or must leave. And if he does leave, he must go somewhere else and start the process over again and work at it again on an indigenous basis." 3) Select and prepare our best young people. "The world mission of the church is really the first business of Christians everywhere and I expect to issue a call, wherever I have the opportunity, that I hope will challenge the best among our young people to take on the biggest of all jobs, of all professions, of all vocations, within the framework of Christian society. . . . I think we Board members need to keep in mind . . . the fact that we have one of the most important enterprises in operation now and it takes the very best in personnel." 4) The great need for Christian literature. "It is imperative to provide more literature and more reading materials for the people whom we are teaching to read. . . . What we are struggling with, I am afraid, is the possibility that . . . we'll find the Christian missionaries teaching the Africans to read and then the Communists furnishing them the reading materials. . . . Somehow we must encourage and facilitate the development and the distribution of things for the African mind to absorb that will foster and cultivate and support and defend the Christian way of life." 5) Better business organization and management. "The CIM has developed within the last few years into what is now big business. These jobs which used to be done in off-and-odd hours by our missionaries - - this matter of book work and accounting . . . is now of such proportions that it can't be done that way. . . . It seems to me that plans and personnel for centralized purchasing and distribution of materials and for adequate accounting are appropriate in the Lord's business if we're going to give a good account of our stewardship . . . ." (8)

With this sort of admonition and counsel coming from the home end, F.J. Enns, in his quiet manner, was effectively at work in Congo. Already in 1950 the decision had been made with African leaders to separate the annual church and missionary conferences so that each would have their own dates, meeting place and program. The first such missionary conference was held in December 1950. The first solo church conference was convened in May of the following year with 46 Africans and 17 missionaries present. As Enns worked with mission/church relations, there were two issues which preoccupied him: the decentralization of church structures and some degree of integration of mission and church. With regard to the first, Enns recognized that the CIM church community needed to be weaned from its tendency to identify with one or the other of the large station churches as the locus of church life and activity of their areas. This tilt was reflected in the African's perception that these centers were the most appropriate setting for receiving baptism, for celebration of weddings and to receive communion. There was the further sense that any decision of consequence affecting the life of the church needed to wait for the annual conference to which each station church sent delegates.

In an effort to change this, Enns came to the African conference of 1956 with a proposal to decentralize church functions and responsibilities. In brief, the concept was to consider each station and the area it served as a district within the broader church and that each district have its own annual conference each with its own locally elected officers and its own particular agenda appropriate to its own setting. Given the large areas encompassed by such districts, a logical next step was the creation of regional conferences within each district structure, each again with its own officers and agendas. Once thoroughly discussed and understood, the plan received the enthusiastic endorsement of all of the delegates present. Consequently, already the following year, conferences in all eight newly created districts were organized and held in the month of April. African Christians took immediate ownership in this new decentralized church structure. It was to become the means of bringing the reality of and responsibility for the Congo Church to the level of the village believers. In time, quite a number of the regions themselves became districts as the church administrators sought to reduce these large areas into smaller units which could be overseen by pastors who had to depend on bicycles or the occasional passing truck for transportation.

The second issue - - and the more sensitive of the two - - was that of initiating some shift in mission/church relations. The socio-political setting of the late 50's was more and more one of rising expectations. Delegates to the annual church conferences were making it increasingly clear to their fellow missionary delegates that the status quo was no longer satisfactory. There was clear impatience and an eagerness to pioneer with some new models of mission/church and missionary/African relations even as was being done in the area of church structures. Although there was some reluctance amidst the broad and rapidly growing missionary family, "Uncle Frank" wisely prodded for action. An initial modest initiative was to invite two African pastors, Kazadi Matthew from Djoko Punda and Ngongo David from Nyanga, to join the missionaries at their annual conference in 1955 where they were invited to sit in on all activities including the business sessions. Following the conference, the two pastors offered a gracious if bland acknowledgment. Speaking for both of them Pastor Kazadi read a short statement in English: "We are happy to be with you in your conference. This is the first time we from the Congo Church have been with you. I thank the people of the Board in America and I thank the missionaries also. Pray for us that the people of Congo will have the power to carry the work of the church to spread the Gospel of our Lord and Savior Jesus Christ." (9)

The following year four pastors were invited to meet with the missionaries. In addition to Pastors Kazadi and Ngongo, Pastors Falanga Elie from Mukedi and Kadima Isaac from Mutena also shared in the occasion. When the missionaries convened for their annual gathering in 1957 at Mukedi, they were joined by eight pastors. While they did not have the right of vote, they were encouraged to ask questions and to voice opinions as they wished. One interesting sidelight of that gathering was a baptismal service held early on a Sunday morning in which 29 local Africans and four missionary children were baptized by three African pastors. (10)

Pastor Kazadi emerges

It was also in 1957 that Pastor Kazadi Matthew began to acquire prominence on the CIM mission/church scene. He was already an outstanding leader in the Djoko Punda district. Born shortly after 1900, the son of a Muluba sub-chief and his eighth wife in a village in the East Kasai some 500 miles southeast of Djoko, he was baptized Catholic as an infant. He later followed a half-brother who was in the employ of CIM missionaries at the Djoko Punda station. At first resistant to Protestant witness because of his Catholic background, he at one point wrapped his meager belongings into a bundle and left the station. In a little dugout canoe halfway across the Kasai River he became aware of what he later described as "an irresistible calling in his heart" which caused him to turn back and go to Rev. Lawrence Haigh (one of the pioneer founders of that station) to seek help in satisfying his heart's yearning. Of that experience Pastor Kazadi later said: "From that time on, I have been a new creature and have never turned back from following and serving the Lord." (11)

During his time on the station at Djoko, Kazadi worked for some ten years for various missionaries while finishing both the primary education and the Bible School training offered at the time. Soon thereafter he became a teacher in the station Bible School and a church worker. While on the station he also celebrated a Christian marriage with a young woman named Elizabeth - - a relationship which was to endure throughout their long, fruitful lives. Ordained as a pastor in 1941, he was sent to a river port to the north of Djoko called Basonga (pr. bah-SAW-ngah) to open a new mission outpost. He was the first African in CIM history to do so on his own. Located amidst a huge oil producing palm plantation established by the British Lever Brothers, he soon came to the attention of Africans and Europeans alike. Not only did he plant a thriving church at Basonga but during his time was able to establish a cluster of outposts around Basonga in care of African teacher/evangelists.

Upon his request he was transferred closer to the Djoko station where he again opened a new regional church outpost in the district. Under his leadership a chapel was built of permanent materials. One Christmas season in the late 1950's, the special offering gathered by his outpost group of believers exceeded that of the older, larger church on the station. By this time Kazadi had also succeeded in establishing a personal coffee plantation in the rich forest soil along the Kasai River. Cultivation and harvesting were done by local people he employed for that purpose. Although he himself was a Muluba, he employed Lulua workmen.

Across the years, as a Djoko Punda pastor, he became a familiar figure at church conferences as the head of his district delegation. A gifted preacher, he was a frequent conference speaker. Tall, slim, possessed of a keen, inquiring mind and a sense of humor, his careful statements and probing questions in conference sessions became an early trademark. When in 1957 missionaries and the home board felt it was an appropriate moment in CIM's history to sponsor the first fraternal visit of a Congo church leader to North America, there was immediate consensus on all sides that Pastor Kazadi should be accorded that privilege. In the course of six months he traveled widely, speaking in churches and gatherings of the constituent conferences, leaving a very favorable impression everywhere he went. (12)

To accommodate his travel schedule, the CIM Board convened its fall sessions a week early. During the sessions he was asked to address the Board on the general topic of the emerging Congo Church. Following are excerpts from his presentation: "The early Christians and early missionaries in our land had very much trouble. . . . Our own people in the villages tried to get us to return to the idols and to frighten us away from the worship of the true God. . . . I went out often to help the missionaries in the villages and it was very difficult to get people to come. . . . But gradually more and more came to accept the Gospel and as we persisted in preaching and in witnessing they saw that we really had an experience in our hearts which helps us and took away our fears, and they also wanted to accept this. . . . Forty people in our mission in the early years made the nucleus of our church. They banded together; they remembered they had now received something worthwhile to worship and which gave them inner peace and a new satisfaction. And soon there were 40 more, and then more. . . . There are still the same difficulties and the same problems today but we who are left who saw the beginning are very happy because we have a larger number and we do not feel so alone."

He then continued by saying he wanted to make six statements regarding his Church in Congo: "l) We worship God and Jesus Christ. 2) We remember that we are a new family, a new tribe, and we always look for new fellow believers. 3) We try to help ourselves in small ways - - building chapels, welcoming/inviting new people to our churches and helping each other as believers in material and spiritual ways. 4) We are becoming stewards; we are learning to give and to tithe. 5) We admonish each other in the things of the Christian life. 6) We are a Church of prayer."

The African pastor then concluded his presentation to the Board by observing: "Many people in America have asked me since I have been here that if the missionaries would have to leave Congo, what would happen to the Church there? I have thought about this very much and my answer is that the Church will always remain in Congo no matter what happens."

Why this optimism and confidence? His summarized reasons were: "l) because Jesus is in our hearts; 2) because the Holy Spirit is in our lives; 3) because the Bible is in our hands and 4) because the Church of Christ in Congo is a fact and it will go on." (13)

Kazadi left the States on January 3, 1958, and returned to the Congo via Ibadan, Nigeria, where he attended the inaugural meeting of an All-Africa Conference of Churches as the delegate from his own Church.

This occasion brought together representatives of the Protestant church from 25 different Afri[c]
of which 60% were Africans. Pastor Kazadi's ecumenical horizons were still further broadene[d]
same year he traveled with missionaries, as delegate of his Church, to the annual meeting
Protestant Council.

the Brussels World Fair

Upon arriving back in the Congo, Pastor Kazadi found excitement running high at the Kalonda Bible
Institute and the Nyanga Teacher Training School. Via the channel of the Congo Protestant Council, the CIM
had been invited to send one of two singing groups to represent the Congo Protestant community at the World's
Fair to be held in Brussels, Belgium, in July of 1958. (14) CIM missionaries Lodema Short and Allan Wiebe
collaborated in selecting a nine-man chorale comprised of seven students from the Nyanga school and two from
the Kalonda Institute one of whom was an ordained pastor. (15) Accompanied to Belgium by Short they sang
three times a day, four days a week at two locations at the Fair and were available for visits in Belgian homes
and for programs in area churches the rest of the time. On one occasion, after listening to a program of song
and witness given by these young men, an observer was heard to say: "This Fair is filled with the wonders
produced by man's hand, but this is what God has done." At the conclusion of their five week visit to Belgium,
they returned to Congo, some to continue their studies in the fall, others to begin their teaching assignments
as graduates of the Nyanga training school. All expenses for their travel and stay in Belgium had been totally
covered by the Belgian government. While all of these events were received with approval and appreciation
on the part of church leaders, both the demeanor and tone of conversation clearly conveyed the sentiment on
their part that still more needed to happen in the area of mission/church collaboration.

old patterns under scrutiny

Frank Enns, CIM field chairman and field board representative, clearly agreed. Already in his 1956
annual report to the home office he wrote: "In the area of church and mission relationships, responsibility and
leadership must increasingly be transferred from the mission to the church. Here we are feeling our way. In the
past the missionary conference and its committees have done the mission business. Beginning last year we have
invited African church leaders to participate in our conference. It may well be that in the not too distant future
we will find it best to have an enlarged mission-church council take over the mission business. At first,
representation from the missionary group would probably be the same as that from the African church but
eventually it would decrease in proportion"

"But there are steps that can be taken now: 1) Have more African representation on conference
committees. 2) Give chairmanship of the church council [on stations] over to church leaders where that has
not yet been done. 3) Have regional church groups take responsibility for adequate participation in church
services and other church activities and in instruction classes of religion. 4) Have these church groups also
become responsible for necessary help to the old and needy in their circle and for the construction of chapels
where that is necessary." (16)

A year later in his 1957 field report Enns wrote: "While the mission carries on activities still too
complex and expensive for the Church to take over, still the two have the same goal: the salvation of souls and
the building of the Church of Christ. The more integrated the two become, the less friction there will be and
the more effective will be our witness. . . . Several of our committees now have African representatives. In
these committees the African contributes considerably to the proper understanding of the problems and the
reaching of a solution. That cannot be said of his part in the large missionary conference with a crowded
program in English . . . ." (17) By the fall of 1958, not only were there church leaders invited to attend the
missionary conference, but some were also requested to sit with missionaries on various working committees
in consultative roles.

Encouraged by the favorable African response and the positive participation in such varied settings,
missionaries in a session of the CIM Field Committee in early 1959 determined to involve Africans in this top-
level policy and decision making body as well. (18) The initial effort was made with one representative from

each of the eight stations on the occasion of the 1959 Congo Mennonite church conference held at Banga. However it was soon realized that this was too small a representation and that there was insufficient time during an already crowded conference program for a meaningful launching of such an important venture. A subsequent decision was made to invite two African representatives from each of the eight stations to meet with the missionaries in their 1959 conference at Kalonda.

Regarding this initiative, Field Chairman Enns wrote: "The subject was introduced . . . the afternoon of July 29 when Waldo Harder led a discussion period on 'Trends and Aims in the Establishment of an Independent Church of Christ in Congo.' In diagrams Mr. Harder showed our missionary conference set-up on the one hand and that of the African Church on the other. The problem now confronting us was how to merge the two into one whole that would allow for the progressive transference of leadership and responsibility from the mission to the African church." (19)

Allan Wiebe, the new Conference Chairman who the previous year had been chosen by the missionaries to replace retiring Frank Enns in this capacity, appointed an ad hoc committee to bring some proposals for action to the conference session. (20) The committee returned offering two possible options: 1) to plan for the creation of an integrated annual conference with African and missionary representation from all departments of each station plus delegates from the regional church centers, or 2) to appoint a standing integration study committee which would report back to both conferences another year. These two proposals clearly reflected the fact that there was no clear consensus within the mixed study committee as to how or how fast to move forward with change nor how radical such change should be.

It is easy from the perspective of elapsed time to reflect critically upon the hesitation and reluctance that many missionaries manifested in the summer of 1959, surrounded as they were by much evidence of rapid, revolutionary change not only within the Congo but across black Africa as well. It should not be forgotten, however, that a majority of the missionaries were by then post-war personnel who had applied to the CIM with a clear sense of call and a readiness to make Christian mission their life's vocation. After work, perseverance and perspiration, they had finally acquired some language skills, had made adjustment to life in a tropical setting and had begun to make a genuine contribution in their areas of competence. In that Congo summer of 1959, they had again met in missionary conference highly motivated and excited about the future. There was yet so much that could be done. This conference, like others before them, had been a high point of the year with wonderful fellowship, stimulating Bible studies, upbeat reporting on all that was happening. A special feature had been the dedication of a beautiful new church that had been finished on the station by Archie Graber and his African crew just in time for the conference. It had been packed with Africans, missionaries and 30 Belgians of the area who had responded to invitations to share in the festivities.

On the broader Congo inter-mission front, CIM's stature was also growing. CIM missionary V.J. Sprunger had just been appointed as interim secretary of the influential Congo Protestant Council. A steady series of financial grants continued to come from the colonial government for CIM's expanding educational and medical services. Furthermore, church growth was surging as mission and church collaborated in a blend of educational and evangelistic outreach. (21) With the roster of CIM missionaries topping 100 adults for the first time, several new initiatives for which both mission and church had been calling now seemed within reach.

An autonomous African Church a clear goal? Of course. A transfer of authority from missionary to African hands an unquestioned objective? Certainly. Working toward the time when the African Christians would be the masters of their own house? Without question. But was this really the time for radical, sudden change? Would it not really be a bit premature to plunge ahead with some of the ideas being bandied about in this conference? Was there sufficient experience and maturity on the part of their African coworkers to assume dramatically heavier responsibilities so abruptly? Was it even fair to propose it yet? What of the Mission's institutions? What of the projects still on the drawing boards?

But it soon became evident that there was a tide of sentiment which required that some clear-cut agreements be reached before the Kalonda conference was brought to a close. The ad hoc study commission was ordered to reconvene for further deliberation. The proposal which was ultimately drafted and approved by the Kalonda conference of 1959 read as follows: "To accelerate church-mission integration, Congolese and missionaries are to have equal representation on administration committees on all levels. The annual missionary conference is to be replaced by a totally integrated conference which is attended by one African and one missionary delegate from each station for each of the main departments of work. This will result in a delegate body of approximately sixty missionaries and eighty Congolese." (22)

"Conference is over and we return to the respective stations to our duties and the opportunities of the coming year." So wrote the annual letter committee. (23) Unstated in the letter but realized by all as they scattered was the fact that they had been participants in a historic event - - the last CIM missionary conference of its kind. In reporting home to the Board, the official correspondence announced that the first newly envisioned integrated mission/church conference was to convene in July of 1960.

That conference was never held. The swift pace of Congo's political events overtook both the Mission and the Church. But at Kalonda, the summer of 1959, directions had been pointed and commitments made which would have unknown positive impact on the future of CIM's work. The decision had come none too soon.

CHAPTER 6   IN ANTICIPATION

"DEE-pah-ndah"

This word, in some form or other, was heard everywhere in the Congo. The magic date had been set. On June 30, 1960, the Belgian flag would be lowered and a new Congo flag would replace it at the top of countless poles across that immense country.

Spelled *indépendance* in French, it came out in a variety of ways in the many dialects of the Congo. In CIM territory, it was "DEE-pah-ndah." An electric excitement and anticipation was in the air - - deep in the bush as well as in the urban centers. No conversation among Congolese during those days was complete without reviewing the latest news about "DEE-pah-ndah." If in better-educated circles there was some grasp of what political independence meant and implied for their country, in the immense rural areas there was much less clarity. On one occasion a cluster of village women were overheard engaged in their typical good natured banter with the cook of a missionary family as they bargained for prices for their basins of tropical fruit. Soon someone brought up the subject which was on everyone's mind. "But," one of the women wondered, "how will we know it when it arrives? Will it be in a bottle like kerosene or in a sack like salt?" But whatever its shape or nature, it indeed was coming and with passing time the anticipation grew. No speculation as to the wonders which would accompany it was too exaggerated to believe; no promise, however wild, was called into question. And, best of all, when it arrived, the increasingly resented ruling hand of the Belgians was to be lifted and they, the Congolese, would at long last be masters in their own household. Why wouldn't everyone be tingling with anticipation?

the building pressures

What, exactly, had brought about this dramatic change in the course of events in the Congo? What had come of the Ten Year Plan so confidently launched a decade earlier by the newly-appointed Minister of Colonies? The Belgians could not be accused of having been half-hearted in pursuing their plan. At great expense they had helped fund rural medical services, often in collaboration with Christian Missions. As a result, little dispensaries dotted the landscape where Africans could receive care and medications for the more common tropical health problems. The Belgian regime had pushed with single-minded purpose the development of an enormous primary school system across the land, this also in cooperation with missionary personnel. As a result, toward the end of the decade of the 50's, the Belgian Congo had one of the highest literacy rates in all of black Africa.

But as laudable an accomplishment as this was, once through primary school, the African student discovered that opportunities for further study were limited to a variety of vocational training courses. While the French and British colonial regimes had long since been forming an educated elite in their colonial areas by providing secondary and university training for gifted African students, the contrasting Belgian philosophy was to bring the general population slowly along together. On their time table, the 50's was the decade of massive extension of a primary school system. There would be ample time in the future, they believed, to develop secondary education for the general population and, eventually, even university level training. (1)

Young King Baudouin visited the Congo in 1955, midway through the Belgian Ten Year Plan. Hosted, among others, by General Emile Janssen, the supreme commanding officer of the *Force Publique*, he told the King that the Congo "was inhabited by 13 to 16 million blacks who were perfectly innocent of political ideas and asked for no more than peace and well being." (2)

In the course of his travels the King was also introduced to a number of the "medal chiefs", i.e., Africans who had been chosen by the colonial regime for their compliance to replace traditional chiefs who resisted the curtailment of their traditional authority. School children were often found along the path of the King's itinerary chanting in French, *"Vive le Roi Baudouin Ier"*, i.e., "Long life to King Baudouin the First." And for those who found the French phrase too difficult, a Kikongo phrase served equally well, *"Buana*

Kitoko," i.e., "Good or Handsome Chief." The Zairian journalist and author, Buana Kabue, in summarizing that 1955 visit of the Belgian King, states tersely that after a visit of 28 days, the Belgian King returned home having understood nothing. (3)

There was, however, a small minority of Belgians who by 1955 were no longer comfortable with their stance in or their reporting of the Congo scene. One such was a Professor Van Bilsen. With the credentials of a doctor in law, he was a member of the teaching faculty in the Institute of Antwerp where courses were given for people destined for colonial service in the Congo. A liberal Catholic, he produced what he called "A 30 Year Plan for the Political Emancipation of Belgian Africa." (4)

While this document stirred tremendously negative reaction on the part of many of his Belgian compatriots within the colonial department, it was received in a much more favorable light in Leopoldville by an organization known as ABAKO (pr. ah-BAH-koh), i.e., "The Association for the Protection of the Culture and Interests of the Bakongo." Originally launched in 1950 as a vehicle for preserving and furthering the interests of the Bakongo people of western Congo, by 1954 its president was a man named Joseph Kasavubu (pr. kah-sah-VOO-boo). Under his leadership, ABAKO soon began to take on clear political overtones. Taking Van Bilsen's document as a point of departure, ABAKO leadership produced its own "manifesto" in which they called for immediate and total emancipation in all areas of their lives. (5) White colonial reaction was one of consternation and calls for the prompt suppression of this radical organization. But the government, wishing to cultivate the collaboration of such emerging politically aware leaders, responded with caution. Other events of political import were not slow in following. On June 16, 1957, there was a soccer match between a white team and a black team in the Baudouin Stadium in Leopoldville. With seating for 100.000 people, the place was packed. The Belgian referee was seen as having favored his white compatriots throughout the match and thus contributed to the defeat of the black team. Angered by this perceived injustice, many cars of Europeans were stoned as they left the area afterward. For the first time, white/black violence had erupted in Leopoldville. (6)

In response, the Belgian colonial authorities opted for a stick and carrot approach. Major armed force maneuvers were mounted in the copper belt region of Katanga to the southeast in August. In October, Belgian naval units appeared for the first time in the estuary of the Congo River. Then in December, municipal elections were held in the major Congo cities. In Leopoldville, it was ABAKO and its President Joseph Kasavubu who garnered 62% of the votes cast. On April 20, 1958, he was officially installed as the Mayor of Dendale, an African quarter of the city. To the dismay of the Belgian officials he made this the occasion to state openly: "The founding of democracy will be a fact only in the measure to which we obtain autonomy. There is no democracy as long as there is not a general vote. We ask for general elections." (7)

The most powerful impetus for political change, however, was likely triggered by the historic itinerary made by General Charles De Gaulle through the French areas of West Africa. Recognizing that the colonial era was coming to a close, he chose to take the bold initiative of offering a clear political choice in region after region: to become participating autonomous member states in a French community "founded upon the equality and solidarity of the people composing it" or to sever all ties with France and to go their independent path. The result was that an overwhelming majority of these former French colonies accepted the offer to become autonomous member states of a new political community with strong diplomatic, financial and commercial ties with France. (8) The dramatic and historic significance of de Gaulle's tour, which at one point brought him to the capital of Congo Brazzaville just across the Congo River from Leopoldville, was not lost on the political activists under Belgian rule.

ten year plans notwithstanding

The 1958 rush of events continued. In that same year Brussels was the site for a World's Fair. No stone had been left unturned to make it a memorable success. Hundreds of Congolese of note were invited to attend, this at the complete expense of the Belgian Government. Among them was a young journalist who had been sent as an observer and reporter by his paper, *Actualités Africaines*, i.e., "African Current Events." His name: Joseph Mobutu. The Congo and the world were destined to hear a great deal about him in the years to come.

But if Joseph Kasavubu of ABAKO was already a well known figure, he was not to have the political arena to himself for long. A tall, slim, energetic man with excellent gifts of communication was also circulating widely in Leopoldville and was making his views known. Originally from Stanleyville in the northeastern Congo, Patrice Lumumba (pr. loo-MOO-mbah) had for a time been a postal worker in that city. There he was much in the public eye and was chairman or secretary of no fewer than seven associations. In particular he was the chairman there of "The Association of *Evolués*" (a term used at the time to indicate "civilized" and upwardly mobile Africans). (9) Thomas Kanza, a Zairian author who probably knew him as well as anyone observes: "He appeared to me as the living symbol of mankind's struggle for emancipation. His powers of observation and oratory impressed all his friends and aroused fear in his critics. . . . His thirst for knowledge was insatiable; he was a voracious reader and to a large extent self-taught." (10)

Charged in 1957 with embezzlement of Post Office monies, he was sentenced to two years of jail by a district court. Upon appeal, his case was transferred to Leopoldville where it came to the attention of influential Belgians of a liberal bent. Whatever the nature of the indictment brought against him, the sentence was reduced to six months which he had already served. Upon his release, Belgian friends secured a public relations position with the Bracongo Brewery in Leopoldville whose product "Polar" was in decline. Turning his gifts of persuasion to his new assignment, he succeeded in turning the commercial fortunes of this drink around, making it the town's most popular beverage. Lumumba's interests, however, extended far beyond the Brewery which employed him. While fully aware of the rising political ferment in Africa and within his country he differed with ABAKO and its president Kasavubu in his convictions and visions. In 1958 he launched what was called *"Le Mouvement National Congolais,"* i.e., "The National Movement of the Congo," which quickly became known by its acronym MNC.

There were immediately some fundamental differences to be noted between the two groups. ABAKO tended to be regional in its focus with a primary concern for the political future of the Bakongo people who had a long, rich tribal history. The MNC cast the political future of the Congo in broad, national terms. Further, ABAKO quickly made clear its pro-Western stance and its sympathetic support of the powerful Catholic Church. The MNC, on the other hand, talked of non-alignment in international affairs and reflected a wariness of the Church if not an outright anti-clerical bias. Very quickly, before any sort of overt political activity was legal in the Congo, these two men and their fledgling parties became opposite poles around which powerful competing and conflicting forces came to swirl, this to the future detriment of that country.

In 1958 Nkwame Nkrumah (pr. nkwah-may NKROO-mah) hosted the first All-African People's Conference at his capital in Ghana. Both Kasavubu and Lumumba wanted to attend but Belgian authorities were not eager for them to go. At the last minute, Lumumba and two companions were granted travel documents. Kasavubu was denied such papers on the pretext that his inoculation certificate was not in order.

Ghana had been granted its political independence by Britain in 1957. Nkrumah lost no time in convening fellow Africans to discuss the revolutionary change which they believed to be imminent in sub-Saharan Africa. Not only did this gathering give him opportunity to meet leaders from outside his country, it also gave him an occasion to state his own opinions: "The Congolese people are aware of the winds of freedom blowing over the African continent. Their long dormant political consciousness is beginning to assert itself and will do so even more in the next few months. The people are solidly behind us in our struggle." (11)

Upon their return to Leopoldville, Lumumba and his traveling companions called a public meeting on December 29, 1958 to report on the Accra Conference. The boisterous crowd which assembled numbered several thousand people. Lumumba seized this opportunity to announce that his organization, the MNC, would now follow a new political program based on the Accra resolutions. He stated, furthermore, that their independence as Congolese people was not to be regarded as a gift from Belgium but as their fundamental right.

It was just a week later on January 4, 1959 that local ABAKO leaders scheduled a meeting at the YMCA building of the Kalamu section of the city. Joseph Kasavubu was to speak. Belgian authorities hearing of the meeting announced, at a late hour, that the meeting was canceled. With no time to circulate word of this cancellation, ABAKO people were posted at all entries to the building to announce the news as people came. This was the spark which lit a powder keg of violent reaction. Over a period of some 48 hours, over 50 people were killed and more than 200 injured. Stores were looted, cars overturned and burned and streets barricaded.

The Belgian community in Congo as well as the government in Brussels were thunderstruck. How could something like this have happened when all their readings of the Congo situation were so optimistic? Locally, in Leopoldville, response was swift. Kasavubu, the ABAKO president, and his entire executive committee were apprehended and jailed - - this for "inciting racial hatred." In Belgium, however, cooler heads interpreted the event for what it was: the bloody signal that, optimistic ten year plans notwithstanding, irresistible change was upon them. On January 13, 1959 the Belgian government issued what was called a *Déclaration Gouvernementale*, a document approved by both Houses of the Belgian Parliament. The crux of the statement was that the Congolese people would be led gradually and progressively toward their independence. A Zairian writer reflecting on that event states: "To the Belgians, 13 January 1959 was a historic and painful day marking their capitulation, the day on which they gave up hope of keeping the Congo indefinitely under Belgian colonial rule." (12)

back in CIM country

As political events tumbled one upon the heels of the other in Leopoldville and Brussels in early 1960, CIM activities were also proceeding at full speed both in Africa and in North America. Under the vigorous leadership of Harve Driver, the CIM headquarters had been moved from south-side Chicago to south-side Elkhart where an office and guest quarters were built adjacent to the campus of the newly founded Associated Mennonite Biblical Seminaries. Vernon and Lilly Bachman Sprunger had just been forced home by her illness. Since the treatment of her cancer promised to be prolonged, Vernon was asked to join the office staff to help cope with the steadily growing volume of administrative work.

And in the Kwilu and West Kasai regions of the Congo, CIM missionaries were hard at work as they sought to come to grips with the far-reaching commitments made during their Kalonda Conference the previous dry season. Committee agendas were now being established in consultation with church leaders and places for meetings were being chosen with a view to travel and hospitality for larger groups comprised of both Africans and missionaries. All the while, daily newscasts from both within and without the country were being closely monitored. While there was a sense that the explosion of political activity in Leopoldville had clear implications for the mission and church community across the Congo, it was all still quite remote. There were other developments, closer at hand, which were of more immediate concern.

smoldering tribal animosity

The Kasai River is more than a diamond rich geographic feature of south central Zaire. For the African population of the area it has also come to be a time-honored tribal boundary between the Baphende, Chokwe and Bashilele people to the west and the Lulua to the east. This occupation of the land had not been without problems. Baphende oral history notes tribal immigration from the southwest into the Kwilu and Kasai as they fled the slave trade along the Atlantic Coast, a migration which had brought them into conflict with the Chokwe people. Compromise, however, had been reached and tribal land rights mutually agreed upon west of the Kasai by the time the first Europeans arrived.

On the east side of the river, a different tribal history had unfolded. The Lulua and Baluba, two major tribal groups of the Congo, had become intermingled all the way from Luluabourg in the east (now known as Kananga, pr. kah-NAH-ngah) to the Kasai River in the west. While both groups trace their histories to a common ancestor and, with slight variations, share the common language of Tshiluba, they nonetheless claim different traditional homelands. As for the Baluba, what is known today as the East Kasai (with its capital

Mbuji Mayi, known as Bakwanga during the Belgian era) is claimed as the land of their forefathers. Meanwhile, the Lulua people lay ancestral claim to a large area in what is known as the West Kasai. Given the shared blood lines and common language, there has historically been much intermingling, something which was considerably accelerated in the mid-to-late 1800's by the Baluba flight from slave raiders who came into the Congo from the east coast of Africa. Added to this was the Baluba tendency to pursue opportunities of education, job training and employment. As missions and commercial activities began to locate along the Kasai River in the late 1800's and early 1900's, the Baluba early responded to the opportunities opened to them. All of this contributed to a growing Baluba population among their Lulua kin. Their attitude had always been: we are of the same blood; there is plenty of room for everyone. In the meantime, however, the Lulua remained by nature deeply attached to their agrarian way of life. They, consequently, tended to remain in their rural villages tilling their fields, tending their livestock and remaining by and large content to let their Baluba kinfolk populate the early mission schools and apply for the early jobs with the white people of the area.

This tribal mix of people of the West Kasai lived together amicably enough under the ordering administrative hand of the Belgian administrators. But once the tribal leaders began sipping the heady wine of promised independence, the inevitable questions were quickly posed: "What will this mean for us as a people? Will our traditional tribal frontiers still be honored? Will we still be able to live in and preside over the earth in which the bones of our forefathers lie buried? Will we still be the masters of our tribal houses?" For none of the tribes of the Congo was this a more burning question than for the Lulua. For generations they had exercised benevolent tolerance toward their Baluba kinfolk from the east. However now they were coming to an alarming realization. If political independence was coming to Congo, this would mean Congolese government officials - - not only in distant Leopoldville and Luluabourg but even in Tshikapa. Realizing that there would be many Baluba candidates for positions in local government service, the haunting prospect of suddenly finding themselves locally under the authority of their kinsmen from the east roused both apprehension and fury. An organization called "*Lulua Frères*," i.e., "Lulua Brothers," mushroomed across the Lulua countryside. With chapters in nearly every village of any size, Lulua youth were meeting to discuss their future as a people. Rapidly a broad consensus emerged in the late 50's: to tolerate the ongoing presence of their Baluba kin among them was to risk humiliation. Something had to be done.

Across the river to the west, the Baphende were also engaged in animated discussion. If independence comes, will we not find ourselves under Lulua authority given the size of their population and their traditional dominance of the east bank? Thus it was that within a matter of months, what had been a tranquil inter-tribal area became a hotbed of secret meetings, rumor and intrigue. Events which began to unfold cut directly across the young, emerging Mennonite Church and its leadership.

missionary readings of the situation

The rapidly accelerating pace of events did not go unnoticed by the CIM missionary team. Excerpts from missionary letters to the home office late in 1959 are interesting. From the perspective of elapsed time, it can be seen that the reporting provided both accurate observations and missionary hopes which subsequent events were to thwart: "There is a tenseness in evidence which appears to be waiting only for a spark to ignite it. . . . The Society of Lulua Brothers, which is an organization in the Lulua tribe and comprises the majority of our local people, is gaining strength and is aiming at political superiority. . . . We have been grieved to see its crippling effect in the lives of many Christians. We need to be much in prayer for them." (13) ". . . We find ourselves in a very different Congo than we have seen heretofore. This land stands in need of your prayers as perhaps never before. . . . The Christian population is praying earnestly for peace in their land and they are faithfully looking unto the Prince of Peace." (14) "A Congo-wide uprising against authority does not seem likely at present. Therefore we have good prospects to be able without much interruption to continue, like Paul, 'Preaching the kingdom of God, and teaching those things concerning the Lord Jesus Christ with all confidence, no one forbidding him'. . . . Missionaries with the proper training, attitude and a Christ-like spirit will continue not only to be welcome, but in demand, I believe." (15) "The riot in Leo[poldville] in January 1959 started Congo's economic downturn. Businessmen are selling out and returning to their homelands. Big companies with extensive interests in the Congo, however, insist they will be able to come to terms with any new

41

government or governments and thus continue operations. . . . It is impossible to know just what the future will bring into the lives of our missionaries for an unexpected turn of events might be in the offing; however it is unlikely that any situation will arise in the foreseeable future which would involve a general evacuation of our missionaries." (16)

seizing the revolution

Harve Driver was a man on the run. Executive Secretary of the Congo Inland Mission, he traveled continually in the interest of the Mission, this with the full support of his wife, Priscilla Liechty Driver, a soft-spoken, courageous woman who was fighting a long, losing battle with cancer. In addition to his administrative responsibilities with the Mission, he maintained his partnership in a turkey processing business. Notes to his Congo missionary personnel came from many places and in many forms; sometimes hastily hand written on note paper, sometimes more lengthy epistles produced on a typewriter. Whatever form they took, they invariably carried messages and admonitions that came straight from both the shoulder and the heart. One such found its way to the field in early 1960 which had for its focus the efforts at serious mission/church integration amidst rapidly escalating instability of the Congo scene. Said Driver: "Let's not hang our harps on the willows but let us seize the revolution and turn it into a day of victory for God and his church." After expressing his love and support for the CIM team he concluded: "I want you to be a winning team. . . . God bless you and keep you victorious and fighting the good fight." (17)

It was in this mood and spirit that the CIM Board decided to send a major delegation to the Congo in late 1959. Composed of R.L. Hartzler, Reuben Short, Orlando Wiebe and Lotus Troyer, it was led by V.J. Sprunger from the home office. A delegation ? Now? In the present circumstances? At what cost? To do what? Even to the Kasai? Such were the questions which quickly began to surface at the home end. Driver quickly responded: "These are all legitimate questions and we are not surprised at their being raised nor critical of you who raised them. The delegates themselves had these same questions on their hearts and minds. The week before leaving disturbing word came with every Congo mail: terrific tribal fighting involving CIM Christians; villages burned at Mutena; at Tshikapa and Charlesville, women and children flee to mission stations and missionaries' homes for refuge and safety; mission hospitals and dispensaries filled with wounded people. BUT MISSIONARIES AND AFRICANS WANT YOU TO COME AND HELP NOW. After reading these heart rending messages there was no holding back of our delegates. Danger, difficulties or peril brought new meaning and urgency to their mission. Not the material matters of property and organization but real things of the Spirit have gained the primacy and urgency. So in this spirit they left their loved ones on January 29. . . . They are in the midst of their mission. Let us continue to be faithful in intercessory prayer for them and their families and for their mission to Africa. And for our Congolese brethren that the prophecy might be true of many of them, 'These are they which have washed their robes and made them white in the blood of the Lamb and have come out of great tribulation.'" (18) The one major purpose of the trip as stated by Board Vice-President and delegation member Reuben Short was "that of effecting some kind of mission-church program relevant to the changing times in Africa." (19)

In preparation for the special "integration conference" which was to take place at Djoko Punda beginning February 25, 1960, a thorough and intense itinerary was laid out for the delegation which would give them opportunity to meet with African church councils and missionary personnel at each of the eight CIM stations and to sit with a newly integrated mission/church administrative committee in a two day working session. At the Djoko Conference, the integration plan worked through at Kalonda the previous July was to be the basic working document for review, evaluation, amendment and eventual approval. Afterward, the delegation members were also to meet with all missionary personnel in a time of review and counsel in the light of whatever decisions and commitments had been made.

It was particularly during the two-day meeting of the integrated administrative committee that enlightening exchanges took place between the delegation and African church leaders. As reported by Board Chairman Lotus Troyer, one exchange went as follows: "At the Mukedi Conference one of the African brethren said that they as Congolese were as our children. In response to the question 'How soon do you anticipate maturity?' they replied, 'It is not when new tasks are first assigned that we see capabilities becoming evident. No one heard much about Joshua's strength and wisdom until after Moses died.'" (20)

Troyer reported a further exchange: "'If we take the proposed path of integration, would you have people capable of assuming responsibilities such as the work of the legal representative, for instance?' we asked. After a brief moment of consultation together they replied, 'We have people ready. We have no one who could step in and do it immediately without help but even Mr. Sprunger and Mr. Wiebe needed help at first in their work. We will need help too, but we can learn.'" Troyer continued: "The meaning of their words was clear and unmistakable. They want position, they want to try their wings but they also want help to pick up the pieces when trouble develops. This is not wrong for it has been a God-given urge in people throughout all history. The directive is clear and the missionary must find himself within new roles which will call for greater understanding and more counseling than the situation has called for up to this time."

When the delegation asked African leaders whether the time had come to recall missionaries from the Congo and reassign them elsewhere, the response was: "Independence gives us a certain amount of fear because we do not realize all it means now and will mean afterward. But the promise of your standing behind us and helping us during this time of independence and afterward gives us strength and courage." Troyer concluded: "As we listened, it became increasingly clear what path it was that we were to take in the mission to the CIM field." (21)

Fellow delegate R.L. Hartzler also recognized the enthusiastic readiness of the African leaders to move ahead, but he also picked up on another dynamic which caused him and the delegation concern. In his trip diary he noted that "eagerness on the part of the Africans and hesitation on the part of the missionaries came into evidence. A way between the two must be found." (22)

Djoko '60

Djoko Punda, known as Charlesville under the Belgian regime, was the site of the first CIM station established in 1912. Not only has it had the distinction of being the historic springboard of CIM work in the Congo but it also became the site for two mission/church consultations both of which had major impact upon the unfolding story of the Mennonite Church there. The first such consultation was that of February, 1960. (23)

Having concluded an extensive itinerary and dialogued with scores of missionaries and African leaders, the Board delegation arrived at Djoko prepared to review the plan for integration already submitted the previous summer. The African Church was fully represented by delegates from all eight of the CIM regions. They obviously came with keen interest and expectations mixed with some apprehension and guardedness. It was, after all, not every day that they had the opportunity to sit with representatives of the home board to express their views and desires. Furthermore, what was being proposed was a radical shift from the patterns of the past.

a question of identity

The integration plan presented by the working committee at the Kalonda Conference of 1959 became the basis for dialogue. While there was considerable discussion on details, the broad thrust and intent of the proposal was never seriously called into doubt by anyone. What did, however, quickly surface was the realization that it was high time for the African Church to face the issue of its own identity and to adopt its own official name. On this question there was early agreement. One after the other the older church leaders rose to speak. Essentially they said: "You have been sent by the Mennonite Churches of North America. You, our fathers and mothers in the faith, are Mennonites. What you have taught us is the Mennonite faith. We can be nothing other than Mennonites." After writing several possible names on the chalk board, "The Evangelical Mennonite Church of the Congo" was adopted as their first formal name. The acronym EMMC was eventually shortened to EMC. (24)

As the consultation unfolded, the African leaders submitted four requests to the CIM delegation: "l) That a document be prepared and signed by the American delegates to commemorate this historic decision. (25) 2) That, eventually, it be envisioned that a mission station be turned over entirely to a Congolese staff. This would mark a first step in the progress of the Church toward final autonomy. (26) 3) That the heavy responsibilities remain, for the present, the responsibilities of the missionaries but that immediate steps be taken to assure an apprenticeship for competent Congolese in all areas of work. 4) That measures be taken to assure a study and drafting of a new constitution of the Church as soon as possible." (27) (28)

As proceedings drew to a close on the last day, delegation member R. L. Hartzler stood to his feet. Capturing both the significance and the emotion of the moment he stated that the delegation felt much as a father giving a beloved daughter in marriage to an eager young suitor. They had watched her from birth, sought to nourish and instruct her and had learned to love her dearly. The delegation was now giving her into new hands. Their only request was that the bride be loved, cherished and cared for as she deserved to be. There was a long moment of silence as the Africans pondered what was both a plea and a prayer adroitly clothed in the sort of allegorical form which they themselves loved to use. What more was there to say? Hartzler had said it all. (29)

In his reporting to the CIM Board, Reuben Short stated: "The Conference closed with a note of triumph, expressions of friendship and goodwill, singing a hymn together each in their own language, and prayer. A new page in the development of the church at home and abroad was now written." (30)

The following July was set as the time for the first conference to be held under the newly integrated mission/church structure. Nyanga Station was to be the setting. Although swiftly developing events in the Congo ultimately prevented that conference from ever being held, the CIM's initiative to introduce dialogue with African leaders on issues dealing with the identity and autonomy of their church was now a matter of record. That fact was to stand both Mission and Church in good stead in the stormy months to come.

CHAPTER 7   THE VOLCANO BLOWS

the Kasai crisis deepens

The optimism and elation of the delegates to the Djoko consultation were quickly tempered by the political realities they found as they returned to their home regions. Particularly was this the case for those returning to areas along the Kasai River. As a matter of fact, Belgian authorities had a few weeks earlier imposed martial law in the West Kasai where Baluba and Lulua villages were intermingled, this in an effort to suppress the growing frequency of violent clashes between tribesmen armed primarily with bush knives, spears, fire and bows and arrows.

Tension had by this time also disrupted the CIM schools in the Kasai. Under mission administration, students and teachers were normally scattered among the stations according to their needs and abilities - - and this irrespective of their tribal identity. Now, suddenly, amidst escalating instability and wild rumors which multiplied from day to day, any student or teacher outside their traditional tribal setting became increasingly fearful. Missionaries consequently found themselves organizing caravans of vehicles to escort Africans back to the safety of their home territories. In some situations during those tense days, it was only the missionaries' presence interposed between angry villagers and fearful students that avoided harm.

Thinly veiled threats against the Baluba population circulated everywhere. The burned villages and deaths which had already occurred were but a prelude to what was coming once the restraining Belgian hand was lifted. The Lulua people were determined to control their own destiny in the uncertain days ahead, whatever the cost. In the midst of the tension, there were already groups of Baluba people who were seeking ways of making the long trek to the land of their forefathers in the East Kasai. A dismal story of the uprooting of a people with all the attendant problems of violence, material loss, hunger, starvation and death was in the making.

on the national scene

While the CIM community was greatly preoccupied with the political tensions of their own area, events at national and international levels were moving at express train speed. No longer was it a question as to whether there would be revolutionary change in the Belgian Congo. There would. The only questions now were those of procedure and timing.

It is not the assignment of this writer to attempt to elaborate on the intricacies and profusion of political developments which erupted on the Congo scene from January through June of 1960. And yet, some understanding of the twists and turns of events of those days provides helpful background against which to view the experiences which befell the CIM mission/church family during those fateful days. It must suffice to simply list some of the events:

January 20 - February 20, 1960   A "round table" dialogue between Belgian government leaders and the key political figures of the Congo in an effort to program events and envision ongoing relations between the two countries. Although an extensive sixteen-point agenda was worked through, all economic, financial, military and political issues were deferred for discussion at a later date.

The high level jockeying for influence and power among the various Congolese political groups represented at the Brussels consultation was intense. Though on the surface all was calm and amicable, between sessions and during the night hours there was much conferring and maneuvering among the delegates themselves as they sought to return to Congo in a position of strength.

April 26 - May 16   A second "round table" in Belgium to deal with economic and financial questions, a consultation in which Congolese interests were ill served. Given the great complexity of financial issues dealt with plus the further complication of the vast internationally-funded mining interests in the Congo, it is not surprising that conclusions were reached which, though advantageous to the western financiers, were not well understood by the Congolese delegates present.

Legislative elections across the Congo in April and May, 1960 in the course of which a variety of political parties forwarded candidates both for the newly envisioned House of Deputies and the Senate. Parties supportive of Patrice Lumumba's nationalist views won a majority of seats. Thus Lumumba was invited to form the first Congolese government.

A fundamental difference in political views quickly became a divisive issue. A majority of parties supported the concept of a single Congolese nation under a strong central government while a minority but influential cluster lobbied for a loose confederation of largely autonomous states, each with a large degree of local authority.

Lumumba pulled together a team of Congolese from across the political spectrum to whom he issued ministry portfolios and with whom he hoped to form a functioning, viable government. He, himself, became Congo's first prime minister; Joseph Kasavubu its first president. Among the thirty-some people chosen to serve as ministers in the newly formed government, there were several with whom Mennonites would become all too well acquainted in the days ahead: Antoine Gizenga, Christophe Gbenye, Pierre Mulele and Joseph Mobutu.

June 30, 1960 was set as the official date for transfer of power and the raising of the flag of the newly independent Congolese State. To Lumumba's great irritation, all matters of protocol for the occasion rested in Belgian hands. King Baudouin of Belgium was invited to grace the occasion with his presence and to make a speech.

the big day

"The Day" dawned amidst tremendous excitement and expectation across the country and in the capital city. A colorful motorcade was formed at the international airport. The King in his limousine was fully dressed in regal attire with a ceremonial sword at his waist. During the leisurely procession of the motorcade toward the city some twelve miles distant, an exuberant Congolese ran beside the royal vehicle and snatched the King's sword from its scabbard. This was only the first of many unplanned events which were to follow.

The official program of celebration of independence called for speeches by the King and by Joseph Kasavubu, the president of the newly born Republic of Congo. When Lumumba learned shortly before the launching of activities that the Belgian organizers had chosen the president to respond to the King's address rather than the prime minister, Lumumba threatened to boycott the entire event! After being strongly counseled by his entourage not to make good on his threat, he decided that he would not only attend but would also make a speech whether invited to do so or not!

Official ceremonies started on time and with much pomp and circumstance. King Baudouin delivered a stirring speech which he began by saying: "The independence of the Congo is the conclusion of a work conceived by the genius of King Leopold II, which he undertook with tenacious courage, and which Belgium has continued perseveringly. It marks a decisive moment not only in the history of the Congo itself, but, I can surely say, of all Africa." (1) The balance of the speech was devoted to an overview of the Belgian accomplishments in the Congo, offers of continued Belgo-Congolese collaboration and his prayer for a prosperous and happy future for the new Republic.

President Kasavubu, in his turn, read a manuscript which had been heavily influenced by his Belgian consultants and which was very conciliatory and appreciative of the contributions made in the Congo by the Belgians in the past.

a departure from printed program

At this point the celebration took a surprising turn. The Congolese chairman of the occasion was Joseph Kasongo, a man who had been elected to the coveted position of President of the Chamber of Deputies thanks to the influence of Lumumba. Being thus politically indebted to him, Kasongo was in no position to deny Lumumba his unscheduled turn at the podium. Striding to the microphone Lumumba launched into a blistering commentary on the Belgian colonial history and the injustices imposed upon the Congolese people. Early in his presentation he made reference to the struggle for independence which led up to that day and then continued: "This struggle, involving tears, fire and blood, is something of which we are proud in our deepest hearts, for it was a noble and just struggle which was needed to bring to an end the humiliating slavery imposed on us by force." This was only a beginning. Much more along the same vein followed before he brought his "speech" to a close. (2)

A shocked King and Belgian community reacted angrily feeling that it had been a deliberate insult directed toward them. Even many Congolese felt that although much of what had been said was true enough it, nonetheless, had been a most inopportune time and discourteous manner in which to address issues which were very important to them.

The irritated King threatened to return directly to his plane and leave for Belgium without even spending the night there. After a flurry of consultations between Congolese and Belgian advisors, it was agreed that the King would remain for the rest of the festivities and Lumumba would later propose a conciliatory toast to Royalty and the Belgians at a banquet to be held in the gardens of the *Palais de la Nation*. A major breach of etiquette was papered over and a potential rupture of diplomatic relations during the first hours of Congo's independence was averted. But Belgians and Africans were provided a startling glimpse of Patrice Lumumba the man: an angry patriot, a charismatic leader, a spell-binding orator and gifted organizer whose naive idealism and inability to adjust to the political realities around him would soon lead to his downfall.

new roads from old graveyards

Meanwhile, up-country, in the Kwilu and Kasai Provinces where the CIM family lived and worked, excitement also mounted as the end of June approached. Among the rural village populations, the conjecture about the nature and meaning of "DEE-pah-ndah" for them had taken some surprising turns. One popular understanding was that one of the immediate and direct results would be an automatic reversal of white/black roles. Whereas before, most of the stores, vehicles and fine houses were in the hands of white people, after independence these all would automatically fall into the hands of Africans. The means by which this was to take place took a variety of forms. Here and there enterprising Congolese were quietly selling "raffle tickets" which after Independence would determine a redistribution of white wives among ticket holders. Other preparations for the day took a turn more in keeping with traditional African beliefs and world-view. From somewhere came the word that all pigs were to be disposed of and any chickens or goats with any white coloring had to be slaughtered. Much carefully reared livestock was thus eliminated over a period of a few months. Any failure to comply with such preparation could mean that "DEE-pah-ndah" might be prevented from arriving.

Further word among the villages had it that any box filled with leaves or grass and set aside would, on the morning of June 30, be full of crisp new money. There was a resultant run on the supply of metal boxes in stores in all directions. When there were no more to be found, boxes were fabricated from wood or split bamboo. The box itself was not important; making provision for independence morning was. And there was more. In some areas there were extensive clean-up projects of traditional burial grounds with wide new roads cleared by villagers leading directly from the midst of the burial areas to their villages - - this in preparation for the return of their ancestors from the dead on independence morning with truckloads of goods which would be divided among them.

On the mission stations, a variety of festivities were organized. One CIM decision had been to give small cash gifts to every individual in the direct employ of the Mission or the missionary. A program for a special church service on each station on June 30 had been distributed and followed. In some places, special festivities were also organized by local government and political leaders to which missionaries and church leaders were invited. Mission representatives were typically received in a gracious manner. On most stations before, sundown on the 30th, a mix of missionaries and Congolese church leaders had a meal together to celebrate the day and to pray together for an untroubled transition into the new Congo ahead.

As notes were compared on July 1 via the mission short-wave radio network, there was word here and there of isolated incidents of Congolese belligerence vis-à-vis the Mission community. At Mukedi, particularly, there had been poor response to the morning church service and a generally surly attitude. (3) In the Kasai, the Tshikapa government representative had asked that given the tribal tension along the river, Nyanga, Mutena and Kalonda stations come on the air five times a day to keep in touch. Reports from other corners of CIM territory reported calm. It seemed clear that where there had been tension or misunderstanding prior to June 30, the activities of the week did nothing to ameliorate them. Where there were good relations, the big day had brought no change.

immediate political problems

While Joseph Kasavubu and Patrice Lumumba were trying to settle into their new roles as leaders of their country, major problems quickly erupted. In all of the pre-independence dialogue which had taken place in Belgium and Leopoldville, one festering irritation had never been addressed, that being the role and command of the *Force Publique*, the armed police force of the country. From its inception, all of its officers at every level had always been white. June 30 came and went without change. This in part reflected an unspoken assumption on the part of the Belgian authorities that in spite of political independence, there would be some degree of ongoing Belgian presence, influence and even authority in some spheres of public life. As a matter of fact, Lieutenant General Janssens, the commander-in-chief of the *Force Publique* went out of his way to underscore his intention to maintain the status quo by inscribing in bold letters on a chalkboard in his headquarters: "After Independence = Before Independence." (4)

It was on July 4 that Lumumba in an early session of the Council of Ministers raised the issue of the grievances of the Congolese armed force and the urgent need for a complete overhaul of the *Force Publique* which clearly implied the dismissal of Lt. General Janssens. Unable to secure a clear consensus on the part of his ministers, an ambiguous communiqué was issued which angered both Janssens and the troops - - Janssens because of the clear implication that drastic change was long overdue, the troops because the change long awaited had not materialized even under a Congolese government.

In a matter of hours there were disturbing rumors that the *Force Publique* was threatening revolt. Lumumba and Kasavubu responded by convoking a special session of the Council of Ministers at the nearby Military Camp, Leo II, in order to meet and dialogue directly with the angry troops. The meeting was convened with a two point agenda: "the Africanization of the leadership in the army and the general maintenance of order." A series of actions were taken. First the troops, invited to elect their own camp commander, chose Adjutant Justin Kokolo. The Ministers then appointed Joseph Mobutu, Lumumba's personal secretary, as Chief of Staff of the army, gave him the rank of Colonel and charged him with the oversight of the reorganization of the army and its command. It was further decided that the Minister of Defense would name a Congolese to replace Janssens who was to be formally dismissed and expelled from the country. (5) Appeals were made for calm and discipline while the Council of Ministers continued to work on the laws and structures for the country's security forces.

While locally the soldiers seemed disposed to respect the decisions made and admonitions given in their camp that day, in Thysville, midway between Leopoldville and the Atlantic coast, and elsewhere, units of the *Force Publique* began taking matters in their own hands. Almost immediately reports began coming in of armed troops apprehending Belgians and other expatriates with varying degrees of menace and demands.

While for the most part reasons given were to search for and confiscate weapons, there were also reports of men being beaten and women abused. Panic quickly followed within the Belgian community. Belgian authorities responded by calling into action special troops stationed at two military camps under their control, i.e., Kamina in the southeastern Shaba area and Kitona situated between Leopoldville and the Atlantic coast. The troops were flown into the major cities across the Congo. President Kasavubu saw this as a regrettable necessity to preserve order. Prime Minister Lumumba, however, viewed this as being an inexcusable violation of the sovereign integrity of an autonomous state.

Barely five days into its newly won political independence, events in the Congo were spinning out of control.

July 10, 1960

It was a normal Sunday morning at Kandala Station. Missionaries and Africans had gathered, as was their custom, in the neatly white washed station chapel for a worship service. Via short-wave radio Kandala people had learned in recent days of unrest among units of the Congolese troops in various distant places. While such reports were heard with concern, no one felt any real apprehension regarding the CIM area. As a matter of fact, the flavor of celebration of independence was still in the air. Everyone was grateful that all had gone so smoothly. Already thought was being given to dry season church activity and the placing of teaching personnel for the coming school year.

It was, therefore, with shock that missionaries and Congolese exiting the church heard the news via the noon short-wave contact of feverish activity at the CIM stations in the Kasai. While the other CIM stations were in rural areas, this was not the case at Tshikapa. The center of the large *Forminère* Diamond Mining Company, it was also the location of an airport, post office and a variety of government offices. As tribal conflict had flared along the River, martial law had been declared already the preceding January and a sizeable contingent of troops brought into the area. During the previous tense months of shuttling Baluba and Lulua teachers and students to safe areas, Kalonda missionaries, Allan Wiebe and Art Janz, had often met military units on the roads and had become known to them.

They, like everyone else, had been monitoring the news casts during those first days of July which told of spreading revolt among the Congolese troops. On Sunday morning, July 10, they decided to go from Kalonda to Tshikapa, across the river, to see what the situation was there. They soon discovered that the large Belgian community was in panic. Vehicles were being loaded as families sought to flee that morning toward the Angolan border some one hundred miles to the south. In the process, some men were being apprehended by Congolese troops and taken into detention.

As Janz and Wiebe sought to return across the river to Kalonda, they too were halted at gun point by soldiers at the bridge. They were curtly questioned. Their vehicle was thoroughly searched. Finally they were permitted to return to the station. Convinced that the local situation had become very unstable and potentially dangerous, Field Chairman Wiebe came on a special 10 AM inter-mission short-wave contact to share their experience of the morning and to direct CIM personnel at all other stations to prepare immediately for possible evacuation. Kalonda and Mutena would need to exit straight south toward the Portuguese town of Ndundu on the Angolan border. All others would need to take the much longer route toward Camaxilo south of Kamayala. This would entail crossing two ferries manned by African villagers but hopefully would risk meeting fewer armed troops along the way.

At Kalonda, as missionary women started packing suitcases and food boxes, missionary men invited Kalonda church leaders for a somber meeting at the Janz home. Sharing their experiences of the morning, they informed the Congolese that they felt it best that they plan for immediate departure - - either yet that afternoon or early the next morning. The station church leaders were deeply troubled at this news and requested a vehicle so they could go across the river themselves to talk with the commanding officer of the Congolese troops stationed there. They soon returned with a Corporal who said he was a Christian. He encouraged them to stay and promised to send several soldiers to guard all their houses that night. Toward evening, however, the Corporal returned stating that the situation across the river was rapidly deteriorating and that he could not assure their safety much longer. He, therefore, advised them all to come across the river in the morning and he would personally accompany them through the city and put them on their escape road toward the Angolan border.

orders to leave

With this development, Field Chairman Wiebe came on the concluding inter-station short-wave contact of the day announcing their departure early the next morning, July 11, and urging any CIM personnel that had not yet made plans to travel to do so immediately. That evening another meeting was held with African leaders at the Wiebe home, this with a noisy contingent of soldiers just outside the open windows on the front porch. It was obvious that they had been drinking. Against the background of their disruptive presence and at the end of a long tension filled day, missionaries, Congolese pastors and station workers tried to come to grips with what was about to happen. Many details needed attention: departmental accounts and cash boxes; keys to buildings, offices, pharmacy; dry season plans for evangelistic efforts with Bible School students as well as continued provision for their rations; church plans for the dry season and school opening in the fall. There was also mention of the first integrated mission/church conference which had been announced for a few weeks later at Nyanga station. What was to happen to that long awaited event? But it soon became clear that the African leaders had but one overriding concern - - the imminent departure of their missionaries. Even though everything was in turmoil and the army officer had urged them to leave early in the morning with his help, was this reason enough to do so, they wondered? Selma Schmidt Wiebe later reported how at one point Pastor Kabangu Tom voiced bluntly what others were thinking: "If you are real missionaries, why don't you stay here and die with us? Would not the Apostle Paul have done that?" (6)

The missionaries shared as best they could their own anguish as they struggled, in that setting, with two primary claims upon their loyalty, i.e., their missionary call and love for the local church on the one hand and their concern for the welfare of their families and particularly their children on the other. "But in the end," Selma wrote, "real love and concern for us was also expressed and the hour of prayer was most heart touching. God was present. Our Congolese brethren left us and we were alone with the drunk soldiers on our porch plus a woman and a crying baby." (7)

Variations of this scene had been played out on station after station during that Sunday in early July, 1960. To the north at Djoko Punda, there had been an early morning mass meeting in the mission village above the station called by a well known local rabble rouser. Missionary Harold Graber called Pastors Kazadi Matthew and Badibanga (pr. bah-di-BAH-ngah) Apollo to share the instructions received that Sunday morning and to seek their counsel.

Reporting on that experience Graber wrote later that "Kazadi was one in whom we could confide and who best understood our situation. After talking with them for some time and seeking the leading of God in prayer together, Kazadi said: 'Yes, I believe it is best that you go and the Lord will bring you back again.' We shall never forget how Kazadi took charge of the situation that Sunday morning. . . . I turned the keys to the various buildings over to the two Pastors and tried to tell them of their new responsibilities and the work they should do until we returned which we expected would be in a few weeks, at least. We told them to move into our houses and take charge of everything. Kazadi assured us that they would do their best. 'We will make mistakes we know but the Lord will help us. We need not do it alone for the Lord is staying with us. You are leaving and do not know what lies ahead of you. We are staying here and we do not know what lies ahead of us. Both of us have the promise of our Master, Lo, I am with you always even to the end of the world. He then committed us to the Lord. He prayed that the Lord would protect us, that He would keep us from sickness and spare our lives.'" (8)

At Banga where the early morning message from Kalonda had been heard, missionaries went to the morning worship service with the knowledge of their impending departure hanging heavily over them. Levi

Keidel observed in later reporting: "The pathos of that Sunday morning worship service is unforgettable. For many of us, funerals had never been sadder. The air was pregnant with the impending grief of a forced separation that nobody wanted." (9)

Keidel further reported that at Nyanga "the pastors (Mazemba Pierre and Ngongo David) were well acquainted with the typical conduct of Congolese soldiers and recommended that missionaries leave for the present." (10)

At Mukedi where the situation had already been tense for months and where a younger group of teachers and medical personnel had become very belligerent in their criticism, the moment of departure produced a mix of responses. Dorothy Bowman Schwartz later observed: "As word spread, the crowd grew. Goodbyes were said. Some were in tears, many were questioning and a few openly hostile. We were relieved to be able to leave in a friendly way and grateful to God for making plain to us the path to follow - - if only for one step ahead." (11)

At Mutena, Lois Slagle would later write: "Both the hospital and maternity were filled with patients. Some needed constant daily care to survive. Additional medicines and medical supplies were in transit but that they would ever arrive, we seriously doubted. For the earnest, understanding and helpful response of our African staff at that time, I shall always be grateful. I shall always have ringing in my ears the question of the African nurses at the maternity hospital, a question that had no answer: 'What shall we do when we are confronted with a case that we cannot handle and the mother will die without help?'" (12)

the exodus

Sunday morning, July 10, found 126 CIM missionary adults and children on Congo soil. 118 of them were scattered across eight mission stations in the Provinces of the Kwilu and the West Kasai. (13) By early afternoon of that day, all missionaries from Djoko, Banga, Nyanga and Mukedi were on the move toward the south or preparing to do so early the next morning. From Kamayala had come word that they would try to stay on long enough to provide a refueling and rest stop for south bound CIM vehicles. And at Kandala, missionaries were scrambling to prepare overnight lodging and food for any who would elect to stay overnight with them.

At Kalonda, the Tshikapa Corporal was as good as his word. Early Monday morning, July 11, he was on the station in a Jeep with a couple of soldiers. He urged missionaries to quickly complete their packing and form a caravan behind him. He seemed nervous and in a hurry. Last minute packages and bags were stuffed into corners and the missionaries followed the Jeep down the hill off the station. In the distance the bridge and military camp, which they would have to traverse, lay plainly in view.

With the Corporal in the lead, they crossed the bridge without incident and began to skirt Tshikapa proper via back streets. Arriving on the main road, they had just begun their southward course when suddenly there was the roar of another Jeep. Passing them it came to an oblique halt in the sandy road ahead of them blocking any further progress. Soldiers jumped out with rifles leveled. Wiebe and Janz got out of their vehicle as did the Corporal. A lengthy and noisy discussion of some 20 minutes followed. The new contingent of soldiers were determined that the missionaries were, in fact, fleeing Belgians and had to be stopped. The Corporal calmly but resolutely insisted that they were not. They, rather, were Protestant missionaries who had brought them the Bible from which they had first learned teaching about independence.

For what seemed an eternity to the missionaries, the stalemate continued - - the soldiers insisting that they turn around and the Corporal insisting that they be allowed to continue. At long last the threatening soldiers removed their Jeep. But twice more the Corporal and his men themselves ordered them to halt their vehicles to discuss among themselves whether in fact they were risking their own lives by aiding the missionaries. It was clear that they were very apprehensive about how they would be viewed upon their return to their camp. At last they reached a point where the Corporal stopped them for a final time. From here, he told them, they would be on their own. "'But before you leave, promise me that you'll pray for us. They'll probably cut our throats when we get back.' The missionaries gave him their promise and also a generous gift for his services." (14) It was with immense relief that after a long tense day the CIM Kalonda staff, hours later, arrived at the Angolan border without further incident.

Mutena missionaries had also left their station that day. Traveling through an area where they were known, they experienced no difficulties. Making a stop at the village of a Mutena district overseer at the last church outpost before crossing the Angolan border, Lois Slagle reported that his prayer, as they parted, would not soon be forgotten: "In his little mud and stick hut we prayed together. In the bewilderment and longing of his heart, he prayed that the Lord would hasten the day when we would celebrate the true independence in the new Jerusalem together. With his prayer ringing in our hearts we crossed over the border into Angola." (15)

The passage of Mukedi missionaries through Kamayala on Monday morning, July 11, triggered uproar amidst the local population. Soon after their departure from the station, Kamayala missionary Mel Claassen was confronted by a mob demanding that he turn over all mission funds and vehicles. Having accused the missionaries of preparing to leave with African property, the local government official came to investigate. He succeeded in calming the crowd but before leaving he advised the missionaries to leave while they could still do so. Reluctantly they too began packing realizing that once they left, no other CIM vehicles would be able to stop for rest or supplies. Angry Congolese threatened that if they tried to leave, they would encounter gunfire. At 9:00 PM that evening they too left. Once off the station, each of the three vehicles were, in fact, fired upon from the roadside brush but the Lord was good. There was no damage or injury.

agonizing decisions

Meanwhile, sunset on Monday evening, July 11, still found a large contingent of CIM personnel at Kandala station in the Kwilu, some 200 miles north of the Angolan border. They were basically the missionaries from Djoko and Banga stations plus one couple from Nyanga. These plus the Kandala staff numbered something over 40 adults and children. All that day the burning question for every adult had been simply: "What shall we do?" The Mennonite Brethren to the west had left their stations that day. The large Presbyterian and Methodist Missions to the east were on the move south into Northern Rhodesia.(now known as Zambia) There was the further knowledge that British and American Embassies were urging their citizens to leave the country. And yet, after much discussion, prayer and consultation with the local Kandala church leaders, the remaining CIM people agreed that barring new developments on the morrow, they would attempt to stay.

On makeshift beds on floor space in different homes, that night passed swiftly for children as they slept the sweet sleep of innocence. But for adults, the night hours passed more slowly as between times of fitful sleep they pondered the implications of the conclusion they'd reached with each other. Periodically through the night there could be heard the roar of Belgian vehicles traveling south along the road skirting the station. At sunrise short wave sets were again switched on. Antennae had previously been hung between palm trees oriented to pick up signals from fellow missionaries now in Angola. Levi Keidel, who with his family was one of the remaining CIM group camping at Kandala, kept a detailed journal of the events of those days. He wrote: "8 AM: Kamayala did not come on the air. Evidently they had left during the night. This meant no gas supply between here and the border. We called for Tshikapa and rejoiced to hear the familiar voice of Art Janz reply, 'We're all safe 100 miles south of Tshikapa. Can't say any more.' Then we heard Dr. Schwartz of Mukedi staff calling us. 'We're at Malange,' he said. 'There are accommodations here for you. Come on.' Good to learn that they were all right. Where's Malange? We found it about 400 miles southeast of us deep into Portuguese Angola. That sounded like a long ways. We decided to sit tight a bit longer."

"10 AM Kajiji (American Mennonite Brethren Station) reported they were pulling out. We put out a couple of calls using the Tshikapa station call letters hoping that Field Chairman Allan Wiebe was listening and would give us some advice. He did come back: 'Get out if at all possible.'" (16)

In view of the missionaries' known hope of being able to camp somewhere temporarily in the Angolan bush and perhaps even shooting some game for meat, someone in low German asked: "What about guns?" Back came the cryptic reply: *Lasse sie dahem*, i.e., "Leave them at home." With that, the signal from the Portuguese transmitter went dead. There would be no further communication with their fellow missionaries south of the border. Those remaining at Kandala were on their own.

There followed yet another round of soul searching as they tried to resolve conflicting sets of responsibilities and loyalties. As children lightheartedly romped on the station under a dry season sun and sky, missionary couples again sat together alone here and there on the station. Once again husbands and wives together searched their hearts before the Lord and prayed for clarity of mind and willingness to accept whatever the Lord's will for them and their families was at that time and place.

In a following meeting with Kandala church leaders, the issue was starkly clear. Both embassies and mission administrators were urging them to leave. Embassy warnings were of small concern. The last instructions received that morning from fellow missionaries and field officers, however, were another matter. At last a painful conclusion was reached: that given all the factors, it was best for the group remaining at Kandala to attempt to follow the others to the border. Keidel again picks up the account: "12 noon. We called several times but made no radio contacts. This meant that all others of our areas had been evacuated. We then announced to anyone who might be listening that we were all preparing to pull out. . . . Kandala missionaries began hastily packing while the first vehicles of the caravan began the 200 mile journey to the border. The one section which gave all of us concern was the Kamayala area where rabid elements were fomenting the villagers against us and at Kamayala's adjacent State Post, Kahemba, where a small contingent of soldiers was stationed."

"The station truck was loaded with fuel, emergency food supplies including several cases of MCC canned beef, extra warm bedding, tools, a few key spare parts, and about 50 suitcases of missionary possessions. . . . Mid-afternoon the Keidels and the Bullers left. (17) The remaining Kandala staff plus the Rockes soon followed in a VW Kombi and the truck. (18) About 20 miles out of Kandala, the Keidels/Bullers discovered that all the leaves but one were broken on a front spring. To continue was to court disaster. Limping back to the station they found all the other missionaries had already gone leaving by a short cut road. Kandala church leaders consented for the station chauffeur, Kamanya Eugene, to load them and their things into the station one-ton pickup and to drive them through the night to a hoped for link up with the rest of the group."

"It was when they reached the border they were informed by soldiers at the barrier that the customs agent was asleep and could not be disturbed. Cars had been going south all night, their drivers demanding his service. He was in a very bad humor. At 7:00 AM we ventured waking him. The soldiers were correct, but by tactful kidding and joking we prodded him to his duties. Forty five minutes later he was parrying with our jokes and completed our formalities. He good-humoredly posed for a snapshot, and as he lifted the gate for us to pass, cried out: 'Be sure and come back soon. We need you.'"

"About three miles across the border we came to a rushing stream. There on the bridge was Glenn Rocke! There in the stream were others, bathing and washing clothes. When they had discovered we were not in the caravan, they became fearful of what might have happened. They decided to camp there on the hillside for the night in hopes that we would still come out. We had a real hallelujah welcome waiting for us. We praised the Lord together." (19)

By nightfall on July 12, with the exception of Bob and Mabel Bontrager in Leopoldville, the entire CIM crew, men, women and children, were scattered in various places in the semi-waste land of north central Angola which was in the grip of its annual dry season.

apprehensive Portuguese hosts

As they crossed the border into Angolan territory, CIM people found sympathetic and courteous help on the part of the Portuguese officials and settlers alike. In some cases they were taken into private homes; in some cases floor space in public facilities was made available. Via short wave radio, officials alerted government posts along the way ahead regarding the evacuating mix of white people from Congo. And, of course, daily reports were going to the officials in Luanda, the seacoast capital of Angola. While Belgians who were also evacuating south in increasing numbers were only interested in the quickest exit west to the coast, the Portuguese discovered to their amazement that the missionaries were in no hurry. As a matter of fact, they were asking if there was not some place where they could set up temporary quarters to await further development in the Congo they had just left. Beyond the fact that there simply was no adequate setting for the sort of temporary refugee camp which they envisioned, there was the further determination on the part of the Portuguese authorities to move all evacuees toward the sea coast as quickly as possible, missionary or otherwise.

They were kind but firm. Their radios were on all day long and at news breaks there were always clusters of Portuguese huddled around the sets with troubled expressions. In the background were also Africans, unobtrusively going about their work, appearing not to notice but alertly taking in the details of the drama unfolding before their eyes. Back at their campfires at night there was spirited discussion of the political events erupting in the country to the north of them which had precipitated this sudden exit of whites. And inevitably someone would wonder out loud when and how something similar would take place in their own country. Of this the Portuguese were only too well aware. They, therefore, were understandably anxious to move the white skinned refugees on their way as soon as possible so their isolated bush communities could once again return to "normal."

But there was a problem, especially for the Kalonda and Mutena personnel. While their route to the Angolan border had been by far the shortest, once in Angola their route west to the coast was much longer and over much worse roads. As a matter of fact, the Portuguese officials told them that from Ndundu west, there were only sand trails on which only large four wheel drive trucks with high clearance could hope to travel. This was disquieting news for the missionaries who were traveling in an assortment of vehicles which even included a little VW sedan.

There was, however, no choice. They could not impose indefinitely on the hospitality of the Portuguese families at Ndundu. There was no question of going back as daily news from Congo revealed increasing confusion. Regardless of the roads, they had to try. Their hope was, like that of their fellow CIMers who had exited via Kamayala, to make it somehow to Quessua, the large Methodist Mission Station some 400 miles to the west near the Angolan town and government post, Malange. Here, it was hoped, the entire CIM family could camp, caucus and make further decisions together.

In the group there were children, some in diapers. Through the day the dry season sun was hot; at night at that altitude the dry season winds were chilling. Scattered along the route they hoped to travel were a few isolated government posts. Otherwise, it was barren waste land. Road-side bushes served as lavatories; small streams became laundromats and bathing facilities. Small primus stoves had to serve for boiling drinking water and for the preparation of simple meals. By late afternoon of the first day, some 20 miles short of their destination, they found themselves hopelessly bogged down on a long, sandy hill. They clearly were unable to go further; turning back was no option either. As they sat exhausted in the roadside sand, they heard the sound of a diesel truck approaching in the distance behind them. In the cab was a short Portuguese man and his African crew. In the manner of frontier men everywhere, he knew something about mechanics, road building, bridge repair and survival amidst harsh surroundings. After learning who the weary, marooned travelers were and their hoped-for destination, he simply cast his lot with the them for the next two days. When a car became imbedded in a sand pit, he hooked on a chain and pulled it free. When a vehicle quit, he got out his tool chest and persuaded it to run again. Small wonder that the missionary group were calling him "their Portuguese angel" by the time they reached their destination.

an oasis in the desert

By Friday, July 15, all CIM people had, in one manner or another, arrived at Quessua. It was also that same day that Bob and Mabel Bontrager had left Leopoldville for Brazzaville across the Congo River. Thus the evening of that day there was not a single CIM missionary on Congolese soil. It being dry season and vacation time, the Quessua Mission students had returned to their villages. The local Methodist missionaries had converted class rooms into sleeping space in preparation for the arrival of the CIM refugees. The missionary women set up community kitchens. Laundry facilities were established at camp water spigots. Men checked over travel weary vehicles. For a day or two, time was principally spent in washing clothes, sleeping, discussion and prayer. What now? Where now? The news from Congo was not encouraging. How long should or could they remain at Quessua? What should be the tone of reporting to the home board? And the most troubling question of all, had they done the right thing in leaving Congo in the first place?

Field Chairman Allan Wiebe had gone on into Luanda from where a series of cables were exchanged with the Elkhart office. American Embassy officials in that center were encouraging a return to North America. There was the further courteous but firm word from the local Portuguese officials that even if temporary arrangements could be made at Quessua, this would not be welcomed by the government.

An emergency meeting of the CIM Board was called on July 20 in Elkhart. There was but a single agenda item - - how to respond to the sudden turn of events in the Congo. After long discussion and troubled prayers, the board members concluded that they should advise their missionaries to return home. Exception would be made for three or four men in the event it was found feasible to remain somewhere in the general area for 60 to 90 days "to view developments and make contact with the field." Action was also taken to authorize the use of certain funds in hand to cover the impending cost of air fare for returning CIM personnel.

In the meantime, American Embassy personnel in Luanda had taken action. In view of the fact that U.S. Air Force Globemasters were airlifting United Nations troops and supplies to Leopoldville and returning to Europe empty, it was arranged for some of these unloaded planes to make the short flight from Leo to Luanda, take on loads of refugees, missionaries as well as others, and fly them to various points in Europe.

Thus it was that between July 20 and 25 three groups of CIM people departed the Luanda airfield aboard these enormous air freighters. They were noisy, unheated and without amenities. Seating was in military-style seats arranged along the sides. The "bathroom" was a bucket behind a curtain. Food and fuel stops were made at U.S. air bases along the way. But after days and nights spent along the sandy trails of Angola, these accommodations were a distinct improvement. Besides, each hour of droning northward through the night skies brought them closer to home and loved ones. The three groups were deposited in Rome, Paris and Frankfurt where arrangements were made to continue to North America via civilian flights. A few Canadian CIM missionaries were taken all the way home by the Canadian Air Force.

The Allan Wiebe and Art Janz families stayed on in Loanda waiting to see if any opportunity would open to make contact with American Embassy or Congo Protestant Council personnel in Leopoldville. As field chairman and treasurer respectively, they needed to transact some mission business in the capital if at all possible before returning to North America. The Bontragers, meanwhile, had gone as far as Accra, Ghana but decided to stay there a few days with personnel of other Congo Missions to see if the way might open for their return. It was not long until the U.S. Embassy in Leopoldville made an appeal to them to return to help fill the void created in the city by the massive exodus of expatriates. By late July the Bontragers had returned to Leo where, among other things, they assumed responsibility for reopening LECO, the inter-mission publishing house to which they had earlier been assigned by the CIM. Before the end of July the Wiebes and Janzes also arrived in the city via air from Angola. Lodging in the LECO building, they attended to a variety of CIM financial and legal matters which, by that time, were largely in the hands of United Nations personnel. By early August these two families also returned home thus, for a while, leaving the Bontragers as the only CIM personnel in the country.

troubled spirits

For most of the CIM folk, their abrupt and unexpected return to North America was a bittersweet experience. Eventually written accounts of their evacuation experiences clearly reflect the emotional turmoil and inner struggle which they experienced in the process. Edna Buller Gerber wrote: "We finally crossed the Congo border. It was a feeling hard to describe. Relief . . . to be sure, but was this the right thing to do? That night I prayed for hours as we were driving in Angola. I prayed that we might return if it were his will. I rededicated myself to the work. I wept as the van slowly moved farther away from the land I felt assured I was called to. I was consoled by the fact that as soon as possible several missionaries would return to contact the Africans. When we left the station we had given all the keys to the Africans with the intention of coming back as soon as possible. Would they think that we ran from the scene as cowards? Reluctantly I stepped onto the plane which started us on our long journey to safety, family and friends." (20)

Another wrote: "In a matter of days we have suddenly been plucked out of our places of service in the Congo and find ourselves in America. We are grateful to be safe. We cannot, however, say that we are happy to be here. Our hearts are in Congo. How we wonder what is transpiring at our mission stations. How we wonder what the Congolese pastors and leaders are facing. In the meantime we are completely at loose ends. We cannot accept that this should be the end of our work in that land. . . . The missionaries left station after station against their will, praying even as they left that the Lord would permit a speedy return. . . If we know our own minds and hearts, we feel that our work in the Congo is not finished." (21)

And Lois Slagle wrote: "Why did God permit such a mass evacuation? Were we led by the Lord to make our way to safety? What would have happened if we had remained at our posts? Questions such as these constantly clamor for attention. Sometimes at night when sleep is far away, or in the first conscious thoughts on awakening in the morning, they beleaguer me. God never makes a mistake. I think we shall see just how this evacuation and subsequent events have again proved that all things work together for good to them that love the Lord for we have been called according to his purpose." (22)

This missionary nurse's words would prove to be prophetic.

CHAPTER 8   HANGING ON

and has God gone too?

The scene was Djoko Punda some weeks after the sudden departure of the missionaries. The setting was one of tension and fear. There had been attacks and counter-attacks as the tribal fighting ebbed and flowed in the area. Fleeing Congolese at various times crisscrossed the station in frantic flight. Often tell-tale plumes of dirty, grey smoke were to be seen on the horizon signaling yet another village being reduced to ashes. The crack of gunfire was frequently heard. But through all of the fear, turmoil and death it was noted that the bell in the chapel tower on the station kept ringing every day at the scheduled intervals as it had for years past.

One day some Congolese came hastening along one of the station paths just as the chapel bell began to toll. They paused, then hurried over to the entrance to find the wizened little bell ringer tugging away with a will. They interrupted him unceremoniously and challenged him: "What's the matter with you? Are you crazy? Why do you ring the bell these days? Who has time to listen or to come? Even the missionaries are gone."

The little man paused for a moment, reflected on their comments, then asked: "And has God gone too?" With that, he turned, gripped the rope firmly and once again bent his back to his task. The bell continued to send its message of rebuke and remembrance across the station and to the surrounding populace.

a response to emergency

The sudden uprooting of over 100 missionaries from eight different CIM stations and their abrupt arrival in North America left the CIM Board scrambling to provide counsel and to project both short and long term courses of action. A special ad hoc group of board members, office staff and returned missionaries was convened in early August at the Elkhart office. Opinions and convictions of those gathered soon converged at the following points: 1) that the sudden events in the Congo in no way exempted the CIM from its ongoing mandate and responsibility for witness in that land; 2) that there remained an array of ministries, services and legal obligations with which the Congo Church would not yet be able to cope adequately if a missionary presence was not renewed; 3) that it was of utmost importance to reestablish contact with the church leaders as quickly as possible to assure them of CIM's continued concern and readiness to again provide help as this became possible; 4) that missionary reentry into the Congo needed to be approached with great sensitivity and with the realization that the familiar framework of missionary/African roles and relationships of previous years had now been swept aside and 5) that while individual needs and circumstances would be taken into consideration, the recently uprooted CIM missionary team be asked to avoid making long-term commitments in North America pending further developments in the Congo. At the same time an appeal would be made for men who would be willing to leave their families behind and return alone for up to a year to reestablish mission/church relations and ministries in that land.

The decisions made proved to be providential for on August 13 a telegram addressed to the CIM home office was posted in Leopoldville as follows: "EVENTS CAUSED REGRETTED DEPARTURE MISSIONARY FAMILIES STOP CHURCH MEMBERS ISSUE APPEAL RETURN SIX MISSIONARIES WITHOUT FAMILIES WHILE AWAITING PEACEFUL STATIONS." (1)

By the time the telegram was received in Elkhart, the first three men to return to the Congo had already been designated - - Allan Wiebe, Elmer Dick and Jim Bertsche. (2) Other men who were also making family arrangements for solo returns of varying durations were Art Janz, Waldo Harder, Loyal Schmidt, Mel Loewen, Archie Graber, Charles Sprunger, Ellis Gerber, Earl Roth, Glenn Rocke and Doctors Merle Schwartz, Henry Hildebrand and John Zook.

change in the home office as well

The dawning of the year 1960 found CIM Secretary Harve Driver a weary man. Invited in October 1949 to serve as an assistant to the then Executive Secretary C.E.Rediger, a year later he was named as his replacement, this on the threshold of the decade of the 50's which was to be one of explosive growth in the work of the CIM. While maintaining his personal business interests in northwest Ohio, he traveled constantly representing the needs and opportunities of the Mission. He saw its missionary roster triple in size and its budget quadruple. He gave impetus and leadership to the moving of the mission headquarters from Chicago to Elkhart. He had inspired and orchestrated the mission/church consultation held at Djoko Punda in February of 1960. What was not as well known was the fact that during the latter years of his CIM service, his wife, Priscilla Liechty Driver, was fighting a courageous, uncomplaining but losing battle with cancer.

Ironically, it was a similar situation which had brought veteran missionaries Vernon and Lilly Bachman Sprunger to the homeland in early 1959. Following surgery, it was thought best for the Sprungers to remain in the United States. In the spring of 1959 "the Board assigned them to duties in the home office." (3)

When in early 1960 Driver's family doctor ordered him to take a break from his administrative duties, the Board complied by granting him a leave of absence effective as of April 19. Two months later, Priscilla Driver breathed her last. At the close of the school year, Driver left with his teen age daughters for a richly deserved time of rest and renewal on the west coast. In the same board session V.J Sprunger was named acting executive secretary. Consequently the events of July 1960, for which Driver sought to prepare the CIM missionary team, found him on leave with Sprunger primarily responsible for the home office.

a returning trio

Wiebe, Dick and Bertsche left the States on August 20, 1960 with straightforward assignments from the CIM Board: 1) to reestablish contact and dialogue with the Congo Church; 2) to assess need/opportunity for further men to follow; 3) to provide information regarding the swiftly changing political scene and 4) to make recommendations as to CIM stance and contributions in the future.

Njili, the international airport at Leopoldville, having being closed to all foreign traffic, the men landed at Brazzaville on August 22 just across the river. Via shortwave equipment of the American Embassies on both sides the men were able to contact Bob and Mabel Bontrager who had already returned in late July to reopen LECO, the Protestant press and book store. It was agreed that the three men would join them as soon as a way could be found.

After a couple of days it was learned that, for a price, an enterprising pilot was ferrying people across the river early mornings via a venerable, canvas-winged, bimotored biplane. He was contacted and a deal made. Soon after sun-up on August 25, the three men and their suitcases were loaded into this conveyance. Props were spun and they were soon airborne. Flying at a low altitude the pilot followed the bank of the river upstream for a few minutes, crossed and returned to land at Ndolo, a small airport used by charter companies and a private flying club. Bontrager, alerted by radio, was there to meet them. Without any formality they made their way to LECO for the first of many rounds of briefing, discussion and prayer which were to follow.

Orie Miller and the CPRA

Already upon arrival at Brazzaville airport, the three men had found Orie Miller, Executive Secretary of the Mennonite Central Committee, waiting for a flight to Europe and home. He had come a few days earlier and found a way to visit the East Kasai with Bob Bontrager to assess the situation of the rapidly growing Baluba refugee population. Conflict along the Kasai River had sharply escalated after the departure of the Belgians. Bakwanga, (pr, bah-KWAH-ngah) the East Kasai capital (now known as Mbuji Mayi), and its environs were being inundated by ragged, emaciated refugees who had by whatever means possible found their way across hundreds of kilometers of forest and savannah. Most of them had endured hunger and privation.

Many had experienced the loss of family members to sickness or violent death. All had left homes and most of their possessions behind; all were uprooted and desperately needy.

Miller had been introduced to the Congo and its large, growing Mennonite Church in the early 50's on the occasion of a trip with CIM Secretary Harve Driver. When in 1960 the Congo fell into political turmoil, he quickly packed his bag. His long experience in dealing with the deadly aftermath of political conflict in other parts of the world made him all too aware of the unfolding tragedy. Having seen the situation for himself, he returned to Leopoldville, met with the Congo Protestant Council's Executive Secretary R.V. de Carle Thompson, CIM's Bob Bontrager and other mission/church representatives available to him at the time.

The August 31, 1960 minutes of the CIM Executive Committee meeting state: "Orie O. Miller reviewed the results and impressions of his recent visit to Congo. 'The Congo Protestant Council formed a relief agency known as CPRA (i.e., the Congo Protestant Relief Agency) of which they appointed Robert Bontrager as Acting Director, Ernest Lehman, Assistant Director, and Roland Metzger as coordinating agent in New York for the boards and agencies cooperating in producing funds and supplies for CPRA.' (4) Brother Miller emphasized that CPRA is called into being by a new and changing structure of the Congo Protestant Council in which the Congo Church is predominating and the missions are assuming an associate status. CPRA has already been assured support by such mission agencies and auxiliaries as Church World Service, World Vision, Christian Medical Society, Evangelical Foreign Missions Association, Independent Foreign Mission Association, Mennonite Central Committee, and others."

The minutes go on to report that the newly formed relief agency was immediately launching two emergency programs; one "Operation Doctor" and the second, "Operation Bakwanga." The success of these proposals, however, would in large part hinge on the availability of qualified personnel to give it direction and oversight. The effort to recruit and place up to 150 doctors on a temporary and emergency basis was to be headed up by Dr. Wm. Rule, a seasoned Presbyterian missionary doctor. As for the relief effort deep in the Kasai, someone was needed who had a first hand knowledge of that region, its people and their language all linked with a genuine heart of compassion.

These demanding requirements narrowed the search considerably. Who was available on very short notice? A name which quickly surfaced was that of Archie Graber. At home on furlough with his wife, Irma, and daughter, Nancy, when the Congo burst into turmoil, they were on hold awaiting opportunity to return. Via cable, CIM was asked if Archie would be willing to leave his family and come immediately. A reply came quickly; he would.

the Congo maelstrom

During the month of July, Congo political events had tumbled one upon the other. On July 11, the day CIM missionaries were evacuating southward into Angola, the copper-rich province of Katanga under the leadership of Moise Tshombe (pr. TSHO-mbay) and the influence of the large resident Belgian community had declared its secession from the central government. The East Kasai with its fabulous diamond deposits soon did likewise under the leadership of Albert Kalonji (pr. kah-LO-nji). In swift succession there then followed further crucial events: July 11, an appeal to the United Nations for technical help; July 12, a goodwill mission from Ghana arrived in Leopoldville sent by President Kwame Nkrumah; July 13, an appeal made to Ghana by the Congo government for support; July 14, an appeal to Russia for help coupled with the rupture of diplomatic relations with Belgium; July 15, a Congo appeal for United Nation troops to help evict Belgian paratroopers who had taken over key urban areas to safeguard Belgian citizens; July 20, the first official Congo delegation arrived in New York under the leadership of Thomas Kanza (5) to represent their country in a session of the UN Security Council.

Given the opportunity to address the Council, Kanza made four requests: 1) that Belgians stop their aggression in the Congo; 2) that the Belgian military units be evacuated; 3) that the U.N. refuse to recognize the political autonomy of secessionist Katanga Province and 4) that the UN provide a wide range of technical help to fill the great vacuum created by the sudden departure of expatriates from the country.

On July 24, Patrice Lumumba also arrived in New York to attend the sessions and to make contact with a variety of U.N. ambassadors from other countries. A key contact which was to influence much of what followed was one with the Russian delegation leader, Vazily Kuznetsov, the first vice-minister of foreign affairs. An invitation was apparently extended and accepted by Lumumba to sometime visit Moscow. This news was promptly circulated by the Soviet news media. Efforts had also been made to arrange a meeting with President Eisenhower but in view of the word from the Russian press, Eisenhower declined, something which Lumumba resented deeply. His several sessions with the U.N. Secretary, Dag Hammarskjold, were not much more successful. Though they met on several occasions, they apparently never did succeed in establishing relations of trust or engage in meaningful dialogue.

In the course of his travel back to the Congo, Lumumba scheduled stops in a variety of places which enabled him to make numerous further diplomatic contacts. In Tunis he not only met government officials but also representatives of the provisional revolutionary government of Algeria "who spoke at length about the sins of French colonialism and the anti-colonialist revolution in general." (6) In Conakry, Guinea, "President Sekou Toure impressed upon Lumumba the advantages of independence wholly without compromise without saying so much of the disadvantages attaching to such a form of liberation. Lumumba was completely hypnotized. In 1960 Sekou Toure was the only French-speaking African leader who could so impress Lumumba and so stir up the anti-colonial in him. After all he had heard from the Algerians in Tunis and the Guineans in Conakry, Lumumba had formed a very definite idea of French colonialism as being all of a piece with the Belgian." (7)

Before returning to the Congo, Lumumba also spent two days in Ghana with President Nkrumah. Together they planned to convene an African summit conference in Leopoldville, August 25-30, with the hope of launching a Union of African States and establishing its capital in that city.

what next?

As it turned out, the three-man CIM team arrived in Leopoldville the morning of August 25, the day that the Pan-African Conference was to open. Though at the time not fully aware of the significance of the date, they nonetheless noted the flurry of activity and the frequent motorcades on the streets.

Back on Congo soil again, how or where were they to start? As they sat in the Bontrager apartment discussing the day's planned visits at government, U.N. and airline offices, there came a knock on the door and in walked Kandha Modial (pr. KHAH-ndah moh-DYAHL), the Congolese who had been sent to the city by Mennonite Church President Kazadi Matthew to send a cable to CIM headquarters requesting the return of some missionary men. Joy was instantaneous and mutual. His information from the Kwilu and the two Kasais was at best sketchy but some essentials were clear: tribal conflict along the Kasai River continued unabated; the Church Conference scheduled for the 1960 dry season at Nyanga had in fact been held; it was the unanimous hope and prayer of the Church that some missionaries could and would return immediately. In the meantime, efforts were being made on all stations to protect that which had been left in their care.

On August 30 Wiebe and Dick flew to Luluabourg. The following morning Bertsche joined George Faul, a Mennonite Brethren missionary, to travel to Kikwit via road. The three CIM men reconvened at Kikwit a couple of days later.

a major surprise

Let a written report dated Kikwit, September 4, tell about it: ". . .the three of us are persuaded that to this point our steps have been ordered of the Lord. One of the great surprises of our lives was to arrive at Kikwit and to discover that an official delegation was here, sent by the Church, to do business. . . . I think none of the CIM missionaries gave any serious thought to the possibility that the church leaders would go ahead with the General Conference planned for August. We thought that in view of the extremely unsettled conditions, road blocks, fighting, ambushes and what not in the Kasai that they would be keeping very close to home. . . . But we arrived to find that Pastor Ngongo David at Nyanga and his people had spearheaded plans, gotten word out inviting the church leaders from seven stations to meet there as planned. (Mutena was excluded as they are Lulua and travel to Nyanga by road at that time would have been risky for them.) It was an abbreviated Conference lasting two days but judging from their report, they got down to work." (8) (9)

Meeting August 24-25, the adopted conference theme was: "Establishing the Church of Christ in Congo." The opening address was brought by President Kazadi based on Acts 1:8 and 2:1. Message topics of other speakers clearly reflected the mood of the gathering: "Are we sufficient?" "In the Hour of Trouble, the Work of God Goes Forward" "He Will Take Care of You to the End." A slate of conference officers was proposed and elected. (10) Much concern was expressed regarding the reopening of schools. In the absence of missionaries, a group of 5 or 6 graduates of the Nyanga Teacher Training School had already called a meeting at Mukedi on August 19. A slate of directors was established and teacher appointments made. This, however, left the problem of staff for the Kalonda Bible Institute and the Nyanga training school.

Another conference concern was the Church's lack of a legal charter. Realizing that without official status they were unable to negotiate directly with the government, the conference body named a delegation to go to Kikwit with the dual assignment to send word to the CIM calling for teachers for the Bible and Teacher Training Schools and to contact the Congo Protestant Council in Leopoldville for help in securing their legal status as a church.

Before leaving Nyanga, Pastor Kazadi told the delegation that they would find missionaries at Kikwit when they arrived! Was it a premonition on his part? Or a sheer exercise of faith? Whatever the case, it proved to be so.

From the joint sessions of the CIM men and the EMC delegation at Kikwit there emerged the following proposals: 1) That we request that CIM send more missionary men to join us immediately; (11) 2) that we request some 1-W boys with mechanical experience; (12) 3) that we do all possible to push legal details in Leopoldville for obtaining a legal charter for the CIM Church; 4) that we open the Bible Institute, Nyanga Teacher Training School and Manual Arts School as soon as possible; 5) that attestations be drawn up for each of the eight stations declaring that mission property is now considered to belong to the Congo Church; [this in the light of rumbles that some local government authorities were threatening to confiscate what they called abandoned property.] 6) that the missionary men return to Leopoldville to pursue various church interests with government offices and with LECO and then seek to reclaim some of the Mission vehicles in storage in Luanda, Angola, before returning to CIM territory; 7) that the missionary men tour the CIM field as soon as possible visiting all stations in the process.

new realities

In addition to the joint actions taken by the group, the three men added a number of observations of their own in their reporting to Elkhart: "We were made to understand in a kind, courteous but firm manner that the Congolese expect to be permitted to do all they can do and want to be trained to do what they cannot yet do. . . . We sensed a strong, new pride on the part of the younger fellows, especially. This is our Congo and we want to grow and develop. They are impatient to be moving. They resent anything that smacks of condescension. Whenever they are faced with the fact of a lack of preparation for a job, their immediate reaction is . . 'And why, after all these years with white people, are we not prepared?' A legitimate question, after all." (13)

As for the mass evacuation of the CIM missionary staff just weeks earlier, "Nothing was directly said . . . but the fact was skirted in conversation at several points. Judging from their comments, they still see no reason why all missionaries should have left all stations. . . . They feel that in many areas there was no reason to leave AND even if there had been reason, were there no missionaries in CIM who were ready to die with them if it came to that!? This is a question which haunts us." (14)

Further painful introspection on the part of the missionary men was triggered when the church delegation asked when they could anticipate the return of missionary families. The report reads: "The risk of such a move, as we view it, is apparently not clear to them. I think we realize a little better just how near the Congolese live all the time to tragedy and how stoic they are when it strikes them. . . . It is useless to talk to them about how a missionary mother feels at the prospect of being left with small children in the African bush with no medical help for hundreds of miles in any direction. Isn't that their situation too?" (15)

Perhaps the most significant observation of the report to the home board was prefaced with the one word caption: RUPTURE. The report reads: "By the very fact that all missionaries left for a few weeks there has been a clean break with the past. Congolese have had to assume new responsibilities and new authority. They have shown new initiative and leadership qualities - - all this only because of the fact that there did not remain a single missionary. . . . A chapter of CIM history was closed when the missionaries left and a new one was immediately opened. No one is now able to leaf back to reopen this closed chapter. More opportunity was accorded our fellow Congolese for self-expression, maturing and initiative in those six weeks of missionary absence than likely would have been the case in a good many months of continued missionary presence. It will be so very much easier now to set up new patterns, organize new programs and grant new responsibilities than it would have been were all missionaries still installed (a better word might be entrenched!) in their familiar places, following their familiar routines, performing their familiar duties. The past 2-3 years of theorizing about integration as compared to the inchworm progress made in actual practice of it offers abundant evidence of how painfully difficult and dangerously slow our progress was along these lines. As a matter of fact, we are beginning to wonder if perhaps God's hand was not in all of this and that missionary evacuation was a blessing in disguise." (16)

The report added an observation regarding future missionary roles. "The African says: "We want missionaries to come to do what we cannot yet do ourselves. But we want the missionary to teach us how and to let us do what we can do.' Human relations will be important. Title, rank, education and color of skin will no longer automatically ensure respect for the missionary. We will have to win the respect of the African and hold his confidence by what we are. Any attitude or action on the part of the missionary that may be interpreted as dictation or attempt to dominate will immediately raise a wall of opposition and resentment. The result will be a clash of wills, misunderstanding and frustration for both missionary and Congolese. . . . The missionary who cannot accept this will find it pretty tough going here from now on." (17)

descent into anarchy

The CIM men returned to Leopoldville intent on getting to Luanda, Angola, to retrieve the assortment of mission vehicles which had been stored with the Methodist Mission there. Upon arrival they learned that theirs had been one of the last flights into Leopoldville before the airport was closed by U.N. personnel who by this time were much in evidence everywhere in the city. Only U.N. authorized air traffic would now be permitted in and out of the capital.

The talked-about Pan-African Conference had in fact been convened in Leopoldville August 25-30 as planned. Prime Minister Lumumba had welcomed the delegations from various countries in an opening speech. On August 27 he left the hosting responsibilities to others and went to Stanleyville in northeastern Congo with several of his ministers including Christophe Gbenye, his Minister of Interior. (18) Lumumba's reason for going to Stanleyville in the midst of the Conference was to be present to receive a flight of sixteen Russian Ilyushin transport planes. In the meanwhile, over 100 Soviet military trucks had been offloaded at the Atlantic port of Matadi, each one accompanied by a crew of "technicians." With these transport resources suddenly at his disposal, Lumumba returned to Leopoldville, met with his military officers and unleashed a military operation against Albert Kalonji and his Baluba secessionist province in the East Kasai.

Thomas Kanza, one of Lumumba's ministers of that era later wrote: "The Soviet Union could hardly fail to be aware of the international implications and repercussions of its offering such aid to the central government. . . . But to Lumumba it was a matter of life and death. He had defied Hammarskjold and the U.N.; he had proof of concerted western action in the Congo's mining provinces and he could really now depend only upon himself, the ANC, (the Congolese National Army) and the Soviet Union - - the one powerful nation apparently prepared to give him the help that he needed in the way of arms, equipment and, above all, transport." (19) It was Lumumba's great hope to be able to effect the quick military occupation and defeat of both secessionist provinces of Katanga and the East Kasai while official delegations from other African countries were still in Leopoldville. The plan had been to convene a "summit meeting" immediately following the Pan-African Conference in an effort to implement some of the basic groundwork planning which could lead to the founding of the Union of African States envisioned by Lumumba and Nkrumah. Time, therefore, was of the essence.

The plan for an armed invasion of the Kasai and Katanga regions was formulated in Lumumba's office and was known only to a few of his closest associates. When the population in general became aware of the attack and the tremendous bloodshed occurring in the Kasai on the Prime Minister's direct orders, "anti-Lumumba circles began organizing themselves more actively around Kasavubu in order to create a constitutional crisis which would divert Lumumba's attention in other directions and hold back his advance into Katanga." (20)

By this time the Congo was surrounded by a web-work of international maneuvering and intrigue. With strong Belgian backing, Moise Tshombe was declaring the Katanga to be an autonomous state, the while casting it as a democratic anti-communist bastion in Central Africa. One of the strongest radio signals received on transistor radios across the Congo at that time came from powerful transmitters in Katanga's capital, Elizabethville (now known as Lubumbashi pr. loo-boo-MBAH-shi). Programming in French, English and major dialects drummed the theme of the communist threat in Africa in general and in the Congo in particular. Russian interest in and readiness to help Lumumba in his efforts to regain political control of the whole of Congo was altogether evident. The U.S. as well as various other western powers were increasingly concerned about the trend of events and were seeking ways of encouraging and helping President Kasavubu and the political groupings loyal to him. By September, tension in Leopoldville was high and President Kasavubu was coming under increasing pressure to assert his powers as the head of state.

Thus it was that the evening of September 5, 1960, the President used the Congolese National Radio to state that he was dismissing Lumumba and six of his ministers. The news had stunning impact upon the population as well as upon the Prime Minister. Within the hour Lumumba also was on the air calling for calm and repudiating the action taken by the President. In his turn, he dismissed Kasavubu from his duties as head of state.

It was in the month of September that the U.N. Security Council submitted the Congo question to the full UN Assembly for plenary debate. It became quickly evident that it was a very divisive issue with delegations speaking for and against both President Kasavubu and Prime Minister Lumumba. It was during one of these September sessions that Russian Prime Minister Nikita Khrushchev pounded a table with his shoe to signal his vehement defiance of western positions taken. The newly-born Republic of Congo had quickly been drawn into the center of an international arena in which the super powers of the day sparred and grappled with each other for influence.

By October 12, 1960, there were two Congo delegations in New York vying for official recognition by the UN, one sent by the President, the other by the Prime Minister. Given the circumstances, the Council refused to seat either one. Thomas Kanza, who at the time led the Lumumba delegation, writes in a mood reflecting both bitterness and sorrow: "So the Congolese problem was discussed in the security council without any contributions from the Congolese actually present. It was almost a mirror image of what was going on in the Congo itself. The Congo's fate was thenceforth to be determined by foreign powers; as for the Congolese people, no one cared too much, since they were, it was said, incapable of resolving their own personal and political problems." (21)

Back in Leopoldville, on September 13, the Congolese parliament had voted full power to Lumumba's government. On the morning of the 14th, President Kasavubu gave the entire parliament a leave of absence. It was on the same day that Colonel Joseph Mobutu, in consultation with the President, came on the national radio and declared the "neutralization of the politicians" and a temporary regime of power by the Congolese Army. In his radio address Mobutu insisted that this was not a *coup d'état* but a peaceful change of government in which no military personnel would be put in power. He called for calm and cooperation assuring the populace that the Army was there to ensure the safety of goods and of the Congolese people. He concluded by saying: "From now till the end of this short revolutionary period, every one of you will learn to be grateful to the Congolese National Army for I hope with all my heart that by then we shall have saved the honor and won the esteem of our country." (22)

With this turn of events, the UN promptly opened all airports and allowed the National Radio to again resume normal programming. As for the government, all Russian and Czech diplomatic personnel were expelled and the military operations in the Kasai and Katanga provinces were called to a halt.

an Angolan excursion

By this time the CIM trió had become a quartet. Responding to the call of the newly founded CPRA to spearhead its refugee program in the East Kasai, Archie Graber had left the States. Arriving at Luanda, Angola, he hitchhiked a ride aboard a UN cargo plane loaded with salt fish. He was noisily welcomed on September 8 as he walked in unannounced on the CIM group in Leopoldville, fish aroma and all.

All four men were eager to be on their way into the interior but first there was the problem of reclaiming the vehicles and goods stranded at Malange and Luanda. What was at first thought to be a fairly simple process proved to consume three weeks of their time. Initially there were needed repairs and the red tape of border clearance. Eventually, by using a mix of Portuguese and Congolese chauffeurs, railway flatcars and river barges, a total of 27 vehicles (17 for the CIM and 10 for the Mennonite Brethren) found their way back to their respective areas.

re-entry into CIM land

By now the CIM contingent had grown to nine men. (23) Graber was already busy with the newly formed CPRA program in the East Kasai. The others were very anxious to leave the capital with its whirling political uncertainty and get back to the CIM area upcountry. To do so meant traveling bush roads. Over some stretches they would be the first white-skinned people to appear since the massive evacuation of expatriates four months earlier. Were the bridges and ferries still intact? Would they encounter acceptance or animosity in the many villages through which they were to pass unannounced and uninvited? And, most importantly of all, what would they find on the eight CIM stations? How would their return be perceived? What would be the first concerns of the local church leaders? There was no lack of questions but all were eager to discover some answers.

Between October 20 and November 14, all eight stations were visited by some mix or other of returning missionary men and church leaders. Receptions from place to place ranged from exuberant and joyful to diffident and cool. Typically, the older people offered a warm welcome while the younger generation tended to be wary and non-committal. It was immediately noted that the tribal conflict of the Kasai was becoming more and more volatile and was spreading to other groups as well. In general there seemed to be a growing polarization of Baluba, Baphende and Chokwe people against the Lulua. All of this was cutting directly across the Congo Mennonite Church isolating the Lulua Christians from the rest of the church body. As the evacuation eastward of Baluba people continued, it was costing the church some of its ablest lay and pastoral leadership of that time.

It also became clear that local church leaders on all eight stations had sought to provide protective surveillance for the buildings and resources left in their hands. In some areas they had experienced affirmation and cooperation of the local populace whereas in others they had come under menace and pressure from surrounding villagers or political groups who much wanted to secure free access to mission supplies and equipment. Consequently, some stations were found essentially as they had been left while on others, houses had been freely occupied, equipment utilized and fuel either used or surrendered to those demanding it.

Withal there was everywhere a pervasive feeling of apprehension. Newscasts were closely followed via transistor radios in even the smallest villages. Rumor and conjecture abounded on every side not the least of which had to do with the missionaries' return and what their intentions, place and roles would now be.

early dialogue sought

Due to its central geographical location and the housing available, Nyanga immediately became a base for the missionary men. Once all of the stations had been visited, an immediate priority was to convene as many members of the church executive committee as possible for purposes of update, orientation, and the establishment of at least some immediate short range goals. Dates were set, travel arranged and the day came. Present were seven Congolese and seven missionaries. (24)

A written report later sent to Elkhart sets the stage: "Pastor Kazadi stood quietly before the semi-circle of church leaders and missionaries. It was November 15, 1960, in the Nyanga church office. It was the first meeting between missionaries and the executive committee of the church since the abrupt evacuation four months earlier. Kazadi spoke: 'We thank God for this day. We've prayed much that we might see this day.' He paused thoughtfully, then continued: 'We've learned much these past weeks. We've learned who among us serves the missionary and who among us serves God.' He moved on to other comments but he had already summed up in one terse sentence significant experience of the Congo Church." (25)

Observing that Genesis 15:1 had been of particular encouragement for him personally in recent days, he commented that the affairs of their country were hanging in the balances and that they could go either way - - for good or for evil. He concluded by saying: 'God has chosen us to serve him and this call is not limited only to times when things go well. He expects us to serve him in difficult times as well. We must never forget that in all circumstances God is with us.'" (26)

The missionaries had submitted a partial agenda, the first item of which was the whole issue of mission/church relations and the integration proposals which had been drafted in February at Djoko Punda. Wishing to be as straightforward and open on this issue as possible, they invited the church leaders to spell out for them "the place and function of the missionaries in the new Congo and specifically in the Church." (27)

It soon became apparent that the Congolese were not prepared to address that broad issue at that time. There were other more immediate concerns with which they were eager to deal. After encouraging the executive committee "to think of the program of the church for a five year period and then present a list of functions for which missionaries would be needed and requested," (28) the committee's attention focused on other matters.

Affirming the general thrust of the recommendations made earlier at Kikwit the committee sought to implement them with a series of decisions: 1) to send missionary/Congolese teams to tour the stations immediately for purposes of counsel and catching up on all disrupted financial matters, including back pay for mission teachers and workmen, and to present token gifts to local chiefs who had cooperated with the station church leaders in maintaining order and respect of property; 2) to relocate and reopen the Bible Institute at Nyanga Station; 3) to reopen the Nyanga Teacher Training School and to begin an immediate transition to a full secondary school status; 4) to relocate and reopen the Industrial School at Nyanga; 5) to temporarily utilize missionaries now on the scene to reopen these schools while making emergency requests of the CIM for the quick return of other men qualified to teach in or direct these schools; (29) 6) to recruit and press into service any Congolese who qualified to teach in these schools; (30) 7) to assign Elmer Dick for ministry and counseling among the Lulua church members from a base at Tshikapa; 8) to approve Dr. Schwartz's placement at the government hospital at Gungu, some forty miles southwest of Mukedi station; 9) to assign Dr. Hildebrand to medical services at Nyanga with regular itineraries to Banga and Djoko Punda; 10) to make Glenn Rocke available to help Archie Graber in his work with CPRA in the East Kasai and 11) to organize a special training session in December for all station church treasurers.

Thus the first official meeting bringing together missionaries and church leaders was in large part devoted to program issues which were of immediate and vital concern to the Congolese. The longer range questions of mission/church and missionary/African partnership in a rapidly changing setting would surface in their own time and in a dramatic manner.

the Lulua folk also meet

The depth of the tribal cleavage that had by this time cut across the heart of the Congo Mennonite Church was highlighted by what was termed a "General Conference" of the Lulua members of the Church held just over a week later, November 26-29 at Tshiela Mata, a regional church center a short distance east of Tshikapa. Meeting on their own without missionary personnel and with a total of 24 delegates from Djoko Punda, Tshikapa and Mutena to which they referred as "our stations," they worked through an extensive agenda. Orderly minutes were kept of all decisions made. Among other things they elected a slate of officers. (31) Missionaries were also listed who were invited back to each of the three stations. Appeals were also addressed to the CIM for a variety of schools to be opened or reopened on these stations. Dates and location were set for their next conference.

This meeting, held on the heels of the executive session at Nyanga, underscored both the wisdom and the urgency of the action taken to designate Elmer Dick as a CIM missionary set apart for the Lulua brothers and sisters within the Congo Church. It was all important to reach out to them in a clear and immediate manner to assure them of the concern of both the CIM and the rest of the Church amidst the heat of conflict which swirled about them. In time, these gestures were to bear precious fruit.

back in Leopoldville

Colonel Mobutu's move to "neutralize" the opposing political factions which had clustered around President Kasavubu and Prime Minister Lumumba was made on September 14. Never known for his timidity, Lumumba declared via his press attaché on September 15: "Colonel Mobutu, Commander-in-Chief of the armed forces, has been corrupted by the imperialists so as to carry out a *coup d'état* against the legal and popularly elected government." (32)

Undeterred, Mobutu established what was termed a "College of General Commissioners" made up of young "intellectuals" most of whom were university students at various points in their studies. To these young and inexperienced hands were to be entrusted the day to day functions of government for several months to come.

On September 20, 1960, the Republic of Congo was admitted as a full member of the United Nations. No delegation was to be seated, however, until the political confusion within the country was cleared up. Meanwhile, in UN circles there was maneuvering and spirited debate regarding the trend of things in that county. Those delegations that had declared support for PM Lumumba were loud in their protests vis-à-vis the recent turn of events. Those who were sympathetic toward President Kasavubu applauded both the roles of the UN in Congo and the moves under way to sidetrack Lumumba from power.

On November 8, 1960, President Kasavubu was allowed to address the UN General Assembly. On November 23 his delegation was officially seated as the legal representatives of the Congo.

In Leopoldville, Lumumba was placed under house arrest. Though prevented from free circulation in the city he still had contacts with his supporters. Having managed to arrange the smuggling of his two oldest children out of Congo to Brussels via a flight of Sabena Airlines, he turned to deal with his own fate.

Lumumba escapes

It was during the night of November 26-27, 1960, that he with his wife and youngest child managed to slip out of the city. With the help of some of his faithful supporters, they soon assembled a convoy of several vehicles. Biographer Thomas Kanza appointed earlier in the year by Lumumba as Congo's first ambassador to the United Nations writes: "There were nine cars in the group altogether and despite various delays and rash actions, all had gone well. . . . The party knew that Leopoldville had alerted every military checkpoint to arrest Lumumba and his companions before they could get to the border of Orientale Province where soldiers sent by Gizenga were waiting to escort them." Although people in his entourage kept urging him to travel as swiftly as possible, he "would let pass no chance of stopping and talking to people in every village."

The day of his arrest, the convoy had reached the Sankuru River and Lumumba had already crossed with most of his entourage. His wife and child, however, were still on the other side when some Congolese soldiers arrived just in time to prevent her from crossing. Although all of his fellow travelers tried to dissuade him, Lumumba returned across the river to rejoin them. Kanza writes further: "It was hopeless; Lumumba would not listen and to the intense disappointment of all those with him, returned to the other bank." (33)

Lumumba's capture and death

He was immediately arrested and taken back to Leopoldville on December 2. He was held there for a while and then imprisoned in the military camp in Thysville some 35 miles southwest of Leopoldville. At one point the restless soldiers were reported to have been ready to release him and reinstall him in power. Alarmed at this news, President Kasavubu and Colonel Mobutu made a hurried trip to the camp to talk with him. It is reported that he was offered the position of Deputy Prime Minister in the government. Seeing this as both a compromise and a demotion, he refused declaring he preferred, rather, to stay in his prison cell. (34)

Shaken by this experience, those in power came to the conclusion that something had to be done. On January 17, 1961, Lumumba and two of his fellow leaders were placed aboard a specially chartered flight which took them directly to Elizabethville in Katanga Province where, perhaps yet that night, all three men died amidst mysterious circumstances.

a rival government declared

In the meanwhile, a number of Congolese who had held key positions in Lumumba's cabinet had managed to make their way to Stanleyville in northeastern Congo, the area from which Lumumba originally came and which remained fiercely loyal to him. Among them were Gizenga Antoine, Mulele Pierre, Christophe Gbenyi, Anicet Kashamura and Joseph Lutula. Already when word was received of Lumumba's capture and imprisonment, Gizenga decided to assume the functions of the head of an opposition government based in that city. It was not long until countries that supported Lumumba sent special envoys with ambassadorial rank to Stanleyville. These included Mali, Yugoslavia, China, USSR, Ghana, Guinea and Egypt. Gizenga made Mulele Pierre responsible for opening diplomatic missions abroad and directed him to install himself in Cairo, a vantage point from which he could easily maintain diplomatic contact with sympathetic and supportive governments.

The CIM family and the Congo Church would unhappily learn much more about some of the men named above as the Congo history of the early 60's continued to unfold.

fireworks within the church camp

Year's end 1960 found the CIM men in Congo hard at work with the responsibilities to which they had been assigned by the executive committee in mid-November. All stations had again been visited with time given for detailed discussions with the church leaders of each place. It was clear that a needed next step was to convene the general council of the Church. This would bring together representatives from as many stations as possible to review with the returned missionaries the plans which had been laid in early 1960 at Djoko but which had been thwarted by the swift pace of Congo events. The question which now preoccupied both missionaries and Africans alike was, "Where do we go from here?"

In anticipation of this meeting, missionary Field Chairman Allan Wiebe had written to the home office proposing that both Harve Driver and Vernon Sprunger make a special trip to represent the CIM Board. Explaining the request Wiebe commented: "A number of underlying policies and principles must be presented to our African brethren in the near future to give both the missionaries and the church leaders direction in the new Congo. With an official Board representation on the field, most of these matters could be settled on the spot." Referring to such concerns as ongoing mission/church relations in the light of the suspended integration plans spelled out earlier at Djoko, ongoing missionary roles, housing, transportation and budgetary questions he continued: "Should we decide to retain the *personnalité civile* [i.e. legal status] of the CIM in Congo, it would be well that some of you be present to present this idea since it was the official board delegation in February that inaugurated the original plan of 'Integration.' I foresee a lot of questions and possibly misgivings in a change of policy in this regard. . . . Since the decisions reached in regard to these questions will set a precedent for our future work in the Congo it would make sense that the Home Board would be represented in any commitments made at this time." (35)

In response Driver stated that it would be "next to impossible" for both of them to come to Congo that quickly but advised that they should have the proposed meeting as planned and should "assure the African brethren that the general principles of the integration conference proposals still stand." Driver also stated that "the revolution and attendant evacuation of all missionaries automatically ushered in a new day that demands further examination and consideration by all concerned, and that, therefore, definite procedures cannot be decided until stability and responsibility is established in the Congo civil government." (36)

In subsequent correspondence it was eventually agreed that V.J. Sprunger would come and that February 14-17, 1961, were to be the dates for the meeting.

the stage is set

Opening day of the EMC General Council meetings dawned with all nine members of the church executive present plus 17 others who came representing the eight stations. (37) After a devotional opening by Pastor Kazadi, the first item of business was promptly introduced - - the legal status of the Congo Church. Where did the matter stand and how soon could the Church anticipate having it? Taking the floor as the representative of the home board, Vernon Sprunger took this early occasion to express CIM's views and concerns. The essential points made were: 1) the Djoko Punda consultation a year earlier had resulted in commitments made in good faith; 2) the radical changes which had taken place in Congo since then had already made some of the plans obsolete; 3) the hopes for a progressive and orderly transition toward mission/church integration had been dashed by subsequent events unforeseen by all; 4) given the great instability and uncertainty of the current scene, it was CIM's judgement that even as every effort was made to secure the legal status of the Church, the CIM should yet for a while retain its legal status before the government; 5) given the sudden drastic reduction of CIM missionary personnel linked with the urgent call for reopening a number of schools, it might be advisable to envision a center where post-primary training programs could be located and the bulk of the missionary personnel clustered.

simmering frustration erupts

What followed over the next couple of days was a colorful mix of theatrics, strategy, counter-strategy and oratory laced with resentment and the energetic release of pent up frustration. It was immediately evident that the suggestions made to delay any change in CIM's legal status and to establish a missionary center of sorts struck them as evidence that CIM was trying to avoid commitments made a year earlier. There then followed a series of carefully crafted "scenes." First, the Congolese requested time to caucus alone. Following this, the missionaries were invited back to the conference room to find the chalkboard carrying a new roster of church officers with all positions filled with missionary names! Pastor Kazadi, a veteran of many head-to-head encounters with Africans and missionaries alike, became the spokesman for the edgy group. His comments were to the effect that they now realized that they were giving us and the CIM Board much shame, that "they now realized that we missionaries had come back to reassume our old positions and that they, the Congolese, were standing in our way. Therefore, they were now stepping down and giving us back our titles and they would take the back seat - - the one they'd been sitting in for fifty years! They would continue to be our helpers since they were untrained, unprepared and altogether incapable of assuming any responsibilities other than those they've already had in years past." (38)

In response, Vernon Sprunger attempted to broaden the context of the CIM stance. He pointed out that while at the Djoko Conference all eight stations had been fully represented, today only seven were represented, this a reference to the absence of Lulua delegates from Mutena. Whatever mission/church relations were to be worked out in the future, CIM felt it must safeguard its freedom to relate freely to and continue to work with all members of the Congo Church family.

It is a telling measure of the supercharged atmosphere of that era that even such an oblique reference to the bitter tribal confrontation of the time prompted Pastor Kazadi to rise and stalk out of the meeting room promptly followed by all his fellow clansmen. This gambit effectively brought this particular session to an abrupt halt!

That evening missionaries attempted to convene just the executive committee members to see what could be done to clear the atmosphere and get the consultation back on track. The response promptly returned: "The missionaries should feel free to meet. Since we are no longer members of the executive committee, the meeting does not involve us." (39)

Next morning, after a less than restful night, both missionaries and Congolese found their way back to the conference room. President Kazadi and Secretary Falanga Elie "made it a point to sit with their brethren in the benches leaving the table in front of us - - the bell conspicuously placed in the center awaiting a missionary hand. We tried once again to present our ideas . . . and the thinking of the Board but added that . . . if they were so sure that our ideas were so contrary to the needs of our work just now, we were not going to insist further. We invited them to take back their positions and asked them to get on with the meeting."

Pastor Kazadi once again became the spokesman for the Africans. From his back bench position among his brethren he vented in the most vehement terms their grievances, irritations and hurts. Injustices and slights, real and imagined, both past, present and future all found ample place in the heated discourse directed at the missionary contingent in general and at Sprunger in particular. At one point he even broadly implied that the Belgians and missionaries were basically responsible for all of the problems they'd experienced in their country. By then some squirming was detectable on the part of some of his fellow Africans. Sensing that by now he was overstating their case, he brought his comments to a close and sat down.

After a long moment of silence, Vernon Sprunger expressed his sorrow for the turn that the meeting had taken and offered his apologies for anything he had said that may have been hurtful to them. Shortly thereafter, one of the Congolese suggested that the chairman and secretary take their places at the table. With yet a further moment of hesitation, the two made their slow and deliberate ways to the empty chairs awaiting them. Before seating himself Pastor Kazadi asked for forgiveness if he'd offended anyone.

But what next? The Congolese again asked that they be granted a time to caucus alone. Returning from this session they brought word that the composition of their executive committee had again been examined and that with the exception of the addition of a second assistant legal representative, a Lulua, the slate was to remain the same. As for missionary membership on the committee, three had been designated as non-voting members. (40)

There then followed some solid working sessions during which a considerable backlog of business was processed. At one point someone wondered where pastors' salaries would come from now that Congo had its independence. Chairman Kazadi entered this discussion with a flat statement: "If we now say that we are independent and want leadership powers, we must also realize that it is time to quit looking to the missionary for everything. This is our own concern. We must help our fellow Congolese in the Church to see and understand this." (41)

The consultation was nearing its end but there yet remained one major hurdle: the filling out of required government forms in order to request a legal charter for the Church. Among the requirements was that of listing each officer by name and function followed by the signatures of all members of the general council as evidence of their approval. It was at this point that a different polarization surfaced which left the missionaries as observers. Why was it, someone wanted to know, that candidates for the most important offices of president and legal representative both came from the same tribe? When it became clear that no agreement would be reached in the large group, a small committee was named to seek further wisdom. Upon their return they reported that they had found no other solution than to support the slate as presented. That said, all were instructed by the president to return in the morning for a closing session and the signing of the documents on the table.

Next morning the Baluba delegates were promptly on hand and proceeded to affix their signatures to the documents. When inquiry was made concerning the absence of the others, it was learned that they had already left for home! The message was obvious to all. They would no longer dispute the choice of people to fill key positions but neither would they sign the papers as required by the government. Suddenly the general council was at an impasse. There was no recourse but to table the whole issue until the executive could meet a month later and seek further wisdom. It was on a subdued note that the remaining members of the council left Nyanga. The non-Baluba members of the Council had struck upon a passive but very effective method to block the approval of two Baluba as key officers of the Church. This effective strategy would, unfortunately, again be used on several occasions by other groups of dissenting delegates to block Church proceedings in the turbulent 60's.

why?

What had contributed to the emotionally charged outburst which had erupted during the council sessions? There obviously were many dynamics at work. First of all, the Congolese leaders came to these sessions in the midst of a period of great tension. Daily news told of bloody conflicts both at a distance and close at hand. The missionaries, who had represented stability, help and even protection, had a few months earlier literally disappeared over night. Comfortable frameworks of life and security had been swept aside. In spite of the euphoria everywhere felt in June 1960, it was all too evident that things were not going well in their land. A further irritant in the mix was the discovery that the Mission and the Church, by now, held differing views as to the meaning of "integration." It was becoming clear that the Congolese had read more into the plans adopted at Djoko Punda than the Mission had realized or intended. The CIM and missionary assumption had always been that, at least during an open ended orientation/transition period, CIM and the EMC would continue to exist side by side each with its own structure and identity. Although nowhere in the integration document spelled out at Djoko was it stated that the Mission was to disappear, the Africans nonetheless had assumed that this was to be the case. It did not now help to be confronted by the harsh realities of the Congo scene which, in any case, made it impossible to make quick, major changes in mission structure or in mission/church relations as had been hoped. Worst of all, there was the stark reality of powerful tribal loyalties which lurked stubbornly just beneath the surface capable of disrupting not only national life but also the life of the Church.

As for the missionaries who had alternately functioned as participants, lightning rods and observers, it all had had an eerie resemblance to the violent tropical storms with which they'd all had frequent experience. Preceded by a heavy, brooding heat, thunder would rumble, clouds darken, lightning flash and suddenly rain would fall in a torrential downpour. Then, gradually, rain would slacken and as the storm front passed, the sky would gradually brighten and the atmosphere would again be clear.

In a sense, the explosion at Nyanga had provided a needed catharsis. It enabled Congolese leaders and missionaries to put unhelpful baggage behind them and to focus together on immediate priority concerns for the Church. The African dream of somehow incorporating both Mission and missionaries into the Church, however, would not be given up. It was simply put on hold as Mission and Church together turned to the myriad of pressing problems which surrounded them in the Congo of 1961. It was recognized that both Africans and missionaries had entered an era of great uncertainty which would see them buffeted by many forces both from within and without the Church. There was the growing realization on the part of all that it was time for renewal of commitment, a time for closing ranks, a time for "hanging on."

other friction points also heat up

After the first delicate and wary encounters between church leaders and returning missionaries in late 1960, a steady stream of CIM people began to find their way back to the Kwilu and the Kasai, this in response to oft repeated requests from the church people at the various stations. By the dry season of 1963, there already were over 70 missionaries back on the Congo scene. (42)

For a high percentage of them, their return was an answer to prayer, a return to places and people and ministries of which they had become a meaningful part in previous years and for which they longed during their enforced delay in North America. One missionary couple expressed it thus upon their return: "O'er mansions and castles though we have flown, be it ever so humble there's a place we call home . . Kamayala." (43)

But it was a radically different Congo to which the CIM team returned. It was also a different mission/church scene into which they were now called upon to fit. It did not take long for the returnees to discover a whole range of new realities which soon became "friction points" with which they had to deal in one manner or another. Notable problem areas for them were: 1) a destabilized rural population in the aftermath of political independence with resultant unpredictable attitudes toward the returned missionaries; 2) neglected maintenance of CIM buildings and equipment which had earlier been put in place by a combination of missionary determination and perspiration; 3) program and policy decisions sometimes made by Congolese in keeping with different values and standards than those followed previously by their missionary predecessors; 4) and frequently, the most frustrating of all, to be legally responsible for government subsidized programs while being unable to control such programs as effectively as before. Whereas under direct missionary supervision, directors and teachers had been placed in accordance with training, competence and Christian character and students had been admitted and promoted in accordance with work done and grades earned, under Congolese control other factors sometimes came into play such as clan, family, friendships or the pressure of expediency.

Excerpts from missionary correspondence of that era clearly reflect this mix of irritations. Telling of becoming bogged down in a sandy washout on a rural road a missionary wrote: "Oh what a day! . . . We forgot to take a shovel along so the village people came and wanted to fix it for 500 francs. A missionary cannot afford that so I asked to rent a shovel and do it myself, and they wanted 100 francs. I told him no, I don't want to buy the shovel, I just want to borrow it. Yes, he replied, it is 100 francs to borrow it. There was no way out so I paid the fare and went to work. But before I was finished with the job, the rent on the shovel ran out. Then he wanted 200 francs to let me have it long enough to finish the job. . . . You know, the Congo just isn't the same anymore." (44)

And from another missionary letter of the time: "Our schools are a headache. The more I see of them the more I long to see the day when the government will take over all the schools and relieve us of the responsibilities of all . . . the sloppy work. Most of the schools are truly independent. To get qualified teachers is becoming almost impossible." (45)

"If I go back to Mutena and I will be the only man there, I will have my hands full, I'm afraid. . . . Most of our stations which have been unoccupied for so long are beginning to look pretty badly in need of repair. . . . The Congolese eyes simply have not been trained to see many things which are common with us." There then follows an inventory of immediate maintenance problems: cracked arches, a crumbling buttress on a church tower, missing window panes, inoperative cistern pumps, fallen electrical lines. "We can neglect these things and find in less than five years a large portion of the station will be non-existent. If that is what we want then we can close our eyes and let her go." (46)

On one occasion the following dry comment found its way into a field secretary report to the CIM Board: "it seems things are normally abnormal!" (47)

And yet another: "The people are very right when they say that their country is sick. Troubles and unrest are on every hand. One sometimes wonders what good we can do in the midst of such confusion. However, I feel that the simple fact that we are here means much. We have not left them in their troubles. We are here to be with them and will do what we can." (48)

But most troubling of all for the missionaries in the early 60's were the mixed messages they were hearing from across the African Church. On the one hand, Congolese who had moved into roles of authority within the church and its various departments frequently reminded the missionaries that it was now a new day in the Congo and that they were to conduct themselves accordingly. But there were other voices also, those of the rank and file members of the Church who were becoming aware of increasing areas of slack, inefficiency and unmet expectations within the Church. It was such as these who with increasing frequency were challenging missionaries: "What are you waiting on to go to work? Don't you see all that needs to be done? Or have you returned to sit on the side lines to watch us stumble and to laugh at us?" (49)

In an increasingly untenable situation for the CIM and its personnel, two corrective measures were over due. First, EMC needed to secure its own legal charter thus enabling its officers to deal directly with its own government in all legal matters touching the Church. Second, it was time for a major consultation between CIM and the EMC to spell out clearly what the guidelines and principles for continued collaboration of the two organizations would be. Both events would take place in due time.

taking counsel at home

Minutes of a CIM Board session held in late February, 1961 record the following joint reporting by Allan Wiebe and Bob Bontrager who had just returned to the States. The two men "emphasized the importance of letting time take its course in the Congo problems in CIM, particularly the tribal problem of the Church, and in the matter of missionary/Congolese nationals inter-relationship. There are enough new ideas confronting them without the Board and the missionaries presenting their suggestions which all seem 'loaded' to the Africans in these days. On the other hand both advised to use all haste in doing the legitimate services which the African brethren want us to do. . . . There is plenty, and more, work than the missionaries can possibly do if they are qualified and willing. Both men emphasized that missionaries must exhibit by their words and bearing calmness, fearlessness, sympathy, understanding, helpfulness. Anyone who is fearful, tense and impatient in the presence of Africans should not consider missionary service now." (50)

Responding to this counsel on the part of Wiebe and Bontrager, the home office soon communicated to the CIM missionary family the following: "We believe it is essential that any missionary who comes to the field should have a definite sense of the call of God to be a part of the program in these critical times. Therefore, as a Board, we do not intend to send out people unless they are certain that God has called them to participate in the mission program on the field at this particular time. There is no duration of length of term given to those who do come." (51)

Meadows revisited

The spring of 1961, Harve Driver was still part of CIM home staff functioning as counselor and resource person for Vernon Sprunger. With the bulk of the CIM missionary staff in North America, the Board felt it particularly appropriate that time and effort be put into the celebration of CIM's 50th anniversary. Driver was asked to see to the arrangements.

Feeling it only natural that this celebration take place in central Illinois, the cradle of the Congo Inland Mission, he went about his planning with characteristic verve and thoroughness. Announcing 1961 to be CIM's "Golden Jubilee Year," the four issues of the Congo Missionary Messenger that year carried a wide variety of historical sketches dealing with home personnel, pioneer missionaries, expanding home constituency, growing inter-Mennonite missionary staff and a steadily developing ministry in the Congo.

Spring Board sessions were set for April 22-25. The Meadows Mennonite Church hosted the gathering and 56 CIM missionaries were present. Greetings from the Congo Church were delivered by missionaries who had just returned. Special tribute was paid to those who had served for 30 or more years. (52) The official 50th anniversary service brought together 600 people from the community on Sunday afternoon, April 23, in the nearby Gridley High School auditorium. H.A. Driver brought the anniversary address.

At the bottom of the program sheet were found the following statements: "Meadows - 1911 marked the beginning of organized cooperation of Mennonites in foreign mission. Meadows - 1961 shall mark a new beginning for advance of the Christian faith in this day." In a two page summary of that special occasion, the following comment is found: "Missionaries rededicated themselves to Christ to make any adjustments and sacrifices necessary in order that His cause be carried forward in Congo." (53) This was not empty publicity. The great majority of the missionaries present at Meadows that spring of 1961 did, in fact, find their way back to the troubled Congo within the following year.

Less than six months later Harve Driver submitted his resignation to the CIM Board. Among other things he wrote: "King Saul went to Gibeah with a band of men whose hearts God had touched. This phrase describes my feelings about the CIM family. I felt there was with me a 'band of persons whose hearts God had touched.' I am hopelessly and forever in debt to each of you, and promise to faithfully serve my God all of my days as I understand His purpose for me." (54) In a Board citation that same spring Driver was recognized "for years of dedicated and self-giving service, much of it under unusually taxing circumstances. He labored with devoted persistence to properly systematize the work of CIM both at home and abroad. He led in a marked expansion of the work with a notable increase in personnel and necessary finance with all the problems incident thereto. He welded the cooperating bodies here at home into an informed, committed and unified supporting brotherhood." (55) (56)

Vernon Sprunger, who had for a year been serving as acting executive secretary, was named CIM's new executive secretary.

synchronizing the sons and daughters of Menno

It should not be surprising that during this era of multiple tensions some efforts also needed to be devoted to dealing with widely divergent views which were represented within the CIM team. Not only were former CIM missionaries returning; but new first term missionaries were also arriving who had no pre-1960 experience or perspective. More significantly still, a growing number of PAX, TAP and VS short term people recruited and sponsored by the MCC were also finding their way to the Congo Mennonite scene.

The MCC PAX program was approved by the MCC Executive Committee already in 1951 "to provide service opportunities for Mennonite conscientious objectors and to facilitate further response to world need." (57) By the mid-1950's the first PAX men were already on assignment with CIM in the Congo. (58) The

Teachers Abroad Program (TAP) was approved by the MCC in 1961 following a trip to Africa by Robert Kreider. (59)

Largely due to the personal interest and concern of Orie Miller, MCC's executive director of the time, MCC involvement in Africa surged dramatically in the 60's. With PAX and TAP structures in place, they became excellent vehicles for channeling increasing numbers of young volunteers to that continent. (60) Young MCC "wine" was being poured into older CIM "wineskins." Some resultant "fizz" was predictable. Reflecting the ferment of the 60's on college campuses at home, some of the young recruits brought the same wariness of and aversion toward established patterns and structures with them to Africa and were ready to question missionary stance, roles and structures on short notice.

There was, further, the idealism of youth which, in this setting, heartily applauded the recent demise of the colonial system of sub-Saharan Africa. There was eagerness to make whatever contribution was possible toward ushering a new African day and a new order of relationships between the mix of white and dark skinned people they found around them. Some were not hesitant to suggest that within the missionary community there was still to be found evidence of a paternalistic and colonial mentality. Elmer Neufeld, appointed in January of 1962 as half-time Peace Section Africa Secretary and half-time MCC Congo Director, gave these concerns sharp focus in a carefully written paper entitled "The Unfinished Revolution."

Opposing perspectives and characterizations slowly came to take shape and were occasionally expressed in less than charitable terms. On the one hand, some young VS folk were tempted to view career missionaries as being by and large provincial, defensive, paternalistic, ultraconservative and as pursuing outdated goals and methodologies. It would be a blessing, some of them were sure, if they could somehow nudge, shove or pull the missionary community into the 20th century! Meanwhile the missionaries, some of whom were in their second and third decade of African service, tended to view the more vocal VS folk as being brash, opinionated, irreverent, uninformed by previous African experience and quick on the trigger with confident answers without being all that clear as to what the questions were. As a matter of fact, CIM missionaries were at times tempted to suspect some prior orientation of attitudes and critiques before their departure from Akron for, it seemed to some, their commentaries were a bit too uniform and too quickly delivered to have been entirely spontaneous on the spot.

All of this is not to say that no change was needed within the missionary camp. Change was indeed needed and, if at times painful, change did come. Furthermore, it became clear with passing time that needed tempering, learning and mellowing was taking place in both camps and, in the process, inter-generational bonds of genuine friendship and respect were forged which in many cases carried across the years which followed.

Viewed overall, the contribution of VS personnel to the work of CIM and the Congo Church was nothing short of outstanding. Typically assigned to construction or repair projects, agricultural and community development efforts, to mission/church schools, transport or mechanical support services, the volunteers of whatever age who served with CIM/EMC left a major impact upon the programs and the lives of the Africans among whom they lived and worked. The fact that many MCC volunteers came to work in the Congo as an alternative to military service was not lost on the Congolese. With passing years this practical, flesh and blood embodiment of a witness against violence and the taking of human life made as great a contribution to the teaching of this historic Anabaptist conviction as anything that was shared in African classrooms and chapels. It was further gratifying to CIM missionaries to note that the Congo experience of a surprising number of youth became a major force in the choice of training and vocations later pursued. CIM ministries were significantly enriched in later years as some former VS folk returned to serve as missionaries under CIM sponsorship.

a burr still under the saddle

While most of the friction of the decade of the 60's within the CIM team had to do with black/white, mission/church relations and the methodology of church planting, there was still another issue of a different nature. Though largely muted in the turbulent 60's, it commanded more attention and critique with passing years as CIM gradually extended its ministry in Africa. This topic was fundamentally theological in nature and had to do with understanding and definition of the core of the Gospel which Mennonites were called to proclaim as they engaged in evangelism and church planting in a variety of distant places in the world. Put another way, "Once planted, what should an overseas Mennonite Church look like, sound like, act like, preach and teach like and live like?" Unlike the issues of the early 60's, this one would prove to have a longer life.

pointing directions; regaining momentum

Although some thorny issues regarding mission/church relations and administrative structures had been tabled, the rush of Congo events and the sheer bulk of work to be done soon found missionaries and Africans collaborating closely in a widening range of church activities. The Bible Institute was reopened with the excellent help of Pastor Kaleta Emile who for years had been respected at Djoko Punda for his teaching ability. The four-year teacher training program at Nyanga was in full transition to a six-year secondary school which would, for the first time, open the door for Mennonite students to university-level training. (61) The Manual Arts School was moved from Mutena and reopened at Nyanga with students gaining on-the-job experience in a renewed building program to house the secondary school. (62)

Elmer Dick was installed in Tshikapa with the blessing of the EMC's General Council to relate to and encourage the Lulua membership of the Church which had been isolated by tribal conflict. (63) A disrupted revision of the Giphende New Testament was revived. Inventories of Christian literature at various stations were undertaken and distribution reactivated. CIM doctors were assuring desperately needed medical services on both sides of the Loange River with Dr. Schwartz traveling between Gungu and Mukedi and Dr. Hildebrand itinerating to Nyanga, Banga and Djoko Punda. Missionaries were working hard to bring files, reports and government subsidy accounts to date. Given the great and immediate need for trained church leadership, the CIM Board was being urged to provide funds to permit the sending of three young Congolese couples to North America for studies there. (64) Regular trips were being made into rural areas by teams of Congolese and missionaries to encourage regional churches, reactivate chapel construction projects, interview baptismal candidates and serve communion.

AMBCF is born

EMC's horizons were also being extended as they sent representatives to the inaugural meeting of what was to become the Africa Mennonite and Brethren in Christ Fellowship which was convened at Limuru, Kenya in April, 1961. Congo Mennonites present were Kakesa Leonard and Glenn Rocke representing the EMC; Nganga Paul representing the Mennonite Brethren Church and Elmer Neufeld who, by that time, was in Leopoldville coordinating MCC personnel and program interests in the Congo. It was Neufeld - - together with missionaries of the Eastern Mennonite Mission Board, based in Nairobi, Kenya - - who served as organizers and conveners of this first meeting.

struggling against the current

Meanwhile, in the midst of all of the tribal conflict in the Kasai, the church leaders and missionaries never gave up efforts to reconcile and reunite all fellow believers from all tribes within the Church. If tribal leaders were politically aligning and realigning themselves against each other with passing time, the consistent and insistent word of the Mennonite Mission/Church leaders was: "We will not allow these conflicts to permanently separate us from our brothers and sisters in Christ. We will not give up in our efforts to reestablish fellowship with our fellow church members, no matter what their tribe, no matter what the claims of political leaders upon us." Even at the height of the fighting in the Kasai, efforts were constantly made by pastors to maintain contact with each other. Thus it was that in the very first meeting of the executive committee with returned missionaries in November 1960, the plan to assign one missionary to relate to and minister among the Lulua Church members was quickly endorsed. Already in early October 1961, through patient effort, eight Lulua and eight Baluba church leaders were brought together on neutral ground at the residence of CIM missionary Harold Graber in Tshikapa. Glenn Rocke, who was present, wrote: "The first part of the meeting went quite well. But before it was over there were some bad offenses going back and forth and we were fearful it would break up the meeting in a spirit of anger. But the Lord answered prayer and we ended with a good prayer and a round of handshaking before they parted." (65)

Determined to build on this breakthrough, opportunity was sought to call a meeting of the EMC General Council as soon as possible which would once again bring together representation from all eight stations and all tribal groups. Of that meeting Vernon Sprunger wrote: "In February, 1962 the long looked-for General Council meeting of the Church was held at Tshikapa. All the different tribes and stations in the entire area were represented and everyone was happy to be together again. The first session was spent in rejoicing in the reality that they were able to fellowship together; testimonies were touching; hymns and prayers were spontaneous. This was an inspiring meeting." Sprunger went on to comment: "The Baphende and Lulua tribes have not yet effected a political reconciliation nor have the Batshoke and Lulua tribes; nevertheless they can meet together face to face in church relationships, pray and sing together. The Church is founded on Jesus Christ and will stand. What can prevail against it?" (66)

Even though still greater tribal confusion and conflict were still to follow in the Tshikapa area, the Church had taken initiative and declared itself. Reconciliation and maintenance of fellowship among members of all ethnic groups was to remain a high priority. It was in this spirit that the disagreements which had so disrupted the Nyanga meeting of the previous November were laid aside and a new slate of officers was elected. (67) This opened the door for the EMC to make formal application to the government for its own legal charter. By May 23, 1962, all necessary documents were in the hands of the government authorities in Leopoldville. Missionaries, furthermore, were clearly demonstrating their desire and readiness to affirm Congolese in new roles of leadership and to partner with them in striving for common goals. As a result the early African wariness began to subside. Times were troubled and the future was clouded. But the Congo Church came more and more to view the returned missionaries not as competitors for roles of leadership but as valued co-laborers in uncertain times.

yet another layer of conflict

In August of 1961, Colonel Joseph Mobutu made good on his promise to return political rule to civilian hands. In collaboration with President Kasavubu, Cyrille Adoula was installed as the new Prime Minister. Whereas his predecessor Patrice Lumumba, a committed nationalist, had sought to maintain the unity of the whole of Congo and thus fiercely opposed Moise Tshombe of the Katanga and Albert Kalonji of the East Kasai, the new regime adopted a more flexible stance. In this setting of political tolerance, a country-wide movement soon became evident which saw a proliferation of political parties and numerous claims for the creation of new "provinces." These initiatives invariably reflected the desires of major ethnic groups for recognition and some degree of autonomy. One such political movement surfaced in the West Kasai and was to add yet another layer of turmoil upon a region already devastated by ethnic conflict. Eventually called *the Unité Kasaiènne*" (i.e., "Kasai Unity"), it was an effort to bring together a mix of sixteen different ethnic groups under a single provincial flag with Tshikapa as its capital. (68) The rich diamond deposits all along the river were viewed as the economic resource to give viability to such a new province.

There remained, however, one crucial question. With its capital to be based squarely on the border between traditional Lulua, Baphende and Chokwe areas, what was to be the place and role of these tribes in all of this? The Lulua people were already engaged in bloody conflict with their Baluba cousins to establish uncontested control in their homeland. They now suddenly saw fresh menace threatening them. There quickly emerged a confrontation which not only heightened the already serious tension between the Lulua and remaining Baluba of the area but also made the Baphende and Chokwe people their adversaries as well. All of this greatly broadened the strains upon the EMC since it claimed membership and pastoral personnel within all three of these groups.

At Djoko Punda, the Lulua had early been forced to move to the east side of the Kasai River leaving station church leadership in the hands of a small group of Baluba including Pastor Kazadi who had not yet joined the migration toward the east. When it became clear to the nearby Bakuba people (69) that a new province was in the making, they one day descended upon the station announcing that if they were going to be included in the new province, they intended to have a mission station of their own and Djoko Punda was it. Pastor Kazadi with his small group of fellow Baluba did all possible to stem the tide but they were menaced by armed men of the chief's retinue. Realizing that the Baluba presence on the west bank of the Kasai at Djoko hung by a slender thread and that resistance could well mean harm to them all, he reluctantly agreed to accompany them to the station for an "inventory" of the buildings and supplies. In the process some looting began to take place. The Mukuba chief then placed armed guards to watch over the station. Although the chief urged Pastor Kazadi to stay, he refused to remain under such circumstances. Turning over what few keys he still held to fellow clansman Pastor Kamba Jean, who would yet make an effort with a few others to maintain Baluba presence and leadership at this station, Pastor Kazadi went to Nyanga. He reported what had happened and requested help to make his way with his wife to join thousands of other refugees in the East Kasai.

In spite of their brave efforts to stay on, Pastor Kamba Jean and his small group soon experienced further menace which forced them to leave also. Arriving at Nyanga he related with great sadness what had transpired and also sought help for their continued journey to Bakwanga. Back at Djoko Punda, full scale looting broke out upon their departure. Subsequent efforts to determine precisely what happened never clarified the story. Some accused the Mukuba chief and his people; others talked of a truck load of soldiers who helped themselves. Whatever the case, Djoko Punda, the first CIM missionary post established in 1912, was the first to suffer major damage and loss in the troubled political era of the early 60's. (70)

in the eye of the storm

At Tshikapa, political maneuvering continued for a year as different leaders representing different ethnic groups vied for advantage and power in the new province which was to be created. In spite of great opposition from the Lulua population in and around Tshikapa, September 15, 1962 was set for the raising of a new flag; the official installation of the new government was slated for September 30. Elmer Dick who witnessed much of what transpired during those days wrote: "The Lulua were determined that the flag raising would not take place and managed to cause enough disturbance. . . that the public ceremony was dropped. However, the officials of the new province were not easily frightened and began moving into Tshikapa requisitioning houses and offices as they needed them. . . . The CIM has also been pressured to give up some of the buildings which we have leased from the mining company."

"While listening to the news. . . on September 17 we were amazed to hear an official declaration of war by Chief Kalamba of the Lulua giving orders that his people must die for Tshikapa. They were to use anything that could be used as a weapon . . . appealing to women as well as the men. . . . The following morning (September 18) the Lulua youth were harassing the policemen who were guarding the new government officials. Somehow they managed to relieve several of the policemen of their weapons. Several hundred Lulua women demonstrated by marching in front of the building occupied by the new government officials, vowing death to the enemy. While the women were carrying on, a number of the Lulua youth began to break into houses occupied by the UK officials. They carried off what they could and destroyed much of the rest."

The same afternoon "a number of us missionary men were called to Rev. Schnell's house for a conference with Kamanga Gregoire, the president of the new province, and several of his aides. He was polite but firm in his demand for some of the buildings being occupied by the Mission. (71) Our reply was that those buildings were officially leased from the mining company and we were under contract for the same. Therefore we could not give them permission to occupy any of these buildings unless we had an understanding with the company to release us from our obligations. . . . At this period of the conference we saw crowds of men pouring off the hill on the opposite side of the Kasai River heading for the bridge. . . . President Kamanga and his aides bid us a hasty farewell and fled to safety on the other side of the Tshikapa River. (72) By the time we were ready to leave, the warriors armed with every kind of weapon imaginable were streaming up the hill past the Schnell house to the Lulua Camp. They displayed no hostility toward us. . . All during the night and the next day we heard the noise of doors being broken down as more property was destroyed and more things stolen. This was mixed with many loud arguments as they were fighting among themselves over stolen goods."

"With daybreak on September 19, open warfare began. The fighting all centered around the Tshikapa River bridge. While some men were occupied with fighting across the river, others were kept busy carrying away more loot as well as their personal belongings. . . . There was no possibility of getting out any word to the outside world as the telegraph system was broken and the missionary transmitters had been confiscated some months before. Late in the afternoon the firing stopped. . . . The greatest loss of life took place in the hospital where some bedfast Lulua were murdered. . . . Thursday morning, September 20, the Congolese soldiers seemed to be in control. Orders had been given for all the Lulua to vacate their camp and move across the Kasai River. It is difficult to picture the confusion and anxiety as everybody to the youngest child was carrying what they could of their belongings." (73)

Meanwhile at Nyanga, tension among the Baphende of the area was running high. Hearing of the fighting between Lulua and Baphende at Tshikapa, a village mob descended upon the station demanding that a truck load of their warriors be transported there immediately. Some of the missionary men sat with the local church council urgently debating how to respond. The council finally concluded that given the wild mood of the mob and their determination to join "the war" at Tshikapa, they might turn their fury on the station and its population if thwarted - - this on the pretext that the Nyanga people were supporting the Lulua.

Since missionary Sam Entz had been planning a trip to Kikwit for a load of school supplies and the route would take him part of the way toward Tshikapa, it was reluctantly agreed to accommodate a truck load of men with a ride as far as the fork of the road where the trip to Kikwit would take the truck in a different direction.

Across the Kasai River at Kalonda, Glenn and Ina Rowell Rocke had just enrolled a new class in the Bible Institute. With Pastor Instructor Kaleta Emile they had just been teaching for one week when hostilities broke out. Rumor spread among the students that all non-Lulua were in danger. Immediately all of the Chokwe, Baphende and Bashilele students "took the footpath to the river and crossed to the other side where their people were in power. All of them started walking to Nyanga 65 miles away with all their children and the clothes they had on their backs." (74)

On September 20, a carload of Belgians from the Diamond Company decided to try to get through to Luluabourg by road which they succeeded in doing. A missionary vehicle which sought to follow somewhat later was stopped about 50 miles out of Tshikapa by a village crowd. Keys were confiscated and the vehicle prevented from continuing. Elmer Dick picks up the story: "Our missionaries endured several anxious hours at the hands of the threatening village men. With the approaching night near, everything seemed rather hopeless when all of a sudden a convoy of Congolese soldiers appeared. The village mob disappeared. . . . Soon one of the policemen brought the keys for the car which had been taken at gunpoint earlier." (75)

It was quickly decided to follow the convoy back to Tshikapa. Alerted regarding the Tshikapa situation, the UN sent a plane with personnel the next day, Friday September 21, to investigate. After a strategy conference, it was decided that women and children would be evacuated to Luluabourg. A few husbands were counseled to accompany their families to a more secure setting. The three missionary nurses, Aggie Friesen, Lois Slagle and Mary Hiebert decided they should stay as did Dr. Zook, Elmer Dick and Mel Claassen. Glenn and Ina Rocke also stayed at Kalonda across the river.

At Nyanga, the day after the departure of the truck, American Embassy personnel from Leopoldville accompanied by Mel Loewen made stops at Tshikapa and Nyanga via an embassy plane. By this time UN personnel was in Tshikapa in force. Dick continues: "Since the UN has been in control here, there has been no more warfare. The tensions mount and recede as new crises develop. We have not been molested and are able to carry on our work under the restrictions resulting from the presently divided situation. . . . We are earnestly praying for the day when tribal unity will be restored and a stable government established." (76)

It took several weeks of UN presence and intervention in the Tshikapa area to reestablish order and impose tribal frontiers. In time, *the Unité Kasiènne* was recognized by the central government. A new flag was successfully raised and the provincial officials duly installed. The temporarily divided CIM missionary families were again reunited at Tshikapa.

There were to follow three years of varying levels of frustration for the mission/church community. Under-equipped, inadequately housed, poorly prepared and often self-serving and short sighted in their approach, the officials of the new pseudo-government tended to view the local mission/church community with ambivalence. At times it seemed the community was viewed as a threat to its autonomy and authority. But for the most part the government saw it as a source of needed help. Thus it was that there were endless demands for supplies, services, housing and transportation interspersed with new provincial regulations and requirements which often struck the local church as having little basis other than pure whimsy. All of this was further complicated by the fact that often local UK authorities would issue regulations which contradicted those received from the central government. Missionaries may be forgiven for having at times sent home exasperated and sardonic commentaries on the local Congo scene, such as this: "If conditions were not so tragically serious, it would be hilariously funny out here. What a hodgepodge of conflicting orders; everyone ordering everybody else around; everybody criticizing everyone else for all the difficulties; . . . new states being born every other week; self appointed ministers a dime a dozen and nobody knows anything!" (77)

When approximately three years later the UK was swept aside by new developments at the national level, the Mennonites of the Kasai breathed collective sighs of genuine relief.

CHAPTER 9   THE STRUGGLE TO SAVE A PEOPLE

a man in a floppy-brimmed felt hat

Although he had already answered the urgent call issued by the newly formed Congo Protestant Relief Agency in August, 1960, preparing logistics took time. It was not until October 4 that Archie Graber first set foot in Bakwanga (pr. BAH-kwah-ngah). This was the name given to the capital of the East Kasai by the Belgians. The name was changed to Mbuji Mai after political independence (pr. mboo-ji MAH-yi, the Tshiluba term literally means "goat water"). The last part of his journey had taken him over war-torn countryside via a small plane and pilot provided by the American Southern Presbyterian Mission of the area. He had a couple of suitcases in his hands, a floppy-brimmed felt hat on his head and a letter in his pocket from Albert Kalonji (pr. kah-LOH-nji), the president of the East Kasai, inviting him to come work among the refugees. (This is the official name of the entire province but was more popularly known as the South Kasai since most of the political and refugee activity was centered in the southern part of the province.) Somewhere between Lobito Bay, Angola, on the Atlantic coast some 1300 miles to the southwest, and Elizabethville some 475 miles to the southeast, were four boxcars loaded with 150 tons of rice that Graber had started on its way before he came inland. He had little else.

First he had to seek food and shelter for himself. For these needs he approached the officials of *MIBA*, the local diamond mining consortium established by the Belgians in earlier years and which was still carrying on its sophisticated extraction of precious stones from one of the richest deposits in the world. They agreed to grant Graber a house and permission to take his meals in the dining hall provided by the company for its expatriate staff.

For transportation he turned to the local government. Prime Minister Ngalula (pr. nga-LOO-lah) allocated two well-worn, battle scarred government trucks which needed some serious repair before they could be trusted with relief supplies on the bush roads

But above all, Graber needed information regarding the scope of the task which lay before him. Already in August some six weeks earlier, Orie Miller had described a rural hospital some 20 miles west of Bakwanga overrun by hundreds of sick, emaciated refugees to be "as pitiful a sight of human misery and suffering from lack of food and medical care as I have ever seen." (1) Scarcely ten days later the troops of Prime Minister Lumumba's central government had stormed their way through the countryside. Armed with mortars and automatic weapons, they swept all resistance before them. Killing and pillaging as they worked their way south toward Katanga Province, they left still greater devastation in their wake. Local food supplies which had already been stretched to the limit by the flood of refugees from the West Kasai were now totally inadequate. (2) To the already sick and starving refugee population there were now added many of the local people who had been injured and whose homes had been destroyed. Another layer of misery had been added to an already desperate situation. What awaited Graber?

the faces of war and famine

Word quickly got around in Bakwanga that a Tshiluba-speaking missionary had arrived who was known to some of the refugees. They called him Muambi Lutonga (pr. Mwah-mbee LOO-taw-ngah, meaning a young teacher or preacher), a name given him by the Africans at Djoko Punda upon his arrival in 1930. As for the small white European community, any source of help in those traumatic days was more than welcome. Even though initially without his own transportation, he was quickly afforded opportunity to travel in the region to make his own assessment of the crisis. But it was the large Presbyterian Mission of the area which became a constant source of help. Via their mission plane and pilot, Graber was able to land on dirt strips in a variety of settings where refugees were congregating and daily growing in number. On one such sortie, he found himself at a village called Kashi (pr. KAH-shi) which, in turn, was seven miles from a larger center called Luputu (pr. loo-POO-too). An army captain at the air strip asked Graber if he wanted to go see the refugees there. He did. His diary, that night, carried the following entry: "Some of the things I saw I would rather forget. The entire town is either burned down or, if built with cement blocks, the doors and windows were broken in. Hundreds of people in the hot sun, with babies crying, with their few things they could get away with, and trying to find a way to leave this place of horror. Filth and dirt everywhere, flies and sickness. Many are hiding in the forest and are afraid to go to their fields for food. This is one place to which I hope to bring some food as soon as I can." (3)

Later that same week he was offered a ride with Mr. Jackmay, an official of the diamond company. He was going to Mwena Ditu (pr. mweh-nah DEE-too), some 90 miles to the south. In his book War to be One, Levi Keidel describes the trip stating that Mwena Ditu "was a transport life line for South Kasai - - the only point for rail shipping goods in and out of the break-away province. He [Graber] seized the opportunity to go along. This trip would give him some first hand knowledge of the scope of human need. Also, he could try to trace the whereabouts of that 150 tons of rice he had shipped from Lobito. He did not foresee that after this journey he would never be the same."

"They left the city and took a gravel road south. The landscape grew more and more bleak and deserted. Here was a burned out abandoned village; there was the blackened hulk of an abandoned automobile. Approaching them on foot was a refugee family - - a man pushing an overloaded bicycle - - a woman steadying a great burden on her head with one hand, leading a small child with the other, and carrying an infant bound by a waistcloth on her back - - a stooped, shriveled old woman with a tiny basin of personal effects balanced on her head, pulling herself onward by careful, measured steps assisted by a crooked walking stick."

"About 15 miles south of Bakwanga the car made a turn to the right. Suddenly Graber saw corpses scattered on both sides of the road. 'Roll up your window fast,' Jackmay said. `Keep out the flies and the smell. This is the village of Tshilenge. About a month ago Lumumba's troops and Kalonji's warriors tangled here. They say about four hundred were killed.' . . . Closed windows kept out the flies, but not the smell. Neither could Graber shut out the visual images. For miles his eyes caught chilling symbols - - shoes and shredded clothing strewn along the roadside - - corpses hastily covered with loose dirt - - a broken spear. For mile after mile the images of horror kept repeating themselves - - the wrecked hulls of vehicles - - the burned and leveled villages - - decaying corpses - - . It was a scene lifted out of Dante's Inferno. The endless lines of straggling refugees were the tormented passing silently, heedlessly, like pre-programmed robots, across the scarred, fetid wasteland." (4)

A fellow CIM missionary who joined Graber some weeks later, wrote of his early encounters with famine: "We had several bunches of bananas along to give to the children. They literally went wild when they saw them and trampled each other under foot in their frantic effort to get something to eat." (5)

a desperate search for food and equipment

Returning to Bakwanga, Graber realized that the 150 tons of rice awaited at Mwene Ditu would be only a drop in an immense bucket of need. Much more food needed to be found - - and quickly. Early reports and requests sent to Leopoldville and New York sought to establish a schedule of monthly shipments. He asked for 100 tons of rice and 100 tons of beans per month plus 500 sacks of salt and 100,000 blankets as soon as possible. At the same time Graber turned to the Presbyterian Mission which responded with an immediate donation of $5,000. This was used on the spot to purchase 20 tons of manioc flour, 3 tons of corn meal, 150 cases of medicated soap and 30 tons of corn. Another $1,000 was given for the purchase of a variety of garden seeds.

As the repair of the two government trucks neared completion, Graber then sent an urgent request for more help. Close at hand the Presbyterians allocated missionary Day Carper. Turning to the CIM, Graber thought of Glenn Rocke, a fellow missionary of other days at Djoko Punda, who also knew the region, the people and the language. Responsible at the time for opening the relocated EMC Bible School at Nyanga, it was agreed he would go to Bakwanga in early December when replaced by Waldo Harder. MCC Akron also received a request for two "mature, emotionally stable young men with mechanical background" who would be prepared to spend long hours on isolated bush roads with the trucks. It was not long till Allan Horst and Abe Suderman joined Graber, the first of a series of MCC-recruited VS people who were to provide invaluable help. (6) Other Presbyterian personnel would also later make major contributions. (7) With the exception of a four month break in late 1961, Graber was the one constant presence and driving force of the nearly five year CPRA saga in the South Kasai.

CPRA goes public

The two government trucks allocated to Graber for use were now on the road. The Presbyterian Mission also offered a VW minibus if it could be repaired. One of the many vehicles which had been commandeered by the Lumumba troops during their bloody passage through the area, it sat stripped along a bush roadside. Towed back into Bakwanga, parts were scrounged here and there including a new motor flown in from Leopoldville. Put back in running order, the CPRA logo was emblazoned on its sides as well as on the doors of the two trucks provided by the government. (8)

The relief team soon fell into an established routine as they made their endless trips into the surrounding area to carry the precious food and supplies. Prior to distribution there were always some brief preliminaries which Rocke describes thus: "Our work so far has been identified as a ministry made possible by Christians from the churches of America. Our aim has been to let them know that we are giving this help in the name of Christ. We speak of this when we leave food with the Africans who have charge of dividing it among the people. We explain that the love of Christ in our hearts makes us want to live in peace with our neighbors and we are even to love our enemies. I am impressed that they listen to these words so attentively. Our prayer is that they will truly discern that Christ makes a difference in our lives and our actions toward others and that they will repent of the hatred and murder that has been in their hearts and brought them so much suffering and poverty." (9)

Following such brief explanations and homilies, prayers were offered, supplies discharged and the trucks moved on. That CPRA, its identity and ministry were was not viewed with favor and appreciation by all in the area was to become all too evident soon enough.

a daily marathon

Surrounded by staggering need on all sides, the days soon began to blur one into the other. Let Graber's diary entries reflect something of the pressure, pathos and exhaustion experienced:

October 14: "I traveled with a Belgian doctor . . . to get all the medicine that a large dairy farmer had. But when we got there, we found all the medicine of importance stolen."

November 1: "Sixty more refugees were flown in from Tshikapa. This makes me wonder much as to how the CIM men were received on their return."

November 2: "Fifteen killed near Lake Munkamba, only a few hundred yards from where we have a distribution center."

November 3: "The roads are very bad. We haul only five tons on each truck."

November 4: "The company let me have a house to live in. But during the war, everything was stolen. Now we are unable to buy at any price kitchen pots, pans or dishes. We were able to trade some corn flour for a pan to have to boil our drinking water. And we found in an African village some 60 miles from here six bowls which will do for coffee."

November 5: "More than 30% of the children will die of hunger within the next six months unless food and medicines will be gotten to them."

November 7: "Some truck trouble. White man from Luluabourg was taken from our dining room to prison today. Much tension."

November 11: "Between 800 and 1.000 children are getting a cup of milk twice a day and a vitamin pill each. (Mwena Ditu) We will begin giving food here this Wednesday, the Lord willing."

December 21: "The two CPRA trucks were the first to distribute food flown in by the UN Planes. . . The CPRA was asked to distribute food to all the hospitals and dispensaries. . . . With the exception of a little milk and food given by the Red Cross, we are the only ones to get food out to the hungry people."

December 22: "Since Ghanaian soldiers are not liked (10) by the government nor the Baluba people, they have a hard time working with them. In order to get out food to some of the needy places, the CPRA was asked to go ahead of the Ghanaian truck and the Red Cross was to follow. . . . We made the trip without any trouble. Praise God for getting an early start distributing food. We are well known in this entire territory."

December 25: "Christmas and how different. The 'Unchanging Star' was the text for the African pastor's Christmas message this morning. When I returned from church I expected to make a cup of coffee and enjoy a quiet Christmas, for I was alone. But a I found a note on the door asking me to go to the UN headquarters as soon as possible. I went at 10:30 and the captain asked if I would drive a CPRA truck out to Miabi with a load of palm oil. . . . A Red Cross truck was loaded, also a UN truck. A special plane was due at 11 AM with news reporters from all over the world. They like many other globe trotters wished to see how we distribute the food, also report on the condition of the people, all in three hours time - - and on Sunday and, besides, on Christmas. . . . The CPRA received a good bit of publicity in a short time today. . . . The officers of the Ghanaian troops asked me to join them in a Christmas dinner. So Christmas passed, but I hope the next one will be different."

December 31: "1960 is history. Life is a one way street. 'Live in the consciousness that you shall not pass this way again.'"

January 1, 1961: "God holds the keys for the New Year before us. It is because of his great love that He does not reveal the future for us. In these days of unrest, tension, strife and fear we know that his grace is sufficient to meet our every need from day to day." (11)

CPRA challenged

The rapidly growing Protestant-sponsored relief program was the object of tearful gratitude on the part of the mushrooming refugee population. The first organization to appear on the scene, it had won the confidence of the UN personnel and consequently became the primary distributor of an ever increasing flow of UN supplies which were finding their way to Bakwanga both by air and rail.

By January, 1961, such had been the publicity overseas of the wretched situation that even direct air freight flights were arriving on the Bakwanga tarmac with such items as tents from Germany, potatoes from Belgium, powdered milk from Denmark. By that time the UN's own fleet of trucks had grown to 30 units. Thus CPRA concentrated on supplying the medical centers while the UN supplied the sprawling refugee camps. As the flow of supplies increased, the estimated area death rate dropped from 200 to 40 or 50 a day. (12)

It was planting time. Seizing the moment, CPRA personnel began to look beyond the desperate race to provide daily sustenance and interspersed basic food stuffs with truck loads of manioc cuttings. They drove through village after village simply throwing off bundles of these cut sticks and metal hoe heads which could be fitted to wooden handles. The refugees were delighted to take the project from there.

But in spite of the superhuman feat of salvaging a people that was in full swing, there were two powerful figures in the region who viewed this unfolding drama with growing resentment. One was Bishop

Nkongolo (pr. nkaw-NGOH-loh) of the area Catholic Church; the second was none other than Albert Kalonji, the president of the province and self-acclaimed "King" of the Baluba people. Why this disfavor and opposition?

By January, 1961, CPRA was surrounded by a tangled web-work of ecclesiastical and political intrigue in the region. Keidel analyzes the setting with skill. Referring to Kalonji he writes: "There was a threat from the west: the Congo central government, with headquarters in Leopoldville, which hoped to topple him. There was a threat from the north. Antoine Gizenga had established headquarters at Stanleyville and had proclaimed himself heir to the arrested Lumumba as rightful president of the Congo. Pro-communist nations were shipping him arms and his troops were making adventurous forays in the direction of the South Kasai. There was a threat from within. Kalonji's title 'King of the Baluba' was a declaration not of right. Traditionally the progenitor of the Baluba peoples had two sons and the right of chieftainship followed the line of his first born. Kalonji was a descendent of the second born. Unquestionably, the primary factor that would determine Kalonji's attitude toward agencies and personnel around him was political survival. He would take the position that would enhance the possibility of his continuing power. He would be alert to lay hold upon anything which would strengthen his position and quick to eliminate anything which threatened it." (13)

With this perspective it was easier to understand Kalonji's gradual shift in attitude. Whereas at first he went out of his way to solicit, encourage and express gratitude for the relief effort within his "kingdom," he now had come to see it as vying with him for the favor and applause of his own people.

Keidel continues: "The descendant of the first born and rightful heir to the chieftainship of the Baluba people was the Prime Minister Ngalula, second in power to Kalonji. . . . How long would he and his people be content in a position subordinate to Kalonji and his clan? The Kalonji-Ngalula alliance was at best tenuous." (14)

Shifting focus, Keidel writes further: "Then there was the Catholic bishop, Monsignor Nkongolo. . . He had announced in public meetings that there was to be only one church in the Baluba Kingdom and he was its priest. He nurtured friendship with government authorities to that end." (15)

To further complicate matters, the local UN peace keeping contingent was composed of Ghanaians and it was known that Ghana was one of the countries which had by this time sent ambassadorial personnel to Stanleyville thus recognizing the Gizenga regime as the legitimate government of Congo! And to rile the waters still further, newly inaugurated American President John Kennedy had publicly declared his support of UN actions taken which called for the expulsion of all Belgian military units from Congo soil, the disarming of all Congolese troops while charging UN forces with the responsibility for keeping peace throughout the land.

Local reactions in Bakwanga came swiftly. Seeing Americans among them as representatives of a hostile American government which had betrayed them, mission planes were grounded, air strips closed and short wave transmitters impounded. Two Belgian mine executives were jailed as was a CPRA African mechanic on charges of fraternizing with Ghanaians.

It was in the context of this increasingly tense setting that Graber received a visit from Mr. Caballero, the local UN official, the evening of January 5. He shared the news that the local Catholic bishop was very displeased with the way CPRA was conducting its work. He was demanding that the CPRA logos be removed from the government trucks loaned to them and that they be allowed to also distribute some of the refugee supplies. Caballero's quiet suggestion was that the logos be removed to placate the bishop. What was important was for CPRA to remain active in the distribution of desperately needed supplies.

By early February friction with the local opposition was reaching flash point. By this time the government had reclaimed the two trucks earlier loaned to CPRA. A young man, full of self- importance and fully attuned to the perspective of the Catholic bishop, had been named the *Commissaire Général aux Réfugiés* (i.e., the Chief Commissioner for Refugees). It was shortly thereafter that Graber went into his office to secure the usual clearance for delivery of several truckloads of UN supplies to rural hospitals. With a flourish the young "commissioner" stroked a ball point across the requisition sheet and announced: "CPRA no longer exists!" When Graber calmly asked why they could not continue supplying rural medical units with food for his own people as had been agreed with the government and the UN months earlier, the commissioner responded by laying down three conditions for any further CPRA activity: 1) the CPRA logos were to be removed from their own trucks; 2) their trucks were to be driven only by African chauffeurs and 3) their trucks would henceforth be driven only in convoy with UN trucks and that only with his express permission.

Maintaining a calm exterior, Graber seethed inside. Months of frustration and hassle all came together that morning. He stood and informed the young official that until such time as CPRA received some explanation for these actions taken, CPRA trucks would stay parked in their sheds. That said, he stalked out of the office.

Early February 1961 was a time of dark anguish for the CPRA team. They went to bed nightly with haunting mental pictures of hungry children and emaciated adults. They knew all too well which dispensaries needed the next load of milk, rice and corn flour. They had no great confidence in the dependability of an ongoing refugee service that would have to function under the direct authority of a department of a shaky local government via temporary UN personnel and equipment. But CPRA could not accept to be forced into becoming just one more impersonal link in a government/UN chain of command. They would not be reduced to simply providing impersonal transport for UN supplies. They had come not only to feed refugees but also to identify with and listen to them, encourage them and witness to them. Furthermore, they carried a special burden for the hundreds of Mennonite refugees who continued to make their way to Bakwanga. That a desperately needed ministry to suffering people could be stopped by capricious decisions motivated by selfish ecclesiastical and political interests was galling beyond description.

Meanwhile, the political situation was becoming increasingly tense. The long standing local animosity focused on the UN Ghanaian contingent now also spilled over on the Americans of the area. It was again Mr. Caballero who came, one day, counseling that CPRA not only keep a low image for a while but that the two PAX men, Allan Horst and Abe Suderman, be allowed to leave the scene. In his opinion, it would be the wisest for CPRA and the safest for them. Reluctantly Graber put them on a UN plane on February 14. On the 15th, Graber removed the logos from the CPRA trucks. On the 16th he was asked to attend a government-arranged conference with all groups involved in refugee ministries the previous three months. At one point a report was circulated which listed tonnage totals of goods distributed by the UN, the government, the diamond company and the Red Cross. There was no mention of CPRA even though their tonnage totals had been larger than any other group. When challenged by Graber, the African in charge used the pretext that CPRA had failed to submit regular reports, something which was totally false. Since CPRA had been declared "non-existent," they were now simply being ignored! (16)

It was in this somber moment of uncertainty that Graber wrote: "Even though the CPRA signs are off the trucks, yet because of our help before the UN came we are known everywhere we go. I believe that God will honor the prayers of his people, that we will be protected and that the CPRA will continue to help these people and strengthen the Church of Jesus Christ in Congo." (17)

Later the same month, Graber reported on a 20 ton stockpile of rice, milk and beans still in the CPRA warehouse: "The CPRA paid all freight on this food and it belongs to us and we expect to have something to say as to how it will be given out. There are many refugees who have not received food as yet. So when we see some of these needy people we give our food to them asking no questions." (18)

CPRA shifts gears

As all those who have lived and worked in Africa can testify, nothing is more certain than change. Just as it seemed that CPRA was being squeezed out of the South Kasai picture, a government official approached Graber requesting help in relocating the ever growing refugee population. No one in government had either the time or the resources to give this urgent problem the attention it needed. This was it! A new door! A new opportunity! The next day Graber and Rocke were off in their VW minibus to check on some prospective areas familiar to them. From February 28 to March 2, they were constantly traveling with two government representatives contacting local chiefs, checking water sources and agricultural potential. In a report Graber sketched a plan that was taking shape: "We will load about 35 people on each truck plus 10 tents. . . . We will take them to one of these new places, set up the tents and leave some food. They are to have the use of the tents just long enough for them to build a shelter for themselves then we will take the tents to another village. . . . We will as much as possible leave an evangelist in each new village. Also Bibles, New Testaments and some Christian literature. . . . Pray that the CPRA may not only help these people in a material way but also in a spiritual way." (19)

CPRA had turned a corner. It was shifting from a short term focus on fighting starvation to a long term focus of resettlement and rehabilitation of a people.

Reports and letters from this time were peppered with proposals for new projects: a trial batch of 200 day-old chicks air freighted from Sunnybrook Poultry Farms of Hudson, NY directly to the Bakwanga airfield. Although the inventory of basic food was gradually improving, there still was a great lack of protein. Might chickens provide a comparatively quick source? The chicks thrived and proved to be the first contingent of thousands more fuzzy, 'cheeping' solutions for a critical dietary problem.

Now that famine conditions were beginning to recede, CPRA staff expressed increasing concern for desperately needed housing. A recently hostile government was also concerned. Over the following months CPRA engaged in a project which would earn the respect and appreciation not only of thousands of displaced people but also of the vacillating government. A builder with years of construction experience in the African bush, Graber set up a workshop and a crew of African carpenters. With the help of the local Presbyterian Mission, the UN and the government itself, nails and hardware were eventually ordered by the ton, lumber and roofing by the railway car load. Standard sizes were established for wooden doors and windows which, over time, were turned out by the thousands and eagerly purchased by the refugees. Hand-operated brick presses were secured. Teams of workmen were trained and adobe bricks began to appear by the tens of thousands. The government purchased a power operated cement brick press and asked CPRA to assemble and place it in operation.

The carpenter shop was soon enlarged and to the production of doors and windows were now added wooden trusses of a standard size which would be hauled by truck to relocation sites where refugees were striving to reestablish homes.

But never losing sight of the undergirding concern for the spiritual welfare of the people, constant effort was made to secure Christian literature in the Tshiluba language. At one point a 5½ ton load of Tshiluba Scriptures and school supplies was air lifted directly from Leopoldville to Bakwanga. Distribution was accomplished via a VW minibus converted into a bookmobile. Book chests were built and stocked and placed in the hands of pastors and teachers in the refugee communities.

With time, as refugee communities harvested their first crops and secured shelter for themselves, constant requests were made for help to replace their little stick and thatch places of worship with chapels in permanent materials. Also, they wanted to assure an education for their children amidst their newly founded villages scattered across the rolling grass lands of the South Kasai. In time, CPRA fielded building crews to construct multiple room school units and to partner with groups of believers in the construction of places of worship. Further chapters of political conflict, bloodshed, road blocks, menace, burned villages were yet to follow with fresh waves of desperate people which would swirl around the CPRA team in that region. But its identity and ministry would never again be placed in doubt by local political or ecclesiastical authorities.

a day at a time

Stressed as they were by the innumerable daily demands upon their time, supplies and strength, frequently they came to the close of a long day with thoughts only of the long list of problems that needed tackling at sunrise the next day. Little wonder that an occasional entry such as this found its way into Graber's journal: "Today was a rat race: truck with broken spring; people coming with sickly, underfed children; others coming for building material and a telegram that 1,000 chicks will be arriving the 29th or 30th." (20)

His journal also frequently reflected their constant exposure to the stark face of suffering of innocent people: "Glenn and I went to see the Lake [Munkamba] area which was completely destroyed by fire on May 9th. It was heartbreaking to see those poor people who were driven from their homes about a year ago and had worked hard to build simple little houses. They were happy to be in their own Baluba territory. Then on May 9th when nearly everyone was working in their gardens about 11 AM the enemy came and destroyed the entire village by fire. Among those who were killed was one from Tshikapa. . . . He had heart trouble and was unable to walk anywhere. I had prayer with him and his family about 2 weeks ago. He was burned to death; no doubt the rest of the family was in the field and he was unable to get out of the burning house." (21)

And again: "Last evening we were told of many refugees coming from Lusambo where Baluba people are being driven out. We went to see if conditions were as bad as we were told. The road that these people were traveling was the short cut from Lusambo to Bakwanga. . . . We passed many graves. One woman who had died 48 hours or more by the looks of things had been stripped from her clothing, a terrible sight; some things and conditions are hard to believe." (22)

But amidst all manner of reasons for discouragement, pessimism and helplessness, the CPRA team often drew fresh courage from their fellow Africans who suffered the most. On one occasion Graber wrote: "One is made to wonder where they get enough courage to keep on going. There seems to be a feeling that if they can get to so or so a place or over this or that road, it will be better farther on. After having spoken to so many this past week, I do admire their courage." (23)

And on another occasion: "I was impressed in the church service this morning when the choir sang SAIL ON, SAIL ON, SAIL ON. Nothing was said in this song about smooth sailing or a rough sea or the condition of the ship, but we are commanded to sail on." (24)

a simmering political pot

Prime Minister Tshombe and "King" Kalonji of the mineral rich provinces of Katanga and the South Kasai continued to figure prominently in the fluid political situation of the Congo in 1961. Early March saw them both go to Madagascar for a meeting with Congo's President Kasavubu. Here the forceful and articulate Tshombe succeeded in selling the idea of a loose confederation of semi-autonomous province/states within the Congo Republic. Later that month Tshombe paid a visit to Bakwanga where he was received with fanfare and made a major speech.

In late April, however, President Kasavubu convened a second major consultation, this time in Coquilhatville, the capital of the Equator Province which was firmly within the orbit of the central government. Here Kasavubu renounced his apparent support of a loose federation discussed in Madagascar and stated that the best interests of the Congo lay in the direction of a strong central government. When Tshombe strongly objected, he was arrested and temporarily detained. Not wishing to risk the same fate, Kalonji paid lip service to Kasavubu's reversal of the Madagascar agreement. The end result of these political flip-flops was to estrange Kalonji and the South Kasai from everyone. Doubting his sincerity, the Congo central government announced a blockade of all commerce with his province. The Katanga population, furthermore, seeing in Kalonji a fickle neighbor began to view the large Baluba population in their own Elizabethville area with a mix of suspicion and resentment.

All of this gave rise to two major consequences both of which had immediate implications for the CPRA team. First was the increased difficulty this trade embargo created in bringing in greatly needed supplies. They were to become increasingly dependent upon UN intervention in the form of sealed railway cars, truck convoys and chartered air freight.

A second consequence was far more ominous. Under increasing political and economic stress, the uneasy Kalonji/Ngalula coalition disintegrated. On July 14 Kalonji dismissed and imprisoned his prime minister along with a cluster of government figures who were loyal to him. This precipitated a whole new chapter of bitter conflict in the South Kasai which was to have far-reaching effects for Kalonji, for the immense refugee population in general and the growing Mennonite community in particular.

Pastor Kazadi arrives

July 11 was a day much like any other in Graber's pressured work schedule. He had gone to the airport with a departing visitor and to meet an incoming TV crew who wanted to do some footage on the CPRA relief program. To Graber's immense surprise, Pastor Kazadi, his wife Elizabeth, and a small son were also among the passengers who descended from the UN chartered flight. Since there had been rumors circulating in Bakwanga that Kazadi had lost his life in fighting around Djoko Punda, it was an emotional reunion between these two men who had known each other and collaborated together for so many years at Djoko Punda. Kazadi was soon to become a major rallying force amidst the refugee population and, with time, would provide critical leadership for the Mennonites who had made their pilgrimage from the CIM area of the West Kasai.

reflections

It would soon be a year that Graber had arrived at Bakwanga. He was eager to see his family back in Ft. Wayne, IN, and needed some rest. Rev. Carrol Stegall, a retired Presbyterian missionary living in Texas, proved to be cut out of the same tough leather as was Graber. Responding to the challenge, he arrived in July to overlap with Graber for a month and to replace him for a short home leave.

As the days passed, a contemplative note crept into Graber's journal entries. Already as early as March and April, the impact of CPRA efforts were becoming visible. It is "very heartening to drive through new Baluba settlements and see miles and miles of corn fields in tassel and manioc plants three feet or more high . . . from seed corn and manioc sticks we gave them last November." (25)

Referring to the problem of fatigue associated with efforts made over long heavy months, it is stated: "we were repaid when we saw some of the families that we had helped with food and tents that had things cleaned up. In fact, one had a few flowers planted beside his little tent." (26)

And on the eve of his departure for Europe and the States, he wrote: "As I look back over the past year I can see how God has answered the prayers of his people. How often planes came swooping down with food like the ravens that brought food for Elijah, as many as 25 planes loaded with food in one day. And how many times God protected us from being numbered with the many we saw dead along side the road, unburied. How many hungry children that were staring in space with swollen feet and faces, all due to hunger, today these same children are playing around their little shelters which they call home. A year that shall never be forgotten, many things we would like to erase from our memories. But with all the miseries, suffering and hardship, there have been many blessings as well." (27)

ominous new trouble further south

In the swirling political tides of southeastern Congo, a large population of Baluba people were in difficulty in Elizabethville, the capital of Katanga Province. Attracted there just as they had been in earlier years to the West Kasai by opportunities for education and employment, many had found their way into responsible positions in the local industry and commerce.

In August, as Graber left for the States, events reached fever pitch in that provincial capital. Although the UN had ordered the departure of all Belgian military personnel from Katanga Province, Tshombe and his government fiercely resisted this proposal since the Belgian presence, in effect, represented for him a major political force. Furthermore, the local resentment toward the large Baluba population in the city had by now degenerated into open animosity.

A 250-man UN Swedish battalion was dispatched to put UN orders into effect. Katangan soldiers seeking to tighten security began to screen, menace and arrest the Baluba population of the city. By August 26, the first Baluba families began to appear at the UN military camp on the outskirts of the city. With growing tension, this trickle of people steadily grew in number. In early September the UN confrontation with local armed forces erupted in battle. By the time a cease fire was effected on September 20, the Baluba population which encircled the Swedish camp had mushroomed to more than 30.000 people. To this mix was added some 350 prisoners who during the confusion of battle in the streets of Elizabethville had rioted, overpowered their guards, escaped and also fled to the UN encampment. Though some were common criminals, upon arrival at the camp they too, like the rest, claimed to be fleeing danger. With no way of knowing one from the other, all were admitted. Thus a hardened criminal element early took up residence within the camp.

Following a cease fire, Katangan government officials asked the Baluba in the camps to again come to work and to reoccupy their former homes. Fearful for their security, they refused. The government, in turn, retaliated by closing all exits out of the camp. Beyond the reach of Katangan security forces, political activists quickly surfaced within the camp loudly stating their opposition to the Katanga regime. Not always agreeing in their aims, these political factions at times fought with each other.

in the shadow of death

Keidel describes the desperate situation which quickly developed as follows: "The camp became a living hell. Hemp smoking youth gangs extended their acts of barbarism at will. Escaped criminals robbed and murdered. Katangan snipers hiding behind ant hills shot into the camp; during September their bullets claimed two hundred victims. In a tribal battle which purportedly began over use of a water tap, fifty were killed. Still, even in this environment, the necessary physical processes of life continued. Over 200 babies were born in the camp every month. Sanitary facilities were confined to a few private latrines. Hunger changed reasonable men into desperados; they slipped out of the camp at night, vandalized businesses, burglarized homes, terrorized the population. Katangan soldiers launched reciprocal attacks against the camp. The climate became such that during every waking hour, defenseless refugees lived on the jagged edge of terror." (28)

The 250-man UN team struggled heroically to cope. The refugee population was relocated in front of the Swedish camp from its original distribution along the sides and back. Barbed-wire-lined corridors were established from the camp to food distribution points. In December armed conflict again erupted between the UN force and Katangan soldiers. As a result still more sought safety at the camp. By Christmas of 1961, this population of miserable humanity was estimated to be 50.000. By now, UN officials entered the camp only with armed escorts and police dogs. Reviled by the Katangese and suspicioned by the refugees, theirs was a truly thankless and impossible assignment. And yet they resolved to maintain their restraining presence and to provide whatever services they could until some solution could be found. To abandon their post would have resulted in a blood bath of unimaginable proportions. But what solution?

It was just after Christmas, 1962, that the Graber family returned to the Congo. Plans were for Irma to stay with their daughter, Nancy, in Leopoldville to serve as house parent for the school age children of a growing number of CIM families who were returning to the Congo. Archie would spend most of his time in the South Kasai while getting back to Leo as often as possible for breaks with his family. Returning to Bakwanga he discovered that the patience, commitment and past record of the CPRA had stood them in good stead. While more and more refugees were being relocated and rehabilitated, the flow of new arrivals seemed to have no end. Under the enormity and the unrelenting pressure of the task, the government which had earlier so airily excluded the CPRA from food distribution was by now only too happy to accept help wherever it could be found. Would CPRA once again take responsibility for distribution of food to hospitals and dispensaries? CPRA would. In such circumstances, the Catholic Church could hardly do other than grant its tacit approval.

It was in February, 1962, while in Leopoldville that Graber was approached concerning the dismal situation in Elizabethville. The Methodist Church had initiated its missionary endeavor in southeastern Congo before the turn of the century. With a large church membership and significant missionary staff on the scene, they were eyewitnesses to the unfolding tragedy of the trapped thousands of Tshiluba speaking Africans on the outskirts of their city. They had heard of CPRA in the South Kasai and of the missionary who had given primary direction to its widely publicized efforts there. Sketching briefly the nature of the emergency in E'ville, they asked if he would be willing to consult with the UN personnel on the scene regarding the horrendous problem they had on their hands. If arrangements for his travel could be made, he would go, he responded.

On February 28 a planning session was held in Leopoldville with UN personnel. On March 19 Graber flew to E'ville. Met at the plane by a UN representative, he was taken immediately for an interview with Nils Gussing, the relief coordinator of the E'ville refugee program. After a briefing on the situation, Gussing suggested that a good starting point might be to determine the extent of the Baluba population inside the camp. At the same time, Gussing was understandably concerned for Graber's safety and offered all help and protection possible for his assignment.

a messenger of hope

Lodged in the Methodist guest house in the city, Graber was invited to preach the first Sunday morning in the Methodist Church of the city. His message, delivered in Tshiluba, was translated. Unknown to him there were a few Baluba from the camp present in the service. The next morning when Graber went to the UN office he found a little cluster of Baluba Christians, some of whom had been in the service the previous Sunday morning. They offered to accompany him into the camp and introduce him to many others of their fellow tribesmen. Armed with nothing other than his deep compassion for a hurting people, his grasp of the Tshiluba language and his complete trust in his newly discovered friends, he slipped into the camp. Of this experience he wrote: "They made themselves small shelters of whatever they could find - - grass piled on top of sticks - - around the outside of the shacks some tied cardboard, others old sacks or pieces of old canvas. The sanitary conditions are awful. Distribution of food is very disorderly, often results in fighting. It takes over 100 tons of food to feed these people a week. They claim that there are some killed in the camp every night. There is fear within the camp and outside the camp. We visited the cemetery where over 900 have been buried since last September." (29)

Invited back the next day, he went with a group of Baluba camp leaders and listened as they poured out their tale of misery and suffering. Graber reported further: "After they finished telling me what they had to say, they wanted me to preach for them and bring some Bibles for them to buy. They said that no one had spoken to them for the past seven months. I thought of what David said in Psalm 142:4: 'No man careth for my soul.'" (30)

Word of the new Tshiluba-speaking white man spread quickly through the camp. Faction leaders sought out the Baluba Christians wanting to know who this man was and what had transpired. Why had he come? Was he to be trusted? Was this a ruse of the Katangese or the UN? To all of this the Baluba firmly responded that he was indeed to be trusted. As a matter of fact, a few among them even knew him many years earlier when they lived in the far distant West Kasai near a mission called Djoko Punda. He even had an African name: it was Muambi Lutonga.

There was no less apprehension among the UN personnel when they learned that Graber had been moving in and out of the camp with neither their knowledge nor their protection. They tried to impress upon him the sort of risk he was taking and that if he insisted returning again alone, they could accept no further responsibility for his safety. Secure in the belief that he and his mission were now known and understood within the camp, Graber thanked the UN staff for their concern but suggested that he simply be allowed to work on his assignment unhindered.

finding a way

The passing days saw a flurry of activity. Surveys of the camp population were taken. It soon became apparent that no amount of talking would persuade them to leave the camp and to seek reintegration into the jobs and society from which they had fled. They, like their kinsmen of the West Kasai, had finally decided that they were no longer welcome or safe where they were. One way or another, they would return to the land of their forefathers. For a large group, this was the South Kasai. For a smaller group, this was Northern Katanga. And for still smaller groups, hoped for destinations lay elsewhere toward the north.

On March 30, Graber made a trip to Bakwanga with a five-man UN team of officials to meet with local provincial government leaders. Visits were made to a variety of area chiefs to solicit land and an invitation for still more of their refugee kinfolk. Both were readily granted. Little by little some pieces of the puzzle were falling into place. One monumental issue, however, remained unsolved. How were the people to be moved? Travel by road through "enemy" territory was simply not feasible. A major bridge on the rail line half way to the South Kasai had been blown up the year before in the regional conflict. Transport by air would be prohibitively expensive.

All of April was devoted to struggling with the evacuation question. Special ID cards were provided for each person in the camp. Even though a UN guard was posted day and night, the camp population continued to grow. Learning that evacuation plans were under way, others were sneaking past the guards hoping also to flee the troubled area. As consultations between E'ville, Leopoldville and Washington continued non-stop via cable and phone, Graber busied himself not only with the E'ville camp but also with the ongoing CPRA program at Bakwanga. He found time to secure a shipment of Tshiluba Scriptures for distribution in the camp. April 22 found him in Leo with his family. A week later he attended a worship service in Bakwanga where he heard Pastor Kazadi preach a moving sermon based on the life of Job.

Meanwhile in E'ville, final agreement on an evacuation plan for the refugees had not yet been reached - - and the camp population continued to grow. Finally, on the afternoon of May 5, Robert Gardiner, the chief officer of the entire UN Congo Operation, plus ten other staff people arrived. A flurry of cables and phone calls were initiated by this group. By evening of that day, a final plan had been hammered out. The refugees would be transported by rail to Kamina, a former Belgian military base, from where they would be airlifted the rest of the way. The next day Graber eagerly returned to the camp. At last he could bring them the news they had waited so long to hear. After bringing a brief message, as was his custom, the Africans led out in the singing of two hymns: "God Will Take Care Of You" and "God Be With You Till We Meet Again."

Three days later, on May 8, Graber was able to write: "3:30 this afternoon, it was a thrill to see the first trainload of 1,028 refugees leave this terrible camp where they have been more or less imprisoned since last September. (31) They were really happy to go. There are more than 30,000 waiting to go. This is a trial trip. They will be traveling through enemy territory. There are two flat cars in front of the steam engine loaded with sand to protect the engine from being derailed. . . . The first car back of the engine is a flat car with an armored car, machine gun and soldiers. In the center of the train there is another such equipped flat car and at the end, a third. . . . We trust and pray that there will be no bloodshed and all will go well so many more can move real soon." (32)

Shuttling between E'ville and Bakwanga, Graber was the coordinator at both ends of the evacuation trail. Rumors and mistrust were still rife in the camp as the refugees clamored for places on each departing train. His presence and counsel were frequently sought by weary UN staff people. And in Bakwanga, CPRA once again was in the foreground of things, meeting, processing, feeding and transporting people to various newly established sites.

By June 5 Graber would note in a report: "From 600 to 1400 refugees are being brought in by plane daily. Up until now there have been only 17,000 refugees flown into the South Kasai. If the program keeps on like the past week, the camp should be cleared in 5 or 6 weeks. A Gospel of John is given to each family as they arrive here. Most of these people will be without work, shelter and food. Having lost everything you may be sure there are many discouraged people around here. Please pray for the Word of God as it is sold and given out. . . . Pray that we who are working with those people may have the needed strength, wisdom and patience that we may show the spirit of Christ in all we do." (33)

By the end of August, the last train load of refugees had been loaded in E'ville and the last tattered, dismal remains of their miserable camp had been bulldozed. A total of 54,000 people had been relocated in the South Kasai with another 20,000 in North Katanga. In the entire process, no new refugee camp was created. Such was the CPRA planning that all found basic preparation already made for them upon arrival. They could put out their own fields, build their own shelters surrounded by people of their own tribe who welcomed them and helped them to the fullest extent of their ability.

voices and symbols of gratitude

A month later, a letter was received in the CPRA coordinating office in Leopoldville. On UN stationary it was addressed to Ernest Lehman, the CPRA administrative assistant in Leo. It read, in part: "Dear Sir, Now that the refugee camp in E'ville has officially been closed, I should like to express to you my deep gratitude and the appreciation of the Secretary General himself for the voluntary workers who cooperated with our staff in the task of repatriating the occupants of the camp to their places of tribal origin. From 28 May until the end of July, over 72,000 refugees were processed and repatriated and we were able to bring this operation to a quick and successful conclusion only with the assistance of voluntary organizations like your own whose staunch and unfailing support was of tremendous help to our small ONUC staff."

"I should particularly like you to convey my thanks to Rev. A.D. Graber who did such fine work preparing the ground in South Kasai for the reception of the evacuees. In the Bakwanga area, the Rev. Stuart [Presbyterian missionary] was of invaluable help to our ONUC representative, Mr. A. Duncan Smith. Their understanding of the Baluba people and the many and varied problems of the refugees contributed greatly to the success of these particular phases of the operation." (34)

The Baluba refugees, themselves, needed fewer words to state their assessment of what had taken place. Typical of the comments frequently heard was the following: "Had Muambi Lutongo and CPRA not come to help us, we would have died as strangers in a foreign land." As a symbol of their gratitude, a cluster of Baluba village chiefs collectively presented Graber with an immense ivory tusk, measuring over five feet in length, with five bands of carved designs - - each a distinct art motif of the Baluba people. Donated to the AIMM by Graber, this tusk today graces the top of a bookcase in the conference room of the AIMM office in Elkhart, Indiana.

still another cloud on the South Kasai horizon

But just as the Baluba people of the South Kasai seemed about to close a long, dark chapter of suffering, still another conflict suddenly erupted in their midst. It was on September 28, 1962, that an MCC delegation comprised of Executive Secretary William Snyder, Bob Miller and Elmer Neufeld visited Bakwanga for a CPRA program review. Together with Graber they had an audience with President Kalonji. He underscored his concern for the spiritual welfare of his people and affirmed the Protestant presence and contribution that he had witnessed. He emphasized their great ongoing needs in the economic, educational and social areas and inquired whether CPRA might be able to introduce oxen for use in agriculture. The time with him had closed on a cordial and appreciative note. Two days later on the 30th, it was a Sunday and the group went to church. In his journal for the day Graber describes subsequent events: "There were five Congolese singing before starting the service. People began running and as I looked out I saw soldiers coming toward the church. They had their guns pointed directly at us and asked what all these people were doing there. I told them we were having a church service. They said that everyone should go to his home at once."

That afternoon the MCC delegation was able to board their departing flight as scheduled. Subsequent events for the rest of Sunday and succeeding days are sketched by Graber as follows: "Now and again we heard gunfire but not until around 7 PM did they really start shooting. It sounded like a town in the States on the 4th of July. . . . At 10:15 there was a blackout. The heaviest firing was about 3:00 AM and it let up about daybreak."

Monday October 1: "No workers showed up and everything was quiet all day. We vaccinated 1500 chicks and worked around the house. There was much shooting all through the night again. October 2: Most of the government officials have been arrested, some beaten up, and some are in hiding. October 3: Workmen were returning to work. Reports that several have been killed 30 miles from here. Cars and trucks are being taken by soldiers for their transport. One family came to CPRA for protection. Others brought their savings for me to keep for them. One told me what to do with his money and things in case of death.

October 5: Five men from the Embassy and two priests and I had a short conference with members of the government. One French phrase was used several times: 'Things are not clear.' How true. October 7: Pastor Kaleta from Tshikapa who fled from there 3 weeks ago gave a heart searching message in the same place we were made to leave a week ago.

October 10: A flag at half-mast always gives one a feeling of loss or sadness. Today it was different than I have ever seen. The South Kasai flag, with its red and green and a large yellow V which stands for victory, was half-mast upside down and the Congo blue flag with its large yellow star in the center and six small stars next to the mast, was proudly waving in the Congo breeze." (35)

There had been a palace coup. King Kalonji and his supporters in government had been overthrown. On October 30, Prime Minister Ngalula Joseph was officially installed as the South Kasai President with the full approval and blessing of the central government. Dreams of stability and peace for that longsuffering region would have to be deferred yet longer. All elements were in place for another tragic round of conflict.

a recurring nightmare

The sudden shift in political fortunes in favor of the other of the two major Baluba sub-clans left many of the supporters of Kalonji furious. Not only had their clan chief been toppled from power but they now would see places of influence and prestige shifting to members of their rival clan. This they refused to accept peaceably. Of this critical political shift Keidel writes: "Village youth brigades fanatically loyal to Kalonji fled to the forest to hide. Within two months they were engaged in full-scale guerrilla warfare against Congolese occupation troops and the government of Ngalula. The war flared, sputtered, and then flared again for months. It engulfed the western half of the province where the village population was of the Kalonji clan. By March, 1963, 300,000 refugees were again homeless; for many of them, this was the third time within the span of eighteen months that they had lost their homes and taken refuge in the forest or high grass." (36)

As has always been the case across human history, in times of armed struggle, it is the innocent and helpless who pay the heaviest price. It was the daily evidence of this dismal fact that was the most difficult for CPRA staff to cope with. There was the case of Kabasele, a friend of Graber's. He writes: "I had seen at once that something grave was troubling him for it looked like he had been crying. He told me the following story: 'When the rebels came burning houses and killing people, five of my seven children ran into hiding with some school teachers. My wife and two small children also escaped through the tall grass. I myself was hiding in the church with seven other men. The rebels came into the church and found us. We were severely beaten and taken out, they told us, to be burned. Someone said: This man is a teacher evangelist and is not in politics so we better let him go. We did escape, but they broke into my house and everything was stolen - - I have only the clothes that are on my back. If I only knew where my children are.' One of the CPRA truck drivers has not heard from his wife and children for more than a month. All of his things were stolen. Daily reports of this kind come to the CPRA staff. By the above news you can see that the South Kasai Province of the Congo has undergone another blood bath. This is all the more discouraging for we had thought that the worst was surely about over and the refugee problem was about to be solved. . . . They tell us that there are still about 200.000 people, men, women and children living away from their villages in tall grass along the river and in the bushes. They are without shelter and this is the season of heavy rains, living without medical care and in constant fear." (37)

Just a month later, the following entry found its way into Graber's journal: "A painting that hung in St. Paul's Cathedral in London, representing a storm at sea and an anxious woman holding a baby looking from the shore to a ship in the distance battling against the angry waves, carried these expressive words written beneath, 'Will the night soon pass?' This picture describes very well the condition of the thousands of families living in fear not knowing where their loved ones are and not knowing how soon they may be attacked by the enemy. . . . I am sure that words like these are often spoken - - 'Will the night soon pass?'- - as they long for the break of day." (38)

CHAPTER 10   CLINGING TO DREAMS

some who persevered

"Nine men of the Congo Inland Mission will graduate this June from our Bible Institute at Tshikapa. . . . This class of Independence days will have many experiences to remember." (1) Behind these simple statements made in the spring of 1962 lay a mix of drama, turmoil, perseverance and answered prayer. Convened as a new class of eleven couples in the summer of 1959 at Kalonda, two of the couples had been forced to abandon their dreams of study shortly thereafter because of tribal conflict. The rest had just finished their first year of study when political independence exploded around them. With the departure of the missionaries, most of them found their ways back to their home areas.

Upon the return of the first missionary men that fall, nine of the original couples were regrouped at Nyanga where their second year of study was pursued in temporary quarters. The following fall, classes were again opened at Kalonda only to see the school temporarily closed by fresh tribal conflict at nearby Tshikapa. Their eventual graduation bore eloquent testimony to their courage and determination, in the face of all odds, to complete their training for a pastoral ministry within the EMC to which they believed the Lord had called them.

In its own special way, this Bible Institute graduation in the spring of 1962 reflected the mood and spirit of the church leaders and returning missionaries. There had been those first tentative contacts between the three missionary men and the Congo Church, first at Kikwit and then at various other places. There had been the frustrating and stormy sessions of the first meeting of the General Council at Nyanga in November, 1960 during which missionaries present had become the subject of heated commentary as pent-up feelings burst loose. There had been the embarrassing closure of that same meeting when the African members were forced to acknowledge that as of that date, at least, they could not agree upon a choice of the church's first legal representative and thus were temporarily blocked in their effort to apply for their own legal charter as a church. And there was the nagging knowledge that even as they were meeting, their Lulua brothers were gathering elsewhere.

But when, with passing time, it became clear to the church leaders that returning missionaries had no desire to reestablish pre-independence roles, the focus of concern quickly shifted to an enormous agenda of church program which had been disrupted or suspended with the abrupt events of the previous July.

a reservoir of good will revealed

By 1962, the Congolese had had ample time to discover that political independence was not the golden password to a problem-free and charmed new life that many had envisioned. As far as the broad church community was concerned, a two-year absence of missionaries had not only given leaders opportunity to try their hand with new responsibilities but also to discover unimagined problems in the process. It was becoming clear that the Church was at a point in its history where missionary presence, training and skills were still essential to the realization of many unachieved goals. And, finally, there was simply the basic fact that across the years many relationships of confidence, trust, respect and love had been knit between missionaries and Africans. Particularly on the stations and in the rural areas, the question was increasingly heard: "When are 'bana betu' (i.e., our brothers and sisters) coming back?" It was striking and reassuring that at a time when some other missions in Congo were entering a period of bitter strife, suspicion and recrimination with their church leaders, CIM missionaries were being urged to return. Even in moments of disagreement and debate with EMC leaders, there was the historic fact of the sessions with CIM Board members held at Djoko Punda in February, 1960, and the basic commitments made to recast mission/church relations. On more than one occasion a Congolese was heard to say: "At a time when we ourselves had not yet thought about such matters, the CIM Board raised the question of the future of our Church. We admit this and we are grateful."

The invitation to return that was extended to CIM missionaries was not unconditional, however. Tshilembu Nicodeme, a trained teacher who was soon to be named the educational secretary of the EMC primary schools, stated it well in a welcoming speech addressed to missionaries in Tshikapa on March 8, 1962, on the occasion of a meeting and meal with Lulua church leaders. Following are excerpts from his presentation: "In the name of the Church of Tshikapa *Cité* (which at the time was a Lulua congregation) and in my own name . . . I seize this occasion to . . . thank you for having accepted to respond to this invitation. Welcome. No one is unaware that since our Congo's accession to its independence, our Church suffers from many illnesses in its different departments. These illnesses are due to human, financial and moral deficits. It is these illnesses which are at the root of all of the difficulties which we presently experience. Desiring to resolve these problems, it is judged to be wise to work hand in hand, white and black, men and women, child and adult. The hour has struck for us to unite in all domains in order to make of this Congo Church a church worthy of its name, a stable church, a church approved not only by human beings but also by its supreme Chief who is in heaven. Our Church has need of people who are honest, dynamic and deserving of supporting it. We must each one work in accordance with his qualities and competence without taking into account his clan, tribe or race. Let us prove ourselves before being given this or that responsibility. . . . To you, our missionaries, we regret, on the one hand, that we no longer find you on each of our stations to help the Congolese to support their own church themselves. On the other hand, we are persuaded that our desire to have missionaries among us touches you. We, therefore, transmit this desire to the CIM Board in America."

"It is not yet time to leave us alone; you must be at our side to help us and to prepare us at the same time. Bring to us still other missionaries who are concerned to help us, to collaborate with us without continually placing us under a yoke of neo-colonialism or minimizing us. Your mission is to help us to raise our religious, moral, intellectual, social and material standing. That is why your presence is helpful among us and that for an indefinite period of time. We must be respected as you are respected everywhere in the world. . . . Thus this little ceremony is organized to symbolize our pleasure in seeing you again among the Congolese and, especially, among us, to work closely with us. This is also an exhortation to us as Congolese toward bonds of collaboration and understanding within our Church. Let us fulfill, whites and blacks, our task without fear; let us follow the example of a shepherd who lives for his flock. God will never forget us." (2)

a surge of response

The trauma of evacuation in July of 1960 had, understandably, been experienced differently by different people. Some missionaries, in all sincerity, felt this to be an indication that the Lord was closing one door of opportunity and calling them to explore new ones. For others, their departure was a heart-wrenching experience accepted only with great reluctance. When it became clear that there was still opportunity for service coupled with a genuine invitation from the Congo Church, response was immediate. Across Canada and the United States from amidst its diverse Mennonite constituent communities, an inter-Mennonite missionary team once again took shape.

At first, it was a few men who returned alone. Shortly thereafter a contingent was sent to Leopoldville comprised of Larry and Alvera Klassen Rempel and Irena Liechty who joined the Bontragers at LECO, the inter-Protestant press. Betty Quiring was sent to help as a translator for Ernest Lehman who had been posted to Leopoldville by the MCC in an administrative role with the newly formed CPRA. Mary Epp returned to teach temporarily in the re-opened American School. By the fall of 1961, Peter and Gladys Klassen Buller became the first couple to return to the Congo interior with children as they accepted an assignment to open a new secondary school at Mukedi Station.

By year's end, 1961, some wives and children had joined their spouses, e.g., Irma Beitler Graber, Ruth Jantzen Roth, Elfrieda Regier Loewen, and Ina Rowell Rocke. In addition were Russell and Helen Yoder Schnell, Harvey and Avril Reimer Barkman and Mrs. Martha Janzen, widow of the Mennonite Brethren Congo pioneer, Aaron Janzen. Martha was assigned as translator to non-French speaking doctors who responded to CPRA's "Operation Doctor." Except for those whose assignments kept them in the city, all others found their way back to the traditional rural CIM regions. By the summer of 1962, a missionary retreat brought together approximately sixty missionaries. Retreat a year later listed a total of seventy.

a variety of pressing needs

Having witnessed the reopening of schools, the re-launching of medical services and pastoral ministries to isolated stations and a formal application for their own legal charter, church leaders turned to other needs. Most persistent was the clamor for new sections of secondary-level education in areas other than Nyanga. The hunger and desire for post-primary education in the early 60's needed to be witnessed to be understood. There was a deeply-rooted sense on the part of the Congolese in general and the youth in particular of having been systematically held back by the Belgian philosophy of colonization. One proof, as far as they were concerned, was the deliberate decision to limit public education - - for years - - to a primary level followed by an array of vocational training options. Secondary education designed to lead to university training was, when available at all, in the hands of the Catholic Church and that for students who declared their commitment to a life's vocation of the priesthood.

Now that the Congo had its independence, the first objective of hundreds of youth from Mennonite families in the Kwilu and the West Kasai was to find entrance into a secondary school. They obviously looked first to the CIM and the EMC for such opportunity. There was a sense of urgency in the air; youth everywhere were in a hurry to make up for lost time. Both missionaries and church leaders were concerned that the CIM and EMC provide, for at least some of the youth of their area, not just a secondary education but ongoing Christian formation as well.

Even as they affirmed the Kalonda Bible Institute as an ongoing training program for rural pastors, the church leaders spoke openly of their concern for the next generation of leadership. From where would they come? How could they prepare and equip some of their sons to one day meet their secondary and even university graduates on an equal footing and proclaim to them the claims of Christ in a credible manner?

The EMC leaders went even a step farther. It was not enough to be concerned only for their sons. It was time to also think of their daughters. If it was part of their responsibility to encourage the establishment of Christian homes, where were the Christian young men with rising standards of education to look for their life partners?

Then there were their bush dispensaries and maternities. They could not always look to the missionary doctors and nurses for help and healing. Where and how could they send students for training in these skills?

And, there was more. The church leaders had always been told by their missionaries that they needed to strive to become a self-supporting church. Their members needed to learn to share their resources to support their own pastors and church activities. But in a rural, subsistence economy, there often was little to give. How could the Church help its large rural membership to better clothe and feed itself and, in turn, have more resources for the support of their Church?

Most important of all, in the midst of rapid change and an uncertain future, how could they be more effective in their ongoing witness in their newly independent land both among the village folk and in the rapidly growing urban centers?

Such was the mix of issues that surfaced again and again in the early 60's as returning missionaries sat with African co-laborers both in scheduled meetings and informal discussions. In spite of local tribal conflict and country-wide political confusion, CIM and the EMC together determined not only to revive ministries that had been abruptly suspended in 1960, but also to launch new ones.

a new home for the Bible Institute

The study of the preceding Bible Institute class having been disturbed and uprooted twice in three years, it was decided to temporarily relocate the school west of the Loange River at Kandala Station. This would take it out of the volatile tribal situation along the Kasai River into what was then felt to be the calm and stability of the neighboring Kwilu Province. This would mean building a whole new temporary complex of school rooms and housing for the new class which was to be brought together from across the EMC area. It would be an expensive and time consuming effort but such was the determination to somehow maintain an ongoing pastoral training program that expense had to be a secondary concern. During dry season of 1963, Loyal and Donna Williams Schmidt were moved across the river to direct a crash dry-season building program. PAX men, Larry Unruh and Alfred Neufeld, joined them. Thousands of sun-dried bricks were made as loads of thatch and building poles were gathered from the surrounding rolling grass lands and valleys. An African work crew put in long hours. By early October, all of the adobe walled buildings were under cover as Harold and Gladys Gjerdevig Graber arrived to assume direction of the Institute. Finishing touches on the building project were to be applied by the students themselves as their first school year progressed.

a new theological school also

In the meantime, inter-Mennonite dialogue in the Congo had been renewed. The Mennonite Brethren missionaries and church leaders were also talking about a higher level of pastoral training in the post-independence era. Having proven in the joint secondary school effort at Nyanga that a shared institution could greatly profit all concerned, the issue of a joint theological program was approached with early enthusiasm. With the earlier decision not to reactivate the inter-Mennonite missionary children's hostel at Kajiji, this freed a set of buildings that seemed suitable for the new school. Some minor remodeling was undertaken and in the fall of 1963, an inter-Mennonite class of sixteen student families was assembled at this station near the Angola border. Peter and Annie Rempel Falk were the first CIM staff appointed to the school. Alfred and Viola Schmidt were the Mennonite Brethren appointees. Alfred was named the school's first director.

Since the academic background and experience of the new students were not uniform, it was decided to first offer an introductory year of preparatory study to be followed by a four year program leading to a diploma. Parallel courses were immediately prepared for the wives as well. Of that period Peter Falk wrote: "The beginning of the school is small and humble. The facilities are somewhat limited. But we are convinced that God can bless and fructify his Word without an elaborate physical plant." (3)

toward university training

In addition to the efforts that were made in Congo, there were also, in the fall of 1963, three Congolese couples studying in the States on CIM scholarships. Having spent one year together in the Freeman, South Dakota community in orientation and language study under the tutelage of Tina Quiring, the men were then enrolled as freshmen in three different colleges - - Ilunga Maurice in Freeman (SD) Junior College, Mbualungu Theodore at Taylor University, Upland, IN, and Ilunga Robert at Bluffton (OH) College.

Within Congo itself there were also new inter-mission initiatives being taken on the educational front. Largely at the initiative of the Methodist Mission active in eastern and southeastern Congo, something called the Congo Polytechnic Institute was brought into being in 1961 which was designed as a pre-university level of training. Former CIM missionary Melvin Loewen had just finished requirements for his Ph.D in political science at the Free University of Brussels, Belgium. Returning to Leopoldville with his family, he became one of the professors. Within two years this Institute became the springboard for the creation of a Free University in Stanleyville in northeastern Congo of which Dr. Loewen became the first *recteur* (i.e., academic dean). This proved to be a fateful development for it took him and his family to that city in the summer of 1963.

re-accenting the printed page

There had always been a major Mennonite emphasis upon the production and distribution of Christian literature in the languages of the tribal groups found in the CIM/EMC area. Already by 1935 Miss Agnes Sprunger's translation of the New Testament into the Giphende language had been published by the British and Foreign Bible Society. (4) In the early 50's a committee was at work on a revision of this translation after which they were to undertake a revision of an existing but unpublished manuscript of the Old Testament which also had been done by Miss Sprunger prior to her retirement in 1953. (5)

Before independence there had already been an inter-mission Tshiluba regional literature committee which had been the clearing house for Christian literature to be published and distributed among the millions of Tshiluba-speaking people of the two Kasais. This committee, reactivated in April, 1962, made a determined effort to create a more systematic distribution of Tshiluba literature once it was printed. These concerns brought the CIM/EMC once again into close collaboration with the Presbyterian Mission with its headquarters in Luluabourg and its own printing press at one of their stations, Luebo. There was, further, the dream of publishing a Christian Tshiluba periodical which could challenge thinking and discipleship of the Tshiluba-speaking Presbyterian and Mennonite Christians alike.

Much of this dreaming and planning came together in an assignment for Levi and Eudene King Keidel. Having been caught up in the missionary evacuation of July 1960, Levi opted to enroll in the Medill School of Journalism at Northwestern University, Evanston, IL. Completing his masters degree in journalism in the spring of 1962, they were ready for reassignment. Funds were raised among central Illinois Mennonite Churches for the purchase of a heavy-duty truck chassis and its conversion into a rugged bookmobile. It was to be used to open and supply a network of book retail points over a large Tshiluba language area under the umbrella organization LIPROKA, i.e., The Protestant Book Store of the Kasai. Keidel also became editor of a new magazine which in the confusion and instability of the early 60's in Congo was appropriately given the Tshiluba name *TUYAYA KUNYI?*, i.e., WHERE SHALL WE GO?

harnessing the transistor

A long-standing dream among CIM missionaries had been that of utilizing the airwaves as a means of witness and ministry in a land that had seen transistor radios mushroom everywhere and where travel was difficult and time consuming. Though talked about before 1960, the press of other activities and mission commitments had delayed this venture. With the upheaval of independence, however, the dream of a radio ministry was revived with vigor.

Important to this new effort were the interest and gifts of Charles and Geraldine Reiff Sprunger. Son of CIM career missionaries, Vernon and Lilly Bachman Sprunger, he had spent his childhood years in the Congo and acquired a love for the land and its people. Though both were qualified as teachers, Charles also had a strong interest in electronics and had acquired considerable practical skill in this area. When he expressed direct interest in gathering taped materials which could eventually be used in a radio ministry, some equipment was made available. Based at Mukedi with classroom duties, he nonetheless began collecting a taped library of music and short devotional messages. Even this modest beginning was wiped out when their home was later gutted in the course of the Kwilu rebellion. Dreams, however, are fire resistant. It was only a few weeks after the evacuation of Mukedi personnel (6) that an important meeting took place in Luluabourg. On March 10-12, 1964, a group of missionaries convened who represented the CIM and the neighboring Presbyterian Mission and who were determined to launch a cooperative recording studio "for preparing taped Christian programs in the Tshiluba language . . . for broadcasting by radio." A subsequent report on the meeting observed: "We have talked and prayed a long time for Tshiluba programs for use over radio and now it is finally materializing. Praise the Lord!" (7)

Initially called CERPROKA, i.e., "Protestant Radio Center of the Kasai," it was hoped to secure adequate facilities and equipment to produce Christian programming on a regular basis for airing over provincial and national radio stations which had offered free air time for such material in the Tshiluba language. At the time it was the only one of four major languages of the Congo for which no Christian programming was available. (8) Given the Sprungers' sudden availability following their evacuation from the Kwilu, it was decided that Charles should be the director of this new inter-mission effort of witness.

The first facilities were modest indeed - - the garage and one bedroom of their rented quarters. The bedroom was converted into a control room. Carton egg flats were attached to walls and ceilings of the garage, a couple of rugs were placed on the cement floor and it was declared a recording studio.

In the meantime, missionaries and Congolese prayed and searched for more adequate quarters. In time, an ideal solution emerged. In the turbulent days of early independence, many expatriates decided that their future in Congo was too uncertain and sought to sell their assets for whatever they could in preparation for their return to Europe. One such was a Belgian citizen who had built a four-plex apartment unit within a short walk of the Luluabourg business district. Approached by the CERPROKA committee, he offered to sell his building at a bargain price. Funds were raised and the location was purchased. After years of discussion and indecision, things suddenly moved swiftly. Remodeling and the accumulation of needed equipment and supplies was pursued in earnest. A bit less than half of the floor space was utilized for living quarters for the director and his family plus a guest bedroom. The balance of the building was converted to offices, recording studios and storage space. In the meantime, the name of the studio was changed to STUDIPROKA (French acronym for "The Protestant Studio of the Kasai") and an air logo adopted - - *Tshiondo Tshia Moyo*, i.e., "The Drum Call of Life." Approximately two years from the date of purchase, the Studio had an excellent permanent home.

But even prior to occupancy of the new quarters, some tapes were coming from the "egg flat studio". Already on December 6, 1964, the first program was aired over the local Luluabourg station. In March, 1965, the first program was featured on the national radio in Leopoldville and in April, programming was for the first time aired over the provincial radio of the South Kasai. In June 1965, radio station ELWA, a powerful transmitter established by the Sudan Interior Mission in Monrovia, Liberia, beamed the first Tshiluba programming into the Kasai region of the Congo. By the time the new Studio was put into service, six or seven 15 minute programs per week were already being aired over this combination of transmitting facilities.

a new sound amidst the "cha-cha-cha"

Commenting on the musical radio fare which was available to the Congolese listeners as Studiproka broke in on the scene, Sprunger wrote: "As one goes through a Congo city or village, one's eardrums are bombarded by blaring 'cha-cha-cha' and other dance music coming out full blast from loudspeakers of cabaret music systems, or from family radios around which the neighborhood may be gathered, or from portable transistor radios being sported by their owners as they stroll proudly down the street or road. As a matter of fact, 'cha-cha-cha' and related types of music make up the highest part of the radio listening diet of the Congolese." (9)

The Tshiluba-speaking population soon discovered the short program segments under the call insignia "Tshiondo Tshia Moyo." It was not long until requests began to come in for cassette tapes of favorite programs - - especially of hymns sung by smaller groups or choirs. When these were made available, they were an instant success and sales were brisk. These tapes gave rise to some startling developments. Always on the lookout for popular music to play for their patrons over their own cassette players, the owners of innumerable bars did not hesitate to alternate the Studiproka tapes with their repertoire of Congo music. As a result one could frequently pass such places with the strains of some well known hymn reverberating through the speakers in a crowded room of people in varying degrees of sobriety.

With time, changes and adjustments took place in the Studio. Congolese personnel were trained and added to the staff. In this process Mr. Muamba Mukengeshayi (pr. mwah-mbah moo-KHEH-ngeh-shah-yi) was named the first Congolese director. Missionary personnel provided technical support while interacting with staff in developing program ideas. In addition to devotional and musical programming, a series of public service programs were done which zeroed in on issues of public health, public morality, alcoholism, divorce, youth problems, child care and Christian marriage. These proved to be very popular.

The flow of mail grew steadily in the late 60's. Questions and requests ranged across a wide spectrum of topics. Questions having to do with the place and role of the Holy Spirit in the life of the Christian were common. Occasional questions prompted smiles. One listener wondered what dialect was used when the serpent spoke to Eve. One student wondered where on the map the land of Paradise was to be found. But for the most part, questions were oriented toward the problems encountered by Christians in the routine of daily life. Every letter received was answered individually by African staff. To help with the increasing flow of correspondence, Pastor Ngulungu (pr. ngoo-LOO-ngoo) Benjamin was added to the Studio staff. When a hymn request program was inaugurated, an overwhelming favorite was the old American gospel song which had been translated into Tshiluba many years earlier, "When the Roll is Called up Yonder."

Across the years, the fortunes of the Studio ebbed and flowed. A pattern emerged in which the CIM/EMC was expected to provide expatriate staff while the Presbyterians provided the majority of operating funds. It was not always possible to replace furloughing or terminating missionary personnel. (10) During such gaps, equipment sometimes broke down; provincial transmitters also sometimes went off the air due to technical problems all of which, at times, restricted outlets for the Studio programs. But at whatever level of productivity, the Studio maintained an unbroken identity among Tshilua-speaking people of the two Kasai Provinces. "Tshiondo Tshia Moyo" has been a constant voice of hope, encouragement and witness to the love and grace of the Lord Jesus. Mail is constant evidence of the fact that it continues to speak to and impact many people for good amidst the discouraging and often chaotic conditions in which they live and attempt to cope.

new pathways by air

In the aftermath of Congo's suddenly-granted independence, the country's road system was an early casualty. The network of bush roads served well as long as there was constant maintenance on the part of hundreds of men with their long-handled shovels. When, with the sudden departure of the Belgian administrators, pay for the road crews ceased, these cross-country trails deteriorated rapidly. In rainy season, they were quickly cut by gullies; in dry season, sand which had washed down the inclines quickly became deep sand traps. Two-wheel drive vehicles which had served well prior to independence soon became useless. Even four-wheel drive, high clearance jeep-type vehicles and trucks soon required constant repair. Spread over an area equal in size to the state of Illinois, CIM/EMC personnel struggled more and more with the problem of inter-station travel and supply.

Already before 1960, preliminary contacts had been made with the Missionary Aviation Fellowship. (MAF) After conducting a survey, MAF administrators stated that, at the time, there were other parts of the mission world requesting help whose problems were more severe and thus needed to receive a higher priority in the allocation of their limited resources. Following independence, however, the Congo and its sprawling mission/church community quickly became a primary MAF concern. Mission/church groups were being encouraged to install landing strips far and wide.

Already by the fall of 1961, a 700 meter dirt strip had been cleared and leveled at Nyanga which permitted MAF planes to fly in and out of that station. Work crews were soon at work at other stations dropping trees, grubbing stumps, leveling ground. With time, strips began to appear at EMC regional centers as well. By 1965, the CIM raised funds to purchase its own Cessna 185. This plane was leased to MAF which, in turn, committed itself to provide both pilots and maintenance of the plane on a replacement basis. Initially based at the government air strip at Tshikapa, both plane and pilot were subject to the scrutiny and whims of government and military personnel. An MAF base was consequently established at Nyanga to which equipment and personnel were promptly moved. CIM/EMC's first two MAF couples were Bob and Edie Gordon and George and Kathy Wall. The high-pitched hum of the single engine Cessna 185s became a familiar and welcome sound to Africans and missionary personnel, alike, in the widely scattered centers of CIM/EMC. With its underslung freight pod, the plane flight logs across the years carried a colorful mix of personalities and baggage. Where in some cases a trip between two points by road required a long, difficult and tiring day via round-about routes, a direct flight of 20 minutes sufficed to cover the bee-line distance on the map.

In the course of its CIM/EMC history, MAF has assembled committee members, transported church delegates and officers, deposited medical and evangelism teams, rescued menaced missionaries, sped desperately ill and injured people to hospitals, ferried missionary children to and from school, carried arriving and departing mission personnel to their destinations and delivered precious mail and medical supplies. Once established and in full service, it became increasingly difficult for CIM/EMC personnel to imagine maintaining mission/church life and activities without it. It soon became a precious service, indeed. (11)

new hands at the Elkhart helm

In the home office of the CIM, once again there was change in administrative personnel. With the departure of H.A. Driver and the appointment of V.J. Sprunger as Executive Secretary in the spring of 1961, George and Justina Wiens Neufeld were invited to serve on home staff, George as treasurer and Justina as headquarters hostess.

Because of the complex post-independence issues that confronted returning missionary staff, Sprunger was frequently urged to make trips to Africa. Having served before 1960 both as field treasurer and mission legal representative, he had an understanding and grasp of historical details that were now invaluable. It was finally decided that Sprunger could make a more critical contribution on the scene in Africa than in the home office.

It had originally been the illness of his wife, Lilly, which had brought him to the States. He laid her to rest in September, 1960. In June 1962 he sought the hand of CIM missionary Irena Liechty in marriage. In the fall of 1963 the CIM Board accepted the urgent pleas of CIM missionary personnel and released the Sprungers for return to the field.

For a replacement, the Board turned to its own chairman, Rev. Reuben Short. First named to the CIM Board as a representative of the EMC/US in 1943, he had served in that capacity for 20 years. He had been a member of the delegation which sat with Congo Church leaders in the historic meeting of February 1960 at Djoko Punda. A graduate of Taylor University of Upland, IN and Asbury Seminary of Wilmore, KY, he came to his new role of CIM leadership having served as a pastor for nine years and as the executive secretary of the EMC/US for fifteen.

Short's approach to his new responsibilities was promptly reflected in early articles in CIM's quarterly, The Congo Missionary Messenger. Referring to the upheaval which came with political independence in 1960 he wrote: "Remember those days? Relatives, friends, boards, and the church had some anxious moments. Reactions ranged from responsibility to complete abandonment. . . . United Nations became involved. Tension was high within and without. Which way should this young nation turn? What kind of government would emerge? Would the doors remain open to the Gospel? Speaking for the Congo Inland Mission, those doors are wide open at present. A new nation is emerging. There is growing hunger for a better life. The call is for knowledge, health, material goods, political leadership and religious understanding. . . . The Congo Inland Mission is first and foremost geared to bringing the gospel of Jesus Christ to them. . . . The Congo Inland Mission has [also] had and continues a policy of helping the total man. Jesus healed the sick, fed the hungry, instructed the illiterate, and pointed the lost to himself as Savior. We can do no less if we propose to follow his pattern." (12)

A comment regarding the place and significance of education vis-à-vis evangelism is also revealing: "A technically trained person, morally unprincipled, spiritually untouched and socially irresponsible, can be very dangerous. Of such is the essence of violence." (13)

With a firm commitment to an inter-Mennonite approach to witness and service in the Congo, he brought a constant pastoral, Biblical and theological perspective to Board discussions and to his correspondence with the CIM missionary team over the next eleven years.

back on the Congo's national scene

By January, 1963, all of the Congo was again at least theoretically loyal to the central government. With the considerable help of the UN, King Kalonji's South Kasai had been brought back into line. The early attempt by some of Patrice Lumumba's former ministers to establish a rebel government in Stanleyville had also been squelched. For a time, Moise Tshombe's secessionist government in ore-rich Katanga Province had held out but after months of skirmishing and maneuvering, UN and ANC forces defeated the Katangese in a final decisive battle waged through the streets of Elizabethville. While Prime Minister Tshombe and some of his ministers were arrested, many of his troops fled across the border into neighboring Angola. They were to become key players in later bloody chapters of Katanga's history.

For the time being, however, Kasavubu and Adoula were savoring a revived dream of their own. After 3½ years of bloodshed, confusion and rivalry, Congo at last was united under a single government. (14) But even though Congo's blue flag with its large yellow star now flew over all of Congolese soil, it quickly became sadly evident that all was not well.

CHAPTER 11   THE EARTH CATCHES FIRE

For several days that January of 1964, it had been unusually quiet at Kandala Station - - unnaturally quiet. No longer was there to be heard the carefree laughter of school children wending their way across the station. They had already returned to their anxious village parents. No longer was there to be overheard the good natured banter of Congolese women vending their garden produce at missionary kitchen doors. They were staying close to their villages. The normal, relaxed, bustling atmosphere of a heavily-populated Congolese community had been replaced by one of uncertainty and vague dread. People stood about in small, uneasy clusters, exchanging the latest spate of rumors in hushed voices. Teachers and church leaders, faces drawn in expressions of worry and concern, drifted past missionary homes - - some to ask questions, some to seek counsel and some just because they didn't know what else to do. Overheard outside a missionary window was the following snatch of conversation: *Mavu etu akuata tshuya; tulenge gio gui?* (Our earth has caught fire; where can we flee?). Some 65 miles to the north at Mukedi Station, CIM missionaries were surrounded by the same abrasive atmosphere.

popped bubbles

June 30, 1960 had been awaited with tremendous excitement and anticipation. There was wild rejoicing as the Belgian colonial rule was formally terminated and newly-elected Congolese political leaders took over the functions of government. Never mind that many of the expectations, particularly in the rural areas, had been naive. What mattered now was the growing, bitter realization that life for most Congolese was worse than it had been before, not better.

As early as January, 1963, a bitter, open letter of protest addressed to Prime Minister Adoula was formulated by the FGTK (General Federation of Workers of the Congo) and the CSCC. (Confederation of Christian Syndicates of the Congo) In part the letter read: "After thirty months of independence, what do we ascertain? The populations of many regions of the country, in order to survive, have been reduced to practicing an economy of subsistence resulting, among other things, in the disappearance of any trace of modern, material civilization in these regions. The rate of infant mortality has increased in the interior of the country in unbelievable proportions and endemic illnesses have reappeared due to the lack of doctors and medicines. The children belonging to families of comfortable circumstances of the country have been placed in boarding schools of the middle class of Europe while hundreds of thousands of children of the people, for lack of buildings, educational material and teachers, are condemned to illiteracy. The whole world stands dumbfounded and powerless before the family quarrels which have divided the leaders of the country and favorized the commitment of monstrous crimes which have caused doubt regarding our political maturity and plunged thousands of families into mourning. In place of giving the example of austerity apt to favorize the cleaning up of public finances which is the base of all economic recovery, the parlementarians grant themselves salaries in the order of 70,000 francs per month and ministers 130,000 francs (1) in a young country where the economy is eternally sick and where the buying power of the laboring masses diminishes from day to day. Profiting from a climate of confusion under which we live since the accession of the country to independence, fishers in troubled waters have built colossal fortunes by dipping into public funds or by exploiting their privilege as politicians."

"But we are determined, at this period of our life, to pursue our campaign of information among the laboring masses of which we are the spokesmen, until such time as all such scabby sheep be removed from our political institutions and public administration and be brought to justice. This is a moral obligation from which we cannot withdraw ourselves." (2)   Kabue, the Zairian historian, goes on to comment that this protest reflected very accurately the feelings of the farmers, the small business people of the rural areas and the people of the street. Even the lyrics of popular singing groups picked up on these themes and developed them effectively - - so much so that alarmed government functionaries complained to the Minister of Justice of the time. Their suggestion? Quiet their protests by throwing them in jail!

From his perspective in the academic community of Leopoldville in early 1963, former CIM missionary, Mel Loewen wrote: "The fact that except for Sector Chiefs the Congolese did not participate in administration is now lamented by Belgians as well as Congolese. . . . Besides the desire common to all men to have a kingdom of their own, local loyalties favored the tribe and the clan at the expense of the nation - - a nebulous term striking no common chord. . . . The fundamental economic problems revolve around transportation, public finances and agriculture. . . . The Congo government will have to face financial responsibility. Too many friends and brothers have swollen the government payrolls. Fat salaries for cabinet members and repeated pay hikes of wage earners have encouraged an uncontrolled inflation which has devalued the Congo franc to 1/5 its former value. . . . Too many well trained teachers and technicians [are] sitting in government offices with secondary positions and not showing the concern for the education of their own younger generation. . . . The total complex political and economic problem in the Congo invariably points to an irresponsible set of values. As leaders realize the [truth of the] old adage 'work before play' and show by example their concern for the well-being of their people, the more developed nations will take renewed interest in helping the Congo. Foreign nations through the UN helped preserve the territorial integrity of the Congo. Before undertaking an expanded development phase they would like to see more serious concern on the part of the Congolese themselves." (3)

Kabue concludes his commentary on this situation: ". . . for certain ranks of the population, particularly in intellectual circles, the failure of men proves that the system is depraved. In their eyes, only a radical revolution can rectify the situation." (4)

Kabue was right.

drying tinder

For the rural people of the eastern third of Kwilu Province in late 1963, there was little grasp of national economics, world marketing problems, deteriorating national infrastructure or the dynamics of inflation. They did, however, know all too well that life was gradually becoming more difficult. Prior to independence, they certainly had never been wealthy but they nonetheless had been able to purchase the necessities of their simple rural life at the thatch-roofed bush stores of their area. There never was any question about being able to buy a packet of rock salt, a new bush knife, a bottle of kerosene, a bicycle tire, a box of matches, a tin of tomato paste or sardines as they needed them. It was also within their ability to secure, now and again, a new, brightly flowered piece of cotton print to be fashioned into a blouse or wrap-around skirt for a wife or daughter, or a new shirt or pair of sandals for the man or son of the household. Roads to other villages or to the government posts and commercial centers were for many people long, dusty and hot. But there were bridges over streams and ferries over rivers. There were also answers and supplies once they got there.

But life was different now. No longer could it be taken for granted that salt or kerosene would always be available at the closest bush store - - and if it was found, it seemed the price had always increased since the last trip. Even though some new cotton prints were sometimes found neatly draped over their bamboo racks, the prices were becoming more and more prohibitive. Some made trips to the closest state dispensary only to find it without needed medicines or closed altogether.

And withal, there were the galling stories that they kept hearing about some of their fellow Congolese in Leopoldville who were riding about in shiny, black cars driven by uniformed chauffeurs, shopping in the big glittering city stores with fully stocked shelves. When they decided to travel to Europe or elsewhere, planes were always available and money was no problem. In the meantime, they in the bush had to make do with ever more faded clothing. Sandals and bicycle tires were patched and re-patched with small slivers of forest vine. With increasing frequency evening meals of mush were eaten with bowls of flat tasting greens for lack of salt. Sitting around their village camp fires at night, more and more irritated comments could be heard such as "*DEE-pah-ndah yetu yatubola*," i.e., "Our independence has gone sour on us," or "*Gouvernement yetu ya athu alabui yafua*," i.e., "Our government of black people has died."

Among the followers of former Prime Minister Patrice Lumumba, who had identified with and supported the short-lived rebel government established briefly in Stanleyville, were two people well-known and honored in the Kwilu Province. The first was Gizenga (pr. gi-ZEH-ngah) Antoine. Born in 1925 in Gungu Territory within 35 miles of Kandala Station, he went to a primary school at the Catholic Mission at Muhaku. He then took 6 years of Latin-oriented humanities in what was called the "minor seminary" of Kinzambi. This was followed by 3 more years in a "major seminary" at Mayidi after which he was for a year in charge of a Catholic Mission post named Mbeno.

Leaving the service of the Catholic Church he worked first, for a while, in the Bank of Congo Belge in Kikwit and then received a position with the colonial administration in Leopoldville. He is described by Thomas Kanza, a Zairian political historian who knew him well, as follows: "He was a thoughtful man, who acted carefully and whose silence and determination won him respect on all sides. . . . I knew him to be taciturn, but determined and indeed obstinate at times; he was also a romantic, and basically sentimental. His great relaxation was playing the guitar."

Gizenga was among those selected to attend the political round tables held in Belgium prior to independence. He took advantage of this opportunity for travel to visit eastern Europe. Kanza comments: "He went to Berlin, both east and west, and Prague and may even have gotten as far as Moscow. Such a journey was not unusual during our fight for national liberation; he was not going there for any kind of indoctrination but to make contacts and to let the socialist world know something of the Congolese people, their aspirations, and the means they were using to rid themselves of the Belgian yoke. He also went to Guinée and met Sekou Touré for whom he had great admiration." (5)

Gizenga became the deputy prime minister of Lumumba's government. Upon its collapse and Lumumba's death, Gizenga attempted to rally his fellow ministers who were loyal to Lumumba and create an opposition government in Stanleyville. When in 1962 the central government succeeded in asserting political control in the region, Gizenga was arrested and jailed.

A second man who was to impact eastern Kwilu even more was Mulele (pr. moo-LAY-lay) Pierre. Born in 1929 in Leopoldville Province, he too had his primary schooling at Catholic missions at Totshi and Kikwit. He, too, studied at the Catholic "minor seminary" at Kinzambi but, after two years, continued his secondary schooling at Leverville. Drafted in 1950, he served in the *Force Publique* for two years, stationed in Coquilhatville, Thysville and Leopoldville. As it happened, he was in the same battalion with Joseph Mobutu. He was demobilized in September, 1952, and entered the colonial administrative service until November 1959.

Appointed by Lumumba to serve in the Ministry of Education and Fine Arts, Kanza describes him in the following terms: "He seemed to have been struck by certain socialist ideas which he had seen in action in Guinée and elsewhere. . . . The Ministry of Education certainly provided him with a handy instrument for revolutionizing the minds of the younger generation of the Congo; he would revise the syllabuses, and renew the authoritarian methods employed in Congolese schools. For that reason alone, Mulele was feared in advance by the missionaries - - particularly the Catholics - - as having communist notions. He lived by the strictest self-discipline and had the will of a soldier. . . . Like Gizenga he was absolutely obstinate, deeply sincere, and intensely anti-colonialist." (6)

By late 1963, the opposition leaders found a favorable political and geographical setting in Brazzaville, just across the Congo River from Leopoldville. The government of Congo Brazzaville, as it was then referred to, had also had its chapter of political shift. At that time there was a regime which was also leftist and anti-Western in stance and which viewed with sympathy the ongoing political aspirations of the remnants of Lumumba's followers.

It was in October 1963 that an opposition group was formed called the National Liberation Committee (NLC) with Christophe Gbenye (pr. gbay-NYI) as its president. Two NLC training camps were established on Congo Brazzaville soil to which young recruits were brought from the Congo for indoctrination and training in the basics of terrorist tactics. It was under the inspiration and guidance of NLC-related leaders that revolutions were to erupt in three widely separated areas of the Congo - - Lomami region to the northeast, Kivu area to the far east and, ominously enough, in the heart of Mennonite country in the Kwilu in south-central Congo.

It is known that NLC personnel found their way from Algiers to China in late 1963, this at the invitation of the local Chinese Embassy. (7) It seems clear that much of the orientation and strategy which was to characterize NLC efforts to overthrow the Congo government in the following year was derived from such contacts and instruction. Destruction and brutal terrorism were to become two earmarks of insurgent activities cross the Congo in 1964

Mulele Pierre, too, had followed the trek to Stanleyville in late 1960 and, after Lumumba's death, was sent by Gizenga to establish an embassy of the opposition government in Cairo. With the founding of the NLC in Congo Brazzaville, Mulele made his way back there and by late 1963 became the one charged to give leadership to the rebel effort in the Kwilu, an area he knew well. Accurately sensing the deep disillusionment and frustration of the Congolese populace, he and a small group of fellow conspirators made their way first to Idiofa, Mulele's home territory, and then began to fan out south and east. Moving quietly about in the countryside, they found their way to the village hearth fires at night where they asked pointed questions and made careful comments. It was not long until they had won a sympathetic hearing - - particularly among the Baphende people between the Kwilu and Loange Rivers. Invoking the name of their tribal political hero, Gizenga Antoine, who had been languishing in prison since being apprehended in Stanleyville, they cleverly tapped a deep current of resentment and animosity toward the central government.

Once confidence was established and a hearing won, they would begin to ask questions about their welfare. When was the last time the men had bought a new piece of cloth for their wives? When was it they last had seen a new bicycle in the village? How far did they now have to go to find medicine for their sick children? Did their wives have salt in their greens that night? Using this approach it obviously did not take long to prime the pump of discontent. Expressions of angry resentment flowed readily enough. The time would then come when the visitors would ask if they were tired and angry enough to do something about it. If so, they had a secret plan to share with them. Their independence had been spoiled by a bunch of thieves in Leopoldville. While they were eating all of the sweet fruits of independence, they here in the villages were not even thrown the peelings. But something could be done about all of this. Their "father" Gizenga and a young man named Mulele Pierre were forming a new political movement to kick out the Leopoldville thieves and to form a new government to finally bring the "DEE-pah-ndah" they had all dreamed of in 1960. Would they support such a movement? If so, they would be back later to tell them more. In the meantime, mum was the word.

whispers in the wind

Village after village was thus visited. Then the time came when, on certain days, young men who normally would be found in the village were curiously missing. With time, missionaries and church leaders noted that some mission teachers and employees were also absent on weekends, sometimes returning to the station about sunset in dusty clothing and obviously tired. As discreet inquiries were made, answers were evasive and uninformative.

With passing time, missionaries in the Kwilu became aware that a new term was cropping up in conversations with African friends: *Jeunesse*. They knew it as a French term meaning youth. But what was its sudden significance now? Little by little missionaries began to piece things together. The term *Jeunesse* was being used to identify and refer to some sort of political opposition movement which was under way. The names of Mulele Pierre and Gizenga Antoine were given as having something to do with it. But how was it organized? What were its goals? Were there any local people who had joined? What was being said about

Christians, the Church and the Mission? Little information was to be had. Trusted pastors and African co-workers even seemed vaguely ill at ease when questioned too closely. And yet the opinion was frequently voiced to the missionaries that they had no reason for concern. If there was a target, it was the corrupt government in Leopoldville and its agents in their area.

Then one day three truckloads of soldiers appeared in the Kandala area making stops in several villages. Chiefs and clan elders were assembled and brusquely questioned. Were there any *Jeunesse* in their villages? Was there a meeting place anywhere close by? To all such questions the village leaders pleaded innocence. There were none around that they knew about. They had heard something about them in some distant villages but not close by. Disbelieving them, the soldiers rounded up some of the village livestock. Throwing it on their trucks they warned them that there would be severe reprisals against them if it was discovered that, in fact, there were *Jeunesse* among them.

At Mukedi, some 65 miles to north of Kandala, the missionaries were even more aware that something was brewing. For them not only was it a matter of rumors but also one of deteriorating inter-personal relations within the station/church community. Here, more than at any other station, there still was a residue of hard-edged criticism remaining from the era of the 1960 evacuation. (8) That the shadowy *Jeunesse* movement had won many Mukedi sympathizers was, by year's end 1963, very obvious. Whereas at Kandala relations with missionaries remained cooperative and cordial, at Mukedi relations had turned sour. School teachers and male nurses were openly agitating for large salary increases, the while broadly implying that the missionaries delighted in their alleged impoverished and disadvantaged lives in mission-directed institutions.

So tense was the situation in early January 1964 that a special meeting of the EMC Executive Committee was convened there. Much time was devoted to listening to delegations of teachers and medical staff spell out their grievances. At the end of a long afternoon with surly, combative African personnel, the committee members sat alone for a while to compare notes and to plot strategy for the next day. At one point, a missionary committee member turned to a Mukedi pastor and asked if there was not some curbing, disciplinary initiative the local church leaders could or should be taking to combat the troubling spirit which was by then so evident on the station. The pastor paused a moment with an anguished expression, dropped his face in his hands and broke into sobs. Through his tears he asked: "Combat these forces? With what strength? With what strength?" It was at that moment that missionary committee members realized that church leaders knew more than they were able to share and that what they knew weighed very heavily upon them.

Next morning, the committee met again with the African delegations. Salary questions were addressed to the best of their ability with promises to pursue unanswered issues with the government. In closing, missionary members openly shared their sorrow regarding the attitudes manifested during the committee sessions. A final observation was made that if the time had come that CIM missionaries were no longer welcome at Mukedi, the CIM was prepared to plan for their reassignment elsewhere. It was on this rather somber and inconclusive note that the sessions were brought to a close. As committee members made their way back to their respective places of ministry it was with a vague sense of foreboding. A feeling of impending change hung in the air in the Kwilu. When would it come? What form would it take? How would it impact the Mission and the Church?

an igniting spark

By early January 1964, the pattern of things had become clear for all to see. The mysterious absence of youth from the villages for hours and days at a time was now understood. They had been meeting in isolated spots for indoctrination in the beliefs and objectives of the new political movement. Known simply as *Jeunesse*, they were to be the force which would overthrow a corrupt government and issue in the happy day of true independence. Theirs was a just cause and one upon which their ancestors would smile as long as they followed instructions of their leaders without deviation. They were told that their new leaders were Gizenga Antoine, a fellow Muphende from the Kwilu, and his friend Mulele Pierre. They might never see Gizenga but some of them just might have the good fortune to meet Mulele in person. These two men had discovered powerful, generous new friends, they were told, whose capital city was named "Mooscoo." They were not at all like the Belgians who had exploited them. They were friends of oppressed people around the world and were happy to help any who were struggling for their freedom and for a better life.

But there was one stipulation: before the people from "Mooscoo" would come to help them, they needed to first overthrow the corrupt government in Leopoldville. They also needed to rid their land of all people and symbols that had any ties with the hated Belgians or with the Congo's present shameful government. This meant inviting and forcing, if necessary, all village chiefs to join and support their movement. This meant destroying bridges and ferries. This meant burning state posts and either killing or chasing away agents of the government. It meant looting and destroying commercial centers and stores. In veiled language there was also reference made to the Missions and missionary personnel scattered through their area. There would be more precise instructions on that topic later. Basically, however, they were to sweep their land clear of all traces of the resented Belgians they had ousted.

In their hideouts, instruction continued. They would operate in teams. Any village of any size would have its own. Large villages would have several. Each team would have its own leader. Team discipline would be firm; obedience absolutely required. When on their "missions," they were to be barefoot. It was important that the soles of their feet remained in direct contact with their ancestral earth at all times. If they did this and respected all other regulations and taboos of the movement, they could move into battle unafraid chanting *meya, meya* (pr. MAY-yah), i.e., "water, water," and the bullets of military arms aimed at them would turn to harmless drops of water. They would be invincible in battle regardless of the odds against them. Dressed in khaki shorts, bare chested, armed with bush knives, bows and a couple of arrows, they were to be the shock troops of the rebellion. To this general orientation were added such details as instruction in the making and use of "molotov cocktails," how to best set vehicles and buildings on fire, how to confuse people who sought to follow their tracks and how to camouflage and hide themselves in various sorts of cover. In brief, the *Jeunesse* bands would be the spark which, given the signal, would ignite the dry tinder of immense popular discontent and resentment. Army patrols came into the area villages with increasing frequency. In spite of manhandling village people and stealing more of their property, the *Jeunesse* were perfectly safe. When questioned, the village elders "knew" nothing." By now an overwhelming majority of the rural population was convinced that the movement taking shape represented a desperately needed political protest and they wished them well.

fire flares

At first, for the CIM missionaries at Kandala and Mukedi, it was mostly a question of rumors of activities at a distance. Organized originally in the Idiofa area of northeastern Kwilu Province, the first blows against authority took the form of night raids upon unsympathetic village chiefs. Striking suddenly under the cover of darkness, they would beat, slash, burn and retreat to their forest hideouts to await the protective cover of another night. But all of that was over 100 miles away.

Then, suddenly, a Portuguese palm oil post was attacked by night only 65 miles away. Appearing suddenly out of the darkness of the surrounding forest they burned equipment, destroyed records. There were conflicting reports: government troops had been wiped out, *Jeunesse* had been put to flight; the ferry had been sunk, the ferry was still operating; the road had been cut, a truck had just come through.

Then it was late December and one morning word was received at Kandala that three school buildings had been burned at Gungu, just 35 miles away. The local population rallied and had rebuilt the stick and thatch shelters in three days but growing apprehension was now in the air. From this point on, each new day brought its fresh spate of stories: a rural government post had been attacked and Congolese government agents had fled; more village schools had been burned to the west of Kandala and the teachers manhandled; a sector chief who had aggressively opposed the movement had rallied his armed police to fight a group in a pitched battle. He and his aides were killed and their families burned alive in their homes. What was exaggeration? What was fact?

Mid-January 1964, at Kandala Station, found Harold and Gladys Graber and Jim and Jenny Bertsche bringing their holiday vacation with their school age children to a close. The children had been flown home in December by a Presbyterian Mission plane to the government airstrip at Gungu to the west of Kandala. They were to be picked up at the same place in mid-January. Word, however, had come from the pilot via inter-station short wave radio stating that he now considered the Gungu airstrip to be too insecure. Could the children rather be taken to Mukedi to the north instead? They could, and on January 13 the two families met the plane there. Hugging their children aboard, they watched them took off on a 90 minute flight to the east to a mission boarding school for their second semester. (9)

The evening of January 15th, the Kandala missionaries stood on their front porches and watched the sky reflect red as the local government guest house was set ablaze just across the Kwilu River down the hill. Next morning, on the 16th, they learned that local Congolese government officials had fled to Gungu in the night. An urgent meeting of the EMC's Executive Committee had been called for the 18th at Nyanga Station. Jim Bertsche, a member, was encouraged to attend. Traveling on the 17th, in order to be at Nyanga for the opening session next day, his was one of the last vehicles to cross the Kandala ferry. That night it was cut adrift. Next morning, the 18th, on the early radio net, Kandala missionaries were requesting his immediate return. Conditions in the Kandala area were deteriorating rapidly. He left right away needing now to detour via the Gungu ferry to the west. Just as he was leaving Gungu in the early afternoon he was buzzed by an MAF plane. A dropped message directed him to return to the government airstrip. Upon arrival, V.J. Sprunger transferred from the plane to the Jeep and continued to Kandala. As mission legal representative and missionary team leader, he had come to verify the situation for himself and to take counsel with the station community, missionary and African alike.

Station people and church leaders quickly clustered about them. What was happening? Who were the people destroying property and setting fires? Would our time come too? Africans of the Mission community, professed ignorance of details. Whoever the *Jeunesse* were, they had to be people from a distance. Surely no local people would be so foolish as to destroy their own local sources of help. Further, it was their optimistic hope that whoever the *Jeunesse* were, they would have no reason to do harm to the Mission with its medical facilities and schools. But even as they talked, there were a few around the edges who observed and listened silently. What did they know that they were not sharing?

The next day, the 19th, was Sunday. Amidst feverish rumor and uncertainty, the chapel bell rang as usual calling believers to worship, prayer and consideration of God's Word. Attendance was good; missionaries and fellow African believers blended voices and hearts in expressions of faith and in prayer for wisdom and courage sufficient for the uncertainties around them. One missionary family, upon returning to reenter their home, paused to look at a little plaque which hung on the wall beside their front door. It read: "In what time I am afraid, I will trust." It was from this station, 3½ years earlier, that the last contingent of CIM missionaries had left on a trek toward the Angolan border which was ultimately to take them home to North America.

This time, they were staying.

On the 20th, Loyal Schmidt from Nyanga and Charles Sprunger from Mukedi arrived with extra fuel for the station. They had passed via Gungu hoping to rendezvous with an MAF plane to pick up a short wave transmitter which could be operated with a car battery. (The one in place on Kandala Station required running a diesel powered generator, something that made quick transmission in an emergency situation impossible.) Bad weather in the area, however, had forced the cancellation of that flight so the two men arrived with fuel only. The morning of Tuesday the 21st dawned bright and clear. The canceled flight of the previous day was rescheduled. Schmidt and Sprunger left to meet the incoming flight at Gungu taking senior missionary Vernon Sprunger with them who took this opportunity of returning to Tshikapa. The two younger men planned to return to Kandala that afternoon.

Kandala is set ablaze

Following are excerpts from missionary journals describing the events of the following days: "It was about 7:30 that evening as missionaries' children were getting into their pajamas that the band struck. Our first warning was the sound of excited shouts and cries out in our mission village. Looking out of our windows we could see flames leaping skyward and against the red backdrop of burning homes the running figures of the attackers brandishing bows and arrows; machetes and torches were clearly visible. In a matter of only minutes the whole village was a mass of flame and the band came screaming toward the station. . . . In a matter of moments they found the missionary group huddled together at the home of the station pastor, Khelendende Pierre (pr. khe-leh-NDEH-ndeh). (10) The first hour was a wild mixture of shrill cries, threats, menacing gestures, accusations and blows. Time and again an excited youth would run up with a notched arrow and drawn bow only to have some other member of his group intervene. A couple of times a honed machete descended only to land flat side across a missionary back. There was the occasional sharp sting of the lash of a whip. There were shrill cries 'tuashiye, tuashiye' ("Let's kill them, let's kill them"). Shoes, socks, watches, glasses were all removed; pockets emptied. We were herded about, pushed and pulled by an endless series of rough hands. 'Where is the gas? Where is the pastor? Why did you call the soldiers? Why do you meddle in politics? Why have you spoiled our land?' And there was the wild eyed youth who, as he shook a razor edged knife in our faces, shrilled at the top of his voice: 'Mooscoo! Mooscoo!'" (11)

In the midst of all of the confusion, a 6 year-old missionary son being carried by his father was softly asking, 'Daddy, where is my puppy?' As if in response the little dog appeared out of the shadows. There was the slash of a bush knife, a couple of yips and the pup fled into the darkness. To the anguish of the moment was added, yet, the particular pain of a little boy's special loss.

Back to the missionary account: "It was a surrealist setting: standing barefoot in the flickering half-light of a mission station going up in flames we heard the excited cries of the destroying bands, the crackling flames, the collapsing roofs, the exploding barrels of fuel, the hiss of a vehicle tire going flat, the blast of an igniting gas tank, the crash of shattering glass, the sound of splintering wood." (12)

And in the distance there was the incongruous sound of the station diesel light plant still running. It wasn't lighting anything anymore but continued to run because no one knew how to shut it off. At one point, a youth appeared with a jerry can of gas and began to pour it on the ground in a circle around the missionary group. "And yet during the hours of greatest confusion, tension and danger there was a quiet reality of God's presence which was a new experience for us all. While all about was uproar, fire and menace, ours was an inner calm of spirit that we shall never forget. Verses which we'd known by memory for years and taken more or less casually for granted suddenly became dramatically relevant and precious: 'Though I walk through the valley of the shadow of death I will fear no evil for thou art with me. - - My grace is sufficient for thee for my strength is made perfect in weakness.'" (13)

Meantime, in the midst of all of the confusion, the pastor at whose house the missionaries had gathered had slipped away into the encircling darkness. Fearful that he, too, would be a target, his wife had pled with him not to risk making her a widow. While attention was fixed on the missionaries he had slipped into the valley below the station. He later would share with the missionaries his night of torment. After wandering about by himself he at last came to a gnarled tree from which a branch jutted out above his head. For a long while Pastor Pierre stood below that branch, his belt in hand, intent on taking his own life. It was not now fear of the *Jeunesse* which drove him. It was rather the deep pain of spirit he was experiencing. He, a pastor of the church, had fled his flock in a moment of danger. And now, up on the plateau above him, flames of many fires leaped skyward. Could he have made a difference had he stayed? And what about the missionaries? Where were they by now? And the Bible School families? But during his hours of dark struggle, the Lord laid a staying hand upon him. He would live to express his remorse and sense of personal failure to the mission family and to continue to give effective leadership in the years ahead.

Back to the missionary account: "Eventually the band's fury seemed to ebb and saner elements began to assert themselves. Two young fellows took us in tow and led us to the edge of the station to a schoolgirl's compound which had not yet been burned. Concern was shown as to clothing, food and water. Selma Unruh was allowed to go back into her house to bundle up a few supplies which would be of help during the night that lay ahead. Then came the decision that the remaining house would not be put to the torch after all and that we could spend the rest of the night there. Hope rose at the prospect of being spared one missionary dwelling and the supplies that it contained. The band gathered about its leader who gave us a final lecture as to the alleged evil deeds we had perpetrated upon their country - - deeds which had precipitated their attack. They then bid us farewell, said they had no further business with us and that only because of their kindness were they leaving us a house. Then they were gone into the night."

"Our relief was short lived, however, for in only a matter of minutes we heard the sound of muffled voices and the shuffling of bare feet. We soon made out the forms of a new group confronting us in single file, bows poised on the ground before them. We immediately realized that we had yet another group to deal with. The first inquiry brought chill apprehension: 'How many women are there and where are they?' Praying and talking at the same time the missionary men engaged them in conversation in Giphende, the dialect of the Kandala area, attempting to divine their genuine intentions. Impatiently the leader snapped: 'If there are no women in the house, you men move over under that mango tree and watch us while we burn the house.' At long last the promise was given not to molest the women and children. As our group moved out and stood among them, the last Kandala missionary dwelling was put to the torch."

"We were then informed that we would go with them through the darkness to their camp in the forest where we would be put on trial before their president. As we began filing off the station, out of the shadows appeared two white clad figures - - - two male nurses who worked in the station dispensary. They intercepted the band and engaged them in conversation on our behalf, an act of highest courage. Unknown to the Kandala missionaries they, like many others, had joined the rebel movement in good faith believing it to be a legitimate political protest. . . . The nurses proposed that we spend the rest of the night with them in the dispensary rather than out in the forest. A heated discussion followed . . . but the decision was finally made that we stay at the dispensary. Lying on our split bamboo mats, the rest of the night was spent in sleepless prayer." (14)

the fellowship of suffering: a precious gift

The dawn of January 22 brought haunting questions: "What had the bush court decided during the night? Were there other bands with personal accounts to settle? Now that the station was burned, were we as missionaries still targets?" In an attempt to learn the answers to these questions, the nurses went out in quest of some rebel leader who would be in a position to reply. In the meantime, people began finding their way to us in the dispensary. There was Eugene the chauffeur; Jacques, one of the pastors; Raymond the gardener; Pauline the slim little widow who was the cleaning woman in the maternity; Louis the carpenter. They came with stunned expressions, tragedy in their eyes, deep emotions in their voices. It was Louis who flung himself flat on the concrete floor, wrapped his arms around a missionary man's ankles sobbing out his grief. Becoming the spokesman for the little group he repeated again and again: "We didn't know this would happen; we didn't know this would happen." With arms about each other, missionaries and Congolese mingled tears of gratitude for spared lives and together prayed for wisdom and guidance for whatever lay ahead.

Making their way outside to the dispensary veranda, they tried to take in the import of the past night's onslaught. Smoke was rising above the remains of buildings here and there. Equipment and supplies were strewn all over the station as they had been taken from buildings and scattered. Here and there groups of *Jeunesse* were loitering about, watching. Looking over toward the station chapel which had for some reason been spared along with the medical facilities, the missionaries saw a group of Bible School students huddled under a tree beside the chapel entrance. Asking permission to join them, they made their barefoot way across the littered station. The students shared how they had snatched children and a few simple belongings from thatch-roofed homes which were being set ablaze and fled into the darkness of the surrounding bush. When with dawn they realized their little Bible Institute village had been reduced to rows of burned out hulks, they noted the chapel still standing and decided as a group to seek refuge there.

After the first exchange of painful news and expressions of joy at still finding one another alive, the refugee students began to take stock of the condition of their missionaries - - women in kimonos, children in pajamas. It was not long until the student couples began to untie the pitiful little bundles of precious belongings which they had salvaged from the fury of the previous night. A woman came to one of the missionary women carrying a threadbare sweater. There were only a couple of buttons left and there was a hole in one elbow. "Here," she said, "take this. The night's are cool. Perhaps it can help keep you warm." And there came a man holding in his hands a battered pair of shoes. The original color was all but gone; heels were badly worn down; one sole had a hole and there were no laces. Offering them to one of the missionary men he said, "Here, *ngambi* (teacher/preacher), take these. You are not accustomed to being barefoot. Perhaps these can help you during these days."

It was an incredible moment of identification, of bonding and of fellowship. It was also, in a profound sense, a moment of truth. In years to come a phrase would be heard in a variety of settings: *Athu awa, tuabalega n'awo mu tshuya; tegedienu mbimbi jiawo* (i.e., "We walked through fire with these people; listen to their words").

case dismissed

Before noon on the 22nd, a message came from the forest *Jeunesse* camp stating that the Kandala missionaries' case had been brought to their "tribunal" during the night. The verdict was that they had been sufficiently punished for all of their wrongdoings. They were free to try to lay plans for evacuation.

For many long hours missionary attention had been riveted on their minute-to-minute existence amidst wild confusion and destruction. Now, for the first time, their thoughts went to the broader CIM missionary family. What had happened to Loyal Schmidt and Charles Sprunger? They were to have returned the previous afternoon. What about Mukedi 65 miles to the north? Had they also been attacked? The Kandala people knew that their own sudden silence on the regularly scheduled inter-station short wave network would soon alert the rest of the stations that something was amiss. But how soon could this be translated into action? Could they possibly all walk out, missionaries and Bible School students, together? It was soon realized that this was an option to be taken seriously only as a last resort. Given the long distance across shadeless savannah and the hazards of strange *Jeunesse* groups which were now constantly crisscrossing the countryside, it was likely that missionaries would quickly become a burden, if not a hazard, to the Congolese. There was nothing to do but wait.

As the sun set, the missionaries made their way back to the dispensary trying to prepare themselves for the uncertainty of another night. A kerosene lamp was provided by medical staff. As they settled in their room, a slight figure emerged from the shadows of the hallway with two bowls balanced on her head and a soot smudged little tea pot in her hand. It was Pauline who kept the maternity ward clean. The bowls contained fresh, hot cassava mush and some greens cooked in seasoned palm oil. The little pot contained hot tea. After expressing heartfelt gratitude for her loving provision of nourishment, the missionaries breathed prayers of thanksgiving for life, fellow believers, shelter and then dipped eager fingers into the bowls of mush and greens. Pauline would yet make several more such trips with food, picking her way through the debris of the station and the milling rebel bands, a veritable angel of mercy.

another hectic night

Regarding the internal organization of the rebel movement, a missionary account reads: "Varying in numbers from the smallest unit of three persons to upward of seventy people depending on the assignment of the night, . . . they form the elusive shock troops of the movement. . . . Traveling at a slow trot they form extremely mobile units and are capable of striking at widely scattered points under the cover of darkness. . .

Each large band has its internal organization comprised of its president, its secretary and its equivalent of a quartermaster. . . . A striking feature of the movement is the choice of terms used among them. Rarely do they call each other by any other term than 'camarade.' In accosting a stranger, invariably there comes the question: 'Are you a partisan?' . . . While obvious effort was made to maintain intra-organizational discipline, one often had the impression that the bands were, in fact, semi-autonomous." (15)

Though little still remained intact on the station, the second night saw new bands arrive, each with their own desire to make their "contribution" to the rebellion. The dispensary became a hub of activity throughout the night. Frequently loud arguments erupted between members of different bands. There was the sound of slamming cupboard doors or the splintering sound of a door being ripped from its hinges. At one point, an investigation was carried out above the ceiling over the missionaries' heads because someone had heard that President Kasavubu was in hiding in the Kandala dispensary attic! Now and again there was the ominous sound of people receiving severe beatings. The method employed was to force the person to lie face down on the ground and to beat the body from shoulders to buttocks with whatever was handy. The consequent sound was that of a huge melon being violently thumped. It was also that night that one of the male nurses who had intervened in behalf of the missionaries the previous night was severely beaten, this for reasons that were never explained.

Suddenly, in the midst of all of the confusion, into the room marched another *Jeunesse* band made up of young teen-age girls. Their male president informed us that they had come "to visit" us. The girls ranged themselves along the four walls around the missionaries, bush knives in hand, with expressionless faces. One of the missionaries present described the scene thus: "The leader placed himself by a table and produced a blurred likeness of Gizenga Antoine. Propping it on the table he entered upon a repetitious, palm-winey harangue on the reasons for burning the Mission and the many failures of the European population which had provoked the attack. Then pausing, he would slowly bend down, hold an attentive ear respectfully to the picture. Finally he would straighten up, pause and declare: '*Mbuta ya muthu udi muzuela gamba*' (i.e., 'The elder is saying this') and he was off again on some lecture and resume of grievances." (16)

It was going on midnight when there was again a commotion outside the dispensary. Suddenly the door opened and Loyal Schmidt and Charles Sprunger were marched in by a rebel escort. They had made it to Gungu the previous day although they needed to lay down planks they had taken along to bridge deepening ditches which were being dug across roads by night. Having seen Vernon Sprunger off on his MAF flight to Tshikapa, they had started back toward Kandala. About ten miles out of Gungu they were suddenly flagged down by a mob of some forty youth who rushed onto the road out of the wayside grass. There followed some thirty hours of extreme tension and menace for them. They were force-marched with hands tied behind them. Passing through several villages, the rebel youth made the most of their opportunity to threaten and menace the people they found. In one village they demanded food. When the chief mildly protested that finding food, on such short notice, would be difficult, they threatened to burn down his village. The elderly chief then got on his knees before the teen-age rebels begging their forgiveness, then went off to find food and water as demanded.

A missionary journal continues: "Just before nightfall we crossed the Kwilu River in wooden dugouts. The cables on the ferry had been cut several days before to prevent soldiers crossing. Our crossing was off in a forested area. . . . As we were walking in the high grass toward their headquarters about 8:30 PM, we saw several flames across the next ridge. Kandala Station was in flames. The missionaries were . . . in the hands of terrorists also." (17)

They were taken to the rebel forest headquarters at about 10 o'clock at night "to be tried" - - presumably the same one toward which the Kandala missionaries had been headed before their interception the previous night. The missionary account continues: "There were no less than 800 faces of 'youth' ranging in age from 12 to 45 years, gloating over our being captured. They shouted threats: 'Let's kill them, let's kill them.'" (18)

There followed a routine repeated several times. With arms in the air, drawn bows and notched arrows held within inches of their faces and knives against the back of their necks, they were presented to person after person in the rebel hierarchy with the explanation of where and how they had been captured. It was further explained that because they had not tried to escape or resist but had gotten out of their vehicles and greeted them, they had not killed them on the spot. Upon being thus informed each one, in turn, questioned the two men and passed them up the line to the next authority. By now ready to drop from exhaustion, they were taken to a small nearby village where the chief was rousted out of bed and ordered to provide food and bed for the two men. The chief's wives eventually brought bowls of chicken and mush. After eating, they were shown into a room of his house containing a narrow wooden bed. With three guards at the door, they spent a fitful night on the slats of the bed.

At "rooster time" they were called and after a three hour walk arrived at a large rebel encampment. Left under guard, several hundred men disappeared into the nearby woods. By mid-afternoon the president sent word that they were to rejoin their fellow missionaries at Kandala. Relieving the men of their rings and watches, they returned their papers and began the trek which brought them to the door of the station maternity near midnight.

outside contact reestablished

Early the next morning the sound of an approaching aircraft was heard. Alarmed by lack of short-wave contact with Kandala, Vernon Sprunger had flown to Kinshasa and contacted MAF personnel as well as American Embassy and UN personnel in the capital. Alerted that Kandala had not been heard from for 36 hours, MAF pilot, Wes Eiseman, took off from Kikwit that morning to fly over the station and area. The missionaries came out of the dispensary and stood motionless in the open while rebel youth hid under palm trees. After circling a couple of times, a note was dropped asking if it would be possible to level an emergency landing strip on the road in front of the station. Lacking tools and not sure what rebel response to such a proposal would be, they signaled nothing. A second pass brought a second note. Did they want evacuation by helicopter? If so, they were to sit down. This they promptly did. With a waggle of wings the plane disappeared toward Mukedi where, unknown to the Kandala group, another drama was unfolding.

The plane was no more than out of sight when the rebel youth erupted from among the trees with shouting and renewed menace. Convinced that the missionaries had succeeded in tricking and endangering them by somehow calling the plane, they began to search their clothing for the hidden "phonee," i.e., transmitter. There was great preoccupation with and fear of shortwave equipment which they knew was located on each station. The first night before setting the missionary homes on fire, they had been ordered to make sure that they first found and disabled the shortwave radio equipment. Consequently they removed hair curlers from Gladys Graber's hair and carried a mimeograph out of the Bertsche home and battered it with bush knives.

The sudden appearance of the plane had been unnerving for them and there followed a period of renewed accusation and threat. When, after a time, they understood that our failure to transmit messages after their attack in and of itself constituted an alarm, the scene became less turbulent. Pointing out that should a plane return it would need a place to land, the missionaries proposed that the road passing the front of the station be smoothed enough to permit a landing. This sparked another round of heated debate. At last it was agreed that some work could be done - - but only if the missionaries did it themselves. Not even Bible School students would be permitted to help. There soon was the entertaining scene of missionary men, women and children in their novel attire swinging short handled hoes under the amused gaze of clusters of *Jeunesse* but to the distress of Mission people and students. Eventually feeling that they had had sport enough, others were permitted to take the hoes and to continue the leveling process. In this informal setting, the missionaries were able to carry on a variety of informative conversations with their rebel supervisors. Questions with regard to their movement, hopes, goals and methods were freely answered.

a glimpse of the rebel mind

Again quoting from a missionary account of those days: "Using the term 'nativistic' in the sense of a rejection of European culture and a return to African values, a number of cases in point were observed. The night the station was burned, missionary purses and wallets were snatched away. A special point was made of taking out the bills and of tearing them methodically to tattered bits before our eyes. Glasses, shoes and watches which were taken from us were thrown on the nearest fire. . . . On several occasions a member would launch into a spirited declaration of the fact that they needed neither the white man nor anything he brought with him. The one thing they needed was their *mavu* (pr MAH-voo), i.e., their ancestral earth. Another theme which began to register with the listening missionaries was an insistence upon scrupulous honesty. "We are not thieves," some insisted. "Government people take things from our people; we take nothing." They explained that their team secretaries kept scrupulous records of every contribution by village chiefs and that, when their movement came into power, the villagers would be fully reimbursed. (19) While these declarations seemed to be born out in some cases, in others they were not. With passing time it became clearer that while some teams destroyed everything and took nothing, others destroyed little and took much.

It was particularly the mix of superstitious beliefs which overlaid *Jeunesse* activity that began to come into focus for the missionaries as they awaited a means of evacuation. Again quoting from a missionary account: "*Jeunesse* arms and activities are bolstered to a great extent by magical beliefs and practices. A case in point are their 'potent arrows'. . . . One youth spent considerable time in showing me his arrow and in explaining that it was far from an ordinary arrow. Indeed it contained at least eight 'cartridges' and in battle it could easily account for several soldiers at once." (20)

"There are both individual and group taboos observed . . . in order to assure success and strength in their campaigns. As groups they sleep only out of doors, changing their camps frequently. The death of a youth in a skirmish with a military patrol is explained on the basis of his failure to observe his personal taboo. . . . Heard repeatedly among them were references to tiny planes that are at the disposition of their leaders for rapid transportation from place to place in their nocturnal activities. The size of the planes is usually indicated by the palm of a hand. By means of these planes leaders are transported instantaneously to any destination desired." (21)

Young, lean, tough, mobile and highly motivated, it was clear that in the hands of rebel leadership they became the ideal and very effective means of unleashing a rebellion that, initially, swept all opposition before it. Around a legitimate core of political aims, Mulele Pierre and his immediate subordinates had spun a clever web-work of ideology and methodology which effectively utilized material and magico-cultural resources available to them in the African bush. In the process they generated great confidence, excitement and commitment on the part of the bare-chested, barefooted and, sadly, expendable young recruits.

an airlift from a soccer field

Friday morning, January 24, dawned with the missionaries hoping that this might be the day their evacuation would materialize. But by this time they were struggling with some fresh anxieties. In conversations they had had with various rebel leaders, some warnings had been repeated. Yes, their superiors had ordered that the missionaries be allowed to leave, but there were some stipulations. First, under no circumstances would central government soldiers be allowed to set foot at Kandala. Should any come aboard the aircraft, their heads would be severed on the spot in the presence of the missionaries. Also, should Vernon Sprunger arrive, he would be taken prisoner. (22) There was, further, the missionaries' major concern for the safety of the Bible School families who had come from the Kasai. How were all of these potentially dangerous issues to be dealt with?

In the dispensary were a couple of barrels of tightly rolled bandages which were used to wrap and keep medications in place on wounds and ulcers. (23) It occurred to someone that they could be used to spell out a message on the soccer field across the road from the station. The following message soon took shape in two-foot high block lettering on the playing field: OK TO LAND   350 YDS   BRING NO SOLDIERS GUNS OR VJ   SAFETY ASSURED

As for the Bible School families, it was agreed with them that missionary and Congolese wives and children would be the first to leave. Men, both missionary and students, would follow as subsequent flights were available.

Missionaries continued the effort to engage their *Jeunesse* guards in conversation. Why had they joined the movement? Answers were widely varied but very personal. For example, "The *secteur* chief put me in jail for 15 days a couple of months ago. We have to help build government houses and we don't get paid. We have no way to earn money but we still have to pay taxes. We have many children who finish primary school but they have no place to study after that. The government people in Leopoldville have 'eaten' all of the money and we get nothing. We are fighting to save our earth from those who seek to spoil it. We want to improve our independence." On and on went the recital reflecting pointed, personal, immediate resentment and frustration. At one juncture, a missionary summoned the courage to ask why the Mission had also been a target. At first there was a flurry of comment such as: "You white people are all friends of the Belgians. You've helped and supported our bad government since independence. We are angry because the government has put 'our father' (i.e. Gizenga Antoine) in jail. The government soldiers come to abuse us and to take our things by force." But it was not long till other voices were heard suggesting that it had all been a mistake. It was small consolation to the burned out missionaries and Bible School students to hear that the two *Jeunesse* bands which had struck Kandala on that fiery night of January 21 had exceeded the orders given by their superiors.

And what of the future? On that topic they were all agreed. Once the state posts, commercial centers and mission stations were all under their control, they would begin to attack the larger government centers. First would be Gungu, then Idiofa, then Kikwit. After that there would be a major drive to take Leopoldville, the capital, and to topple the hated central government. They had much work yet to be done. That's why they wanted the missionaries out of their way.

It was mid-morning when the sound of approaching aircraft was again heard. Coming in low over the river, two helicopters operated by Scandinavian UN crews settled on the soccer field while a small plane circled overhead. Alerted to the exploding rebellion in the region, the UN had quickly established a base at Tshikapa. This was one of their first flights into rebel territory. Doors were thrown open and the crews motioned vigorously toward missionaries to enter. A missionary man scrambled up the crew ladder on the side of one of the copters in an attempt to explain to the pilot the plan to evacuate women and children first. The rotors were whirling, the sand was flying. Trying to speak above the exhaust noise was further complicated by the fact that the crews spoke neither French or English well. Discussion of plans, under the circumstances, was impossible.

Suddenly, the crews jumped down from the cargo doors and began to literally throw the missionaries, bodily, into the copters. Unknown to them, a large group of *Jeunesse* visible to the commanding officer overhead, was approaching the soccer field through the high grass from three sides. Fearing an attack, he ordered the crews to get the missionaries on board and to lift off immediately.

It was at this moment that the tense drama was extended still further. In the confusion, both copters lifted off not noting that Charles Sprunger was still on the soccer field held by the wrist by a *Jeunesse* leader. He was pressing Sprunger to stay behind because, he insisted, this was the only way to ensure that the helicopters would return to take out the Bible School families as well.

And who was this leader? The same one who had been in charge of the rebel band which had earlier taken Sprunger and Schmidt captives on the Gungu road. He was also the one who had shown some concern for their welfare during the long, exhausting march to Kandala Station. In conversation with him Sprunger learned that he had been a former student at Kandala. Upon graduating from 6th grade, his scores had not been high enough for entry into the Nyanga secondary school. He had thus become one of the unemployed,

120

frustrated youth that Mulele Pierre's recruiters found in his home village who became persuaded that their movement was legitimate and held genuine promise for him.

As he seized Sprunger by the wrist that day of drama at Kandala, was he speaking sincerely? Was it an honest effort to help the Bible School families still among them who were also strangers in their area? Was it somehow a reflection of influences he experienced on that station in calmer, gentler days as a student? Was it an effort to inject some compassion into a scene of mindless destruction? Or was it a ruse to keep at least one missionary in their hands during the uncertain and violent days ahead of them?

In the swift pace of events that question was never answered. Quickly discovering that one missionary still remained on the ground below, one of the copters again landed. Cargo doors flew open revealing a couple of crew members who were urgently motioning, loaded automatic rifles in hand, for Sprunger to get in. Wrenching free of the young man's grip, he ran over to the open door with bloody fingernail scratches on his arm.

Across the river, at a nearby Catholic Station, three sisters and two priests were being held. One helicopter landed in front of the sisters' residence. The *Jeunesse* surrounding the sisters hesitated when menaced by the helicopter crew. Seizing the moment of indecision, the sisters ran to the copter and were quickly airborne. The plan was to return for the priests that afternoon.

Arriving at Tshikapa, the missionaries sought out the commanding UN officer and explained their deep concern for the Bible School families left behind. He promised that upon refueling they would return a second time to Kandala. Given a list of their names, he promised to do his best.

As good as his word, they did return. But upon arrival they found the soccer field strewn with debris. No sign of life was to be seen anywhere. Understandably doubtful that the aircraft would return, the entire group of some 50 adults and children had already left for the river intent on crossing yet before dusk. Led by the local pastor, Kindumba (gi-NDOO-mbah) Jacques, and Kipoko (gi-POH-goh) David, the Nyanga member of the Giphende New Testament revision team that had just been assembled there, they were beginning a pilgrimage which would become a gripping story all its own.

Returning to the Catholic Mission, one copter landed in front of the priests' residence. They stood on the porch but were blocked by a solid wall of shouting and menacing youth ranged across the front of the house. When an arrow found its mark in the shoulder of a crewman, there was the chatter of automatic weapons in response. A gap was opened in the wall of young men and the priests ran off the porch, over fallen bodies and into the copter. Later reports had it that three of them died while a number of others were wounded.

The Kandala missionaries who were part of the dramatic events of that day remain forever grateful that their evacuation transpired without loss of life or injury to anyone.

massacre at Kilembe

It was early morning, January 23rd, at Mukedi Station. Missionary Peter Buller's account reads as follows: "There was a voice on the veranda. Dr. [Arnold] Nickel called, 'Pete, it is an emergency.' A messenger had come with a letter signed by the Mother Superior of the Catholic Mission at Kilembe. It read: 'Sirs, Please come over and help us. Last night all of the priests of the Mission were massacred. Terrible! Please come get us to take us, if possible, on to Idiofa.'" (24) (25)

Mukedi, established in 1923 as the first CIM station to the west of the Loange River, was the first Christian presence and witness of that area. A decade or so later, the Jesuits opened their first post in that region some 10 miles to the northeast of Mukedi at a location called Kilembe (pr. ki-LEH-mbeh). In 1931 the post was taken over by the Oblate Catholic Order. (26) Staffed primarily by Belgian personnel, their militant loyalty to their Orders and their Church was quickly felt by the Mukedi missionaries and Congolese. Many were the emotional stories that were related across the years by earlier Mukedi missionaries which reflected the high level of confrontation that flared with unfortunate regularity. It is undoubtedly not too much to assume that, on their part, the priests and nuns also had an ample supply of their own to share with their compatriots.

But on this tense January morning in 1964, this history of conflict meant nothing. It had been just five days earlier that a vehicle had come to the station from Kilembe bearing a priest who had damaged his knee in an accident. Dr. Nickel had applied a plaster cast and given instructions to be followed for further care. Little did the doctor imagine that the priest would become the tragic victim of violence in just a matter of days.

out of the night

The evening of January 22 had been like many others that had preceded at Kilembe. The man with a plaster cast on one leg and two fellow priests were in their quarters for the night preparing for the next day's activities. They, like everyone else in the area, were fully aware of the seething political ferment all about them but, like mission personnel in general, they had no particular anxiety for their safety or that of the mission. Over at the maternity, an African woman had died shortly after childbirth and one of the Catholic sisters had taken the baby to her residence for initial care.

Suddenly, rocks began to fall on the metal roof of the priests' dwelling. When one of them went to the door, he was seized and forced out into the yard. When the second priest came out to investigate, he too was taken. By that time others had entered the house, found the priest with the cast and dragged him out as well. All three were set upon with bush knives. Not only were they killed by the multiple slashing wounds inflicted but they were also mutilated. Morning light would reveal missing fingers and hands. Before disappearing into the surrounding bush, the attackers ransacked the priests' quarters and then set it ablaze. The nuns, though not attacked, spent the night in terror and prayer.

an errand of mercy

The Catholic school director, having carried his message to Mukedi, waited on the missionary veranda. The missionary men knew they had to respond to the desperate plea for help that had come. About this there could be no doubt. But what should be the plan? A flurry of consultations followed. It helped nothing, in the process, that it had already been 36 hours without any radio contact with Kandala. As a pickup truck was being readied, questions followed questions. Who should go? How many? With what in hand? To do what? Buller and Nickel soon made their decision. They would both go and leave immediately. As they were driving off the station with the Kilembe school director, they were intercepted with a message from the Mukedi church leaders: "It is too dangerous to go to Kilembe but the *Jeunesse* might not kill a doctor. Therefore Mr. Buller should get off the truck. Dr. Nickel would wear his operating gown and leave alone after painting red crosses on the truck doors." (27)

Pausing a moment to reflect on the message, the two men put their truck in gear and continued their trip as planned. Perhaps an operating gown might even be mistaken as the garb of another priest. Buller's written account continues the story: "Four miles out of Mukedi we saw a mass of people approaching on the road. 'The youth gang,' we thought, 'and coming our way'. . . . To our relief, the people on the road proved to be the Catholic Mission students returning to their villages. For them the school year was over, at least for this school year, and likely for much longer. Their faces tense and sober, they were trudging homeward, carrying on their heads the remains of their broken education: a few notebooks, some texts, a slate and a small bundle of clothes. The villages along the road were deserted except for occasional stragglers who eyed us fearfully. Turning into the Catholic Mission driveway, we glimpsed a life-sized statue of Mary holding, with a stone hand, the stone hand of an African child. Next the Catholic station church came into view. About fifteen yards in front of it three Africans were digging a common grave some three yards square. Nearby clustered seven women, six hooded nuns and a woman from Belgium who was teaching in the girl's school. We dismounted from the truck and shook hands with the stricken nuns. Then we turned to the three iron cots upon which lay the shrouded bodies of the three priests who had paid us a visit only a few days before. What a ghastly massacre. Mutilations - - corn knife cuts on face, neck and body. The man with the cast, his foot swollen grotesquely. Legs broken. Some hands chopped off above the wrist leaving only a bloody stump." (28)

Although three men were digging, a hole that size would still take time. The men suggested to the nuns that to gain time they go load their luggage on the truck. One of the nuns came out carrying the tiny infant orphaned the night before. Buller continues: "We return to the burial service. I help lift the leaden bamboo stretcher into the too-shallow grave. An African man stands with his face turned away; he is crying and says over and over, 'God! God! God! This is terrible.' The Congolese student priest chants a short burial service and the nuns, joined by the half-dozen Africans present, say the liturgical responses. Then each picks up a handful of dirt and throws it onto the motionless forms. As we turn away, a rock crashes onto the fallen roof of the dead priests' residence. Startled, we look back. . . . The Mother Superior, referring to the crashing stone says, 'That is the way it started last night.' Quickly we mount the pick-up and bounce the ten miles back to Mukedi, the one nun tenderly cradling in her arms the newly born African infant." (29)

decisions amidst crisis

Back at Mukedi, in the meantime, missionary Harvey Barkman had been busy at the station shortwave transmitter. Messages had been sent alerting both Vernon Sprunger and MAF personnel in Leopoldville, regarding the Mukedi situation. An MAF plane would leave immediately and would fly to Mukedi via Kandala to see what had happened there. When the pick-up truck returned, the Catholic sisters were temporarily lodged in the home of the Nickels. There were further consultations with the station church leadership. More and more information was becoming available. The story of Kilembe was now common knowledge. Flying over Kandala, MAF pilot West Eiseman had radioed the news of a burned out station.

Who were these *Jeunesse* who so suddenly had begun such bloody and destructive activity? Why did they target priests at Kilembe? Were there grudges that had been settled? Or had they in recent weeks inadvertently stirred anger by some innocent but ill-advised comment, attitude or action? What chances were there that Mukedi or some of its missionary personnel might also be on some *Jeunesse* leader's grudge list?

Consensus quickly emerged that at the very least the women and children needed to be flown out of Mukedi yet that day. (30) By that time the incoming MAF flight was touching down on the Mukedi strip when, suddenly, full power was applied and the plane lifted up and veered over the station. Seeing a crowd of bare chested youth approaching the airstrip, the pilot decided to return aloft for further reconnaissance. When missionaries also appeared at the strip, he landed and the first load of people was quickly put aboard. (31) But before the pilot could prepare for takeoff there was suddenly the sound of a second larger plane circling for a landing. Recognizing it as a government plane, pilot Eiseman ordered that the Mission pickup truck be quickly driven to the middle of the airstrip. Making a low pass, the plane left. One can only conjecture what might have transpired had it landed and armed government officials had stepped onto the sandy turf of the Mukedi airstrip amidst hundreds of *Jeunesse*.

As the first MAF flight took off, the missionary men again conferred with the deeply apprehensive church leaders. Their response was brief and to the point: "This thing is completely beyond us. We have no way to guarantee your safety. You are free to leave." (32) It was not long until a second MAF plane landed and the next contingent of missionaries was loaded without incident. (33)

enter Chief Nzamba

No sooner had the sound of the departing MAF plane receded when word came that the nuns in the Nickel house were being menaced. By this time, Mukedi village chief Nzamba (pr. NZAH-mbah) had appeared on the scene with a cluster of his sons and his prized European-manufactured twelve-gauge shot gun in hand. A respected chief among the Baphende of the area, he had pledged his support for the brewing political movement. But he also took pride in the thriving mission station and missionary staff adjacent to his home village. He proceeded to impose his authority and control upon the growing crowd of excited youth. He let it be known that he had made two decisions. First, the Catholic nuns were to be allowed to depart unharmed. Second, all the flights planned for that day to evacuate their missionaries were to take place with no further interference from anyone.

The day wore on. First Eiseman, then Gordon Fairley, the second pilot, returned. Flights three and four were reserved for the nuns and the teaching lay sister. Writes Buller: "They are gone and alive! Arnold, [Nickel] Harvey [Barkman] and I breathe a sigh of relief. All women and children are off the station. . . . We await Gordon at the airstrip. He is overdue having been blown off course by a strong north wind. With us are Chief Nzamba, the local pastors and church leaders. Gordon finally lands. The Chief shakes our hands and says: 'I will preserve Mukedi station with all my strength and we want you to come back.' The church leaders likewise express their regret over our departure and assure us we are wanted at Mukedi. . . . We climb into the plane. The motor warms up briefly. Overloaded, we start sluggishly down the air strip. Will we ever break ground? The strip slants downhill into a deep valley and when we do break ground we continue in level flight while the hill drops away from underneath our wings. Slowly gaining altitude, we turn toward Kikwit circling back over Mukedi. There it lies below, deceptively toy-like and peaceful under the waning tropical sun. It has been a long day. It seems an eternity since Dr. Nickel called out, 'Pete, it is an emergency.' But through this day too, God has been faithful. He specializes in emergencies." (34)

In the Lord's design of things, quiet-spoken Chief Nzamba had emerged as a key figure in the course of that historic day. Unschooled in any formal sense, he nonetheless had a bearing which reflected great innate leadership qualities and which commanded respect. Unknown to him or those around him that day, he would later play a major role in the eventual defeat of the *Jeunesse* movement in the Kwilu.

a CIM declaration

It was February 11-15, 1964, barely two weeks after the evacuation of the Mukedi and Kandala missionaries, that the field mission executive committee met for extended consultations in an effort to take stock of the sudden new situation and to state itself with regard to the future. Out of these sessions came a set of recommendations and decisions which were to characterize CIM's stance amidst the aftermath of the Kwilu rebellion.

Following are some excerpts: "For the second time within the space of four years, we in CIM have seen revolutionary change move across our field, sweeping mission personnel before it, leaving destruction and death in its wake. Once again we have witnessed the disruption of program, the scattering of Congolese personnel and the loss of property. And, once again, we in CIM have been brought up abruptly, confronted by the necessity of attempting to sort out our new circumstances and to re-plot our course in a troubled and changing environment." (35)

In addressing itself to the issues at hand the committee drafted some basic premises: 1) Congo, the land to which Mennonite missionaries were led 50 years ago, is a focal point of interest in today's world and has become yet another theater of strife between the conflicting ideologies of our time. History is being written daily and the need for Christian witness is a continuing and imperative one. 2) In a revolutionary setting such as ours, the likelihood of sudden change and the need for adaptability must be remembered. 3) The evacuation of or even permanent loss of parts of our traditional area of work must not in itself be construed to signal the termination either of our work nor of our responsibility as concerns the rest of our field. The forced abandonment of some particular area or of some particular phase of our work may in actuality be the hand of God nudging us toward new avenues of service rather than the tragic result of a blind turn of violence. 4) Even should work in our CIM area, as we think of it, become impossible, we must remember that ours is a mission to the whole of Congo, not just a small part of it. For as long as opportunities of witness are open to us within the Republic, we stand involved and responsible before God, our constituency and our Congolese fellow believers.

The committee then turned to the drafting of some guiding principles: 1) In an effort to keep personal contact with the major tribes of our CIM area, Nyanga, Mukedi and Kamayala stations should be re-occupied by missionary personnel as soon as conditions make it possible and advisable. (36)   2) Our continuing emphasis should be in the areas of spiritual counseling, leadership training, medical service and technical assistance with particular reference to agriculture, literature and radio.   3) In view of the likelihood of continuing instability in rural areas for some time to come and the growing strategic importance of urban centers in today's Congo, specific steps should be taken to explore avenues of witness open to us in such centers as Luluabourg, Kikwit and Leopoldville.   4) We should continue the policy of seconding qualified and requested personnel to sister organizations in Congo which are pursuing goals consonant with our own.   5) We should continue our recruitment and training of new personnel for service with the CIM.   (37)

There then followed a series of actions that had largely to do with the temporary placement and/or alternate assignments of CIM missionaries evacuated from Kamayala, Kajiji, Kandala, Mukedi and Nyanga. A concluding minute read: "That we express our deepest thanks and appreciation for the way in which our CIM missionary staff has cooperated and helped in supplying accommodations and emergency supplies for displaced members of the CIM family." (38)

It was clear that this time around, CIM personnel would not be quickly or easily dislodged from the soil of Congo.

CHAPTER 12   THE FIRE SPREADS

Stanleyville, in the spring of 1964, was deceptively peaceful. Located in the midst of equatorial forest with its heavy rainfall, lush vegetation and riot of tropical flowers, it was named for the famous explorer, H. Morton Stanley, and situated on the Congo River at the farthest navigable point from Leopoldville.

LECO, the Protestant press and publishing house in Leopoldville, under the direction of CIM missionary Bob Bontrager, had chosen to convene a Congo-wide consultation on Christian literature there the first week in May. In June of the previous year, LECO had opened a major new supply depot and bookstore in that city which had, within one year, racked up encouraging sales.

The consultation had been marked by enthusiasm and optimistic planning both for the northeast area of Congo and the country as a whole. Strong consensus emerged on four key points: 1) to seek funding for larger offset printing equipment for the LECO press to make maximum use of the printing expertise offered by the newly arrived CIM couple Henry and Tina Weier Dirks; 2) the creation of a central office which could serve as a clearing house for Protestant literature projects country-wide while providing a manuscript library and a translation service; 3) the creation of new regional literature committees in two major language areas where literature work, untill then, had been carried on in an uncoordinated manner; and 4) the call for the reviving of a French language Christian magazine for the whole of the country.

Not only was Stanleyville the focus of a strong new thrust in Protestant literature supply and distribution, it was also to be the site of a new *Université Libre* (Free University), this in addition to a Catholic institution in Leopoldville and a state sponsored university in Elizabethville far to the southeast of Congo. The new Stanleyville campus was also to house a Protestant School of Theology under the academic umbrella of the university. Upon concluding his doctoral studies in Belgium, Mel and Elfrieda Loewen and their five children took up residence in this city where Loewen was appointed the University's academic dean. They were soon joined by MCC sponsored PAX men, Jon Snyder and Gene Bergman, who were assigned to maintenance and support roles on campus.

There were, furthermore, two EMC student couples already resident in the area at a theological school opened only two years earlier by the Unevangelized Fields Mission at their station, Banjwadi, situated some 40 miles north of Stanleyville. Mayambi (mah-YAH-mbi) Sosthène and family had arrived from Nyanga already in the fall of 1961. They were joined a year later by Bapatuila (bah-pah-TWEE-lah) John and his family who came from Mutena.

In a letter to Elkhart, one of the CIM missionaries attending the Stanleyville literature consultation commented that Stanleyville "is one of the oldest European communities in the whole of the Congo. There is a fascinating blend of blood in the local population that dates back for more than 80 years to the time of the slave trade when locally-established Arab traders took African wives thus creating an Arabized strain both as to physical characteristics and religious faith. We visited a little mosque in the process of construction in a suburb . . . entirely the project of the local Congolese who descend from Arab fathers generations ago. Then there are the numerous Indians and a large Greek community which has come progressively to replace the Portuguese as commercial men. . . . Then, too, this is the home stomping ground of the former Congo Prime Minister, Patrice Lumumba . . . . And now there is a life-sized photographic likeness of him behind plate glass on a V-shaped corner where two angling streets meet near the center of town. Politically things are quiet. It seems the National Army sent one of its ablest officers, General Leonard Mulamba from the Luluabourg region, and he has really succeeded in keeping his troops in hand and in holding the respect of his fellow countrymen if not their affection. But there is always the undercurrent of hope that one day a shift in fortune will bring to power those who are of the same mind and persuasion of their local hero." (1)

The "undercurrent" referred to in the letter was to become all too apparent in a few scant months. And the flower-bordered area in front of the photographic likeness of the martyred Lumumba in the heart of the city was soon to be transformed into a blood-drenched memorial to his memory and the scene of ferocious barbarity.

the *Simbas*

In the far eastern reaches of the Congo in 1964, names, languages and topography were different from those of the Kwilu, but the deep social unrest and bitter resentment against the central government and its rough-handed national army were exactly the same. In the Kivu Province, bordering beautiful Lake Kivu, and in the Maniema area of northern Katanga Province, bordering Lake Tanganyika, the long-awaited independence from Belgian rule had turned to ashes between the teeth of the simple, rural population of the area. This Maniema region, as it was popularly called, was no stranger to suffering and violence. During the previous century, it had been ravaged by the slave trade which decimated entire villages. Uncounted thousands of people were yoked together in long caravans and force marched eastward toward the Indian Ocean for shipment to slave markets in the Middle and Far East. For those who sickened or whose strength failed, they were simply abandoned along the wayside. In time, their sun bleached bones became markers along trails that were followed by successive caravans. The callous brutality of those who were part of the slave trade was angrily documented by Stanley in his exploratory travels. In one instance, he noted the remark of a trader who said: "Slaves cost nothing. They only require to be gathered." (2)

But there was one significant way in which the situation of this east Congo area differed from the Kwilu. It was the home area of the Batetela (pr. bah-teh-TAY-lah) people. A proud, hardy tribal grouping of sub-clans, they had a history of aggression and of domination over other smaller ethnic groups of the region. It was from this tribe that Patrice Lumumba had come. In the course of his brief three months of political leadership following independence, he had become a towering folk hero among his fellow countrymen. His death at the hands of political enemies festered like a deep-seated ulcer. Small wonder, therefore, that the powerful core of leadership and supporters of the *Simba* rebellion took shape within this tribal group.

Nicolas Olenga

The initial outbreak of opposition to Congo's central government took place in Albertville, a port town on Congo's eastern frontier on Lake Tanganyika. At first it was simply a case where social unrest among unemployed townsfolk reached flash point. Storming government offices, they soon took over control of the port town. Hearing of the action, unemployed politicians and those of the area who harbored animosity toward the central government quickly made their way to the lake-side town to join the insurrection. Among them was a man named Nicolas Olenga. A Mutetela, like his fellow clansman Lumumba, he too had worked at one time for Belgian employers, had also been accused of pilfering and was jailed for a couple of months. When in 1961 Gizenga Antoine attempted to set up an opposition government in Stanleyville, Olenga was among those who made his way there and, for a time, filled a minor role in that regime. When Gizenga's effort collapsed, Olenga made his way back south to his home area at Kindu at the head of the rail line which linked that town with Albertville to the east on the lake.

Sensing that the Albertville public uprising offered him an opportunity, he quickly imposed himself upon the scene and gave it dramatic leadership. He was described as "a striking figure. He was in his early thirties, stood nearly six feet tall with a lean, hard body . . . He carried himself with the grace and ease of a man who knew that he was born to command. Olenga had a handsome, intent face, with dark, piercing eyes." (3)

Bestowing upon himself the military grade of "Lieutenant Colonel", he began recruiting for what he called "The People's Army." The popular term adopted to identify themselves was *Simba* - - the word for lion in the local dialect. There were basically three key strands which ran through the *Simba* rebellion from beginning to end. First and foremost, the powerful dynamic of popular unrest and resentment nurtured by the steadily deteriorating situation of their daily lives. This was significantly heightened by the bitter memory of the assassination of their fellow tribesman, Lumumba. There was, further, the rhetoric of Communist ideology. Leaflets extolling the blessings of life under leftist governments in various parts of the world quickly began to appear among the people. Later on, other Congolese politicians joined the movement who were known to have access to Chinese sources of arms and funds. This was, at least in part, a contributing factor to the strong anti-American tone which early permeated the movement.

But most significantly, in the *Simba* movement, as among the *Jeunesse* in the Kwilu, there was a heavy reliance upon the powers of witchcraft. It was this more than any political ideology which provided a common basis of operation for rank and file members. The *Simbas* created an elaborate initiation process through which they put their recruits. After making cuts on foreheads and chests, charcoal was rubbed into the wounds which, upon healing, would create permanent welts of scarred tissue. They then typically threw an animal hide over them and ordered them to walk away while a gun was fired in the air. Called back they were told that they now were *Simbas*. They were assured that via this process they had acquired powerful "dawa" (pr. DAH-wah), i.e., the local term for occult, magical power. This power, however, was not unconditional. It would protect them only if they carefully respected the taboos placed upon *Simbas*. Among the things prohibited were sleeping with women during daytime hours, eating food prepared by pregnant women. And above all else, when going into battle, they were never to look either to the right or the left; they were only to stare fixedly straight ahead. If they respected these instructions, their newly acquired "dawa" was guaranteed to make them bullet-proof in battle. Sometimes there were extra embellishments to the process such as attaching a bit of fur to their hair which purportedly would protect them from attack by air. In some cases it was even reported that new recruits were sprinkled with "holy water."

Whether for psychological reasons or because of his own personal belief in the efficacy of "dawa," General Olenga made sure that he too was covered. To assure this, he secured the services of an aged sorceress of that region known as Mama Onema. Widely known and feared for her powers of sorcery, General Olenga attached her to his personal retinue thus assuring that her considerable prestige was firmly associated not only with him personally but with the *Simba* cause as well. All in all, Olenga demonstrated a canny ability to utilize cultural dynamics for his own ends. With the "dawa" his motley bands of followers were infused with a fearlessness which they otherwise would not have had. And with the taboos he created a means of exercising some degree of discipline. (4)

Olenga made his first move west out of Albertville in July. Accompanied by his tattered followers, he was preceded by sorcerers waving palm fronds who fixedly looked straight ahead. They almost immediately overran the town of Kasongo from which the soldiers of the national government fled in panic. Rounding up some 200 Congolese who were to any degree educated or functionaries of the central government, they assembled them in a public place and beat them to death. Thus was set a grisly precedent which was to be followed again and again, with various refinements, as they began their march northward toward Stanleyville. Equipped now with vehicles, they moved toward Kindu, the capital of Maniema Province. Here again, the army fled ahead of them and they took control of the town without resistance. And here, too, suspected sympathizers of the central government were publicly assembled and executed.

By now word had spread far and wide via the jungle grape vine. They were moving north, the *Simbas*. Their final destination was Stanleyville. They had powerful *dawa*. They could not be stopped. The bullets of any rifle turned to harmless drops of water when fired at them. Under the leadership of Olenga, who had by now conferred upon himself the title of Lieutenant General, it was clear that they were invincible. None heard the news more clearly or with greater fear than the government army contingents scattered ahead of them along the route they were following.

Stanleyville is taken

That summer of 1964, Mel and Elfrieda Loewen were settled in Stanleyville with their family where Mel was busy with his academic responsibilities at the newly opened University. That the provincial government was eager for the new institution to be opened there is evidenced by the facilities they had made available free of charge. A large complex of buildings had been constructed prior to 1960 by the Belgians to house a secondary school for white children. These facilities provided ample space for dormitories, library and classrooms, dining hall, kitchen, storage and office space. The local government officials had further promised free additional acreage as more space might be needed. As for housing, a set of new apartment buildings abandoned after independence some three miles from the school was also at their disposal for university staff. The 1963/64 school year had been a rather impromptu arrangement due to considerable Congolese pressure. Some 20 students had been enrolled in what was considered a preparatory year of study with a teaching staff that had been hurriedly recruited. But this was simply a beginning. Both government and populace applauded the new academic venture among them. Stanleyville was to have its own university.

From their vantage point within the city, the Loewens, like all of the other 1,600 expatriates, had also been hearing about the *Simbas*. They were concerned, of course, but many of them had weathered other troubled days in the Congo and did not feel there was reason for exaggerated alarm. As a matter of fact, in late July word had been sent ahead to the white community by Lt. Olenga urging them to stay and remain calm. Their expertise and services would be needed by the new regime once it was established in Stanleyville. So it was said.

But for the Congolese population and, particularly, for representatives of the central government, it was another matter. Let the Loewen journal describe what happened: "On Monday, August 3, [1964] the army called a curfew for 3:30 in the afternoon. Officers and men were nervous. Military trucks and jeeps were moving all over Stanleyville. Reports had the rebels within 20 miles of the city. I drove to army headquarters at 4:00 to check on developments. Intelligence was sketchy. The Congolese officers and their few Belgian advisors were trying to form a total picture of where the rebels actually were and what measures to take to defend the city. But the conflicting messages of the soldiers who had run in fear for miles were of little help. They babbled incoherently about attacks on this bridge and that village. Nobody could stand against the rebels, they said. Their only hope was to run and flee from terror. Considering the equipment and ammunition at their disposal, the soldiers were a bunch of cowards. And yet, seeing later the daring and cruelty of the rebel hard core, I could understand their fear." (5)

Monday night was calm. Workmen came to their jobs as usual on Tuesday morning but were obviously tense and fearful. Most asked permission to return to their homes early to be near their families. During the day on the 4th of August, several UN planes came in to evacuate the UN personnel. The previous evening SEDEC, a large commercial enterprise, had chartered a flight to lift out women and children of its staff families. The US Embassy had also brought in a small plane to take out non-essential Stanleyville staff. Loewens as well as resident Americans were notified that the following Wednesday another plane would be sent aboard which they could leave if they wished. The Loewens declined.

They later described the events of Tuesday August 4 as follows: ". . . at four as we went home from the office, soldiers were all over the uptown area, some running and hitching rides to the airport which would be a major target of attack. Others sat around the city square, waiting for something to happen. Wives of soldiers were moving out of their houses at the military camps carrying children on their backs; cots, bedding and sewing machines on their heads, shouting, running everywhere in the hot humid afternoon. The city was in panic and fear drove the people not knowing where." (6)

Their "moment" came when the first *Simbas* put in their appearance. Emerging from the tropical rain forest which surrounded Stanleyville on all sides, they began their slow, measured progress along the main boulevard of the city. In the lead was a *Simba* sorcerer. Bare to the waist and armed only with a palm branch which he waved from side to side, he calmly walked down the middle of the street, eyes fixed straight ahead. Behind him, evenly spaced, came bare-chested *Simbas*, each waving their own palm branches and also staring straight ahead. Heavily armed ANC troops had long since taken flight. It was psychological warfare at its best. Though there was sporadic gunfire both day and night, by Friday, August 7, the rebel takeover of Stanleyville, its three military camps, its banks, its large commercial enterprises and some 1,600 white people had been accomplished. (7)

The Loewen account continues: "The rebel victors whooped it up on the weekend. Officially all was sweetness and light. Everyone was told to return to work. Prices would go down, wages up. The people cheered the liberators who came in the name of Lumumba. At last the oppressors from Leopoldville were driven out of their land. A new day had come. The bodies lying in the streets were picked up and dumped in the river; elections were held by cheering in the city stadium. Former administrators were executed together with an assortment of thieves at the foot of Lumumba's monument and left to lie for a while as a public lesson of instant judgement to all who opposed the new regime." (8)

But with regard to the white population, the regime was all smiles at the outset. "We were welcome and appreciated as necessary technicians in the building of a new nation. We would be protected as well as our property. This revolution was a matter between Congolese and had nothing to do with the foreigners. But woe to any foreigner who got involved and by some indiscretion aided the political parties of the opposition." (9)

It was not long until some administrative structure began to take shape. Christophe Gbenye (pr. gbeh-NYAY), an original minister of Lumumba's short-lived government and the late president of the NLC group at Brazzaville, turned up in Stanleyville and was declared president. On the military side, another Mutetela surfaced as the second in command. He was Colonel Opepe (pr. oh-PAY-pay). Described as in his 50's, short and rotund, he had enlisted in the Belgian *Force Publique* and later served in the ANC as chief-of-staff in Stanleyville. He had retired in 1963 and soon after joined the *Simbas*. A devout Catholic, he also proved to be an alcoholic. During the days of *Simba* control of the city, he would become something of an enigma to the white population. At times he seemed genuinely concerned for them. At other times he could be brutal and despotic. (10) With passing time it became clear that the lives of people, both white and black, would literally lie in the hands of emotionally unstable men such as he.

On September 5, the *Simba* movement declared itself to be a "People's Republic." On September 25, Thomas Kanza, Lumumba's former ambassador to the UN, was declared its foreign minister. He left the Congo to begin a circuit of some of the world's capitals charged with the assignment of pleading their cause and seeking acceptance and support. Kanza would not return to Stanleyville again. Subsequent events were to overtake the *Simba* cause which he sought to represent.

spreading fear

The Mennonite missionary and church community in the Congo had already been shaken by the impact of rebellion. In the Kwilu, Mukedi and Kandala missionaries had been evacuated. In Stanleyville, the Loewens and two PAX men, Gene Bergman and Jon Snyder, had elected to stay and were now trapped. But there was more to come. On the heels of the *Simba's* quick victory in Stanleyville came immediate plans to take remaining centers in the east and to begin probing toward the west. In the east this meant attempting to take Bukavu, a town on the shore of Lake Kivu which was the last center of any importance still held by government forces.

To the west and southwest there were Lusambo and Luluabourg which, if taken, would open the way to a march across the two Kasai Provinces to link up with the *Jeunesse* in the Kwilu. In a matter of days, rebel patrols had moved west from Kindu and entered an area where Methodist missionaries had been at work since the early 1900's. Burleigh Law, one of their pilots, flew to Wembo Nyama on August 5 to check on the situation at that large station. No more than landed, he was surrounded by *Simbas*. Refusing to turn over the keys to his plane, he was shot. He died that same day in surgery in the hospital of that station. Two days later, missionaries at Wembo Nyama sent the message via radio that the rebel leaders would allow missionary women and children to be flown out. On August 7, two planes flew in. After lengthy negotiations, wives and children were evacuated but the men were kept in rebel hands.

At Luluabourg, these events found the Presbyterian Mission staff in their annual conference. By this time CIM missionaries Levi and Eudene Keidel had settled there, as well, to give leadership to the production and distribution of Tshiluba Christian literature in the two Kasais. Harold and Gladys Graber had also been relocated in Luluabourg. Burned out eight months previously at Kandala, they had been reassigned to help in translation of a backlog of manuscripts which had accumulated. Invited to join the Presbyterian missionaries in their conference, they were part of that fellowship when news of events in the Methodist area to the east arrived. But that was not all. By August 12, a Presbyterian pilot flying to the north over Lusambo, a major center on the road leading to Luluabourg, reported that this town was already in rebel hands. Flushed with the confidence of their imagined invincibility, *Simba* forces had sent word ahead to Luluabourg: "We are coming. We will arrive on Saturday, August 15." Elsewhere General Olenga was laying plans to attack Bukavu on Lake Kivu four days later.

It was amidst such a tension and emotion-laden setting that the missionary conference at Luluabourg was drawing to a close. All that week radio sets had been tuned to the mission network frequencies from sunup to sunset as effort was made to monitor the swift pace of events. The close of the conference took the form of a communion service. All during the week contingency plans for evacuation had been drawn and redrawn. Now they stood in semi-circles around the serving table oblivious to denominational identities. All that mattered were the individual decisions they were making in the recesses of their own hearts regarding their individual courses of action in the next days.

Given their recent experience at Kandala and a large concern for their five school age children, it was the group consensus that the Grabers ought not stay longer. The Keidels were struggling with their personal schedule. Levi had promised to lead special literature workshops in Malawi and Ethiopia in September. For the time being, any further travel in the Kasai bush country for literature distribution was out of the question. It was decided that Eudene would join their four children at the Presbyterian Station Lubondai, to the south, where a new school year was soon to begin. If evacuation became necessary in Levi's absence, she and the children would leave with others of that same station.

In the midst of these missionary deliberations, there was frenetic activity in the city. The UN sent a large plane to evacuate its technicians from the city. Driving to the airport to put the Graber family aboard this flight, Keidel found "soldiers were dug in all around the airport, foxholes bristled with guns at the ready. Preparing to leave were two jeep-loads of camouflaged soldiers with grass tied around their helmets and European officers, destination unknown. Others had taken positions on roofs of airport buildings." The route to the airport also took Keidel past the military camp. In the light of later events, the following observation had particular significance: "Five big double-dualed US army trucks were piled high with about 40 soldiers each and all their personal effects and weapons. . . . They soon moved out taking the road toward Lusambo." (11)

Back in the Kwilu, the area taken in the rush of events in mid-January was now solidly under rebel control. *Jeunesse* patrols there were also probing in various directions. Ben and Helen Reimer Eidse, CIM missionaries at Kamayala in southern Kwango felt the growing tension. There, as in the far east of Congo, fantastic stories of the growing rebel threat were heard on all sides. CIM and Catholic stations to the north had already been hit and evacuated. In consultation with the local church leaders, it was agreed that they should leave for a while. On January 25, they had been airlifted by MAF to Leopoldville. Fifty miles to the west at the Mennonite Brethren station of Kajiji, CIM missionaries Peter and Annie Falk were settling in as staff for the newly-launched inter-Mennonite theology school. Before the end of January they, too, had felt it wise to evacuate to Leopolville with other MB staff from that station.

At Nyanga, barely 25 miles to the east of the Loange River which had become a porous frontier between rebel-held and government-held ground, missionaries were weighing the situation from day to day. It soon became clear that frequent rebel forays were being made across the river under cover of darkness in the heart of CIM land. One time it would be a small bridge which bore evidence of tampering. Then it would be some burned houses on the fringe of an isolated village. And always there were the wild rumors which circulated from day to day. Could it be the *Jeunesse* were really serious about trying to take Tshikapa some 50 miles to their rear? Should this happen - - or even if only the Lovua River ferry halfway between were to be cut adrift - - the Nyanga missionaries would find their evacuation route to the east cut. With great reluctance the Nyanga staff, too, had packed bags and left their station on February 3. (12)

And from the politically unstable south Kasai came yet another unsettling report: "Pastor Kazadi came with a troubled look on his face to greet us with the sad news that 75% of our South Kasai CIM Christians have been driven from their homes once again. "The area which had been particularly hard hit was Kabeya Kamuanga (pr. kah-BAY-ah kah-MWAH-ngah), some 35 miles west of Bakwanga, which had become a center for many of the Mennonite Baluba refugees who had fled the West Kasai in 1960-61. Their local pastor was Kabangu (pr. kah-BAH-ngoo) Tom who had formerly served so effectively at Djoko Punda and Tshikapa. They had dug in with a will and in three short years had thriving fields and a permanent chapel under construction. Many of them had a good start on new homes in permanent materials. Arriving at Graber's door Pastor Tom said: "I come with only my new typewriter tied on my bicycle; my dog followed me and these clothes I have on. When I went back to lock our home, the soldiers started shooting. My wife whom I left to wait for me got scared and ran. It is now four days. I have not heard from her. Our church was growing. A little over two weeks ago we had a large baptismal service and gathered around the Lord's table. We were so happy. Now here I am with a bad cut on my foot, my wife is lost and our things are stolen . . ."

In the murky political setting of the South Kasai in mid-1964, inter-clan conflict was generating its own regional fear, destruction and bloodshed. The Graber journal from that month comments only: "The present upheaval in South Kasai is the result of increased rebel activity in the rural regions around Bakwanga. The National Army tries to suppress it and fighting and plundering begin." (13)

filtered news

Wherever rebel control was established, links of communication with the outside world came under strict control. The *Simbas* to the northeast, with their access to the former provincial radio facilities, quickly turned them to their own purposes and daily broadcast a mix of anti-Western, anti-government *Simba* propaganda. In the Kwilu, the *Jeunesse* movement, not having access to such equipment, was largely content to allow a blanket of silence to descend upon the areas under their control. News from or about the occupied area of the Kwilu was limited to word of mouth stories leaked around the edges of their frontiers.

For the broad missionary and church community of the Congo, there was the keen realization that they had suddenly been cut off from many of their fellow believers whose lot it now was to discover the price of faithfulness to their Lord and their Church under the savage grip of rebel regimes. It made it no easier for missionaries who had been lifted out of danger's way to recognize that it had been primarily because of their status as expatriates that they had been provided opportunity for evacuation. This was a luxury denied thousands of Congolese Christians during those fearful days of *Simba* and *Jeunesse* rule. Small wonder that during those troubled months of early 1964, fitful sleep came late and fled early for CIM missionaries in their temporary quarters here and there in the Congo.

CHAPTER 13   THE FIRE IS QUENCHED

March 1964 was not a good moment in Congo's history for President Kasavubu and his Prime Minister Adoula. Not only was there openly expressed discontent on every hand, but more ominously still was the fact that this discontent had taken a violent turn in the Kwilu. In spite of repeated orders from Leopoldville, the efforts of the national army to suppress the rebellion had been totally ineffective. The *Jeunesse* had developed a very effective strategy for dealing with the hated military patrols. Allowing them to pass on the outbound portion of their foray, they then dropped a tree or dug a deep trench across the road camouflaged with sticks, grass and sand. Returning later in the day, the truck of soldiers would find themselves immobilized. As the *Jeunesse* signaled their presence from the surrounding brush, the fearful soldiers would often fire wildly and blindly. When their ammunition was exhausted the *Jeunesse* would cut them down in hand-to-hand combat.

But most troublesome of all for the central government was the information that Moise Tshombe, the former prime minister of the restless province of Katanga, was profiting from his exile in Spain to court support from sympathetic Belgian officials. There was further word that he was quietly ordering a group of his former Katangese troops to assemble just across Congo's southern border with Angola. A report of UN General Secretary U. Thant, published March 16, stated that approximately 1,800 former Katangese gendarmes were training there in company with some twenty white mercenaries. (1)

Adoula resigns

Prime Minister Adoula was coming to the end of his term. Unable to suppress the *Jeunesse* in the Kwilu and menaced by a possible incursion from forces loyal to Tshombe from the south, he submitted his resignation. Confronted by a deteriorating situation within and threat from without, President Kasavubu made a decision which not only astonished the world but angered many of his fellow Congolese. Recognizing that Tshombe represented not only a threat to his regime but also a power base which he desperately needed, Tshombe was invited to return to the Congo as its new prime minister! So it was that on July 10, 1964, what was called the Government of Public Welfare was officially installed by the president. And Moise Tshombe, the former archenemy of the central government and best known champion of regional autonomy, became the Congo's new head of government.

strange bedfellows

Knowing better than most the opposition he was facing, Tshombe immediately began a round of trips attempting to placate opponents of the new regime. Trying twice to go to Brazzaville to talk with the leaders of the NLC (the group that was masterminding the Kwilu rebellion) based there, he was rebuffed by the authorities across the river. This did not prevent him from negotiating with that group via other channels. NLC president Christophe Gbenye set unacceptable conditions for their cooperation and discussions broke down. Nonetheless, Tshombe did make highly publicized trips to Stanleyville and Bakwanga in efforts to strengthen central government ties with these outlying areas.

He knew, however, that his immediate and most pressing responsibility was to suppress the Kwilu rebellion. To make matters worse, although barely installed he began to hear rumors of something called a *Simba* movement in the far eastern reaches of the country. Knowing the ineffectiveness of the national army, he turned to the only other source of help available to him - - his former Katangese troops and a small core of professional mercenaries. The information reported by the UN Secretary earlier in the year proved to be very accurate. Quiet recruitment was indeed going on in Europe and southern Africa. Inbound flights to Leopoldville's international airport soon began to off-load small groups of "soldiers of fortune."

carnage at Gungu

Immediately incorporating Katangese officers into the Congo military structure, the army focused on the eastern Kwilu. Already before the Kandala missionaries had been evacuated, *Jeunesse* bands holding them had confidently stated that once all rural government posts came under their control they would amass many teams from the region for concerted attacks on Gungu, Idiofa and Kikwit. (EMC and Mennonite Brethren Churches and schools were located in two of the three centers - - Gungu and Kikwit.)

As good as their word, the time came when *Jeunesse* bands from far and wide began to converge on Gungu. They were about to attack their first major outpost of government authority. Alerted regarding the *Jeunesse* preparation out in the rolling grasslands to the east, the military garrison was supplied with extra ammunition by air drop and instructed to take up a defensive position on the dirt airstrip just adjacent to the town.

The day came. From a distance they could be seen coming from all directions toward the soldiers hunkered down behind their circle of dug-in machine gun emplacements. Marching bare breasted and bare footed, brandishing their bush knives and chanting *meya, meya* in cadence with their measured steps, they came, their eyes fixed on their targets. Holding their fire until the *Jeunesse* were in easy range, the machine guns began to chatter. Desperately repeating the magical words they'd been taught to trust, they walked into a lethal hail of lead.

The bullets did not turn into water.

Informed about what had happened, representatives of the International Red Cross made their way there a few days later. Aghast at what they found, they quickly realized that burial of so many corpses was impossible. Ordering barrels of fuel to be brought to the airstrip, they fashioned mounds of dead youth, saturated them with gasoline and set them aflame. It was soon learned that during the same period, assaults were also mounted in the Idiofa and Kikwit areas which were likewise bloodily repulsed.

Such was the tragic end of countless young men. They had believed deeply in the justice of their cause as well as in their invincibility and fully expected the ultimate rewards promised them by their leaders. No major government post in the Kwilu was again seriously threatened by the *Jeunesse*. They began to withdraw and concentrate on consolidating their control over an area between the Kwilu and Loange Rivers (where CIM stations Mukedi and Kandala were located) while awaiting further developments of the *Simba* movement in the far northeast. With rebel expansion checked in the Kwilu, the central government was content for several months to simply seal off the area while awaiting an advantageous moment to push pursuit across the Kwilu River. Among those isolated by this government decision were thousands of Mennonite Africans.

Bloodied by crushing defeat, the myth of *Jeunesse* invincibility shattered, Mulele Pierre hastened to strengthen his grip upon the population between the two rivers. The Baphende people in general and the Mennonite Church in particular were yet to learn the full implications of the tightening rebel rule.

at Bukavu the tide also turns

Lt. General Olenga's march into Stanleyville had been ridiculously easy. Out-manned and out-gunned by the national army at every turn, so massive was the popular excitement and so paralyzing the fear which gripped the representatives of the central government that waved palm fronds and bare chested youth shouting *mai, mai* (i.e., "water, water") had been enough. Yet Olenga had a problem. In his sweep from south to north along the main road, he had left one major government center on his eastern flank, Bukavu, the capital of Kivu Province. Instinctively he knew that as long as this port city remained in government hands, he was in constant danger in Stanleyville. But he saw no reason why he should not storm that final center as he had all the rest. The government officials were no problem. The army units there were comprised of a mix of soldiers who had already been put to flight in other encounters and had taken refuge there.

But there was one critical difference. At Bukavu, the Congolese Army officer was Col. Leonard Mulamba. Short, stocky and taciturn, he disciplined himself and imposed discipline upon those around him. Originally assigned to Stanleyville following the overthrow of the short-lived Gizenga government there, he had been temporarily ordered to Bukavu where Olenga found him on August 19 when he attacked the city. Serene in their confidence in their *Simba* magical powers and now better equipped with automatic weapons found in Stanleyville, they slowly pushed the government troops back, block by block, in the direction of Mulamba's headquarters on the tip of a peninsula which jutted into the lake. With the water at their backs and sides, the government troops could retreat no further. The peninsula also now concentrated the approaching rebels into a single body. Leading his troops, Mulamba charged and the rebel approach faltered. Nightfall brought a lull in the fighting. Via short wave radio Mulamba alerted Leopoldville of his situation and called for reinforcements. Three American turbo-prop transport planes flown by American crews lifted off in Leopoldville well before dawn and deposited 150 Katangese troops across the lake in Ruwanda, a few miles from Bukavu. Reinforced by this unit, Mulamba took the offensive. By evening the rebel force had been decimated and scattered. *Simba* General Olenga had experienced his first defeat.

Retreating to Kindu, he gave shrill orders via shortwave to his government in Stanleyville to start rounding up all Americans and Belgians. They had been attacked and defeated in Bukavu by American planes and mercenaries. All Americans in Stanleyville would now be held as political hostages, a decision which would, in time, make the name of missionary doctor Paul Carlson a household word around the world. The *Simba* story in Stanleyville was entering a new chapter that was to spell terror not only for American consular staff and the missionary community but also for the hundreds of other expatriates trapped there.

Lima I and II

It took all of September and October for Prime Minister Tshombe's mercenary force to take shape. Arriving first in Leopoldville, they were then airlifted to the huge Belgian-built Kamina military base in Katanga Province, the same base which had served as a shuttle point shortly before for the Graber-led UN evacuation of the Baluba refugee camp at Elizabethville.

Over the ensuing weeks, the group at that base came to number a total of 120 mercenaries and 150 Katangese. The caravan which was assembled was comprised of some 50 trucks and vehicles to transport the men, fuel and military supplies. Three nondescript armored vehicles had been salvaged and rebuilt from a local military junk yard and led the caravan which arrived on November 1 at Kongolo, a railway town which had been among the first to be overrun by Olenga and his *Simba* forces earlier in the summer. Under the over-all command of Michael Hoare, who had fought for Prime Minister Tshombe during his break-away attempt in Katanga, the column was under the direct command of Albert Liegeois, a professional soldier on loan to the Congo government. (2) They would be followed a bit later by a second column under the command of Robert Lamouline. Both officers' names started with the letter L, thus the code names Lima I and II. (3)

Poised at Kongolo, their orders from Prime Minister Tshombe were brief and clear: "Take Stanleyville and crush the Simba rebellion." Their objective lay 470 miles to the north. The only access was via mud and sand roads snaking their ways through the equatorial rain forests.

Kindu and the mercenaries

As the lead column moved north, they encountered only occasional and light resistance. It was at Kindu, the capital of Maniema Province, where on November 5 the *Simbas* chose to make a determined stand. It was also here that the mercenaries making up the column would quickly demonstrate who they were and for what reason they had come. It was here that the personality and mind-set of professional soldiers for hire came sharply into focus. The group that came together in Eastern Congo under the command of Michael Hoare represented a broad mix of nationalities, backgrounds and personalities. They tended to be around 30 years of age. Most of them came from laboring class families and had limited education. That the pay offered for their services against the *Simbas* was attractive to them was obvious. It clearly represented a financial bonanza - - if they survived.

They held, however, one more key characteristic in common - - their readiness to shoot and kill when ordered to do so, and this without hesitation or pangs of conscience. One writer who researched the Stanleyville operation commented that when asked why they had come to Congo, they would assure him that they had come to fight Communism. "Then they would burst into laughter. . . . The mercenaries operated in a cruel and merciless world. . . . Mercy and compassion were unknown. Only death meant anything, and it meant a lot; it was ever close at hand." (4)

At Kindu, random mob savagery collided with organized savagery. The *Simbas* paid a frightful price. When the roar of automatic weapons ceased, Lima I had taken control of the town. In the process they rescued some 125 Europeans who had been held prisoner since July 22. When personnel of Lima I burst into one area of the town, they found 24 local European men lined up against the wall of a building awaiting execution. Only minutes earlier *Simba* guards had been inviting a flock of children to suggest various ways in which different ones of the semi-dressed captives might be put to death. Lima I had arrived before the *Simba* guards had time to carry out the childrens' suggestions. There was no official count of the dead. Most were simply dumped into the Lualaba River which flows past the town. One of the few *Simbas* to escape across the river was General Olenga.

Making his tattered way to Stanleyville he discovered that there was more bad news. *Simba* forces which at one point had gotten as far downstream as the river port of Lisala, some 300 miles to the north of Leopoldville, had been repulsed by yet another small group of mercenaries who were making their way upstream. By now they had come as far as Bumba, a river town just 225 miles from Stanleyville. And there was still more. *Simba* troops, by now, were supposed to have taken Luluabourg. Instead, several truckloads of *Simbas* had been ambushed in the forest between Lusambo and Luluabourg by government troops and most of them had lost their lives.

And at Kindu, Lima I was waiting for Lima II to catch up. Time was spent repairing equipment and resting in preparation for their final push on their ultimate goal still some 250 miles to the north.

Stanleyville under siege

In Stanleyville, Canadian-born Mel Loewen, his American wife Elfrieda and their five children, along with American PAX men Gene Bergman and Jon Snyder tried to follow as normal a daily routine as possible. All were on university staff: Loewen as dean, Bergman as a builder and Snyder as a bookkeeper. But with passing time, in the midst of the worsening fortunes of the *Simba* cause, this became increasingly difficult. In his chronicle of their days under rebel rule, Loewen wrote: "In the twilight of freedom and fear, most Europeans continued to go to their jobs, either on bicycles or walking. Since in the first few weeks the rebels were still advancing it became apparent that the occupation could be long unless some reconciliation were effected. . . . The thousand or so Europeans in the city were constantly stocking food. . . . All felt insidiously threatened by scarcities and the gnawing fear drove them into groups pledged to survival. By back doors and devious ways common to all war situations they laid up for the long haul. Few suffered from starvation but after a while the diets of rice and sardines held no attractions. . . . For three months we moved about from home to town to the university with only occasional incidents . . . showing our identity papers or placating some begging rebel with a tip. No mail and telegraph connections from the outside reduced our university correspondence to a few exchanges with firms in the city. . . . Mostly we were putting in time and waiting; waiting for something to happen. We hoped for reconciliation of some sort with the Leo government and thereby avoid going through another battle. Yet, as the weeks passed, it became evident that neither side was ready for compromise and the only solution was military. And so we waited." (5)

At first the five members of the American Consulate headed by Consul Michael Hoyt, who had elected to remain in Stanleyville, experienced freedom of circulation. This soon changed and after two or three weeks, they experienced constant detention, menace and abuse. What early triggered the fear and wrath of the *Simba* leaders was America's role, real and imagined, in the unfolding story of their shrinking domain. Loewen writes; "Every loss - - Bukavu, Uvira, Kindu - - was blamed to American aerial interventions. Stanleyville radio ranted day after day about the imperialist, neo-colonialist Americans. And as the regular army continued to advance toward Stanleyville, all were informed that the rebels were no longer fighting the Congo Army which had surrendered long ago, but foreign troops led by the U.S." (6)

What was less well known was the vicious turn that *Simba* rule had early taken vis-à-vis their fellows Africans. In the early rush of *Simba* victories, government representatives, soldiers and educated people who were captured from place to place were summarily killed. But once control was established over their territory, the wisdom of showing a more benign face would seem self-evident. But this was not to be. Avowed supporters of the movement, as long as they demonstrated total obedience and performed whatever service required, were able to survive in Stanleyville. But the "intellectuals" - - clerks, teachers, small business people or artisans who had in any way previously served the central government - - continued to be marked for extermination. Furthermore, as rebel fortunes dwindled and discord erupted among top leaders, a simple rumor sufficed for any African to lose his life. Thus, tragically, the very people upon whom any chance of success for their movement was dependent were systematically hunted down and destroyed.

the Lumumba monument becomes a grisly altar

One of the dominant *Simba* personalities of the regime was a hulk of a man named Alphonse Kinghis. Standing well over six feet and weighing better than 200 pounds, he was known to the Europeans of Stanleyville "as a madman and as the fanatic leader of an anti-white, anarchistic religious cult. The cult, known as the Kitawala movement, was a weird mixture of teachings of the Watchtower group and African paganism. Kinghis . . . was the bishop of the Kitawalists." (7)

The *Simbas* had found him in prison in Stanleyville and had released him. He had a history of being in the forefront of bizarre and violent activity. In 1960, as political independence came to the Congo, he and his followers had toppled several monuments which had been erected in the memory of early explorers and Belgian colonial personalities. They then went to the Catholic cathedral where Kinghis declared a statue of Christ to be King Albert of Belgium and ordered the mob to topple it as well. Intercepted by a Congolese priest, they left the statue with a broken hand. Some time later it was Kinghis who circulated the information that Americans had contaminated all 20 *franc* notes. Due to its radioactive nature, it was dangerous to sleep in the same room with such a bill. (8)

As long as General Olenga was in Stanleyville, he was able to keep the excesses of such rabble rousers in check. But in mid-August, when Olenga left the city for his ill-fated attempt to take Bukavu, Kinghis saw his chance. Assuming authority over *Simba* forces in the city he ordered a dozen or so Congolese prisoners to the Lumumba monument in the middle of the city. For the most part they were men who had played minor roles in the local government in the past. Haranguing the assembled crowd he accused the hapless prisoners with all manner of crimes committed against the *Simba* cause. Then, ordering the first victim to the monument, he shouted to the mob: "Guilty or innocent?" "Guilty" roared the crowd. "The *Simbas* riddled the man's body with bullets. They kept firing in a frenzy until the entire body had been cut to pieces. Blood spurted onto the monument, onto the clothes of the *Simbas* and the civilians." (9) This process continued for about an hour until all twelve bodies lay in a shredded heap on the ground before the photographic likeness of Lumumba behind the plate glass. In a gory sense, what had been erected as a monument to his memory had become an altar of execution in his honor.

With passing weeks this happened so often that finally revulsion surfaced even among the fanatical *Simba* populace. Sensing this, in later days rebel leaders disposed of their victims in a quicker, less public manner by taking them to the edge of town, tying them hand and foot and throwing them off a bridge into the Tshopo River and the rapids just downstream. (10)

the last eight days

November 16 marked the beginning of a final whirlwind of international activity which would have Stanleyville as its focal point. Having repeatedly declared over the radio that the *Simbas* were now fighting American mercenaries, Olenga was desperate to come up with some proof. While most of the mercenaries were English-speaking, the U.S. government had been very explicit in forbidding any American involvement in the military operations of Lima I and Lima II. In their frustration the *Simbas* finally decided to fabricate charges against some American already in their hands. For whatever bizarre reasons it may have been, it was decided to accuse missionary Dr. Paul Carlson of actually being a major in the American military and of spying for the American government.

From Culver City, CA, the son of a Swedish immigrant father, he joined the Mission Covenant Church as a teenager. After serving two years in the Navy he enrolled in North Park College in Chicago and then finished an undergraduate degree in anthropology at Stanford in his home state. Married in 1950 to Lois Ludblom, he moved to Washington State where he entered the medical school in George Washington University.

Graduating with distinction in 1955, there followed an internship and residency. By 1960, at age 32, he volunteered for a five month term of service with the Mennonite-prompted CPRA in the Congo. Part of that time was spent at a bush hospital at Wasolo, to the northwest of Stanleyville, which was jointly sponsored by his Church and the Evangelical Free Church. After a short time of private practice back in the States, he longed to return to the Congo. In 1962 he and his wife made their decision. After studying tropical medicine in Liverpool, England, and French in Paris, they returned to Wasolo.

When the *Simba* rebellion erupted and spread, he took his family to the safety of Bangui in the nearby country of Congo/Brazzaville and returned to his work at Wasolo. It was there he was eventually taken captive by the rebels and accused of being an American spy because of the inter-mission short-wave transmitter which he had in his house. (11)

Shrill *Simba* broadcasts repeatedly made these charges against Dr. Carlson and stated that, as a spy, he would be executed. There were the further frightening declarations that all expatriates now in their hands were considered to be prisoners of war and that unless the American government called off the advancing columns of mercenaries and ceased giving aid to the central government, these prisoners would also be executed. Recognizing that they were losing the cause militarily, the rebel leadership now desperately sought a diplomatic means of staving off defeat.

Of those last days Loewen wrote: "The rebels played with our lives as a leopard with a child. They could mash us in an instant but they toyed before the kill. And the outside world didn't know which way to attack the leopard lest they hurt the child." (12) Loewen's imagery of leopard and child was given full credence by a statement of *Simba* President Gbenye which appeared in their newspaper, *The Martyr*, during those last hectic days. The article used precisely this language as it announced that *Simba* forces held "in its claws" over 800 Belgians and 300 Americans. While they were being held in "secure places," they would be immediately "massacred" at the slightest threat of an attack on the *Simba* stronghold. It was further declared they had all written their last wills and testaments which were soon to be forwarded to their respective destinations. Unless the Belgians and Americans ordered the withdrawal from Congo soil of those who continually massacre our people, "we will make fetishes with the hearts and dress ourselves in the skins of the Belgians and the Americans." (13)

Mennonites to the monument

It was mid-morning on November 18 that U.S. Consul Michael Hoyt, four other consular staff people, Dr. Carlson and the two Mennonite PAX men, Gene Bergman and Jon Snyder, were put in two vehicles.

"'Where are you taking us?' Hoyt asked one of the *Simbas*. 'To the monument,' the *Simba* replied. And they added in a matter of fact tone, 'to be killed.'"

The monument was a short three blocks from the hotel where the men had been kept under guard. The sidewalk grapevine had long since spread the word that there was to be another public trial at the monument. This time, however, was special for there would be white men lined up before the portait of Lumumba. As the vehicles slowly made their way along the street, there were crowds everywhere. Thousand had already preceded them to Lumumba Square where they awaited the spectacle.

Finally the vehicles arrived at their destination where all eight men were jammed into a covered Jeep. The mob surged forward. Hands thrust into the back groping for bodies. Beards were pulled, burning cigarettes pushed onto bare skins. Other jabbed sharp objects into backs and arms. Now and again the word "mateke" (pr. mah-TEH-keh) was shouted in their ears, i.e., the local term for margarine or oil. But in the chaos and menace of that hour, a secondary meaning of the word took on fearsome relevance - - "meat." Indeed, several of the *Simbas* kept repeating: "we're going to eat you."

Gene Bergman, the PAX man, would later recall hoping amidst din and danger that his death, whenever and however it came, would be mercifully swift.

The scene of savagery continued unabated for about fifteen minutes. Then all eight men were told to get out of the Jeep and line up before the monument. When the white skins became visible to the crowd, an immense roar rocked the square. The men were made to stand single file before the monument. But before the *Simbas* could give any further orders, General Olenga suddenly came elbowing and pushing his way through the mob. Ignoring the white men he went straight to the *Simba* in charge. A heated argument ensued. Though the Americans were unable to get the gist of the exchange, they could see that the *Simba* officer was resisting. Suddenly General Olenga lashed out and knocked the *Simba* to the ground. The men were ordered back into the Jeep and were taken back to the hotel. Olenga had canceled the execution. (14)

a general roundup of whites

From the perspective of their apartment on the fringe of the city, the Loewens tried to keep track of events via whatever means available. Mel wrote later: "Our first warning of arrest was given by a small boy who said, rather casually, that all whites were being taken as prisoners and some would be executed. There were many rumors going the rounds, so we dismissed this as another wild one. . . . But next morning four rebels came to our house to take us uptown for a check of passports. . . . At the *Hotel des Chutes*, which served as the rebel control center that day, we were told to line up by two's. One of the *Simbas* began to look at our passports. He looked at my Canadian passport first and while he was momentarily distracted I slipped my wife's American passport in my pocket. It was apparent that they were seeking out Americans and Belgians. Perhaps they would be satisfied by seeing only my passport. Next I was referred to the infamous Colonel Opepe, rebel commander of Stanleyville, who looked at my passport and wondered in what part of the world Canada might be. A rebel nearby said it was in South America so Opepe let us go. Last in line were the two PAX men, Gene Bergman and Jon Snyder. These two were held because they had American passports. The German professor of mathematics and his family were next but also released. So our two families returned to their homes and the PAX men were held together with other Americans and hundreds of Belgians."

"Those of us who were held in Stanleyville yet free to listen to foreign newscasts were caught in our own dilemma. For our own safety we wanted to have a negotiated peace and thus be spared another battle. And yet, to negotiate on these terms and to give recognition to these evil men was equally revolting. So we braced for the battle which could not be long in coming for the army was now within striking distance of the city." (15)

While mercenary columns were now making steady progress toward Stanleyville from the south and west, their time of arrival could not be fixed with certainty. Furthermore, even though they would undoubtedly be able to defeat the rebel defenders upon arrival, they would in the last hours still have time to make good on their repeated threats to massacre the hostages they had in their grasp. The only plan that seemed to offer any hope was one of a surprise drop of para-commandos upon the city and that before the mercenary columns could arrive. Thus was born Operation Red Dragon, a joint Belgian-American rescue effort.

Ascension Island

It is a British-owned speck of land nearly 2,000 miles out in the Atlantic Ocean off the mouth of the Congo River. It is only 34 square miles in size but holds a large air strip built by the American government during World War II as a fueling station for bombers which were ferried from South America to Africa. (16) With permission of the British government, this island was to become a link in the chain of events which was being forged in round-the-clock consultations in Washington and Brussels during those November days.

Already as early as November 8, the Belgian Foreign Minister, Paul-Henri Spaak, had over a lunch in Washington discussed possible eventualities with W. Averell Harriman of the American State Department. Foreseeing the likelihood of a worsening hostage situation in Stanleyville, groundwork was laid which would enable swift action later in the month. Knowing that no African countries would grant permission to overfly their territories, any aerial movement would need to skirt the immense western bulge of the African continent before arriving in Congo air space. Ascension Island was the answer.

America would furnish the necessary air transport; Belgium would provide the paratroopers. By Wednesday, November 18, some 350 Belgian para-commandos were swimming, fishing and doing calisthenics on the beaches of Ascension Island awaiting further orders. Meanwhile, world attention was increasingly fixed on that city in Congo's equatorial rain forest and the unfolding hostage drama which had come to be so dramatically symbolized by Doctor Carlson. As the *Simba* pronouncements became increasingly agitated and threats ever more violent, a message was flashed to the island out in the Atlantic for the commandos to get in the air as quickly as possible. Their destination was Kamina air base in southeastern Congo, nearly 2,500 nautical miles distant. The flight was to be made non-stop. The first plane lifted off in the early morning of Saturday, November 21. Traveling through the night and into early morning of Sunday November 22, the line of flight of the transport planes took them across CIM territory in the West Kasai.

a Sunday morning at Nyanga

After the evacuation of CIM missionaries from Mukedi, Kandala, Kamayala, Kajiji and, finally, Nyanga, the month of February had been spent in restless anticipation of the opportunity to return to their places of service. By late March, both the Falks and the Eidses had returned to their stations at Kajiji and Kamayala. By mid-May, the first contingent of Nyanga missionaries had returned and by June had been followed by the rest. In October it was decided that the Bertsches should make Nyanga their base as well, Jim to continue the revision project of the Phende New Testament and Jenny to give direction to a new preparatory year of study for girls who desired to enroll in the EMC secondary school on the station.

November 22 fell on a Sunday and it was a special one at Nyanga. A group of believers was to be baptized in the early morning after which there would be a full day of church activity. While the missionaries and Nyanga Christians alike looked forward to this day with joyous anticipation, there was nonetheless a brooding, somber mood among them for they were well aware of the drama that was being played out at Stanleyville. Much prayer was being offered for the people trapped under rebel control and especially for the Christians there.

In the course of that day one of the Nyanga missionaries typed an airgram addressed to the Elkhart office. In part it read: "This morning before daylight we began to hear the sound of planes passing west to east in the distance to the north of us. Sounded a lot like turbo-prop engines but not sure. What it's all about we'll hear sometime. We do know, as do you, that things are coming to a head fast at Stanleyville. . . . In the remotest bush, people are very aware of what is going on and the people around here, via their transistor sets, keep tab on what is developing. In general, a morning of tension among the people - - not because of anything imminent right here, but because they sense that some sort of history is being written these days in their land."

"But at daylight, things were stirring. By 6:30 a group of sixty-odd baptismal candidates were already lined up in front of the Nyanga Church answering a roll call read by a pastor and his assistant. After prayer, minutes later they were making their way single-file accompanied by friends and relatives. Singing hymns we began a long walk under cool, cloudy, Sunday morning Congo skies along a gradually descending path bordered by the fresh green foliage of rainy season to a spot surrounded by trees where a small, clear stream meandered its way around a bend. After an introductory prayer, the candidates made their way two by two into the stream to the missionary and Congolese pastor who, side by side, baptized them in the name of the triune God as a witness to their faith in Christ. There was quiet broken only by the sound of fresh running water, the splash of feet entering and leaving the water's edge and, off in the distance to the north, the periodic whine of turbojet motors moving across the sky toward the east."

"9:15 found us in church. By the time the opening 30 minutes of preliminaries were attended to, the church was packed to all doors. It was baptism Sunday and a special program had been planned including many special numbers. The message of the morning was based on Zechariah 7:8-14 with particular emphasis on verse 12. The subject the missionary gave to his message was: *Mitshima Yabua Seso*, i.e., 'Hearts Become Stone.' Three points were made: 'The heart that has become as a stone within the breast of a person is one that feels no fear before the wrath of God, that feels no shame before the sin of the world and feels no hunger for the things of God.' Each one present was invited to apply these measures to his or her own heart and come to their own conclusion as to where he or she stood. There was the final quiet of the closing prayer and the congregation dispersed. This afternoon there is to be a communion service. At 6:00 there will be clusters around radios to hear the latest report from Leopoldville and at 10:00 missionaries will be dialed to the Voice of America to see if there will be some word as to what has transpired this day in this land."

"In the shadow and under the sound of conflict, revolution and snarling hatred, the cause of Christ continues to be upheld, the Word of God continues to be preached and there is, on the part of many a heart, searching that is new, serious and refreshing. Should it be within the purpose of Divine providence to stay the hand of savage aggression, it may well be that we shall soon be able to see that the wrath of man has been made to praise the Eternal God and that this period of suffering and bloodshed has been an instrument of revitalization of which the Congo Church is so much in need. God grant that it be so." (17)

discussions around a zebra hide

During those last frantic hours, not only were European diplomats part of the negotiation but some African leaders as well. "State department and Pentagon officials held one meeting after another. In Leopoldville, the American and Belgian Embassies maintained a twenty-four hour vigil. Newspapers emblazoned the Stanleyville story in headlines. And millions of ordinary people waited, with dread, to hear news of the fate of Paul Carlson and the other hostages." (18)

For a brief moment the world's attention was shifted to Nairobi, Kenya. The United States and Belgium were making one last effort to solve the hostage crisis without violence. As a matter of fact, it was word of this impending diplomatic effort that had sent General Olenga to the Lumumba Monument the morning of the 18th to rescue the eight American men who were at the point of death. The American Ambassador to Kenya had been ordered by President Gbenye to meet with someone delegated to secure the release of the hostages. Gbenye had chosen Thomas Kanza. He had also asked that Jomo Kenyatta, Kenya's head of state, and Diallo Telli, the Secretary General of the Organization of African States, take part in the proceedings.

On Saturday the 21st, Ambassador Attwood arrived at Kenyatta's home to find him and Telly there but not Kanza. The word was that he was somewhere in northwestern Uganda. This being in the proximity of the Congo border led some to believe that he was attempting to arrange shipments of Communist armament to the *Simbas*. (19) Talking with the two men in the absence of Kanza, Telli expressed the strong opinion that neither he nor Kenyatta had any business getting involved in the Stanleyville "problem." By the next day, he had left Nairobi.

Around a table draped with a zebra skin, Kanza, Attwood and Kenyatta quickly laid out their positions. Kenyatta said there would have to be a cease fire. Kanza declared he expected to discuss "the whole Congo problem" and to negotiate the halt of advancing mercenaries. Attwood countered that his instructions were clearly to negotiate the safety of the hostages and nothing else. After a couple of rounds in which each participant restated his position, Atwood declared that "since we're not authorized to talk about the same thing, I will have to seek further instruction from Washington." The U.S. State Department's response was sent that evening to the effect that Kanza's proposals were "outrageous blackmail." Attwood was told to break off the talks. (20)

parachutes over Stanleyville

It was the morning of November 24, just as daylight was breaking, that the hum of turboprops could be heard and the opened canopies of Belgian paratroopers could be seen dropping on the airport from end to end. The American Consul personnel, Dr. Carlson and the PAX men were by this time among the 238 white hostages who were being held in the downtown Victoria Hotel of which 200 were Belgians and 17 Americans. About 100 of them were women and children. The Loewens were still permitted to live in their apartment on the city's outskirts. Those who had radios tuned in to the local station heard an announcer screaming: "We've been stabbed in the back by Belgians and Americans. Take your machetes and kill the white people. Kill the white people." (21)

By 7:00 the paratroopers were starting their move toward the center of the city. Their all-consuming concern was to find where the hostages were before it was too late. Suddenly there were *Simbas* in the hotel halls banging on doors: "*Kwenda*" was the curt order given in doorway after doorway, i.e. "Walk."

As they came out of their rooms they were ordered out into the street in front of the hotel where they were met by a dozen or so *Simbas* each holding an automatic rifle. In all the hostages numbered about 250. Some were women with babies in their arms. About 50 others had managed to stay behind in the hotel - - some in closets and cupboards, some on the roof. The *Simba* officer in charge was colonel Joseph Opepe. He wore a sport shirt and slacks. Over his shoulder hung his rifle. Given the drama and impending disaster that morning, he presented a strange appearance. Those who had gotten acquainted with him scarcely knew hm. He seemed quaint, haggard and worried. (22) The hostages were ordered to line up three abreast which made a total of about 80 ranks. Opepe then gave the order to march. It appeared he intended to take them in the direction of the airport. The other armed *Simbas* walking along on either side began to urge Opepe to kill them immediately. In the distance they could hear the gunfire of approaching commandos. Opepe kept refusing. First he said they could be used as human shields against the approaching paratroopers. Or if the attackers started to drop bombs, the foreigners would die under their own bombs. Coming to a major intersection, the column of refugees had about half turned a corner when the order was given to sit on the street. In the meantime, the sound of approaching gunfire grew louder.

It seems it will never be known exactly what happened next. Some say the armed *Simbas* finally defied Opepe and began to fire. Another word is that *Simbas* fleeing the commandos rounded the corner, saw the seated whites and began to fire. Whatever the case, a number of people soon fell to the pavement either dead or wounded. Those remembering that moment comment that after the first fusillade of bullets, all was strangely quiet except for the moans of the wounded. Among those on their faces on the street were missionaries Paul Carlson, Al Larson (23) and Charlie Davis. (24) MCC volunteers Jon Snyder and Gene Bergman also were there. When the *Simbas* hesitated, many of the hostages jumped to their feet and bolted for the nearest possible place of protection from further fire. Seeing them scatter, the *Simbas* again opened fire in all directions. Carlson, Larson, Snyder and Davis ran toward a small yellow house across the street from them which had a five foot high cement wall along the porch. Larson, Snyder and Davis vaulted over the wall, broke down the door and took refuge inside Carlson too had run with them but chose to skirt the side of the house apparently hoping to find shelter behind it. Encountering an armed *Simba* he turned around and ran back to the front where he succeeded in getting one leg over the top of the wall. As Davis reached out to help pull him to safety, the *Simba* began shooting. Dr. Carlson, whose name had for weeks been in the headlines of the international press, lay in a crumpled heap at the base of the wall - - dead. (25)

A moment later the first commandos burst around the corner of the street. The *Simbas* quickly fled the scene. Davis, Larson and Snyder came out of the bungalow. Gene Bergman had survived the slaughter lying still on his face in the street throughout the onslaught. After welcoming the commandos, Davis went to look for Carlson. Jumping the porch wall he found Carlson's body lying where he fell as he tried to scale the wall. He was riddled with rebel bullets. Twenty-two people lay dead or dying in the street. Twenty were Belgians, two were American missionaries: Phyllis Rine and Paul Carlson. (26) (27)

The Loewens, thanks to Mel's Canadian passport, lived those last days in hiding in their apartment on the edge of the city. In an adjacent apartment were Dr. and Mrs. Lampe, fellow university staff of German nationality. Of those concluding hours Loewen wrote: "A few minutes after the [commando] drop John Snyder, one of the PAX men held as a hostage uptown, called to say the paratroopers had come. We knew then that this was the day we'd been waiting for. We collected a few of our things and waited." (28)

At 9:00 the Loewens received another phone call from a friend downtown stating that the paratroopers now controlled the center of the city but that before they reached the hostages, there had been gunfire and two missionaries had been killed. All other American missionaries and the PAX men were safe. At noon came another call telling them that plans were now formed to come to their northwest corner of the city to get them. The minutes ticked by. The Loewen account continues: "At two I called back to remind the rescue headquarters that the *Simbas* were all around our two houses - - the only two white families in that corner of town. . . . Two thirty, still no troops. At three I tried to call again and the phone was dead. We were completely shut off now. . . . Four o'clock and we began to wonder whether we would have to spend another night in our houses surrounded by rebels. Then, at twenty minutes to five, there was a burst of machine gun fire nearby. . . . From upstairs and looking out a window we saw three army trucks and with the soldiers, a former American consul who had been transferred to Washington a few weeks before the rebels came. We had been wondering how these soldiers would be able to find our two houses among the many of our suburb. The State Department had flown back this friend for this day of rescue operations. And he knew where we lived. . . . It was a moving experience to realize that so many lives had been risked to save a few of us."

In concluding their evacuation story, Mel highlights one of the mysteries which preoccupied so many in the days following the violence when he writes: "Yet so many of our missionary colleagues were killed at this time. Thousands too had prayed for their safety. We recalled with humble hearts the prayer of our professor neighbor when he said: 'Dear Lord, if you have more work for us to do you can get us out. And if not, it's all right too.'" (29)

It will likely always remain a mystery as to what Colonel Opepe's real intentions were during those final fateful moments in the streets of Stanleyville. His disheveled, gaunt appearance gave every indication of a man under keen emotional stress. Though a committed *Simba*, he was also a devout Catholic. He must have many times struggled with his conscience as the two basic systems of values and beliefs, of which he had become a part, came into unyielding collision. Had he been looking for a way to save the lives of the group of hostages which had fallen into his hands? Or had he continued to play the *Simba* psychological cat-and-mouse game to which they had all been so long subjected? Whatever the case, in his own way Opepe was also a tragic victim of the hurricane of violence in which he became trapped and from which he had no escape.

a tug-of-war

While the paratroopers and their commanders pled for time to move out from Stanleyville into surrounding towns where more hostages were known to be held, the Western governments which had staged and equipped the airdrop of Stanleyville were under intense international pressure. Reaction from across all of Africa and from leftist regimes around the world was loud and angry. The rescue operation was characterized as an outrageous exercise in renewed colonialism and the unforgivable violation of the sovereign territory of an independent African nation. Upon the urgent request of 18 African countries, a special session of the UN Security Council was called. Among the speakers was the foreign minister of the former French Congo who said: "The famous humanitarian operation of Stanleyville has now proved to us that a white, especially if his name is Carlson, or if he is an American, a Belgian or an Englishman, is worth thousands upon thousands of blacks. Thus . . . the most ruthless and most scandalous aggression of our era has just been committed." (30)

With these kinds of angry statements being made in an international forum, the US and Belgium were understandably eager to bring the rescue effort to a swift close. The original time frame set for the operation did allow for one major sortie. Two days after securing Stanleyville and its airport, seven planes took off for Paulis, a major center 225 air miles to the northeast, where it was known several hundred hostages were also being held. Coming in on a dirt air strip in dense fog, the town was quickly abandoned by the *Simba* defenders. Learning that some were being held at the local Catholic Mission and that twenty had already been killed in response to rebel orders given by radio the morning of the paratroop drop, the commandos raced to the Mission. They found 50 men still alive. Patrols into the surrounding towns throughout the day found more. Next day search was renewed at daybreak. By noon a total of 355 people had been found. But they were operating under a deadline. Transport planes would begin arriving at noon. By air the Belgian major pled for an extension so as to at least be able to get to a plantation 40 miles out where it was known other hostages were being held. But such decisions lay in the hands of others far outside Africa. Orders were orders. The first evacuation plane touched down exactly at noon. By 3:00 the last plane had lifted off with the paratroopers and the last freed hostage. Within moments the *Simbas* reappeared out of the surrounding forest to reclaim the town. It would remain for the two columns of mercenaries and national army units approaching from the south and west to seek out all who were left behind and would survive until their arrival. (31)

a tragic residue

With passing weeks the military units of the central government made their way into the remotest corners of northeastern Congo. Slowly the total picture emerged. During those last frantic days of rebel rule, over 300 hostage whites were killed. Eight of those were Americans. There had been a particularly heavy toll among Catholic priests and nuns. Methods used ranged from a quick merciful end via rifle bullet to others which are best left undescribed. But a far greater tragedy of human suffering and loss of life was that inflicted upon the Congolese themselves. There likely will never be any detailed statistics. It is only known that losses of African life numbered in the tens of thousands. As David Reed so sadly states it: "The northeast of Congo had become one vast graveyard." (32)

As for the *Simba* leaders, Gbenye had early slipped out of Stanleyville and north across the border to the Sudan. General Olenga remained in Aba, a town in the extreme northeast of Congo on the Sudan border where he apparently hoped to be re-armed by countries sympathetic to him and his cause. There he remained till a few hours before a contingent of mercenaries arrived. He then also slipped across the border.

Like a tornado, the *Simba* movement had torn through Congo leaving suffering and devastation in its wake. As a political force, it had been crushed. The basic dynamics which had spawned it, however, still remained basically unchanged.

Banjwadi, a postscript

The dramatic November 24 rescue of the white population of Stanleyville left four Congolese Mennonites and their children behind, some 40 miles to the north of the city. They were Mayambi Sosthène and his wife Koloma Pauline from Nyanga, and Bapatuila Jean and family from Mutena. Arriving first in 1961, warm and outgoing Mayambi and Koloma soon won acceptance and trust not only among their fellow students but also within the local church at Banjwadi. Evidence of this was the decision of the local church to name Mayambi as their representative to the annual meeting of the Congo Protestant Council which was convened that year at Stanleyville. Alert and informed, he saw the significance of Prime Minister Tshombe's widely advertised visit in July of 1964 in his effort to heal the long-standing breach between northeastern Congo and the central government. Mayambi traveled to the city to hear his speech made at the time. It was only four days later that the *Simba* forces took over the city.

Hurrying back to Banjwadi he found that mission vehicles had already been confiscated. After the initial flurry of activity, station life settled back into routine. But as the early advance of rebel forces was stemmed and rumors of defeat began to circulate, the early cocky *Simba* rule gave way to surly domination. In October, a systematic round up of foreigners was begun. One day a team appeared at Banjwadi and ordered the missionaries still on the station to pack their suitcases. Mayambi's open association with them to the last minute raised rebel suspicions and they consequently ordered him into the vehicle with them. In Stanleyville he was placed under house arrest under the nominal authority of the Congolese Catholic bishop of the city. After 3 days of detention, Mayambi went to the bishop, explained who he was and how it was he came to be there. That evening he was allowed to slip out of the compound. In a matter of hours he was back with his family at the mission station.

In a written account of his experiences, the following is found: "Tension was high. All were apprehensive and uncertain but the theology students continued to conduct services in the station chapel. Sunday morning, November 8, 1964, it was Mayambi's turn to conduct the service and preach. The preliminaries were over and he had begun his message when they suddenly realized that the church had been completely surrounded by rebels. Presently two or three of them made their way in the door, guns in hand. Upon seeing them, Mayambi paused, then sat down. The rebels quickly came to the front, seized Mayambi and his fellow student, who was with him on the platform, and launched into a tirade of accusation. 'You are against the rebellion; you pray to your God that we may be defeated; you meet in church to conspire against us; you are lovers of the central government' and before they could even respond, the leaders set upon them with clubs and gun butts beating them unmercifully. After lecturing the fearful audience and threatening them with more severe reprisals if they continued meeting for services, they departed with the second student leaving Mayambi to limp to his home." (33)

Unnerved by the sudden display of hostility, most of the station population fled in the next few days leaving the theological students largely alone. News of the commando drop on Stanleyville on November 24, 1964, spread in all directions. Indeed planes could be seen and heard from Banjwadi station. Panic reigned as rebel leaders attempted to round up the rural populace in mass and force march them toward the north away from the city. It was amidst this confusion that the Mayambi and Bapatuila families managed "to slip away to the nearby river, paddle across and strike off along twisting foot trails deep into the dense equatorial forest. After traveling some hours, they left the beaten path and picked their way through the tangle of brush and vines until they felt they would be safe from detection. Here it was that they made crude bark and leaf shelters and began a refugee existence, living on roasted cassava roots that they dug from abandoned fields and on whatever else they could glean from the surrounding jungle. Here it was that, at times, they crouched motionless in their shelters as roving bands of gorillas detected their presence and frightened them with their guttural challenges. Here it was that they hid, prayed, and waited." (34)

In spite of every precaution, the day came when they were discovered and forced to return to Banjwadi which had become a rebel zone command post. Discovering that Mayambi could type, he was forced to join their clerical staff in return for food rations for him and his family.

In early June, 1965, there was greatly increased activity of government forces in the region. Planes overhead were frequently seen and heard. Fearful of a military operation, the *Simba* leaders once again ordered a mass evacuation of the population and once again the two EMC couples were able to edge away into the surrounding forest. This time, however, they built their little shelters near the main road for they had determined to take the risk of giving themselves up to the government forces if they had the opportunity. It was only a few mornings later, on June 8, that they heard the sound of vehicles in the distance. "Mayambi hurried from their forest shelter, hid in the roadside brush and when the patrol was upon him, stepped out, hands high, in a sign of surrender. This was an act of decisive courage for the patrol was deep in rebel territory and the jeep-load of soldiers had automatic weapons at the ready, fingers on triggers. Often they shot first and inquired later. But the lead vehicle stopped and under the menacing muzzles of many rifles, Mayambi swiftly told the officer his plight. He was then told to return in search of his groups and any others who would be willing to accompany him. They would continue their patrol further and upon their return would pick up at this spot all those who were waiting for them. . . . Back in the forest shelters the story was quickly and quietly told with hurried furtive trips to other nearby friends. The last minutes were given to gathering up of what by this time were pitifully few possessions - - and then the beginning of their vigil at the designated spot. Would the convoy really return? Might they be discovered at the last minute by *Simbas*? 'Please Lord, you've helped us so often. Please help us this one more time.'" (35)

By mid-afternoon they did again hear the sound of vehicles. By night they were safe in a military refugee camp. Here they remained until mid-July when they were permitted to go to Stanleyville. There, on August 21, Koloma Pauline gave birth to a son. With the African flair for wry commemoration of life's troubles and trials, the new son was named John Baptist Misery.

From Stanleyville they were eventually flown to Leopoldville where CIM and EMC officials made arrangements for their to return to Tshikapa and their home mission stations. In conversation with missionaries, a few days later, Mayambi was asked what he had to say about all of his experiences. After some moments of reflection, he said: "We are here because of the love and grace of God. I know that nothing happens to any of his children without his knowledge. Truly I had planned for four years of study at Banjwadi. I went to school for four years, all right, but the fourth year of study was much different than I had expected. The Lord decided to give me a year of schooling in the forest instead of in a classroom. It was a hard year but the Lord saw I needed it and I give him thanks." (36)

CHAPTER 14　　　POST-REBELLION ECHOES

a wolf's pelt becomes wormy

"We cried to have a wolf's pelt; it turned to worms in our hands." With the African's great gift for distilling life's learnings and experiences into proverb and allegory, it was thus that Kakesa Samuel summarized the experience of the Kwilu population under the banner of the *Jeunesse* movement.

Striking as it did across the western area of the CIM and the EMC, it impacted many hundreds of church members, leaders and lay people alike. Little by little stories were pieced together of their experience. Some were stories of courage and heroism while others were stories of fear and failure. Some had to do with the preservation of the Church amidst fires of persecution while others had to do with people who were swept from the moorings of their faith. Some had to do with sacrificial love while others had to do with crass personal profiteering. Some had to do with efforts of spiritual nurture of fellow believers at great personal risk, while others had to do with the settling of old personal animosities and grudges. Familiar stories, all of them, which have endlessly played themselves out across human history in times of upheaval, crisis and anarchy. This time, the setting was eastern Kwilu in 1964-65. The telling of all of the stories is impossible. A few snapshots of what transpired must suffice.

a contemporary Joshua

When the CIM missionaries were lifted off the Kandala soccer field that January 25, 1964, they had told the Bible Institute families to await return flights. But the helicopters had no more than left and the *Jeunesse* rose as a man out of the surrounding bush and scattered debris over the field, thus signaling plainly that a second landing was not welcome.

During the ensuing excitement, the refugee student families quickly gathered their meager belongings and started a journey which they hoped and prayed would eventually bring them to safety. It was the same afternoon, while crossing the nearby Kwilu River in dugout canoes, that they for the second time that day heard and saw helicopters whirling overhead. Moments later they also heard the chatter of machine gun fire up the hill in the direction of the Catholic Mission. That evening at dusk, as they entered the first village, they heard wailing and saw corpses being carried and mourned. The machine guns heard earlier that afternoon had not been fired in jest. It was also that first evening that they encountered their first hostile stares and heard the first muttered threats for they were strangers and, in the confusion of that day, strangers had killed their fellow clansmen.

Huddling in crowded quarters grudgingly shown them by night and walking the limit of their physical endurance by day, they made their apprehensive way among hurrying bands of rebels. Often they were stopped and questioned and, at times, menaced. With each such incident, two men stepped out to place themselves between the huddled group of fearful student families and the challenging rebels to answer, explain and intercede. One was Pastor Kindumba Jacques (pr. gi-NDOO-mbah), from Kandala station. The other was a church layman named Kipoko David (pr. gi-POH-goh). He had just moved his large family to Kandala in late 1963 so as to join a committee which was working on a revision of the Giphende New Testament, the language of his people. (1)

And now it was Sunday, January 27. A written account picks up the story: "There were endless conflicting rumors. 'The soldiers were approaching. People were fleeing to the forest. The *Jeunesse* ahead were killing all strangers they met. Some had tried to escape and had failed. The only solution was to join the rebel bands and to travel with them.' What was true? What was false? The group made its way along a winding path and, then, there was a fork. They came to a weary halt. A decision had to be made. Among the 56 members of the party there were 22 adults, 20 children old enough to walk and 14 so small they had to be carried at least part of the time. Scattered about was a curious assortment of salvaged possessions: here two or three chickens tied together by the legs, there a bicycle or two, yonder a portable sewing machine and, along the path, variously shaped bundles of clothing, pans, blankets, cooking pots and sleeping mats." (2)

As for Kipoko himself, the one thing he had been able to salvage, beside a bundle of cooking utensils, was a portable typewriter. This was entrusted to his oldest son to be carried on his head during their entire trek toward safety. This, in a remarkable manner, symbolized his deep commitment to the revision project of which he had been a part from the beginning and of which he was determined to remain a part for as long as it took to put a revised New Testament into the hands of his people.

There was yet another dramatic dimension to the story of the fleeing refugees. Two of the women were pregnant, one of which was his own wife, Gin'a Laurent (i.e., the mother of Laurent, her first-born child). She was within days of a full term pregnancy.

But there was no time to worry about such details. They stood at a fork in the path. Should they bear to the left and pass through a populated area which would perhaps afford possibility for shelter, food and water or should they turn right and continue across the wide, hot, thirsty and comparatively uninhabited plain? Voices edged with irritation and fear soon rose in argument. After some moments of hesitation Kipoko called for silence. "True," he said, "to the north are villages and people, shelter and food but there are also rebel bands. The Lord has been good to us and heard our prayers thus far, but why invite trouble? To the right are wide plains; the sun is hot and we will be very weary and thirsty but it is the short cut to the Kasai, our land, and in that path we will meet the least people. We must do what we can to help ourselves. After that we pray." (3)

A decision made, Pastor Jacques bid them farewell, wished them a safe exit from the Kwilu and said that he needed now to return to the station. It was only later that it would become known that unlike his fellow pastor, Khelendende Pierre, Pastor Jacques had joined the *Jeunesse* cause. A flood of questions come to mind. What had been his motives to secretly join this movement? Did he see it as a needed and responsible endorsement of a protest of corrupt government? Did he feel that as a member he would be better placed to represent or defend the interests of the Mission and his Church? Why was it that over a year later, as the rebel movement began to crumble, he decided to flee with the rebel leaders taking his family with him into the wild hill country along the Loange River? And especially, why was it, when the time came that he could easily have slipped across the river and be met at river's edge by fellow EMC Pastor Ngongo David from Nyanga, that he hesitated and returned to rebel-controlled territory? The answers to these questions will likely never be known since Pastor Jacques and his entire family were eventually buried in unmarked graves in the rebel wilderness, the victims of illness and malnutrition.

Their decision made, the travelers deposited children and bundles on hips, shoulders and heads and began their trek toward the east. Now, they were on their own. The sun hung low in the west that evening as the first members of the group approached a village. Beyond it, the terrain would gradually begin to drop toward the Loange River in the distance. As others caught up, adults helped each other put down bundles and children that had been carried throughout the heat of the day. But even as food and drink was brought by village people, a group of young men approached, watched silently for a while and then stated flatly: "We don't know who you are but if there are any Baluba or Lulua among you" - - and there were - - "they will never cross the river." Thus to the fatigue of the day was now added the chill of scantily veiled threat.

Squaring with the sudden new danger, Kipoko set out to find some common ground upon which to deal with it. After some inquiry he discovered that the village chief belonged to a clan of the same name as his own which signified that, back somewhere in their tribal history, both he and the chief traced their blood line to a common grandparent. Hope stirred quickly in his heart as he made his way to the chief's house and pressed upon him his claims of hospitality and mercy for all his fellow-travelers that night. The chief told him to return to his group. During the night he would gather his clan elders for a consultation. Returning, Kipoko found the travelers huddled together; many had already yielded to the slumber of exhaustion. For Kipoko, however, there was no sleep. As he kept watch, he prayed. Finally the sound of footsteps was heard and the figure of the chief took shape in the darkness. Greeting Kipoko he said: "It has been decided. You can sleep in peace. I've persuaded my elders to allow your whole group to leave in the morning. I do not want the blood of the friends of my kinsman on my head."

The next morning, after food and drink had been provided, the group resumed travel which by mid-afternoon brought them to the river's edge. There, in typical African fashion, bargaining set in over fees for being ferried across the river in dugout canoes. Though the decision had been made in the last village to allow their safe passage to the river, this did not exempt them from extortion at the hands of the canoe men who had no hesitation about taking advantage of the hapless strangers who had fallen into their hands. Realizing that no amount of protest would help, little bundles were untied as each couple bartered parts of their last earthly goods for passage across the river.

time out for gratitude

When the last canoe load had traversed the river which marked the frontier of rebel control, Kipoko promptly summoned everyone and announced a service of thanksgiving. After they sang a couple of hymns from memory, he said: "We call this river the Loange but for us, it has become our Jordan. The Lord truly has brought us out of a land of death and across this stream. We must praise Him. We still have a long path before us and we do not know what awaits us. We have no stones here on the river bank with which to build an altar, as did the Israelites, but our prayers of thanksgiving are the offering we lift before his face." After prayer, they shared what little food they had left among them and resumed their journey.

During the late afternoon they walked in the rain. Toward evening they arrived, wet and weary, at a village whose chief refused them shelter and food. So near was the rebel frontier that he was afraid that any kindness shown to fleeing refugees might be interpreted as lack of support for the *Jeunesse* cause. Forced to press on, it was after dark when they reached the next village. They experienced the same suspicious reception. It was only after extended pleading that they were at last allowed to stay the night. With much grumbling, space was shown here and there under thatch roofs to throw down their sleeping mats.

Next morning, unmindful of empty stomachs and damp clothing, they set out at sun-up toward a distant village located on a road where they knew they would find an EMC teacher/evangelist placed by the Nyanga Church District. They knew that if they could just make it that far they would be met with love and care by fellow Mennonite believers. Although they knew they would still be over 60 miles from Nyanga Station, word could easily be sent from there about their escape and arrival in EMC territory.

With only brief stops for rest in sparse shade of scrubby trees, they pressed on. Finally, after dark, on the night of January 29 they made their way into the flickering glow of friendly village hearth fires and the sound of shouted welcomes of Christian friends. As children were taken from aching arms and weights lifted from bodies trembling with fatigue, the weary party slumped gratefully upon stools and mats. They had at last crossed the perimeter of safety.

Early the next morning a message was sent to Nyanga via bicycle. By evening of the following day, the entire group arrived there by truck. Forty-eight hours later, in the Nyanga station maternity, Gin'a Laurent, Kipoko's wife, gave birth to a son. In the colorful manner of the African people, Kipoko named the infant son Gikenene (pr. GIH-keh-neh-neh), i.e., Sorrow or Distress, thus commemorating the traumatic experiences which surrounded them at the time of his birth.

a critical warning

Back at Nyanga, Kipoko and the Bible Institute students were besieged with questions. "Is it true that rebels are immune to soldiers' bullets? Is it true that rebels can turn themselves into palm trees so that soldiers cannot see them? Is it true their leaders can travel long distances through the air at night? Is it true they will soon take over Leopoldville? Is it true they kill all who oppose them?"

In this atmosphere of anxiety and apprehension, Kipoko's voice was raised with resolution: "What I have seen is evil. If we stand idly by, the *Jeunesse* will soon be among us also. We must warn our village chiefs and elders, our relatives and, above all, our Church." Rallying to his challenge, a mass meeting of area chiefs and village elders was held in the station chapel. Kipoko rose before them and described with emotion what they had witnessed and experienced. "We can oppose the *Jeunesse* if we will," he insisted. "But if we don't, we will suffer just as our brothers and sisters on the other side of the river are suffering now."

Alerted by his warning and stiffened by his resolve, the chiefs returned to their villages with ultimatums to their people and, particularly, to their youth. "We, too, have heard the promises the *Jeunesse* have made to our fellow tribesmen across the river. We, too, have thought that their promises were good. We have been hesitating between two paths. But if the real purpose of their movement is to do what they are now doing across the river, we want nothing to do with it. From now on, any strange face seen among us is to be reported to us. We will have no one from our villages going to secret meetings in the valleys and forests. Any suspicious activity in our areas will be reported immediately to the government office at Tshikapa."

They were as good as their word. While nighttime forays were still made for a while across the river from the Kwilu side with minor damage inflicted on bridges and isolated villages, the *Jeunesse* movement never succeeded in getting a foothold on the east bank of the Loange. Denied the protective screen of a cooperative and sympathetic population behind which to organize, theirs was a lost cause in the Kasai. In a real sense, Kipoko David, a dedicated Mennonite layman, had single-handedly blocked the eastward progress of the *Jeunesse* movement at the Loange, his Jordan River. (4)

Pastor Wayindama amidst the flames

Slight of build, of medium height and gentle spirit, Pastor Wayindama (pr. wah-yi-NDA-mah) and his family had also come to Kandala, late in the fall of 1963, to join the teaching staff of the relocated Bible Institute. An excellent student himself, Wayindama had earlier graduated from a two-year teacher training school and then from the Tshikapa Bible Institute. A Muchoke from Kamayala Station, some 125 miles to the south, he brought both a good mind and years of successful pastoral service to his new teaching assignment at Kandala.

The fury of the *Jeunesse* attack the night of January 24 fell on his household just like all others on the station. Realizing that their thatch roof house had already been set ablaze from the outside, they quickly attempted to carry a few things outside hoping thus to salvage at least something. Rounding the sides of the house, the attacking youth fell upon the pastor. First they threw the things they had just brought outside back into the flaming house. Then they turned on Emmanuel, ordered him to remove all his outer clothing and to kneel before them as his wife and children stood by in terror in the flickering light of their burning home. There followed a period of beating alternated with questions and accusations. Asking that he at least be allowed to wrap a blanket around himself, the answer was that such things came from President Kasavubu and thus needed to be destroyed.

Hit from behind with the wooden arc of a rebel bow while menaced in front by an arrow notched, drawn and aimed at close range at his bare chest he protested: "You have no reason to kill me. I've come here only to preach the Gospel of Christ." His protest was swept aside by loud cries: "You're lying. You are guilty. We want to kill you. You have meddled in political affairs. Your missionaries have called the soldiers. You people eat (profit from) Kasavubu's money." Resuming the beating the rebels said they wanted one of his daughters. Emmanuel responded: "I cannot do that even if you kill me." (5)

Angered even more by this refusal, they ordered him to hold out his arms so they could cut off his hands. To this new threat the Pastor responded: "If these hands of mine are guilty of evil you may cut them off, but I have done nothing other than preach the Gospel." Blows continued to fall on the slim, bare body of the kneeling pastor. Summoned elsewhere on the burning station by their leader, they left him with the order to remain as he was until they returned. Before long, they were back seemingly perplexed that he was still there.

Asked one, "You're still here! Aren't you afraid?" "No," he replied, "I'm not afraid. You cannot kill me because the Lord will help me."

Distracted for a moment from their continuing abuse, the pastor's wife quietly reproached him for what he'd said: "Why anger them even further by using the name of the Lord?" He replied: "Who is it that will help me if it's not the Eternal One? I must honor him to the death." After one more whipping, the rebel band left him and his family beside the glowing rubble of their destroyed home. Miraculously, his ID card had somehow been flipped into the nearby grass and had survived the night of flame. Gratefully he slipped it into his pocket. Gathering a few remains into a bundle they made their way to the station chapel where other students had taken shelter.

After two days the missionary staff was evacuated. Fearing that the helicopters would not return again as promised, the pastor's wife and a student couple from their same area insisted that they leave immediately on foot toward the south even as they had seen other students from the east leave the station that same day. There followed a full week of travel by foot. Intercepted and interrogated on several occasions, they were always able to continue. Arriving at last in their home territory they slipped, one night, into their home village only to learn that government soldiers were nearby and that they were very suspicious of any new arrivals in the village. Knowing he had nothing to hide, he went next morning to present himself. Immediately they seized him. "Aha," said they, "your name is on one of our lists of wanted *Jeunesse* leaders. Here it is: Muatshidiata Emmanuel!" Without further discussion he was arrested, despite his protests, and had a rope tied around his neck. Providentially, there was an officer among the military unit who knew him. Although he was able to remove the rope, he could not prevent his imprisonment. To his weeping wife and children Pastor Wayindama said: "Do not weep; I will see you later somewhere along the road." Taken to the nearby government post at Kahemba, he was put in jail with others suspicioned of being *Jeunesse*. The word to them all was: "Tomorrow you will be executed."

During that night Pastor Wayindama prayed: "If I am guilty, oh Lord, then may I stay in this prison; but if I am your servant, then show your power and free me from this prison." The next morning he was brought out of the jail and ordered to sweep the courtyard, a menial task designed to humiliate him publicly. He had no more than started when the officer who had recognized him the day before called him to his house, asked for his ID card and went to find his superior officer. After a couple of hours, he returned to inform the pastor that he was a free man and loaned him his own bicycle to make the last 10 kilometers of his long journey to Kamayala station. As he pedaled home to rejoin his family and fellow believers he sang a hymn that was often used in the Kamayala Church and was a favorite of his: "Jesus Has Proven His Love for Me." (6)

Kakesa Samuel and Mulele Pierre

Compared to the *Simbas* who flared onto the world scene and commanded international attention for four dramatic months, the *Jeunesse* movement was a "pocket rebellion." Cut off from outside contacts and help of any significance, there was much less international awareness of it. While the *Simbas* at first overran center after center and, for a brief moment, menaced half of Congo's vast interior, the *Jeunesse* were never able to take a single government center of any size and were always limited to the area between the Loange and Kwilu Rivers.

While the *Simbas* took over a provincial radio station and an excellent airfield which became vital for purposes of communication and supply, the *Jeunesse* never were able to plunder anything more significant than bush stores. The mission air strips scattered through their area were quickly rendered useless by digging trenches across them. While the *Simbas* secured increasingly more and better armament and equipment with passing time, the *Jeunesse* relied almost exclusively on their bows and arrows and bush knives. While the *Simbas* secured sympathetic support of leftist world governments, the *Jeunesse* had no such direct supportive links.

153

But for the village people and the Mennonite believers of eastern Kwilu, the menace, the destruction, the terror, the desolation, the isolation, the bloodshed, the anguish of spirit and the struggle with conscience were no less real for that. It is interesting to note further that while the *Simba* rebellion was turned back by a sophisticated, expensive and internationally orchestrated military intervention, the *Jeunesse* movement came unglued because of dynamics and forces which were at work within the movement itself. Fanned by proud Mukedi village chief, Nzamba, the regional and tribal loyalties of the Baphende people eventually brought them into conflict with other tribal groups within the *Jeunesse* movement. It must also be noted that Mukedi Station, with its staff of teachers, nurses and church leaders together with hundreds of baptized believers of the surrounding villages, eventually became a bone in Mulele's throat which he was never able to dislodge.

In a fascinating kind of way, the murky currents of the Kwilu rebellion threw two strong-willed people together at Malemba (pr. mah-LEH-mbah), the bush headquarters of the rebel movement. In their head-to-head struggle with each other over a period of months, they mirrored the broader battle of a people to free themselves of a yoke of bondage which had settled about their necks.

Kakesa (pr. kah-KEH-sah) Samuel was the son of first generation Christians, Kasala Jacob and Kavunji Rebecca. Jacob served for years as the steady, even-tempered foreman of the Mukedi station work crew. Trained as a midwife, Rebecca served for years in the Mukedi Station maternity hospital with faithfulness, efficiency and compassion. After graduating from the Mukedi primary school Kakesa was among a select few chosen to enter the new four-year Teacher Training School opened at Nyanga. Not only an apt student, he early demonstrated marked leadership qualities. Upon graduation he married Kafutshi Françoise, also the daughter of first generation Christian parents, Mulebo Samuel and Sona Henrietta. His father-in-law, with only primary school training, had made his way up through the administrative ranks of the *Compagnie du Kasai*, a large commercial enterprise of the area, and held a key position in its regional office when the rebellion erupted. Also possessed of unusual leadership gifts, Kafutshi complemented Kakesa's abilities in many ways. They quickly became a talented and forceful lay couple who, with passing time, provided key leadership within the Congo Mennonite Church.

Following graduation at Nyanga, Kakesa was assigned to Kamayala Station as a school director. After the church executive committee had twice been unsuccessful in installing a legal representative, (7) Kakesa became their choice. While in 1963 the EMC still did not have its own legal charter from the government, the CIM by that time had already entrusted to him the major responsibility of distributing monthly government subsidy monies for the EMC schools in the Kwilu. The rebellion in January 1964 found him and his wife based at Mukedi.

The day the CIM missionaries were evacuated from the station, Kakesa had played a key role in protecting the Catholic nuns and in securing their safe departure with the others. As they left, one of the nuns is reported to have said to him: "Had we had someone like you at our Mission, perhaps the priests would not have been killed." In recognition of his status as a member of the EMC Executive Committee, church leaders agreed that all station keys be left in his care, something which further brought him to the attention of all.

Initially, rebel rule was benign enough. A rebel command post was established some six miles north of the station with a *commandant du zone* named Fimbo Antoine in charge. Early rebel instructions were for mission activities to be carried on as usual. Schools were to be open; medical services were to function; Christians were to go to church as was their custom. But instinctively Kakesa suspected that he would soon be hearing more from the rebel leaders. He was not wrong. One day there was a small delegation at his door sent by the nearby *commandant*. They said it was known that he had a radio transmitter in his home. The rebel movement needed it and invited him to "donate" it to the cause. Realizing that it was useless to resist, he showed them where it was and they took it.

A few days later another delegation came. This time they gave him a lengthy lecture on the goals and glory of the *Jeunesse* movement. They concluded by urging him to join them as a *partisan*. Pleading his need for time to discuss this with his wife, they left. A few days later they returned with the same proposal. Kakesa again requested time. The next time they came just at dawn, nearly 200 of them. The message was curt. For a last time he was "invited" to join them. If he again refused, they were to take him by force. "Then take me," was his answer. They pounced on him, beat him, tied him and made off with him to the area command post. Ushered into the presence of the *commandant*, Kakesa was told of reports coming to their ears that he was counseling people not to cooperate with their cause. Furthermore he had received many letters accusing Kakesa of bad things. It was for his own good that he had been brought to the camp. Here he would be safe! He was untied and shown a hut. He was free to circulate in the camp but under surveillance. He was not to return to Mukedi. Visits from his father would be permitted to bring news from his family.

Limited to the rebel camp, Kakesa queried his father on successive visits as to what was happening at Mukedi. It had become clear that the rebels were not about to adopt a "hands off" policy vis-à-vis the large station on the plateau a scant six miles away. Already word had gone out that church members should keep their services short. Also they should not ring the church bell since it was "distracting" people who had other more important things to do. And as for the medical services, the *commandant* expected that the staff would henceforth submit regular reports to him regarding their work.

And how were the Mukedi people taking all of this? With resentment and resistance. Kakesa rejoiced at this news and sent word via his father that they should never forget the reason for which the station had been built. *Commandant* Antoine soon sensed the passive resistance of the mission people. Things were not going as he'd planned. Some of his subordinates quoted him a proverb: "It's not the ill-smelling herb in the distant valley which is disturbing the people; it is the sorcerer who lives next to you." (8) Having made this oblique reference to Kakesa, they urged the *commandant* to simply dispose of him and thus remove this insolent young man within his own camp who refused to respect him or to support their cause. He however realized that Kakesa had strong support among the Mukedi people. He nonetheless had a plan of his own. "We'll send him to our central headquarters," he announced. "Our Supreme Leader Mulele Pierre can deal with him as he may decide."

It was in early June of 1964 and the evening of the fifth day of walking that Kakesa and four armed guards arrived at Malemba, the hideaway headquarters of Mulele Pierre. CIM missionary Levi Keidel who traces Kakesa's experience in his book Caught in the Crossfire describes Kakesa's arrival and first experiences as follows: "Four long straight rows of huts formed the four sides of a square enclosing the camp. Three larger houses dominated its center. Toward the far end of the square beneath a tree a man was lecturing a group of about thirty rebels seated on the ground before him. Kakesa [alias Stephen in Keidel's book] followed his escort toward one of the larger houses where a man a bit older than he was seated behind a worn table. To his left was a long, shed-like structure with a one-way roof. Through the high open front one could see secretaries busy at typewriters."

"The man at the table was dressed in khaki shorts, an unbuttoned shirt and a two-corner military 'overseas' cap. . . . Muscles in his smooth lean face were taut; his frame was spare and sinewy. He was tense, like an animal poised to spring. One of Kakesa's guards took a position in front of the man, stamped his right foot on the ground, snapped a salute, gave his report, and stepped to one side. Kakesa was nudged into the guard's position. He stood before the man whom he now knew to be Pierre Mulele."

"Hmmm, so you are the big friend of the Americans from Mukedi," Mulele observed. "I've been told about you. Now that the Americans are gone, I hear you are still giving people hard heads to resist the revolution. . . . Take this man away. Give him food and a place to sleep. We will take up his case again in the morning." (9)

The next day Kakesa again stood before Mulele. This time the rebel leader had a file open before him on the table containing a packet of letters which he said had been sent to *Jeunesse* leaders accusing Kakesa of all manner of "crimes" - - from helping the Americans escape to being a spy for President Kasavubu to "eating" the teachers' salaries to encouraging Mukedi people to resist the rebellion.

It is a sad phenomenon that has occurred again and again in circumstances of political instability and revolt. There are always people who surface eager to curry favor with a new regime. The temptation for some is irresistible. On the one hand they can settle old grudges and on the other they can "prove" their unwavering loyalty to the new authorities by revealing its "enemies." This was the situation which confronted Kakesa as he stood before Mulele.

Pushing the packet of letters across the table he asked Kakesa to take them with him and to study them carefully. He was then locked in a small windowless stick and thatch enclosure under guard. Suddenly his situation was clear. He was a prisoner and on trial for a lengthy list of "crimes" against the new regime. For a week nothing happened. By listening intently and peeking through cracks in his little locked shelter, he became aware of the daily rebel routine around him: indoctrination classes, drills, camp maintenance and a continual stream of delegations from the corners of rebel occupied land, some for consultation and decisions, some for trial and acquittal, others for punishment or death. A week was more than sufficient time for Kakesa to verify for himself that the tales of rebel brutality vis-à-vis prisoners condemned of crimes against the rebel regime were indeed true. The sound of people being put to death weighed upon him like a deadly shroud.

One day two men arrived from Mukedi. They had a packet for Kakesa sent by his parents. Guards allowed them to visit with him a bit. News from Mukedi and his family was precious. When they left, he opened the package; it contained a pair of trousers which would now replace the shorts he had been wearing since leaving the station. Under the trousers he found something else wrapped in smudged paper - - a Bible! During the long hours of his ongoing isolation he turned to the Scripture in his hand in the seclusion of his cell with a sense of spiritual need he'd never known before.

missionary voices heard in the rebel camp

One morning, across the open area of the rectangular camp, he heard the sound of distant voices which were strangely familiar. Indeed, they sounded like the voices of his fellow Mennonite church leaders and missionaries! Was he losing his mind? Then, suddenly, he understood. The rebels had installed the Mukedi transmitter taken from his house and had happened upon the frequency used by the EMC leaders and missionaries in their daily short-wave communications. Then, using the same transmitter and frequency, he heard someone in the camp proclaiming the praises of the rebel movement to whomever might be listening.

After an initial emotional rush of memories stirred by hearing the voices of close friends in this improbable place, a plan began to form in Kakesa's mind. Yet the same day he requested to have a word with Mulele. His wish granted, Kakesa referred to their initial conversation at which time Mulele had said he was waiting for further evidence to either prove Kakesa's guilt or innocence. If tomorrow morning Kakesa could prove that the letters accusing him of embezzling teacher's salaries were not true, would Mulele then be satisfied? Agreeing that he would, Kakesa then proposed that he be allowed to speak with Tshikapa personnel next morning via their own transmitter and the entire camp could listen in on whatever conversation would follow. Stating that he needed time to discuss this startling proposal with his subordinates he promised to give his answer before sun-down. The minutes seemed like hours as Kakesa sat in his little stick and thatch cell. True to his word, Mulele sent a messenger before darkness fell. He would be permitted to speak to people at Tshikapa in the morning.

vindication via Missavia

Immediately following World War II, CIM missionaries had attempted to establish an inter-station short-wave communication network with war surplus equipment. It was better than letters via bicycle but not much. Their range was limited and any atmospheric disturbance made messages unintelligible. In the early 60's, with the arrival of MAF personnel and aircraft, it became imperative to have short-wave equipment that would enable CIM and EMC personnel to keep contact with the main MAF base in Leopoldville as well as their planes in flight. Thus Missavia short-wave transceivers were installed at all of the CIM stations. And, in the progression of events, the Mukedi set with its six volt battery eventually found its way to the rebel's bush headquarters.

Next morning when Kakesa was released from his hut, he was taken first to Mulele. Holding Kakesa's eyes he said: "I've decided to grant you opportunity to talk with your missionary friends at Tshikapa but I'm sending my armed guards with you. If the missionary asks questions to trap you, you will remain silent. In your talking, if you say one word which betrays us, you will die on the spot. And remember, I'll be listening to everything."

Walking across the camp compound surrounded by armed guards, Kakesa was silently praying that this morning, of all mornings, response from Tshikapa would be prompt and that communication would be clear. Arriving at a little hut, he entered and immediately spotted the familiar transceiver perched on a table. Noting that the switch had already been flipped on, Kakesa picked up the microphone which he had so often cradled in his hand in better days back at Mukedi. Keidel picks up the narrative: "'9TX63. I am calling 9TX63.' He waited praying that his missionary friend [V.J. Sprunger] would answer. He called again, and a third time, waiting. 'This is 9TX63.' The voice of his white friend was strong and clear. 'Who are you?' 'This is Kakesa Samuel.' 'Kakesa Samuel!' Is that really you? Or is someone impersonating you? We heard that you were dead. Where are you?' The prisoner hesitated. 'I'm in the hands of soldiers,' he replied. It was a half-truth designed to satisfy those watching him. How are things there?' 'Everything is going well here. The big matter is that of teacher's salaries. I have four months of salary money to give you. It is urgent that the teachers be paid or they will stop working. Do you have a way to come here and get it?' Kakesa was dumbfounded. Before he had even raised the issue, the missionary had proven in the hearing of them all that teachers' charges against him of embezzlement of funds were false. His purpose for broadcasting was achieved. 'I'm not able to come,' he replied. 'It is necessary that you yourself go with the money to Mukedi and pay them.' 'There is much fighting between here and Mukedi; no one can get through. But in as much as you are in the hands of soldiers, explain the situation to them. The government does not want the schools to close. Soldiers will escort you there.' 'There is no way for me to come,' Kakesa repeated. 'Then arrange with your local government man to come with soldiers and meet us halfway along the main road to the river' his friend rejoined. 'You set the time and we will meet you there.' Kakesa struggled to conceal his anguish. 'My situation is very difficult. I cannot come.'"

"The missionary paused. Suggesting his suspicion he asked: 'Whose transmitter are you using?' 'It belongs to the soldiers.' 'I'm not reading you very well on this frequency. Change to channel number two.' Kakesa suspected the request was calculated to disclose what kind of transmitter set he was using. The guards watched unsuspectingly. He changed channels and thereby confirmed that he was using a familiar mission transceiver. 'One other matter', the missionary added. 'You have been chosen to go to Belgium for study. Your scholarship money is waiting for you. We want to arrange your travel plans. How soon will the soldiers bring you out?' The missionary's questions, shot at him like hunter's arrows, were coming perilously close. His emotions buffeted him mercilessly. He feared losing self-control. 'Give the scholarship to someone else. I stand between life and death.'"

"With that last exchange, Kakesa laid the microphone on the table and responded no further. Emotionally spent, he waited a moment still surrounded by the guards. Then came word: 'Mulele is calling for you.' Still seated beside his radio in his house, Mulele said: 'Today I accept that your words are true. You did not raise the matter of the teacher's salaries. The missionary himself did. You are vindicated." (10)

Kakesa assigned duties at rebel headquarters

Mulele declared Kakesa a free man but with the stipulation that he not leave the central headquarters. Since he was there, he could help in many ways. For starters, he would join the secretarial crew. Thus in following days he found himself seated at a table typing whatever was handed to him such as warrants for the arrest of accused persons; carbon copies of excerpts from Communist writings for distribution to various rebel training camps. He also typed the official minutes of court proceedings which continually went on around him.

157

While immensely grateful that his own life had been spared, he soon found himself engaged in a deep personal struggle of conscience. He was revolted by the arbitrary judgments he saw meted out from day to day and by the endless cruelty. Sometimes Christians would be brought in or people he knew. Often he would seek to intervene for them. Once a well-known Mennonite commercial man from Mukedi area was brought in for trial. His crime: he had operated a store and had protested too vigorously when nearly everything was taken from him. He was condemned to death. Kakesa prevailed on Mulele to revoke his sentence.

One day a packet of new material was handed him to be typed. For a while his fingers roamed automatically over the keyboard. Suddenly, it registered that he was typing portions of a guerrilla handbook describing how to make incendiary fuses from materials of the bush and how to lay booby traps in foot paths. What was this he was typing? What if someone's home was reduced to ashes with the help of this sheet? What if some innocent person lost his life as a result of his work?

Then his assignment took an even worse turn. Because of his familiarity with the languages of the area and his experience with the short-wave transceiver, Mulele decided that he would make an excellent "voice" for the rebel cause. The scripts would be prepared for him by others but he would read them from day to day. Kakesa assumed this new role with a tormented spirit. Although he knew that fewer people were likely hearing their transmitted messages than the rebels imagined, it was nonetheless his voice that was sending out the propaganda, much of it condemning and scorning the very values and causes in which he so deeply believed. One day, at the close of a broadcast, he secretly damaged the transceiver fuse making it inoperable. No one in the camp knew enough about electronics to discover what had happened.

a Bible in the camp

As the days passed, Kakesa spent more and more time with his Bible. He was searching for help for his inner turmoil which was becoming ever more intense. He longed for news from his wife and family. But how could he ever return to Mukedi, to the Mission and the Church to resume his role as a lay leader? To have remained really true to his conscience here in this evil place could well have demanded a price he was not sure he was prepared to pay. So, the answer seemed clear. He'd been tested and found wanting. He would not return. He would plot his personal course in some other direction like so many others around him were doing. His ties with and responsibility toward the Mission and Church were costing him too much.

But in spite of himself he was driven again and again to his Bible. At first he was careful to read it in secret as he could find moments alone. Then on day, the inevitable happened. A group in the camp happened upon him as he read. Asked what it was, he answered honestly. Some expressed surprise stating that they'd left their Catholic prayer books at home when they joined the *Jeunesse* cause. While some made inquiry about the passage he was reading, a couple slipped away to inform Mulele of their important "discovery" with the agitated comment that those who read the Bible are the ones who oppose the revolution. At the time Mulele made no comment. The secret now found out, Kakesa determined to make no further effort to hide his reading times.

Then the day came when Kakesa, his day's work finished, sat with his Bible in his hands, reading. Hearing a footstep, he looked up. It was Mulele Pierre. Pausing for a long moment, the rebel leader turned and walked away. Neither that day nor any other did he make reference to Kakesa and his Bible. What had gone though his mind? What had stayed his hand? Were memories stirred of his own earlier years in a Catholic seminary among other youth who were studying for the priesthood? Was there recognition, in that moment, that even in the bush headquarters of the rebel movement it was appropriate, at least this once, to recognize a higher power?

It was not long after this encounter that in one of his reading times Kakesa heard what seemed to be a voice clearly saying to him: "Go back to Mukedi; go back to Mukedi." His immediate reaction was a mix of astonishment and resistance. Again he heard the voice and the same words. At last he prayed: "Oh Lord, if this is your voice and your command, I accept. If you'll open the way for me to go, I'll go." (11)

a prayer for illness granted

Kakesa had already been struggling for some time with the diet available in the rebel headquarters. He ate the food as did everyone else but the meager fare of cassava mush and greens supplemented with little else left him with steady weight loss. Unknown to him, family and friends back at Mukedi had been praying that Kakesa would become so ill in the camp that they would allow him to leave to secure medical help. In addition to weight loss, Kakesa now began to experience swelling of his ankles and lower legs. Before long the swelling extended to his thighs. Increasingly concerned, he one day called his condition to Mulele's attention adding that he feared for what lay ahead of him if he could not find help. Pressing the point, he asked Mulele to have mercy on him and allow him to go to the Mukedi hospital, the only place in the entire rebel controlled region where there was any hope for help.

After a moment of silence Mulele responded: "'Perhaps your idea is good. We need you, but you are not able to help us in such a condition. When you are healed, will you return to help us?' Searching for an obliging response which would be short of an outright promise, Kakesa responded: 'Aren't you the ruler of our land? Why would I despise your authority and refuse to return?' 'Very well, Speaker of God. You are a man of true words. I will prepare a letter instructing the director of the hospital to take good care of you. I will put you into the hands of two men who will accompany you.'" (12)

Given the letter and two men in the morning, he set out for home. Though each step was painful and a long trying journey lay ahead of him, he was deeply grateful that the Lord had opened an unexpected way for him to escape from the bondage and torment of the previous six months.

twin babies along the path

Kafutshi, Kakesa's wife, had had her own valley of shadow to walk during the months of their separation. When Kakesa was taken by force from their home, he left her four months pregnant. Although her husband was no longer on the station, those who wished him ill reflected their animosity toward her as well. Concerned that some irresponsible person might do her harm, family members took her toward the south to a cluster of villages where fellow Christians would care for her.

Anxiety concerning the welfare of her husband weighed heavily upon her. Suddenly a second fear was added. She was now six months pregnant and she was losing blood. As the condition became more pronounced, she began to fear for the life of her unborn child. Sharing her concern with other mothers, it was decided to send a message to her father-in-law at Mukedi to explain her plight. A couple of days later Kasala Jacob appeared on his bicycle. He was dressed in shorts with a bush knife slipped through his belt. It was his hope that this attire would help him move across the rebel controlled countryside without delays or prolonged questioning. Realizing that walking was out of the question for Kafutshi, he secured a sturdy bamboo chair from the villagers, fashioned a stick platform on his luggage rack and securely tied the chair to it. Knowing that he could not possibly pedal his bike through the loose sand of the trails ahead and still maintain his balance with his top-heavy load, he prepared himself for the taxing prospect of walking his daughter-in-law atop his bike to Mukedi - - some thirty-five miles.

Kafutshi watched the proceedings with mixed emotions. She hadn't heard from Kakesa in many days but she had managed to have her small daughters brought to her from Mukedi. Now, suddenly, she herself was in desperate need and would have to leave her daughters with Christian friends. Her heart swelled with gratitude toward her compassionate father-in-law who had dropped everything to come to her aid as soon as he had heard of her dilemma. She longed to be in the Mukedi maternity where she would be among loving friends and in the skilled, practiced hands of the Mission midwives including her own mother-in-law. But two long days of travel teetering on top of this bicycle? What if - - ?

Strong hands eased her up onto the wicker chair on the back of the bicycle. She bid her fellow Christians farewell entrusting her children to their care. Kasala took a hitch in his belt, gripped the handle bars and began what would have been a daunting prospect for a man half his age. The walking of such a distance would be simple; it would be the constant struggle to keep his bicycle erect while steering it around the holes, washouts and up and down slopes of that long sandy trail ahead which would be very difficult.

The first day passed without incident. There was still some loss of blood but nothing that alarmed Kafutshi. Next morning as they set out again Kasala sought to comfort her. If they traveled as far today as yesterday, after a second night along the way they would be at Mukedi by mid-morning the following day. They traveled a couple of hours after which their path began to take them across an expanse of grassland without shade or shelter. Suddenly Kafutshi felt a sharp pain. Startled she breathed a silent prayer: "Oh Lord, not now." Her situation could hardly have been more difficult and less appropriate. But within moments, there it was again and she knew that she was going into labor there in the middle of the bleak expanse of that prairie atop a bicycle with no one to help except her father-in-law. When she shared her disturbing news with him, he calmly stopped, helped her off her chair, cut some grass to lay a padding on the path side, spread a cloth and eased her down upon it. Having done all he could he walked away a few paces, anguish and fear in his heart. Meanwhile Kafutshi tried to face her own situation. What was she to do now? How could she survive what lay ahead without help?

Suddenly in the distance Kasala saw a white speck bobbing along just visible above the top of the plains grass. Instantly he recognized it as a white enamel basin atop the head of a woman. Crying out to catch her attention he started toward her. For a moment she paused ready to take flight. Might this strange man not be a rebel who wanted to harass her? But across the distance Kasala shouted the news: A woman in childbirth - - the universal language of motherhood. Casting caution to the winds, the woman and her companion came toward him. They were older women who had often helped with village births in the past. Best of all, as it turned out, they were Christians. Providentially, one of them had just filled her enamel pan with fresh water. Before long, the first of what proved to be twin girls was born - - but without life. Moments later a live baby was born. One of the women then rose to her feet stating that she would go to the village for help while her companion stayed with Kafutshi to tend to her new baby. Kasala, meanwhile, would bury the tiny, dead infant. Soon the second woman returned with two men. They had brought a sturdy bamboo pole and a blanket. Carefully placing it around Kafutshi, they knotted the ends round the pole fashioning a hammock in which they carried her to their village.

The trauma and loss of blood had taken its toll. For days Kafutshi lay in a comatose condition. Beginning to despair for her life, Kasala determined to again leave on his bicycle, this time to search for Kafutshi's own mother. Making his way through a countryside crisscrossed by rebel groups, he found Sona Henrietta and, after a couple of days, brought her to the village where her daughter lay. It proved to be the comfort and inspiration she needed. Rallying physically and emotionally, they were soon able to take Kafutshi the rest of the way to Mukedi. Shortly after, her new-found Christian friends brought her daughters to her there.

rebellion within rebellion

The trip back to Mukedi had been long and painful but one day Kakesa hobbled the last mile onto the station and made his way over familiar terrain to his own home. He was thin, dirty, bearded, wearing tattered clothing and limping on his badly swollen legs. So changed was he in appearance that Kafutshi at first did not recognize her husband. Then with a cry of delight she rushed to welcome him. Word spread quickly. Kakesa was back. Fellow Christians came to greet him with joy and some exclaimed "Praise the Lord. He's answered our prayers. He's granted Kakesa a sickness which has brought him home - - just as we prayed."

Kakesa soon discovered that much had changed at Mukedi during the months of his absence. In brief, Mukedi-area people, Christians and non-Christians alike, were having serious second thoughts about the rebel movement. There had been a series of events, one after the other, which were rousing increasing resentment. An early experience which planted the first seeds of suspicion was the decision of the rebel leaders to impose non-Baphende authorities over the Mukedi area. To his surprise and chagrin, Chief Nzamba learned that a local

Jeunesse zone commander was to be installed just six miles from Mukedi and that he was a member of a small clan situated between them and the larger Ambunda tribe to the northwest. Furthermore, in the broad rebel scheme of things, the Mukedi area was to be lumped with two neighboring sectors, one made up predominantly of Ambunda people and the other of a group of Baphende with whom Chief Nzamba had a running dispute over boundary lines. This meant that they found themselves under a non-Muphende rebel commander and were administratively thrown in with people with whom they had a history of strained relations and among whom they now stood as a minority.

Furthermore, it had by now become clear that full-fledged members of the movement comprised a privileged "elite" who were to be served and obeyed by everyone else. The *Jeunesse* lived in their "bivouacs" in valleys and forests away from their home villages. Their only reason to return home was to carry messages, give orders, recruit labor, command food and visit relatives. Any word or attitude which was interpreted either as being critical or derisive was swiftly met with harsh reprimands if not physical punishment. With passing time disciplinary actions gave way more and more to violent death. Through vicious experience villagers soon learned that it was wise to remain quietly passive, to observe all regulations laid upon them and to show a constant attitude of respectful appreciation for the leaders in particular and the rebellion in general.

Another grating facet of the emerging rebel scene was the reversal of social standing. While the *Jeunesse* did not unleash the mindless slaughter of educated and trained people which characterized the *Simba* rebellion, the *Jeunesse* nonetheless increasingly singled out such people for scorn and intimidation. They were told that they had "grown fat" on the money and favors of the hated central government while they, the *Jeunesse*, had gone naked and hungry. Now the tables were turned. The social order was reversed. Those who had been the elite before were now the *penepe* (pr. PEH-neh-pay, a Gimbunda term of scorn and insult). One mission teacher told of being taken in hand by a group of his former students. His trouser legs were cut off, he was made to kneel in the middle of the village for three hours, arms in air, the object of boisterous comments. Later he was forced to carry large enamel pans of mush on his head from the village out to the rebel camp. This being the traditional work of women, he was greeted with ribald comments, laughter and general disdain. At first, some hardier individuals took it upon themselves to go to rebel leaders to protest such insults only to discover that a rebel could do no wrong and was automatically vindicated no matter what the charge.

Furthermore, Mukedi-area people had had sufficient time to compare their experience under rebel rule with what they had known before - - and the comparison was not favorable. In spite of all of the rosy promises made, things were not getting better. They were clearly getting worse. The most basic commodities were beginning to disappear one by one. Then came the time they began to experience the armed confiscation of carefully hoarded savings and material resources in home after home.

But for the Mukedi area Mennonite community, the worst of it was the continual effort made to extend control over their Church. Particularly ominous was the rebel announcement that given the heavy loss of life experienced in their bloody defeats at places like Gungu and Kikwit, they needed now to try to "repopulate their earth"! Thus one day it was declared that young rebels could now claim girls in the villages through which they passed and take them back to their camps with them. Each *partisan* was to have a "wife." Most villagers, though angered by this, were too fearful to oppose the edict. For Mukedi Christians, however, it was another matter.

Christmas day 1964

It was not long after Kakesa's return to Mukedi that Mukedi pastors Falanga Elie and Kidinda David and two church elders were summoned to Malemba, the rebel headquarters, where Kakesa had just spent six months. Upon their arrival they were lectured at length on their place and role in the rebellion as leaders of the Mukedi Church. Preaching would still be tolerated but from now on they were to preach in a manner to aid the rebellion and not hinder it. After all, their Bible was full of excellent texts. Did not the Israelites revolt against their slavery in Egypt? Jesus himself was a rebel in his time. He gave his life to overthrow established, unfair practices and to oppose entrenched, corrupt rulers. Excellent sermon material - - all of it. And to be sure that

161

they were heeding these "suggestions," someone would be in the Mukedi Church services from then on to monitor and report on their sermons.

And one more thing: upon their return, they were to advise the Mukedi people, in general, and chief Nzamba, in particular, that the tracing of the rebel administrative zones had been decided long ago and that nothing would be changed.

Whether by design or by happenstance, on their return journey the four Mennonite church leaders were accosted by a band of rebels and taken prisoner. They were beaten and bound and thrown into "jail." Word was then sent to Mukedi setting a price in animals and goods for their release. Their wives scrounged the required ransom from relatives and church folk and went to the place where their husbands were being held and secured their release. This was in late 1964.

Christmas was near, traditionally a time of festive celebration, chorales, worship, pageants and the taking of a major community offering as a special gift for the work of the Church in the name of the Christ Child. Still carrying the marks of their beatings, the four leaders met with the local church council in early December. The single question which hung heavily over them was simply: "What, if anything, do we do this year?" After all, this was no ordinary year at Mukedi. But it was the four recently ransomed leaders who asserted themselves: "We refuse to spend this Christmas as though we'd never been taught anything about Jesus. We will spend Christmas day as we have all others in the past - - in the house of God. Our message will not have to do with rebellion and hatred but will tell of love, forgiveness and redemption. If we are killed, we will be killed in our chapel and in the name of Christ whose birth we intend to celebrate as is our custom."

And gather they did, supported by the community which responded to their courageous leadership. The church bell rang; the old beloved Christmas songs echoed cross the station and in the midst of their poverty they honored the tradition of their annual Christmas offering - - all of this amidst the brooding rebel presence around them. And there was no reprisal.

flash point

It was early in January 1965 that a scrap of paper fell into the hands of Chief Nzamba at Mukedi. It was a rebel "hit list" of fifteen Mukedi area people. The first name on the list was his own. Shortly thereafter, he was invited to the rebel zone headquarters some six miles away "to discuss" the situation in the Mukedi area. The chief and his elders decided to decline the summons and to rather invite the rebel leaders to come to the station instead. In keeping with a tribal custom to exchange messages between hostile camps via an adolescent girl, they sent their proposal in this way. To signal their anger, the rebel leaders killed the girl.

That was it. Chief Nzamba rallied his village men and stormed the rebel zone camp. Buildings were burned and the rebels put to flight. Hearing of this in his bush headquarters, Mulele was outraged. Mukedi people knew it was only a matter of time and they would be counterattacked. In preparation, they sent their women and children to villages of fellow tribes people to the south and sent word to the men to prepare for war. Reluctantly, Kakesa and Kafutshi sent their children with others.

Rebel response was not long in coming. For two days Nzamba and his men skirmished in the area and finally, once again, the rebels were force to retreat. By this time Mulele Pierre was alarmed. He was discovering that the unleashing of a rebellion had been the easy part of his venture. Controlling and turning the rebellion to his own ends was proving to be another matter. Coming secretly to the Mukedi area, he personally called in thousands of Ambunda tribesmen from the villages to the west. He apparently also had a couple of grenade launchers and a few automatic rifles. In the pre-dawn darkness of a mid-March morning, he succeeded in surprising Chief Nzamba and his people. The entire village and mission/church community took flight toward the south. Having routed the local population, the *Jeunesse* began to sack and destroy parts of the station. The hospital, a school building and some of the houses were put to flames. Benches were stacked in the middle of the chapel, doused with fuel and set ablaze. Houses were entered and whatever of worth remained was carried

162

off. Surrounding villages known to be loyal to Chief Nzamba were also put to the torch. Mulele Pierre and his men had carried the day. They were still in control but his victory was to be short-lived.

In the mass flight southward, those who went to further villages found themselves in the general area of Kandala. Here they were in another zone of the rebel network. The *commandant* was also a Muphende and thus shared a blood link with the refugees who had fled from Mukedi. It was no secret that by this time Chief Nzamba had had enough of the rebellion and was looking for some way to signal his readiness to cooperate with government forces situated across the Kwilu River. Realizing that some Mukedi people might well attempt to do just that, Mulele gave orders to seal off the approaches to the river. Anyone caught attempting to cross was to be put to death without further question.

Knowing the price that would be paid if they were discovered, there was initially but a trickle of people - - one here, two there - - who managed to elude the guards and slip into the water. They were mostly young Mennonite men who had worked at Mukedi in one capacity or another and who were bitterly disillusioned with what they'd seen and experienced.

Kandala revisited

It was mid-May, 1965, and the onset of dry season. Missionaries and church leaders at Tshikapa and Nyanga had known for some time that government soldiers had retaken control of the south bank of the Kwilu at Kandala. A small military garrison was reported to be located just off the station. Via short-wave radio, plans were put in place for a four-man CIM/EMC delegation to fly to Kikwit to meet representatives of the Mennonite Brethren Mission/Church and, together, seek a way to make contact with Mennonite Christians in areas recently freed from rebel rule. (13)

The mission/church delegation soon learned that their only hope of getting to Gungu and Kandala was to drive a mission truck in a military convoy. One was scheduled to leave Kikwit soon with fresh troops and supplies for new forays into rebel-held territory across the river. It was not the way they'd hoped to make their first visit but there was no choice. The government refused permission for the team to try to make the trip alone. They would travel in a military convoy or not at all.

The CIM/EMC men arrived at Kandala late the afternoon of May 16, having left the MB men at Gungu en route. The sun rose the next morning over a somber and dismal scene. In a report of the visit it is said: "The station was completely deserted. Where only months before there was a Bible School camp, there were now only eroding sections of mud brick walls jutting above the top of high, yellow, dry season grass. Under foot, nettles caught at socks and pant legs and twice a snake was killed. . . . The store room that had contained more than two tons of Giphende literature now was roofless and completely empty except for a soft mat of paper pulp underfoot, literature that had succumbed to months of successive sun and rain. But near the entrance there was still a legible fragment from a Giphende Gospel of Luke which read: 'Why call ye me Lord Lord and do not the things that I say'?. . . And on a patch of wall beside a doorless entryway to the chapel a sardonic message was scratched with charcoal: 'You little thieves, yours is a revolution of lies.' All that remained of the former place of worship was a shell of masonry open to the hazy, dry season sky." (14)

As they continued their slow walk across a station which had been battered and burned on that fiery night 16 months earlier, in the distance across the river they heard the hollow thump of mortar shells which marked the advance of the military patrol with which they'd travelled just the day before. As the little group arrived at the charred remains of what had earlier been home for a missionary family, the account reads: "In rummaging through the debris there came to light such fragments as half a saucer bearing the partial likeness of the *Hotel de Ville* in Brussels, Belgium; a pyrex measuring cup that had been melted flat in the fierce heat of that rebel night; a rusted picture frame; the flame spreader of a Coleman kerosene lamp; the battered tray of a slide projector and the handled fragment of a brightly colored teacup." (15) A short distance off the station was found a burned-out rebel camp. A displaced station light pole, which had served as a rebel flag pole, stood in the center of a circle of chapel benches. Nearby, some orange trees were beginning to litter the ground with their ripe, unsought fruit.

A handful of emaciated and tattered refugees had already come out of hiding and were in little grass and stick shelters along the road in front of the station near the small military camp. To their disappointment, the CIM/EMC team found no one they knew from the mission/church community. Next morning they would need to join the returning convoy to Kikwit. They did distribute food and blankets to the few people they found and left the balance of their supplies with the commanding officer to be distributed as others would decide to risk coming out of hiding. They also left a list of area church leaders with the officer in charge suggesting that he make inquiry about them as people began to emerge from hiding in the forest. On the list were the names of two Kandala pastors, Khelendende Pierre and Kindumba Jacques; male nurse Konda Bernard (who interceded for the Kandala missionaries the night the station was burned); elder and translation committee member Kimbadi Paul; and Kakesa Samuel though they had no idea where he was at the time.

Before sundown, the delegation walked down the hillside toward the river and a little village where a small group of people were rebuilding shelters. Recognizing the white men as missionaries, a village elder hurried up to pump their hands and stated flatly: "Our earth is sick. We've experienced suffering such as we'd never believed could come to us." Another toothless old villager grasped a missionary hand and said: "Thank you, thank you God. Truly God is there. None of us believed we'd ever see the face of another missionary again." Next morning, as the little huddle of refugees along the roadside were handed some tinned food and blankets, one was heard to observe to another: "This affair of God is a powerful affair. These are the people whose houses we burned down and we caused to suffer. Today they return and give us covering for our naked bodies and food for our empty stomachs." (16) After a brief roadside service with the refugees and soldiers, Pastor David closed with a prayer for the speedy return of peace and they were on their way. Unknown to the CIM/EMC men at the time, with the amazing speed of the African bush news grapevine, word of their brief visit at Kandala had already reached Pastor Khelendende in the isolation of the refugee camp he had organized in a forested valley of the area. While they were debating what to do about the astonishing news, the trucks had already begun their return trip to Kikwit.

It was particularly at the Gungu government post that the mission/church delegation secured the most information for it was there they found the very first half dozen young Mennonite men who had risked their lives by slipping past rebel guards and giving themselves up to government forces. In a report of that encounter this is found: "There was Andrew, the young, spirited teacher who had worked at Kandala Station until the week of the rebel attack. He sat, elbows on knees, slowly shaking his head and repeating over and over: 'Nous en avons assez', i.e., "We've had enough of it."

"There was Alexander . . . who was employed at a state dispensary at Idiofa and had lived through the destruction of the rebel siege of February 1964. Looking at us with eyes that were darkened with shadows of memories and responsibilities far beyond his years, he urged on us passionately the necessity for continuing the struggle to save Mukedi Station and the witness of the Gospel among his people. And there was the Mukedi teacher Evariste, who had been among the more outspoken critics of Mission policy and personnel, who now was prepared to quietly admit: "At first we thought the rebellion was a good and just cause. By the time we found out it wasn't, it was too late."

"And there is the reported emphasis of Mukedi pastors who are known to be alive and in hiding in the villages toward Kandala: 'We've seen and experienced nothing about which we were not warned long ago by our missionaries.'" (17)

Even though the trip was limited to a few hours and contacts with fellow believers were limited, the mission/church delegation came away from the experience with several insights into the dynamics and causes which were rapidly spelling defeat for the Kwilu rebellion: - There was a deep, bitter resentment against their tribal political leaders who, they now realized, had persuaded them to support a rebellion the true nature of which was carefully kept from them until it was solidly launched. - There was furious resentment at the treatment they had received at the hands of generally poorly-educated, braggart and fanatical rebel leaders. - There was the painful realization that they had allowed themselves to be persuaded by the propaganda of a leftist political movement and had suffered consequences about which they'd been forewarned. - There was the abrasive fear of what the end results of the rebellion would be for them, their people and their Church if it was not stamped out. - There was, finally, the will to combat and resist the movement and to reclaim their home areas from the rebels.

If the four-man CIM/EMC delegation had to return home without the detailed sort of information they had hoped to find, they had nonetheless seen and heard enough that they were prepared to make some clear recommendations. Writing to the home board and constituency they said: "Where does all of this leave us - - we the missionaries and constituency of the Congo Inland Mission? In terms of material assets, we've taken tremendous losses. It is all the harder to accept since the destruction has been wanton, unjustifiable and blind. It is also true that our counsel and suggestions in the past have at times been deliberately spurned and misquoted. But if all indications can be believed, we have before us a spectacle of a people fighting to pull back from an abyss; a people struggling to salvage their country, their way of life and their faith. Were we a commercial firm, we would undoubtedly write the Kwilu off as a bad gamble and forget it - - exactly as some are doing now. Were we an unsympathetic neighboring tribe not directly involved in the rebellion we might with some logic wash our hands of the Kwilu Baphende, precisely as some are doing, and say, 'They asked for it, let them enjoy it.'. . . But we are neither of the above. We are among those who name the name of Him who said: 'It is more blessed to give than to receive,' and who also said, 'Be not overcome of evil but overcome evil with good.'" (18)

CIM/EMC soon spelled out a series of responses to be implemented as soon as possible: "- a ministry of material aid to an uprooted and homeless people; - a ministry of reconciliation among a people torn by hatred and bloodshed; - a ministry of guidance and help to a people seeking to reassemble the fragments of a disrupted life; - a ministry of spiritual restoration for those who have been swept from the moorings of their faith; - a ministry of consolation and strengthening for the Church." (19)

a martyr's roll is begun

There was an early idea of the damage done to mission/church buildings and equipment. It was not long until the field administrative committee was able to send preliminary estimates of material resources which would be required to reopen schools and medical services. A much more somber reckoning was the slowly lengthening list of EMC members who had lost their lives amidst the violence of the previous years. While it would be many months till anything like complete information could be tabulated, by the close of 1965 there was already some information in hand - - particularly from the Mukedi area where the rebel grip was early broken.

There was Kituku (pr. gi-TOO-goo) Jacob, a portly, gifted evangelist who had a striking ability to illustrate Biblical messages with Phende proverbs, history and folklore. His command of a Baphende audience as he preached was outstandingly effective. He apparently was overtaken and killed while in flight from the *Jeunesse* attack on Mukedi Station and village in March 1965.

There was Mabula (pr. mah-BOO-lah) Matthew, a slim man of medium height, a shopkeeper, a member of the Mukedi Church Council of many years and a lay preacher who often accompanied evangelistic teams into the outlying areas of his home district. He was reported to have been trapped near his shop the day the rebels swept over the station.

There was Mutshimba (pr. moo-TSHI-mbah) Philippe and Katoko (pr. kah-TOH-koh) Timothy, long-time members of the Mukedi Church who, as the rebel movement broke into the open, were trying to help establish a Kimbanguist group just off the station. (20) When they defied orders to cease their meetings and activities as a Kimbanguist group, a rebel team was sent to their site and they were put to death on the spot.

165

There was the loss of Matangua (pr. mah-TAH-ngwah) Constant, a soft spoken, gifted male nurse who had served for years with Dr. Merle and Dorothy Schwartz in the Mukedi hospital. Dr. Schwartz often had him scrub up and work with him across the table in surgery - - particularly in doing hernia repairs and caesarian sections. With the forced evacuation of the missionaries, Constant calmly stepped to the other side of the table and performed scores of such operations during the months that Mukedi was under rebel rule. When in June, 1965, the government forces approached the station accompanied by Chief Nzamba and his men, Constant was forced to flee with the rebels. They considered him to be "their doctor" and demanded that he follow them into the rugged bush country along the Loange River where they sought to make a final stand. Some months later, a military patrol surprised a rebel encampment in the bush. Among those who fled the gunfire was the Mukedi medical assistant. Struck from behind, Constant fell mortally wounded.

There was Kabanga (pr. kah-BAH-ngah) Jacques, a quick-mannered, alert teacher who had often been among the more vocal personnel in criticizing mission policies. Jacques quickly came to recognize the rebel movement for what it was and became more and more vocal in his dissent. One day he overstepped his bounds and was condemned to death for his "disloyalty" to the cause.

Particularly poignant for one former Kandala missionary family (21) was the news of the death of their former cook, Kamuangu (pr. kah-MWAH-ngoo) Pascal. Having heard the rumor that missionaries and church leaders had visited Kandala and passed one night there, he determined to cross the Kwilu River to learn for himself the truth of the matter. He was fully aware that local rebel leaders promised death for anyone who dared to cross that boundary. But such was his longing for news from "the outside" and about the missionaries for whom he had worked for years that he determined to take the risk. He slipped away, did visit Kandala, talked with people there to verify what he had heard and what had transpired since the missionaries' departure. Retracing his steps, he was betrayed by some fellow villagers. Enraged at this disregard for their authority, rebel leaders seized him along with the village chief, his uncle, and two of his brothers. All were tied hand and foot and thrown into the river he had recently crossed in search of information he had desired to know. (22)

a cry for forgiveness

"We must get rid of our burden of guilt" was the heart of a message sent to Kandala by a cluster of Christians at Shakenge. (23)

The first EMC/CIM team to visit Kandala after rebel control had been broken quickly sensed that several major areas of need were opening before them. There was the immediate need for material help. Then there were those who had stood fast in their faith who hungered for reassurance and the nurture of God's Word. But there were also those - - many of them - - who had found either the allure of rebel promises or the fearful pressure of rebel tyranny to be too great and had compromised their commitments to the Lord and their Church. Many of them now cried out for opportunity for confession and restoration. And, furthermore, there was great need for a ministry of reconciliation among brothers and sisters of the Mennonite Church who had not been faithful to one another and who, in some cases, had even betrayed one another. The cry "we must get rid of our burden of guilt" was not an idle one. It was the cry of tormented spirits.

It was late in July 1965 that arrangements were made for Ngongo David to return to Kandala. A seasoned pastor, an astute listener and an animated preacher, he was an ideal man for that delicate assignment. By that time Pastor Khelendende Pierre had led hundreds of Kandala people out of hiding to return to the station area. Pastor Ngongo also found Kakesa Samuel and his wife Kafutshi there. They had joined the Mukedi people in their wild flight southward in mid-March. When in mid-June Chief Nzamba and his people linked up with government forces and began their trek back to drive the rebels out of their home village and territory, Kakesa and Kafutshi had to make a decision. Would they join the migration back toward Mukedi or would they stay behind and attempt to escape across the river to Kandala? In spite of Kafutshi's great apprehension, Kakesa slipped away alone one morning at daybreak and prayed as he walked. He slept under a crude leaf shelter where nightfall found him. Next day he continued his apprehensive way until he happened upon a military outpost which had already been established on his side of the river. Surrendering to them, he was at first seriously menaced. Upon finally being able to prove his identity and relationship with the nearby Mennonite Mission due to his command of a variety of area languages, they asked what his intentions were. First he asked permission to return for his family. Offered a military escort, he begged them to allow him to return alone - - this for fear that they might encounter opposition, use their weapons, and Kafutshi would flee with the children.

Once again the Lord granted him safe travel through an area which was still partially under rebel control. Finding his family still waiting, they tied their little refugee bundles and returned to the military outpost and crossed the river to Kandala. There it was that Pastor Ngongo found them a few days later.

In the first public meeting that was held, Pastor Ngongo brought a simple, straightforward message from God's Word underscoring the dual facts that while God punishes sinners he welcomes all who come to Him in penitence and meets them with loving forgiveness. Suddenly someone stood in the audience and lifted his voice in prayer with tears upon his cheeks. Almost immediately a second person joined him in audible prayer. The two men were Kandala's pastor Khelendende Pierre and Kakesa Samuel. Before long, the entire refugee group packed tightly into the roofless station chapel were caught up in a swell of voices as individually people began to pour out their anguished hearts to the Lord.

Later, as Pastor Ngongo gave opportunity for individual times of conversation and confession, clusters of people waited patiently for time with him or Mandala (pr. mah NDAH-lah) Solomon, the Nyanga church evangelist who accompanied him on his trip. For many it was a time of desperately needed catharsis. Many Kandala Christians had witnessed, experienced, endured and participated - - whether willingly or unwillingly - - in activities for which they now felt repugnance and shame. A time of healing was urgently needed. Amidst the burned-out shambles of Kandala Station, such opportunity was provided and seized upon with immense gratitude.

It was in late August 1965 that Kakesa became a member of the first EMC team to visit Mukedi Station. National government forces were now in control of the roads and principal villages but rebels were still a threatening presence in the surrounded bush country. There were four of them in the party. (24) As they bounced their way slowly northward from Kandala toward Mukedi, all were aware that Kakesa would again soon see some of the teachers whose letters of false accusation he had found in the folder Mulele Pierre had handed him months before in the rebel bush headquarters. Samuel's own description of that encounter was later reported by missionary Ben Eidse as follows: "When I confronted the teachers at Mukedi I asked them: 'Are you convinced, now, that I did not eat your money?' They answered, 'Yes, we did wrong. You were innocent.' They were penitent and I forgave them. I'll be glad to work with them again." (25)

Sensing the crucial timing of ministry among the refugees coming out of hiding, further teams were sent. On two different occasions groups of students from the Theological School at Kajiji were transported to the Kandala and Mukedi areas. Again and again they ministered to gaunt, ill-clad fellow Congolese who had come through nightmarish experiences and were seeking emotional and spiritual equilibrium once again. Peter Falk who accompanied his students on one trip wrote: "The roofless chapel at Kandala was filled on Sunday morning, September 19, and the message, based on John 8:31-32 was well received. . . . One is moved with deep compassion at the sight of a pastor with marks of beatings upon his body, living in a little shack because his house had been destroyed, eating with fingers from a common dish because all of their dishes and necessities of the household have been confiscated and destroyed. Some had managed to hide away their Bibles and hymnbooks but those were only few. . . . There are acute problems confronting the Church. Some people have been molested, beaten, tied up. Their lives have been threatened and their earthly possessions have been destroyed at the hands of their fellow men. Now they are to forgive them and minister to them." (26)

That this process of restoration was not easy - - or even possible - - for all is suggested by another experience related by Kakesa. "There was one Kandala teacher who personally tried to take me to Malemba for execution. When I met him at Kandala, now, he looked as if he carried around a burden. It seemed as if he wanted to tell me something but no words came out. The Lord has helped me to forgive him." (27)

167

Thus was played out, on a painful individual basis, the aftermath of the *Jeunesse* movement within the Mennonite family of the Kwilu. While an overwhelming majority welcomed and seized upon opportunities given to confess failure, to seek cleansing and renewed fellowship with their Lord and other believers, there were also those miserable souls who came through their time in rebel hands twisted and disoriented to a degree that seemingly left them incapable of responding to opportunities offered for healing and rehabilitation - - the tragic aftermath of brutalization carried one step too far.

at Bakwanga CPRA closes shop

By spring of 1965, it had become clear that the crisis in the South Kasai had passed. At long last there was reason to believe that political calm had been restored and that the Baluba refugees were on the way to recovery. Fields covered the rolling countryside; adobe brick or cement block houses were cropping up everywhere. School rooms, whether in permanent or semi-permanent materials, were appearing and children were back in school. And little chapels were scattered across the landscape marking spots where Christians regularly met for worship and prayer. The refugees, who had endured so much, were putting down roots. In the process, the CPRA team "had constructed fifty-two school buildings plus churches and medical units. It had distributed some twenty thousand baby chicks. Twenty-four of Graber's workmen had built their own homes of permanent materials. Sixteen of his carpenters had bought their tools and started private businesses. By means of a profit sharing plan, the black foreman who had been responsible for the CPRA carpenter shop, its power equipment and supplies, completed payment of a $45.000 purchase price and went into business on his own." (28)

The South Kasai effort to salvage a people had been a successful inter-mission effort. The local Presbyterian Mission had given unflagging support in supplies and personnel. CIM missionaries and MCC voluntary service people had given major leadership. Sizeable shipments of MCC tinned meat and ground wheat had found their way into the large stream of emergency supplies which came in from many overseas points of origin. At times it had been done in the face of the most formidable and frightening odds but always in the name of Christ. The Lord had seen fit to overshadow his servants on their rounds of mercy. The CPRA team would take its departure with the knowledge of an enormous task well done. After time in Leopoldville with CPRA administrators and some vacation travel, the Grabers anticipated arriving in the United States in mid-July. They were to remain there, however, for a shorter time than they realized.

a different setting; the same story

The summer of 1965 saw the Kwilu *Jeunesse* forces in retreat. Ragged, skin and bones people were beginning to slip out of the forested hills and valleys, which had once been under rebel control, and to make their weary way to places like Kandala, Gungu, Idiofa and Kikwit. By this time, William Snyder had succeeded Orie Miller as the executive secretary of the MCC. He had just visited Leopoldville, Kikwit and Nyanga in the Congo where he had held discussions with the Mennonite Brethren representative John Kliewer, and CIM representatives V.J. Sprunger and Art Janz with regard to the new refugee problem swiftly taking shape in the Kwilu. In a letter dated October 25 and posted in Nairobi, Kenya, Snyder said of his Congo consultation: "All of us felt the relief needs in the Kwilu require urgent attention for the next nine months to one year within which time it is hoped that the people can begin planting and somewhat developing their food producing potential. . . . I feel that we should invite Archie Graber to come to Congo for one year on MCC support for service with CPRA. . . . CPRA is declaring Kwilu as one of its emergency areas and I believe it will be able to provide almost as much goods as Archie and the others can distribute. . . . I suggest that you work out the arrangements even before I return. . . ." (29)

In an MCC memo dated December 20, 1965, it is said in part: "MCC and CIM will loan Archie Graber, veteran Congo relief worker, to the CPRA for one year to direct the relief program in the Kwilu province. Archie will arrive in the Congo approximately February 1, 1966 and will be joined by his wife and daughter in June, 1966. . . . Base of operation for Archie Graber will be Kikwit." Among those associated with this new effort was John Gaeddert who, by that time, had followed Elmer Neufeld as MCC country director in the

Congo, Malcolm McVeigh, the new CPRA country coordinator, and PAX workers Al Dahl, Mark Weaver and Elmer Beachy.

a survey of need

Graber arrived in Leopoldville on February 9. Seven days later he, Gaeddert and McVeigh set out for Kikwit via road. On the 18th, MAF picked them up for a tour of eastern Kwilu. The air strips at Mukedi and Kandala having by then been repaired, they were able to visit both of these stations which had seen so much violent rebel activity. Huge crowds of people flocked to both airstrips eagerly providing information and making pleas for hoes, bush knives and supplies of various sorts. But the most urgent requests had to do with the reopening of their schools, the return of their missionaries and the restoration of their severely damaged stations.

Since their trip coincided with an EMC pastors/school directors conference which was being held across the river at Nyanga Station, the men touched down there also. Although Graber welcomed the opportunity for fellowship with many Congolese friends and coworkers of other years, uppermost on his mind was his need for a translator. In the Kasai his command of the Tshiluba language had enabled him to range far and wide without communication problems. In the Kwilu, however, it would be another story. Kituba was the trade language and Giphende a major tribal dialect. Explaining his need to the pastors gathered at Nyanga, it was decided to appoint Mukedi Pastor Kidinda (pr.ki-DI-ndah) David as his collaborator. A graduate of the Kalonda Bible Institute in earlier years, Pastor David had added Tshiluba to his language inventory. They quickly became an effective team.

Immediately visiting refugee camps which had already been established by the government in Kikwit and Idiofa regions, they began to understand the bitter toll which refugee life in the forest had taken. There were no families which had not dug lonely graves - - especially for children and the aged. Malnutrition and disease had relentlessly claimed its suffering victims. And many of those who survived to emerge from hiding would always carry the stamp of starvation. Walking through the camps hacked out of the bush, the places carried different names but the scenes were tragically the same - - children with pipe-stem arms and legs, skins tight over skeletal rib cages, stomachs bloated and hair carrying a reddish tinge - - all signs of prolonged protein deficiency. Gaunt adults, clutching frayed remains of clothing about them, extended bony hands in supplication for food, clothing and blankets.

Concluding his first report, Graber wrote: "We trust that this report will encourage you to join us in prayer for guidance, patience, strength and supplies to meet these many needs. His grace is enough and to spare for us all." (30)

the face of suffering

In the city of Kikwit itself, CPRA again found itself amidst many Mennonites. Since this was the administrative center of the Mennonite Brethren for the region, there were both EMC and MB people in great numbers. CPRA felt that the services of churches and the state hospital should be utilized for food distribution in the city thus freeing CPRA to concentrate on needs in the surrounding rural areas where neither church nor government personnel was available. They were soon to discover, however, that the local hospital and pastors were unable to cope. They were being inundated by a sea of human need.

Realizing that the feeding program set up in the city was not meeting the need as they had planned, CPRA quickly swung into action. Graber wrote in a May report: "Grass and brush were cleared away and ten days later the [pole and thatch] building 18' x 65' was complete and a short dedication service held. The children began coming. In only a few days the news spread and more and more children came. At present we are feeding 120 children daily and 1,400 families have cards that get weekly rations. . . . What do we give the children to eat? We have a shipment of U.S. surplus wheat flour. For as long as this lasts we will be baking 115 loaves of bread from each sack. This bread is cut in good sized pieces. It is given with a little MCC meat or a little Heinz baby food for a spread; this with a cup of milk to each child. We also give them some cooked rolled oats and bulgar, a wheat product served with milk. For the family rations, they receive according to the size of their families. Milk, bulgar, corn meal, when we have it, rice when we have it, and rolled oats are given out. Meat is very scarce. What little we get we try to save for the undernourished children. Services are held each morning before we begin giving out food."

But in spite of superhuman efforts made, it was frequently not enough. "Friday, May 13, returning from getting our truck out of the river, [where it had broken through a pole bridge] a man was lying in the center of the road about 50 miles from here. We tried to make him talk but of no use. We gave him some bread, but he would not eat. We lifted him in our Land Rover, covered him with a blanket, and brought him into the hospital here at Kikwit. The next morning the doctor called and said the man died. This is like many others coming out of hiding." (31)

the fear of getting used to it

From sunup to sundown, day in and day out, they were surrounded by the sights, sounds, odors, facial expressions and pathetic gestures of hungry and often hopeless people. For the relief workers, black and white, there was a constant, personal, emotional struggle to walk the fine line between compassion which, on the one hand frequently brought them to tears, and cool professionalism which, on the other hand, enabled them to continue to move and function efficiently amidst unrelenting and endless need. The reports of the CPRA Kwilu team so clearly reflect this struggle: "A family of seven fled out the forest from the rebels. Three of the five children died of hunger and exposure. The daughter, age twelve, came to the large hospital here in Kikwit very ill and her body covered with sores. The father came to the missionaries and asked them to pray much for his daughter who meant so much to him. One day she asked that her father would come to see her. This is what she told him: 'Look at me well and for a long time for I will soon leave you.' Shortly after this her suffering was over and she went to be with Jesus whom she learned to love and trust.' Like Rev. McVeigh said during his recent visit to the Kwilu. 'What if that were my child?' Many of us said the same thing. Yes, there is danger of becoming used to it. May the following be a prayer for each of us as we continue laboring together: 'Give me a heart sympathetic and tender, Jesus like thine, Jesus like thine; touched by the needs that are surging around me, And filled with compassion divine.' Anon." (32)

helping them to help themselves

The CPRA experience in the South Kasai had taught Graber that the shortest route to rehabilitating the uprooted, starving population of the Kwilu was to enable them to help themselves, and this as soon as possible. Thus it was that, by September, monthly reporting was carrying paragraphs such as these: "The final details were all finally attended to and we were lined up to leave for our second plowing project. It was quite a sight! The camper built on a 5 ton Deutz truck all equipped for camping near the field projects plus a ton of seed corn and rice seed for planting. The new Ford tractor followed the camper, then the new 7 ton Deutz loaded with food, clothing and chicks for distribution among the refugees. Bringing up the rear was a small Red Cross Jeep loaned to us for use in the work here. Quite an impressive CPRA convoy." (33)

plow repair via parachute

Scarcely a week into their plowing project, a critical part on their equipment broke. We pick up the story from the report: "Just as they were removing the broken part and wondering to themselves how they would ever get it repaired, a car drove up. The boys [PAX volunteers Mark Weaver and Elmer Beachy] confessed that at that moment to have a car drive up to them and someone get out who spoke American English to them was almost more than they could fathom. An American doctor and three other men associated with the Army had come to one of the nearby towns by plane. They had been driving through the area to visit refugee camps. They were so interested in our project that they offered to take the broken part to the capital city that afternoon and return it by parachute drop on Thursday. [48 hours later] Mark said, 'Talk about answer to prayer. This is one!' Before they call I will answer . . . ." (34)

the struggle for protein

Having proven the feasibility of air freighting chicks from North America during their years in the Kasai, this method was again utilized. Over time a total of 20.000 chicks were air lifted to the Kikwit air field and scattered through the refugee communities as "seed" to re-start their own flocks again. But while this was a comparatively quick method of producing at least limited sources of protein among the people, Graber was seeking other means that might provide a more ample and longer term supply. In November, 1966, a CPRA report carries the following observation: "We have been able to purchase 15 head of cattle and are trying to interest people in cattle raising. These are divided into three herds of five each, one bull and four heifers. The Kwilu with its thousands of acres of pasture land makes the project possible. We hope that the interest of the church leaders and Christians of the province will make it one of the most profitable of the rehabilitation efforts. It could supply meat for food, help the economy of the country, help support underpaid pastors and many other church needs." (35) In the course of CPRA's sponsorship of this project in the Kwilu, an additional 200 head of cattle were provided - - primarily through MCC funding. (36)

CIM/EMC calls again

In the midst of the pressure of his work load among the refugees of the Kwilu, Graber found time to help the EMC people of Kikwit to secure a parcel of ground on the plateau overlooking the river. It was along the main road between the city and the air field and was ideally located for the construction of a church. A building fund drive conducted by the EMC refugee congregation plus help from the CIM resulted in the construction of EMC's first permanent chapel in that city. It was a particular source of satisfaction for Grabers that they were able to bring their two years of service in the Kwilu to a close with the dedication of this new place of worship. In his last report as project director he wrote: "Meetings and more meetings, finishing business and packing. Thank you for your prayers and support during the past two difficult years. We have seen much hunger, suffering, sorrow and death but by God's grace, His love and mercy, the conditions have improved much. . . . We leave for Tshikapa where we expect to be engaged in evangelistic work and visiting churches." (37) (38)

Based at Tshikapa, the Grabers divided their time during the following six months between village itineration and a variety of building/repair projects which included a new dispensary at Kandala, a new chapel in Luluabourg and a variety of maintenance projects at Kalonda and Tshikapa.

By summer of 1968, they once again packed their bags. CIM needed to provide more adequate hostel facilities for its missionary children attending the American School in Leopoldville. CIM missionary house parents Harold and Joyce Ediger Harms were doing a heroic job in make-shift, crowded quarters to make a home away from home for a growing group of children but the time had come to expand the facilities. Grabers accepted the challenge and arrived in late May 1968 to take this project in hand. They were joined by VS workers Arlo and Leontine Raid of Denmark, IA. (39) The progress of the project and the functional outlay of the building soon became the talk of the expatriate church community of the capital. Before leaving the city, Graber was drafted to oversee the carpentry phase of a large building project to house a newly-created inter-mission theology school just a few minutes' drive away from the CIM hostel grounds. Setting up a production line system with crews of African carpenters, he soon was turning out a steady flow of windows, doors and roof trusses for a project that had fallen far behind its original construction schedule.

By this time, in his late 60's, Graber thought each new assignment would surely be his last. There would, however, be one more.

CHAPTER 15   A NEW POLITICAL FORCE

a resented victor

Moise Tshombe had followed instructions laid down by President Kasavubu when he was installed as Congo's Prime Minister in July 1964. He had crushed both the *Simba* and the *Jeunesse* rebellions. He had done so the only way he knew how - - by seeking the help of white-skinned mercenaries and by incorporating some of his former Katangese troops into the National Army. While he had publicly protested against and condemned the paratroop drop on Stanleyville in November 1964, many of his fellow Congolese remembered that earlier he had not hesitated to seek such outside help during his days as head of the break-away Shaba Province.

Such were the dynamics of the African political scene late in 1965 that just when Prime Minister Tshombe hoped to turn from his victory to a growing role of leadership on the Congo national scene, he found that decisions he had made during the first weeks of his regime contained in them the seeds of his political demise.

A missionary letter of the time carried the following observation: "The attitudes of many of the African leaders toward Tshombe show clearly that the single most powerful dynamic at work in political and racial relations is that of violent and even hysterical reaction to the specter of colonialism, white domination and exploitation by 'imperialist countries.' So deep is this resentment and so alive this fear that everything else is subordinated to it. Because Tshombe has stooped to the sacrilege of employing white mercenaries to shoot down Africans, he is deeply resented and hated and all other issues become secondary." (1)

Fully aware of the violent opinions swirling about his Prime Minister both on the national and broader African scene, President Kasavubu attempted to dismiss him from his post in April 1965, shortly before new elections were to be held for the national senate and house of representatives. There followed weeks of maneuvering in high places. Though Tshombe managed to block the President for several weeks, Kasavubu eventually succeeded in installing a new Prime Minister of his choice named Evariste Kimba. Ousted as Prime Minister, Tshombe promptly announced that he would run for president in the upcoming national elections. It was recognized by many that this was no idle threat. Tshombe had a considerable power base within the Congo because of the military units scattered through the army and across the country who were loyal to him.

It was early the morning of November 25, 1965, at the occasion of the first news cast of the day, that the Congolese and the country's international community heard the startling news: "Joseph Kasavubu and Evariste Kimba have been dismissed from their positions as President and Prime Minister. Lt. General Joseph Désiré Mobutu is assuming the constitutional prerogatives of head of state." The Congo had come to a major turning point in its history. Africa and the world would become increasingly aware of this man with passing time.

"for love of country"

Under the guise of a regular meeting with the high command of the army, Lt. General Mobutu had invited the 13 regional commanders of the National Army to meet him at his home the evening of November 24. In the course of the night it was agreed that while the military situation in the country was satisfactory, there was complete failure in the political domain. While thousands of refugees were in desperate need in the aftermath of two rebellions, the principal politicians showed no concern about them. Instead, they were engaged in a sterile political battle between themselves for the control of the government. If this situation was allowed to continue, it was concluded, it was very possible that more blood would flow as a result. The Congolese Army had never sought to impose a military regime upon the country and did not propose to do so now. However, given the crisis, a number of decisions were made to be put immediately into effect. Among them were: - the removal of Joseph Kasavubu as President of the Republic; - the dismissal of Evariste Kimba as Prime Minister; - the installation of Lt. General Joseph Désiré Mobutu as Chief of State; - the maintenance of the constitution of August 1, 1964; - the continued membership in the United Nations and the Organization of African Unity; - the respect of all existing agreements with States friendly to the Congo; - the pursuit of peace and understanding with all other African states; - the rejection of all exterior meddling into the internal affairs of the Congo; - the freedom of the press; and - the liberation of political prisoners not having been involved in recent rebel movements within the country.

Appealing for the support and cooperation of all Congolese and the normal functioning of all commercial enterprises and government offices, Mobutu then made his first appointments as Head of State: - Colonel Leonard Mulamba, the hero of the Bukavu battle with the *Simba* forces only a few months earlier, as Prime Minister; and - General Major Louis Bobozo as the Commander in Chief of the Congolese National Army. (2)

There followed in swift succession a series of events which would eventually culminate in the new president's firm political control over the entire country. On December 12, he convened his first mass meeting. The "20th of May Stadium" was packed with people. Themes of his speech included: - condemnation of a political system which had brought the Congo to the edge of an abyss; - denouncement of a public administration which was corrupt and inefficient at all levels; - criticism of a judicial system which handled cases in a deplorable fashion; and - the observation that the social, economic and financial situation of the country was in a catastrophic condition and that the export of agricultural products was in rapid decline. Observing that politicians had destroyed the country in five years, he proposed, with the help of the Congolese people, to rebuild it again in the next five years.

Early on, as the elected Parliament realized that Mobutu was asserting himself in an unusually forceful manner, there were some rumbles of reaction and resistance. Knowing that he needed their support as well as the support of the tribal groups they represented, he moved diplomatically. Refraining from flexing military muscle, he rather appealed to popular support via the news media. He furthermore went to great lengths to court the support of traditional chiefs. On a rising wave of popularity, he turned to the Parliament and obliged it to share legislative power with him as the Head of State. This meant that he would in the future be able to issue governmental decrees as formulated by the small select group he established around himself. Using the national radio as an immense public address system, Mobutu began to impose himself and his decisions upon a Congo that was literally on the brink of disintegration. Slowly he began to bring his country back from the edge.

a fishing village named N'Sele (pr. NSEH-lay)

By far the most significant initiative on the part of Mobutu in the early years of his rule was that of convening the leaders of all of the political parties of the country for a meeting that was to have historic significance for decades to come. The spot chosen for the gathering was not Leopoldville, the capital, but rather a fishing village on a large bay of the Congo River roughly fifty miles southwest of the capital. If those invited were puzzled as to why a meeting of this nature should be called in such an isolated and unpretentious corner of the country, the organizers soon gave clear answers. The new regime intended to renew its roots in Congolese soil and culture. It was determined to reunite the urban intellectuals and the mass of village folk which at that point comprised 80% of the population. The new regime was intent on reorienting Congo's future independently of the Belgian past which was so forcefully symbolized by the city of Leopoldville.

It was on May 20, 1967, that the assembled political leaders were invited to listen to the reading of a prepared document which came to be known as the *Manifeste de la N'Sele*, i.e., "The N'Sele Manifesto." As it was slowly and deliberately read, it gradually dawned on those gathered that a new, single political party was being founded. It was to be known as *Le Mouvement Populaire de la Révolution*, or simply the MPR. And what was more to the point, they all were invited to become part of this new national movement. The message was clear: there would be no further political activity or identity tolerated apart from this new party. As a matter of fact, every citizen of the Congo would now automatically become a member of this new party. It was to be a new revolutionary nationalism in which even the simplest and most isolated villager was to have an important role. It would touch every area of national life and demand the total loyalty and cooperation of every Congolese.

As the reading of the manifesto progressed, the assembled participants heard reference made to the emancipation of Congo's women, the organization of Congo's youth, the honoring of Congo's cultural and artistic traditions, the restructuring of Congo's educational system, and the organization of compulsory public service. It was announced that the different provincial police would be reorganized and all brought under a centralized national administration. Representatives of different labor unions were "invited" to unite as a single union which would come to be known as the National Union of Congolese Workmen, or the UNTC.

As for international affairs, Congo would remain a supportive and active member of the UN and of the Organization of African States. As to its political orientation, it would follow neither the Chinese, nor the Russians nor the Cubans. Its revolution would be pragmatic and, above all, Congolese in inspiration and objectives. To underscore the fact that in the new Congo everyone was to go to work, it was observed, during the sessions, that Mobutu's wife sat with other wives, on a little stool under a palm tree, helping to prepare food for the daily meals.

The N'Sele gathering was brought to a close by inviting all those present to approve the manifesto and to approve the newly-founded political party as the seat and source of all authority in the country. Members of Parliament would henceforth be known as *commissaires du peuple* (i.e., "commissars of the people") and would work for the best interests of the entire country and not for personal or regional interests alone. It was further agreed to hold a national congress five years later at the same spot to take an inventory of progress made. After five years of stabilization, the priorities of the next five years of the Congolese revolution would be further determined. (3)

implications of the N'Sele Manifesto

There can be no doubt that among those attending the first N'Sele gathering in May 1967 there was a wide range of impressions. Some were undoubtedly slightly bewildered, others bemused while many were excited and enthusiastic. Few had any idea of the long-range impact of the principles laid down and the directions pointed. One thing, however, was clear to all: the helm of Congolese government had fallen to the hands of a visionary and charismatic man. Wholesome, reasonable principles and goals had been adopted. Curiously, it seemed that many of the ideals for which Patrice Lumumba had so fiercely and ineffectively fought less than six years previously were now being adopted and championed by the man who had toppled him from power.

The Mennonites of the West Kasai did not have long to wait to experience a major benefit from the N'Sele meeting. When Mobutu came to power, there were already twenty-one different provinces recognized with a number of other tribal groups clamoring for the authorization to form still others. Seeing this as just another evidence of a splintering country, Mobutu and those around him decreed that these mini-provinces would all be canceled and rolled back into eight major provinces. It was with applause that much of the population of the West Kasai heard the news that the chaotic *Unité Kasaïenne* was to be dissolved and that the provincial seat of government for their area would once again revert to Luluabourg.

There was a sense of excitement and expectation in the Congo air in 1967. The sweep, promise and even nobility of the goals set at N'Sele would make the later history of Congo all the more tragic.

CHAPTER 16   A SECOND MENNONITE CHURCH EMERGES

arrival at stage three

Pastor Kazadi was not a person who long remained unnoticed, whether at Djoko Punda in the West Kasai or at Bakwanga in the South Kasai. An able student of the Bible, a skilled preacher and a natural leader, people began to gravitate toward him soon after his arrival in mid-1961. Knowing his pastoral skills, people soon found their way to his door amidst the trauma of their early refugee days. In addition to Mennonites, uprooted Presbyterian and Methodist believers also were attracted to his preaching as were people of no faith. All alike hungered for some word of comfort and assurance in those days of menace and suffering. Renting a partly-finished structure originally intended to serve as a tavern, Kazadi began ministry to a mixed congregation soon after his arrival.

When in 1963, the owner decided he now wanted to pursue his original project further, the growing congregation brought their accumulated offerings to Archie Graber asking for his help. It was decided to first construct a building which could later serve as a school. When they had sufficient funds they would then construct a chapel.

Mennonite refugees, while supporting this emerging congregation led by Pastor Kazadi, were pondering their own future in the area. A delegation eventually sat with him, raising the issue of their Mennonite identity and their future in this region to which they had fled. Pastor Kazadi promptly promised them that if they would raise funds to build their own place of worship, he would be their pastor. It was not long that both a site and enough funds to start construction were in hand. They christened their hill top terrain *Diulu* (i.e., "heaven" in the Tshiluba language). With the help of CPRA workmen, they also put up a school building as an initial place of worship and Pastor Kazadi began leadership of the first Mennonite congregation in the South Kasai.

In his characteristic energetic style, he began contacting fellow Mennonite refugee church leaders throughout the region (1) and sent them out "to survey the area and compile a complete list of names and locations of Christians who had emigrated from the CIM field. Believers planted in new villages, established by Graber's refugee relocation program, began gathering people for regular worship. Soon new churches were cropping up like fresh, green sprouts from a burnt-off grassland. Kazadi subdivided the area and assigned each refugee pastor a parish of village churches." (2)

An observer of that pioneering effort, Graber wrote of an experience in which he shared: "It was on January 19, 1964, when a carload of our CIM church leaders and I left early to travel over 40 miles of very bad road. We parked the car and walked the balance of the way for one and a half hours, high grass switching us on the faces as we walked up and down hills, crossed a hanging bridge which was made from forest vines and sticks. As we were nearing the large village at the foot of the famous Dilunda Hill, where people ran for their lives and suffered so much but a few months ago, we heard singing in the distance. Many people returning from a nearby river where 104 precious souls redeemed by the blood of the Lamb were baptized. Two of the songs they were singing, as they marched slowly toward the thatch covered chapel, were 'There is Power in the Blood' and 'Glory to his Name.'. . . It was encouraging to hear testimonies. Some told how the Lord spared their lives and others were thankful for the food they received from CPRA. Pastor Kazadi said: 'What we see here today rejoices our hearts. We have reached the third stage in our development. The first stage was before we could read or write. The second stage was being taught to read and write and do various things by the missionaries. We depended upon the missionaries to help us. Now here we have reached the third stage [which] is to do things by ourselves such as we see here today.'" (3)

we are Mennonites

Fully aware that the CPRA emergency relief program would soon come to an end and that the expatriate team would be withdrawn, the South Kasai Mennonite leaders began to press the Grabers about their status and their future plans. Cut off from their Tshikapa brothers and sisters by both distance and political turmoil, what was to be their status? To whom could they turn for help? Could he not simply stay and work with them there even as they had for so many years when they had all been together at Djoko Punda? Through all of the questions and discussions there came a clear message: "We were Mennonites before we were uprooted and forced to come here as refugees. It is impossible for us to even consider joining any other church. We are who we are. There were no Mennonite Churches when we arrived here but there are now because we are here. Had CIM forgotten them now that they were no longer in the West Kasai near the CIM stations?"

Wanting to be sure that the CIM Board heard their concerns, Pastor Kazadi sent a personal letter to Elkhart, IN. Written the summer of 1963, it read: "Dear Rev. Sprunger and Board members: Greetings to you in Christ's name. We are your children of the Congo Inland Mission. We have come from various parts of Congo and gathered in South Kasai. We are writing you this letter about two important things. First, we want to thank you that in all things that have happened to us since we received our independence you have prayed for us and you have accepted that missionaries stay with us during this difficult time. This showed us how much you loved us. You know that confusion caught the whole of Congo after Independence and was especially bad in the [West] Kasai Province, [but] surpassing in the South Kasai. Thus all of us Congo Inland Mission people coming from other parts of Congo, when we arrived in South Kasai we found Muambi Lutonga [Archie Graber] who had been sent by CPRA to help the refugees coming from the different areas. And all the things which you have gathered together in your country with which to help the refugees surpassed to make them happy. This work which Rev. Graber was doing became our deliverance."

"The second thing . . . all of us, your brothers in the Church of CIM who live in South Kasai, we counted to see how many there were of us. We saw that we were such a large number we could not join another church. Thus in our prayers and in our services we have decided that we want to have a Congo Inland Mission Church in this area of our forefathers. . . . Thus we beg you, we ask you with humble hearts to accept that Rev. Archie Graber stay with us in South Kasai. . . . Because of your love toward us, we know that you will accept for him to stay with us. II Cor 13:14. All of our group send greetings with hope of a good answer to our request. God bless you. In the name of the committee of the Mennonite Church of Congo in South Kasai. Pastor Matthew Kazadi." (4)

a prickly question of comity

In the meantime, Graber had not been silent about the struggles and hopes of the Mennonite Christians who surrounded him. His concern for them surfaced regularly in his correspondence with the CIM office in Elkhart. But his reporting also clearly reflected his awareness of the long history of presence and work of the Southern Presbyterian Mission throughout the area. Via the good services of the Congo Protestant Council decades earlier, an inter-Protestant agreement had been established regarding boundary lines between Mission and Mission across the land including those between Presbyterians and Mennonites in the West Kasai. Suddenly, the comity lines so carefully drawn in an earlier day were thoroughly scrambled. What now?

It is readily understandable that, particularly at the outset, there was a certain wariness all around as Presbyterian and Mennonite pastors began encountering each other. Sensitive to what was transpiring around him, Graber wrote: "As far as we are personally concerned, we feel that it was definitely God's leading that we could be here in the name of CPRA to give help and encouragement to the CIM Christians. . . . However in the growth and administration of the church, we have purposely tried to stay in the background. We have been able to help them in other ways, but in finances and also in the field of administration - - we just have not. All of the growth and advance have been made because they themselves have felt the need. Always we have encouraged them but on the other hand advised them to be courteous and fair especially in their relations with the Presbyterians. . . . We are happy that up to this time the two groups have been able to work together in reasonable harmony and a good spirit of cooperation. . . . I'm sure it will take time and tact on the part of the Church and the Mission to work things out, but I'm also positive that the EMC is in the South Kasai to stay, even though we have had CPC comity [agreements]. . . ." (5)

But for Pastor Kazadi and his fellow Mennonite refugees, questions of Mission comity were of little concern. Such boundaries, after all, had been the invention of the missionaries. While such agreements may have served some useful purpose in an earlier time, they felt them in no way relevant to the situation in which they now found themselves. This, however, did not mean that he was indifferent to the African Presbyterian Church all about him. He sought opportunity to attend several Presbyterian meetings and, as the occasion came, to raise the issue of the new Mennonite presence and identity among them. Detecting, at first, considerable reservation, he did not insist on an early agreement but patiently presented his case. On one occasion he said: "From my childhood all the way to my present old age, I've been taught by the Mennonites. I've matured and ripened in their beliefs and traditions. If I go into a new church now, I'll return to my infancy to learn all over again its different way of doing things. Accept for us to be among you and to do our work by ourselves." (6)

Although it required a few more such meetings, eventually agreement came. With the acceptance of their Presbyterian fellow Christians, they were free to pursue their own dream of planting a Mennonite Church in the South Kasai.

still other problems

If questions of former mission boundary agreements were soon resolved, there were other problems confronting the South Kasai Mennonites which would prove to be much more difficult. One had to do with their ongoing ties with the EMC of the West Kasai from where they had been forced to flee. What would now be their relations with their mother church? On this the EMC leaders at Tshikapa were clear. They often expressed their sorrow for the events which had taken place and the suffering experienced by their fellow Baluba believers. But now that they were there and putting down roots, they were invited - - indeed expected - - to simply organize themselves as a new district of the EMC and thus become an extension of their mother church in their new location. This would mean remaining under EMC jurisdiction and administration even though separated from Tshikapa by many miles of barely passable bush roads and the disruptive political turmoil of the time.

Although the Mennonite refugees carried deep emotional ties with the EMC of the West Kasai, Pastor Kazadi had misgivings about the workability of accepting district status under the distant Tshikapa offices. They had already learned that for the nitty-gritty of daily life, they had to work out their own problems and solutions with the local government.

A second question had to do with the refugee's relationship with the CIM. They early and constantly declared their loyalty to the Mennonite faith and their desire to establish direct ties with the Mission and missionaries with whom they had worked in the past. CIM Board and staff people, for their part, found themselves struggling with a dilemma. While there was great sympathy and concern for the Mennonite refugees, there was still, in the mid-1960's, much concern about the "good neighbor policy" which had characterized Mennonite and Presbyterian interaction from the very beginning of CIM presence in that part of the Congo. The Board did not want to give the impression of a unilateral dismantling of years of cordial co-existence by directly sponsoring a new Mennonite presence in the heart of "Presbyterian country."

But there was an even more troublesome dimension to the picture, that being the repeated, firm cautions voiced by the Tshikapa EMC leadership warning CIM not to open direct ties with the South Kasai refugee group. They reminded the CIM that the EMC was a large church with believers scattered over an extended area. The EMC counted believers from among half a dozen major tribal groups, each in their own traditional region, some of which also were located long distances from Tshikapa. Were CIM to open direct administrative ties with the Baluba refugees of the South Kasai, would this not be sending a message to other groups who might also at some time like to by-pass their own church offices and open direct ties with CIM's American office? This argument fell on sympathetic CIM ears. Their was great hope within the Board that the EMC could survive this era of violent political upheaval and remain a single, united Mennonite body.

Consequently the CIM encouraged Pastor Kazadi and the Bakwanga group to maintain its identity as an extension of the EMC while working out their local ecumenical relations on a church to church basis. It was thought that this, then, could leave the CIM free for indirect supportive roles via the Tshikapa church administration.

Yet a third major issue confronted the South Kasai Mennonites and this one would prove to be the most difficult of all: the deeply rooted clan and political division which split the entire South Kasai Baluba population into Kalonji and Ngalula factions. From the beginning, their Mennonite identity and common refugee experience had held them together despite the angry factions which swirled around them. In his early travel, encouragement and planning, Pastor Kazadi's interest was to preserve their inter-clan unity in the South Kasai just as they had back at Djoko Punda and Tshikapa. But even as they were attempting to sort out their relations with the CIM, with the EMC and with each other across the barrier of local political cleavage, events were in the making which would overtake them and exert a powerful negative impact upon the shape of things to come.

we must educate our children

Determined to preserve their identity, the Mennonite refugee community knew that it wasn't enough just to plant their own churches. They also had to have their own schools where they could gather their children and influence and instruct them in the ways and beliefs of their parents. Well acquainted with the church-administered school system they had left in the West Kasai, they sought now to establish their own in their new location. But there was an immediate, crucial problem - - their lack of legal identity as a church in their province. While the local provincial government was sympathetic toward them and their desires, they could not authorize local monies or recommend funds from central government for a group without legal status. Even if they were to seek recognition as a new district of the EMC, this would take time since government subsidy for the EMC schools was designated for the West Kasai and Kwilu Provinces only. To wait for solutions which might or might not one day take shape, the South Kasai Mennonites had neither the time nor the patience. They had children, hundreds of them, whom they wanted to put in school immediately.

There followed a series of emergency negotiations with the local provincial government and with the Presbyterian Church leaders. The first step was to open two Mennonite primary schools, one at Bakwanga and the other at Kabeya Kamuanga. Some government funds were promised to help with the cost of teacher pay and some school supplies. The channel for forwarding the funds would be the local Presbyterian Church. For Pastor Kazadi, this was at best a stop-gap measure. As long as this arrangement continued, the new schools, though in their hands, would still technically remain Presbyterian. A way had to be found to have their own.

Unfortunately for the future unity of the Baluba Mennonite community, already at this stage the Ngalula/Kalonji clan conflict was exerting poisonous pressure. Pastor Kazadi and the Bakwanga Mennonites were primarily of the Ngalula wing. With Prime Minister Ngalula being of their group, they found it convenient and efficient to seek to speak for the entire Mennonite group even though they themselves were based in Bakwanga and directly represented refugees of the Ngalula clan. Meanwhile the refugee community at Kabeya Kamuanga, composed largely of Kalonji clan members, felt they should be represented in any consultations with government as well. When their requests for such representation went largely unheeded, frictions quickly set in. It was amidst this simmering discontent that the last round of political fighting exploded in the Kabeya Kamuanga area. When Kalonji dissidents attacked and destroyed a series of villages of Ngalula loyalists, government forces retaliated. The Kabeya Kamuanga Mennonites were caught in the cross-fire and experienced, yet once again, near total destruction of their material goods. In all of the upheaval, not only was their school closed but they were also cut off from any further government school funds.

When in mid-1964 the inter-clan fighting was finally stopped, a new provincial prime minister was named who happened to be a son-in-law of Pastor Kazadi. Sensing that the time was favorable for the Mennonites to seek their own legal status as a church, Pastor Kazadi and those around him made the decision to apply to the central government for their own legal charter. Their name? "The Association of Evangelical

Mennonites of the South Kasai" which resulted in the French acronym AEMSK. The church's president was Pastor Kazadi; its legal representative was a fellow clansman, Ntumba Kalala (pr. NTUH-mbah kah-LAH-lah). It was on July 29, 1966, that a charter granting legal status to the Bakwanga Mennonites was signed by President Mobutu; this was confirmed two months later in a government publication. This, then, opened the door for the AEMSK to seek and sign its own educational convention with the central government, open its own bank account and function in all respects as an autonomous church in its own right.

bitter repercussions

The official recognition of a second autonomous Mennonite Church precipitated sharp reactions at the EMC offices at Tshikapa where the news was greeted with hostility. Viewed as a deliberate rupture with the mother church and, to some extent, a repudiation of the EMC leadership and fellowship of which he had been such a significant and productive part for so many years, Pastor Kazadi and the new Mennonite Church he headed entered a decade of strained relations and abundant misunderstanding vis-à-vis the EMC.

On the local scene, the Kalonji wing Mennonite community based at Kabeya Kamuanga saw this development as final evidence that they would need to determine their own future independently of the newly-formed church. It must be believed that Pastor Kazadi and those around him did not deliberately seek to exclude their refugee brothers and sisters of the Kalonji clan or to create a new church comprised exclusively of their fellow clan folk. Yet given the trauma of bloody clan confrontations of the early 1960's and the fact that the key leadership of the new church came from one side only, it is at least understandable that the Kabeya Kamuanga cluster of Mennonites were not inclined to make any further effort to find a meaningful place within the AEMSK.

Realizing that no case could be made either with the provincial or central governments for the creation of yet a second church among the Mennonite refugees, they turned to the EMC leaders at Tshikapa for counsel and help. As political stability and more dependable communications were gradually reestablished, it became feasible for them to follow earlier suggestions from Tshikapa and organize themselves as a new district of the EMC. After several rounds of negotiations with government offices, division of school subsidies were worked out between the two groups. A regional EMC structure was put in place and delegates from the EMC region of Kabeya Kamuanga began to attend sessions of the EMC Executive Committee and General Assemblies. Thus, with time, the EMC did gain a presence and identity in the South Kasai.

But for years to come relations between EMC and AEMSK, on one hand, and the two Mennonite refugee communities within the South Kasai on the other, would remain strained and distrustful. CIM and its missionaries could only accept bitter reality and pray that healing would come with passing time.

CHAPTER 17   A SUBDUED MOOD

July, 1964, found the EMC in General Conference sessions at Mutena Station without a complete roster of delegates. Mukedi and Kandala areas were still in rebel hands. Little was yet known at that time about the situation or fate of fellow church leaders from those regions. Though invitations had been sent to their refugee brethren in the South Kasai, no one had accepted to come. While travel arrangements could have been made via air, such was the political tension around them that summer that they feared to leave home for even a few days.

shattered hopes

For the Africans it had now been four years since the jubilant celebration of political independence with all of the euphoric anticipation which surrounded it. There had been the early brash confidence across the land that, with the departure of the white-skinned foreigners, they could at long last assume all of the roles and enjoy all of the material comforts which had previously been inaccessible to them. There had also been the great confidence that once political power fell into the hands of their fellow Africans, the government of their land would be one of understanding, benefit and benevolence for all.

But something had gone tragically wrong. There had indeed been black governments, but it gradually became clear that they either were unconcerned for or unable to do anything about the steadily deteriorating quality of life of most of their fellow citizens. But for the delegates of the EMC gathered at Mutena the summer of 1964 this was not all. To the overall decline of general national welfare there had been added, in the Kwilu and the two Kasais, the brutality and destruction of tribal and rebel conflict. As regarded the EMC itself, the legal charter which had been applied for nearly 2½ years earlier still had not been granted. There was the further sobering realization that not all church departments and services, which had so confidently been taken over after the July 1960 departure of the missionaries, were doing well. There had, furthermore, been time for reflection on some of the principles and patterns to which they had seen missionaries adhere in earlier days, the reasons for which had become clearer with passing time. In brief, it was with a certain emotional and spiritual fatigue that the EMC delegates who were able to attend their conference that year arrived at Mutena.

sore missionary shins

The previous four years had not been easy ones for the missionaries either. Initially surprised by and caught up in the massive evacuation of whites in July 1960, the CIM staff in Congo had by the summer of 1964 again grown to some seventy people. Before leaving North America, they had been carefully warned by the CIM board and office staff that they were returning to a different Congo than the one they had left. The missionaries, of course, felt that they understood this. Now and again they admonished one another to regard the "earthquake" of 1960 as a blessing in disguise. What might well have taken many days to achieve under ordinary circumstances had suddenly happened over night. Returning now, they were to make themselves available for assignments as might be worked out between CIM field staff and EMC leaders. Those early assignments had seemed obvious enough. There were post-primary schools to be reopened, medical services to be reestablished, government-related business galore to be updated. The primary schools and general church activities, however, were now considered to be basically the responsibility of the Africans themselves.

These lines which initially seemed so clearly drawn, however, began to blur and change for both Africans and missionaries. The Africans, for example, soon discovered that it was not the Church but the CIM, with its legal charter and educational convention signed with the State, that was legally recognized by its own government. Consequently CIM personnel gradually were drawn back into the mainstream of day to day school activity, whether desired by missionaries and Africans or not. What made this situation all the more difficult was the fact that although the Mission was legally responsible for the total school system, it could no longer exercise total control. With little knowledge of or concern for the need for long-range planning, enthusiastic school directors in the isolation of their regional centers frequently rushed ahead with the installation of new classes in their schools. When informed by a missionary supervisor that there was neither government authorization for the class nor government funds to pay the teacher, angry letters would not be long in coming. What was now to be done with the students already registered and the teacher already at work? In the heady days of early independence, it is not difficult to see how misunderstanding and resentment quickly began to gravitate around such missionary personnel.

Even touchier issues had to do with questions of discipline and maintenance of standards. African directors, wanting to make as good a showing in their schools as possible, looked for candidate teachers with the strongest credentials and classroom experience. Under the pressure to round out teaching staffs, some directors found it easy to overlook such problems as questionable personal conduct or obvious indifference with regard to the church. And, at times, in the flow of church life itself, missionaries soon realized that some personnel decisions made had more to do with clan loyalty and the pressure of a hostile environment surrounding it than with Scriptural teaching on a given topic. In such circumstances, what was the missionary to do? To register protest or to attempt to initiate change frequently sparked sharp repercussions.

Added to all of this was the further reality of the difficult position in which missionaries frequently found themselves amidst tribal conflict on the one hand, and brewing rebellion on the other. In the super-charged atmosphere of rumor and animosity, missionaries frequently were misunderstood, misquoted and falsely accused. In effect, amidst the turmoil, danger and deep frustration experienced by many Africans in the early 1960's, the missionary shins often served as a convenient target for well directed though largely undeserved swift kicks. It was thus understandable that missionary delegates to the 1964 EMC General Conference arrived with a certain weariness and wariness of spirit. On a variety of occasions in previous years, such gatherings had been the occasion for vehement oratory directed toward Mission policies and personnel. Given the Congo setting and pressures of the summer of 1964, what would their experience be this time?

having put a hand to the plow

Arriving at Mutena, both missionaries and Africans discovered that the adopted Tshiluba theme for the week was: *Ndiba dia Kudima* (a literal translation: "The time to hoe for the planting of seed"). The conference theme text was Luke 9:62: "No man having put his hand to the plow and looking back is fit for the Kingdom of God." Present were 57 delegates from six stations which were comprised of 46 Congolese and 11 missionaries. Present also was Rev. Reuben Short, CIM Executive Secretary, Elmer Neufeld, MCC country director and Peter Falk, staff member from the Theology School at Kajiji. (1)

It did not take long for all to sense that the theme was a particularly appropriate one for that time and setting. Hands, both black and white, had long since been put to "the plow" of CIM/EMC. If due to the buffeting of events the furrows recently cut had become less symmetrical, and the grip of some hands had become uncertain, there was a solid sense that the time had come for all to be reminded of the immense task which still awaited and challenged them all.

Some substantive agenda, reflecting a hard-eyed look by Congolese leaders at their own performance, was processed in different commissions and reported back to delegate sessions for approval. Among the more significant conference actions taken were: - the election of EMC's first general treasurer, Bukungu François, a school director from the Bashilele region of Banga; (2) - the maintenance of Kakesa Samuel as legal representative even though he was at that time still blocked somewhere in rebel territory in the Kwilu; - the reelection of Pastor Ngongo David of Nyanga to another three year term as EMC President; - the decision to begin putting the newly-drafted EMC constitution into effect even as they continued to wait for their own legal charter from the government; - the call for uniform Christian education materials to be drawn up by the EMC educational secretary Tshilembu Nicodème and CIM legal representative V. J. Sprunger; - the decision to enroll a new class of students in the Bible Institute that fall and to establish its first school board; (3) - the affirmation of a principle of matching CIM/EMC funds in a central EMC account for funding projects of church-wide concern; - the appointment of Pastor Kazadi, though absent, to accompany Elmer Neufeld on a fraternal visit to fellow Mennonite Churches in East Africa; - the appointment of school director Lamba Gerard as an EMC delegate to a meeting of the African Mennonite and Brethren in Christ Fellowship planned for January of the following year in Bulawayo, Southern Rhodesia; (now known as Zimbabwe) - the call for the opening of a vocational training school at Djoko Punda as soon as possible under the direction of Wilmer Sprunger; - the decision to fire all teachers who were guilty of "selling grade cards and documents" in their schools; - to drop from service any church overseer who was not diligent in visiting his assigned areas of responsibility; and - the call for a conference for pastors and school directors in January, 1965, for purposes of consultations and mutual strengthening of the Church's ministries of evangelism and Christian education. (4)

an African look inward

The conference came to a close and delegates scattered to their respective places of responsibility. But the imagery of the white and black hands together grasping a plow seemed to have set a certain new tone. While missionaries were invited to scrutinize their roles and contributions within the Church, the Africans also reflected a new readiness to engage in an honest self-assessment of their own. This was soon to be borne out in a variety of different contexts.

In February 1965, as hoped, a conference of pastors, school directors snd several missionaries was convened at Djoko Punda. There was more than a little eagerness to see how this station and church had weathered the tribal fighting of 1960-61. What sort of leadership was now in place? How would the local church go about hosting and feeding a group that would run to some 70 delegates? A missionary letter written following the conference provides some informative glimpses: "For some missionaries it was the first visit since the evacuation of 1960. For the Bakwanga people it was the first visit since the frantic flight from tribal fighting. For the odd delegate, it was the first visit ever. . . . Food was ample, well prepared and on time. While at the Mutena General Conference the previous summer, Pastor Mpanda Jean (pr. MPAH-ndah JOHN) had been the 'floating foreman,' at Djoko it was tall, lean Badibanga Apollo (pr. bah-di-BAH-ngah ah-PAW-loh), the Lulua pastor from the church center across the river. . . . Our conference theme was 'The Church Amidst Trial.' It seemed to fit the mood of the pastors for it was often referred to during our time together. I clearly had the impression that the men came looking for help, for refreshing, for guidance and challenge."

"Archie Graber had the series of Bible studies and at every session there were open Bibles, notebooks and pencils. It was fascinating to watch the group during those hours as they followed the messages. . . . For me the high point came Saturday forenoon at the close of Archie's last message. With the deft touch of a man tuned to spiritual needs and moods, he suggested quietly that perhaps we'd like to spend some time in prayer together. With one reaction the delegate body went to its knees and there followed a time of spontaneous prayer and song - - and thus it went for over 30 minutes without a break. Prayers were short but to the point as pastors and school directors shared alike. Sunday morning Pastor Kabangu Tom, from Kabeya Kamuanga in the South Kasai, brought the message. He chose Mt 5:43-45 for his text and his subject was: 'Love Those Who Hate You.' Big Tom, as he is affectionately referred to by missionaries, is graying on top and some of the spring has gone out of his step. . . . But he found it in his heart to stand in the Djoko pulpit in the area where some of his fellow tribesmen had been killed and where most had been harried away by ill-will in recent years, and urge upon that Sunday morning congregation that it was their duty and privilege to love those that despise them because l) Christ had first done so and 2) in so doing we may show that we are truly God's children." (5)

In early March 1965, the second meeting of the Africa Mennonite and Brethren in Christ Fellowship was convened in Bulawayo, Southern Rhodesia as planned. EMC school director Lamba (pr. LAH-mbah), Gerard from Nyanga area was the official delegate from the EMC. In the course of the several days of fellowship, each delegate was invited to report on the life, activity and experience of the church and country he represented. When it came Lamba's turn, he presented a comprehensive and honest report. Referring to the mix of tribal conflict and rebel movements which had slashed across his land and his Church, he listed some of the painful results, e.g., disrupted communication between stations, destruction of files and records in some places, loss of some of the ablest and best-educated church leaders either through death or flight as refugees, heavy loss of property. He then went on to cite some of the aftermath of these years of conflict, e.g,. deteriorating roads, neglected public services, shortage of basic supplies, declining national productivity, inexperienced people in public office, resurgence of fear of witchcraft, and the weakened faith of some church members as well as leaders.

Turning from a recital of problems Lamba insisted that, in spite of everything, there remained a faithful core of people within the Church who were persevering in their faith and in their work in the name of Christ. In the midst of all of the instability, a high EMC priority was leadership training in two different theological training schools. Amidst hatred, the Church was doing all it possibly could to show an example of Christian fellowship and love.

He then concluded by saying: "The Mennonite Church of Congo still has great need of missionaries at each of its stations as was the case in the past. Teachers and doctors are being requested all the time. It is our hope that the Mission will dedicate itself completely to the development of the Church in Africa." (6)

And yet another voice was heard in the fall of 1965, this time from EMC layman Tshilembu Nicodème who at the time served both as the assistant legal representative and the inspector of primary education for the EMC. In an article entitled "The Responsibility of Being Free," he shared, in part, the following convictions and admonition: "The Congo becoming independent, her coming to her sovereignty brought many consequences to the country as you all know. . . . Unfortunately, the mission fields also did not escape that situation. During the absence of missionaries, the Congolese groped about here and there until the return of the missionaries to the country. Many efforts and steps were taken and finally the Church obtained her *personnalité civile*" (i.e., legal charter).

"Now what sort of autonomy has the church obtained? Having become autonomous, what must she do? . . . This autonomy, we say, is organizational rather than spiritual. For we all know that as believers we are already freed by the blood of Jesus Christ and this the very day of our repentance. Since the Lord who has redeemed us was and always will be free, his servants (his Church) are likewise free. . . . Jesus Christ guarantees us that liberty and no one can take it from us so long as we continue to serve Him honorably."

"We speak of the responsibility in the ministry of the Word and responsibility in the administrative direction of the Church organization. The situation which now prevails in the world and especially in the Congo gives rise to many imperative needs to preach the Gospel to a population that is disoriented, whether by materialism, by some foreign influence, by false doctrines or traditions or by any other influence. In short, the population is vacillating . . . . The Church has a capital task of evangelizing the people in order that they may know the truth. Jesus Christ alone is truth. . . . However, the acquisition of this autonomy signifies something else for some. No more discipline in the Church, one may conduct oneself as may seem good. Others let it be known that one may revise the doctrinal points which, according to their point of view, were too much enforced by the missionaries. Among these one makes allusion to marriage, divorce, the tithe, and others. For them the Church must adapt herself to the age. . . . This is to say, in a word, that the Church becomes more or less independent. Such is the conception of some on this subject."

"Being fully aware of this, must not the church redouble her efforts and remain vigilant in order to convince such thinkers that the Church is never of human inspiration (missionary, pastor or other) but, on the contrary, the Church is the work of God accomplished by the Holy Spirit? It is at the heart of the Church that the divine will is felt, is manifested and . . . is completed. By this fact, any attempt to substitute human desire or any other human interpretation for the teaching of the Bible must be purely and simply repulsed. . . ."

"Being autonomous or independent implies hard work, well-ordered and conscientious, and this without excluding the moral, material and spiritual support which this young Church needs in order to develop. . . . We need capable persons (whatever their position) who are determined to serve the Lord without any reservation. We need funds and the necessary equipment. . . . We need sometimes the counsel of the mother Church. Finally we need above all the guidance of the Holy Spirit in order to intensify all these activities to the glory of God by his Son. We take into account that in spite of our own efforts, in spite of the good equipment, all will be destined to failure unless first of all we seek the Kingdom and the righteousness of God. (Mt. 6:33)"

"We can all rejoice in autonomy. Some rejoice for the birth of the new organization. Others for being more or less unburdened. But this is not all. One must yet be concerned for the young Church's evolution and especially as to what her future will be. We are thankful particularly to the mother Church for the support which she assures us and will continue to assure us. We are anxious to promise that we will try to work within the framework of the planned program of which she will be kept informed. May she now receive our very profound gratitude. May God bless us all." (7)

a call for missionary response

Given the evident shift in African mood and attitude, a response from the missionary community was clearly needed. This took the form of a letter addressed to all CIM personnel by the field chairman of the missionary team of that time. Having missed several consecutive church conferences due to evacuations and furloughs, the Mutena Conference of 1964 gave him opportunity to reflect on changes he noted and to make some comparisons with conferences of earlier days.

Commentary, in part, ran as follows: "The impact of four years of independence was clearly evident. Though not said in so many words, one can sense in attitudes and tenors of conversation that some bitter lessons have been learned these past years. In national, school and church life, they've had ample opportunity to see the high price that is paid for having inept and unprepared people in places of responsibility and authority."

As the letter to fellow missionaries continued, the field chairman highlighted what he considered to be three major problem areas for the Church at that point. First ". . . the massive conditioning to which the Congolese have been subjected by . . . years of paternalistic colonial rule. [For decades the] Congolese have lived in a social and political framework where, in many contexts, the dark-skinned man received . . . heavily subsidized schooling, medicine and housing. . . from the white-skinned man. This paternalism under which they've lived has deeply conditioned their thinking, their values, their expectations, indeed their view of life, of themselves and of their fellow men. How could they have any other? It is all they have known. . . . We must strive to help them to understand that the world in which they would take their place as a newly independent nation doesn't operate thus."

A second basic problem, as viewed by the field chairman, was that of clan and tribal loyalty. "The Bantu social structure has profoundly deeper roots than we are generally aware of and command surer loyalties than we are prepared for. It would seem that this is an area in which the leavening influence of the Gospel has yet to exercise its fullest redemptive work."

There was also a third area highlighted in the letter: "There is often a confusion in the minds of our Congolese leaders between what comprises the Church and what we as missionaries see as supporting and contributing ministries, i.e., medical services or specialized training programs. Given their experience and orientation, it is not an easy distinction to make. . . . Somehow we must help them to see that the Church is not necessarily booming because there are 50 babies a month born at the station maternity nor are we trying to 'kill the Church' if we cannot grant them the request of some new school somewhere."

Turning then to a review of some of the troublesome issues which confronted the CIM itself at that point, the letter went on to enumerate a list of things such as: " . . . a snarled backlog of administrative, legal and financial questions. These have been compounded by rebellion, loss of records and oft changing missionary personnel between 1960 and 1963. . . . The multitudinous administrative complications inherent in having to work in four different Congo Provinces at once. If that is not our fault, neither is it the fault of our fellow Congolese with whom we work. . . . The irritation of a long delayed legal charter for the Church. . . . The eternal pressure for new schools which we cannot possibly meet. . . . Our reduced medical personnel coupled with the staggering load of medical services to which we have committed ourselves."

The open letter yet addressed a final topic - - that of mission/church, missionary/African, white/black relations. On this issue it was said: "Rightly or wrongly, some of our Congolese feel that with the coming of independence, some missionaries gave up some of their responsibilities grudgingly and have since taken a certain cynical satisfaction in seeing the Congolese stumble and blunder their way along with new and unaccustomed tasks. Especially resented are the times when the Congolese requests help and is told '*Bualu buebe mpindiu*' (i.e., "It's your affair now!") or something similar which to him implies that the missionary is washing his hands both of him and the work for which he is now responsible. . . . When a Congolese who is trying to carry his load comes with an honest and legitimate request for aid or counsel, this aid must be given. Good faith must be met with good faith - - always."

The letter concluded with the acknowledgment that the role of the missionary was not an easy one in the Congo of the early 60's. It was then further observed: "Congolese Christians have now lived through four years of frustration and disillusionment. The majority of things they had hoped for and been promised in the rosy days of 1960 have not materialized. For reasons most of them only partially grasp, high hopes have gone sour; ambitions have been frustrated. It is but human nature to want to lash out in accusation at someone or something and it so happens that the missionary is often the most readily available target. This, probably, is of all irritations and disappointments of contemporary missionary life the most difficult to accept with Christian grace. To be justly accused is one thing. To be falsely maligned is something else. . . . Nonetheless, when slandered, scorned, misquoted or even manhandled, let us always strive to see the experience against the broader context of the Congolese' own suffering and try by the help of our Lord to love, as said Dr. Walter Shelly, (8) 'our often unlovely neighbor.'"

And then, a concluding comment: "At Charlesville in 1960, we voted for total integration of Mission and Church. The events of succeeding months brought us to the conclusion that a progressive transfer of autonomy was a wiser strategy to follow. . . . In the meantime, let us be very sure that our policy of progressive transfer is in actuality made to be a strategy of progress and not an excuse for delay and stagnation." (9)

CHAPTER 18   INTEGRATION: A PERSISTENT THEME

The annual Church Conference held in June 1965, at Kalonda Station was as joyous and upbeat as the one the year before at Mutena had been subdued. The rebel grip on eastern Kwilu Province was shrinking. Enough people had been able to slip past rebel guards and into freed territory that both Mukedi and Kandala regions were able to send a couple of delegates to the conference. Though many of their fellow Christians were still in hiding, it was now clear that for the rebel cause, it was only a matter of time. (1)

at last, a legal charter

A major contribution to the air of festivity was the knowledge that on November 11, 1964, after 2 1/2 years of waiting and uncertainty, the central government had finally authorized and issued a *personnalité civile* for the Church, i.e., an official charter which gave it legal identity and rights as an autonomous organization.

In keeping with a decision made in 1960, its adopted name was *Eglise Mennonite au Congo* - - "The Mennonite Church of the Congo," or EMC in its acronym form. (2)

Overshadowed by the conference theme "The Church in her Independence," expressions of joy and thanksgiving throughout the conference days were numerous and genuine. The reality of their legal status cast a whole new light on the activities of the week. Amidst their pride, discussions and decisions took place which reflected a fresh sense of responsibility for their newly-recognized Church.

busy commissions

Early on, commissions were composed and assigned lengthy agendas with instructions to come to plenary sessions with recommendations. That the different commissions took their assignments seriously is reflected by the following excerpts. The Evangelism Commission recommended that a requirement of formal Bible training, as a pre-requisite for the ordination of pastors, be maintained; - that the pastors of the Tshikapa region divide the area among themselves for ministry rather than all residing together in the same place; - that each district help with the support of their students who were at the Bible Institute; - that church funds be held by lay people and not by pastors; - that school teachers understand that they too carry responsibilities within the Church (they were called upon to do away with the notion that they could misbehave because they were in the pay of the State); and - that women plan for a program of their own at the next annual conference.

, From the Educational Commission came recommendations that school directors organize free seminars for their teachers during the summer vacations; - that a four-person committee arrange for time with the CIM Legal Representative to learn all of the details of the granting and use of government subsidies in the school program; and - that any interested teachers be encouraged to volunteer to work in the South Kasai where our schools are greatly in need of help.

The Administrative Committee brought proposals for the creation of several standing working committees and a slate of appointments for secondary school teachers for the following year. It was further proposed that the airstrips at Kandala and Mukedi be repaired as soon as the local situations would permit; - that Ilunga (pr. i-LUH-ngah) Robert (3) be sent as the EMC delegate to the meeting of the Association of Evangelicals of Africa and Madagascar which was being planned in 1966 in Kenya; and that station councils everywhere conduct audits of all station funds including those of the medical departments.

the EMC Executive Committee once again complete

It was on August 30, 1965 that the glad word flashed across the EMC/CIM area that Kakesa Samuel and his family had escaped rebel territory. They had arrived safely in Kikwit. This happened just in time for Kakesa to attend a meeting of the EMC's Executive Committee. (4) President Ngongo David opened the session in a manner which reflected the African's gift for allowing Scripture to speak to everyday life. Against the background of the Kwilu rebellion and Kakesa's recent escape, committee members listened as he read from John chapter 1 in his Giphende Testament: "At the start the Word was there, that Word was with God, that Word was God truly. He was with Nzambi (the creator God) at the start. All things were created by Him; there is not one thing that was not created by Him. In his breast was life, that life was the light of people of on the earth. . . . That light was a true light which makes things bright for every person who comes on the earth. He was among those of the earth; those of the earth were created by Him but they did not know Him. He came to his very own people but they did not accept or welcome Him. But those who did accept Him and leaned upon his name, He gave to them power to become children of God."

A long day of discussion ranged over a number of church-related concerns. Among actions taken was a school director called to an accounting for supplementary school fees collected from his students; - the call for the reopening of post-primary classes at Mukedi and Kandala; - the placement of Mbualungu Theodore and Mayambi Sosthène recently returned from study in the States and at Banjwadi in the Stanleyville areas; - the approval of a cash contribution to the Kikwit EMC congregation for the purchase of an urban plot of ground for a chapel and school; - a request addressed to missionary Ben Eidse to visit Kandala and Mukedi as soon as possible and to report on his findings; - the proposal that EMC's legal representative, Kakesa Samuel, come with his family to live at Kalonda as soon as arrangements could be made; and - plans to send a delegation to Luluabourg to seek agreement from the Presbyterian Church for the planting of an EMC church in that urban center. Of particular additional note was a minute which read frostily: "That the Legal Representative of the EMC write to the Minister of Justice of the Central Government to inform him that according to our statutes, our Church extends all the way to the South Kasai and that there has never been any division within our church until now; that the Minister forward to us a copy of the proposed statutes of the supposed Mennonite Church of the South Kasai [AEMSK] to help us adopt an eventual stance in this regard." (5) Thus, early on, it became very evident that the EMC would view Pastor Kazadi's initiative to establish a second autonomous Mennonite Church in the Congo with disfavor.

EMC/CIM for how long?

By the fall of 1965, the CIM missionary roster had again reached significant size. Invited and urged by the EMC to again seek to place missionaries at all of the eight major stations, both former missionaries and new recruits were responding to the call. (6) In the very nature of things, the CIM personnel and field officers found it easy to take initiatives and to make decisions regarding the EMC program responsibilities they had been given, with or without consultation with EMC officers. At times it was a bit too easy. After all, the acronym EMC/CIM clearly reflected dual organizations with agendas which, though often overlapping, were rarely identical. If EMC now had its legal status, CIM also still had its own. For a time, missionary initiatives which overstepped the guidelines of EMC/CIM relations as spelled out in a trial draft of an EMC constitution that was under consideration, were allowed to pass without comment.

But a meeting of the CIM Executive Committee held at Kamayala on November 11, 1965 without an observer from the EMC Executive, sparked sharp reaction. The fact that flight logistics and weight limitations imposed by the MAF plane and pilot made it impossible to include a member of the church executive committee made no difference. The proposed EMC constitution, which at the time was under study and tentative application, called for EMC Executive observers at CIM committee meetings. Although a Kamayala church leader had been coopted to sit in as a substitute, that was not how the draft of the constitution read.

In a matter of days a letter of three short paragraphs was addressed to the CIM field chairman by the church's legal representative. A man who had withstood and survived the pressures of Mulele Pierre's bush headquarters did not hesitate to make his concern clear to the missionaries. In a blunt, straight-from-the-shoulder manner he said: "I do not want to engage you missionaries in a long discussion but I want to call your attention to an article of the constitution. You are a member of the CIM executive committee and you are also the one who participated in the work of writing the constitution. . . . The examples we've had of disrespect of the constitution are sufficient for us. We do not beg to meet with you in your missionary conferences and gatherings but I simply point out to you that there are several articles of the constitution which we must strike out."

While on the surface it might appear that this was much ado over an exceedingly minor issue, it was symptomatic of a far larger concern which was carried by the Congolese Church leaders, that being the ultimate shape of EMC/CIM relations. If the uneasy sparring of the early 60's had by now been replaced by a growing and productive missionary/Congolese partnership in many areas of witness and service, still the dialogue on the topic of integration of mission and church which had been opened in 1960 at Djoko Punda had never really been reactivated. True, many adjustments had been made in such matters as composition of committees, commissions and the delegate body at annual conference. It was also true that the CIM was eager to transfer responsibility for all primary school work to the Church now that it had finally secured its own legal charter. But the basic reality of dual entities still remained untouched. There were two organizations, two legal charters, two sets of officers, two executive committees, two treasurers, two budgets, two annual gatherings - - two of everything, and this was not what the Congolese understood the meaning of integration to be.

It was against the background of the contested Kamayala committee meeting that the CIM field chairman addressed a letter to the other three members of the CIM executive who had been there: "I think we should learn something from this - - a lesson in human relations, in diplomacy. The proposed constitution has been in hand for some time now and in theory we are working toward putting it into effective use. In theory also we are working toward eventual integration of church and mission. But we'll have to remind ourselves continually that the burden of proof lies with us. . . . The initiative for the implementation of integration will have to be ours. And the Congolese are watching us all the time for indications that we are serious about this. Our recent meeting at Kamayala was taken, rather, to be an indication to the contrary, i.e., a move away from integration, a move to preserve the status quo, and I think it is on this basis that the energetic reactions can be explained and best understood. It is so very easy to do what's always been done and not take the time to examine ourselves and our activities in the light of our continually changing scene. . . . This should serve as a lesson and if we learn from it what we should, it probably will have been worth the trouble." (7)

a solid African quartet emerges

With the escape of Kakesa Samuel from rebel hands in the Kwilu and his arrival at Kalonda, a capable and stable EMC administrative team was taking shape. To facilitate access to President Ngongo David, he was also brought to Tshikapa where he was assigned a congregation of the area. The balance among the four men was unusually good. Ngongo, as president, brought age and years of pastoral experience to the team. Kakesa, Tshilembu Nicodème and Bukungu François were respectively the EMC Legal Representative, Inspector of primary education and General Treasurer represented the Baphende, Lulua and Bashilele tribal areas. (8)

All four were the products of the CIM's own training programs. Pastor Ngongo, years earlier, had graduated from a three-year Bible program at Nyanga. Kakesa and Tshilembu had graduated from the four-year Teacher Training School at Nyanga. Bukungu had taken a specialized two-year training course. With political stability again returning to the land and with this energetic team of church officers in place, the year 1966 witnessed a surge of church activities.

February of that year saw a gathering of church officers with EMC pastors and school directors who came from all EMC/CIM areas. With Kandala and Mukedi areas fully represented, it was once again possible to think and act in terms of the total church. The theme set before the group was: "Let's Move Ahead". Against the background of recent hostility, division and violence, the conference theme text of Philippians 3:13-14 had striking relevance: "forgetting those things which are behind and reaching for those things which are before I press toward the mark for the prize of the high calling of God in Christ Jesus."

A total of 57 delegates, of whom six were missionaries, produced 46 actions which ranged across the EMC school and church scene. Among the decisions made were several of particular significance: - that a small committee be created within the larger church administrative committee empowered to meet and act on short notice as might be required; - that plans for an EMC fraternal delegation to North America during the year 1967 be made and that the people chosen be our delegates to the Mennonite World Conference to be held in Amsterdam; - that all budget monies allocated to the EMC by the CIM be transmitted to the church via the general treasurer starting with the current budget year; - that an official EMC stamp be designed and produced; - that a committee be named to study how increased donations may be secured for the central administration fund; (9) and - that the religious education material furnished by our Tshikapa office be utilized and followed in all our schools.

As the conference of pastors and directors drew to a close, it was with a new sense of purpose and optimism that the delegates scattered to their home areas. In a new sense, they were functioning and planning as an autonomous church.

Christ For All

Not only in the EMC/CIM community was there a sense of new beginnings. There was a similar stir all across the Congo. Having all come through the trauma of political upheaval and loss of the previous five years, many mission/church communities felt the need for a restatement of purpose and a revitalization of spirit and commitment. Willys Braun, a talented missionary evangelist serving in the lower Congo under the Christian and Missionary Alliance Mission, was possessed of the conviction that the Congo was ripe for a dramatic new effort in basic evangelism. After a series of consultations with fellow pastors and leaders of both mission and church, a new evangelistic thrust was spelled out. Patterned after the well-known model of Evangelism in Depth of the 1960's which had been conceived and used with much success in Central America, it was launched in Congo under the caption *Christ Pour Tous* (i.e., Christ For All).

Andrew Rupp, a missionary of the EMC/US who had served several terms in the Dominican Republic, had had firsthand experience with this approach in his area. When inquiry came from the home CIM office as to whether EMC/CIM would be interested in having Rupp come to the Congo to conduct seminars for missionaries and African leaders alike, response was immediate. This proposal meshed perfectly with the newly proposed effort in the Congo.

First joining the CIM missionaries in their annual retreat in July at Nyanga, he then met with the delegates to the annual EMC conference a week later at Banga. In both places he spelled-out the philosophy and structure of the E/D program as it had been used elsewhere. Combining prayer cells, house to house visitation, publicity and public campaigns, it focused with intensity upon human need on the one hand, and grace, forgiveness and peace found in Christ, on the other. Conference delegates arrived at Banga to discover a program developed around the theme "This is our Task," with an accompanying theme text from I Cor. 15:58: "Therefore my beloved brethren, be ye steadfast, unmovable, always abounding in the work of the Lord, for as much as ye know that your labor is not in vain in the Lord."

Following several sessions in which Rupp spelled-out the format and objectives of E/D program elsewhere, the first item of official conference business was to name a five-person organizing committee to plan and implement a similar campaign for EMC/CIM under the national Congo banner *Christ Pour Tous*. (10) Other conference actions were to elect a new vice-president, Pastor Muadilu Philip; - to discipline and de-frock an EMC pastor who ha taken a second wife; - to invite and welcome a home board delegation interested in coming to the Congo early in 1967; and to name Pastor Ngongo David and Tshilembu Nicodème as the EMC fraternal delegation to the Mennonite World Conference in Amsterdam and to North America.

The new "Christ For All" committee met immediately after the conference to lay plans for the launching of the newly-authorized campaign. Mayambi Sosthène was named full-time coordinator. Memories of his escape with his family from *Simba* territory north of Stanleyville were still fresh in his mind. It was with a mix of personal gratitude and high motivation that he turned to his new appointment. Personable, articulate and enthusiastic by nature, he was well equipped for his new role. The term *Christ Pour Tous* became a byword in EMC/CIM areas for months to come. Travel schedules were established for Mayambi and reports were regularly filed which listed striking figures of people in attendance at meetings, new professions of faith and renewal of commitments to the Lord. The basic thrust of this effort carried over a two year period. It was concluded by an extensive tour of EMC/CIM regions with African personnel from the national "Christ For All" committee with public rallies in the urban centers.

Father of John returns

Supplementary to the new thrust of evangelism was another significant ministry provided by veteran CIM missionary Frank Enns. Having officially retired in the summer of 1960, Frank and Agnes Enns returned to their home community in Inman, KS. When in the fall of 1965 his wife suddenly died following surgery, "Uncle" Frank, as he was affectionately known by a generation of younger missionaries, was a lonely man. Although he had maintained a lively correspondence with the Nyanga Church leaders after his retirement, this was not enough to fill the new void in his life. When in the fall of 1966 it was suggested that he return to the Congo for a pastoral ministry in the villages of Nyanga region, he responded with enthusiasm. So it was that 71 year old *Sh'a Yone* returned to his beloved village people among whom he had lived, moved and worked for so many years. (11) Dusting off a couple of camp boxes and a folding cot, he began a ministry which was to last for three years. Returning periodically to the station for rest and refreshment, he would be taken out in another direction and left with his bush outfit and a bicycle. His emphasis was on organizing cell groups of worshiping believers wherever he found them. Encouraging them to faithfulness in witness in their village settings, he sought to nurture an understanding of their importance in the broader church of which they were a part. So much appreciated was his ministry by Africans that requests soon came from the Mukedi and Kandala regions across the Loange River as well. Enns moved easily across the river and continued his teaching and pastoral ministry among people of the same dialect, village Christians who were struggling in their pilgrimage of faith in the aftermath of the rebellion years. It was in the summer of 1969, at age 74, that *Sh'a Yone* departed the Congo for the last time. His ministry left an indelible imprint upon the EMC of Nyanga district even as his life became part of the legend of CIM in that land.

preparation for the CIM delegation

Already in the summer of 1966, references to the delegation visit planned for the following year were creeping into correspondence with the home office. In June, in a letter from the field chairman, the following was found: "Among the priority items for discussion and decision during such a visit are the following: guidelines for the continuing transition from mission to church; questions of property and maintenance of same; . . . spelling out more specifically the relation of the missionary to the Congo Church. Also the lines of administrative authority both in CIM and EMC might well be reviewed . . . ." (12)

And a couple of months later, the following comments found a place in correspondence relative to the visit anticipated early the following year: "One of the impressions I received from the Banga Conference [the previous month] is the strong groundswell of feeling on the part of the Congolese that it is again time to sit down and discuss this whole matter of mission/church relations and the future patterns of our work with them and among them. This theme came up repeatedly and was stated or implied in many manners. The attitudes were friendly, open and even cordial throughout the conference but there was no mistaking what is on their minds. It is . . . the opportune time to move in this atmosphere of good will and to sit down with them to talk over in the frankest and most open manner all they have on their minds. The key word, of course, is integration. . . . There has been integration on the part of some of the mission/church groups in Congo. While no one has much specific detail or very much of a grasp as to what all this term may mean, still they are sure that they want to be 'ONE.'" (13)

In late September there was still further effort to provide orientation for the planned delegation. "Today's thinking and planning must of course take place against the background of what has preceded. There was the February 1960 conference at Djoko which culminated the visit of the last CIM board delegation to the field. Here the decision was made for integration - - whatever all may have been read into the term at that time - - and some general administrative framework was drawn up. Before we had time to put anything into practice or to spell out any detail, July 1 came along and everything blew up. . . . They [the Congolese] had to take over in our absence and are only to be commended for the way in which they rose to the occasion. . . . But time has passed; Congolese governments have succeeded each other at all levels and generally with the same results. Tribal warfare has taken its toll, rebels have risen to destroy and kill, everyone has felt the pinch of inflation and withal the Mission, its history, its program, its image and what it stands for have all come to be seen in a new light. Once again there is talk about 'integration' but now, as I sense attitudes, there is no longer the flavor of attack and criticism but rather an attitude of honest inquiry, an invitation to discussion."

"There is suspicion and even fear of dual organizations or dual entities, i.e., Mission/Church, projected into an indefinite future. These fears seem to be of three kinds: 1) Some see the maintenance of the Mission and its organization as a propagation of pre-independence Congo - - i.e., power, resources and status wrapped in white skins. There is always the uneasy feeling on the part of some that insisting upon the identity and legal status of the Mission is in reality a camouflage for the maintenance of favored position and retention of power in missionary hands; 2) There are others who see in dual organizations the implication that we as missionaries are not quite ready to accept them as fellow human beings or on an equal basis within the fraternity of the Christian faith and Christian service. They see the Mission as something of a preferential umbrella out from under which we hesitate to step. This creates for many a real problem of identification - - the identification of the missionary with the Church he has had a share in raising up. 3) And there are those who fear the plan of dual organizations" because it might make it too easy to turn over new responsibilities "without the sort of commitment that they know is necessary on the part of the missionary personnel and the Mission resources they will need to carry the load. They react quickly and emphatically to any suggestion that it is OUR Mission and THEIR Church or that something is YOUR problem! They are seeking assurance that as responsibility is turned over, we will continue to stand by and with them, giving them every support, counsel and encouragement we can. But the insistence upon the maintenance of two organizations with its 'ours and yours' implications calls the whole point above into question." (14)

the topic is tackled

The CIM Board approached the pending dialogue with EMC leadership with thoroughness and care. A five-man delegation was chosen: Executive Secretary Reuben Short, and Board members Milo Nussbaum, Allan Wiebe, Maurice Stahly and Elmer Neufeld (who was also chairman of the General Conference Mennonite Commission on Overseas Mission). Blocking out a total of six weeks, they devoted nearly a month to a wide range of contacts with other mission/church groups also at work in the Congo. Before their arrival at Tshikapa for the joint EMC/CIM sessions slated for February 9-14, 1967, they wanted to be sure that they would have a good sense of what was transpiring among the mission/church groups elsewhere in the land as well as within the EMC/CIM family.

Upon arrival at Tshikapa, the delegation found EMC leadership assembled with high anticipation. The moment for what they had come to term as their "integration conference" had arrived. While there were endless details and ramifications of the topic at hand, it soon became evident that the entire issue could be summarized in one simple question: In ongoing mission/church relations, was it still to be CIM/EMC or simply EMC? If at first the full import of this formulation was not completely apparent, it became clear soon enough. As the church leaders began to express their hopes and dreams, it could be seen that they had come to view these double and single terms as symbols of two entirely different relationships. They very much wanted the first; they were very much opposed to the other. As a matter of fact, as discussions proceeded, the delegation became aware that the Africans were really implying that the CIM should cease to exist legally in the Congo.

In the time-honored pattern of African "palavering," there followed during that week alternate joint and divided meetings which gave both delegation members and Africans opportunity to meet separately to compare notes and to take counsel together alone. As board members and missionaries met alone, it soon became apparent that there was no openness to the idea of annulling the legal charter of the CIM in the Congo. This struck everyone as being extremely premature and unwise at that point. CIM, after all, had a wide range of interests and concerns in the Congo which were not the immediate concern of the Church and which they ought not be expected to assume. There was the growing cluster of institutional involvements; there were the post-primary school responsibilities carried by CIM; there were the sprawling medical services which required doctors, supplies and equipment; and there were the mission shares in various inter-mission projects.

Furthermore, what of the freedom to take possible future initiative in the Congo independently of the EMC should need and opportunity arise? No, CIM must still retain its legal identity and a certain freedom to act on its own should it decide it wise or necessary to do so. But it was equally clear that some major adjustments needed to be made in EMC/CIM working relations. For instance, was there any reason why all CIM budget monies destined for the Church should not be channeled directly via the EMC General Treasurer? Was there any reason why all ground, buildings and equipment directly related to the work of the Church should not be turned over to the Church? Was there any reason why the mission program which in any way touched the Church directly should not be officially carried on in the name of the EMC? Was it not time to be very clear that any and all decisions touching on the life of the Church should be made in committees and commissions of the Church? And what about the missionaries? Was there any reason why they should not be absorbed into the Church and continue to work as they had - - but as members of the Church who were allotted assignments within the Church by the Church and not as appointees of the Mission which stood apart from the Church?

As the week moved along, board delegation and EMC leaders began to spell out a framework of ongoing partnership in which the profile of CIM would be sharply lowered, EMC prerogatives clearly defined and missionary roles spelled-out. Recognizing that there were still, at the time, well-founded reasons for resisting the dissolution of CIM as a legally registered organization in the Congo, the EMC leaders did not press the issue further.

As the consultation drew to a close, a concise set of minutes was drafted and jointly issued as the record of what had transpired. Running a total of twenty-one articles, a diagram was appended which attempted to portray the new EMC/CIM relationships and responsibilities which had been agreed upon. Six of the articles summarized the core of the discussions held and agreements reached: " l) That the work of CIM and EMC become a single work and that this be carried on under the name of the EMC; 2) That the missionaries who work in the midst of EMC become members of EMC; 3) That all official correspondence take place between CIM Elkhart and EMC Tshikapa . . .; 14-15) That all educational subsidy funds . . . [and] all financial aid given by CIM Elkhart for the EMC be channeled through the office of the EMC treasurer as of January 1, 1968; and 18) That all the above propositions be applied during a three year period after which they are to again be reviewed by another delegation from CIM Elkhart in collaboration with the EMC Administrative Committee." (15)

The consultation came to a close with an African sense of having come to grips with basic issues which had been drifting for seven years. The delegation returned to North American convinced that some needed shifts had been made. In a written report following their trip, Reuben Short reflected on the new policies adopted: "It is anticipated that it will take time, patience, and longsuffering to enact the program. Local groups will undoubtedly react according to how they are directly affected. . . . Difficult as the adjustment may be for the Congo Church, it may well be difficult for the CIM constituency as well. For many years our concept of MISSION has been to send a missionary to evangelize - - this by direct encounter or through so-called secondary channels of medical, agricultural or educational services. Such were usually supervised directly by the Mission or the missionary. Now supervision is designed to be by the Congo Church. We will be serving as assistants. We will need to understand this role as well as practice it." (16)

It remained in large part for the CIM missionary team, of course, to implement and adjust to the new structures which had been agreed upon. It would be less than candid to suggest that the new shape of things did not stir some apprehension. Recognizing and understanding this, some effort was made by field leadership to orient and encourage the missionaries to enter the new era of EMC/CIM partnership in good faith and with every intent to make it work to the benefit of the Church. An example would be an article which appeared following the integration conference which was circulated both in Congo and in North America which was entitled: "Are We Understanding Each Other?" An introductory paragraph read in part: "The decade of the 1960's has been as dramatic as it has been historic. A colonial era has been brought to an abrupt end as across vast expanses of Africa the role of the white-skinned man has been emphatically and irrevocably changed. Africa, that dormant giant, has in the 1960's begun to break out of the shroud of western imposed ideas, values and control and has begun the monumental effort to assert itself as a land of free peoples with their own claims to dignity and their own reasons for pride within themselves. And in the midst of these changes which are so basic and so revolutionary - - there we stand as missionaries and as a Mission. Whereas we have through the years been mostly talking and the Congolese mostly listening, the Congolese are now also talking. There are now two all-important questions we must ask ourselves: 1) Have we arrived at a point where monologue has truly become dialogue? i.e., are we listening as well as talking? 2) If so, is there truly communication between us? i.e., are we understanding each other?"

After summarizing the contrasting agenda concerns which missionaries and Congolese had brought to the Tshikapa consultation, the article continues by underscoring the great importance of striving as missionaries "to make the transition to our new roles within the Congo Church a gracious one. We have been accustomed in the past to the roles of teachers, preachers, decision makers and disciplinarians. Whether we have played these roles well or not, history moves on. The time is here for us to share these responsibilities if not relinquish them entirely. Let us be ware lest these roles be relinquished suspiciously, reluctantly, grudgingly, apprehensively or even cynically. Should we do so, our attitudes will be unerringly sensed and resented."

The article concludes by observing that "we need to intercede much for them as they assume new and increasingly heavier responsibilities. And they also need to pray for us as we seek to guide them into their new duties. For it is in praying for one another that we arrive at truly loving one another. And it is in loving one another that we most easily arrive at understanding one another." (17)

trainee relationships established

With the framework of agreements reached during the integration consultation in hand, CIM and EMC officers set to work with a will to implement what had been decided. The obvious point of departure was to make it possible for Congolese officers to have access to their missionary counterparts on a day-to-day basis for consultation, training and explanation of the multitudinous details of CIM's wide-ranging involvements and commitments. Questions were invited, files opened, financial accounts and bookkeeping methods explained. It took time - - in some cases, much time - - but progress was steady.

For Kakesa Samuel, the EMC Legal Representative and Tshilembu Nicodème, the Inspector of Primary Education, the missionary resource person was Vernon Sprunger who for years served in both capacities for the Mission. The two Congolese were based at Kalonda, and Sprunger just across the Kasai River at Tshikapa. Access to each other was easy; trips back and forth across the bridge were frequent.

Bukungu François, EMC's first General Treasurer, initially spent much time with Art Janz as a trainee. By the time the integration consultation had taken place, Janz had been replaced by Herman Buller who, in turn, became Bukungu's mentor. There developed between these two men a most remarkable relationship of trust and respect. Bukungu, a totally honest and incorruptible layman, had by this time won the confidence and respect of all - - African and missionary alike. After the integration agreement, Bukungu's office became the conduit for hundreds of thousands of dollars in government educational funds plus the CIM budget monies allocated to the Church. While taking full responsibility for his office and his position, Bukungu openly welcomed Buller's accounting expertise and counsel in the day-to-day conduct of his work. The two made an excellent team. Various audits of the EMC books during Bukungu's tenure always found his accounts in order. This was all the more remarkable given the fact that during his years as EMC treasurer, graft, corruption and dishonesty in the use of public funds and resources were steadily increasing in the society around him.

President Ngongo David found it easy to partner with Jim Bertsche who had been chosen by the Congolese at the integration conference to serve a term as EMC's first Vice President. (1) Both being based in the Tshikapa area made them available for committee work as well as for frequent consultation. In keeping with the integration agreement, official correspondence between the EMC and the CIM began to pass between EMC officers and the Elkhart office co-signed by their missionary counterparts.

church officers under siege

The newly constituted Congolese/missionary church executive committee was no more than in place than a veritable avalanche of requests began to arrive from across the EMC landscape. Above all else, there were pleas for more schools. For Mennonite families in the Kwilu and the two Kasais, the only choices for the education of their children were Mennonite, Catholic or the occasional state school. They, of course, turned first to their own Church for help. In the more isolated areas, the requests were for complete six-year primary schools. In established EMC regional centers, the requests were for at least a two-year orientation course leading to a four-year secondary program. And on the stations where these two-year courses were already offered, impassioned pleas came for additional classes of the upper cycles.

At Nyanga, the transition had by now been made from a four-year teacher training program to a full six-year secondary school with two academic tracks, one in teacher training and the other in biology/chemistry both of which opened the door to university level training for the ablest students. Each fall standardized entrance exams were given at each of the stations and the five or six candidates receiving the best grades at each station were admitted. Under mission direction and with a mix of Congolese and missionary teaching staff, the Nyanga Secondary School had come to be regarded as one of the best of its kind in the country.

For the privileged few students who made it through this stringent sifting process, it was with pride and elation that they journeyed to Nyanga to continue their education. But for the disappointed and frustrated rural families whose children did not meet the standards for enrollment at Nyanga, the obvious solution was to open more schools - - many more. Unfortunately, it was not as simple as that. Under severe financial stress, the central government was hesitant to authorize new schools, particularly in the rural areas. Meanwhile the cost in buildings, equipment and support of qualified African staff involved in opening new schools was far beyond the means of the EMC/CIM.

While there were a few state schools in the urban centers, these too were overcrowded and not nearly able to meet the clamor for enrollment which came from every side. The unfortunate result was that each year there were more and more young people who were unable to continue their education. Under this sort of pressure, it was tempting indeed to yield to the pleas of parents who argued that any sort of school of whatever quality and standard was better than no school at all. As a matter of fact, enterprising Congolese did step into this partial vacuum and opened some "private classes." Charging the desperate parents fees and hiring their own teachers, they always had plenty of candidates for entry. With no supervision either from the Church or the State, such classes had no official recognition. Although their students were allowed to write standard exams at the end of the year, results as a rule were disappointing. Missionaries involved in the EMC/CIM schools came to dread the fall of the year as decisions were made regarding the enrollment of new students. The verandas of their homes were often the scene of poignant encounters as pleading village parents stood with baskets of chickens or rolls of frayed Congo money in their worn, calloused hands and a son or a daughter standing beside them. "Our time for learning is past," they would say, "but this is the time for our children. You just have to find a place for them in your school. If you fail us, what are we to do?"

no more dirty hands?

While the hunger for an education and the ferocious determination to go to school somewhere was perfectly understandable and praiseworthy, there was nonetheless a troubling under-side to this coin. One of the disturbing legacies of the colonial presence and massive primary level education system it fostered was a growing perception on the part of the rural Congolese that to become educated was to become "civilized." Believing that being "educated" was somehow related to clean clothing, clean hands and employment which provided a desk, paper and a ballpoint pen, increasing numbers of young people began to resist routine tasks of village life which seemed menial and beneath their newly acquired dignity. This view of things tended to speed the drift of young people from the rural areas toward the mushrooming urban centers.

This migration early became a topic of concern for missionaries and church leaders alike. It was a troubling trend for several reasons. First of all, it tended to demean rural people and their agricultural way of life. It also contributed to a false sense of self-importance on the part of students and a naive belief that basic literacy entitled a young person to lay claim to being an "intellectual". It further contributed to the tendency of graduates and school dropouts to find their way to relatives in urban centers to pursue their dreams of further education or employment amidst the excitement of city life. Unfortunately, most of them simply contributed to the growing ranks of the unemployed and the financial burden of the clan members with whom they stayed.

The CIM had long been aware of and concerned about this crucial problem. It had from its earliest years believed that the "Good News" of the Gospel of Christ, if correctly interpreted and applied, had something to say to the totality of human experience and need. Already prior to political independence, Arnold and Elaine Waltner Regier had been recruited and placed at Mutena Station with a view to initiating new experimental poultry and agricultural projects. This effort was cut short by the upheaval of political independence. In the early 1960's Melvin and Martha Buhler Claassen had been assigned to oversee the farm and livestock briefly acquired from the *Forminière* Diamond Company at Tshikapa with the hope that it might become a training and supply base for rural Africans of the area. This initiative, too, fell victim to the tumult of the early years of independence.

As political stability returned in the late 1960's, this issue of the well-being of rural Mennonites again surfaced, but this time with the added impetus of African voices which had joined the discussion. What could the Congo Mennonites do to attempt to counter this growing negative trend in their area? It was agreed that whatever was attempted should seek to address three goals: 1) to underscore the dignity and value of rural life and the ongoing provision of food supply for a newly independent country; 2) to introduce new ideas and methods to rural people which would enable them to more adequately feed, clothe and educate their families and to better support their church; 3) to utilize such a demonstration of practical compassion and concern as a means of witness, evangelism and encouragement of church members.

The Mennonite Central Committee, by that time, had a growing contingent of PAX men and VS personnel in the Congo and took keen interest and active part in these discussions. Out of this EMC/CIM/MCC dialogue was born the concept of a model farm where experimentation and pilot projects in both agriculture, poultry and animal husbandry could be undertaken. Nyanga Station soon emerged as a logical location for such an effort. Not only was it centrally located to the entire EMC/CIM area, but there was also a plot of ground adjacent to the station which had years earlier been solicited by missionary Frank Enns from the local chiefs and government authorities for the purpose of school fields for the growing student body of his day. Following independence this plot of ground had fallen into disuse. But if a suitable location for a farm was available, the problem of qualified leadership for the project remained.

It was at this point that Fremont and Sara Janzen Regier entered the picture. Fremont had already been in the Congo as a single PAX man in the mid-50's assigned to a construction project at Mutena Station. Returning home to Whitewater, KS, he married his waiting fiancee who, by that time, had completed her nurses training. In addition to his experience of growing up on a farm, Fremont had added training in animal science and nutrition. Their combined qualifications quickly came to the notice of the CIM and they were approached about the hope for an experimental church sponsored farm in the area of Congo which Fremont knew well. With good memories of his Congo days, the appeal was great. Arriving at Nyanga in the mid-60's, they were shown an expanse of tropical brush adjacent to the station and given a free hand to pursue a shared dream. Bringing with him his African name *Kasonga Mule* (Kah-SAW-ngah MOO-lay) bestowed upon him as a young PAX man at Mutena, (2) his wife was promptly called *Mama Sala*, the African version of "Mother Sara."

With CIM-sponsored missionary personnel and significant MCC program funding, this venture in church-sponsored rural development was to make a major impact upon the Mennonite area of the Congo and beyond. Initially, it was called "Congo Mennonite Agricultural Service" with the acronym COMAS. (In time it was given the French name *Service de Développement Agricole*, i.e., "Agricultural Development Service" with the acronym SEDA.)

Early publicity given to this new venture stated: "COMAS is experimenting with feed and livestock. Seed, breeding stock and knowledge are then made available to prospective farmers. An extension program is planned." The commentary continues: "Agricultural Missions is a crusade against nutritional illness, the employment of idle hands, an aid to better living, a method of averting hunger and a form of Christian witness." (3) The underlying philosophy of COMAS also soon came to the fore: "Our program must be geared to produce producers, rather than to produce products." (4)

Over the years a wide variety of experimental projects were undertaken at this center. In a land where the menace of the tsetse fly had been an effective barrier to the use of horses and cattle as beasts of burden or for traction power, an effort was made to introduce teams of oxen and two-wheeled freight carts. In a land of chronic protein deficiency, there were experiments in cross-breeding native pigs and goats with European stock. In a land where dry season disease constantly wiped out flocks of half-wild village chickens, there was experimentation in the introduction of improved stock plus vaccination services. Experimental flocks of geese and ducks were tried. In the seed plots, new varieties of cassava and beans were planted. Forage crops with high nitrogen-building qualities were sought and tried. A supply depot was opened providing isolated village folk a place to purchase basic items such as nails, hinges, screws, hoes, knives, wire netting and kerosene at reasonable prices.

But central to the program was always a strong emphasis upon extension services. A steady stream of PAX men were assigned for this effort by MCC. (5) Extension routes were established which were covered via bicycles on a scheduled basis. These hot, sweaty, exhausting trips always had three objectives: 1) to mix with the rural African populations in their own setting and at their own level in an attempt to hear and understand what they were saying and feeling; 2) to encourage and facilitate efforts being made, from village to village, to reproduce projects they had witnessed at the Nyanga farm center; and 3) to share personal Christian faith and to encourage village Christians met in the course of their circuits.

In the early years, the COMAS program developed two major thrusts - - poultry and rabbits. Fences, shelters and cages were built largely of materials available to the village people from the surrounding bush. Laying flocks and incubators were established. A hammer mill was installed and large amounts of local produce were purchased from area farmers and converted into starter mash. The pattern was to sell a dozen or so six-week-old vaccinated chicks with a required bag of mash to supplement their initial foraging in the village. Response was massive and continuously outstripped the supply. Sadly, the poultry scheme eventually had to be closed because of the impossibility of securing adequate protein concentrates for the mash.

The single most successful venture was that of raising rabbits. It was demonstrated that they could be bred and cared for in cages made from local materials and could be basically fed with palm branches and greenery from the surrounding bush. At a point there were literally hundreds of rabbits in cages in the villages of the Nyanga region and beyond. Not only could they provide tasty meat for the family cooking pots, they also represented a ready source of cash for the heads of families. But it was also discovered that success, over time, was limited to those who saw in this scheme sufficient value to make the commitment of daily maintenance and care which was necessary for healthy animals.

With the growing popularity and success of the COMAS program at Nyanga there were increasing pleas for similar services from other more distant EMC regions. In an effort to respond, periodic seminars were conducted to which representatives from distant EMC areas were brought for observation and training. In time, both expatriate and African extension personnel was placed at several other stations.

With the coming of the autonomy of the Congo Church, sponsorship of the COMAS program became that of EMC/MCC. The CIM continued to appoint administrative personnel while MCC continued to provide short term workers and a major share of the funding. When, after 12 years of leadership, the Regiers terminated their services, Ngulubi Mazemba (pr. ngoo-LOO-bi mah-ZEH-mbah), his understudy, was installed as the first African director. The son of Mazemba Pierre, a greatly respected local senior pastor, he had worked with Regier for several years and had made a trip to North America with him to be introduced as his successor. A bright, witty young man with some university training in veterinary medicine and a broad knowledge of the Nyanga area, he seemed an ideal choice to become the first Congolese director. Unfortunately, this venture of Africanization of staff at the farm did not work out as hoped. Pressures and expectations of Mazemba's clan members and friends were such that he found it all but impossible to maintain the professional impartiality and detachment vis-à-vis SEDA's resources and inventory so critical for such a role. EMC leadership eventually decided that a change needed to be made and new CIM administrative personnel was installed. This brought Arnold and Grace Hiebner Harder on the scene, a CIM couple who had already for a number of years been associated with COMAS and who at the time were in charge of SEDA activities at Mukedi. (6)

This failed effort of Africanization of administration at the Nyanga center weighed heavily on both missionary and Congolese church leadership. When, with time, similar experiences were registered in some other church departments, a basic question emerged as to the appropriateness, compatibility and long-term value of Western-oriented institutional programs under the umbrella of the Congo Church. While COMAS became a publicized model of church-sponsored community development in the African bush, its continuation under direct African supervision proved to be problematic. This problem, also experienced by other mission/church groups elsewhere, was to generate much debate in Congo mission/church circles during ensuing years.

also a call for saw and hammer

As important as it was for EMC and CIM leaders to seek to affirm and encourage a time-honored agricultural way of life among rural Mennonites, they well knew that there were other skills which could be used in a rural setting and which could be of great help in the community and the Church.

Just prior to independence, the CIM had opened a vocational training school at Mutena with a focus on masonry and carpentry under the direction of Loyd Brown. With the return of the first missionary men, the class was transferred to Nyanga where, under the guidance of Loyal Schmidt, their two-year cycle of study was finished. Their practical work assignment was to help in the completion of a new dormitory for the secondary school. When in the summer of 1961 Schmidt was transferred to Leopldville, the school was suspended. The reopening of a vocational training program was a high priority for the church leaders in the late 60's.

Wilmer Sprunger, son of long-time CIM missionaries Vernon and Lilly Bachman Sprunger, had done his PAX service in the Mutena school and had demonstrated his skill in carpentry and wood working. Returning to the States, he finished his college studies, married Kenlyn Augsburger, a graduate nurse from Berne, IN. Together they applied to the CIM for assignment in the Congo. Serving an initial term at Nyanga where Wilmer taught in the secondary school, they were invited back for a second term, this time to go to Djoko Punda to re-launch a vocational training program for EMC at that location.

By the year 1969 Dr. Ralph and Fern Bartch Ewert had already taken up residence at the same station with Glenn and Ina Rowell Rocke. They were first expatriate personnel to return to that station following the missionary evacuation of a decade earlier. The welcome extended to all returning CIM personnel at Djoko Punda was enthusiastic for the local population was, by this time, very desirous to see this historic mission post reactivated. With the departure of Pastor Kazadi in 1961 and the eventual flight of all other Baluba folk, station leadership had fallen into much less qualified hands and both the station and the church had paid a heavy price. Joined by MCC VS personnel Wilbur and Elizabeth Becker Hershberger and later by CIM recruits Wayne and Annette Jost Albrecht, Sprunger and his associates quickly set a high standard of craftsmanship for their Congolese students. While he secured some mechanized equipment, the focus was clearly on the skilled use of hand tools which, for most of the graduates, would have great value in the absence of mechanized power in a rural setting. Securing mill-sawn lumber when they could, but also using rough hewn planks brought in from the forest by village pit saw crews, the students began to produce sturdy, functional furniture which was immediately in great demand. When upon graduation from the two-year training program these young men began to set up their own simple workshops in their home areas or in small urban centers, church leaders quickly expressed their satisfaction.

have you forgotten our daughters?

But there were still other casualties of the political upheaval of 1960. Irena Liechty had just opened a new girl's school at Djoko Punda when political independence exploded on the scene. That first class was small, made up of selected girls from a few of the stations. The focus was on the art of homemaking and the role of a Christian wife and mother in the African home. In the hectic atmosphere of the early 60's, though talked about, no effort to resurrect this new program for girls was possible. With the return of political stability, however, the church leaders became more insistent. They all clearly remembered their early struggles to bring village girls to the station boarding schools established for them. While the village parents and elders had come to see the value of some education for their sons and nephews, the idea of education for a girl was seen as sheer foolishness. For what reason would they need to learn how to read and write or work with numbers? Their village mothers and grandmothers could teach them all they needed to know in order to take their place in the clan as wives, mothers and the providers of food for children and husbands. But the missionaries had persevered and, at last, some girls were grudgingly allowed to depart for the stations but with the firm warning that as soon as they were of marriageable age, the study nonsense would come to a quick end. Consequently girls in their early teens were sometimes found in the first two or three years of primary school. Even though they rarely finished grade school before marriage during that era, the great value was that most of them professed faith in Christ while at the mission and thus brought a commitment to Christ and to the Church into their marriages which usually was with Christian young men.

But times had changed. Boys were now moving beyond primary school and starting to graduate from secondary schools. Some were going on to university. There was a rapidly growing gap between the educational levels of their sons and daughters. EMC leaders fretted that while they discouraged Christian young men from marrying girls who were barely if at all literate, who then were they to marry? Seeking Catholic girls was, from their standpoint, no better solution.

By the mid-60's, a few girls were found in the Nyanga secondary school, but they were clearly exceptional young women. Not only did they have to hold their own academically with the male students but also had to have firm personal commitments to their own education and future - - this at a point in their lives when an overwhelming majority of their age group were already married. Frequently they had to put up with an undercurrent of resistance from their fellow male students. If their ability to study and complete school at a secondary level was questioned, that was one thing. But what caused far greater hurt were the frequent accusations that they were scorning and betraying the time-revered role of women in their society, that of marriage and child bearing within their respective clans. A solution had to be found. (7)

Already in the fall of 1965 it had been decided to try to gather all girls from every station who had successfully finished primary school the previous spring and bring them to Nyanga Station. A special dormitory was planned for them where they were to live under the care of a Christian Congolese couple. A special year of pre-secondary orientation study was created for them with a view to preparing them for full secondary level schooling the following year. Jenny Bertsche, who had been asked to supervise this new project, wrote: "Since the girls came from many different tribes and language areas, it was decided to conduct the school in French. The girls made surprising progress. New confidence developed as they began to recite and express themselves in a classroom all their own. . . . During the final exams in June, a few girls were in the top grading bracket along with the boys who had studied from the same text books with separate classrooms. . . . Another encouraging trend has taken place recently among the Congolese. A recent influx of educated young men have been coming from far and wide to ask to become engaged to the girls from this special class. In other words, the future school teachers, clerks, pastors and government officials want better trained women for their wives. . . . Whereas just two decades ago Congo chiefs and elders would scarcely send a girl to the mission school, now the young men of Congo are seeking educated and trained girls for wives. . . . We're on the way! There is hope." (8) This special class became the forerunner of a major EMC thrust in girls' education - - a full-blown four year girls' high school which was launched in the decade of the 70's.

a clamor from the Kwilu

As the rebel grip on eastern Kwilu Province was gradually broken and thousands of people began to reoccupy their villages, cries for help began to come to the EMC/CIM leaders at Tshikapa from Mukedi and Kandala stations. Damage to buildings and equipment at Mukedi had been heavy but a significant amount of the station's resources had escaped intact. At Kandala, however, destruction of the station had been nearly total. From both areas came pleas for help, help of all kinds. Buildings needed major repair; schools needed to be reopened which called for supplies and teaching staff; medical facilities had been demolished; and pastors and church leaders needed encouragement and, in some cases, rehabilitation. From both stations there were repeated calls for the return of missionary personnel.

As soon as the roads were again safe for travel, early teams had gone back to both station areas with CPRA supplies of blankets, powdered milk, rice and tinned beef in an effort to help meet some of the early, pressing needs of a refugee people seeking to reoccupy the areas from which they had been driven.

But the longer range rehabilitation needed at both stations represented great cost. EMC legal representative Kakesa Samuel. who had lived through the fire and horror of the rebellion, lobbied energetically for immediate major response on the part of the CIM. Missionary and board response, however, was not automatic or instantaneous. There clearly was some question on the part of the Mission as to how quickly and at what level new personnel and funds should once again be invested in the two *Jeunesse*-ravaged areas.

In the end, it was Mukedi which became the recipient of the earliest and the most help and this for several reasons. An older, larger station, it had a broader range of ministries and services at the time of evacuation as well as a larger missionary staff. Whereas at Kandala all residences had been burned, some remained intact at Mukedi. At Kandala the chapel was totally unroofed; at Mukedi a major part of the roof remained intact. At Kandala school units were all in shambles whereas at Mukedi some classroom space still remained.

But what was most significant in influencing the pace and amount of mission/church response was the attitude of the people themselves. While at Kandala the local people seemed inclined to wait for mission/church initiative to begin reparation and rehabilitation, at Mukedi people set to work on their own. Furious at the way in which they had been used and betrayed by a movement in which they had put their hope and trust, they went to work as soon as they were able to reoccupy their station. By the time the first missionaries were able to visit them, they found that local teachers and directors had already had meetings, enrolled students and in a community effort were putting up shelters of temporary materials in which to open a new school year. Work was under way to repair the dug-up airstrip. The medical staff had salvaged what it could and was doing for the sick whatever was possible amidst the circumstances. In the presence of such spirit and determination, ways were sought to help. In December 1966, Archie Graber spent several days at Mukedi working with church leaders to repair a large hole burned through the roof of the chapel. Other help was soon to follow.

the Schwartzes start again

Perhaps nothing better embodies the sort of commitment and forgiving spirit that was required on the part of missionary and African church personnel alike in the aftermath of rebellion than the return of Dr. Merle and Dorothy Bowman Schwartz to Mukedi. Merle, a farm boy from the Carlock, Illinois area, sat as a teenager in a service in his community when the urgency of missionary medical personnel in the Congo was shared. At a point in his life when he was casting about for a cause to which to devote himself, he carried the challenge home with him. After consultation with family and conference leader R.L.Hartzler, he left for Bluffton College in the fall of 1929. The fall of 1934 he enrolled in the University of Illinois School of Medicine in Chicago. Four years later he not only graduated with his degree but was also engaged to Dorothy Bowman, a student nurse he had met at Bethany Hospital where she was in training. Married in June 1940, they applied to the CIM as WW II was exploding in Europe. They gathered an outfit and left for the Congo aboard an Egyptian freighter improbably named the "*ZAM ZAM*." Spotted in its trans-Atlantic travel by a German raider, the "*Zam Zam*" was shelled. Damaged, it halted dead in the water. The passengers and crew were off-loaded with the clothing on their backs. After four days during which time some baggage was salvaged, their boat was sunk. The next day they were transferred to the German ship "Dresden" which became their "home" for nearly a month. Eventually running the British blockade, they were disembarked in occupied France and transported to Portugal from where they finally returned to the States.

They located temporarily at Sideling Hill, PA, a camp where scores of young Mennonite men were doing their alternative war time service. When in the summer of 1942 an opportunity suddenly came to book them on a boat destined for the Congo port of Matadi, there was instant acceptance. In a note left for family and friends they said: "As we sail once more for His chosen field for us in Congo, we go with full resignation to His will knowing both from experience and promises from His Word that He is able to care for us. . . . Remember us in your prayers that we might always do His will." (9)

In late September they at last set foot on Congo soil and began their career as medical missionaries with the CIM which was to stretch across a period of 35 years. Stationed at Mukedi they found a small, thatch-roofed dispensary/hospital built of field stones laid up in red mud mortar with external cement pointing. Internal walls were also of red mud plaster with a coating of whitewash. Small bamboos tied together with split forests vines served as ceilings. Bringing a farm boy's familiarity with tools to his assignment, a medical complex slowly grew under his guiding and innovative hand. A major boost came in the form of a large maternity hospital built in the post-war years with a government grant. Ward space was gradually enlarged. Along the way equipment was scrounged and fabricated. Improvisation was the name of the game amidst a continual struggle to keep pace with a steadily growing patient load. A high point was reached just months before independence when a spacious new hospital was dedicated which, for the first time, afforded adequate space for a pharmacy, a surgical area plus such luxuries as a doctor's office and storage space. (10)

Now, nine years later, they were being asked to return to the shambles of what once was Mukedi's medical facility. The maternity and hospital stood unroofed; equipment was scattered and destroyed. Would they accept? They would. The task was daunting and disheartening. No one knew better than they how difficult it would be to start again. But two things remained unchanged for them: the medical needs of a large Congolese population and their commitment to serve in the name of Christ regardless of the circumstances. Teamed with Don and Naomi Reimer Unruh, they returned in the fall of 1969, the Unruhs to work with the Church and the Schwartzes to begin picking up the pieces of a shattered medical work. (11)

In the fall of 1970, the two couples were joined by Arlo and Leontine Schlecht Raid who had come for a year of VS service. A resourceful lay couple from southeastern Iowa, they both were well acquainted with hammer, saw and paintbrush and soon endeared themselves to the Mukedi population. In the fall of 1972, John and Olga Unruh Klaassen arrived to lend a hand in the secondary school. A missionary presence was again reestablished at Mukedi. With the enthusiastic participation of the Africans themselves, the time came when the only notable evidence of the ravages of rebellion were the eroding stone and mud walls of a small garage which were allowed to stand as a mute symbol of dark days and to follow its own timetable of demise under the tropical rain and sun.

At Kandala, funding was gradually provided for such projects as the re-roofing of the station chapel and the erection of some new school rooms. In collaboration with funds raised by the local church, some dwellings and other smaller buildings were repaired. A new dispensary was also built with funds given in the States as a memorial to Kornela Unrau, a long-time Nyanga nurse who served her last four years at Kandala before her retirement in 1960. Although often requested by the Kandala Church, it never worked out to place resident missionary personnel at that post again.

upgrading the shepherds

Amidst the rapid change of independent Congo, demands made upon pastoral leadership were also changing. Pre-1960 formats and levels of pastoral training were no longer adequate. Already in 1962 the Congo Protestant Council had sounded an alarm and asked member churches to seek to establish a theological school in the capital. In 1964 a special consultation was held in Luluabourg. This meeting "underlined the fact that a scattered individual effort at training church leadership by various groups was resulting in much unnecessary duplication of effort and expense. There were at that time twenty professors for forty-nine theological students throughout the Congo! The consultation recommended, in part, that to better respond to the needs of our churches in personnel and in ministry we study the possibility of uniting certain schools of pastoral training." (12)

But it remained for the governing board of a widely-known and respected School for Pastors and Teachers in the lower Congo to take a decisive step toward the creation of such a new theological training effort. Based on the American Baptist Station at Kimpesi and known by its French acronym EPI, this school was already a joint effort on the part of two Protestant Missions of the lower Congo. Though recognized as being in the forefront of Protestant church leadership training, its directors were also feeling the urgency of somehow establishing a broader-based, higher level training program in the country. It was in May, 1966, that the EPI board made the decision to close the pastoral training section of this school and to propose that a "school of theology open to all churches desiring to participate in its creation be founded in the capital city of Kinshasa" [formerly Leopoldville]. (13)

It was nearly a year later on March 5, 1967, that an organizational meeting was held in Kinshasa in which missionary Ben Eidse participated as CIM's representative. Rev. Wes Brown, director of the closed Kimpese pastoral training school, spoke on the topic "A Call to a Common Task." In the course of presentation he reviewed the advantages of forming a united training institution for Christian workers. He then made the following observations: "There are difficulties, dangers, and sometimes risks when one works together. There is the question of the basis of cooperation. Admitting that our churches have been influenced by their mother churches, they have inherited traditions and interpretations which separate us if we defend them in detail. But what is really important? The faith communicated in our Savior Jesus Christ, based on the Bible, the inspired Word of God, unites us. I hope that we will be able to put our suspicions aside and see objectively if there is a basis of cooperation which could unite us in our task. Since questions of church structure and eschatology divide us most frequently, I propose that in a united school the diverse positions be presented freely without any intentions of proselytizing from another association." (14)

A total of twelve mission/church groups were represented at this meeting of which ten had signaled their intention to become partners in the new venture. Among them were the CIM/EMC and the Mennonite Brethren Mission/Church. Thus, in effect, two existing schools, the inter-Mennonite one at Kajiji and the one at Kimpese, were to be merged with their separate staffs, libraries and students into a single, new institution. Classes were scheduled to begin the following September (1968) with a teaching staff of seven professors including two well-trained Congolese who had studied overseas. A student body of 55 was projected. Parallel to a curriculum for the men would be a three year set of courses for women. The name of the new training institution would be *Ecole de Théologie Evangélique de Kinshasa*, i.e., "The Evangelical School of Theology of Kinshasa" with the acronym ETEK. Later, in keeping with changing terminology in usage in the Congo, the name would be changed to *Institut Supérieur de Théologie de Kinshasa*, i.e., "The Superior Institute of Theology of Kinshasa" with the acronym ISTK.

Advised of the new Protestant initiative envisioned for the city, President Mobutu signaled his affirmation and support by allocating, cost free, a choice 35 acre plot of ground at the edge of the city along the major Kinshasa/Matadi road. Fund raising was launched, administrative personnel designated and the project was begun. Realizing that it would be impossible to build enough of the new campus to accommodate the new school within one year's time, arrangements were made to conduct the first year of study (1968-69) in temporary quarters at Kimpese. Following this decision CIM/EMC professor couples Peter/Gladys Buller and Peter/Annie Falk took up residence there for one year. The original class at Kajiji having graduated in the spring of 1968, four new EMC couples joined the Mennonite professors to begin their training there.

It was not long until it became clear that the massive building project in Kinshasa was lagging behind schedule. In a report to the CIM Board in the spring of 1969 the following is found: "Shortly before New Year's, the outlook for this project was extremely bleak. Time was slipping by, money was being spent and the building project on the new Kinshasa site was practically at a standstill. The ETEK program temporarily housed at Kimpese for this year was advised that it would have to be moved this coming summer without fail. A special committee was formed, accounts examined, building plans re-examined. Two Mennonite builders were then pressured into temporary service - - Archie Graber of CIM and Jake Nickel of the Mennonite Brethren. Work gangs were organized, piece work systems set up, uniform building plans adopted and suddenly the project began to move. It now appears that there is every chance that the ETEK program can be housed at the new site by next September." (15) This optimism proved to be well-founded for the 1969/70 school year was in fact launched on the new campus even as final stages of construction continued around the students. The official inauguration of the grounds and facilities took place on March 1, 1970 in the midst of the annual sessions of the Congo Protestant Council which were held that year in Kinshasa. Rev. Jean Bokeleale, the CPC Executive Secretary, brought the inaugural address.

Early statements regarding the stance and objectives of the new pastoral training school were clear. A brief doctrinal statement was adopted which read: "The Evangelical Theological School of Kinshasa confesses its faith in Jesus Christ, Son of God, who is the only Savior, who died on the cross, was resurrected, and who will come again. The school believes that the Holy Scriptures of the Old and New Testaments contain all that is necessary for salvation and that they are the supreme authority of our faith. The Bible calls us to believe in God the Father, God the Son and God the Holy Spirit who dwells in us and leads us on the path of truth and love. The School believes that the church is the body of Christ the Lord and the assembly of those who are saved and called to serve Him in the world." (16)

Peter Buller, who was associated with the school from its inception in 1968 until his retirement in the fall of 1988, summarized the vision and purpose of ETEK's founders thus: "In a word, the Evangelical School of Theology of Kinshasa is dedicated to training leaders for the various ministries of the Church of Christ, who are firmly grounded on the Word of God, and who under the guidance of the Holy Spirit will be able to interpret and apply that living Word in and to the African culture. ETEK must be a living and constantly developing institution that changes even from year to year as old needs are met and the emerging needs of the Congo Church become known. It can never think of itself in a static sense, but must ever turn its eye to the future while it addresses a prophetic voice to the present and listens to the past." (17)

Initially, when the idea of a new inter-mission pastoral training center was proposed in the capital of the country, some concern was expressed by missionary personnel in the isolated rural areas. After three years of exposure and orientation to "the big city of bright lights," would the student couples be so uprooted that they could not or would not want to return to serve in the rural churches which had selected and sent them for training? Such apprehension was shared by CIM missionaries as well. This concern, however, was soon laid to rest. It is true that the early graduates did tend to make stipulations as to their assignments, given the level of their training. But as ISTK graduates became more numerous, they increasingly found their way into rural church settings for service. Frequently associated with the church school programs at regional centers, they served dual pastoral and educational roles which proved valuable for the church.

CIM/EMC were to maintain a major presence in this inter-mission school across the years. Always sending a full quota of students, once the full three-year program was in cycle, CIM/EMC nearly always had a dozen couples in resident studies there. Both CIM and the Mennonite Brethren Mission provided solid teaching support as well. For the first 20 or so years of its existence, there were Mennonite members on the teaching and/or administrative staffs. So consistent was this presence that, at times, some of the other member groups became a somewhat restive feeling that the Mennonite profile on campus was a bit high. However, as more Congolese began to return from overseas with doctoral degrees, there was a gradual replacement of non-African staff. The governing board likewise came to be increasingly comprised of Congolese and thus debate and decisions regarding policies, priorities and the filling of staff openings became the responsibility of Congolese church representatives.

This transition of ISTK administrative direction to African hands, unfortunately, was not trouble free. In 1985, after several years under an African director, the school board made an urgent appeal to Peter Buller to assume this role, an assignment which was accepted with great reluctance for a two year period. As had been the case in other programs and settings, the use and allocation of institutional funds under the pressure of regional and family expectations eventually discredited the African director. This troubling experience raised yet once again, in the post-independence era of the Congo, a sense of uncertainty as to the compatibility and viability of Western-style institutions in an African setting.

Mennonites organize in the capital

Meanwhile, a very significant result of the CIM/EMC involvement in ETEK/ISTK was the start of EMC church planting activity amidst the exploding population of the capital city. For many years there had been a steady migration of Mennonite church members into Kinshasa. In the process they had kept track of each other. Typically, people from the same home areas clustered in the same suburbs of the city. Under the original inter-mission polity arrangement which pertained in the city, they found no Mennonite Churches and thus worshipped in other Protestant congregations they found on the scene.

A group of former students of CIM/EMC schools in the Kwilu, Kwango and the two Kasais had nonetheless formally organized and met on a regular basis for fellowship and for exchange of news from their home areas. When EMC students in ETEK/ISTK began to receive practical work assignments, it was only natural to begin with such an organized cluster of Mennonites. Over time, with the leadership and encouragement of EMC students and professors from ETEK/ISTK, new EMC congregations were planted here and there across the sprawling expanse of the city and became the forerunners of an established EMC presence in the capital of the country. (18)

CHAPTER 20   EXPERIENCING NEW EXTERNAL PRESSURES

an amazing turn of events

Not only was the newly integrated EMC African/missionary leadership team confronted by an array of needs and challenges within the Church, it was also experiencing a variety of new pressures from outside the church community.

For years the *Forminière* Diamond Company had maintained an all-encompassing and dominating presence along the Kasai River of south central Congo. Not only was Tshikapa its administrative center; it also had built its diamond picking/sorting plant there plus large camps to house its 25,000-man African labor force. Clusters of residences overlooking the river were provided for officials and a roomy hotel/restaurant/bar/recreation facility was at the disposition of European mining personnel who sought to retreat from the rigors of the bush for times of periodic relaxation and rest. But that was not all. Nearby, along the river, was a company farm where poultry and livestock were raised for their restaurant and for sale to their personnel.

Furthermore, across the Tshikapa River (a tributary stream which joins the Kasai River at that location), a sprawling complex of medical facilities had been built including a 300-bed hospital and a 150-bed maternity wing to ensure the health care of its thousands of African employees. This was in addition to a small 6 bed "white clinic." All of these facilities were under the care of European doctors and Catholic sisters. Then, on a bluff, overlooking everything, was a large Catholic Mission with its schools, its cathedral and its European and Congolese staff. Considering this as their chaplaincy for their work force, *Forminière* had contributed generously to the building costs.

To round out the picture, local government officers were located on the east bank of the Kasai where fellow Belgians in the employ of the colonial government exercised their administrative functions. It was a cozy, self-contained economic, political and religious community which had successfully excluded Mennonite missionaries and African pastors for several decades.

Then came the explosion of political independence which shattered the *Forminière*/Catholic Mission/Belgian administrative grip on the Tshikapa area and its people. Suddenly the Belgian government officials on the east bank were gone. The company officials and the Catholic missionaries up on the bluff suddenly found themselves the object of a mix of deep resentment and overt hostility. Amidst military mutiny Belgian families joined in the massive exodus of white people which swept with it the CIM missionaries of the area as described earlier in this account (cf. ch.7). The few company officials who stayed behind were taken under armed custody and experienced menace and scorn as local Congolese gleefully exploited the sudden reversal of roles and authority.

Company officials in Belgium and in Leopoldville scrambled to maintain some semblance of control of their enterprise but, as months slipped by, it became increasingly apparent that there would be no return to the privileged days of the past. Drastic moves were needed in the face of the new reality. In a <u>Congo Missionary Messenger</u> article of the time entitled "Opportunities Unlimited," the following is found: "Missionary Elmer Dick reports that a flourishing post-independence diamond black market has undercut profits of commercial mining operations. He says company officials believe it will become profitable to legalize private diamond marketing and buy the gems directly from enterprising Africans. The Company is holding only a few of its European personnel in Tshikapa and closing its facilities." (1) (2)

With the shutdown of its normal mining operation, the Company no longer had need of its large Congolese work force. Thus plans were soon announced to close its medical services in the area. It was at this point that V.J. Sprunger, the CIM Executive Secretary at the time, approached *Forminière* officials both in Congo and in Brussels about the possibility of renting or leasing some of their Tshikapa facilities for the needs and purposes of the CIM and EMC. Negotiations were encouraging and by early 1962 CIM staff in Elkhart was able to report: "For you who pray for the Congo, the Company's . . . reply is an example of Jeremiah's promised 'great and mighty things which thou knowest not' (Jer. 33:3). The Company offered to lease us l) Its fully equipped hospital and maternity ward, the only hospital between Luluabourg and Kikwit equipped to handle most any medical problem. 2) Its 6-bed European hospital with operating room and dental equipment. 3) Its modern 180 acre farm with dairy barn, pig barns, . . . feed mill and mixer, 16 chicken houses and incubator, all with modern facilities. 4) Twelve dwellings for missionaries or national staff. 5) Four office buildings. 6) A large workshop with three forges, several lathes, power planer and saws; ideal to use as a professional school for carpentry and metal working." (3) For the use of this extraordinary array of facilities in the bush of the West Kasai, the Company proposed the token figure of $1,000 a month.

As regarded plans for the farm, it was stated that it would be "operated jointly by the CIM and the MCC. Christian farmers can study animal husbandry and get starts of livestock. This will afford them economic opportunity that will mean more money for a self-supporting church. It will also supply much needed protein in village diets. Missionary Mel Claassen has come from Kamayala Station to be general manager of the farm. Arthur Augsburger of Middlebury, IN and Gordon Liechty of Berne, IN have gone out under MCC to supervise livestock and poultry programs." (4)

In the same article it is further explained that Dr. Ralph and Fern Bartsch Ewert and Aganetha Friesen had moved to Tshikapa from Nyanga to work in the hospital and that Dr. John and Jean Pierson Zook would soon join them there. (Other CIM medical personnel who, in time, were moved to Tshikapa to help staff this large medical facility were Lois Slagle, June Friesen, Merle and Dorothy Schwartz, Elda Hiebert and Anita Janzen.) On the administrative side, Russell and Helen Yoder Schnell had moved the CIM field office to Tshikapa which put it in close proximity to the government airstrip, post and telegraph offices.

Throughout the article there is a tone of exuberant excitement: "By an amazing turn of events, opportunities to serve Jesus Christ in the city of Tshikapa have suddenly been offered us which well nigh outstrip our resources. . . . The possibility inherent in these facilities for the Kingdom of Christ defy the imagination. What a center for soul winning! What a laboratory for teaching Christian students practical work! Without undertaking a building program, we can proceed at full speed in training Congolese for leadership in church, school, medical and administrational work. None of our four tribes will have to come far to take advantage of our type of training offered. . . . From what was once a closed city will now issue a stream of living water. Hidden in His heart are the things He hopes to accomplish with what He has so clearly placed in our hands. . . . Pray for your missionaries. May eternity reveal that through them God was able to accomplish all His purposes for these needy people in the diamond mining area of [the] Kasai." (5) Home staff, field missionary personnel and African leaders all shared in the excitement of what appeared to be a wide, new door dramatically opened before them. An African pastor was overheard commenting: "Does not the Bible talk about the last being first and the first being last?"

defenders of the Diamond Company?

But in spite of the early optimistic dreams of establishing a broad new range of Mission/Church ministries and witness in the newly-leased diamond company facilities, it was not to be. In all of the planning and negotiation, it had been taken for granted that sufficient political stability would be restored that legal lease arrangements would be binding and respected by all concerned. This did not prove to be the case. The first casualty was the farm and its livestock. Between the problems of thieving and the frequent requisitions of military and government officials, it soon became evident that it would be impossible to maintain herds or flocks of any consequence in the name of the Mission or Church.

Another early casualty was the idea of establishing a vocational training school in the company maintenance and woodworking shops. Once again the missionaries and church leaders found themselves in conflict with military and government personnel who clearly saw these facilities as part of their legacy from the former diamond mining operation and were not impressed with any formal arrangement which may have been agreed upon between white people.

CIM and EMC were, however, able to occupy a number of residences and some office space for a time. One benefit of this arrangement was the establishment of a book store at Tshikapa which under Tina Quiring's tireless direction became a major source of Christian literature and school supplies. Local government offices also came to depend on this store for many of their needs. There was also significant sale of Bibles and Testaments in several languages from year to year. In time, this central book shop became a supply depot for several smaller shops both in the Tshikapa area and on some of the CIM stations.

But the housing and the office space also eventually became an abrasive issue which generated irritated discussion. With the advent of the short-lived mini-province called the *Unité Kasaiènne*, various provincial functionaries required housing. Eyes immediately fell upon company houses occupied and maintained in good condition by mission personnel. Whenever Mission/Church leaders were approached with demands to yield these facilities, discussion inevitably revolved around the legality of the lease drawn up with the Company, something which the Africans, in the unsettled times of the early 1960's, considered to be nothing more than a subterfuge designed to help the Company retain control of part of its assets.

All of this gradually gave rise to growing uneasiness within missionary ranks. While some were inclined to stand on legality and demand that official lease arrangements be respected by the new Congo government, others wondered what the long-range implications of such a stance might be. A commentary dated April 30, 1965, addressed to the home office read: "Our whole posture at Tshikapa has caused us concern these past months. . . . The Tshikapa government resents the *Forminière* . . . for what they've done in the past and for what they are now doing. They feel that this diamond company 'milked' them and their land through the years. . . . In our situation there, we've consistently been backed into the same corner with them and have been maneuvered into defending, to a certain extent, the interests of the company. . . . True, we've had a legal contract and previous occupation all on our side, but this the government has chosen to disregard arguing that this is their ground and their diamonds and that everything now standing at Tshikapa was built by revenue from their natural resources and therefore they now have a right to them. . . . We've come to the place where we must choose between convenience and our witness and influence in the area." (6)

healing under duress

Reluctant to yield the dream of what might have been, CIM/EMC leaders nonetheless came to the place by the mid-60's where they realized that Tshikapa simply would not afford the opportunities for expanded witness and service that were earlier envisioned. There yet remained, however, the large hospital which was staffed and operated by the Mennonites. Immensely popular amidst the rapidly growing population, it was at the same time a constant target of criticism and envy on the part of local government officials. It was unthinkable, they said, that a "province" should not have and maintain its own medical services. When pressed as to how they would staff and operate it if the Mennonites withdrew, there were vague references to plans to recruit qualified personnel elsewhere. Unconvinced, the local population constantly urged CIM/EMC leaders to simply ignore their agitation and to continue to provide the medical services which they trusted and valued so highly.

With the eventual demise of the *Unité Kasaiènne* Province, local government functions fell to the hands of new Congolese personnel appointed by the central government. Instead of dealing with local authorities, there were now the representatives of a new bureau simply called "The Office" which was charged with the oversight of former *Forminière* assets. By this time CIM/EMC occupation of former Company property had been reduced to a few houses, a book shop and the hospital. Now pressure on the Mission/Church medical personnel took a different tack. Alternating between accusations of "sub-standard" medical services and the "pilfering" of medical supplies and "profiteering" at the expense of the general public, the demand to yield the medical services to the government was maintained. In addition to all of this, there were efforts to sharply increase the cost of renewed lease agreements for the few buildings which were still occupied. Unstated was the naive belief that the large hospital and the thousands of people cared for from year to year represented a lucrative source of revenue which, if controlled by the local bureaucrats, would mean significant income for local government and/or individual coffers.

When repeated efforts to sign some sort of long-term lease arrangement with the local officials met only with indifference and lack of understanding, CIM/EMC leaders at long last made the reluctant decision to turn the hospital over to the provincial medical authorities. This was done knowing that it would inevitably mean a decline in the quality of service offered and a major increase in the medical load at the small Mennonite mission dispensary and maternity across the Kasai River at Kalonda Station.

A general memorandum, dated November 27, 1969, was drawn up and broadly distributed in the Tshikapa area. Though couched in conciliatory language it nonetheless stated plainly the problem of indifference and misunderstanding encountered during the previous years. It further declared the intention of the EMC/CIM to enlarge the medical facilities across the river at Kalonda, to place a missionary doctor, to build an air strip and to serve any and all who sought help there. By year's end, 1969, the transfer was complete. Though there was a flurry of last-minute activity as government officials began to feel the ire of the local population, there was no turning back. Missionaries and church leaders alike had had enough. They would in the future seek to establish witness and service in an area based on their own terrain. Having unsuccessfully tried to create a major service and training center at Tshikapa, such efforts and its medical personnel would again be distributed among the stations and urban centers where such help was welcomed.

A long series of missionary doctors eventually served the Tshikapa area from their base at Kalonda including Elvina Martens, Jim Steiner, John Byler, Dennis Ries, Richard Hirschler, Gary Groot, John Grasse and Glenn Rediger. (7) Among the missionary nurses who worked beside them were Eudene Keidel, Leona Entz, Hulda Banman and Marilyn Derksen. Donna Colbert played a major role in organizing and stocking the first central pharmacy which served outlying dispensaries in all directions. Anita Janzen also served for a time as a lab technician. An outstanding African nurse known to all of these medical missionaries was Kabundi Jacques (pr. kah-BUH-ndi JAHK) who faithfully served both as a nurse and as an African administrator of the station medical services over many years.

The government-operated hospital across the river soon encountered problems in securing adequate supplies and qualified personnel. As the quality of service declined, it was more and more deserted by the population which walked past it to the Mission/Church hospital further on across the river. Eventually, missionary doctors again helped at the government facility, on a part time basis, but Mission personnel never again accepted administrative responsibilities for that establishment.

the IMCK is born

There still remained, however, the question of a medical training center and referral hospital. What was the solution to be? An earlier decision to affiliate with the large inter-mission medical center at Kimpese in the lower Congo had not proven to be a feasible arrangement. In the meantime, the Presbyterian Mission had taken steps to develop a similar center just outside Luluabourg some 100 miles east of Tshikapa. Just prior to independence in 1960, the Belgian administration had erected a complex of buildings on a site adjacent to a little village called Tshikaji (pr. tshi-KAH-jee), aboute eight miles outside the city, with the intention of making it a training center for the sons of traditional African chiefs from across the country. They would be brought there, it was thought yet even at that late date, to be oriented and groomed to replace their fathers and to cooperate willingly and knowledgeably with the colonial authorities in their ongoing efforts to create what they termed a Belgo/African country in the heart of Africa.

Political independence erupted just as the campus was nearing completion. In the early aftermath of independence, the buildings had been partially occupied by squatters and the grounds had largely grown up in weeds. Seeing this as a possible site for a major Protestant medical center, the Presbyterians began negotiations with the government at both local and national levels. It was finally stipulated that in order to secure government approval, the envisioned center would need to be sponsored by more than a single mission/church organization. Having already earlier approached CIM/EMC with a proposal of partnership in the project, the government stance gave fresh impetus to the dialogue between the two mission/church groups. While existing buildings would suit well for purposes of dormitories and class rooms, medical facilities, as such, would need to be built. This would require significant financial outlay.

By this time Mennonite/Presbyterian relations dated back over several decades and it had become common knowledge that Mennonites were typically "short" on cash but "long" on well-qualified personnel. With major Presbyterian funds available in the States, it was agreed that the Mennonites would make a nominal capital investment in the new enterprise while providing some key medical personnel. The earliest CIM/EMC couple to take up residence at the new center were Dr. John and Jeanne Pierson Zook, a highly-trained and energetic couple. He, a board surgeon, and she with her master's degree in nursing arts, quickly meshed their considerable abilities with those of Presbyterian personnel in the development of what was to become known as "The Christian Medical Institute of the Kasai," i.e., IMCK in its French acronym form. Arriving in the fall of 1969, the Zooks served there for eight years.

In January, 1972, Sam and Betty Jane Regehr Ediger of Hesston, KS were recruited to give 2 1/2 years of service. Sam, an experienced building contractor, accepted the assignment to supervise the construction of a series of inter-connected pavilions which would form the core of a new hospital complex. For the best part of a year CIM missionary Henry Braun also helped with this construction project. Other CIM personnel who served at IMCK were Anita Janzen, a lab technician, Margie Neuenschwander and Hulda Banman, teachers of nursing arts and Marilyn Carter Derksen as a floor supervisor of student nurses.

In time, the Institute offered training both in nursing arts and laboratory techniques. A large outpatient and maternity service soon developed. Eventually, services in ophthalmology and dentistry were also added. As Zairians began to graduate from the school of medicine in Kinshasa, IMCK assumed even further significance as a facility where they could come for an internship working beside missionary doctors. With passing time, IMCK became a medical center of renown throughout the country where Africans and non-Africans alike were cared for with skill and compassion in the name of Christ.

authenticity: a battle cry

As frustrating and disappointing as was the experience of withdrawing from the Tshikapa hospital, there were other forces taking shape on the Congo national scene that were to have far more serious repercussions not only for the EMC/CIM but for the entire Christian community of the country.

Joseph Mobutu proved to be a man of his word. Having set out some clear goals at the founding of a new national political movement at N'Sele in May of 1967, he promptly set out to achieve them. Already a year earlier, even before the launching of his *Mouvement Populaire de la Révolution*, the country's currency of the *franc* left by the Belgians had been replaced by a new national currency called the *zaire*. (8) The rash of splintering provinces had been rolled back into a total of twelve country-wide. The armed forces and police had been reorganized and unified. The multiple political parties had been regrouped in a single political movement.

Having dealt with some of the most pressing internal political problems, Mobutu turned to the major source of foreign power and influence still entrenched in the Congo, that being the multi-national copper mining industry that had been developed over the years in the mineral rich southeastern Katanga Province under the umbrella term *Union Minière du Haute Katanga*, i.e., "The Mining Union of High Katanga. During the short lived efforts of Moise Tshombe in the early 60's to lead this area in secession from the control of the central government, Belgian "counselors" had been active behind the scenes. Even now that a new political regime was in place in Leopoldville, there still was no lack of confidence, either in Belgium or in the Katanga region, that continued white control of the mining enterprise would be maintained.

But in a series of clever and well planned moves in 1966-67, the Congo government forced the immense mining conglomerate to accept an entirely new agreement which, among other things, moved the headquarters of the mining operation from Belgium to Leopoldville and granted the Congo government a much more advantageous share of operating control and revenues from the sale of its copper overseas. By 1969, the final details of the nationalization of the enormous mining operation of Katanga had been agreed upon. In 1974 the Zaire victory was complete in that the Belgian monopoly of the sale of Zaire's copper was also terminated. As of that date, both production and sale of its own ore would be entirely in Zairian hands.

There was, yet, a power bloc of another sort within the country to which Mobutu now turned his attention - - the Catholic Church. It was his conviction that the Congo's political and economic independence would be meaningless if they did not succeed, as Congolese, to rediscover and reassert themselves as Africans with their own history, traditions, culture, gifts, art and tribal strengths in which they could justifiably take pride. For too long they had attempted to copy the white-skinned strangers among them. For too long they had been made to feel that their traditional ways of life were somehow inherently inferior to those of the Western world. For too long they had been apologetic about their supposed short comings as an African people vis-à-vis their colonial rulers. Speaking in a variety of settings and to a variety of audiences, Mobutu's theme was everywhere the same: "We have a right as Congolese to be who and what we are and not what others may want us to be." Seizing upon the theme "authenticity," he was heard to say in a speech at the United Nations: "Authenticity is universal, it is the mark of every people, it is a cultural constant, a permanent feature of civilization. . . . It is, in effect, in the measure that we will be ourselves, strongly rooted in our own culture, that we will be able to profitably assimilate contributions from the exterior and adapt them to our mode of life. . . . Authenticity is a sober decision of the Zairian people to return to their own roots, to research the values of their ancestors in order to appreciate those which contribute to their natural and well-proportioned and harmonious development. It is the refusal of the Zairian people to blindly espouse imported ideologies. . . . The pursuit of authenticity is not a narrow nationalism, a blind return to the past. . . . It is not only a deepened knowledge of our own culture but also a respect for the cultural legacy of others. . . . The return to a traditional heritage permits us to integrate the socio-cultural experience of our elders into modern Zairian society. . . . It is not a question of a simple adoption of antique village customs but rather a continual search for certain transcendent values which are unique to our people and which, in a way, constitute their genius." (9)

So far, so good.

With this basic commitment to rediscover and revalidate themselves as Congolese came a cascade of events and changes. For one thing, an article of the constitution adopted in June, 1967, declared Congo to be a secular state. This, then, meant that there was no state religion. This seemed innocent enough. But for the powerful and all-pervasive Catholic Church, this decision carried troubling overtones. Though the Catholic faith had never been a national religion in an official sense, practically speaking the Catholic Church was accustomed to exercising a dominant force in the country and had been all but an official church. Under the Belgians, Catholic holidays had been incorporated into the official calendar and were observed across the land. State functions were typically preceded by special celebrations in the local Catholic Churches. Within Congo itself, there had been no particular reaction at the time the constitution was drafted since relations between the new regime and the Church were cordial. President Mobutu was himself, after all, a baptized Catholic and the product of Catholic schools. It was known that influential people of the Church had played a major role in the drafting of the Manifesto of N'Sele. The government had even paid some reparations to Catholic Missions for damages inflicted during the years of rebellion. (10)

But in 1970, at a special congress of the MPR, it was declared that the MPR was the "supreme institution" of the country and that all other institutions were to be subordinated to it. What was more, since MPR was a movement of the people, every citizen was automatically a member including Catholic Priests! It was also in 1970 that the Congo was officially renamed the Republic of Zaire. This set in motion a wholesale trend of renaming towns, rivers and places all across the country. The Congo River became the Zaire River. Leopoldville reverted to Kinshasa, the original name of the little fishing village which once was found on the river bank where the capital was now located. In EMC/CIM territory, Charlesville reverted to Djoko Punda, Luluabourg to Kananga, and Bakwanga to Mbuji Mayi - - all original pre-colonial names for these places. (11)

By this time Vatican figures in Rome had contacted the Zaire Catholic Church hierarchy sounding a note of warning. In response, an eleven-person permanent committee was formed in Zaire which included two Belgian bishops and was headed by Cardinal Malula, the Archbishop of Kinshasa. Malula had earlier been outspoken in his opposition to Lumumba during his brief tenure as Congo's Prime Minister. Once convinced that Mobutu and the MPR were also moving on a threatening course, he did not hesitate to say so. To make his concerns clear, he chose a moment of maximum exposure - - June, 1970, on the occasion of the celebration of a decade of Zairian independence. A special service was held in the Catholic Cathedral in Kinshasa with King Baudouin from Belgium present along with President Mobutu and top ranking officials of the capital. In the course of his sermon Malulu painted a negative picture of recent events stating that he detected some "dictatorial tendencies" on the part of the regime. As an example he cited the demand of the government that all youth movements and particularly those of the Church be incorporated into the youth wing of the MPR, i.e., *La Jeunesse du Mouvement Populaire Révolutionnaire*, which quickly came to be known by its acronym JMPR.

The same year all three universities in the country were unified into a single academic entity with three campuses. This meant that *Louvanium*, the prestigious Catholic University at Kinshasa, would no longer be under the direct control of the Church. (12) More serious still, there was talk of government plans to take over all primary education across the nation.

The honeymoon between the Catholic Church and the MPR was over.

In 1971, the church/state confrontation escalated rapidly. In a public speech President Mobutu made reference to the various monuments scattered across the country which had been erected in honor of the colonial rulers and suggested that they be taken down. In the same speech he gave the theme of authenticity new meaning by stating publicly he was abandoning his "Christian" name of Joseph Désiré, given at the moment of Catholic baptism, and was taking family names which had meaning and significance in his clan and country: Mobutu Seso Seko Kuku-Ngbendu Wa-Za-Banga. (13) Following his "suggestion," Christians all across the country, Protestant as well as Catholic, felt pressured to drop their foreign names, which were often Biblical, and to adopt clan and parental names. Furthermore, Zairians were now to address each other not as Mr., Mrs., or Miss but rather as *Citoyen* and *Citoyenne*, i.e., the French masculine and feminine terms for fellow citizen. In Zaire's church communities, the name change was at best half-hearted. In Protestant circles, at least, if the new titles were used in addressing letters and in conversation with strangers in public places, in private and among friends the Biblical names taken at baptism were largely retained.

Western dress styles also came to be frowned upon. Neckties were to be discarded and short-sleeved, open-necked jackets became the mode for men. For a time, liquor imported from overseas was prohibited with the explanation that every village had its own alcoholic beverages which sufficed. Women were enjoined to quit using western cosmetics and to wear their hair in its natural, kinky form.

Confrontation with the Catholic Church came to flash point over the issue of the JMPR youth cells which the government demanded be organized in schools across the country - - including Catholic institutions at all levels. To draw a line, Archbishop Malula declared there would be no such political youth cell in the large Seminary Jean XXIII in Kinshasa. MPR leaders promptly responded by closing the school! Furthermore, there were to be no more meetings of the Council of Bishops of the country; religious magazines and religious radio programs of whatever faith were suspended.

For Zaire Mennonites, the harshest impact of this period was the forced creation of political youth cells in all its schools. A popular feature was a 15 minute "rally" each morning, before entering the class rooms, which featured the raising of the MPR flag and the shouting of political slogans supportive of Mobutu all of which was accompanied by singing and dancing. Meanwhile the youth were called upon by Mobutu to serve as the "eyes and ears" of the revolution. It is not difficult to understand the deep anxiety felt by both missionaries and church leaders as they often witnessed the daily political hubbub created on their stations and at their regional centers. In a few instances, mission and church personnel were reported to MPR officers for lack of enthusiasm and even for alleged opposition to the movement. (14)

Sensing that the situation was becoming volatile, Vatican officials called Cardinal Malula to Rome "for consultation." In his absence, local clergy called upon their faithful to pray for their Cardinal in Rome and that "the Holy Spirit might enlighten the president." (15) Hearing of this, the MPR responded that there were to be no more references to the Chief of State in public religious services. Furthermore, it was decided to wipe all religious holidays from the official calendar - - including Christmas and Easter!

The effort to ban Christmas as a holiday backfired badly for the government. Instead of a celebration concentrated around a single day, special evening activities were organized at the close of the work day by church leaders, both Catholic and Protestant, which were spread over a solid week. Support for the call of a return to authentic African values was one thing; tolerating outright suppression of the Church and its freedom of worship was clearly another issue altogether.

Both the Church and the State knew instinctively that things had gone too far and this to the detriment of all concerned. There followed a series of face-saving maneuvers on the part of both power blocks and in due time normal church activities were gradually resumed. JMPR youth cells, however, were maintained in all schools. In the process it was made clear that Zaire would indeed be a secular state which would not be as responsive to Catholic agenda and pressures as had been the established pattern under the colonial regime.

Mobutu had hit on a popular theme. The proposed return to African values, in the aftermath of the oft repressive and oppressive colonial years, stirred quick response among the populace at large. He rode the crest of growing popularity and influence both inside and outside the country during the 1970's.

the ECZ is born

One government ruling which was to have particular implications for the Protestants of Zaire was the decision to limit official recognition of religious faiths within the country to six groups: Catholics, Protestants, Jews, Muslims, Greek Orthodox and Kimbanguists. (16) This government edict, which seemed to call for some form of united Protestant entity in the country, was not lost on Reverend Jean Bokeleale (pr. jah boh-kay-lay-AH-lay). A member of the Disciples of Christ Mission/Church which had for years made Mbandaka (pr. mbah-NDAH-kah) in northwest Zaire a center of its activity, he came through their schools demonstrating both marked scholastic and leadership abilities. Upon graduation he was given a scholarship for theological studies at the Free University of Brussels, Belgium. His diploma earned, he returned to Zaire and served for a time as the first African field secretary of their group. In 1968 he became a candidate for the position of executive secretary of the Congo Protestant Council which, like the mission/church groups which formed its membership, was in process of undergoing fundamental change.

The first recorded inter-Protestant gathering in the Congo took place in 1902 in Leopoldville. With intermittent gatherings, the sixth session was called in 1911 at the Disciples Station of Bolenge. A primary concern, by that time, was to "implement the findings of the Edinburgh Conference on World Mission held in 1910." (17) Thought to be the first missionary response to that Conference, it was decided to constitute a Congo Continuation Committee and to start a periodical for circulation among Protestant missionaries in the Congo. The first issue of the Congo Mission News appeared in November 1912.

It was in 1925 that the Continuation Committee met for the last time to approve the creation of the Congo Protestant Council which replaced it and which for many years thereafter was popularly known by its acronym CPC. From its inception, it was regarded and organized as an advisory council of missions which met annually "to unify and develop work of Protestant Evangelical Missions in the conventional basin of the Congo; to foster the Church of Christ in Congo and to relate the Protestant community effectively to the authorities and to the Christian bodies in other lands." (18) All Protestant Missions were encouraged to join the newly founded Council. The only requirement was to have secured a legal charter from the Congo government. (19)

Under steadily growing pressure from the Catholic Church, it was felt to be of critical importance to establish a CPC office in Leopoldville and to name a full time secretary authorized to speak before government in behalf of the broad Protestant community in the country. In 1928 such an office was opened. Dr. Emory Ross, of the Disciples of Christ Mission, was the first executive secretary. (20) Constituted originally as a Council of Missions, delegates for many years were obviously missionaries. CPC sessions were consultative in nature; actions passed were recommendations only and had no binding power upon Mission members. By the late 50's, some missionary delegates were taking some of their church leaders with them to CPC sessions as observers.

The CPC meeting of February 1960 marked a critical turning point in the history of this organization. It was convened at a conference center named Kumbya on the shores of scenic Lake Kivu in eastern Congo. Composed of an equal mix of missionaries and African church leaders, (21) there was a tingle of excitement in the air. Political independence was just a matter of months away. A CIM missionary who was a delegate wrote later: "From the first there was an undercurrent of expectancy - - an awareness that there would never be another CPC meeting exactly like this one. Everyone sensed that during this week the closing paragraphs of a wondrously colorful chapter of Congo Missions would be written and the first blank page of a new chapter eagerly turned by ebony hands. . . . From the Kumbya conference room there is a matchless view of Lake Kivu. Though it is some forty miles wide at this point, three volcanoes loom massively on its distant shore. Geologists long have pondered the herculean subterranean forces which underlie this great Rift Valley. Though they stand currently silent like three great brooding sentinels, they have been erupting sporadically over the years and are capable of exploding into life again at any time, a striking backdrop for the 1960 Kumbya Conference." (22)

Speaking of the mood of the African delegates he suggested that it had perhaps been best summarized by a pastor who said: "'We face the future with apprehension because we know things will change greatly. We don't know in what way we may be tested or exactly what problems we will face. But we as church leaders cannot permit ourselves any other thought than that of marching forward. Our country is changing but our God and our work does not change. We call upon our missionaries to share with us this new experience and to work side by side with us. We ask that the Mission and the Church may now in reality become one and that all the little barriers of past days be removed.'" (23)

Before the Kumbya Conference came to a close, Rev. Pierre Shaumba (pr. shah-UH-mbah) ,a long-time leader of the Zaire Methodist Church, was elected to serve as co-general secretary of the CPC for the year 1960-61 with the missionary secretary of the time, Rev. R.V. de Carle Thompson. It was stipulated that after one year of transition, Rev. Shaumba would function alone as the head of the CPC. Rev. Shaumba represented an older generation of African church leadership. While serving as an effective spokesman for the CPC community in the troubled 60's, he never viewed the CPC as anything other than it had been founded to be, i.e., a Protestant Council whose primary functions were to provide opportunity for fellowship, mutual support, counsel and some joint inter-mission/church projects. In his view, its nature remained consultative; it exercised no authority over member mission/churches.

It was on the occasion of the 1968 annual meeting of the CPC that Rev. Jean Bokeleale was elected to succeed Rev. Shaumba as general secretary. A representative of a younger, more visionary generation of African church leadership, it soon became evident that he had some new ideas as to how the many Protestant Churches scattered across the country should view each other and their Council. During his first two years in office, Rev. Bokeleale and a small group of associates led an aggressive campaign which was to result in a radical re-casting of both the Council and the Protestant community of the land.

The March, 1969, meeting of the CPC was the first following Bokeleale's election of the previous year. Entitled to two delegates that year, EMC sent a missionary and a Congolese. (24) Writing to the Elkhart office during the CPC sessions, the missionary delegate observed: "John Bokeleale is a forthright, well-educated man with broad background. [He makes frequent references to] "the shame of Protestantism today in Congo, i.e., divisions within established churches, friction between missions and churches, little sects everywhere. He makes references to a parallel with the political history of this country and whereas before there were also many groups with friction and fighting, now there is one party, one army, one objective - - and there is peace. He has directly or by implication let us understand several things: 1) the bishop system of ecclesiastical authority is good for Congo; 2) the period of missions is past; 3) it is our duty to collaborate closely and in every manner possible with the present government; 4) Scripture teaches us the ideal of unity; 5) until we have a single church, people will not believe that we are serious about our religion or that we love either the Lord or each other; 6) Protestantism is at an impasse in Congo because of its internal struggles; 7) drastic action will have to be taken if we are to save the day." (25)

In a further note written from Kinshasa toward the close of the CPC sessions it is remarked: "There are numerous (CPC) minutes which touch our interests and concerns: 1) All member mission organizations are to fuse with their churches, i.e., become one with a single legal status. 2) A clear, frank drive toward some form of unity in the Congo Church. This is all still nebulous, no guidelines spelled out, but the basic commitment is there nonetheless. . . .[This is not necessarily envisioned] within the framework either of the World Council of Churches or the Evangelical Alliance here in Africa. As a matter of fact it is . . . stated that these are foreign quarrels and they don't want to have any part of them. 3) There is also a move to try to concentrate ecclesiastical control in the hands of the CPC officers which of course immediately poses the question: What is the CPC finally? - - an organ of service for the church community or an ecclesiastical entity in itself?" (26)

In a field report to the CIM Board in its 1969 fall sessions, the following comments are found: "A key meeting is scheduled for the Executive Committee of the CPC before the end of this year when the details of organic union of the Congo Protestant Community are to be discussed and spelled out. This sort of talk has stirred some foreboding in some quarters, particularly on the part of those who aggressively support the Evangelical Alliance here in Congo and Africa. They foresee in this move the beginning of the end. . . . A great deal hinges on what the Executive Committee comes up with in the way of proposals for church union out here. If it is some sort of loose, top-level affiliation which allows for autonomy and independence of action at the individual church and mission level while permitting a single authentic voice at the top before government and the Catholic Church, this of itself is not necessarily bad. We must recognize that the Congo has its own particular situation, its own particular historical peculiarities in which the Protestant Church must find its way and seek to assure its future. We must as strangers in the land be cautious about attempting to impose upon them pat, made-in-America attitudes and structures. We are very reluctant to start shouting that CPC is a lost cause and to charge off seeking a new and conflicting affiliation. However, should the Executive Committee come out with proposals that would in reality curtail the freedom of individual church/mission groups and subject them to some type of imposed, autocratic rule from on high, the whole picture would immediately take on a different cast." (27)

"fusion": also a battle cry

In the 1969 Assembly of the CPC, Jean Bokeleale and his staff had come to the delegates with two new concepts - - the fusion of mission and church and the creation of a single, country-wide "Church of Christ" of which all existing churches would become members known as "communities." A year later, on the occasion of the 1970 Assembly sessions, CPC staff was ready to spell out both proposals in detail and to push hard for final adoption. With the African flair for celebrating official occasions with pomp and circumstance, the opening session was marked by the presence of government representatives and by religious figures including Catholic Cardinal Malula and Joseph Diangenda, the head of the Kimbanguist Church.

As regarded the proposal for fusion of mission and church, expressions of reservation and concern were few and those came primarily from missionary delegates who sought to raise issues of ongoing freedom of missionary endeavor and the future of the many mission institutions across the country. A pastor delegate perhaps best summarized the African view and mood when he said: "This is our country; grant us the right to make our own decisions and value judgements whether political, cultural or spiritual. . . . The missionary has brought us the Holy Scriptures and the Gospel. We are forever grateful. Now allow us to adapt and incorporate this Book and this Good News into our life and culture in this our period of Congo history. . . . If the missionaries cannot wholeheartedly join us in all our proposals, may they at least allow us the freedom to shape the future of our church in this our land without interference." (28) When the call for fusion was submitted to the delegates for a vote, it was passed by an overwhelming majority.

The second proposal, that of creating a single Congo-wide church, met with more resistance. This time, reservations were openly expressed by missionary and African delegates alike. For some there was a problem of legality, if not logic, in attempting to transform a consultative council into a single national church. For others, an overriding concern was that of identity. What would be the results of becoming "communities" within the proposed national church structure? What freedoms would be threatened? What efforts to dictate doctrine and practice? CPC staff repeatedly insisted that the concern and need were for a national "image" and a single, authoritative voice to represent and defend them all before government and the powerful Catholic Church in the land. At the local level, freedom to pursue church life would remain just as in the past. It was finally proposed that the concept of a single Protestant Church be approved in principle but that detailed bylaws be drafted and distributed for study. At whatever point the bylaws were approved by a future CPC Assembly, the Church of Christ of Congo would become a reality. It was this motion which, at 2:00 AM on a Sunday morning, finally secured a 2/3 majority vote. As willed by the delegates to the Assembly of 1970, the historic Congo Protestant Council was on its way to becoming the Church of Christ of Congo (ECC in its acronym form; after the country was re-named Zaire, the acronym became ECZ).

The 1970 CPC Assembly held still further significance for the Zaire Mennonite family. For years Pastor Kazadi had attempted to secure CPC recognition for the autonomous Church he had founded but had met with resistance both from EMC and CPC leadership. But in the drive to bring into being a broad church structure across the land, CPC staff, in the spring of 1970, were courting friends and support. Thus the AEMSK was recommended and accepted for CPC membership. With the subsequent change of CPC terminology, Kazadi's group came to be known as the *Communauté Evangélique Mennonite* or, by the French acronym, CEM.

Fusion. Suddenly it was a word heard in Protestant communities all across Zaire. It also was a word that appeared with persistent regularity in correspondence between field mission leaders and their home office staffs. Reporting to the CIM board in its 1970 spring sessions, CIM's field chairman sought to spell out what fusion meant for them: "the cancellation of the legal charter of the mission; - missionaries becoming members of the church with full rights and privileges of a member; - all property and equipment of the mission passing to the church; - a single budget for the field and all funds passing through the church-appointed treasurer; - direct relations between the Church and the overseas Mission Board without an intermediary."

As regarded the newly voted constitution of the CPC, newly named the ECC, the report to the board pointed out that " - the CPC as a consultative body is changed into the national assembly of a church; - the Kinshasa secretariat becomes the apex of the ecclesiastical hierarchy of a church; - the General Secretary and Legal Representative of the Kinshasa CPC office become the General Secretary and Legal Representative of a church. Remain unchanged: - the general composition of the assembly commissions and their responsibilities; - the autonomy of the local churches in matters of doctrine, polity, organization, tradition, program and emphasis; - conditions of membership, of dissolution and exclusion, etc."(29)

On the part of missionaries who attended the 1970 session, there were some reservations and negative reactions to what was viewed as pressure of CPC staff people prior to and during the sessions for immediate approval of their recommendations as submitted; - the growing emphasis upon organization and bureaucracy; - the proposed concentration of power in a small group of people in Kinshasa; - the rough-handed and sometimes distorted evaluation of missions and missionaries that came out on occasion; - and just the concept of what was felt to be an imposed church union and an imposed fusion of mission and church bodies in the country.

Field reporting to the home board in the spring of 1970 on this topic was concluded by observing: "We must remember always that this is their country and their church. We must grant that they have the right to struggle, now, with the problems of their day and there time. We must strive to analyze as honestly as we possibly can our own attitudes. To what extent are our opinions validated by Scripture and to what extent are they shaped by our own American Mennonite cultural and religious traditions? We must believe that the Spirit of God can work through today's Congolese leaders to bring about his purpose in the Church we have had a share in bringing into being. We must never forget that if the Congo Church is to take root and become a viable part of the Congolese life and culture, it will be because it has been appropriated and adapted by the Congolese themselves to the needs, concepts and realities of this their land as they see them, feel them and live them." (30)

Like many other delegates, those from the EMC returned to Tshikapa with some genuine reservations regarding the proposed country-wide church union which was being pushed by the ECC leadership. They, like others, were reserving judgment until they could study the eventual bylaws which would spell out the freedom of action and degree of autonomy reserved for member "communities." But they, like others, responded enthusiastically to the proposal of fusion of mission and church. After all, long strides had already been taken in that direction in their 1967 consultation with a CIM Board delegation. The fusion now proposed by national church leaders was but a final, logical conclusion of a process already begun.

In North America, plans were already underway for another Board delegation to travel to Zaire in early 1971. In 1967 the delegation had found a theme of integration which focused on bringing mission/church resources into a single joint effort. This time, the burning issue would be the desire to fuse CIM and EMC into a single, legal entity - - a very different and revolutionary proposal indeed.

CHAPTER 21   STRUGGLING WITH NEW INTERNAL TENSIONS

The EMC/CIM community was a beehive of activity in the late 60's. 1967 had seen the travel of EMC's fraternal delegation to North America. Composed of EMC President Ngongo David and Assistant Legal Representative Tshilembu Nicodème, the trip had done much to heighten mutual awareness and appreciation between the church in Congo and churches in North America. Integration patterns agreed upon in 1967 were being implemented. Africans were filling new roles and responsibilities with a sense of excitement and purpose. The EMC officers had all been located at Kalonda/Tshikapa. Quickly accessible to each other, consultation was easy. Meetings of the newly created executive committee were frequent. A variety of commissions and sub-commissions had been formed. Annual conferences had become times of well-organized discussion, planning and decision making. The General Conference held at Mukedi, July 8-15, 1968 is a case in point. The first church-wide EMC function to be hosted in the Kwilu following the rebellion, the thought-provoking theme "Come and See" was adopted with an accompanying theme verse John 1:46: "Can any good thing come out of Nazareth? Philip answered, 'Come and see.'" The Mukedi people clearly intended to show that they had not only survived the fires of rebellion but were ready and eager to again take their place in the EMC family.

The literature committee met twice in 1968 in long working sessions resulting in more than 40 separate actions related to literature production and distribution within EMC territory. Three actions had to do with the writing and translation of a pamphlet entitled "Who Are the Mennonites?" Plans for the writing, printing and distribution of Sunday School lessons and daily devotional reading guides across the area were put in place. Numerous pamphlets were approved and assigned both to missionaries and Africans for writing. A new edition of the Giphende song book was requested.

The "Christ for All" campaign had reached a peak of activity in the course of 1968 with extensive itineraries made by Mayambi Sosthène and his team. Detailed reports of travel, meetings held, attendance and people dealt with were submitted to the EMC officers. Of particular note were the mass rallies held at Tshikapa, Kananga and Kikwit assisted by Jean Perce Makanzu, a gifted preacher who had been commissioned by the CPC of the time as a national evangelist. Many thousands of people had attended meetings in the course of these campaigns in EMC territory and hundreds responded to invitations for counseling and prayer. Year-end statistics in 1968 indicated that the EMC primary school population was approaching 20,000 students with over 700 secondary students.

Concerned that there be the broadest and most mature representation of the church within the administrative committee, action was taken in January of 1970 to enlarge it to 13 members. The roster was made up of people from every area where EMC was at work and included both lay people and experienced pastors, Congolese merchants and church officers plus two missionaries. (1)

By year's end 1970 the CIM roster of missionaries on active status was again approaching one hundred adults. (2) Their places of assignment and ministry ranged across the following locations: ETEK, LECO, the CIM children's hostel in Kinshasa; an inter-mission hospital at Kimpese in western Congo; IMCK, Liproka and Studiproka at Luluabourg; and Tshikapa, Kalonda, Nyanga, Mutena, Mukedi, Kamayala and Djoko Punda stations. And overshadowing all was the country-wide ferment among mission/church groups generated by the universal African expectation that some form of mission/church fusion would be worked out before long.

But amidst the buzz of expanding EMC/CIM activity, there were internal rumbles which were becoming increasingly audible. There were three primary issues which were generating discontent and dissension within the Church itself. The first was rooted in the South Kasai.

EMC/AEMSK Frictions

Under the able leadership of Pastor Kazadi, the Evangelical Mennonite Church of the South Kasai (AEMSK) had become a reality despite the opposition and resentment manifested by the EMC and its leadership. Confrontation and friction between these two Mennonite Churches was a constant reality in the late

60's and this at two levels. First, there were the persistent AEMSK requests for their share of the *patrimoine,* a French term for legacy or inheritance. By this time the CIM had given many chapels, schools and material resources over to the EMC. The AEMSK was also made up of sons and daughters of the CIM. When were they to receive some of this same largesse at the hands of the Mission?

Not only was there dispute between the two Churches at a national level but also at a regional level in the South Kasai itself. As explained earlier, the political cleavage of the region, rooted in the two major Baluba clans, had finally divided the Mennonite refugee community. The one, under the leadership of Pastor Kazadi, had ultimately sought and obtained government recognition as a new autonomous church. Those belonging to the opposing clan decided to maintain ties with the EMC based at Tshikapa. The relations between these two South Kasai refugee groups, which had always been tenuous, were further strained by conflict over access to and allocation of government subsidies for their respective schools.

On one occasion the EMC appointed a special commission to go to Mbuji Mayi in an attempt to sort things out and to establish some equitable solution. They were met by government representatives and were lodged under what amounted to house arrest. Next morning they were ordered to leave without having made contact with EMC loyalists of the area! (3)

Against this background of quarreling, it is not surprising that the differences between the two Churches came sharply into focus at the EMC General Conference of 1967 held at Djoko Punda. Mutangilayi Norbert had come as a representative of the AEMSK to officially press his Church's claims. As regarded the *patrimoine* issue, EMC's stance was made clear enough in a conference minute which read in part: "It is impossible to do this since the separation was not caused by the EMC. We suggest that the AEMSK rejoin the EMC." (4)

Muambi Lutonga: once again an agent of peace

It was in the midst of these tensions between the two Churches that Archie and Irma Graber were preparing for their return to the States for retirement. This news became an agenda item for the EMC Administrative Committee which held sessions in January, 1969, at Kalonda station. Recognizing the outstanding impact of Graber's ministry across the years among the Tshiluba speaking people of the two Kasais and beyond, a special planning committee was named to organize an event of recognition and celebration. (5) Meeting shortly thereafter, the committee called for a weekend in May, suitable to the Grabers, to which delegations would be invited from the various areas where they had served in the past. At one point in the planning, the missionary member of the committee suggested that an invitation be sent to Pastor Kazadi and the AEMSK at Mbuji May as well. While the African committee members expressed skepticism that anyone would come, they did not oppose the proposal.

The first weekend in May was set. Friday would be the day for arrival of all guests. Saturday there would be an open air feast with those who had come from a distance. On Sunday morning Graber would be invited to preach in the in the Kalonda church which he had built. Sunday afternoon there would be a tea primarily for local people. Opportunity would be given on both social gatherings to address expressions of appreciation to the Grabers.

By Friday evening all was in readiness; the Grabers and all the delegations had arrived, or so it was thought. But there was a surprise in store for all. Author Levi Keidel portrays it as follows: "About 2 AM on the morning of the special day, Bertsche was awakened by a tapping on his front veranda door. He got up and opened the door. The scene was bathed with light from a full moon. Out front he saw a worn, mud-splattered Landrover; in the shadows of the veranda he recognized the tall, slender silhouette of Pastor Kazadi. 'I'm sorry to trouble you at a bad time like this,' Kazadi said. 'We started out yesterday morning. The roads are terribly bad; we had lots of trouble. We kept getting stuck in the mud. Had someone not helped us, we never would have arrived. But now we are here. We are tired and dirty. Can we find a place to sleep? There are five of us.' It was the first time since the rending events of 1960 that a Muluba church leader had returned to the AIMM

(CIM) field to make his appearance among those who had expelled the tribe. The respect Kazadi had for Archie overcame the qualms he had about the kind of reception he would encounter. [Kalonda church] leaders who had been skeptical of his coming were now rousted from bed to arrange sleeping quarters for their guests." (6)

Among the many tributes paid to the Grabers by the assembled Africans on Saturday, none were more eloquent or heartfelt than those presented by Pastor Kazadi in the name of the large Mennonite refugee community of the South Kasai. The written statement prepared by the group and read in the presence of all said: "We experience a deep joy to testify to this generous family of our total gratitude for the service so richly deserving of praise which they rendered to the Congolese during their stay among us in Congo - - particularly in the Kasai and the Kwilu. In effect, he was not satisfied to limit his activities to preaching activities only as so many do, but succeeded in setting a standard which is very difficult for many preachers of this world to attain, a standard which is nothing more than the application of the supreme commandment of our Lord and Savior Jesus Christ - - LIVE WHAT YOU TEACH!"

"Many Congolese and particularly those from the martyr regions, among whom we ourselves find our place, are not ready to forget the total disregard for self and life that was shown by Rev. Graber in order to bring help both material and spiritual to the poor populations that were victims of the experiences that our country lived through during the years 1959-1964. More than once you risked death in stepping high over piles of dead bodies in order to bring help to those who still lived while arms were exploding all around you. In this benevolent sacrifice of yourselves for us, we ask you, Rev. Graber and family, to accept our immense and infinite gratitude." (7)

Keidel again picks up the account: "Tables were prepared under a spreading mango tree. There was a big feast that day, and speech-making and singing and reminiscing. Archie was overwhelmed with a sense of unworthiness. AIMM missionaries had left their distant posts to come join the festivities. Kazadi and his friends had sacrificed so much to come. Still, Archie recalled, the church was split. While conversing with Kazadi that afternoon, he felt prompted to broach the subject. 'You've been telling people today that you are unable to finish your indebtedness to me.' 'Yes, that's the way it is.' 'In my heart I feel there is a debt you have to me which you can repay.' 'What kind of debt?' Lutonga weighed his response. It was strong medicine but he believed his old friend would take it. 'How can I return to my home country and retire in happiness when I remember that part of the AIMM (CIM) church is split off to itself, estranged from the mother who gave it birth and from her other children? Will it stay that way forever? That is the debt I want you to finish.'"

"Kazadi was moved deeply. What Lutonga had said was more than an appeal; it was a commission."(8)

It was the late afternoon of that same day that Pastor Kazadi and Elder Ntambue Paul, a Djoko Punda Bible School teacher of other days and a fellow AEMSK leader, came again to the Bertsche home. In a letter to the mission office in Elkhart, the encounter is described as follows: "Kazadi underlined two things: 1) 'We want you and the board at home to know that we have always been and will always be children of the CIM. 2) We'll always be Mennonites and want very much to find some way of opening fellowship between ourselves and other Mennonites of the Congo.' I don't know what may finally come of all this but it might just possibly be that Archie's farewell provided the spark to reopen contacts with the Mbuji Mayi group." (9)

For the first time a ray of hope had broken through the somber clouds which had for so long hung over CIM's inter-church scene. Tensions would still continue to be serious for some while to come, but there had been a glimpse of possible eventual healing of the wounds. With continual efforts on the part of CIM personnel and church leaders on both sides, better days were, in fact, on the way.

static from the bleachers

By the spring of 1970, another source of discontent within EMC was also becoming clear. By then several classes had graduated from the Bible Institute. More significantly still, the first class of the inter-

Mennonite Theological School at Kajiji had also finished their studies and returned to EMC land. While their academic achievements were duly applauded and admired as they returned to their home church districts, they soon discovered that the EMC leaders and veteran corps of older pastors were not overly impressed with these young, somewhat brash and self-confident men and the new diplomas they held in hand. While strongly affirming the schools and programs from which they had graduated, the wisdom of age suggested that this new generation of prospective church leaders needed to prove itself worthy and capable of assuming growing responsibility within the church just as an older generation of pastors, in an earlier day, had had to do. Thus new graduates were discovering, to their disappointment and chagrin, that their diplomas did not mean automatic prestige or ordination as pastors within the EMC.

With the impatience and hyperbole of youth the world around, a letter dated March 31,1970, was drawn up by the seven EMC Kajiji graduates and addressed to the Congo Inland Mission, the EMC students studying in ETEK at the time and to the members of the full EMC Administrative Committee. Under the heading "Manifestation of Dissatisfaction," the letter said in part: "Dear Brothers in Christ: It is with the greatest regret that we ascertain as a result of actions taken toward us, that the EMC has no need of theologians. It is this attitude which permits us to write to you for the first and last time in order to explain to you how fed up we are with the inhuman acts which we encounter with the EMC. We ask that you be willing to lighten our yoke." A series of grievances were then listed which the drafters of the letter obviously felt would substantiate their complaints. They then concluded the letter by urging that "a remedy for the deplorable situation be found within a period of no more than two months. Otherwise we will be obliged to confirm our schism from the EMC on the occasion of the General Conference at Kalonda." (10)

In a classic example of African indirect response to a brewing problem, the program of the general conference held three months later at Kalonda was liberally sprinkled with the names of the offended Kajiji graduates. One was given a series of Bible studies; another was assigned a topic for exploration with the conference delegates; others had opportunity to demonstrate their theological insights in early morning devotionals with the conference delegates. It was not long, despite their agitated letter, that the Kajiji graduates found their way into significant roles of leadership and ministry within EMC.

tabled for lack of agreement

There was, however, a third focus of friction within the EMC, at the close of the decade of the 1960's, which was much more deeply rooted and was much more of a threat for the life and future of the Church. Fundamentally, it had to do with distribution of roles of top leadership and representation of the widely-scattered major tribal groups within the top circles of EMC decision making administration.

In the late 1950's and early 60's the senior, more experienced pastoral EMC leadership tended to come from the Baluba personnel of the pioneer station Djoko Punda. In early 1961, right after the return of the first CIM missionaries and at the occasion of the first meeting of the administrative committee, efforts were made to approve a slate of officers and a set of bylaws in order to apply for the Church's legal charter. In keeping with the pattern of the time, the candidates for the two key positions of president and legal representative were both Baluba. Seeing this as a concentration of authority in the hands of a single ethnic group within the Church, delegates from other tribes blocked proceedings by refusing to attend a final session where the legal forms were to be signed. The effectiveness of this strategy was not lost on the Baluba members. The time would come when they would employ it as well with equally paralyzing impact upon conduct of church business.

With the explosive impact of the tribal conflict in 1960-61 and the consequent migration of Baluba eastward to their ancestral homeland, a vacuum in top EMC church leadership was created which was soon filled by Baphende candidates - - Nyanga pastor Ngongo David as president and Mukedi layman Kakesa Samuel as legal representative. While members of other tribal groups completed the top leadership, it was this Baphende president/legal representative team which provided leadership during the period when the Church secured its legal charter, drafted its first constitution, forged the CIM/EMC integration plan, and launched a series of new programs.

With the accession of Joseph Mobutu to national power, the return of political stability and the clustering of EMC officers at Kalonda/Tshikapa, the question of a permanent EMC headquarters began to surface with regularity. As early as 1965, administrative committee discussions reflected this concern and pointed a tentative direction: "That our EMC/CIM office be built at Tshikapa/Kalonda. To this end the legal representative should submit a request for the enlargement of the present Kalonda concession." (11) (12)

Partially due to the fact that there was no response from the provincial government regarding the request and also due to the fact that the EMC officers continued to be housed in very crowded living and working quarters, the officers began investigating the possibility of securing a concession for the Church across the river in Tshikapa proper along the main road leading south out of the center and just adjacent to the government airstrip. By late 1968 the officers were optimistic enough that in an executive committee session they took the action to consult Archie Graber "concerning a logical plan for the construction of our administrative center." (13)

A month later during sessions of the full administrative committee, however, there was less optimism that the government would accord the Church such a choice parcel of ground. After lengthy discussion and debate, it was decided to renew the EMC request to enlarge the existing Kalonda concession if for no other reason than to accommodate the growing mission/church program at that station. But when some of the committee members urged that specific plans be laid to construct the church headquarters at Kalonda as had once been proposed, there was immediate opposition on the part of other committee members. This stalemate was clearly reflected in the minutes of those sessions: "That in view of our lack of agreement concerning the location of our administrative center for the EMC we table, for now, the matter of the construction of this center." (14)

The EMC General Conference of July 1969 was held at Kabeya Kamuanga, which in and of itself was a remarkable achievement. Though the transportation of delegates to this southeastern corner of EMC territory represented a formidable logistical task, there was a unanimous desire to respond to the invitation extended by their refugee brethren of the South Kasai to convene the first conference of this kind in that area. Upon arrival it became quickly apparent that these former refugees were intent on hosting their fellow delegates from the Kwilu and the West Kasai with a flourish amidst an atmosphere of joy and thanksgiving. Unfortunately, a sour note of discord was to surface before the conclusion of the gathering.

It was at this conference that the questions of church leadership and the location of an EMC church center came to be linked as equally volatile issues. It was by this time known that the government had refused to grant land in Tshikapa proper. Located on a neutral wedge of terrain between the converging Tshikapa and Kasai Rivers, it would have been an acceptable spot for all had the government seen fit to grant it at that time. But to reintroduce new requests, it was felt, would only be a further waste of time. Thus two rival points of view quickly surfaced within the delegate body: one which held that the center should be located at Kalonda Station east of the Kasai River (and in traditional Baluba/Lulua territory), and another which advocated locating it at Bena Nshimba, a rapidly growing suburb of Tshikapa on the west side of the river (and in the traditional Baphende territory.)

Complicating delegate sessions even further, that year at Kabeya Kamuanga, was the uncertainty about the inauguration of a new a cycle of elections for church officers as stipulated in EMC's first constitution which had just been approved at that same conference. (15) Those from east of the Kasai River felt that an election of a new president should be held without further delay. To their disappointment and irritation, a majority opinion prevailed to defer this election until the next conference which was scheduled for Kalonda the following year.

When it became clear to the delegates east of the Kasai that there would be no decision regarding the location of the proposed headquarters nor a vote for a new president, they stalked out of what was to have been the concluding delegate session. Taking the Coleman pressure lamps with them they left the remainder of the delegates sitting in the dark! Needless to say, the conference was brought to an abrupt close. The only reference to this episode in the conference minutes is the following: "Because of a lack of a 2/3 majority vote, it is impossible for us for the present to determine the location of an administrative center. The problem will be reviewed again later on." (16)

While the divisive debate regarding the placement of EMC's central offices commanded much time and attention among the church leaders and members in the late 1960's, there was yet another source of internal discontent. Though less clearly recognized and articulated, it was rapidly becoming clear that the far flung districts of the Church were finding it difficult to relate to a highly centralized church administrative structure. The delegate body assembled in an annual conference represented and exercised the ultimate authority within the Church. Between such gatherings, however, it was the administrative and the executive committees which made interim decisions. Frequently when issues arose needing quick attention out in the church districts, the answer was either that they had to wait for the next meeting of the administrative committee or even until the next general conference for discussion and decision. Under such conditions it was easy for remote church districts to feel both hampered and isolated in their work.

both tense and busy

The 1969-70 church year was in many ways a strange one. Some good things were happening. A packet of questionnaires was worked out and distributed to all pastors in the first serious effort to gather church statistics in the post-independence era. Various church committees met for scheduled meetings and worked through lengthy agendas in a businesslike manner. EMC delegates also traveled to represent their Church in meetings of boards which had the oversight of inter-church endeavors. (17) A final 6th year of study was scheduled to open at the Nyanga secondary school in fall and the search was on for supplies and qualified teaching personnel. Pastor Kabangy Moise, who had served as the Kandala Station pastor since his graduation at Kajiji, was slated to join the school staff in fall as the student chaplain. The Kalonda Bible Institute had graduated a class in the spring and the process was under way to select from among the many applicants those who would be enrolled the following school year.

Word had been received from the central government that special subsidies would be made available to the EMC/CIM to reactivate schools that had been closed during the Kwilu rebellion. A university student home on vacation in the Banga area had asked if there was some contribution he could make to the work of his Church. It was suggested that he undertake the translation of the Gospel of Mark into his mother tongue, Kishelele (pr. ki-sheh-LAY-lay). The expectation was that before his return to school in mid-October he, in consultation with two fellow Bashilele tribesmen at work at Kalonda, would have a typed manuscript to submit. When accomplished, this would be the first draft of a New Testament book in their language. (18)

Genuine effort was being made by EMC leaders to more directly involve its broad membership in EMC projects. Specific Sundays were set on which offerings were invited for such projects as the development of ETEK, the new joint theological school in Kinshasa and for IMCK, the new medical center outside Luluabourg. Calls were also being issued by leadership challenging the EMC districts to make systematic contributions toward the cost of the central administration of their own Church.

It was also in the spring of 1970 that EMC leaders named a special three man committee which was instructed to study the newly-issued CPC call for fusion of mission/church bodies in the Congo. They were "to come with their report to the next general conference" which was scheduled four months later at Kalonda. (19)

But amidst the busyness and bustle of mission/church activity that spring of 1970, there continued an undercurrent of tension which needed little provocation to manifest itself. The cleavage of opinion which had disrupted the Kabeya Kamuanga Conference the previous dry season was also present within the executive and administrative committees. This unresolved agenda tended to color other issues. Sharp exchanges in committee sessions and curt notes exchanged between offices were not uncommon. Though unresolved agenda had been tabled at the last conference, fundamental discord continued unabated.

In a field report to the CIM board in its 1970 spring session, a missionary reviewed a series of substantive decisions made by the Church's administrative committee. There then followed a further observation: "But a couple of issues gingerly touched upon only served to highlight the basic regional and tribal struggle which exists within our Congo fellowship. While some decisions made in January have dropped the pressures considerably, the problem remains very real nonetheless. The role of the missionary in all of this is not easy to discern. . . . One thing is certain: in confronting these issues we deal directly with the life and future of our church. A God-given spirit of charity and wisdom is needed by all." (20)

an impasse prolonged

Early July 1970 found the EMC officers and local Kalonda church leaders busily preparing for the year's annual conference on their station. By the evening of the 7th, most of the delegates had arrived either by truck or by MAF plane. The conference was to officially open on the morning of the 8th. The planning committee had injected an optimistic note into the program by the adoption of the conference theme "Forward Together" accompanied by a theme text from I Cor 12:14: "The body is not made up of one part, but of many."

The committee which had been discussing the issue of possible fusion of CIM/EMC had done its work and had recommendations to submit to the delegate body. The administrative committee had also announced early in the year that an election for a new president would be held during these sessions. Who knew? Might this also be the time to come to agreement on the prickly issue of a location for the greatly needed church headquarters?

Sessions got under way smoothly enough. Following early morning sessions of Biblical study led by recent Kajiji graduates, the time was used either for hearing department and district reports or for dividing the delegate body into a variety of working commissions. Early in the proceedings the fusion study committee brought its report. The response was an enthusiastic and unanimous call for EMC/CIM to pursue the issue further. To this end, a special commission was appointed which met during conference sessions and came up with a sketch of the major concerns that would have to be studied and details that would have to be worked through. (21) The delegate body then further instructed the commission to meet in August or September to prepare a document clearly spelling out the Congolese point of view - - this in preparation for the arrival of a board delegation promised for January 1971.

It was on Monday evening that the delegates finally came to the point in the printed program which called for "various votes." It was intended at this point, among others, to hold elections for a new president who was to replace Pastor Ngongo David. It was also intended that the much discussed issue of the location of a church headquarters be resubmitted to the delegate body. After considerable discussion it was decided to address the headquarters question first. In a letter to the home office, one missionary described the ensuing scene: "After repeated restatement of various positions and arguments, it became clearer and clearer that there would be no agreement on this. Finally about midnight, the Mbuji Mayi folk told President Ngongo David that he could stay in his presidential chair, that they were leaving, that this was their last general conference of EMC, that they would no longer consider administrative committee minutes to be binding upon them and that they were prepared to run their own church affairs in their area. Following this cue, the Lulua folk expressed themselves in somewhat similar terms and also walked out. This left the Baphende, Batshoke and Bashilele delegates." (22)

Efforts next morning to reassemble the delegate body for a concluding session of the conference failed. Following breakfast, the delegates from the South Kasai called for their truck. As they clambered up the sides and into the back of their conveyance, their spokesman, a slim, energetic pastor, clamped his nondescript hat on his head and, as the chauffeur eased into first gear, declared in clipped Tshiluba: "Unless there are some changes made in EMC we won't be back." (23) For the second year in a row, a general conference of the EMC had ground to a premature close in an atmosphere of acrimony and clashing wills.

Despite the vehemence of their parting shot, however, some of them were to return in just a matter of weeks but only in response to a major intervention on the part of EMC leadership.

On Tuesday morning, July 14, there was to have been a seven o'clock communion service followed by breakfast and the departure of the delegates for their home areas. Instead, there had been the departure of a truck load of delegates from the eastern districts leaving the balance of the Africans and missionaries standing about in little clusters on the station. Reactions were varied. Some Africans expressed hurt and sadness and wondered out loud what was to become of their beloved Church. Other Africans, especially the younger men, carried on animated conversations punctuated with stabbing fingers and sweeping gestures of arms and hands. Snatches of phrases could be heard across the intervening distances between groups: "Two years in a row! No more respect than that for the Lord's table? Will we allow this to block our work in the western districts? And we all just voted for fusion! What will the CIM Board members think? How much longer do we put up with such actions?"

Missionaries, too, were talking here and there. What was to be made of all of this? Was there more beneath the surface than met the eye? Comments reflected a mix of disappointment and uncertainty. Even those who had been the most supportive of the proposal for fusion of Mission and Church were heard to voice some misgivings. A missionary letter written to the home office from Kalonda two days after the breakup of the conference reflected this uneasiness: "It is indeed anomalous that in the same conference that so unanimously and enthusiastically endorsed the idea of a fusion of EMC with CIM, the separatist tendencies among the Congolese themselves should crystalize in such clear fashion. I asked a number of them in the closing hours of the session just whom they proposed that the CIM fuse with? There seemed to be no ready answers!" (1)

In the same letter the missionary ventured some opinions as to the dynamics which underlay the disrupted church conferences two years hand running: "After having mulled and slept over all of this for a day or two it seems to me that we will have to admit that we have in reality been advocating a centralized administration that makes a lot of sense to a westerner - - efficiency, delegated authority and responsibility assuming impartial and fair service on the part of those named with pin-point statistics and neatly marshaled columns of figures and percentages. But all of this implies a long range subsidy from overseas to cover heavy travel expenses of officers and the meeting of large commissions and large conference groups - - even the building of a rather extensive set of offices with adjacent living quarters."

"There is a nagging realization that has been growing in the back of our collective missionary minds the last while, i.e., that the real, viable level of autonomous, self-propagating church administration is the district level and not the level projected in the new constitution. Something like a provincial level grouping of districts could be accomplished with a minimum of financial help from overseas. So, perhaps we've come to the point where we need to recognize that we've been trying to run the whole thing through the wrong model of sausage stuffer! The valid ingredients are all there but apparently our Congolese brethren here have some ideas of their own as to the model of stuffer they want to use with which to package the ingredients!" (2)

a rump session

Unknown to the missionary as he typed his letter to the home secretary, a significant meeting had just been closed at Nyanga Station. As it happened, the travel arrangements for all delegates west of the Kasai River, with the exception of those from Kikwit, scheduled them for an overnight stay at Nyanga Station. From there, next morning, they would fan out south, west and north to their home areas. Seizing upon the opportunity, an impromptu session was called of all delegates present. They totaled 27 people, including two missionaries, and represented seven different EMC districts - - Banga, Kamayala, Kandala, Mukedi, Nyanga, Shamuana and Bena Nshimba. Absent but declared to be supportive of the proposed agenda were four delegates from Kikwit.

Electing Pastor Kabangy Moise as their chairman, they set to work. Although they were limited for time, they turned out a formal record of the actions taken which ran to 17 articles. In a preamble it was stated, in part: "In view of numerous difficulties and misunderstandings caused by the rigid structure of our association known as the Mennonite Church of Congo (EMC); in view of the lack of unanimity among the members of the above mentioned association which caused the failure of our conference at Kabeya Kamuanga as well as the conference recently held at Kalonda; in view of the fact that our decision and plans for work must be approved by the general conference; we, the above named members of the EMC gathered together at Nyanga, July 15, 1970, declare our firm attachment to the Mennonite Church of the Congo. However, to bring an end to the anarchy which our association is experiencing and especially in the interests of efficiency, we make the firm decision to change the old structures of the EMC which no longer correspond to present realities and to replace them with others which grant a larger autonomy to regions which want to group themselves together in order to work well." (3)

Later in the statement it was proposed that the EMC be divided into different zones called conferences; that each conference be free to organize and direct its own evangelistic and educational programs under the legal jurisdiction of the EMC and its legal representative; that other regions and districts of the EMC have the liberty to organize themselves into conferences as well "to take in hand their own destiny instead of wasting their time and ours in further futilities. To this end we wish them good luck and success." (4)

A variety of further details were covered including some preliminary budget assessments, dates for the first district conferences under the newly proposed structure and the appointment of some educational personnel for the coming year. Officially adopting the name "The Conference of the North Zone," a final article read: "The present decisions go into effect as of today." (5)

the EMC executive acts

It was the evening of July 17 of the week of the disrupted Kalonda Conference that members of the EMC Administrative Committee resident in the Tshikapa area met to take counsel together. By this time they had word of the actions taken at Nyanga two days earlier by homeward bound conference delegates and realized that events were threatening to spin out of control.

During the evening, a number of decisions were made which were subsequently shared in a letter drafted and circulated throughout all of the EMC districts. Dated August 5, it stated among other things that "even though the delegates to the General Conference at Kalonda left without finishing their agenda of business and without solving many of our problems, we as members and officers of the EMC cannot accept that this situation remain confused." The letter then went on to state that three basic actions had been taken: 1) to issue an official set of minutes of the Kalonda Conference which would reflect major discussions held, opinions expressed as well as reports given and approved; 2) to assure the normal functioning and activities of the EMC in spite of the disarray created by the incomplete conference and 3) to call an emergency meeting of the complete administrative committee to be convened at Nyanga on September 1 "in order to take a tour of the horizon of our current problems together." (6)

The letter went on to state that there were three major areas of concern which would need to be addressed at the September meeting, i.e. 1) the sort of administrative structure now to be envisaged by the EMC "in view of the desire expressed for a larger regional autonomy." 2) How to "defend and present the proposal of fusion to the delegation from Elkhart expected in the month of January 1971." 3) "The burning question of organic union of the Protestant Churches of Congo about which everyone was talking but which was not even touched during our conference."

The circular letter concluded: "You will certainly agree with us that these are very basic problems which touch directly the future of our Church which must be resolved without any delay whatsoever."(7)

a second rump session

The initiative taken by the EMC Executive Committee came none too soon. Hearing of the Nyanga meeting held July 15 by overnighting delegates from the west, there was a flurry of response as representatives from seven of the EMC districts from the other side of the Kasai River were convened at Luluabourg on August 21-22. A total of 24 people were present.

Pastor Kadima Isaac was elected chairman. A theme adopted for the two day consultation was: "Where there is no possibility for man, there is possibility before God." In his opening remarks the chairman insisted that their gathering was not called simply to imitate what others had done at Nyanga after the Kalonda Conference but rather to try to see what could be done to redress the situation. (8) Early in the record of the two-day session it is stated: "Since the Congolese State does not accept the sort of division that is coming from our brethren of the north which is based upon languages and tribes; since the Congolese State hopes for a united people; since the Church of Christ of Congo (ECC) refuses categorically all divisions; since the ECC hopes for the unity of the churches and for the fusion of the churches, we, effective members and representatives of the EMC, forming the group outside the one that calls itself the Conference of the North, solemnly declare our loyalty and attachment to the Mennonite Church of Congo and particularly to its constitution and statutes." (9)

There then followed, in the record of the meeting, references to a series of incidents which they felt indicated either lack of concern for or deliberate maneuvering against the welfare of the EMC districts which they represented. Frequent references were made to "neglect and lack of integrity on the part of the group in power and in the majority." The document goes on to observe, however, that "in spite of everything, a conference remains a conference and we remain a part of this conference. . . . We maintain our position for the unity of the EMC and ask that after the meeting of the administrative committee at Nyanga that the general conference and the missionaries, the saboteurs of fusion, gather together for good discussions in order to review the major problem of the administration of the Church." Some attention was also given to school concerns and lists of teacher placement in schools of their districts were drawn up. The minutes were concluded with the phrase, "For a renewed contact." (10)

which way?

As the members of the full administrative committee made their ways from different directions toward Nyanga the last day of August, 1970, there was no need to underscore for anyone the heavy agenda and responsibility which awaited them all. A missionary reporting on the proceedings sent later to the home board observed: "There was an all-pervading sense of gravity as the meetings got under way. Conjecture was rife on all sides as to what the final outcome might be. Every committee member seemed to realize all too well that our Congo Church stood at a fork in the path." (11)

Assembled next morning in the Nyanga church office, a room which had been the setting for many another EMC gathering, President Ngongo David observed that there were still two members missing due to the fact that their truck had arrived at Tshikapa too late the previous day to be picked up by plane. But since MAF pilot George Wall had promised to make the 20-minute flight to get them as soon as the morning fog lifted, we would get started. Pastor David then called for a time of prayer. Bringing the period to a close some minutes later, he prayed for a spirit of peace and for courage to tackle the issues which lay before us. In concluding, he referred to the early morning flight to be made to bring the missing committee members. With the direct, uncluttered faith of the African Christian he prayed: "You know how it is up there in the air, Father God. When we enter that little plane there is nothing to hold on to. So please keep your hands under the wings of that little bird and bring our people to us safely."

There then followed a moment of drama described to the home board as follows: "We were already gathered for our opening session when the Nyanga community heard the familiar sounds of the Cessna's Continental engine warming up out at the hangar. Soon there came the roar of full power as the plane began speeding down the dirt strip when, suddenly, there was an abrupt and ominous silence. Missionaries and Congolese alike jerked to startled attention and paused apprehensively wondering what had happened. Out at the farm (COMAS), Fremont Regier jumped on his Honda motorbike and raced along a winding foot path leading to the airstrip. Upon arrival he saw the plane [known by its short wave code name of Charlie Mike

Zulu] (12) on the ground near the end of the strip, the prop turning slowly as the pilot attempted to restart the motor. Eventual inspection revealed a small defective plastic gear in the fuel pump of the newly installed engine which, at the moment of take-off, suddenly malfunctioned and shut off the fuel supply. Thanks to the extra long Nyanga strip, our pilot had time and room to set the plane back down and to brake to a halt without damage. Had this happened on any of the other shorter bush strips which he used the previous day gathering committee members, there would not have been sufficient room." (13)

As the story became known, it is not at all surprising that during a prayer time in a subsequent committee session expressions of thanks were lifted to a Father God who indeed "had kept his hands under the wings of the little plane."

It was against this rather sobering background that an already somber consultation got under way. In typical African fashion, there was a preliminary period of cautiously testing the waters as members from east and west tried to assess the spirit and attitude of fellow committee members.

The missionary report continues: "It was with a tremendous sense of relief that we soon discovered that, in spite of everything, there was broad agreement within the committee on the basic issues before us. As discussions began, the following points of agreement fell into place: 1) Whatever the nature of the problems and decisions before us, EMC is a reality and its unity must be preserved at whatever cost. 2) The minutes and decisions of both rump groups are to be canceled and ignored out of hand. Any decisions made by the groups are to be considered as illegal and therefore invalid. 3) To preserve the unity of the EMC and to provide for future cooperation and fraternity, some form of decentralization must be envisaged allowing for greater autonomy in the life of the church at regional levels." (14)

Once the basic ground rules of agreement were laid there followed days of intensive work. The church constitution, which had been adopted only a year earlier, was reexamined in the light of the 1969 and 1970 general conferences which had ended in disagreement and ill will. A basic concern throughout the working sessions was to find some way for allowing greater regional freedom while still preserving EMC's overall integrity and unity. A working document was eventually produced which, in effect, proposed the insertion of provincial-level conferences and administrative organization between the existing district and the annual conference levels. Time was given to a discussion of top EMC administrative posts with final recommendation that there be three - - General Secretary, Legal Representative and General Treasurer. The continuing prerogatives and responsibilities of the central administration were spelled out. The EMC Executive Committee was then instructed to spell everything out in detail in a document which was to be submitted for approval at a meeting of the EMC General Council (i.e. the administrative committee supplemented by senior pastors from all stations) prior to the anticipated meeting with the CIM delegation in January 1971.

As regarded the issue of EMC/CIM fusion, the study commission earlier appointed at the Kalonda Conference was instructed to finish its assignment of preparing a detailed document for the EMC which was also to be submitted for approval to the General Council prior to the EMC/CIM fusion consultation.

A bit wary as to how the CIM Board at home might view or interpret the recent series of events in the Congo Church, the missionary reporter felt it appropriate to insert the following paragraphs in his review of what had happened: "We may well wonder what manner of lack of brotherly love has brought on this development and tend to regret this departure from field administration 'à la CIM.' However, it is easy to overlook the frequent American and Canadian communities where there are to be found an astonishing array of different Mennonite Churches within a ten mile radius whose reasons for being go back to obscure historical roots and whose relations with each other through the years have consistently been somewhat less than warmly cordial! True, regional and clan loyalties and rivalries are playing a powerful role in EMC developments just now. But the positive side of this development is that it will place new responsibilities upon Congolese Christians for their own church at a level closer to where they live. . . . In the meantime, there is much rustling among the mulberry leaves as laymen and pastors alike discuss just what all the implications of the newly proposed EMC administrative structure might be." (15)

As for the members of the administrative committee, the specially-called consultation came to a close with a mix of physical weariness and emotional relief. There had been long, intense work days. But there was the deeply shared sense that, as responsible church leaders, they had risen above formidable pressures and had together sought a path of common good and were pointing some new directions for their Church

CHAPTER 23   THE LEAP OF FUSION

clear signals from the Congo

"We cannot understand why missionaries would give their lives to build a house in which they do not now care to live." Such was the observation of a Congolese member of the special commission which had been named to spell out an official fusion proposal to be presented to the CIM Board for study prior to the planned arrival of its delegation in January 1971.

Viewed from an African standpoint, particularly in the Congo of 1970, the call for fusion of mission and church made perfect sense. In the pioneering days, it had been the mission which had existed and stood alone. With passing time, a church began to emerge and, for years, stood side by side with the mission. Now that the church was planted and had its own corps of African workers and leaders, it was time to grant it the preeminence and the rights of an autonomous organization. As the Congolese had at first collaborated with the missionaries within the program and structure of the mission, they now invited missionaries to collaborate with them within the structure of the church as well. No African was suggesting that the missionaries had served their purpose and should prepare to return to their homeland. On the contrary, they were being urged to continue their various ministries but under the sponsorship and jurisdiction of the church.

The study commission appointed by the EMC had taken its assignment seriously. Comprised of eight Congolese and three missionaries, some long hours were put into combing through both mission and church constitutions and bylaws. This done, attention was turned to drawing up a trial draft of a CIM/EMC fusion agreement. A document running to six typewritten pages, it dealt first with a revision of the Church's own statutes in the light of the hoped-for fusion with the Mission. A second section presented a series of twenty-one articles which traced procedures, principles and actions proposed to the CIM as a means of achieving a fusion of the two organizations.

Understanding full well that the adoption of the Congo Church proposals by the Mission was not a foregone conclusion, the CIM field secretary in his report to the home board in its sessions the fall of 1970 wrote: "CIM comes to this encounter via a familiar and authentic route. Even before the Congolese themselves thought of political independence, CIM under the persistent prodding of H.A. Driver was talking with its Congolese church leaders about their autonomy. Then, a little over 10 years ago, a CIM delegation came to the field. In a well-remembered meeting at Djoko Punda, symbolic papers were signed and handed over to Pastor Kazadi, the President of the EMC. The administrative sketches calling for equal missionary/Congolese participation in the government of EMC affairs were never implemented because just four short months later, Congo was plunged into the chaos of political independence. But CIM's gesture was a matter of history and a remembered fact."

"Missionaries gradually came back upon the scene and in the turbulence of the times had to take up places of authority again to hold things together. But with gradually restored calm and a maturing Congolese leadership, the 1967 CIM delegation found the Congolese Christians talking much about 'integration.' As a result . . . a plan for integration was traced which 1) outlined a genuine transfer of administrative authority and responsibility to Congolese shoulders, and 2) began the transition of the missionary from his role of pilot to co-pilot. And now, once again, a CIM delegation looks toward the field. Once again they are awaited with anticipation and once again there is a word on every tongue, i.e., 'FUSION.'" (1)

There then follows a copy of the complete document as proposed by the EMC-appointed study commission. There also follows further commentary: "At first flush, this may strike us as a rather drastic and revolutionary document. But in actuality, our plan for integration of CIM and EMC agreed upon in 1967 and implemented since then has taken us in giant strides along the path toward the final step of fusion now spelled out and recommended - - indeed urged upon us. EMC officers have come into a place of leadership in fact as well as in name and in the process have proven themselves abundantly worthy of the trust placed in them." (2)

After highlighting some of the implications of the document of which both missionaries and board members needed to be aware as the fusion consultation approached, the report was concluded: "Let it simply be noted that we are living in challenging, eventful days in Congo. Our missionary predecessors of other decades worked toward and prayed for the decade we are now privileged to share in - - the decade of an emerging, autonomous Congo Church. May we have the wisdom, the sensitivity and the Divine guidance which will enable us to contribute wisely and positively to the young Church of which we are now urged to become, in a new way, an integral part." (3)

another board delegation: composition and stance

The CIM Board was very aware of the ferment at work in Congo as the decade of the 70's swung open. This awareness on the home end was reflected in various ways. On an editorial page of the spring 1970 issue of the Congo Missionary Messenger, there was reference to the 48th session of the Congo Protestant Council held in March of that year in Kinshasa and the "released pent-up feelings about a new innovation. Fusion with diversity was suddenly the conversation. Organizational machinery was established to work out details. The desire is deeply imbedded for fusion of the church into one unified organizational structure allowing for diversity. What all this will mean is uncertain. A CIM board delegation to Congo is scheduled for 1971 with this pending innovation as part of the agenda. . . . Congo is continuing to change and we seek to understand the process." (4)

In an article in the same issue of the Messenger, Board Chairman Milo Nussbaum observed: "One of the last things we would wish on the Church of Congo is the multiplicity of divisions with which we are acquainted in America. . . . But if we love them in the Lord, we will wait to share with them our lessons learned from our own failures. We have nothing about which to boast and we certainly have no example to share. So it seems that the best we can do is humbly to turn to the Word and see if together we can discover what the Lord wants to say to us and to them at this time. . . . We must be ready to encourage and participate in any union of believers which will cause the Lord's will to be done today. No other motive is big enough." (5)

Accurately sensing that the board delegation to the Congo in January 1971 would be expected to have authority to negotiate with the EMC leaders and to make commitments on the spot, the Board responded by naming its executive committee comprised of Milo Nussbaum, president, Elmer Neufeld, vice-president, Heinz Janzen, recording secretary and George Loewen, treasurer. They would be accompanied by Reuben Short, CIM executive secretary and Howard Habegger, the newly-appointed executive secretary of the Commission on Overseas Mission of the General Conference Mennonite Church.

In an editorial comment in the last issue of the Messenger prior to their departure, it was said: "Plans are to send the above delegation to Congo in January 1971 to share in restructuring the Congo Church from central to regional autonomy . . . . Consideration will be given to fusion of Mission and Church. . . . The delegation will be required to work out ways and means of fusion including a certain amount of transfusion of material aid and personnel from CIM. . . . Change either pushes us or is made by us. The Board has a record of providing leadership and thus a delegation to Congo for the negotiating of this next important step." (6)

fusion: the nitty-gritty

The significance of what was being so enthusiastically urged upon the CIM was not lost upon the missionary team. Some felt that while fusion of Mission and Church represented a step into the unknown, it was nonetheless an idea whose time had come, a logical conclusion to more than 50 years of presence and ministry in that land. Others openly voiced their reservation and apprehension. Would this really be in the best interests of the work of which they had become a part and to which they had made deep commitments? And what if, in the future, they were assigned to a department or a station for which they felt unqualified or where their personal priorities could not be respected? And what of their futures? What was to become of their sense of call to service in Africa as a life's work? Meanwhile there were still others who kept their thoughts to themselves as they awaited the scheduled consultation.

One thing was clear to all: the fusion of Mission and Church would inevitably impact traditional missionary status and roles and impose a process of self-scrutiny and adjustment upon every member of the team. In an article written for the <u>Missionary Messenger</u>, Peter Buller observed that the situation of the Congo missionary in 1970 was not unlike that of John the Baptist when he began to hear reports of the advent of Jesus upon the scene. Buller wrote: "The analogy is far from perfect but in Africa where the Church, Christ's body, is finding new and fuller expression, the missionary must be willing to take a subordinate place. In failing to do so . . . we set ourselves upon a collision course with our African colleagues." (7)

Pursuing the parallel, Buller suggested several areas in which missionaries would need to "decrease" in a conscious and deliberate manner. Developing his theme he wrote: "Withdrawal of ourselves, our personal aspirations and prerogatives, though it is perhaps the most evident and seemingly simple act that is required of us, is yet the most difficult."

Moving to a second sensitive area he wrote of "our pride and assurance in the correctness of our philosophical and cultural presuppositions. The fact that the writer, after years of service in Congo, must admit to a lack of understanding the philosophy of the people with whom he works is in itself a judgement which underlies the point being made. . . . At some point we must tune in on the African philosophical and cultural wave length and then together we must listen to what the Spirit of Christ has to say to both of us."

The article was concluded by suggesting that in the face of the impending fusion of Mission and Church, the missionary would need to be prepared to "decrease theologically. This is the most difficult for us because in theology we <u>know</u> that we are right and we have been trained to root out heresy. . . . I touch here upon the intriguing question of the Africanization of theology. The church in Congo must remain free to interpret the Gospel of Christ within its culture, to let the Gospel transform African culture into Christian-African culture according to His will, and not ours. African church leaders are insisting upon this right of theirs, often to our consternation." Buller concluded by stating that the example of John, our Biblical predecessor, "is part of the challenge facing the missionary in Africa today. It is a challenge that we must meet in intertwining personal cultural and theological areas. Our finding answers to it under the direction of Christ's Spirit will aid our confronting each other with the person of Christ and help avoid a collision of personalities and views that could only fragment His body, the Church." (8)

If the missionary team had ample cause for questions and reflection, it was no less the case for the board delegation once they arrived on the scene. As they interacted with leaders of other missions and churches as well as with CIM personnel in various settings before the fusion conference, the list of questions seemed to get longer with each passing day. The emergence of a large, autonomous Mennonite Church in the Congo was a cause for rejoicing on the part of all. But did that necessarily mean that the CIM, as such, should disappear? What were they to make of the two previous church conferences which had ended in acrimony and disorder? What about the eight large CIM mission stations scattered across south central Congo? How were they to be utilized and maintained? What about the significant mission institutions which had been so painstakingly developed across the years at great cost of material resources and human effort? What was to be their future? What of the medical service with its network of station hospitals and bush dispensaries where no one was turned away and where people of all tribes were received with equal compassion and care? What was to be its future? What of the secondary schools where Christian professors maintained standards and records with scrupulous care? Would there be the same concerns for ethical standards once they passed from direct mission control?

What of the historic and single-minded focus upon evangelism and church planting which had characterized the work of the CIM across the years and which had resulted in a multi-tribal Mennonite Church? Would the commitment to outreach across tribal and regional boundaries still be maintained? What of the whole issue of financial support? Would continuing mission funds be anticipated even though the Mission no longer existed? And, finally, what about CIM's missionary team? How were they to be called, recruited, and placed? How were their assignments to be determined? How were they to be housed? What of their transportation? What of their relationship with the Congo Church? What would be their role? their voice? their place? What would fusion mean for the CIM's ongoing role and mission elsewhere in the Congo - - or elsewhere in Africa?

And the list went on.

If few such specific questions had been addressed by the delegation before leaving North America, the basic dynamics and principles which underlay them had nonetheless been faced. In an article written prior to the delegation departure, board Vice President Elmer Neufeld discussed the issue of fusion which awaited them in the Congo. After tracing something of the colonial history within which Protestant Missions had worked and planted churches, he wrote: "What does all of this mean for the tensions that still exist in mission and church affairs in the Congo today [or] for the unreconciled aspects of mission and church life? It means that we must first of all try to understand ourselves and our African brethren in light of the histories in which we stand. We must try to understand that some of our own western points of view do not make sense in Africa and we must try to understand as far as possible how some of our opinions and practices appear to the African in light of his own past experiences. Thus when our African brethren say almost unanimously that they want fusion of mission and church organizations in the Congo, we must understand that they are speaking from a long history in which a separate mission organization with its separate budget and direct channels to America meant paternalism and foreign control. . . . Why shouldn't workers from America be an integral part of Congo Christian Churches, including church membership, just as a Mennonite family moving from Kansas to Chicago would transfer church membership to become completely involved in a local congregation? . . ."

"We should be deeply grateful that there are thousands and thousands of Congolese Christians who are committed to the Church of Christ and deeply concerned about her future. We should be further grateful that they wish to continue a fellowship of service together with western Christians, though clearly in ways different from the past. We should be asking ourselves in the West what we may learn from our African Christian brethren. And above all, we should have faith in God as we know Him in Christ that He will continue to build his church both in Africa and in the West." (9)

A long list of unanswered questions notwithstanding, it was in the spirit of the Neufeld article that the board delegation entered upon its dialogue with the church leaders regarding the merging of CIM with the EMC.

Djoko Punda once again

The very first site chosen by CIM pioneer missionaries in 1912 and the location for the pre-independence 1960 consultation regarding the autonomy of the Church, Djoko Punda was again chosen as the place for what everyone knew would be the most significant mission/church dialogue of all.

A broad mix of missionaries was present who reflected a diversity of concern and opinion. Representing the Church was the general council composed of the full administrative committee plus senior pastors from each of the stations. And there was the six man delegation from the CIM Board.

No one was quite sure what to expect. Some of the missionaries had heard about similar mission/church consultations elsewhere in Congo where board delegations had negotiated directly with African leaders and entered into agreements in which the missionaries had no voice, this much to their irritation and apprehension. The EMC leaders, on the other hand, were well aware that there were some mission/church groups in Congo who were still far from ready to enter into the sort of dialogue which was scheduled for them the morning of January 12, 1971. And there was the CIM delegation from North America which felt the dual burdens of onrushing Congo events and the responsibility for the ongoing well-being of both a young emerging Church and a large missionary team.

But early in the proceedings it became clear that an overwhelming majority of participants had approached this day with a great deal of prayer and a deep desire to arrive at an understanding to which all could give genuine assent and support. Discussions were unhurried, wide-ranging and marked with openness and candor. From the mission side there were certain themes which emerged: gratitude for God's blessing and enabling hand across 60 years of missionary presence and effort; gratitude for the devoted collaboration of many Africans who were largely responsible for the evangelizing of their own people; thanksgiving for the thousands of African believers and an established, autonomous Mennonite Church; recognition of plans laid and commitments made a decade earlier which had been sidetracked by the swift pace of events; the desire to affirm the Church and its leaders both in the present and the future; the desire to continue collaboration with the Church as this might be needed and desired in the future.

From the African side there also were clear themes which soon emerged: gratitude for the initiative of the CIM and its pioneers to come into south central Congo with a witness to Christ; appreciation for the many sorts of mission ministry and service developed across the years; recognition of the troubled history of the preceding decade; the conviction that the Church must now more fully take responsibility for its own future; the ready recognition that they still needed help in many areas of church life; appreciation for the missionary staff in Congo and a plea for their continued presence and full collaboration with the Church in the future.

And there was the missionary team. They would, after all, be the ones directly involved and would feel the major brunt of any agreements made. What stance did they bring to the Djoko consultation? The tone had already been set during the weeks leading up to the arrival of the board delegation and was perhaps best reflected in a letter sent to the home office a couple of months earlier: "As I sense the feelings and attitude of the missionaries, I believe it can be said that a very great majority of them accept the principle of fusion and are prepared to move into this new relationship with the EMC. If we had our 'druthers,' we would go slower on such items as phasing out CIM legally right away, drastic decentralization of the church administration . . . but I doubt that any of us feel strongly enough about any of these to resist to a point of risking estrangement, bitterness and loss of communication - - something that we have seen happen around us out here in the broad mission/church community. In brief . . . our basic concern is that whatever is wisest and best for the future of this young Church, in its unique Congo setting and history, be done." (10)

By evening of the third day, January 14, agreement had been reached and a document signed by the board delegation, church leaders and representatives of the missionary team. The final agreement was essentially the one hammered out by the Congolese/missionary working committee late the previous year. Embodied in this document was a drastically new set of principles and commitments which were to serve as the framework of CIM/EMC and missionary/Congolese partnership in the years ahead. In a preamble to the document it was stated: "In keeping with its own policy of development and the recommendation of the General Assembly of the Church of Christ of Congo, the CIM decided to give to the Mennonite Church of Congo the responsibility of administrating its own work and of placing the missionary personnel sent to Congo by the home missionary society. These responsibilities were accepted by the Mennonite Church in Congo. Nevertheless there is a mutual desire on the part of the missionary society and on the part of the Mennonite Church in Congo to follow a policy of collaboration in the pursuit of the goals of the association." (11)

The goals of the Church had been spelled out in the restructured constitution which also was approved during the Djoko consultation. They were five - - "evangelization, medical work, education, literature production and social help."

The theme of intended collaboration was repeated in the first article of the convention which read: "The purpose of the two parties to this agreement is to continue together in the mission of evangelization in the Congo." Regarding mission/church relations in the future, no room was left for ambiguity: "The Congo Inland Mission of Elkhart recognized the Mennonite Church in Congo as an autonomous church which directs its own affairs under the guidance of the Holy Spirit." (12)

All official correspondence would therefore now pass directly between the headquarters of the two organizations. Given the problem of language, either English or French could be used. (13) As regarded the missionary staff, the hope was clearly stated that the CIM would continue to recruit and to make available missionary personnel qualified to serve in the various departments and programs of the Church. Missionaries, however, would in the future be sent only in response to formal invitation. Once in the Congo, they would be placed and assigned responsibilities by the Church and serve under the administration of the Church. The Church assumed responsibility to look after all legal matters which might arise as a result of their presence and service in the Congo. The CIM would continue to be entirely responsible for missionary support and education of their children. While the ultimate right to engage and terminate the service of missionaries remained with the CIM, the Church reserved the right to request the recall of a particular missionary in the event of a problem.

Missionaries would automatically be considered to be full members of the Church and would be expected to exercise the same privileges and assume the same responsibilities as Congolese members. No formalities of transfer of church letter from North America was necessary. An experienced missionary would be elected by the missionary group, with the approval of the home board and the church administrative committee, to serve as a counselor for fellow missionaries. Such a person was to work closely with the general secretary of the EMC and would deal primarily with such matters as missionary travel, family needs and possible friction between missionaries and the Church or between missionaries themselves. Missionaries would be allowed to have annual retreats under the auspices of the Church to be conducted in their own language for purposes of fellowship and spiritual nurture. (14)

The CIM would continue to make the needs of the Congo Church known to the North American constituency and to provide help in material resources and personnel as it was able. The CIM would proceed to take formal legal action with the Congo government to transfer legal titles for all its holdings in the country to the Church, i.e. the mission stations and the properties owned in Kinshasa. The mission would also transfer to the EMC any shares it had acquired across the years in inter-mission organizations and enterprises. (15)

All mission-owned vehicles were to be registered with the government in the name of the Church. Privately owned vehicles were to be respected as such. All equipment and machinery of the mission was to be recognized as belonging to the Church. (16)

The Church was to submit annual treasurer's reports to the Elkhart office as well as detailed annual budget needs and requests. (17)

Ratification of the convention was contingent upon the approval of the EMC General Conference and the CIM Board. Initiative to modify the convention could be taken by the administrative committee of the Church and by the CIM Board. Any changes would need to be mutually approved before going into effect. The convention was declared to annul all previous agreements between the CIM and the EMC and would go into effect the date it was accepted by competent bodies of both groups. (18)

Unspecified in the convention, but clearly implied, was the understanding that the time would come when the CIM would take formal action to annul its charter with the Congo government and cease to exist as a legal entity in the country.

pleasantly surprised

"Matala (pr. mah-TAH-lah) David, our Congolese transport director, was very surprised when informed that the fusion meeting was over in three days and he had to go from Kalonda to Djoko to get delegates. 'It's not possible,' he said. 'How can such a big church round table conference end in just three days? It must not have been a good meeting.'" (19) Thus Ilunga Robert opened his article of commentary on the Djoko Punda consultation. A graduate of Bluffton College, Bluffton, OH, he with his wife had been one of three young couples sent to the States in the early 60's to secure a college education. At the time of the Djoko consultation, he was a school director at that station and a delegate to the sessions. He continued: "Contrary to the imagination of this brother, our meeting was very good. Being a Christian conference and non-political, it had no reason to fail. The uncertainties as to the success of this conference were multiple. The Congolese thought that the CIM delegation would not sign the fusion plan because other Congolese churches who had already fused experienced an exodus of missionaries to America. Some of our missionaries were afraid of what was happening elsewhere and had told friends that they were prepared to fight the endorsement of the fusion plan by the Board and go back home to serve the Lord there. The Congolese were somewhat divided among themselves not only along tribal lines but also as to the success of the fusion. The younger generation was very much in favor of it but the older people were reluctant."

". . . The confrontation predicted to take place at the fusion meeting did not materialize. The Christian spirit of brotherhood prevailed. There was a good free discussion of the fusion plan to avoid a misunderstanding in the future. We do not wish to see what happened to other churches (the exodus of missionaries) touch our EMC. The fusion plan was adjusted to satisfy everyone so I feel it ought to work well. The delegation from America was very open and made some revelations to us on matters never told us before. Everyone was amazed for the willingness of these men to make the fusion of CIM and EMC a reality." (20)

Kidinda (pr. ki-DI-ndah) John, son of Mukedi pastor Kidinda David and at the time a school director on that station, was also a delegate to the conference. Asked to comment on the consultation, he first made reference to "disagreeable consequences" which stemmed from the creation of dual associations side by side when in 1964 the Church received its legal charter. He then continued: "Because the Church is of Christ and not of the Congolese or of the missionary, it is necessary that we come back to the word of the Apostle Paul in Ephesians 2:19: 'Now therefore ye are no more strangers and foreigners, but fellow citizens with the saints, and of the household of God.' This, then, is the objective that has called us to fusion." Referring to the Djoko consultation he observed: "An atmosphere of calm and confidence prevailed. Both parties were convinced of the necessity of such action and dealt with the problems in a Christian rather than a political context." (21)

From Kakesa Samuel, the legal representative of the EMC who played a major role in the drafting of the original document, there came these comments: "We do not cease to be thankful to the CIM Board for sending the delegation to make the final contract with the EMC at Djoko. . . . We accept the agreement in good faith. There was not a person who was not a bit fearful of the Djoko days, but by God's grace everything was done. . . . For the future of the EMC, it will be necessary to multiply contacts between the CIM and EMC." (22)

And from CIM Board President Milo Nussbaum there came the observation: "After spending a month with leaders of the Congo Church, one comes away with deep assurance that the church is there as a part of the Body of Christ. The Lord still gives gifts to individuals and gives these individuals to the Church. The Congo Church is blessed with men of outstanding ability." (23)

it looks good on paper

Amidst the mood of elation and optimism following the consultation, however, there were also sounded notes of realism and caution. In an editorial note, Executive Secretary Reuben Short observed: "We have chosen to relinquish all authority to the Congo Mennonite Church. . . . This does not imply abandonment. Responsible parents do not abandon children. But they do let them be free to choose - - even to fail if by improper choice or misfortune." (24)

George Loewen, a delegation member and business man from Steinbach, Manitoba observed: "There is no easy answer. I believe we must work together. . . . The Church will not be able to do this alone." (25)

In further reflections on the consultation, Ilunga Robert wrote: "How will this new plan affect the work of the EMC in the future? The plan itself, as stated above, looks very good on paper but its application is another thing. For this plan to work, Congolese and missionaries ought to practice it as drawn up and signed. Their interpretation of every article must be the same. Both Congolese and missionaries must adjust themselves to it. . . . Each one of us has to consider the other as a man, otherwise the fusion will just mean confusion!" (26)

Kakesa Samuel also stated simply: "What remains for us to do is to implement the things we have put on paper." (27)

School director Kidinda John reflected further: "Though the question of property was the greatest subject of discussion, other points were no less important because it is these that will keep the locomotive on the rail prepared by CIM. The one who inherits the property must find ways to properly maintain it and also construct new rails to accomplish the task ahead. . . . The principal purpose of the church is evangelization whether that be in the education program, medical program or any other program of the Church. The objectives are clear. We are convinced we must study in detail how we can best carry out that which the agreement says."

"First and most important is ourselves. Since we accepted the responsibility to direct the work of the Church, we should no longer look to others from the outside to do the work. Our success depends upon ourselves. Because of this the members of our young Church will need to be informed that the proper functioning of the Church will depend on their contribution, not on others. . . . Sad to say, there is a condition in our young Church that causes tension between lay people and church leaders. . . . Because of this we have need for an internal fusion (laity and church leaders) so anyone from the outside can see the Church has a real sense of direction. . . . We all know of the life of a child. The most important and most dangerous days are when it begins to stand and tries to walk. At this time the role of the parent is most important because when making a mistake the child could put its life in danger. It is because of this that CIM cannot underestimate the importance of needed cooperation. . . . For us, for our brothers in America, and for all who have the goodwill to help us, the task will be a difficult one and the road will be a long run. There will be joy when we accomplish our Christian duties well to enlarge the Church of Christ in Congo and in the whole world. Mt 10:37-38." (28)

from paper to action

On the heels of the Djoko consultation there came a flurry of activity. There was much work to be done. Before the end of January, a special three-person committee named by the Church executive met to review a variety of issues having to do with EMC financial needs. (29) Major attention was focused on efforts to standardize the collection and transmission of district contributions toward the costs of EMC's own central administration.

In March there was a gathering of EMC educational personnel numbering fifteen people of whom two were missionaries. (30) Major time during the two day session was devoted to dealing with the clamor for additional post-primary classes in nearly all of EMC's districts. Response required new government subsidy, materials and qualified teachers - - all of which were in very short supply.

Encouraged by the Church Administrative Committee, Leona Schrag organized a first ever workshop for student leaders who were active in the "Youth for Christ" movement which had been introduced by Lodema Short in the Nyanga secondary school and had spread to other EMC schools as well.

In April, the full commission on evangelism met at Kamayala numbering 20 people of whom 5 were missionaries and two were Congolese women. (31) The agenda for the sessions was lengthy. Some of the actions taken were: to require two years of service within the church by IB and ISTK graduates before considering them for ordination; to instigate a search for Congolese qualified to join the staff of the Kalonda Bible Institute; to recommend three new areas to the next general conference for approval as new EMC districts; to call for the organization of a special retreat for all EMC pastors to provide opportunity for fellowship, Biblical instruction and discussion of mutual cares and concerns. There was also reference to an impending meeting between EMC and AEMSK representatives at Luluabourg at some time during the year with the counsel that EMC people of the Mbuji Mayi area be adequately consulted ahead of time.

The month of May saw a gathering of seven EMC medical people of whom three were CIM doctors. (32) Major attention was given to requests to open new bush dispensaries in isolated rural areas where tens of thousands of people, including many Mennonite believers, had no other source of help.

In brief, by the summer of 1971, there was a stir of activity and optimism within EMC in which missionaries were fully involved. The EMC's fondest dream had been realized at the Djoko Punda fusion consultation. The decentralization of EMC structures was in the process of being worked out. Dates for the next general conference were set and this time, all were assured, the election of a new president would indeed take place.

And in addition to all else, there was a name change. Following President Mobutu's declared change of name for the country and the decisions made to transform the Congo Protestant Council into a national church with member "communities," the Evangelical Mennonite Church of Congo (EMC) became known as the Mennonite Community of Zaire or 'CMZa' in its French acronym form.

Clearly, 1971 marked the opening of a new era in the history of the Zaire Church and in CIM's ongoing partnership with it.

CHAPTER 24   A MAN NAMED KABANGY

a busy hoe is noted

It was a weekday afternoon on Mukedi Station in the fall of 1951. The classroom schedule for the group of 6th-year boys was finished and they were rounding out their school day on a work detail hoeing weeds in one area of the station on which their school was located. Armed with typical short-handled African hoes, they were synchronizing their chopping strokes with the cadence of a song one of them had started. Some distance away a missionary mother stood in the partial shade of a palm tree observing the group. (1) Rainy season was approaching and it was time to make preparations for planting her garden. She was looking for a student who might be interested in making a bit of pocket money by using his hoe in her garden at odd hours through the week.

The musical chant which had been setting the tempo for their swinging hoes had come to an end. Since their supervising teacher had temporarily left them on their own, temptation was great to indulge in banter and joking up and down the line. Soon hoes were lying scattered about on the ground. Here and there one had been upended, the broad, flat hoe head making a convenient little stool. One student was experimenting with tossing his in the air attempting to catch it by the handle as it came back down. The weeds, for the time being, were safe but for one exception. At the far end of the line the missionary mother noted one student who had not joined his classmates in their self-granted work break. Though the supervisory eye of his teacher was momentarily removed, he continued his work as he and all of them had been instructed to do.

Making her way to the end of the line, the missionary mother greeted the young man: "Wabanda?" (pr. wah-BAH-ndah.; a typical greeting of the Baphende people, it posed a question , literally asking "Did you sleep?") "Ai, ngabanda Mama" came the reply, i.e., "Yes, Mother, I slept." She continued: "When you've finished your work, would you come to my house? I would like to talk with you." "Yes, Mother," came the reply, "I will come."

Later that afternoon he appeared at the missionary veranda. He had bathed and groomed himself and was dressed in neatly pressed khaki shorts and shirt. Soon a free-flowing conversation took place and the missionary mother began to fit together a mental profile of the young student before her. His name was Kabangy Moise (pr. kah-BAH-ngee mo-EEZ or Moses). The first was the name given him at birth by his village parents; the second he himself had taken in its French form the day of his Christian baptism.

Born to non-Christian parents in 1932, he was enrolled as a seven year old in a thatch and stick village school sponsored by Canadian Baptist missionaries Percy and Rosalind Near from their station Kandala, some two miles distant. His early education was frequently disrupted. It was nearly 10 years later that he moved to the station to enroll in their fourth and fifth year classes. It was also there, in 1949, that he made a profession of faith in Christ, was baptized and became a member of the church.

By this time a serious student with a yearning for further education, he was among a handful of young men chosen by the Nears to be sent approximately 65 miles to the north to the Mukedi Station of the Congo Inland Mission where he was enrolled in the sixth year of elementary school. Under the Belgian colonial regime this was the terminal year of primary education. It was shortly thereafter that he and his hoe came to the attention of the missionary who was looking for a helper in her family truck-patch.

Kabangy encounters Matthew 28

Upon graduation he returned to Kandala where he taught in the lower grades. Based on the station, he also soon became increasingly involved in the local church. In 1957 he married Kimbadi Bertine, (pr. gi-MBAH-di bair-TEEN) the daughter of a Kandala church overseer. This marriage, in time, was to be blessed with eight children including two sets of twins. Thus, in the cultural tradition of his people, he came to be known as Kabangy Sh'a Pasa (pr. shah PAH-sah), i.e., Kabangy, the father of twins.

It was in his capacity as station Sunday School superintendent that he one day found himself preparing his teachers for an upcoming lesson which was, in part, based on Matthew 28:19-20. Later that week this text kept coming to his mind and he found himself wondering: "What do these words of Jesus mean in my own life?"

In 1961 his local church voted to present him to the next general conference of the Congo Mennonite Church as a pastoral candidate. Meeting at Kamayala in the dry season of that year, he was approved by the delegates and was ordained by a pastoral committee composed of Pastor Kazadi Matthew, Pastor Falanga Elie and Harold Graber. (2) Following his ordination, his first pastoral assignment by the Kandala Church was among the Chokwe people of the southern region of their district. When in 1963 a new inter-Mennonite theological school was opened at Kajiji, he was among the applicants approved for enrollment. His first year of study barely begun, the Kwilu rebellion engulfed his home territory and for many months he was cut off from his family and home church. He later stated that during this time of anxiety and anguish, he turned to Nehemiah chapter one for comfort and strength.

emerging gifts

It was also during those lonely days at Kajiji that Kabangy's pastoral gifts began to surface in a notable way. Although they were all pastors or pastoral candidates, life in the classroom and the close quarters of the residential camp did sometimes spark friction between members of a widely diverse group which had been drawn together from a variety of ethnic backgrounds. Kabangy's gifts for careful listening, tactful intervention and counsel in heated confrontations soon became apparent. During his years as a student he was called upon with increasing frequency to intervene in situations of stress as a peacemaker.

Upon graduation in 1968, he returned to Kandala where he was elected to serve as the station pastor, a position known by the French term *chef de poste*. In a setting and among a people still bearing the scars of the bloody Kwilu rebellion of 1964-65, he set in with vigor and a will to rebuild his beloved home station and to renew the spiritual vitality of his home church. An interesting insight into his innovative spirit was gained by a missionary who visited Kandala soon after he had assumed his new responsibilities. Entering a small thatch-roofed shelter, the missionary was shown a chair after which Kabangy seated himself behind his "desk," the hollow frame of a Servel kerosene refrigerator which had survived the fires of that wild night in January 1964 when the station had been put to the torch by *jeunesse* rebels. Laid lengthwise on the floor, the missing door provided a pigeon hole for his knees while the flat side afforded ready made desk space! With a broad smile he welcomed the missionary to Kandala and with a sweeping gesture of his hand said that they were making the best of what was left and that by God's help they would move ahead from there. (3)

Pastor Kabangy was by this time known beyond the borders of the region of Kandala. The summer of 1970 found Earl Roth, the missionary director of the church high school at Nyanga, looking for someone who could serve both as dean of students and a spiritual counselor on campus. In discussion with school staff, it did not take long for a consensus to emerge. A request was sent to the Kandala church council and, in the fall of 1970 Pastor Kabangy was released to move to Nyanga with his growing family.

His arrival at Nyanga coincided with a time of great ferment and tension within Zaire's Mennonite Church. There had been two annual conferences in a row which had ended in acrimony and abrupt termination. In spite of loud calls for the election of a new president, for a variety of reasons elections had not been held at either conference. The last one had been followed by widely-publicized rump sessions of disgruntled delegates which had precipitated emergency sessions of the EMC Administrative Committee. Among other things, it was promised that a new president would indeed be elected at the next general conference which was slated for June 1971 at Nyanga.

Thus Kabangy, as his first year on staff at the Nyanga High School drew to a close, found himself in the midst of excitement and conjecture as preparations were made to host the delegates to the much-anticipated and hotly-discussed sessions of the next conference. Already there was a word circulating among the Nyanga people that there was one man who would be a particularly strong candidate for the position, none other than their own high school chaplain. There were a number of factors which contributed to this sentiment. He was a graduate of the Kajiji theological training program; he had served as teacher and pastor at Kandala; he had already been named as a member of a three man fraternal delegation to be sent to North America in the fall of 1971, this in response to an invitation given by the CIM delegation earlier in the year at the fusion consultation held at Djoko Punda. (4) But most of all it was the positive impact he had had during his first year in the station high school which gave special weight to his name.

election by acclamation

After two stormy and rancorous general conferences of the Church, it was as though a great calm descended upon the delegate body of 1971 gathered at Nyanga. The official minutes of the conference simply read: "This plan [for the creation of new central and provincial level administrations] was unanimously voted and the people whose names follow hereafter were elected: Kakesa Samuel Legal Representative, Kabangy Moise General Secretary, Bukungu François General Treasurer and Herman Buller Associate General Treasurer." (5) The vote for these four officers took the form of a standing acclamation on the part of the delegate body.

For the first time in three years, a cherished tradition of closing general conferences with a communion service was again honored. The conference theme "May God be Praised in All Things" had been drawn from I Peter 4:11b. It was with a sense of great relief and thanksgiving that the conference delegates, missionary and African alike, dispersed. Another time of tension and struggle within the Church had been traversed. With new optimism attention was now focused on the future and the implementation of the new fusion plan worked through only five short months earlier.

a personal profile takes shape

With the transition of leadership from greying Pastor Ngongo David to newly-elected Kabangy Moise, a new chapter was opened in the life of the Church. Until that point, an older generation represented by Kazadi Matthew and Ngongo David had held the top positions. They had been colleagues of the missionary pioneers. They had trekked with them on foot, had encountered early resistance and hostility of villagers, had witnessed the conversion and baptism of the first handfuls of believers. Their understanding of the Gospel and of the Church had been conditioned much more by their interaction and close collaboration with their missionary colleagues than by formal classroom training. Although legal, educational and financial accounting responsibilities within the Church had already fallen to younger hands, with the election of the new general secretary the transition to a new generation of leadership was complete. What difference would it make? What commitments, understanding, values, priorities would Pastor Kabangy now bring to his new position? How might they impact the Church and the missionary team? It was not long until some indicators began to surface.

Only days after his election, in a conversation with a missionary with whom he had worked closely he said: "God and his people have placed a heavy burden upon my shoulders. I have so much to learn. Please take me by the hand and lead me as I learn my new responsibilities. I want to do my best for my church." (6)

Elected in June, by mid-August he was caught up in a whirlwind tour of North American Mennonite communities as a member of a Zairian fraternal delegation. In the space of six weeks they made stops in such widely separated areas as Indiana, Kansas, California, British Columbia, Saskatchewan, Manitoba, Ontario and Pennsylvania. There were moments of fatigue and bewilderment as they experienced a massive dose of exposure to a culture and church scene largely strange to them. Amidst the rush of activity, however, there came moments of dialogue with missionaries traveling with them which provided glimpses of their struggle to assimilate what they were seeing and hearing. On one occasion, after having spent a couple of hours with an urban Mennonite fellowship which was experimenting with team leadership, Kabangy asked a missionary: "What manner of sheep are these that feel they have no need of a shepherd?"

After visiting a series of Mennonite-financed retirement centers, Kabangy commented: "These buildings are all very nice. But these grey headed, frail Mennonites we see in these places, have they no blood relatives? No children? No grandchildren? Why are they put in places like this if they have their own kin who could care for them?"

And toward the end of their tour, there was the comment: "You Mennonites in North America, the Lord has blessed you with so much, so much. Your missionaries have left much to bring the Gospel to us and we are truly grateful. But please remember that there is still so much that we as Zairian Mennonites must do in our homeland. We will continue to do our best with the little we have but please continue to work with us, continue to strengthen our hearts and our hands."

A year later in conversation with CIM missionary Waldo Harder, director of the Kalonda Bible Institute, Kabangy perhaps summarized most clearly what was to be the focus and spirit of his years as the general secretary of the Zaire Church: "Doors are open awaiting our entry. Opportunity is unlimited. The call to reapers resounds equally to you there [in North America] as to us here. Today there are no Zairians. There are no missionaries. There is no difference . . . for we advance together in the name of Christ. We are laborers together in the great harvest field of our Lord." (7)

CHAPTER 25   A TORN MENNONITE FABRIC MENDED AT LAST

Historic events had taken place within the CMZA. Fusion documents had been signed in early '71 by CIM delegation members and top church leaders. The Church had chosen a new general secretary a few months later at its annual conference at Nyanga. Decentralization of church structures had been enthusiastically acclaimed by the delegates. Agreement had been reached to build a church headquarters on a plot of neutral ground at Tshikapa on a wedge of land between the Kasai and Tshikapa Rivers. There was an air of anticipation and much discussion of things to come.

In the South Kasai, the Baluba refugees settled around Kabeya Kamuanga had strengthened their ties with the CMZA administration at Tshikapa. The larger group, however, which had settled in and around Mbuji Mayi under the leadership of Pastor Kazadi, had solidified their position. As they entered the decade of the 70's, they were legally recognized by the government as the CEM (the French acronym for the Evangelical Mennonite Community), an autonomous church independent of and separate from the CMZa based at Tshikapa. They had their own schools, were receiving their own educational subsidies from the government and had been admitted as members of the ECZ.

But a sad fact remained clear to all. The fabric of the Mennonite family of the two Kasais had been ripped into two segments and remained so. As for the CMZa, its leaders maintained a rigid position. If the Mennonites of the South Kasai were concerned about renewed fellowship with the people of the land they had fled in the early 60's, the solution was simple: "Cancel your legal status and rejoin the CMZa as a southern region under its name, legal charter and constitution." On the CEM side, such curt admonition was viewed as an insulting repudiation of who they were and of what they had achieved. Hurts, suspicion and ill will abounded on all sides. When perchance members of the two groups met, civilities were exchanged in cool, guarded fashion and conversations were brief.

And yet, there was the memory, on both sides, of the Graber farewell held at Kalonda in May, 1969. Graber's plea for reconciliation addressed to Kazadi, as they parted, had been broadly shared by word of mouth. It was also known that before leaving Kalonda Kazadi had expressed to local missionaries his hope that some way could be fond to dismantle the barriers which at the time stood high between the two groups. On the occasion of the visit of the CIM Board delegation of December '70 - January '71, there had been discussions with both sides. Once again Kazadi voiced his hope that festering wounds might be healed.

But how? Time was slipping by and the rift between the two seemed as wide as ever. Though longing to do something about it, missionary hands were tied. CMZa leaders repeatedly warned that any missionary approaches to the new South Kasai Church would quickly be interpreted as Mission approval of the seceded group and thus encourage other distant regions of the CMZa to consider similar initiatives.

Le Plan Short

Correctly sensing the stalemate, the CIM Board and its Executive Secretary Reuben Short determined to take some initiative in an effort to move the two Mennonite Churches off dead center. Short proposed a joint meeting at some neutral spot to which delegations of both Churches could come for open ended dialogue regarding the hurts of the past and their hopes for the future. After several rounds of correspondence, it was agreed that such a meeting would take place at Luluabourg on June 7-8, 1971 and that there would be four representatives from CMZa Tshikapa, four from CMZa of the South Kasai and eight from the CEM. Rev. Kabeya Paul, the ECZ Provincial President, would be invited as an observer and Reuben Short would chair the sessions. CIM missionary Charles Sprunger would be asked to serve as translator.

Sunday evening, June 7 found all groups on hand. (1) Short spent the evening in sessions with each of the two groups alone seeking to assess the mood and to determine how to move into the next day. In these first encounters it became clear that the CEM concerns revolved around the hope of recognition and help from the CIM while CMZa's focus was on a desire for the reunification of the two groups. Under Short's guidance it was finally agreed to work with a four point agenda: 1) an opening devotional and time of prayer; 2) a sharing of what God had done within the respective fellowships in recent years; 3) an honest review and discussion of unresolved issues between them "if the spirit of the meeting justified it" and 4) a listing of issues for possible future consideration. An overriding stipulation was that the meetings would not be permitted to degenerate into an exercise of bitter recrimination.

After an opening devotional, the first joint session began with a period of verbal probing and shadow boxing. The CEM delegates seemed particularly suspicious that the CIM Executive Secretary had come from Elkhart with decisions ready made in their regard. When it became clear that this was not the case, attention shifted to dialogue between the delegates themselves. Some of the more telling exchanges went as follows:

CEM: "We are happy for this opportunity to meet this way. We have no problems to discuss. All has already been settled."
CMZa: "Oh? Settled to what point?"
CEM: "Yes, we consider all our problems with CMZa to be settled. Our questions are addressed to CIM."
CMZa: "If that's the case, why are we here?"
CEM: "We see no point in digging up the past. Once manure has been buried, it is best left buried."
CMZa: "Look, we're just talking in circles to please Rev. Short because he instructed us to be nice to each other. We are in his hands. What are his words for us?"

Soon thereafter the group was dismissed for lunch with the understanding that Secretary Short would return with some proposals to lay before them. Reconvened, Short submitted a series of recommendations: 1) that a future conference be planned with larger representation from each group to determine the next concrete steps to be taken; 2) that in the meantime, they agree a) that each Mennonite Community be responsible for its own affairs, finances and program; b) that each Community have the right to address its needs and requests for help to the CIM with the condition that CEM route its requests via CMZa Tshikapa and that CIM channel its financial help to CEM via the CMZa General Treasurer; 3) that CMZa/CEM relations be encouraged for mutual benefit to all and that CIM stand by to help facilitate such relations; 4) that a long term goal be the eventual close collaboration between the Churches in the work of the Lord and 5) that a carefully-chosen commission be appointed to discuss and seek solutions for unresolved issues between the Churches.

Implicit in the list of proposals was a de facto recognition of CEM as an autonomous Church by both CIM and the CMZa. Secretary Short had frankly laid the issue on the table.

The CEM delegates quickly responded in the affirmative. They declared "the Short Plan" to be a good one and stated their readiness to proceed on such terms. CMZa delegates, however, quickly raised caution flags. "Is the Secretary from America trying to unite us or divide us? This proposal is nothing to play with. If we accept these suggestions, we will remain divided forever and open the door to other groups within our Church to try to do likewise."

Pastor Kazadi had been largely silent in the discussions of the day. Standing, now, he asserted his authority as the leader of his own group and said: "We from the CEM have two words. Rev. Short's suggestion of a conference bringing us and others of our brethren together again is a good one. We support it. In order to accomplish this, we urge that some plan be made here before we leave so that such a conference will actually take place. We can then take up all of these other matters and discuss them further."

With some of the more volatile questions thus tabled, the balance of the time was devoted to discussing the next proposed gathering. By evening of the second day it had been agreed 1) that the suggested gathering take place in January 1972, at Lake Munkamba; 2) that a joint six-man committee plus a missionary work out details of exact dates, program, travel and funding (2) and 3) that each Church be represented by 18 delegates plus the members of the organizing committee. CIM would pay half the cost of the consultation.

In the concluding moments Secretary Short underscored CIM's unwavering love and concern for both Churches, expressed CIM's sorrow for the bitter and bloody history which had separated them and stated CIM's intention to help the CEM with some modest financial help in the coming year. Their requests were to be channeled to Elkhart via CMZa Tshikapa.

A circle was formed and a closing prayer was offered. Much of the bitter agenda between the two groups still remained unresolved. But for the first time since the fury and suffering of the early 60's, official delegates from the two Churches had sat together and begun a process which would, further down the road, lead to genuine reconciliation. In the meantime, something called *le Plan Short* had been launched. The phrase would be heard often in the months ahead with both positive and negative connotations depending on how the individual using it viewed and interpreted it. What was of crucial importance was that Secretary Short's intervention had jarred loose a log jam. Positive change was in the making.

Lake Munkamba, 1972

The planning committee named in June '71 did meet the following November but almost immediately ran into problems. Without the steadying hand of an older generation, discussions soon became bogged down in debate as to what had actually been said and agreed upon in the previous sessions. "The Short Plan" was frequently invoked with the CEM representatives praising it and the CMZa people expressing clear resistance toward it. In the end, no official minutes of the planning meeting were issued. Via consensus, however, dates for the envisioned gathering were set (January 19-22, 1972) and agreement was reached on details of travel and individual fees to be paid by the participants. CIM missionary Levi Keidel was to be invited to lead the group in two studies of Mennonite history. They would convene at Lake Munkamba, a lovely setting roughly half way between Luluabourg and Mbuji Mayi, which for years had been a conference ground for the Presbyterian Mission/Church. Beyond that, little else had been agreed upon. While there was to be another CEM/CMZa meeting, what was to happen at that time was far from clear.

Keidel himself later wrote: "On January 11, 1972 about twenty [CMZa] Africans with light baggage pitched and bounced in the rear of a Tshikapa transport truck headed east toward the frontier of South Kasai. In exactly the same way thousands of fear-stricken refugees had made their 200 mile trip twelve years earlier, fleeing the tumultuous events which then were ripping the fabric of society to shreds. Now this group of Africans was traveling the same road, this time hoping to stitch some of the pieces back together again." (3)

Earl Roth, one of the CIM missionary participants, commented on the opening session. CEM took the initiative and "presented a program for the conference, well written and stenciled, complete with an agenda for discussion. CMZa refused this program. For a while things were nip and tuck. After scrambling and floundering, we were able to get the [organizing] commission together and an entirely new program was worked out. Kakesa [Samuel], having been moderator of the previous meetings and chairman of the commission, opened the conference. . . . A moderator and three secretaries were elected." (4)

Regarding the election of the moderator of the Munkamba meeting, Keidel wrote: "Of the three nominees, Pastor Kazadi won by a comfortable margin. To the missionaries this was remarkable. Kazadi was elected only because some of the [CMZa] delegates had voted for him over their own nominee. Obviously the Holy Spirit, though unseen, was also present and taking active part." (5)

Following an opening devotional by CEM delegate, Kumbi Zecharie, based on Saul's Damascus road experience detailed in Acts 9:3-6, Keidel presented his first study of Mennonite history. Kazadi then formally opened the consultation. It very quickly became evident that the two groups were still far apart in their views and that old hurts and animosities were still deeply rooted. The primary concern of the CMZa delegates was that of reunification of the two Mennonite Communities into a single body, i.e., their own. As for the CEM folk, their driving concern was to secure formal recognition from both the CMZa and the CIM [AIMM] and to establish lines of communication with Elkhart. Consequently they viewed what had come to be known as "the Short Plan" with enthusiastic support. The CMZa, on the other hand, viewed it with alarm.

251

Against this background Keidel continued: "A large number of delegates participated in carefully calculated parleying. From the missionaries' viewpoint, it seemed as if the delegates were all treading gingerly around a fused mine, hunting for a handle by which to defuse it before it exploded. The torrent of words appeared to contribute little to the proceedings but Kazadi apparently felt that their talking had important cathartic value." (6)

The morning wore on, with always more hands in the air requesting the moderator's permission to speak. Finally, ignoring still other hands, Kazadi slowly stood to his feet before the assembled delegates. In a manner so characteristic of him, he simply stood silently - - looking alternately at them and down at the table behind which he stood. Then with a soft voice and a slow, deliberate manner, he began to speak. Keidel picks up the account: "'When I first arrived down-country in the AIMM field as a child, I was known only as Kazadi Lukuna. . . . It was there that I became known as Pastor Kazadi. My love, for most of the years of my life, was planted down-country. Who can be happy to leave a place after working there for forty years? If I died today, people at Charlesville, Tshikapa, Nyanga and Mukedi would all say, 'Pastor Kazadi has died.' People of South Kasai where I now live would only say, 'They're burying another refugee.'"

"'What happened in 1960 started a fire that raged completely out of anyone's control, When those things happened, I was terribly surprised; I saw some of our AIMM Christians stirring up the fire. We lost everything we had down-country; we fled as refugees to South Kasai. What one of you here would want to carry all the responsibility I was carrying at that time? There's not one of us here who would want to give account for all that happened then. When I was setting up our own church, was I happy to be cut off from you? I longed with all my heart for a meeting such as this. . . . When a fire stops burning, and smoke subsides, and eyes stop hurting, people begin to hunt for ways to repair things. Everyone knows the great work missionary Lutonga [Archie Graber] did for us when we were starving refugees in South Kasai. When I heard he was about to go home to retire, and they were having a farewell meeting for him and his wife at Tshikapa, I said, 'I must go in the name of my people and tell him how indebted we are to him.' When I talked to him alone at the meeting, he said I had a debt with him that I must finish. I asked him to explain what he meant. He asked me, 'How long will the children of one mother be broken apart? When will the quarreling and fighting end? When are you going to do like Jesus said and start showing love one for the other?'"

"'We are here to finish that debt, . . . It is time for us to again find unity in the Church of Jesus Christ. Each of us has been speaking his mind about the purpose of this conference. In my thinking, its purpose is clear. It is to heal our divisions and to reestablish our friendship and oneness in Christ.' The assembly sat in silence, absorbing the impact of his words." (7)

It was at this key juncture that another voice was heard. At the Luluabourg meeting in January, Kabangy Moise had not yet been elected as the new general secretary of the CMZa. But now, in January '72, he was the leader of the CMZa delegation. He too had been quiet during the morning of heated exchange. He had already during the previous months traveled to Mbuji Mayi. Though his primary reason for his trip had been to contact the CMZa folk there, he made special effort to also call on Pastor Kazadi. Although separated by age, an early bond of understanding and pastoral concern quickly emerged between these two Mennonite church leaders. Kabangy, too, longed for an end to the bitterness which had for so long wrought havoc within the Mennonite family of his land.

Keidel picks up the account of Kabangy's intervention in that session as follows: "'We will all disappear from this earth. We will leave behind us our children, and for them, the Church. What kind of Church do we want to leave for them? It is also for their sakes that we must rebuild what has been destroyed, correct our mistakes, and heal our divisions. The purpose of this meeting is to reconcile us again to our oneness in Christ.' Kazadi asked all those who agreed to stand. The vote was unanimous. Someone said it was a good time to pray. Everyone bowed his head. Someone led in prayer. Then another, then another. . . . The tension which had prevailed a short time earlier dissipated and was supplanted by a sacred sense of unity in the Holy Spirit. After several had prayed, Kazadi adjourned the meeting for lunch." (8)

The afternoon session was opened with another devotional time, another study of Anabaptist chur history and a variety of reports from the two groups. It was a time of learning for everyone. The refuge listened attentively to news from the West Kasai areas which they once had known so well. As for the Tshika people, it was difficult not to be impressed with the remarkable record of perseverance, endurance and growth of the CEM amidst suffering, loss and death. A further evidence of their self reliance not lost on the CMZa folk was the large CEM diesel truck parked outside under a palm tree which had provided their transportation and had been purchased without the help of foreign funds. All went to their cots for the night with a tumult of memories and reasons for praise chasing about in their minds and hearts.

But the next day, painful history attempted one last time to raise its ugly, disruptive head. Younger CEM delegates followed each other on the floor repeating hurts and accusations rooted in the past while broadly intimating that the Church they represented was entitled to some sort of indemnity from CMZa/CIM for all the losses they had sustained as refugees. CMZa delegates quickly responded with vehement counter statements of their own. Kazadi sat in his quiet manner, listening to everything. It was becoming clear that the spirit of unity which had been achieved the day before was now being dissipated by renewed controversy.

Yet once again the aging Kazadi took matters in hand. "'My friends . . . we don't restrain anyone from talking at this conference. Anyone can say whatever his heart desires. At the same time, the first day Pastor Kabangy and I both said that the purpose of this meeting is to put out the fires so that we can start building together again. You all stood to your feet showing that you agreed. Yesterday we all sat for a sufficient period of time to hear your opinions. We must act like mature men who know how to pursue an objective we've set for ourselves. Since we agreed on what we want to achieve, we must ask ourselves, are the words we speak now designed to keep on stirring the ashes so the fires stay alive or do they work to help us put out the fires once and for all?'. . . Then a neutral delegate rose to make a motion: 'We agree that because of terrible events that happened in our country, we treated each other badly. But beginning today, we are forgiving each other of all those things and are leaving them behind us and we will move into the future together.' The motion was adopted."

"The groups agreed that while maintaining separate administrative structures, they would begin immediate collaboration in church activities. Discussion became animated: 'What will we do with the Short Plan?' 'It talks too much about money. If we begin talking about those things now, it may ruin everything. The big thing now is to rebuild our spiritual unity.' 'When can we meet again?' 'Whenever you want us to come to see you; . . . you just let us know. We'll sweep our pennies together and find a way to pay the truck to get us there.' 'Where should our next meeting be held?' 'Make it somewhere in the CIM area,' Pastor Kazadi said. 'Let us drive up and down those roads in the land where we matured. When people see us there, gossip in their mouths about division will be finished.'" (9)

Before bringing the consultation to a close, a few decisions were officially recorded; 1) that we acknowledge that we have sinned and are now reconciled; 2) that we continue contact through correspondence; 3) that we hold another conference together in 1974; 4) that we seek cooperation but yet maintain our separate organizations." (10) These brief minutes agreed upon, the delegates circled the room, joined hands and sang an old hymn which, though American in origin, has nonetheless found its way into the hearts and usage of Zairian Mennonites, "Blest Be the Tie That Binds".

another healing step

As early as 1969, the idea of an all-Mennonite Pastors' Conference somewhere in Congo was under discussion. William Snyder, MCC Executive Secretary of that era, had suggested the idea while outlining three general objectives: 1) to afford spiritual refreshment and challenge, 2) to provide opportunity for serious discussion of needs, problems and discouragements common to them all and 3) to leave some new materials in their hands which would be helpful to them in their continuing work in their churches. As a board member of the Schowalter Foundation, he suggested that a formal request be submitted to this organization for a grant to cover travel costs for such a gathering. He also suggested that MCC be approached for funds to provide some Christian literature for the pastors.

Although there was immediate interest among African pastors and missionaries, it was clear that in 1969 CIM/EMC had more pressing agenda to deal with. By the spring of 1972, however, the situation was very different. An organizing committee was convened in Kikwit on March 15. (11) Minutes resulting from this planning session set the dates for July 7-15, 1973, and selected Nyanga as the place where those attending would be housed and fed in the secondary school facilities. A tentative program was sketched and special speakers named. A flyer announcing the conference was broadly circulated which concluded with the comment: "We hope for the success of this fraternal and spiritual gathering which will be the first such event in the Mennonite history of Zaire. Let all three church offices (12) do their best to communicate this information in good time to all their regions. The presence of all Mennonite pastors is indispensable as we seek to learn to know each other in a spirit of fraternity in 1973 at Nyanga."

The following months brought moments of uncertainty to the planners as political tension threatened to make a gathering of this size impossible. But at the last moment government permission was secured and the long awaited Pastors' Conference took place. In all a total of 108 people from the three Mennonite areas were registered. (13) Each day was closely scheduled with a variety of sessions featuring studies of the book of Revelation, lectures on pastoral life, Mennonite history and doctrine, the development of an authentically African church, church administration, evangelism and the maintenance of the pastor's own spiritual life. As requested, the Showalter Foundation did cover all travel costs and an MCC grant translated into a much appreciated credit for each attendee at a well-stocked book table that was set up for the week.

During the conference many enthusiastic comments were heard: "Whatever word shows joy which surpasses all joy, that is what we have felt." "Trees clustered together in the forest can withstand the heaviest storm." "Unknown to us, missionaries who left CIM 50 years ago to start their own work in fields west of us took some of our tribesmates as their helpers. Today we have met their offspring, relatives whom we never knew existed." (14) "As pastors at our separate places of work, we sometimes feel alone. Only today we discover who the others are who stand with us and how many we are. It makes us feel strong enough to withstand the storm." (15)

But the highlight of the entire week clearly was the closing evening. After viewing an hour long film entitled "The Life of Christ," host Pastor Kabangy gave opportunity for testimony or, if appropriate, personal confession. There promptly followed a flow of unbroken sharing. A missionary who was present later wrote: "A pastor from Port Francqui (a river port on the Kasai River on the northern fringe of AIMM territory) got up and unburdened his heart to his fellow pastors concerning the difficulties of his work. A local pastor who had ably translated the Bible studies all through the week got up and said he'd been in front of them translating but what they didn't know was the way God's Word had been at work in his own heart all the while. He asked for prayer for himself and his work . . . ."

"A pastor from Kalonda stood and said he was not in right relations with a fellow pastor from his station whereupon he asked him to join him at the front, took hold of his hand before everyone and pledged that their relations, when they returned home, would be what they should be as church leaders. A CMZa pastor from Kikwit stood revealing that he was out of fellowship with a CEFMZ pastor there. He then walked halfway across the chapel, took him by the hand and asked his forgiveness. (16) One of the CEM men from the South Kasai rose observing that this was the first time since the days of tribal fighting that they were in a service together with opportunity to take the Lord's Supper with former colleagues and neighbors. His plea was that this be done with full understanding of its significance and with a genuine spirit of forgiveness and commitment to the Lord's work and to each other. After 90 minutes Kabangy regretfully had to bring the sharing session to a close for it truly was getting late."

"The service was then turned over to Pastor Kazadi to conduct the time of communion. In spite of the hour he could not resist the opportunity for some personal sharing. He reminded them that their split up did not come because of personal desires but because of warfare, something nobody wanted. He talked about all of the things that had been said and written on one side and the other during the intervening years. There were times, he said, when he wondered when, if ever, they would again have the chance to demonstrate that they still held their brethren of the CMZa in respect and to reknit the bonds of love. Said he, it seems that we have finally found that moment. He too then urged that all taking the bread and the cup that hour do so with sincerity and with full recognition of the implications of what they were doing. It was about midnight when a final word of prayer brought the conference to a close and we made our way out of the Nyanga chapel under a full moon. This was a key point in the history of Kazadi's group. While they already were recognized by the State and the ECZ, this now was tangible evidence that they were also recognized as Mennonites - - by Mennonites - - here in Zaire. This probably is the most cherished of all achievements as far as Kazadi is concerned." (17)

That week during one noonday break, while other delegates were taking a brief siesta in the heat, Kazadi made his way to a missionary home to ask a number of questions about the functioning of AIMM in North America. He was particularly interested in the way different Mennonite groups cooperated within a single board to maintain a shared ministry in Africa while retaining their own autonomy and separate programs in other areas. It was clear that he was thinking of the future of the broad Zaire Mennonite family in which he and his Church had now found a place, and of how they might best contribute to it.

the last stitches

At the level of fraternal relations and renewed friendship within the broad Mennonite community of Zaire, progress was enormous. The Pastors' Conference at Nyanga had afforded dramatic proof of that. But there remained yet one thorny issue to be tackled. There was now a rectangle of four Mennonite bodies - - CMZa with offices in Tshikapa; CEM with headquarters in Mbuji Mayi; a regional grouping of CMZa churches, also in the South Kasai, clustered around Kabeya Kamuanga, and AIMM with headquarters in Elkhart, IN. How the four could and should relate to each other was till far from clear in the summer of 1974. CMZa still clung to its insistence that it be the official link between AIMM and the country of Zaire. CEM made it increasingly clear that as long as this was the case, their autonomy was not fully recognized or honored by either CMZa or AIMM. And to further complicate matters, the CMZa folk of the South Kasai still insisted that any concessions made to the CEM would betray them - - they who had also experienced the misery of the refugee years but still had sought to maintain ties with their Tshikapa based mother Church in the West Kasai. As a matter of fact, two CMZa pastors from the South Kasai had been conspicuously absent at the Nyanga Pastors' Conference, an absence which was broadly interpreted as signaling their discontent with CMZa/CEM negotiations under way.

When in the summer of 1974 another AIMM Board delegation was assembled for a trip to Africa, (18) it was clear that CMZa/CEM/AIMM relations would have to be reviewed and brought to some resolution if at all possible. It was for this reason that time was blocked out for what was referred to as a "tripartite consultation" at Tshikapa. It was on Monday, June 10, that the AIMM delegation and the CMZa Administrative Committee welcomed a group from Mbuji Mayi at the local government airstrip. (19)

In an opening session Pastor Kazadi, in his direct, clear manner pointed out that while AIMM and CMZa had signed a fusion document in which clear guide lines were established for their continued partnership in ministry, CEM thus far had been denied any such recognition. Kazadi stated their desire that AIMM either sign a similar statement of understanding with them or rewrite an agreement which would include both CMZa and CEM.

In response, the AIMM delegation drew up a proposal the first evening which focused on CMZa/CEM relations at large but which said nothing about the relations between the two Mennonite groups in the South Kasai itself. Presented next morning, it sparked much debate and, in the end, was rejected. In the process it had become clear that the real problem now lay not between CMZa and CEM at a national level but rather between representatives of the two groups in the South Kasai itself. Thus a second proposal was drafted which attempted to spell out their future relations there in that region and their ongoing channels of communication with Tshikapa and Elkhart. Seeing that this bypassed his own basic concerns, Kazadi objected.

By this time it was midday. The CEM delegation had reservations to return home via an *Air Zaire* flight scheduled early that afternoon. Describing the scene at that juncture, AIMM delegation member Howard Habegger later wrote: "There was a keen sense of disappointment which could be seen on Kazadi's face. Now he must return to Mbuji Mayi without an agreement." (20) Writing in a similar vein, delegation member Elmer Neufeld commented: "With this impasse we finally went on to other business. . . . I am sure that many persons were deeply disappointed by Tuesday's impasse and that there was much prayer for some resolution." (21)

Then, just as the CEM delegation began packing their bags for their departure, word came: "The *Air Zaire* flight was canceled! There was to be another flight next day." The much-maligned Zaire airline had done what it so often did - - cancel flights without warning. But this time, for the group of Mennonites in session at Tshikapa, the disruption turned out to be providential. There would be more time, after all, for the inter-Mennonite negotiations which seemed stalemated. Seizing upon the opportunity, the AIMM delegation urged the CMZa folk to take a turn at drafting a proposal. This was done but still met with no better success. By that time the CMZa Administrative Committee was becoming restless. They had already devoted more time to this issue than had been scheduled and they had their own major concerns yet to review with the AIMM representatives including the re-reading and clarification of the AIMM/CMZa fusion document drawn up three years earlier.

That night, after the day's activities had come to a close, Kazadi and Kabangy looked for each other. Surrounded by the sounds of a tropical night they sat talking quietly. They had already on earlier occasions met to share their sorrow regarding the bloody history which had separated them and their longing to, in some manner, achieve full reconciliation. They had both hoped so much that this June 1974 meeting in Tshikapa would be the time to finally lay the last vestiges of the bitter past to rest. Were they about to allow this golden opportunity to slip through their fingers? No. There must be some way. There had to be. They soon invited a few others to join them as they talked and prayed into the night. Before they disbanded they had agreed on their own proposal which they would submit to the entire group in the morning. The Lord willing, they would still find a way to resolve the disagreements among them before the delayed flight arrived.

Describing the proposal they brought next morning, Neufeld commented: "The compromise was in effect a joining together of two earlier proposals. It included recognition of the CEM as an autonomous sister Church with the further phrase that 'AIMM would aid the CEM group as it intends or wishes.' While there would still be coordination of the requests of the two South Kasai Mennonite groups, . . . AIMM response to them would be handled directly through the appropriate channels for each group. The whole conference group was greatly relieved and grateful for this further step toward reconciliation and clarification of relationships."

"The compromise was entitled 'A Convention for the Normalization of Relationships Between AIMM, CMZa and CEM.' When agreement was finally reached, there was a joining of hands around the circle and a time of prayer together. Then the meeting broke up for official signing of the new convention by the representatives present. . . This was clearly a high point in the Tshikapa meetings. It was truly wonderful that the departure of the Kazadi group later on Wednesday could be in a spirit of reconciliation and brotherhood rather than with the complete impasse reached Tuesday evening." (22) In his reporting Howard Habegger also observed: "It was a dramatic moment and we felt as if the Spirit had broken through in a marvelous way." (23)

The ultimate proof that a historic reconciliation had been achieved at Tshikapa on June 12, 1974, would come four years later when, with full CMZa blessing, a two-man Zairian delegation was invited for a fraternal visit to North America. The two men: Pastor Kazadi of the CEM and Pastor Kabangu Tom, a leading pastor of the CMZa group of the South Kasai. The torn fabric of the Zaire Mennonite community had, at last, been made whole.

CHAPTER 26   ASCENTS TO PEAKS OF POWER

Using the "Manifesto of N'Sele" hammered out in 1967 as a springboard, Joseph Mobutu launched a whirlwind of change in Zaire. During the early 70's the list of achievements was growing steadily longer. He met the entrenched western mining conglomerate head-on and in the process extracted major concessions to the great benefit of his country. He took on the powerful Catholic Church and its institutions and clearly emerged from that encounter holding the upper hand. Brooking no political opposition, all former parties were incorporated into one single political entity known as the *Mouvement Populaire de la Révolution,* or the MPR in its French acronym. To ensure control of the undergraduate student scene, the three universities of the country were melded into a single state university with three campuses. Out of a hodgepodge of provincial police forces and armed units he created a single national army of which he was the Commander in Chief. Fully aware of the low level of skill of the average army unit, he proceeded to create an elite para-commando force which was trained by Israeli military officers, a training course in which he himself also participated. This special group was directly answerable to him.

tokens of opulence

Copper on the world market was commanding a good price. This plus the steady flow of diamonds from the two Kasai regions assured a strong financial base. Intent on making Kinshasa a show place on the African continent, he ordered the construction of a series of very costly and ostentatious projects such as a multi-story trade center, an enormous communications center and a sprawling, luxurious conference facility for those occasional times when Kinshasa would be the venue for pan-African or international gatherings.

Perhaps the most dramatic example of an ill-advised, grandiose venture was the effort to erect, in Kinshasa, the highest man-made construction on the entire continent of Africa. On a wedge of land along the boulevard leading from the city out to Njili (pr. NJEE-lee), the international airport, four cement columns with an interlinking steel framework began to rise. At first it was rumored that it was to be a monument to Patrice Lumumba, Zaire's earliest patriot. Later the circulating word was that it would memorialize MPR, the political party or, perhaps, even Mobutu's own mother. Whenever it reached its ultimate height, a revolving restaurant was to cap the structure. Such was the scale of the venture that its demands upon the cement supply resulted, for a time, in shortages and delays for other construction projects in the city and the surrounding area.

INGA

While there was a clear focus of energy upon making Kinshasa a capital of renown, one enormous development project was undertaken outside the city, a project which would make the name INGA (pr. IH-ngah) a familiar term across central Africa.

Zaire, a great sandy basin, collects its annual rainfall via a network of tributaries which eventually pour their growing volume of water into the Zaire River. Flowing placidly through Stanley Pool with Kinshasa and Brazzaville situated opposite each other on its southeastern and northwestern banks, the river soon thereafter begins its twisting and plunging course through endless rapids and, eventually, through the Crystal Mountains before entering the Atlantic Ocean. The volume of output at its mouth is second only to the Amazon River of South America.

As early as 1885 Belgian pioneers had recognized the river's incredible potential for generating hydroelectric power. Although various technical studies were conducted during the Belgian colonial era, no effort was made to tap this immense resource. Early in his speech-making, Mobutu referred to the plight of underdeveloped countries which, like Zaire, were condemned to supply raw materials at world market prices over which they had no control only to buy back manufactured goods made of these same raw materials, this again at prices that were dictated to them. Before Zaire could entertain any thought of creating an industrial complex for the processing of its own natural resources, the problem of energy had to be resolved.

Already in 1967 feasibility studies and blue prints were pulled from files left by the colonial administrators and a decision was made. What had for long been only a topic of discussion was to be translated into reality. An Italian engineering firm was engaged. Zaire itself would come up with 60% of the financing; the Italian government would make a loan for 25% of the cost and a European Development Fund would cover the rest. (1) Not only was the hydroelectric potential immense, but more astounding still were the geologic formations at an isolated rural spot in the mountains 125 miles downstream from Kinshasa known as Inga. At 700 feet above sea level the contours of the twisting course of the river were such that the engineering project could easily be undertaken in three progressive stages. The estimated total capacity of output should all three stages be realized? Three hundred seventy billion kilowatts per year, a figure which in 1971 represented more than double the total energy production of France and Italy combined! (2)

The Zairian government was clear. The first stage was to be finished by November 24, 1972 as an anniversary celebration of the Zaire revolution. Among the barren, unpopulated hills around Inga a community of 13,000 people quickly took shape; work was carried forward on a 24-hour-a-day schedule. Excitement grew. At every political meeting reference was made to Inga. Popular musical groups across the country picked up on the theme and sang the praises of MPR, Inga and their leader Mobutu. And, as stipulated, on November 24, 1972, in the presence of twelve different African heads of state, "Little Inga" was inaugurated. "Big Inga" still lay in the future as projected in the plan.

But there was more. Zaire's rich copper resources lay in Shaba Province over 1,100 miles to the southeast of this new source of power. Ignoring earlier findings that new sources of energy for that distant mining complex could easily be developed locally at much less expense, Mobutu determined that its power needs would be supplied by a direct current high line which would be strung across his country from Inga. It would come to be known as the Inga-Shaba project. (3)

Strangely, except for Kinshasa, the electricity would benefit none of the rural areas or urban centers along its 1,100 mile track. Eventually cutting directly through Mennonite territories in Bandundu, West and East Kasai Provinces, bemused Africans and missionaries alike watched as surveying crews hedgehopped their way cross-country via helicopters laying down great white X marks of plastic sheeting. On their heels came road crews and, eventually, construction crews. To the consternation and anger of village folk, sometimes the heavy equipment bulldozed its way directly through fields of ripening millet and maturing manioc which had been laboriously cultivated with short handled hoes. There were government promises of compensation for any such loss incurred but no one believed it. Personnel on Mennonite stations in the bush became accustomed to helicopters dropping onto their soccer fields bringing white crews in search of companionship or a bit of green produce or fresh eggs from missionary gardens and chicken pens.

In the heady days of the early 70's in Zaire, the Inga-Shaba venture made great press. It was a remarkable engineering feat by any standard. Furthermore, it was a striking example of a former colonized African country racing to catch up with the industrialized world by tapping and developing its own resources. It was a heralded demonstration of African initiative and resolve. So read much of what was written at the time.

But why incur the astronomical cost of such a line to deliver power to the distant Shaba Province if, indeed, its needs could be met locally for a fraction of the Inga-Shaba project cost? And why, if built, should it be done with no benefit to any of the populations, rural or urban, along the way? Persistent conjecture quietly made its way among the people of the country. Perhaps at some future date it would benefit ordinary people but for now the creation of the power line was politically motivated. Shaba Province had a history of political restlessness dating back to earliest post-independence times. Mobutu, it was said, wanted to supply a source of needed power to that area which he could control. Whatever the case, many an evening Nyanga Zairians and missionaries alike pondered the mysterious political quirks which left them to light candles and kerosene lamps in full view of sagging power cables silhouetted against the sky on a hilltop just to the north of their station.

travels, speeches and evolving ideas

As Mobutu's regime gathered momentum, he and his projects in Zaire were coming to the attention of an ever broader circle of interested governments both in and outside Africa. Invitations began to come for visits from a variety of countries. Seizing on these opportunities he traveled with increasing frequency explaining his political goals in Zaire and expressing his views regarding events transpiring on the international scene. Places he chose to go and topics he chose to address in his speeches shed revealing light on the beliefs he held and the goals he pursued. In Dakar, Senegal, during a visit in 1971, he discussed the political movement which he headed. Addressing his Senegalese audience he stated that although MPR was referred to as a political party, there was a fundamental difference between his movement and political parties elsewhere. Whereas traditional political groups had as their objective to eradicate opposition in order to impose themselves upon people, MPR was a national movement of all Zairians which implied a radical break with the political ideas and methods which had failed before he took power. (4)

In the course of a speech made at an MPR Congress in 1972, he referred to criticism that the movement he headed amounted to a single-party system of government. He countered by pointing out that MPR was born out of a process which was fundamentally African. MPR's adopted philosophy of authenticity could not easily accept the existence of several conflicting political parties at the same time. "The family has only one head in the village and the village clans cannot have two chiefs since for us as Africans, two or three heads on a single body constitute a monster." (5)

As the theme of authenticity was drummed in the press, via radio and in public addresses, public response sometimes ran ahead of what was intended. On one occasion, when party leaders suggested it was time that some of the Belgian monuments scattered around town be removed for preservation in a museum, an exuberant crowd took matters in their own hands. An AIMM missionary passing through the city at that time wrote: "Enthusiasm ran high and most of them were badly damaged in the process. Stanley's famous likeness on the bluff overlooking the river toward the east broke between the knees and ankles leaving two jagged empty boots still bolted to the base. King Leopold suffered the indignity of coming down head first and being buried to his shoulders in the flower bed directly below him." (6)

a trip to China

The year of 1973 perhaps best portrayed Mobutu at the crest of his prestige and influence both as a national and international figure. In January of that year he made an extended trip to Asia which included several days in China. For a time Zaire had had diplomatic relations with Taiwan but during this visit Mobutu saw various similarities between this enormous country and his own. China also was underdeveloped. It also had had unpleasant experiences with domineering western powers. It too had a large rural population. And yet, via a disciplined harnessing of its massive labor force, it was feeding itself and achieving much progress using intermediate technology appropriate to its situation and needs.

Opening diplomatic relations with that country Mobutu praised its government in a subsequent speech. After criticizing the various sorts of technical aid provided by western governments which were proving costly for Zaire he commented: "For Chinese technical assistants we pay for no plane tickets and we make no transfers of funds to their home country for salary. The Chinese experts adopt the life styles of their Zairian counterparts. The Chinese travels, houses and nourishes himself exactly like his Zairian partner. In the domain of financial assistance, China has accorded us an important credit at very long term without interest. There, in my opinion, is a beautiful example to be followed if one wants to help an under-equipped country." (7) (8)

In the course of this same trip Mobutu also made a stop in India. When invited to make a speech at a state function, he made a number of statements: The British had tried to make Indian Englishmen out of them just like Belgians had tried to make African Belgians out them; both countries had been humiliated, exploited and had experienced the imposition of strange dress, a strange language, strange customs and strange beliefs; in both countries foreigners had reaped the benefit of cheap labor while the laboring man reaped all the hardships. He concluded his comments by praising Mahatma Gandhi as an Indian apostle of non-violence and as the author of basic concepts which were guiding the non-aligned nations in their growing collaboration.

at the United Nations

It was in October 1973 that Mobutu had occasion to address the General Assembly of the United Nations in New York. Taking full advantage of this opportunity he sought to make himself heard on a wide range of issues which he felt to be important for him and his country in an international setting. Beginning with his battle cry of "authenticity" he explained: "Authenticity is the determination of the Zairian people to return to their own roots, to examine the values of their ancestors in order to evaluate those which contribute to their harmonious and natural development. Authenticity is the refusal of the Zairian people to blindly espouse imported ideologies. Authenticity is the affirmation of the Zairian man or, more basically, of man himself, there where he is, as he is, with his own mental and social structures."

Turning to the international scene he protested the term "third world" which was commonly being used to categorize countries such as his. "In Zaire we challenge this appellation . . . which for us has no meaning. . . . It is impossible to justify this term on the basis of geography or of population. The 'third world' does not constitute a third of humanity but rather two thirds." (9)

He went on to observe that such a term made no economic sense either because among such countries there were some following a capitalistic system whereas others were communal in nature. The term "Eastern and Western blocks" was not helpful either because all others who did not belong to either group were tossed into a single basket called "third world." What was even worse was the use of such terms as "backward" or "underdeveloped" to describe countries like his own. All such terms carried for them a tone of scorn and were therefore resented, inappropriate and needed to be dropped from international vocabulary. He then stated that as far as Zaire was concerned, they would freely acknowledge being "under-equipped" in comparison with other countries, something which has no shame. He concluded his discussion of the topic by stating: "The world is divided into two camps; those who are dominated and those who are the dominators; those who are exploited and those who are the exploiters. Countries are not poor because of congenital incapacity; they are poor as a result of history which saw certain countries which dominated, exploited and pillaged others in order to enrich themselves. And it is but mathematical logic: when the rich exploit the poor, the rich become more and more rich and the poor become more and more poor."

Turning to other issues before the UN Assembly, he spoke of "cultural pillage" which his and other African countries had experienced. Observing that as westerners cherish the pieces of art produced by their cultures so do also the Africans. Pointing out that during the colonial period great amounts of African handcraft and art had found their way into museums around the world, he requested "that this General Assembly pass a resolution requesting the rich powers to return part of them so that we can teach our children and grandchildren the history of their country." (10)

But Mobutu was not yet done. Pressing ahead, he touched on the issue of world-wide ecology. "In Zaire we are flattered when we are considered as champions in the protection of nature. But what does this performance help . . . if our efforts are annulled by people located at a distance of thousands of kilometers from us?" He went on to propose that the UN Assembly sponsor a world-wide study of all kinds of pollution and the best manner to combat them. Then he added: "Logically this study should be financed by the rich countries, not only because they have the resources but also, and above all, because they are the greatest polluters." (11)

Turning momentarily philosophical Mobutu observed: "In our opinion there is a difference between poverty and misery. We are called 'poor countries' because some of our fellow countrymen walk bare footed, lightly dressed and sleep in rudimentary dwellings. But the modern life of sophisticated countries reveal millionaires who leave their Cadillacs in the garage and make long trips to our countries to walk bare foot, sleep under the open sky and burn themselves under the sun. Without doubt they are searching for simple happiness and true joy in life." (12)

There was also Zaire's views on the international scene to be spelled out and on this he wanted to be clear. Referring to the minority white regime in power in South Africa, he roundly condemned them as well as the white minority which at the time was still trying to cling to power in Southern Rhodesia (now Zimbabwe). He then quoted African author Frantz Fanon who had written: "Africa has the form of a revolver whose trigger is placed in Zaire." In other contexts Mobutu was also heard to declare that when Zaire was sick, so was Africa and as Zaire becomes strong, so does Africa. Employing Kennedy-esque rhetoric he brought this portion of his speech to the following conclusion: "My country is ready to confront this sacred battle whatever sacrifices may result from it. We will never retreat no matter what happens, no matter what the cost." (13)

Under Mobutu's regime, close ties had been forged between Zaire and Israel. His appearance at the United Nations, however, coincided with an escalating Israeli-Arab confrontation. With a certain flair for theatrics Mobutu chose this moment to make an announcement: "Zaire finds itself at an hour of decision. . . Zaire must make a choice between a friend, Israel, and a brother, Egypt. Well, between a friend and a brother the choice is clear. . . . Thus I announce, before the world, the rupture of diplomatic relations with Israel until such time as Egypt and the Arab countries concerned regain their territories presently occupied." (14)

Back in Zaire after his world travels, for Mobutu it was full steam ahead. Before a congress of the MPR at N'Sele in October of 1973, he reported on what he perceived to be Zaire's growing stature in the international community. He reminded his audience of MPR faithful of Zaire's commitment to the Organization of African Unity. He explained: "That means that the Chief of State of Zaire has a permanent mandate, without consultation either with the people or the national legislative council, to commit the Zairian State to whatever strengthens the unity of Africa." (15)

Referring to the white/black confrontation in southern Africa, he pictured Zaire as being on the forefront of a protective African line of defense against the assault of imperialism. Reporting on the break of diplomatic relations with Israel, Mobutu expressed surprise and hurt at the violent reaction of the Israeli government following his public announcement earlier in the year in New York. He added that it was difficult for Zairians to understand why a people who had so often been humiliated in the past should be precisely those who were humiliating the Arab people.

But it was the developments on the Zairian domestic front which were of greatest import that November of 1973. Under the theme of "Zairianization", drastic proposals were in the making. Under the umbrella motto of authenticity, Mobutu was intent on taking possession of his national house on every front. Political independence had been won. Economic independence, however, had been only partially won. With MPR leadership it was decided to announce the takeover of much of the commercial enterprise of the country. The rationale? "The legitimate desire of the Zairian citizen to feel himself to be master of his own country and to manage his own material inheritance." (16)

Thus it was announced that within three months time the State was going to oversee the transfer of all small and medium-sized commercial holdings and of even a few of the major business concerns to Zairian hands. This raised an immediate cluster of questions, but none were more troubling than these: How were the Zairians to be chosen who would be the beneficiaries of such a windfall? And what about recompense for the expatriates who across the years had painstakingly built up their commercial ventures? It soon became evident that these "plums" were not necessarily going to fall into hands of Zairians who had particular business experience but rather of those who had good MPR connections. As for settlement with the non-Zairian business people whose assets were simply being taken from them, there were vague promises of eventual reimbursement by the State.

The year 1974 saw still further international travel including a return trip to China plus a stop in North Korea. In late December, Mobutu went into a huddle with his MPR leadership on the Zaire River aboard his presidential yacht. In the course of three days of dialogue ten problems seen as plaguing Zaire at the time were defined: 1) liberty vs. license; 2) the agricultural crisis; 3) unemployment; 4) inflation; 5) the drift toward becoming a consumer society; 6) inadequate education of youth; 7) a costly military; 8) social injustice; 9) social problems; 10) egotism in high places.

January 4, 1975: Mobutu addresses the nation

The people of Zaire heard soon enough about what had been decided on the river and what Mobutu and the MPR proposed to do about the problems they had identified. Calling a mass meeting at the "May 20th Stadium," so named in honor of the official founding of the MPR as a political movement, Mobutu began by observing that 1975 marked the 10th anniversary of the Zairian revolution and that very much had indeed been accomplished. He stated further: "Zaire which yesterday was Congo, the joke of the world and the shame of Africa, is today respected everywhere on our planet. At first our revolution aroused skepticism, then criticism, and finally admiration. It has been recognized by serious men who record revolutions which mark the history of men." (17)

Referring to his constant travel both outside and within his country, he described the Zairians before November 24, 1965 (his moment of accession to power) as a "people who did not know where to turn their heads for there were too many prophets and too many miracle workers. The Zairian people who had known the nightmare of colonial exploitation and of imperialist domination, civil wars and disorders without number, were but a shadow of themselves." But, he continued, "Today, if our political theory [of authenticity] is perfect, it is also necessary to recognize that our practice does not yet match our theory. We must avoid acting like Pharisees who preach what they do not practice." (18)

He then launched into an inventory of Zaire's problems and the impending changes he envisioned. Agriculture and the Zairian rural people had been neglected and Zairian production of food was declining. "A new agricultural plan is imperative. As of today, a popular mobilization is decreed in order to create productive agriculture units and cooperatives of a new type." (19) Unstated but implicit in the announcement was the idea of regrouping scattered rural villages into agricultural cooperatives somewhat in the Chinese pattern. And, if there was to be increased agricultural production, major improvement of roads would be necessary. This, it was explained, was to be accomplished by construction companies which Zaire had already nationalized. Given all the new work initiatives planned, Mobutu predicted that unemployment would soon be unknown in Zaire.

Turning to the topic of Zaire's youth who were "the Zaire of tomorrow," he stated that for the building of a harmonious society, it was imperative that all children receive the same education, the same political instruction and the same military training. He continued: "In order to achieve this, all children must receive their formation within the same system." (20) Though stated in veiled terms in the stadium that day, what was in fact being announced was the nationalization of all schools in the country. This, of course, meant that school systems which had been painstakingly created and maintained across the years by both Catholic and Protestant Missions were to come under direct government control. Shock waves from this decision immediately rippled across the mission/church communities of the country.

As for the international scene, it was stated that Zaire was taking its place firmly within the non-aligned block of nations. Zaire would seek to be the friend of all nations regardless of their political stance but would not tolerate interference in its internal affairs from any country. He cautioned that this statement was to be taken as an official warning to all foreign embassies present within the country.

Turning in his speech to the topic of Zaire's military, he stated that its role was being redefined. Referring to its traditional stance as a force of attack in case of danger, it would henceforth enlarge its mandate and take its place beside the working population of the country to make its own contribution to the country's development.

But before concluding his speech in the packed stadium, he yet turned his critical attention to those within his own MPR hierarchy: "At the beginning of the tenth year of our revolution, I have unfortunately discovered that many among you have not taken my reflections seriously. We are now before a major shift in direction. Shilly-shallying is no longer possible. If someone wants to know if citizen Mobutu works for the people or for the party leadership, I respond: 'I work for the people and not for the party leadership.' . . . Thus it is that I am asking all of my collaborators to return to the State the holdings acquired when business enterprises were taken over by the Zaire government about a year ago. . . . I now confront them with a clear choice: that those who love the people give up everything to the State and follow me. In plain words, I am declaring war against the privileged class of our country. You the leadership of the MPR, keep your hands clean. Keep a clear conscience and work for the people and only for the people. . . . That which I ask is simply that which the MPR preaches, 'To Serve and Not To Be Served.' . . . This is the price of social justice for I cannot tolerate in my country the rich who are too rich and the poor who are too poor. As always I ask you to place your confidence in me. I will never betray our revolution. It is with public service, self sacrifice and solidarity that we will build a great country and will always be young and dynamic in the heart of this continent, a model of discipline, liberty, prosperity and happiness." (21)

It was soaring rhetoric and Mobutu had been at his charismatic best. Response was tumultuous as the crowd erupted in cheers, chants and applause. He was at the peak of his popularity and power.

In an interview later that same year Mobutu matter-of-factly made a series of statements: "The MPR is nothing other than the nation organized politically and it is one and the same as the State. . . . In such a system the President, elected by direct national election, is invested with his power by the masses and not by pressure groups or a single pressure group. . . . Thus the keystone of the edifice is the President of the MPR whose powers are very broad. He is President of the Republic. He chairs the political bureau, the executive council, the legislative council and the judiciary council. In a single word, he is the chief according to our Bantu conception of things. In effect, the Bantu soul is not satisfied with abstractions. It postulates one chief and one only . . . . The President of the party is the incarnation of MPR and thus of the nation." (22)

a second power structure also takes shape

Elected as the new general secretary of the Congo Protestant Council in 1968, Jean (French form of the name John) Bokeleale early made his leadership skills felt. After only two years of planning, lobbying, cajoling and pressuring, he and his staff were able to secure general assembly approval for two revolutionary proposals which drastically changed the Protestant landscape of Zaire: 1) an insistent call for the fusion of all missions with the churches they had planted and, 2) the transformation of the historic Protestant Council into a single national church called *L'Eglise du Christ au Zaire* (i.e., The Church of Christ of Zaire or, simply, the ECZ in its French acronym). The former proposal meant the legal dissolution of the missions which would yield to this call. The latter meant that churches across the country would cease to refer to themselves as churches but would become, instead, "communities" of the ECZ.

Already in the early 70's, amidst its confrontation with the Catholic Church, the government had issued a ruling that among the six religious communities granted official recognition was "the Protestant Church." At this point the government made itself clear. By "the Protestant Church" it meant the ECZ. To ensure recognition and ongoing freedom of activity, Protestant mission/church groups in the entire country were "invited" to regularize their membership within the ECZ. Any declining to do so would be required to disband and to cease their activities.

For many Protestants of Zaire, this ruling coincided in a striking manner with the ECZ's push for a single church. Coming as they did from the same northwestern region of Zaire, it was easy to wonder if there had been some consultation - - if not outright collaboration - - between President Mobutu and ECZ General Secretary Bokeleale in coordinating these parallel and complimentary events.

making a case for the ECZ

If President Mobutu manifested charisma and conviction on the speech making circuit, Secretary Bokeleale demonstrated no less skill in using interviews and platform appearances to good advantage. A

263

journalist in the employ of a Kinshasa newspaper, *Le Courrier d'Afrique,* sat with Secretary Bokeleale to do research for an article which appeared in his paper under the dateline of January 1, 1972. Regarding the move under way to establish a single Protestant Church in Zaire, Bokeleale commented: "Christianity is above all a religion of love, of reconciliation; a religion which brings salvation to mankind. It is not a religion of individualism but a religion of fraternity, one of family; a religion of a nation of people just as was the case . . . in Judaism from which it derives. Christianity coincides exactly with the Bantu conception of the family." (23)

In an article for the October 1973 issue of International Review of Mission entitled "From Missions to Mission," Doctor Bokeleale (24) gave the following background to the birth of the ECZ: "Missions had always been regarded as close allies of colonialism because they came to Africa together, they collaborated with one another and the one was considered to be the agent of the other, always in the long run for the benefit of the colonizing power. But apart from that, an institutional mission which lasts 25 years, 50 years, a century even, destroys the real development of a young church. . . . Further, at the time Zaire attained its political independence in 1960, a number of missions had in fact begun granting 'autonomy' to their corresponding communities in this country. Many of them, however, still retained the mission as a separate identity. Not only did this in many ways make a mockery of the so-called 'autonomy' but it also made it difficult if not impossible for the Zairian churchmen, leaders of the local communities, to really lead and develop their work in a manner suited for their country's new circumstances."

In the light of the new law governing religious bodies in Zaire Dr. Bokeleale observed that "Protestant Missions, as such, are no longer legally recognized in Zaire. . . . The stage is now set for the ECZ and its member communities to develop naturally, to become the Church rooted in their own society and to look to the future to play their particular role in strengthening the Church of our Lord as a whole everywhere in the world. If the Church in Zaire started by attacking the mission as an institution, it was because it was the classic, indeed the only relationship between the young churches and their sister churches in the West. The purpose of this relationship was theoretically to assist the development of the church. But since aid was always channeled through missionaries and mission institutions, it could only be concluded that this help was conditional on the presence of missionaries of the same nationality as the sending churches."

Turning to issues of financial support, Bokeleale stated that much of mission funding at that point continued to be channeled to mission projects "which do not produce anything but which rather condemn the young churches to eternal dependance on aid from the rich. . . . The young churches today have among their members more and more people who are highly qualified and whose presence is essential for their development. But they often cannot employ them because at this stage they are not economically strong enough to do so. Are the western churches ready to divert funds to support these people, instead of continuing to spend thousands upon thousands of dollars on Western personnel who are often less qualified and who have difficulty in understanding the innermost soul and the customs of the people to be evangelized?"

Concluding his article on a conciliatory note, ECZ Secretary Bokeleale wrote: "There is no intention of putting an end to the sending of missionaries as fraternal workers who have the right qualifications and are sincerely ready to collaborate under the chosen leadership of the young churches. On the contrary, this is desirable because their presence is the sign of the universality of the Church and of its unity. For the Church belongs to the Lord and not to any particular race, culture or nation. . . . Can we not all agree that Jesus Christ is the Lord of all, that the all-powerful God is our Father and that we are all called to be brethren through his love? Such a faith, sincerely held, can orientate all our new fraternal relations." (25)

a power base is developed

The vision of the ECZ leadership was clear but needs and hindrances were many. Staff was growing as the ECZ attempted to deal with multitudinous issues which confronted it, but office space was a problem as were funds to meet monthly payrolls. It was also felt that to be an effective force across the country, a structure of provincial level ECZ offices and secretaries needed to be developed but, once again, funding was a problem.

While ECZ delegates had early agreed to maintain the policy of non-alignment with international ecumenical bodies established by its predecessor, the Congo Protestant Council, member communities of the ECZ were nonetheless granted the freedom to join such bodies if they so desired. Dr. Bokeleale's Zairian Disciples of Christ Church early took this step. Naming him as an official representative to meetings of the World Council of Churches was a logical action. Once on the scene in Geneva, Switzerland, he quickly became known as the dynamic pioneer of an innovative new thrust in ecumenism in Zaire. It was not long that he was named to the WCC executive and in that capacity began to make regular trips to Europe.

As the shape and nature of the ECZ cause came to be known to the WCC bureaucracy and, particularly, to the West German Protestant leadership, increasingly significant funding was earmarked for ECZ purposes. There followed a series of impressive achievements. Securing a choice piece of ground from the government near the imposing Ministry of Justice building in Kinshasa, a multi-storied double winged ECZ administrative building began to take shape. Once finished it was to provide a chapel, conference rooms and office space not only for all ECZ departments and supportive staff but also additional space for rental to some of the para-church organizations at work in the country.

Once the construction of ECZ's national headquarters was well launched and its administrative structure worked through, Secretary Bokeleale turned to the forging of a network of provincial level offices. This meant the appointment of provincial ECZ secretaries who could be counted on to solidly support ECZ philosophy and plans for the future and to represent these views in a forceful and articulate manner within the Protestant communities of their respective regions. After considerable travel, there came a series of pioneering consultations in province after province where the representatives of the Protestant communities were gathered. They were invited to affirm the spreading ECZ structure and to elect from among their leaders the first ECZ provincial secretaries.

Invariably, in the course of such consultation, questions of office space, salaries and means of transportation for their newly-elected secretaries would arise. While local communities were strongly encouraged to contribute generously to the cost of these new joint ventures, the quiet word was that the new structure being created would not be allowed to falter for lack of sufficient funds. (26)

a rumble of dissent

This swift pace of ECZ events was not lost on the broad Protestant community of Zaire. Reaction was not long in coming. Methodist Bishop John Wesley Shungu (pr. SHOO-ngoo) soon emerged as the key personality and voice of a growing opposition movement. As head of the largest Protestant "community" in the country, he was vehemently opposed to an emerging ECZ structure which he saw as threatening to the autonomy of his Church. There quickly gathered around him some thirty other mission/church groups located mostly in the eastern half of Zaire. Meetings were held and a name was adopted - - "The Council of Protestant Churches of Zaire," or CEPZA in its French acronym. A missionary report of that era summarized developments as follows: "Motivations for affiliation with CEPZA are varied: for some it takes on overtones of a power struggle between Bishop Shungu and Secretary Bokeleale; for some there is the element of regional and tribal competition; for many there is fear of the leanings of the ECZ toward the World Council; all have misgivings concerning the mushrooming bureaucracy that characterizes ECZ and its apparent desire to create something of a 'super church' if not a national Protestant Church for Zaire with all of the implications of control from the top down, infringement upon local church authority and freedom." (27)

Having connections in the Zaire Judiciary of the time, Bishop Shungu explored the possibility of securing legal status for the newly formed Council. Apparently receiving some encouragement, official papers were submitted. A meeting was then called in early January, 1972, by the Minister of Justice to which representatives of all Protestant groups in the country were invited. The understanding was that in the presence of the minister each group would be asked to declare publicly and finally which of the two groups their church wanted to identify with. But before the announced date arrived, there came a second word. The minister would still meet with church representatives but only with those who were seeking to form a new council.

ECZ influence is revealed

Upon arrival at the Ministry of Justice, the church representatives were convened in the presence of the Minister and were brusquely told that the law was the law. The ECZ had already been recognized as the one covering organization for all Protestants in the country. This, therefore, left no room for questions or debate. Their choice was either to submit to the government ruling or to disband their churches. It was widely believed among the apprehensive Protestant leaders that ECZ leadership had been able to bring sufficient pressure to bear upon the Ministry of Justice to cause the Minister to reverse himself.

Suddenly left high and dry, the dissident group immediately went to Secretary Bokeleale and requested that an emergency assembly of the ECZ be held so that the tense situation could be dealt with. Instead, the ECZ Secretary convened a meeting of his executive committee. Recognizing that all avenues had been effectively blocked for them, the representatives of CEPZA began to return to their home areas. Shortly thereafter, the ECZ submitted a list of its membership to the government including all members of the aborted CEPZA group.

In a striking fashion, the ECZ had demonstrated the power and stature which it had already acquired in Zaire. ECZ pulled no punches. In a variety of ways its views regarding the political scene, on the one hand, and the dissident church group, on the other, were made quite clear. Regarding President Mobutu, the MPR and its theme of authenticity, Secretary Bokeleale observed: "Christianity such as we've come to know it here among us seems to be a religion imported from the West. There are therefore many things which do not mesh with our customs and traditions. The Church must sanctify that which exists here among us. But there are, furthermore, many traditions and beliefs which constitute already a base for Christianity. For example, following ancestral tradition, there is a profound communion between the dead and the living. The Zairians believe, therefore, in eternal life. The Zairian theologians must study our traditions and our customs in order to clarify them in the light of the Gospel. Furthermore, when we fight for unity, and when we condemn division, we are making a special effort to instill a spirit of family in the church. This is a return to our sources, a return to the Bantu conception of community." (28) (29)

In a New Year's message addressed to the Zairian people, Secretary Bokeleale made ECZ's stance vis-à-vis Zairian political power very clear: "Were there competing political parties in Zaire, it would not be wise for the ECZ to identify with any single party. But in Zaire there are no political parties. There is simply the movement of an entire people to build its country and to better its lot in the face of tremendous difficulties and odds. Since every Zairian is part of this movement, every church member obviously is too and thus the Church itself is part of the movement. The goals of the MPR are straight from the Gospel, i.e., honesty, justice and work, with emphasis upon helping the average man and living in peace with all men. Thus in supporting the movement [MPR] one is in reality supporting some of the goals of the Church itself . . . for in many ways they are one and the same." (30)

As for the failed effort to establish a parallel Council of Churches, the ECZ Secretary placed blame as follows: "The divisions and conflicts provoked in the midst of the ECZ by a minority of foreign missionaries are contrary to the Biblical spirit and to the conception of society. . . . Foreign missionaries who destroy the unity of the Protestant Church in Zaire apply a diabolical policy: divide so as to rule. They sow hate where there is love; mistrust where there is mutual trust; disorder where there is order and tension where there is peace." (31)

Mennonites amidst the powers

Residents of central Zaire, Mennonites had early been approached by leaders of the ill-fated effort to create a second Zairian Church Council. While sympathetic toward both the member groups and some of their concerns, CMZa and CEM leaders recalled that in an earlier era, CIM missionaries had decided to remain members of the Congo Protestant Council during a time of similar tension. It was consequently decided to maintain ECZ membership in the hope that, by so doing, Mennonites might at least in some small ways find it possible to play counseling and conciliatory roles within the organization.

As for the swirling political waters in which they found themselves immersed, one missionary described the CMZa attitude as one of "wary uneasiness." There were MPR youth cells in all of their communities while all church-related youth activity had been forbidden. Pictures of President Mobutu were in all church school classrooms. His larger-than-life images were found at airports and other public traffic arteries. All church school centers experienced the daily hubbub of morning flag raisings accompanied by drumming, dancing, the shouting of political slogans and the singing of songs praising the MPR and its founder. There were even the disquieting rumors of a government takeover of all church schools. Religious broadcasting and religious publications had been suppressed. There were rumors of a plan to uproot scattered rural village populations (including Mennonites) for regrouping into "agricultural production units." There was also talk of creating village based "road brigades" which would be required to contribute "volunteer labor" for the repair and maintenance of roads which had fallen into drastic disrepair. China, they learned, had for years been harnessing rural manpower for the common good; why not Zaire too?

One report of that era to the AIMM Board was concluded with the comment that "everything is overshadowed by the swift pace of events round about us. In the meantime we work, watch and pray." (32)

CHAPTER 27   THE CIM TAKES INVENTORY

The year 1971, both in Zaire and in North America, had about it the sense of a turned page of hi
The CMZa had at long last achieved a goal it had pursued - - the signing of a fusion document with a board
delegation from America. After a couple of years of growing internal tension, new administrative structures
for the Church had been welcomed and Kabangy Moise had been unanimously elected as the new general
secretary. Church statistics in 1971 counted 51 ordained pastors on active status who collaborated with 73
overseers and 231 teacher/evangelists widely scattered through rural villages.

A missionary team which had gradually grown in size since the traumatic events of 1960 and 1964 had
reached a total of 86 adults dispersed across eight mission stations and in several urban centers. Another
fourteen young MCC volunteers were at work in school rooms and in agricultural or construction projects. All
mission personnel now took their place under the umbrella of the Zaire Church. For the Zairians there was a
clear sense of achievement mixed with optimism as to the future.

In keeping with the fusion agreement signed at Djoko Punda in 1971, the CIM had pursued legal steps
for its own dissolution in Zaire. In a letter dated February 23, 1972, written by Vernon Sprunger to a
missionary on furlough, there was a terse five line paragraph: "Have drawn up papers for the dissolution of the
CIM and have taken them in to the Justice Department and they have OK'd them. Now I will type them out
in seven copies and send them around to be signed and then turn them in to the Justice Department, and the
CIM will have gone out of existence in Zaire." (1)

It was less than three months later when on May 8, 1972, Jim Bertsche and Vernon Sprunger,
respectively legal and assistant legal representatives of the CIM at the time, made their way through the marble
corridors of the Belgian-built Ministry of Justice building of Kinshasa and laid a packet of material on a desk.
A brief covering letter addressed to the Minister of Justice said simply: "We the undersigned, Bertsche, J.E.,
Legal Representative and Sprunger, V.J., Assistant Legal Representative of the not-for-profit Association called
the Congo Inland Mission with headquarters at Tshikapa, have the honor to bring to your attention that the
effective members of this Association of which we are the officers have made the decision to dissolve the
Association known as the Congo Inland Mission."

"Please find here included a copy of the decision made and supported by its effective members who
have attached their signatures to it."

With the customary flourish of formal French correspondence the letter concluded: "We ask that you
accept the assurance of our most distinguished esteem." (2)

The two men exited the building in silence, each deep in his own thoughts.

Meanwhile, back in North America, the events of the early 1970's in Zaire had been followed with
keen interest. The delegation which had traveled to Zaire to help draft the fusion agreement with CMZA had
returned with favorable reports. Not that all problems had been solved; some issues remained which would call
for ongoing consultation, struggle and prayer. But it was abundantly clear to all that a dream of many years had
been realized. For six decades inter-Mennonite teams of missionaries had followed each other in a wide range
of ministries and witness. There had initially been times of struggle under a tropical sun with meager results.
There had been times of financial crisis as the American economy collapsed in the late 1920's. There had been
times of great anxiety as emergency missionary evacuations were carried out amidst bloody revolt and tribal
warfare. But in the face of formidable odds, a large, growing, enthusiastic Mennonite church community had,
by God's grace, become a reality.

now what?

It would have been easy in the early 70's for the CIM Board to have settled back into a supportive, fraternal relationship with the Mennonite Churches which had resulted from its sixty years of witness in Congo/Zaire. It would have been understandable if, at that point, board members had wondered out loud if perhaps the CIM had accomplished the purpose for which it had been brought into being six decades earlier.

But as the board and its executive committee continued to meet, a clear consensus quickly emerged. Africa was an immense continent. There was no terminal date attached to their mandate for Christian mission. Opportunity and need for ongoing mission in the name of Christ was limitless. There could be no question of relaxing; it was rather a question of re-tooling. In the bare bones manner of official minutes, this early round of discussion was noted as follows: "No sentiment for terminating CIM was expressed though most favored substantial changes at home and new ventures overseas." (3)

A starting point was to name a constitution revision committee. (4) At the outset committee members recognized that two basic board concerns had prompted their appointment: 1) the need to spell out ways of relating helpfully and constructively to an emerging African Church to which full autonomy had been granted and in reference to which legal dissolution of the Mission had been accepted, and 2) the need to rethink and redefine its ongoing intent and purpose in Africa.

In an initial committee session three basic assumptions were made: 1) that whatever the organization was eventually to be called, it must remain inter-Mennonite in nature; 2) that given the intent to probe new ministries in Africa, it must seek to expand its supportive base and 3) that in the midst of impending change it must remain Anabaptist/Mennonite in creed and character. It was within these adopted parameters that the revision committee worked and eventually arrived at a series of recommendations which were submitted to the CIM Board in its spring sessions March 23-24, 1972: 1) that the name be changed from the Congo Inland Mission to the Africa Inter-Mennonite Mission; (5) 2) that the stated dual purpose of the Mission be expanded by a third, i.e., "to demonstrate Christian love through service ministries. Mt 25:34-40; John 10:25" (6) 3) that regarding the geographical focus of ongoing ministry the Mission look beyond Zaire to other "carefully selected countries of Africa." (7)

The revision committee also had a proposal relative to the composition of the board which for some years had been comprised of 17 members drawn from three partnering conferences plus an 18th member-at-large. (8) The suggestion was to reduce the board to 13 members while creating a category to be known as advisory members who could be selected by board action to represent any church group "maintaining missionary work through the organization but not having the right to select board members." (9)

what did you say your name is?

Other sections of the constitution having to do with the internal workings of the organization were also reviewed before its final adoption. But nothing more clearly summarized the newly adopted stance of the Mission than its new name, The Africa Inter-Mennonite Mission. A bit long and, at first, a bit awkward on the tongue, it for a time elicited some puzzled inquiries and expressions. But the choice had been a deliberate and intentional one. In a variety of ways it embodied the basic changes the organization was in process of making.

First, there was a shift of focus from Congo to Africa. After sixty years of preoccupation with a single African country, the intent was now, while maintaining close working relations with the Zaire Churches, to look beyond that country to possible new opportunities of ministry. Next, the historic inter-Mennonite nature of the organization was now being unmistakably highlighted and the implication was clear. The CIM had not been a quirk of Mennonite history. A joint partnership in Africa had been intentional from the beginning and was now being reaffirmed. It had been an enjoyable and fruitful venture. After 60 years, this cooperative venture on the part of a variety of the sons and daughters of Menno was not only going to be maintained but broadened if possible. And, finally, Mission; an unabashed statement of the conviction that the mandate for witness in the name of Christ was just as fresh and compelling in the early 1970's as it had ever been.

By coincidence, the year of constitution revision and renaming of the Mission was also its 60th anniversary year. This was an opportunity too good to ignore. Plans were laid for a celebration. The spring sessions of the board which normally were scheduled in April each year were in the spring of 1972 delayed until June at which time a Zairian lay couple would be traveling in North America as fraternal visitors while en route to Curitiba, Brazil, as delegates of their Church to the Mennonite World Conference of that year. The couple: Kakesa Samuel and his wife Kafutshi whose dramatic story of survival in the midst of the Kwilu rebellion, a decade earlier, had become widely known. An offer from the EMC/US Brookside Church in Fort Wayne, IN, to host the board sessions was accepted. Sunday afternoon, June 18, was devoted to a service of celebration and an AIMM rally was held in the large General Conference Mennonite Church in Berne, IN, that evening. Public response to these open meetings was broad and enthusiastic. Kakesa was invited to meet with both the AIMM Board and Executive Committee. The recently-signed fusion agreement with the African Church bulked large in the discussions. Executive Committee minutes described the encounter with Kakesa as being "very open, frank and cordial."

changes in the home office

George and Justina Wiens Neufeld joined the home staff in the summer of 1961 in the aftermath of the massive evacuation of CIM personnel the summer before, George as office accountant and Justina as the headquarters hostess. When the Neufelds reached retirement age in 1969, Art and Martini Reimer Janz were invited to join the home staff where Art took over the role of office accountant and treasurer. Shortly thereafter Martini became his part-time assistant.

Reuben Short, who had been named executive secretary in 1963, was nearing the end of his second five year term. Already in 1972 he had called the attention of the board to this fact and suggested that a replacement be found. When in 1973 the board was not yet prepared to name a replacement, Short accepted to remain at his post for one additional year on the condition that he be allowed to terminate in the fall of 1974. Short had given solid leadership to the CIM. Though describing his years in the AIMM office as rich and rewarding for him personally he noted, however, that changes had taken place which led him to conclude that it was time for a new secretary in the home office. A decade earlier when he had accepted the position, the board was relating to and planning with a mission organization in Congo with missionaries in roles of leadership. A decade later, a Zaire mission structure had been dismantled and the home office was suddenly corresponding with Zairian church officers who relied on French to express themselves and to submit their proposals. Beyond the question of language, Short also felt that it was time that he be replaced with someone who had African experience and who had been part of the unfolding history of the African Church.

With this in mind the AIMM Executive Committee began its search and eventually opened dialogue with Jim Bertsche. The Bertsches registered large reservations about the proposal to come to the Elkhart office. Leaving the States the first time in 1948, Africa had by this time in a very real sense become "home" for them. Language proficiency had gradually been achieved across the years. Deep friendships had been forged with a variety of African church leaders at the different stations where they had been assigned. They had had time to watch a generation of their students establish families and emerge in roles of leadership in their Church. They had fully supported the move toward fusion and had increasingly become a part of the African church life there. Each succeeding term was becoming more personally satisfying for them. There was genuine reluctance on their part to return to the States for an indefinite period of time. Furthermore, they had some large reservations as to their qualifications for the proposed role of leadership in a radically new era of the Mission's history.

Belief in and commitment to the AIMM, however, were deep. In an article written for the spring 1972 issue of the Zaire Missionary Messenger (for many years known as the Congo Missionary Messenger and later renamed the AIMM Messenger) Bertsche reflected on the impending 60th anniversary celebration and wrote, in part: "It is clear that during the first decade of its existence, the courageous faith of a few men from central

Illinois/Indiana was all that stood between CIM and a premature death. If there ever was an example of piteously inadequate loaves and fishes being entrusted into the hands of the Master, surely this was it. . . . In the first decade of struggle it would have been so very easy for those first board members to reckon the mountain too steep and to dissolve the fledgling organization. But theirs was an abiding conviction that they had a divine task. The Mennonite Church of Zaire is today an eloquent vindication of their vision."

It was then asked how succeeding generations of missionaries had "succeeded in planting a church? Certainly not because they were all well trained in the dynamics of cross-cultural relations. Neither was it because they were all saintly folk. On the contrary, missionaries are very earthy vessels with all manner of flaws and blemishes. But they do not go to proclaim themselves. They go to bring a Word - - a Word that became flesh, a Word that speaks directly to human needs and problems and fears and aspirations as ancient as man himself. And there has been response, not to the missionary as such, but to the Word that he brought. People of Africa have been drawn to the risen Lord, have been touched and have become and are still becoming new creatures in Christ."

Touching on the turmoil of Zaire he continued: "Occasionally Zaire missionaries have been heard to wish out loud for less troubled circumstances in which to work. But . . . even a moment's reflection will remind us that Christ himself lived in troubled times and that the Apostolic Church was launched in the midst of intense nationalism, colliding religious systems and political insurrection in the making. Perhaps we all need to relearn the lesson that although troubled times spell insecurity, they also spell opportunity for the committed."

Turning to the inter-Mennonite nature of the Mission, he observed that AIMM pre-dated MCC by a decade and had from the beginning served as a coordinating and channeling agency for Mennonite missionaries. Having felt the call to serve in Zaire, "they plunged into the same work, sharing the same dreams, carrying the same burdens and preaching the same Word of life. American geographical and conference origins quickly became highly irrelevant. Most significant of all, these missionaries from varied American communities set to work to bring into being not replicas of their own particular home groups but, rather and simply, the Mennonite Church of Zaire, a Church which is neither defensive nor apologetic about its name." (10)

The AIMM Board took official action in the fall of 1973 to invite Bertsche for a three-year assignment at the AIMM headquarters. The move was made in the fall of 1974 and after a one month overlap with Reuben Short, Jim assumed responsibilities as the new executive secretary on September 1, 1974. (11)

probing new frontiers

A special AIMM brochure was prepared for distribution at the time of its 60th anniversary celebration. Entitled "Mileposts Across Sixty Years", it traced some of the high points of its work in Africa. On a back flap a concluding paragraph read: "And what of the future? The . . . Board is seeking to relate positively to the Zaire Mennonite Church. Our continuing purpose remains one of proclamation of the Gospel coupled with Christian service. Adjustments in method are currently under study and require negotiation with the overseas Church. Plans are in progress for outreach to other parts of Africa."

The "plans in progress" referred to in the brochure had their origins in a succession of events which dated back to 1967. Although the Brethren in Christ had already established a missionary presence in the Rhodesias (presently known as Zambia and Zimbabwe) before the turn of the century, neither they nor any Mennonite mission agency had undertaken any activity in southern Africa beyond these two countries.

In 1967 Robert Kreider, under the auspices of the Mennonite Central Committee, made an investigative trip to Botswana in the interest of the Teachers Abroad Program (TAP) which had been created earlier in that decade in conjunction with the Council of Mennonite and Affiliated Colleges. Vern Preheim, MCC Africa Secretary of that era, made a follow-up trip in 1968 and by September of that same year, the first TAP teachers were in place in that country (cf ch 47).

It was in May of that same year that in the course of a meeting of the Council of Mennonite Board Secretaries (COMBS) it was decided to sponsor "a study of needs and opportunities in South Africa." Further directives stipulated "that we counsel with MCC regarding their entry into Botswana and over-all objectives; that the study team formulate a clear rationale in terms of strategy if any program proposals result and that the total report be brought back to COMBS for review and evaluation." (12)

It was not until early 1970 that this COMBS initiative was finally implemented. By this time there had been other meetings and the original proposal had been changed to read: "That COMBS sponsor a study assignment for southern Africa in consultation with MCC and the Africa Mennonite and Brethren in Christ Fellowship (13) with the following goals: a) a review of pertinent information regarding population, social, educational and economic developments and other statistical data that would enhance the total understanding of this area; b) a survey and analysis of present mission and church development; c) a projection of potential strategy and program opportunities for consideration of Mennonite agencies." (14)

It was further decided to approach the Schowalter Foundation for a grant to cover the travel and living costs of a team of three people to be made up of two missionaries and an African representative of the Brethren in Christ Churches in Rhodesia/Zambia.

It was, finally, in April 1970 that the long-discussed investigative trip was made. Appointed to the project were Don Jacobs who, at the time, was based in Nairobi, Kenya, under the sponsorship of the Eastern Mennonite Board of Missions and Charities (now known as Eastern Mennonite Missions) with offices in Salunga, PA, and Jim Bertsche who represented the Congo Inland Mission and the Congo Mennonite Church based, at the time, in Zaire at Tshikapa. The hope to have Bishop Philip Khumalo join the team as a representative of the Brethren in Christ Church of Rhodesia/Zambia was thwarted by scheduling and visa difficulties.

Their itinerary took the two men to the Republic of South Africa, the Transkei, Swaziland, Lesotho and Botswana. Concluding their travel in Bulawayo they spent some time in consultation with Bishop Khumalo and in formulating their findings which were circulated to the sponsoring organizations the following month.

A brief paragraph in a foreword perhaps best summarizes the tone of the reporting. Having sketched something of the gross injustice experienced by Africans under the white minority government of the Republic of South Africa and the resultant volatile racial friction, it was said: "We finish this investigation, analysis and report with the clear conviction that we must begin to participate in life south of the Zambezi. (15) May God give courage and wisdom, men and money, infinite patience and compassion as we roll up our sleeves and take up the challenge for Christ Jesus and His Kingdom." (16)

Response was swift. Before year's end a second trip was made by Vern Preheim, Harold Stauffer, Paul Kraybill and Jacobs representing respectively MCC, the Eastern Board, COMBS and the Africa Mennonite and Brethren in Christ Fellowship. (AMBCF) The first of a series of general recommendations read: "That the Southern Africa planning continue in line with the general principles as outlined in the Bertsche/Jacobs May report." (17)

In a special year-end meeting of the CIM Board on December 16, 1970, Paul Kraybill shared his personal impressions and made some tentative suggestions. The CIM record of the meeting reads in part: "Paul Kraybill visualizes three or four agencies coordinating their work though not having a joint board. MCC-TAP might work in Botswana along with the Brethren in Christ. He suggests CIM might work in Lesotho in relief, agriculture and sending of teachers. Eastern Board might work in Swaziland. Possibly all would work to strengthen Independent Churches." (18)

In April 1971, Don Jacobs and Harold F. Miller traveled to South Africa and focused their attention on Swaziland, the Transkei and Namaqualand, the latter two being "black homelands" created by the government of the Republic of South Africa. Out of this trip came specific proposals for Eastern Board involvement in Swaziland with a focus on agricultural development.

With all of the travel, reporting and recommendations regarding southern Africa as a background, the AIMM Board began to make immediate preparations for fielding its first missionary personnel in the little country of Lesotho (cf. ch. 49).

A radically new and different chapter of AIMM history was being opened, a chapter which, as it unfolded, would involve AIMM in a ministry in southern Africa which in the spring of 1972 was unforeseen.

Pastor Kabangy and the fusion plan arrived on the mission/church scene the same year. Although he had not yet been in a role of church leadership at the time it was worked through and signed, he wholeheartedly shared in the vision and spirit which surrounded the forging of this agreement in January 1971. He was well aware of the political and ecumenical pressures which had surrounded the fusion decision. He also knew the views of some of the younger church members who joyfully asserted that now, at last, they had achieved their freedom from the mission and were finally in a position to take possession of their inheritance. Indeed Kabangy too made it clear, as he assumed his role as the new general secretary of the CMZa, that he would not remain silent in the event any missionary made an effort to undercut the fusion agreement. He would not look kindly on anyone who might still cling to paternalistic attitudes.

But at a deep personal level Kabangy viewed the fusion agreement as a happy and logical culmination of sixty years of Mennonite missionary labor among them. When he said that he viewed the AIMM missionaries as brothers and sisters in Christ, he meant it. When he said they were welcomed as colaborers and fellow members of the CMZa, he meant it. When he said he wanted missionaries to take full and active part in the life and activity of the Church, he meant it. When he said he would look at qualifications and gifts and not color of skin in appointing people to commissions, committees and special assignments, he meant it. While he would insist on the training and orientation of Zairians to gradually replace missionaries in key positions and responsibilities, he did not foresee a time when at least a small missionary presence would no longer be needed or welcome. In conversations with missionaries he frequently would state why the CMZa wanted an ongoing missionary presence. His reasons were basically four: 1) to serve as trainers and the providers of technical skills which the Zairians could not yet provide for themselves; 2) to partner with them in their ongoing ministries of witness and service; 3) to counsel and encourage the leaders of a newly-autonomous Church and 4) to model the truth that the body of Christ is universal in scope and made up of all tribes, tongues and nations.

In a circulated statement he on one occasion discussed the meaning of the term "autonomy" as it related to missionaries among them. He acknowledged that in their context of Zaire this term sometimes became a pretext for breaking relations with former friends. He then went on to say: "The CMZa searches ways of developing even closer fraternal cooperation [with its missionaries] in order to utilize the spiritual gifts which the Lord Jesus has given his Church which, led by the Holy Spirit, recognizes neither color nor race." (1) It was in this spirit that Kabangy and the CMZa approached and sought to integrate the missionary into the life of the church during his years of leadership.

For the AIMM missionary family in Zaire in the early 70's, the fusion agreement did indeed represent a radical change. Agreeing to a plan sketched on paper was one thing. Seeking to fit into it on a daily basis in the Zaire bush was another. A member of the 1971 AIMM delegation demonstrated keen insight in this regard. Reporting to the Board he wrote: "Missionaries will need to shift their psychological gears under the fusion structure. . . . There remains apprehension especially with regard to vehicles, finances and housing. Because of changing roles and relationships, a few missionaries may be unable to work happily or effectively under fusion. . . . There is also the distinct possibility that the EMC of Congo will not invite certain missionaries to return after their first term of service. . . . The expression 'a little frog in a big pond' aptly describes something of the new role and relationship of our missionaries in the Congo. It calls missionaries of the present and future to Christian maturity and the 'optimism of grace' which views church/mission fusion not as a threat but as a promise. President Kaunda (pr. kah-OOH-ndah) (2) makes a pertinent observation which missionaries in Africa may well take to heart. 'Modern Africa is no place for the uncommitted. Life here demands cool nerves, perpetual optimism and a great faith in human possibilities.'" (3)

In a letter to the home board one missionary wrote: "We are getting into the nitty-gritty of fusion and this is easily detectable among the missionaries. While an overwhelming majority of our people approved the Charlesville agreement signed with the Church, the working out of it has inevitably created some friction points. One sees that it is possible to accept fusion at a rather superficial intellectual level only to find it much more difficult to accept at much deeper emotional and psychological levels. Some are moving well with the transition; some are struggling with it and will make it; a few are struggling and probably won't make it." (4)

It was against the background of a certain level of stress within the missionary team that the AIMM Board held its spring 1973 sessions at the EMC/US Church Camp on Bankson Lake near Lawton, MI, and invited all missionaries at home at the time to join them for discussion, meditation and prayer. Out of this encounter came a statement which read in part:

> We, the assembled missionaries and board members of AIMM have confidence that the Lord of the church will guard his people in Zaire and in North America in the various trials and changes that may come.

> We affirm a) our trust in our brothers and sisters in Zaire to carry on faithfully the work God has entrusted to them; b) our respect for the autonomy of the Mennonite Community of Zaire and c) our relationship with the Church as Christian brethren and sisters.

> We willingly continue to send and support missionaries to serve in Zaire with the Mennonite Community in all of its ministries upon invitation by CMZa as long as missionaries can remain faithful to the stated purpose of AIMM.

> We recognize that there may be times and places when a missionary's presence may be more important than the specific job he does. In such a situation he may not be able to find fulfillment in his work because his talents are not being fully used. We encourage him to be there as a Christian servant realizing that in being there as a brother or sister he or she may be making his or her greatest contribution. This does not mean, however, that the church, missionary and board shall not make every effort to find a meaningful and fulfilling assignment for every missionary under the guidance of the Holy Spirit.

> We of the Board support missionaries who continue to serve there. . . . We will also be supportive of those missionaries who for sake of conscience may be unable to continue there. (5)

CMZa ordains a missionary pastor

But for CMZa leadership, it was full steam ahead. A sprawling, growing Church which had personnel, program, membership and institutions separated in some cases by hundreds of miles of tropical bush, there was both a sense of exhilaration and excitement. Indeed they found a striking way of highlighting their identity and prerogatives as an autonomous church during the visit of the delegation in January 1971.

Don and Naomi Reimer Unruh were at the time serving their first term with AIMM at Mukedi Station. Envisioning before his arrival that his primary ministry would be in the Mukedi secondary school as a teacher, he had not sought ordination before leaving North America. (6) When the local Church began to involve Unruh more and more in pastoral ministries, they had a ready answer as to his clerical credentials. They would recommend him as one of their pastoral candidates to be ordained at the time of the AIMM delegation visit to their station.

A member of that group later wrote of this occasion: "On January 26, 1971 at Mukedi two hogs and six ducks were butchered before dawn. The day closed with a traditional tribal dance. Between these two events the first ordination of a Mennonite missionary by the EMC of Congo took place. A festive spirit filled the air. Beautiful African flowers and palm branches decorated the entrances to the church. Tribal chiefs came in their colorful paraphernalia. School students came in bright uniforms. Congolese women came in multi-colored head dress all of which added an authentic African touch to the impressive service. . . . Jim Bertsche, (7) the only missionary to participate directly in the service, preached . . . . Pastor Kidinda David (8) led the service with dignity and was in charge of the ordination prayer. Donovan Unruh knelt for the laying on of hands. . .

. It was black hands that were predominant. . . . Everyone realized that the first missionary had just been officially ordained by the Congolese Mennonite Church. The event was proof that church-mission fusion was not just words on a document but held within them the ring of reality. . . . It was a day to remember." (9)

Muambi Lutonga responds one more time

Already in the late 60's the African Church's executive committee had struggled with the problem of a church headquarters. A younger, competent and energetic leadership team had by the early 70's appeared on the scene and was pushing hard for a solution. (10) Housed in cramped, inadequate quarters at Kalonda Station, efforts to secure agreement on a building site had been stymied by the same regional rivalries which had earlier brought two successive annual conferences to disorderly conclusions.

Legal Representative Kakesa, however, had continued to work behind the scenes and had quietly secured permission of the local government to salvage burnt bricks from a variety of crumbling buildings in former workers camps which had been built in earlier years by the *Forminière* Diamond Company. Kakesa also secured permission to haul gravel from an abandoned mining site along the Kasai River nearby. When, after repeated appeals, the local government finally granted the CMZa a choice piece of neutral ground directly across the road from the government airstrip and its near by post office and telegraph service, Kakesa and the CMZa were poised to act.

Land was finally in hand. Building material was available for the hauling. AIMM had promised a grant for the headquarters project as a token of good will and affirmation toward the newly autonomous Church. But a builder with experience in Africa was needed. Who else could better fit the bill than Muambi Lutonga? Even though the Grabers had retired a second time in the States, might they not hear their appeal for help yet one more time?

The answer was "Yes!" On February 12, 1972, six days after his 71st birthday, Archie and Irma Graber again boarded a plane bound for Africa. Taking up residence in a Zairian pastor's small brick cottage adjacent to the building site, the Grabers were noisily and joyously welcomed back by church leaders and work crews alike. Fourteen months later, having erected three residences for the church officers and a building which provided a mix of office and meeting space, the Grabers left Zaire for what they thought for sure was their last time. (11)

a missionary in the church treasury?

The CMZa post of general treasurer was a major concern for both Mission and Church as the fusion plan was put into effect. Bukungu François, a school director from Banga Station, had come to the attention of CIM field treasurer Art Janz during the early 60's for his punctual and accurate reporting on Banga District church funds. His outstanding record as a district treasurer was a major factor in his election as CMZa's general treasurer in 1964. As an understudy to Janz, he over a period of a couple of years acquired a solid grip on principles of accounting in a mission office through which mission and government monies passed in the hundreds of thousands of dollars each year. With the forging of the fusion agreement, the general treasury passed to Zairian hands. Enormous responsibility descended upon the shoulders of Treasurer Bukungu.

But not only did he bring a thorough grounding in accounting to his new position, he also brought an unwavering commitment to his Lord and his Church. Now that CMZa stood on its own, would any further missionary presence in that office be appropriate or desired? The CMZa's quick response was "Yes." Since in June 1969 the Janz family had been obliged to return to North America because of health concerns for a daughter, a new CIM recruit had been found to take over the mission field accounts. Herman and Ruth Lehman Buller came from a business background. Having served as business manager of two different hospitals before applying to CIM for service, Herman brought obvious competence to this position with the Mission. A quiet, soft-spoken man with unusual sensitivity for those around him and unfailing attention to detail, he early won the confidence of church leaders. With the inauguration of the fusion plan, Herman Buller was voted the associate general treasurer of the Church with the understanding that he would be available to Bukungu on a day to day basis.

The potential for misunderstanding and trouble in their joint assignments in the treasurer's office was immediate and real. All of the possibilities for missionary/African, black/white frictions were in the very nature of things present. Particularly was this the case due to a mission stipulation that there be an annual audit of the use of AIMM funds contributed to the Church, a concept which was basically foreign to rural tribal culture.

It is to the everlasting credit of these two men that an enduring relationship of mutual trust and respect was forged that carried across the years of Bukungu's service in that capacity. CMZa would have its share of personnel problems as an autonomous Church but none were to arise from the handling of church funds during the era of these two men. (12)

don't do our work for us

In his commitment to move his church forward in all areas of ministry, General Secretary Kabangy pressed into service all qualified Zairians available to him. But when the need arose, he did not hesitate to appoint missionaries to roles of leadership within the Church. Reflecting his lifelong concern for evangelism, Levi Keidel was named National Coordinator of Evangelism at CMZa's General Assembly of 1973. In personal conversation with Keidel, Kabangy made it clear that he did not want missionaries to do anything that Zairian pastors should be doing themselves. The missionary pastor's role, as he saw it, was to work with the pastors in enabling, training and counseling roles. Thus the Keidels began a program of itinerating seminars using rural church centers as bases. They spent long weekends with rural leaders from the surrounding areas in times of intensive Bible study, discussion of pastoral problems, health concerns and prayer. In the process regional evangelism coordinators were chosen and oriented to their responsibilities.

On the heels of this appointment came Kabangy's naming of a four-missionary study commission to review and evaluate the Church's performance not only in evangelism but also in Christian education and the production and distribution of Christian literature. Thus it was that Leona Schrag, Tina Quiring, Earl Roth and Levi Keidel met at Djoko Punda November 30 - December 1, 1973, for an intensive two-day consultation. Out of these sessions came a cluster of recommendations which, upon submission to CMZa leadership, were soon implemented. Of particular note were the proposals to create a CMZa manuscript committee to be composed of representatives from the three major languages of the CMZa area, i.e., Chokwe, Tshiluba and Giphende; to merge the Christian education endeavors into the evangelism department; and to review and upgrade uniform Christian education materials for use in all of the CMZa church schools and to inaugurate plans and materials for vacation Bible Schools.

It is of interest to note that when the newly-constituted manuscript committee first met some months later, early in the proceedings a minute was passed to request that a booklet entitled "Who are the Mennonites?" written by Levi Keidel some years earlier, be restocked in all of the CMZa book shops. (13) During the frenzied public support for Mobutu in the early 70's, because of its emphasis upon non-violence and separation of church and state, CMZa leaders had feared political repercussions in the event copies come into the hands of political leaders. But by October 1975, the mood of the church leaders had shifted and there was a clear call for the redistribution and sale of the booklet. Mobutu and his political movement notwithstanding, this booklet was also, in time, followed by translations of several of J.C. Wenger's well known series on Mennonite history and distinctive beliefs.

oh ye of little faith!

And there was more. CMZa leaders had talked for years about their desire to create a post-primary school for the teen-age girls of their Church. Secretary Kabangy determined to generate some movement on this long-debated and long-stalled project. An intermediary step had been to add a two-year post-primary *coupe et couture* section (a French phrase used to designate training in the art of design and sewing of garments). But for CMZa leaders this was only a stopgap measure. They wanted a full blown girls' high school which would open the door for apt students to pursue their education at a university level. This caused most missionaries to blink. Where would the funds and equipment come from not to mention qualified staff? These were all hurdles to be sure, the Zairians admitted, but they could be cleared with determination and faith. A special commission was named by the CMZa Executive Committee in February, 1972. Just a bit over four weeks later it was convened at Nyanga made up of Legal Representative Kakesa Samuel, Kangu Sualala, the director of the Nyanga Secondary School, and career missionary teacher Lodema Short.(14)

Clearly carried along by their vision and their deeply-shared conviction that the CMZa had to make a major investment of effort and resources in the future of their teen-age girls, a clear-cut and far-reaching set of proposals were forged in the name of their Church for study and action by the CMZa Executive Committee.

The envisioned purpose of the school was first addressed - - "To provide a livelihood for young women who desire to integrate themselves into the economic structure of their country or to establish themselves in their own enterprises . . .; to prepare young women to fulfill the role of home maker/wife whether in a rural or urban area while pursuing their general education."

Then there followed a series of eighteen specific proposals among which were: That it be a four-year post-primary school; that selection of the first students be made via entrance exams; that the first year class be limited to 20 students; that the secondary school director immediately prepare a list of supplies that would be needed; that the AIMM accept to fund the building of a duplex to house teaching staff and that entrance fees be set for parents of all girls who are to be enrolled. A blueprint was annexed to the minutes. The date proposed for opening the school was September 1973 - - within six months! The first slate of instructors proposed was Laverna Dick, director; Frieda Guengerich, associate director and Jenny Bertsche, instructor.

On the back of a set of minutes sent to Martini Janz, the coordinator of the AIMM Women's Auxiliary of the time, there was an optimistic and matter of fact note: "Mrs. Janz, I am sending you a copy of propositions for a girls' school. We are waiting the approval of the [church] executive committee. Muabanda. Kakesa" (Muabanda, pr. mwah-BAH-ndah; a traditional Baphende salutation literally meaning "Did you sleep well?"). (15)

Out of the bold initiative of this three-member commission there ultimately emerged a four-year girls' high school which was eventually named *Lycée Miodi* (the French term *lycée* denoting a high school; Miodi the name of a small lake just down the hill to the east of the school grounds). In time a long series of MCC and AIMM personnel made their contribution to the development of this school. A mix of AIMM Womens' Auxiliary grants and government funds made possible a gradual building program. Before long well-qualified Zairian personnel became available who more and more assured the ongoing life of the school. Among the Zairian staff none would become better known or win broader confidence and respect than Professor and eventual Director, Ibwa Pang (pr. EE-bwah PAHNG). Originally recruited by Lodema Short to teach courses in graphic arts and design, he soon demonstrated both teaching skill and solid Christian integrity. Such was the esteem he won from local parents and church administrators that when it was no longer possible to provide a missionary director for the school, he became the unanimous choice to be the school's first Zairian director. It was a striking tribute both to him personally and the CMZa Banga District from which he and his family came.

new life on the farm

There was still more. Launched in 1965 by CIM, MCC and the Congo Church, COMAS (The Congo Mennonite Agricultural Service) was a clear reflection of the shared conviction that Christian mission amidst poverty and malnutrition needed in some way to address the needs of both soul and body. Under the gifted direction of Fremont and Sara Janzen Regier, an experimental farm on the south edge of Nyanga Station soon became a beehive of activity. Undergirding the laying out of experimental agricultural plots, the breeding of rabbits and the development of poultry flocks were five stated goals: 1) to improve nutrition, 2) to facilitate economic development, 3) to demonstrate stewardship of natural resources, 4) to instill love and appreciation for the soil and 5) to witness to "saving faith in Christ by living, working and serving through an effective Christian life among the Congolese always bearing in mind and trying to witness to the fact that Christ and not better economic life is the answer to man's deepest needs." The entire effort was to be a service arm of the African Church. (16)

In 1968, Ngulubi Mazemba (pr. ngoo-LOO-bi mah-ZEH-mbah), a son of widely known and respected Nyanga Pastor Mazemba Pierre, joined the SEDA team with training in veterinary medicine, agriculture and youth work. (With the name change of the country, the former term COMAS was changed to Agricultural Development Service or SEDA in its French acronym form.) He was named associate director in 1973 and director in 1975. While well qualified for his position in terms of technical skills, of equal importance was the deep grounding in faith he'd acquired as a youth in the home of his pastor father. He wholeheartedly affirmed a basic guiding principle which SEDA staff had adopted: "A development program which does not point men to Christ is not complete. Christ, and not a better economic life, is the answer to man's deepest needs, i.e., Christ as seen in his life, death and resurrection." (17)

Secretary Kabangy's call for renewed efforts of evangelism and spiritual nurture fell on sympathetic ears at SEDA. It was after several rounds of discussion that a new effort of outreach and ministry was launched. It was called "New Life for All." Director Mazemba explained it as follows: "Actually, this program is an effort to put together all the resources at the Church's disposal in a team effort to bring new life to rural families. SEDA provides an agricultural-extension agent and the pickup truck for transportation. The Nyanga Church provides an evangelist. The hospital sends a public health nurse and the women's group adds a lady to the team. The CMZa bookstore sends a book seller with a trunk of books and a youth singing group completes the team. . . . During the course of the weekend, team members visit sick people, folks in mourning, new converts, baptismal candidates and livestock projects and farms. The climax of the weekend is the Sunday morning evangelistic rally where sometimes up to a thousand people attend. The most exciting thing about the program [is that] . . . the local church can feel that it is their project. . . . One of the most important results we see is the fact that people in remote villages realize that the Church cares." (18)

Along with the heightened SEDA activity around Nyanga, great effort was made to extend its ministry to other CMZa districts which were clamoring for similar services. Seminars were organized at the farm for representatives from other areas for orientation and training after which they returned to their home regions. In some instances they were accompanied by MCC VS workers who played a major role in the SEDA program from its earliest days.

By the mid-1970's, the SEDA venture had come to the attention of mission/church groups beyond the Mennonite area. Visits were not uncommon as delegations came to observe, ask questions and take notes. In many ways, the Mennonite effort to forge a genuinely holistic ministry of witness and service in the Zairian bush country reached a high water mark in the 70's.

During this same period there were many other AIMM missionaries who, with lower profile, were also serving in places and manners designated by the Zaire church. The AIMM missionary roster for Zaire in the summer of 1975 numbered 58 adults on the field or at home on furlough. Among them were seven doctors, nine nurses, five pastor evangelists, 15 teachers and a variety of technicians and support personnel. They were distributed across six rural stations, three urban centers and two inter-mission training hospitals. All served under the sponsoring umbrella of the Mennonite Church of Zaire. (19)

It is not without significance that at this point the CMZa Executive Committee recommended "that in the future new missionaries receive orientation given by the administrative staff of the CMZa before beginning their work." (20)

CHAPTER 29   A SHEPHERD AT WORK

It was in January 1973 that the CMZa Administrative Committee passed the following recommendation: "To stimulate the spiritual life of the Mennonite Community, the Administrative Committee asks the General Secretary in the capacity of the spiritual leader of the Church to visit in the region of CMZa to counsel and encourage the leaders." (1)

This was no small assignment. "The region of the CMZa" referred to in the minute was very extended and included a broad mix of ethnic groups. Scattered over a geographical expanse roughly equivalent in size to the State of Illinois were over a dozen tribal groups (2) with which Mennonite missionaries and Zairian evangelists had had contact across the years and among most of whom, in varying degrees, converts had been won. Widely divergent in cultural patterns and dialects and fiercely loyal to their own groups, they represented a very mixed "flock" indeed for Mennonite "shepherds."

Reflecting on this reality, a missionary of that era wrote: "If for non-Zairians, clan-based tensions within the Zaire Church are clearly discernible, it may come as something of a surprise to learn that the North American Mennonite communities, when viewed through African eyes, appear also as so many 'clan groups'! For are not these various groups also often traceable to different 'ancestors' in different lands? Did they not also come to North America via different migration routes amidst many privations and hardships? . . . To be sure, the traditions and interpretations held to by each of our American fellowships are extremely significant to and for each one. But make no mistake, it is no less the case in Zaire. There is, however, one significant difference between North America and Zaire. Whereas pressure of tradition and culture and nationality were allowed to determine the shape of the multiple Mennonite fraternities in the first case, the struggle is on, in the second, to melt and mold widely divergent elements into a single new fellowship, a single new clan. Just as there is continual need for the gentle moving of the breath of God's Spirit across our North American brotherhoods, so it is also greatly needed among our Zairian brethren . . . particularly at this juncture in the history of the Zaire Church as it seeks to find its way as a living part of the body of Christ and as a newly autonomous member of the world's Mennonite community." (3)

No one understood this better or carried any more concern about it than CMZa Secretary Kabangy.

CMZa circuit riders

Calling on church treasurer Bukungu François and evangelism coordinator Levi Keidel, a team was formed. Travel schedules were planned which would involve 1,000 miles of travel and visits to each of the CMZa's sixteen district church centers. Announcements and copies of schedules were sent in all directions. The declared purposes of the trip were four: 1) to strengthen ties between local church leaders and their CMZa officials; 2) to cultivate a deeper sense of responsibility on the part of the district leaders with regard to pastoral leadership and the handling of church funds; 3) to hear grievances and 4) to try to resolve problems found which were troubling the local church. (4)

In conversation with a missionary co-worker, Kabangy cast the purpose of his travel in more colorful terms. Their team travel was to offer "laundry and mending services" to the district church leaders. In each place they'd be invited to lay their "church linens" out on the table for scrutiny. If there were torn places, they would seek to mend them. If there were spots or smudges, they would seek to scrub them clean.

Of both tears and smudges there was no lack in the district church "linens" they came to examine. Most of the problems encountered fell into one of four categories: 1) real or rumored financial irregularities; 2) conflicts between leaders; 3) refusal of medical and educational personnel to submit to the authority of the local church councils and 4) sexual misconduct. Then there were the endless complaints and requests: "We've been begging all these years and you haven't yet sent us a missionary. Thousands of people living here have no place to get medical help. Can't you give us a dispensary? You give us work to do, but no tools. We want a transmitter so we can communicate with other district church centers. Evangelists are quitting because they never get paid. Pastors are discouraged because of low salaries." (5)

Reflecting on the itinerary and what he had observed, Keidel wrote: "Pastor Kabangy and Elder Bukungu have squarely shouldered responsibilities we missionaries were carrying fifteen years ago. They defused volatile confrontations and parried loaded questions with consummate skill. When it became necessary to confront church leaders with personal failures, in almost every case they accepted it graciously and were willing to make amends. . . . Remarks of several District Chairmen reveal the depth of their spiritual life. I contemplated upon what they once were, and what they are today, and marveled. 'Every Saturday night at midnight my wife and I have prayer for our family and the work of the coming Lord's Day.' 'My wife is my strength. She's brought into our home what she learned in the home of her parents.' (They were among the earliest CIM evangelists.) 'Where do I get peace from? The One I kneel before.'" (6) (7)

Such was the response and success of the 1973 itinerary that another was undertaken in dry season of the following year. To the original trio were added the CMZa's women's president and the evangelism coordinator of each region visited. New questionnaires were prepared and materials assembled to be left with each district chairman. A routine was established which was followed at each place. The women met separately while the rest of the delegation met first with the district chairman alone, then with all pastors and, finally, with the total district church council.

Commenting on this second itinerary, Keidel observed that the previous year they had been "dropped into a unique slough of long undisturbed and gradually thickening problems. Last year's experience enabled us to plan for a high level of success this year." (8) That their visit and counseling ministry the previous year had born fruit was early discovered. One district chairman said: "'We're happy to see you this time; we're still together in a single path like when you left us.'" In another center: "'You heard of our badness before you arrived last year; while you were here, you didn't eat well because of it. But your scolding us did a great work. After you left, not a tongue wagged. We're still following the standard you left us. . . . What new instructions do you have for us this year?'"

But not all news was uniformly good, of course. Here and there problems worked with a year earlier still remained stubbornly rooted and triggered another round of counseling and attempted discipline. In some cases there was resistance to the systematic reporting which was now being required from the leadership of each district. "'All that extra work they make us do, what do we get for it? Why do you need a report of what I do? How can we get around our areas if you do not provide us transportation?'" (9)

Though the missionary member of the team had to drop out of the second itinerary because of other responsibilities, President Kabangy pressed ahead with his fellow Zairians and once again brought a complete circuit of the far-flung CMZa districts to completion. Commenting on this second trip Keidel wrote: "These trips are expensive . . . but have contributed tremendously to strengthening the witness of the Mennonite Church Community in Zaire. They have extricated districts from a bog of problems and returned them to the business of evangelism and Christian nurture. They have introduced them to a greatly increased sense of self-discipline, order and leadership responsibility." (10)

Unmentioned, but no less important, was the fact that two years in a row, CMZa district pastors in isolated corners were sought out by CMZa leaders and given face to face opportunities . . . irrespective of their tribal affiliation . . . to express their needs, problems and complaints while being assured that they were a part of and important in the broad framework of CMZa.

Though Pastor Kabangy continued to visit CMZa districts, due to restraints of cost and time, such complete circuits unfortunately had to be dropped. But for the remainder of his years as the leader of his Church, the time and effort invested in those trips stood him in good stead. In the most distant corners of CMZa land, he was known and his pastoral heart had become apparent. There was the sense that there was someone in distant Tshikapa who knew them and cared about them.

pastoral letters

Knowing full well the isolation, temptations and problems confronting his fellow pastors in CMZa, amidst his travels and duties Kabangy occasionally circulated a pastoral letter. One such was apparently used as a handout during one of his trips through the sixteen CMZa districts. Under the heading "pastoral objectives" he listed four: 1) to create a community rather than an organization; 2) to build a church rather than institutions; 3) to form a holy people and not just individual saints; 4) to form a mature and committed people and not just a people instructed in religion. By way of commentary he stated: "The church is a living and dynamic organism and can never be simply an organization. The best organization is never, in and of itself, a church nor can it be the source of a church. . . . Institutions, if they are not an expression of faith, of love and of unity of a Christian community, are . . . empty of sense."

Concluding the letter by a discussion of attitudes and comportment appropriate to pastoral ministry, he underscored the need for pastors to consider themselves as "brothers among brothers" who do not "pursue their personal interests." The letter then ended with an observation: "The beginning of all new life in the church is always a return to the Word of God. The Holy Spirit said to the famous church of Ephesus: 'Remember the height from which you have fallen! Repent and do the things you did at first. . . .'" (11)

Another letter which reveals much about his stance as a leader was circulated in April 1975, in response to the Zaire government's takeover of all mission/church primary schools. There was within the church consternation, on the one hand, and a certain spirit of defeatism and laxity on the other. Seeking to counter these trends he wrote, in part: "Dear Zaire Pastors, leaders, missionaries and faithful friends of our Mennonite Church Community: We greet you all in the name of Jesus Christ our Savior. . . . All of us recognize that this is a very crucial period as regards the Church. We know the change which has been put into effect regarding the educational program. Since January 1975 the Zaire government has taken charge of it. This comes as no surprise as they have been talking about doing such for a long time. One may ask the question, 'Because the church once occupied itself with so much of the educational program, what will now replace it?' We affirm to you that evangelization remains our fundamental and most important task. The new situation will give you the opportunity to put yourself to this task. . . ."

"Others are asking, 'How does all this affect our work as a Church?' The answer is easy. Most of you Zairian pastors have in your hands the calendar of evangelistic activities outlined. Continue to purposely carry on these activities as in the past. Our Christian education team is in the process of drawing up a new program which will be sent to you soon. As regards the abolishment of religion courses in our public school programs, the Church will develop a program of Christian education which makes the local Church the hub of spiritual instruction. . . ."

"We are also aware that the morality of many Christians is faltering and discipline in our parishes leaves much to be desired. This is sad. However, dear brothers, THE CHURCH IS MUCH MORE THAN A PUBLIC EDUCATION PROGRAM. . . . We enthusiastically congratulate the Pastors and their helpers who give themselves day and night for the cause of the Church and in preaching the Good News of the Savior. With all of our hearts we thank God for you. May the Grace of our Lord Jesus Christ be given to you abundantly. Amen. Your brother in Christ, Kabangy Djeke Shapasa." (12)

confronting conflict

It is ironic that at a moment when Kabangy was rallying loyalty and support for CMZa among its multi-ethnic, grass-roots membership, he was encountering growing tension within his own executive committee. Kakesa Samuel, the legal representative and Tshilembu Nicodeme, the assistant legal representative and the CMZa's educational secretary, were increasingly at odds. Both were intelligent, gifted and deeply committed to their Church. As to personalities, Tshilembu tended to be literary, reflective and philosophical in make-up. Kakesa was an activist with boundless energy and a readiness to move in keeping with his convictions. Both had demonstrated over the course of years their readiness to make personal sacrifices in order to carry out their church responsibilities. Both had courageously defended their Church and its interests before indifferent villagers and hostile government agents. They both took pride in the obvious progress of their Church and the contributions they each were making to that progress. They both had their own ideas about the future. Clear cut, contrasting personalities, they did not always see eye to eye and, at times, their ideas clashed.

They also came from different regions and major ethnic groups within the Church, Kakesa from Bandundu Province in the west and a member of the Baphende tribe; Tshilembu came from the Kasai in the east and the Lulua were his people. Increasingly they had come to be viewed by their own respective "constituencies" as key representatives in circles of CMZa influence and power. Increasingly they were subjected to pressures from their own people to make sure that their interests were not only represented but defended and promoted. With increasing frequency sharp debate took place between the two in sessions of the church executive and administrative committees. It was also with increasing frequency that issues had to be tabled for lack of agreement.

Pastor Kabangy viewed the steadily growing friction between these two key leaders with mounting concern. Fellow members of the executive committee shared his concern and had, at times, sought to counsel the two men to exercise greater tolerance toward each other in the best interests of the Church. Such concern found its way into committee records in August of 1972: "That a way be found to work in good collaboration between the Legal Representative and the Assistant Legal Representative." (13)

In administrative committee minutes of January 1973 there was again reference to the problem as effort was made to spell out in some detail the division of responsibilities and authority between the two officers. (14)

Pressures upon and friction between the two men were of such a nature, however, that admonition and committee minutes did little to defuse the mounting confrontation. Kabangy knew this and agonized over it. In a conversation with a missionary colleague he once poured out his heart. "What am I to do? I go to bed at night only to toss and turn. These men are both my friends and colleagues in the work of the Church. They are gifted men and very valuable to CMZa. I respect them both. The departure of one or both would be a great loss for us. But if we continue as we are within the walls of our own church headquarters, our lack of brotherhood is known to all. How can we expect our church members to heed our admonition to respect and love each other when we as their leaders are unable to do so?"

As the CMZa prepared for its general assembly in the dry season of 1973, Kabangy knew that in some manner or other this festering problem would have to be dealt with. The question was how? Wanting to establish an appropriate opening tone for the assembly, he asked a missionary colleague to bring an opening address which would "speak to our situation". In the address the missionary likened the CMZa to a large dugout canoe in shallow water with two groups of people at opposite ends yanking and whipsawing the boat between them. With the sound of argument filling the air, the boat was being immobilized. Meanwhile a growing number of people stood on the bank, Christian and non-Christian alike, with hands over their mouths viewing the scene with a mix of bemusement and distaste. (15)

Early in the proceedings Kabangy, as the CMZa's president, took the floor. Before getting into the details of his report to the delegates he made some preliminary remarks, the first dealing with the fusion of Mission and Church recently effected. "This fusion for which we all can rejoice groups the missionaries and Zairians together in the Church of their Lord Jesus of which He is the head."

Referring then to the opening of their assembly he continued: "May God our Creator be praised that He has made this gathering possible. As we are all gathered here, we have opportunity first of all to humble ourselves before God and to forgive each other. We have opportunity to admit our weaknesses for, as Christians and light of the world, our quarrels and our divisions, . . . dear brothers, create a scandal for people and for many Christians who regard us as models . . . . May the Lord grant us all his forgiveness. May He help us to bear with one another so that we may love each other as He first so loved us. . . . As Christians before the world and before God, never has our responsibility been so great or so enormous. All of our acts are registered and our conduct observed. Without peace and agreement, we cannot proclaim the good news, the news of salvation. Let us be one in order that the world may believe." (16)

Though couched in general terms, all delegates realized full well the problem to which he was referring and the reason for his call for a spirit of humility and reconciliation. The question, however, still remained: How was the thorny and potentially explosive issue to be addressed during the few days they were in session at Banga?

Some early sessions of the administrative committee were held but when "the problem" was once again raised, it soon became evident that this group would have no more success then than it had had in the past in resolving the impasse. Meanwhile precious time was slipping by.

It was at this point that Pastor Kabangy took the situation in hand. Dipping into rural African culture, he called into being an ad hoc "commission of wise ones" and instructed them to meet until they were prepared to come to the full delegate body with proposals for dealing with the long standing dilemma. Selected was a fifteen-member group with careful representation from all across the CMZa area which included four missionaries. Then alongside he named four additional people as "counselors" who would have no vote but who were invited to participate in the discussion. Upon meeting, the first three hours were devoted to hearing each man tell, once for all, his side of the story. Then about midnight both were excused and another two hours of discussion followed.

Consensus soon emerged on three essential points: 1) both men were recognized for the valuable service they had given to the CMZa; 2) they had allowed themselves to become enmeshed in a controversy which had made them, willingly or unwillingly, the key figures in a growing polarization process within the Church; 3) given the situation there was no alternative but to recommend the termination of the services of both men with CMZa. Given the fact that Tshilembu had been offered a position as government inspector of schools, he was to be released immediately. Given the complexity and volume of legal work, it was proposed that Kakesa remain in office yet for one year thus allowing time for an orderly transition of personnel in that office. Ilunga Robert (17) was proposed as Tshilembu's successor. No one was suggested to replace Kakesa since there would still be time for this decision later. Presented next morning to the full delegate body, the commission proposals were adopted by a voice vote.

In the closing moment of the Banga Assembly, a moving scene unfolded. As recorded in the assembly minutes by the Zairian recording secretary, Kabeya Kidiongo, it reads: "The General Secretary speaking in the name of the whole Community expressed praise and appreciation for the work of Mr. Tshilembu in the Community. He expressed his regret at his departure but being unable to do anything else wished him successful work and much courage in the future. Concluding he said, 'May God bless you.'"

"Responding to the wishes expressed to him, Mr. Tshilembu, after thanking the General Secretary, confirmed that he would keep his faith and that he would remain the Christian he had always been. He promised that he would bring no legal complaint against the Church or engage in any sort of conflict with the Church. After a prayer, the General Secretary declared the Assembly closed. Upon leaving the church all the delegates formed a circle, hand in hand, and sang a hymn of farewell after which they took leave of each other in the blessing of God." (18)

Subsequent efforts to select and install Kakesa and Tshilembu's successors were yet to encounter some difficulties. But at the Banga Assembly, a general secretary with a pastoral heart had led his flock through very troubled terrain and there was gratitude. Among parting delegates one was heard to comment: "People now know that our Church does have a 'father' after all. We can now go back with light hearts." (19)

As for the missionaries on the scene, one commented: "In all of this, Pastor Kabangy is the emerging key figure in CMZa leadership. . . . His concerns are clear and he has a way of putting his finger on basic issues. Throughout there was the theme of insistence that the spiritual welfare of the Church is the issue of issues. In this we support him wholeheartedly and with much appreciation." (20)

two Banga Assembly footnotes

The action taken in the conflict between CMZa leaders had so dominated assembly sessions that delegates talked of little else as they made their way back to their home areas. Much other church business, however, had also been processed during those days. Embedded in the forty-two assembly actions listed in the official minutes were two which had major implications, one for the Church and one for the missionary personnel on the field and for AIMM at home.

It was traditional at annual assemblies for the commission on evangelism to submit a list of pastoral candidates with recommendation for ordination. At Banga the list submitted and approved by the delegates was comprised of nine names. In the dry season of 1973, there was little to distinguish one from the other. With passing time, however, two of the nine were to emerge as key figures in the ongoing history of CMZa and were to play major roles in a tragic drama that was to unfold. One was Mukanza Ilunga (pr. moo-KAH-nzah i-LOO-ngah) from the Kandala District; the other was Mbonza Kikunga (pr. MBOH-nzah gi-KOO-ngah) from the Nyanga District. (21)

Another assembly minute which was to have major implications read: "Given the financial crisis which the CMZa is experiencing, the General Secretary is authorized to solicit financial aid from sister churches outside our country." (22) While the intent of this blandly worded minute was apparently known to members of the CMZa administrative committee, it had escaped the missionary delegates present.

From the earliest days of the mission/church fusion agreement, the AIMM Board had been gently but firmly indicating to the CMZa leadership that with autonomy also came growing responsibility for the funding of its own activities. This responsibility, it was pointed out, included a greater share of the cost of maintaining its administrative center at Tshikapa and travel costs for its own officers and the assembling of members of committees, commissions and delegates for church-wide gatherings.

CMZa leaders did not dispute this. In conversations there was frequent agreement that, in principle, they needed to assume a growing share of their costs but, they added, they needed time. When, however, with each passing year CMZa budget requests for administrative costs were increasing rather than diminishing, the Board decided to put a cap on its contributions in this regard. With expanding program and inflationary pressures, this limit soon began to exert a financial pinch.

This all was taking place against the background of dramatic expansion of the ECZ under Secretary John Bokeleale's aggressive leadership. It was well known to the CMZa administrative committee members that much of his financial support came via the Geneva office of the World Council of Churches in Switzerland. It was also known that the WCC was actively courting applications for membership from the broad mix of Zaire churches. It was particularly the younger members of the CMZa administrative committee who saw the WCC as a possible source of new funding. Reminding one another that they were now an autonomous church free to make their own policy decisions, Kabangy was strongly urged to probe possible new ecumenical ties overseas. On the heels of the assembly action in July of 1973, official CMZa correspondence was addressed to WCC offices in Switzerland asking for information regarding application for membership.

CMZA, AIMM and the WCC

But there was a problem. In an ironic coincidence of events, it was this same year in North America that the AIMM Board had decided to apply for membership in the Evangelical Foreign Missions Association (EFMA) which, in turn, was an affiliate of the National Association of Evangelicals (NAE). This was not a precipitous action on the part of the Board. The issue of possible EFMA membership had surfaced in a couple of earlier meetings but had been tabled for further investigation and discussion. When resubmitted as a proposal in AIMM's semiannual board session in April 1973, it was approved with eleven votes and two abstentions. (23)

Response to the news of CMZa initiative to probe WCC relations was low key. In a letter from the AIMM executive secretary in December 1973 it was observed: "We were accepted as full members by unanimous vote at their [EFMA] meeting just about ten days ago. . . . While deeply concerned, I think the problem [i.e., CMZa's inquiries about WCC affiliation] can be resolved by careful and prayerful negotiation." (24)

In Zaire, however, reaction from the missionary contingent was more spirited. There were two issues at stake from their point of view, one theological and the other relational. With regard to the first, many missionaries carried genuine reservations regarding the World Council and its activist political agenda, on the one hand, and its bland theological stance on the other. There was the further reality, for many of them, of a supporting constituency at home which fully shared their reservations. To suddenly learn that the CMZa with which they whole heartedly served was exploring possible WCC membership was genuinely unsettling.

But there was a second concern which was equally troubling for them. They felt that the resolution passed at the delegate session at Banga had been worded in a manner to camouflage its intent thus avoiding any cautionary comments which might have otherwise been triggered on the part of missionary delegates. Having in good faith accepted and supported the fusion plan, they now felt that there had been a breach of good faith. This mix of feelings and reactions found expression in a joint letter addressed to CMZa leadership.

In opening paragraphs the series of steps by which the CMZa had arrived at its autonomy were reviewed. It was further observed that there had been missionary affirmation at each point which culminated in their signing a document of dissolution of AIMM in Zaire. The letter continued: "We did this because we understood that we were becoming full members of the CMZa with full right of voice and participation. In brief, in accepting the project of fusion, we committed ourselves to the life, the destiny and the future of our Church in Zaire believing that we are accepted within the Church as brothers and sisters in Christ. This we continue to hope for."

"Understand us clearly. In no way do we contest the right of the CMZa to face up to its own future and to take action as an autonomous Church. The CMZa is autonomous among its sister churches in Africa as well as among its sister churches overseas. It is free to affiliate itself whenever and wherever it decides while keeping in mind its traditions, its beliefs and its priorities. It is, however, not always wise to do everything one has the right to do."

The letter then proceeded to state three problems which concerned them: the first was the procedure used to adopt article 20 of the Banga Assembly. Expressing both surprise and sadness the letter went on to comment: "It seems clear to us that the article in question was worded in an ambiguous fashion to hide from your missionaries its true import. . . . If we are really full members, let it be permitted to us to at least express ourselves with regard to decisions which touch the future of all of us. Whether or not the views expressed by your missionary partners are taken into account is not important. What is important is to maintain an atmosphere of open dialogue and mutual respect. Since Banga, however, we your missionaries feel a certain uneasiness . . . . What, now, is our place within CMZa?"

A second concern expressed had to do with how CMZa's move toward WCC affiliation might be viewed and interpreted in North America at the moment that the AIMM Board itself had just opted for membership with the EFMA.

A third raised a question as to CMZa's ecumenical orientation in the future. It was granted that the WCC did not intervene in the doctrinal matters of member churches. But it was also clear that the CMZa seemed in process of making a decision between the WCC and the World Evangelical Alliance which had also established a presence in Africa. The letter wondered what the implications of this might be for the future.

287

Concluding the letter it was said: "We attack no one. We criticize no one. But we would be grateful to you for clarification with regard to these concerns. . . . In the meantime the CMZa is also our community. Its joys are ours; its problems are ours; its victories are ours and its failures are also ours. We pray continually that God our Father may be at work among us in order to achieve his will for CMZa and that all of us, Zairians and missionaries, may be his instruments to that end." The letter was signed in the name of all of the missionaries by the missionary counselor, Earl Roth. (25)

For Pastor Kabangy, the year 1973 was a heavy one. Mid-year he had struggled with a conflict which pitted two fellow church administrators against each other. Having finally found a way through that he now, at year's end, suddenly found himself facing an issue which saw his missionary colleagues challenging a course of action urged upon him by his Zairian church colleagues.

Given the heady political atmosphere and the rapidly growing structure of the ECZ in the early 70's, it would have been very understandable had Kabangy elected to adopt the sort of hard line that some of the younger church laymen were urging upon him. But once again his shepherd instincts came to the fore. Always known for the open door at his office, he invited missionaries to come and discuss with him the concerns expressed in their letter. After one such time of dialogue one missionary commented to the home secretary that "in spite of some of the tension that has developed over budget pressures and, more recently, the WCC issue, Pastor Kabangy is certainly conciliatory about things and has a couple of times gone out of his way to say that this was a hasty step and is to be reviewed." (26)

Kabangy did take the missionary letter to his administrative committee at his first opportunity. As a result, a five-member Zairian delegation was appointed to dialogue with the missionaries "in order to clear up the suspicions which are seeking to establish themselves between the CMZa and its missionaries." The same minute also instructed Secretary Kabangy to seek full information regarding the Evangelical Alliance and to bring a report to the next general assembly. (27)

In the end, CMZa did not join this ecumenical group. For some years WCC personnel in Geneva continued to send correspondence to the CMZa leaders seeking to formalize their membership, but the mailings remained unanswered. (28) With time CMZa turned increasingly to the Africa Mennonite and Brethren in Christ Fellowship (AMBCF) and the Mennonite World Conference for interaction and fellowship outside Zaire.

leadership from a hospital bed

July 1975 marked the first administrative trip of AIMM's new executive secretary to Africa. Accompanying Bertsche was Allan Wiebe, a board member and former AIMM missionary. Upon arrival in Kinshasa, they were informed that Secretary Kabangy was hospitalized in town following emergency surgery and was eager to see them. Making their way to the sprawling Mama Yemo Hospital complex, they found Kabangy immobilized with a large plaster cast on his left leg. After warm greetings, explanations quickly followed. He told of having had chronic pain high in his left thigh for months but that tests had been inconclusive. Surrounded by needs on all sides he persevered in his work schedule until one day he collapsed as he was walking. His left thigh bone had snapped near the hip. He was flown to Kinshasa. Surgery revealed a bone tumor at the point of the break. He would be on crutches for several months. He spoke freely of his experience with intense pain, anxiety and the testing of his faith. He also said that in the midst of his anguish it was his *Mukanda wa Nzambi* (pr. moo-KAH-ndah wah NZAH-mbi, i.e., his Book of God) that had been his primary source of strength.

Conversation, however, quickly moved beyond his physical incapacitation to the Church, its needs and problems, the AIMM delegation visit and plans that had been laid for an itinerary among the CMZa districts. He regretted deeply that he would not be able to accompany the men but urged them to follow through on the travel plans. "Our people are waiting for you. Visit our districts. Eat with our people. Hear what they are saying. Meet with our executive committee. Seek ways of encouraging our Church. I will wait for your visit and report when you come back through this city."

There had been a number of new developments with CMZa during the previous year. When efforts to select a successor for Kakesa Samuel as the new legal representative proved to be unsuccessful, the general assembly had decided in the summer of 1974 to combine the posts of general secretary and legal representative, something that several other Zaire church groups had already done. The same assembly had elected Kabongo Bukasa (pr. kah-BAW-ngo boo-KAH-sah), a pastor from the South Kasai, to the newly created post of assistant legal representative and associate general secretary. While this effectively put an end to the rivalry which had developed between two factions to name the next legal representative of the Church, it had also doubled Kabangy's work load.

There was more. Factions had again surfaced in the South Kasai, this time among the CMZa folk themselves. Kabangy's best efforts to the contrary, he had not yet been able to effect reconciliation -- something which weighed heavily upon him. And there was negative fall-out from the government's nationalization of the church schools. Some teachers whose loyalty to the Church had always been marginal now saw this as an opportunity to flaunt church discipline and to stop their financial support. Amidst the aggressive stance that Mobutu had taken against the Catholic Church and his repeated calls for African "authenticity," people with axes to grind with the Church were coming out of the woodwork. Often finding local tribunals happy to rule in their favor, CMZa had not been spared. A disgruntled male nurse from Nyanga had successfully extracted a large settlement in court pleading an infringement of some technical detail of the government's labor laws. All of this vexed Kabangy much more in his hospital bed than did the plaster caste on his leg. His parting comments to the AIMM delegation came from his heart when he said: "Go, sit with our people. Seek ways of encouraging and strengthening the Church in these difficult days."

Arriving in the West Kasai, the AIMM men made contacts in a variety of church districts along the way finding former colleagues both missionary and Zairian. It very soon became evident that the CMZa was feeling the pressure of aggressive government measures. There was much talk about the schools which had been removed from their control, the consequent defection of some of the teachers, the drop in giving to the church box. Repeatedly there was heard the phrase, *Mobutu a dit*, i.e., "Mobutu has said." Others frequently complained: "The ECZ seems to be marching in step with Mobutu." Everywhere was the comment: "There is too much change." Completing their travel, the delegation came to Tshikapa with the clear impression of a Church off balance.

Beginning a series of working sessions with the CMZa Executive Committee, the delegation suggested that perhaps it was a good moment to review and restate what the Church saw as its fundamental goals and then to engage in some brainstorming as to what strategies might be used to attain these goals in the midst of the gales which were buffeting the Church. This seemed to strike a responsive chord and there followed several working sessions with a chalk board. Put forward that dry season of 1975 were five priority concerns: evangelism, leadership training, Christian education, humanitarian service and projects for self-financing of the Church. Each priority was broken down into considerable detail with parallel columns in which strategies were sketched. In some cases existing commitments were simply restated. In others, some new directions were indicated. A case in point was the statement of concern for evangelism at both national and international levels. This was the first time that a church document specifically stated CMZa's concern about witness beyond its national borders. The listing of Christian education as a priority of the Church echoed a statement earlier given out by Kabangy insisting that CMZa could and would find ways of providing spiritual nurture for its youth, public schools or no public schools. The mention of projects of self-finance was an obvious reference to the financial constraints they were experiencing.

On their return to Kinshasa, the delegation again sought out Kabangy on his hospital bed and handed him a copy of the executive committee minutes. After reading through them, he said with enthusiasm: "This is not a set of committee minutes you have brought me. This is a 5 year plan of attack and work for the CMZa." (29)

Before leaving Zaire, the AIMM Secretary contacted Dr. Cal Johnson, the surgeon who had operated on Kabangy's leg. In essence he said: "We have determined that Reverend Kabangy does have a form of myeloma. The immediate prognosis is good. The long range prognosis is poor."

CHAPTER 30   A MAN AND A COUNTRY IN DECLINE

In many ways, the year 1975 marked the high water mark of power for Joseph Mobutu and his political movement, the MPR. The ten year anniversary of his accession to power became the occasion for much fanfare and bold prediction of things yet to come. That he had made a dramatic impact upon his country and his people was undeniable. Upon seizing power in 1965, he found a country literally coming apart at its multitudinous tribal seams. Imposing himself and ruling essentially by decree, he pulled a nation back from the brink of disintegration. A confusion of political parties was merged into a single movement. A variety of police and military units were brought under a single command. International financiers who controlled the huge mining interests in his country were forced to renegotiate the terms of exploitation and marketing of the country's raw materials. Launching the theme of "authenticity," he had drummed into the Zairian people the proud message that they, as Africans, had much of which to be proud and that there was much of value in their cultural heritage which merited preservation. He had even made some headway in his drive to educate the Zairian people to think first of their nationality and then of their tribal origin. They were repeatedly told, "If someone asks you who you are, answer first with pride, 'I am a Zairian.'"

In 1974 there had been a constitutional reform which, among other things, stated that Mobutu's political movement, the MPR, was the only political institution in the country and "Mobutuism" was the only approved political doctrine. The reworked constitution also recognized a political structure which amalgamated a political party and state government into a single whole. Thus government appointees at all levels were at the same time the official representatives of the MPR. Party and government had become one. A consummate politician, Mobutu had brought into being a structure where all people in government were doubly answerable directly to him as the head both of the state and the political movement. To be sure that no one in government had opportunity to form local followings, he regularly shuffled people in high government posts from one region to another.

Having gained the upper hand in a power struggle with the Roman Catholic Church, he decided to underscore the secular nature of his government by removing all primary and secondary education from the jurisdiction of mission/church bodies. This, it was said, would ensure the proper indoctrination and education of a new generation of Zairians in the goals and philosophy of the MPR. Political youth cells known as JMPR were installed everywhere to serve as the "eyes and ears of the Movement." To underscore that Zairians had attained both their political and economic independence, the business enterprises of many expatriate commercial people had been simply expropriated and handed out to "deserving" Zairians.

Mobutu's pictures were everywhere. Musical groups vied with each other in creating new lyrics of adulation and praise of their national "Father and Guide." Newspapers, radio and TV programming all portrayed him as a heroic, larger than life figure worthy of their adulation and lavish gratitude, (1)

On the international scene, his avowed anti-communist stance had long since come to the favorable attention of the United States and other Western governments. Seen as a dependable ally in central Africa during the tense days of the cold war, grants in cash and aid came easily and frequently from the western powers. There were, furthermore, individual banking consortiums which were willing and even eager to grant multi-million dollar loans to this ore-rich country. Viewed from Mobutu's perspective in 1975, there seemed little reason for anything but great optimism and self-confidence with regard to the future.

Unbeknown to Mobutu, two economic trends were already in the making in world markets which would have a catastrophic impact on Zaire. The first was a precipitous decline in the value of raw copper ore; the other was a surge in the price of petroleum products following the successful effort of OPEC countries to curb the flow of crude oil from their wells. While Mobutu certainly was not responsible for either of these events, they nonetheless laid bare two lethal flaws in his leadership of his nation.

flawed judgements

As long as the flow of funds into public coffers was strong, these flaws remained more or less camouflaged. But as submerged seashore debris is exposed at low tide, so also some of Zaire's crucial problems began to come to light as the flow of revenue was sharply reduced. There had been a long series of grandiose schemes designed to make Kinshasa the show place of Africa. Fortunes were being spent in developing such projects as a luxuriously appointed conference center; a nineteen-story combination communication, office and restaurant complex; a multi-story trade center with a cavernous marble floored lobby featuring elaborate panels of ebony carvings from floor to ceiling. And there was the unnamed memorial construction project midway between the city and its international airport which punctuated the skyline.

Meanwhile, as enormous energy and resources were being poured into these prestigious projects, the interior of the immense country was for all practical purposes abandoned to its own devices. The fragile road system left by the Belgians soon became, with neglect, a network of deep sand pits and impassable gullies. Isolated ferries rusted and became unusable. Bridges made of forest poles yielded to decay and termites and became unsafe for anything but light vehicle and pedestrian traffic. Plantations which once produced coffee, tea and palm oil gradually were reclaimed by the surrounding forest.

When at last the Zairian political leaders realized that their country had regressed from the status of an exporter of agricultural products to that of an importer of basic food supplies, there was a flurry of publicity urging rural populations to plant larger fields as a service to their country. In some areas there was temporary response to this call followed by disillusionment. After enlarging their fields with their bush knives and short handled hoes and cultivating additional crops, they discovered that frequently there was no commercial outlet for their hard-earned extra produce in their isolated areas. They were the victims of a decaying infra-structure which the Zairian government had inflicted upon them by a combination of neglect and the liquidation, in early 1971, of an intermediate level, rural, commercial community which had for years been provided by expatriates. (2) As they departed the Zairian scene, lines of credit, capital for maintenance of inventory and commercial expertise departed with them.

In brief, after riding a crest of inflowing revenues, grants and loans for several years, Zaire was suddenly bankrupt. There followed a scramble of responses as western financial institutions tried to reschedule loan payments on which Zaire was defaulting. It was one measure of Zaire's financial crisis that in 1979 the government swallowed its pride and issued a plea to the former expatriate owners of the confiscated business enterprises to return to Zaire to renew their commercial activities. Some actually did respond but found little more than empty buildings. But such was their confidence in Zaire's enormous potential that in spite of the injustice and loss suffered they were willing to try again.

Katanga revisited

Mobutu's ill-advised political decisions were not confined to internal concerns alone. By early 1975 he had already become involved in a bloody civil war in Angola just across his southern border. There had been sporadic guerrilla activity against the Portuguese in that country as early as 1961. The conflict gradually escalated in the 60's as three separate Angolan political parties emerged: The National Front for the Liberation of Angola or FNLA; The Popular Movement for the Liberation of Angola, or MPLA; and the National Union for Total Independence of Angola, or UNITA. All were committed to the winning of national freedom just as their Zairian neighbors to the north had done in 1960. (3)

Determined to maintain its grip on its African colonial empire in the face of the powerful tide of freedom which was moving all across Africa, the Portuguese committed more and more troops and weaponry not only to Angola but also to Mozambique and Guinea Bissau. As hit and run guerrilla attacks increased, the Portuguese stepped up their campaign of terrorism in the rural areas in an attempt to cow the population into submission. It was bloody, it was ugly, it was merciless. The Portuguese, of Catholic orientation, early came to view Protestants, both missionaries and Angolans, with suspicion. Arrests of Angolans were frequent; interrogations were brutal. Missionaries were frequently ordered out of the country. (4)

Strangely enough, it was the Portuguese military that tired of the senseless bloodshed and the mindless effort to delay the inevitable. Under pressure from its own military establishment the government signed a pact with all three Angolan groups and a joint interim government was put in place in January, 1975. By June fighting broke out among the three factions and by August the interim government was disbanded. The confused situation notwithstanding, the Portuguese granted political independence in November of that same year with MPLA and UNITA having set up rival governments.

It was the era of the cold war. For some years both the United States and Russia had been providing modest help, respectively, for the FNLA and the MPLA. The sudden collapse of Portuguese rule left both super powers scrambling to counter each others influence in Central Africa as well as that of China and South Africa. Turning to Mobutu, the United States secured permission to establish a supply base on Zairian soil. Mobutu not only agreed to provide a base but in mid-1975 he also committed Zairian troops to join the FNLA guerrilla force in northern Angola.

Better trained and better led, the MPLA troops routed the Zairian/FNLA forces in early 1976 forcing them back into Zaire. In the process they captured large amounts of American military hardware. With this, the FNLA disintegrated as a political force and the MPLA turned to what was to become a protracted and bitter struggle with the Jonas Savimbi-led UNITA forces. Mobutu's intrusion into the Angolan political struggle was not kindly viewed by MPLA's leader Agostinho Neto. His resentment was soon to find expression to Mobutu's embarrassment.

In the early 60's it had taken United Nations forces to quell the effort of the copper-rich Katanga Province to repudiate the authority of the central government. When the tide of battle went against them, the Katangese troops took refuge across nearby Angolan borders to the southwest. They and their leaders had been thwarted by the central government in their bid for autonomy but they refused to abandon their dream. It is understandable that the Angolan government chose to turn a benign ear to the reports that clandestine training camps had been set up along its distant eastern borders with Zaire. In March of 1977 ex-Katangese troops moved across the border along two routes with Lubumbashi, the capital, as their intended goal. For the first month their progress was little hampered by small units of the Zaire military. Caught unawares, Mobutu issued an urgent cry for help to the western powers. Concerned to preserve their Zairian ally, the United States, Belgium and France conferred. Ultimately French air transport flew Moroccan troops to southern Zaire. The Katangese advance was repulsed.

There followed a flurry of activity as Mobutu struggled to re-polish a badly tarnished image. Top ranks of the Zaire military were purged in June. July saw the reorganization of his political cabinet and the announcement of economic reform. The Governor of the Central Bank was dismissed and the Prime Minister was accused of treason. At the end of the year, national "elections" were held in which Mobutu was unopposed.

In January 1978, Mobutu flew fresh Zairian reinforcements to the Katanga area. March saw highly publicized trials of 91 people accused of plotting against Mobutu and his regime. Thirteen were convicted and executed.

But the end was not yet. Licking their wounds and nursing their hatred of the Zaire government, the defeated Katangese had once again retreated across the Angolan border and sought to regroup for yet another effort to topple the Mobutu regime. This time, they declared, it would be different. Trained and oriented by Cuban advisors in classic guerrilla warfare, a process of infiltration was begun. Caches of arms and ammunition were secreted, bit by bit, in a variety of rural areas in Zaire. Katangese fighters in civilian dress gradually took up residence amidst the surrounding population which wished them well. In May 1978, in a matter of hours, Kolwezi, a key railway center west of Lubumbashi with a sizeable white population, was surrounded and overrun by the infiltrators. Once again Mobutu and his security forces had been caught unawares. Once again he had no other recourse than to appeal to his western allies for help. French and Belgian paratroopers were flown into the area. American air transport brought ammunition, fuel, vehicles and supplies. Once again the tide was turned against the attacking forces. This time, however, the price in human lives and destruction exacted before retreat was much higher. Although a unit of French Foreign Legion Commandos were dropped into the center of Kolwezi, forty-four Europeans were killed before they were able to retake the city. Hundreds of other expatriates were evacuated. The mining operation in the entire area was brought to a halt. If there had been any doubt on the part of anyone as to the shaky nature of the Mobutu regime, the second incursion into Katanga Province and the Zairian Army's total inability to deal with it made things abundantly clear. In spite of all the rhetoric and speech-making, the Zairian political regime was revealed, by that time, to be a flimsy edifice at best.

flawed morality

As costly as some of Mobutu's unwise political decisions proved to be, none were as devastating for the well-being of Zaire as the events which set in motion the dismantling of morality in public life. An early casualty were the primary and secondary schools which had been taken over the fall of 1974 amidst much political fanfare. MPR leaders asserted that it was time to free the education of children from the influence of mission/church groups in order to instill into the minds and hearts of a new generation of Zairian citizens the philosophy of "authenticity" and the ideology of the political revolution. In the takeover the government acquired a far-flung network of rural schools which had been laboriously and sacrificially brought into being across the years by mission/church personnel including buildings and equipment. Most important of all was a corps of Zairian directors and teachers, trained and supervised by church personnel, which worked hard at maintaining some standards of integrity and credibility. Great effort was made to ensure enrollment and graduation not on the basis of tribal origin but upon the basis of individual qualification and academic achievement. Effort was continually made to handle and distribute government funds, including teacher pay, exactly as allocated and intended.

It took less than three complete school years under government supervision for the educational system of the country to be reduced to chaotic shambles. Teaching staffs which had been assembled by mission/church administrators were often scattered by reassignment or termination by government appointed directors and inspectors. Didactic materials, which at best were sparse, disappeared. Benches and tables found their way into the homes of school personnel leaving starkly bare class rooms. Broken windows, sagging ceilings, discolored walls, leaky roofs, doors without handles remained unrepaired.

Although an enormous amount of government funding was allocated for the direct administration of the school system it had attempted to take over (approximately 20% of total national budget during that period), it was discovered that government educational funds were not reaching their intended destinations. Passing through several administrative levels between Kinshasa and isolated rural areas, there was "leakage" at every juncture. The end result was that rural teachers typically were paid late, often at a figure below the salary figure written into their work books and, sometimes, were simply not paid at all as monies intended for them were siphoned off along the leaky government pay pipe line.

The deteriorating system in which they sought to work steadily ground down teacher morale. Instruction became perfunctory at best; absenteeism was common as teachers sought to supplement their meager income with other pursuits - - sometimes even during school hours. When confronted by parents or village elders, there was the sardonic response: "To survive these days in Zaire, we are forced to put article 15 into effect." (Article 15 was something of a code term for the French phrase *Débrouillez-vous*, i.e., fend for yourself, paddle your own canoe, find your own way!)

But the most shattering impact came from the steady decline of ethical and moral standards within the educational system itself. Caught between steady inflation on the one hand and sporadic, inadequate salaries on the other, directors and teachers found it all too easy to turn to the exploitation of the vulnerable student population under their control. Parents coming to enroll their children in the fall learned that a few chickens or a goat would greatly improve the chances of admission of their sons and daughters. And as year-end exams approached, once again the less than subtle message went out that "gifts" to the teacher or director would have a major bearing upon the ease or difficulty with which their children would be promoted to the next year of study. And, of course, between times, the school personnel always appreciated contributions to their cooking pots on holidays. And, tragically, it became more and more common to hear of cases where teachers were pressing female students for sexual favors so as to "guarantee" passing grades.

The broad deterioration of the country's school system had not gone unnoted by the Zairian people. It did not take long to discover that rather than being educated, their children were being victimized. Especially was there anger on the part of the Christian families who had benefitted so much in the past from mission/church schools and who now saw their children being not only short changed but also frequently exploited. Rural delegations began to find their way to Kinshasa demanding of political leaders that something be done. Ever the pragmatist, Mobutu realized that the taking over of the schools, like the confiscation of small business enterprises across the country, had been a colossal mistake. In neither case had there been adequate qualified personnel or the commitment to ideals of public service required to make the ventures work for the public good.

Thus it was that in 1977, with a roll of drums, the government announced its decision to return primary and secondary schools to the jurisdiction of the mission/church groups of the country. In early negotiations with church representatives, the Council of Catholic Bishops laid down three stipulations: 1) freedom of religious instruction, 2) the handling and channeling of all government funds destined for schools under their administration and 3) the right to hire and fire its own educational personnel. When an original draft of a "convention" was submitted by the government omitting the third stipulation, church authorities refused to sign. Knowing there was no other option, the government backed down and accepted the conditions as laid out by the church representatives.

It was on February 26, 1977 that the government Secretary of Education convened personnel of his department and representatives of the Catholic, Protestant and Kimbanguist Churches. In an opening speech the Secretary made reference to the historic collaboration between government and church in education which went back as far as the colonial era, a collaboration which had been praised by "the Guide Mobutu Sese Seko" as recently as the previous December. Mobutu congratulated the Churches "for having provided, in unity, their contribution to a special effort of national development especially in the domain of education." In continuing his speech he also congratulated the Churches for the spirit which continued to animate them and "for their readiness and availability to collaborate closely with the State in the work of educating the youth of the country." The Secretary then concluded by observing that the Churches of Zaire could congratulate themselves, upon signing the new convention, for having realized, materialized and concretized the will of the Father of the Nation who had approved the terms of the convention and authorized his signature." (5) Thus, with a flourish of flowery French, a discredited government education system was returned to the Churches of Zaire. The disastrous experiment had lasted less than three complete school years.

a political slogan reversed

In the light of the fiasco of government intervention into commerce and education, it is ironic to note that already in late 1974 Mobutu was sounding an alarm. In a meeting with his MPR cabinet in December he said there was mounting evidence that efforts to attain their economic independence were not going well. A Zairian historian wrote of this era; "The motto of the party 'To Serve and Not To Serve Oneself' had literally been applied in reverse. A lack of conscience, greed and even incompetence of many beneficiaries risked putting in doubt the most elementary principles of the Revolution." (6)

In a mass rally held in a Kinshasa stadium in early January 1975, Mobutu took the occasion to rail against what he called "multiple deviations" which had exploited his initial projects and promised radical measures to correct the situation. Spelled out, these new measures would forbid any further commercial activity on the part of political authorities. They were to be free, said he, to devote themselves completely to the achievement of the revolutionary goals adopted by their political movement.

Sadly, however, it was gradually becoming known among the Zairian populace that even as he made his speeches calling for loyalty and sacrifice on the part of ordinary citizens, Mobutu and a growing group of privileged people around him were quietly becoming wealthy and were emerging as a class of privileged elite. Efforts were made to conceal it. Anyone foolhardy enough to voice public criticism soon found himself in prison. Nonetheless it was becoming common knowledge that numbered bank accounts were being opened in Switzerland; luxurious villas were being purchased and staffed with family members in Europe. Air Zaire, which had secured a Boeing 747, understood that this aircraft was to be readily available for personal trips for Mobutu and any specially favored people he might invite to travel with him. There even was the word that for a family vacation to Disneyland in the United States, a French Concorde plane had been chartered. Slowly it became painfully clear that whatever the political and economic fate of his country was to be, Mobutu was intent on becoming enormously and flamboyantly wealthy at the expense of his own people.

An evil virus had been let loose in the political body of Zaire which slowly but surely began to filter from top to bottom infecting every level and every area of public life. By the spring of 1979 an expatriate journalist would write: "Not long ago this young nation of 29 million people was basking in prosperity, apparently recovered from the chaos that followed its independence in 1960. For the last three years, however, the country has been going downhill. Zaire has amassed foreign debts totaling 3.5 billion dollars that it can't pay. Production has declined 4 to 6 percent every year since 1975. There are serious shortages of almost everything the country needs. . . . The copper industry, Zaire's biggest money producer, is in a mess. Much of the country's limited foreign exchange earnings are squandered on luxuries. . . ."

"Behind these problems lies a web of public and private corruption. While common in many developing countries, corruption here ranks among the most blatant to be found. . . . The President himself says, 'In our country, anything can be sold, anything can be bought.' Bribery is everywhere. Minor officials demand payment - - first to find the proper form, then to sign it. Hotel desks lose reservations, only to locate them when money is passed. Police fine drivers for trumped-up offenses. . . . According to a knowledgeable foreigner here, even the government often must bribe customs officials to get its own imports into the country. . . . Diamonds are smuggled out of the country and proceeds banked abroad. Coffee is deliberately under valued and the exporters keep the difference between the declared and the actual price. Changing this system will require massive shifts in attitudes because bribery, called *matabiche*, is an accepted way of life here. . . . Also behind the corruption is the fact that most Zairians cannot live on what they are able to earn honestly." (7)

Fully aware of Zaire's steady decline and Mobutu's callous abuse of power, Western powers, including the United States, turned blind eyes and continued to support him. His excesses notwithstanding, his pro-Western anticommunist stance was firm. Thus he continued to be a "valuable ally" who needed to be kept in power.

Meanwhile, along the four-lane boulevard leading to the international airport outside the city of Kinshasa, construction on the unnamed memorial had long since ground to a halt. The four towering, unfinished concrete pylons stood in a patch of weeds with rusting construction equipment scattered about their bases. Though unintentional on Mobutu's part, it stood as a starkly appropriate memorial to a political regime fatally flawed by unwise decisions and moral decay.

CHAPTER 31   A SHEPHERD'S LAST YEARS

Released from the Kinshasa hospital, Pastor Kabangy made his way home to his family and his office on crutches. He was impatient to get back to work. Earlier, while still immobilized by his surgery, he had greeted with enthusiasm the set of priorities which had been proposed by the CMZa Executive Committee in consultation with a visiting AIMM delegation. His promise to make them the heart of a "five year plan of action" for the CMZa had not been idle talk. The moral decline in public life was glaringly obvious on every side. Financial pressures on the Church were real and growing. Kabangy believed that the adopted priorities could serve as a rallying cry and as a means of keeping the Church focused on issues fundamental to its nature and its ministry. Thus there was frequent reference to "our five priorities", i.e., evangelism, leadership training, Christian education, social services and fund raising. Over succeeding years deliberate efforts were made to implement them all in the life of the Church.

rewriting the CMZa bylaws

Beset by adverse influences of all kinds, Secretary Kabangy convened a meeting of the CMZa's general council in his home district Kandala in April of 1976. Provided for by the CMZa constitution, this was an enlarged administrative committee which could be assembled between general assemblies to deal with major immediate concerns. In all there were 31 delegates including four missionaries (1) drawn from the entire CMZa landscape. The agenda was lengthy and ranged all across a sweep of church concerns. Minutes eventually contained record of 54 separate actions taken which covered such issues as qualifications required for ordination of new pastors, the defrocking of three pastors for conduct unbecoming to them and their Church, the utilization of budget monies accorded to the districts, occupation and rental fees of housing on the stations, formation of a special commission to deal with officers' salaries, an offer to establish savings accounts at church headquarters for pastors, changes in titles to be used for church officers (e.g. the secretary and associate secretary general would henceforth be known as president and vice-president), the nomination of new regional assistant legal representatives and a strong affirmation of CMZa's ongoing collaboration with AIMM.

One action taken at Kandala which had far reaching implications read as follows: "Given the confusion created by the proliferation of statutes of the CMZa, the General Council annuls them all and adopts the statutes annexed to these minutes as the only ones legal for the governing of the CMZa as decided by the effective members." (2) This was followed by a recommendation asking the administrative committee to adopt the new statutes and to bring them to final approval at the next general assembly of the Church. The final draft of the statutes was left to a four man committee composed of President Kabangy, Vice- President Kabongo, Treasurer Bukungu and Deacon Mpoyi Tshienda. In its final form, it was a document which effectively centered much authority within the body which had just met and, furthermore, made it a self-perpetuating group.

Just three months later, the CMZa convened in its general assembly at Ilebo, a river port on the extreme northern edge of CMZa territory. In an opening address, President Kabangy greeted the assembled delegates with the following statement: "This General Assembly is going to place a particular accent on an analysis of the spiritual and moral life of the people of God beginning with his servants. We must undertake a self-examination of our manner of life as Christians and then extend this analysis to the life of each member of our Church. . . . A church attached to God by Jesus Christ, whose faithful members give evidence by their lives of their attachment to Jesus Christ, is a church which will live from one generation to the next. That is what we hope for the Mennonite Church in Zaire." (3)

In his report Kabangy went on to underscore what he called the five "priorities of priorities" adopted by the CMZa and his determination to pursue them. After highlighting some of the new program developments undertaken by the Church, he concluded his opening remarks by saying: "We rejoice that good relations exist between the CMZa and the AIMM. We request the AIMM to double its efforts in the future . . . to cooperate in a spirit of brotherhood with the CMZa in the work of the Lord." (4)

In the official record of the gathering was a brief minute which read: "The General Assembly unanimously voted all the articles of the Minutes of the General Council held at Kandala . . . as the fundamental directives for the new structure of the ECZ/27'CMZ." (This sequence of letters and numbers was the shorthand identification of the CMZa within the broad national structure of the ECZ. All other ECZ members also had assigned combinations to identify them.) (5)

At the time Kabangy undoubtedly viewed this action as a needed correction to enable a small body of church leaders to sail a tighter ship in what promised to be increasingly troubled economic and political waters. With passing time, however, as copies of the revised statutes were more freely circulated and studied, they were to become the object of growing discussion and irritation amidst grass-roots membership.

putting priorities in gear

Though aware of the possibility of reaction to the drastic revamping of CMZa statutes, President Kabangy and his team plunged ahead in an effort to put CMZa's adopted agenda into action. In the area of leadership training, an AIMM scholarship made possible the departure of Mukanza Ilunga for studies at the Associated Mennonite Biblical Seminaries at Elkhart, IN.

He was born into the village home of a simple rural teacher/evangelist who served under the sponsorship of Canadian Baptist missionaries based at Shakenge Station some fifty miles southwest of Kandala. He began his quest for schooling via a path followed by many a rural African child, i.e., first in a rustic grass and stick shelter in his home village, then on to the nearby mission station. Finishing primary school he was chosen to enroll in the Mennonite High School at Nyanga. Like many others, he too came to faith in Christ and requested baptism during his student days. Following graduation he married a lovely girl named Mbongela (pr. mbaw-NGEH-lah, i.e., one who pleases). After teaching a while they were selected by CMZa to pursue theological studies at ISTK in Kinshasa. It was after serving as CMZa's provincial secretary in Bandundu Province for three years that he was granted the AIMM scholarship for further study in America. Given the sudden loss of their schools at government hands, the CMZa was urgently addressing the challenge of the Christian orientation of its children without the familiar structure of its own school system. Mukanza was encouraged to pursue the Christian Education track available at AMBS with a view to assuming CMZa leadership in this field upon his return.

In the meantime, however, Leona Schrag had been moved from Mutena to the new church center at Tshikapa where she was assigned full-time duties in the preparation of religious education materials for the Church. Working with the CMZa Literature Committee, material turned out took a variety of forms including daily devotional reading guides in two languages, Sunday School lessons also in two languages, program ideas for pastors for special Sundays in the year, translation and distribution of tracts in a variety of dialects. Beside this there were the unflagging efforts of Tina Quiring who supervised the stocking of a bookstore in Tshikapa while supplying outlets in several places with Bibles, New Testaments and paperbacks on a variety of themes having to do with Christian faith and life.

CMZa had people in training both in North America and at ISTK in Kinshasa. But church leaders by now had taken a new look at their Bible Institute at Kalonda. There had been a tendency, for a while, to downplay its role and significance given the fact that the diplomas issued upon graduation were not recognized by the Zairian government. However with President Kabangy's renewed emphasis upon evangelism, church planting and the nurture of believers, it became clear to all that the Institute remained a steady source of pastoral candidates who were prepared to return to the rural areas from which they had come to serve their own people. Some modifications of Institute curriculum were consequently made in an effort to better equip its graduates for their intended rural ministry. Recognizing that village Christians were not able to completely support a pastor and his family, students were introduced to some crafts which permitted them to provide at least partial self-support. In collaboration with MCC and SEDA, students were introduced to the breeding and care of caged rabbits and the rudiments of carpentry. For a time some even received instruction in the basics of photography.

But the needs of rural CMZa believers were vast and the pastoral candidates from the Bible Institute and ISTK came slowly. Thus it was determined to reactivate a TEE (Theological Education by Extension) program which had lain more or less dormant for some years. Rudy Martens, who had served as the Institute director for four years, was replaced by Earl Roth (who after two years relinquished the post to Malembe Tshingudi, pr. mah-LEH-mbeh tshi-NGOO-di, the first Zairian director of the school). Martens, in turn, was asked to organize and renew the TEE thrust as an extended training arm of the school. With fresh materials and clear structure, the response was immediate. ISTK graduate Kabasele Bantubiabo (pr. kah-bah-SEH-leh bah-ntoo-BIA-boh) was assigned to partner with Martens in this program and brought invaluable help as a translator of materials and as associate director. Early titles which found their way into printed lesson form were:"Prayer," "The Work of a Shepherd" and a 200-page manual which brought together Tshiluba translations of J.C. Wenger's two studies entitled "How Mennonites Came To Be" and "What Mennonites Believe."

While CMZa leaders viewed with concern the caution signals the AIMM Board was sending with regard to future subsidy of Zaire church programs, there was genuine desire to face their own responsibilities. When AIMM offered to send someone to conduct workshops with CMZa leaders to study Biblical principles of stewardship, there was quick acceptance. In response AIMM Treasurer Art Janz was present at the July 1976 general assembly after which some seminars were organized in regional centers. Interest was good; response was positive. There followed an increase in giving in several districts thereafter. But while this was most encouraging and helpful at district levels, the problem of achieving self-funding of a costly central administration remained largely unsolved.

Protestants in Zaire had long been aware of a Catholic tradition in the country of creating revenue producing projects such as live stock, handcraft or agricultural schemes. CMZa leaders often questioned Protestant hesitance to engage in such endeavors. With the CMZa headquarters situated on the banks of the Kasai River which downstream wound its way through great stands of tropical forest, the idea of a church owned saw mill began to surface with increasing regularity. Response of AIMM personnel was less than enthusiastic for two reasons: first, there was some understanding of the enormous capital outlay which would have been involved in attempting to set up a traditional lumbering operation. There was also great reserve based on principle. AIMMers felt strongly that to encourage church-sponsored profit making schemes would be to cloud years of teaching regarding the responsibility of individual members to support their own church.

It was just at this point that news came of a revolutionary device developed by a professional lumberman in Oregon. Instead of creating a stationary saw mill which required heavy equipment to drag logs to it, this man turned the process around. Why not take the saw to the trees? He proceeded to make this feasible by developing a portable saw powered by a Volkswagen motor which could "walk" a geared track mounted on the sides of the felled trees in the forest. This equipment could be disassembled, carried by hand and reassembled anywhere that crews dropped trees. The sawn lumber could also be carried out by hand to a road for transport by truck. If this invention did not address the second missionary concern, it did effectively wipe out the first.

MEDA representatives were contacted. A loan was arranged for the purchase and shipment of this new equipment. MCC recruited Darrel Martin, a young man with mechanical skills from central Illinois, who was challenged by the sort of project that was taking shape. In due time government lumbering permits were secured, a bush camp established and the whine of a saw mingled with the staccato exhaust of a VW motor were to be heard echoing among the towering forest trees. A storage shed was built at the church headquarters. Demand for precision cut lumber was instantaneous. There were CMZa districts building chapels which immediately placed orders. Some CMZa departments were wanting to repair and enlarge their facilities.

A troublesome problem soon developed, however. Situated amidst the rapidly growing center of Tshikapa, demand for the locally produced, precision sawn lumber was insatiable. People were building houses. Commercial people were building stores. Others wanted to purchase lumber by the truck load for transport to distant Kananga where it could be sold for a very attractive profit. Soon Zairian entrepreneurs began arriving at church headquarters pressing bundles of ready cash upon church officers as down payments on orders for lumber. In the process CMZa's own departments and districts found it more and more difficult to secure needed wood for their own needs. While for several years the church sawmill did indeed produce considerable lumber for the area and did generate significant funds for CMZa, in time the enterprise was to create some serious difficulties for the Church.

chickens: for aid or for profit?

As for CMZa's commitment to ongoing social services in far-flung rural areas, the long established medical service was there. Over time many dispensaries and maternity units were established. As simple and rudimentary as they were, for literally thousands of villagers, these church-sponsored facilities manned by Zairian staff were the only source of health care for many miles in any direction. In the fall of 1978 AIMM missionary doctors Elvina Martens and Dennis Ries were both stationed at Kalonda. They plus missionary nurse Leona Entz and a corps of Zairian personnel staffed CMZa's referral hospital to which critical patients were brought by air and road for diagnosis, surgery or special care. By this time graduates from the medical school at the University in Kinshasa were looking for places to do their internship. Anxious to find opportunity for work with missionary doctors, some were finding their way to Kalonda as well. From the hospital pharmacy there was a continual flow of packets of medical supplies to the Zairian medical personnel in the bush. With the arrival of Dr. Richard and Jeanne Simpson Hirschler, efforts in public health earlier launched by Dr. Ries were greatly strengthened. Consensus was clear. The healing services offered under CMZa sponsorship were critically important, gladly provided and widely acclaimed.

There was less consensus among CMZa leaders, however, regarding the purpose of SEDA, the experimental farm at Nyanga. The "New Life for All" program was warmly affirmed by the church leaders. There were, however, also rabbits, chickens, supplies and services which were eagerly sought by the surrounding population. With the church administration under financial stress, it was understandable that questions were raised as to how this agricultural center and its thriving activity could contribute financially to the overall CMZa budget needs. AIMM and MCC staff people, on the other hand, kept reminding church administrators that from its inception SEDA had been a non-profit enterprise with the dual goals of Christian witness and the improvement of diet of protein starved village populations. Any "profit" extracted from this program would literally be at the expense of the very people it was intended to help. For years this difference in perspective generated debate between missionaries and Zairian church leaders.

our schools on our terms

The government return of primary and secondary schools to the mission/church groups of Zaire was viewed with mixed feelings. In one way the government takeover had been a relief. The hiring of hundreds of teachers, records for thousands of students, handling of large amounts of subsidy monies had been a huge administrative responsibility. But the opportunity to freely conduct religious instruction in scores of classrooms had been greatly missed. The freedom demanded by church representatives in negotiation with government officials to once again include religious instruction in the curriculum, hire and fire its own personnel and to handle its own subsidy funds were heartily endorsed by CMZa leaders. The transfer once effected, however, President Kabangy well knew the enormous task which again confronted the church. Making the school system one with which CMZa would again want to be identified would not be a simple matter.

These concerns were early reflected in a meeting of the CMZa Administrative Committee in January 1978. Ben Eidse, a member of the committee, afterward reflected the spirit of the sessions: "Now that we again have the school mandate, every effort should be made to have as solid a spiritual input as possible in the class room. Teachers must be encouraged to a greater commitment to Christ, a greater dedication to meet the spiritual needs of students. Courses should be worked through more thoroughly, made more relevant to life and culture. . . ." (6)

The committee took direct action and requested AIMM missionary Betty Quiring, a trained teacher with graduate study in religion, to work full time at establishing a revised curriculum of religious studies for

CMZa schools at every level. Once again President Kabangy hit the road and began a systematic circuit of many of the CMZa districts. His objectives were three: 1) to review area church problems and needs; 2) to spell out clearly to district leaders the terms under which the CMZa was again assuming responsibility for schools in their areas and 3) to screen available educational personnel and to make clear the educational and Christian qualifications they would have to meet in order to be employed by CMZa.

In early 1978 two documents were released from Kabangy's office spelling out what he had been saying in his travel. The first was a seven-page statement outlining the conditions of employment which would apply for all who sought positions in CMZa schools. The usual details of required credentials, salary rates, hours, punctuality and medical card were listed. Amidst the material were other details of particular significance. In the list of legal holidays, Christmas was reinstated. One short paragraph read: "Since the CMZa is a religious association, every person desiring to obtain employment by it promises in writing to respect the doctrines, moral standards and regulations of the Community." (7)

On the heels of this mailing came a letter dated January 30, 1978, which became very specific in its focus. With copies sent to regional government educational offices and all CMZa school personnel, he made reference to the survey of educational facilities and personnel which had just been undertaken. He then continued: "In the census of personnel it was ascertained that several of our teachers and directors had been the object of polygamy during the period which we can describe as having been temporary. A spiritual call has been issued to all leaders of the community to counsel our brothers to come to their senses. The result has truly been satisfactory and encouraging to a large degree." (8)

In a concluding paragraph he stated that those among the CMZa educational personnel who insisted on maintaining polygamous relationships should prepare themselves for CMZa disciplinary action in keeping with Article IV of the convention they had just signed with the government, an article which granted churches the authority to require "public morality" with respect to "the principles of ecclesiastic instructions regarding matrimonial life." (9)

A missionary observer of the scene wrote: "In the past month or so, the [church] central educational office has been a flurry of activity. The veranda continued to remain crowded with directors and teachers all vitally interested either in their pay or in their placement. From what we have seen . . . I've been generally positively impressed with the spirit of our educational personnel. Directors and teachers in general welcome the school takeover. Through the experience of the past few years they seem to have developed a new appreciation of the Church." (10)

"trouble shooters" appointed

Two key people became simultaneously available to the CMZa in the summer of 1977. Mukanza Ilunga returned from the United States having earned an MA in Christian education at AMBS, Elkhart, IN. Levi and Eudene King Keidel also returned to Zaire that summer following a three year leave of absence during which Levi finished three book manuscripts for publication. (11) Before either of them had arrived in Zaire, Mukanza had been named Director of the Department of Evangelism with Keidel to serve as his counselor. (12) To facilitate their collaboration, both were placed at Nyanga.

Once on the scene, their mandate was soon broadened. As members of the CMZa Administrative Committee, Mukanza and Keidel began to contribute their views and dreams to the discussions. Out of this interaction was born a Commission on the Life of the Church to which they were to give leadership. In a record of that discussion it is noted: "The principle objective of this section is to edify and cause growth of souls in the knowledge of Christ and in spiritual maturity through the united ministry of all of the departments of the Community . . . ." (13) In committee discussion this assignment was interpreted to mean responsibility for dealing with church disputes, orientation of new pastors and the counseling oversight of CMZa's Christian Education department, Bible Institute, TEE, book shops and women's work. And the net was thrown even more broadly still by indicating that the commission was also to look in on other church departments such as SEDA, the medical services, education, transport and saw mill to assure that they functioned in a manner so as to make a contribution to the life and witness of the Church.

This extraordinary blanket assignment reflected at least three things: 1) President Kabangy's abiding concern for the well-being and ministry of the Mennonite Church of Zaire, 2) his deep confidence in the two men who were asked to give leadership to this newly created commission, and 3) his eagerness to have qualified people shoulder the burdens of church leadership with him.

As Mukanza and Keidel worked into their assignment, regional seminars for CMZa leaders become a basic feature of their program. Team members were chosen for each trip who could bring to bear knowledge of the people and area in question and provide Bible studies as well as presentations in public health and nutrition. A radical addition to the team was Kafutshi Françoise who by this time was president of the CMZa women's group. She was at first reluctant to address predominantly male audiences at these seminars on topics she knew would be controversial. But encouraged by Mukanza, the Keidels and particularly her own husband, Kakesa Samuel, she took the plunge. An articulate and spirited speaker, she began to address such topics as the sacredness of Christian marriage, the Christian home, shared parental responsibility in child care, the rights of wives within the circle of the Christian family. Her presentations did frequently stir agitated response as defensive men sought to justify themselves in some of their traditional attitudes. But Kafutshi had both Scripture and CMZa leadership on her side. And, interestingly enough, as word got around about her presentations in the itinerating seminars, church leaders from other districts began to write requesting that she be a member of the team when they came to their areas. Though her teaching at times was strong medicine, they knew that it was both appropriate and needed.

gravel in the hammer mill

To picture the decade of the 70's in the history of the CMZa as a decade free of blemish would be to ignore reality. Amidst stories of success and progress there were also struggles with stubborn problems.

Some of the problems were external in origin. After the euphoria of the early 1970's came the sudden skid in Mobutu's political fortunes and the abrupt decline in Zaire's economy. Spiraling inflation meshed with a steady devaluation of the Zairian currency. Basic goods across the country gradually became more scarce and more expensive. Tshikapa, a growing diamond mining/vending center, came more and more to resemble a frontier town of the early American west where money and liquor flowed freely, prices for everything were high and public morality was fluid.

To all of this were added the reverberations of the Katanga invasions of 1977 and '78. Situated a scant 65 miles from the Angolan border to the south, Tshikapa was the site of beefed up military units which roared back and forth along the road skirting the CMZa office complex. Heavy gun emplacements were dug in along the mission air strip across the river at Kalonda Station. Gun crews made up of chronically ill-paid military units became frequent callers at station homes seeking hand outs of "beer money." In the grips of a disintegrating national economy, salaried church personnel gradually found themselves unable to feed and clothe their families with their salaries alone. They were increasingly being forced to supplement their income in one manner or another. With the creeping decline of public morality which was evident all about them, it was enormously tempting for some church personnel to trim some ethical corners as well. Missionary members of the church family also felt the impact of economic deterioration in a variety of ways. As basic supplies and services became more scarce and problematic, life, of necessity, became simpler. Although under the mission/church fusion agreement the CMZa had accepted responsibility for providing adequate housing for missionaries invited to work with them, there frequently were breakdowns in the implementation of the agreement which left missionaries to improvise on their own.

After visiting Zaire in 1977, the following notes regarding the Zaire missionaries were found in the AIMM Secretary's reporting to the Board: "Living more simply than in the past; pantry supplies skimpier; fewer conveniences and extras; basic goods often in short supply and expensive; intriguing varieties of morning porridge; charcoal/gas barrel ovens; an old ferry cable poured into a foundation in lieu of reinforcing iron; scare water doing multiple services." The report went on to observe that what few missionary complaints had been heard had not touched on personal inconveniences but rather with frustration over work being curtailed amidst the shortage of supplies: "TEE hampered by shortage of paper, then ink, then stencils; building hampered by shortage of cement, then transport; medical work being hampered by shortage of the most basic drugs." (14)

But aside from the external pressures which were impacting the Church there were also problems which were simply inherent within the Church itself. That there even was a Mennonite Church counting membership in three different provinces and from a dozen or so different ethnic groups was in and of itself a miracle.(15) Just below the surface of African church life there has always lain the volcanic power of regional and tribal loyalties which can erupt given the right provocation. Representation named to committees and commissions were always closely scrutinized. Appointments to positions and assignments given out always were reviewed with an eye to regional and ethnic representation. Whenever real or perceived discrimination took place, letters of protest quickly found their way to CMZa headquarters. President Kabangy demonstrated extraordinary pastoral gifts of patience, understanding and compassion when it came to dealing with hurting people and conflicts within the Church. But when letters came attacking him personally, as they did with increasing frequency across the years, and accusing him of malfeasance, tribalism or other sins which he knew to be unfounded, Kabangy at times demonstrated a short fuse. This, on occasion, led to ill advised exchanges of hot letters with his accusers. In the process there were some cases of alienation.

One case in point was a temporary estrangement between Kabangy and Kakesa Samuel. As details of Kakesa's formal severance with CMZa were worked out, there had been some difference of opinion. Strong leaders both, differences flared into unhappy exchanges which for a time led to strained relations between them.

There was also Muhaku Boniface (pr. moo-HAH-koo). He had been a fellow classmate in their student days at Kajiji, in the early 60's, and soon rose to a post of leadership in his home district at Nyanga. After a while he became embroiled in a series of disagreements with the local district council over policies and church funds. Transferred to Kananga, the capital of the province, he was appointed to both a pastoral role and the position of educational coordinator. Before long disagreement over policies and handling of funds again erupted. This time President Kabangy was involved and exchanges became heated. As a result Pastor Muhaku left the CMZa and made a short-lived attempt to launch a separatist group which he chose to call "The Anabaptist Mennonite Church."

There were still other layers of tension within CMZa in the 1970's. For instance, there were the increasing number of younger, better educated pastors who at times became impatient with a senior generation who were in no hurry to relinquish their authority. And with gradually rising levels of education, a lay movement was under foot which was becoming more and more vocal about what they saw as the domination of "the theologians" in the life of their Church within a centralized system of administration. Kidinda Shandungo, the son of Mukedi District Pastor Kidinda David, had with AIMM scholarship help done doctoral studies in the United States. Returning to Zaire he became an instructor of education in the National University. (16) As a Mennonite layman he became a perceptive spokesman for this group when he wrote and circulated an 18-page study document.

Early in the paper he pointed out the "tall type administrative structure" of CMZa while admitting that it did have some advantages. "Composed of members from many ethnic groups and occupying a vast area . . . in Zaire, [the Church] needs on the one hand a certain centralism to hold its members together and a certain bureaucracy with its impersonality necessary for a just treatment as opposed to favoritism, personal whim, tribalism and regionalism. On the other hand there is an increasing call for decentralization which can be interpreted as a reaction against the growing impersonal structures and a sense that the church members are having less and less control over the Church." (17)

There then followed a concluding observation: "Church leaders are not there to make decisions for their followers but decisions should be made by those who will be effected by them. . . . If we [church

303

members] cannot communicate with mutual understanding we will remain strangers [something] which will be prejudicial for a voluntary association such as the Mennonite Church of Zaire." (18)

the pain of stumbling

Woven into the very fabric of the plan of mission/church fusion was the understanding that, over time, Zairians would be oriented to fill all key positions within the various departments of the Church. By the mid-70's much progress had been made on many fronts. Church legal matters, the general treasury, oversight of schools, the chairs of a long list of committees and commissions had long since passed to Zairians. In a few departments which required specialized skills, the transition had taken longer but were also eventually realized. Two such were the church farm at Nyanga and CMZa's literature department. In both cases there had been specialized training for Zairians chosen to succeed missionary directors. In both cases there had been on- the-scene orientation. In both cases, administrative roles involved the oversight of considerable inventory, cash flow, supervision of personnel and the ordering of supplies. In time, both departments came to grief under Zairian administration.

It was a bitter pill for all concerned. For CMZa leaders it was painful to have to accept clear evidence of the failure of fellow Zairians who had been entrusted with major roles of leadership within the Church. For missionaries who had invested much time and energy in grooming their successors, there was keen disappointment - - and even a certain sense of betrayal. It made it no easier to know that CMZa's experience was not an isolated one. From here and there across Zaire there were other stories of comparable collapsed church departments under Zairian direction.

In an October 1978 meeting of the CMZa Executive Committee with representatives of MCC and AIMM present, (19) these problems were addressed. In the flat language of official minutes it was simply said that the SEDA Director was removed from his functions and that he was to assume responsibility for a newly created sub-department of extension. (20) AIMM and MCC were asked to find someone qualified to take over the administrative direction of SEDA.

In a second action, it was stated that the director of LIMEZA (the French acronym for the Mennonite Bookstore of Zaire) be removed from his functions and that legal procedures be initiated in his regard [for recovery of lost assets] and that Miss Leona Schrag be designated as the director of this department. (21) (22)

What had gone wrong? In both cases there had been a rising tide of complaint and criticism over deteriorating services in the two departments. Caught, as they were, in the general collapse of the Zaire economy around them, they could not be held accountable for providing supplies which simply were unobtainable. But in each case there had also been incomplete inventories, unexplained disappearance of department funds and equipment. For this they definitely were responsible. If there were any explanations, what were they?

In a letter addressed to missionary Ben Eidse earlier that same year, the AIMM Secretary wrote: "Even though we work in the face of overwhelming graft and dishonesty, we cannot yield to the tide. But the question remains nonetheless, Why? . . . Is it the hunger for material gain that only those know who have so recently broken out of a subsistence level of life? Is it the pressure of the endless list of unsatisfied wants? Is it clan or family pressures? Is it the thirst to move or demonstrate one's status or prestige in African society? Is it the Bantu tradition which grants the clan chief the right to dip into the clan kitty, no questions asked? Is it the tradition which assumes the chief's right to require tribute and gifts from those under him? Is it failure on our part to successfully teach a Christian ethic which makes honesty an integral part of Christian faith and life?" (23)

Reporting to the AIMM Board later in the year the AIMM Secretary, after describing what had happened, commented: "It becomes more and more clear that in order to make a program of Western orientation and conceptualization function, it is necessary to bring to it a cluster of presuppositions and values which are simply not shared by the average Zairian, i.e., welcoming regular audits; sensitivity to the problem of possible conflict of interests; sharp delineation between personal and program resources; regular, clear reporting on program. . . . Overlying all of this are the tremendous pressures of clan loyalty and expectations coupled with the need we all share of continual growth in grace." (24)

August 1978 found President Kabangy in the States as a CMZa delegate to the Mennonite World Conference at Wichita, KS. Not being able to attend the general assembly of the CMZa which was convened the same month in Zaire, he sent a written message in which he did not mince words. Referring to the decline of morality in society all about them and to specific problems within the Church, he underscored the Church's ongoing responsibility to evangelize and preach the Word of God. He then observed that the best preaching was done "by our lives and our conduct as Christians. . . . We are going to correct certain habits, theft, corruption in all domains, in the schools, in our work - - and in our administration. We must, in the love of the Lord, correct this situation at a moment when the roots are not far spread. In spite of all, I have confidence in God and in our people." (25)

Indeed Pastor Kabangy's upbeat note was justified. Some cases of failure notwithstanding, there were many Zairians who carried responsibility within CMZa with distinction. In the face of enormous pressure and temptation, the wonder is not that some succumbed but rather that many maintained their integrity and Christian witness.

President Kabangy attended the sessions of the Mennonite World Conference of 1978 in Wichita, KS as the vice-president for Africa. His wife Kimbadi (pr. gi-MBAH-di) accompanied him as the representative of the Mennonite women of Zaire. Also part of the delegation representing the CMZa were Pastors Falanga Elie and Mayambi Diakande respectively from from Mukedi and Nyanga Districts and Elder Mpoyi Tshienda from Mbuji Mayi in the South Kasai.

It was immediately obvious as he deplaned at O'Hare Field in Chicago with a cane that he was walking with much discomfort. Arriving at Hesston where he attended a pre-conference consultation on Mennonite World Mission, a pair of crutches were secured at the campus clinic. He attended all sessions there and at Wichita as well moving slowly and quietly about. Between sessions and during free time he frequently would be found in a dormitory lounge, leg propped up on a chair. Reservations had already been made for their return in time to attend the sessions of the CMZa General Assembly at Kikwit the third week in August. In consultation with AIMM personnel, however, it was decided that Kabangy and Kimbadi would delay their return so as to allow time for a stop at Elkhart for a bone scan and consultation with Dr. William Pletcher, a Christian oncologist. Bone marrow was drawn and sent to a laboratory.

recurring malignancy confirmed

Next day Kabangy returned to the doctor's office to learn the results of all that had transpired. The doctor summarized his situation in a few brief statements: there was renewed malignant activity at the point where the bone had been pinned in previous surgery; no spread of malignancy was found elsewhere; the blood count was surprisingly good; a series of four fifteen- to twenty-minute cobalt treatments were to be given on successive days; increased oral chemotherapy dosage was to be continued upon his return to Zaire; treatments received plus oral medications would arrest further growth for a while. Pausing, the Christian physician then quietly added with compassion that the long-range prognosis on the basis of medical science alone was not good.

They returned to the home of Art and Martini Janz where they were being hosted. Soon after supper that evening Kabangy and Kimbadi excused themselves and retired downstairs to their guest bedroom. Before long there was heard the sound of sobbing as, at long last, the couple was free to vent their disappointment, sorrow and apprehension triggered by the information given them that day. They had known the nature of his illness ever since his first surgery. But they had often prayed committing their burden to the Lord and requesting healing if it pleased Him. But in recent months there had once again been the nagging, worsening pain; and now, today, the verdict shared by a kindly doctor. What of the future? What would happen to their ten children? Was his work with the CMZa really finished? Slowly the anguished sounds from the bedroom downstairs subsided and, finally, all was still.

Next morning they emerged from their bedroom, subdued and yet serene of spirit. In the night hours they had committed themselves yet once again to the Lord's purpose for them. They were ready to return to Zaire.

the Kikwit General Assembly

Delayed by his need for medical care, Kabangy was unable to participate in the CMZa General Assembly the summer of 1978. In his absence the sessions had been formally opened by the CMZa Vice-President Kabongo Bukasa. By this time the broad membership of the Church had had time to read and ponder the thrust of the Church's bylaws which had been reworked two years previously by the CMZa General Council at Kandala. The church at large did not like what it discovered. While the council members at the Kandala meeting had seen their actions as efforts to strengthen the hand of the CMZa central administration amidst troubled times in their country, the rank-and-file membership saw the new bylaws rather as a ploy to concentrate a large degree of authority in the hands of a small group of people. What was worse, the new bylaws envisioned a small, self-propagating group which could make a variety of major decisions for the Church while largely insulated from the voice and vote of the people of the CMZa districts which by now had grown to a total of 25.

Kabangy's absence notwithstanding, the delegates determined to assert their prerogative as the ultimate authoritative body of CMZa and to rescind a number of the decisions earlier made at Kandala. Of particular note were their decisions to fix April 30, 1980, as the end of term for the officers of the central administration; to hold elections during the general assembly of 1979; to inaugurate biennial general assemblies thereafter; to ask for public reporting on the operation of the new saw mill project; to stipulate that the districts elect their own district leadership rather than allowing this decision to be made by the CMZa Administrative Committee; to make clear that district contributions to the cost of central administration be made according to their ability and resources and not the 20% of district receipts stipulated by the Kandala minutes; to insist that proposals for the hiring and firing of educational personnel originate with local church councils rather than with the central CMZa educational office.

Another action laden with significance was the assembly's rejection of Bukungu Mishumbi's offer to resign as CMZa General Treasurer. Amidst the take charge mood of this assembly, this action was a notable vote of confidence in and appreciation for this remarkable ex-school director from Banga District who had demonstrated unquestioned integrity in a highly sensitive role in the life of CMZa. (1)

Upon his return to his office in Tshikapa, the Kikwit minutes made startling and troubling reading for President Kabangy. How was he to interpret the actions of the assembly delegates in his absence? Had their earlier work at Kandala really been that misguided? Was this a repudiation of his leadership? Or was there genuine wisdom in what had been done? And what was he to make of the call for the election of officers at the next general assembly?

little time for pondering

After an absence of several weeks from his office, there was little time to dwell on what had transpired in his absence. There was a stack of work on his desk that clamored for attention. In early October AIMM Secretary Jim Bertsche came through Tshikapa on an administrative trip. In sessions with the personnel at the church headquarters, Kabangy placed heavy emphasis upon the necessity for discipline and integrity within the Church in the face of a steadily deteriorating Zairian society around them. A meeting of the full CMZa Administrative Committee ten days later reflected his stance. It was in these sessions that disciplinary action was taken vis-à-vis failed Zairian leadership at the Nyanga farm and in the CMZa literature department. A list of seventeen pastoral candidates were reviewed and approved for ordination. Among them was a young man from the Kamayala District of Bandundu Province named Chibulenu Sakayimbo (pr. tshi-boo-LEH-noo sah-kah-YI-mboh). The CMZa was to hear much more from this pastoral candidate in the future. It was also in these sessions that plans were laid for another administrative circuit through CMZa districts to be led by President Kabangy. As it turned out, it was a trip he was never able to make.

In the meantime, Kabangy was continuing chemotherapy via oral drugs. Though uncomplaining, it was noted that he gradually came to lean more heavily on his cane. It was clear that the pain in his left leg, which had nagged him so often in the past, was again returning. Forewarned by the American doctor, he recognized what was happening but continued his schedule of work to the full limit of his energy.

Christmas and New Years are traditional times of celebration for Zairians. Even as the Kabangy family, like others around them, celebrated once again the birth of Christ and prayed for God's blessing on the year ahead, Kabangy carried some troubling private agenda. He was estranged from a couple of key CMZa leaders. There had been differences of opinion and the exchange of sharply worded letters. Relations with them had broken down. He was not at peace. Via a traveling missionary he sent word to Kakesa Samuel in Kikwit that he longed for reconciliation. It is a measure of both men that, in response, Kakesa made a personal trip to Tshikapa to sit with Kabangy. In spite of their differences and the heated exchanges which had passed between them, they respected each other. Before Kakesa returned home, genuine reconciliation was achieved.

In the meantime Pastor Muhaku Boniface, the alienated CMZa pastor who had tried to establish a splinter church, lay ill in a hospital some sixty miles to the north of Tshikapa. Not only had his effort to found a new church collapsed but he had now been told that his sustained fever was an indication of an advanced state of tuberculosis. Calling a friend, he dictated a letter to President Kabangy. In a weak voice, frequently interrupted by coughing, he sketched the events and personal decisions which had led them on different paths and had eventually brought them into conflict. He freely admitted his error and his regret and asked for reconciliation with the CMZa and for personal forgiveness from Kabangy. By now obviously in failing health himself, Kabangy promptly acknowledged the letter and assured him that the sought for reconciliation was joyfully affirmed.

In early February, Kabangy became aware of a growing mass on his rib cage. Taken to the Kalonda hospital across the river from the church center, a biopsy was taken. Incurring tetanus in the process, he slipped into unconsciousness. With intensive care he rallied enough to regain consciousness.

final words of admonition and a dream come true

He then called his family and some of his closest associates around his hospital bed and made three basic statements which were widely circulated in the following months: "I am not afraid of death because I know that Jesus is my Savior. I hold no one accountable for my illness nor do I want anyone else to do so. Should I die, I accept it as the will of God for me. When my time comes to leave you, I want all of you to remain at peace with one another and to do all you can to strengthen and to carry on the work of our Church." (2)

It was not long after this final exchange with coworkers and loved ones that he once again slipped into unconsciousness. At about 5:00 AM on Wednesday February 28, 1979, Pastor Kabangy breathed his last.

Later that same day, Pastor Muhaku stirred on his hospital bed and signaled for his wife to come near. In a voice barely above a whisper he told her: "I've had a dream that fills my heart with joy. I've learned that I've been invited to a feast with Pastor Kabangy tomorrow. I've seen the banquet robe that's been prepared for me. It is beautiful beyond any clothing you and I have ever seen here in Zaire - - a robe we would never have enough money to buy. But the robe is ready for me. I've seen it and tomorrow, Thursday, I'm going to wear it at a banquet with Kabangy." (3)

That was on a Wednesday. That night Pastor Muhaku died. Some sixty miles to the south at Kalonda before the sun came up that same day, Pastor Kabangy had also died.

And the next day was Thursday!

burial at Kandala

Word went out in all directions via the Church's network of short wave transmitters. At Kandala the local church made a quick decision as to the burial site. Kabangy would be laid to rest midway in the wide path leading up to the chapel doors on the station. At Kikwit, Kakesa supervised the building of a coffin and arranged for its immediate transport to Kandala via truck. At Tshikapa a memorial service was held Thursday morning, March 1, in the chapel adjacent to the church headquarters after which his body was carried across the road to the airstrip where an MAF pilot waited to fly directly to Kandala.

Missionary Ben Eidse, who had worked very closely with President Kabangy in his last three years in his role as missionary counselor, picks up the account: "Some 1,000 people gathered at Kandala many of whom were obviously grief-stricken. The night vigil consisted of singing Christian songs, short sermonettes, typical Phende dancing and chanting and conversation around a number of *nkunyi* [wood] fires. Pastor Nkulu [regional ECZ secretary] came to assist at the funeral together with the Bandundu army chaplain."

A number of people were invited to reminisce and to make observations at the funeral. "Some points emphasized: he was man who liked to smile; a man of courage; a man whose great concern was the spiritual welfare and unity of the Church and who managed to hold it together in most trying circumstances."

Kakesa, who himself was ill at the time, had sent "a touching letter which went something like this: 'Dear Kabangy, you and l had our differences but these were all straightened out. We had a good long visit at Kalonda. I will do whatever is in my power for your family. Go well, Kabangy, we will meet again.'"

Regarding the committal service, Eidse yet added: "Kimbadi and four of her sons gathered around the casket and sang their goodbye - - very touching. Kimbadi did so well throughout the activities singing along wholeheartedly in so many of the songs. . . . We've shared so much these last three years; some affairs very difficult and trying, others beautiful and rewarding. The last verse I gave him was, 'Be still and know that I am God.'" (4)

In a circular newsletter addressed to fellow missionaries a month later Eidse reported further: "In keeping with Bantu custom, night vigils were observed with members of the family at Tshikapa, Mukedi and Kandala. At Kandala the people sat around a dozen fires. Close by, under a palm leaf shelter, the body lay in state. . . . Many Christian songs of assurance were sung. Mama Kimbadi, the widow, joined in these with feeling. The most frequently sung hymn through the night was 'Christ Arose' which obviously gave assurance of Kabangy's future resurrection. From time to time the Pastor would give sermonettes and pray. . . . From remarks heard from various parts of the CMZa area it is clear that the Church feels a great indebtedness to him. Concerns have been expressed about the future of the Church now that he is gone. What I cherish most in our relationship were the times we had counseling people together. At such times his sensitivity to peoples' feelings and his dependence on the Lord for guidance were an inspiration to me. I was also impressed with the courage he showed in making some particularly weighty decisions." (5)

Without question Eidse spoke for many, both white and black, when he wrote: "For myself, I feel a deep personal loss." (6)

CHAPTER 33   MIRACLE CAMP 1979

It was in 1971 that the AIMM had recommitted itself to an ongoing inter-Mennonite effort in Christian mission in Africa and set in motion a process of investigative travel both north and south of the equator. The spring of 1979 found the AIMM not only poised on the doorstep of the decade of the 1980's but also newly involved in regions of Africa far beyond the borders of Zaire. Within the space of five years, AIMM had placed missionary personnel in three new countries. To the south, AIMM was seeking to find its way in a ministry among African Independent Churches in Lesotho and Botswana and this in the shadow of a minority white government in the adjacent Republic of South Africa which was brutally applying its socio-political ideology known as "apartheid."

To the northwest in Upper Volta, on the fringes of the Sahara Desert, AIMM was having its first experience with the powerful, all-pervading influence of Islam. And in Zaire, where AIMM had served for many years, the emergence of autonomous Mennonite Churches and leadership was posing a whole cluster of different issues which needed to be faced. With each board meeting and each administrative trip to Africa, there was a growing sense that the time had come for the AIMM to engage in a thorough self-study. It was time to review AIMM's understanding of Christian mission, its definition of "the good news" and the assumptions which had undergirded its ministry across nearly seven decades of witness and service in Africa.

Preparation for the self study was thorough. Questionnaires were prepared and circulated probing experience and views of all AIMM missionaries on active status, one for Zaire and a different one for southern Africa. Five major study papers were assigned dealing with the five areas felt to be most germane to AIMM's work in the decade ahead. (1) In addition to the seventeen-member AIMM Board and staff, (2) there were also invited eight furloughing AIMM missionaries, Ray Brubacher representing MCC, Bill Wiebe from the Mennonite Brethren Board of Mission and Services (BOMAS), Hershey Leaman from the Eastern Mennonite Board of Missions and Charities, Vern Preheim and Bryce Winteregg from the Commissions on Mission of the General Conference Mennonite Church and the EMC/US. From Africa came Pastor Kazadi of the CEM. Given President Kabangy's death, the CMZa-appointed Mukanza Ilunga as its representative. In addition there were another dozen or so people invited for purposes of counsel and participation in the sessions of the working groups including two former AIMM Executive Secretaries, Harve Driver and Reuben Short.

The dates were set for April 20-23 which were to be followed by a brief session of the AIMM Board. The place chosen was a church facility named Miracle Camp on the shore of Bankson Lake in lower Michigan owned by the EMC/US. (3)

a backdrop traced

In an opening session the AIMM Executive Secretary sought to place the self-study exercise in context. He traced first what he considered to be some of the key decisions that the CIM/AIMM had made to that point in its history - - to resist early pressures to become an inter-denominational "faith mission" and to remain an inter-Mennonite organization; to probe west across the Loange River in the Congo after World War I in an effort to evangelize the hardy Baphende people; the decision to early join the Congo Protestant Council and thus to affirm, at least implicitly, its focus upon the concept of a Congo-wide Church of Christ with a concomitant soft-pedaling of denominational tradition and emphasis; to accept, after World War II, government subsidies for medical and educational programs thereby opening a decade of extraordinary expansion on several fronts as well as an influx of people into the Church for what proved to be a mixture of motives; to probe to the northwest of Djoko Punda in an effort to plant churches among the traditionally resistant Bashilele people; to broaden the constituent base in North America and to formally incorporate representation of a third Mennonite Conference (the General Conference Mennonite Church); to move to meet the revolutionary changes which were gathering force in the late 1950's in the Congo and to instigate dialogue with Congo church leaders concerning their autonomy; to stand with the Congo Church during the turbulent and bloody years of the early 60's at the expense of separating missionary families and sending men back alone; to undertake a joint experimental rural development program with the MCC which opened the door to a steady

311

flow of gifted Paxmen and VS people assigned by MCC to this and other development efforts; to begin, in 1967, a systematic, deliberate process of transition from Mission to Church by training a cadre of African leaders to replace missionaries in a gamut of leadership roles; to reach out to an independent Mennonite Church which had emerged in the South Kasai out of bitter tribal conflict and to give leadership to efforts to heal wounds and to re-knit bonds of respect and love; to forge and sign with Zairian Church leaders a document known as the fusion agreement; to adopt a new name in 1971; to probe opportunities for service outside Zaire and to extend official invitations to the Evangelical Mennonite Conference of Canada and the Mennonite Brethren for collaboration in Africa; to place missionary personnel in southern Africa and in sub-Saharan Africa ; and , "finally, after placing missionary personnel in three new African countries within the space of five years, the decision - - indeed the necessity - - of meeting in the consultation which is beginning here today." (4)

Moving beyond the listing of what were considered to be significant CIM/AIMM decisions of the past, the AIMM Secretary then attempted to highlight what he considered to be "some basic assumptions implicit in this series of decisions and stances adopted by CIM/AIMM across the years - - that Christian mission is not an option to be accepted or rejected but rather a timeless mandate; that the emerging global body of Christ is the objective of true Christian mission everywhere and the eternal reality to which we ultimately want to make our contribution; that when it is our privilege to be the first to witness to people in the name of Christ we anticipate the emergence of communities of believers who will be Mennonite in name and in their understandings of the meaning of Christian faith and discipleship; that where we minister to already established churches, the opportunity for sensitive sharing of our understanding of the Scriptures and the Christian faith is also a legitimate part of Christian mission in Africa and that we engage in such ministries without ulterior motives; that to nurture and encourage African believers to probe the meanings of true discipleship in the context of their own society and culture is of utmost importance everywhere; that it is God through the power and instrumentality of his Holy Spirit, his Word and the ministry of his servants who builds the Church and that it is first and above all else his Church - - not Protestant, Catholic, Coptic, Baptist or even Mennonite; that a joint effort in mission makes possible the realization of goals which would be beyond the possibility of any single group alone; that the Gospel as proclaimed by Christ our Lord and as illustrated by his life has reference and relevance to the totality of human experience and need; that to attempt to isolate human spiritual need from human physical suffering within the context of Christian mission is to propagate a false dichotomy; that to address ourselves to one area of need to the denial and exclusion of the other is to preach a truncated and impoverished "gospel" which falls grievously short of the example set for us by our Lord; that in the light of his example, the one can neither be separated from the other nor can the one displace the other; that a mission organization, per se, is not an end in itself but a means to an end; and that the missionary is not a permanent fixture or indispensable to the emerging Church but can and should be replaced as qualified national Christians become available."

Having sketched this series of assumptions, the secretary invited the delegates to the consultation to review them for accuracy and to evaluate them "to determine the extent to which they need to be reaffirmed, amended, changed or supplemented as we look toward the decade of the 80's." (5)

In concluding his presentation he referred yet to ongoing AIMM and MCC relations in Africa. There was their mutual history in Zaire which although overwhelmingly positive still had, on occasion, sparked differences of opinion as to what a Mennonite presence in that land should look and sound like. Now, once again, AIMM and MCC service tracks were intersecting, this time in volatile southern Africa where the seething social confrontation was coloring and impacting all else around it. Once again it had become clear that AIMM and MCC views as to how to respond in that setting in faithful witness and discipleship did not always mesh. Seeking to address this issue early in the proceedings, the secretary observed that "CIM/AIMM's affirmation of the social dimensions of a full-orbed Gospel is by now a matter of record. It is furthermore my sincere hope that as we work during these days . . . we can make it abundantly clear that AIMM also carries genuine concern for peace and justice in a world and, more particularly, a continent that is so cruelly torn by hatred, brutality, exploitation and greed. But I also hope that this statement will leave no uncertainty as to our ongoing and unswerving commitment to witness to the fact that God was in Christ, reconciling the world unto

Himself and to seek to be agents and facilitators of that reconciliation which is a prior and enabling reconciliation for all others that we may seek to effect." (6)

a document hammered out

There followed three days of intensive interaction on the part of the broadly-representative Mennonite group gathered at the Camp. Central to the discussions was the goal of spelling out yet once again AIMM's self view as well as its priorities and strategies for ongoing witness and service in Africa.

Coordinated by board member Howard Habegger, all participants were divided into work groups to deal with the five core issues which were presented in a series of five study papers. Working sessions were alternated with plenary sessions during which there was feedback from the groups for testing with everyone. Final recommendations were presented to a findings committee chaired by Elmer Neufeld which, in turn, presented a final draft to the entire group. With some amendment and minor changes the document was unanimously adopted by the group as a statement of its findings and recommendations to the AIMM Board.

Mimeographed during the night, the results of the Miracle Camp sessions were submitted to the AIMM Board which convened the following day. An eight page document, it covered a wide range of issues. The following excerpts summarize the heart and thrust of the recommendations:

AIMM's understanding of Christian mission:

- The Bible is the final authority in all matters of Christian faith, life and ministry.
- Christian mission originated with God. It is his work and his people are called to participate in his mission.
- The core of the good news which the church is to proclaim is that in his death and resurrection, Jesus Christ has overcome 'principalities and powers' providing salvation for all who believe.
- Jesus Christ is the Head of the Church. Believers of every race, color and nationality are part of the universal church of Jesus Christ.
- We identify with the Anabaptist heritage which includes believers' baptism and fellowship in a local body of believers, the new community where the new life of Christ is visible.
- The Christian life can be lived only by a person who has entered into a personal and vital relationship with the Lord Jesus Christ brought about by the work of the Holy Spirit in conversion and sanctification.
- The new life in Christ leads to new life in the world. As a member of God's new community and empowered by the Holy Spirit, the believer earnestly seeks to live a life of servanthood in word and deed, calls others to the new reality of God's Kingdom and renounces violence of every kind, lives in peace with all men and identifies in caring and sharing ministries with those who suffer.

AIMM's stance in southern Africa:

- AIMM will give priority to the further development of Bible teaching/leadership training among African Independent Churches (AICs).
- Regarding the issues of justice and oppression, AIMM believes God created people to live in communities of love and acceptance. AIMM is opposed to both structural violence which holds people in poverty, illiteracy and powerlessness and to military violence by which national armies or guerrilla movements endeavor to impose their wills upon others.
- AIMM calls its workers to be more sensitive to the needs and aspirations of the oppressed. We also affirm the validity of a ministry to alleged oppressors as well as to those who maybe victims of ideologies such as apartheid and communism.
- The ministries of both AIMM and MCC in southern Africa are affirmed while acknowledging the unique perspective of each in the body of Christ.

- AIMM and MCC are encouraged to coordinate criteria in selecting personnel for areas where both are working. Such criteria shall include commitment to Jesus Christ, his purposes and his Church.

AIMM's stance vis-à-vis the AICs:

- AIMM's basic aim is that, through its involvement, both the AICs and the churches in North America should grow in maturity.
- In AIMM's ongoing efforts it is intended that more personnel be appointed in Botswana and Lesotho; that within the next five years possible ministry to AICs in the Transkei, Bophuthatswana and Namibia be explored and that the life and witness of AICs be carefully interpreted to the sending constituencies in North America.
- As for AIMM's ministry among AICs per se, effort is to be made to meet people where they are; to emphasize the person-to-person approach; to maintain teacher/learner attitudes; to work with people, not for them; to develop Christian education materials which are appropriate in method and content to the people being taught; to be open to discussions about development programs that are locally initiated; to encourage and provide for AIC ministries to North American churches; to encourage AICs to relate to each other and to mission churches in a spirit of love and understanding and to share our concern for AIC work with other mission agencies.

AIMM's stance vis-à-vis Zaire's autonomous Mennonite Churches:

- AIMM underscores concepts of equality and mutuality as being crucial in ongoing mission/church relations. In Christ we are all equal. In Christ we all have gifts to give one another. The need to find ways of sharing our gifts with each other is affirmed.
- As the Zaire Churches seek to make their way from a stance of dependency to one of inter-dependence, AIMM sees that the following areas of cooperation will need particular attention and study: church funding of its own administrative costs; ongoing roles for missionaries within the Church; two-way fraternal visits; mission outreach by Zaire Churches beyond their own national borders; leadership training and the genuine contexualization of the Gospel within Zairian culture

AIMM's stance as an inter-Mennonite organization:

- As to its organization, it is agreed that AIMM add an additional staff person for purposes of promotion, publicity and public representation; that the AIMM Executive Committee be expanded to include representation from each AIMM-related conference; that warm working relationships be sought with MCC and MEDA wherever our interests intersect.
- As to its identity, AIMM sees itself to be more than the simple extension of any single one or combination of its member groups. AIMM is also more than the simple sum total of its constituent parts. While each member group makes its own clear contribution and would be greatly missed were it not there, the end result of the confluence and admixture of varied gifts, resources and strengths is a ministry which is immensely different on the one hand and immensely enriched on the other. (7)

Before leaving the Miracle Camp grounds the AIMM Board took the following action: "That the document of the AIMM self-study be approved as a basic statement of guidelines for AIMM with the understanding that more specific study and proposed action will be on the agenda for the next AIMM Board meeting." (8)

fresh directives plus a mood

The Miracle Camp consultation clearly closed on an upbeat note, a note which was r' AIMM staff editorial a few months later. Reflecting on the experience it was observed: "In on. assignment is clear enough. Some directions have been pointed. Some recommendations have been in. Some guidelines have been sketched in a forthright manner. From a purely administrative perspective, it is now a question of beginning to implement the directives and to try to follow through on the courses of action which are implicit in the document. . . ."

"There was, however, another aspect of the four-day experience at Miracle Camp which hopefully can also be preserved as we face the decade of the 1980's. This entails the capturing and nurturing of a certain mood which pervaded the sessions of study, dialogue and prayer. There were at least three ingredients of the Miracle Camp mood which might best be characterized as conviction, commitment and confidence. Perhaps the most precious . . . was a quiet confidence that the Lord's grace is sufficient for whatever assignments He has in store for us in the unpredictable decade ahead on the immense, troubled continent of Africa. The recommendations are in hand in writing. The impact of the mood is still fresh in heart and memory. We are grateful for both the directives and the mood. Even as we begin our efforts to implement the former, may we carefully nurture the latter. They are indispensable to each other - - and to us." (9)

"In conformity with the resolutions taken at the last General Assembly at Banga, especially in the article of the Assembly minutes relative to the imminent vacancy declared in the post of the Legal Representative of the CMZa, I have the honor to present myself to you and to propose to serve [CMZa] validly, honestly and faithfully before the State and other parties. . . . General Secretary, the first to support my candidacy will be you: that is my conviction!" (1)

Thus began a letter addressed on November 21, 1973, to Pastor Kabangy, the general secretary of the CMZa. The letter continued in part: "At the University I was taught to read the Bible before philosophy and to place the heart above the brain, to be humble, obliging, and to cultivate fraternity and peace within the church. Upon leaving the University, you ordained me a pastor. I believe you accepted to ordain me a pastor not because I am an intellectual but because you were above all convinced that I was a child of God, a man capable and worthy of the Gospel of our Lord which he was not ashamed to preach at the door of the paternal home at Nyanga . . ."

"A third generation Mennonite, it is needless to remind you of the sacrifice with which I've always proposed to work for the Mennonites, Africans as well as non-Africans, pastors as well as lay people." The letter was brought to a close: "In conclusion Rev. General Secretary, please believe in my constant attitude of prayer for you, for the administrative committee and the district church leaders. I ask you all to accept in advance my thanks for your confidence in your son of 31 years who is ready to devote himself for you." The letter was signed Pastor Mbonza Kikunga, Chaplain of the IMCK. [The Christian Medical Institute of the Kasai.] (2)

a bright student from the Kasai

Who was this young man who with such confidence submitted his candidacy for a key position of leadership in the Zaire Mennonite Church? Born in 1942 to Christian parents in the Baphende village of Kipoko on the banks of the Kasai River some 10 miles to the east of Nyanga Station, he began his quest for education, like many other rural children, in a little bush primary school in his home village. Staffed by the nearby CIM station with Christian teachers, he early heard about Jesus, a loving God and the Christian faith and committed his share of Scripture passages to memory in Giphende, his mother tongue, under the tutelage of his village teachers. This influence eventually led to his personal acceptance of Christ as his Savior and his baptism upon profession of faith.

He early demonstrated a quick mind and moved from class to class in his village setting with ease. Finishing the schooling available there he joined other youth of his area and enrolled in the central primary school at nearby Nyanga Station. Terminating the six year primary cycle of the Belgian system, he was enrolled in a two-year junior high where his growing command of French soon became evident. There followed four years in the station *Ecole de Moniteurs*, the Mission's top teacher training program of that era.

By this time it was becoming clear that student Mbonza's intelligence was linked with an independent spirit. He loved to ask probing questions in the class room and to debate issues with his class mates. He did not mind taking controversial positions now and again and sometimes needled his fellow students by cheering for a visiting soccer team at a match with his own school team.

an early influence

An early influence in his life was the senior pastor on the station, Rev. Mazemba Pierre who came from his own clan. Respected by all for his knowledge of Scripture and his deep commitment to his church, student Mbonza frequently found his way to the pastor's court yard. There he sat and listened as the aging leader spoke of his experiences and his love for his people and his Lord. Separated by age and by a widening gap of education, Mbonza nonetheless recognized in this man a depth of faith and wisdom which he both admired and respected.

But at the senior pastor's home there was yet a further attraction - - his youngest daughter, Dimuka (pr. dee-MOO-kah) Ana, whose demure manner and shy smile had not been lost on Mbonza. When upon graduating from the four year teacher training program he was given a teaching post on the station, he was well placed to maintain contact with the pastor and his family. The year Dimuka turned eighteen, Mbonza sent her a personal note proposing marriage. She responded by suggesting that he approach her father on the subject which he soon did. In the custom of the culture, his proposal was accepted and sealed in sharing a drink with the parents.

The following year their paths diverged. Mbonza left Nyanga to enroll in a pre-university orientation year of study at Kananga while Dimuka journeyed to Kajiji, the Mennonite Brethren station far to the southwest near the Angolan border, where she enrolled in the first year of a nurses training program. A year later, during vacation, Mbonza formalized marriage plans by the passing of a dowry to the parents. In fall he traveled to Kisangani to enroll as a first year student at the University in its school of theology. Meanwhile Dimuka stayed at home to spend a year with her mother who tutored her in the art of Christian homemaking in an African setting. The summer of 1968 she and Mbonza were married and she returned with him to Kisangani for three more years of study. It is interesting to note that in partial fulfillment of his graduation requirements he wrote a dissertation dealing in part with the issue of the separation of church and state - - a theme which was hardly popular in the Zaire of the early 70's.

Upon his graduation in the summer of 1971, they returned to Nyanga where they soon became familiar figures. He was the first member of the CMZa to graduate from a university level theological school. He was immediately given a mix of teaching assignments on the station which not only took him back into the secondary school from which he had earlier graduated but also into a new girl's high school which by that time was in formation at Nyanga.

Tall and slim, Mbonza enjoyed dressing in an immaculate fashion and using an excellent French that he had polished well during his years at the University. It was clear that given his academic accomplishments, he considered himself one of the first intellectuals of the CMZa. (3)

It was two years later, in 1973, that he was invited to attend the general assembly of the CMZa at Banga and was approved for ordination. Two months later the Nyanga District church leaders arranged for a special day of recognition for him and a fellow pastoral candidate from the same district, Muizu Kabadi (pr. MWEE-zoo kah-BAH-di).

ordination with a flourish

The African love for celebration seizes upon any occasion. After the formal service and ordination ceremonies came to a close in the station chapel, the fellow clans folk of the two candidates took over as they exited the church door. There was singing, clapping and dancing punctuated by the unique, high pitched trilling of feminine voices reserved for occasions of special joy.

The two candidates had arranged ahead of time for a joint feast to which a total of nearly 500 relatives, friends and missionaries were invited. In the midst of the festivities, a relative from his nearby home village appeared to place a beaded chief's hat on Mbonza's head and to drape him with a voluminous raffia cloth normally regarded as chief's attire. His fellow pastor was treated somewhat less flamboyantly and his gifts were less pretentious.

After abundant food and drink had been served it was time for speech-making. In a well prepared presentation Rev. Mbonza made a number of statements that were worthy of note: "I did not know the word 'vocation.' It is clear that today I finally have understood the word. Before, I sought its meaning with my brain without understanding that real comprehension of the meaning belongs to the heart. . . . The church made the decision concerning my ordination; my own church has made me a pastor. Men have made me a pastor. But I am convinced of having been called by Jehovah who chose me and anointed me today. I was a pastor before I became a pastor. I therefore consider the past as having been a time of preparation . . . for a sacred ministry to all."

"We consider, furthermore, that a Christian pastor is a cosmopolitan. He has no home town. He has no family. He is a friend of everyone. He has no enemy except sin. He has no favored group. He's not white. He's not black. He's not Catholic nor is he Protestant and even less Kimbanguist. He is a Christian pastor in as far as he is a friend and disciple of Christ. I believe firmly in Jesus Christ as my Savior and my Lord. For this reason we fight with force against the tendency to construct for the pastor any sort of throne."

"We affirm that the pastorate is a service among men for Jesus Christ. As such, this work manifests itself in simplicity and frankness, in availability for service everywhere, whether at home or elsewhere, there where there is need of the Lord, in the city as well as in the country. I hope to serve the church of Christ and to serve my country with greater effort and devotion and effectiveness than in the past." (4)

Ringing words, laudable goals, commendable insights all of which were all the more remarkable given the humble rural setting from which he had come. It would with passing time become increasingly difficult to mesh such early language with what was to become CMZa's unfolding story.

The next day Rev. Mbonza and Dimuka boarded an MAF plane at the edge of the station for an hour's flight to the east to Tshikaji, the site of IMCK (the Christian Medical Institute of the Kasai), the joint Mennonite/Presbyterian medical service and training center. Rev. Mbonza had been invited to become the first full time chaplain of that institution where AIMM missionaries John and Jeanne Pierson Zook served on staff as a physician/nurse team. It was from there that, two months later, Rev. Mbonza addressed his letter to General Secretary Kabangy posing his candidacy for the post of CMZa's legal representative.

Rev. Muizu Kabadi, the other young man who was ordained the same day with Rev. Mbonza, prepared himself and his family for a long journey to the southwest of Nyanga station to an isolated area of the district along the Loange River where he was assigned to serve as a supply teacher and itinerant pastor. A graduate of the Kalonda Bible Institute, his appointment and departure was surrounded with much less fanfare but he too was to find sheep who needed a shepherd.

a persistent dissident

At the general assembly of 1974 held at Kalonda, it was decided to combine the CMZa posts of general secretary and legal representative and that Pastor Kabangy should assume them both. Pastor Kabongo Bukasa, (pr. kah-BOH-ngo boo-KAH-sah) from the South Kasai, was elected as his associate in both roles. Thus the office for which Rev. Mbonza had submitted his application no longer existed.

Rev. Mbonza settled into his role as the IMCK chaplain with considerable skill. With passing time it became clear that he was not someone who left people around him without opinions as to his work. While there were soon those who were eloquent in their appreciation and praise, there were also others who were equally vocal in their reactions to him as a personality and a key leader on campus. Few people were neutral.

In the meantime circular letters written by Rev. Mbonza began to appear across the CMZa landscape addressed to district leaders in which he deplored what he saw to be poor CMZa leadership, lack of vision and, above all, lack of discipline and integrity on the part of those in places of responsibility and leadership. Such letters also typically carried the further comment that the CMZa was at a point in its history when it needed leaders of a high level of training and competence to lead it back to a level of spiritual health from which he maintained it was drifting.

319

In 1977, after four years of service as the IMCK chaplain, Rev. Mbonza left that post. In spite of his frequent negative commentary regarding CMZa administration, President Kabangy named him regional inspector of CMZa's secondary schools in the West Kasai and offered housing at Djoko Punda.

A couple of years later he was offered a similar post by the provincial government which he accepted. A move to Tshikapa in his new position placed him close to the CMZa headquarters and staff. Relations between them became steadily more strained with passing time.

After President Kabangy's death, the administrative committee convened in a special session on March 12, 1979, and officially authorized Vice-President Kabongo Bukasa to function as CMZa's President and Legal Representative until the next general assembly which was scheduled to meet in early 1980 at which time there was to be an election of officers. (5)

1979: a busy year in CMZa

Though it is in the nature of interim administrations to serve as bridges from one era to another, Rev. Kabongo was clear as to his personal vision and commitment. Less than a month after his installation as Pastor Kabangy's successor, he wrote: "Kabangy has died but his work and his philosophy will continue for as long as we who worked with him are still at the head of this Church as its leaders. Pray much for us and especially for our Church which is passing through such a difficult moment of its history. Pray also for a large family of ten children he left to be cared for and fed." (6) (7)

Official minutes of the CMZa's Administrative Committee revealed a wide range of activity and concern during the year. In a session during the month of June, disciplinary action was initiated regarding a pastor at Ilebo and a school director at Nyanga. Measures were taken to assure ongoing leadership at SEDA. A new printing of a Tshiluba hymnal was ordered and a new set of Bible lessons for children was encouraged. (8)

In an October meeting the committee responded in detail to five different regions where clusters of CMZa believers were requesting district status; sought to ascertain and provide for the cost of sending a CMZa delegate to a Pan-African Consultation for evangelists scheduled for Abidjan, Ivory Coast; requested the Department of Evangelism to do its best to establish statistics of actual CMZa membership; authorized the installation of five new dirt air strips in isolated CMZa areas; amended and approved a proposed CMZa budget for the following year; approved grants for roofing for three different CMZa chapels which were under construction; decided to delay official recognition of an Angolan refugee congregation in Kinshasa until such time as they could return to their homeland and there demonstrate their ongoing interest in and commitment to their professed Mennonite identity; encouraged Leona Schrag to pursue the idea of a first ever Youth Bible Camp during the upcoming school vacation; made a special request of AIMM for missionary couples to serve in evangelism and TEE in the urban centers of Kinshasa, Kikwit, Kananga and Mbuji Mayi. (9)

It was also in the fall of that year that the CMZa's eleven-member Medical Council (10) met for a major consultation. An opening item of business was to clarify and restate the basic objectives of the Church's medical service. Stated in the minutes of the meeting were the following: 1) fostering of spiritual growth of medical staff; 2) evangelization of those who come for medical care; 3) public health and 4) curative medicine. There then followed a series of 37 separate actions which ranged across issues of discipline and placement of personnel, opening of new rural dispensaries, supervision and supply of existing ones and overall budget concerns for a department which by this time was self-funding.

all eyes on Kamayala

But as the year ran its course, the press of church activity notwithstanding, increasing attention and discussion throughout the CMZa districts came to be focused on the impending general assembly scheduled for Kamayala. Far to the south, it had frequently been the location for small CMZa committee meetings but had never had the opportunity to host a general assembly. After repeated invitations, 1980 was to be the year. The dates: March 25-30. Given the harsh logistics of transportation, the delegate body was limited to two people per district plus three from Kinshasa and the fourteen-member administrative committee. It had been just over a year since President Kabangy's death. Who would now be chosen? No one within the CMZa family posed this question with greater interest than Rev. Mbonza who was now based in Tshikapa due to his position with the government department of education.

Following his arrival there, he and his wife Dimuka had chosen to identify with one of the newer CMZa congregations of that growing center which had adopted the name of its urban locale, i.e., Biantonde. (pr. Byah-NTOH-ndi.). Their services were held in temporary quarters just a mile from the CMZa church center. The group was under the energetic leadership of a talented layman named Mupemba Mulenda and Pastor Mutombo Simon, a Bible Institute graduate (pr. moo-PEH-mbah moo-LEH-ndah and moo-TOH-mbo). With some charismatic leanings the group featured energetic and spirited worship services. When in January, 1980, an administrative trip took Jim and Jenny Bertsche to Tshikapa, an early invitation was received from the Biantondi Church urging them to pay a visit to their group during their time in the area.

When the day came, the itinerating AIMM couple was met at the roadside by a delegation from the congregation and slowly escorted to their meeting place with swishing palm fronds, singing and dancing. Arrived at the palm branch shelter which served as their place of worship, they were greeted by the congregational leaders and escorted to seats before the assembled group. There were thoughtful presentations of various family units and individuals including the first adult Mennonite convert from the Babindi (pr. bah-BIH-ndi) people whose traditional tribal area lay to the southeast of Tshikapa.

Called upon for a brief meditation, Rev. Mbonza first read from Acts 14, then went on to comment that the AIMM representatives had not been invited so they could make requests for hospitals, schools, cow meat or an airplane (an obvious reference to requests often encountered by traveling mission delegations). No, the people of the Biantondi group had simply invited their guests to rejoice with them in the Lord. Following the service, a sumptuous African meal was served the visitors in a nearby member's home.

It was as the guests were later being escorted to their lodging for the night that further agenda surfaced. The Biantondi leaders had much they wanted to discuss with the AIMM couple. What time could be arranged? A long evening was subsequently spent with them during which they spelled out in detail what they perceived to be the shortcomings and evils of the CMZa administration of the time. They further left the clear impression that one of their number, i.e., Rev. Mbonza, would be qualified and happy to provide the needed correctives for CMZa were he given the opportunity.

In due time the CMZa headquarters circulated information detailing how the delegates to the impending Kamayala Assembly were to be gathered and transported. Many from the West and South Kasai were to rendezvous at Tshikapa from whence a large group would be put aboard a CMZa truck for the long trek to the south. On the appointed morning, Rev. Mbonza was among those who presented themselves for boarding. Since he was not an official delegate from any CMZa district nor a member of the administration, he was politely but firmly denied a place. Determined to be present at the assembly one way or another, he and Kandaiz a Kitamba (pr. kah-NDEZ ah gi-TAH-mbah), a maternal uncle, made arrangements for a truck and chauffeur on their own and followed the others to Kamayala. Though late, they arrived finding the assembly at work.

Under the adopted theme "The Church, a Community of Discernment," the opening session featured greetings and welcomes from Rev. Kabongo Nawej (pr. nah-WEHJ), the regional CMZa representative, Rev. Chibulenu Sakayimbo (pr. tshi-buh-LEH-noo sah-kah-YI-mboh), the chairman of the hosting Kamayala District and by Rev. Kabongo Bukasa, the CMZa President who in the course of his opening remarks called for a moment of silence in memory of President Kabangy. Former CMZa officer Tshilembu Nicodème from Kananga was elected chairman to whom were added a vice-chairman and two recording secretaries. All delegates were assigned membership on one or another of the working commissions. Plenary sessions were interspersed with Biblical messages from Kabangu Thomas, a gifted pastor evangelist from the South Kasai, Malembe Tshingudi, the Kalonda Bible Institute director and AIMM missionary Levi Keidel.

Though the assembly schedule was a demanding one, the delegates from the various areas still found time to caucus periodically to compare notes and to discuss what candidates were to be submitted for the elections at the end of the week. Those from east of the Kasai River strongly supported the incumbent President, Rev. Kabongo. Those west of the Kasai were mentioning two names - - Rev. Mukanza Ilunga and Rev. Mbonza Kikunga. Although there were frequent references made in public sessions to the conference theme of "discernment" and public prayer was often offered for the Lord's guidance in this process, many of the delegates were keeping their own shirt-pocket tallies as the various district delegations confided what their vote would be. Overall there was a growing undercurrent of intense lobbying on the part of delegates from west of the Kasai for the election of a president who, as they phrased is, "had the training, the poise and the intelligence needed to lead CMZa into a new decade of its history amidst a politically and socially volatile Zaire. Our church is now our responsibility. We must face up to it and elect our best qualified candidate," it was insisted.

This emphasis was without question timely and of genuine importance. Unfortunately, the behind-the-scenes debate which was taking place the spring of 1980 at the Kamayala Assembly stemmed primarily from tribal and regional loyalties. (11)

On the first ballot cast, Rev. Mbonza won by a slim margin over incumbent President Kabongo. Rev. Mukanza Ilunga was third in the balloting. Realizing this meant that he was again being asked to serve as CMZa's Vice-President, Rev. Kabongo declined the post. Rev. Mukanza was then declared as CMZa's new appointee to that position. General Treasurer Bukungu François had at the outset of the assembly submitted his resignation. Recognizing that they had just elected two men from the western area of CMZa territory, Bukungu was told that he would be allowed to step down only when a valid candidate could be proposed by the eastern CMZa districts and he had had opportunity to orient his successor to his new office.

a talented new leadership team

In terms of its leadership, CMZa clearly had turned a new page of its history. Their two key officers now were by far and away the best trained and most knowledgeable of any who had preceded them. They now had a president with a degree in theological studies from the University of Kisangani, Zaire, and a vice-president who held a degree in Christian Education from AMBS in Elkhart, IN.

In reporting to the home constituency at a later date, the AIMM Executive Secretary described what he called four distinct successive sets of CMZa leadership in the following terms:

a) The first gray heads symbolized by the Kazadis and the Ngongos who were accomplished evangelists/pastors who had benefitted from on-the-job training working side by side with their missionary colleagues and manifested a tendency to defer to their judgement in matters relating to the church.

b) The transition team, Kakesa, Tshilembu and Bukungu who were directly oriented and trained by missionary counterparts and who worked with them closely on a day-to-day basis but who began to make independent decisions in keeping with their responsibilities.

c) Pastor Kabangy and his team who had specific theological training at a post-primary level. A step removed from direct missionary roles in church administration, they nonetheless frequently sought missionary counsel and advice.

d) Rev. Mbonza and his associate Rev. Mukanza who have the highest training of any of their predecessors. With a broad grasp of Zaire's problems they have clear opinions as to appropriate roles for their missionary collaborators within the church and are not averse to challenging both mission and missionary. A bit thin-skinned, they long for true AIMM/CMZa interdependence and yet are forced to recognize their ongoing need for support in missionary personnel and budgetary grants. (12)

In truth, as the Kamayala Assembly delegates trekked and bounced their ways back to their far-flung districts of origin, it was with a sense of having put a "blue ribbon" set of leaders in place. Though the votes had been close and energetically contested, there was nonetheless now a consensus among them that they would be represented and led by unusually qualified and accomplished men.

Gifted and trained they were. They also offered a dramatic contrast in personalities and temperaments. If they would jell into a working team, CMZa had every reason to anticipate a time of extraordinary vitality and ministry. But if not, the potential was also there for extraordinary problems.

It had been "like a picture of hell" said one who had witnessed the scene. A tall, tower-like bamboo structure was completely enveloped in flames. People were being roughly herded and shoved into a tight perimeter around the base of the fire, nude except for their loin cloths, jumping about and crying out in fear as their bare skins were showered by glowing embers in the fierce heat. Safely outside the reach of heat and flame was an immense crowd shouting their condemnation and expressing their glee at the sight of the "guilty" being punished for their evil deeds. The fiery night was the culmination of several days of an intense anti-witchcraft movement designed to reveal and punish those who were in any way believed to be involved with the practice or paraphernalia of occult power. And, of all places, the scene was situated just off the edge of Nyanga Mission station in what was commonly referred to as the Christian village.

life viewed through African eyes

Traditional religious beliefs and practices of Africans vary greatly from one ethnic group to another. There are, however, some views broadly shared all across black Africa. There is, for instance, the common belief in an all-powerful God who created and put all things into place. While the name used for this God varies from tribe to tribe, the general belief in this God as the source of all things is broadly shared. In the CMZa territory, the term used to refer to God is Nzambi (pr. NZAH-mbi) or some variant of it. But there is a second belief also generally held, namely, that this creating God - - for whatever reason - - has withdrawn from his creation and remains aloof, largely unconcerned and basically unapproachable except in special circumstances and then only by special clan leaders.

On the heels of these traditional African views there follows yet another one. If the creator God has basically disengaged from the day to day routines of human life, there is a very real supernatural, nonmaterial world in which the African is literally immersed from birth until death with which it is crucially important to come to terms.

For lack of a better word, the term "animism" has frequently been used to describe this African understanding of his/her world. Originally coined by British anthropologist Edward B. Tylor in 1866, it was derived from the Latin term *anima* and carried the connotation of "breath" or "breath of life." Pursuing this concept further, Tylor expressed the opinion that in preliterate societies "soul stuff" is not limited to human kind; that both animate and inanimate objects have their own particular "power" or "force." (1)

A variety of African scholars have expressed their discontent with both the term and its usage in anthropological and missiological literature. There is nonetheless agreement that in traditional African societies there is the perception that spirits "are ubiquitous; there is no area on earth, no object or creature, which has not a spirit of its own or which cannot be inhabited by a spirit." (2) There is, further, the concept of a gradation or hierarchy of power: 1) God as the ultimate explanation of the genesis and sustenance of all things; 2) spirits; 3) human beings; 4) animals and plants; 5) inanimate objects. (3)

Regarding the spirits, the African defines three basic kinds: 1) a multitude of minor divinities; 2) ancestral spirits and 3) evil spirits. (4)

The first category are considered to have their origin in a creating God and can serve as his emissaries. Though they can be capricious at times, they are generally benign and exercise great power in a wide range of human affairs. (5)

The ancestral spirits are frequently referred to as the "living dead." This is an apt description as they are literally viewed by the African as clan members who remain present in the village in disembodied form after death. They are the unseen observers of ongoing village activities and the unseen listeners as conversations ebb and flow around the hearth fires. If honored and remembered in day to day clan activity, they can respond by providing good fortune and blessing. If forgotten or slighted or vexed, they can act in malicious ways causing misfortune or calamity for the clan.

The last category of spirits is considered to be "entirely evil, constantly seeking to distress mankind." (6) While there is no uniform explanation in African society as to their origin, there is complete agreement as to their perverse nature and the constant danger which they pose for human beings. Some ethnic groups explain that evil spirits have their origin in people who lived evil lives before their death. Others believe them to be the spirits of people who died abnormal deaths; still others hold that they are deceased witches. Whatever their origin, in Africa there is universal belief in and fear of these supernatural beings.

nothing "just happens"

The context of daily life, then, as viewed by the traditional African, is one in which there is constant interaction between spiritual powers which can at any moment impact the individual for either good or evil. The large mountain with an unusual profile, the deep forest, the noisy waterfall, the hovering disembodied ancestors, the lurking evil spirits all represent supernatural forces to be reckoned with. The spirits present in nature must be respected. The "living dead" must be honored and placated. Protection must be found against evil spirits.

Thus it is that footpaths which crisscross the countryside between villages will sometimes skirt certain areas even if it means a longer walk. Thus it is that cups of palm wine or food offerings are ceremoniously offered to clan spirits. Thus it is that the confectioners of protective amulets and charms and potions do a brisk business as people seek to secure something which will ward off potential harm. This traffic in charms is fed by the belief that it is possible for evil spirits to take possession of humans with resulting depletion of vital life forces causing illness or deranged mental capacities or even death. It is not coincidental that typical greetings among the Baphende people are "Muakola?" i.e., "Are you strong?" or "Ngolo jiji?" i.e., "Is there strength?" In Kituba, the far-ranging trade language of western Congo, it is the same question: "Ngolo ikele?" Among the Tshiluba speaking people a universal greeting is simply "Muoyo wenu," i.e., literally "Your life." Among the Chokwe people, a favored greeting is also "Mwoyo," i.e., "Life to you." In brief, there is tremendous preoccupation with the preservation of inner spiritual force and well-being in the midst of a potentially dangerous world of spirits and the agents of occult power.

The African's world is intricately interconnected. The African sees himself as an inextricable part of a web-work of life which englobes both the seen and the unseen, the material and the spiritual, the living and the "living dead." Out of this context grow two realities: First, life is of one piece, woven of a single fabric. For the African "his world is spiritualistic as opposed to materialistic. Any distinction between the religious and the secular is meaningless. Whatever happens in the physical world has its spiritual coordinates and whatever happens in the spiritual world has its physical coordinates. There is an interconnectedness of the whole of the universe through the animation of 'will' and 'power' contained in both animate and inanimate objects. Everything man does, handles, projects and interacts with is interpenetrated with the spiritual. His socio-cultural structures, to their finest details, come under the control of spiritual powers or forces. Nothing in man's environment escapes the influence or manipulation of the spirit world. The world is more spiritual than physical, and spiritually upheld." (7)

For the African there is yet a second reality. For everything that happens, there is a cause. Regarding this perception Stephen Ezeanya comments: "The world of men and the world of spirits are not two independent worlds for the one signifies nothing without the other; they are complimentary. Man has need of the spirits; the minor spirits, on the other hand, have need of men to rejoice their heart and to nourish themselves with their abundant offerings. But the fact must be underlined that between the world of men directed by spirits, and the world of spirits, there is order which reigns and not chaos. The spirits can upset the order of the universe in order to punish human fault but man has the means to prevent such disaster and to restore order when it is upset. . . . This is why nothing happens by chance." (8)

two key people of the traditional African world

Given this "cause and effect" view of human experience, every misfortune, disease or death is viewed with deep suspicion. Hanging over all trauma is the haunting question, "Why?" (9) Particularly is this the case in the event of a severe accident, a lingering illness or an abrupt death. In African society there is no such thing as a natural death. Except for tiny infants and the very aged, all death is caused somehow by someone. For an answer they go to a diviner. They explain their experience in detail and then wait for an explanation. What they have come to find out is the source of their trouble. Has it befallen them because one of the "living dead" is displeased with them? If so, they know what to do for there are tribally prescribed amends to be made to regain their favor. Or is their trouble due to evil spirits? If so, the individual knows that he or she must seek out those who can fashion protective charms or fetishes to keep such spirits away.

But frequently the verdict of the diviner is that the questioner or his clan have been the object of sorcery. In this case the person who has sought him out demands to know who is responsible. Eventually the diviner will provide a name. In such a case, anger and a desire for revenge come powerfully into play. Though dreaded and hated in African society, a sorcerer is nonetheless sought in order to secure some sort of punitive response to be directed in return toward the individual declared responsible for the clan's misfortune. A deadly cycle of accusation and counter accusation, attack and counter attack is ever in process - - much of it shrouded in secrecy but the subject of endless suspicion and rumor.

African perceptions of how a sorcerer can operate vary from tribe to tribe. An occult attack on someone else, it is believed, can take one of two forms - - 1) the creation of a powerful, destructive fetish which is given to the individual seeking revenge which can be "activated" at the will of the owner or 2) via a direct action of some sort on the part of the sorcerer. This, in turn, can take a variety of forms. Among them are the pronouncement of a curse causing a lingering, debilitating disease, a fatal accident or an unexplained sudden death. There is also common belief that the sorcerer is capable of transforming himself into animal or bird form, travel at night and waylay the intended victim. Still another perception is the sorcerer's ability to simply "eat" the inner, vital life powers of an individual leaving him or her to simply waste away. On more than one occasion a missionary doctor has observed an African village patient slowly deteriorating in spite of repeated exams and tests which revealed nothing physically wrong. Missionary doctors have also had occasion to witness the recovery of such people when clan elders took over, diagnosed the problem as deriving from a "curse" and resorted to cultural methods of "lifting" it from the victim. Once reassured that this had been done, the dying person began to recover.

the phenomenon of anti-witchcraft movements

Such anti-social and destructive conditions tend to feed on themselves. Social tensions finally build to a point where one of two things happens: Either clan groups which are caught up in such tensions split into smaller groups and move away from each other or some dramatic anti-witchcraft movement erupts designed to "cleanse" entire areas. Such movements serve a variety of purposes some of which are to reveal openly the sorcerers among them, to verify those who have secured and launched sorcery against others, to discern and free those who have become the victims of sorcery and, finally, to gather and destroy all objects of whatever nature that are related to destructive occult power.

AIMM missionaries have had opportunity to observe such social convulsions in African tribal groups in the past. During the 1950's, two such movements erupted in the Mukedi region. Both were associated with local Catholic priests who in effect became key players in the process. One movement came to be identified by the term "lusampulu" (pr. loo-sah-MPOO-loo), i.e., the local Giphende term for holy water. Whatever its origins, the word began to circulate that the priests could come into a village, round up all objects of sorcery, cleanse the village and leave each household with a little bottle of "lusampulu" which would protect the inhabitants from further danger of sorcery and, especially, from lightning, a common and destructive occurrence in tropical Africa.

The movement quickly gathered momentum. Delegations of village chiefs and elders came from far and wide to the Catholic Mission pleading for the priests to visit and cleanse their villages of sorcery. Recognizing an unusual opportunity, the priests soon laid down a set of conditions for each delegation: the construction of a chapel, class rooms, housing for their teachers and the inscription of a certain number of new children in their village school. Villagers turned out en masse and worked from dawn to dusk to meet the conditions laid down. If in order to meet their imposed quota of new students they needed to withdraw a few from the local Mennonite school in their village, that was fine. A day would be set and the priest arrived with a flourish. Newly built facilities were inspected and new students lined up for enrollment. A place was then designated in the midst of the village and all were ordered to go to their homes and return with all their charms, fetishes and objects related to sorcery. A growing mound of objects soon began to take shape. The priests were not easily satisfied and villagers were sent back to bring what they had "forgotten" the first time. When finally assured by the chief and elders that the village was "swept clean," the heap of paraphernalia was doused with kerosene and set ablaze.

Large enamel pans were then produced and the villagers were ordered to fill them with spring water into which some rock salt was sprinkled and stirred. Then they were invited to come with little bottles to each receive their portion of protective "lusampulu." As the day drew to a close, the villages were given a final warning. The potion they now held in their hands was very powerful. If anyone attempted to again bring objects of sorcery under the same roof with it, there would be dire consequences for all in the house. And, they were reminded, it was particularly effective against lightning. Such scenes were replayed in village after village in the area until one day lightning hit a home in one of the villages already visited. A couple of people were killed in spite of their bottles of "lusampulu." Understandably, the number of village delegations to the Catholic Mission rapidly dwindled thereafter.

A few years later another movement surfaced in the same area and once again the Catholic priests were integral parts of it. The demands for housing and school children were the same and the routine of gathering and burning objects of witchcraft were the same. Only this time the villagers were left with a large wooden cross erected at the edge of the village which was to be the symbol of their cleansed status and the assurance of their safety. In time the trusting villagers were once again disillusioned as illness and death continued in the village as before, the towering crosses at village edges notwithstanding.

In the euphoric atmosphere which characterized the period leading up to political independence in June, 1960, the word was that if any object of witchcraft was sheltered by anyone, independence would not come. In eastern Bandundu Province there came a wave of massive pressure to eradicate all animals and fowls which were black in color. To this were added certain trees which carried particularly dense foliage and consequently cast solid shade. There followed an incredible slaughter of precious livestock and the felling of beautiful, useful trees. The color black, it was declared, indicated likely shelter for evil spirits among them. Until these were removed, independence would not arrive.

In the early 1970's in the area west of Tshikapa, a different sort of movement emerged which also had as its focus the combating of witchcraft. In village after village small grass and stick huts were constructed. From the roof of each a wire was strung leading to the top of nearby palm trees. These were declared to be "antennae" via which movement leaders kept in communication with their peers in other locations. Information was said to be exchanged concerning the status of witchcraft and its practitioners across the region. Meanwhile the huts and their "antennae" stood as warnings in the villages that any further trifling with the occult would immediately be detected and exposed.

Although there is great diversity in such movements, there are nonetheless some common denominators which unite them all - - an unwavering belief in the reality and menace of witchcraft, recurring cycles of efforts to expose its presence and practitioners and to deal with both in an effort to relieve destructive tension within the society.

the Manesa story

Early in 1980, the Nyanga region was the scene of high drama. There were two key players, i.e., a local resident named Kasongo Pusa (pr. kah-SAW-ngah POO-sah) and a stranger from the Bandundu region known only as Manesa. (pr. mah-NEH-sah) Kasongo was an influential man in the area. An early convert and long-time member of the Nyanga Church, he had in his earlier years traveled with missionaries as a supervisor of rural mission schools. Tall, well built, alert, quiet spoken, he had a commanding air about him. He also had administrative and leadership gifts which served the Nyanga district school system well. He furthermore had a gift for business. Even while he worked for the Church, he maintained a small retail shop beside his home. Carefully saving and investing his earnings, the day came when he was able to purchase his own truck which he used to expand his commercial interests. When better-trained educational personnel became available, he was replaced in his role after which he devoted full time to his commercial enterprise. By early 1980 he had been appointed as mayor of the local Nyanga community and simultaneously became the principal representative of Zaire's political movement, the MPR, in the local township in which Nyanga station was located. Thus his status as a successful business man was further enhanced by his appointment as a lower echelon political figure.

Faithful in his church attendance and generous in his giving, Kasongo, however, decided to go against the grain of the teaching of his Church in one area of his personal life. He took a second wife. It was not long after this that she began to experience a mild epileptic condition with occasional seizures. This was very troubling both to her and to her husband. They sought counsel and help from the local church medical personnel. They were told that while medications could be given to control it somewhat, there was no known cure.

It was then, in early 1980, that the Nyanga area people began to hear about a Zairian man named Manesa. At first said to be an *Abbé* (a French term used for one category of Catholic cleric), he was traveling about the countryside wherever he was invited to expose and eliminate witchcraft. Hearing that he was able to determine if an illness was due to evil power, Kasongo sent his wife to consult him. Upon appearing before him she was told that in order to deal with her problem he needed first to begin in the house of her husband for it was "full of spooks." Hearing this, Kasongo determined to bring Manesa to his home which stood just a short distance from the border of Nyanga Station.

A mix of news and rumor spread like wildfire. Manesa has come to Nyanga. He can reveal both those who have been the unknowing victims of witchcraft and those who have actively engaged in occult practices with resultant suffering for others. Soon people began arriving from surrounding villages converging on Kasongo's house and yard. Some came out of sheer curiosity while others came to consult him regarding their personal illnesses or fears. There soon emerged a procedure which was followed with many hundreds of people. As inquiring individuals came they were placed, one by one, before Manesa. He would gaze intently at their foreheads and the backs of their heads. There then would be one of three verdicts: 1) "This person has neither been hexed nor has s/he initiated any such activity vis-à-vis others; 2) yes, this individual has been hexed. Go, slaughter a chicken, cook it and eat the heart. You will then fall into a trance and utter the name of a person. That person is the one who has exercised witchcraft against you. 3) Yes, you have been guilty of practicing witchcraft." For those declared guilty, whether by direct accusation or via names revealed by those who had eaten a chicken heart, they were brought to an area where they were forced to walk between a double line of local political youth cell members while being pummeled and loudly castigated on all sides. Arriving at the end, their heads were shaved clean. They were then warned that when they were later summoned, they were to return without fail for their final cleansing.

As the process gathered momentum, there was soon a shift from dealing with volunteers to one of growing coercion. Tallies of people who appeared before Manesa were being kept. Before long people from the area were being accosted with the question: "Have you gone to Manesa yet?" Very soon failure to do so was interpreted as evidence that the individual in question had something to hide. Enormous social pressure built very rapidly. Mixed with this were the names whispered to Manesa of people thought to have practiced witchcraft in one form or another. Members of the local political youth cell were then quickly dispatched to bring the accused people to stand before Manesa and to await his verdict. In this supercharged, near hysterical atmosphere, the wildest rumor became instant fact. "A 'witch tree' had been discovered in someone's back yard. It was, in fact, a 'witch hotel,' a gathering place for witches from far and near where they met periodically to plot their deadly nocturnal activities." The "witch tree" was chopped down on Manesa's orders. "A hole had been dug in the dirt floor of someone's house who practiced witchcraft. A big granite pan of fresh, clear water had been found under the dirt floor with a live fish swimming about in it. A village chief renowned throughout the area for his powers of witchcraft was on his way one night to engage Manesa in a test of occult power. En route he encountered a violent storm and was forced to return to his village defeated." (As a matter of fact, there had been an unusually violent tropical storm in the Nyanga area one night during Manesa's stay.)

While a large majority of those who came or were brought by force were villagers from the surrounding region, some church members were also experiencing increasing pressure. When they protested their innocence, the stock response was: "If you are innocent, Manesa will know. If not, we intend to find out." Before he leaves we want to reveal everything and everyone who has any link with witchcraft in our community. When he leaves, we want to live in peace and without further fear. Pressures to conform, on church members and non-members alike, were enormous. The marvel is not that some professed Christians finally allowed themselves to be brought before the diviner. The marvel was rather that some defied all efforts to coerce them. Typical of these was gray-haired Pastor Mazemba Pierre. He later would calmly tell a missionary: "I rejected all of this business years ago when I accepted Jesus as my Savior and my *Fumu* (pr. FOO-moo, i.e., my chief); I have had nothing to do with witchcraft. To appear before a man like this it would require being dragged there by a rope around my neck. I would never go of my own free will. I'm an old man now. I've lived many years. I've made my peace with my *Fumu*. I now only wait for his call to join him in his village above." (10)

There were also other Nyanga Christians who stood their ground, unmoved amidst the hurricane of public pressure which surrounded them. Among them were Mavule Kikunga (pr. mah-VOO-leh gi-KUH-ngah), a station pastor of a younger generation, and Dr. Makina, (pr. mah-KEE-nah), a Zairian physician and director of local church medical services of the time. (11)

As the Manesa episode drew to a close, things took a curious turn. Host Kasongo typed up and distributed copies of a "program" for the conclusion of activities. Missionary Levi Keidel was invited but understandably declined. After consultation with Keidel, however, Pastor Kikunga Mavule decided to accept an invitation to speak to the crowd at the closing ceremonies. The final night, all those who had been found "guilty" were assembled with shaven heads. They wore only loin cloths and were grouped around a tall bamboo framework. The interior was stuffed with dry grass. Around the base were heaped dry wood and mixed with all of the objects of witchcraft which had been gathered during the previous days. As the structure was set afire, the accused were forced to stand close to the flaming structure where they were showered with falling embers amidst the heat of the flames. When the fire began to die down, Pastor Kikunga was invited to bring a brief message. He chose themes of repentance and the consequences of sin. Before dispersing the crowd, Manesa invited all to scoop up small amounts of the ashes created by the fire and to carry them to their homes. They were to keep the ashes both as a remembrance of what had transpired and as "protection" for the future. Those with shaved heads were to sleep on their floors for two weeks after which they were to return to a normal routine of life. They were also admonished to go to church and to sin no more. At some later date he promised he would return to see if instructions had been respected.

Next morning, Manesa left Nyanga.

the aftermath

The Nyanga Church was left with some deeply troubling issues to deal with. Well over 2,000 people had either come voluntarily or been pressured to appear before Manesa. Four hundred forty-eight had been accused of some sort of involvement with witchcraft. The most troubling of all for the church council was the fact that among those declared by Manesa to be guilty were twenty-one church members including six in roles of leadership.

Feelings in the area ran high. "Aha! If unbelieving villagers were found guilty, that was one thing. But professed Christians too? That was inexcusable. What was the Church going to do about that? If no disciplinary action was taken, they might as well quit ringing the church bell because no one would again come to the services." The church council convened a special session to which all twenty-one members accused by Manesa were summoned. Pastor Kikunga, as council chairman, invited all to make statements of admission and repentance for any sins committed. The response was mixed. One person said that he finally took a packet of medicine to Manesa to get the people off his back. The medicine? Something he had purchased for his high blood pressure! Declared to be "witchcraft," it was added to the growing mound of confiscated items which were part of the closing night bonfire. Most of the accused resolutely denied any wrong doing no matter what Manesa had said. Given the supercharged atmosphere in which they were then meeting, the council finally decided to suspend the membership of the accused people until such time as they could be worked with individually in calmer circumstances.

Pastor Kikunga immediately set up a schedule of teaching sessions in each of the neighborhoods which surrounded the station in an effort to help Christians both to process what had happened and, more importantly still, to learn from the experience through which they had just come.

It was just a matter of weeks after the Manesa story that a traveling AIMM delegation visited Nyanga. As can easily be imagined, questions from this AIMM group regarding the Manesa story were many. (12) What, in reality, had happened? What had been fact, what had been fiction? And what about Manesa? Had he actually in some instances revealed witchcraft and its practitioners or was he primarily the clever stage manager of a hoax? African opinion differed widely. As for the African village community as a whole, there was a wide spread sense of relief. An emotional and psychological abscess had been lanced. People declared to be evil doers among them had been revealed and punished. Their dangerous fetishes had been exposed, gathered and destroyed. For a while, at least, they could breathe more easily.

And how did the church community view what had happened? First of all, Kasongo Pusa resolutely defended himself for he was under considerable local criticism for having precipitated such stormy days at Nyanga. Even though his second wife's health had not improved, he nonetheless insisted that he had done the area and the Church a great favor by bringing the diviner into their community with the resultant destruction of so much witchcraft. In the process of his defense he let it be known that he was disappointed that the missionaries on the station had not given their public support and approval for what he had instigated.

Among Nyanga Christians, something of a composite of views eventually emerged: "Yes, there is witchcraft among us Africans. Yes, there are people who have mysterious, dangerous powers. Yes, it is possible to direct such powers against innocent people. Yes, Manesa had genuine divining ability. How else, as a stranger and outsider, could he have exposed certain people who have long been known to practice witchcraft among us?"

Frequently the question was posed: "If, truly, he had the divining powers he claimed and seemed to have exhibited, were these powers from God or from Satan?" A common response was: "We do not know. But is it not true that even in Bible times God sometimes used evil people to punish his own people for their sins?"

"Are Manesa's accusations against a handful of Nyanga Christians true?" Some commented: "It is possible because we know that many of our fellow believers follow Jesus with two hearts. They come to church faithfully. They know the songs and Bible verses by heart. But in times of great sickness, suffering, fear or death, it takes a single heart and a pure faith to resist the pressures of our tribal elders and chiefs to stand in the name of Jesus alone. Whatever the case, it is a shame for us as a Church that a stranger using we are not sure what sort of power needed to come to expose and rid us of this sort of evil. Yes, powers of sorcery among us are real. Yes, there are powerful fetishes, but the power of our God is greater than all of this. If all our church

331

leaders were really doing their work and we Christians were all living and trusting Jesus as we should, there would be nothing for someone like Manesa to do among us."

fact or fiction?

The men of the AIMM delegation left Nyanga with most of their questions unanswered. In later reporting to the AIMM Board, the executive secretary observed: "We as westerners are clearly out of our element as we struggle to understand what we saw and heard at Nyanga this past summer. Perplexing from our perspective are the facts that there was near total belief in the guilt of all those accused; that there was no readiness to entertain the idea that at least some may have been innocent of wrong doing and thus were falsely accused; that the local Church simply accepted the validity of the list of names submitted to it by Manesa and acted upon the authority of his judgment. . . . Whatever else may be said, the African Church understands very well what Paul talks about in his letter to the Ephesians when he states 'that we wrestle not against flesh and blood but against principalities, against powers, against the rulers of the darkness of this world, against spiritual wickedness in high places.'" (13)

Recognizing this gulf between African and western world views, African scholar John Mbiti comments: "Myriads of spirits are reported from every African people but they defy description almost as much as they defy the scientist's test tubes in the laboratory. . . . Whatever science may do to prove the existence or non-existence of the spirits, one thing is undeniable, namely that for African people the spirits are a reality and a reality which must be reckoned with, whether it is a clear, blurred or confused reality. And it demands and deserves more than academic attention." (14)

With passing time, teaching in the Nyanga Church District took a more prophetic turn. Frequently preachers would state that "we've been put to shame. God will tolerate sin in the camp only so long. We need not marvel that we've been tested as by fire and found wanting. God has always called his people to repentance. He calls us as well."

Hearing continual reports and complaints about Manesa and his activities, the Catholic Church of the region formally disavowed any connection with him or approval of his activities. As he promised, some months later he revisited Nyanga. He again met with some people but there was neither the interest nor the wild acclaim he had earlier received. He soon left the area.

And there is, however, a melancholy postscript to this story. Less than a year after the Manesa experience, Kasongo Pusa was buried. He died in the IMCK hospital outside Kananga of cancer. It goes without saying that in the minds of many Nyanga area people there reverberated the haunting question: "Why?"

For the AIMM delegation that was scheduled to travel to Africa in the summer of 1980, the Zaire stop on their itinerary held particular interest. (1) It would be the first opportunity for AIMM Board personnel and staff for direct contact with the new CMZa leadership team elected earlier in the year at Kamayala.

There was no less interest in Zaire. Detailed travel was arranged for the American visitors which enabled them to stop at a number of CMZa districts before arriving at Nyanga where they would find the CMZa Administrative Committee already meeting in preparation for the joint sessions to follow.

In opening the first joint session, President Mbonza prefaced his remarks with the reading of Hebrews 13:14-21 which interestingly combined a reference to the transient nature of humankind, admonition to believers to be submissive to those responsible for their spiritual oversight and a well-known apostolic benediction. President Mbonza then went on to make a number of observations: This first joint consultation with the CMZa's new leadership team will determine much regarding future relations; in speaking of AIMM/CMZa we are in reality talking about the Church of Christ and if Christ is not present and honored in our deliberations, we will waste our time; CMZa "is your son, your daughter" and we are proud of that; the ties which unite us are precious and special; our discussions must be carried out in a spirit of sincerity and love. In conclusion he posed what he termed "a little challenge." He had observed that missionaries, like Zairians, tended to consider their personal church to be located where their parents were located. It was his hope, he concluded, that during the consultation which was beginning, the focus of discussion and thinking would simply be on the Church of Christ as such.

The sixteen members of the administrative committee included two missionaries (2) and represented CMZa districts all the way from Kinshasa to the west to Mbuji Mayi in the South Kasai. For those acquainted with an earlier chapter of CMZa leadership struggle, it was a joy to see Kakesa Samuel and his wife Kafutshi as well as Tshilembu Nicodème present as members of the new committee as it had been reconstituted at the general assembly at Kamayala earlier in the year.

Speaking for the committee, Vice-President Mukanza Ilunga then observed that the major concerns which they as committee members were bringing to the joint consultation might best be summarized under five general headings: 1) the spiritual needs of the Church, 2) service ministries among the needy people all around them both in rural and urban areas, 3) church leadership training, 4) financial problems and 5) their ongoing partnership with AIMM and its missionaries. Indeed, these general topics well covered the hours of dialogue and planning which followed.

discerning the spirits

President Mbonza and his newly-constituted leadership team had assumed office at a time when the CMZa was being buffeted by two different and powerful spirit movements. On the one hand was the Manesa phenomenon which had hit the Mukedi and Nyanga Districts among the Baphende people with such whirlwind impact. Arising, as it did, out of their own culture, the CMZa leaders were well aware of the dynamics which had spawned it. With regard to Manesa and his activity, there was no hesitancy. Condemnation was categoric and a call went out to CMZa district leaders everywhere to be watchful and to oppose it and anything like it. Evidence of this attitude was a minute of the committee in October, 1980, which read: "It is urgent that the President send out (3) pastoral letters to encourage and console the Church which is menaced by various pagan religious movements." (4)

When in early 1983 Manesa made a brief reappearance in the Nyanga area, the CMZa administrative response was even more vehement. A minute from a meeting of the CMZa Executive Committee read in part: "The Executive Committee, having heard the report of the Commission of Evangelism on the Manesa affair in the Nyanga District, declares itself as follows: It reminds the Church with insistence that Manesa symbolizes a diabolical current which circulates in our regions already for some time. . . . It finds no error on the part of

Reverend Mazemba Pierre but rather praises him for his attitude toward this diabolic power and proclaims him as an example of courage of the Christian faith to be imitated. . . . It has decided that this district should multiply prayer cells and evangelistic efforts to help and strengthen the life of this Church. . . . It requests the Department of Evangelization and Life of the Church to provide a Bible study based on the power of God and the Lordship of Jesus Christ." (5)

There was, however, another powerful spiritual movement also gaining attention during the same time which was far more widely spread and with which the CMZa leadership had less experience. There consequently was less certainty as to how to respond. Surrounded in the late 70's and early 80's by a crumbling economy and deteriorating social structure, the Lord saw fit to unleash some unique demonstrations of his grace and power in the lives of specific individuals and the Church as a whole. There were various strands in this movement.

Within CMZa, some of the earliest experience was centered in the city of Kikwit. AIMM missionaries Don and Naomi Reimer Unruh were stationed there for a time during this era for purposes of Kituba language study. While there, Don became aware of an inter-confessional, interracial Bible study/prayer group led by a Catholic Father. Don made inquiry and was warmly welcomed into the group. Later moving to Mukedi, the Unruhs found that word of this group had preceded them and Don was invited to give leadership to a similar gathering there. Mildly charismatic, the emphasis was clearly upon a search for deepened faith which would enable Christians to remain firm and fruitful amidst a Zairian society which was becoming more troubled and insecure by the day.

It was also at Kikwit that a young man named Miteleji Kibatshi (pr. MEE-teh-leh-ji ki-BAH-tshi) was based. Originally from Mukedi District, his commitment to his Church as an active layman and teacher in the CMZa's secondary school at Kikwit had come to the attention of church leaders. He was consequently appointed the president of the CMZa's chapter of Youth for Christ in that growing center. He plunged into his new role with enthusiasm and much success. Meeting him early in 1980, the AIMM Executive Secretary invited him to put something of his vision and experience in writing.

"We and our children is a topic which troubles and preoccupies me. There is among us a lack of conscience, irresponsibility, corruption and immorality. These are all sins which destroy people. They are a scourge among us for which only the Gospel is a remedy. The Lord holds me responsible before our present situation. Woe is me if I do not preach the Gospel. Thus it is that the Lord has organized through my efforts seven Bible study and prayer groups. We have also organized seminars. We are convinced that the Lord loves us and that He loves all the world. Because of this we launched our first campaign of evangelism here in Kikwit August, 5-8, 1979. . . . In the course of this campaign a total of 2,213 people attended of which 313 professed conversions to Christ. . . . A second campaign was held here in Kikwit during the holidays from January 3-5, 1980. The themes emphasized were: Prepare yourselves to meet the Lord; this generation is accused of crucifying Jesus a second time; be prepared and ready. The Lord himself was at work during those days for a total of 2,144 people attended the rallies of which 789 were brought to Christ. If together we believe in faith, Africa will be saved. Pray for us that the work of the Lord may spread and be put in application among us." (6)

Another significant contribution to the CMZa youth ministry was made by Charles Buller, son of long-time AIMM missionaries Peter and Gladys Klaassen Buller. Completing his college education in the spring of 1991, he applied for two years of voluntary service in the city of Kinshasa where he focused on the youth of the CMZa congregations of that city. Living simply, traveling with and sharing the diet of his Zairian peers, he was instrumental in organizing a series of youth groups in that sprawling urban center. The focus and concern was the same everywhere - - translating Christian faith into faithful witness, Godly living and supportive, caring fellowship. This pattern also spread and there soon were similar youth groups in some of the traditional CMZa districts up-country.

But the most far reaching spiritual impact stemmed from a renewal group which took shape on the campus of Louvanium University in Kinshasa. A key figure in the formation of this group was a remarkable Zairian named Nzash Lumeya (pr. Nzahsh loo-MAY-ah). A member of the CFMZa (Zaire Mennonite Brethren Church), he had received a scholarship which permitted him to study at *Vaux sur Seine*, a Protestant Theological School on the outskirts of Paris, France. Earning his degree in the mid-70's, he returned to Zaire where he was appointed as one of the Protestant chaplains on the campus of the University. A gifted, energetic man with a deep love for his Lord, he plunged into his new ministry with zeal. Encouraged by Dr. Aeschliman, a professor of urology in the medical school, Nzash succeeded in putting together a group of university students who found their way to deeper understandings of the Lordship of Christ in their lives.

A Mennonite student at the university early touched and influenced by this group was Makina a Nganga. After finishing primary school at Nyanga he began his secondary education elsewhere but transferred to the Nyanga secondary school for his last two years. Gifted with a good mind and armed with high grades he was able to secure a government scholarship for six years of study in medicine in the University at Kinshasa. He described himself as an "average Christian" who knew the teachings of his Church, some Scripture and who attended church services as convenient. Hearing of a Christian student group on campus he began to attend their meetings and soon discovered an intensity of spiritual fervor and commitment which was foreign to him. When on one occasion the discussion of the evening focused on the imagery used in Luke 9:62 of a plowman who looked back, it struck home. He recognized himself as being among those who though professing faith did not have Christ as the fixed focus of their lives. He experienced what he termed "a miracle" as he encountered Christ in a new way. Upon graduation he was assigned to Nyanga Station. As the medical director of the station's health services, he plunged into the life of his home church offering his time and services in such roles as volunteer chaplain at the secondary school, Sunday School superintendent and teacher of a class of secondary students. Established at Nyanga when the Manesa storm hit, he told one and all, "Sure there is sorcery but God's power is greater."

It was during the special Kikwit meetings described by Youth For Christ President Miteleji Kibatshi that a Mukedi secondary teacher named Kianza Nolisa-Nola (pr.KYAH-nzah no-LEE-sah NO-lah) was on vacation there. A professor in the teacher training section of the Mukedi school, he had left the station under a cloud of suspected adultery. Drawn to one of the public meetings in Kikwit, the word of God impacted him with life-changing power. In his testimony regarding his past life he said: "I was baptized. . . . I sang all the hymns but I didn't believe a word!" He had now experienced God's grace in a dramatic new manner. Not knowing what awaited him at Mukedi, he returned after vacation where he made public confession of his sin and sought forgiveness - - an electrifying event. Students began to flock to him for counsel, confession and prayer. Parents began to note changes in the life style and attitude of their children. News of his testimony spread and soon invitations came from other CMZa districts. Subsequent journeys took him to Kandala and Kamayala. When a storm forced a detour of an MAF return flight and caused a layover at Nyanga, Professor Kianza asked permission to meet in the station chapel at 4:00 PM one day with station secondary students. What followed was totally unexpected. After simply giving his personal testimony as a church member who had professed faith with his tongue but denied that confession with his life, he challenged the large group of students to examine their own lives. What had been scheduled to be a meeting of an hour or so eventually became a nine hour marathon of prayer, public confession of sin, pleas for forgiveness, reconciliation with both God and fellow students, singing, testimony and praise.

By this time, news of such events were spreading in all directions. What was happening? How were these kinds of events to be understood? What were they to be called? A French term *renouveau* meaning spring time or renewal or revival was pressed into usage. AIMM missionary Don Unruh, by then based at Mukedi, had become part of a team including Mukedi Professor Kianza which was holding seminars in various places as they were invited. At one point their travel took them to Kalonda for a series of study sessions which drew people from all directions some of whom walked long distances. President Mbonza went across the river with a delegation of people from the Biantondi congregation for each session. It was contacts such as these plus frequent conversations with Charles Buller which convinced President Mbonza that the *renouveau* movement reflected a genuine working of God's Spirit in many lives and that it represented a spiritual potential for the good for the church.

But not all CMZa leaders viewed these activities favorably. It was especially the older generation of pastors who split into two camps of opinion. While some rejoiced saying that they had been praying for years for a renewing demonstration of God's power among them, others insisted that this movement with its strong charismatic overtones comprised a threat to the stability of their church. Indeed, the young people who were active in these cell groups had a disconcerting way of pointing out what they felt to be the short comings and inconsistencies of some of their older pastors as well as the weaknesses and sins within their church. As a matter of fact, there were instances of pastors being defrocked after being exposed in personal sin by renewal groups. Being thus challenged in their leadership role, it was not surprising that some reacted negatively and exerted considerable energy in attempting to combat it.

This is not to say that the movement was trouble-free. As it spread, it began more and more to attract people of all ages. As the groups multiplied, frequently leadership roles fell to people who had inadequate understanding both of the movement's history and of Biblical teaching regarding the person and work of the Holy Spirit. Occasional irregularities and excesses became inevitable.

CMZa leaders, meanwhile, wisely decided to recognize and affirm the movement, as such, recognizing that if owned by and channeled within the Church, it truly contained a dynamic which could result in great benefit for the CMZa. Already in July of 1980 a minute of the administrative committee reflected a positive tone: "The Committee views the 'spiritual renewal' as an activity of our Church and wants to encourage the brothers and sisters who are responsible for it." (7)

During the general assembly of 1983, the entire CMZa delegate body took action both to encourage and to exert some control over it. It was voted "that the pastor or congregational leader be the sponsor of 'spiritual renewal' in his parish and that each group choose its own leader who must be approved by the local church council." (8)

CMZa and human services

In their joint meeting with the AIMM delegation in July of 1980, Vice-President Mukanza underlined CMZa's human services as another area of concern for the new administration. In making his point he observed: "Evangelism in our context also means fighting hunger, sickness and poverty." To this President Mbonza added: "People are waiting to see what CMZa with its new leadership team is all about. It is time that we preach by our acts as well as with our words."

This was not a new topic. In one form or another it had often surfaced in previous committee meetings and in conversation between CMZa administrators and AIMM missionaries. CMZa concern for ministry for a needy population which lay on every hand was genuine. The Church leaders deeply believed that "the Good News" they sought to preach had to say something about empty stomachs and hollow hopes as well as empty hearts. It was the working out of this dual good news which often proved problematic.

A far-flung network of primary and secondary schools was in place. This clearly was one significant facet of CMZa presence. The many dispensaries and maternity facilities scattered across historic stations and rural church centers also provided invaluable aid to hurting people. But there were other CMZa-sponsored endeavors where there was less clarity. Chief among them was SEDA, the farm and community development center at the edge of Nyanga station. Launched originally as a joint AIMM/MCC undertaking, it had become a joint CMZa/MCC project after the mission/church fusion agreement was put in place. Under increasing financial stress, CMZa leaders had difficulty in accepting that the farm center should function as a non-profit enterprise. The potential in its livestock and farm supply store for significant profit was great, profit which some felt should be tapped for CMZa's broader needs.

Then there was the saw mill. The original rationale in requesting such equipment was to supply wood at reasonable costs to CMZa church districts for building chapels, to CMZa members for building homes and to the CMZa administration for sale as there was a surplus. In the diamond-driven economy of the Tshikapa area, however, commercial demand for the lumber was instantaneous and unrelenting. Caught between such a lucrative market, on the one hand, and very real CMZa budget pressures on the other, the temptation was deadly. Reports on inventories and the sawmill account became somewhat sporadic and vague. While some funds were credited to specific CMZa projects and needs, it became nearly impossible to secure lumber, as such, for CMZa-related building projects, this to the increasing frustration of CMZa district leaders and missionary personnel alike. This tension between stated ideals of human services on the one hand, and the temptation to view and operate the church mill as a lucrative revenue producing project remained a largely unresolved dilemma.

our future lies with the leaders we train

In his resume of CMZa priorities in the 80's, Vice-President Mukanza became most animated when he addressed the burning issue of CMZa leadership training. On one occasion he was heard to declare: "A church which does not train leaders for the future is already preparing for its death." A perceptive observer of the Mennonite scene of North America during his two year stint at AMBS, Mukanza returned to Zaire in the fall of 1977 carrying not only a graduate degree in Christian Education but also a conviction that Mennonite pastoral training needed to be lifted to a new level in his homeland. The Kalonda Bible Institute was in place. Its level of study had gradually been lifted across the years and the curriculum expanded from a three-year to a four-year program. But the focus clearly remained on training pastoral candidates for ministry in rural settings where traditional culture and social structures were still firmly in place and the language used was the local dialect of the people. Reverend Mukanza, however, felt that CMZa by now needed its own theological institute which would provide training at a higher level. While AIMM/CMZa were founding members of ISTK, Mukanza feared that Mennonite graduates would always be too few in number due to scholarship restraints. There was the further impossibility of providing a predominantly Anabaptist perspective for Mennonite students in an inter-denominational school.

With Pastor Kabangy before his death, Mukanza had found an early sympathetic ear. Their agreement became clear in a meeting of the CMZa Administrative Committee in January of 1978. Formal committee action was taken to propose the creation of an *Institut Supérieur Théologique* in collaboration with the other two Mennonite Churches of Zaire. A study commission was created to pursue the matter further and to formulate recommendations. (9) (10)

The newly-appointed commission wasted no time in pursuing their assignment. In a meeting one month later at Kalonda they produced a document which, first of all, sought to provide historical perspective on the comparatively low Mennonite profile of the earlier years in their country. Given as reasons were: 1) general interest of missionaries to first spread the basic message of salvation through faith in Christ; 2) certain aspects of the colonial era which did not favor Mennonite doctrines, and 3) the fact that Protestant Missions needed a solidarity to resist Catholic rivalry and domination. They then pointed out what they felt to be conditions which by then favorized an aggressive teaching of Mennonite distinctives: 1) the fact that a basic message of the Gospel had been proclaimed, 2) the "ardent desire among Christians called Mennonite to discover the historic origin of their faith," and 3) the desire to "define our identity as Mennonites in Zaire."

Turning to their proposal to withdraw from ISTK, the inter-denominational theological institute in Kinshasa, a variety of reasons were given: 1) diverse doctrines taught there, 2) a lack of knowledge of Mennonite doctrines, 3) a lack of instruction adapted to the actual needs of our local churches. The further opinion was expressed that if there was a Mennonite Institute, curriculum could be altered to allow for some vocational training along with the academic courses, this to equip future pastors to help support themselves and their families. It was also thought that for the same money invested each year at ISTK to train a handful of Mennonite students, a significantly larger student body could be in training in a Mennonite institution.

The commission then divided itself into two subcommittees. One would travel to the South Kasai to contact the CEM leaders and the other to Kikwit to dialogue with the CEFMZ people. In the event of a favorable response, a larger tri-member study commission would be organized to carry the study process forward. (11)

By June 1978 the subcommittees had traveled and met with their fellow Mennonites to the west and east. In a letter addressed to President Kabangy Rev. Mukanza summarized what had transpired. Citing the CMZa as the original moving force behind the idea, he reported both interest and enthusiasm on the part of the other two Mennonite Churches and a readiness to pursue their joint vision further. He concluded his letter by suggesting that it was very probable that the enlarged study commission proposed in their recommendations would be meeting before the end of the year. (12)

President Kabangy had represented the CMZa at an international consultation on world mission held at Hesston, KS, prior to the Mennonite World Conference in Wichita the summer of 1978. During these sessions Mennonite church leaders from various parts of the world strongly emphasized their desire for the establishment of Anabaptist training centers in the major cultural areas of the world where there was a significant Mennonite population. As the representative of the CMZa, Kabangy not only quickly affirmed this proposal but added that the Mennonites of Zaire had already taken some initiative in this regard.

It was in response to all of this that the AIMM organized two major consultations in Zaire on theological training for the Mennonite churches of that country. The first was held in Kinshasa August 2-3, 1981. Present were representatives from all three Mennonite Churches and the Kalonda Bible Institute plus BOMAS, AIMM and MCC. (13) It quickly became apparent that the CMZa delegation was prepared to urge withdrawal from ISTK, the interdenominational school of which Mennonites were a part, and the establishment of an inter-Mennonite Institute of their own of comparable academic level. Basic reasons advanced were: 1) the spiritual tone at ISTK leaves much to be desired; 2) there is no clear Mennonite instruction; 3) urban life tends to disorient students for work in rural areas; 4) it is costly to send and maintain students in the capital; 5) Mennonites are numerous in Zaire; our membership and our prestige require such a school; 6) our future is insecure until we have our own school where we can determine our own staff, curriculum and discipline.

Response from others reflected a more cautious stance. It was particularly CEFMZ delegates who voiced reserve about early severing relations with ISTK and striking off on a new inter-Mennonite path. The fact that the ISTK director at the time, Kikweta Mawa (pr. ki-KWEH-tah MAH-wah), was a member of the Mennonite Brethren Church likely was a major influence. Some comments voiced: 1) True, there is much which needs improvement at ISTK; 2) true, a Mennonite school at this level is needed. If such a school were possible it would be to our honor. 3) But to attempt the creation of a new school would be much more expensive than remaining partners in ISTK. 4) It would furthermore add yet another costly institution to others with which we are already struggling. If we were assured that to the building funds would be added long range subsidy for the operation of the new school, we woould all be for the idea, but we doubt seriously that this would be the case. 5) Mennonites have invested heavily in ISTK. By a gradual process of default on the part of other founding member groups, the school offers growing opportunity for Mennonite presence and influence. 6) We live in uncertain times in our country. For now, at least, we favor seeking ways to change what we can at ISTK and to strengthen our Mennonite presence and role there. It was this last proposal which finally provided the focus of following sessions.

At the close of the consultation five recommendations were agreed upon for submission to the two Mission Boards: 1) That the two Boards be asked to recruit a professor of Mennonite studies for ISTK, at the Boards' expense, to teach elective courses dealing with Mennonite history and Anabaptist distinctives; 2) that both Boards help to establish adequate Mennonite resource material in the ISTK library; 3) that both Boards seek to make scholarships available to the Zaire Mennonite Churches to enable carefully-selected candidates to do doctoral studies in a variety of disciplines with a view to becoming a teaching corps for the future; 4) that some writing by Zaire Mennonite leaders already done be gathered and reproduced for distribution in Zaire and to any others outside Zaire who should have access to it; 5) that another such consultation take place for further discussions. Though approved by the CMZa delegation, it was clear that in their thinking these were acceptable only as interim measures.

As proposed, a second consultation was held in Kinshasa February 14-15, 1983. Once again there was representation from all three Zaire Churches, two schools, both Mennonite Boards and MCC. (14) This time the scope of discussion was broader. Reflecting discussions of a similar nature which had by then taken place at a meeting of the Africa Mennonite/Brethren in Christ Fellowship, some time was devoted to a discussion of Mennonite presence and witness in Africa as a whole and the feasibility of some sort of pan-African Mennonite leadership training effort. An immediate question of language arose with the firm opinion expressed that given the preponderance of Mennonites in French speaking areas, such a program, if created, would most appropriately be located in Zaire.

At one point the suggestion was floated of seeking to establish a "Mennonite Studies Chair" in an existing institution such as ISTK or a recently launched theological school in Bangui in the neighboring Central African Republic. As conversation moved from one focus to another, Mukanza Ilunga would occasionally underscore his convictions: "A church that does not prepare for its future is a church which is already preparing for its demise."

Some of the concerns of the 1981 consultation were revisited, such as the heavy Mennonite investment of funds and personnel in ISTK; the enormous cost involved in attempting to establish a new school; all the long-range problems associated with the creation of another institution of this magnitude; and the negative impact upon ISTK in the event of Mennonite withdrawal.

As this second consultation drew to a close, the proposals of the 1981 gathering were maintained while several new actions were taken: 1) to name a continuing study commission with representatives from all six groups; (15) 2) to recognize that varying levels of pastoral service required different levels of training and that existing Bible Institutes be affirmed, upgraded and curricula re-worked in keeping with heightened Anabaptist concerns; 3) to seek to establish an inter-Mennonite news sheet for circulation in Zaire; 4) to pursue the MCC suggestion of a series of inter-Mennonite pastoral seminars led by Mennonite theologians from Europe and North America; 5) to explore the possibility of establishing a core collection of study materials for translation and distribution among all Mennonite Churches of Africa.

These two consultations did produce some results. Considerable Anabaptist-oriented material was secured and presented to ISTK for the creation of "an Anabaptist shelf." Million Belete (pr.beh-LEH-teh), a member of the Meserete Kristos (Mennonite) Church of Ethiopia and based in Nairobi with the International Bible Society, took leadership in assigning the writing of some syllabi for distribution among African Mennonite Churches. A few scholarships were provided for graduate studies overseas. The continuing committee named at the second consultation met yet that same year at Kikwit hosted by the CEFMZ. Moving resolutely ahead in pursuit of their dream it was proposed to open a first year class of a new inter-Mennonite school in the fall of 1984 in temporary quarters offered by the CEFMZ and an appeal was launched to both Mennonite Mission Boards for qualified professors, funding and equipment.

This proposal never found serious support on the part of either Board. The North American consensus seemed to be that while the idea was not without merit, it was too costly and that ways should be found to make the existing Mennonite Bible Institutes, ISTK and other available training options at least part of the answer. In spite of admirable vision and initiative on the part of Zairian Mennonite leaders of the time, the proposed project was stillborn.

extended horizons

Even as the newly-elected CMZa leadership team was attempting to come to grips with their local assignments and agenda, events of their time were opening international doors of opportunity for them. Named as the CMZa delegate to a meeting of the AMBCF in Nairobi, Kenya in December, 1979, Rev. Mukanza Ilunga was, in turn, named with Million Belete as the two African representatives on an International Mennonite Peace Committee which was being formed under the auspices of the World Mennonite Conference. This became a springboard for a widely enlarged ministry for Rev. Mukanza. Given his education, his command of both French and English and a sunny disposition, he quickly became a valuable asset to the committee.

Just prior to the AIMM/CMZa dialogue at Nyanga in July, 1980, he had attended initial meetings of this committee convened in Managua, Nicaragua and Bogota, Colombia. In a report written after his return to Zaire he commented: ". . . the situation in these two South American countries is not so different from what some African countries are experiencing. Many African countries are under dictatorship governments using violence, oppression and corruption to maintain themselves. How can we as peace churches cooperate with these regimes? What will be the content of our message and witness to them? How can we contribute to correction without hurting and compromising? These are the kinds of questions that our churches need to meditate upon under the guidance of the Holy Spirit." (16)

Upon his return to Zaire, Mukanza immediately began to lay plans for a "seminar on non-violence" to be conducted in Zaire in August of 1981 to which thirty key people from the three Mennonite Churches were invited.

New doors of opportunity also opened for President Mbonza. AIMM made arrangements for ten weeks of intensive study in a specialized English language program in Brattleboro, VT. Upon terminating the course he was joined by his wife Dimuka Ana for a six week fraternal visit to a variety of North American Mennonite communities which had historic ties with AIMM. Invited to attend the spring sessions of the AIMM Board, President Mbonza emphasized that the Zaire Church, though presenting impressive statistics, (17) was still young and inexperienced and needed the ongoing support of AIMM and its missionaries. In his remarks the President also underscored the lack of adequate instruction in the past as to Anabaptist distinctives and called for this to be corrected. He concluded by questioning AIMM's expanding ministry among African Independent Churches in southern Africa. He wondered what inferences CMZa was to draw from this surrounded as they were, in Zaire, with all manner of independent groups as well. (18)

His wife, Dimuka Ana, often had occasion to address women's groups during their travels. Her open, disarming and warm manner made a special impact everywhere. On one occasion she spoke of her great apprehension to undertake travel from Africa alone to join her husband. As she boarded her flight in Kinshasa she simply prayed: "I'm going to Brussels, Lord, and I expect you to meet me there!"

Upon leaving the States, President Mbonza left a two-page letter to be shared with "my brothers and sisters, members of the AIMM." After briefly reviewing some of their experiences and impressions as they traveled, he summarized the message he had attempted to leave wherever he spoke or had conversations with American mission and church leaders: 1) The Church of Christ is holy, universal, one and indivisible. All members of this Church are brothers and sisters in time and space. 2) Christian love, which is the sign of the love of Christ, is unselfish, without limits, calm and deep. 3) Supported by its Lord the Christ, the church survives thanks to the life of its members, their faithfulness to the Master, their comprehension of their responsibilities as Christians and as church members."

He continued: "We hope that fraternal visits for mutual encouragement organized within a framework of exchange between our respective churches may become ever more frequent. . . . We leave you assured that you will pray without ceasing for us, prayers which are the result of your pain and sleeplessness in our behalf. And, finally, we will faithfully inform your brothers and sisters in Zaire concerning everything we have seen and experienced among you. We will convey to them your many salutations. We will ask them to pray for you for, as human beings, you also face difficult problems. You too are weak, prone to evil, prey to discouragement and inclined toward the temptations which characterize the world community in the midst of which we all live as we await the return of the Christ." (19)

It was a perceptive letter which conveyed a breadth of concern and understanding and, as can be imagined, was well received in North America among those who had met and interacted with him. Traveling back to Europe together, Dimuka returned to Zaire to her family while President Mbonza went to Nairobi where he with his Vice-President, Mukanza, attended a meeting of the General Council of the MWC. It was while there that President Mbonza was named to replace former President Kabangy as the African representative to the MWC Executive Committee, an appointment which would open for him subsequent opportunities for broadened contacts and extended travel.

For Vice-President Mukanza, the occasions for travel and interaction with the international Mennonite world became avenues for personal growth and ever expanding service. Unfortunately, for President Mbonza, this did not prove to be the case.

In the July 1980 meeting at Nyanga which for the first time brought the new CMZa officers into dialogue with an AIMM delegation, CMZa spokesman Vice-President Mukanza outlined what for them at the time were five fundamental priority concerns. Beyond those of the spiritual welfare of the church, leadership training and human services, there also were the concerns of financial resources and ongoing relations with AIMM.

a "papa/child" relationship

In his introductory remarks in the first joint session, President Mbonza made oblique references to the financial pressures they were experiencing as a Church and their underlying assumption that, as in the past, AIMM would continue to be a generous donor to their annual budgets. At one point he observed that "whether we or you like it or not, ours is a papa/child relationship. We are the result of your faithful work of many years among us. Although we are entering a new era in our relationship, our needs remain many." Though stated in typically indirect African style, the President's meaning was nonetheless clear. An energetic new leadership team with many dreams of growth and expansion assumed that the AIMM would take seriously its "father role" vis-à-vis the "offspring church" and be appropriately liberal with its ongoing financial support.

This stance took on early substance when in preliminary sessions of the administrative committee it was proposed that a request be submitted to the AIMM delegation for a grant of five new British Landrovers, rugged four wheel drive vehicles which had long since proven their worth on bush roads all across Africa. They were also expensive. By the time the joint CMZa/AIMM sessions were held, the initial proposal had been trimmed down to two Landrovers and three bush motorbikes. Tempered by further dialogue, a concluding proposal was to buy one vehicle for the needs of the central administration and motorcycles for each of the three regional representatives. CMZa would cover half the cost.

But if capital investment in needed church equipment was obviously justified, the spiraling growth of CMZa's annual operating costs and the excessive dependence upon AIMM funds to meet them was another matter. This issue had been earlier discussed with CMZa leaders in President Kabangy's era but little headway had been made in improving the situation. CMZa's problems were admittedly real. There was, first of all, the fact that CMZa administrative structures had either been inherited from the AIMM or been imposed by the Zairian government. Furthermore CMZa districts were scattered across an immense area. Separated by hundreds of miles and in some cases readily accessible only by air, there simply was no inexpensive way for church leaders to travel. More and more the planning of commission and general assembly gatherings entailed complicated logistics and major expense. With a large rural membership which was caught in the brutal squeeze of wild inflation and the steady decline of Zairian political and economic structures, the first concern of district church leaders, understandably, was to raise from their people funds to assure their own immediate district church programs. Though continually reminded of their responsibilities and obligations toward their central administration in Tshikapa, the raising of funds to support both their local church activities and the country-wide CMZa administrative structure became steadily more difficult.

A further complicating issue was the fact that church leaders at both the national and regional levels typically lived at an economic level that was considerably higher than that of the average village church member, something which was known to all. A final problem was the great hesitancy of the CMZa officers to provide annual detailed accounting regarding the AIMM and government funds which passed through their offices and the ways in which they were utilized in the interests of the church. A certain level of consequent indifference on the part of rank and file members toward repeated calls for increased contributions to the Tshikapa office was understandable.

As the decade of the 80's opened, this whole issue had become a painful dilemma for the AIMM Board. On the one hand, there were genuine affection and respect on the part of the Board for many of the CMZa leaders. There was understanding of the worsening economic crisis in Zaire. But the Board also held some deeply-rooted missiological convictions not the least of which was the belief that the growing dependence of the CMZa upon AIMM funding for its operating needs constituted a danger both for its integrity and its future.

So it was that during the July 1980 consultation at Nyanga the new CMZa leaders were warned that the AIMM saw this juncture of CMZa history as the moment to institute a new policy. Rather than assume that their perceived parent/child relationship would automatically translate into open ended increase in subsidies for annual CMZa budgetary needs, AIMM would, on the contrary, seek some way of gradually reducing, not increasing, such support. In its fall sessions that same year the Board took action and instructed its executive secretary to advise President Mbonza and his staff accordingly. A short time later a letter from Elkhart read, in part: "You remember (at the July consultation) that we said that the Board is more and more concerned because the administrative costs of the CMZa continue to grow while the church at the level of the districts seems little concerned. We asked ourselves around the tables as to the reason for that. Several . . . explanations were advanced. Finally it was agreed that, sooner or later, the CMZa must seriously concern itself with its own administration and its own officers."

"Thus it is the Board has adopted the principle of reducing its contribution to the expense of central administration by 15% a year during a four year period after which it envisages another consultation with the CMZa . . . . The motive which has moved the Board to take this initiative is a profound concern for the well-being of the CMZa in the future. The more dependence there is on overseas funds for the administrative functioning of CMZa, the more one builds upon sand. The Board is convinced that a moment has arrived - - especially now when a new administrative team launches upon its work - - to invite the CMZa to face up to its own responsibilities as regards its own administration and its own officers. [AIMM] does not want to act in a precipitous manner. It wants to allow time for study, evaluation and dialogue with the district church leaders and pastors everywhere as well as with the thousands of lay people who are found wherever CMZa is at work. . . . We are convinced that even if this news causes you to shiver a bit at the first hearing, we believe that after serious reflection you will agree with us that we enter with you upon a path which leads to the maturity of the CMZa." (1)

While the response to this news from CMZa leaders was muted, with passing time it became clear that President Mbonza increasingly questioned why the new AIMM financial policy should have coincided with his arrival on the scene as CMZa's chief administrative officer. It is, therefore, understandable that with passing time expressions of displeasure and frustration surfaced in a variety of ways.

new ventures in CMZa/AIMM collaboration?

In the July '80 consultation, it was particularly in relation to possible future models of CMZa/AIMM collaboration that popcorn popper sorts of discussions took place. There already was a tradition of the exchange of fraternal visits between Zaire and North America. Much appreciation was expressed for these experiences made possible by AIMM help. It was strongly urged that such exchanges be continued and even increased in frequency.

The proposal of a joint effort in mission in Upper Volta, initially probed in the late 1970's, was revisited. What had been the discussions? What had been the obstacles? Why had the project been tabled? Once again information was requested and possible patterns of oversight of a joint venture in West Africa were explored. Eventually the new team of leaders came out where the preceding Kabangy administration had, stating that there were candidates for such appointment (2) but that commitment to sharing financial responsibilities for their service was impossible. Once again, an idea which stirred so much tantalizing discussion with AIMM representatives and excited conjecture among rank-and-file CMZa membership foundered over such mundane issues as travel costs, housing, health care and basic support.

But even as these discussions were going on, a companion idea also surfaced - - that of CMZa having the opportunity to name an official delegate to the AIMM Board. Both President and Vice-President Mbonza and Mukanza had had opportunity to visit North America and to attend AIMM Board sessions. They quickly sensed the significance of these gatherings for the African Church. They also rightly suggested that often it would be helpful and instructive to have a Zairian voice and perspective present as discussions took place and decisions were made. But once again the dollar sign raised its disruptive head. Such Zairian presence and perspective was contingent upon periodic inter-continental travel which, in turn, was contingent upon funds. And, yet once again, the Zairian assumption was clear. Such travel, like so much already funded by AIMM within Zaire, could be made possible by AIMM resources.

Early sensing the harsh impact which the enormous imbalance of economic resources continually had upon CMZa/AIMM dialogue and interaction, AIMM Board member Jim Juhnke observed at a Zaire missionary retreat with a mix of frustration and sadness: "Our relations to Africa will more and more be colored by this fact. Economic dependence inevitably limits independence of mind and spirit. We in the West can't/won't give without requiring accountability. Our aid is not unconditional like the grace of God! So how can we really talk of mutuality?" He then continued, "We must nonetheless search for viable contributions they can make to us while facing our ongoing responsibility before God vis-à-vis the 'have nots' of the world. Liberation theologians speak of the unholy alliance between rich minorities of the West against the poor of their countries. We can have the best of intentions vis-à-vis the under privileged and run afoul of structural problems" (3)

Dialogue regarding possible new formats of CMZa/AIMM collaboration the summer of 1980 took yet some other directions which offered more promise. By this time a CMZa presence of one degree or another was to be identified in an unbroken string of urban centers starting with Kinshasa the capital in the west. Moving eastward and, eventually in a southeasterly direction, there was Mennonite activity in Kikwit, Ilebo, Tshikapa, Kananga, Mbuji Mayi, Kolwezi, Likasi and Lubumbashi. Strung as they are basically across the rolling savannas of the southern third of Zaire, they also lie in the heaviest population belt of the country. An early generation of pioneering AIMM missionaries settled in areas which later became strategic regions from which it was easy to move outward. This challenging prospect was not lost on the new CMZa officers. There was frequent reference to the need to give supervision and leadership to new Mennonite ventures in church planting in this lengthening list of growing centers. They well understood AIMM delegation member Jim Juhnke when he on one occasion warned: "We must do more than gather together our migrants in the centers and sing the old songs." A key ingredient to significant ministry in the urban centers, it was realized, would be deliberate efforts to minister among the rapidly-growing community of university students and to pursue aggressively the establishment and nurture of small prayer and Bible study cells.

But there was still more. Following the reports of AIMM's approach to the evangelization of unreached ethnic groups in Upper Volta via language analysis teams based in isolated areas, President Mbonza proposed that AIMM give serious consideration to recruiting comparably qualified and motivated candidates to do the same sort of pioneering work among the ethnic groups on the fringes Zaire's traditional "Mennonite area" whose response to the Gospel preached in tongues other than their own had been minimal.

When toward the conclusion of the 1980 Nyanga dialogue, President Mbonza declared the desire of CMZa to collaborate with the AIMM in the building of the world Mennonite community, it clearly was the expression of a sincere hope. There is every reason to believe that had Zairian circumstances in the following years been more stable, some of the visionary ideas which surfaced in the 1980 dialogue would have been seriously pursued.

"things are about normal here"

"The sun is just sinking into the Kasai and the evening is beautiful. We wish you were here. Things are about normal here. The truck is two days over due from a Kinshasa trip. The Chevy pickup is down for repairs. The Ford truck went to the sawmill yesterday and came home last night with what looked to be a broken front spring. The light plant is still not running and the cistern down at the spring has filled up with sand."

With his trademark wry sense of humor, Jim Christensen thus opened a letter to the AIMM office in the spring of 1983. He and his wife Jeanette Myers Christensen were voluntary service personnel at Kalonda Station where he was in charge of the CMZa garage and transport system. Members of the Glennon Heights Mennonite Church in Denver, CO, they were a lay couple who had nurtured a lifelong dream of one day serving in some capacity somewhere in Christian mission. Learning in early 1978 of an urgent need for someone in Zaire with broad background in mechanics and general maintenance, they both applied for early retirement, he from his trade as a machinist/mechanic and she from her position in the credit department of J. C. Penny Department Stores, and began packing their bags. Fearful that they were being led into a stressful role for which they were not adequately prepared, AIMM staff painted the difficulties which awaited them in rather graphic terms. Their only response was: "How soon can we go?"

Jim continued his letter: "Two weeks ago we took two students into the garage on a training program that is to last six weeks. They are going to school [in industrial arts] at Djoko Punda. . . . They have had a lot of class room work but no experience. If there is one thing we can give them here, it is experience! Last week we had to repair the water pump on the Toyota. We had to convert a Ford pump seal to a Toyota. We also put a new clutch in the Toyota and adjusted the bearings in the differential, so they are getting some experience. Now they will get to take a front spring off a Ford truck. That is a fun experience. This week they will probably get a chance to shovel sand out of a cistern. That may not be mechanical, but it is an experience."

The letter lay unfinished on Jim's desk for a few days and then he continued: "I am sure that there were a lot of good things happening today, but not in the garage. It started early. The Ford truck was to go for a load of gravel. Well, it wouldn't start. They [the garage help] had tightened the battery clamp and somehow managed to pull it against the post. The battery was dead, the clamp was melted and the rubber on the battery had a hole in it. Eventually it got on the road. On the ten o'clock radio net I got word that the Bedford truck was at Idiofa with a dead tire. . . . This afternoon I lost my keys somewhere in the garage. . . . That meant change all the locks. So went the day. . . . We will try again tomorrow." (4)

It would be difficult to find material that would any better capture the experience and spirit of AIMM personnel that was at work in Zaire in the early 80's. For Jim Christensen it was a question of struggling with constantly malfunctioning CMZa mechanical equipment and the battle to secure scarce repair parts and fuel. Other missionaries faced their own shortages of supplies and their own problems unique to the particular department to which they had been assigned.

A major contributing factor was the steady deterioration of Zaire's public services of the time. Chuck Fennig, son of missionaries in Kenya, applied to AIMM for a stint of voluntary service upon graduation from college. He was assigned to serve as a purchasing agent for the Church and Mission in Kinshasa. On one occasion he wrote a short article for the AIMM Messenger in which he observed: Patience is "a pleasant sounding word to many Christians. . . . Since I have come to Zaire with AIMM . . . the Lord has been teaching me what 'real patience' is. I had always thought of myself as a Christian who had this particular fruit of the Spirit if nothing else. My work in Kinshasa . . . has exposed me to situations that have strained my 'uncomplaining endurance' and brought me to that imaginary line where patience breaks down into anger or defeat. . . ."

"Buying supplies may seem as easy as walking into the nearest department store, and licensing a car might mean a ten minute visit to the local license branch. In Zaire, however, it may mean waiting days, weeks or months. As an example, I recently spent five consecutive mornings waiting for some licenses for church vehicles, standing in a sweltering office packed with people. The paper for one motorcycle having been lost must be found. This means more time spent - - waiting. We are [also] waiting for a barrel of alcohol which was ordered several months ago for our hospital at Kalonda. A couple of months after ordering it, we are informed that our license for buying and using alcohol was invalid and that we would have to obtain another one. This meant another week-long process."

It was of no help to AIMM and CMZa people like Chuck to know that a "lost" form could be found immediately upon passing an under-the-table "gift" to a clerk or that an "outdated" purchase permit could suddenly be updated with an appropriate behind-the-scenes "donation" to the one who had the rubber stamp in his desk drawer. It was even more difficult to keep a serene disposition when problems relative to their assignments stemmed from ineptitude, carelessness or simple lack of conscience on the part of people within the church itself who had too hastily been thrust into roles of responsibility.

And yet in the midst of the aggravation, this young man found it within himself to ponder what God's purpose was in all of his frustration for him personally. His conclusion: "He is really showing me that He wants me to depend on Him completely for everything. I have learned that I certainly do not have the patience needed. As I let Christ live through me, He gives me the endurance I need for every situation." (5)

The pressure and circumstances under which AIMM personnel worked under CMZa authority in Zaire did not go unnoticed by North American travelers. On one occasion, after a visit, an AIMM Board member was heard to say something to this effect: "Any new candidates for Zaire will have to convince me of a very loud and a very clear, direct call from God along with a special measure of dedication and grace."

The AIMM missionary team in Zaire in the late 70's and early 80's, however, was a group that had largely come to terms both with the crumbling Zairian setting which surrounded them and, more importantly still, with the plan of CMZa/AIMM fusion which had been agreed upon in 1971. By this time a full decade had passed and some changes had taken place within the missionary team. Some had reached retirement age and said their farewells to a land and people to which they had given much of their lives. A few other missionaries of the 70's had been frank to express their reservations about the new plan and their hesitance to continue their service in Zaire. Their concerns were honored by the Board and they were freed to seek avenues of service elsewhere. But to a core of continuing people were added new recruits who affirmed the concept of a merged mission/church structure. In spite of the mix of frustrations and handicaps which came to characterize the Zaire setting, the AIMM Zaire team gradually grew in size. Whereas in the summer of 1980 there were twenty five people listed on active status, by 1984 the list had grown to 41.

Some stood in classrooms from day to day before future pastors and church leaders. Some sat in receiving rooms of dispensaries and hospitals day in and day out meeting and ministering with compassion to desperately ill and destitute village folk. Some walked through experimental patches of cassava plants and struggled to introduce the strange new concept of teams of oxen as a source of animal power. Some spent long hours at tables with fellow Africans translating Scriptures or Christian materials in a variety of tongues. Some bounced over sandy trails with African pastors in shepherding tours of distant flocks. Some spent many long hours on hard benches in church committees in a common search for solutions to lengthy agendas submitted to them.

But if, for visiting guests, all of this had the appearance of exceptional hardship, for those involved, there were genuine rewards. For one thing, working within the church under the appointment and authority of that church provided a unique opportunity "to walk where they walked" and to share intimately and authentically in the joys and sorrows, the achievements and failures of that Zairian segment of the body of Christ. To be named by the church to its committees and assemblies with full voice and vote provided a striking opportunity to enter into the life of the church and to demonstrate concern, affirmation and love for that church. There was clearly something special and uniquely rewarding about the opportunity of serving in the name of Christ as an integral part of the African Church.

An excellent insight into the mind and heart of the AIMM Zaire missionaries of that era is provided by excerpts from some "Psalms of Life" written by Kalonda missionaries as an exercise for a group Bible study which was convened once a week:

> "Oh Lord, my Lord, how excellent is thy name!
> You loved me when I had not asked to be loved.

You chose me when I had not asked to be chosen.
You placed me in a place to be nurtured where I had
        not asked to be placed.
You gave me the fellowship of Christian believers
        for which I had not asked.
You placed me in a place of responsibility where I
        did not want to be placed.
You gave me wisdom beyond my understanding.
You allowed me to stray but kept me within your reach.
You gave me weaknesses and failures enough that I
        am reminded of my constant need of you.
You give me joy and peace by the assurance of
        your presence.
Therefore with joy and humility I bear witness to thy
        saving grace, sustaining power and the presence of
        thy everlasting arms.
Oh Lord, how excellent is thy name in all the earth." (6)

For as long as there were CMZa leaders who had been part of the 1971 fusion dialogue and had experienced its mood of mutual trust and affirmation, missionaries were welcomed and affirmed in their multitudinous roles. Vice-President Mukanza on one occasion said: "We need and welcome experienced, seasoned brothers and sisters in Christ who are prepared to live and work among us, share our dreams, achievements, problems and heartaches as fellow members of the body of Christ."

With his gift for colorful imagery, Kakesa Samuel at one point compared the missionary to cream and sugar. There was a time in an earlier era when the missionary was the "cream in the coffee," i.e. very visible and changing the appearance of our "coffee." Now was the time for the missionary to be the "sugar," i.e., not quickly apparent on the surface of things but making a needed and unmistakable contribution to the life and well-being of the church.

For as long as this attitude was maintained by CMZa leadership, there was AIMM personnel ready to serve within the African Church in spite of the deep frustration of endless problems experienced in a crumbling nation. With passing time, however, attitudes of CMZa leadership vis-à-vis its missionary personnel underwent subtle changes. This shift also coincided with a variety of powerful dynamics which were at play on the North American scene at the time: budget shortfalls among constituent AIMM conferences; greater emphasis upon upgraded church buildings and growing salaried staffs; and uniformly negative reporting of Zaire news in the American media. In the face of all of these factors, the AIMM Board found it easy to become tentative in its recruitment for new personnel for Zaire while being considerably more positive and emphatic in its recruitment for new areas of ministry which had opened elsewhere in Africa.

another AIMM anniversary

Nineteen eighty-two marked another decennial year in AIMM's history. Plans had been in the making. A number of converging events promised to make it a memorable occasion. A delegation of Mennonite business men plus a Mennonite pastor were to travel in Africa early in the year accompanied by AIMM staff member Art Janz. (7) They would bring to the subsequent anniversary celebration fresh news and their perspectives as professional people. It was also a time which saw a growing cluster of AIMM missionaries who had reached retirement age. All those who had served under AIMM for twenty or more years would be the guests of the Board at a testimonial dinner in their honor at which appropriate plaques were to be presented to them. In addition to the fifteen-member Board and AIMM staff, furloughing missionaries plus first-time candidates for service would also be brought to the meetings. To round out the special guest list, invitations were sent to former AIMM Executive Secretaries Harvey Driver and Reuben Short and to Rev. R.L Hartzler, a long-time member of the Board of earlier years then in retirement in the area.

As planning progressed, the Carlock and North Danvers Mennonite Churches of central Illinois offered to host the gathering. This was a happy initiative for it meant that AIMM's 70th anniversary celebration would take place in the very geographical area where this inter-Mennonite venture in Christian Mission had first been conceived and launched.

The weekend of April 30 - May 2, 1982, consequently saw a total of eighty people gather for the festivities including open board sessions. During a weekend of high activity there were two special occasions. The first was the evening testimonial banquet offered for AIMM retirees. A total of seventeen were present whose combined time of service totaled 488 years - - a moving testimony to the sort of career missionaries which had enabled AIMM to maintain its presence and witness in a distant land which frequently had thrust hardship and menace in their path. (8)

A second high moment was the Sunday evening AIMM rally held in the Carlock Mennonite Church. A packed sanctuary of people listened to a series of presentations. The evening was capped by an address by Board Chairman Jim Juhnke entitled "Out of our Quarry" which took as its point of reference a passage from Isaiah 51:1: "Look to the rock from which you were hewn and to the quarry from which you were digged." A trained historian, he sketched in quick strokes the background of an "Amish quarry" from which the initial AIMM building blocks had come, blocks which along the way were joined by other Mennonite stones from other quarries as well. Tracing in broad outline some of the major challenges encountered and decisions made by the growing inter-Mennonite mission organization, he concluded: "We face an uncertain future but we are inspired by the courage and faithfulness of those who have gone before. God expects no less of us than he did of them. We face our future with our eyes open, using the wisdom God has given, to understand the needs of our world and the missionary mandate it has been our privilege to inherit. We bear the inescapable marks of our Amish and Mennonite heritage, and pray that God will give us the wisdom to mine and to use the best from that heritage. We press on toward the mark, grateful for the rock from which we were hewn and the quarry from which we were digged." (9)

There was evidence in the official minutes of that anniversary weekend that Board President Juhnke's commitment to carry AIMM's work forward was not idle rhetoric. Among the new candidates approved for service were Larry Hills, and Dan and Kathy Fluth Petersen. Hills was to become the first AIMM person to establish residence in the Transkei, a black homeland nestled against the Indian Ocean on the southern tip of Africa. The Petersens would join a team being formed along the fringes of the Sahara Desert to the north in Upper Volta.

Seventy years after its birth the AIMM was very much alive and well.

Blessed with an alert intelligence, President Mbonza's years at the University of Kisangani had served to sharpen his gifts for analysis and debate and his command of the French language. Those years also served to deepen his personal conviction that he was gifted beyond many of his fellow Zairians and that he was consequently destined to roles of leadership among his people. It was with a growing sense of self-confidence that, upon graduation, he returned to his home area in the West Kasai and reestablished contacts with his church, the CMZa, which elected him president in the spring of 1983.

an early impact

Installed in the CMZa headquarters in Tshikapa, it very soon became evident that there was a new personality at the helm of the Church. Carefully crafted letters began to circulate among regional CMZa leaders spelling out new instructions. Headquarters staff quickly learned that schedules were established to be followed and that correct and orderly records were to be kept of all meetings. "Discipline" became a word that was heard with increasing frequency and, with passing time, credentials and performance of educational and pastoral staff came under review. When irregularities came to light, efforts were made to correct them. Failing that, people were frequently dismissed from their CMZa-related functions and replaced by others. At such times President Mbonza not infrequently had candidates of his choice to propose as replacements.

As the new president had occasion or need to make calls in government offices or to appear in public settings, he was always immaculately dressed, erect in posture, deliberate in manner and reflected his command of both the language and procedures of government protocol. A man possessed of the courage of his convictions, he did not hesitate to press an issue energetically if he felt the CMZa was in some manner being denied its rights. In the person of its new president, the CMZa soon came to realize they had someone who could represent them with uncommon ability and flair.

In the early years of his leadership, President Mbonza turned regularly to the missionaries among them seeking, as had his predecessors, to incorporate them into the day to day life of the church. Though his plan never materialized, he early proposed that a single missionary serve as his personal receptionist and secretary. (1) There were regular requests forwarded to the AIMM Elkhart office for a gamut of missionaries, particularly for the schools, medical department and for specialized ministries in agriculture, production of literature, radio programming and theological training. A striking example of this early openness toward AIMM personnel was the appointment of second-term missionary Rick Derksen to replace Vice President Mukanza in the key CMZa post of Coordinator of Evangelism and Church Life. Rick and Marilyn Carter Derksen had spent their first term on the isolated CMZa station of Mutena where they came under the tutelage of seasoned African church leaders like Tshiaba Muanza (pr. TSHAH-bah MWAH-nza), Mushimbele Ikutu (pr. moo-shi-MBEH-lay i-KOO-too), and Mayindama Kasay (pr. mah-yi-NDAH-mah kah-SAH-yi), a dedicated couple on staff at the Mutena dispensary, and fellow missionaries Elmer and Esther Quiring Dick who, at the time, were serving their seventh missionary term with AIMM. The Derksens quickly demonstrated both their gift for language acquisition and their empathetic openness to the African people around them.

Having been thrust into a role which would bring him into constant contact with CMZa pastors from district to district, the question of Derksen's own ministerial credentials quickly surfaced. Though he held a degree in Biblical studies, he had not seen himself as qualified or gifted to fill what he considered to be a traditional pastoral role and thus had not sought ordination prior to coming to Zaire the first time. To these reservations the CMZa leaders had a quick response. They witnessed to his pastoral skills, his uncommon ability to communicate in the Tshiluba language and to his perceptive, affirming manner in relating to them as Africans. As for his credentials, that was no problem. The CMZa would ordain him. (2)

Thus in June, 1983, Derksen became the second AIMM missionary to be ordained by the African Church. Joining three other Zairian candidates in a service of ordination to the Christian ministry in the station chapel at Kalonda, (3) he moved into the mainstream of CMZa pastoral and administrative responsibility, a position which would eventually bring a period of acutely painful heart-searching for him.

but there was more

While the new president's sharp awareness of the shape and dynamics of government structure around him served CMZa well in its relations to the State, with passing time it became clear that this same awareness was coloring his view of his Church and how its administration should function. Evidence of this was to be found in some of the language which began to creep into usage. There were, for instance, references to "the Presidency of the CMZa" and to the "President's Cabinet." There were increasing references to the necessity of following the "hierarchical lines of communication" in addressing letters or requests to the president or his fellow officers. Appointments with the president were secured via his secretary and were then referred to as "audiences" with him.

But if a certain language of secular government was being adopted, so also were some views of administration. Under the former President Kabangy, CMZa bylaws had been rewritten which centered great authority in a group known, at the time, as the general council in which the administrative committee wielded great influence. The Mbonza administration proceeded to utilize these powers in a variety of ways. There was, for instance, the matter of processing new pastoral candidates. Traditionally, recommendations for ordination were brought by district leaders to CMZa General Assemblies. Their qualifications and performance were first reviewed by the Commission on Evangelism which, in turn, brought formal recommendation for those approved to the full delegate body. Only after this process of evaluation and approval were plans made back in their districts for their ordination.

However as early as October, 1980, just seven months after the election of a new president, it was the administrative committee which began to occupy itself with such matters. In a series of three actions, new educational stipulations were established as preconditions for ordination; (4) seven candidates were selected from a longer list for immediate ordination; a four-man Commission of Consecration was established to review and make decisions regarding the remainder of the candidates and to proceed with their ordination with eventual reporting back to the committee. The president and vice-president were declared to be permanent members of this commission. While the desire of the administrative committee to establish clear criteria for the future ordination of its pastors was praiseworthy, the feeling of CMZa district church leaders was nonetheless that a new "filter" had been installed by which their proposed pastoral candidates would now have to be screened.

Then there was the matter of constant requests for the establishment and recognition of new CMZa districts. Here again, such questions had traditionally first been submitted to the Commission on Evangelism during general assemblies for study and subsequent recommendation to the entire delegate body for discussion and action. By late 1980, however, this issue had also found its way into the agenda of the administrative committee. One minute of that October meeting created two new CMZa districts in the city of Kinshasa while stipulating their boundaries and their member congregations. (5)

The broadening of centralized authority within the administrative and executive committees in time also infringed upon the work of CMZa's medical services. While across the years CMZa administrations had asked for regular reporting and the opportunity to study major changes before they were put into effect, it was traditionally recognized that medicine and healing were highly specialized areas in which doctors and nurses needed a large autonomy of decision and action to best serve the Church and the needy populations around them. With the advent of the new administration in 1980, however, committee minutes soon began to appear in which decisions and directives were being issued for the medical work and staff.

When in 1981 the Medical Council submitted the request to be recognized as a department in its own right so as to practice its traditional freedom of action, the following comments appeared in committee minutes: "The Administrative Committee confirms the spirit of the General Assembly of Kamayala which instituted a

Department of Social Services under which the medical service is recognized as a sub-department. The A.C. calls attention [to the fact] that the Medical Council is a consultative body and not one of decision. This Council, established by the Church for the interest of the Church, must work in conformity with the aspirations and norms of the Church. The A.C. makes the Legal Representative responsible to pursue an investigation to discover the points which have led the Medical Council to want to withdraw from the Department of Social Services." (6)

Perhaps the clearest indication of the early drift toward an authoritative "top-down" approach to church administration was the decision to order the transfer and/or exchange of what were known as *chefs de districts* (a French term literally meaning "district chiefs" but used to designate what in American usage would be known as district pastors or presidents). This was a sharp departure from a long established CMZa pattern in which district level leadership was both elected and placed by the districts themselves. Now the new administrative committee was assuming the authority to move these key district church leaders from place to place and this with or without the approval of the districts involved.

The rationale spelled out by President Mbonza seemed reasonable enough. In one report he said: "Today there are numerous pastors and evangelists who work with joy and courage far from their families and villages. They belong, as do we, to the Church of Christ which not only sends [workers] out into the world but also confirms that the prophet is not respected at home. The transfer of functionaries and agents of [secular] societies and especially of the servants of God defies regionalism, tribalism and clanism. Indeed regionalism, tribalism and clanism are grave social maladies in the church in Africa which suffocate the Gospel of love and handicap its promotion to the point of canceling a ministry of many years. We have furthermore observed with satisfaction that the servants of God who had been scorned and discredited in their home areas carry on a remarkable work among their brethren in Christ of other tribes and clans." (7)

While, in fact, a number of transferred pastors were freed from local prejudice and enjoyed successful ministry in areas other than their own, there were also others so placed who encountered unrelenting resistance and problems. With passing time local districts came more and more to view such unilateral action on the part of the CMZa central administration as being in conflict with their local autonomy. It was over this issue of district rights that a crisis would eventually develop between President Mbonza and the leaders at Kalonda, just across the Kasai River from CMZa headquarters.

As the profile of the new administration further came into focus, it gradually became evident that behind the new terminology, the new penchant for protocol and the new assumptions of authority lay some new attitudes which were to become more and more troubling. For instance, official minutes of the administrative and executive committees occasionally took on a sharp, sardonic edge. As early as August, 1980, a minute of the administrative committee carried the following comments: "The AC reminds [everyone] that the reunions of councils in which divorced people, declared polygamists, professional quarrelers and career drunks take part are not Mennonite reunions. Consequently faithful members are asked to help their district and congregational leaders to correct this deplorable situation where it persists." (8) While there undoubtedly were problems at district levels which needed to be addressed, one wonders what corrective pastoral impact the language of this minute might have had.

It was in the same minutes that the following action was taken: "As regards the discourteous letter of the head of Kamayala District addressed to the [CMZa] Legal Representative with copies sent all over, the AC responds to him with censure and asks that a disciplinary file be opened in his name." (9) (Opening a disciplinary file was the language used to indicate the official notation of grievances required by Zaire labor laws as a prerequisite to the dismissal of an employee.) A year later in a meeting of the AC, it was stated "that all correspondence of a subversive nature be discouraged and that their authors be dealt with in a manner to make them an example." (10)

Minutes of such a retaliatory nature became more frequent through the first term of the new administration. It is certainly true that the new CMZa officers received a constant flow of requests, suggestions

353

and criticisms mixed with accusations as had all previous administrations. It is also true that criticisms and accusations were often based on a mix of fact and fiction. It goes without saying that the CMZa leaders needed to respond with efforts to counter negative influences and to seek ways of disciplining those who were guilty of disruptive and evil conduct. In time, however, a deep seated weakness became gradually apparent, that being an unwillingness or an inability to receive and deal honestly with sincere dissent or well intentioned critique. In the new authoritarian scheme of things, criticism of the new president and his collaborators was not well received. Any expression of differing points of view or discontent with decisions made were either attributed to ignorance and thus unworthy of response, or to ill will and thus "subversive" and calling for disciplinary retaliation. Though not stated in so many words, a perceived message began to take shape among rank-and-file CMZa people: "Within the CMZa we are your superiors. Our titles are to be used. We are to be respected and our directives are to be put into prompt and unquestioned application."

Presidents Mbonza and Bokeleale collide

By the year 1982, Reverend Bokeleale, President and Legal Representative of the ECZ, was able to view a nation-wide administrative structure well in place. By this time there were offices in every one of Zaire's regions headed by regional presidents whom he had installed following election by an assembly of representatives of the churches of the region. He himself had by this time been consecrated a Bishop and was making the same status a condition for those serving as ECZ regional presidents. (11)

In 1979, the Protestant groups of the West Kasai voted Rev. Bakatushipa (pr. bah-kah-too-SHEE-pah), the Legal Representative of the Presbyterian Church of the region, to serve as their ECZ regional secretary. Affirmed by Bishop Bokeleale, he was installed and consecrated a bishop - - this in spite of considerable resistance on the part of the Presbyterian Church. (12) His new ecclesiastical status was finally accepted by the Presbyterians on the condition that he would not attempt in any manner to function as a bishop within his own Church.

Problems nonetheless soon developed as Bishop Bakatushipa attempted to carry out his dual and frequently overlapping roles. Conflicts of interest and power gradually became apparent with the result that two years later, his membership and pastoral credentials with his own Church were revoked. This being the case, a special session of the regional ECZ Synod was convened in February, 1982. The basic issue before the group was: Since Bishop Bakatushipa had been excommunicated by his own Church, how could he continue as the president of the regional ECZ? Although advised of the meeting and invited to attend, Bishop Bokeleale declined. In a carefully worded document of proceedings, the history of the situation was spelled out after which a number of actions were taken chief of which were 1) to revoke Bishop Bakatushipa as well as his vice-president and 2) to name a transition committee to be responsible for ECZ regional concerns until they could reconvene to elect a successor. President Mbonza represented the CMZa on this committee and was appointed committee chairman.

Response from ECZ Bishop Bokeleale in Kinshasa was swift. He stated that he would not accept their actions and that as far as he was concerned, Bishop Bakatushipa remained the head of the regional ECZ. Ignoring his letters, a regional synod was convened just two months later. Once again Bishop Bokeleale was invited and once again he refused to come. The urgent issue before the delegates was the choice of a new regional president. Controversy was by this time swirling on all sides. It was well known that whoever would be elected would immediately come into direct conflict with Bishop Bokeleale in Kinshasa. After some canvassing of various church groups, a delegation approached President Mbonza. Would he allow his name to be presented for a vote? He would. Thus it was that the president of the CMZa was elected to this contested post. Word was flashed by short-wave radio to Tshikapa where celebrations were held in his honor upon his return. The festivities, however, proved to be premature. Word came from Kinshasa that the election was considered null and void; that President Mbonza was not recognized and that Bishop Bakatushipa remained the regional ECZ head all actions to the contrary notwithstanding.

There followed a year of confused stalemate. Finally another regional synod was set for January 15, 1983. This time Bishop Bokeleale came accompanied by a team of staff members from the ECZ national headquarters. There followed four days of confrontation featuring debates over the seating of delegates, the interpretation and application of ECZ's own bylaws and the rights of regional synods to elect their own officers. Bishop Bokeleale was determined to reinstate the former regional head regardless of the charges which had caused his expulsion from his own Church. The assembled delegates of the major church groups of the West Kasai were just as adamant in their refusal to allow an ECZ team from Kinshasa to impose its will upon them.

Rumors of all descriptions flew day and night. The controversy was already being interpreted by some journalists as having political overtones, i.e., Bishop Bokeleale represented the national political regime in his efforts to promote ecumenical stability. The regional church groups, in defying Bishop Bokeleale, were, in effect, defying higher political authority of the country. So tense was the situation that President Mbonza sought night lodging in the home of AIMM missionaries Henry and Tina Weier Dirks who, at the time, were supervising the completion of a new mission printing facility in the city of Kananga. (13)

By the afternoon of the fourth day, it had become obvious to all that the meeting was at an impasse. Finally Bishop Bokeleale walked to the podium and stated that, given their unwillingness to submit to his wishes, he as of that hour declared the regional ECZ to be suspended. Since there was no longer such an organization, there obviously was no need for officers. Each church group was to carry on its activities under their own bylaws and officers as in the past. Turning, he led his delegation out of the assembly hall and shortly thereafter they boarded their flight for Kinshasa.

In the confrontation there had been no winners, only losers. Among the latter was President Mbonza. During the four tense days of those January 1983 meetings, he had come to symbolize the defiant opposition of the West Kasai church community toward the national leadership of the ECZ. The time would come soon enough when President Mbonza and the ECZ Bishop would once again confront each other in conflict.

Mbuji Mayi 1983

Five weeks after the stormy Kananga meetings found the CMZa gathered in its general assembly in Mbuji Mayi, the setting where some thirty years earlier Archie Graber had led a Mennonite team of volunteers in an effort to keep thousands of ragged and emaciated Baluba refugees alive. Neither the city nor the people bore much resemblance to those of the early 60's. The town had grown rapidly. The hardy Baluba refugees, given help, had plunged with a will into their own rehabilitation. Indeed, it was a measure of their confidence and pride that they had offered to host the CMZa General Assembly of 1983. An interesting facet of their planning was the place of meeting which had been arranged - - a large, airy Presbyterian Church which housed a growing congregation under the skillful pastoral care of a former Mennonite refugee, Rev. Kaleta (pr. kah-LEH-tah) Emile. Known and respected by CMZa people prior to independence as an able preacher and Bible teacher at the Kalonda Bible Institute, his gifts quickly came to light after his forced migration to the South Kasai. His delight in being able to serve as the host pastor for his former Mennonite colleagues was apparent to all.

In preparation for his first general assembly as president of the CMZa, Rev. Mbonza had left no stone unturned. Detailed instructions for travel for all delegates from thirty-three different districts were circulated well in advance. Eighty official delegates arrived to find a registration line where credentials were verified and the status of financial contributions of their respective districts toward CMZa central administration were reviewed. For those with serious arrears, arrangements were required on the spot. Upon clearance, each delegate received a name tag and a large handbook which contained, among other things, department reports, copies of some of the presentations they were to hear, statistics, an official roster of active pastors listed district by district, budget information, two study papers on the topic of the Holy Spirit (14) and copies of the voluminous report President Mbonza would himself present to the assembly.

a remarkable morning

The opening session of the assembly was marked by careful protocol. Preliminaries featured hymn singing, a Biblical meditation, the official seating of delegates, approval of agenda and rules of order and the voting of officers. There then followed, what on the program was called, "the solemn opening" of the assembly. There were some numbers by an excellent church choir. President Mbonza then took the podium attired in his clerical garb. After recognizing a variety of visitors, representatives of government and other church communities including Andy Rupp and Jim Bertsche of the AIMM, the assembly was declared officially opened.

That done, President Mbonza began working his way through his 37 page report which was truly impressive by any standard. It was, in effect, a "state of the church" address to the assembled delegates. The editorial patterns of his report quickly became evident. Drawing upon materials which had been submitted to him by various department heads, he underscored whatever progress had been realized. He then also highlighted weaknesses and failures which he followed with personal observations and personal recommendations to the delegate body for discussion and approval. The scope of his treatment was broad. His proposals for action reflected much thought on his part.

For example, in the area of Christian Education he observed that there was a lack of interest in the Sunday School materials offered to all districts in the CMZa book store. He then went on to comment: "If this lack of interest is due to a weakness on our part in the Department of Evangelism, let us correct this weakness. If it is due to the fact that such a program does not address the cultural and socio-economic reality of this country, let the Christian Education [department] propose another way of educating the children in the Christian faith." (15)

Commenting on the Kalonda Bible Institute he pointed out, with obvious satisfaction, that for the first time three women were enrolled in the men's section and doing their studies in French. He then defined two problems: the inability of rural churches to fully support their pastors and the insufficient number of graduates coming from this Institute. Regarding the first problem, he urged the renewal of some basic vocational training in conjunction with their Biblical studies. As for the latter problem, he proposed either the creation of special courses for those who demonstrated obvious pastoral gifts or to admit a class into the Institute every two years instead of every four thus doubling the output of students - - a proposal which obviously meant more classrooms and student housing.

In a section of his report entitled "projects for the future" he listed, among others: 1) to achieve a CMZa administrative budget entirely supported by the members of the CMZa; 2) to realign CMZa's regions so as to reflect its ecclesiastical realities rather than the political boundaries of our country; 3) to do more to nourish the bodies of our believers as well as their souls; 4) to recognize the city of Kinshasa as a fourth region of the CMZa; 5) to prepare missionaries of the CMZa to serve in other regions of our country, in neighboring countries as well as more distant countries." (16)

Turning to the life of the Church and its pastoral ministry, he commented on "the authoritarian, inflexible, legalistic, unorganized and tribalist manner in which certain district leaders direct their work." He then followed with what he termed "a vision for the future." Citing the life of the early church as described in Acts 2:42-47, he said: "It is thus that the prayer of the Lord 'Thy kingdom come, thy will be done on earth as it is in heaven' was realized. My prayer today is that the reign of God may come and that his will may be done in the Mennonite Community as in heaven. This vision cannot be realized by a good administration or by some program at the level of central CMZa administration. It is necessary that we ask God to manifest himself among us every time that we pray. It is also necessary that we begin to live this shared life which was seen in the first Christian community. I know well this must begin with me. If I start to put this vision in practice with a few brothers and sisters around me, perhaps others will do it too."

"I see [envision] more groups of Christians who gather regularly not only to pray and sing and read the Word of God but also to talk about their social and economic problems . . . and to analyze their economic, political and spiritual causes. I see small groups of Christians who are not afraid to speak and act differently than the mass, who are not afraid to speak out against and to refuse all injustice. I see small groups of Christians who always defend the poor and the oppressed with the courage of prophets. I see little groups of Christians who are able to discern and employ the gifts of the Holy Spirit. And I see little groups of Christians who manifest all the fruits of the Holy Spirit in their daily lives. Such groups of Christians certainly do not hesitate to call others to come see what Jesus has done for them. And the Lord will also add disciples each day to those communities of Christians. That is evangelization." (17)

It truly was a remarkable statement of vision, Biblically grounded, drawn in imaginative terms and crafted in moving language. The assembled CMZa delegates were given much to ponder as they settled into the schedule of activities for the rest of the week.

and yet - - -

The CMZa General Assembly of 1983 at Mbuji Mayi was exceptional in many ways. The preparation and organization, entirely in Zairian hands, was outstanding. All thirty-three CMZa districts were represented; among the eighty delegates only three were missionaries. (18) While there was a sprinkling of gray heads among the delegates, a clear majority were from a younger generation who were proficient in French and took active part in both commission meetings and the plenary sessions. There was a spirit of freedom as issues were ably debated and brought to a vote by Assembly Chairman Kakesa Samuel.

There were some notable assembly decisions, e.g. 1) the decision to respond to Kafutshi Kakesa's spirited plea to raise the CMZa women's work to the level of a full department of the church - - a striking accomplishment in an African male-oriented culture; 2) the decision to apply for affiliation with the Association of Evangelicals of Africa and Madagascar; (AEAM) 3) the formal recommendation to enroll and graduate students from the Kalonda Bible Institute every two years instead of every four; 4) the establishment of some criteria for the recognition of new CMZa districts; 5) the granting of district status to four new areas bringing the CMZa total at assembly time to thirty-seven; 6) the authorization of the CMZa South Kasai leaders to open a program of evangelization in the copper rich region of Shaba; 7) the adoption of President Mbonza's proposal to recognize the city of Kinshasa as CMZa's fourth region. (19)

And there was an update on CMZa statistics, a significant piece of work in and of itself. In his report to the delegates, President Mbonza cited a total of 113 primary schools and sixty-six secondary sections scattered across CMZa territory. He also stated that at assembly time, CMZa counted 472 ordained deacons and maintained some degree of ministry among as many as twenty-five different tribal groups. (20) There was an updated listing of all CMZa district presidents and a roster of all 106 ordained pastors, per district, who at assembly time were active and in good standing. (21)

And yet, amidst the sights and sounds of a large church seriously at work, there were some muted signals of attitudes on the part of President Mbonza which were to become more and more pronounced with passing time. There were, for instance, his introductory remarks in the first session. After thanking all those who had worked closely and faithfully with him during his first three years as CMZa's president, he continued: "Although there were within the work team which [God] entrusted to me some sons of the Evil One who resembled their father (hypocrites, lazy, bitter, dissatisfied, opportunists, etc.), he reserves for his church men and women of faith, prophets, workers who are conscientious, diligent and honest, men and women of peace and love." (22)

Referring briefly to the tempestuous sessions of the regional ECZ meetings of Kananga through which he had just come, he commented: "I would have functioned [as the next President] if there had not been incomprehension between the synod of the region and the General Secretariat of the ECZ." (23) Referring to the ECZ President, Mbonza then added: "I can forget everything regarding President Bokeleale but I will not forget his salutations to the communities which characterize his letters." (24)

Regarding CMZa relations with AIMM, the following obscure comment was made to the delegate body: "Relations with the AIMM are very good; that is why we even have among us today Brother Andrew Rupp, the President of their Board and Brother Jim Bertsche, the Executive Secretary of the organization. Unless it is because of our laziness, we digest [or stomach] badly [or poorly] their very good decision, one full of instruction and lessons, to diminish their contribution to the budget of the administration of the Community [CMZa]. We would request either [the AIMM] review its decision or the [CMZa] districts and parishes who have need of officers' visits to augment their contributions to the central treasury." (25)

Prior to the assembly, President Mbonza had basically stopped written communication with the AIMM secretary in Elkhart. Letters from Elkhart addressed to him remained unrecognized and unanswered. During their limited time at the Assembly at Mbuji Mayi, the AIMM secretary managed a few brief working sessions with the CMZa president. On one occasion the issue of unacknowledged AIMM correspondence was raised, correspondence which at times was copied to his vice-president or others whom the contents directly involved. His response made it clear that he did not appreciate his letters being copied to anyone. As long as this remained the practice, those who received copies were free to answer in his place!

It was in this same conversation that President Mbonza informed the AIMM secretary that one of the veteran missionaries who had overseen a long series of building and remodeling programs across the years was no longer viewed by CMZa as "competent" to direct any further such projects for them. When asked the reasons for this decision, the president declared the results of his last project to have been "deplorable." Pushed for further explanation, he cited a ceiling in a room which had fallen. Henceforth capable Zairians would be assigned to work with this missionary to be sure that further work would be acceptable to the CMZa. Unrecognized was the fact that the termite-riddled fallen ceiling had - - due to pressure of time - - been installed with scrap lumber because the quality lumber repeatedly requested from the CMZa sawmill was diverted elsewhere by CMZa officials. Unspoken but clearly underlying such combative attitudes was a festering resentment toward the AIMM for the gradual reversal of the heavy subsidy granted for costs of Zaire church administration.

And there were the CMZa's ongoing relations with its missionaries on the scene. In the opening comments addressed to the assembly delegates, President Mbonza conveyed "the warm greetings of all those who love you and think of the community." Mentioned specifically were the collaborators and staff of the church headquarters; members of the administrative committee; their brothers and sisters of North America and Belgium whom he visited in 1981; your brothers and sisters of the world gathered in August of the same year at the meeting of the MWC General Council in Nairobi. Mentioning yet their fellow Christians from other church groups across Zaire as well as fellow Mennonites from all of the CMZa regions and districts, he concluded with the observation: "God gave me a wife who carries the Church in her heart and who asked me to greet you." It was a touching and richly merited tribute to Dimuka Ana, his wife." (26)

It was, however, not without significance that in this extensive roll call of people and groups whose greetings were so carefully conveyed to the delegate body there was no reference made to the nearly fifty AIMM missionaries who were either present in Zaire or preparing to return there from North America who were deeply interested in and concerned for the assembly sessions. It was elsewhere in his reporting that the president took up the issue of CMZa/missionary relations. In a section entitled "a review of problems and propositions," he referred to a lack of agreement [or understanding] between CMZa and its missionaries. In response to this situation he proposed "that there be a serious orientation of missionaries during the first days of their Zairian stay; that there be regular communication between [CMZa] staff and missionaries and that some missionaries be sent home in the event of impossibility of adaptation."

A specific problem cited in this part of his report was "a lack of participation of missionaries in the life of the church and confusion of roles, i.e., with whom and for whom they work." This observation was followed with the proposal: "In the future let us invite 'missionaries' under the title of 'mission partners,' i.e. ,[those] who are not supported by AIMM but rather by other groups, whether by the local church or by their own means. See Mt. 10:10. Once here they will have no further connection with AIMM. They will be completely dependent upon CMZa for direction and support." (27)

It was a further measure of an undercurrent of CMZa headquarters staff discontent with its missionary collaborators in the spring of 1983 that an ad hoc committee was named to meet during the assembly sessions. Called simply a "special commission," it in fact was a small group convened to review the performance and attitude of CMZa's missionary personnel.

As the Mbuji Mayi General Assembly drew to a close, it had become very clear that some friction was developing between the new CMZa administration and the AIMM and its personnel. In his reporting to the board the AIMM executive secretary stated that warning flags were clearly snapping in the Zaire wind. It was now twelve years since the 1971 consultation at Djoko Punda in which the fusion of mission and church had been worked through. New CMZa leaders were now in place who had not been part of that dialogue and who had their own ideas and views as to what fusion should mean and the missionaries' place within it.

For their part, many of the missionaries viewed some of the shifts in language, stance, procedure and attitude with genuine misgivings. And, it must be admitted, on the part of some missionaries working in some of the CMZa departments, such misgivings at times resulted in language and demeanor vis-à-vis CMZa leaders which bespoke discontent, lack of support and even outright resistance.

It was high time to lay plans for another AIMM/CMZa round table discussion.

CHAPTER 39   THE SHADOWS DEEPEN

President Mbonza and his fellow CMZa staff members returned to Tshikapa after the Mbuji Mayi Assembly weary but with a sense of having conducted a businesslike gathering which had dealt with a wide ranging church agenda. Introductory comments in the official minutes carried praise for the president's work and his reporting to the delegate body which, it was said, was greeted by prolonged applause. But as busy as they had been, much pressing work awaited them. Minutes from a flurry of committee meetings revealed a church busy in a variety of areas. In the first post-assembly session of the executive committee CMZa delegates were named to two world gatherings: 1) a Conference for Itinerant Evangelists which was being organized that summer in Amsterdam by the Billy Graham Association, and 2) the Mennonite World Conference scheduled the following summer in Strasbourg, France. In the same sessions it was decided to create an administrative board for the Kalonda Bible Institute. Continuing a tradition begun by the new administration, four new CMZa district presidents were appointed. (1)

During succeeding months in meetings of the executive and full administrative committees, official records revealed further facets of church life, e.g., a lengthy minute dealing with "the financial situation of the community." In attempting to grapple with their administrative budget short fall in 1983, it was decided that all members of the AC assume the responsibility of sensitizing the members of their respective areas regarding their responsibility toward the CMZa 1983 budget; that a serious effort be made to establish an accurate census of CMZa members in each district; that a circular letter be issued listing the contributions to date from each district. The detailed minute concluded by stating that in the event these efforts did not result in adequate response, each staff member was to make proposals for cut backs in their own departments. (2)

The issue of the place of lay people in the Church was addressed; a call for prayer was issued to CMZa at large for "the sad situation which continues to exist within the regional synod of the ECZ." (Given the confrontation with President Bokeleale, the Methodist and Presbyterian Churches were threatening to withdraw from the ECZ and to create an independent council in the region. CMZa's stance was to discourage this and to support efforts of reconciliation.) Official approval was given by CMZa for doctoral studies for Vice President Mukanza if a scholarship could be arranged via AIMM. Referring to voices of dissent among the CMZa membership of the South Kasai and a call for some form of autonomy vis-à-vis CMZa administration at Tshikapa, a minute read: "In the Lord all believers form a single indivisible body. All clan and tribal particularities are to be subdued. Our salvation is in our one and only Lord and Creator." Regarding the hiring of teachers for the coming school year, it was warned that this was to be done "under the eye of the church councils in conformity with the norms of the [CMZa] community . . . ." (3)

In another action, recognizing their earlier imprudence in attempting to administer the CMZa's sprawling medical service, it was decided to raise the medical service to the administrative rank of a department, an action which granted a much larger degree of freedom to its missionary and Zairian staff to carry on their work.

a series of firsts

In the ongoing life of the Zaire Church far beyond the walls of the central offices, some exciting things were happening. In the summer of 1984, CMZa's first woman graduated with honors from ISTK, the pastoral training institute in Kinshasa. Furthermore, she was the first married woman to earn a diploma from the pastoral track of this school.

But being first was not a new experience for this remarkable lady. She was born in the village home of Kandala District Pastor Khelendende Pierre (pr. keh-leh-NDEH-ndeh). A gifted preacher, she had early heard the Gospel spelled out by her father in Giphende, her mother tongue. In early life she gave her heart to the Lord. A sister died at a young age leaving her the only child in the pastor's home.

Pastor Khelendende had always longed for a son with the dream that he might follow in his footsteps and also become a pastor in the Zaire Mennonite Church. When it became apparent that this would never happen, he one day came to see an AIMM missionary friend and said: "It has always been my dream to have a son to give to my Church. The Lord has not chosen to give me a son but he has given me a daughter whom we love with all our hearts. She learns quickly and has always been obedient in our home. I now give her to you and to the Lord. Care for her and train her as you would your own child. Perhaps my hunger to see a child of mine serve the Lord in our Church may yet be realized, in some manner or other, through our daughter." (4)

Upon finishing junior high, Leonie Khelendende was enrolled in the Nyanga Secondary School. Her pastor father was right. She was a bright, disciplined student. In June of 1971 she became the first CMZa girl to graduate from the school. Her study track had been in elementary education. The CMZa honored her by naming her the first woman director of a CMZa primary school, this back at her home station, Kandala. Along the way she met Lwadi Nari (LWAH-di nah-REE), a graduate of a humanities section of a state school in Kikwit. Marriage followed and together they continued in church teaching assignments.

It was in 1981 that after much prayer and discussion they both applied for CMZa scholarships to enroll in ISTK. How would her boldness be viewed by the CMZa administration? How would they feel about a couple enrolling in the same pastoral training program together? What of their four children? Could she really carry the heavy study load and adequately care for her family at the same time? The CMZa administration was prepared to grant her husband a scholarship but was hesitant about one for her. There were so many candidates and their scholarships were limited. How could they grant two for a single household? Hearing about this, the AIMM Women's Auxiliary offered to provide funds for her, a grant which was joyfully accepted.

There followed three full, grueling years. Children were sometimes seriously ill. Food rations were sometimes barely adequate. But Leonie not only held her own but did so with distinction. Graduation day in 1984 was a day of triumph. A written account later read: "What a celebration! Khelendende's letters to AIMM during those years have been full of humility recognizing her need of the Savior, his help and his guidance. She freely expresses sincere gratitude to all who have helped her, who have prayed for her, who have given her scholarships and who have taught her. Surely our heavenly Father will hover near and keep his hands upon this 'second time she's a first' woman as she ministers to her people in Zaire." (5)

Upon graduation Leonie was named the director of the secondary school of her home station Kandala which, upon her arrival, had an enrollment of 238 boys and 132 girls. She was also welcomed home by her parents. In ill health, her aging father had lived to see his heart's desire, a child of his trained in Bible and a leader in his beloved church. (6)

Another CMZa "first" was scored that same summer in that same class in the persons of Mr. and Mrs. Sambi (pr. SAH-mbi). Coming from the isolated village of Karuru among the Banjembe (pr. bah-NJEH-mbay) people of the West Kasai, their tribe had long been resistant to change of any kind. It was only after years of faithful witness on the part of both missionaries and Africans that the first converts were won -- and this primarily through the simple bush schools which were made available to their children. Commenting on the challenge which lay ahead of the Sambis in the summer of 1984, AIMM missionary and ISTK staff member Gladys Buller wrote: "How well we remember our 'evangelistic forays' into Karuru . . . some thirty years ago! . . . 'Uncle' Frank Enns, a pioneer missionary, had a great burden for the Njembe tribe. Now we have the first graduates from there, a young man and woman, sincere and dedicated to God. But going back and finding acceptance will be no lark. Every graduate must give proof that his faith is genuine and he will be tried in many ways for Gospel and culture inevitably clash. Back in the bush, it's survival of the fittest in a spiritual sense as well as physical." (7)

And there were still other "firsts" in CMZa circles. Dr. Makina a Nganga, a Zairian Mennonite doctor was enrolled in Tulane University in New Orleans, LA (1983-85) in a master's program in public health with a view to returning to Zaire as the administrator of CMZa's ministry in this field.

In the rapidly growing city of Kikwit, AIMM/CMZa were involved in their first cooperative effort with the widely-renowned Habitat for Humanity organization. A sizeable terrain had been donated by the local government and an organizing committee was in place headed by Kakesa Samuel. Habitat was ready to begin this new project but was looking for someone to oversee building crews. Glen and Phyllis Thomas Boese of Avon, SD, enabled AIMM/CMZa to step into this gap. Trained respectively in industrial arts and home economics and in their mid-50's, they saw this as an opportunity for overseas service they didn't want to miss. Thus another dimension of human service was undertaken under a Mennonite mission/church flag.

In the fall of 1984 there were 37 AIMM missionaries listed on active status for Zaire with three additional couples under appointment to that country. There was the bright light of activity and opportunity on all sides but there were also growing pockets of shadow.

if you were honest

An early focus of concern for both the CMZa administration and the AIMM Board following the Mbuji Mayi Assembly was the scheduling of another major AIMM/CMZa consultation. A centerpiece of that dialogue was to be a detailed review of the mission/church fusion agreement which had been worked through in 1971 at Djoko Punda. Dates were set for December 10-12, 1984. As the time approached, a certain frostiness became apparent on the part of the CMZa administration. For many years it had been a tradition to view AIMM delegation members as fraternal visitors as well official board representatives. Thus it was that a prelude to consultations had always been extensive travel among the districts for preliminary contacts with both church leaders and missionaries.

In 1984, however, when it was again proposed that the delegation (8) visit various areas before the official meeting, AIMM was informed that the CMZa saw no need for such contacts ahead of time. But if the delegation insisted, stops en route to Tshikapa would be scheduled. In each case, however, the delegation would be accompanied by President Mbonza or a member of the CMZa staff. The message was clear. The travel and contacts of the AIMM group of late 1984 would be limited and more closely monitored than had others of the past.

President Mbonza opened the first joint session with a meditation based on the theme: "The knowledge of truth sets us free." He observed, with good insight, that "we tend to make finances the basis of our relationship. Jesus wants to wave a red flag before us. May the language of our consultation be not that of the world but that of the church." (9) It was an excellent opening. The delegation responded assuring the committee members that it was in this spirit that they wished to work through the agenda and to deal with any misunderstandings which may have accumulated.

Early in the sessions Vice President Mukanza Ilunga raised the issue of possible new models of AIMM/CMZa collaboration. Might CMZa in some way join other AIMM member conferences based in North America? It was an intriguing idea and one which sparked considerable discussion. But the pursuit of the topic, like several others, inevitably brought the group to the hard realities of budgets and financial resources. A sketch of AIMM's own priorities for the 1980's had been mailed ahead including reference to AIMM's planned involvement in areas of Africa outside Zaire. Referring to this announcement, President Mbonza observed at one point: "CMZa has become vast and its needs are growing. If the AIMM were more honest, it would dispense more of its resources in Zaire than anywhere else in Africa." He then distributed a handout in which it was stated that CMZa saw all phases of its program as efforts in evangelism. The president then concluded: "If evangelism is really a high priority for the AIMM, CMZa can offer many opportunities in Zaire." (10) Clearly CMZa leaders took a dim view of AIMM's announced intention of expanding its ministry on the continent of Africa while trimming back on its support of the operating costs of the Zaire Church.

But it was discussion regarding missionary personnel that took on the sharpest edge. As a matter of fact, the CMZa Executive had reworked the 1971 fusion agreement and had its draft ready for distribution to the AIMM delegation. It was somewhat shorter than the original, and this for two reasons. First, some articles had been shortened or combined. It was further discovered that all references to missionary roles and relations within CMZa had been dropped. In ensuing discussion the delegation was told that missionary loyalty to the church was in some cases questionable. To resolve this, CMZa was now proposing that missionary membership in the Zaire Church would henceforth be subjected to clearly established formalities which would mean formal application, the presentation of a letter from their home church overseas and the termination of all ties with such churches. Under such circumstances, they could become members of the Zaire Church like Africans themselves and there would be no need for any reference to them in the revised fusion agreement. As for the position of "missionary counselor" spelled out in the original document, this position would be retained only if it was made very clear that such a person's responsibilities lay with fellow missionaries alone and that this individual in no way spoke for the missionaries nor for the AIMM in North America.

In further negotiation, some of the articles dealing with missionary housing, retreats and education of children were reluctantly reinstated but the mood of the CMZa administration was clear enough. It expected - - even demanded - - respect and submission on the part of all. Such demands of unqualified loyalty to the CMZa leadership had already for some time been addressed to Zairians. Similar demands were now also being addressed to missionary personnel.

As the consultation wound down, the AIMM delegation expressed appreciation for the willingness of the CMZa leaders to share their views and frustrations in an open manner. If AIMM at times had been perceived to work unilaterally or without sufficient prior consultation, it was only out of a desire to help and to stand with the Church. There had never been any thought or desire of bypassing the Church and its administration. To this Kakesa Samuel responded with his gift for descriptive speech: "It is not that we do not welcome AIMM help. We do. But we want that help to come through our front door and not through a side window!" (11)

The consultation came to a close with a general feeling on the part of the AIMM representatives that dialogue with a feisty new CMZa administration had gone reasonably well and that essential agenda had been dealt with in an open, frank manner. There was, nonetheless, a vague feeling of uneasiness which stemmed not so much from things actually said as from body language, expressions and attitudes observed and sensed around the tables during those days - - particularly on the part of CMZa office staff that had been part of the negotiations. There was a nagging sense that within the CMZa at year's end 1984, all was not well.

the Tshikapa General Hospital revisited

The sprawling general hospital built in the 1940's with *Forminière* Diamond Company money had gone through several chapters of its existence. Originally staffed by Belgian doctors and Catholic Sisters, it was abandoned by the Company shortly after political independence was achieved in 1960. At that point the AIMM negotiated a rental arrangement and continued to operate the medical facility with missionary and Zairian medical personnel, this to the delight and appreciation of the local population. When, by the late 60's, local government officials mistakenly saw it as a gold mine of revenue, a period of pressure and rumor mongering was concluded by the Mission's withdrawal of its personnel. Although the government did assign its own staff, the hospital began a slow decline. There were frequent shortages of medications and supplies. Government staff, furthermore, rarely brought to their service the compassion or ethical standards that had been maintained by AIMM. The little mission hospital and maternity across the river at Kalonda were consequently inundated with patients.

President Mbonza considered this situation to be an opportunity for the CMZa to assert itself and to upgrade the medical services of the rapidly growing Tshikapa community. He spent a great deal of time and energy in visiting the provincial medical offices soliciting the administrative transfer of this hospital to the CMZa. Long known for their major presence and contribution to public welfare in the Tshikapa area, the promise of Mennonite personnel and expertise proved to be convincing and in early 1984 a five year preliminary agreement was signed by President Mbonza and provincial medical authorities. (12)

The news of the transfer of the hospital back to Mennonite hands was greeted with great enthusiasm by the local populace. As a matter of fact, squads of volunteer labor were recruited by the Kimbanguists (a local congregation of the largest African Independent Church in Zaire) as well as the Muslim community of the area to help cut down patches of weeds and to scrub down abandoned pavilions. From the beginning, however, there was lack of clarity as to how the hospital was to be operated. While appealing to the State for the hospital in the name of CMZa and its medical department, once the papers were signed, President Mbonza began to make unilateral assignments of CMZa staff to the hospital. Even more troubling was the fact that while he required the central pharmacy at Kalonda to provide medications and supplies for the newly acquired medical facility, he resisted all efforts of the CMZa medical department to secure either reports on services rendered or accounting for its finances. With passing time it became clear that the general hospital staff was answerable to CMZa's central administrators and not to its medical department.

an angry "tug-of-war"

The issues of the exercise and balance of power are as old as the human race itself. Whether in secular or religious circles, lines have been repeatedly drawn and redrawn to indicate the boundaries between central and regional authority. This was an ongoing process with the CMZa from its earliest days. With powerful tribal and regional loyalties always lying close to the surface, there clearly needed to be some form of central church authority. In peaceful times it resembled a delicate balancing act. In times of discord, it more resembled an angry "tug-of-war." Given President Mbonza's clear administrative gifts, his deep rooted dislike of disorder and his inclination to retaliate against those who overstepped boundaries or displayed lack of respect for CMZa central administration, it was inevitable that serious friction points would materialize.

The CMZa region of the South Kasai had always enjoyed a somewhat larger autonomy vis-à-vis the central CMZa offices at Tshikapa than the other regions. Separated both by long distances and the memories of the bloody early 1960's which saw Baluba Mennonites flee for their lives from the tribal clashes which exploded along the Kasai River, they tended to draw their own lines between CMZa central authority and what they considered to be their regional prerogatives and rights. Under the alert leadership of Regional Representative Mpoyi Tshienda (pr. mpoi TSHEH-ndah), they had succeeded in deflecting repeated efforts of previous CMZa administrations to impose fuller accountability for their activities as a CMZa region. When in 1984 division once again lifted its head between the two major clan groups which comprised the regional CMZa community of the South Kasai and complaints were addressed by one of the groups to Tshikapa, President Mbonza saw this as the moment to step in and to try to bring this freewheeling regional church administration into line. A special five-person investigative commission was named to go to Mbuji Mayi and to bring back recommendations as to the measures to be taken. The commission was to be headed by President Mbonza himself. (13) Notified of their arrival and the purpose of their visit, local CMZa leaders found a sympathetic ear in government offices. Seeing such a trip from distant Tshikapa as a violation of their hard-won autonomy, the MAF flight was met on the Mbuji Mayi tarmac by immigration agents. Within 17 short minutes the plane was again air borne and on the return leg of its trip with all commission members aboard!

They were not amused. The clipped language of the minutes of this commission reflected their irritation. After listing in detail the misdemeanors and complaints which had accumulated around him, action was taken "to suspend Brother Mpoyi Tshienda Bitekete from his functions of Regional Representative and asks the General Assembly to exclude and to excommunicate him for the innumerable abuses of which he has been guilty." A second article stated that "all the powers of the ex-Regional Representative are temporarily entrusted to the Presidency of the CMZa until the next General Assembly." Further action was taken to name new presidents of the five CMZa districts of that region. The minutes went on to comment on the "broader autonomy" requested by the region stating that the issue would be referred to the next general assembly to be settled once for all. In the meantime, the special commission "condemned with energy all autonomous behavior before a final decision of the next General Assembly." And, finally, it requested that the CMZa President bring all those actions to the attention of appropriate political authorities. (14)

But still another confrontation was in the making at Kalonda Station, just across the Kasai River from the Tshikapa CMZa headquarters, which was to have a major impact upon events which were to follow. Kalonda Station was the church headquarters of its district and was experiencing troubled times with its district leadership. There had been great jubilation of the local Lulua membership when, in 1968, one of their own young men, Loena Pierre, (pr. LOH-nah) graduated from the newly created inter-Mennonite theological school at Kajiji. Recommended for ordination by his district, he then taught in church schools and eventually was elected district president in which role he served for several years. In 1979 he was replaced by Pastor Tshalu (pr. TSHAH-loo), also a member of the local ethnic group. Within two years there was also discontent with his leadership. It was in 1981 that the CMZa Administrative Committee (AC) adopted its policy of appointing district presidents irrespective of their district of origin. Thus it was that Pastor Djare (pr. DJAH-ray) Jeremie arrived at Kalonda.

Originally from the Banga area, he was an energetic, vibrant pastor who took his role as district president seriously. He had vision for the Kalonda Church and did not hesitate to tackle problems or to address wrong doing. It was not long until his forthright manner as an "outsider" began to stir reaction. By the time the Kalonda District Conference of 1984 rolled around, there was a rumble of discontent. Not having unanimous support, the dissident delegates waited until the conference had been concluded and then held a rump session of dissidents who voted to oust President Djare and to replace him with Shamuimba Mbombo (pr. shah-MUI-mbah MBOH-mboh), the son of a venerated senior pastor at Kalonda, Mbombo Daniel. A graduate of ISTK, Shamuimba was at the time director of the CMZa primary school at Mutena Station.

Hearing of this irregular action, the CMZa AC declared the action null and void and President Djare continued as the district head though with mounting opposition. It was at this point that the tense situation was greatly aggravated by the meddling of an area village chief. A non-Christian but a member of Shamuimba's clan, he began to visit the station. An irrational and noisy man, he attempted to impose himself and his demands on behalf of his fellow clansman upon the station church. Hearing of this, President Mbonza recognized that a new element had been inserted into an already tense situation over which he as a church officer had no control. Going to the local government authorities he reported what was going on. Thus yet another exterior element was drawn into the already confused Kalonda Church scene. A local government agent sought out the chief and threatened him with jail if he sought to intervene any further.

There then followed a swift succession of events: In January 1985 the Kalonda District Council met and contested the ruling of CMZa's central administration by affirming its support of Shamuimba as their own candidate for the position of district president. In March Shamuimba himself came from Mutena and convened a session of the district council at which time it was decided that he should simply move to the station and assume that position.

By this time there were several levels of dynamics within the mounting confrontation taking shape. A first and obvious level was one which opposed the will of CMZa's central administration against that of the Kalonda District leadership. At another level there was tribal friction as the Kalonda District sought to replace an unpopular non-Lulua president who had been assigned to them instead of one of their own local sons. At still another level there was resentment vis-à-vis President Mbonza for his authoritarian approach and for bringing government authorities into the picture. And, finally, there was the approaching CMZa General Assembly which was to be held in the summer of 1985 at which time election of officers was to take place. It was no secret that there were other districts which shared Kalonda's growing disenchantment with the central administration and that a movement was under way to field a strong candidate to oppose President Mbonza in the elections. Thus the controversy over the issue of the Kalonda District President was, in fact, also a controversy over votes at the coming general assembly.

Palm Sunday 1985 saw all of these conflicting dynamics merge into an explosive mix. Plans had long been laid for a baptism service early that morning down the hill in the Kasai River with worship and communion services to follow up in the church on the station. But with station church leadership under contention, who would officiate on Sunday morning in all of these special activities? AIMM missionary Rick

Derksen, a member of the CMZa Administrative Committee and a resident at Kalonda, was deeply involved in these unfolding events as he sought to play counseling and mediating roles.

Unknown to President Mbonza across the river, Derksen had succeeded in working out a compromise which removed Shamuimba from any leading role in the program for the day. Early Sunday morning, as the baptismal service at river's edge was coming to a close, from the tall grass there suddenly emerged two soldiers led by President Mbonza's personal secretary. They asked for Shamuimba to be identified and arrested him. Derksen followed them and found the vehicle from CMZa headquarters parked at the edge of the road with President Mbonza seated at the steering wheel. Under the false impression that Shamuimba was defying central CMZa administration that morning by participating in the baptismal service, he had again gone to local state authorities. This time it was to seek government help to force CMZa's will upon one of its own members. There he received the usual response: "If you need our help, you must provide transportation. We have none of our own." President Mbonza did not hesitate. He himself would take the official and his military escort to the baptismal scene. A tragic precedent was being set. Although he would later protest that "I was only a chauffeur," it had become clear that CMZa's President was willing to call upon government force to maintain his authority.

There followed a day of confusion and menace on Kalonda Station. The village chief reappeared and led a popular protest which verged on a riot. Finally a delegation of village chiefs went to the local government offices demanding Shamuimba's release. They, in turn, were also jailed for their trouble. Derksen's first appeal to President Mbonza that evening to request Shamuimba's release fell on unreceptive ears. The request repeated next day was acted upon and he was released from custody, a chagrined and anxious young man who had been pulled into a vortex of events beyond his will or control.

When the dust of the events of Palm Sunday had settled, word came from CMZa headquarters that Pastor Djare was suspended as the Kalonda District President and that the district could elect a qualified replacement of their choice at their next conference. Shamuimba, however, could not be a candidate. As for Rev. Djare, though suspended as District President, he would still head the district delegation at the upcoming general assembly!

the Nyanga General Assembly of 1985

News of the Palm Sunday events at Kalonda spread swiftly across the CMZa countryside and contributed much to a feeling of malaise as the dates of the assembly approached. It was to be an elective assembly. Word had already gotten around that the CMZa Administrative Committee favored the maintenance of the incumbent officers with the exception of Vice President Mukanza who had been approved for doctoral studies overseas if funding could be found. In the meantime, however, he had been approached by the leadership of a number of CMZa districts requesting that he allow his name to be put in nomination for the position of CMZa President. All of this was done quietly. The vice president remained noncommittal until just shortly before the convening of the assembly at which time he gave his consent.

From the very outset, tension was in the air. Delegates began to arrive to find a large contingent of people from nearby Kipoko, President Mbonza's home village. Some of them carried their old fashioned, muzzle-loading flintlock muskets, this to celebrate Mbonza's reelection, they explained. (In rural Zaire gun blasts are traditional parts of celebration at special events such as weddings, graduation feasts and are even used to mark the burial of people of note.) Not all delegates, however, were put at ease by these explanations.

It did not help that President Mbonza himself arrived on the station air strip via an MAF flight accompanied by a government official from Tshikapa who, in turn, was accompanied by an armed guard. President Mbonza promptly accepted to be taken to private quarters where he ate and slept entirely separated from other delegates and fellow officers during the days of the assembly. His public appearances were limited primarily to delegate sessions in the station chapel. All of this being the case, a brooding sense of intrigue and uneasiness descended upon the assembled delegates. And yet, many carried the expectation that when it came time for the presidential vote, Vice President Mukanza's name would be on the ballot.

An opening session was devoted to the usual protocol of the official opening of the assembly by President Mbonza, remarks of the government official, words of welcome from the local Nyanga District President and an opening Biblical meditation given by missionary Rick Derksen. This time there were a few sets of dual delegations from dissident districts both contesting delegate seats at the assembly. In each case the dissidents were sidelined in favor of those officially recognized by and loyal to the central administration. There were also, from the beginning, large contingents of partisan local people filling the rear of the chapel following carefully all that took place and noting the comments of all those who spoke. Beyond this there was their disconcerting way of approaching delegates between sessions to quiz them concerning their comments and in some cases to confront them point blank with the question: "Are you for or against Mbonza?" And, day after day, there was the unaccustomed sight of the government official conspicuously seated among delegates in assembly sessions.

Yet in spite of all of the unsettling abnormalities, the first couple of days were conducted in a businesslike fashion. Kakesa Samuel was once again installed as assembly moderator with Pastor Djare from Kalonda as vice moderator. Among the delegates were three AIMM missionaries who were present by virtue of their functions within the CMZa: Herman Buller as the associate treasurer, Rick Derksen as the coordinator of the Department of Evangelism and Life of the Church, and Leona Schrag as missionary counselor. In addition Peter Falk, an ISTK staff member, was invited to present a study on the proliferation of false prophets and cults. Don Unruh and Kinshasa youth director Kanku Kele (pr. KHA-nkoo KEH-leh) were also invited to give a leadership to worship devotionals and music.

maneuvers behind the scenes

While the assembly sessions continued with a surface appearance of calm and order, there was intense activity between sessions and at night as various delegates sought each other and dialogue continued with Vice President Mukanza regarding the impending elections. Meanwhile some members of the administrative committee, learning of Mukanza's last-moment willingness to be a candidate, quickly expressed their irritation and opposition among the delegates. They accused him of subterfuge in that he had openly sought and secured CMZa approval for further study. Why, now, had he suddenly become a candidate? While some cast their opposition in terms of ethics and procedure, others clearly opposed his candidacy because they knew that if elected he would bring a new stance to the central administration and that they might well at some point lose their appointments in CMZa service. Withal, tension was building rapidly.

At last assembly moderator Kakesa and regional representative Luingo Mudinda (pr. LWI-ngo mu-DI-ndah) sought Mukanza and urged that he withdraw his candidacy. They underscored the building tension among the delegates and insisted that it was becoming explosive. Things needed to be defused and only Mukanza had it in his power to do that. He, however, insisted that before he respond he have the opportunity to speak directly with President Mbonza in their presence. This confrontation took place. Exchanges were frank and harsh. Mbonza accused his vice president of dishonesty in his dealings with him and the AC over the issue of the study proposal. Furthermore, said the president, in allowing his name to be put in nomination, he was in effect being a traitor to him personally. Mukanza, in turn, told the president he was blindly pursuing an autocratic and egotistical style of leadership that was rapidly alienating larger and larger segments of the CMZa family. It was in recognition of this growing crisis within CMZa and in response to the pleas of increasing numbers of district leaders that he was prepared to set his hopes for further study aside and to serve his Church if that was the will of the majority of the assembled delegates.

At this point Kakesa addressed Mukanza and asked that he state clearly what his real preference was: to pursue his studies, to remain as CMZa Vice President or to run for the post of president. Mukanza, in turn, asked Mbonza if he would accept to work with him another term if he remained as vice president. To this the President replied: "This is not my decision to make but if it were, I would refuse." (15)

Whatever the tenor of the remaining exchanges between the two men in that closed session, it was apparently of a nature to convince Vice-President Mukanza that to pursue any leadership role with CMZa was no longer a feasible option for him. It was shortly thereafter that the men went to the Nyanga chapel where the delegate body was assembled and wondering about the prolonged delay in program. Moderator Kakesa then announced that as far as the elections were concerned, the office of vice president was open since Rev. Mukanza had reaffirmed his intention to pursue his studies. While the delegate body sat in shocked silence the moderator directly opened the floor for nominations for president. Taken completely by surprise, the cluster of delegates who had urged Rev. Mukanza's candidacy were left with no time or opportunity to caucus regarding a possible alternative. Though the opportunity for nominations was extended for some time, none was forthcoming. Nominations were then opened for vice president. Two names were submitted - - Pastor Chibulenu Sakayimbo, the Kamayala District President and Pastor Kituku Kibula (pr. gi-TU-goo gi-BOO-lah) from Mukedi District. It was then announced that the actual elections would take place later in the assembly.

While the sudden turn of events did noticeably relieve the tension among the delegates, it also left many of them with a sense of simply going through the motions. Some felt that the assembly had been taken out of their hands and that they were little more than observers. Nevertheless assembly business did continue and brought a few more controversial issues to the floor for debate. One was the report and recommendations of the special CMZa commission which had made a seventeen-minute visit to Mbuji Mayi the previous December in an ill-fated effort to investigate the division within the CMZa ranks of the Mbuji Mayi region. Over the caution urged by some of the delegates it was decided to affirm the retaliatory proposals of the commission and to excommunicate the Regional Representative Mpoyi Tshienda and two of his fellow regional leaders. As for their request for a broader autonomy, the assembly minutes rejected this as "incomprehensible." (16)

Another issue that had been generating opposition in the West Kasai was President Mbonza's effort to have the CMZa regional office of that province moved from Kananga to Tshikapa. This was resolutely opposed by several districts as it was seen as an effort to bring this office and its handling of regional educational monies to Tshikapa where the president could have a direct role in their dispersal. At the specific recommendation of the CMZa Administrative Committee, this proposal was also endorsed by a majority of the delegates. (17)

And there was also the controversial issue of the proposal to change the length of term of CMZa's officers. The church bylaws at the time of the Nyanga Assembly stipulated four year terms. The administrative committee had come with a proposal that terms be lengthened to six or seven years. In floor discussion it was even suggested that terms of officers simply be open ended altogether. After considerable debate, six year terms were agreed upon. (18)

The formal election of officers was held in abeyance as the last official agenda item of the assembly. All the business was finally cleared by Sunday at 1:30 AM. The moderator then proposed that since no other candidate had been proposed for president when earlier called for, the sitting president simply be reelected by acclamation. In a confused setting, with many non-delegates in the back half of the chapel, a mixed chorus of yeas and nays was heard whereupon President Mbonza was declared reelected for a new six year term. Outside in the darkness Mbonza's fellow villagers began priming and firing their muzzle loaders in celebration. In a close ballot vote, Pastor Kituku Kibula from Mukedi was elected the new vice president. This meant that CMZa's two top officers now both came from the same ethnic group. The election of the other candidate, Pastor Chibulenu Sakayimbo from the Kamayala District, would have brought a member of the large southern Chokwe tribe into the CMZa executive circle. Though narrowly defeated in the election, Pastor Chibulenu would soon be heard from again.

The Nyanga Assembly was brought to a close with a Sunday morning worship service. The speaker was elder Pastor Muatende (pr. muah-TEH-ndeh) Pierre from the Mutena District, a man who had long amazed missionaries and Africans alike with his ability to quote Scripture in the course of his preaching. Unimpressed with the protocol and fanfare which had surrounded the activities of the week, in a blunt, straight-from-the-shoulder message to the delegate body and its newly elected officers he said: "There is sin among us and we have not repented." Lifting his text from Matthew 3 he stated: "The axe is ready to cut down the tree at the roots; every tree that does not bear good fruit will be cut down and thrown into the fire."

The official minutes of the assembly once again described proceedings in enthusiastic terms. While acknowledging that there had been a temporary time of tension since it was an election year, this all had changed and the assembly had become "a veritable place of welcome, repentance and spiritual revival." (19)

Upon his return to Tshikapa, President Mbonza was met at the airport by a group of his supporters. They made their way across the road to the chapel for a victory celebration in the course of which he observed "how thankful he was for the peace and communion which had characterized the assembly." He commented further that it had been the will of the delegates to extend his next term from four to six years and that "all returned home strengthened." While he was describing the days at Nyanga in glowing terms and was receiving the adulation of Tshikapa supporters, many of the nearly 100 delegates were fanning back out across the CMZa countryside with a totally different reading on what had happened and they carried with them a mix of sadness, frustration and anger.

Meanwhile the former Vice President Mukanza quietly began preparing his family for their departure from the Tshikapa CMZa headquarters. Their paths were about to part. Tragically the extraordinarily gifted leadership team of the Zaire Mennonite Church had been torn asunder. Little did President Mbonza realize that even as he received the applause of his supporters, the departure of Vice President Mukanza and the installation of Rev. Kituku in his place were fueling flames of opposition which were soon to grow into a conflagration within the CMZa that would engulf him.

CHAPTER 40   CMZa: A SIMMERING CAULDRON

business as usual

If the CMZa Administrative Committee had sensed any warning signals at the Nyanga General Assembly, it was not readily apparent. Official minutes continued to bristle with ongoing "top-down" attitudes and directives. There were numerous examples. "The Executive Committee warns [five people named] for having been the principle promoters and leaders of the confused situation at Kalonda. [The Committee] consequently recommends to their employers to take appropriate disciplinary action in their regard. . . . On the same subject the EC makes the Vice President and the Regional Representative of the West Kasai responsible to supervise the election of a new District President which must take place in accordance with article 21 of the April 1985 AC." (1)

In administrative committee minutes a few weeks later the following is found: "The AC strongly advises pastors not located at their proposed posts to go there before the end of the year. Beyond that time they will be considered deserters and will see their pastoral dignity removed. The Coordinator of the [Department] of Evangelization and Life of the Church is made responsible for the execution of this article." (2)

And with regard to letters addressed to the CMZa central administration, the AC had long been clear. Already in a meeting just prior to the Nyanga General Assembly there is reference to a specific letter addressed to the president which had been returned to the district from which it had come. There follows the further comment: "As for other authors of other biased, circular writings both present and future, the AC asks their Districts to counsel and warn them while advising those involved that they will be excommunicated in case of a second offense. Nevertheless the AC reminds its members near and far who are desirous of contributing morally and materially to the construction of the CMZa to make themselves heard via the channel of their respective councils or to contact church leaders at all levels in following the hierarchical path." (3)

letters, letters, letters

Letters there were. Some were sharp and combative. Many more were thoughtful, probing, reasonable letters which sought to engage the top CMZa leaders in dialogue regarding trends within the Church. Already a full year before the Nyanga General Assembly of 1985 there came a letter from the District of Banga. Early paragraphs were devoted to reminding President Mbonza of his own personal pilgrimage, his early calls for change in CMZa, his election at Kamayala with the help of district delegates such as theirs. They underscored what they saw to be a systematic discrimination against Banga people in matters of discipline, employment and placement by the CMZa central administration. After some sharply worded criticism of President Mbonza's regime, the letter concluded on a conciliatory note: "The Reverend Mbonza Kikunga must at least for the rest of his time consider all Christians - - lay people, deacons and pastors of the Districts as children of God and work with them in peace and true love." The letter was signed by thity-five district church leaders. (4)

Just before the Nyanga Assembly there came a letter from Pastor Tshilembu Kashikisha from Kananga. A former CMZa officer and long-time member of the administrative committee, he had been dropped from that committee upon his ordination on the technicality that his original appointment was as a lay person. When in early 1985 the CMZa administration dictated Kananga District delegates to the upcoming Nyanga Assembly depriving Rev. Tshilembu of a seat in the process, he wrote a carefully-worded letter which embodied a striking pastoral tone.

It read, in part: "It is far from my inclination to nag you for I respect myself. But you will agree with me that whenever there has been something which was wrong, I have never beaten around the bush. I have always raised my voice either at the local, community or national level especially when it is a question of the Body of Christ of which we are all members." Referring to the CMZa administration action to choose assembly delegates from Kananga contrary to the wishes of the local people, Tshilembu wrote: "The executive proves abundantly its tendency to dominate, crush and undermine the carefully thought out decisions of the local churches while disdaining even the Regional Assemblies. This . . . does not conform to Mennonite principles. We must review our attitude and ask ourselves what we really are: the chief of the church or a servant of the Lord. It is very regrettable and even dangerous if we are chiefs! Rather let us listen to and respect our local churches for they are our employer."

"I have never acted as the devil's advocate. . . . You will agree with me that the whole of CMZa is agitated. Here and there are very serious problems. For this large remedies are necessary . . . . I have wondered as I have noticed that the Executive Committee plans measures of retaliation against certain brothers who have expressed their opinions regarding the health of our community. . . . How much better it would be to receive and analyze criticism both constructive and negative and to perform an autopsy of the denounced situation, take note of the points raised and to invite the authors to a dialogue, an exchange of views in order to dissipate misunderstanding. You know that well-organized societies place boxes where the public place criticisms and suggestions. They improve their way of working thanks to these criticisms. And we who are the light of the world, what do we do? Let us be open to criticism, opinions and suggestions without always reacting with condemnation and discipline. . . . We should rather pray the Lord that he might work in our hearts in a manner that we may see, reason, act or react in a manner worthy of a faith in our Lord Jesus Christ. . . . Verse 9 of I Peter 2 has long inspired me and I often share it with my brothers in Christ in our church gatherings. . . . I remain convinced that this small observation of fact will help you toward a more profound reflection in order to attack the very causes which produce difficulties within the CMZa. . . . May divine goodness cover us always. Your brother in Christ." (5)

It is a moving tribute to the pastoral spirit of this man that such a letter was written just four weeks before the 1985 General Assembly where he was denied a delegate status in favor of someone more amenable to the wishes and agenda that the CMZa administration was bringing to the assembly for approval.

It was after the Nyanga Assembly, however, that letters really began to flow from all directions. Some passed between district presidents as they sought to compare notes and impressions and to assess what had actually happened during those days. Some were addressed by districts to the CMZa headquarters many of which protested and/or condemned what had happened. And there were letters from non-delegates who, upon hearing an account, wrote general letters addressed to delegates condemning them for having allowed things to transpire as they had. There were also letters from Zairians addressed to missionaries asking for counsel or asking why AIMM was allowing such things to happen. Some also found their way to the AIMM office in Elkhart. One writer couched his views in a tribal proverb: "We put an egg in our pocket only to discover it contained a scorpion." Some were bitter verbal assaults on the CMZa administration in general and President Mbonza in particular.

Remarkable, amidst the furor, was an open letter addressed to "The Legal Representative of the CMZa and his collaborators with regard to the life of the Church" from a group of lay people of Kahemba, a sub-district of Kamayala far to the south near the Angolan border. Clear in language, moderate in tone, it provided a view of CMZa life and administration from that distant geographic and tribal perspective. Early in their letter it is stated: "It is in humility that we offer our critique. In a spirit of sincerity we will not be in the wrong to address ourselves especially to the elite of the community and to those who are not afraid or ashamed of the Gospel of Christ."

Speaking for ethnic groups of their area (largely Chokwe and Lunda), they underscored the heavy predominance of Baphende that had in recent years secured appointments at national and regional levels within the Church, this to the practical exclusion of candidates from their area. Attention is then called to the gradual changes which had been effected in the CMZa bylaws to accommodate those in power and the authoritarian manner in which the church officers dealt with church leaders at district levels. Having made these essential points they continued: "In all sincerity this injustice risks to one day be the cause of a separation between the Mennonites of South Bandundu and the others. We consider this fact as being a shame which should not be experienced at the level of a great community such as ours." And, finally, it was said: "In brief, this message is simply a reaction against the inequalities within the community. It is also a warning and a mirror for the leaders of the community who love honor and not ecclesiastical submission." (6)

Though in low-key and even oblique language, there is was. For the second time in the history of CMZa, the specter of a church split was rearing its head. The first time it had come about due to external pressures which scattered Baluba Mennonites in the early 1960's. This time it was due to rapidly growing internal tensions which swirled around its own leadership.

Bukungu Mishumbi, the widely trusted and respected former general treasurer of the CMZa, was known as a man of few words. Having resigned his post after years of faithful service totally free of rumor or suspicion, he settled at Ilebo, a port town on the Kasai river on the northern edge of CMZa territory. In due time he was ordained a deacon in his local church and became a solid source of counsel and material resource for the CMZa. Not given to writing letters, he listened, observed and pondered. The time finally came when he felt he needed to break his silence. In a letter addressed to President Mbonza with copies to all district leaders, the ECZ and AIMM, he clearly stated his concerns and fears. In part he wrote: "Our community . . . was one of the large well-known Protestant communities which merited a certain sense of pride and honor. Soon after 1981 our community began to be contorted with an illness; it is an illness of cancer. Cancer is a sickness which ravages numerous human lives. When it is not treated, the tumors slowly grow with a tendency to spread in the organism; finally it is death."

"From April 10 to 14, 1985, CMZa presented itself before the doctor who was the General Assembly held at Nyanga with the hope of being healed. The doctor failing in his diagnosis prescribed a medicine which seems to further the sickness." Bukungu then lifted a quotation from one of President Mbonza's own letters circulated widely in the late 1970's when he was presenting himself as a presidential candidate: "'Who will lift the CMZa out of this deep ravine?' I do not hesitate to express to you my sentiments of great sorrow regarding your decisions which slowly and surely are leading our loved community toward its decline. Although to state this truth is to make me your enemy, I will never make of myself a hypocrite and allow the truth to die hidden in my heart."

In his letter Bukungu then proceeded to list a series of incidents to illustrate his concerns. He then concluded: "Certainly these serious situations within the Community have agitated all of its members. The General Assembly, which once was a decision-making body, has lost its importance and the Administrative Committee has become the occupation of a single person. Where can we appeal for help? It is true that some biased people seize upon the cries of alarm on the part of the Mennonite mass for reasons of personal ambition; [as for me] far from that. The time for patience approaches its end. I cannot suppress this truth any longer for the benefit of your esteem. The faithful throughout the [CMZa] Districts which have been suspended dismiss the action with laughter and will continue to worship together in autonomy. With my cordial salutations in Jesus Christ." (7)

And from an influential Mennonite layman active in a local CMZa congregation at Tshikapa came the following commentary in a letter to Elkhart: The General Assembly of 1985 "plunges us into inexpressible and inexplicable perplexity. These are things very complex and difficult to explain for we had absolutely not hoped for them. That which impresses us the most was the intrusion of village chiefs, the tribal vigilance, the insecurity of the delegates and above all, the lack of electoral democracy caused by the camouflaged menace of armed people reported to be members of the extended family of Brother Mbonza Kikunga." (8)

It was not only Africans who were expressing their concern. After the Nyanga Assembly, there were also some deeply troubled missionaries. Committed to the fusion plan and sincere in their commitment to and loyalty toward the CMZa and its elected officers, the stance of most missionaries typically had been one of sympathetic support. Decisions and policies were not always to their liking but they reminded themselves that the CMZa was an autonomous Church and had the right to make its own decisions without interference from the missionaries invited to work within the Church.

But some of the events and trends leading up to the Nyanga gathering had been genuinely disturbing and the assembly itself had left missionaries with great uneasiness. This was reflected in some of the correspondence with the AIMM office. For instance: "Regarding the rosy account given by CMZa officers at Tshikapa when they returned from Nyanga, I personally struggle with this kind of reporting. Everyone knows much of the calm was on the surface only. Not all return home strengthened. Even the final Sunday morning message stated this clearly. Was all that happened in God's perfect will - - including our way of getting to these results? I would like for a shepherd to notice that some of his sheep are weak and hurting rather than to insist without adequate basis that all are fine." (9)

Another wrote: "The president's report included much of the reports of the commissions and the regional representatives, making it a valuable comprehensive report of 51 pages. . . . I went to the meeting of the Evangelism Commission. I felt it was conducted in line with the President's report. The most crucial issue was the CMZa attitude toward the seceding group at Mbuji Mayi. Although some of us recommended efforts of reconciliation, the Commission recommended to the delegate body that the seceding pastors be excommunicated. .. . We cannot speak of a Christian election, we cannot even speak of a democratic election. . . . I think the results of the Assembly will need to be observed closely and careful evaluation of the ministries will be necessary." (10)

Whatever the language used, it was increasingly clear that, after five years, the Mbonza administration was being seen by more and more people as one characterized by favoritism, ethnic bias, an unfeeling authoritarian manner, harsh discipline, egotism, an unforgiving spirit, quick retaliation against dissenters and a readiness to utilize government force, if necessary, to achieve desired ends.

the President goes to Lombard, IL

In his capacity as vice president for Africa, President Mbonza became a member of the executive committee of the Mennonite World Conference. The summer of 1985, Executive Secretary Paul Kraybill convened this committee in Lombard, IL. Following these sessions, President Mbonza was invited to come to Elkhart where time was spent with AIMM staff between other travel. Interaction with him both in Lombard and Elkhart resulted in mixed reactions. While there were various expressions of appreciation and affirmation, there were also puzzled observations. University-trained, he entered freely into discussions and reflected a probing mind. Regarding the World Mennonite family and the Zaire Church's place in and contribution to it, he asked: "But what does it mean to be an African and a Mennonite Christian at the same time?" Not many of his fellow Zairians were asking such questions.

In dialogue in the AIMM office he sketched the thorny problems confronting the Church ranging over such issues as leadership training, pastoral support amidst poverty, evangelism via ministries of compassion, models of more equitable partnership with AIMM, the desire for direct relations with the Mennonite Churches of North America and Europe, the African reality of witchcraft, how to meet CMZa administrative costs amidst a crumbling Zaire economy on the one hand and AIMM's reduction of subsidies on the other, the tension felt by CMZa leaders in striving for true autonomy while inevitably dependent upon expatriate personnel and financial help. These were excellent questions and clearly had to do with issues at the very forefront of CMZa concern.

And yet, mixed though such discussions were other troubling and disruptive incidents which were hard to evaluate and fit into place. In the Lombard sessions, the CMZa President persistently sought to insert specific CMZa agenda into the discussions apparently feeling that this was an appropriate time and place to make appeals for help and services for his Church, appeals that were completely out of context and foreign to the nature and purpose of the gathering. (11) Among others things, it was during these sessions that he pressed European Mennonite representatives for an ambitious tour of their churches at their expense. Given as a reason was that of a fraternal visit which without question was genuine enough. Though not stated it was clearly sensed by the European Committee members, however, that the requested trip was also seen by the President as an opportunity for soliciting financial help for the CMZa.

Upon arrival at Elkhart he quickly informed AIMM office staff of his plans to visit friends in Colorado and Maine. When asked how air fare to these distant places was to be covered, he responded with aplomb that he was sure his friends in both places would be happy to cover any costs involved. The AIMM Secretary consequently spent a couple of days on the phone contacting the people in question. An itinerary by air was eventually worked out with stops in Denver, CO, Newton, KS, Hartford, CT and Akron, PA. This was all accepted by Rev. Mbonza as being only normal response to the wishes of a visitor of his status.

During a morning in an MCC retreat setting at a church camp south of Elkhart, he was invited to address the group. To the startled chagrin of all present, he saw this an occasion to air his irritation and criticism regarding some VS folk who had displeased him in Zaire, this while expressing no appreciation whatever for the scores of MCC-sponsored folk who had made outstanding contributions to both CMZa and the AIMM across the years.

For AIMM staff during those days, there developed the eerie sense of dealing with two totally different people on different days and in different settings. It seemed to have something to do with the dress of the occasion. On days when he was clad in sport shirt and slacks, he was affable, relaxed and could smile. But whenever he was dressed in his clerical collar and garb, it was as though he had also donned the persona and demeanor of "the President" and all seemed to be focused on playing that role - - as though he saw himself as having just stepped from behind a curtain on stage. This seemed to mean, for him, being erect in posture, unsmiling in demeanor and correctly precise in language. He was in this "mode" when AIMM staff drove him to O'Hare Airport in Chicago for his flight home. As the boarding call came, wishes were expressed to him for safe travel and for the Lord's blessing as he returned to his work in Zaire. It was also requested that he convey the greetings and love of the North American Mennonite family to the CMZa. He responded with a perfunctory nod and stiff handshakes, then turned and strode to the boarding gate.

On the way back to Elkhart AIMM staff spent much of the trip sharing impressions and attempting to integrate Mbonza, the man, with Mbonza, the President.

one last trip

AIMM Secretary Jim Bertsche prepared for his administrative trip to Africa in late 1985 with mixed feelings. He had always looked forward to opportunities to return to the African continent where he and his wife Jenny had made many friends across the years. It held extra emotional loading for him, this time, because it was to be his last as an AIMM administrator. And, furthermore, given the swift pace of events within the Church in Zaire, he had some apprehension as to what he might find.

He did not have long to wait. Arriving in Kinshasa he learned of a confrontation between the CMZa Regional President Kakesa Mulume (kah-KEH-sah MOO-loo-may) and the Tshikapa administration regarding Kandaiz a Kitamba (pr. kah-NDEZ ah MOO-loo-may), a local pastor and a maternal uncle of the President Mbonza, who had been unilaterally named the leader of a local city congregation by the CMZa Executive Committee. In the troubled atmosphere of early 1986, he let it be known that he was responsible only to his president-nephew in Tshikapa and that he would henceforth ignore the local regional CMZa leaders. Although this ran directly counter to the oft-repeated demands of the Tshikapa office that echelons of church administration be strictly respected, President Mbonza not only accepted but encouraged his uncle pastor in this relationship. When regional officers suspended him from his pastoral duties, President Mbonza, in turn, suspended the Kinshasa Regional President. Coming to Kinshasa, President Mbonza attempted to call a meeting of the CMZa Executive Committee but was unable to gather a quorum. It was this stalemate which the AIMM Secretary found upon arrival.

At Kikwit on the way inland the Secretary was given a little hand-written note stating that "a delegation" from the southern districts of Bandundu Province were requesting to meet with him. A time and place were set - - and they were there, seven CMZa leaders representing four CMZa Districts. (12)

a message from Kamayala

The leader and spokesman of the group was Pastor Chibulenu Sakayimbo from the district of Kamayala who, with passing time, was emerging as one of the key dissenting voices vis-à-vis CMZa trends. They were a subdued - - even somber group. Their words were carefully chosen and spoken with sadness. After thanking the AIMM Secretary for granting them the opportunity to meet, they said in essence: the four districts they represented were making plans to officially declare their secession from the CMZa. This was a painful decision and one that had not been easily or quickly made. But there were reasons among which were the geographic distance which separated them from Tshikapa, the lack of visits to their area by central administrators, the growing realization that people from their area would never be granted a place at upper levels of church administration, the growing sense of domination of a single ethnic group within the church.

The last straw, they said, was the Nyanga Assembly of the previous year which, for them, was the ultimate proof of a central administration that had gone astray. They spoke of the sense of intimidation they had felt while there and their perception that much of what transpired had been the result of behind-the-scenes manipulation. Before 1980, they said, they had felt they had a place within CMZa and that they were welcomed by the Church. All that was now changed and they no longer felt either welcome or even wanted.

In response to all of this, the AIMM Secretary attempted to put some of their grievances into perspective and tried to counsel patience on their part. To this they responded: "We made this long trip because we wanted to sit with you face to face. We wanted you to hear from our mouths an explanation of what we are planning to do. We stand vis-à-vis the CMZa as did Abraham before Lot. We too are saying that CMZa should choose the path it desires to go and we will go another. We sincerely appreciate all that the AIMM has done for us in the past. We will always remain Mennonites. If in the future the AIMM will see fit to continue to relate to us in some manner or other, we will greatly appreciate it. If not, we will remain brothers in Christ and will do our best in our isolation to faithfully serve our Lord." (13)

It was with a sense of foreboding that the traveling Secretary led in a closing prayer and bid his friends from the south farewell. Events were clearly gathering momentum within CMZa. Did President Mbonza really understand? There was quick evidence that he did not. Attending a special reception organized by the Kikwit CMZa Churches for the President and the AIMM Secretary, the southern delegation walked quietly onto the church grounds. Approaching the President they greeted him courteously. His only response was a curt inquiry as to why they were in town!

with the CMZa Executive Committee

Continuing his Zaire travel, the AIMM Secretary eventually arrived at Kalonda where he was invited to meet with the Church officers at their headquarters across the river. After pleasantries were exchanged the visiting secretary was invited, in the time-honored African tradition, to "tell his news." He seized on this opportunity to frankly share some of the impressions, observations and concerns he had gathered along the way from Zairians and missionaries alike. When, upon concluding, he turned to them and invited them also to "tell their news," President Mbonza replied: "You've already told our news. There is nothing left for us to tell."

After a long moment, newly elected Vice President Kituku Kibula broke the silence. The son of a gifted evangelist from Mukedi District of an earlier generation who had lost his life in the Kwilu Rebellion, he carried some of his father's sensitivity toward people and a genuine concern for his Church. Addressing the visitor among them, he asked if he did not have some counsel to offer the CMZa Executive Committee given the difficulties they were encountering.

Offered this opening the secretary expressed his sorrow for the tension and obvious disarray in which he found the Church and then made four suggestions: 1) Make an effort to walk in the sandals of those who are criticizing you and your administration; 2) try to look past their criticism which admittedly, at times, is harsh and not always well-informed, in an attempt to hear and understand their legitimate concerns and hurts;

3) seek opportunity for genuine dialogue with dissidents, not as officials but as brothers who are ready to admit mistakes and who genuinely want to hear their views and, 4) deal honestly and in humility with their complaints and seek to meet at least some of their requests. He then concluded: "In Africa strong church leadership is needed, yes; and sometimes a firm word and disciplining action is necessary for the welfare of the church. But sometimes wise leaders realize that it is an extended hand of brotherhood and reconciliation which is needed much more. In my opinion, this is such a time in the history of the CMZa."

Response to these comments was mixed. While some expressed appreciation, others were quick to point out that district leaders did not understand their problems as church officers. Furthermore missionaries, at times, complicated their work for them. A concluding note was firmly made - - that the AIMM had a responsibility to speak up against the chorus of dissident voices and to support the CMZa administration without reservation.

Before leaving Zaire, the AIMM Secretary had yet one more painful encounter. Back in Kinshasa en route to other points in Africa, he was informed of a special meeting of the CMZa leaders of the city to which he was urgently invited. Called into order and presided by Kakesa Mulume, the CMZa Regional President, an opening devotional meditation drew heavily upon Paul's Philippians passage in which he likened the Christian's experience to that of a race which is to be run with determination and commitment to the end. The chairman then observed that the AIMM had for long years worked to plant a Mennonite Church in Zaire. Thanks to the faithfulness of missionaries and the Lord's blessing, a Church had indeed been planted. For this they were deeply grateful. He went on: "The Bible tells us that we are to do the Lord's work with joy. This is what we are trying to do but you find us at a moment when we are without joy in our work. Excuse us for our words but we must tell you that the CMZa is on fire. There is fire in all of our regions and it is spreading. We regret that you need to return to North America on this sort of note but it is true. We pray that AIMM will not just passively look at us in our struggle and hopelessness. Help us. Pray for us. Although events seem to be beyond our control we know that the Holy Spirit is powerful and can do whatever He wants in and for his church."

It was against this background that the AIMM Secretary was invited to respond both as a friend and former missionary and as the official representative of the Mission. He attempted to convey two messages. As a former missionary he looked into many familiar faces around the room and shared in their anguish as their beloved Church was being shaken to its foundations by internal dissent. But as a representative of the Mission he had to remind them that even if it were possible for the AIMM "to step in and take matters in hand," as some were urging, AIMM would be doing them and their Church a disservice. That there was a crisis there was no doubt. But the tumult of the hour confronted the rank-and-file members and leaders scattered across their thirty-plus districts with the challenge to assert themselves and to take ownership in and responsibility for their Church in an entirely new manner.

In the AIMM mission guest house in Kinshasa his last evening on Zairian soil, the secretary wrote a personal note to President Mbonza. In part it said: "Dear Brother in Christ, I leave Zaire with a heavy spirit and with many questions. I've made the effort to meet with a large range of people and I've listened to a great variety of comments and points of view. It is clear that the CMZa, as we've known it in the past, is in great difficulty. I can only repeat what I've already said several times while I've been among you, i.e., official and purely administrative actions no longer suffice. What is now needed above everything else is a pastoral ministry, a very special effort of reconciliation which is clothed with true humility and which is prepared to admit whatever faults there may be - - something which is difficult but which is clearly necessary at this time. Our prayers are with you and the staff at Tshikapa." (14)

This brief letter was never acknowledged or answered.

as good as their word

It was the soft-spoken men from southern Bandundu Province who first translated their discontent into action. It was in the minutes of their annual district conference that the following appeared: "The District Conference decides that two pastoral candidates . . . be ordained." The same action put in place an ordination commission and dates were set for each pastor. (15) And there was more. "The District Conference informs the [CMZa] Administrative Committee that the contribution of [this] District to the budget of the Community for the year 1985 will be utilized for the development of [our] District." (16)

The delegates to their district conference could hardly have been clearer. They were taking their district church matters of finances and the ordination of pastors into their own hands thus bypassing the Tshikapa administration. A scant two months after having sent a delegation to Kikwit to intercept a traveling AIMM Secretary, the four southern CMZa districts became the first to make a public statement of repudiation of the Tshikapa administration. In a document dated February 2, 1986, the following was stated: "We, representative members of the Districts of Kamayala. Shamwana, Tshitambi and Mukoso declare that we've broken relations with the CMZa as of February 2, 1986. We remain Mennonites and continue the work of the Lord in our Districts while awaiting the full decision of the ECZ." (17)

In the meantime, in Kinshasa, the entire CMZa Region had met in a special assembly and adopted "the suspension of its administrative relations with the central administration of the CMZa until the next General Assembly of the CMZa." (18) Two months later two more similar documents appeared, one from the District of Kananga in the east and the other from the District of Ilebo to the north. (19)

overtaken by events

It was in early March that an ordination commission headed by President Mbonza made its way to Mukedi to consecrate two local pastoral candidates. (20) It was their intent to continue their travel to Shamwana and Kamayala Districts to ordain a new pastor in each place. Before leaving Mukedi, however, news of the four southern districts announced break reached them. It was the strong concern of most of the commission members that they carry out their travel plans while reconstituting themselves as a commission of inquiry. President Mbonza accepted the idea but refused to accompany them. Thus Rev. Luingo Mudindu, Rick Derksen and Don Unruh left on a week's journey which would take them to each of the separated districts. They sat with leaders, they listened, they took notes.

In a joint report established after their return, there was candid reporting of the complaints and grievances they had heard including direct criticism of President Mbonza and his administration. In the light of what they had sensed and heard, the commission made three proposals: 1) that Pastor Chibulenu Sakayimbo be named Coordinator of Evangelization and Life of the Church after a year's training; 2) that a General Council be convened to provide for equitable representation of the southern districts in the administrative committee and 3) that the same Council review the decision of the Mbuji May General Assembly to suspend the recognition of new districts. (21)

They were wise and needed recommendations but they came too late. A groundswell of events was already under way which would quickly make the commission recommendations irrelevant.

It was in June of that year that, for the first time, a certain sense of alarm became apparent at CMZa headquarters in Tshikapa. A special meeting of the administrative committee was called to which a variety of non-committee members were invited including a number of older pastors. Also invited were representatives from the southern districts - - none of whom accepted to come. There was a lengthy agenda and the sessions carried across five days. A different person presented a devotional meditation to open each session. Given the troubled context in which they met, the local Pastor Mutombo's topic was both startling and moving. Based on Luke 2 he clustered his comments around the theme: "Let us return for He is no longer among us." No less striking was a meditation given by CMZa staff member Ngongo Muteba based on II Corinthians 5 and entitled: "Reconcile yourselves with God and with your neighbor."

The minutes of these sessions reflected a heavy agenda but no committee actions were more significant than those addressed to their own president. For the first time official minutes reflected sharp committee disagreement with their president and corrective action in his regard. Aware that he had already once refused to go in person to seek out the dissident district leaders in the south, the committee ordered him to go with a delegation to all of the districts and areas which had declared their autonomy "to enter into dialogue with these churches in order to resolve the different problems which are present." A companion action was to instruct the president to annul some recent correspondence and "to withdraw all complaints against certain brothers lodged in Kinshasa courts." (22)

Once again it was a case of a desperately needed initiative which came too late. More and more the tenor of conversation and correspondence which was flowing across the CMZa districts was that of enduring the status quo until they could again meet in a general assembly which was scheduled for the first quarter of 1987. The next time, the district delegates vowed, things were going to be different.

Summer's dry season slipped by and the first rains of a new growing season began to fall. In spite of the growing storm which surrounded the central Church offices, church life at the grass roots district levels continued unabated. Believers met for worship, prayer, fellowship and the making of decisions that stemmed from their church life. Baptisms, marriages and holy communion were being celebrated. Missionaries were busy in their appointed places of service. But as New Years came and went without any indication of plans for the next general assembly, questions and rumors began to fly. Why the silence at CMZa headquarters? Why had no dates yet been set? Why no discussion as to where it was to held? From the president's office there finally came word that due to national elections which were being planned in early 1987 it would not be wise for the CMZa to convene an assembly in the first quarter of the year. While there was some merit in what was said, the CMZa at large was in no mood for delay. Seeing this as an excuse to obstruct due process in their Church, voices were heard on all sides demanding that another assembly be held before the end of March 1987 just as had been stipulated by the delegates of the previous Nyanga Assembly.

It was in the midst of this uncertainty that President Mbonza lost a major block of support. Meeting in Kikwit in mid-December, the staff of the Bandundu Region drew up an inventory of the failures of the central administration as viewed from their perspective. A three-page document sounded such themes of protest as, clanism, indifference to district level problems, authoritarian style and lack of compassion. (23) Though protests of this sort had already been heard with frequency in other CMZa quarters, this was different for now it was Baphende leaders publicly leveling criticism at their fellow tribesman president, a very telling indicator of the level to which discontent within the church had risen.

an open letter from the missionaries

It was a time of anguish for the AIMM missionaries in Zaire. They had kept official silence amidst the rising controversy around them, but among themselves there were often spirited and even heated discussions. All were supportive of the fusion plan and wanted to see it work. There was a strong consensus that at this point in its history it was proper that they serve under the direct sponsorship and administration of the Church. They also felt that the Church should be allowed to make its own decisions without missionary pressures.

Nonetheless they had also been the troubled observers of events and recognized, in late 1986, that a church administration was deteriorating before their eyes. Zairian friends constantly sought them out and bombarded them with questions: "Don't you see what is going on? Don't you understand? Don't you care?"

For none of the missionaries was the situation more painful than for Leona Schrag, Herman Buller and Rick Derksen who, by virtue of their responsibilities within the Church, were assembly delegates and members of the administrative and executive committees. Because of their roles they were in closer and more intimate contact with the Tshikapa CMZa staff than other missionaries. It had also been made clear to them that as the president demanded unconditional loyalty and support from his fellow Zairians, so he also expected loyalty from missionaries on his staff. They had ample opportunity to witness the angry responses directed against any who presumed to question or criticize him. The three knew full well that if they added their voices of protest, they and their fellow missionaries would be the targets of intense presidential displeasure.

Nevertheless, given the fact of a rapidly worsening situation, it was finally decided that further silence would surely be interpreted as ongoing missionary support of an administration which was being repudiated by its own Church. While they were not sure if, somehow, the president still did not grasp the depth and scope of the opposition that was building against him or if he was aware but determined to cling to power at any cost, the missionaries all agreed that the time had come when they needed to clearly declare their views and concerns.

In consultation with fellow missionaries, Derksen and Schrag drafted a mildly worded letter addressed to President Mbonza which was signed "for the missionaries" by Schrag in her role as missionary counselor. The letter was dated January 22, 1987 and was co-signed by all thity-two AIMM missionaries in the country at the time. Copies were also sent to all members of the CMZa Administrative Committee. It read, in part: "We, the missionaries of the AIMM serving the Lord Jesus Christ with the CMZa, come with this letter to express to you our anxiety regarding the state of our community since the General Assembly of 1985. Our greatest hope is to see reconciliation and unity in place of conflicts and divisions which presently hold sway so that the Gospel of Christ, which we preach to others, may manifest itself with power in us."

"It is our opinion that it is necessary to convene representatives of all the Regions and all the Districts including those who have already declared themselves autonomous to give them the occasion to express themselves openly and together find solutions for the problems of the CMZa. . . . We already approach the end of January and there has not been a single notice regarding a General Assembly. Why this silence? We pray God to show you his will in this situation. May the peace, grace and love of God be with you." (24)

There was no immediate response but when it came, it was furious. In a meeting of the executive committee with Schrag and Derksen present, the missionary letter was a major agenda item. Comments took on a sarcastic and bitter tone as they discussed their "supposed [missionary] collaborators" who would stoop to writing such a "subversive letter." "You know that we condemn and reject all such letters from wherever they come. Why is reference made to the next General Assembly? This letter implies that our administration is in error. Missionaries are at the base of many of our problems. We don't need missionaries like this. Shall we require them to retract the letter?" After lengthy discussion as to the ways in which the letter was a violation of various clauses in the fusion agreement, the topic was finally dropped with the stern order that no such letter should ever be written again. (25)

In a letter written to the AIMM office in Elkhart shortly thereafter, President Mbonza stated that he was lifting excerpts out of the minutes of a recent CMZa Executive Committee meeting and was forwarding them to the AIMM without comment: "The Executive condemns with the utmost energy the circular petition of the missionaries of the AIMM prepared by Leona Schrag . . ." There then follows in the minutes several references to the fusion document none of which well fit the case in point. Then a minute from an earlier date is cited in which all subversive letters are condemned. President Mbonza concluded by stating that this minute certainly applies since the missionary letter in question is "extremely subversive." (26)

Sadly, nowhere either in the record of committee meetings or in correspondence with Elkhart was there the slightest indication of introspection or self-evaluation. So intent were CMZa office staff on maintaining their grip on power that even a gentle word of counsel was rejected as subversive and traitorous.

a solemn declaration

In the CMZa administrative structure, the first echelon of authority below the central officers was that of the four regional presidents. By March they had enough. Dated March 2, a sparsely-worded single sheet document appeared. It was entitled: "A Solemn Declaration of CMZa Representatives regarding the Convocation of a General Assembly of the Community addressed to the President and Legal Representative, Reverend Mbonza Kikunga." In part it stated:

> We the regional ecclesiastic representatives of Bandundu, West Kasai, East Kasai and Kinshasa, conscious of the catastrophic situation which prevails currently in the CMZa . . .

> In view of the manifest incapacity of the administration of the CMZa at the headquarters in Tshikapa to restore peace . . . [and]

> Considering that this deplorable situation which has continued for a long time only worsens by reason of the unreasonable measures and decisions which the administration does not cease to adopt . . . [and]

> Given that this administration remains insensitive to numerous letters of concern which are continually addressed to it by members asking that it find a solution for the reconciliation of the children of God . . . [and]

> Considering the non-convocation of the regular General Assembly envisioned for the first quarter of 1987 as a dilatory maneuver destined to maintain this sad situation . . .

> We declare what follows:

>> 1) the urgent convocation of the General Assembly in keeping with article 26 of the 1985 General Assembly of Nyanga with a view to facilitate the reconciliation of the daughters and sons of the CMZa.

>> 2) If the time set by the General Assembly of 1985 passes, we will see ourselves as obliged to recommend a special session of the General Assembly.

The document was signed by all four Regional Presidents of the CMZa and copies were sent to all members of the Administrative Committee. (27)

In the midst of conflict and pain, the CMZa was asserting itself as the body of Christ.

CHAPTER 41   AIMM EXTENDS BOTH ROOT AND BRANCH

For the AIMM Board in North America, it was once again time to celebrate an anniversary. This time it was to be the 75th. In one of the two full-color AIMM Messengers which were published in 1987 to celebrate the occasion, there was a full page sketch of a large tree which revealed a network of labeled roots and branches, the former representing a growing North American constituency, the latter the AIMM's expanding involvement on the continent of Africa.

As for AIMM's partnering members, there had been steady growth across the years. The enterprise was launched in 1912 as the Congo Inland Mission by two small conferences - - The Defenseless Mennonite Church (now known as the Evangelical Mennonite Church) and the Central Conference of Mennonites. After providing missionaries for a number of years, the Evangelical Mennonite Brethren (now known as the Fellowship of Evangelical Bible Churches, or FEBC) became an official partner in 1938. When in 1943 the Central Conference merged with the Central District of the General Conference Mennonite Church, the General Conference became an AIMM partner. As early as 1953, the Evangelical Mennonite Conference of Canada (EMC/C) had sponsored missionary candidates Ben and Helen Reimer Eidse for service with the CIM. At first the EMC/C sent observers to board meetings but later responded to the invitation to appoint a board member. In 1975 the Mennonite Brethren affiliated as associate members. While they had their own historic work in Zaire and related to their own Church there, they were interested in becoming part of AIMM's new work among African Independent Churches in Southern Africa. (In 1993 the Mennonite Brethren became full members of AIMM.) In 1984 the EMC/C took action to place the AIMM on an equal footing with its own mission involvements elsewhere. Shortly thereafter a second board member was appointed as well. In 1986 the Evangelical Mennonite Mission Conference (EMMC) became a second Canadian group to affiliate with AIMM bringing the total of AIMM member conferences to six. (1)

EMEK also

European links were nothing new for the AIMM. During its very first decade of work, several European candidates applied for service due to the energetic recruitment of Alma Doering. (2) Again in the late 1940's and early 50's there were four missionaries of Swiss nationality who came under the AIMM umbrella (CIM at that time) in the process of the post-war disbanding of the Unevangelized Tribes Mission.

It was also in the early 1950's that a new inter-Mennonite mission organization emerged in Europe. The catalyst had been the Indonesian accession to political independence, an area in which the Dutch Mennonites had for decades maintained a mission endeavor. Representatives of the Mennonite mission committees from Holland, France, Germany and Switzerland met to discuss common interests and to counsel together as to the future. Out of this initial contact was eventually born the "Europaisch-Mennonitisches Evangelisations Komittee," or EMEK in its acronym form. Aware that even prior to the formal organization of this European committee French Mennonites had been at work in the African country of Chad, AIMM sought opportunity for dialogue with this group. The first meeting took place in the summer of 1981.(3) Information was shared regarding the origins, structures and program philosophies of the two bodies. The meeting was concluded by stating that while there were some differences which would have to be worked out in the event of collaboration in Africa, there was definite interest on the part of both groups in further exploration of such a possibility.

This interest was heightened when, in 1984, the French Mennonites were approached by Martine Ehrismann, one of their own members, who was training in linguistics and who expressed strong interest in an assignment to Upper Volta in northwest Africa. It was in the spring of 1986 that negotiations finally culminated in a formal three-way agreement between EMEK, Wycliffe Bible Translators and the AIMM. Martine and her husband, Paul Solomiac, would be supported by EMEK and appointed by Wycliffe for service with the AIMM team in Upper Volta. Thus, as AIMM prepared to observe its 75th anniversary, it could be said that it had once again established a link of partnership with the European Mennonite community.

Zaire and beyond

For sixty years Congo/Zaire had been the unique focus of CIM/AIMM's ministry in Africa. But as the Zairian Mennonite Churches acquired their autonomy and AIMM's support base at home was broadened, there was aggressive exploration of opportunities for witness and service beyond Zaire's borders. This initiative took AIMM into a remarkable decade of expansion with establishment of personnel and program in Lesotho in 1973, Botswana in 1975, Upper Volta (now Burkina Faso) in 1978 and the Transkei in 1982. The move into southern Africa brought AIMM into a totally new sort of ministry as ways were sought to relate to and work among African Independent Churches. In Burkina Faso, AIMM for the first time undertook work in an area that was under major Muslim influence. There was the further challenge of a cluster of unreached ethnic groups in an isolated corner of that country. In a sense, after a presence of more than six decades in Africa, AIMM had come full circle. Just as in 1912 a first generation of pioneer missionaries hacked out a clearing in riverside forest in south central Belgian Congo among unreached tribal groups, so in 1978 a new generation of pioneers sought to establish a beachhead among a cluster of unreached people on the fringes of the Sahara Desert. A spirit of venture and of commitment to a timeless mandate for Christian mission was alive and clearly evident within AIMM in the decade of the 1970's.

A further reflection of this exploratory stance was AIMM's participation in a joint Mennonite venture of support of a study center based at Selley Oak Colleges in Birmingham, England. Dr. Harold Turner, a New Zealander by birth, had as a young man gone to England in search of employment. Learning of teaching opportunities in West Africa, he and his wife subsequently spent seven years in Sierra Leone followed by three in Nigeria where he came in contact with a large, active African Independent Church named "The Church of the Lord Aladura." This sparked an interest and a research direction which was to absorb his considerable energies for the rest of his life.

First he compiled a two volume documentation of the history, beliefs and practices of this Church he had encountered. He then began seeking information regarding similar churches and movements elsewhere. Over time he amassed the largest such collection of documentation anywhere in the world. First he took his collection to the University of Scotland in Aberdeen with the hope of establishing a permanent depository. When satisfactory long-term arrangements could not be made, he took his material to a consortium of church-related colleges occupying a joint campus in Birmingham, England. His collection installed in a new setting, he continued his travel and research. As the volume of his material steadily grew, he proposed the idea of moving his project beyond the status of a simple archival resource to becoming a training center for missionaries assigned to or already at work among ethnic groups which featured renewal movements of which the AICs were a prime example.

In 1984, while presenting a paper at a symposium on AICs in southern Africa, Dr. Turner met Stan Nussbaum who also was a presenter. Assigned by AIMM in 1977 with his wife Lorri Berends for ministry among the AICs of that little country, Nussbaum had along the way enrolled in a doctoral study program in missiology at the University of South Africa under the guidance of faculty members M.L. Daneel and David Bosch. Learning of the Mennonite interest in and approach to such ministry there and elsewhere in Africa (notably the pioneering work of Ed and Irene Weaver in Nigeria under the sponsorship of the Mennonite Board of Missions a decade earlier), Turner began efforts to secure Mennonite help to bring his dream for his center in Birmingham to reality.

Over the next two years there were contacts between Turner and various Mennonite Mission Board staff people both in North America and on site at Birmingham. In such contacts he kept alive his proposal of the Nussbaum's appointment to his Center although they had by this time terminated with AIMM and Stan was acting director of the Program of World Mission of the Fort Wayne (IN) Bible College. All of these contacts finally came into focus in the spring of 1986 when, under the umbrella of the Council of International Ministries, five organizations formed an appointing committee - - AIMM, COM/GC, Eastern Mennonite Board, Mennonite Board of Missions and MCC. In this highly inter-Mennonite venture, the EMC/US made Nussbaum available to this committee via the AIMM for appointment to the Selly Oak project which by this time was known as CENERM, i.e., the Center for the Study of Renewal Movements Among Primal Societies. (It was later renamed INTERACT Research Center.) When shortly after this Dr. Turner retired and returned to New Zealand, the new Mennonite appointee became the director for the new enterprise. Under his innovative leadership a variety of projects and study programs were launched for both missionary appointees and national church leaders from various parts of the world including major pan-African consultations sponsored in various places on that continent. (4)

transition once again in the AIMM home office

Planning for the celebration of AIMM's 75th anniversary coincided with a search process for a new executive secretary. Nineteen eighty-six not only marked twelve years for Jim Bertsche in that role but also his retirement age. After screening a number of possible candidates, the Board called another Zaire missionary to serve in the home office.

As young missionary candidates, Earl W. and Ruth Jantzen Roth had originally thought they were en route to India, but with their teaching credentials they were diverted to Zaire in the early 1950's by the GC Commission on Overseas Mission. Their years of service took them into a wide range of assignments in that country. They served on a number of isolated bush stations as well as in the urban centers of Tshikapa and Kinshasa. Earl had experience both as an itinerant evangelist/pastor and as a teacher/director in several mission/church schools. In later years he served as missionary counselor and as a member of CMZa's Administrative and Executive Committees. In later years, he and Ruth filled key roles in Kinshasa among university students, in church planting and as a church/mission liaison person with government offices. By 1986 he knew many of the CMZa and CEM leaders personally and was very well versed in the details of the evolving Zairian church scene.

In preliminary conversations with the AIMM search committee, Roth sketched his views as follows: "The mission of the church is to proclaim the Gospel of the Lord Jesus Christ throughout the world through word and deed and to provide opportunities for Christian fellowship and spiritual growth in the Body of Christ. AIMM has performed this task very well through evangelistic efforts, Bible teaching, education, medical services and agricultural development. Its performance is evidenced by the exciting, living Mennonite community of Zaire, . . . the renewal movement among youth and the interest for spiritual growth and practical Christianity among Zaire lay people, the number of people who are accepting Christ in Burkina Faso and the response to Bible teaching in Southern Africa. . . . I view the AIMM as an inter-dependent mission agency sponsored by six Mennonite mission organizations in partnership, yet independent of any one of these organizations. I view this partnership as a vital witness to unity within the body of Christ; as a strength in the common responsibility to make disciples of all nations and as fundamental to the existence of AIMM." (5)

The spring board meeting of April 1986 was Bertsche's last as executive secretary. In a moment of reminiscing he spoke for himself and Jenny: "Our years with AIMM have been immensely rewarding years. We've been blessed, enriched and, at times, tested. Occasionally there has been pain as well, but always there has been fulfillment and reward. We have no regrets. We have only praise and thanksgiving to the Lord for having granted us the opportunity of attempting to serve him in overseas mission and particularly that, in the process, He directed our steps to Africa."

"That great continent and its people will ever remain a part of us. They have contributed so much to us. We've learned from them, been challenged and humbled by them. We can truthfully say that we have been the benefactors for having spent a part of our lives among them. We've learned much about life, about joy, sorrow and contentment. We've also learned something about the value of friendship and about fellow human beings. . . ."

"This is the 75th year of CIM/AIMM. There has never been any doubt in our minds that this inter-Mennonite venture in witness and service on the African continent was raised up by the Lord and has been nurtured and blessed across the years by a divine hand. Opportunities for ongoing ministry in Africa are limitless. It is our prayer that AIMM may continue to be an instrument of his purpose both in Africa and here in North America for as long as there are unmet spiritual needs in that immense land." (6)

a sense of family

Whereas former AIMM anniversary celebrations were centered about a single event and location, it was decided that the 75th would feature a number of separate AIMM rallies in church communities which had across the years supported its work. The first was held in Steinbach, Man, in October 1986, in conjunction with the regular fall board meetings. On the heels of this one there came three more in November in the three states which held AIMM's original supporting constituency in 1912: Illinois, Indiana and Ohio. Later in 1987 another three were held in Mountain Lake, MN, Fort Wayne, IN, and Harleysville, PA. The format everywhere was similar. Featured were the introduction of former and active missionaries and board members of each area, a multi-media presentation of some of the historical highlights of AIMM's 75 years of ministry, special music provided by local churches, the introduction of Earl Roth, the new AIMM Secretary and the singing of a 16th century Anabaptist hymn used in commissioning services of missionaries of their time. Discovered and translated from German by Hans Kasdorf (7) the first of four verses read:

"As God his Son was sending into this world of sin;
His Son is now commanding that we this world should win.
He sends us and commissions to preach the Gospel clear;
To call upon all nations to listen and to hear." (8)

Each rally was followed by a fellowship hour featuring anniversary cakes baked by local church members colorfully decorated with African motifs and lettering to spell out the reason for the evening. As these celebrations were brought to a close at place after place, there clearly was a feeling of festivity and family celebration in the air as old timers and new recruits, spanning three generations, mingled with local people who had a knowledge of AIMM and its ongoing identity and ministry.

Indeed, the term "family" was not a misnomer when used to describe the AIMM team of the first 75 years. For the first 60 years, AIMM had worked in a single country. Everyone literally knew everyone else. Across years of service on different stations many missionaries had occasion to work side by side with a variety of AIMM people in these settings. Out of this grew a genuine *corps d'esprit*, a sense of belonging to one another and of being accountable to and for one another. This is not to say that there were no frictions or rivalries between people or stations. There were. But there was the solid bottom line of a sense of ownership as regarded AIMM and its efforts in Africa and a deepening awareness that membership in this unusual inter-Mennonite family, drawn together by the Lord from many churches and backgrounds across the United States and Canada, was a special experience to be treasured. Conference affiliations in the homeland soon receded in importance. The reality for them was the high profile identity of the AIMM and a shared dream - - the planting of a Mennonite Church in central Africa.

It was, therefore, not surprising that when home staff was recruited from among missionary personnel, this same sense of team and family was carried with them into their new positions. Many letters from the Elkhart office to missionary colleagues in Africa carried a message of identification with them and the expression of a readiness to do whatever was possible on the home end to undergird and facilitate their work.

Consequently a number of services were provided from the home office not all of which were typical of other mission organizations. There was, for instance, a long tradition of providing bandages, gowns and medical supplies for the mission hospitals. Rolled and sewn by women's societies in Mennonite churches across North America, they converged upon the home office where they were packed in barrels and eventually shipped to Africa often via the much-appreciated services of MCC Akron. Having themselves experienced life in the isolation of the African bush, Elkhart staff responded sympathetically to frequent requests for help with securing supplies, repair parts and food which were all but impossible to find in Zaire. Return trips of Zaire missionaries were often planned via O'Hare Airport in Chicago where they were met by AIMM staff people with van and pickup loads of accumulated footlockers and cartons of supplies which were shipped with them as accompanied baggage.

AIMM home staff of the early 1980's was comprised of three former missionary couples and one secretary. Among them they provided work time the equivalent of 5½ full time people. In the absence of policy to the contrary, the Board of the time accepted and even encouraged spouses to help in the office as needed given the valuable overseas experience and perspective they could bring to the home base. As AIMM approached its 75th anniversary, headquarters bookkeeping was still done manually while correspondence and reporting was turned out on typewriters. Office procedures were truly labor intensive but, as someone put it, they were also love laden.

As AIMM program began to spread beyond Zaire, this sense of family became more difficult to maintain for no longer was it possible for all new recruits to meet AIMM's entire missionary team. Nonetheless much effort was made in the home office to nurture this sense of oneness, common identity and common cause even across the miles and political boundaries which now separated AIMM folk.

from *freundschaft* toward *gemeindschaft*

As generations of missionaries followed each other overseas, so also generations of board members followed each other in seats around the AIMM board tables. And just as new waves of missionary recruits brought questions to their overseas assignments, so also new board members brought questions to their early board sessions. What, exactly, was AIMM? What had brought it into being? Why were things done as they were? How did they and the conferences they represented fit into the picture?

As AIMM's 75th anniversary year rolled around, there were new and younger board members who came from church offices which were already computerizing their operations and which had detailed handbooks regulating staff policies and office procedures. They also came from a background of seminars where the language of "cost efficiency, administrative streamlining, chain of command, interfacing and adapted software" was familiar and much used. For some newcomers on the AIMM Board, the 75th anniversary celebrations came at a time of a growing perception on their part of a kindly, folksy, family sort of enterprise which had served well enough in the past but which, by now, was rather antiquated and probably inefficient as well. With the appointment of a new AIMM Executive Secretary, it obviously was an opportune moment to engage in a thorough going self-study. An initial executive committee minute read: "That AIMM evaluate the administrative structures and patterns at the Elkhart office utilizing an outside resource person . . ." (9)

Implementing this recommendation, Dr. Ben Sprunger was secured to lead the AIMM in this exercise. A former president of Bluffton College at Bluffton, OH, he at the time was serving as a management consultant with the Quest National Center in Columbus, OH. In subsequent executive sessions it was suggested that his study focus particularly "on utilization of staff, division of responsibilities in the home office, prioritization of staff responsibilities, interrelations between staff, executive and board, AIMM identity vis-à-vis member conference identity, imbalance in size and resources of partnering conferences and appropriate management style." (10) Sprunger's assignment, as it was fleshed out, was a broad one. If an AIMM administrative review was to be undertaken at all, the AIMM Executive Committee intended that it be thorough.

In his reporting to the AIMM five months later, Sprunger's observations and recommendations included the following;

The reading of AIMM background material and reporting since coming to Elkhart left me excited and enthused about a topic which had been part of my awareness and interest since childhood. It has been a pleasant and educational experience for me.

There is plenty for the AIMM staff to do; in many ways the AIMM home office is understaffed. Some more 'efficiencies' may be achieved but staff carries a heavy load.

AIMM's expansion into new fields and new programs has clearly increased administrative responsibilities in Elkhart. AIMM has made a good start in upgrading office equipment but there is room for considerable improvement.

There has been continuity of staff while there has been considerable change within the Board. This has sometimes resulted in some redirection of policy and program with some frustration for staff. It is not always clear where policy setting ends and administration begins.

Sprunger then made a few specific suggestions:

Increased automation should be a number one priority. Lines of authority should be clarified. Board/staff relations need clarification. Some grievance procedures should be put in place before they are needed. Clarification of staff spouse policy. (11)

But clarifying administrative procedures and staff job descriptions was one thing. Sorting out the ongoing identity of AIMM vis-à-vis its affiliated conferences was another. Some dynamics were already at work which were to have powerful impact upon the profile and program of AIMM.

a gradual shift in a delicate balance

It had been a common experience of AIMM executive secretaries. In mission seminars which brought them into contact with administrators of other mission organizations, they frequently were asked to describe the composition and structure of AIMM. As it was explained that a cluster of Mennonite denominations of North America were engaged in a partnership in mission in Africa directed by a single, joint board, looks would become puzzled and questions uncertain. It was clear that for those unacquainted with the organization, it sounded something like the proverbial bumblebee - - something which, on the face of things, couldn't be expected to fly!

From its very inception as an inter-Mennonite venture in Christian mission, the issue of the identity of CIM/AIMM vis-à-vis that of its sponsoring groups was one that had to be faced. Born before the era of highly developed denominational headquarters, the early CIM/AIMM leaders went directly to the churches with their vision, challenge and needs. A direct result was a clear cut identity and a high profile for the newly created inter-Mennonite Mission. This pattern peaked in the 1950"s during H. A. Driver's years as executive secretary. Coming to the scene during an era of explosive expansion and unlimited opportunity in Zaire, he barnstormed Mennonite Churches of North America raising funds and recruiting new missionaries. This was done with the encouragement and blessing of partnering conferences for he was adept at helping them raise their own commitments of candidates and funds for the joint venture. The profile and identity of the AIMM was high and clear. No less clear was its autonomy as an organization.

The decade of the 1960's and 70's, however, witnessed ferment of various kinds which was to have long range impact upon the North American church scene and, in turn, upon ongoing support of Christian mission around the world. There was, first, a broad move toward more activity at the various Mennonite Conference headquarters. More salaried staff was gradually added as conference ministries were diversified and expanded. There was, further, a trend toward the establishment of unified budgets within which all conference fund raising and fund allocations needed to find their place. It became increasingly clear that, in the new scheme of things, AIMM's former freedom to make unilateral appeals for its projects and program among the local churches was steadily being curtailed. AIMM had to find its place among other mission commitments of the different conferences. Even special AIMM reports and displays, which had for years been traditional at annual and triennial conventions, were gradually incorporated into the overall reporting of the mission secretaries of the respective conferences.

There were still other dynamics at work. There was the marked post-World War II trend on the part of local congregations to expand local salaried staff and to upgrade worship, educational and social facilities.

This was typically done at the cost of sizeable mortgages incurred by the congregations in question. As budget percentages for local programs climbed, budget dollars allocated for outreach frequently declined. When in the late 1980's and early 90's the American and Canadian economies slumped, AIMM's member conferences began to experience budget shortfalls which quickly translated into a new mood of caution around the AIMM Board tables in semiannual sessions. After three decades of steady expansion, AIMM Board members found themselves more and more having to make painful decisions to curtail growth.

Perhaps the story of AIMM's magazine best highlights the gradual lowering of its North American profile. Known in the early years as The Congo Missionary Messenger, it in later years was renamed The AIMM Messenger. Published in the early years as a monthly, then a bi-monthly, it eventually settled into the format of a quarterly. With passing time, the Messenger became a rich repository of first-person accounts of its history which were widely read. So clear was the view of AIMM's own identity and autonomy as an organization that in 1981 it was thought necessary to add a Director of Communications to the Elkhart staff to devote full time to the AIMM quarterly, publicity materials and news releases. To fill this new position, AIMM turned to Bob and Joyce Stradinger Gerhart who, at the time, were AIMM missionaries in Maseru, Lesotho. Assigned in 1974 to a pastoral ministry in the Maseru United Church, Bob's artistic and communication skills had become quickly apparent. Joining the Elkhart staff, Bob's creative gifts quickly became evident both in the format and art work of the quarterly and in the brochures and displays created for presentation in the churches.

But under the mounting financial restraints of the late 1980's, AIMM's publicity costs soon came under review. By 1987 the AIMM Messenger was cut back to two issues a year. In 1988 the staff position of a Coordinator of Communications was dropped. In 1990 the Messenger was reduced to a single edition per year. To compensate for this, it was said that each member conference would highlight AIMM in its own denominational periodicals. But with no one at the AIMM office to provide a steady supply of written releases, AIMM coverage in denominational publications tended to be spotty. And, when something regarding AIMM was reported, its identity was frequently not clear.

Furthermore in Board sessions of the early 90's, AIMM board members occasionally lapsed into discussions about "your missionaries" in country X and "our missionaries" in country Y - - language which earlier generations of board members would have found perplexing.

Sensing this gradual shift as he concluded his time in the AIMM office, Jim Bertsche made the following comments in his final board session in the spring of 1986: ". . . in recent years we as staff have at times, rightly or wrongly, felt ourselves to be in the curious position of defending AIMM before its own board and executive."

"As your outgoing secretary I affirm the current administrative analysis which is under way. It is time that AIMM restate once again its self-understanding and its ongoing reason for existence and ministry. It is time to review how AIMM issues are conceptualized and eventually brought into the form of adopted policy statements. It is time that we look at how staff, executive and board interrelate. It is time that home office functions and job descriptions be reviewed and re-sketched. If, in this whole process, valid reasons are found for sharply lowering AIMM's identity and curtailing its roles vis-à-vis the partnering groups, let it at least be done with a clear understanding of the fundamental shift which is under way and of the clear, long-range implications such a shift will have both in North America and overseas."

"It is my hope that as we engage in this process of review of AIMM program and partnership in mission, we will emerge from the exercise prepared to commit our collective energies and resources in a new way to an inter-Mennonite ministry in Africa. May our self-evaluation result in renewed commitment to an affirmation of each other in a shared ministry in which we all deeply believe." (12)

As the decade of the 1990's opened, AIMM found itself in an odd situation. At a time when it was experiencing the most extended presence and ministry of its history in Africa, it was also experiencing the lowest profile and identity of its history in North America.

hearing but without understanding

Back in Zaire, the missionary letter of January 1987 and the March "declaration" of the four CMZa Regional Presidents had become common knowledge. To these were added yet a third voice, that of Rev. Jean Bokeleale, the Archbishop of the ECZ. In a brief, carefully worded letter addressed to President Mbonza, he made reference to the petitions already circulating and the fact that the first quarter of the year had almost passed. He then wrote: "Thus I beg you to immediately convene the General Assembly in order that you may conform to your [1985 Assembly] decision. . . . You must submit to the decision of the supreme body of your community. This Assembly will have the goal of bringing love, peace and harmony within your community." (1)

Although the CMZa Executive had met in late March, there was no mention in the minutes of an assembly. There was, however, some interesting news. For some time the CMZa headquarters had been receiving correspondence from a cluster of groups in far southeastern Shaba Province who had declared their desire to be recognized as Mennonites. Vice President Kituka with AIMM missionary Rick Derksen had been sent to make contact with these groups. Upon their return Kituku reported having baptized 97 people and having received nineteen more by transfer from other churches. Twenty marriages had been "blessed," five elders and one deacon were consecrated to their ministry. Three four-day seminars were held dealing with the topics: "Who are the Mennonites?" "The Life of the Christian" and "The Home of the Christian." In less troubled times such reporting would have been the cause of general rejoicing. Sadly, such was the situation in the spring of that year that the only comment found in the minutes is the following phrase: "In short, the church which is being born in Shaba is alive even though it does not have a single pastor for the moment." (2)

There clearly was other agenda for the day which bulked larger in the minds of the committee members: "the *dossiers* [i.e. files or cases] of missionaries finishing their terms." A total of three single missionaries and five couples were on the list for review. There were clearly two "files" which were the focus of attention - - those of Rick and Marilyn Derksen and Leona Schrag. Members of both the administrative and executive committees, Schrag and Derksen had been the object of angry tirades in a session of the executive the previous month. This time committee discussion of their future service with CMZa was couched in bland language. Upon their return from furlough, Schrag would be transferred to Bandundu Province and the Derksens to either Banga, Djoko Punda or Kananga as they might choose. For both of them it meant a move away from Tshikapa and its church offices and a removal from both the CMZa Executive and Administrative Committees. The sort of punitive CMZa administrative action with which Zairian church workers had long been familiar had now also been applied to missionary personnel. (3)

It was just two weeks later that the full administrative committee met in Tshikapa. Of the eighteen members, five were absent - - those from Kinshasa and Bandundu Province to the west. All had written notes and offered excuses. Among them were Kakesa Samuel and his wife Kafutshi at Kikwit, a couple that had in the past lent their unswerving influential support to the administration of President Mbonza. These and all other notes were critically reviewed in an opening committee session. Four of the five were rejected as being invalid reasons for their absence. A more perceptive group of people would have recognized that their absence was a clear signal of serious trouble to come. But for President Mbonza, even at that late date, it was business as usual. He and his fellow officers were the authorities in the Church. They held power in their hands and they intended to continue to use it even as they had in the past.

The record of the sessions of the administration committee that April of 1987 abound with bristling entries and familiar references to threatened discipline. For example, it was noted that two suspended CMZa pastors of a suspended district in Kananga, Tshilembu Nicodème and Ntumba Batubenga "continued their anarchic ordination of pastors in their illegal organization and this always in the name of the CMZa. The AC maintains the suspension imposed upon them by the Executive Committee and promises the lifting of this measure as soon as they repent." (4)

There was also bitter reference to the "solemn declaration" which had been circulated early in March by the four Regional Presidents. Once again, instead of pondering the storm signals this document so clearly carried, President Mbonza and his entourage dismissed it as a subversive document born of an illegal meeting and issued by people who had "betrayed" both their regions and the "supreme body of the Church" of which they themselves were members. Given the abuse of the powers entrusted to them and given the delicacy of the entire matter, the CMZa President was made responsible to carefully prepare their files for presentation to the next general assembly. (5)

And there was more. In two earlier sessions of the executive committee, missionaries Derksen and Schrag had been harshly criticized because of their January open letter which expressed their concern regarding the trend of events. In March Derksen had written a second letter to all members of the administration committee taking exception to the manner in which the executive had handled some recent issues. He then concluded his letter by observing: "In all of this, that which saddens me the most is that our single and only reaction to the problems which surge within CMZa is to condemn . . . those whom we take to be evildoers. . . . Let us be more ready to listen to everyone because it is together that we can best discern the will of God in each situation. In the AC of June 1986 I openly said that we, that is the central administration, must change its attitude and manner of directing. Unfortunately I do not see change and the situation of the CMZa is more serious now than last year. I am also saddened by the false and injurious accusations contained in some letters addressed to the central administration. All of this must cease because it is only the Devil who profits from it to win the victory." Derksen's letter was concluded by quoting Philippians 2:2-5. (6)

In response to this letter there was the following entry in the committee record: "Given that in spite of the counsel given to our missionary brethren and sisters . . . the Rev. Richard Derksen has written a second letter . . . only five days before the meeting of the full AC; given the number of copies and the character and the psychological effects of the letter in question; considering, on the other hand, the good work of Rev. Derksen at the head of the Department of Evangelism and Life of the Church during the past years; the AC warns him for the last time against the writing of any similar letters in the future. Along the same line the AC warns that any missionary who directly or indirectly compromises himself from now on by propagating subversive writing of a circular and biased nature will be declared undesirable by the CMZa." (7)

This article was then followed by another which stated that since, in an earlier executive meeting, Derksen had been designated for a different assignment upon return after furlough, he would be relieved immediately of his church functions. Until a replacement could be prepared, responsibility for his department would be attached to the CMZa presidency. (8)

As for CMZa's relations with the AIMM, in his opening remarks President Mbonza stated his opinion that AIMM was not content with the convention signed with CMZa in December 1984, particularly as it had to do with the autonomy of the Church. He went on to wonder what this AIMM attitude had to do with a situation in which demands for autonomy were coming "in torrents" from nearly every level of the church. (9)

But it was also in these same committee minutes that there appeared the first official word regarding a general assembly. After observing that 1987 was an election year in the country, the dates were set for June 9-14, 1987 (they were later changed to June 23-28). CMZa headquarters at Tshikapa were designated as the location. There then crept into the minutes a wistful note. The assembly theme was to be: "God has reconciled us with himself in Christ." An outside speaker was to be found to be in charge of the "spiritual direction" of the assembly. It was recommended to all CMZa congregations to designate Wednesdays as a day of special prayer that the next assembly "might be a true gathering of the children of God animated by a single spirit of reconciliation and a single love." (10)

In the committee minutes it was also stated: "The AC asks all the districts or regions which have wished to withdraw from the unity of the Church to come with all their problems to the next GA of Reconciliation where all the dirty laundry will be washed within the family of the children of God." (11) It was a tone and invitation which had been desperately needed for a long time on the part of the central administration. Tragically, it was too late. Much too late. Convinced that the time for drastic action had come, the four Regional Presidents had already announced the convening of an emergency general assembly for the end of May 1987, in Kikwit.

President Mbonza early learned of the plans which were under way. As a matter of fact, he had been invited to attend. He sought, rather, to block the gathering. Sensing, perhaps for the first time, that his credibility and authority within his church were rapidly eroding, he once again sought help from the government. In a letter dated May 18 1987, addressed to the government authorities in Kikwit, he stated that the impending gathering was illegal and politically dangerous since its objective was "the destabilization of the Mennonite Community in particular and the menace of the security and peace in general." Naming the well-known layman Kakesa Samuel and the Regional President Luingo Mudindu as the ringleaders, he asked that they be stopped and the meeting canceled by government order. (12)

Four days later President Mbonza addressed a letter to the two men he had just denounced to local government authorities plus Kinshasa Regional President, Kakesa Mulume, and layman Kidinda Sh'a Ndungo. After pointing out their errors and the "illegality" of what they were proposing to do, he urged them to drop their plans. Rather they should come to the assembly he was planning for Tshikapa in June where they could bring all the problems which troubled them and "to resolve them with due process and in the love of the children of God . . ."

The CMZa leaders of the Kinshasa and Bandundu Regions, however, had done their homework. ECZ Archbishop Bokeleale had been alerted to the plans which were underway and he had given his tacit encouragement. In Kikwit the CMZa leaders had fully briefed the local government officials. When President Mbonza's letter arrived attempting to sound a political alarm, it was simply ignored. The response of the Kikwit Church leaders was to send yet one final invitation to Mbonza to join them in the special assembly they were convening. There was no response. The die was cast. There was no turning back.

Assembly I

They converged on Kikwit the last week in May. They came from all corners of CMZa territory by whatever means of transportation was available to them not knowing when or if they would be reimbursed for the high travel costs involved in coming from isolated areas as many of them did. (13) In all, a total of sixty-eight delegates arrived from twenty-seven of CMZa's thirty-plus districts. Seven additional people were invited to attend, all of them influential laymen. AIMM missionary and ISTK professor Peter Buller was invited to bring a series of devotional messages centered around the adopted assembly theme: "Unity in the Faith" and its associated text for the week, Ephesians 4:3.

The mood of the gathering was immediately clear, a mix of excitement and determination. Memories of the Nyanga Assembly of 1985 were still fresh. After months of frustration and indecision, CMZa, at its grass-roots level, was reacting. After years of enduring an increasingly heavy handed, top-down central administration, they were asserting themselves. They had enough.

The preamble of the official record of the Kikwit Assembly expressed their mood well: "The CMZa since May 1985 is passing through a generally deplorable situation characterized by conflicts, discrimination, anarchy, dictatorship, irregular suspensions and revocations of members, a total absence of Christian dialogue between members and the central authority . . . . Numerous letters addressed [to the central authority] to request the urgent convocation of an assembly were treated as subversive. . . . Anxious to save the Community in order to allow peace and unity to reign, the members of the CMZa recommended via their declaration a special GA at Kikwit." (14)

In the assembly discussions and actions taken, a high level of concern was evident for the repair of damage done and for reconciliation and reversal of the splintering process which was under way. Special commissions were named to go to the South Kasai and to Kinshasa to seek to resolve the divisive disputes that had erupted among the districts of those two areas. A number of pastors who had been defrocked by the central administration were reinstated. Special concern was evident with regard to CMZa members and AIMM missionaries who had experienced harsh treatment. One of the assembly actions read as follows: The assembly asks both our "national and expatriate brothers and sisters who have been hurt psychologically by such inhuman decisions to recommit themselves to the hands of the Lord to serve in peace and order." The assembly "calls back the members who may have left the CMZa for personal reasons to rejoin their Church in order to each bring their building stone to the edifice." (15)

To this was added yet a further assembly action: "All punitive measures taken against certain missionaries are annulled. The Assembly asks these missionaries to feel at ease and to work each one where they formerly were." (16)

Another major concern for the delegates was the CMZa structures which had permitted the excessive centralized authority they had experienced. Determined to effect some needed changes, a special commission was authorized to review the CMZa constitution and bylaws with a view to curbing central authority while granting larger freedom of action at regional and district levels.

In dealing with their absent CMZa officers, there was no equivocation. While the theme of unity was often referred to, there was no sentiment to try further to engage their president in dialogue. Too many pleas addressed to him in the past had been either ignored or haughtily rejected. Even their invitations to join them at Kikwit met with silence. Official action was taken to discharge both President Mbonza and his Vice President Kituku Gibula from their functions as officers of the CMZa. Regarding the president further action was taken to suspend his pastoral credentials and to excommunicate him from the church. (17)

a new team of officers elected

The election process was carried out amidst freedom of nomination and spirited flow of debate. In an interesting turn of events, an early and strong candidate was Kamayala District President Pastor Chibulenu Sakayimbo. Early in Mbonza's time as CMZa President, Pastor Chibulenu had been heard from. It was he who early questioned new terminology adopted to refer to CMZa officers. He suggested it was inappropriate to borrow terms from government for use in church circles. It was he who early raised the troublesome issue of non-representation of the ethnic groups of his southern area either at regional or national levels of church administration. It was he who early had expressed his sorrow and alarm regarding the conduct of the Nyanga Assembly in 1985. It was also he who had given leadership to the first announced withdrawal of a cluster of districts from the CMZa. At first largely ignored, Pastor Chibulenu's repeated calls for fairness addressed to the Tshikapa office came to be viewed as a prime example of biased provincial views which were to be rejected and condemned as "subversive."

Born in a rural Chokwe village in the Territory of Kahemba in which a teacher/evangelist had been placed by missionaries from Kamayala Station, Chibulenu came under his influence at an early age. He later wrote of those years: "Mornings before school or evenings after school he organized meetings. Those who took an interest gathered in a semicircle around him to hear him sing, pray and preach. At the end he invited people to accept Jesus and to seek baptism. This sort of ministry continued over time. Eventually those who accepted were taught further in preparation for baptism. . . which was granted as an exterior sign of a changed heart. In order to grow in faith, the converted person needed to meditate on the Word of God. . . . The Bible constituted at one and the same time the source and the authority of the faith professed. Among the Biblical passages used as preaching texts at church, John 3:16 predominated. That passage, I believe, led more people to Christ than all others . . . . Those who believed in Jesus Christ followed the model of his life and sought to live according to his teachings. . . ."

"Among the teachings emphasized were nonviolence [this within an ethnic group with a pre-colonial history of warfare and slave trading], simplicity of life, and honesty." In concluding comments Chibulenu said: "These teachings and the manner in which they were applied in daily life impressed me very much.

Proclamation of the Word and the witness of the lives of Christians are the origin of my faith. When I discovered my Mennonite identity, I regretted neither my baptism nor the teachings I had received." (18)

Finishing his primary education at Kamayala Station, he was soon chosen as one of a small Kamayala contingent of students for enrollment in the CMZa secondary school at Nyanga. Having successfully finished his third year of study, his home church district was eager to send one of their own sons to ISTK. Having met the academic requirements of that epoch for enrollment, he responded to their pleas and transferred to that pastoral training school in Kinshasa.

There followed a bitter chapter in his life. Although he successfully concluded his studies and graduated from ISTK, he in the meantime had made friends with a few fellow students who insisted that "Christian freedom" meant that temperate indulgence in alcoholic beverages was their privilege. Finding this an exciting concept as compared to the firm stance of abstinence with which he had grown up back at Kamayala, he began to experiment. To be sure it was his intent to be moderate and controlled in his drinking but he soon began a steady descent into an enslavement which was to bring him to the brink of disaster. At first welcomed back at Kamayala with congratulations and applause for his completed studies, he was given a series of church assignments each of which was withdrawn as his addiction to alcohol became increasingly apparent. Even a teaching position in a government school also came to naught as his addiction continued to rule his life.

In desperation, church leaders arranged that he leave his wife Constantine and their children with relatives in her home village and that he return to Kinshasa to spend time in the home of a Chokwe pastor of that city. It was here that Chibulenu literally came to the end of himself. Finally admitting the steady unraveling of his life and the progressive loss of everything and everyone dear to him, he turned to God in desperation, penitence and prayer. He later would describe this as a dramatic encounter with Christ the Lord. Receiving the power to break with his addiction, he began "rebuilding his life on the old foundation, apprenticing himself to this pastor for nine months. When he returned to Kamayala, he was a very humble man and a totally committed believer. People marveled: 'How can a man change like that?'" (19)

Re-establishing a home and family life he was welcomed back into the church where opportunities for ministry quickly succeeded one another culminating in his eventual election as District President. It was against the background of this pilgrimage of personal pain and faith that he was chosen, at the specially convened Kikwit Assembly, to replace Mbonza Kikunga as president of the CMZa. Elected as vice president was Kabasele Bantubiabo, a member of the large Baluba tribe so many of whom had experienced the bitter migration of the early 60's as refugees to the South Kasai.

Remarkably, in the setting of the Kikwit Assembly where drastic change was the order of the day, incumbent CMZa Treasurer Tshimowa Bisosa was re-elected to that position. Also a Muluba, this meant that for the first time in the history of the CMZa there was not a Muphende within the circle of CMZa's national officers.

In a concluding worship service of the assembly, the newly elected president was consecrated to his new task by prayer and the laying on of hands. Peter Buller, a participant in the ceremony, reported that President Chibulenu took his response from Luke 1:38 "saying like Mary, he in his unworthiness took a task imposed upon him by the Lord and asked for our prayers." (20)

Assembly II

Although the Kikwit Assembly had stipulated the people who were to be present on the occasion of the official transfer of personnel in the Tshikapa headquarters, no attempt was made to set a date. The delegates instinctively knew that this would not be a simple process. Having been unable to prevent the Kikwit gathering, President Mbonza plunged into preparation for the assembly which the CMZa Administrative Committee had set for June 23-29 at Tshikapa. With the support of a minority group still loyal to him and the use of influence and resources available to the incumbent administration, President Mbonza was able to rally a total of sixty-five delegates from twenty-four Districts. It was a clear indication of the uncertainty of some of the district leaders amidst the power struggle that twelve districts that had sent delegates to the Kikwit gathering four weeks earlier also sent delegates to the Tshikapa assembly convened by Mbonza. In addition to the official delegates, there were eleven members of the administrative committee, four regional evangelists, two women's coordinators, six invited guests including missionaries Maurice Briggs and Tim Bertsche from nearby Kalonda Station, six observers and seven members of the headquarters staff.

In an opening address President Mbonza expressed thanks to all those who had responded to the call to come to Tshikapa. "Your presence here witnesses to the importance that you attach to the well-being of our Church inherited at the price of the blood of our Master and Savior Jesus Christ." The cloud of controversy under which the Tshikapa assembly was convened quickly was reflected in his ongoing comments. Our assembly meets, he observed, "during an agitated moment when the community is experiencing an explosive situation of attempted divisions which causes unbelievers and Christians of little faith to tremble. The Lord speaks to us about this in I Corinthians 11:19 and says: 'No doubt there must be divisions among you so that the ones who are in the right may be clearly seen.' We must understand that the Christian church is a human society that is characterized by a thirst for the Word of God, by his love, by a fear [of him], by a knowledge of and respect for laws and precepts, divine and human, as well as by respect and obedience of human authorities. I ask that you take the time to redress the prejudice caused toward the Community by the torrent of injurious, insolent and subversive letters courageously written and circulated by these ordained Reverend Pastors and their faithful members."

Having thus expressed his displeasure with the rising tide of dissidents within CMZa, he concluded his address on a strangely tentative and uncertain note: "It is necessary that we arrive at a clear definition of the autonomy that certain groups demand, and spell out their status. If that is the will of God, we must bow before his sovereignty." (21)

The official minutes of the assembly ran a total of forty-five different articles, a clear reflection of the many responsibilities which faced the incumbent administration. There was recognition of some new CMZa districts; there was serious discussion of the chronic problem of a church membership which was out-stripping CMZa's supply of pastoral candidates; there was an article calling for spiritual retreats for the pastors of the Community; there was discussion of CMZa's financial problems; the president was encouraged "to multiply contacts with different churches and organizations of Europe, America and Asia [with reference to] public health, agriculture, leadership training, rural development and transportation." (22)

but still more retaliation

In spite of the large legitimate CMZa agenda which needed attention, it was obvious that the Tshikapa Assembly met under the shadow of the dissident Kikwit gathering held just four weeks earlier. How were they to respond? This soon became clear since over half of the Tshikapa Assembly actions were related in one manner or another to reactions of the central administration toward those who were absent. Early in this block of minutes there was the comment: "The GA regretted the absence of the leaders of these discontented groups even though they were invited." Referring to correspondence from AIMM proposing an early consultation with CMZa regarding recent developments, the delegates affirmed the idea while instructing the CMZa President "to prepare the files of missionaries presumed to be undesirable and to forward them to the Executive Secretary of the AIMM before the next CMZa/AIMM consultation."

There was a series of minutes dealing with specific dissident CMZa leaders which became increasingly shrill in language. Regarding Tshilembu Nicodème and Ntumba Batubenga of Kananga, "The GA revokes all their ecclesiastic activities and lifts from them their pastoral dignity. The President is requested to do whatever necessary to see to it that this measure is respected." Nowhere in the official minutes did the anger of the central administration come through more clearly than in the references to the four Regional Presidents who had convened the Kikwit Assembly the previous month. After reviewing their refusal to respect central administration warnings and the "illegality" of what they had done, they were all denounced as "incompetents and as traitors of their regions as well as of the Supreme Organ of the Community." In another context there was reference to "incompetence and high treason." Actions then followed to replace them all in their positions with new CMZa personnel.

The retaliatory action of the Tshikapa Assembly did not stop there. A number of other changes were made at regional and district levels in an attempt to replace people who had been supportive of the Kikwit gathering with others who would be loyal to the central administration.

Missionaries also came under critical review. In the minutes it was stated that "in conformity to the law of the country and the standards of the ECZ and given the present situation in the CMZa where certain 'missionaries' are directly or indirectly implicated, the GA decides that in the future no 'missionaries' will have a seat in important meetings of the CMZa . . . ."

And there was yet another assembly action which clearly reflected the defensive mood of the delegates: "Given the complexity of certain judicial cases which oppose the Community against third parties and against certain of its rebel members . . . the GA accepts to secure the services of a legal council and makes the President responsible to contact an attorney immediately after the close of this Assembly for the orientation of our different judicial cases." (23)

It was on this somber and joyless note that the Tshikapa Assembly drew to a close. As the delegates dispersed, the sad reality was that within four weeks time there had been two CMZa General Assemblies. As a result there were now dual sets of officers, dual sets of Regional Presidents, dual sets of minutes and conflicting actions and dual sets of correspondence being addressed to the AIMM office in Elkhart.

It is ironical that while both assemblies talked much about pursuing reconciliation within the CMZa, the two factions within the Church were clearly on a collision course.

a different voice

It was in the early aftermath of these two assemblies that a significant letter arrived in Elkhart addressed conjointly to Earl Roth and Art Janz. It was from Kakesa Samuel at Kikwit. He was a layman who had been a key figure in the earlier years as the transition from mission to church was worked though. He had been the first fully functioning legal representative of the CMZa. He had survived the Kwilu rebellion of the early 1960's with a mix of courage, daring and personal faith. After being replaced by others, he and his wife, Kafutshi, had waited for further opportunity to serve their church. Before long they were again integrated into the life of the CMZa at both local and national levels. He had played a powerful role in supporting Rev. Mbonza's early candidacy for the presidency. He had also been an intimate observer of the disintegration of the Church to which he had given so much of his energy and life.

Now, dated July 8, 1987, came his letter which read in part: "Dear Brothers Roth and Janz: In this very difficult moment which the CMZa in general and I in particular are experiencing I want to write you a few words of encouragement. . . . I know that you are also touched and staggered by what is happening here. Samuel told Saul that obedience is worth more than sacrifices. CMZa is sick and has sinned against God. May God truly forgive us. . . . I do not want to say that the special GA at Kikwit was totally right since I participated in it but I think it is necessary to count on it. Why? The Assembly agenda had two points: the reconciliation and the restructuring [of the CMZa.] I think that if the former President had come to Kikwit he might have been able to keep his position. . . . Do not be discouraged, do nothing to withdraw the missionaries but let us submit ourselves to the will of God. . . . Above everything else that we can ask of you, PRAY for us. Fraternally yours in the Lord, Kakesa Khakha Kasala."

President Mbonza and the Mennonite World Conference

In his capacity as vice president for Africa, President Mbonza was a member of the MWC Executive Committee. In the summer of 1986, the Committee was hosted by the Mennonite Churches of Taiwan. Transportation schedules had been meticulously worked out months ahead of time by Executive Secretary Paul Kraybill thus benefitting from special rates. On the day of his scheduled departure, President Mbonza failed to take his flight out of Kinshasa. Thereupon the only solution to ensure his arrival for the Taiwan meetings was to travel first class, something which obviously resulted in sharply increased costs. When later asked about the missed flight he nonchalantly explained that he had been "too busy" that day to take the scheduled flight.

Once in Taiwan, he became insistent on rerouting and reticketing his homeward travel so as to spend several days in Japan, changes which again would have resulted in greatly increased air fares. These requests were politely but firmly refused by the MWC Secretary.

In July of 1987, another MWC planning meeting was scheduled. This time it was to be a larger group known as the MWC General Council and it was to be hosted by the Mennonite Churches of Paraguay, South America. To this broader gathering the CMZa was entitled to send two representatives in addition to President Mbonza, as the MWC Vice President for Africa, and Rev. Mukanza Ilunga, as chairman of the MWC International Peace Committee.

Fully aware of the growing controversy which was swirling around Mbonza, MWC Secretary Kraybill was confronted with a painful dilemma. Should he move ahead with processing travel papers and air tickets for the controversial president or should he prevent his participation in the Paraguay gathering by the simple expedient of denying him the necessary documents? Neither alternative was a pleasant one. After much consultation with people close to the Zaire Mennonite scene, he decided to withhold the papers.

When it became clear to Mbonza what had happened, he addressed a letter of protest to Kraybill. In his letter he said in part: "Contrary to my will, I have not come to take part in the General Council of the MWC because the letter of guarantee for the visa for Paraguay, which you promised, has not arrived even as I write these lines." He then stated that the men who had traveled to Paraguay (24) could in no manner represent the CMZa because they had all been removed from their positions with the Church by the General Assembly held the previous month in Tshikapa. Thus, he observed, "they come to defend their own interests or those of the ones who made possible their travel. They can no longer speak in the name of the Church for they are no longer its representatives."

The letter then concluded: "If Mennonite Churches belong to Jesus Christ, we will see each other in sessions of future meetings. If they are purely and simply human societies, it is possible that we will never see each other again." (25) Mbonza and Kraybill never did see each other again though not for the reason he suggested in his letter.

Assembly III

Archbishop Bokeleale of the ECZ had been far from a passive observer of the escalating CMZa conflict. Already in the summer of 1985, following the controversial elective assembly at Nyanga, the ECZ had used its influence to block government approval of the new slate of officers - - this in spite of repeated efforts on Mbonza's part to secure official recognition. When there was a delay in convening the 1987 Assembly, Rev. Bokeleale addressed a personal letter to Mbonza reminding him that according to CMZa's own delegate body action, it was time to do so. When the four CMZa Regional Presidents informed him of their decision to convene a special assembly in May at Kikwit, he raised no objection to their proposal.

It was in the course of a meeting of the ECZ Executive Committee the end of July that the sad CMZa situation was reviewed and firm action was taken. Following the session, a letter was addressed to the four CMZa Regional Presidents. After tracing some of the history and the holding of dual CMZa Assemblies neither of which was able to achieve reconciliation within the Church, the Archbishop informed them that both assemblies were considered as null and void; that both Mbonza Kikunga and Chibulenu Sakayimbo were suspended as CMZa officers; that the CMZa would temporarily function under the supervision of ECZ Regional Presidents in the four areas where CMZa was present and that the ECZ was convening a special assembly for the CMZa September 28-30, 1987, in the city of Kinshasa. There would be two items on the agenda - - "the reconciliation of the children of God and the election of new leaders."

The letter concluded by appealing to the four Regional CMZa Presidents for their support in this venture "in order to permit us once and for all to finish this sad problem." (26) On the same day a second letter was addressed to the AIMM office in Elkhart soliciting a special contribution toward the cost which this special assembly would incur.

For a third time within the space of four months, CMZa delegates began their treks from near and far to attend an assembly of their Church. This time it had been planned and organized by ECZ personnel. A total of seventy-seven delegates representing four regional offices and thirty-three CMZa Districts were present as the gathering was formally opened by ECZ national staff. Though this group still did not account for all CMZa districts, it was a broader representation than had been achieved by either of the preceding gatherings. In the absence of President Mbonza and staff, Dr. Makina a Nganga and AIMM missionary Rick Derksen were seated to represent CMZa's central administration. Specifically invited to attend the Kinshasa meeting, the Mbonza administration had countered by drawing up a document of withdrawal from the ECZ. They furthermore called a session for CMZa district presidents at Ilebo, far to the north of Tshikapa, at the same time as the Kinshasa gathering. While this likely prevented a few district presidents from going to Kinshasa, in most cases their districts were represented in Kinshasa by others.

ECZ personnel opened the first session with a Biblical exposition on the theme of reconciliation and love within the body of Christ correctly pointing out, in the process, that nonviolence is recognized as a fundamental Mennonite creed. It was only after being led in an exercise of introspection and reconciliation with each other that the CMZa delegates were allowed to elect their chairman and recording secretaries. (27) This done, ECZ staff withdrew to the sideline roles of observers and consultants. Two major working commissions were then formed, one to deal with the critical need for reconciliation and healing within the CMZa; the second to serve as a nominating committee.

As the assembly drew to a close, the official actions taken clearly reflected much of what had been said and done in the Kikwit Assembly four months earlier - - to reintegrate a number of CMZa leaders who had recently been removed from office by the Tshikapa administration; to organize meetings of healing in all four CMZa regions as soon as possible; to seek ways of restructuring the CMZa administration so as to curb the powers of the Tshikapa office.

As regarded the team of officers at Tshikapa, assembly actions this time were somewhat more temperate. Though President Mbonza, Vice President Kituku and Treasurer Tshimowa were all three removed from office, they were placed at the disposition of their home districts for other pastoral functions. As for the supposed withdrawal of the CMZa from the ECZ, all who co-signed the document were also removed from office. (28)

When it came to the election of officers, the delegates held firmly to the decisions made at Kikwit. Rev. Chibulenu Sakayimbo was again elected president by a vote of seventy-four with four abstentions. Kabasele Bantubiabo was maintained as vice president. Whereas at Kikwit the incumbent treasurer Tshimowa Bisosa had been retained, at Kinshasa he was replaced by Kabeya Kanda. In addition, the four regional presidents were maintained in their posts.

A final act of business was to set October 15, 1987, as the date for the formal transition in leadership at the CMZa headquarters in Tshikapa. A special, broadly-based commission was named to oversee this event. (29) Meanwhile ECZ personnel in Kinshasa promised to push energetically for prompt recognition of the newly elected CMZa officers by the government's Justice Department.

The Kinshasa Assembly came to a close on September 30. The next morning, October 1, the newly-constituted CMZa Administrative Committee met in its first working session. Two concerns predominated the discussions - - new appointments of CMZa personnel and ongoing relations with AIMM and its missionaries. Missionary appointments were made in the light of missionary training and preferences. Plans were also laid for an impending consultation with AIMM and MCC at Nyanga in November. But overshadowing all else was a concern for the scheduled transition of leadership in the central offices in Tshikapa occupied by an increasingly defiant Mbonza and staff. How and under what circumstances would it take place? They were soon to find out.

episodes of shame

Respecting the October 15 date set by the Kinshasa Assembly, members of the appointed commission began to converge on Tshikapa several days before. In preparation for the day, members of the commission paid a courtesy call at the office of the local government official known as the *Commissaire de Zone* where they explained the reason for their arrival. Although courteously received he warned them of the belligerence of the incumbent CMZa officers and their readiness to resist with physical force any effort to replace them in the church headquarters. This being the case, the local *commissaire* said he was not prepared to become involved in a potentially explosive situation without direct orders from his superiors. In the meantime, CMZa staff members whose loyalty to the Tshikapa administration was in question had already been forcibly evicted from their offices by Mbonza's personnel.

There followed weeks of travel and negotiation as commission members made trips to Kinshasa and to the provincial capital at Kananga trying to secure the authorization and help needed to effect the installation of the new officers in their church headquarters. Although the local state official continued to pay lip service to the proposed change, it became increasingly evident to the commission that he, in fact, supported President Mbonza and would continue to seek ways of thwarting the new officers.

All during November some members of the commission remained in the Tshikapa area housed and hosted across the river at Kalonda station. All efforts to move the process forward met obstruction on the part of local authorities who, by this time, had made it clear where their sympathies lay in the dispute. Suddenly the news came. With unaccustomed speed the Department of Justice had acted on the decision of the Kinshasa Assembly. A "decree" had been issued dated December 1, 1987, officially recognizing the new CMZa slate of officers. There was instant jubilation on the part of the commission encamped at Kalonda. A further hopeful sign was the unexplained transfer of the local *commissaire* and the appointment of a different man. Contact was immediately made with the new appointee by members of the commission with the new government decree in hand. Ordered by the provincial governor to proceed, the new official set December 15 as the day for transition of CMZa personnel at the church headquarters.

Convening everyone concerned in his office that morning, he explained what his instructions were from higher authorities and that he would proceed that day with the ordered transition of personnel in the church offices. Reaction from the incumbent officers in the room was immediate and angry. The commission report later described events as follows: "The former team [of officers] categorically opposed the voluntary transfer as the commissaire . . . had requested. As a result he made the decision to order a forced transition . . . . From each team three members were designated to be present for the operation on the site. Thus for the exiting team the delegation was composed of the President/Legal Representative, the Vice President/Assistant Legal Representative and the General Treasurer [i.e. Mbonza Kikunga, Kibula Kituku and Tshimowa Bisosa.]. The new team would be represented by the Vice President, the General Treasurer and the former General Treasurer" [i.e. Kabasele Bantubiabo, Kabeya Kanda and Bukungu Mishumbi].

". . . Upon arrival at the administrative center, the former President did not want to pass over the keys of the offices until the authorities threatened to force the doors. During the discussion concerning the keys, the new team was attacked." (30) For some reason President Mbonza was particularly incensed by the presence of Bukungu Mishumbi, the former CMZa General Treasurer who had been named a member of the transition commission. Standing calmly and impassively in front of the office doors which had for so many years been his place of work he endured, without response, the menace and insults of the president and, finally, his spittle. Meanwhile partisan family and clan members surrounded the other two men and rained blows and invective upon them.

In the midst of this abuse, both the new team and the local government agent demonstrated amazing restraint. The *commissaire* later rightly observed that had he given orders for the police present to take harsh counter actions, it could well have worked against the long-term best interests of the new team. Given the extreme tension, he decided to have the offices locked and to pursue matters further at a later date.

That night the church center offered a strange, disquieting scene for passers-by. The soft glow of kerosene lamps indicated the presence of the deposed officers with their families in their homes while nearby a detachment of police stood guard over the padlocked headquarters of the Zaire Mennonite Church.

A few days later Mbonza Kikunga went to Kinshasa leaving the church center and former staff members behind. Unknown to all and perhaps even to himself, it would be many long months before he would again see or assume responsibility for his wife and children.

The New Year came and went as well as most of January. The church offices were still padlocked; the families of the former officers still occupied the houses at the center. The commission members charged to oversee the transition were still circulating in and out of Kalonda Station. The whole issue had once again become embroiled with conflicting and overlapping local government offices. In spite of all that had transpired and clear directives from central and provincial government offices, some local authorities sympathetic to ex-President Mbonza were engaged in a last-ditch effort to derail the long awaited transition.

Tiring of the local politics at Tshikapa, the commission sent yet another delegation to Kananga to again seek help from the Governor. This time there was prompt action. On February 3, 1988, a delegation sent by the Governor representing the Judiciary, the Department of Security and the Military arrived by plane. Arriving at the local government offices, they summoned representatives from both groups. They had few words. They had come with clear instructions - - "to execute without fail the decision of the Justice Department approving the new team." (31)

The leader of the delegation, however, spoke not only in terms of legal requirements but commented pointedly about the tragic situation he had found at Tshikapa: "This is not worthy of a church which should always preach by examples to be followed."

Going to the CMZa center, a large partisan group was again found on the scene made up primarily of members of Mbonza's clan. In his absence Vice President Kituku became the spokesman for the staff still occupying the center. He cooperated in opening his own office as requested. Other staff members were less cooperative and responded only under duress. There were again moments of tension as young people began hurling insults and stones. Again there was extraordinary restraint. Two or three of the more violent protesters were taken in hand as office after office was entered and inventories taken. Before leaving the center that afternoon, the families were given orders to evacuate within forty-eight hours. In succeeding days bank accounts were checked; the local hospital and the CMZa sawmill operation visited.

It was February 9, 1988, that for the first time the new officers were able to visit the center alone. Homes were checked and cleaned with the excited help of local church members. The commission report described the next day as follows: "Wednesday the 10th of February remains an unforgettable date for the new CMZa, the first day and first night at the administrative center. This first night was passed in song and prayer

401

with all of the pastors of Kalonda District. . . . The following morning was consecrated to a service of thanksgiving in front of the offices and homes of the officers." (32)

AIMM missionary Maurice Briggs with his wife Joyce Suran was stationed at Kalonda during those difficult days, was frequently pressed into service as the chauffeur of a church jeep transporting commission members, government personnel, mail, messages and needed supplies. He kept a log of those tumultuous days. On February 11, the entry reads: "Happy, relaxed atmosphere at the CMZa headquarters today. A welcome change that has been a long time in coming. There's a lot of work ahead but the first major hurdle . . . has been completed. The Lord has answered many prayers to get us this far along and I'm sure He'll continue to assist as long as we look to Him first in everything. Throughout this whole ordeal I have found the new CMZa leadership to be steady and patient. They made it a practice to have devotions and a time of prayer together each day. The change of administration was to have taken place October 15 and finally became a reality nearly four months later. We are now at the end of the beginning." (33)

To be sure there was a widespread sense of relief all across the CMZa landscape as the new team of officers was at long last able to occupy the church headquarters at Tshikapa. But the sense of relief was tempered by a certain sense of failure as well. It was clear to all that CMZa had not been able to resolve its internal conflict on its own. It had required varying degrees of intervention on the part of the ECZ, the AIMM and even the government, interventions which clearly cast a shadow over CMZa's claims of autonomy, its integrity and its testimony in Zaire.

CHAPTER 43   LOOKING TOWARD THE FUTURE

reaching out to scattered sheep

In a letter addressed to AIMM Secretary Earl Roth soon after his installation in the CMZa headquarters, President Chibulenu summarized his stance and that of the new administration when he said: "I write to you here from the center and we greatly glorify the Lord our God for this. There is much work to be done . . ." (1)

As to "the work to be done," nothing loomed larger for the new CMZa leaders and the AIMM than the call for a ministry of reconciliation. With the news that AIMM Secretary Roth and board member Lawrence Giesbrecht were planning a trip to Africa that spring, President Chibulenu laid detailed plans for the extensive travel of an AIMM/CMZa team to CMZa church centers far and near. Trip reports submitted after their return home provided something of the flavor and tone of these visits.

At Mutena, as at all other church centers, an official letter of welcome was read to open the meeting with local leaders. This letter contained the following paragraph: "We know very well that this is the very first time since accession to authority that the central administration has organized a visit of consolation of brothers and sisters in Christ. We can also say that this visit is the point of departure of real expansion for it will prepare the leaders to combat false doctrines and ideas which invade our [efforts of] evangelism and orient people on the good path of salvation." (2) To this President Chibulenu responded: "We are here to see together what is needed to redress [our situation.] We need to regroup and establish again a sound base for evangelism." (3)

In a written report to fellow Board members, Giesbrecht observed: "At Kasadisadi, a government military post close to the Angolan border, we were enthusiastically welcomed and ushered into the partly finished, partly roofed church, built around the steel frame of an otherwise destroyed storage building from the pre-revolution diamond mining era. Chibulenu spoke on reconciliation after a letter of greeting was read."

At Mukedi there was " . . . a tumultuous reception complete with the usual greetings punctuated with musket fire salutes. . . . With over 600 in attendance the usual letter of greeting was read. Vice President Kabasele addressed the congregation . . . using II Corinthians 5:17-20 to call the people to reconciliation."

At Kamayala " . . . from where Pastor Chibulenu was called to become President of CMZa, he was greeted like a native son who had come home a hero. . . . People filled the building [station chapel] beyond capacity. The usual letter of greetings was read to the visitors. Part of the letter contained what was probably the longest list of requests addressed to AIMM and CMZa." After dealing with a number of specific items the new president pointed out to his fellows clansmen that in seeking solutions for their needs "we do not start with the Legal Representative or with the delegation but each of us has to start on his own. You first have to start with local resources and with yourselves and afterward look for external help." (4)

At Djoko Punda the traditional letter of greeting contained the following comments: "Before all else we first give thanks to the eternal God the all powerful One for having given us this day the occasion to welcome you here in this original and first district of the CMZa. It is for us a very great joy for this visit encourages us to put behind us the difficulties of the period of inhibition by which the entire Mennonite community has passed." (5)

And at Kananga, a letter of welcome carried the following sentiments: "Your visit . . . is a comfort and encouragement among us for, as the saying goes, after the rain comes clear weather." (6)

new language, new perspective

It was dry season of 1988 when the first meeting of a full-blown administrative committee was held. Anyone familiar with the last meetings of the previous AC was immediately struck by some obvious changes. For starters, there was the theme verse adopted for the sessions by President Chibulenu - - Nehemiah 2:17-18:

"See what trouble we are in because Jerusalem is in ruins and its gates are destroyed. Let us rebuild the city walls and put an end to our disgrace . . . and they got ready to start the work."

Then there was the composition of the newly formed committee. Among the members and six specially-invited nonvoting participants were several who in the last months of the previous regime had been ostracized as subversives and, in some cases, been excommunicated. Notable among them were Kakesa Samuel and his wife Kafutshi, Tshilembu Nicodème, Mpoyi Tshienda, Bukungu Mishumbi and Dr. Kidinda Shandungo, son of a Mukedi pastor who, with an AIMM scholarship, had earned his doctorate in comparative education. Though frequently offering his opinions and help to the previous administrations, he had consistently been ignored. A look around the circle of the convened group quickly revealed the deliberate effort made to assemble people as broadly representative of CMZa's regions and membership as possible.

Perhaps most revealing of all was the language of the official minutes of their first work sessions. Dealing with a heavy agenda, there were a total of forty-two separate actions taken. Whereas the committee minutes of the concluding months of the previous administration frequently used language of command, scorn, warning and retaliation, this group used a different terminology. The very first official action was to express gratitude: "The AC thanks all the brethren and sisters in Christ who have contributed spiritually, morally, materially and financially to the recovery of the CMZa and ask the President/Legal Representative to write them to this effect." (7)

A perusal of the record of following actions reveals the use of such words and phrases as "requests, as it is possible, approves, delays, recommends, encourages, establishes, gives responsibility, decides, authorizes, invites, reconstitutes, accords, takes knowledge of, reminds and reinforces."

A number of special commissions were named to deal with such issues as the increasing number of groups who were requesting to be recognized as new CMZa districts, the auditing of CMZa accounts, the urgent need to hold district conferences throughout the South Kasai in an effort to achieve reconciliation in a CMZa region which long had struggled with disagreement between two factions, the review and evaluation of all CMZa pastors who had been ordained during the "period of conflict," as well as CMZa pastors at work who had been ordained in other churches, the review and revision of CMZa's bylaws in the light of the principles of "separation of powers, decentralization, reinforcement of the unity of the CMZa, democracy and non-violence," the review of the many requests for scholarships along with the funding sources available and the revision of the existing AIMM/CMZa convention in preparation for meeting with the next AIMM delegation the following year. (8)

Other actions pinpointed still other concerns such as "the integration of women in all of the activities of the Church;" encouraging "the initiative of the creation of a National Inter-Mennonite Committee" to which former CMZa Vice President Mukanza Ilunga was by this time giving leadership; to review and evaluate CMZa's ongoing participation in inter-mission projects in Zaire; to send the new president to Shaba Province with two or three others "to regularize the situation of the CMZa in this region and to perform pastoral activities;" to extend an invitation to a series of missionaries plus requests for new candidates for other positions; and to name the new CMZa President as the replacement of their former President as a member of the MWC General Council. (9)

Incontestably the new CMZa Administrative Committee had taken their theme text from Nehemiah seriously. By actions and initiatives taken, they were clearly saying: "Let us rebuild the city walls." It was only days later that President Chibulenu wrote to the AIMM Secretary at Elkhart in the following terms: "At the conclusion of the work of the AC this past August, all of the members expressed their satisfaction for the support, material as well as moral, which the AIMM accorded our Community during the period of sad memory. They also asked me to address our most fraternal thanks to you yourself and to the brothers and sisters who participate in this work. May your will to help us not grow weary. The difficulties which the CMZa has known mark a particular period and are inherent in every work undertaken under the control of the flesh. We will, however, strive by the grace of God to consolidate the unity acquired so that this should not occur again in the future." (10)

AIMM again examines mission/church relations in Zaire

AIMM missionaries, Board and staff had experienced deep anguish during the months of angry confusion within the Zaire Church. At first, not always sure how to separate fact from fiction, the only course of action open to them seemed that of standing by in prayer and continuing agreed upon contributions of missionary personnel and material resources for assignment and utilization by the central administration. When, after the specially called General Assembly of Kikwit in May 1987, it became abundantly clear that the incumbent administration had in fact lost the respect and support of a large majority of the church members, the AIMM Board suspended all further contributions to the CMZa's administrative budget - - an action which drew sharp protest from President Mbonza in his last months in office. Following this suspension special AIMM contributions were channeled to Zaire to help cover some of the cost of the Kikwit Assembly and, later, the one in Kinshasa under ECZ sponsorship. Help was also given to the new team of officers during their prolonged efforts to occupy the church headquarters. With the return of some stability to the Church, the Board early expressed the desire to schedule a major consultation with the new Zaire leadership team.

There was, yet, a further concern. Direct contributions to the CEM, the Church pioneered by Pastor Kazadi, had also been suspended because of a power struggle which had erupted within this group in which the aging pastor had been unseated as president. There was growing uneasiness on the part of AIMM with this rupture in relationships. Thus, when in late 1989 a four-person delegation was named (11) to travel in Africa, their Zaire agenda carried two major concerns: to review an ongoing partnership with CMZa and to review ties with the CEM.

As for the CMZa, for some years the concern of AIMM Board and staff members during visits had been to try to negotiate and counsel with a church leadership that was increasingly discredited and repudiated by its own church. Now that change had taken place, a new focus of concern was AIMM's ongoing partnership with the Church itself - - and there were concerns. For one thing, there was the fusion plan that had been agreed upon with the CMZa some eighteen years earlier. While in 1971 there were powerfully compelling reasons for the adoption of this plan, there had been sufficient time to test this relationship and to highlight some of its disadvantages for the AIMM. Particularly was this the case during the years of a CMZa administration that had become increasingly possessive and bellicose regarding its missionary personnel.

Especially troubling for the AIMM was the restriction the fusion plan placed on any and all AIMM initiative within Zaire independent of the CMZa. Over time it had also been noted that under CMZa administration, missionaries' primary gifts and training were not always taken into consideration in their assignments. There was, furthermore, the chronic, thorny and persistent problem of the CMZa's dependence upon AIMM subsidy to carry its operating budget. While church life at the level of its, by then, nearly forty districts was being carried on almost totally at the initiative and with the resources generated by local church members, the CMZa was heavily dependent upon the AIMM for funding the costs of its central administration as well as some of its departments and institutions. The issue of the Church's financial responsibility for its own activities and officers had come up repeatedly across the years in correspondence and face to face dialogue. The response was always the same - - "Yes, we accept that this should be our own responsibility and a goal we should work toward." But always there would be the reminder that a great majority of its members lived in deepening poverty amidst the crumbling Zaire economy, an observation that was tragically true. And, furthermore, there was the stark reality that most of the costly institutions and programs the Church had inherited from the Mission had not been self-sustaining under the mission administration either. The problems were real; the realities were harsh.

Already in 1988, however, the AIMM Board had debated its stance and future vis-à-vis the Zaire Church and had drawn up a tentative position paper which had foreseen a partial restructuring of the fusion plan which would make place for an intermediate "missionary advisory body" in Zaire comprised of two missionaries and "an AIMM country representative." Implicit in this document was an effort to reestablish some degree, however low in profile, of AIMM identity and freedom of action within Zaire.

The tension experienced by all mission organizations with long term presence in underdeveloped and poverty stricken areas of the world was clearly reflected in this document. Under a section dealing with strategy, it was proposed that AIMM test with the Zaire Churches the missiological premise "that it is possible for the church to exist and minister in any social, political and economic context utilizing existing resources without outside assistance." But in the same document it is also clearly stated that "Biblical values including interdependence, mutuality, partnership, collaboration, cooperation and reciprocity will characterize AIMM's relationship with Zaire Mennonite Churches in whatever structure is agreed upon." (12)

The much anticipated roundtable discussion took place at Nganda (pr. NGAH-ndah), a Catholic Conference Center in Kinshasa. CMZa was represented by its executive committee. There was an immediate spirit of warmth and cordiality established. For the AIMM representatives it was particularly gratifying to meet once again with church leaders in an atmosphere of openness and mutual respect. Early in the proceedings, however, it became apparent that the CMZa representatives intended to make the AIMM/CMZa fusion agreement, as amended in 1984, the basic framework of discussion and planning. The church leaders were very clear on a number of issues. As far as missionaries were concerned, they were welcomed into full membership in the Zaire Church without formality. As a matter of fact, CMZa wanted more, not fewer missionaries. That said ,they presented a ten-year plan which outlined the sort of missionary personnel desired and the placements envisioned for them. There was even the unrealistic dream of once again having AIMM personnel establish residence on all of the historic bush stations. (13)

With evangelism renamed a core concern of the Church, CMZa leaders explained that in their view "the Good News of Jesus" in the African context needed to touch all aspects of human life, not only the spiritual. There was also a strong appeal for the reactivation of fraternal visits between the African and North American Churches.

When the AIMM delegation posed the idea of establishing a position of an AIMM country representative, caution was immediately evident. In his report to the Board Executive Secretary Roth later wrote: "There was fear that an organized parallel administration would be preoccupied with new mission concerns [which] might emerge. There was also discomfort in the fact that AIMM might broaden its base to build relationships with other groups, perhaps even African Independent Churches in Zaire." When the delegation informed the CMZa leaders that for the following year AIMM would limit its contribution to CMZa's declared budget needs, one reaction was: "You have loved us, but you must love us still." The fusion agreement, as amended in 1984, was again reviewed article by article. Roth observed: "There were no major changes in the content but some words were changed to express a cooperative attitude and to eliminate negativism." (14)

While the time of dialogue had been a heartening and rewarding experience in many ways for all, the fact remained that most of the missiological issues with which the AIMM Board had struggled prior to the consultation were still largely on the table. If there was to be a basic recasting of AIMM's profile and role in Zaire, or if there was to be any new light shed upon CMZa's struggle to maintain its enormous spread of programs and institutions, it would have to happen at another time.

CEM revisited

Of all the African church leaders who had visited North America, there probably was none who made a more distinct impact or was more widely remembered than the first one - - Pastor Kazadi. Tall, spare in build, keenly observant and a man who chose his words carefully, his trip in late 1957 had been a memorable learning experience for him as the president of his Church and for the American constituency of the AIMM.

Caught up in the havoc of the post-independence struggle of the early 1960's, he had fled with thousands of other Baluba refugees to their tribal homeland in the South Kasai where he soon rallied fellow Mennonites around him. Over time, his leadership culminated in the founding of what was first known by the French acronym AEMSK, i.e., the Evangelical Association of Mennonites of the South Kasai. Official recognition was granted by the Zaire government in 1966. By that time the Baluba refugee community had been caught up in the grip of a major political cleavage between its two major clan groups. Unfortunately this eventually impacted the Mennonites as well with the result that the AEMSK was primarily composed of one clan group while a second group, clustered around the center of Kabeya Kamuanga, maintained its ties with CMZa Tshikapa. In 1971, in keeping with the evolving structure of the ECZ, the name AEMSK was changed to the CEM, i.e., the Evangelical Mennonite Community.

With the hunger and horror of the refugee experience behind them, they turned with a will to the building of their newly established Church. Under Pastor Kazadi's leadership, pockets of Mennonite refugees were quickly formed into worshiping communities. Through persistent effort, government subsidies were finally granted for the support of their own primary schools. At the same time they had education of another kind on their minds. Worshiping congregations were taking form much faster than they could provide trained pastors. Isolated from the CMZa, their mother church and its training schools, they determined to create their own Bible Institute. Choosing the village of Lukelenge (pr. loo-keh-LEH-ngay) some ten miles outside the city of Mbuji Mayi, they erected temporary buildings and enrolled an entering class, this in the fall of 1966. The man chosen to serve as director was Nkumbi Mudiayi (pr. NKUH-mbi moo-DYAH-yi), a member of the CEM Executive Committee. (15) Though he had not had formal pastoral training, he was an alert, articulate man with teaching experience who had pursued some personal Biblical studies via correspondence.

Another key figure in this newly founded Church was Ntumba Kalala (pr. NTUH-mbah ka-LAH-lah), a young man handpicked by Pastor Kazadi to serve as the Legal Representative and Educational Secretary of the Church. An aggressive and resourceful person, he gave energetic leadership to CEM's efforts to expand its school system. For the first decade of their history, these two young men were valuable colleagues for Pastor Kazadi. In due time the first graduates emerged from the Bible Institute most of whom were quickly ordained and appointed to CEM congregations.

But there was trouble brewing. Pastor Kazadi began hearing reports of some strange teaching in some of the Institute Director's own classes, teachings that apparently viewed the Old Testament patterns of polygamy with a sympathetic eye. When efforts to counsel and correct his teachings failed, the CEM General Council acted in 1976 not only to remove Mr. Nkumbi as the Institute Director but to excommunicate him from the Church as well. In the same council sessions a new director was named (16) and the school was moved to Bipemba (pr. bi-PEH-mbah), a location within the city of Mbuji Mayi.

Former Director Nkumbi did not look kindly on this disciplinary action of his Church. Not daring to challenge the venerated Pastor Kazadi directly, he rather launched an attack upon the Church's legal representative, Ntumba Kalala, accusing him of lack of competence and misuse of the Church's educational funds. Thus was born a bitterly divisive struggle within the Church. When President Kazadi stood with Ntumba, his legal representative in the emerging conflict, the former Bible Institute Director took his case into the local court. There followed three years of bitter charges and counter charges.

It was eventually the local court which stepped in to seek a solution for the Church. With many fellow Baluba in the judicial system, it was to their credit that they viewed the drawn-out conflict with growing concern. Local government officials finally convened an assembly of CEM delegates and, in the interest of peace, urged them to hold an election of officers. In this meeting Ntumba Kalala was set aside and a Kazadi grandson, Mundeke Kalawu (pr. muh-NDEH-keh ka-LAH-woo), replaced him as legal representative.

It was with a sense of great relief that both Pastor Kazadi and the AIMM concentrated again upon the CEM's ongoing efforts of church extension. As contacts of various kinds were made between the aging church leader and the AIMM, a basic set of requests were often repeated: 1) missionary personnel to help in leadership training, 2) the upgrading of their Bible Institute, their girls' school and a church sponsored dispensary and 3) contributions to their annual operating budget. Though AIMM early expressed a live interest in placing missionary personnel at Mbuji Mayi, such was the complicated history that it was felt unwise to place inexperienced, first term people there. Efforts to assign older missionaries who could bring firsthand knowledge and a command of language to the still tense setting were unsuccessful. In the meantime, however, AIMM continued to make a modest annual contribution to CEM via the CMZa General Treasurer at Tshikapa and provided several scholarships for study at ISTK in Kinshasa and at the CMZa Bible Institute at Kalonda. AIMM and MCC also collaborated in bringing the new CEM Legal Representative, Mundeke Kalawu, to North America in January 1983 for a fraternal visit and a period of formal English instruction.

But in spite of an outward appearance of calm, not all was well. Mr. Nkumbi, the ousted former Bible teacher, was quietly at work behind the scenes. Rallying a group of his former students around him, he succeeded in gathering a bloc of support among CEM members. Though always careful to honor Pastor Kazadi as their "Moses" who had led them through their own wilderness wanderings and who had the courage and resolve to unite them into a new Church, Nkumbi also pointed out his age and suggested that in the early 1980's the Church really needed new and better educated leadership.

In a manner that is not clear, he eventually was able to prepare documentation in the name of a majority of CEM members which declared the election of a new slate of CEM officers among whom Nkumbi was designated as the legal representative. (17) It was clear that he had laid the groundwork well. As the new slate of officers was submitted to the Justice Department in Kinshasa for approbation, the ECZ promptly lent its approval and support. In spite of Pastor Kazadi's protests, there followed a swift series of successes for the newly declared CEM leadership: the new officers were announced in the November 5, 1982 issue of the ECZ news bulletin. On May 21, 1983, Archbishop Bokeleale signed a document recognizing Nkumbi as the legal administrator of CEM's schools. The government officially approved the new officers by publishing an ordinance in its gazette of November 15, 1983. (18)

In an attempt to counter what had happened, Pastor Kazadi moved to Kinshasa and filed a suit in the Supreme Court contesting the legality of the newly recognized set of officers. It was at that point - - December 1984 - - that a traveling AIMM delegation met with him. (19) After probing his memory regarding some of the events of AIMM's early years in his country, conversation turned to the events which had brought him to Kinshasa. In his quiet, reflective manner he said: "We are in prayer. We wonder and we pray: 'God, what are you asking us to do? Are you asking us to follow affairs with the government courts or did you send us here to preach the Word of God?'. . . Maybe after this whole matter is finished, then God is going to give us good days to spread the Good News of Jesus Christ. We pray that God will give us peace. The Mennonites are people who talk a lot about peace and we are in accord with this. We have now gotten into affairs such as this which certainly don't show very much peace. We ask God to help us in this matter very, very much."

At one point, a member of the delegation raised a question about trying to resolve church matters in the courts. Kazadi responded: "Our affair needs now to be straightened out with the government so we know who is in charge of the Church. No village can have two chiefs. Later, relationships between people are going to be mended. . . . This is not the Lord's work we are engaged in now; this affair has been taken into the courts and that is where it will be finished. . . . I want to get this all behind us so we can get on with the work of the Lord." Glancing at his wife Elizabeth seated nearby, whom he had married in 1924, he added: "We feel very lonely sometimes here in Kinshasa." (20)

Once again the AIMM Board was in a quandary. They had known and admired Pastor Kazadi for many years. While AIMM was perfectly willing to respect a decision by the majority of CEM members to make a change in its leadership, there was Pastor Kazadi's troubling, adamant insistence that irregular means had been used to unseat him. Thus it was that the AIMM Board decided to suspend financial contributions to the CEM until there was greater clarity as to what had actually happened.

Legal Representative Nkumbi, however, saw no justification for this. He insisted that all had been done legally and in order. He further underscored, correctly, that he and his new team of leaders had been fully recognized both by the Zaire government and the national staff of the ECZ. He too honored Pastor Kazadi as the pioneering founder of their Church and as his own spiritual father, but it was a new day. Enormous work remained to be done and they were eager to get on with it. For what reason would AIMM withdraw support at this point?

It was in the midst of this tension in the fall of 1984 that Executive Secretary Jim Bertsche received a packet of photocopied documentation from Rev. Nkumbi underscoring the legality of the new CEM leadership team which he headed. In attempting to summarize the AIMM stance, Bertsche wrote in part: "1) The AIMM maintains a continuing live interest with regard to the life, activities and well-being of CEM; 2) the AIMM regrets the misunderstandings and quarrels which have exploded within CEM in recent years, something which does not mesh easily with the teachings left us by our Lord; 3) the AIMM continues to hope to be able to renew relations of friendship and brotherhood with the CEM which will exclude no one who is a member of this community; 4) for the AIMM at this hour, the greatest concern . . . is to encourage an effort of reconciliation which can result in the possibility of collaboration with all of our brothers and sisters in Christ who desire to affiliate with this Community." (21)

The following year a letter was received from the Nkumbi administration submitting a cluster of requests for AIMM scholarships for three different training institutions in Kinshasa. Once again the executive secretary responded with reserve and concluded his letter by stating: " . . . until there is assurance of being able to negotiate with a group which represents the entire CEM, we regret that we must still await the moment when God grants us our prayer for reconciliation between the brothers and sisters of the CEM. May that be possible very soon." (22)

The response to this letter was one of anger and invective addressed both at the AIMM Secretary and the AIMM Board. (23) It was on this painful note that Bertsche approached his retirement as AIMM Secretary. Not wanting to leave this last exchange of letters as the final trace of correspondence between them, Bertsche wrote yet once more: "I do not want to close my days here in the office without at least acknowledging the reception of the letter in question. It is evident that it was written at a moment of anger and agitation of spirit. While such letters hardly promote relations between Christian pilgrims, I believe that I understand you all the same. I understand that the reservations of the AIMM manifested following the request for a series of scholarships disappointed and frustrated you. To be the spokesman for an organization is not always easy. . . . But what is most important is the future. . . . It is impossible to change history. The CEM, as the CMZa, is an outgrowth of the same CIM/AIMM root. One, like the other, is deeply Mennonite. The AIMM will never turn its back on either one. It is my prayer that the misunderstanding which, for the moment, complicates our relations will soon be resolved so that we may together address ourselves to the work of the Lord in Zaire which remains enormous to this day." (24)

allowing bygones to be bygones

With passing time it gradually became clear that Pastor Kazadi's hopes for vindication in the courts were not to be realized. True, there was a small core of supporters who still remained loyal to him, particularly the older grey-headed pastors who had lived through the traumatic refugee experience with him. They welcomed and responded with appreciation to any efforts made by AIMM personnel to maintain contact with them and always insisted that, with time, the High Court would rule in their favor. But the years were beginning to take their toll. Though his memory remained keen, Kazadi's vision was dimming and he needed help to raise his tall, spare frame from a chair. Meanwhile Rev. Nkumbi and his administration were broadly recognized as the *de facto* leadership of the CEM. MCC personnel in Zaire had along the way begun to work with him. In Mennonite World Conference material he and his fellow officers were listed as the heads of their Church. When in late 1989 the AIMM Board sent a delegation to Zaire, they not only went to meet and dialogue with the new CMZa leadership which had at last been installed in the CMZa center in Tshikapa, but also let it be known that they were prepared to meet with the officers of the CEM who were long contested by Pastor Kazadi.

Already in 1988 the AIMM Board had made a gesture toward the Nkumbi administration by offering four $500 scholarships thus enabling four CEM men to be enrolled in the "International Center for Evangelism" in Kinshasa. (25) In May of that same year, MWC Secretary Paul Kraybill traveled in Zaire and recognized the Nkumbi administration of CEM. All of these gestures were observed by Pastor Kazadi and drew letters of carefully worded protest. But it was clear that the sequence of events set in motion years earlier had by now reached a point of no return.

The 1989 AIMM representatives met with a five-man CEM delegation headed by General Secretary and Legal Representative Nkumbi Mudiayi in a conference room at CEDI in Kinshasa. It was a historic meeting in a double sense, first because it was the first official contact with the leadership contested by Pastor Kazadi and also the first unilateral AIMM/CEM contact independent of CMZa. AIMM Secretary Roth described the meeting in the following terms: "The consultation began with expressions of goodwill, hope, challenges and scriptural edification. CEM called itself 'the eternal first fruits of AIMM, converts who were abandoned in their mission of preaching.' They looked at this meeting as 'the return of the forgotten converts.' Contact with AIMM has been reestablished and will continue. The past is to be forgotten. AIMM expressed regrets for the hurts CEM has felt . . . . They were assured that their Church has been in our prayers; to dwell in the past would only weaken our relationships." (26) Another AIMM delegation member observed that " . . . relationships were cordial. The [CEM] officers were moved to the point of tears at the aid granted (27) and the establishment of an official relationship." (28)

A one page "Memo of Understanding" was drawn up between AIMM and CEM in which it was basically stated that "AIMM and CEM mutually recognize each other as autonomous associations working under the direction of the Holy Spirit as partners." The primary concern in this partnership was the proclamation of the Gospel, the edification of believers, Christian education, leadership training and material development. In making requests of AIMM for future help, such requests are to be accompanied by an indication of local participation of its own members. (29)

Later in their visit, the AIMM delegation made its way to Mbuji Mayi in the South Kasai where they were received by CEM people in a wildly enthusiastic manner. AIMM Secretary Roth commented that the delegation plus CEM pastors Nkumbi and Mukengeshai were honored at a celebration organized at an urban church which he characterized as "a true Baluba cultural expression of joy." Roth further observed that "it was encouraging to observe the ministry of the CEM which is carried on independently of AIMM and to learn about their vision for future ministry." (30)

And vision there was. CEM leadership was projecting the planting of a congregation in each of the twenty sections of the city within five years. In this connection a plea was made for AIMM missionaries to help them in this effort not only within the city but beyond. Already a year earlier AIMM had placed Gordon and Jarna Rautakoski Claassen in Mbuji Mayi in response to oft repeated requests from the CMZa people of the area. When the AIMM delegation made it clear that they would be happy to make the Claassens available to CEM as well for church-related ministries, the offer was readily accepted. In the course of 1990 they began moving freely among both CMZa and CEM congregations of the area while experiencing a warm welcome everywhere. What had been unthinkable amidst the bitter tension between the two churches some twenty years earlier was now, at last, possible.

CONIM: a Zairian inter-Mennonite vision

It was amidst the murky atmosphere which surrounded the CMZa General Assembly at Nyanga in 1985 that Rev. Mukanza Ilunga was replaced as the vice president of the Church. In less than a month thereafter he had turned over his keys and files and had quietly moved his family back to his home province of Bandundu. By this time his credentials were impressive. He was fluent in three Zairian languages plus English and French. He held diplomas in theology and Christian education. Named to the International Peace Committee of the

MWC already in 1981, he traveled outside Zaire on a number of occasions and broadened his contact with and understanding of the international Mennonite family.

His departure from Tshikapa came at a time which found administrative personnel of the Missionary Aviation Fellowship (MAF) in Kinshasa searching for a Zairian to fill a key public relations role for them. With a number of planes and pilots based across the country, a major maintenance and supply center in the capital and a rapidly expanding program, they had great need of a knowledgeable Zairian to serve as a liaison person with government. Hearing of Mukanza, contact was made and soon thereafter he was in their employ. He immediately demonstrated his value for MAF. For many long months they had been seeking authorization from the government to do commercial flying, as there was space aboard their aircraft, between points not linked by other Zairian air services. Such additional financial resource was sought as a means of maintaining air service for mission/church personnel at the lowest levels possible. The best efforts of expatriate MAF personnel to secure such authorization had proven to be futile. In less than six months after Mukanza joined the organization, the long-sought authorization was secured to the great benefit of the mission/church community across the country.

Based in Kinshasa, Mukanza soon came to the attention of another international para-church organization known as RURCON, i.e., Rural Development Counseling for Christian Churches in Africa. Instigated by Peter Batchelor, a widely-known British Christian agriculturalist, its African base was in Jos, Nigeria. Its philosophy was that of emphasizing small self-help, rural based projects utilizing whatever resources were available locally while teaching why Christians should be involved in helping to raise their own living standards as well as those of people around them. RURCON had established branch offices in a number of African countries and wanted to do the same in Zaire. It was not long that Mukanza was named director of RURCON's francophone office in Zaire. With this new dimension of service opened to him, an agreement was reached to devote 70% of his time to MAF and 30% to RURCON.

There was another horizon beckoning this Zairian Christian leader and it had to do with his dream of bringing into being some form of inter-Mennonite structure within his own country. While studying at AMBS from 1975 to 1977, he had gained insight into the broad-based partnership in Christian mission portrayed by AIMM. He had been an active participant in the early inter-Mennonite consultations held in Kinshasa in 1981 and 1983. In frequent contact with MWC and MCC personnel, there were many conversations which confirmed his conviction that some sort of inter-Mennonite body within Zaire could serve a variety of mutually beneficial purposes. All of these contributing strands finally came together on December 11, 1987, in the creation of what came to be known by its French acronym CONIM, i.e., *Comité National inter-Mennonite* (National Inter-Mennonite Committee). Official membership was comprised of the three Mennonite Churches of Zaire (31) plus MCC/Zaire.

Two early brochures spelled out the focus of the new organization in some detail. Objectives cited were the promotion of the Anabaptist Mennonite vision of peace, love, justice and work both in the church and in society; the strengthening of unity and mutual aid among the member communities; and the promotion of socio-economic activities of the member communities. Under the heading "Program of Activities" were listed: research, documentation and promotion of the vision of a church which is both Mennonite and African; the education, training and the sharing of information regarding the Anabaptist/Mennonite vision of the church and society; and help for member communities in matters of mutual aid and development. An office was established in Kinshasa with four staff people. Rev. Mukanza was named executive secretary. (32)

There was early enthusiasm both within and outside Zaire. There was something new under the inter-Mennonite sun. Having a framework within which to discuss common problems and to think together about a broad Mennonite presence and witness in their country was an appreciated privilege.

As for the international Mennonite community, CONIM was seen as an excellent vehicle for the promotion of Anabaptist concerns. Traveling in Zaire in 1988, MWC Secretary Paul Kraybill expressed his pleasure and support regarding the new venture. MCC personnel in Zaire were enthusiastic and committed financial support. A number of significant events were organized under CONIM auspices including country-wide peace seminars, the distribution of MCC relief supplies following Kinshasa riots in the early 1990's and the organization of a pan-African Mennonite Women's Conference in Kinshasa. Very clearly there also was fostered a heightened awareness of each other among the three Zaire Mennonite Churches which, by this time, counted a composite membership approaching 100,000 people.

Over time, however, two problems emerged, one structural and the other financial. In his leadership, Rev. Mukanza sought to establish CONIM as the primary channel of international contact for Zaire Mennonites as well as the conduit for reception and distribution of outside help that might be forwarded to them. Leaders of the three Churches soon viewed this as an infringement upon their autonomy and freedom to seek their own international contacts. There was the further issue of meeting CONIM's budget needs. Early contributions were sought and provided from each member church which, in turn, were generously supplemented first by RURCON and then by MCC/Zaire. AIMM and BOMAS were early approached by their respective Zaire Churches to make contributions as well. Wishing to foster the three Churches' sense of ownership in and commitment to their own organization, a matching plan was adopted to supplement their own financial contributions.

In an effort to exert more control over CONIM, the three Churches restructured the organization instituting three department heads who functioned as a decision-making executive committee while retaining Mukanza as their executive secretary. As for funding the CONIM budget, by early 1993 church and, consequently, mission board contributions had dropped to token levels leaving MCC/Zaire nearly total financial responsibility for the organization.

At its birth, CONIM had been welcomed enthusiastically by Zairians and expatriates alike as a needed and visionary development. But like so many other laudable overseas projects initially kept afloat by foreign funds, CONIM in 1993 faced an uncertain future. Eventually it would be the three Zaire Churches which would decide if and in what form the organization was to remain a part of their Mennonite experience.

CHAPTER 44   **AMIDST THE RUINS**

As the decade of the 1980's was drawing to a close, the long-suffering people of Zaire were finding it steadily more difficult just to survive. Long gone were the days of euphoria of the late 1960's when the celebrated N'Sele Manifesto, with its soaring idealism and rhetoric, had been established as a national set of guidelines by which a prosperous and happy new Zaire was to become a reality. Instead, particularly for the masses which had migrated to the urban centers, life had become a grim daily struggle just to keep body and soul together. What had gone wrong?

greed trickled down

It had been popular in the first couple of decades following the 1960 declaration of independence to explain any and all difficulties as the nasty legacy of the former Belgian colonial regime. It was easy to find articles in that era, by both black and white journalists, which were quick to exonerate Zairian politicians and government figures of any responsibility for any post-independence problems which surfaced.

It is true that the economy of Zaire, like those of all underdeveloped countries of the world, had been rocked by sharp increases in the costs of petroleum products and the fluctuating prices paid for its raw materials on the international commodity markets. It is true that Western bank consortiums had rushed in after Zaire's independence encouraging unwise loans which eventually contributed heavily to Zaire's growing debt. Caught in the grip of economic forces over which it had little control, it is true that Zaire experienced the brutal impact of steadily devaluating currency on the one hand and steadily spiraling inflation and unemployment on the other.

But there was more. By the late 1980's it was evident to all that something had gone drastically, criminally wrong at the very top of Zaire's political structure and that its deadly effect had seeped down through the whole Zairian socio-political body like a poisonous waste polluting everything in its path. As the decade drew to a close, no longer did an international press attempt to put a good face on a bad scene but rather sought to lay bare the tragic irresponsibility in high places which had triggered the steady disintegration of a promising land. There are many examples.

Two journalists of Africa News wrote in February, 1988: "President Mobutu Sese Seko is perhaps the only head of state who could pay off his country's crippling foreign debt - - $5 billion - - from his own pocket. Everyone here [in Zaire] generally agrees that Mobutu and other national leaders have enriched themselves at public expense for the past quarter century. . . . Social scientists have coined a word to describe a political economy like Zaire's: 'kleptocracy' - - government by thieves! Their example is followed, by inclination or necessity, at every level of social interaction. . . . Paid as little as [the equivalent of $3.75] a month by the government, civil servants routinely support themselves by stealing. . . . Nurses demand bribes to tend the sick, police set up impromptu roadblocks to shake down motorists and soldiers sell their weapons on the black market. . . . Hospital patients must bribe doctors, nurses, even supply clerks if they hope to survive." . . . One person complained that even bribes don't always work but a patient who has paid nothing to anyone "can scream until she dies and no one will lift a finger to help."

Another witness interviewed told of a funeral mass being delayed for eight hours "while the bereaved family raised money to pay off the driver of the state-owned hearse." Commented a Catholic priest: "Respect for the dead is the most African of values. When that disappears, it means the whole social order has collapsed." (1)

It is not that there were no voices of protest raised along the way. Already as early as 1976 the Catholic Archbishop of Lubumbashi wrote in a pastoral letter: "The thirst for money . . . transforms men into assassins. Many poor unemployed are condemned to misery along with their families because they are unable to pay off the person who hires. How many children and adults die without medical care because they are unable to bribe the medical personnel who are supposed to care for them? Why are there no medical supplies in the hospitals while they are found in the market place? How do they get there?"

"Why is it that in our courts justice can only be obtained by fat bribes to the judge? Why are prisoners forgotten in jail? They have no one to pay off the judge who sits on their file. Why do government offices force people to come back day after day to obtain services to which they are entitled? If the clerks are not paid off, they will not be served. Why, at the opening of school, must parents go into debt to bribe the school principal? Children who are unable to pay will have no school . . . . Whoever holds a morsel of authority or means of pressure profits from it to impose on people and exploit them, especially in rural areas. All means are good to obtain money or to humiliate the human being . . . ." (2)

a "clear conscience!"

Presiding over the steadily growing suffering of the Zairian people was Mobutu Sese Seko, a name which according to one source could be translated as meaning "Mobutu Himself Forever." (3) The same writer continues: "Under any name, he has been robbing his country blind for two decades . . . . Estimates of Mobutu's fortune run from upwards of $2 billion to more than twice that. . . . He has extracted these vast sums from a greed shattered $4.7 billion GNP economy maimed still further by mismanagement and the kind of grandiose visions that are called prophetic only when they work, which in this part seems to be never." (4)

In this climate there emerged a favored elite which had access, under Mobutu's benevolent eye, to the levers of power and the country's revenues. One observer put it this way: "A high government post here is not simply political patronage, a cushy job for backing the right man. . . . No, it's more like a license to steal. There are 47 corporations in the government portfolio and the top jobs work on a revolving door basis, allowing the occupant enough time to make his fortune until someone else can be shifted in. . . . Such a system hardly encourages honesty or hard work among the subordinates who, understandably, match the boss' grand larceny with a little larceny of their own. . . . It is the Zairian in the street who is doubly the victim here: first, because theft higher up brings him close to starvation; second, because it forces him to become a thief as well." (5)

Perhaps nothing quite highlights the growing disparity in fortunes which existed in the early 90's between the wealthy elite and the poverty stricken Zairian masses like this vignette: while multiplied thousands walked long, hot, dusty miles day by day in search of work and food in cheap, plastic sandals, Kinshasa boasted the largest Mercedes Benz agency in all of Africa! (6)

In addition to his multiple overseas holdings in costly real estate and unnumbered bank accounts, Mobutu ordered a "palace" to be built for him in his home tribal area in northwestern Zaire at a place called Gbadolite (pr. G-bah-doh-LEET) surrounded by his ethnic group, the Ngbandi (pr. Ng-BAH-ndee) people. Those having had occasion to see it speak of marble halls and furnishings air-freighted from overseas directly to the special jet strip built near by to accommodate his personal arrivals and departures and those of his family and entourage.

It was in the midst of this growing opulence surrounded by the deepening suffering of his fellow Zairians that Mobutu was interviewed by two correspondents for <u>Africa News</u>. They pressed him on a wide front of issues. With haughty aplomb he defended himself and his record at every turn. At one point, when the conversation turned to violations of basic human rights, he responded: "I can say . . . without equivocation that I have a clear conscience." (7)

a bolt out of the blue

It had been with a sense of relief that, in the fall of 1987, CMZa President Chibulenu and his fellow staff members turned to their responsibilities. The third CMZa Assembly of that single year had resulted in his official recognition by the ECZ and the Zaire government. It was therefore with shocked disbelief that Tshikapa staff learned in August of 1990 that the same Justice Department which had recognized Chibulenu as CMZa

President had now annulled its own previous action and had issued a new ruling reinstating President Mbonza as the CMZa President!

It was a telling measure of the instability of the government services of the time that such a reversal was possible. According to information widely circulated in CMZa circles, Mbonza had profited from the influence of a fellow clansman who had risen through the ranks of Zairian political influence finally securing an appointment to the staff of UNESCO in Paris, France. In Zaire on a family vacation in the summer of 1990, it was alleged that he used his influence with the Minister of Justice herself, a Madam Muyabu (pr. moo-YAH-boo), to secure the reversal. The ECZ-sponsored assembly decisions in September 1987 were declared "invalid." Until Mbonza could once again be installed in the CMZa headquarters at Tshikapa, Madam Muyabu ordered the CMZa center there closed!

With his freshly issued document in hand, Mbonza made his first trip back to Tshikapa in over two years. Presenting himself to the local government authorities, he asked that they oversee his reinstallation in the CMZa headquarters. To his irritation he discovered that now the authorities were no more eager to help him than they had been two years earlier to help President Chibulenu and his colleagues. When, after several months, it became apparent that the local officials were not going to cooperate, he returned to Kinshasa to once again press his case with the Justice Department. Finally the Minister of Justice issued written orders to the provincial Attorney General to see that the change was made. This time Mbonza was accompanied by the Minister's personal emissary, the Justice Department's own Director of Church Affairs.

There followed a sad reenactment of a scene of confrontation which had first been played out at the CMZa headquarters two years earlier. The officials arrived with Mbonza to discover a large crowed of CMZa members demonstrating with chants and placards declaring their opposition to Mbonza's return while asserting their support for President Chibulenu. Recognizing that the overwhelming tide of public opinion was against them, the authorities retreated and subsequently reported to the Minister in Kinshasa that to have proceeded according to her orders would have risked disturbing the peace of the region, this much to Mbonza's obvious chagrin. (8)

an AIMM delegation sees the Minister

It was at this juncture that AIMM Executive Secretary Earl Roth and board member Erwin Rempel's African travel brought them to Kinshasa. All discussion with missionaries and CMZa personnel was heavily overshadowed by the rekindled controversy over CMZa leadership. At the urging of both missionaries and CMZa Vice President Kabasele Bantubiabo, a meeting was sought with the Minister of Justice. (9) One major reason for prompt action was the possibility of a change in Ministers at any time. There had been four of them in the space of three years in the that department.

A meeting was granted. On the appointed day AIMM missionaries Arnold Harder and Rick Derksen and AIMM Board representatives Erwin Rempel and Earl Roth presented themselves at the Ministry of Justice. For an hour the Minister shared her views regarding the long, enduring controversy over CMZa leadership. She made several points. She was weary of the problem and much wanted to find a solution; she did not view the ECZ with favor, feeling that she'd been insulted by this organization; and she had no problem with the CMZa as such. She then spelled out what she considered to be essentially two options she had before her vis-à-vis the problem: 1) that CMZa still recognize Mbonza as its president and that he, in turn, call a general assembly where another election would be held, or 2) that CMZa decide to annul both the Mbonza and Tshibulenu administrations and call yet another general assembly to elect its officers. She then added that if neither option pleased CMZa, she did have a third - - to simply dissolve and put an end to the CMZa!

Assembly IV

Confronted with these options, CMZa leaders quickly responded. If there was no alternative other than to convene yet another CMZa Assembly, they were ready to do so. This time it was to be held in the presence of personnel from the Justice Department. Once again roles of district delegates were established. Once again word was sent out across the countryside. Once again AIMM provided partial funding to help meet the heavy costs of bringing people to Kinshasa from near and far.

The morning of March 18, 1991, found a total of 63 CMZa delegates present at Nganda, the Catholic Conference Center in Kinshasa in which they had already met once before under the auspices of the ECZ for the same reason. They represented the thirty-three CMZa districts which had comprised the official roster six years earlier in 1985. Present also were two representatives of the ECZ and two from the Department of Justice, both of whom had been earlier present at Tshikapa and witnessed Mbonza's failed effort to reoccupy the CMZa offices.

An opening meditation was brought by ECZ representative Dr. Diafwila dia Mbuangi on the adopted Biblical text of the day which carried the rather pointed injunction from Romans 13:14: "Do not think about how to gratify the desires of the sinful nature." Rev. Mukanza Ilunga was elected moderator (10) and a four-point agenda was adopted: amendment of bylaws, election of officers, updating and validation of a new list of district level officers, and the choice of date for the next general assembly.

Obviously the agenda item which commanded the total attention of all was the election of officers. This time, to be sure that there could be no doubt as to the will of the assembled delegates, two slates of candidates were presented - - the incumbent team of Chibulenu Sakayimbo, Kabasele Bantubiabo and Kabeya Kanda plus the former team composed of Mbonza Kikunga, Kibula Kituku and Tshimowa Bisosa. President Chibulenu and his colleagues were reelected by a overwhelming majorities. (11)

A twelve-person committee was chosen to study and rework the CMZa bylaws. Once again action was taken to excommunicate former President Mbonza. District leaders everywhere were asked to be alert so that former members of the Mbonza administration not engage in any activities which could further disturb the peace within the CMZa and to seek to reintegrate them into the life of the Church in their home districts.

Grass-roots representatives of the CMZa had spoken yet once more, this time in the presence of officials of both the ECZ and the central government. But for the issue to be fully settled, the Minister of Justice needed yet to issue an official document legalizing assembly actions. Until that happened, CMZa was still in limbo. Days slipped by with no word from the government. Apprehension grew in CMZa circles in Kinshasa. Had their sense of relief been premature? Was the Minister still delaying the final legal step? Was she once again experiencing pressures to sidetrack the legalization process? What if, in her delay, she was suddenly replaced? With whom, then, would they have to deal?

Increasingly concerned, another CMZa delegation was organized to seek still another audience with her. But what was left to say that had not already been said? What influence could they bring to bear which had not already been summoned in previous encounters? CMZa leaders took counsel and decided to use a pastoral approach to someone who would be viewed first of all not as an adversarial government official but rather as a fellow Zairian who had her own spiritual needs.

The audience was set for 10:30 on April 11, 1991. They were finally summoned into her chambers at 1:00 PM. (12) They first requested permission to open their audience with her with prayer. They then presented her with a French Bible and a one volume commentary which she willingly received. President Chibulenu than updated her briefly on recent events in some CMZa areas which revealed continuing uncertainty and unrest. He then expressed his concern that such incidents might well increase in the absence of official confirmation of the church officers which had yet once again been elected under her own direct sponsorship.

Calling in an aide, she learned that the legal forms had not yet been typed up. Offering an apology for the delay she promised that they would be issued shortly. As good as her word, the document legalizing CMZa's reelected administration was issued four days later on April 15.

On a Sunday morning two weeks later at Ngaba (pr. NGAH-bah), one of the CMZa Churches in Kinshasa, President Chibulenu was heard to say: "No man is the head of the church, only God is. Leaders come and go. What remains and is important is the church whose responsibility it is to please God and to do his will." He went on to add that CMZa "can remain strong if all tribes find their place within the Church and make their contribution to the church as a service done unto the Lord."

a ticking time bomb

In spite of his bravado in interviews with foreign journalists, Mobutu's personal life style belied his claims of a "clear conscience." Known in his earlier years for his frequent trips into the Zairian interior to greet and talk with officials and common village folk alike, by the early 90's such trips were only a distant memory. Even within the city of Kinshasa where he had formerly opted to travel the streets in noisy motorcades, he now travelled overhead by helicopter. Where before he lodged in a presidential residence overlooking the Zaire River surrounded by a zoological garden and fenced in wild animals, more and more his location - - particularly at night - - became a secret. With passing time it became known that he often retired to his presidential yacht anchored in the river upstream of Kinshasa, a helicopter poised on the deck. It seemed unlikely that its location near the international airport of Njili was simply coincidental. Among the ragged unemployed of the capital city, the sardonic phrase "our aquatic president" was more and more heard in street corner conversations. (13) The time finally came when for reasons of security he withdrew more and more to his presidential palace at Gbadolite, his home area, surrounded not only by his tribal group but also by elements of the SPD - - his Israeli-trained Special Presidential Division of commandos who also were made up principally of young men from his own ethnic group.

But if he was becoming more reclusive and cautious as to his personal life, he was no less determined to maintain his grip upon his country. Controlling the elite armed force, the banks and the news media, he was just as capable as always of taking ruthless action against those who dared oppose him. For example, when his secret service informed him of political dissent being fomented among the university students in Lubumbashi in the distant southeastern reaches of the country in the spring of 1990, he ordered retaliation. On June 11 police stormed dormitory rooms and attacked students with knives and bayonets. While the government reported one person died, opposition activists insisted that more than sixty students had been massacred with many more injured. (14)

Long since alarmed by the worsening situation in Zaire and Mobutu's adamant refusal to make any political concessions, Belgium, France and the United States had cut off all but humanitarian aid which more and more was channeled via non-government organizations. The International Monetary Fund, which had been striving to move Mobutu toward some monetary and economic reforms, also suspended help. Experiencing genuine financial pressure, Mobutu first cut back on public services. Hospitals slowly ran out of supplies; government-subsidized schools slowly shut down across the entire country. Then it was the regular army which began to feel the pinch. Never well paid, they now found themselves paid only sporadically, if at all. Mobutu's dwindling government revenues were being used to pay his elite SPD units and to meet the needs and demands of those who were unquestionably loyal to him.

And yet, in the midst of growing international demands for political reform in Zaire, the United States still did not speak out with a single, clear voice. While angry demands were made in Congress and by private groups for action against Mobutu, the US State Department was still equivocating. For decades Mobutu had been favored and strongly supported because of his resolute anti-Communist stance and the ideal base of operations his country provided the US for efforts to curb Russian expansionist ventures in Africa. This being the case, the US had for years found it politically expedient to maintain an unhearing ear vis-à-vis persistent reports of chronic human rights violations in that country. As late as January 1991, the US State Department was still treading softly. As President George Bush was rallying support for Operation Desert Storm, a UN Security Council rotating system had brought the Zairian delegate to the position of Council Chairman. His "performance" in this key position at that critical point was of great concern to the US. Thus any State Department references to the worsening conditions in Zaire of that time were couched in very bland terms.

Far from the circles of international intrigue the shanty town dwellers, who surrounded Kinshasa, struggled to survive in a deadly, tightening grip of misery. It was not a pleasant scene. There was for literally hundreds of thousands the daily specter of hunger, malnutrition and disease. There was massive unemployment and a wildly inflationary economy which frequently saw goods marked up in price between opening time in the morning and closing time in the evening. The rate of inflation in February, 1991, was estimated to be 35% per month! (15) The zaire (local currency) which in the early 1970's had been issued at the exchange value of $2, was by now being quoted at about 2½ million per dollar. Commercial people had long since given up trying to count it. A standard method adopted was to tie different denominations into bundles and then place them on scales. Money was no longer counted, it was weighed! Clerks sat behind cash registers with open drawers, stacks of bundled bills behind them on the floor watched over by a guard. Back rooms were stacked to the ceilings. And stories were more and more frequent of city families assigning their children their days to eat - - some on odd days, the rest on even days. Medicine was only available in the great public markets and typically at prices beyond the reach of the average Zairian. All the while, however, the government controlled media continued to proclaim the blessings of life under Mobutu's enlightened leadership, proclamations which were more and more greeted with open scorn and sullen resentment.

then it happened

Monday morning September 23, 1991, found unpaid units of the regular army stationed in the Kinshasa area as hungry and resentful as most of the civilians around them. Among them were 3,000 paratroopers stationed near Njili, Kinshasa's international airport. They would signal their grievances, they decided, by a peaceful march of protest. Once the march was under way, the chemistry soon changed and what was to have been a disciplined demonstration quickly turned into looting.

Word instantly spread through the city. When civilians realized that they could join the soldiers without reprisal, they poured out of the deprivation of their shanty town lives by the hundreds of thousands. There followed three days and nights of raging riot. One source estimated that half of the four million inhabitants of Kinshasa were involved in the melee. Reuters News Agency reported on September 25 "that looters had stripped homes, shops and one hotel of all transportable items including carpets and light fixtures. They also ransacked the headquarters of the government party and raided several car dealerships stealing hundreds of vehicles." (16)

AIMM missionary Henry Dirks stationed at CEDI, the inter-church printing press along the Zaire river just downstream from the heart of the capital, wrote from his vantage point on September 23rd: "The situation in Kinshasa is very tense today. There is shooting all around us. Even as I am typing out this message there are shots very close by. . . . this 'peaceful' march has resulted in many, many stores being looted this morning. We can see people walking by on the street with TVs, bicycles and motorbikes, rolls of electric wire, toilet fixtures, roofing, even fridges, etc. etc. There seems to be a free-for-all down town. . . . The General Motors assembly plant has been broken into and destroyed . . . many vehicles burned. The American Embassy garage has been broken into and all their vehicles taken. The Mercedes garage on the boulevard has also been broken into and all the Mercedes have been commandeered." (17) Almost immediately vendors were to be found along street sides in many places offering looted goods for sale. It soon became common knowledge that most anything could now be found and purchased at the military camp. By week's end there were also reports of similar rampages in other Zairian centers across the country.

Response from France and Belgium was swift. Provided the use of several American transport planes, they both had troops on the ground in Kinshasa by late Tuesday afternoon where they secured places for their nationals and began bringing them across the river to Brazzaville for flights home to Europe.

wheeling and dealing

Confronted by a massive explosion of civil unrest on the one hand and an intense flurry of international diplomatic pressure on the other, Mobutu began to make some conciliatory noises. He was corrupt and ruthless but he was also pragmatic. For over 25 years as Zaire's head of state he had developed the political art of "give and take" to perfection. Knowing full well the growing frustration within his own country and feeling the increasing criticism of the outside world, already in April 1990 he had announced the end of single party rule in Zaire and invited opposition leaders to join him in dialogue. These contacts quickly became embroiled in sharply differing views and stalemate soon followed. In March of 1991, something called a National Conference was finally officially planned which was to be an open forum for political discussion and the formation of new government policy. But dates for the opening sessions were repeatedly postponed or canceled.

On September 29, six days after the eruption of rioting in Kinshasa, Mobutu announced that he was open to discussions with opposition leaders with a view to establishing a coalition government. For the first time, Mobutu appeared ready to share the power he alone had held since 1965. The first step was to be the convening of a large consultative group which would be representative of a broad sweep of Zairian society including the church communities. An eventual delegate list of 2,300 people was established including Presidents Chibulenu and Nkumbi of CMZa and CEM as well as a representative of the CEFMZ.

Early on this group came to be known as the Sovereign National Conference. Already prior to the convening of this body a major political coalition had taken shape known as the Sacred Union. Comprised of a reported 129 opposition groups, a key leader was Etienne Tshisekedi wa Mulumba (pr. tshi-seh-KEH-di wah muh-LUH-mbah). He quickly became a predominant force in the events which followed. A burly, courageous man trained in law, he was a Muluba from the South Kasai. He had at one point been a cabinet member serving under Mobutu but fell out of favor because of his outspoken manner.

Mobutu tried and failed at the outset to stack the Conference with candidates loyal to him and thus early provoked a political polarity pitting himself against the newly constituted popular Conference. After a series of postponements the first session was finally opened on December 11, 1991. Chosen to preside over the sessions of the Conference was a respected Zairian churchman, Catholic Archbishop Mosengwo Pasinya (pr. moh-SEH-ngwo pah-SI-nyah).

There followed over the ensuing two years an incredible mix of proposals/counter-proposals, initiatives/counter-initiatives and decisions/counter-decisions. Under unrelenting pressure both from within and without his country, Mobutu played a skilled game of cynical politics. Yielding when he needed to, retreating when he had to, conceding when it served his purposes, he paid lip service to the ideal of democratic reform in his country but worked doggedly behind the scenes to hamstring any real progress in that direction.

The first major outcome of the Conference sessions was to declare itself an interim government and to elect Tshisekedi as its Prime Minister who, in turn, selected his cabinet. Mobutu at first accepted this decision but within two days rejected it because of Tshisekedi's insistence that he and his Cabinet were the only legal authority in the country. Mobutu, in turn, named his own Prime Minister who, in turn, named his own cabinet. (18) There followed months of political maneuvering which played out in an infinite series of twists and turns. Tshisekedi's access to TV and radio coverage was granted and/or withheld at Mobutu's whim. Tshisekedi and his cabinet members were on occasion placed under surveillance in their homes. The Conference at times met while the building was surrounded by units of the military.

Crucial to the political struggle was control of the Central Bank and the military. Realizing this, Tshisekedi early made open appeals to the regular army for support. He also attempted to install a new team of directors in the State Bank. Mobutu blocked this move by the simple expedient of surrounding the Bank with troops loyal to him. As for Tshisekedi's appeal to the regular army, though pledges of support were forthcoming, he knew that this meant little. Not only were regular army units poorly equipped but, across the country, morale was extremely low and the chain of command had all but disappeared in the political chaos of the early 1990's.

with Bibles and rosaries

In the face of Tshisekedi's persistent efforts to assert himself as the Prime Minister of a legitimate and functioning interim government, Mobutu suspended the National Conference. Tshisekedi simply ignored Mobutu's actions and continued to speak and act as he had in the past. Angered by this Mobutu declared in April 1992 that Tshisekedi was "dismissed' and, in turn, appointed yet another man as his newest choice for that post - - Faustin Birindwa (pr. fo-STAN bi-RI-ndwah), a former Tshisekedi supporter from eastern Zaire.

The church communities across Zaire, both Catholic and Protestant, followed the evolution of the political scene with the greatest concern. They saw the National Conference as their only hope for a platform of open debate and as a de facto parliament which gave authenticity to Prime Minister Tshisekedi and his transition government.

Then word began to spread among Christians in Kinshasa. On Sunday, February 16, Catholics and Protestants would leave their churches at the close of services and meet to stage a peaceful demonstration calling for the reconvening of the stalled Conference. Numbered in the thousands, the group formed and began to march. Hearing of their intentions, a unit of the Special Presidential Division took up a position in the path of the marchers. A Spanish Catholic priest, Father Rodriguez of one of the Catholic parishes of Kinshasa, wrote of the incident as follows: " The soldiers began to shoot and we threw ourselves to the ground. The crowd got to its feet again and we began to sing and pray. It was very moving - - prayer against rifles. We then tried to move past the [military] barrier and they began to shoot again. The crowd was seized with panic and I was nearly trampled."(19)

Over forty Zairian Christians, who less than two hours before had sat in the pews of their places of worship, now lay dying in pools of blood in the street, some clutching their rosaries, others their Bibles. Over 100 were helped from the scene having sustained gunshot wounds. Mobutu's callous determination to remain in power no matter the cost had been starkly etched in blood on a Kinshasa boulevard that Sunday.

It was a measure of both the courage and the desperation of the Zairian Christian community that this loss of life did not cow it into silence. It was promptly announced that another peaceful demonstration would be held two Sundays later on March 1. Said one spokesman: "They might as well shoot us. We are dying of hunger anyway." The massacre of peaceful demonstrators that Sunday created such a furor in the international press that Mobutu rescinded his order and the National Conference was allowed to reconvene.

The Zairian year of 1992 offered a dismal political scene. A pugnacious man, Prime Minister Tshisekedi and his Cabinet kept taking aggressive action in an attempt to validate themselves as a functioning transition government while awaiting national elections. On one occasion Mobutu's party, the MPR, was accused of misappropriation of public funds and ordered to refund them to the State. It was proposed to change Zaire's name back to its original name of Congo. A commission was working on a new draft of a constitution. Meanwhile Mobutu was backing his own "government" and sought by all means possible to harass Tshisekedi's regime which by this time was recognized and affirmed by many countries of the international community. All the while there were reports of sporadic looting by military units scattered across the country over which neither Mobutu nor Tshisekedi could exert any control. The only schools still open and the only medical services still available were those sponsored by churches or by individuals as private enterprises.

a five million zaire bill

As early as April of 1982, it had been rumored that Zaire's banks would have to be closed because of a lack of cash. Mobutu's response to this was simply to order the printing of more money. But with the wildly skyrocketing inflation and devaluating Zaire currency, the printed bills needed always to be of a higher denomination.

In December 1992 Mobutu announced the issuance of a new bill. It was declared to be worth five million zaires! At the rate of exchange of the time it could be traded for less than two American dollars. Tshisekedi condemned this move as simply further fueling an already out of control inflation. He publicly declared the new bill as illegal tender in the country and called on the commercial community and the public in general to reject it.

In January 1993 military personnel received their pay in the form of the new bills. Going into the markets and stores, the bills were refused. Angered, the soldiers once again erupted in violence. Here and there shop keepers and vendors in the markets were shot on the spot. The tense situation once again degenerated into general looting accompanied by the steady sound of gunfire in the sprawling business and government center of Kinshasa. The toll of death began to mount.

Once again, in a matter of hours, French para-commandos arrived in this dismal city to protect their citizens and to oversee evacuations across the river to nearby Brazzaville. Infuriated by this newest outburst of violence on the part of regular army units, Mobutu gave orders to his elite troops to take reprisal. Over the next several days there were pitched battles between the two forces which culminated in the SPD surrounding a military barracks. Outgunned and out-manned, the barracks became a scene of carnage as soldiers and their families were indiscriminately cut down by automatic weapon fire. There were some long, tragic hours during which resumed pedestrian and vehicle traffic along Kinshasa's thoroughfares wound past abandoned khaki clad bodies in rain drenched gutters.

In early 1993, Zaire was a bleeding country with two Prime Ministers, two sets of cabinet officers and two supposed governments locked in struggle. More and more it was becoming evident that in the confrontation, Mobutu held two key cards in his hand: control of the Central Bank and control of the only functioning, disciplined military units in the country. To this confrontation Tshisekedi and the National Conference could only bring the weapons of moral suasion and the knowledge that they spoke for an overwhelming majority of their fellow Zairians who cried out for change.

Mobutu Sese Seko, a man who in 1965 was the charismatic symbol of shining hope for a newly independent country, had by 1993 become the blood-stained symbol of despotism and despair.

Mbonza tries one more time

It was in the setting of the Zairian socio-political chaos of 1992-93 that ex-CMZa President Mbonza determined to make yet one more attempt to vindicate himself. Seemingly obsessed by a compulsion to reimpose himself upon a Church which had emphatically and repeatedly repudiated him and his leadership, he turned to the only avenue of pursuit left to him, the Zaire Supreme Court. Finding a Kinshasa barrister with credentials for pleading cases before this Court, he filed a dual suit of complaint against CMZa President Chibulenu and against the Republic of Zaire! Regarding the former, his argument was always the same - - "illegalities" in the general assemblies which had elected President Chibulenu three times in a row. As for the Republic of Zaire, his complaint was that its Department of Justice, after having temporarily reinstated him as the CMZa President, reversed itself and ruled against him.

There was a flurry of legal activity prior to the formal examination of his case. Although Mbonza had secured his own legal counsel, he still felt it appropriate to address a personal letter to the Chief Justice in which he sought to instruct him on the sort of evidence which would be appropriate or inappropriate in his case. (20) The ECZ, once again, took interest and used its channels of communication with this High Court to be sure that the judges were fully aware of all the history which had preceded this case.

This litigation finally came to the Court docket in late April. Early on, Mbonza took it upon himself to correct his own lawyer in his presentations before the Court. In a second session, his interruptions became so frequent that the Chief Justice finally turned to ask him: "Who is presenting your case, you or your lawyer?"

It was on May first that all parties were again summoned to the Court chambers. It was announced that the Court had reached a decision. In a two-page document, Mbonza's basic allegations were systematically reviewed and refuted. The ruling concluded by stating that his suit was found without justification and was thus rejected; that the defense presented by President Chibulenu was found to be accurate and thus was affirmed; that the disputed recognition of Chibulenu as the President of the CMZa was maintained and that Mbonza was responsible to pay for all court costs related to the trial."

It was with a tremendous sense of relief and gratitude that the CMZa delegation turned to exit the court chambers. For a long moment Mbonza stood silently looking at the judges and then he too turned to leave. It did not help that a member of the CMZa delegation of that day was Mukanza Ilunga, his former vice president whom he had one day scorned as unworthy of being reelected to serve as his associate.

Gifted with a profusion of natural talent, educated beyond the level of many of his fellow church members, given the opportunity of making an enormous contribution to his Church, tragically Mbonza somehow missed his way. In spite of his education, he seemed unable to rise above ethnic bias and loyalty. Though holding a university degree in theology, he seemed never to understand what it really meant to be a pastor. Though quick to underscore and condemn the failures of others, he seemed incapable of recognizing his own shortcomings or of bringing himself to admit that he had largely contributed to the tension which had shaken the Church he sought to serve. Though keenly aware of the governmental structures and political dynamics at work about him in his country, he never seemed to grasp that they were not appropriate models to be followed within the church as the body of Christ. Though well versed in Anabaptist themes including those of humility and a servanthood stance within the church, he seemed never to comprehend that this teaching had any relevance for him personally during his years as the president of the Zaire Mennonite Church.

CHAPTER 45   ECHOES OF 1960

The explosive violence of September 23, 1991, found AIMM with ten missionary couples and sixteen children on Zairian soil. Nine of ten couples were based in two major cities of the country. Rick and Marilyn Carter Derksen were in Kananga, the capital of the West Kasai where Rick served in pastoral counseling roles among CMZa congregations and university students in the city and gave guidance to the Zairian staff of the inter-church recording studio known as Studiproka. Marilyn taught nursing arts at IMCK, the large inter-church training and health care center a short distance outside the city. Also in Kananga and only recently arrived were Steve and Janet Sinclair Plenert and Delbert and Susan Mast Dick. Newly recruited to work in the joint Mennonite/Presbyterian ministries in the city, the Plenerts were to provide administrative help in the Press and Book Store while the Dicks were to provide technical and administrative support in the Studio. In spite of the somber Zairian scene of the early 90's, the arrival of two AIMM couples new to the Kananga scene was ample testimony to the AIMM's ongoing commitment to that troubled land and its people. Still another couple, Gordon and Jarna Rautakoski Claassen, had just left in late August from Mbuji Mayi, some 100 miles to the southeast, where they had just concluded a term of ministry among the CMZa and CEM churches of the area, Gordon in pastoral and relief work, Jarna in women's work.

In Kinshasa there were six couples: Henry and Tina Weier Dirks were giving technical and administrative direction to CEDI; Arnold and Grace Hiebner Harder were providing coordination of services for both mission and church in the city; Dick and Marilyn Dissinger Steiner were serving on the staff of the International Center for Evangelism of the city; Steve and Pat Wicke Nelson were house parents in the AIMM Hostel; Maurice and Joyce Suran Briggs, at the time, were on loan to the MAF for support services in their large maintenance and supply base in the city. Also in Kinshasa were newly-arrived Dr. Glenn and Pauline Gima Rediger. Having already served one term at Kalonda they had now returned to Zaire with plans to join the medical staff in the West Kasai at IMCK just outside Kananga. The only AIMM personnel who were still based in the Zairian bush at that time were Glen and Phyllis Thomas Boese at the historic church post Nyanga where they were contributing leadership to SEDA, the CMZa's farm and community development center.

eerie resemblances

Across its eight decades of ministry in Africa, AIMM and its missionaries had not been strangers to danger and potential harm. Particularly was this the case in the early 1960's which had witnessed the upheavals of political independence and the rebellions centered in northeastern and south central Zaire. Although in 1960 there were nearly 100 AIMM adults situated largely on isolated mission stations as compared to only twenty adults in 1991 eighteen of whom were located in large urban centers, the experiences of the two teams separated by three decades of time were startlingly the same.(1) In both cases there had been a growing, uneasy awareness on the part of missionaries that serious trouble was brewing and yet, when explosion came, there was stunned disbelief at what happened. In both cases, once unleashed, the fury of violence knew no bounds as mobs of people abandoned themselves to mindless destruction of all that lay in their path, actions which resulted in even greater suffering for the participants.

In both cases missionary personnel turned to their shortwave equipment to keep in touch with each other and to take counsel together. In both cases they were bombarded by a daily mix of truth, half truth and pure rumor which enormously complicated their efforts to evaluate what was happening and to make responsible decisions. In both cases they were early pressured by American and Canadian Embassy personnel to consider and prepare for early evacuation. In both cases there were expatriate friends and members of the broader missionary community who made early decisions to leave and who urged them to do likewise.

And there were further resemblances. In both cases there were hours of anguished turmoil of spirit. In both cases there were missionaries who - - after lengthy preparation and much prayer in their homelands - - found themselves in Africa with no doubt whatsoever that they were where the Lord wanted them. Now what? In both cases there were missionaries who had paid their dues in terms of tedious language learning and acculturation and who felt poised to begin making a genuine contribution in their own right. Now what?

In both cases there were somber conversations and prayers with perplexed and anxious Zairian friends and colleagues. In both cases there were nights of fitful sleep interspersed with repeated moments of prayer beseeching God for wisdom, guidance and "a still small voice" of guidance.

In both cases there was no other turmoil of spirit like that felt when moments of decision approached and they found themselves balancing one commitment against another, one loyalty against another, one responsibility against another. In both cases there were husbands and wives who, as children slept the sweet sleep of innocence, talked quietly into the night trying to weigh responsibility for their work in Africa against their responsibility for the safety and welfare of the little ones God had entrusted to them. In both cases there was the struggle to balance faithfulness to their sense of call against real risks for their safety. And, in both cases, there were the questions which came endlessly to mind for which there seemed no clear answer. "Has the current violence spent itself or is there more to come? Will we help our church most amidst this uncertainty if we stay or if we go? What will we teach to or model for our fellow Zairian Christians about faith and discipleship if we stay? If we go?"

In both cases, once decisions for evacuation were made, MAF provided incalculable service. And, finally, in both cases there were unforgettable experiences of God's grace, presence and protection. Once again in the early 1990's, as in the early 60's, AIMM missionaries were surrounded by real potential for injury and death. In both cases AIMM personnel was spared serious harm.

sharing at the Travelodge

As the sun was setting Friday evening, September 27, a specially chartered "Evergreen Airline" 747 was being readied on the Brazzaville tarmac across the Zaire River from Kinshasa to airlift a load of Zairian missionaries to the United States. Among the 457 passengers who eventually boarded the aircraft were most of the AIMM missionaries. (2)

During a night refueling stop in the Canary Islands, an interesting meeting took place aboard the aircraft. Seven members of the Board of Twelve of the International Protestant Church of Kinshasa (IPCK) were on the plane. AIMM missionary Henry Dirks, chairman of the committee, wanted to convene the group in an emergency planning session before they arrived in the States. Securing permission from the crew, the seven met in the "bubble" upstairs in the nose of the 747 and laid some interim plans for the church group which had been scattered to the four winds in a matter of days. "It was a very sad meeting . . . trying to make decisions for a Church that [had suddenly ceased] to exist."(3) Arriving at Andrews Air Force Base in Washington, D.C. on Saturday morning, the missionaries were soon booked on a variety of flights and by evening were reunited with family and friends across North America.

Concerned not only to learn from their experiences but also to help their suddenly uprooted missionaries process their experiences, the AIMM Board convened the evacuees at the O'Hare Travelodge in Chicago for debriefing/sharing sessions on October 15-16, 1991. Pastor Bryce and Karen Short Winteregg were asked to give leadership to this time of reflection and sharing. (4) The missionaries seized this opportunity with eagerness and appreciation. In verbal sharing in the motel and in written testimonies later given to AIMM staff by a few who could not be present, a mix of themes immediately came into clear focus.

themes of personal turmoil

"Shortly before leaving Kinshasa for North America I heard reports of people both in the Christian and also the secular communities criticizing missionaries for leaving while many business people stayed on solely for financial gain. Why did so many who claimed a higher allegiance and gave lip service to protection from above leave so quickly?" (5)

"We were hearing of the destruction and couldn't believe what we were hearing. . . . It was frightening to think that we might be the only ones [expatriates] left in our area. . . . We made a quick stop at CEDI once more. . . . Our workers cried and so did we. . . . I will never forget the sight as we drove down the streets that morning. There always are lots of Zairians standing along the streets but that morning they seemed to stand in a daze, many standing at the gates and doors to buildings and residences which their expatriate employers had left." (6)

It was a "great disappointment to be leaving Zaire just when things seemed to be coming together for us. That Monday we had just hired an excellent house worker and I had my first Tshiluba lesson. On Thursday Delbert was to have become the official director of the Studio." (7)

"It wasn't long before we began hearing the ominous sounds of angry mobs of rioters and gunfire in Kintambo, a small commercial area near us. Huge military vehicles rumbled by in the streets carrying armed soldiers. The kids took turns sitting in the trees outside our house so they could look over the concrete wall which surrounds our compound . . . . Merchandise of all kinds, large and small, was seen leaving the area as more and more of the stores were shot open and looted. It was a scary time as we wondered if our houses would be next. Sharing with and supporting each other was important during this time and in the evening another missionary family joined us for tea by candlelight since we weren't sure how much light we should have on in the house. The kids shut themselves in their bedrooms and played a tension-relieving game of Balderdash."

"About midnight the Embassy called and asked us how many of our missionaries would leave if it became necessary to leave. Reality hit at that time making me realize that evacuation was a real possibility. I did not get much sleep that night as thoughts raced through my mind as I wondered what I could take if we would have to leave with only one small suit case. Would we even be safe till morning? What would happen to our Zaire friends? Thoughts going through our mind along with the constant gunfire outside our compound and sometimes hearing the stray bullets whiz through the trees kept us awake most of the night. . . . I prayed a lot [the next day] asking the Lord's guidance in making the right decision in what seemed a monumental step to take. . . . Were the Embassy people becoming alarmed sooner than necessary? . . . I thought I was not materialistic but at a time like that I realized how much I wanted to hold on to my possessions! . . . I remember asking the Lord many times what He had in mind through all this while through faith doing what we felt led to do." (8)

"It was a very difficult decision to leave. . . . SEDA staff did not have much to say. They were also in an 'I don't believe this trance' the same as myself. . . . [Our MAF pilot] Jerry Krause was visibly shaken when he arrived. [From Kinshasa] He reported all food and fuel destroyed and that he would be leaving himself as soon as fuel ran out and/or evacuation was complete. He told me I should go while there was a chance, at least as far as Kikwit to be with Glen. . . . [But] we are not presenting the incarnate Christ when we leave our Zairian people to suffer alone." (9)

themes of abiding concern

"Many tears were shed on that flight as our whole way of life, our mission, our church community, our school, our work . . . everything was torn apart and gone . . . maybe never to return. Our prayer is, as it has been for so long, that Zaire might be given a new government that would really have the good of the people at heart, and that God will strengthen and sustain his people in Zaire." (10)

"Zaire, Kinshasa will never be the same again. There has been tremendous damage done to the infrastructure. The economy, the political [system] and the church - - all communities have been badly affected. The Zairians are resilient and patient people. We need to pray that the Lord will help them come out of this yoke of suppression that the Mobutu regime has imposed on them." (11)

"For some Africans this [looting] seemed like a big holiday, others who could see beyond today saw the seriousness of the behavior and were very concerned. Most expatriates, knowing the dire economic situation of the country, could understand why this happened but were saddened by the short sightedness of this . . . destruction not only of material goods but also of the moral fabric of society . . . ." (12)

"I was still wondering if we were doing the right thing. As we drove along the highway everything seemed so normal until we looked into the business areas and saw the results of the last few days of looting and destruction. Where do the Zairians go from here? In just a few days provisions and security were torn away from them, leaving many destitute. . . . I wondered what could be the Lord's purpose in all this. I thought of our Zairian friends who could not leave and who were left to face the realities of hunger and desolation. I felt a sense of guilt for abandoning them." (13)

"My concern for the church as a whole in Zaire is how they view the situation. Now that most of the missionaries are out of the country I pray that they will shift their dependency more on God and not on what aid we can send over when the situation becomes a bit more normal." (14)

Though not specifically mentioned in the missionary reporting, a major concern of the entire church community in Zaire was the catastrophic loss suffered by MAF in Kinshasa in the September rioting. It so happened that it coincided with an annual meeting of pilots and maintenance technicians which consequently placed most of the planes in the country at Kinshasa's Ndolo airport. AIMM missionary Maurice Briggs, who was on loan to MAF at the time, described what he had witnessed as follows: "On the way to the airport we saw quite a mess. Stores trashed and completely looted, litter strewn all about and scavengers still looking for anything of value to take. Burned and/or stripped and smashed vehicles were left in and by the roads and at Ndolo, utter chaos. Hangers completely trashed, tools and parts gone and several aircraft damaged. (15)

In an October 21 memo Max Meyers, MAF chief executive officer based at their headquarters in Redlands, California, revealed losses "of at least $1,220,000 in furnishings, personal effects and equipment in Kinshasa and damage to nine of our aircraft in the country. This is one of the most devastating setbacks to our work in many years. But what is most important about these losses is that they have greatly hampered our ability to minister to more than 35 million desperately hurting people."

themes of comfort

"I remember being especially comforted at hearing the singing of birds as dawn began to break. Their singing was never more beautiful than on that morning as it mingled with the eerie silence and the intermittent sound of gunfire. It was a promise to me that even amid the chaos of our situation the Lord cared for me. . . . The prayer given on my daily calendar that day seemed very appropriate: 'Lord, help me give to you today the thing I fear most.' Through it all, despite the uncertainties I felt a sense of peace - - a result, I'm sure, of many people praying." (16)

"In my personal devotions the Lord led me to Psalm 27. Verses 1-3 and 13-14 really spoke to me and through them the Lord gave me courage to face what was going on. . . . Verse 13 kindled in me a real hope that God would see us through this and that we would still be able to fulfill the work to which He had called us in Zaire." ("I know that I will live to see the Lord's goodness in this present life.") (17)

themes of commitment

In the midst of immense loss and destruction, the MAF memo went on to declare: "All of us at MAF remain committed to the church and the people of Zaire. We are determined to regroup and renew our work there as quickly as we can. . . . This is a considerable challenge. But the stakes are too high not to respond."

MAF was not alone in declaring its determination to maintain its presence and ministry in that strife-torn land. The AIMM Board was also looking to the future. The question was not if missionaries would return but rather when and on what conditions. In consultation between AIMM staff, returned missionaries and the AIMM Executive Committee, a six-point set of guidelines was circulated in January 1992, designed to help evacuated missionaries work though their own recommitment process. Two issues were held to be of critical importance for each individual: 1) a clear, personal sense of God's leading to return to Zaire and 2) an invitation from the Zaire church to return. (18)

The sharing in October 1991 at the Travelodge, however, reflected that some of the evacuees had already worked through this process. "I definitely want to return to reassure the people we left behind and work until termination having things in order and people prepared to continue on their own. There is much unfinished business that needs orderly transition for the project, [SEDA] the churches, the school [in Kikwit] and the many people to feel that they have not just been abandoned." (19)

"For me personally I hope that through this experience I have learned to be more sensitive to the Lord's leading, that I will be more open to His working in my life and that my eyes will be open to see His hand at work in every situation. I hope that it will be possible to return to Zaire even if I could not return immediately to the Studio. My desire is to be able to be involved with helping the people to whom the Lord has called us." (20)

"[The] impact of events on people . . . is a tragedy. . . . [Our] personal hopes [are for] peace so that we can soon return and continue the school ministry." (i.e., in the Evangelism Resource Center in Kinshasa) (21)

"I hope to return to Zaire early in '92 for a short time, and then would like to return with our family as soon as it is feasible. . . . The Lord did not, to the best of my knowledge, say that following Him would be easy, but he did say that we were to follow and to go where He would send us and that He would always be with us and never fail us. Praise the Lord." (22)

CHAPTER 46   IF IT WERE NOT FOR THE CHURCH - -

It was Sunday morning at Sanga Mamba (pr. SAH-ngah MAH-mbah), one of the CMZa congregations in Kinshasa. Perched on a slope overlooking a stream below and the sprawling, ever spreading growth of the city beyond, the church terrain was crowded with constructions of various kinds. On one side was a bare cement block building which housed a primary school. On the other side was a large stone and cement foundation which was to carry, at some point in the future, a chapel built of permanent materials. Wedged between was a rectangular palm leaf shelter where the services of this church family were held.

As the sound of singing carried through the irregular rows of housing above and around the church plot, people were seen threading there way along sandy footpaths around house corners, skirting piles of refuse, washouts, tiny fenced garden plots and an occasional rusting hulk of an abandoned, stripped-down vehicle.

Under the dried palm branch shelter the crowd was growing in size. Some were perched on little stools or folding chairs they had brought with them. Others sat on upended cement blocks or on split bamboo mats thrown on the ground. The "church benches," fashioned of poles suspended at either end in tree crotch supports driven into the dirt floor, had long since been filled to capacity by children and early arrivals.

In the Kinshasa of 1986, food was already expensive, jobs scarce, school fees high and medical care too costly for ordinary illnesses. Life already at that point, for the Mennonite families congregating in their little temporary place of worship, was a day-to-day struggle for survival. The cotton print shirts and skirts on the men and women reflected many washings and dryings under the tropical sun. Handed-down garments of the children "fit" to varying degrees, some baggy and loose, others barely covering the essentials. For a western observer, simplicity was hardly the word to adequately describe the scene. Poverty was more like it.

But the service was now in full swing and the tempo was quickening. Hymns were numerous and largely sung from memory led in an animated fashion by enthusiastic choristers. Announcements were detailed revealing much about the activity and concerns of this particular Mennonite congregation. There were special numbers of various kinds. No matter how long the service would eventually be, no offered special number was refused. There was also an offering. A battered enamel wash basin was placed on a table in the front of the shelter and as the congregation launched into an animated singing of a "giving song," people came forward by age groups to file by the pan to deposit their gifts. It quickly became apparent that all were expected to give something. The day to day struggles of the people to meet their own personal needs were not a good enough reason to ignore the chipped enamel "offering plate" on the table in front.

Then before the message of the morning, still another special number. This time it was a group of young mothers, some with babies on their hips or in cloth slings on their backs. Their song was not one to be found in Mennonite hymnals in North America but one born out of the rigor and struggle which they experienced from day to day. It had a number of verses which, as they unfolded, proved to be a musical commentary on daily life - - its needs, its pain, its battle to survive, but after each verse there was the same refrain which said: "But if our Father in heaven can feed the birds of the air, we know that He can also feed us."

Engaging several of the young mothers in conversation after the service, the visiting AIMM Secretary commented on the beauty and message of their special number. After a momentary pause, one of them responded: "If it were not for our church and our faith in God, we would have nothing; nothing at all."

distant light in the tunnel?

For the Zairian population in general and the Zairian church community alike, the steady deterioration of their country's economy, infrastructure and moral fabric was a painful, bitter and sterile experience. Though endowed with a riot of natural resources which far exceeded those of many other African countries, the Zaire people saw themselves plunged ever deeper into need and suffering as the Mobutu regime pursued its politics of corruption and greed.

For the CMZa and CEM there was added the special distress of deeply divisive power struggles which threatened both their unity and their legal status with the government. In a very real sense, the late 1980's and early 90's had been a wilderness experience. But in the fall of 1993 was there any glimmer of light at the end of their dark tunnel? On the national scene, would the sputtering, oft thwarted efforts of the National Conference to initiate democratic reforms finally achieve some success? Did the scene in the chambers of the Zaire Supreme Court finally mark the closure of the bitter leadership struggle within CMZa? Did AIMM's memo of understanding drawn up with the CEM signal a new era of harmony in the history of this refugee founded Church?

As for Zaire, given the political morass into which it had sunk and Mobutu's dogged determination to cling to power, it was difficult in the fall of 1993 to view the immediate future with any optimism. Was their only option to somehow endure until his demise?

And what of the two Mennonite Churches? At the level of the church as a legal entity with its administrative structures, bylaws, officers and institutions, it is very likely that ethnic and regional loyalties will again and again generate pressures which will necessitate further constitutional amendments and structural adjustments in an ongoing search for fair representation and participation in the life of the sprawling, growing churches.

But it is nonetheless clear that whenever and wherever in Zaire there have been islands of integrity, stability and contentment, the church - - as the body of Christ - - has invariably been found at the center. It is this form of the church, independent of its broader administrative and legal structures, which has long since been planted in Zaire and which continues to speak to the hunger and longing of African hearts. It is at this level that people gather, weep and sing together, worship and pray together, listen and take counsel together. It is at this level that the Gospel continues to be preached and that people experience redeeming grace. It is at this level that the challenge to accept the lordship of Christ is lifted and people gather to celebrate holy communion together. It is at this level that people are empowered to function as light and leaven in the abysmal setting which surrounds them. This is what the young mother was talking about that Sunday morning at Sanga Mamba when she told the traveling AIMM Secretary, "Were it not for our church and our faith in God, we would have nothing."

the African body of Christ

There has been abundant evidence of Christ incarnate in his people in Africa from the earliest days of missionary effort. Stories abound of sacrificial service offered, prophetic words spoken and faithful lives lived in his name.

On the broad Zairian scene, there was Inkima John (pr. i-NKEE-mah), an African layman who was trained by early pioneering missionaries to pilot their supply boat up and down Zaire's rivers in the 1930's. In a message once delivered to his African crew he said: "[Our boat] the *Oregon* is unlike all other boats on the river. She does not run to carry state men nor company officials. She operates for only one purpose - - to transport missionaries and African evangelists on their mission of good will. She is a gospel boat. [It is] that our people may know the love of God, our heavenly Father; that they may be released from the dreadful fear of spirits, the strong bonds of ignorance, of superstition, of sin; that they may receive instruction which will lift them up to better living physically, mentally, morally and spiritually that the *Oregon* steams up and down these rivers. And as her purpose differs from that of other boats, so must her crew differ. I expect every man to live as best he can in accord with that higher purpose. If our lives belie the message that the teachers bring to the people, do you suppose the people will believe? Unless our lives conform to the message, then the evangelists are carrying water in baskets . . . ." (1)

* * * * *

There is the moving story of "The Singing Pastor of Burundi," that land of sad renown because of its repeated rounds of bloody tribal conflict. The pastor had acquired his name due to his love for music, his excellent voice and his habit of frequently underscoring a point in his message by singing a verse or two of a familiar hymn. An outgoing, loving man, he was loved in turn and respected by many as a compassionate shepherd of his sheep.

Then came the night that a squad of armed men of the opposing tribe knocked on a series of doors in his village including his own. He and others had their hands tied behind their backs and were marched into the nearby forest. Untied, they were handed shovels and ordered to dig a trench. Their task accomplished, their hands were again tied behind them. Lined up, their backs to the trench, they were each asked if they had any final message to leave for the living. When it came the singing pastor's turn he said, "Yes, I do have a message to leave." "And what is it?" his captors asked.

Looking toward heaven he lifted his voice in song yet one more time. The hymn? In the English version known in the Western world, the verse is: "Out of my bondage, sorrow and night; Jesus I come, Jesus I come. Into thy freedom, gladness and light; Jesus I come to thee."

The commanding officer then gave the order to his squad to fire. Not a rifle moved. The men stood transfixed before the demeanor and the message of the Pastor. Again the officer commanded that they fire. Again, not a move. In anger the officer drew his own side arm and fired. The singing pastor crumpled backward into the open trench and in a moment of time stood in the glorious presence about which he had just sung. The pastor was gone, but his influence and the beauty of his witness remains as the story of his life and death has been told and retold in countless settings since.

* * * * *

There was Mawesha (pr. mah-WEH-shah) Apollo of the Belgian Congo. A powerfully-built bear of a man, his riotous life of alcoholism in his earlier years brought him one fateful day in 1944 into a violent confrontation with Belgian security personnel in which he clubbed one of them to death. He was brutally trussed, ankles to elbows by chains for ten days, a procedure which resulted in deep infections and scarring. At his trial he was sentenced to life in prison. Through contact with a Protestant fellow prisoner he was led to faith in Christ. Through his own study of portions of Scripture smuggled into the prison and through personal prayer he experienced a dramatic conversion. His total transformation of attitude and conduct led to the suspension of his sentence after nine years of imprisonment and his release. He made his way directly to the Presbyterian Station at Luebo in the West Kasai where he enrolled in their Bible School. Upon graduation in 1956 he began an enormously effective life as a pastor and evangelist. (2)

On one occasion, in the troubled aftermath of the Kwilu Rebellion, he was invited by CMZa to conduct meetings at Bena Nshimba (pr. MBAY-nah NSHI-mbah), a suburb of Tshikapa. An AIMM missionary attending some of the meetings later wrote: In a packed chapel "every eye is on him as he makes his leisurely way along the aisle. Dressed in a knit shirt, his heavily muscled shoulders and torso are clearly visible. . . . There is the easy and lithe tread of a strong man in the prime of life. But above all it is the scars which hold the attention and the eyes of the watching audience. Great ridges of deformed tissue lying under shiny, brown skin circle his arms at the elbows; lesser but still noticeable marks are also visible at mid-forearms and wrists. . . . To one and all Mawesha Apollo hammered home the theme of that evening: 'You cannot serve both God and Mammon. You may be trying it but don't fool yourself. The Book of God says it can't be done.' And his audience sat listening to him intently, the man with the scarred arms, and knew that what he told them was truth."

Invited to speak to AIMM missionaries on one occasion at nearby Kalonda Station, he spotted an African painting on the living room wall of the missionary home. Taking his departure from that familiar scene he observed that "we - - we missionaries and he, a Congolese servant of God . . . we are not our own. As the Congo dugout canoe is at the command of the skilled oarsman balancing in its stern, being turned, maneuvered and propelled according to his will, so we must also be controlled and directed by the Spirit of God, responsive and submissive to his directive will." (3)

*   *   *   *   *

There was Mr. Tusanduka (pr. too-sah-NDOO-kah), the personnel manager of CEDI who that explosive morning of September 23, 1991 in Kinshasa addressed his fellow workers. AIMM missionary Henry Dirks described the moment as follows: "Only 23 of our 65 workers showed up for work. . . . There were no buses or taxi-buses for the workers. . . . By 9:00 o'clock that morning the few workers were asking to go home to be with their families. We held a prayer meeting with all present asking for God's protection over them, their families and CEDI. . . . Before leaving Mr. Tusanduka told the workers they should go straight home. They were not to enter any shops or stores that had been broken open and take any materials. He told them not even to pick up anything on the streets, not even if it was money. We do not want to be part of this widespread looting that is taking place." (4)

*   *   *   *   *

There was Dr. Mengi of the ECZ who addressed a congregation of fellow Zairians in a service in Kinshasa the first Sunday following the September riots. In the course of his message he stated bluntly that some seated in his audience had personally profited from the previous days of destruction and looting and that in so doing, they had sinned. In a voice quivering with emotion he called for repentance. There followed an extended prayer service in which many participated in open prayer of penitence. Among them was an elderly woman who with wet cheeks prayed: "Father God, we the mothers are crying out to you. We are really crying for it is we the mothers who gave birth to the looters; it is we the mothers who gave birth to the soldiers. We don't understand what has happened. Please forgive them, our sons. Please forgive us, their mothers." (5)

the body of Christ in its Mennonite form

Set within the broad Zairian mission/church scene, the body of Christ in its Mennonite form early made its appearance. There were Nsongamadi (pr. nsaw-ngah-MAH-di) Joseph and his wife Baba Naomi, two names which will forever be associated with pioneering, first generation evangelism and planting of the Zaire Mennonite Church. Baluba by birth, it is part of their record to have brought an early witness to the Gospel of Christ in three different tribal settings other than their own. After some Bible training at Djoko Punda, they were first placed among the Bashilele to the west of Djoko. As they met with determined resistance, it must have seemed to them that the seed they sought to sow fell on extremely hard soil. Eventually moved to a Lulua area, they nonetheless lived to see the first converts from the Bashilele people among whom they had pioneered.

When in the early 1920's the missionaries decided to explore possibilities of extending ministry among the Baphende people to the southwest, Nsongamadi was chosen to itinerate with them. Settling on Mukedi village across the Loange River as a possible site, Nsongamadi and Naomi were left there to provide a vanguard of witness. When in 1923 the Mission was able to place the first missionary personnel, they found the faithful couple at their post. All they could show for their efforts, at that point, was an orphan girl who had professed faith in Jesus. But they had broken some stony soil and had again sown the first seed. In due time Mukedi was to become the site of a mission station and the district headquarters of a large church.

Nsongamadi spent his last years as the chaplain of the Djoko hospital. After his death, Naomi responded to the invitation from AIMM missionaries in Kananga to minister to patients in the city's large hospital. Her loving, caring manner became her trademark in that setting where she came to be known fondly by hospital patients as "that woman with a Bible." She remained faithful in that role until ill health and death overtook her. (6)

*   *   *   *   *

There is the story of another Muluba evangelist placed among the Bashilele folk by Djoko Punda missionaries in the early pioneering years of the Djoko Punda station. Rev. Lupera David, a present-day CMZa pastor from that ethnic group, describes what happened: "When I was ten years old our neighboring village had a teacher from the Mission [Djoko Punda] for several months. Besides teaching 'books' this man also taught about God and his son, Jesus. He told how people were raised from the dead and also that Jesus came back to life again after being dead for three days. The people of this village were not at all happy to have this teacher who was sent by the white folk at the Mission. They often threatened his life. They told him to go back to his Baluba tribe at the Mission. But he persisted in teaching children 'books' and about God and Jesus."

"One day a villager died and was awaiting burial. Some of the old fathers got the idea that they were going to put this teacher from the Mission to a test. If his God can raise people from the dead we will now see if this be true or not. They caught the teacher and tied him with strong vines to the dead man who was to be buried at sundown. He was told to bring the dead man back to life. If he failed to do so before sundown, he and the corpse would be thrown in the grave and be buried together. The dead man and the teacher were left lying in the sun just next to the grave. Every person in the village and people from neighboring villages were gathered near by in the shade to see what would happen."

"Two hours before sundown the villagers began to hear noises of a crowd of people approaching. The fathers sent young men to find out what was going on. Soon they came running back breathlessly with the news that a Belgian State Official was coming with his police to check on the population of the area. Everyone knew that the Belgian Official would be seeking out the Mission school teacher for a place of lodging and to provide a place where he could conduct his business. The village fathers lost no time cutting the vines off their hostage and putting things back in order before the official arrived."

"The fact that amazed me most was that this Muluba teacher did not run off after this had happened to him. The next day he was teaching his children 'books' as usual. I thought, 'This teacher must have something of great importance to teach my people, otherwise he surely would have run off after dark and never showed up again.' I was determined to find out why this Muluba man stayed at his work. When the opportunity came I also learned 'books.' I listened to the good news about God and his Son, Jesus. I learned that Jesus had lived in this world and about his teachings, his death and his resurrection. I became a believer and was baptized." (7)

*   *   *   *   *

There was Baba Mimbembe (pr. mi-MBEH-mbeh) and her teacher husband Toma. They had come, bare-foot children from near by villages, to Djoko Punda Station in the early years of its history, drawn by the opportunity of education. Like many others, they experienced conversion to faith in Christ during their student years and in time were baptized and taken into the Church at Djoko. After a couple of years of rudimentary teacher training and Bible study following their primary education, they exchanged vows in a Christian wedding ceremony in the station chapel, vows which they both took to heart.

Seeing them as a young couple with a lot of potential, the missionaries and church leaders approached them about serving as a teacher/evangelist couple. They accepted and soon found themselves in an area village with no Christians. Total strangers, Mimembe had an early concern about making at least one friend with whom she could make fields, gather firewood, carry water and talk in confidence as a young bride. Her prayers were soon answered in the person of a young woman of the village, roughly her same age, who befriended her and showed her great kindness.

One day Mimbembe's husband said "I hear that the husband of your friend has some fresh wild meat for sale. Here, take this money and buy some for our cooking pot this evening."

433

Taking the money, Mimbembe made her way along familiar paths to her friend's house only to discover that she was not there and that her husband was at home alone. Standing at the doorway Mimbembe called out to announce her presence and to inquire about the purchase of a piece of meat. "Yes," came the response from inside the house, "I have meat for sale. Come on in." Sensing immediately the man's intent in the absence of his wife, she replied: "No thank you, I don't need to come in. I just want to buy some meat." The man persisted: "It is good meat and I will sell you a piece. But you should come in and see it before you buy." Realizing that he was attempting to lay a trap for her, she turned and returned home empty handed.

When her husband later inquired whether she had purchased meat from her friend's husband, Mimbembe replied: "No, I did not. The price was too high!"

It was some time later while in the same village that Mimbembe walked to a small crossroads bush store where simple necessities of life in a village setting were for sale. She needed a piece of cotton print to make herself a new blouse and wraparound skirt. Selecting a piece that pleased her, she sought to make payment to the man who operated the shop. Eyeing the young woman for a moment, he said in an ingratiating manner: "Oh you need not pay for it; just take it. I don't need any money for it!"

Knowing immediately that the older man would one day soon invite her to repay him for his kindness by accompanying him into a shuttered back room of his store, she turned on her heel and returned to her simple village home and to her teacher husband to whom she had pledged her faithfulness and love in a Christian wedding at Djoko a couple of short years before.

With passing time God blessed Mimbembe and Toma with several children. Assignments to other villages followed. On one occasion she and some of her daughters sat on a mat before her little mud and thatch kitchen scraping the brown, brittle skin from sun-dried manioc roots which were to be pounded into flour for making their evening ball of manioc mush. Upon finishing she instructed the girls to carefully gather the scrapings into a basket.

"Why Mama?" one asked. "I hear there is a man down the road who is buying these scrapings. He uses them to brew *mayi a kapia*. (a literal translation of the Tshiluba is "fire water," a term used for an alcoholic drink)

After a moment came yet another inquiry: "But Mama, we don't drink *mayi a kapia* and Father tells people all the time they shouldn't either." Mimbembe and her children then engaged in a frank discussion of the issue. Extremely limited in resources and cash income, even the smallest coins were welcome in their family purse. Any additional income, however small, was a big help. But, they decided, they could not not do this at the price of compromising themselves and their influence in the village.

The discussion was brought to a close when Mimbembe instructed her daughters: "Take the basket of scrapings and dump them in our compost hole in the corner of our courtyard. Ours will not be for sale." (8)

*   *   *   *   *

There was Badibanga (pr. bah-di-BAH-ngah) Valentin born in the late 1930's. After finishing primary school and a two year teacher training course at Djoko Punda, he enrolled in a two-year commercial course at Vanga, a large educational center of the American Baptist Mission to the west of Mennonite territory. The following story was provided by a Baptist missionary who learned to know this young man: "Two years ago the missionaries made a special effort to reduce certain unchristian social habits which were prevalent among the boarding students. One of the things [the missionaries] did was to mix students up in our commercial school dorms instead of following the usual class divisions. The students attempted to intimidate their class juniors. . . . Because Badibanga had no [local] tribal ties, he was in for it particularly. This went on for several weeks and finally ended one night in their throwing him out of the dorm, taking his suitcases and dumping their contents on his bed and bedding and then pouring ink all over them. In all of this . . . he kept at his studies and

434

refrained from responding in kind to their taunts nor did he let it embitter him in his relations with his fellow students."

"You can understand that it would be normal not to have much love for the people here after that. This Christmas past a woman had been given up for the worst at the hospital due to complications which followed delivery and surgery. Her baby was in good health but she got lower and lower. Her relatives refused to offer blood and left her to die. The station personnel refused also. Because she seemed to be hanging on, we thought perhaps if we would get some blood that might change the tide. The missionaries were typed but none matched so . . . we appealed to the older students on the basis of Christian concern the day before Christmas vacation. The students objected on the basis that they would die if anyone took their blood. We thought that no one would offer as a result but after a few minutes Badibanga stepped forward. As a result of his example nine others stepped forward and we found two who matched. The woman recovered. We feel that this act of his for a person he had never seen and with whom he had no tribal ties was an example of real Christian perception, particularly in the light of some of the things which he suffered from their people last year." (9)

In a note of his own to his friends at home he wrote: "It was sad because this woman didn't have anyone who could help her. In hearing about this from our missionaries I thought of the verse in the Bible which says: 'Love one another as I have loved you.' I accepted to give my blood to help this woman. Give thanks to God because she is alive." (10)

*   *   *   *   *

There was a man named Kibuza (pr. gi-BOO-zah) Joseph who was already an adult and the husband of two wives when the pioneer missionaries of the CIM arrived to establish a new mission post adjacent to his village Mukedi in 1923. One account of his life goes as follows: "As understanding and comprehension of the Gospel grew, the time came when Kibuza made a simple but profound personal commitment to Christ. Believing that in Christ was to be found not only forgiveness for sin but a source of joy and peace, he embraced his new-found faith with an enthusiasm which was to characterize his entire life."

"Unschooled and illiterate, he nonetheless set himself to the memorization of a variety of Scripture passages which had to do with the basic themes of faith, trust and hope of the Christian life. Armed with these passages plus many hymns that he also memorized, he began to share his new found faith with fellow villagers totally unconcerned that he did not know how to write his own name. . . . As a medical service was developed at Mukedi Station, the need was felt for a hospital evangelist. With his infectious fervor and his obvious love for the Lord, the hospital grounds and pavilions became an ideal area for Kibuza's witness and concern for others. . . . When Kibuza died, the Mukedi Church lost a rich spiritual resource but was left with the memory of a life which had been uniquely blessed and used of the Lord among them." (11)

*   *   *   *   *

And there was Mufuta (pr. moo-FOO-tah) Ana. Slight of build and short of stature she had come to Mutena Station as a girl. She was quiet but a good student. By the time she graduated from primary school she had come to the attention of Mutena missionaries. Asked if she would like to learn the skills of a midwife and work in the Mission maternity, she quickly responded. She was steadily given more responsibility and eventually she became a key person in whom the missionary nurses placed great confidence.

Then came 1960, the year of political independence. Mary Hiebert, a missionary nurse at that station, picks up the story: "Word had been received on July 10, 1960, that all CIM missionaries were to leave the country following the sudden Congo-wide post-Independence [military] mutiny. With heavy hearts we cycled over to the Maternity to discuss these matters with the staff."

"To whom would we give the keys, and along with them the responsibility of directing the newly-built Maternity? None other than Mufuta Ana, a staunch Christian woman who had been with the Mission since her childhood. Her Bible training in Christian principles by the pioneer missionaries laid the foundation for further services."

"Her experience as counselor in the Girls' Home, as a Bible teacher in women's meetings and Sunday School classes, as well as instructor in Grammar School, coupled with . . . training in midwifery, prepared her for such an emergency."

"Mufuta Ana was now in charge. Her heart was heavy as she, her staff, and a puzzled group of new and waiting mothers waved their sad farewells to the evacuating missionaries. As she looked into the anxious faces of her patients she keenly felt the weight of her new responsibilities."

Hiebert continues the story sketching a series of events in a deteriorating situation. Left with a staff made up of people from four different tribes, Mufuta needed the help of them all to assure the normal functioning of the large maternity work which had been left in her care. But the tribal fighting they had been hearing about in the north along the Kasai River was steadily coming closer. Rumors were flying all about them and tension steadily grew. One morning she discovered that two of her helpers had run away during the night. Now there was no one to wash the clothes or to scrub floors. A week later a trusted assistant joined her relatives to leave the troubled area. That left the full burdens of the maternity to Mufuta Ana and one other long time colleague Kashiba Beneke (pr. kah-SHEE-bah BEH-neh-keh). But as fighting approached closer and closer, Beneke also made the painful decision to leave the area. Now Mufuta Ana was completely alone at the maternity.

Hiebert continues the story: "More and more people were vacating their homes including the pastors and other church members. . . . Conditions were grave. Mufuta felt uneasy. The dispensary personnel had long since gone away. Mufuta alone was on call. In fact, she was the only woman on the station which was being guarded by three sentries. Even her closest friends from the nearby village had deserted her. What ought she to do? Should she leave her post of duty? The words of Psalm 102 were a source of strength to her: 'Hear my prayer, O Lord and let my cry come unto Thee . .' She received her answer and decided to follow her friends."

"Quickly and carefully she stored all the supplies, foam rubber pillows and mattresses, bedside tables and baby cribs, linens and chairs, not forgetting the portable Singer sewing machine, into the office and securely locked the door. That night her niece, a mother of seven children, walked five miles to come for her. Before the break of day they were hurrying along a dark path to safety."

They were hidden under a canopy of trees in the forest but Mufuta Ana was miserable. "Sleep did not come at night as she spent the long hours singing softly 'Ask the Saviour to help you, comfort, strengthen and keep you. He is willing to aid you. He will carry you through.'"

"Everyone rejoiced when the local chief sent word that they could return to their villages. The fathers, husbands and sons had been given orders to stop fighting. Once more the weary refugees set out to cross the river. . . . The returning Mutenites received a hearty welcome from the three lonely sentries who had guarded the station since the exodus. Mufuta hurried over to the Maternity and found everything as she had left it some six weeks ago. She praised the Lord for answering prayer."

"In anticipation of the first delivery she set up her department. Her first patient came, then her second, and gradually the number increased. . . . She had no helpers. Besides her regular duties of delivering, caring for babies, charting and recording births, she scrubbed the floors, tidied the wards and did the laundry at the nearest stream. . . . What did she do when difficulties arose? Let us hear what she has to say: 'Mama, I never prayed so hard. There was . . . the Pastor's daughter who gave birth to her first baby. All went well until she hemorrhaged profusely. Her mother began to sob and mourn. Other women came in and made much noise. Things were getting out of hand. I had done all I could. I called the pastors over to pray for her. God answered prayer and spared her life.'"

When in the mid-1960's it was again possible to place a missionary nurse at Mutena, what did she find? "She [Mufuta Ana] remains the director of the Maternity. You may find her at her desk recording births, charting, or signing birth certificates, discharging patients. You may see her in the delivery room or bathing the babies. You will see her whole-hearted interest in the regular [devotional] services in the ward and at clinics. She is the consultant to her domestic staff and comforter to her patients, always willing to listen to their problems." (12)

*   *   *   *   *

While there are many more beautiful facets of the Zairian Mennonite body of Christ of the past, there are others to be described in the present tense.

There is Pastor Mayele (pr. mah-YAY-lay) Isaac, a lifelong rural pastor of the CMZa. Of medium height, a ready smile and infectious optimism, his commitment to his faith and his Church early became apparent. Already serving as an overseer of rural catechist/teachers he was enrolled in the 1956 class of the Kalonda Bible Institute and graduated three years later. With passing time he became the embodiment of the very vision of that school, i.e., the equipping of Zairians from rural areas to serve as shepherds of the Lord back in the rural areas from which they had come. At a time when people of training often expressed preference for assignments at the Mission stations or at established regional church centers, Pastor Mayele remained open to placement wherever the Church needed him.

For years the Nyanga District had been unsuccessful in efforts to establish a church at Katanga (pr. kah-TAH-ngah), a large village in their area about halfway along the road to Tshikapa. The influence of a nearby Catholic Mission was strong and the village elders had remained uncooperative. It was during the sessions of a Nyanga District Conference one year that district leaders turned to Pastor Mayele and asked: "Pastor, do you think you can plant a church in that village?" Without hesitation he replied: "No, I can't, but Jesus can!" Shortly after he and his family were moved and he began his ministry of presence and witness among the people there.

It was only a few years later that a missionary based at Kalonda received a letter from Pastor Mayele. In the letter, dates were set for a big Sunday of celebration. Some new converts were to be baptized early in the morning. There then was to be a worship service followed by communion. Would the missionary come to preach and to rejoice with them for what Jesus had done?

It was truly a day for rejoicing. Recent converts, enthusiastic in their new found faith, were individually introduced with obvious affection by Pastor Mayele. The morning service, presided by the Pastor in a rumpled, slightly frayed jacket, exuded a mood of celebration and optimism. As the special activities of the day came to a close in mid-afternoon, Pastor Mayele insisted that the missionary stay long enough to be served something to eat. Ushered into their humble stick and thatch, dirt-floored home, he was seated at a small wooden table which needed to be shifted a couple of times to achieve stability. After a moment Mrs. Mayele entered carrying a small enamel saucer on which was one hard boiled egg over which a spoon of peppery palm oil sauce had been poured. In her kitchen larder that Sunday afternoon, this was all that was available. But what she had was served with grace, dignity and love. It was a special "Sunday dinner" that the missionary would never forget.

It was not long after that Pastor Mayele was approached by a delegation of Baphende elders from his home village. Their chief had died and they were in search of a new one. They had decided that Pastor Mayele was their choice. After thanking them kindly for the honor they sought to bestow on him he explained: "There are many people who would like to be chiefs but there are not many who want to be pastors and tell people about Jesus. God has not called me to be a chief, he has called me to be a servant, a servant of the Lord Jesus and his people." (13)

*   *   *   *   *

There is Pastor Muatende (pr. mwah-TEH-ndeh) Pierre of the CMZa Mutena District. Born to a Lulua chief in 1914 he found his way as a teenager to Kalamba, an early post of the CIM along the Kasai River to the south of Tshikapa. His study in primary school was interrupted by his father who opposed any further schooling for his son and demanded that he return to his home village, take a wife in the traditional manner and settle back into village culture and life. Missionary intervention finally prevailed in his behalf and he was able to return to the Mission with his wife, Luanganji (pr. lwah-NGAH-nji), where he finished his primary education and eventually graduated from the Station Bible School in 1937.

In 1938 he was appointed a village teacher/catechist and placed for his first assignment in a village of the Badinga (pr. bah-DI-ngah) people, a neighboring ethnic group. This was truly a pioneering effort for Muatende since he encountered a different language, different customs, a determined resistance to all outside influence and a deep distrust of the stranger among them. But Muatende persevered and eventually won acceptance for both himself, his wife and his message. Later ministry took him into a variety of areas including a refugee camp of some ten thousand people during the political turmoil of the early 1960's in the West Kasai.

Across the years, his phenomenal ability to memorize and quote Scripture became known beyond the borders of his home church district. This coupled with his natural ability as a preacher led to his appointment as a CMZa regional evangelist in 1971. It was in this role that the depth of his resource for his Church became ever more apparent. A literal walking Scripture concordance plus a rich repository of African idiom, proverbs and folklore, he held audiences in his hand as he led them along the pathway of Scriptural truth, rebuke, admonition and encouragement.

In later years, as a younger generation of CMZa leadership struggled with difficult problems, they would at times invite a small group of gray heads to meet with them. At such times Pastor Muatende was often present. With the experience of many years of working with people, he would sit quietly listening as the younger men sought solutions. At an appropriate time he had a way of dipping both into African proverbs and Scripture and with an economy of words lay bare the heart of a problem which younger and supposedly better-educated fellow pastors had either ignored or failed to recognize. (14)

*   *   *   *   *

There is Ntambue (pr. NTAH-mbway) Paul who was born to Baluba parents in the area of Djoko Punda in 1912. Enrolled as a boy in the school of the nearby Mennonite Mission Station, he early came to confess Christ as Lord and Savior. As a student in the Station Bible School he soon demonstrated a rare ability to study on his own, something which proved to be a lifelong trait. It was not long that he was appointed as an instructor in the Station Bible School and also became a deacon in his home church at Djoko. Using his notes from student days as a spring board he prepared much of his own material and was often found at his home studying his Tshiluba Bible on his own in preparation for his classes and ministry on the station.

Ntambue came to play a major role in the life of his local Church as he gave increasing time as a member of the church council. A large man with a resonant bass voice, he spoke slowly and deliberately in a manner which clearly reflected his grasp of a problem at hand and his careful reflection before speaking. He often underscored local tribal customs and then sought to apply Scriptural principles as he understood them. He gained the respect of both Africans and missionaries for his unbiased approach to issues and his firmness in dealing with problems.

Caught up in the fury of the tribal conflict of the early 1960's, he joined many others of the Djoko area in flight to the South Kasai. Once there he quickly supported Pastor Kazadi in his efforts to rally and shepherd the scattered Mennonite refugees. When the CEM was officially recognized, Ntambue was one of the first to be ordained a pastor within the new Mennonite Church and became a source of strength, stability and wisdom among his uprooted fellow Mennonites. (15)

438

*   *   *   *   *

There is Kake (pr. KAH-khe) Elizabeth, a tall, lean Muphende woman. Life had not dealt kindly with her. Orphaned at an early age she was cared for by a grandmother. At school age she was enrolled in a simple village class which at the time was taught by Ngongo (pr. NGAW-ngo) David who was later to become a widely known pastor of Nyanga District and had a enduring impact for good upon her life. Noting her bearing and ability to learn, she was selected as one of nine girls to go to the station school across the valley to continue her education there. Hesitant village elders warned her that this was dangerous for a little girl but encouraged by her teacher she insisted on going. Once on the station she come under the further influence of Frank and Agnes Neufeld Enns and Pastor Mazemba (pr. mah-ZEH-mbah) Pierre.

When at first hearing the story of Christ's love, she assumed that such a gift was surely intended only for white folk. But as she talked with her Zairian teacher and Pastor Mazemba she came to realize that God loved her too. Upon making her own profession of faith, she sought baptism and made a commitment to the work of the church and the mission which was to become the lifelong focus of her devotion. In typical African custom, she was sought in marriage in her teens by a young man who also had finished school on the station. The early years were years of joy for Elizabeth. Her husband was employed as a teacher and she was busy as a mother and provider for their growing family which eventually numbered seven children. Along the way she had come to the attention of missionary nurses Leona Entz and Kornelia Unrau as a mature, energetic mother and a faithful Christian on the station. When they needed more help at the station maternity hospital, they offered Elizabeth the opportunity of on-the-job training, an offer she quickly accepted. It soon became evident that she was determined to master the skills of midwifery to the best of her ability. In the late 1950's she took state exams and won government certification. In the evacuation of missionaries after independence in 1960, all keys and responsibilities for the maternity hospital were left in her hands.

In 1970 life took a somber turn for her. She had been aware for some time that her husband was distant and evasive. Suddenly he left her and her family to take another woman as his wife. To make matters still more difficult, it had by then become evident that a son, still at home with her, had become mentally unstable due to an attack of cerebral malaria. None of these heartaches, however, deterred her from her work or her involvement with her beloved Church. No hour was too late or too early for her to be roused from her bed if a prospective mother needed her help. The tribe or social status of the woman made no difference to Elizabeth; they were all her sisters and they all received her sacrificial and loving care alike. Across the years countless babies were ushered into the Zairian world via her calloused, gentle hands.

Unless prevented by her work at the maternity, she was always present in the church for services and meetings of the women's group. For the annual women's harvest festival offering, she always had her own woven hamper of hand-threshed millet grain to give as an offering, millet she somehow found time to plant, cultivate and harvest in the midst of her busy life.

Bearing her personal heartaches and disappointments with courage, Elizabeth submerged herself in service for others and for her Lord. To know her was to admire her, to be inspired by her and to love her as a sister in Christ. Ultimate proof of the respect in which she is held in the CMZa District of Nyanga unfolded one Sunday morning in October 1987 when she became the first woman in the history of that district to be consecrated a deaconess.

An article written about her in the late 1980's comments: "Because of her health Kake Elizabeth no longer goes to the fields or carries heavy loads so she spends her time in supporting ministries of the church, visiting and encouraging the sick and mourning. Most recently she's taken responsibility for the high school girls in the 'girl's fence.' . . . Her chief pursuit in life is to glorify Christ whom she loves and serves. Her children know that when she dies she wants her *masaka* [pr. mah-SAH-kah, meaning traditional mourning time] to [instead] be a celebration of new life in Jesus Christ."

439

Elizabeth has stipulated that a favorite hymn of hers be sung at her funeral (English title, "Shall You? Shall I?"). The Giphende translation speaks of entry into heaven at the end of life. The fourth verse is: "When one day our time of death comes, we want to go in peace. Others of our number have gone ahead; when we find them again in heaven our hearts will rejoice." (16)

*   *   *   *   *

There is Shamuimba Mbombo (pr. shah-MWI-mbah MBO-mbo) who in March 1988 was named director of the CMZa's program of Theological Education by Extension (TEE) which is designed to provide opportunity for guided Bible study for rural church leaders and lay members alike at rural church centers. A graduate of the Ndesha Theological Institute near Kananga, he served for a time as a school director for the Church. During the stormy confrontation of early 1985 between Kalonda District and the central administration, he had been thrust into the foreground by these events as a spokesman for his district. It was after the transition to a new CMZa administration that he was assigned his new responsibility with the TEE program.

He was well known in the Tshikapa area since he was the son of a long-time and widely known Kalonda Pastor Mbombo Daniel. Though he suffered in his later years from a chronic stomach disorder and was limited to a very restricted diet, aging Pastor Mbombo never faltered in his role as the hospital chaplain on the station and in his stabilizing influence as a member of the local church council. It was a source of personal comfort and pride for him that one of his sons was following him in service devoted to his Church.

In a letter addressed to AIMM Secretary Earl Roth dated August 4, 1988, son Shamuimba wrote in detail of his work as head of the TEE department and the personal effort he had invested in visiting some of the teaching centers at a distance from Kalonda. In the summer of 1988 he listed fifty-eight teaching centers, forty-five volunteer teachers with 822 students enrolled in the program of whom 205 were women.

Moving beyond statistics he shared the problems and difficulties he encountered in pursuing his work. In addition to a minimal budget there was the further problem of transportation. Since his department provided no means of travel, he reported having gone on foot to some centers which were more than sixty-five miles distant from Kalonda. Renting a motorbike, he had taken a trip in another direction which totaled 340 miles over sandy bush trails.

He went on in his letter to underscore also the difficulty he was having to provide for his family in the Tshikapa diamond area on the very modest support which the CMZa was able to grant him from the central budget monies. He admitted that this problem particularly had given him moments of much concern and discouragement. "God is great and all things are possible for him. But how is it that his servants must suffer?" He admitted to moments of temptation to simply leave his work with his Church and search other means of earning a livelihood as others had done. But always, as these thoughts came to him, the word of God "condemned him." And what was the "word" to which he referred?

During the last months before his father's death, he had often sat and talked with him. On one occasion his gray-haired pastor father took his Bible and turned to I Kings Chapter 2. Appropriating the opening verses as his own to his son, Pastor Mbombo read: " When David was about to die, he called his son Solomon and gave him his last instruction: 'My time to die has come. Be confidant, be determined and do what the Lord your God orders you to do. Obey all his laws and commands as written in the Law of Moses so that wherever you go you may prosper in everything you do. If you obey him the Lord will keep the promise he made when he told me that my descendants would rule Israel as long as they were careful to obey his commands faithfully with all their heart and soul.'" (17)

*   *   *   *   *

And there is Pastor Kuamba (pr. KWAH-mbah) Charles. Born of Lulua parentage along the Kasai River he was drawn to the CIM station of Djoko Punda by the opportunity of education. Though by nature a quiet person he had strong musical gifts and soon became an active layman in the station Church teaching classes in the Bible School and directing a variety of choirs. His patience and perceptivity equipped him well to serve as a language tutor for new missionaries who were assigned to the station across the years.

Kuamba's faith commitments were deep. They were never more severely tested than during his first marriage. Although he and his wife greatly desired children, they lived in deepening disappointment. Furthermore his wife became ill at an early age and experienced steadily declining health. Childless and burdened with a wife who eventually became an invalid, his fellow clansmen frequently came urging - - even demanding - - that he return his wife to her people and take another in order to ensure children for himself and their clan. In spite of the powerful pressures he experienced, he resolutely refused and lovingly cared for her until her death. Following a period of hesitation he again proposed marriage. This union, to his great joy, was blessed with a total of eleven children.

During the political upheaval of the early 1960's in Zaire which in the West Kasai brought his Lulua people into bitter conflict with the Baluba, Pastor Kuamba was one day confronted by a delegation of his fellow tribesmen. They said: "We have noticed that you are strangely quiet amidst the conflict of these days. Today we want to know to which tribe you give your allegiance."

After a pause he replied: "If amidst the hatred and bloodshed all around us you are asking which tribe I belong to, my answer is that I belong to neither one. Years ago when I gave my life to Jesus Christ, I joined a new tribe - - his tribe. If today you ask me who I am, my answer is simple: I am a Christian and I seek to follow and serve Him." (18)

*   *   *   *   *

The story of AIMM and of the two Mennonite Churches that have issued from its efforts of witness and ministry across the years has often been one of struggle and pain. But, thank God, it has also be a story of God's marvelous grace at work in the heart of Africa.

441

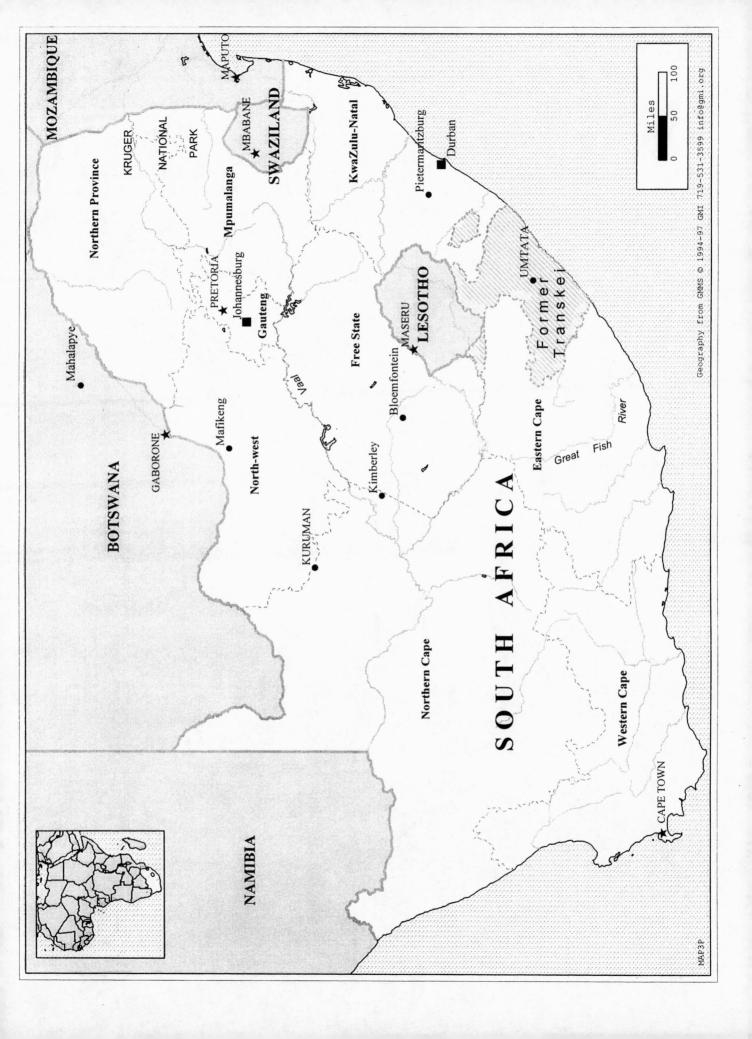

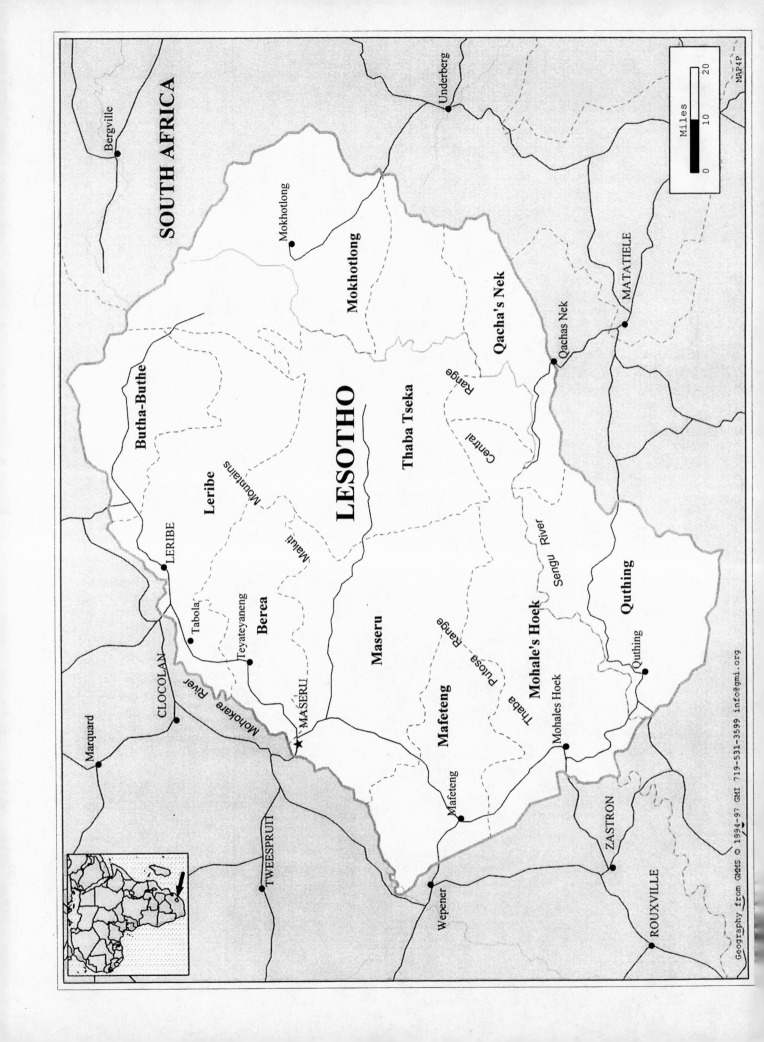

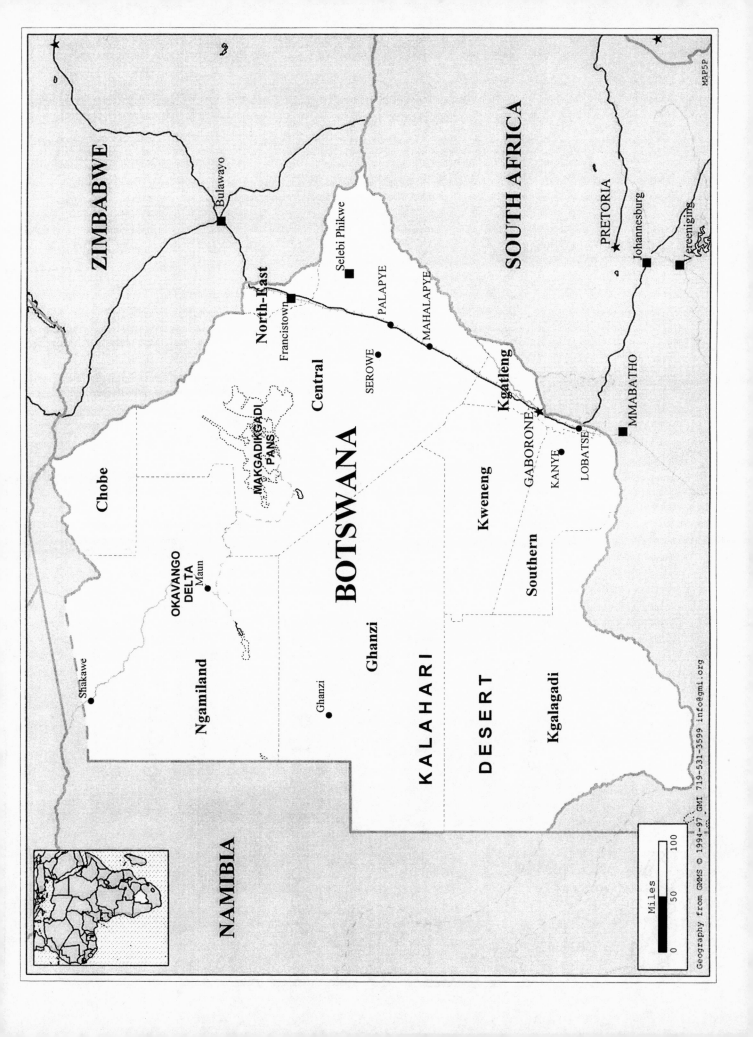

ZIMBABWE

SOUTH AFRICA

PRETORIA

Johannesburg

Vereeniging

Bulawayo

Selebi Phikwe

North-East

Francistown

PALAPYE

MAHALAPYE

MMABATHO

Central

SEROWE

Kgatleng

BOTSWANA

Chobe

MAKGADIKGADI PANS

GABORONE

KANYE

LOBATSE

Kweneng

OKAVANGO DELTA

Maun

Ghanzi

Southern

Ngamiland

Shakawe

Ghanzi

KALAHARI

DESERT

Kgalagadi

NAMIBIA

Miles

0   50   100

Geography from GRMS © 1994-97 GMI 719-531-3599 info@gml.org

MAP5P

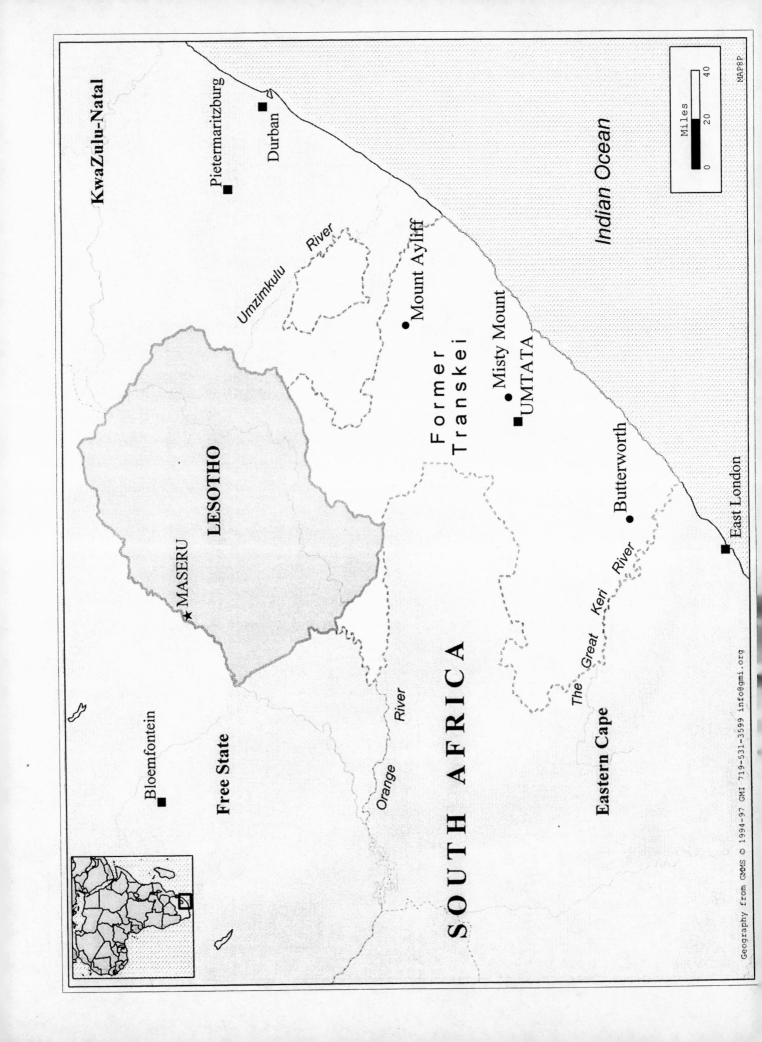

CHAPTER 47   MENNONITES CROSS THE LIMPOPO

Mennonite and Brethren in Christ missionary presence on the continent of Africa is traceable as far back as the late 19th century. In 1890 Eusebius Hershey, a member of the Mennonite Brethren in Christ Church (today the Missionary Church), went to Liberia on his own. Though he soon sickened and died, the challenge of his example stirred his home church. By 1920 the MBC organized the United Missionary Society and sponsored work notably in Nigeria.

In 1896 Miss Mathilda Kohm was sponsored by the Defenseless Mennonite Church (now the Evangelical Mennonite Church, or EMC/US) for service with the Christian and Missionary Alliance Mission near Boma, just inland from the mouth of the Congo River.

In 1898 a Brethren in Christ missionary party of five people arrived in Capetown, South Africa, to seek opportunity and place for the founding of a BIC witness in Africa. They were: Jesse and Elizabeth Nisley Engle, Hannah Davidson, Alice Lehman and Barbara Swanson. Upon seeking the counsel of the legendary British empire builder, Cecil Rhodes, they were encouraged to proceed northward and to establish a presence and ministry in Southern Rhodesia (now Zimbabwe). To facilitate the launching of their missionary endeavor, Rhodes made generous grants of land upon which mission installations could be built and agricultural and livestock projects could be undertaken. By 1910 the BIC had also placed their first missionaries in Northern Rhodesia now known as Zambia.

In 1900 the Defenseless Mennonite Conference sent Mathilda Kohm back to the Congo for a second term accompanied by Alma Doering. This time they worked with a Swedish Mission further inland between the Congo and Kasai Rivers.

In 1906 the Central Conference of Mennonites sent Lawrence B. Haigh and Rose Boehning to serve with the Africa Inland Mission in Kenya.

In 1907 the Defenseless Conference also sent a team of missionaries to East Africa to work with the Africa Inland Mission. They were: Amos and Julia Oyer, Anna Zimmerman, Alma Doering, Marie Schneider and Emil Sywulka. The Oyers were assigned to develop a new work in the Kenyan highlands at a place called Matara among the Kikuyu people.

In 1907 the Central Conference sent an additional four recruits to East Africa: Jesse Raynor, L.S. Probst, Laura Collins and Miss Schoenheit.

In 1912 Lawrence and Rose Boehning Haigh and Alvin Stevenson were the first missionaries of the newly-founded Congo Inland Mission (now Africa Inter-Mennonite Mission, or AIMM) to arrive in south central Congo.

In 1934 the Eastern Mennonite Board of Missions and Charities (now known as Eastern Mennonite Missions, or EMM) placed their first missionaries, Elam and Grace Stauffer, and John and Ruth Mosemann in Tanganyika in East Africa (now Tanzania). This was the beginning of a mission endeavor of this Board which, in time, spread into Kenya, Ethiopia, Somalia, Swaziland and the Sudan..

In 1954 Raymond and Suzy Eyer became the first French Mennonites to work in Africa when they were sent to serve under the auspices of the Sudan United Mission in the country of Chad.

And, by 1957, the Mennonite Board of Missions had placed S. J. and Ida Hostetler, Erma Grove and Ruby Hostetler in West Africa in the country of Ghana.

But in spite of steadily growing Mennonite/BIC program and ministry elsewhere in Africa, as the decade of the 1960's dawned, southern Africa remained a frontier which had not yet been probed. There were, however, developments afoot in the Mennonite world which were soon to change this.

The late 1950's and early 1960's were volcanic years in sub-Saharan Africa. Within the space of a few years, all but a few isolated remnants of vast colonial empires had crumbled. Country after country had rushed to claim its political autonomy and, simultaneously, began to clamor for many forms of help including scholarships for study overseas and for revamped and upgraded educational systems at home. There was quick response as a number of western governments, universities and foundations sought to design teacher training and aid programs for Africa. In the United States, 1961 found the government putting the finishing touches on a new volunteer program called "The Peace Corps." At the same time the Council of Mennonite and Affiliated Colleges was actively discussing the idea of the training and assignment of Mennonite personnel in underdeveloped countries for work in the field of education. (1)

MCC soon joined the dialogue. For a time it was thought that this new Mennonite venture might in some manner be associated with the newly-founded Peace Corps program. But when it became apparent that the new service corps would function as an arm of the US government, Mennonites studying the question soon determined to explore opportunities for service on their own.

Tim Lind, commenting on this turn of events, wrote: "Immediately subsequent to the decision not to work with Peace Corps, MCC and the Council of Mennonite and Affiliated Colleges agreed to co-sponsor a tour of Africa by Robert Kreider to investigate possibilities for increased Mennonite service involvement in Africa. Kreider's subsequent report urged the creation of a 'Teachers for Africa' or 'Teachers Abroad Program.' The proposed program was approved by the MCC Executive Committee in December 1961 . . . ." (2) The term "Teachers Abroad Program" was adopted and the acronym TAP quickly became part of Mennonite terminology.

Initially TAP programs were recommended for East, West and South Central Africa. In 1967 Kreider was again asked to travel to Africa and to assess the possibility and need for TAP volunteers in the southern part of that continent. Upon his return he specifically recommended that a TAP program be undertaken in Botswana. Thus it was that in 1968 the first Mennonites took up residence and initiated ministry in south central Africa.

AIMM indicates interest

The new initiatives in southern Africa on the part of the MCC/Council of Mennonite Colleges did not go unnoticed by Mennonite Mission Boards in North America. In a spring 1968 meeting of the Council of Mennonite Board Secretaries (then known by its acronym COMBS, and now known as the Council of International Ministries, or CIM) the minutes carried the following entry: " . . . agreed that we approve a study of South Africa . . . to be carried out by a team of at least two people; that we counsel with MCC regarding their entry into Botswana and over-all objectives." (3)

In the October COMBS meeting of the same year, the issue of Mennonite presence in southern Africa was again discussed and the pending COMBS study of the region was further spelled out: "Moved that COMBS sponsor a study assignment for southern Africa in consultation with MCC and Africa Mennonite Fellowship [Africa Mennonite and Brethren in Christ Fellowship known as AMBCF] with the following goals: a) Review of pertinent information regarding population, social, educational and economic developments and other statistical data that would enhance the total understanding of this area; b) Survey and analysis of present mission and church development; c) Projection of potential strategy and program opportunities for consideration by Mennonite agencies; d) That a request be made to Schowalter Foundation for a grant of up to $2.500 to finance travel and living costs for a team of three people, to include Don Jacobs as leader, plus an African representative of the Brethren in Christ Churches in Rhodesia/Zambia, and one additional person; and e) The date for the study is to be October, 1969." (4)

AIMM, a member of COMBS, had followed these discussions with particular interest. For years the AIMM Board had periodically discussed the feasibility and/or advisability of probing opportunity for service somewhere in English-speaking Africa. Working exclusively in francophone Africa had not been without complication and additional expense. For many new AIMM recruits, six months to a year of intensive French study had to be inserted into training programs at some point prior to their arrival in Zaire. Work in English-speaking Africa would clearly simplify some aspects of recruitment, training and provision of resource materials. AIMM in the late 1960's, furthermore, was moving rapidly toward the granting of full autonomy to the Zaire Church which had emerged out of its years of ministry there. AIMM was ready to explore new opportunities for witness and service elsewhere in Africa. From its perspective, the new COMBS initiative was well timed.

the Jacobs/Bertsche investigative trip

The exploratory trip proposed by COMBS finally took place in April of 1970. Don Jacobs, serving at the time under Eastern Mennonite Board of Missions auspices in Nairobi, Kenya, and Jim Bertsche of AIMM, located at Kalonda, Zaire, met in Johannesburg, South Africa and began a trip which was to cover the best part of three weeks. Traveling essentially by road and rail, their route took them to Swaziland, Lesotho, Botswana and Zimbabwe while crossing intermediate areas of the Republic of South Africa in the process. All along the way every effort was made to seek contact with and information from mission/church and Christian Council personnel as well as lay people both white and black. Original plans had been to travel part of the time with BIC Bishop Philip Khumalo. When administrative commitments made this impossible, Jacobs and Bertsche arranged to conclude their trip in Bulawayo at which time the Bishop provided insight and perspective which helped greatly in shaping the views and recommendations of the team.

A written report of findings submitted to COMBS was clear in its thrust. In an introductory statement it was simply said: "This report recommends involvement." This "involvement" was spelled out in the following terms: "While the evils of the apartheid system are clearly recognized and while desiring that this system be changed so that all men may be treated as people with God-given dignity where they are now oppressed, the authentic goals for Mennonite involvement are the encouragement of the growth and nurture of the Kingdom of Heaven within the situation, and authentic signs of the love of Christ in particular settings. This means that involvement shall produce Christian disciples who carry a concern for the total condition of man as did their Lord."

"It is therefore not enough to be in southern Africa simply as an expression of American or European Mennonite interest in a crucial area of the world. We are and ever will be interested in the development of fellowships of believers who will together seek God's way from within a situation."

"We may be tempted to 'do good' in southern African for the next twenty years but the 'do gooding' would simply be an extension of affluent white concern. This we must do, of course, but only in conjunction with an enlightened program for the encouragement of the fellowship of disciples."

"Said in another way, we must think in terms of total church involvement which, in Mennonite parlance, means the Word and the deed producing believing communities."

"This will not be easy in southern Africa where there is already 'mission activity' in the traditional sense of the word. We should be reluctant to be another one of these. However, we would be denying our very nature if we as a believing community would be satisfied to apply a 'band aid' and run. If we are going to get involved, we must take the plunge and be all things to all men so that the Kingdom may be extended." (5)

There followed a series of background and interpretative articles on the areas visited. Each was concluded by a listing of existing programs or possible new initiatives in which Mennonite personnel might conceivably become involved.

Further travel to southern Africa by other mission board/MCC delegations followed (6) over the next two years. Each new trip added still further to the growing mix of Mennonite observations and opinions regarding the situation on the southern tip of that continent and tentative suggestions as to how Mennonites and the Brethren in Christ might become involved. It was clearly time for all interested groups to take counsel together.

the Maseru consultation April 30 - May 1, 1972

In a memo addressed to AIMM, Eastern Mennonite Board of Missions and MCC offices, Vern Preheim, the MCC Africa Secretary of the time, proposed a meeting on the scene in southern Africa "to review where we are, where we've come from and where we're going in Botswana, Swaziland and Lesotho and to plan further Mennonite witness and service in Southern Africa." (7)

Delegated by their respective organizations to participate in the meeting were Don Jacobs and Hershey Leaman from Nairobi, Kenya and Maynard Kurtz from Mbabane, Swaziland, where he and his family had recently been assigned (Eastern Board); Ray Brubacher from Akron, PA and Jim Juhnke from Gaborone, Botswana where he was at the time serving as country program director (MCC); and Jim Bertsche (AIMM).

The consultation revolved primarily around a three-point agenda: Biblical meditations led by Jacobs; two study papers prepared by Juhnke, and the sharing of updates and learnings from the three organizations represented there. Juhnke's two papers were entitled "White Politics in Southern Africa" and "Mennonites in Southern Africa: Dilemmas and Prospects." The first focused on the harsh realities of the minority white rule which was firmly entrenched in the Republic at that time. The second discussed some practical and ethical issues which needed to be addressed if, in fact, Mennonites were serious about seeking opportunities for involvement in that part of the world. This was an appropriate focus for, at the time, there was sharp debate going on among personnel of mission boards and voluntary service agencies regarding the morality of any sort of involvement with South Africa at all. While some called for a boycott of the country and refusal to assign personnel in whatever capacity, others urged the approach of dialogue and influence from within the scene to whatever extent this was possible.

Recognizing the polarity of opinions on the one hand and the growing sentiment among Mennonites in the early 1970's for some sort of involvement on the other, Juhnke wrote: "Mennonites who have spent a good deal of their history attempting to escape from worldly involvements and compromises need to be reminded that there is in fact no escape. South Africa is a microcosm of a shockingly unjust and exploitative world. We would gain nothing whatsoever in the way of moral purity by refusing to become involved in the agonizing dilemmas of identifying with the problems of people in countries such as South Africa. Indeed, the strategy of withdrawal can partake of a kind of moral arrogance which contradicts the spirit of Christ." (8)

It was clearly in this mood that the six participants in the Maseru consultation drew up a set of eleven observations and recommendations for submission to the three organizations which had sponsored the gathering. In the light of AIMM's involvement which was to unfold progressively over the following years, four were of particular significance: "Given the vigor of the Swaziland independent churches and the expressed desire of at least one Swazi church leader for a structured training program for independent church leadership in that country, we recommend that someone be invited to visit Swaziland to attempt to determine the receptivity of these leaders to dialogue, biblical training and spiritual fellowship across the borders of their own particular groups. In view of its previous experience in relating to independent church groups in Africa, we recommend that the Elkhart Board [Mennonite Board of Missions] be invited to propose someone qualified to undertake the exploratory mission sketched above."

"We encourage Jim Juhnke to contact Bishop Khumalo in Bulawayo to explore with him the possibilities of implementing the recommendation made in the Jacobs/Bertsche report (p.29), i.e., 'that the pastoral evangelistic arm of the [Botswana Mennonite] program be undertaken by the Brethren in Christ Church from Zambia and Rhodesia."

446

"We feel that Lesotho as well as Botswana and Swaziland offers opportunities for Mennonite service and witness. We therefore encourage the CIM [i.e., AIMM prior to its name change] to pursue aggressively its current investigation and to determine in conjunction with the MCC the wisest plan for entry and the best assignment of the first Mennonite personnel in that country."

"We recommend that an effort be made to respond to the requests of the Transkei Christian Council for a Mennonite qualified to serve as a technical advisor to a Xhosa layman recently appointed by the Council to head a development program." (9)

As the participants in the consultation scattered, the best summation of their views vis-à-vis a broadened Mennonite/BIC presence and witness in southern Africa was to be found in the "Report of Proceedings" which came out immediately thereafter: "The focus of questioning among our people by this time seems to be less on the IF but more on the HOW of Mennonite involvement. You can only do what you can do. Our Mennonite 'thing' through the years has been involvement. Given our deep and credible involvement in other areas of Africa, the correct question regarding South Africa now would seem not to be WHY but rather WHY NOT?" (10)

CHAPTER 48   IN THE SHADOW OF *APARTHEID*

It was a spring evening in 1970 in the restaurant of a motel on the border of Kruger National Park up in the northeast corner of the Transvaal, South Africa. Not only was it on the fringe of the famed African game park; it was also in the heart of Afrikanerdom. (The Dutch South African settlers were first known as Boers, their own term for farmers and, eventually, as Afrikaners. Their language came to be referred to as Afrikaans.)

Two white men (1) had entered and were seated at a table dressed with a spotless white cloth and wrinkle-free napkins. A quiet African of medium height and averted gaze had taken their orders and in due time began to serve their food. Early efforts at conversation had drawn only short, noncommittal, bland answers. Although hovering nearby for purposes of service required of him, he clearly was not anxious to be engaged in conversation with the white strangers.

But the white men were in no hurry. They had all night. Eventually the African waiter learned that they were nonresident Americans paying a brief visit to southern Africa and that they had been sent by their North American churches to see if there might be ways of helping the people of his land. The waiter pondered this information as the meal ran its leisurely course. Eventually, over a final cup of coffee, he approached the table, looked about to be sure that he was out of earshot of his white employer and then said in a flat, stoically unemotional low voice: "My grandfather before me suffered; my father also suffered; I am now suffering and my children after me will also have to suffer."

Shortly thereafter the two white men made their way along flower bordered paths to their nearby room. Their waiter, however, walked to a bus stop where he began the return leg of a daily 38-mile round trip between his home and his place of work. Although he had formerly lived within a few blocks of the motel, new government regulations had forced him to move to the nearest "location" which had been allocated to "blacks" in order to leave the motel and its environs "white."

An issue of <u>Newsweek</u> purchased in Johannesburg, as the men began their trip, provided a somber supplement to what they had just heard in the dining room that evening. In an article which traced the spiraling racial confrontation of South Africa of the time, an educated black man was quoted as saying: "I try not to think too much about that part of my life that is ruled by fear - - fear for the future of my children. Will they lose their pride, their right to be thought of and treated as people? Perhaps there is some reason for a little hope. Without it, I don't know what I'd do. With the certain knowledge that we had been definitely condemned to a futureless existence, I would drink myself to death or go mad." (2)

Afrikaners: who are they?

Any understanding of the southern Africa into which Mennonite missionaries and VS personnel began to venture in the late 1960's and early 70's must begin with the descendants of the Dutch immigrants who by then traced their presence on the southern tip of the African continent back for more than 300 years.

It was in 1488 that the seafaring Portuguese first rounded South Africa's southern cape. By 1600 the English, French and Dutch were doing likewise as they followed the long sea route to the spices and exotic products of Asia and the Pacific islands. In 1652 the first Dutch people established residence on the Cape as representatives of the Dutch East Indies Company. The objectives, as stated by one source were to barter for meat with local "Hottentots," (3) provide supplies for Dutch ships passing the Cape, build a fort to secure the area, and keep peace with the local population. (4)

In 1658 a Portuguese ship carrying slaves was intercepted and its human cargo was added to the growing community. By 1670 the first Dutch settlers were already engaged in agricultural projects of their own. By 1700 the community saw still more immigrants as more Dutch citizens made their way to the Cape as well as some 150 French Huguenot refugees. Most of these people, both Dutch and French, were fleeing religious persecution in their European homelands.

It was in the early decades of the 1700's that the ingredients of an Afrikaner culture began to jell. Already in the late 1600's a Dutch farming community was taking shape just inland from Capetown. To their agricultural pursuits the Dutch pioneers soon added the breeding and grazing of cattle. As need for pasture land increased, they pushed steadily further into the hinterland. Although fellow Dutch people were in charge of the Dutch Indies Post at the Cape, some friction had developed over questions of outlet for their produce and issues of their personal welfare.

With growing families and herds, they slowly expanded their community eastward along the southern rim of the African continent. In growing isolation from the outside world, these immigrants began to coalesce into a close-knit society. In the way of pioneering frontier people everywhere, there emerged a deep loyalty toward and accountability for each other surrounded, as they were, by the frequently inhospitable African bush. Dialect variations which brought together linguistic strands of Dutch, Flemish, German, English, French and even Portuguese gradually merged into a common vernacular which eventually came to be known as Afrikaans and which became a prized and distinctive feature of their culture.

But above all, it was the Dutch Reformed Church (known in Afrikaans as the Nederduitse Gereformeerde Kerk, or NGK) which exerted a powerful, unifying and shaping force upon the Afrikaner culture which was being forged in their African setting. A deeply religious people, Sundays were reserved for rest, worship, preaching, family and visiting neighbors. The Bible, the rifle and the plow increasingly came to symbolize who they were and what they were about.

By the late 1700's the frontiers of their expanding domain reached the Fish River roughly at mid-point between today's cities of Port Elizabeth and East London, some 400 miles east of Capetown. It was here that the Afrikaners made their first contact with a hardy, proud Bantu tribe known as the Zulu who were also in process of migration into South Africa from the northeast. While these early contacts were comparatively peaceful, over time the Afrikaners and the Zulu found themselves locked in mortal combat. (5)

Meanwhile, back at the Cape, there were other events taking place which were to have traumatic impact upon the growing agrarian Afrikaner community. In 1795 the Cape was occupied by a British expeditionary force, an event which marked the end of Dutch control of the Cape. In 1820 the British government sponsored a migration of some 5,000 of its people. Over the next 40 years another 35,000 British citizens journeyed to the Cape area to take up residence. In this whole process, British Cape authorities began a deliberate effort to bring the Afrikaner minority under their influence and authority.

It was not a gentle process. Viewing the Afrikaners as stubborn and uncouth on the one hand and potentially a political problem on the other, discriminatory policies were gradually put in place. Their language was disqualified for use in courts and government offices. Consequently Afrikaners themselves were excluded from jury service. Black servants, however, were encouraged to give evidence against their Afrikaner masters in court. The decision was made to impose English as the language of instruction in their schools. The ultimate outrage was the British effort to impose English-speaking pastors upon their congregations.

the great trek of 1835 - 1838

Recognizing that the growing influence and power of the British in the Cape area meant long-term harassment and suppression for them, the great majority of the Afrikaner population determined to put as much distance as possible between themselves and those they viewed as their tormenters. Packing their families and as much of their household goods and supplies as they could into rugged Conestoga-type wagons, they inspanned their teams of oxen and began a long, hazardous journey toward the north and northeast intent on finding a place where they could live and worship unmolested by others.

Estimated to have been ten or twelve thousand total, they traveled via a variety of routes in varying sized groups moving slowly both to accommodate their sizeable herds of livestock and to allow small parties of men on horseback to ride ahead to scout the terrain and to seek the best possibilities of passage for the following caravans. But even as they hoped they were leaving British oppression behind, they soon discovered that a new kind of menace lay before them.

Southern Africa of the early 1800's was a scene of immense human upheaval and turmoil among the large Bantu ethnic groups of the area. Famed Zulu chief Shaka had risen to unquestioned power among his people and had consolidated them into a feared fighting force. Showing genius for organization, discipline and battle maneuver, he succeeded in defeating one tribal group after another in pitched battle. While expanding the Zulu Kingdom, he was simultaneously provoking domino-like migrations of other tribal groups as they fled from his marauding Zulu forces. (6)

Not only was Chief Shaka very intelligent; he was also very brutal. He had learned to use terror as a powerful weapon against the people he sought to conquer and as a means of maintaining control over his expanding kingdom. His ruthless manner, which for so long served him so well, finally led to his undoing. It was in 1828 that Chief Shaka was assassinated by one of his principle cohorts, named Dingaan, who immediately installed himself as Shaka's successor. If somewhat less bloody in his methods, Dingaan was no less determined to defend and expand the kingdom he had usurped from his illustrious fallen predecessor.

It was at this juncture in Zulu history that the first probing caravans of Afrikaner immigrants began to make contact not only with them but with other ethnic groups which had been destabilized by the Zulu forces. Conflict was inevitable. The further the Dutch and their herds penetrated these Bantu areas, the more frequent became the armed skirmishes in which there was loss of life on both sides. Encountering growing opposition in the north, one large group of Dutch folk determined to turn to the east. Under the leadership of Andries Pretorius, the group found its way through the Drakensburg Mountains and attempted to enter the heart of Zulu land in what today is known as Natal Province.

The new Zulu chief Dingaan recognized immediately the threat this posed for him as chief and determined to crush the white-skinned invaders. Alerted to the news that he was raising an army of thousands of Zulu warriors, the Afrikaner caravaners chose their terrain carefully. Following the small Ncome River, they found a spot where it looped back on itself providing an oblong area basically surrounded on three sides by water. Pulling their caravan into this area, they established what, in their dialect, was known as a *laager*. Lining their sturdy wagons in close rank into a solid, circular wall they effectively blocked off the narrow neck of land. People and cattle then settled inside the perimeter of their *laager* to await the coming attack.

During a daylong effort the Zulu warriors attempted to overrun the Afrikaner encampment. Armed only with their animal hide shields and their spears, they first charged the wagon barricade. Hunkered down behind them with rifles the white defenders methodically shot down the charging bare-chested warriors at point-blank range. Realizing that the wagons presented a formidable obstacle, others attempted to attack on the flanks by crossing the water and climbing the embankments. But here too they encountered the same lethal fire from the Afrikaner perimeter. As the day waned, the water of the Ncome River literally ran red with Zulu blood. Toward sunset chief Dingaan gathered his remaining men and retreated. He and his army had suffered a crushing defeat. It was later reported that some 3,000 Zulu men had been killed. The Afrikaners had not suffered a single casualty. That day, December 16, 1838, was to become enshrined in Afrikaner legend. The Ncome River came eventually to be called the Blood River in their history. Above all else, the devout Dutch immigrants emerged from this day of bloody encounter convinced that the Lord had delivered them from "their enemies" and that a long sought homeland lay before them.

the long arm of the British

Retreating to the north with his followers, Chief Dingaan left a vacuum in the south of Zululand. Into this opening stepped a half brother named Mpande (pr. MPAH-ndeh). Having observed the awesome power of the Afrikaner riflemen, he chose to negotiate a political settlement with the newly-arrived whites. There resulted something called the Republic of Natal declared in 1839. British reaction was not long in coming. In 1843, by the simple expedient of annexation, the British brought the infant Republic under their jurisdiction.

Refusing to accept reimposed British rule, the Afrikaners loaded their wagons, rounded up their livestock and once again began a slow journey toward the north. Those from Natal were eventually joined by others who had temporarily remained on the west side of the Drakensberg Mountains and all moved northward till they came to the Vaal River. While some stayed to the south, others crossed and moved still further north.

Once again the Dutch migrants attempted to establish autonomous homelands. In 1852 a large area south of the Vaal River was declared to be the Orange Free State. Two years later an area of similar size north of the river was named the Transvaal Republic. When officially recognized in the 1850's by the British, the Afrikaners felt that at long last they had found a place to call home.

But there was more to come. In 1867 a fabulous deposit of diamonds was discovered at Kimberly in the western reaches of the Orange Free State. Recognizing the enormous significance of this find, the British attempted to bring the Free State under the British flag. This time, the Dutch settlers decided to resist. Organizing themselves into highly mobile commando units, the Afrikaner horsemen developed "hit and run" strategies of combat. In what came to be known as the First Boer War, there were a number of battles from which the Dutch emerged victorious.

When in 1886 the famed gold deposits of Witwatersrand (in the present day Johannesburg area) came to light, the British decided to bring these rich natural resources under their control at whatever price. Mounting and equipping an expeditionary force in England in 1899, the British unleashed what came to be known as the Second Boer War. There followed a bitter and protracted conflict. Though the British fielded a larger and more heavily armed fighting force, the mobile and determined Dutch commando units initially fought them to a standstill. When the British finally resorted to a scorched earth policy, however, the tide slowly turned against the Dutch. Burning fields and homesteads as they advanced and taking women and children as prisoners, the Dutch forces were slowly but surely deprived of help and resource. The end finally came in 1902. The Afrikaners had paid a terrible price for their resistance. One in seven of the men had died as victims of combat. Their homesteads lay in ruins. Many of their women and children had died of malnutrition and disease in the British prisoner of war camps. To the dramatic triumph of Blood River there was no sequel.

a smoldering dream

Denied political autonomy by their military defeat, the Afrikaners had no option but to submit to British authority. Under the British flag there soon emerged four self-governing areas: the Cape, Natal Province, The Free State and the Transvaal. In 1910 these four areas were declared to constitute the Union of South Africa which, in turn, became a Dominion of the British Crown.

In the early going, men of good will from both sides sought to achieve a reconciliation and blending of the two hostile groups. Led by General Louis Botha and General Jan Christiaan Smuts, the United Party was created. It is a measure of the positive view of European powers of that era that, after World War I, the Union of South Africa was granted an administrative mandate over the former German colony of South West Africa, today known as Namibia.

But as early as 1918 there was clear evidence that the Afrikaner spirit was alive and well for it was in that year there came into being something called, in Afrikaans, the *Broederbond*, i.e., "a band of brothers." A shadowy and highly secretive organization made up of Afrikaner men, it became a rallying force and a vehicle for generating and coordinating economic and political power within their community.

By 1924 two key political leaders had emerged who clearly embodied the deep-rooted differences which remained unchanged. They were General Jan Smuts of the British community and Afrikaner General James B. M. Hertzog. By 1926 the two groups were again on the verge of a political split. Already at this time General Hertzog was formulating and advocating a philosophy of "segregation of races." For a time the world depression of the 1930's forced the two factions to work together for the economic survival of their country.

But when their economy again rebounded, Hertzog led a strong dissident wing within the government and was able to initiate and secure passage of two significant acts - - "The Bantu Representation Act" which took the franchise away from black people in the Cape and set up indirect representation of blacks via whites in government. A second action was to pass the "Bantu Trust and Land Act" which laid the guidelines for the concept of "black homelands" and set in motion a process of acquiring land with this goal in mind. If a homeland sought by the Afrikaners by retreat and armed conflict had eluded them, perhaps there was another avenue open to them.

Then came 1938, the centennial year of what had by now become a hallowed event in Dutch history, the Battle of Blood River. Almost spontaneously the word spread across the Dutch farmlands. We are going to recondition our wagons, hitch up teams of oxen and make our way to a high bluff overlooking the city of Pretoria. And they did. Coming from all directions they converged on that bluff in their creaking, ox-drawn wagons to look out over the city of Pretoria below. A variety of dissident and dissatisfied Afrikaner orators rang the changes on themes of their pioneering history, their suffering and their ongoing hunger to one day be masters in their own house.

The oratory tapped deep wells of loyalty, patriotism and pride. As the rally came to a close and the wagons began to lumber their way back across the African countryside, there was a sense on the part of many that the embers of a smoldering dream had been fanned into flame.

When World War II erupted, it was over stiff Afrikaner opposition that Jan Smuts swung the support of the South African government to the Allied cause. In the national elections of 1948 in the aftermath of the war, Jan Smuts was defeated and a new government was headed by Afrikaner Prime Minister D.F. Malan. Heading a political group known as the National Party, it didn't take long for the new head of government to declare himself. Early in his regime Prime Minister Malan was quoted as accusing the previous government of "indifference towards and ineffectiveness in dealing with the color problem; of over taxation; neglect of overseas trade and of weakness in handling communism, the most dangerous of South Africa's enemies." (7)

It was further stated that the pivotal point of his new regime would be "a formula for political and social separateness or 'apartheid' for the White, Colored, Indian and Bantu population groups, to ensure the maintenance, protection and consolidation of the white race as the bearer of Christian civilization in South Africa and to enable it to fulfill its function of responsible trusteeship to guide the other groups toward eventual freedom in a peaceful manner." (8)

In brief, Prime Minister Malan stated clearly that he was going to reverse what he considered to have been the drift of the preceding government toward racial integration. He also was going to identify communism for the dangerous evil that it was and to declare any efforts to support it to be illegal in South Africa.

He was as good as his word. There soon followed an avalanche of legislation which focused on the issue of race relations: 1949 - - "The Group Areas Act" which authorized and plotted residential segregation based on race; 1950 - - The creation of "A Population Register" which introduced the passbook system and forbade mixed marriage; 1951 - - "The Bantu Authorities Act" which established a hierarchy of authority in the "black homelands;" 1953 - - "The Bantu Education Act" which placed all education of blacks in the hands of government thus removing missions and churches from the arena of public education; 1954 - - "The Bantu Resettlement Act" which authorized the forced relocation of blacks to what was considered to be their rural "tribal areas." It was explained that this was done in order to bring together those who "belong together."

After an interim period of leadership on the part of Prime Minister Johannes G. Strijdom, the elections of 1958 brought Dr. Hendrick F. Verwoerd to the powerful role of Prime Minister. It was he who more than any other was to develop the far reaching social philosophy of *apartheid* to its ultimate extreme. Under his leadership South Africa declared itself a republic and in 1961 the decision was made to withdraw from the British Commonwealth. Early in his regime he declared: "We see ourselves as a part of the western world, a true white state in Africa while not withstanding the possibility of granting a full future to the black man in our midst. We look upon ourselves as indispensable to the white world." Referring then to the necessity of friendship between white nations and the black states of Africa he added:" We are the link. We are white but we are in Africa. We have links with both and that lays upon us a special duty and we realize it." (9)

apartheid: its theory

An Afrikaans word meaning separateness, *apartheid* came to be an identifying and rallying term for a socio-political system methodically developed by the Afrikaners across a period of some four decades. Although the seeds of this concept were already present in the earlier era of the Union of South Africa, it was Prime Minister Verwoerd who began to develop the idea of racial separation as an all-encompassing political philosophy. Assassinated by a demented colored (i.e., mixed blood) clerk in 1966 after eight years as Prime Minister, he was succeeded by Balthazar J. Vorster who during the next eighteen years devoted all his energies to the implementation of the racial philosophy elaborated by his predecessors.

At first flush, given the historical and racial realities of southern Africa of the time, the concept of *apartheid* did not seem all that radical. The popular reasoning ran something like this: "The events of three centuries of history in southern Africa have placed us all, a mixture of peoples, where we are. We cannot rewrite the history of these past 300 years. This is the homeland of us all. We all have the right to order our own lives in the light of our own culture, language, traditions, beliefs and gifts. We all should be allowed to do so at our own tempo unhindered by others and in harmony and respect for one another. This being the case, we want to delineate geographical areas which are clearly designated as "homelands" for each of the major tribal groups as well as for the whites so as to permit independent life and pursuit of happiness for each group to take place."

apartheid: its theology

In many ways the Dutch Reformed Church had served as a rallying center for the Afrikaner people during their pioneering years of harsh conflict with the British and the fiercely resistant African tribal groups with whom they came in conflict. When in 1948 general elections swept Afrikaners into political power and they began to forge the political dogma of separateness, Dutch Reformed Church theologians of South Africa were also at work crafting a supportive theological platform to undergird it.

Steeped in the Dutch Reformed theology of John Calvin, the theme of predestination was part of their understanding of God's dealings with mankind across time. One student of this South African Church scene put it as follows: "Afrikaner Calvinists refer back to nineteenth century Dutch Church history to identify the stem of their philosophy, and beyond that time to the Synod of Dort in 1618-19 to locate the taproot of their faith. Here the doctrine of election was written into Dutch Reformed theology for all time." (10)

In all fairness, it must be stated that the South African Dutch Reformed Church has never taught that the black races are inherently inferior or even under "the curse of Ham" and thus should be relegated to roles of subservience. Nor is it true that the Church has ever taught that the Afrikaners are in some sense the "new Israelites" who have been ordered to occupy a "new Canaan" while driving out the "new black Canaanites" before them. There are, however, some clear DRC views regarding Scriptural teaching on race relations much of which is based upon creation narratives and the history of Genesis 1 - 11. John de Gruchy, a native-born South African lecturer in religious studies, speaks of two dominant themes in DRC teaching: "The first is that the Scriptures teach and uphold the essential unity of mankind and the primordial relatedness and fundamental equality of all peoples. The second and subsidiary conviction is that ethnic diversity is in its very origin in accordance with the will of God for this dispensation. Babel is the consequence not just of God's judgment on sin, but also of his preserving mercy (cf. Acts 17:27) effecting the fulfillment of his saving purposes. Thus while the unity of mankind is always the basic reality given in creation, there is also a given differentiation in creation. Furthermore, because of human sin, the unity of mankind has been seriously affected and can only be restored through God's redeeming grace in Christ. The ultimate restoration of this unity will only occur at the final coming of the kingdom of God." (11) De Gruchy observes further: "The theme of unity and diversity which is described initially in terms of Old Testament passages, is also developed on the basis of the New Testament. In specific circumstances and under specific conditions the New Testament makes provision for the . . . separate development of . . . various people in one country." (12) He then summarizes: " . . . the DRC rejects racial injustice and discrimination in principle. Equally clearly, the DRC accepts the policy of separate development." (13)

With such confluence of political and theological underpinnings, it is not surprising that the rhetoric of government leaders soon took on a crusade-like quality as church and nation came to be intermingled in Afrikaner thought. On one occasion Prime Minister Verwoerd stated: "Perhaps it was intended that we should have been planted here at the southern point within this crisis area so that from this resistance might emanate the victory whereby all that has been built up since the days of Christ may be maintained for the good of all mankind. May you have strength, people of South Africa, to serve the purpose for which you have been placed here!" (14)

apartheid: its reality

All of the altruistic language of church and national leaders notwithstanding, it soon became clear to all but the Afrikaners themselves that there was a rapidly widening and tragic gap between *apartheid*, the benign theory, and *apartheid*, the harsh reality.

The concept of separateness being the corner stone of Afrikaner political philosophy, there were many immediate implications for the black population. First, if people were to be grouped together according to their ethnicity, every person in South Africa needed to be classified as to race and, in the case of the African, by tribe as well. Thus there emerged four basic categories of people: white, black, colored (i.e., mixed blooded) and Asian. Meanwhile the government was busy in the process of determining where each group of people was to live. Seated at desks with maps before them, the architects of *apartheid* determined by pen strokes who was to live where. In urban areas, sections of towns were declared white, colored or Asian. As for blacks, the methodical Afrikaners designed what were called "townships" or "locations" at varying distances from the towns or cities in which black employees were obliged to live and from which they needed to commute daily to work in largely white owned business establishments and industries.

But for those blacks without employment, a massive forced relocation process was put in motion to what came to be known as "bantustans" or "black homelands." The dismal routine soon became all too familiar. One day a government representative would appear in a community issuing papers to all inhabitants informing them that their area had just been allocated to some other racial group and that they had a certain number of days to move to their new "location" or, if unemployed, to their new "homeland." Not infrequently, those served such notices were living where their parents before them had lived. There was land available for the cultivation of food and the grazing of their livestock. Furthermore it was land in which the bones of their forefathers lay buried. None of this made any difference. If on the appointed day the black residents had made no preparations, police simply entered homes, removed all belongings to the street upon which people and their possessions were loaded into waiting trucks and transported to their newly defined "home areas." If, as frequently happened, there was protest and opposition, simple homes were bulldozed and people removed by force. Upon arrival at their destinations, they were unceremoniously removed from the trucks often - - amidst bleak, arid surroundings. They typically found a row of latrines, rudimentary shelters, a water source at some distant stream, well or faucet and little else. The cavalier manner of the authorities seemed to say: "There, we have brought you to your own homeland. Enjoy!"

It did not take long for the stark injustice of the homeland scheme to become apparent to the whole world. First, the better farming and grazing areas of rural South Africa had long since been occupied by white settlers. Creating "homelands" for the African was all right with them as long as they and their acreage were not disturbed. The end result was that those areas eventually designated as "black" became a scattered, often disconnected jumble of inked in areas on the map. Not only were many of the homelands not contiguous, they also were in regions of marginal possibilities for sustaining life. Even rudimentary medical and educational facilities were often lacking. More harsh still was the lack of local employment and consequent inability of fathers to provide for their displaced families in their new locations.

It was the statistics which reflected most clearly the ghastly inequality of the entire scheme. Once the redrawn maps had been finalized, it was clear that if fully carried out, the homeland plan would one day try to cram 70% of the population into 13% of the land leaving 30% of the population (white, colored and Asian) to occupy 87% of the land. To this geographic imbalance was added the fact that the white areas englobed the best farming and grazing regions, the seaports and, above all, the country's industries and mineral wealth,

But this was only the beginning. Since the blacks were now "citizens" of their new "homelands," this meant they were no longer citizens of South Africa. Thus to travel outside their "countries," they required identity papers which came to be known as "passbooks." These had to be in the possession of every black person whenever he or she entered a "white" area. Not only did they include photos, complete identification and legal addresses, they also were required to contain an explanation for the black person's presence in a white area. The reasons were many. While the white minority wanted to move the black majority into homelands which frequently were distant from them, still they needed black laborers by the tens of thousands to work in the mines, in industry, in business places, and in their own homes as cooks, caretakers of their children and janitorial personnel. To accommodate such a labor force, black locations or townships were developed within commuting distances from the urban centers. By bus or train the black labor flowed into the centers in the morning and flowed back to the locations in the evening. They could rent but not own living quarters in these locations. At whatever time their passbooks no longer carried proof of local employment, they were liable for removal and forced return to their homeland. Many a suburban residential area made the calm assertion: "We are white by night."

In these large townships the government did make an effort to provide some medical and educational facilities under the motto "Separate but equal." Separate they were; equal they were not. In medical emergencies, white access to South Africa's skilled medical care was quick, efficient and sure. For blacks it often was a laborious, time-consuming process of waiting in lines and suffering indignities of scrutinized passbooks, required papers and abrupt questioning. White schools were well-staffed and well-equipped. Black schools frequently were overcrowded and poorly equipped. To this was added the irritating requirement to not only study Afrikaans as a language but, for a time, to even endure the aggravation of instruction in that language rather than in English. In this regard the Afrikaners exhibited a short memory. Their own forebears had earlier rebelled against English authorities in the Cape over the issue of language. Now they were demonstrating the same sort of arrogance and insensitivity vis-à-vis African students in their schools.

And in the workplace, black folk soon found the long arm of *apartheid*, as well. Separateness meant that there were certain categories of employment to which they could not aspire because they had been categorized as "white positions." Education, experience and seniority of black personnel were all simply ignored as young whites were catapulted through the companies' ranks ahead of them. And, in those rather frequent situations where blacks and whites were doing comparable work with comparable skills, the blacks discovered that under *apartheid* there were also black salary scales and white salary scales, something which made it impossible to receive equal pay for equal work.

To this South African labor scene was added yet another powerfully disruptive ingredient. The reefs of the famous gold deposits of the region do not lie parallel to the surface of the earth but rather slant gently to ever deeper levels. This, in turn, results in ever greater heat and danger for the mining crews. The mining corporations need a large, constant source of cheap labor. To keep up their reservoir of supply, thousands of men are hired in adjacent countries such as Lesotho, Swaziland and Botswana. Although the wages offered are low by international standards, compared to the local economies of their own countries, they are still attractive enough that men will accept the shriveling heat and constant danger to sign up again and again for six-, nine-, and twelve-month labor contracts. Once in South Africa, however, they are housed in "bachelor dorms" on the mining complexes. Separated from wives and families for extended periods of time, social problems of every description abound, not the least of which are prostitution, abuse of alcohol and ethnic clashes.

apartheid: its mindless bureaucracy

Externally, world outcry against *apartheid* in the 1970's and 80's was mounting as more and more governments condemned the system. Here and there boycotts were taking shape, some with a focus on the sports world, others upon the provision of military and scientific equipment and petroleum products. Internally African protest was also rising in intensity. As pressures mounted, the Afrikaner determination to resist grew apace. Orators increasingly made reference to their troubled history, their sufferings and their ultimate triumph over all odds. They had pulled their wagons into *laagers* before; they would do so again if need be.

Driven by a deeply ingrained Dutch penchant for thoroughness and their commitment to a philosophy of separateness which they saw as their only hope for preserving a homeland for themselves, enormous effort was invested in trying to make the machinery of separateness work. Since racial identification was a key ingredient to the whole endeavor, meticulous and methodical efforts were made to determine the genealogy of every nonwhite in the country - - even to the registering of l/16th or 1/32nd of black blood which, in turn, placed the individual in question into an all encompassing social category. But it was a process shot through with absurdities and arbitrary decisions. In a Time magazine cover story from the era, it was reported: "Chinese are classified as a colored sub-group; the Japanese in South Africa who are mostly foreign business men, are regarded as 'honorary whites' - - thereby illustrating the comment of Frantz Fanon, the black radical writer, that 'you are rich because you are white but you are also white because you are rich.' [The same concessions were made for diplomats from independent African countries.] A black beauty queen who won a holiday at a Cape hotel was refused accommodations because the hotel did not have international status. In a reshuffle of Durban's elaborately segregated beaches, Indians took over a formerly white beach but discovered they could not use the restaurant there; its designation had not been changed." (15)

Over time, 300 separate pieces of legislation were crafted to spell out *apartheid*'s response to every conceivable contingency. The interpretation and enforcement of this maze of laws lay largely in the hands of Afrikaner bureaucrats for whom the high-flown language of their political and church leaders had scant import. Maligned by the international community and all too aware of the building resentment of an overwhelming black majority around them, they regarded *apartheid* not in philosophical or theological terms but as a bastion constructed for their protection and their preservation as a people. Thus they sat behind their desks in their crisply pressed uniforms, stony-faced and hard-eyed. No matter what the indignity, hardship, frustration, injustice or outright havoc and suffering wreaked upon the helpless Africans standing before them, the response was always the same: "This is the law and you will abide by it."

apartheid: its efforts to maintain control

With mounting external outcry and growing internal pressure, a siege mentality began to set in. More and more it was claimed that the intrigue of foreign powers was largely responsible for South Africa's internal problems. International communism and Russia, in particular, became the ultimate enemies. It cannot be denied that during the cold war era Russia did have more than passing interest in the great mineral resources of southern Africa and its strategic location on the tip of the African continent. In that climate it became easy for the South African government to falsely characterize African protest of whatever kind as communist inspired agitation in their midst. To counter these dangerous forces, real and imagined, a sophisticated security force was developed with a network of informers both black and white. Arbitrary arrest and detainment became more and more routine. Prison populations grew steadily and police interrogations became increasingly more brutal and bloody.

In the whole process, Robben Island became a term which stirred increasing dread in African hearts. A small rocky island just off Cape Town, it was made a center for long-term incarceration of political prisoners. Treatment of the detainees varied from time to time as prison administrators and guards were rotated. Humiliation, menace, abuse and starvation were at times used to torment and cow prisoners into submission as vindictive Afrikaner personnel served terms of service there. Across the years of the *apartheid* regime, a long series of African political leaders were confined there. Among them was a young man from the Transkei who, with keen intellect and immense courage, succeeded in making his island cell the heart of political resistance and influence which eventually led to the demise of *apartheid*. His name: Nelson Mandela.

apartheid: its walls

In their investigative travel in the spring of 1970, Don Jacobs and Jim Bertsche traveled by road through the Transvaal and the Orange Free State, the heart of Afrikanerland. One day, lunch time found them passing through a small, rural town. The center piece of this village was the church. High walls in red brick were capped by a high peaked roof and a slim steeple reaching up toward the blue sky overhead. It was set in a large green lawn which showed obvious signs of careful clipping, watering and grooming. Around the entire church grounds were evenly-spaced low brick pillars from which were draped white painted lengths of chain to mark off the terrain. Ample parking area was carefully laid out near the sanctuary entrance.

It was not a Sunday but evidence was on every hand that this was a revered and oft frequented hub of that Afrikaner community. Scattered in all directions from that little country town the members were out on their farms and in their places of business. But on Sunday mornings they came to their church - - scrubbed, carefully dressed, Bibles in hand to worship, to pray and to listen to serious and often lengthy sermons in their cherished Afrikaans language. They were pious people who took their religion seriously. Evidence of this commitment to church and faith is the fact that even while defending the socio-political concept of racial separateness, they nonetheless were also committed to mission outreach. Proof of this is the large number of DRC missionaries who were commissioned and supported across the years to minister in African, colored and Asian communities. It was in response to this energetic and faithful outreach that there came into being large DRC synods in all three of these communities.

But while the fruits of their labors were greeted with joy and gratitude, their brothers and sisters in Christ needed to organize, meet and worship "separately." *Apartheid* cast its long shadow over the body of Christ as well. To be sure they were all "one in the Lord" in a spiritual sense, but there were "practical matters" which made it wise and even necessary to remain apart in the flesh.

Passing the beautifully-kept church grounds, the two white travelers pulled up in front of a little combination cafe/grocery store. Walking up the steps they were immediately confronted by two doors. Though unmarked, it was perfectly clear which door they were expected to use. Entering the right hand door they stood in a pleasant, brightly painted tea room with grocery items ranged on shelves along the wall. Little tables were covered with crisp linens, china and silverware. After being seated, a white waitress pleasantly took their order. While waiting for their food, the screen door opened and in walked a resident of the little country town. Clothed in a carefully ironed cotton print dress, her gray hair was neatly swept back into a bun behind her head and topped with a straw hat adorned with a floral motif. Her arms and face were sun tanned and her hands eloquently reflected their acquaintance with long years of hard work. She carefully checked the prices on the shelved food items, placing a few in her little market basket while returning others.

As Bertsche sat observing her, there came to mind the image of his Aunt Lizzie whom he had known as a growing boy amidst the flat farmland of central Illinois. They both projected images and personalities which bespoke integrity, fortitude, frugality and great self confidence. Aunt Lizzie was a Mennonite whose roots went back to Alsace on the French/German border in Europe. The elderly lady, shopping in the rural South African tea room that day, was Dutch Reformed whose ancestry undoubtedly took her to Holland. The migration of their forebears were similarly-rooted in religious convictions and the longing to find a place where they could worship as they wished. Aunt Lizzie's ancestors had migrated to North America. The ancestors of the self-possessed Afrikaner woman in that little tea room, that day, had journeyed to South Africa.

Lunch finished and paid for, the two men stepped back out on the porch and lingered long enough to take a look through the door on the left. A long wall separated the rectangular building reaching back to the single kitchen. Along the rear was a bare wooden counter; along the two walls were backless benches. Just at that moment a black man received a platter of food unceremoniously shoved to him across the bare counter.

Without comment from either the server or the recipient, he took his plate, retreated to a spot on a well-worn bench and proceeded to eat in silence. His food and ours had come from a common source but we had each eaten it in the starkly dissimilar and unequal circumstances imposed upon us by *apartheid*.

the *Voortrekker* Monument

The same high bluff overlooking Pretoria which had been the gathering point for oxen-drawn wagons in December 1938 to commemorate the centennial of the Battle of Blood River became, in time, the site of a towering edifice of masonry known as the *Voortrekker* (i.e., pioneer trekkers) Monument. Standing high against the skyline of the countryside, it was designed and built to be an enduring memorial to Afrikaner history and spirit. It is approached by a wide flight of steps which give entrance, first of all, to an exterior plaza surrounded by a low enclosure carrying in chiseled relief the likeness of covered wagons and teams of oxen. Entering the edifice, one stands immediately in a circular rotunda. Once again there are presented, on the interior walls, a series of marble engravings depicting key events in the history of the Afrikaner people. At the center of the floor there is a large opening which affords a view of a lower level the predominant feature, of which, is an enormous black block of stone mounted on a low base. High overhead, in the curving vault of the roof structure, is a slot through which, each December 16, rays of the sun fall directly upon the memorial block below. Again there is a series of tableaux depicting key events in the history of the Afrikaner people - - - this time in needle craft, the handiwork of eight women done over a nine year period using 130 different shades of yarn. Off to a side in a crypt a flame flickers representing the Afrikaners' undying remembrance of who they are and what they intend to remain.

Perhaps nothing captures better the spirit and aura of the lower level of that shrine than the first verse from the South African national anthem of that era: "Ringing out from our blue heavens from our deep seas breaking round; Over everlasting mountains where the echoing crags resound; From our plains where creaking wagons cut their trains into the earth, calls the spirit of our country, of the land that gave us birth. At thy call we shall not falter, firm and steadfast we shall stand; At thy will to live or perish, O South Africa, our dear land."

haunting parallels

Across a plaza from the memorial is a museum. For a Mennonite, a visit to this place is an arresting and sobering experience. The entire display could be picked up and set down in Steinbach, MB, or Henderson, NE, or Wichita, KS and it would fit perfectly. All the artifacts of a rugged, difficult, pioneering era of an agrarian people are there: pitch forks, shovels and mauls fashioned from wood; the battered high wheeled wagons; the paraphernalia required for harnessing animals to work implements; plows and wooden toothed harrows; an anvil bolted to a hardwood stump; the cradle scythe, the wooden churns, bowls and ladles of a frontier kitchen - - and leather bound Bibles.

It is perfectly clear. The Mennonite pioneers of North America and the Afrikaners of Southern Africa have shared many common traits and experiences. Jim Juhnke, the MCC program director in Botswana in the early 1970's, reflected on these similarities in a perceptive paper: "Mennonites, more than most people, ought to be able to understand the Afrikaner folk who have established their homeland in South Africa. Both the Mennonites and the Afrikaners are hard working rural folk who trace their history to the Protestant Reformation in 16th century Europe. The durable virtues of Mennonite life are likewise the strength of Afrikaner culture. Both Mennonites and Afrikaners are religious minorities who left their place of origin. The Mennonites or Anabaptists were left wing reformers starting in Switzerland and the Netherlands who were driven out by an intolerant religious-political establishment. The Afrikaner were originally a Calvinist minority in the predominantly Catholic southern interior provinces of the Netherlands. . . . The Afrikaners, like the Mennonites, have a history of migrations. Time and again they have been led to pull up stakes and move to new frontiers where they could live out God's will as they understood it." (16)

In his paper Juhnke went on to name a number of major similarities in the early history of the two peoples: the family as a crucial institution; worship a family affair led by a patriarch; outsiders accepted into ethnic communities if they adopted the prevailing way of life, language and religion; the family the teacher of strict moral values; deeply religious people who believed their piety set them apart from a sinful world; a keen sense of difference between the church and the world; the shared trauma of trying to cope with the impact of an increasingly urbanized society and an economy which they could not control; and the gradual migration of youth toward the glitter of the cities leaving parents and grandparents with the fear that they might "barter their honorable heritage and faith for a pot of urban glitter and material profit." (17)

But if there were striking similarities in their experience and histories, there also were fundamental differences. Juhnke highlights some of these as well: "The Afrikaners succeeded in developing a successful nationalist movement while the Mennonites have remained a fragile and homeless religious-ethnic group. The Afrikaners engaged indigenous peoples in bloody combat to establish a homeland. They created their own language and literature." (18)

apartheid; its ultimate tragedy

A small, white minority, the Afrikaner people had sought a way to preserve a future and homeland for themselves and their descendants in a part of the world to which their forebears had come hundreds of years earlier. It was not that they were an inherently evil people who had deliberately set out to create an evil system. But with passing time, they found themselves increasingly trapped within a prison of their own making. If *apartheid* had its flaws, they could envision no alternative. Furthermore they were greatly influenced by the government-controlled media which constantly produced programming with carefully crafted versions of news which shielded the South African white population in general from the harsh realities of *apartheid* while continually casting South Africa as a beleaguered bastion of white Christian civilization on the tip of the African continent.

So with dogged determination and ever increasing brutality they sought to enforce their "solution" to the utmost of their ability and resources. In the process, *apartheid* became a vicious, two-edged sword which cut in both directions deeply wounding the spirit and psyche of both blacks and whites. With passing time sheer self-interest and fear more and more became the driving force. Simultaneously the white population in general and the Afrikaners in particular became increasingly rigid, unfeeling and unwilling to face the reality of the dehumanizing havoc they were inflicting upon the black population all around them, an overwhelming majority of whom, ironically, also professed a Christian faith.

For the millions of blacks upon whom this "solution" was thrust, it was becoming more and more insupportable with each passing day. Allan Boesak, a widely-known leader of the black DRC of South Africa, said it well: "Whatever grandiloquent ideal this ideology may represent for white people, for Blacks it means bad housing, being underpaid, pass laws, influx control, migrant labor, groups areas, resettlement camps, inequality before the law, fear, intimidation, white bosses and black informers, condescension and paternalism; in a word, Black powerlessness." (19)

An even deeper tragedy was that the Dutch Reformed Church became enmeshed in the same system of injustice. One observer of the scene put it starkly as follows: " Today . . . after a half century of Christian nationalism, we stand before the terrifying reality of an Afrikaner nationalism which also controls the religious life of the Afrikaner instead of the other way around." (20)

As the Mennonites started arriving on the scene in southern Africa in the late 1960's and early 70's, they found an entire nation in which whites and blacks seemed in the grip of a vortex which was slowly but surely sucking them all into what appeared to be an inescapable abyss. More than one arriving Mennonite had occasion to ponder out loud: "For what reason is it that the Lord has seen fit to guide our steps to the southern tip of Africa at such a time as this?"

CHAPTER 49   LESOTHO: A PLACE TO START

the land of King Moshoeshoe (pr. moh-SHWAY-shway)

In the reporting done by Don Jacobs and Jim Bertsche after their first trip to southern Africa in the spring of 1970, the little country of Lesotho (pr. lay-SOO-too) was described in the following terms: "Lesotho, a country of rugged beauty, is the product of an interesting chapter of the tumultuous flow of southern African history over the past 150 years. Sitting on a high hill overlooking the little capital town of Maseru [pr. mah-SAY-roo] is a monument bearing the bronze likeness of King Moshoeshoe I who is honored as the founder of the present Sotho [pr. SOO-too] nation. During the murderous military expansion of the famed Zulu tribesmen under their Chief Shaka in the early 1800's, Chief Moshoeshoe elected to lead his people northward into the broken terrain of the Maluti Mountains where, in 1824, he chose a towering, flat-topped butte as a site around which to form his new kingdom." (1)   Known in the Sotho language as Thaba Bosiu (pr. TAH-bah boh-SEE-yoo), meaning "mountain of night," it could be scaled only by a few, easily defended steep footpaths. It quickly became an unassailable fortress for him and his people.

His fame spread and soon other chiefs came requesting to become part of his kingdom. A man of great innate wisdom, the King realized that the future of his people lay not in armed conflict but in peaceful cohabitation with those around them. Desiring to inculcate in his people a true love for peace, he sent word requesting Christian missionaries. In 1833 a three-man delegation, representing the Paris Evangelical Missionary Society (PEMS) arrived at his mountain fortress. Led by Eugene Casalis, the PEMS soon established its first mission post on a tract of land given them by the King some 25 miles to the south at a place called Morija (pr. maw-REE-jah). Casalis forged a friendship with Moshoeshoe which was to endure for the King's lifetime. The French missionary came to play not only the role of a trusted counselor but, eventually, functioned as the King's de facto minister of foreign affairs.

But on the heels of the missionaries came other less welcome Europeans. Wishing to escape the influence and control of the British in the Cape area, increasing numbers of Dutch settlers were joining the historic northward trek across the veld of south central Africa and soon Moshoeshoe's kingdom was surrounded by these Dutch folk who were intent upon establishing a new nation of their own. Friction between the two groups was inevitable since they both sought to control and use the same low lands. After a series of clashes, King Moshoeshoe requested British protection. In 1868 a proclamation was issued stating that henceforth Basutoland, as it was known at that time, was to be regarded as a Protectorate of the British Crown. Having at last secured a promise of stability for his Kingdom, Moshoeshoe two years later turned his chieftainship over to his son Letsie (pr. lay-TSEE-ay).

For the aged King there yet remained one major desire - - to bear public witness to his Christian faith. Encouraged already for years by his missionary friends to make a public profession of his faith, he had hesitated. Now relieved of his responsibilities as king, he set a day for his baptism. Invitations went out to his people to congregate for the momentous event. Sadly, the venerable leader died the morning before his baptism was to take place. Many people who arrived anticipating an occasion of joy participated, rather, in the funeral and burial of this remarkable man on his mountain top.

Sam Mohono

Given the political uncertainty and the complicated church picture in the early 1970's in Lesotho, it was all-important that Mennonites proposing to begin work there should find someone who knew the country and its people well and who would respond frankly to their questions. Fortunately, such a person was found immediately.

A towering, large-framed, balding man with a gray-flecked beard, a deep rumbling voice and a slow, deliberate manner of speech, S.A. Mohono was found on Jacob and Bertsche's first visit in the modest office of the Lesotho Bible Society in Maseru. Born in Lesotho, educated in the Republic of South Africa and married to Emily, a very able and articulate Zulu wife, he had for some years served in the Republic of the South Africa Sunday School Union and a Youth Hostel Association. When the South Africa Bible Society sought for someone to serve as secretary for a branch office in Maseru, Sam Mohono was invited to assume that post. (The Lesotho office eventually established its autonomy vis-à-vis the South Africa Society.)

Articulate, well-read and deeply committed to his own people, he was equally at home in the saddle of a Lesotho mountain pony and at a conference table with Bible Society personnel in Capetown. These two worlds easily intersected in his office under his administration.

In the manner of his people, he was most gracious and yet reserved in the initial 1970 meeting with Mennonite personnel. In the way of the African everywhere, he was unobtrusively observant and in the course of conversation was forming opinions of the white visitors who had arrived unannounced in his office. After all, the name Mennonite meant little to him.

In 1972, after the April 30 - May 1 consultation in Maseru, Jim Bertsche and Ray Brubacher stayed on for further investigation of possible openings for MCC and/or CIM ministry in the country. Once again Sam Mohono was sought out. This time he spoke of a Christian Council in the country and arranged a meeting with its officers in his own office. (2)

As a result of these discussions, a tentative set of agreements emerged: "That there is interest in and opportunity for Mennonite witness and service in Lesotho; that Mennonite entry into the country should be under the auspices of the Christian Council rather than under any particular church group; that the three churchmen with whom we had held discussions would report to the full Council and press for action; that a first priority for MCC should be teacher placement at the LEC's [Lesotho Evangelical Church; the outgrowth of the historic work of the PEMS in the country] trade school at Quthing; that CIM's first placement should be at the LEC's youth camp *Mophato* (pr. moh-PAH-toh), at their station Morija, if someone with training for youth work could be found; and that any further negotiations would await official correspondence from the officers of the Christian Council." (3)

In a concluding paragraph of a report to the AIMM Board it is stated: "If we feel that we are looking for a place where we can enter under our own flag and begin immediately with a program of evangelism and church planting, Lesotho does not seem to be the place. But if we share the interest and concern of the broader Mennonite household for that troubled, tense and strategic part of Africa, and if we are prepared to regard the first term of CIM personnel in that country as an exploratory term where even as they pursue an unhurried investigation of the possibilities of long-term CIM involvement . . . they plug into local church life, Lesotho . . . seems like a good opportunity." (4)

AIMM's first missionaries in Southern Africa

Even before the April/May 1972 Maseru consultation, AIMM staff had been in touch with Allen and Marabeth Loewen Busenitz, a new candidate couple who expressed keen interest in an assignment to Africa. Allen had served three years in Tanzania as a TAP teacher. While in graduate school, they both had been active in the local chapter of Inter-Varsity Christian Fellowship. Both had their teaching credentials. Following the conversations with Christian Council officers in Maseru about a possible opening at *Mophato* adjacent to the LEC station of Morija, planning for the Busenitz assignment was soon under way.

Preparation on the home end, however, soon ran ahead of the ecumenical process in Lesotho. In spite of the encouraging dialogue which had been held with Christian Council of Lesotho (CCL) personnel, no correspondence was forthcoming. Letters addressed to them from Elkhart remained unanswered. One final effort was needed. En route back to Zaire in the fall of 1971, Jim Bertsche was asked to revisit Lesotho and to pursue further the discussions held earlier that same year. It was soon discovered that while sincere and well meaning, the Council officers had overstepped themselves in suggesting an AIMM placement with the LEC.

If such a placement was to happen, the LEC leaders would do their own negotiating and issue their own invitation!

This time opportunity was sought to meet with the LEC Executive Committee. It was indeed true that they had a lovely youth camp situated at the edge of Morija Station which had been built with funds donated by the World Council of Churches. There was large dorm, dining and activity space but at that time it was largely unused since their previous director of youth activity had served out his contract. As the qualifications and gifts of the AIMM's candidate couple were reviewed and they were offered to the LEC with all support costs assured, an invitation was promptly extended and housing promised.

It was in January 1973 that Allen and Marabeth Busenitz arrived in Lesotho and settled amidst the surroundings of a station whose history went back to the founding years of that mountain Kingdom. As they began their pioneering role with AIMM, Allen - - at the request of MCC - - also served part time as the first country representative for MCC personnel who were placed in the following months.

searching for a focus

If the immediate assignment for the Busenitz couple in early 1973 was clear, there was considerable less clarity as to AIMM's place and role on the broader scene in southern Africa. To be sure, interest and motivation were high. The ominous escalation of racial tension was frequently headlined in the world press. Stories and statistics poured out of that region detailing in stark clarity the inhuman impact of the system of apartheid upon the black population. If any place in the Africa needed a witness to God's healing and reconciling love, surely this was it. And since it was not possible to secure residence or ministry permits within the Republic, Lesotho seemed an excellent opening. An autonomous country totally embedded within the Republic of South Africa, (RSA) it offered opportunity for AIMM personnel to live and work literally within the sight and sound of the powerful neighbor which surrounded it on all sides.

But establishing an AIMM presence in Lesotho was one thing. Discerning and articulating a longer range direction was something else. Underlying all of the preliminary discussion and planning for AIMM arrival in southern Africa was the assumption that its ultimate objective was the planting of a Mennonite Church. After all, was this not the reason for which AIMM had been brought into existence in the first place? Had this not been the centerpiece of its work across the years in Zaire? Once on the scene, however, the discovered reality of a South African Christian presence which dated back literally hundreds of years quickly gave rise to a persistent, troubling question: In that setting and at that point in its history, was it AIMM's mission to seek to plant yet another church among the many already on the scene or, rather, to adopt a servanthood role vis-à-vis the churches and Christian organizations found there? Determined not to make hasty judgments, AIMM counseled the Busenitzes to work as closely as possible with the Lesotho Evangelical Church in their youth program while observing and assessing other possible needs and opportunities for ministry within the country. That there were a variety of needs quickly became apparent.

the Lesotho Evangelical Church

Perhaps nothing quite symbolized the tradition and self-understanding of the LEC at the point of AIMM arrival like its historic red brick church at Morija. Set amidst towering pine trees on the rolling acreage of the station, it pushes its sharply pitched red roof and high steeple toward the blue southern African sky. Inside, at one end, an elevated platform and pulpit immediately catch the eye. A choir loft overhangs the rear of the sanctuary at the other end. A double row of high, rough, wooden pillars march the length of the edifice carrying the weight of the roof. They are the masts of sailing ships which were salvaged at the Cape during an earlier pioneering era. Though about a thousand miles to the southwest of Morija, they were nonetheless laboriously transported across the intervening distance via teams of oxen.

Early AIMM missionaries who attended worship services in this venerable setting were quickly struck by the enduring imprint that the French Reformed missionaries had left upon this Church across more than a century of ministry. Liturgical patterns of worship, European hymns and the use of books of prayer were much in evidence. Whereas, in the 1970's, church leaders across black Africa were enthusiastically seeking ways of making their worship experience more African, it seemed that the LEC leadership was intent on preserving the mood and form of worship brought to them over a century earlier. Along with the formality of worship there was an established clergy and church hierarchy which seemed much concerned to maintain and exert firm authority over the Church and its membership.

Across the long years of its history, the LEC had also acquired an impressive array of institutions. To start with there was *Mophato*, the youth campground at the edge of Morija to which the Busenitz couple had been assigned to give leadership. The choice of name, meaning "circumcision" in the Sesotho language, in and of itself reflected an imaginative approach to a church-sponsored youth program within that culture. Believing, like many other African church leaders, that traditional rites of circumcision served some valuable purposes for African youth, effort was made to tap into this tradition in the layout of the camp and in the sorts of teaching and training offered there. (5) Built primarily with funds from the WCC it was hoped that it could serve not only the needs of the LEC itself, but also serve as an ecumenical center for youth ministries for groups both within and outside the country.

But this was only a beginning. The first AIMM visitors in the early 1970's discovered other LEC installations at Morija as well: two high schools, one for boys and another for girls (the boys school has the distinction of being the oldest educational institution in the entire country); and a theological institute intended for the formation of church leaders and a training school for evangelists. All of these schools were short on qualified teachers.

Morija also was the site of a widely-known and respected medical center called Scott Memorial Hospital. Staffed by a mix of European and African personnel, the institution drew people from far and wide which typically resulted in crowded facilities and overworked personnel. Also on the grounds was a busy press which provided printed materials both for the LEC and other organizations both within and outside Lesotho.

Seventy five miles to the south, at a town called Quthing (pr. koo with a click - TING), was another historic LEC institution known as Leloaleng (pr. LAY-luah-LENG). Originally a British government post, it was taken over by the French missionaries in 1879 and more buildings were added. This was the site of an LEC trade school which across the years had offered Basotho youth training in mechanics, leather work, wood working and other vocational skills. It, like the schools at Morija, was in need of more staff and equipment.

In addition to its training centers, the LEC also sponsored a network of primary schools which lay all through the valleys and across the mountains of Lesotho. Harking back to an earlier era of remarkable vigor and growth which made the Church a household word all across the little Kingdom, by the 1970's many of these rural schools needed repair and new equipment.

The LEC eventually offered AIMM yet another intriguing window of opportunity, this being the periodic appointment of a Protestant chaplain to the campus at Roma, the country's small university. Founded originally as a Catholic institution, it was nationalized at the time of political independence. While a Catholic chaplaincy was maintained on campus, the government also stipulated that there be Anglican and Protestant counterparts. LEC being by far the major Protestant group in the country, it was granted the privilege of naming people of its choice to this post. Across time the appointee had come to carry three primary responsibilities: teaching some classes in the school of religion, providing pastoral leadership for an area LEC parish and part-time teaching at the LEC theological school at nearby Morija.

Added to the burden of its institutions, the AIMM found the LEC much impacted by and involved in the smoldering political situation of the time. A deep political cleavage separated the Basotho into two opposing camps which saw the influential Catholics backing Leabua (pr. lay-ah-BOO-ah) Jonathan, the incumbent Prime Minister. Originally elected to power in 1966, he ran again in the elections of 1970. When it became apparent that he and his Basutoland National Party would not again receive a majority vote he cancelled the elections and held on to power suspending the country's constitution in the process. Protestants, meanwhile, were largely supportive of the opposition group known as the Basutoland Congress Party which was seen by the government not only as political opponents but as subversive, as well. LEC leaders consequently were typically viewed with suspicion by authorities and were frequently placed under surveillance.

All in all, the AIMM found in the LEC of the early 1970's a large church with a long history of which it could justifiably be proud. It literally was woven into the very fabric of Sotho society and its birth as a nation. Possessed of a dynamic spirit of evangelism in its earlier years, it had blanketed the little Kingdom with its message and ministry. But by the 1970's, some 140 years into its history, there was the clear impression of a church which was suffering battle fatigue. Much of its vitality and resources were concentrated in keeping its institutions and church structures afloat. It was steeped in tradition but was no longer a growing church. Rather there was something of a siege mentality, a tendency to see itself menaced both by the government and the Catholic hierarchy of the country. (6) If AIMM was looking for opportunities to meet need in Lesotho, the LEC offered a variety of openings.

the Christian Council of Lesotho (CCL)

One of the AIMM's earliest contacts in Lesotho had been with this body. Organized in 1964, it brought together representatives of the six principal Christian groups of the country. (7) In early AIMM encounters with this body, discussions were both informative and visionary. Council concerns were particularly expressed regarding the need for joint church ministry to prisoners, refugees from the Republic of South Africa next door, alcoholics and the handicapped. Also high on their list were the growing numbers of unemployed youth and migrant workers who were absent for long periods of time from their homes, something which placed immense strain on Basotho families and marriages.

With some modest funding obtained from outside sources, small office space was secured and some headway made in refugee services. Caught in the social and ecumenical pressures of the time, however, much of the ministry envisioned at its inception simply remained on paper. As a matter of fact, AIMM's early plan to enter the country under Council sponsorship had proved to be unworkable. There was, however, one Council initiative which had, by the early 1970's, achieved considerable prominence - - the *Thaba Khupa* Ecumenical Training Institute (pr. tah-bah KHOO-pah). It was born of the deep concern of the Council for young students who were annually culled out of the country's schools due to insufficient grades. Without vocational skills their only alternative was to look for jobs in the neighboring Republic of South Africa in its mines, factories or homes of white South Africans as domestic help. Failing that, they simply joined the already swollen ranks of the country's unemployed.

A major conference was held in 1970 at the instigation of the Christian Council. The focus of the envisioned training program was to be on intensive farming of vegetable and fruit plots, fruit preservation, the creation of fish ponds and training in a variety of handcrafts. Funding was secured from a variety of overseas sources; buildings were erected at a place called *Thaba Khupa* and the first students were enrolled. Critical to the success of this venture were staff people who could bring the required enthusiasm and skills to the training venture. It was not long after AIMM's arrival in the country that inquiry was made as to possible Mennonite help in staffing this pioneering venture.

the African Federal Church Council (AFCC)

For the AIMM, an early key African figure in Lesotho was Sam Mohono. Always courteous, always well informed, always available and helpful, always a careful listener and a careful respondent to questions, he had been of tremendous help to the early AIMM delegations which visited Lesotho. Soon after their arrival, the Busenitzes also made his acquaintance and regularly found their way to his modest office in Maseru where he served as the Secretary of the Bible Society of Lesotho.

While welcomes to his office were always warm and genuine, getting to know this gifted man well took some time. He, after all, was gradually forming his own assessment as to who Mennonites were and what had really brought them to his country. But as friendship grew and confidence deepened, a clearer profile emerged. He was well-educated, well-traveled and had a broad variety of experience in church related service both in the Republic and in Lesotho. He was a talented conversationalist and speaker. A weekly radio program had provided him voice and name recognition across his country. He met people easily and had a gift for relating to any audience. He derived as much pleasure from leading a group of school children in choruses as he did in sitting at a table with church leaders discussing Bible Society issues and the distribution of Christian literature. He had a gift for inspiring and enabling others for service. No fellow African was so humble, no new missionary so insecure but that a time of conversation with him left them encouraged and renewed for their task.

Eventually the time came when Mohono shared with his AIMM friends that he was the son of the cofounder of a "spiritual church" in Lesotho named "Moshoeshoe's Berea Bible Reading Church," or as it was commonly known in its shortened form, *Kereke ea Moshoeshoe*, i.e., "The Church of Moshoeshoe." He and his wife were members of this Church. In a biographical sketch of the founder of this church written by Mohono the following information is found: Its origins go back to 1907 at which time there appeared a prophet named Walter Matitta (pr. mah-TEE-tah) within the church of the Paris Evangelical Missionary Society. He said he had been ill for nine months and then died. He returned from death in that same year and thereafter began a ministry of preaching and healing which drew large crowds. In 1914 he founded a "Nazarite Association." In 1916 they produced their own constitution.

Hundreds joined this association and were described as "sincere, humble, all loving and they studied the Bible enthusiastically and were steadfast in prayer. They sang freely and wept freely. They were charismatic." By 1919 the PEMS church no longer tolerated them. When Matitta was expelled, one thousand believers followed him. Among them was R.M. Mohono, Sam Mohono's father. Thousands more had been followers as well but due to various PEMS pressures, they decided to remain within the mission church. For over a year Matitta and his followers were without a church home. In 1921 it was decided to organize a church of their own. After deliberation they decided to call themselves "Moshoeshoe's Berea Bible Readers Church." The church was officially organized in January 1922, and in time established branches in the Republic of South Africa in the Free State, the Transvaal and the Natal and Cape regions. In 1917 Matitta organized the "African Federal Council of Churches." He died in 1935. (8)

The time then came when Mohono revealed to AIMM personnel that the Council of Churches founded by Matitta was a continuing organization in Lesotho. There were numerous other African Churches in the country beside the one co-founded by his father. Some of them were members of this Council and held annual meetings to worship together and to share their experiences, problems and hopes with each other. There was much they wanted to accomplish individually and together in their country but their needs were many. Might their cause be one in which the AIMM would take an interest?

the Maseru United Church

Almost immediately after their arrival in Lesotho, the Busenitzes began hearing of a small church in Maseru, the little town which served as the capital of the country. It was made up primarily of English-speaking expatriates who were in Lesotho under contract with a variety of businesses and government services. By 1973, the Busenitzes discovered, church activities were limited primarily to weekly Sunday evening services. Making their way to Maseru one weekend the Busenitzes found a small chapel built of artistically hand cut local stone in a neatly maintained parcel of ground surrounded by a low stone block wall. At the rear stood a second building which served as a hall for special gatherings. Situated on a well-known thoroughfare named Constitution Road, it was adjacent to Maseru's main street and business district. They were warmly greeted by the small group of worshipers. Following the service, inquiries were made as to what had brought them to Lesotho. Learning that they were newly arrived personnel of a mission organization, they were not only urged to return again but Allen was invited to speak some Sunday evening soon. After speaking several times, the church group asked if the AIMM would consider allowing him to preach for them on a scheduled basis.

The origin of the Maseru United Church dated back to the mid-1800's. In 1834, a Wesleyan Methodist Mission post was established just across Lesotho's western borders with South Africa near the town of Ladybrand on what was then known as the G.D. Hobson farm. Hobson was a man with a vision and played a leading role in establishing a "United Church" in the little town of Maseru a few miles to the east. Known for several decades as "the Tin Tabernacle," it eventually became the joint project of three different churches in the Republic - - the Wesleyan Methodists, the Orange River Presbytery and the Dutch Reformed Church. It was in 1948 that the beautiful stone chapel was erected. The hall to the rear was added in 1957. For years there were approximately 100 active members most of whom were Presbyterians and Methodists.

With the advent of political independence in 1966, the expatriate community of Maseru began to dwindle as did attendance at the MUC. When in 1971 the Dutch Reformed Church decided to withdraw from the joint venture, the other two church partners were left to carry on as best they could. It was agreed that the Presbyterians would be responsible for two services a month, the Methodists for one, leaving other Sundays to be arranged for locally by the membership.

The Sunday evening in 1973 that the Busenitz couple dropped in found the church reduced to ten active members. The future of the once active Church was clearly in doubt. It was not surprising that question was quickly raised as to Allen's willingness to preach for them with some regularity. Further inquiry as to possible AIMM interest in providing full-time pastoral leadership was equally understandable.

AIMM and MCC gradually became aware of still other opportunities for service in Lesotho. Inquiries at times came from totally unexpected quarters. Once a chance encounter in the Maseru airport brought together a travelling AIMM Executive Secretary and Canon Desmond Tutu, the head of the Anglican Church at the time in that country. Stating that he had come in contact with Mennonites in his travels and was impressed by their approach to witness and service, he went on to ask if AIMM would consider providing staff to teach Christian education courses in some of the schools for which he was responsible in the country. (9)

But if widening circles of opportunity were opening for AIMM, Busenitz was accurate when, in October 1973 he commented in a bimonthly report to the home office that things were "far from sorted out" as far as AIMM priorities in the country were concerned.

There was, however, an event that was soon to take place elsewhere which would serve as a catalyst in AIMM's ongoing search for a unifying focus for its presence and ministry - - not only in Lesotho, but in southern Africa as a whole.

CHAPTER 50   BOTSWANA BECKONS

It was a late June morning in 1974 in Gaborone (pr. hah-boh-ROH-nay), the newly chosen and rapidly growing capital of the southern African country of Botswana (pr. boh-TSWAH-nah). A meeting was under way which was to play a major role in sharpening AIMM's focus of ministry in southern Africa. The setting was a neatly maintained chapel situated on carefully swept grounds. Over an exterior doorway was painted a large, blue circle with the lettering SPIRITUAL HEALING CHURCH. At the center was a white cross with a dove resting on its peak.

has our prayer been answered?

The chapel was laid out in the form of a cross. Solid wooden benches were arranged in parallel blocks facing a small raised platform. Seated on a front bench was an AIMM delegation composed of AIMM Board Chairman Elmer Neufeld and Executive Secretary-elect Jim Bertsche. Opposite them were four church leaders. Bishop Israel Motswasele (pr. moh-tswah-SEE-leh) was seated at a small table. Behind him, in a semicircle, were three fellow churchmen.

This meeting had not been abruptly planned. As a matter of fact, it was the result of several years of prior Mennonite contact with the Bishop and his Church. Jim and Anna Kreider Juhnke had served as MCC country program directors from 1970 to 1972. Living in Gaborone, they had noticed this chapel and the many activities which took place there from week to week. Their curiosity stirred, they began to make inquiry in the expatriate community as to the nature of this group. When they were unable to secure much helpful information, they determined to find out on their own. Walking into the church unannounced one Sunday morning, the leaders and worshipers concealed their surprise and warmly welcomed their light-skinned visitors. Impressed both by their welcome and the exuberant worship they observed all around them, they returned on a regular basis for the remainder of their term of service in Botswana.

During this time the Juhnkes became increasingly impressed with the people they met, with their spiritual vitality and the practical application of their faith to daily life. As the time drew near for the Juhnkes' return to North America, it was their turn for a surprise. A very special Sunday was planned in their honor by Bishop Motswaseler. Amidst a recounting of their unexpected appearance in their church and the growing friendship which had developed between them, they were especially commissioned as their representatives to America. In this capacity they were asked to look for people who might be willing to return to Botswana to accept them as the Juhnkes had, and to work with them on a long-term basis.

The Juhnkes did not take their assignment lightly. It was not long after their return that Jim was appointed as one of the General Conference representatives to the AIMM Board. From that vantage point he began to share his experiences with the Spiritual Healing Church in Gaborone and his conviction that this group represented a special and different opportunity for ministry in Botswana in particular and, perhaps, in southern Africa in general. When the Board indicated a willingness to at least consider this possibility, via correspondence Juhnke arranged for a meeting between the Bishop and an AIMM delegation. That June 1974 morning was the culmination of that planning.

Some time was initially given to greetings, introductions and a review of the previous events which had brought the six men together there. On the table before the Bishop was an album-like register through which he began to leaf. From their vantage point nearby, the AIMM representatives could see that each page was divided into three sections. Each section carried some notations and a small photo. As he slowly turned the pages of the register, the Bishop explained that it contained pictures and brief biographical sketches of every person who carried any kind of leadership role in the Church he headed. Among them, he went on to explain, there were only two or three who had ever had any sort of formal Bible training.

After a pause he closed the register, folded his hands on it, looked at the two AIMM men and said: "For years, now, we have been praying that the Lord would send us some people who would be willing to accept us as we are and to help us as we seek, as a Church, to serve our God." Again there was a pause and then a question: "Is it possible that this day our prayer has been answered?"

who are these people?

The phenomenon of religious renewal movements is one that has been witnessed and studied worldwide. Nowhere, however, have such movements appeared in such numbers and such wide diversity as in sub-Saharan Africa. Typically referred to by scholars as "African Independent Churches" (AICs), this term serves as a huge umbrella under which fall literally thousands of separate groups. A considerable body of scholarly work already exists on this subject. (1)

Efforts have been made by several people to work out descriptive categories under which to cluster the many groups to be found in Africa. Some of these schemes have become quite complicated as researchers have sought to highlight the great variety of belief and practice to be found among them. Many students of these groups have found it helpful to simply approach them in terms of two broad categories: Ethiopian and Zionist Churches.

The origin of the term "Ethiopian" is traced back to an African Wesleyan Methodist pastor Mangane M. Mohone who in 1892 opposed his church's decision to create two separate conferences, one for whites and one for blacks. Viewing this as discrimination, he protested and called for a single church and a single conference. When he realized that his pleas would go unheeded, he broke away from the Wesleyan Church and founded what he called "The Ethiopian Church." Taking Biblical passages such as Psalm 68:31 and Acts 8:27 as points of departure, he believed that Africa was to be evangelized via the efforts of Africans themselves. He was joined in 1896 by another Methodist pastor, James Dwane, who also had disagreed with his Mission. He was chosen the same year to travel to the States to seek affiliation with the African Methodist Episcopal Church. This linkage was accorded and in 1898 AME Bishop H.M. Turner visited South Africa and ordained sixty-five ministers. This movement eventually experienced many ramifications but a basic terminology had been established for such breakaway groups. (2)

"Zionist Churches," the second broad term, also traces its origins to events before the year 1900. It was in 1896 that a man named John Alexander Dowie founded something called "The Christian Apostolic Church" with headquarters at Zion City near Chicago, IL. Soon declaring himself to be the First Apostle of Jesus Christ, he established divine healing as one of the tenets of his new church along with taboos against pork, alcohol and tobacco. In 1896 he began to publish a monthly called "Leaves of Healing."

In the meantime, in southern Africa there was a man named Johannes Buchler. His Swiss parents had experienced revival in their country in 1860 and formed a group of friends who all claimed to have received the Holy Spirit as promised by Christ. Eventually viewed as unbalanced by their Swiss neighbors, they gave away their belongings and migrated with some thirty others of their group to South Africa where they settled at Johannesburg. During his schooling Buchler discovered that he enjoyed preaching. He was accepted as "pastor to the Coloreds" and in 1893 was ordained to the ministry of the Congregational Church. Buchler, however, found this Church's practice of infant baptism hard to accept. He eventually resigned his pastorate over this issue and encouraged his congregation to build a chapel of their own. They called themselves "The Zion Church," possibly influenced by the Moravian hymn book they used entitled *Zions Liedere*. (3)

Always an avid student, Buchler one day came across the magazine "Leaves of Healing" published by John Alexander Dowie of Zion City, IL. He became a regular reader and found himself charmed by Dowie's emphasis upon "Jesus as Savior, Sanctifier, Healer and Coming King." In poor health himself, the healing theme of Dowie's teaching had special appeal for him. After extensive correspondence with Dowie, he sought to establish a ministry of healing of his own in Johannesburg. Dowie pursued relations with Buchler "thrilled by the new possibilities that his contact . . . seemed to open up, on Zion's behalf, in Johannesburg and in Africa as a whole." (4)

Visiting Zion City, Buchler quickly became disenchanted with Dowie. Returning to South Africa he disavowed any further relationship with him. By this time, however, Dowie had wide enough support in South Africa that he determined to send his own emissary, Pastor Daniel Bryant. An educated and skilled man who had come under Dowie's spell, he served effectively for four years establishing a Zion community in Johannesburg. During his time there he traveled widely seeking out other white religious leaders of similar views. It was during these itineraries that the first "Zion baptism for Africans" took place.

Showing increased evidence of mental instability in his later years, Dowie died in 1907. He was briefly replaced in his leadership role by another man, W. G. Voliva. The movement as such, however, had peaked and was soon to fade as a major influence both in North America and in Africa. Stan Nussbaum comments: "The inability of the church to finance any more missionaries was what led to the 'independence' of the South African Zionists, setting them free to develop their own theology and worship after an initial, short introduction to Dowie's version of the Gospel." (5) It nonetheless had wielded a key influence at a time of religious ferment among South Africans at the turn of the century. Some of its themes as well as the name were to linger among African Independent Churches for years to come.

In summary, then, the term "African Independent Church" is used by students of these groups to designate an African fellowship of believers - - whether well organized or loosely knit - - which has been organized through the initiative and leadership of Africans themselves.

As to descriptive terminology, the term "Ethiopian Church" is used to designate groups which typically are break-aways from established mainline churches while retaining many of the characteristics and structures of the former church. The head of the church tends to function in a manner which reflects the traditional cultural role of an African chief.

The term "Zionist Church," on the other hand, is typically used to refer to groups which have evolved independently of any previous tie with an established church. (It should be noted that the Zion, IL-based Christian Catholic Church claims a large following in South Africa to this day; these groups would be an exception.) Such churches tend to incorporate much more traditional African style into their worship and a stronger emphasis upon healing and prophecy. The head of the church typically is quite charismatic and fills the role of a prophet-healer rather than that of a chief.

It must be realized, however, that such categories are far from water tight or exclusive. Unconcerned about researchers and their efforts to fit them into neatly drawn categories or charts, they blithely go their ways doing what seems best and most rewarding to them whether they fit into the researchers scheme of things or not.

why?

It is one thing to discuss the AICs in terms of categories. It is an entirely different matter to understand the powerful dynamics which have given rise to these churches all across sub-Saharan Africa. Like mushrooms after a warm tropical rain, they have erupted everywhere and especially in southern Africa. What are the forces at work which give rise to them? How can their appearance and numbers be explained?

A wide variety of theories have been advanced across the years. One which has been popular among anthropologists and sociologists has been that the thousands of AICs are symptoms of an African culture under stress. It is pointed out that both geographically and historically, there is remarkable coincidence between the establishment of a massive colonial empire in black Africa and the rise of African renewal movements. As tribal leaders lost authority and as traditional practices were frequently curbed or suppressed, social scientists see the AICs as camouflaged ways of reaffirming and nurturing traditional world-views and values which underwent the onslaught of powerful colonial regimes.

Other students of these church groups have suggested that they provide outlets for Africans whose aspirations to leadership were otherwise blocked. Under the colonial regime, in general, and under apartheid, in particular, the black man had no political role to play. Indeed, leadership roles of any kind in the African's socio-political setting were extremely limited. But via the AICs, men and women with leadership gifts found a place to exercise them. A man who, through the week, quietly went about his tasks as a white employer's "garden boy" could, on Sunday, don his robe and function as the bishop of the church he had brought into being. A man who, during the week, was voiceless and powerless in his work-a-day world could, on Sunday, bring his church members under the sway of his charismatic gifts. A woman who, through the week, was a "nanny" or a "maid" in the home of white people could, on Sunday, fill roles of influence among her peers in her little church. Such is the explanation offered by some.

There are, however, still other observers of these movements who suggest that a major reason for their appearance is the insensitivity with which Christian mission was frequently carried out in Africa. If, at first flush, such a suggestion seems exaggerated or unduly harsh, there is nonetheless some truth in the assertion. Early generations of missionaries who came to Africa under the rule of colonial governments were deeply committed people. Spurred by a clear sense of call and urgency, they were prepared to give their lives if necessary in their effort to bring a witness to the hundreds of tribal groups of that immense continent.

It is also true, however, that they frequently brought some presuppositions with them of which they typically were not all that aware, e.g., that a non-technological society is, in some sense, a backward society; that a nonliterate society is, in some sense, a less intelligent society; that a "civilizing mission" was a legitimate and even necessary part of the broad task of evangelization; that preferential treatment accorded the white-skinned stranger was somehow appropriate; or that different, strange cultural practices needed to be viewed as suspect, if not downright evil, simply because they were strange. Given this innocent mind-set on the part of many early missionaries, it is understandable that they employed a rough broom as they attempted to sweep aside many tribal beliefs and practices which they attributed either to ignorance or to evil power at work among the Africans around them.

Beyond this, it must also be admitted that a strong note of paternalism often characterized mission history. At a more benign end of the spectrum it took the form of delay in moving toward the autonomy of the African church and the passing of reins of authority to black hands. At the more evil end of the spectrum this attitude took the form of *apartheid* and the insistence that Christians be consigned to racially segregated churches.

Discussing the situation which existed in his country, South African born John W. de Gruchy has written as follows: "There were three ecclesiastical alternatives for black Christians in South Africa by the turn of the twentieth century. They could be members of mission churches whose membership was wholly black but which were under the control of white missionaries . . . . A second possibility was that they could be members of multi-racial denominations, those churches largely of British origin, where the line between settler and mission church had not been clearly drawn. But here, likewise, the black members were dominated by white leadership, . . . discrimination and a great deal of paternalism. . . . There was a third option. They could leave the mission and the multi-racial churches and initiate their own." (6)

In a hard-edged article reflecting on the coming of Christian missionaries to southern Africa, Sipo E. Nzimela, a black South African, on one occasion wrote: "In South Africa, as in most parts of Africa, Christianity quickly caught root despite the fact that those who preached it did not usually practice what they taught. . . . There are at least three reasons for this rapid growth. First, the African did not need to be persuaded about the existence of God. He already knew about this long before the missionaries came. Secondly, the Africans firmly believed in life after death. They believed that God was with them throughout life here on earth and that they would go to him after death. Thirdly, the world of the African is a world full of things that are spirit . . . . These basic beliefs provided favorable conditions for the acceptance and rapid growth of the Gospel."

Turning to a critique of the missionary endeavor in southern Africa, Nzimela wrote further: ". . . before the year 1900, it had become abundantly clear to some African church leaders within the missionary churches that the Christianity preached to them was irrelevant to the African way of life and way of thinking. For them it was incomprehensible that the missionaries could preach from the same Bible which bears the message of love, brotherhood and reconciliation and yet show no interest in putting any of these into practice."

Referring to the often bitter competition between different denominational missions for converts, and the typical emphasis upon "sin and the commandments," the writer concluded: "Above all, the refusal on the part of the missionaries to accept the Africans as brothers in the Christ they preached disillusioned the Africans and partly contributed to the rise of the African Religious Movements . . . ." (7)

In attempting to pursue still further the "why" of the dramatic rise of African Independent Churches, there is another area even more fundamental than that of insensitivity in the missionary's approach to the African and his culture, that being a certain degree of inadequacy in the presentation of Christ as sovereign Lord vis-à-vis the African's spirit world. In a paper presented to the General Conference Commission on Overseas Mission in 1985, the AIMM Executive Secretary commented as follows: "In the midst of a remarkable and sustained expansion of the Christian faith in Africa there has been, to use Dr. Paul Hiebert's term, 'an excluded middle' - - an area of belief/concern in the African world-view which western missionaries have been ill equipped to understand or deal with."

"The African's belief in the reality of an immediate, largely malevolent spirit world and the consequent necessity of finding effective ways of dealing with that world for years prompted varying responses of amused and bemused disbelief on the part of the western missionary. Finding it easy to attribute such beliefs either to superstition or to inadequate education, the tendency was to dismiss such notions and to wait for the time when adequate education and maturing faith would lead to the discarding of such pernicious beliefs and the liberation of the African Christian from such groundless fears."

"The African, however, his profession of faith notwithstanding, has continued to believe in the spirit world close at hand. In the ongoing teaching of the missionary, on the other hand, a certain vacuum of instruction remained. It was into this vacuum that the African Independent Churches moved. Taking their stance squarely within the traditional African world view they say: 'Of course there are evil spirits close at hand; of course there are practitioners of the occult; of course there is danger in the night but we have the answers. We can help you.' It is small wonder that with such an emphasis these groups have had an enduring appeal to African Christians and non-Christians alike for the greater part of this century." (8)

Having recognized all of the above dynamics as partial explanations for the appearance of AICs in such dramatic numbers, our search is not yet complete. It is not enough nor is it accurate to simply explain the AICs as being the result of the African's frustration with and reaction against some forms of Christian mission among them. At a very deep level, the AICs reflect the innate spirituality of the African and the questing of the African spirit for an intensely personal encounter with the God of grace and power who will meet and satisfy their deepest needs. As Nzimela puts it: "The African Religious Movements are providing a much longed for Spiritual Home for Africans and for this reason they have come to stay." (9)

some AIC characteristics

As observed earlier, AICs which have their origin in a secession from mission established churches (Ethiopian) tend to follow rather closely the churches they left in matters of creed and organization. Their leaders tend to be better educated.

"Zionist" Churches, on the other hand, i.e., those who typically appear independently of any missionary role, have a strong charismatic flavor. Their services are usually lengthy with much spontaneity and singing frequently interspersed with drumming and dancing. There is among them, as AIMM missionary Jonathan Larson puts it, "a lively awareness of the Holy Spirit." There is the practice of group prayer, and times designated for healing are a regular feature of worship services. The AICs understanding of healing goes far beyond physical ailments. Members are also invited for prayers for "healing" for literally everything that is troubling them and their lives, e.g., healing of relationships, healing of memories, healing of troubled marriages, healing of blighted aspirations and dreams. Job hunters, students about to write exams, people experiencing difficulties of whatever sort are also invited for prayer for "healing" by their church leaders.

Zionist Churches also find the Old Testament to be intriguing terrain. Taboos on certain foods, especially pork, are common. Some require that shoes be left at the door of places of worship. Some offer sacrifices of one sort or another guided by the Old Testament practices of the Hebrew people.

There are still further widely-shared traits: leaders who typically have come to their roles via some sort of traumatic personal experience; taking African culture and world view as their frame of reference and their point of departure; addressing issues that matter greatly to Africans in the routine of their daily lives; working with themes of power and healing; joyous, celebratory worship with everyone participating; a high level of member involvement in the life and activity of the church; histories of ostracism and discrimination at the hands of both mission church leaders and government officials; a hunger for acceptance, affirmation and status; a deep desire for church institutions of their own; the readiness of members to give sacrificially of their time and their resources for the cause of their church.

some AIC problems

Although they have been generally characterized by dramatic growth and excitement, the AICs have not been without their share of problems. One that soon comes to the attention of the observer is the high level of rivalry and competition which frequently exists between such groups. As dramatic reports of new healings or new manifestations of the Spirit circulate regarding this or that group, it is not uncommon for members of others churches to drift toward the new attraction.

A strong note of legalism is also found among the AICs. Regulations regarding diet, dress and schedules of church activity can be rigid. As a result, it is easy to associate salvation with doing what is required by the church leadership. Another major problem for many AICs is very loose organization and administration. Records are often poorly kept with financial accounting that is spotty at best.

But the most prevalent problems have to do with AIC leadership. The typical leader has very little formal education and Bible training. But with flamboyant personalities they often depend upon personal charisma to attract and hold a following. Some groups tend to become cults centered about strong leaders. When such leaders die, struggles frequently erupt between new candidates for leadership roles. In such situations, splits are often the result as contenders go their own ways with their own followers.

The most serious problem of all is that of the ever present danger of syncretism. With minimal Biblical instruction, on the one hand, and the unabashed affirmation of African cultural beliefs on the other, it is easy for leaders of some AICs to come up with a mix of teachings and practices which clearly take them well outside the boundaries of Biblical Christianity.

the powerful appeal of the AICs

Such problems notwithstanding there is a broad mainstream of Independent Churches which exerts tremendous influence within African society and which has enormous appeal for literally millions of Africans. This appeal has several parts. There is, first of all, the obvious fact that AICs are purely and simply African in their origin, leadership and perspective. Africans can take justifiable pride in the knowledge that they were brought into being without help from overseas or from the white-skinned expatriates among them. What they have is due to their own vision and their own efforts.

There is the further reality that many (particularly the Zionist Churches) make a complete break with the occult and the demonic world. While affirming the reality of these forces, these Churches offer a perceived shelter from their power via prayer, potions and group solidarity. Put another way, the AICs are talking about things and dealing with problems which are of tremendous importance in the every day life of the average African. So powerful is this AIC attraction that there has been steady leakage of members across the years from mission-established churches, something which has contributed greatly to the friction and animosity which has often characterized relations between them. As a matter of fact, this tension has frequently led to Africans applying for dual membership in order to safeguard the benefits of both churches. Mission churches offer the opportunity for formal education, medical care and employment. The AICs offer an understanding of the innermost hunger of the African heart. On more than one occasion such an individual has been heard to say: "In the morning I go to the mission church because they know how to teach and preach. In the evening I go to the independent church because they know how to pray."

Another facet of the appeal of the AICs is their simple acceptance of Biblical teaching as truth to be believed and applied to life on a daily basis. One South African observer of both the mission-planted churches and the AICs writes: "Members of these movements see mission Christianity as irrelevant because of the failure to penetrate their lives. For them mission Christianity is nothing but a set of rules to be observed; some vague promise about the future; something to be forgotten six days a week and thought about perhaps for an hour or so on Sundays; something confined to a church building. To all this the African says 'No.' The Gospel is part of his life. They generally accept the basic doctrines of the church. The Bible is held to be the sole authority for them and their interpretation of it is usually literal and their theology is accordingly Biblical. They accept such mysteries as the Trinity without pretending for a moment that there are arguments for or against. For them the Trinity and all other mysteries are facts. Period. There is no room for such debates as the 'Jesusness of Christ' or the 'Christness of Jesus.' That there are inexplicable mysteries is accepted without resentment. That there are human beings who have answers to these mysteries is rejected without further ado." (10)

Yet another facet of AIC life with strong attraction for the African is the great emphasis upon worship, prayer and church life in general as a corporate experience. As the AICs gather to worship, there are no observers, no passive bystanders. Group participation is carefully structured into AIC worship. Even offerings become lengthy occasions for song, dance and celebration of all those present. Preachers are regularly interrupted by spontaneous song. Prayers typically are group prayers in which the entire congregation, on its knees, is invited to participate.

In this regard Nzimela observes: "The way Africans worship makes it clear that for them the Church is an organic and corporate fellowship. . . . There is an emphasis on the wholeness of God's people as opposed to the western idea of dividing this wholeness into clergy and laity. The African wants to belong to a fellowship where his whole personality is at home . . . . There is a great urge to have some place where he can feel at home." (11)

And, finally, there is the appeal of the AICs emphasis upon the person and power of the Holy Spirit. With a major accent upon healing, as understood in a broad sense, many Africans join AICs following an experience of healing in their lives. Indeed, AIC leaders see their healing ministries as a prime means of evangelism and outreach. These leaders, furthermore, believe that they are under the constant guidance of the Holy Spirit and that direction and instruction can come to them via dreams, visions, trances and extraordinary experiences which befall them. Church members anticipate and give testimony to this same sort of guidance in their lives. This being the case, it is common to find women not only in roles of leadership among the AICs but even as founders of new churches. If the Spirit has chosen and called her, who is to question it? Such is the emphasis upon being Spirit-possessed and Spirit-led that they refer to themselves not as "Independent Churches" but rather as "Spiritual Churches."

An African observer of the AIC scene from Zimbabwe has summarized the matter well: "Whether we like it or not, the African Independent Churches have erupted upon the continent in great numbers. Though there are great differences in the extent of their influence, . . . they are a response to Christianity in African terms and a reality to account for." (12)

but how does all of this fit into "Christian Mission"?

Bertsche and Neufeld came away from their meeting with Bishop Motswasele, that June morning in 1974, impressed by the warmth and candor of their encounter. They were also convinced that the invitation to provide missionary personnel to work with the Spiritual Healing Church in Botswana was genuine.

A set of recommendations drawn up and submitted to the AIMM Board in their fall meeting that year read as follows:

1 - That Africa Inter-Mennonite Mission seek to appoint a missionary couple with African experience for an initial one-to-two-year assignment to explore and initiate a Christian leadership training ministry in cooperation with Independent Churches in Botswana, and that this appointment be made as soon as possible.

2 - That the persons appointed to this ministry be expected to work in consultation with the appropriate Botswana government representatives, the Botswana Christian Council, the denominational church leadership and that they work in cooperation with the MCC team in Botswana and other Mennonite mission workers in Southern Africa.

3 - That Africa Inter-Mennonite Mission recruit an additional couple with seminary training and pastoral experience and help them secure some additional training for a ministry among Independent Churches in anticipation of assignment in Botswana, or possibly Lesotho, or some other part of Africa. (13)

There were immediate questions.

Who are these Independent Church folk? Are they even Christian? What do they believe? What are their practices? Do we have any idea what this sort of involvement might get us into? If working with them in Botswana is such an opportunity, why has no one else already started to do so? What would we seek to accomplish? How would we approach them - - as Christians or non-Christians? - - as people needing salvation or nurture? - - as errant seekers needing correction or as fellow believers needing fuller understanding of the Scriptures?

But the biggest question of all was one that had to do with missiology. Was not Christian Mission first and above all else a call to evangelism and church planting? And as Mennonites, had it not been our objective for over sixty years to plant a Mennonite Church in Africa? So where, now, did the business of African Independent Churches fit into our understanding of our role in Africa? If we decided to try to engage in ministry among them, what would be our objective? - - to seek to bring them into the Mennonite fold or simply to accept and affirm them as we find them while trusting joint study of Scripture to accomplish God's intended work among them?

As time came for board action on the set of recommendations, few of these questions had found a clear answer. And yet the Board found it impossible to turn a deaf ear to a call for help which had such a "Macedonian" ring. The following minute was consequently proposed and passed: "That AIMM delegation to Africa recommendations 1, 2 and 3 on Botswana be approved." (14)

Though little was known, at the time, of the far-reaching implications of this Board action, a direction was pointed which was to become increasingly the focus of AIMM's ministry in southern Africa in the years ahead.

CHAPTER 51   FINDING OUR WAY

Israel Motswasele and the Spiritual Healing Church

Who was this man who, that June morning in 1974, invited the AIMM to help his Church in its ministry in Botswana? Who were the people of the Spiritual Healing Church (SHC) who extended such a warm hand of welcome to the Mennonites?

It was in 1923 that revival broke out in an isolated village named Matsiloje (pr. mah-tsi-LOH-jay), twenty-five miles east of Francistown just on the Botswana side of the border with Southern Rhodesia (now known as Zimbabwe). An itinerant South African prophet named Harry Morolong visited the village and his ministry had dramatic impact upon the people including a man named Jacob Mokaleng Motswasele (pr. moh-koh-LENG moh-tswah-oh-SEE-leh). Interestingly, Prophet Morolong, in turn, had been strongly influenced by the Prophet Walter Matitta of Lesotho. Morolong conducted public meetings characterized by singing, Scripture reading, prayer, preaching and prophetic messages revealed by the Spirit. A song which was particularly moving to the young people and was sung frequently at the meetings was the chorus known in English as "Where He leads me I will follow." (1)

Matsiloje, a village which had previously been known for the riotous and undisciplined life of its young people, experienced dramatic change. After the departure of the Prophet Morolong, the youth of the village continued to gather for prayer meetings which frequently were led by the youthful Jacob Motswasele.
In time, like many others his age, Jacob left home to seek employment in the Republic of South Africa. Following the pattern of migrant workers, he took a variety of jobs while returning once or twice a year to his home village. At such times he would revive prayer meetings but when he left, they tended to cease.

While in the Republic, he came into contact with the St. John's Apostolic Faith Mission founded in 1937 by Mrs. Christinah Nku who was simply known as Mma Nku (pr. mmah NKOO) in AIC circles of southern Africa. Seeking baptism by a minister of this church, Jacob joined in the late 1940's. Shortly after his baptism Jacob experienced a time of spiritual struggle. "He felt that the Holy Spirit was not allowing him to continue working in South Africa and that he was called to prophesy. He had several visions in which he was instructed to return to Matsiloje permanently. In this crisis he sought the counsel, blessing and prayers of Mma Nku . . . . It was Prophetess Nku who commissioned Mokaleng for his work in the Protectorate [i.e. the Protectorate of Bechuanaland now known as Botswana] advising him to return to Matsiloje and there follow the leading of the Holy Spirit. She told him, 'You have been ordered to go to Bechuanaland and to serve the people there. You have been given the country of Bechuanaland.'" (2)

Returning with his family in 1949, he quickly resurrected the prayer services he had earlier conducted as a young man. It was not long, however, that he again experienced inner turmoil. He isolated himself in the hills in prayer. "When he came back to Matsiloje he was filled with the Spirit and began to prophesy. People began to come to him for prayer and healing." (3) Word concerning the prophet of Matsiloje spread swiftly and the size of the crowds coming to seek his help steadily grew. "Within a year he was conducting a full-time prayer meeting with healing as its central focus. . . . A great number of ill, crippled and blind people went to the prophet for healing; he was also sought out by people with special problems, e.g., those who were unemployed or who could not have children. Mentally ill people were brought for healing, some of such violent behavior that they had to be handcuffed. People who had lost touch with a relative . . . asked the Prophet to pray for that person's return . . . ." (4)

By this time a fuller profile of the Prophet was emerging. There were many who paid tribute to his charisma, his concern for people, his gift for healing and his "gift of sight," i.e., the "ability to diagnose the cause of a person's illness, to divine a person's motives, to interpret dreams and visions and to foretell the future of events." (5) While he was widely reported to heal by faith and prayer, he would at times refer people to hospitals for medical treatment or for surgery. On still other occasions he would state that an illness did not have Pa physical origin but was rather spiritual in nature. Such were counseled to seek baptism and to join the church.

So large were the crowds that many either pitched little tents for shelter or simply lay their sleeping mats on the ground under the stars. The Prophet eventually constructed a large shelter in which the prayer services were held. In his healing ministry he usually used water and prayer with occasional salt and ashes. Prayer services typically were begun in early morning and continued till midday. He frequently spent the afternoons alone and would then resume prayer services in the evening.

Along the way the Prophet became a prosperous pastoralist and farmer. Herdboys tended his cattle and family members helped care for the crops in nearby fields. Sometimes people who came to him stayed for long periods of time. They too would help in the cultivation of the fields from which they, in turn, were fed. Sundays were the high point of each week. "They involved preaching, prayers for the sick and much singing during which individuals were sometimes possessed by the Spirit. When Prophet Mokoleng was possessed of the Spirit he would sing for one or two minutes, then calm down and pray." (6)

The crowds and activity at this isolated little village did not go unnoticed by government officials or by leaders of mission established churches of the area. The former found it easy to read subversive political overtones into the activities at Matsiloje. The latter, well aware of the tremendous appeal and growing influence of the prophet, found it just as easy to view the whole thing as a suspect movement heavily colored by pagan belief and practice. Even though the Prophet always urged the people who came to him to return to and faithfully support their own churches, white suspicions were not allayed. If a certain freedom was allowed the prophet in his home village, it was made clear to his followers that any effort to spread their activities to other areas would not be tolerated.

Experiencing the increasing disfavor and suspicion of both government and established church personnel, more and more requests came to the Prophet to create his own church, a church to which they could belong and in which they could feel at home. At first he resisted this pressure but eventually he agreed as he saw the prejudice and ostracism his people were experiencing. It was on October 10, 1952, that he and his followers officially formed what was at first referred to as the "Apostolic United Faith Coloured Church," a name that was to undergo several changes. Prophet Harry Morolong was invited to return to Matsiloje to conduct the first baptisms which took place on April 16, 1953. Two hundred people participated in the mass baptism on that day. Soon after that it was decided that all church members should wear a distinctive attire and that baptism and communion would be observed once a year. In 1955 the building of a church was begun. Prophet Morolong was once again invited to come and share in its official dedication. The ties of mutual respect between the two men were enduring.

A daily observer of the hum of activity at Matsiloje was the Prophet's oldest son named Israel. Always a man of vision, the Prophet recognized that one day his Church would need new and younger leadership. He prepared for that day by sending his son to the pastoral training school at Morija in Lesotho. Upon his return in 1966, the Prophet-father presided over his ordination. By this time there was already a group of church members who had gone to the rapidly growing center of Gaborone in search of work. Loyal to their prophet and their church, they were meeting under the leadership of a young man named Benjamin Moilwa who had earlier been the prophet's assistant. Meeting wherever they could, they engaged in prayer, singing and preaching. Known at first simply as "Mokaleng's Church," people started to come in from distant villages to attend the services. Eventually Benjamin started new groups in the villages from which they came so they would not need to travel to Gaborone to worship.

A movement was under way in southern Botswana. Leadership was crucial. The prophet's son had come back none too soon from his studies in Lesotho. Upon his ordination at the hands of his father, he was sent to Gaborone to take charge of the expanding membership of his church in that region.

Coincidentally, 1966 was also the year that Botswana acquired its political autonomy from Britain. A man of purpose and action, Israel Motswasele promptly took advantage of the new religious freedom which was theirs, under the new constitution, by purchasing a plot of ground in the town in the name of his Church. Construction was started in 1967 with funds raised from the membership. The church was officially opened in 1968. It was the first Independent Church building in Gaborone and, indeed, the first church building of any kind to be built in the newly-designated capital of that new nation. It was by this time clear that Israel, the prophet's son, had become the administrative head of the Church. Jacob, the father, remained the revered Prophet and spiritual force of the Church until his death in 1980.

When in 1972 the Botswana government passed "The Societies Act" designed to curb the proliferation of Independent Churches which erupted after independence, Israel Motswasele was unimpressed. Rather he forged ahead in his efforts to see his church officially recognized by the government of his country. His efforts were rewarded in April 1973. It was just over a year later that the AIMM delegation sat with him, his register of church personnel and his three fellow church leaders in the front of the newly built chapel and heard him ask if the Mennonites might be the answer to their prayer for help.

Even as the AIMM decision was made to respond to this appeal, it was known that finding the right kind of candidates was crucial for this new undertaking. Where could AIMM find people with the training, experience, temperament and attitude which this assignment would require?

enter the Weavers

Irene Lehman was born to missionary parents serving in India under the sponsorship of the Mennonite Board of Missions. Pursuing her education at Goshen College, she came to the attention of fellow student, Edwin Weaver from Newton, KS, who was working toward a degree in Bible and theology. Married in 1933, Ed was ordained to the Christian ministry. For two years they gave leadership to a Home Mission project in Chicago. In 1935 they were accepted as candidates for service in India, an appointment which took them back to Irene's "homeland." They served there over a period of twenty years. Much of this time Ed filled the role of Bishop in the Indian Mennonite Church. By 1956 they felt that it was time to lower the missionary profile in the Indian Church and asked to terminate their services there. Invited to Hesston College in Kansas, they served on staff there in a counseling ministry.

Meanwhile the Mennonite Board of Missions had been sponsoring an international broadcast of the Mennonite Hour. Unknown to MBM staff, the broadcasts were being followed with uncommon interest by a cluster of African Independent Churches in southeastern Nigeria around a village center known as Uyo (pr. OO-yoh). In 1958 letters arrived in the MBM office stating that the Biblical teaching they heard on the broadcasts were similar to their own beliefs and they now wanted to declare themselves Mennonites. In response to this news J.D. Graber, the MBM missions secretary of the time, asked S. Jay Hostetler, an MBM missionary on assignment in Ghana, to travel to Nigeria to seek out the church groups which had sent letters to Elkhart. Within a year Hostetler made four different visits. During this time he "officially received seventeen congregations with a total of some 500 members" into the Mennonite fellowship. (7)

This done, MBM sought seasoned missionary personnel to initiate ministry among these newly received congregations. It was in late 1959 that the Weavers, former career missionaries to India, arrived at Uyo. They eventually wrote of their experiences there with a refreshing mix of humor and candor. (8)

It was not long after their arrival that the import of their situation struck home. They were, they said, neither sure of what they had gotten themselves into nor if they were capable of carrying out the assignment they had been given. This was not India! Furthermore, in spite of the names they carried, these were not like any Mennonite churches they had ever seen. But, after an initial period of indecision and misgivings, the Weavers settled into a learning, teaching, counseling relationship with the churches around them which was to carry over a period of eight years. By the time they were evacuated in 1967, due to the Biafran Civil War, they had not only pioneered Mennonite work among AICs but, in the process, had also forged some convictions and hammered out some working principles which were later to impact similar kinds of work far beyond southeastern Nigeria. In 1969 they again returned to West Africa under MBM sponsorship, this time to Ghana where they continued a similar ministry among AIC folk there. (9)

In 1973 they were again sent to Africa, this time to Swaziland on the tip of the continent to give leadership to a survey of AICs in that little country for the Eastern Mennonite Board of Missions. Returning to their retirement apartment in Hesston, KS they thought that, at last, they could put their traveling bags in permanent storage.

But in AIMM's search for a couple qualified to launch its new venture in Botswana, the name Weaver quickly surfaced in board discussions. There was no doubting their ability and experience. But could they be enticed out of retirement by a Mennonite mission board that was new to them? A two-man AIMM delegation went to visit with them one morning in their apartment. Over cups of tea the newly envisioned venture was laid before them. Would they consider giving initial leadership for a year or two? The AIMM representatives were prepared to suggest that they take a few days to think about the proposal. This, however, proved to be unnecessary. Their only questions had to do with details of preparation and travel schedules! African Independent Churches had, in a profound sense, become a part of them. This was another opportunity too good to miss.

drawing upon earlier Mennonite experience

The Weavers arrived in Gaborone in January 1975, at a time when AIMM was looking at the same mix of questions and uncertainties that they and MBM had confronted fifteen years earlier in Nigeria. Though separated by thousands of miles, it quickly became apparent to them that the AIC landscape of southern Africa bore many similarities to what they had previously observed in West Africa.

AIMM correspondence flowed between Elkhart and Gaborone. Out of these exchanges, plus the reading of their writings and other MBM materials, AIMM began to establish some base lines for its work. First of all, a rationale. Back home some inquiries were being heard among AIMM's partnering conferences. "What's this business about African Independent Churches? Why get involved with them? What qualifications do Mennonites in general or AIMM in particular have to justify such an initiative?"

To this set of questions the following answers gradually took shape: - As newcomers on the South African scene, Mennonites were in the unique position of not being encumbered with previous historical baggage which tended to complicate relations with AICs for some of the other church groups already present for decades. - As Mennonites we have had our own harsh experience with oppression and rejection by hostile governments and influential church bodies. - As Mennonites we have also sometimes been known as "people of the Book" who seek to take its teachings seriously and to incorporate them in daily life. - As Mennonites we, too, have often found ourselves at odds with and critical of contemporary culture around us. - As Mennonites we, too, have a long tradition of lay leadership within a believer's church with a preference for local congregational government and decision making via consensus. - As Mennonites we, too, have in the past often responded to oppression or government efforts of coercion by nonviolent, passive resistance. - As Mennonites we perceive AICs as one facet of the disenfranchised black population which experiences discrimination and exploitation at the hands of entrenched power structures. - But above all else, as Mennonites we see the AICs as a direct encounter between Africans and the Christian faith without the intervening "filter" of a mission established church. They are seen as being in search of understandings and practices which permit them to be both genuinely African and genuinely Christian. - As Mennonites we believe that whatever the eventual shape of African Christianity proves to be, the AICs will have made a major impact upon it. (10) And, finally, AIMM saw the opening to work among AICs as an exciting new opportunity to serve in Africa apart from an established mission structure, program and denominational goals.

But from the AIMM constituency there were still other questions, such as "If, as Mennonites, we feel a certain empathy for and understanding of the AICs experience, how does AIMM propose to approach ministry among them?" It was especially in this regard that AIMM drew upon the long experience of the Weavers. When their counsel was sought, their response was clear: - We must not approach the AICs in a critical, corrective manner. While we will find some beliefs and practices among them which are strange and even troubling for us, we must reserve judgment until we understand the reasons for them. - We must approach the AICs not as their instructors but rather as fellow students of God's Word who, with them, seek a better understanding of the Scriptures and what they have to say to both them and us about faith and life. - We must not try to dictate to them what they ought to study but rather seek to elicit from them the areas of their own needs and then seek together with them what light the Scriptures shed upon them. - In our studies we must focus on the Bible rather than on books about the Bible. - We must guard against a mind-set in which we see ourselves approaching the AICs with our "Biblical pruning shears" in hand. Rather we must believe that the Scriptures are what they themselves claim to be - - light, salt and leaven which can work to accomplish God's purposes among them in His own time and manner.

There was one more thing: we need to enter our ministry among the AICs fully prepared to allow them to remain who they are - - African Independent Churches, not Mennonite Churches. We owe it to them and to ourselves to work among them without ulterior motives. While we must be open about the North American Church which sends us and to which we have made deep commitments, we want to enable and to equip our students to better serve and lead their own churches. We are not coming to introduce yet another denomination amidst the already cluttered ecclesiastical landscape of Botswana in the mid-1970's nor are we coming to proselytize. We come in the name of Jesus to help them as best we can. And in the process, we are prepared also to learn from them.

at first, nothing much happened

Already in 1971, in their exploratory travels, Jim Bertsche and Don Jacobs had encountered polite skepticism in Botswana on the part of mission/church representatives with whom they talked. When they were informed that Mennonite concern was to ascertain opportunities for service rather than possibilities for carving out a new denominational beachhead, disbelief was evident. While MCC had already established an appreciated presence as a service agency, Mennonite mission boards were something else again. Who ever heard of a mission agency sending people halfway around the world for reasons other than the planting of their own churches?

Arriving in 1975, the Weavers found much the same attitude, i.e., a polite reception but a guarded manner which clearly reflected a "wait and see" stance on their part. There even seemed to be a bit of ambivalence on the part of the MCC team. A sizeable group scattered in a variety of government teaching posts and agricultural schemes, there seemed to be some uncertainty as to the reason or need for an AIMM presence in the country. But for the Weavers, the most puzzling was the initial passive stance adopted by the local AIC leaders. Soon after their arrival in Gaborone, they visited the Spiritual Healing Church where the Juhnkes had worshiped and where the AIMM delegation had met with Israel Motswasele. The reception was warm and joyous but there was no talk of Bible study. As they sought out and worshiped in other churches in the city, it was much the same - - a warm welcome and not much else.

But the Weavers had wisdom born of long experience with AICS to simply adopt a stance of availability. In early reporting to the home office they wrote: "Developing relationships and finding fellowship is a very important part of adjusting and being happy in one's new home in a foreign country. This takes time and a lot of doing. In cultures such as this, the initiative must come from us. We must show ourselves friendly and interested in people. We must go to them, and not expect them to come to us . . . . Our getting adjusted to our new MCC house on 5119 Leruo [Street] was more than learning to accept a house, finding a shelter. Both of us need feeding of body and soul. Irene needs to fix up a house that expresses feelings and need of creativity. All who know Ed know he needs a garden with flowers and vegetables to feed both body and soul. We are now eating vegetables from our garden and a few roses are beginning to bloom, where only a few months ago the grass was three feet high. But flowers and a creatively arranged house are not enough. Somewhere God has to come into the picture." (11)

Meanwhile, if there was minimal direct contact with the people of the Spiritual Healing Church, they were far from disinterested. In the typical manner of the African, they were discretely observing this new Mennonite couple who had been sent to work with them.

Then one day, a number of weeks after their arrival, there was a knock at the door. It was Israel Motswasele accompanied by a second man. Invited into the tiny living room of their prefab house, tea was served. Then the Bishop explained the reason for their visit. The man with him, J.C. Tshwene (pr.TSHWAY-nay), was a trusted, long-time teacher and member of his Church. The Bishop had a dream that one day his Church would have its own Bible School. When that time came, he would name Mr. Tshwene as its teaching director. "I give him into your hands," he said. "Teach him how to study the Scriptures so that he, in turn, can teach others."

The visit was an answer to prayer. The proposal reflected both acceptance of and trust in the Weavers. Furthermore, as they set up a schedule of Bible study with Rev. Tshwene, he in turn could provide invaluable help as an interpreter of the culture around them and precious insight into the history and life of his Church. Before leaving, the Bishop had still another word. The Weavers were asked to reserve Sunday, July 13 on their calendar for a special day of celebration at his Church. There would be more details later.

In subsequent correspondence the Weavers described that special weekend as follows: "The day [Saturday] was ending and soon it would be dark. As we came near we could hear the sound of music: 'The sun rises in the east and sets in the west but the Spiritual Healing Church will live forever!' Over and over again the refrain was repeated, accompanied by the waving of white handkerchiefs. Prophets, ministers, evangelists, preachers, deacons, elders and laymen of the Spiritual Healing Church had come to Gaborone from as far away as Maun by the Kalahari Desert to take part in the next day's celebration. Ed and I had known about it far in advance. 'Be sure to keep that Sunday open' Rev. Motswasele had told us at least three months earlier. By Saturday evening, nearly all coming from a distance were assembled in the church. At dusk we, too, came to greet them and present ourselves before the Sunday morning service. We came by Rev. Motswasele's invitation. It seemed something that culture required. Someone brought a candle and placed it on the altar rail. There was no other light. So in the light of one little candle we were faced with the welcoming crowd. They were beautiful. And so was their song."

"Sunday morning, July 13th, was bright and crispy. It seemed that everyone was aglow with the spirit of the day. Seven hundred thirty-nine people crowded into the church for the morning service. For many there was only sitting room on the floor. As the service began we sang, we clapped, we knelt to pray. Suddenly there was a hush, a pause in the worship. The whole congregation rose and burst into song to honor the aged Prophet who was entering the church. Prophet Jacob Motswasele, Founder/Head of the Spiritual Healing Church, had come from his home village at Matsiloje, near Francistown, for this special occasion. He is an old man now, and in ill health. With great effort he came to the meeting and sat in his place of honor at the front of the church facing the congregation. This special service was one more step for the fulfillment of his vision. Many years had gone by since God had first spoken to him in a vision. Addressing the church he said, 'I have given everything over to my son. He will now be your leader.' As he spoke from the pulpit, I saw the old father look down lovingly on his son Israel who was sitting with the elders of their Church. The son, Rev. Israel Motswasele, was in charge of the service. Using Scripture passages from Gen 1:1-2 'In the beginning God said let there be light' and Luke 18:35-43 'Lord, let me receive my sight' Rev. Motswasele explained the theme of the service. . . . "

The lengthy service moved along and Irene continued her account: " . . . as Ed and I were kneeling on a rug in the church, the aged Prophet and Rev. Motswasele, in an act of consecration, laid their hands on us and prayed. We were surrounded by the throng of people who had come to receive us as a partner in the development of their training school. As the ministers and leaders came forward one by one, we felt the congregation's throbbing response in song. To me the singing is one of the most beautiful parts of the Indigenous Church worship service. In a healing service, as the ministers lay hands on and pray for the sick and others who are kneeling, the congregation embraces these persons in beautiful, appropriate singing.

Whenever a child is blessed, a marriage consecrated, or a layman consecrated for some special work, always there is the embrace in song. It was so today. . . . "

"Very wisely the church council had chosen and called Mr. J.C. Tshwene, a primary school principal, from near Francistown in the north, and seconded him to work with us. . . . He, too, today was presented to the church and consecrated for his new duties. Again the aged Prophet came forward to lay hands on Brother Tshwene along with Rev. Motswasele and Ed. The Church considers today's event historic, leading to tremendous possibilities for church growth and development. For all of us who took part it brought a solemn realization of great responsibility. It was another step in the fulfillment of a prophet's dream."

"It was now after 2:30 and time to close. 'We will sing again our Church Song before we close' said Rev. Motswasele. For another ten minutes we sang: 'The sun rises in the east and sets in the west but the Spiritual Healing Church will live forever.'"

"We went home to ponder over the events of the day - - and to pray." (12)

The time of tentative waiting had come to an end. A wide door of opportunity had been dramatically opened to the Weavers. Others were soon to follow. The special activities of that July weekend at the Spiritual Healing Church in Gaborone had not gone unnoticed by the broader AIC community. The AIC grapevine in the country was buzzing: "We hear that there is this white couple that has recently arrived in Gaborone who are neither commercial people nor missionaries of any of the missions we know. We hear they have come to help us, we the people of the Spiritual Churches. We hear they are already attending the SHC in Gaborone and may even have joined that Church. Is there a possibility that they would also be willing to help us?"

Gradually knocks at the front door of the Weaver's little home became more frequent. Instinctively they knew that there soon would be many more requests for ministry than they themselves could meet. Based as they were in Gaborone, a primary concern for them was Francistown, the next largest center in the country located along the railway some 280 miles to the northeast. Perched on the eastern edge of the Kalahari Desert, it was a thriving commercial center and the staging point for safaris into the rich game areas of the vast Okavango Swamps another 300 miles to the northwest. But there was more. It was also the location of a cluster of AICs who had organized themselves into what was known as "The Botswana Spiritual Christian Churches" (BSCC). They had already made themselves known to the Weavers and had expressed interest in Bible study.

Word soon arrived in Elkhart from the Weavers that it was time to recruit more help for the new undertaking in Botswana.

The spring of 1975 found Harry and Lois Riehl Dyck in Elkhart, IN, where Harry was finishing requirements for his M.Div degree at the AMBS. They were already in conversation with COM Newton and AIMM staff people about possible service in Africa. As information about AIMM's new horizon of ministry was shared with them, interest quickly grew. By August they were already in Botswana and shortly thereafter were situated in Francistown as the first AIMM missionaries in that part of the country.

meanwhile in Lesotho

While a focus of ministry was taking shape in Botswana, AIMM relations with the Lesotho Evangelical Church were not working out particularly well. It was slowly becoming clear that the LEC leadership had some expectations for this relationship which were not being met. Over time, two areas of growing LEC discontent emerged. The first had to do with what they saw as their administrative jurisdiction over the Busenitzes and their work. Although early dialogue had left AIMM under the impression that they sought someone to give broad direction to a youth ministry within their Church, upon arrival the AIMM couple rather found themselves assigned a variety of custodial, maintenance and clerical work, something which obviously was both disappointing and frustrating for them. Furthermore, when the LEC leadership became aware that Allen was carrying some minimal administrative and investigative responsibilities for AIMM and MCC within the country, LEC leaders made it known that this was unacceptable. They expected that their time and energy be devoted exclusively to the LEC and its needs.

Gradually AIMM became aware of a second complicating factor, that of finances. Though never verbalized in conversations with AIMM, there apparently had been an LEC assumption that with the AIMM personnel would also come some funding for LEC's many program needs. A country-wide church with a variety of institutions and programs, budget problems were real. It was further true that, in the past, expatriate personnel from Europe and Canada had typically became sources of overseas funding for their church needs. When it became clear that AIMM did not fit into this pattern of support, LEC disenchantment grew.

It was in the midst of this less than cordial relationship that the AIMM Board began to actively pursue other opportunities for witness and service in that mountainous, pocket-sized kingdom.

the little chapel in downtown Maseru

As a result of the Busenitzes' early contacts with the Maseru United Church, an AIMM delegation had met with its management committee already in 1974. (13) It quickly became evident that there were concerns on both sides of the table which needed to be addressed. Though struggling to keep the Church open and eager for qualified pastoral help, the MUC representatives wondered if they would be required to become Mennonites in the event an AIMM missionary were provided for them. The quick answer was "No."

For their part, the AIMM representatives had two basic questions: - Would a Mennonite pastor be free to teach and preach according to his beliefs and convictions? "Yes." - Was the church group ready to open its doors to and fellowship with people of all races? Again the answer was affirmative. Convinced that the MUC offered a startling opportunity to seek to bring into being a multiracial ecumenical worshiping fellowship literally within the shadow of *apartheid*, the delegation recommended the placement of a missionary pastoral couple at the MUC.

Among candidate files of that time were those of Robert and Joyce Stradinger Gerhart. They had had ten years of experience in pastoral ministry behind them during which their strong creative gifts had been well demonstrated. Upon Board action their credentials were submitted to the MUC and they were promptly accepted. It was in October 1974 that they arrived to begin AIMM's partnership in mission with that unique group. Over a period of nearly two decades there was to be steady growth both in membership and scope of impact. AIMM involvement with the MUC was nonetheless to become the focus of some controversy within the broader South African Mennonite team. Was not AIMM involvement with the MUC an act of solidarity with the white power structures of South Africa? Was AIMM not generating mixed signals amidst the tragic racial confrontation of the region? Such critique sparked periodic and thorough AIMM evaluation of its pastoral ties with MUC. In each case there was reaffirmation of its commitment to this strategically located little church. With passing time, the growth, composition and impact of the church vindicated the AIMM stance.

the AFCC

In his affable, sensitive manner, Sam Mohono was always available to provide AIMM with helpful information. AIMM initially was under the mistaken impression that he was a member of the LEC. It was only as AIMM's interest in the AICs became clear that he made known his membership in the Church of Moshoeshoe of which his own father had been a cofounder. He further explained that his father had also been the cofounder of an affiliation of AICs in the country originally known as "The African Independent Federal Church Council" which was later abbreviated to "The African Federal Church Council," or AFCC. Although its membership was rather limited in the mid-1970's, there was a tradition of an annual festival which brought together representatives of the member groups for a time of celebration, worship and mutual encouragement.

Mohono was quick to suggest that this organization could easily serve as a sponsoring and coordinating body for AIMM's entry into ministry among them. In Lesotho, as in Botswana, there was ready admission of great need for systematic Bible study among the church leaders. In Lesotho, as elsewhere, there had been a history of friction between the AICs and the mainline mission churches. In Lesotho, as elsewhere, they had never encountered a mission which was prepared to take them seriously or to work with them sympathetically. If AIMM would consider working with this organization, they were delighted and ready.

As AIMM was soon to discover, Sam Mohono was a man of vision who had all manner of ideas and projects to propose. Among them were: - the launching of a program of Theological Education by Extension; - hopes for a residential AIC Bible School; - the dream for a joint AIC administrative center accompanied by a prayer/healing center manned by AIC personnel possessed of the gift of healing; - an AIC-sponsored rural development program with a focus on better care and use of Lesotho's extremely limited agricultural land coupled with an emphasis on vegetable/fruit farming and food preservation (with his gift for phrasing concepts, he liked to talk about "working with both soil and soul"); - the granting of scholarships to a few carefully-selected AIC candidates in areas of theology and church administration. Beyond all this, he spoke of the great need for youth work among the AICs and a program designed specifically for the needs of AIC women. As for the sparse AIC membership in the AFCC, Mohono was sure that if this organization - - with AIMM's help - - became the sponsoring agency for visible and valuable ministries for AIC groups in the country, more churches would apply for membership soon enough.

Persuaded that in Lesotho there was also an open avenue for ministry among the AICs, recruitment was begun at home for possible candidates. One day AIMM board member Andrew Rupp approached a young man on the subject who, at the time, was director of Christian Education in the headquarters of the EMC/US in Ft. Wayne, IN. It was a seed which bore quick fruit. In March 1977, Stan and Lorri Berends Nussbaum arrived in Maseru. Degrees in philosophy, church history and theology (14) coupled with a quick mind equipped Nussbaum unusually well for the innovative leadership he was invited to provide for AIMM's work among the AICs of Lesotho.

an early disaster narrowly averted

Meanwhile in Botswana, AIMM people were encountering a pronounced tone of skepticism on the part of mainline mission personnel regarding the AICs. Although it was granted that there likely were some sincere and dedicated leaders among them, it was also their opinion that there were many unscrupulous opportunists whose so called "churches" were but a camouflage for self-serving interests of all kinds. AIMM personnel, newcomers to the scene that they were, took note of such commentaries but privately tended to regard them as evidence of a general prejudice against the AICs existing in the country. It was not long, however, until AIMM discovered that in Botswana there was at least one such "opportunist."

Once word of the Weaver's arrival in Gaborone had gotten around, an early caller at their home was a portly, articulate and determined man named W. R. Gulubane (pr. goo-loo-BAH-nay). With a wide smile and hearty handshake he introduced himself as the founder and leader of the St. Philips Faith Healing Church with headquarters at Palapye (pr. pah-LAH-pyeh) located approximately half the distance along the main road to Francistown. He had come to greet and welcome them to Botswana in general and to his own Church in particular. He was eager to get better acquainted. He urged them to set a weekend to visit him at his church headquarters to worship with them and to see firsthand the many projects which he was developing, projects for which he was sure the Weavers and the AIMM would be happy to provide much needed personnel and funds.

Pleased for such an early enthusiastic invitation to the headquarters of another Botswana, AIC the Weavers agreed on a time for a weekend visit. Concerning those eventful days the Weavers later wrote: "No one could miss the church site. The sign on the church wall can be seen from quite a far distance. The people were waiting for us. . . . What a welcome! Banners, songs, soft drinks and a tour of the compound. This was Friday before Palm Sunday so already the ministering women of the Church were coming to the compound in preparation for the festivities of Easter. Our host, thinking we would not like to stay among them for the night, arranged for us to have our evening meal and first night at the station [town] hotel. Every detail was graciously and thoughtfully cared for."

"But Rev. Gulubane was not going to let us rest till he had launched what was uppermost in his mind. He knew we were the answer to his great need. He needed money, and needed it now for the enlarged Secondary School which he is planning to build. . . . Very clearly Ed began to tell Rev. Gulubane that we were not prepared to help in this way. We offered to help with Bible teaching, supplying teachers and giving of ourselves. Gulubane would be glad for teachers for his Bible School, but he needed money for the Secondary School. . . ."

"To lodge in the station hotel was defeating our purpose. We needed to be among the people of St. Philips Faith Healing church, available at all times for dialogue. We needed to hear what they were saying. So on Saturday morning we moved out of the hotel onto the compound of the Church. The next two nights we slept in Rev. Gulubane's camper. . . . Everything we needed was there. . . . A new latrine had been put up back of the camper. As we prepared for the night, our host said to one of the ministering women: 'Go and get that chamber. These people will not want to go out in the dark with the witches.' . . ."

"Rev. Gulubane spent hours with us. The students and the church people were all around us. Rev. Gulubane still kept pressing us for money. All day Saturday and most of Sunday we continually tried to get across to him that people are more important than buildings; that love and acceptance and personnel to help in the Bible School were more important than money. Even through the services in the church, Gulubane assured his people that Rev. Weaver would not fail him, and would supply his need."

The Weavers then described the closing service: "Ed spoke about what it means to follow Jesus. . . . At the close he gave an invitation for anyone to come forward who wanted to rededicate his life. Many came forward - - almost everyone. Ed was ready to end his part of the service when Rev. Gulubane came forward and knelt alone. At the close of the prayer, as Gulubane was getting up from his knees, Ed kept hold of his hands and exchanged places with him. Now Ed was kneeling and Rev. Gulubane was praying for him. . . . As we were leaving the next morning, our host said: 'I am going to be very lonely when you are gone.' We replied: 'Rev. Gulubane, love and acceptance are more important than money.' 'Yes,' he said." (15)

Feeling that they had, in fact, established a new ground of understanding with this ambitious church leader, recommendation soon came to the home office to give serious consideration to recruiting a mature, experienced pastoral couple for the newly-opened Bible School at Palapye.

It was, therefore, quite a surprise when shortly after their weekend at Palapye, Rev. Gulubane appeared at their door in Gaborone to announce that he was going to the States to personally meet with the people who had sent the Weavers . . . . A man of considerable personal resources, airfare for a round-trip ticket to North America was no deterrent. He clearly believed that financial contributions would be forthcoming when he personally made his appeal in overseas Mennonite circles. All he needed from the Weavers was the names and addresses of Mennonite church leaders in North America!

Taken aback by his determination to make his case for himself overseas, the Weavers quickly sent word to the AIMM Secretary in Elkhart. Making reference to their reporting on their weekend at Palapye, they continued: "Though we were able to persuade him not to press Mennonites for financial aid for his schools, we did not convince him that there were not funds . . . in America that could be tapped . . . . You will note that I have given the names of persons who might act as contact people. In the Elkhart-Goshen area I have given your name. I realize that this may come to you as a tremendous surprise. . . . I hope it will work out well." (16)

Rev. Gulubane did make his trip. Making the basement guest facility of the AIMM Secretary's home his base of operations, arrangements were made for contact with a variety of Mennonite denominational leaders. No stone was left unturned in his effort to tap the funds he believed to be available. But as his time came to a close, he discovered that Ed Weaver's information had been accurate after all. The Mennonites were indeed interested in offering people and their skills but were not interested in providing financial grants.

Undaunted by his failure to secure financial help, he returned to Botswana to keep close contact with the Weavers. In the summer of 1975, in the course of an administrative trip by AIMM board personnel, (17) Gulubane made sure that the itinerary included an extended stop at Palapye, his Church headquarters. There he escorted the delegation on a tour of the grounds and buildings already erected while explaining projects still on his drawing boards. In their discussions he frequently underscored his theme: "We've only begun. Much remains to be done. We need your help."

An entry in the AIMM Secretary's journal at this point reads: "He travels much. His means of locomotion, a recent model one-ton, four wheel drive Ford pickup. . . . They have been granted three plots of ground by local authorities; the one where the headquarters is being built, the one where he hopes to build a complete secondary school and a third some distance outside the village where he wants to develop a vocational training school. . . . He is looking first and above all to American Mennonites for help to realize all of these projects. . . . For funds he is now looking to MCC and other organizations. For personnel he is looking to both AIMM and MCC."

A second memorable delegation encounter with Rev. Gulubane, during that trip, was in the setting of a special evening meeting in Francistown with a large group of AIC leaders organized by an AIC group identified that evening as the "Inter-Spiritual Christian Church Council." At this point the journal entries observed: "Rev. Gulubane, as Secretary of Public Relations, pretty well engineered the evening and its happenings. He circulated photocopies of the evening agenda and we were launched. In an opening speech by Bishop Monyatse (pr. moh-NYAH-tseh) of the Eleven Apostles Healing Spirit Church, the following points were made: From I Kings 5:1-6 it was observed that King Solomon was only able to build the temple as he received aid from his friends. For a long while the AIC leaders had been dreaming of building 'their temple.' It now appeared that God had, at long last, sent them some 'friends' to help them in their task."

It then came Rev. Gulubane's turn to take the floor. Among his comments were these: "I went overseas, I met these our friends. We are not members of the Botswana Christian Council (made up primarily of mainline churches). We were discriminated against by the Registration Act. We fought a 'Christian war;' finally the great majority of our churches were registered. The churches of the Botswana Christian Council are old, wealthy, influential and powerful. We are young, poor and without much power but we are going to continue our struggle until we replace the BCC. We've come through a time of spiritual bondage and suffering. But we don't like to think about that. The BCC is composed of foreigners and refugees. We are the indigenous children of this country. Your arrival among us renewed our spirits. In the past the church overseas has not known about us, but your visit indicates that we are now known. We now believe that we'll be able 'to build our temple.'"

Arriving at the point in the program which called for comments from the AIMM delegation, thanks were first expressed for the hospitality and warm welcome extended them. The delegation then made several statements: - Our primary interest is in the area of Bible instruction. - We want to help as many AICs as possible. - We will not be a part of anything that would tend to further divide or split the church community of Botswana; on the contrary we are much interested in reconciliation. - We seek together with you to discover what God's purpose and will for us in Botswana now is.

Regarding the closure of the evening there was yet a journal comment: "The evening was finally concluded by what Brother Gulubane referred to as a 'truly apostolic song. We spiritual Christians clap and dance when we are happy,' he explained, whereupon he proceeded to lead out on a number, clapping and doing a brisk two-step in a sidewise circular fashion in the front of the hall. It was not long before he was joined by others. The circle enlarged, the tempo quickened, a syncopation of beat found its way into the clapping and a cloud of dust partially obscured the glow of the light bulb hanging from the ceiling. Some twenty minutes later

Brother Gulubane, glowing with pleasure and perspiration, brought the evening to a close. After a benediction everyone in the hall filed by to shake our hands, to thank us for coming and to wish us well." (18)

As the delegation pondered the events of that colorful evening with the Weavers, it was clear that there was a great deal which was still unknown about the AICs of the country. It was also clear that the forceful Gulubane remained something of an enigma. And yet, after some earlier weeks of biding their time in Gaborone, suddenly there was a rush of AIC doors which seemed to be swinging wide before the AIMM. With the Weavers in Gaborone and the Dycks in Francistown, would not the opening at the Palapye Bible School be a reasonable placement for a third AIMM couple? When in subsequent conversations with Gulubane he gave assurance that adequate housing would be provided on his campus for such a couple, AIMM turned to the recruitment of qualified candidates.

Among those in North America who had been following AIMM's new ministry among AICs were Irwin and Lydia Guenther Friesen. Long-time missionaries to Zaire under the Mennonite Brethren Board of Missions they had returned to the States in 1971 for several years of church related ministry. After discussion both with them and the MB Board, they arrived in Botswana in November, 1976. Their assignment: to teach in the Bible School founded by Rev. Gulubane in the name of the St. Philips Faith Healing Church.

It was just six months later that a visiting AIMM Secretary found all manner of warning flags snapping in the Botswana breeze. Things were not going well with Rev. Gulubane at Palapye. First of all, assurances to the contrary, the Friesens arrived to find that the housing promised was not ready for them. A student roster for the Bible School was not clear either. Renting other housing in the general vicinity, the Friesens had begun Bible classes with interested AIC people on their own while observing the Palapye campus at close hand.

Meanwhile, MCC had been trying to reach an understanding regarding the vocational training school Gulubane wanted to open. Larry Fisher, the MCC country director of the time, was clearly interested in securing some qualified personnel but had made the stipulation that a school board be established composed of people of the area to which MCC could relate. Considering the proposed school his idea and his project, Gulubane saw no need of a board. Thus the project was at a stalemate.

Furthermore, some troubling snippets of news had begun to surface about this flamboyant man. He was a former civil servant who was dismissed when it was discovered that some of the activities in his office went beyond his jurisdiction and authority. His sympathies for a political opposition group in the country had also become known. He was in debt with a local construction firm for supplies he had ordered by cable during his trip to the states. His marital status was not clear either. There was no resident wife at Palapye. Meanwhile it was quietly rumored that the functions of some of the "ministering women" at Palapye could be broadly interpreted.

Most significant of all, there was the slowly growing realization of the guarded manner in which the broad AIC community of the country viewed him and his Church. It had become clear that the Bible School had no administrative board either and that it was answerable to him alone. Not assured of impartial welcome or treatment as students, there were no candidates for study from any independent church other than his own.

A moment of decision had come for AIMM.

It was on a June morning in 1977 that the AIMM Executive Secretary, accompanied by Irvin Friesen, made a last official call at the church headquarters at Palapye. It was explained that it had become clear that his operating guidelines for his school did not mesh well with AIMM's hopes for ministry to the broad AIC community of the country. In view of the fact that requests for Bible study were now starting to come in from various other churches, we felt it best that the Friesens develop their own program in the area, a study program to which the people of St. Philips would be most welcome if they cared to come.

The enterprise at Palapye was led by an immensely gifted and visionary man who was possessed of an enormous drive to achieve. Tragically, he was also a deeply flawed man. AIMM had come to understand this just in time - - and stepped back. There were by then many other AICs in the country led by people who, if less gifted, were nonetheless genuine in their concern for their churches and who sincerely sought help from the AIMM. It was such opportunities that AIMM sought.

CHAPTER 52   "MENNONITE MINISTRIES" IS BORN

Isn't a Mennonite a Mennonite?

By the time the Weavers arrived in Botswana early in 1975, MCC had already been in the country for seven years under a technical assistance agreement with the Botswana government. Under this arrangement the usual formalities of entry were waived. As MCC personnel was recruited for placement in government sponsored schools and development projects, it sufficed for the MCC country director to submit their names and qualifications to secure clearance for their arrival in the country.

When the Weavers were preparing to leave the States they were advised to simply apply for residence papers upon arrival. When asked at the airport by officials their purpose in coming, they explained that they were assigned to work with Botswana Churches under the sponsorship of the Africa Inter-Mennonite Mission. "This is a Mennonite organization?" "Yes, a Mennonite organization."

For the civil servants at the airport, a Mennonite was a Mennonite. News by this time had gotten around that these were people who were welcome in their newly independent country. They brought many skills and, furthermore, truly wanted to help them in their task of nation-building. If the Weavers also were Mennonites, they were welcome.

With passing time, however, as they went about the details of establishing residence, purchasing a vehicle, seeking driver's permits and, eventually, alerting the immigration office of more people to follow, authorities more clearly understood that, in fact, they were dealing with two separate Mennonite organizations, one of which was a Mission. Thus people who were arriving under the auspices of the Mission must be regarded as missionaries and subject to regular visa requirements. Furthermore, as a Mission organization, there were stipulations for registration which also had to be met.

There followed months of conversations with government officials. At times there was talk of deadlines for regularizing the presence of AIMM personnel already in the country. Sometimes dates were set for the completion of all legal requirements only to be postponed. Eventually AIMM's legal situation became clear: as soon as there were ten or more AIMM missionaries in Botswana, AIMM would be required to file for registration as a new organization in the country. That time was already fast approaching. By the end of 1976, there were already four couples in the country. One more couple would put the AIMM team at ten people. (1)

Registration, as such, was no problem. The procedure, once understood, was straightforward and uncomplicated. There was by this time assurance that such an application would be favorably received by the authorities.

Mennonites: how many kinds?

But there was a lurking question which kept surfacing with regularity in the conversations among AIMM personnel, both in Botswana and at home. With a positive Mennonite identity already well established in Botswana, what would be the implications and repercussions of pursuing AIMM registration? Would this not, at the very least, cause confusion in the minds of the people? If Mennonites in Botswana truly shared common goals there, what then was the necessity for two different organizations?

The decade of the 1970'sseventies found administrative personnel in the Akron and Elkhart offices who had earlier served in Africa. (2) In the mid-70's Jim Bertsche and Ray Brubacher had traveled together in Lesotho and had attempted to assess the needs and opportunities for ministry there for the organizations they represented. By this time, MCC had already worked out a joint administrative program in East Africa with Eastern Mennonite Board of Missions and had found it to be a mutually beneficial experience. As the two men traveled in Lesotho, there was ample opportunity to wonder out loud about the possibility of some similar AIMM/MCC arrangement in southern Africa.

Early on, MCC Akron staff let it be known that there was live interest in exploring such a relationship. This interest was quickly translated into action in Lesotho as, at MCC's request, AIMM's Allen Buzenitz during his first term served as part-time MCC country representative. As the need for AIMM registration in Botswana loomed, Akron personnel again suggested that some sort of joint arrangement there might merit consideration. The AIMM Board at that point, however, was largely oriented toward pursuing its own course. By January 1977 there was already a tentative draft of a constitution for "AIMM Botswana" being studied by the AIMM Executive Committee. (3)

As the AIMM involvement in Botswana unfolded, however, the personnel count leveled off at nine for a couple of years. Discussions about registration consequently proceeded at a more leisurely pace. It should be noted that some new AIMM voices had joined the discussion. When in April 1977 the Weavers concluded their term of service, a search for new team leadership was underway. It was in May 1978 that John and Ruth Fast Kliewer arrived in Gaborone. Long-time missionaries in Zaire under the sponsorship of the Mennonite Brethren Board of Missions (now known as MBMS International), upon their return to North America they served as representatives of their Church both to the MCC and the AIMM Board.

Yet another voice was added to the mix. Ronald Sawatzky had completed a three year term in the summer of 1975 as a math teacher in a government school under MCC auspices. Committed to longer-term service in that country, he applied to and was accepted by AIMM in 1977 for reappointment to continuing service as a Christian teacher in a government teacher training school. Having served with both organizations, he became an enthusiastic advocate of some kind of unified Mennonite stance in the country.

But for every voice supportive of some new form of inter-Mennonite venture in Botswana, there was another which counseled caution. When in October, 1980, there was a proposal for both a joint AIMM/MCC registration and a joint program in that country, there were quick reservations: "Is it in fact possible for one person (a joint country director) to adequately administer both programs? Since it (AIMM) is smaller and more recently arrived in the country, is it possible that AIMM may lose its identity and sense of direction? Is there danger that the AIMM will be overshadowed or dominated in this relationship and that we will be hampered in maintaining our emphasis upon evangelism and spiritual nurture? Clarity is lacking in some respects. Will we eventually be the losers?" (4)

Reservations, however, were not limited to the AIMM camp alone. In a paper presented by MCC country director John Eby in February, 1980, he correctly suggested that there were some questions which needed to be faced seriously such as: "Do AIMM and MCC work from the same theology and philosophy? Can both . . . work with the same administrative philosophy and style in Botswana? Is it possible to include in one program the divergent specialties now represented by the current AIMM/MCC programs?" (5) These were legitimate concerns in which other MCC recruits also shared.

In spite of evident inter-Mennonite jitters all around, there emerged a conviction that in Botswana AIMM and MCC found themselves in a unique situation. Jointly confronted by an unusual mix of problems and opportunities, the challenge seemed clear to summon the will and faith to plow some new furrows of inter-Mennonite collaboration. On one occasion the AIMM Executive Secretary observed: "If AIMM and MCC intend to try to close ranks somewhere sometime in Africa, Botswana is the place and the time is now."

In his study paper Eby not only highlighted possible problems but, also, underscored good reasons for moving ahead with some form of joint ministry, e.g., "The Biblical imperative to be in mission includes both word and deed integrally interrelated. Our structures for doing programming should reflect that unity. Two Mennonite . . . programs in Botswana are unnecessarily confusing to local people. Our witness will be enforced by unity. AIMM must soon register with the government. It seems better to register only one Mennonite program. There would be administrative efficiencies if there were a more unified program. Local programs would more likely include both word and deed in integrated ministries to the whole person." (6)

The Eby paper further suggested some principles to be followed, some possible next steps and a diagram of a possible organizational model. There was a concluding notation: "This paper is jointly prepared by John Kliewer (AIMM) and John Eby (MCC) in Botswana. Together we recommend a) that we proceed with joint registration as soon as possible using the organizational model above and, b) that serious discussion continue in both North America and Botswana leading to additional steps toward a joint program . . . as the nature of such steps becomes clear." (7)

In the same October 1980 board meeting, where AIMM reservations about a joint program in Botswana were discussed at length, the following action was eventually proposed and passed: "That the AIMM Board approve a conjoint country administrator in Botswana with MCC; that AIMM recruit such a person if this is mutually acceptable to MCC and that such a person be under AIMM support arrangements with 50% carried by each party; that such an arrangement be subject to review within two years." (8)

It was on this rather guarded and cautious note that AIMM gave its approval to an effort to bring something new into being under the Mennonite sun.

things take shape

The time to initiate legal proceedings in Botswana came at a point when two key people were approaching the end of their terms. June 1981 found John Kliewer, AIMM field coordinator, within a couple of months of returning to the States. John Eby, MCC field director, was starting the last year of his term. They nonetheless vigorously pursued their project of drafting a joint constitution and bylaws in consultation with government officials. There was no end of questions. First of all, what should this new joint AIMM/MCC organization be called? Someone suggested "Mennonite Ministries." Why not? That said it as well as anything for it was indeed the desire of both organizations to pool their respective experience, personnel and expertise in a common, shared ministry in the name of Christ in Botswana.

Then there was the question of intent. What would be the stated purpose of the new inter-Mennonite body? An eventual four-point statement was incorporated into the constitution: 1) to extend the Gospel of Jesus Christ; 2) to provide a Bible teaching ministry to existing churches, groups and individuals; 3) to carry out ministries of benevolence and service in areas such as education, development, agriculture, social service and other areas of human need; 4) to provide personnel, funding and other kinds of assistance to local organizations working in development. (9) In the manner of constitutions everywhere, other concerns such as membership, officers, powers, quorum, amendments and dissolution were spelled out, as well.

Dated June 12, 1981, the long-awaited government approval arrived. Sparsely worded it marked the successful conclusion of months of dialogue, effort and prayer: "Enclosed please find registration certificate CR 062 issued in respect of Mennonite Ministries in Botswana. Your application has been successful; and your Society is registered under the Societies Act."

Both AIMM and MCC recognized that, long-term, nothing was more crucial to the success of their new venture than the recruitment of their first jointly-appointed leadership personnel who could bring maturity, previous African experience and deep commitment to the historic concerns of both parties to the new venture. Even as the final stages of government registration were under way, administrators in the States were in dialogue with Fremont and Sara Regier. If they accepted, they would bring strong qualifications to this sensitive new assignment. Fremont had served as a single man with AIMM under the MCC-sponsored PAX program in Zaire. After marriage, they had both served a short term with MCC in Mexico. Thereafter they accepted AIMM appointment to Zaire where they worked for three terms developing an innovative church related AIMM/MCC sponsored program of rural development.

Accepting AIMM/MCC's invitation to provide administrative leadership for the newly-created MM program in Botswana, they were sent to Gaborone in the summer of 1981 for a year of language study and orientation. This was possible due to John Eby's presence and willingness to serve as MM's first legal representative during his last year in the country. In this role he provided invaluable groundwork for the Regiers who picked up their new responsibilities in the summer of 1982.

negotiating potholes in the MM path

The early going in the new MM venture was not friction-free. First of all, there were some people in both camps who viewed the new enterprise with some misgiving. Skeptical that MM could be made to work, the stance of some seemed to be: "We'll wait and see but we don't expect much!" AIMM and MCC, it was said, were too diverse to be brought together in a smoothly-functioning, joint venture. AIMM recruited people for long term service, MCC for short terms. This usually resulted in "older" and "younger" recruits with all of the differences in views, values and concerns such age differences implied. AIMM and MCC support patterns were drastically different. Furthermore AIMMers tended to work via consensus while maintaining close contact with their home office in Elkhart. MCCers, on the other hand, engaged in many meetings and in lengthy annual "planning sessions." AIMM's historic focus had always been evangelism and spiritual nurture whereas MCC's had been more in areas of responses to disaster, community development and, in recent years, issues of peace and justice. To all of this was yet to be added the often sharply divergent views on what constituted Christian identity and faithful discipleship in the context of brutal racism in southern Africa. How do you mix all of this together, some wanted to know, and expect it to work?

All important to the birth of MM and its steady development across the years has been an unswerving conviction on the part of more and more people that, at least in the context of Botswana, this was a venture that was right, an idea that had found its time and place. When differing opinions arose and consensus proved elusive, it was important that these shared convictions were frequently reaffirmed. A case in point is a letter addressed by the AIMM Secretary of the time to MCC Africa personnel in Akron in 1985. Before addressing the issue specifically at hand, he first reflected briefly on the frictions which had characterized some Mennonite mission and MCC personnel relations in overseas settings in the past which "generated more smoke than illumination. In such settings, it was easy indeed to categorize one another in uncomplimentary terms and to lay program plans, at best, independently of each other and, at worst, at cross-purposes with each other. It has always been our conviction that as Mennonites overseas, we are called to higher ground than that!"

Moving to AIMM's vision for MM, the AIMM Secretary went on to write: "It continues our hope that through MM we can strengthen a process of regular intra-team dialogue and cross-fertilization as to its *raison d'être* in Botswana and southern Africa; nurture a sense of accountability to each other within the team and a sense of ownership in the efforts and ministries of fellow team members; continually affirm the diversity of gifts, skills and training brought together by the AIMM/MCC team members; field a more broadly equipped and diverse team than either of us would be able to do alone or independently of each other. "

Moving to another topic the letter continues: "AIMM approaches its partnership in MM with the expectation that both AIMM's and MCC's historic concerns, experience and expertise will continue to find outlet for ministry within the MM partnership; that these concerns will not stand in competition or conflict with each other within MM but will rather supplement each other and enhance overall Mennonite presence and impact for good within the country; that it be the vehicle of a truly holistic team ministry." (10)

With passing time, word about MM began to get around both in Africa and in North America. Both Elkhart and Akron began to receive inquiries from possible candidates who were attracted by the new model of ministry in Botswana. In orientations they needed no convincing but rather arrived already persuaded that it was a program of which they wanted to be a part.

Perhaps the single most significant contribution to the development and progress of MM was the creation of several standing committees each of which focused on some particular area of service. With AIMM's continuing preoccupation with the AICs, the committee of particular interest was the one which focused on Bible teaching and Christian education. Comprised of both AIMM and MCC personnel plus AIC representatives, the committee in its regular sessions became a vehicle for the sharing of ideas, concerns, questions, problems, success and failures. Other committees, with other focal points, had much the same experience. In such settings, AIMM and MCC profiles diminished sharply as committee members freely talked, debated and prayed about MM agenda and its ministry in which they all shared.

Since its creation MM has steadily acquired an identity of its own in Botswana. In 1994 Eric Fast, the MM co-country representative wrote: "Overall the positives [of the MM arrangement] have far outweighed the negatives. The long-term AIMMers are a hundred percent behind the Mennonite Ministries concept. The MCCers don't know much about the differences between themselves and the AIMMers and they don't really care to know. We're all seen as MM workers. This is really the key to making the Mennonite Ministries concept work." (11)

MM: a broad umbrella

If a few civil servants in offices of government had acquired some understanding of AIMM and MCC as separate entities, for the rank-and-file people of Botswana, their acronyms were meaningless. All they knew was that some white-skinned expatriates were among them; that they called themselves Mennonites and that they were open to serving in a wide variety of service roles in their country. This stance of availability resulted, over time, in a startling variety of requests for help. From the government side, there was a standing invitation for qualified teachers for a network of government schools scattered across the land. Via MCC recruitment, many young American volunteers found their way into Botswana classrooms.

The government was also looking for qualified technicians to help operate a variety of vocational training programs and development schemes such as poultry projects, dry land agriculture and vegetable gardening under net shelters. One particularly successful innovation was the creation of a "tool bar" by MCC volunteer Eric Rempel. The concept was a basic, simple, steel frame mounted on two wheels which could be pulled by two donkeys and be equipped, with minor changes and attachments, to haul two barrels of water, plow or cultivate crops. Everything was fabricated locally except the wheels. When later MM began to disengage from government programs, some innovative schemes were developed in partnership with area AICs.

a place called Xanagas

One of the most intriguing MM involvements in which MCC took the lead was a government resettlement project for the legendary Bushmen people. Known among anthropologists as San or Basarwa, the large Kalahari Desert of Botswana is one of the few remaining areas where the Bushmen have still been able to pursue their nomadic gathering and hunting style of life. Two major factors have come into play which have increasingly squeezed these diminutive people out of the arid areas which for many generations had been their homeland - - recurring times of severe drought and the steady encroachment of cattle ranchers who have been in need of more and more grazing land for their herds.

It is to the credit of the Botswana government that the crisis of this tiny ethnic minority in the country was recognized. Official response took the form of efforts to relocate the Bushmen in settlements on the fringes of the desert while trying to help them make a transition to a sedentary life style based around a driven well, a few head of cattle and garden plots. It was for one such resettlement project that MCC recruited personnel who became part of a fascinating expatriate team effort.

The Black Dutch Reformed Church of South Africa had been looking for an area for mission outreach beyond its own national borders. This was at a time when Rev. Willie Cilliers was serving the black Church as its Secretary for Evangelism and Mission. A descendent of Huguenot ancestors who had fled religious persecution in Europe and sought refuge in South Africa many generations earlier, Cilliers was among a restive minority of pastors within the white Dutch Reformed Church who, already in the mid-70's, were condemning apartheid and were seeking ways of allying themselves with their black brothers and sisters across the artificial racial barriers enforced by their white Church.

Interested in attempting mission outreach among the displaced Bushmen of Botswana, the black Church had recruited missionary candidates to send. Cilliers realized that there also needed to be other members of the envisaged team if the complex issues of resettlement were to be addressed. Having already served as a resource person at a Mennonite retreat, he had become acquainted with MCC personnel and the Mennonite approach to service in southern Africa. At his initiative, MCC was approached about placing a couple to work with the rural community development side of the scheme. Thus, as the new MM organization took shape in the early 1980's, one facet of its outreach was at a place called Xanagas (pr. KAH-nah-hahs) on the arid western fringes of Botswana. The improbable team of expatriates was comprised of the Black Dutch Reformed Church Pastor Joshua Seklohe, the white pastor Johan Schmitz and their families plus Randy and Roxie Flaming Ewert, the MM appointees. Over time, other MM appointees followed.

It was not an easy assignment. Government concern notwithstanding, prejudice against the Bushmen within the general population was deep rooted. Often obliged by hunger to hire themselves out as herdsmen to cattle ranchers, they were typically treated with less concern and care than the animals they herded. The tug of their traditional, nomadic desert life furthermore was powerful. The way of their forefathers was not easily uprooted. It was not uncommon for families to simply disappear from the settlements for weeks at a time only to eventually reappear driven back by thirst or hunger. The invitations to place their children in school and to cultivate gardens was a radical departure from the life that had been theirs for generations past. Under imposed idleness, their pride and self-esteem tended to erode and alcoholism became a scourge in their new unnatural surroundings. The efforts of the team at Xanagas was truly one made in the interests and defense of a voiceless, powerless, exploited group of people.

This effort did not go unnoticed in the broader world. At one point, a team from Time magazine appeared on the scene. Viewed by the reporters as people engaged in a curious, atypical assignment for church-related personnel, the Ewerts appeared, soon thereafter, on the cover of an issue of that magazine. (12)

an opening at Radio Botswana

On the AIMM side of the Mennonite Ministries equation, an equally intriguing service opportunity presented itself early in the game. Soon after achieving political independence in 1966, the government established a Department of Information and Broadcasting. One facet of this department was Radio Botswana. Eager to avail themselves of this new avenue of communication, a variety of Churches approached the government via their Botswana Council of Churches (BCC) seeking air time for religious programs. It was eventually agreed that Radio Botswana would grant up to 5% of its total air time for free religious programming if the Council could come up with someone qualified to oversee and organize such programming for them.

After some initial searching, a German national was secured from Swaziland for this post but personality clashes soon emerged and his services were terminated. Into this opening then stepped the Dutch Reformed Church (DRC). Providing personnel and equipment for a studio in Gaborone, programs of professional quality were soon being produced. Having nothing else, the BCC and Radio Botswana put these tapes on the air. But in view of the rising social and political tension of the times, the DRC link was becoming an increasingly sensitive issue both for the Council and the government. It was not long after the arrival of the Weavers that inquiry came from the BCC. Was this an area of ministry in which the Mennonites might take an interest? When the Weavers indicated that the Mennonites would at least be prepared to give the opening consideration, further dialogue quickly followed.

They were not looking for a technician. Radio Botswana had its own technical staff. What was needed and wanted was someone with experience in religious programming, as such, who could bring organizational and administrative skills to his appointment. Such a person would, in effect, serve as the Council's coordinating liaison person between the Churches and the radio voice of their country. Conditions were few and straight forward: the programming was to be nondenominational in thrust and nonpolitical in nature. Programs were not to be offensive to any of the religious groups in the country. And serious effort was to be made to train a

Motswana to eventually replace the expatriate in this role. Aside from these few stipulations, the religious programmer being sought would have large leeway in the nature and scope of the programs put on the air.

It was in a February 1976 meeting of the Southern Africa Task Force, a subcommittee of the Council of Mennonite Board Secretaries (now known as the Council of International Ministries, or CIM) comprised of Board representatives who had program interests in southern Africa, that this opening was presented for discussion and evaluation. There was clear consensus that the matter ought to be pursued further and that the AIMM should take the initiative.

The working out of an assignment to this remarkable opportunity in Botswana became an interesting exercise in Mennonite networking. An early inquiry for counsel went to Ken Weaver, the executive director of Mennonite Broadcasts, Inc., of Harrisonburg, VA. Not only did Weaver consider the Botswana opening to be challenging, he also had a person to suggest for the opening - - Rev. Norman Derstine. A man of both teaching and pastoral experience, he had earlier worked at Mennonite Broadcasts. At the time of writing he was on their Board and serving as the Director of Church Relations at Eastern Mennonite College. Not only was he well qualified but was anticipating a sabbatical leave of absence for the following school year. Norman and Virginia Martin Derstine arrived in Gaborone in June of 1976. In consultations with the College, an original nine-month leave stretched into twenty-four months with partial support from the school. An eventual total support package was fashioned with contributions from three different denominational sources. (13)

As they do in Africa, the Derstines discovered upon their arrival that "things take time"! First, a key person in the radio department was out of the country. Then it was someone in the Council who was traveling. In the meantime, Derstine could only wait. On one occasion his "musings" found their way into a letter to Elkhart: "People are more important than programs: programs do not begin at the appointed hour; programs are not 'programmed'; programs without western agendas; programs, assignments . . . slow in developing; time seems to merge into eternity; time seems to be 'awaiting'; time: past-present-future not clearly defined; time is neither slave nor master; time is more plentiful than anything else. Frustrated with frustration, I muse ; does the pendulum need to swing this far, Lord? Does the concern for 'program' really mean less concern for 'people?' Conversely, does concern for 'people' mean less interest in 'program?' Are western people who have been schooled in efficiency not useable here? People are more important than programs. Forgive, Lord, my recurring frustrations. You too believed that people were important, more important than manmade programs." (14)

Eventually all of the pieces fell into place and Derstine began putting together a schedule of programming. An early happy development was the allocation of a time slot just before the first morning newscast for a daily devotional meditation. At a time when the whole country was stirring and preparing for the day and awaiting the first news, there was opportunity to focus the listeners' attention on issues of faith and their spiritual welfare. An early centerpiece of Derstine's programming was the theme "No Man is an Island," around which he developed a long series of related Biblical meditations. Later, as racial conflict steadily rose in the neighboring Republic of South Africa, he developed a series around the general theme of "Strength to Love." Drawing on materials from Martin Luther King, among others, he opened and closed the meditations with appropriate Scripture passages. Once assembled, he added an African touch by having a local pastor read the materials.

In addition to the daily devotional slots, time was added for general church news, sacred music and regular Sunday worship services in which various local pastors were invited to bring messages. By the time the Derstines approached the end of their two year stint, a clear profile of religious programming had emerged. Listener response was growing. Expressions of appreciation from both the BCC and the Radio Botswana staff were frequently heard.

With this apparent success, AIMM was eager to recruit and send replacements to continue the radio ministry just begun. The spring of 1978 found Henry and Naomi Zacharias Unrau in Goshen, IN where Henry was finishing his studies for a BA in communications at Goshen College. He had served from 1970 to 1972 as a PAX man in Zaire with AIMM and had demonstrated strong gifts in music and youth work. Would they be interested in an assignment in religious programming with Radio Botswana? A positive answer was prompt in coming.

Quickly settling into the general program formats that Derstine had worked out, Unrau began to introduce innovations of his own. Early in his first term he chanced upon an African Lutheran pastor named Oswald Dipheko (pr. di-PEH-koh) who listened to the daily programs and was much interested in them - - so interested that he offered to serve as translator or speaker if Unrau welcomed the help. There quickly developed a team relationship that was to carry across the years of Unrau's service with the BCC and Radio Botswana. With this linguistic help available, the regular format of the 10 minute morning Biblical meditation was changed to allow for a 3½ minute meditation in English followed by 4½ minute version of the same meditation by Rev. Dipheko in Setswana, the primary language of the country. With opening and interspersed music, it made a ten minute package just before the first news of the morning which drew an increasing audience across the Texas-sized country of Botswana.

Adopting an overall theme "A Closer Look," a variety of topics were explored in some detail, e.g., "The Way to Happiness" (a study of the Sermon on the Mount); The Proverbs (which were interspersed with relevant African proverbs); "Love in Marriage" (which prompted a sharp increase in letters addressed to the Unrau/Dipheko team); "Stories for Children;" "God's Letter of Love" (a N.T. survey); "Bible Teaching for Parents;" "The Parables of Jesus;" "Choices for Today;" and "Independence and Freedom."

Along the way there was special seasonal programming for Christmas, New Year's Day, Easter and national holidays. Slowly but surely the program and the featured voices of Unrau and Dipheko were gaining national recognition and influence. While there was some critique in the flow of letters, the great majority carried messages of appreciation.

Such was the esteem in which the Unrau/Dipheko team was held that upon the death of Seretse Khama, the country's first and revered president, all normal programming was canceled and Radio Botswana personnel came to them asking that they take charge of air time with whatever they deemed appropriate for the country in its time of deep loss and sorrow. There followed a mix of music, Scripture readings and "open microphone" sessions in which pastors, country leaders and ordinary citizens were invited to the studios to express their personal appreciation for their departed president as well as their grief.

stepping on sensitive toes

It was in early 1984 that the Unrau/Dipheko team decided to do a series of morning devotionals on the general theme of peace and justice. In this series, as in all others, they sought to relate their messages to the daily life and experience of their listeners. And, as in the other series, they invited reactions and comments from their radio audience. Letters were not long in coming, letters which raised questions about such issues as inequities in government policies; the preferential treatment of influential people in the courts; the rising problem of alcoholism while many liquor stores were owned and operated by government figures; and the widespread exploitation of the Bushmen people.

Realizing full well the sensitive nature of what they were doing, Unrau and Dipheko struggled to arrive at a decision. Would they retreat into vague, safe generalities or would they continue to be specific enough to make the issues at stake perfectly clear? Upon consultation with Radio Botswana personnel and church leaders, they decided to remain specific.

Thus it was on March 28, 1984, that a Western Union telegram arrived in the AIMM office in Elkhart stating: "Most religious broadcasting including Henry's own program permanently suspended. Searching for direction."

On the scene in Botswana, although there was no written form of the order, the end result was all too clear. Except for routine daily morning and evening prayers and some Sunday worship services, the bulk of the religious programming developed by the Unrau/Dipheko duo, including their immensely popular early morning meditations, had been wiped from the air.

What had happened?

Unrau eventually learned that it was particularly the Minister of Public Service and Information, under whose government department Radio Botswana operated, who was irritated with the thrust of the series and eventually issued orders for the suspension of a block of programming until such time as "an acceptable format would be established." The word was that he was particularly irate that such issues as alcoholism (he himself operated a liquor store), the treatment of employees, Basarwa questions, and inequities in the courts should be discussed and exposed on government radio.

Response from across the country was quick. Irate inquiries came from all directions. It is interesting to note, however, that the only formal written protest lodged with the government by a church group was that of the AIC Botswana Spiritual Council of Churches. Their letter was hand delivered to government authorities by Otsile Ditsheko of the Spiritual Healing Church. Their courage notwithstanding, people in power had been embarrassed by the "peace and justice" series and had reacted. In spite of widespread protest, there was no way for government figures to retreat without losing face. Although some of the former programming was eventually reinstated, the Unrau/Dipheko "A Closer Look" series never was.

This chapter in MM ministry in Botswana obviously stirred a lot of discussion both among MM workers and AIMM Board members. An ancient missiological dilemma had been revisited: in the presence of obvious injustice and evil, should expatriate missionaries remain silent and safe or should they be prophetic and risk retaliation against their ministry and perhaps even expulsion from the country?

On the part of one key church leader on the scene, there was no uncertainty. In conversation with the visiting AIMM Secretary a few weeks later, the Archbishop of the Anglican Church of Botswana said: "The church must be the conscience of society. That Henry had to raise issues of ethics and justice as an expatriate is a reproach to the Botswana churches. The idea that religion should be divorced from politics is folly. Any government minister who so insists is misguided and narrow in spirit and must be challenged." His closing comment on the Radio Botswana incident was: "Thank God for Henry Unrau." (15)

it's a long way from Karl Barth

"I applied for an assignment as a Bible teacher. It even says that on my prayer card: 'Assignment: Bible teaching with African Independent Churches.' When I first read the job description while at seminary, I pictured myself sitting around a conference table with several articulate ministers, discussing the theology of Karl Barth or the finer points of higher criticism. 'A nice job,' I thought to myself. 'I like the academic life.'"

"I spent four weeks in the small rural village of Pitseng counting cattle, goats, pigs and chickens. I found that there are 1,389 cattle but not a single pig. Next week I'll spend several days adding up the figures for chickens, plows and two-wheeled carts. It's a long way from Karl Barth." (1)

Such were the reflections of Don Boschman, an AIMM recruit for work among the AICs in Botswana after having volunteered to help do an evaluation of an MCC-sponsored rural development project. In one manner or another, all AIMM missionaries sent to work among AICs were early confronted with disparities between the ministry routine they imagined, before their arrival, and what they actually experienced. Other comments equally as colorful as Boschman's kept turning up in reporting to the home office as the reality of constant surprise and required flexibility became the common experience of them all.

"Thunder rumbled in the distance. The service continued. A louder, closer thunderclap got everyone's attention, and the minister left. 'Why did the minister go out during the song?' I wrote in my sheet of notes so I wouldn't forget to ask him later. Soon he came back and began a ritual I had never seen before. He took what appeared to be very fine white corn meal and sprinkled it all over the floor of the small church building. Then he gave a pinch to each person in the congregation, starting with the man on my right. When he got to me at the end of the circle, I politely received whatever it was with both hands, licked it and swallowed it like everyone else."

"It was then that I came to the painful realization that the stuff was not cornmeal at all. It might have been corn once, but since then it had been through a cow and a fire. The minister told me that they use four kinds of ash in church rituals - - some from coal, some from sacrifices, some from wood and some from cow dung. He said that what had been used that day was coal ash, but he either was trying to make life a little easier for his white visitor or he got the labels on his ash pouches mixed up."

"The explanation of the ritual? Quite simple. The ash applied to building and worshipers was to protect it and them from being hit by lightning when the approaching storm passed over the village. It is a substitute for the protective medicine which can be purchased from the traditional doctor (or 'medicine man') with whom the church people will have absolutely nothing to do now that they have been 'converted.'"

"I would not have taken part in the ritual if I had known what it meant, but I did take part because it was one of those 'what do I do now?' situations." (2)

As the AIMM made the AICs the primary focus of its ministry in southern Africa, recruitment of new personnel moved at a steady pace. By the year 1992, a total of eight couples and three single people had served or were still at work in Botswana. (3)

In Lesotho by that year, a total of six couples had already served or were still on hand for ministry among AICs of that country. (4) And by 1992 there had also been placement of AIMM personnel among AICs of the Transkei. (5)

At the same time the Eastern Mennonite Board of Missions had also placed personnel among AICs in nearby Swaziland where their experiences were very similar to those of the AIMM people elsewhere. It is small wonder that opportunities were sought to exchange experiences, compare notes and to take counsel together regarding the intriguing and often perplexing ministry which they had undertaken. Some consultations were of an impromptu nature and of short duration, e.g., during annual retreats for Mennonite personnel in southern Africa. Others were the result of major planning accompanied by significant funding and carefully prepared input. A prime example is the consultation which took place in the summer of 1981.

The Gaborone Consultation, July 27-31, 1981

By this time, a growing roster of AIMM personnel had been at work among the AICs for over six years. There was a clear consensus that it was time to step back and take careful inventory of efforts made, approaches employed, materials developed and used, lessons learned, unresolved questions and plans for the future. The intent was to bring together as broad a mix of people as possible representing a variety of AIC leaders, AIMM and MCC personnel on the scene plus home board representatives. Also invited were two Mennonite scholars - - anthropologist Paul Hiebert and missiologist Don Jacobs. To help cover costs the Schowalter Foundation of Hesston, KS made a much appreciated grant of $10,000. Housing, meals and meeting rooms were secured on the campus of the University of Botswana.

The opening session found over forty people present. Among them were AIC and mainline church leaders as well as MCC and missionary personnel from Botswana, Lesotho, Swaziland and the Transkei. Present also were North American representatives of the Eastern Mennonite, Mennonite Brethren and AIMM mission boards. (6)

Early sessions were devoted to basic presentations by resource people, e.g., "Contrasting World Views" by Jacobs; "Anabaptist Traditions Meaningful to Mennonites" by John Eby; "Spiritual Church Distinctives Which Are Precious To Us" by Sam Mohono; "Dealing with Symbolism and Ritual in Cross-Cultural Ministry" by Hiebert; "Dealing with the Problem of Adaptation and Contextualization in Cross-Cultural Ministry" by Jacobs; and "Fundamental Issues of Sickness, Medicine, Healing, Crisis and the Ancestral Spirits" by Hiebert.

Both Jacobs and Hiebert did excellent jobs of sketching, for the consultation participants, the radical differences between Western and African world-views and the ways in which they came into sharp focus in the ministry that Mennonites were attempting to carry out among the AICs. Both men underscored the fact that for the African, life in its totality is a single fabric. Religious beliefs are incorporated into daily life. Throughout everything runs a dominant theme of power encounters with spiritual forces which are believed to surround every person from birth until death. Hiebert particularly pointed out that rational westerners have problems in understanding and addressing these power encounters. This results in what he termed "a neglected middle" between this world, as perceived by Africans, and the spiritual realm as understood and taught by missionaries.

It was against the background of these formal presentations that careful effort was made to allow participants to relate to and discuss with each other the issues at hand. At times, Africans and expatriates met alone. At other times they were divided into mixed groups to deal with assigned sets of questions. It was out of this mix of sharing, discussion and eventual plenary sessions that the most valuable results of the entire consultation emerged.

In a session by themselves, some missionary concerns and frustrations were voiced, e.g,: - the uncertainty about the meaning of some symbols and rituals used; - the handling and use of the Old and New Testaments; - the view and use of time; - the attitude toward dreams and visions; - understanding and dealing with spirit possession; - legalism/works vs grace; - incidents of payment of fees for AIC services rendered; - hierarchies within the churches; - concepts and understandings of holiness; - the tendency toward Biblical literalism.

In their session alone, the AIC leaders also provided some revealing feedback, e.g.,: - missionaries do not listen enough; - why do missionaries always want to know why!?; - sometimes all records and finances regarding our work together are kept in missionary hands; - sometimes missionary men and women sit together in church and sometimes missionary women come to church bare headed and bare armed.

In group sessions where expatriates and Africans met together, some specific questions were given for discussion, e.g.,: "What sort of overlap is there between Mennonite and Spiritual Church emphases?" Some responses were: - a strong sense of peoplehood; - choice of leaders from within congregations; - sometimes too much authority granted to leaders; - use of symbols and rituals; - faith in Christ; - prayer for healing, though with different approaches; - the Bible very important with some tendency toward literalism; - adult baptism; - shared histories of persecution, migration and minority status; - love of singing and music; - tendency toward dictated regulation of daily life patterns.

What can Westerners learn from AICs? - tolerance and openness; - the daily practice of faith; - the joy of fellowship; - meaningful prayer ministry; - freedom and spontaneity in worship; - the use of song, dance and music; - recognition and confrontation of evil powers; - mutual concern and help; - the reality of the spiritual dimensions of life.

What can AICs learn from Western churches? - more complete and balanced Biblical understandings; - techniques of administration; - dealing with succession in leadership; - handling church finances; - Christian education and youth ministries; - teaching and training methods; - preaching and sermon preparation.

What have Mennonites done among you so far that has been of particular help to you? - accepting us in genuine friendship; - bringing us together locally, nationally and internationally; - helping us with administration; - leading our elders to maturity in their faith through Bible study.

As the consultation drew to a close, effort was made to pull together a broad group consensus on a variety of issues that had surfaced during the five days together. Regarding AIMM's stance vis-à-vis the AICs, there was clear affirmation of the following: - no plans for Mennonite church planting; - a nonjudgmental, accepting attitude; - an inclusive, bridge-building approach involving as many AICs as possible; - avoiding agenda and curriculum prepackaged in North America; - a wariness of becoming a divisive force among AICs; - non-imposition of ourselves but responding to invitations; - the candid admission of our Anabaptist roots and frank recognition that this colors our approach to the Bible; - a "fellow learner demeanor" in our teaching ministry; - readiness to recognize and build on Biblical truth which has already been discovered and incorporated into AIC life and practice; - seeking to develop a personal piety as much in line with that of the AIC people as possible; - offering authentication to church groups which have experienced ostracism and discrimination at the hands of both governmental and ecclesiastical authorities; - openness to expanding ministry to other countries of southern Africa.

Regarding questions of methodology, there was affirmation of inductive study as our basic approach to Scripture; - allowing study themes and topics to arise out of interaction with AIC students themselves; - the traditional TEE approach as a basic model with adaptations as needed; - generous use of local cultural themes and skills such as writing of poems, composing of songs and story telling; - use of/collaboration with local African consultants; - seeking to learn to know a few individuals at a deep level; - specialized training for a few selected AIC leaders; - inter-country visits for selected trainees; - teaching within the context of celebration; - to search for alternatives to typical western classroom teaching formats.

Regarding curriculum content, there was affirmation of a continuing focus on basic tenets of the Christian faith; - Old Testament studies approached as a bridge to the New Testament; - a focus on Christology as often as it is relevant and appropriate to the study at hand; - readiness to work with other topics and themes that may be requested by students. It was also recognized that more effort needed to be made to deal with the issue of "power encounters" and with natural phenomena which constantly impinge on the life and experience of the African.

In a concluding session, Jacobs admonished the assembled missionaries to allow for large areas of mystery and to be prepared to accept that there are some things which are simply unexplainable; - "to go further than you think you can when confronted by practices about which you are unsure." - to seek to teach in the context of celebration; - to seek to teach less in classroom settings and more in church settings; - to not be satisfied until the students real questions and concerns emerge. "Ask yourselves frequently: 'Are our questions in our teaching materials actually their questions?'" - to be wary of "tests" over the material taught. "It's possible for them to feed back 'capsules of truth' without having digested them or having drawn any nutrient from them." - to remember that "you as western missionaries, too, are bound by your own world-view. We too have symbols important to us and rituals we cheerfully follow."

It was along this same line that Hiebert suggested three kinds of tests which can help us evaluate how well we are communicating in our teaching: 1) the cognitive test, i.e., what has been understood of what we have said? 2) the feelings test, i.e., are emotions stirred? 3) the impact test, i.e., what change has taken place in the lives of the students? Both 1 and 2 are essential if 3 is to be realized.

And, scattered through the sessions and informal conversations during tea breaks, there were snippets of African comments which found their way into missionary notebooks to be pondered later, e.g.: "We cannot separate preaching from healing" (J.C. Tshwene, Botswana). "We don't talk about our faith much, we live it" (Isaac Dlamini, Swaziland). "In Botswana we love our President and thus we 'hear' his words to us. We must also love the Lord in order to 'hear' his words to us. Without loving him we cannot understand him" (Bishop Monyatsi, Botswana). "One sick man goes to a herbalist. Another sick man goes to a spiritual leader. A third man goes to the hospital to a western doctor. Who among the three men has sinned?" (Tshwene).

"The foundation of the Christian church was laid in Asia. The walls of the church were raised in Europe and the west. It now remains for Africa to add the roof but, there is a problem. The walls on which we seek to build a roof are badly cracked by divisions and dissensions. This is a pity. But the door which gives entrance to the church remains the same regardless, the door Jesus Christ. . . . Can we together come to roof the Church of God and in the process see that the cracked walls are properly repaired so that the Church will stand sure? There are signs all over the world of the Lord's returning soon and when it happens it will be because his Church is complete" (Mohono).

"Africans accept Christianity but they often refuse the structures that accompany it from overseas. Africans want freedom in worship. If Africans are sick or have a problem, they want help then. Africans enjoy clapping, singing, dancing, spontaneity; they find western reserve and stiffness in worship to be strange. Africans don't pray in church because the bulletin says it's time to pray; the African bathes his life in prayer" (Mohono).

"We are sometimes called 'independent churches,' but I don't know why. In fact, we are the most dependent churches anywhere because we must trust God for everything!" (Mohono). "Western history books say that the black man was discovered by Livingstone, Stanley and others but we black people didn't know we were being discovered. In any case, this discovery brought with it hardship and suffering for many black people" (Mohono).

And the poignant comment of an African participant made as we sat a short distance from the border of the Republic of South Africa: "We look forward to heaven so much because there won't be any jails there" (Dlamini). (7)

One AIMM participant later wrote: "To understand any consultation or conference, you have to read between the lines, looking at the informal personal interaction among the participants. I for one can't think of a group of people, both African and missionaries, that I would rather be serving with. We weren't perfect or perfectly harmonious but there is among us a deep sense of common commitment and a lot of good people putting their commitment into action. This is the team to be on." (8)

One of the resource people later wrote a letter of appreciation to the Schowalter Foundation and said, in part: "For me this was the first time to have had the occasion to share in fellowship and discussions with a number of such [AIC] leaders for an extended period of time in what I consider to be one of the first and best examples of a post-colonial model for new mission. Too often such discussions are hurried, or they occur in what is a survival of an old colonial model of missions characterized by a sense of western superiority and power. At Gaborone I felt a real meeting of minds and spirits on a level of equality, trust, openness on hard issues and a willingness to respect one another's differences. . . . The results were solid on both sides of the discussions. I believe the prophets representing the AICs were able to express, after the first day of trust building, their deeper concerns and to put on the table their own agenda rather than only responding to those of the mission. . . . The missionaries, on their part, were also able to express fears to one another and to seek help by outside input, as well as sharing, to deal with what are often difficult cross-cultural and multi-theological problems. The greatest gain was a building of understanding, trust and fellowship between participants in the conference."

"But a second and more important consequence of the meetings was bringing together a number of the AIC leaders for the first time. . . . I sensed in Gaborone the trust and equality of spirit that allowed for frank openness and discussion on matters of theology that makes possible a searching of the Scriptures together to find God's call for our time. For me, it reaffirmed the belief that the international church will need to rediscover our Anabaptist theology of the priesthood of the believers. We need not western theological colonialism nor multi-cultural theological relativism, but a gathering of people from all parts of this world around the Gospel and sharing and correcting one another as a single body, the Church." (9)

For AIMM, the Gaborone consultation of July 1981 was in many ways a defining experience. Far-reaching in its agenda, broad-based in its selection of participants, open in its approach to discussions and planning, its findings and recommendations were to serve as fundamental points of reference for AIMM's ongoing work among AICs for years to come. (10)

Not that all questions were resolved or that a final methodology was set. Far from it. There were many more times of discussion and sharing to come. But fundamental issues had been honestly recognized by both missionaries and Africans. Even more important, mutual commitments were made to continue a joint search for guidance and instruction from the Scriptures which spoke to them in their settings and needs.

CHAPTER 54   A BLACK HOMELAND TOO?

"Having received the report of the ad hoc committee on Bible Training . . . this special meeting of Division III [of the Transkei Christian Council (TCC)] accepts its recommendations, and decides to request the Mennonites to appoint two of its members to confer with four representatives of the TCC of whom two are African Independent Church leaders, to be fully responsible for organizing the Extension Programme envisaged for Biblical training of the African Independent Church leaders."

Thus read article 94 of a copy of official minutes of the Transkei Christian Council's Division III received in the AIMM office June 14, 1982. On an adjoining sheet the Council explained that for the sort of ministry they envisioned for Mennonite personnel, it would be important that they be mobile, have a good working knowledge of Xhosa, the local language, have the ability to translate materials, the ability to put ideas into new thought forms and have "a patient, listening ear."

A door of service was swinging open to Mennonites in still another area of southern Africa but there was a long series of significant events which had preceded this formal written invitation.

Transkei, the first "black homeland"

For the Afrikaner-dominated government of South Africa in the 1970's, the capstone of the grand scheme of *apartheid* was the sorting out and allocation of all black people to regions designated specifically for them according to their tribal identity. In this process, it was insisted that Africans were simply being returned to their original "ancestral grounds." In other words, they were being helped to return home!

Well aware of the angry opposition of the black population to this plan, methods used by South African authorities to create the first homeland were thorough, though not straightforward. For their pilot project, the Pretoria regime settled on the Transkei region. Bordering the Indian Ocean to the southeast and Lesotho to the northwest, it encompassed a cluster of tribal groups popularly referred to as "Xhosa speaking people," although only one of the tribes was authentically Xhosa in origin. Already in the early 1960's the white government had hand-picked two paramount chiefs as cohorts in the unfolding political scheme, this over the protests of the rightful traditional chiefs. When some of them became vehement in their opposition, they were arrested and condemned to twenty years penal servitude on Robben Island.

Picked were the Mantanzima brothers, Kaiser and George. In 1967 a vote was held regarding the acceptance or rejection of the eventual status of a homeland. Knowing that many fellow Transkeians did not support the idea, the Mantanzimas effectively squelched disagreement by jailing those who were too vocal in their opposition. "Approval" of the scheme thus secured, there followed a carefully orchestrated transition toward the status of a homeland which was officially celebrated in October 1976. Under the watchful eye of South African security agents, the brothers were installed in places of power, Kaiser as President and George as Prime Minister.

reality sets in

The white South African government pulled out all the stops in an effort to publicize this first step toward the creation of independent homelands where the blacks would be totally free to pursue their own destinies according to their own traditions, cultures and desires. And from the offices of the new Transkei authorities, there also came enthusiastic announcements. At last, the end of *apartheid*! No more passbooks, no more identity checks by stone-faced white police, no more off-limit beaches or public facilities. They were at last masters in their own house.

Three realities, however, soon became all too clear for the ordinary blacks of the Transkei. First, they discovered that if South African security forces had a much lower profile, they were far from gone. With headquarters in their capital city, Umtata (pr. oom-TAH-tah), they continued to be a powerful, all-pervasive presence behind the scenes. The Transkei Police, it was soon discovered, were but a black front for the real white political power behind them. Even worse, although black, they were no more kindly disposed toward suspected political opponents than their white predecessors had been. Fearing that the African National Congress (ANC) might seek to establish a base of operations in this new supposedly independent homeland, South Africa's security agents made sure that the Transkei Police arrested, detained and interrogated any and all, of whatever color, who were suspected of pro-ANC leanings. AIMM personnel were later to experience the impact of this poorly camouflaged South African security system.

A second reality which began to dawn for the Transkei people was that, in spite of all the propaganda, the only government which recognized them as an independent state was their creator, the Republic of South Africa. Not a single embassy was opened in Umtata by any other country in the world. On the contrary, there was a rising storm of condemnation as country after country of the international community roundly condemned and rejected the homelands scheme.

And, finally, what hurt the most was to witness the regular arrival of their fellow tribesmen who were systematically being ferreted out in the urban centers of the Republic and deported by force to their new "homes" which were gradually becoming overcrowded and where means of livelihood were extremely limited. It was of this harsh economic pressure that an AIMM missionary later wrote in the following terms: "It was a chance encounter: he leaning against a wall near the bus depot in Umtata, I wandering about looking for likely candidates with whom to practice speaking the Xhosa language. 'Molo, Tata' (Hello, Father). 'Molo, Mhlekazi' (Hello, Sir). We exchanged extended greetings. He was in his fifties, poorly dressed, but with an alert look about him. I saw that he wasn't one of the many alcoholics lounging around the market and bus depot."

"'I've been in Umtata three months now looking for work,' he told me. 'It is not to be found. This city is full of people looking for work. Some are hungry and steal. Others drink to forget their sorrows.' 'Where do you live?' I asked. 'In the location.' I knew the location he meant. It is the part of Umtata which was reserved for blacks before the Transkei received its 'independence' from South Africa. The situation is little changed today although there are no longer *apartheid* laws on the books in Transkei. However, it is a typical South African township with thousands of tiny houses crowded into a small area having all the attendant social problems."

"'Where did you work before coming to Umtata?' I asked. 'I worked in the coal mines as a machine operator and driver near Johannesburg. I've had a license for 24 years. Now my contract is expired. We blacks from the homelands aren't permitted to stay around looking for work when our contracts expire. I've been going to the recruiting agencies every day but no one wants me.'"

"I thought of the agencies operating in Umtata and other cities in the Transkei recruiting migrant labor for the mines. I knew that normally one is hired on a contract of six months to a year, and when the contract is up one returns home, often to try for another contract. The men rarely return home during the time of the contract. Of course their families are not permitted to accompany them as the accommodations are single-sex dormitories. In spite of the hardships there are dozens waiting for any expired contract. There are few job opportunities in the Transkei and those which exist pay little in comparison to wages in the mines. I understood why a high percentage of the able-bodied men work in the Republic."

"'What about your family? How are they getting food now? Did you have some savings from when you were working?' 'I have a wife and four children,' he replied. 'No, five,' he added quickly. 'My daughter, aged 20, gave birth to a child and she has no husband. She has left the child with my wife and we don't know where she is. They live at Engcobo (100 kilometers from Umtata). Our relatives are sharing food with them. I did have savings but we've used it all.'"

"I assured him that our family would be praying that he would get a job soon. I handed him some money for food for the day, said 'Sala kahle' (farewell) and went my way pondering his situation. No doubt a majority of the hundreds of people I observed around the market and bus depot would have similar stories to relate. What does our faith in Christ compel us to do about these overwhelming problems of *apartheid*, poverty, and migratory labor?" (1)

overtures toward the Mennonites

As has been the Mennonite experience in a variety of places in Africa, it was MCC personnel who made the first contacts in the Transkei. It was already in early 1976, before the official inauguration of the Transkei as a homeland, that MCC received a request to provide assistance after its soon-to-be-granted independence. It was in response to this invitation that an MCC representative paid an extended visit in mid-1976. It was subsequently recommended that MCC place people in a secondary school at a Lay Training Center, and a rural development advisor for the Transkei Christian Council (TCC). Another MCC representative, trained in economics, was sent who, after research, also recommended placement of personnel. He suggested expansion of MCC involvement by seconding personnel to the government Departments of Agriculture, Forestry and the Transkei Development Corporation. (2)

Ray Brubacher, MCC's Africa Secretary of the time and all other Mennonite mission administrators with personnel in southern Africa, struggled to find their way through a thorny thicket of clashing views. There were influential individuals and organizations in both the secular and church communities who heatedly condemned any gesture of support toward the Transkei which had become "exhibit A" of an unfolding evil racial philosophy. Some of the arguments forwarded were: It is impossible to become involved in the Transkei without some collaboration with its government and, by extension, with the government of South Africa. Involvement of any kind there would imply a tacit recognition of the status of the homeland and, thus, at least indirect approval of South Africa's racial policies. Helping Transkei to become more viable was to play into the hands of the South African government which desperately wanted the Transkei venture to succeed. By helping the Transkei we might well improve the lot of some people sufficiently to diminish their resistance. And, finally, how would a Mennonite presence in the Transkei be interpreted throughout the world? Might we not risk being seen to be on the wrong side of a volatile issue? (3)

But it was in the face of such a galaxy of arguments to stay out of the Transkei that other voices were also heard: The weaker the Transkei, the more helpless it is before the dominating power of South Africa. The more the Transkei is helped to be economically viable, the less cheap migrant labor will flow from it to the Republic. The Transkei affords a significantly new kind of context within which to work - - a new place within the South African scene which has long been denied Mennonite personnel.

On a philosophical note, John Howard Yoder was quoted as saying: "If we say we will only work when the basic structures come above a certain level of tolerability, then we mean that we will consistently not serve the people who are worst off and that our need for a relatively good conscience in having opposed evil regimes is more important to us that the physical and educational needs of the people who are worst off." (4)

a Mennonite presence is established

Amidst a swirl of counsel to the contrary, a Mennonite consensus for involvement had emerged and there was prompt action. Dave Neufeld was the first MCC appointee to arrive in the Transkei. In the course of his first term he was joined by Bob and Judy Zimmerman Herr who served as MCC country representatives. In 1978 the Herrs were replaced by Tim and Susanne Hilty Lind who were seconded to the Transkei Christian Council. In addition to being country representatives, Tim was assigned to serve as a full-time consultant on rural development issues and Susanne to work part-time on a study of the South African homelands scheme.

For Mennonites to relate to and affirm the TCC in its ministries was not without some risk. It was soon discovered that Transkei authorities viewed the TCC as a controversial organization and this for several reasons. First, it had direct ties with the South Africa Council of Churches (SACC) which by this time had adopted a critical stance regarding the Pretoria regime in general and the philosophy of *apartheid* in particular.

Furthermore, the TCC was heavily dependent upon SACC subsidies for funding its programs, one of which was the seeking out of families and dependents of men who were under long-term detention on Robben Island. In this process both legal counsel and physical sustenance were being provided. All of this was condemned as subversive by South African security personnel who, in turn, leaned heavily upon Transkei authorities to at least harass the Council, if not ban it completely. There consequently followed years of surveillance, summons for questioning, occasional detainment and unannounced inspections of Council files. At one point, the TCC was ordered to sever all ties with the SACC and was forbidden to receive any further funds from this organization. Transkei Council personnel refused to obey these orders and quietly continued to serve as the channel of SACC monies for its ministries. This resulted in something of a standoff with the authorities and a contest of wills. While the TCC was never closed down, Council personnel demonstrated daily courage as they continued their work under the continual menace of intrusion and interrogation.

One visiting Mennonite journalist portrayed TCC ministry and spirit in the following terms: "The headquarters of the Transkei Council of Churches are located in a nondescript building in downtown Umtata. Next door is a church with an expanse of lawn where workers come to eat their lunches. Inside the TCC headquarters . . . they seem friendly, relaxed, without fear. It's funny how everything and everyone exudes an air of normalcy. After all, this is South Africa."

"But once I begin to talk with the staff, I immediately sense something else. As strong as their voices may sound, these people have not had an easy time. To start with, they are constantly watched by the local security police. Several years ago, when a burglar alarm company moved in on the same floor, one of their video cameras was invariably pointed in the direction of the TCC offices. The result of this not-so-subtle surveillance was a marked decline in visitors. Even though the company moved out about two years ago, staff members say they still are working at rebuilding people's trust. . . . 'We keep on,' says TCC office manager Winnie Tshangela [pr. tshah-NGEH-lah]. 'We put up with the harassment because we are committed. There is nothing illegal in what we do.'. . ."

"The council's work with detainees is most likely what attracts the attention of the security police. Ntombentle Zungula (pr. ntoh-MBEH-ntleh zoo-NGOO-lah) spends most of her work hours on the road, traveling to the homes of detainees and their families. 'No one is in prison here because of Transkei politics. They are all involved in organizations fighting against the South African situation,' she says. 'I am not allowed to visit the detainees in prison, but when they get out I ask them what kind of torture they received,' says Zungula, 'then I try to disperse the information to the local churches and the press, if they are interested. The problem is that papers are censored.'. . . 'The worst part, though,' says Zungula, 'is the uncertainty. The detainees wait for a long time in prison. They don't know what their charges are or if there will be a trial. There is a lot of confusion and depression. It is a sad situation.' . . . Still Tshangela remains optimistic about the future of her people. . . . 'We need to keep raising their awareness about their rights,' she says. 'We must be prepared for the era of post-*apartheid*.'" (5)

AIMM also becomes involved

There were a number of factors which combined to open the way for AIMM's entry into the Transkei. There was, first of all, an effective AIC "grapevine." Early on, the AIC leaders of the black homeland began hearing about Mennonites next door in Lesotho who were providing opportunity for Bible study for some of the AICs of that country. News they heard about this ministry from fellow AIC folks was positive. In the meantime, they were getting acquainted with Mennonite personnel in their own country who were working with the TCC. If Mennonites could provide opportunity for Bible study in Lesotho, why not also in the Transkei? As the Linds' term of service drew to a close in early 1981, they reported to Akron their perception that at least some of the AICs of the country would welcome the opportunity of Mennonite-directed Bible study. MCC staff shared this information with Elkhart and encouraged AIMM to take leadership in probing this apparent opening.

It was while the Linds were still in Umtata that the first formal discussions were held. It was an intriguing mix of people who sat together in the office of the TCC that early January day of 1981. From Lesotho, representing AIMM, came Stan Nussbaum accompanied by his father Rev. Milo Nussbaum. (6) Tim Lind represented MCC while Dr. Hennie Pretorius sat in for the TCC. From the Transkei AIC community were Rev. Dikwa and Rev. Tsofela (pr. DI-kwah and tsoh-FEH-lah). It was particularly in the person of Dr. Pretorius that the Mennonites had found an unexpected friend and ally in Umtata. An ordained minister of the White Dutch Reformed Church of South Africa, he was in the early 1980's one of a courageous minority of DRC clergymen who were beginning to openly voice their condemnation of the philosophy of *apartheid* in general and their own Church's affirmation of it in particular. He was serving under the appointment of his Church as a teacher at Decoligny, a theological training school of the Black Dutch Reformed Church on the outskirts of Umtata. While the White Church related to the TCC only as observers, the Black Church was a full member and had named Dr. Pretorius as one of its official representatives on the Council, an appointment which bespoke the respect with which he was viewed by the Black Church.

He, like many others, had at first greeted the Mennonite newcomers with considerable reserve. After all, for what reasons would a mission board send its personnel to the Transkei if it was not to try to establish still another denomination? But once he was persuaded that the Mennonites' declared interest in helping the AICs was genuine, he became an invaluable source of information and counsel. On one occasion he was heard to say: "I live in a permanent state of amazement that you are willing to work with Independent Churches. After all, isn't mission about members?"

Reporting to the home office after the Umtata meeting, Stan Nussbaum wrote: "The consensus was that the two AIC ministers should present the matter to the next meeting of the TCC Committee on Church Development . . . and see if there is interest in holding a weekend seminar bringing a number of AIC and mission church leaders together to discuss the possibilities. An AIMM representative would be invited . . . to discuss the formation of a Bible Teaching program under the auspices of the TCC. Basically I think we just now need to wait and see if the two AIC leaders have contagious enthusiasm or quarantined enthusiasm." (7)

It was just six months later that the AIMM consultation on AIC ministries took place in Gaborone. One of the participants was Father Patrick Kotta, an Anglican priest from the Transkei and also a member of the TCC. Favorably impressed by what he heard and sensed in those sessions, he invited Nussbaum to come to the Transkei again, this time to meet with full representation of the TCC. During January 1982 two such consultations were held in Umtata under the jurisdiction of what was known as Division III of the Council which occupied itself with matters of church development and congregational life issues. This division, in turn, created a "Bible Teaching Sub-Committee" to which the envisioned Bible teaching ministry would be responsible. (8)

Nineteen eighty-two was a busy year for AIMM missionary Jim Egli who, in addition to his responsibilities in Lesotho, made frequent trips to the Transkei to lead Bible teaching sessions there. It was becoming apparent to all that the growing teaching ministry could not for long be carried on by AIMM personnel commuting via an eight hour drive from Lesotho. It was at this point that the official TCC letter arrived in the AIMM office in Elkhart requesting that missionary personnel be recruited for the Transkei itself.

yes, but who?

The AIMM Board was very much aware of the complexity of the Transkei scene and the consequent need for careful screening of candidates to become its first appointees there. Yet once again AIMM was to discover that as ventures of faith were decided upon, people of God's choosing were already waiting just off stage.

In this case it was a young man named Larry Hills. Born to American Baptist parents in the state of Maine, he took an undergraduate degree in psychology and sought a position as a teacher. Serving first in an urban setting in New Jersey, he changed to a position in rural Maine and, eventually, to a one room school on an island off the coast of Maine. Summers he supplemented his income by signing on as a hand on coastal lobster boats. Eventually returning to his home area to help his family, he encountered an enthusiastic young Baptist pastor who was instrumental in leading him to a reaffirmation of his faith and a commitment of his life to Christ the Lord. (9) Soon, thereafter, he enrolled in a study program in Gordon-Conwell Seminary.

Toward the end of his first year he became aware of some Mennonite church leaders and their writings. (10) Desirous of learning more, he transferred to AMBS in Elkhart in the fall of 1981 where, in turn, he for the first time heard of the AIMM. He eventually returned to Gordon-Conwell to take his degree but not before beginning candidate procedures with AIMM. As dialogue continued, Larry sensed a "tug" toward southern Africa and AIMM's Bible teaching ministry among AICs. Returning to the Elkhart area in the summer of 1982, he was both ordained to the ministry and commissioned for missionary service by the Silver Street Mennonite Church some five miles east of Goshen, IN, a Church which he joined. (11)

In communication with the AIMM home office in June of that same summer the Transkei Christian Council had underlined the importance of sending someone who could be mobile, who could put ideas into new thought forms and someone who could bring to them "a patient, listening ear." In Larry Hills, they were to discover such a person.

a bishop from Misty Mount

An early assumption of Mennonite personnel on the scene was that the new AIMM arrival would best be located somewhere in Umtata, the capital, from where he could move out into the surrounding areas. It was soon discovered that housing for expatriates in Umtata was tight. Initial accommodations were finally found in a mobile home park. It was not long, however, until Hills began to chafe with this arrangement. He was in a part of town to which AIC folk did not normally come. Furthermore, in the capital city, everyone expected to talk with him in English. How was he to make serious progress in his language study? Sharing his concerns with AIC leaders, it was tentatively agreed that he would at least move to the fringe of the city where he could be part of a black neighborhood. But, even as negotiations were under way to find a place, a remarkable African woman intervened.

The name Muriel Manyadu (pr. mah-NYAH-doo) was known to AIC people both within and outside the capital city of the Transkei. Located in a shanty town fringe of the city, she had established a church and a following amidst a highly unstable setting. Though the streets around her at night regularly witnessed a variety of crimes, she was known both for her fearlessness and her power in prayer. Africans frequently sought her out for counsel and help. She had at first been supportive of the proposal for Hills' move into her general area. Then one night she had a vision in which she was warned against such a move. When she shared her vision with some of the AIC bishops, she was taken seriously and the idea of a move within Umtata was dropped.

It was at this point that yet another unusual AIC leader stepped forward. His name was Bishop Mphehla (pr. MPEH-lah.). His home and church headquarters were situated at a place called Misty Mount. In an area which often experienced marginal rainfall, there was a swath of green which through a quirk of wind currents off the Indian Ocean regularly resulted in fog and mist in the early morning hours providing continual moisture for the landscape. It was in this area that Bishop Mphehla had established his base and regularly rallied his faithful around him for worship. Approximately fifteen miles from Umtata, he had followed news of Larry Hills' arrival and search for living quarters with a lively interest. Although Hills by this time was busy with a regular schedule of Bible classes, nothing was happening regarding new living quarters for him. It was only later that he learned that the AIC leaders were having great difficulty in believing that he, a white man, was really serious about leaving the city and establishing residence somewhere in a rural setting among them. But while others were immobilized by their doubt, Bishop Mphehla decided to check things out for himself. Since Hills at times scheduled Bible classes at his Church, the Bishop on one occasion opened the subject with him.

Pointing to his courtyard he suggested that there was plenty of room to build a place for the missionary Bible teacher. His church members would gather the necessary materials from his surrounding land. But there was one problem. Since they had no electricity or running water, they could not provide the sort of toilet facilities to which white people were accustomed. Hills' response was as pragmatic as it was unambiguous. "Dig a hole!" Finally convinced that Hills would indeed settle into his family courtyard if arrangements were made, he turned to yet other concerns. Hills described his uncertainty at that point as follows: "At first he could not believe that such a thing could ever be legal. He has spent his life living under the Group Areas Act. And the notion of whites and blacks living together seemed strange to him. But he was sufficiently intrigued by the idea to want to pursue it with the authorities. He checked first with the government where he was told that those laws are no longer in effect in the Transkei; that was followed by a meeting with the chief and the district magistrate, both of whom gave their blessings to the idea. Under the leadership of Bishop Mphehla, his Church decided to work together to build a house where I could live. This house is located within the Mphehla family compound. And, except for the window and the door, is being constructed entirely with materials gathered from the bishop's land with the labor supplied by the church people." (12)

As Hills prepared to take up residence in his newly constructed quarters, he sought to raise the issue of some sort of rental arrangement. This time it was the Bishop's turn to be brief and to the point: "Brothers do not rent to brothers."

Eventually they worked out an arrangement which was more in keeping with African custom. "I am considered a member of the family and, as such, contributions from me in the form of seeds, food, materials is welcomed. I try to contribute what I feel is a fair amount in goods rather than in cash. I think this makes for a more human and African way of working things out. Regarding meals, I cook breakfast and lunch and eat supper with the rest of the family." (13)

Although anguishing difficulties lay just ahead, Larry could truthfully write home in the spring of 1984 in the following terms: "My work and relationships with the Independent Churches constitute the most rewarding thing I have ever done. As I reflect on the past months, I would characterize my relationship with the church leaders as one of a growing sense of mutual trust. The bishops are becoming more and more open in sharing their needs and the needs of their churches. I find that I am also opening up more of my life to the people of the Independent Churches. So I see the bonds of openness and trust becoming stronger among us as we seek to understand God's Word and to discern His will for our life together in the Transkei." (14)

seminars become a useful tool

Even though the AIMM early made a Bible teaching ministry among the AICs the central focus of its ministry, AIMM also sought to be responsive to other needs as expressed by AIC leaders. It was this openness which soon led the MM workers into sponsoring a variety of special seminars for their benefit. One of the earliest issues addressed in Botswana was the deep desire of all AIC leaders to secure government authorization to function as marriage officers - - especially within their own churches. While most pastors of mainline churches were automatically authorized on the basis of their training in mission-founded schools, AIC leaders were denied this pastoral status. While the government rationale given was the general lack of formal education among AIC pastors, it was also true that this was another convenient way of reflecting government disapproval, if not outright disdain, vis-à-vis these leaders and the churches they represented.

Coming to realize the deep frustration and embarrassment AIC leaders continually felt as they had to refer their own church members to pastors of other churches for the solemnization of their wedding vows, AIMM missionaries sought out government officials to make inquiry in their behalf. They were soon assured that the government was prepared to grant the longed for status to AIC leaders who could pass a written test. If AIMM was interested in conducting training seminars for them, the government would allow them to write an exam. Those who passed would be granted the certification they so much desired.

Across the years a number of such training seminars were held especially for AIC leaders. Over time more and more have been able to pass the exam with the result that recognized marriage officers, within AIC ranks, have steadily increased in number. In this process AIMM and, later, MM have gained the abiding gratitude of the AICs involved.

As African leaders were further encouraged to share their concerns, there were frequent expressions of fear regarding the future of their youth. Alcohol addiction and sexual promiscuity were growing problems in their society as a whole, problems from which their young people were not exempt. Frightened by the talk of the rapid spread of AIDS in Africa, they urged their Mennonite partners to find a way to address this issue with them. Having already found the seminar approach a productive one, might this not be an option? After several rounds of discussion, Mennonite and AIC leaders determined to sponsor open seminars to which mainline church leaders and government officials would also be invited. One such was held in Francistown, Botswana's second largest city. (Located near its northeastern border with Zimbabwe, the city - - with passing time - - became home to a series of AIMM missionaries.) (1)

A written missionary account of this event reads, in part, as follows: "On December 12, 1990, [representatives of] 32 churches in Francistown, Botswana, gathered together at the Civic Center to participate in a one-day AIDS awareness seminar. The 75 delegates, representing 23 African Independent Churches and nine mainline churches, were evenly divided between men and women. . . ."

"The workshop was opened by the town mayor at 8 AM with a frightening presentation on the statistics of HIV positive carriers and AIDS cases presently recorded in Botswana and in neighboring Zambia and Zimbabwe. He stressed that the churches must take up the case along with government for instructing its members about AIDS if this disease is to be curbed. . . ."

"The speaker was Mr. J. Ndaba (pr. NDAH-bah), a pastor from the Seventh Day Adventist Church, who works under the Association of Medical Missions in Botswana. He has been given the task by the government of addressing all churches in Botswana about the problems of AIDS. . . . He began with a true and false quiz highlighting some of the myths about AIDS. The quiz was repeated later in the day to check whether there had been any progress in the delegates' understanding. He than explained what AIDS was and dealt at length with how it is transmitted."

Following a question and answer period conducted by two nurses regarding the nature and transmission of AIDS, Mr. Ndaba conducted another session in which he addressed "the issue of sexual promiscuity as the leading cause for the swift transmission of AIDS. He gave a Biblical presentation stressing the idea that if Christian people will respect, teach and obey God's laws, the spread of AIDS could be drastically reduced. . . . Mr. Ndaba did not mince words nor was he afraid to step on anyone's toes. His presentation served to inform and stir up a response. One woman sitting beside me exclaimed at one point: 'AIDS is a killer. I am afraid of it. I am not going to get AIDS!' If other delegates felt the same way, the seminar was a grand success."

The report continued with the observation: " . . . no expatriate that I know could have done the presentation better than Mr. Ndaba. He knew the subject, he had experience, and he could speak 'deep Setswana.' As a Motswana, he understood the social relationships, the cultural innuendoes, and the use of appropriate body language necessary for a successful presentation. He provided the posters, pamphlets, the lunch and even the lapel buttons '1 husband plus 1 wife = NO AIDS!'" The report concluded with the observation that it had been a rewarding experience to play a behind-the-scenes role of a facilitator and to see the large participation of the area AICs in the event. (2)

Another burden shared by AIC leaders was that of creeping alcohol addiction abroad in their land. While they were indeed concerned for their own youth, there was equal anxiety for the welfare of their country as a whole. This issue, however, was a politically sensitive one since influential people in the government were known to own highly profitable "bottle stores," the term used in southern Africa for liquor stores. A few were even suspected of having vested interest in the liquor industry itself. (In Lesotho the government had a 51% stake in the brewing industry of the country.)

But the impact of alcohol addiction upon Botswana society was grim and growing. There was increasing conviction on the part of church leaders, both main line and AIC, that the problem needed somehow to be addressed in a forceful, public manner. Commenting on this situation, an AIMM missionary at one point wrote: "Alcohol abuse is clearly a hot issue in many communities at the family level as well as in public forums. Family violence associated with alcohol abuse, appalling carnage on the public highways and the debilitating effects of alcohol on job performance are fervently discussed."

"Mennonites last year [1987] invited a cross-section of Christians to an informal gathering here [Gaborone] to consider the potential for joint church action. Fifty representatives from 25 churches ranging from Baptists to Catholics, both African Independent Churches and mission-founded churches, evangelical, liberal and charismatic met last October to ask if this could be taken up as a joint challenge."

"A key element in strengthening this impulse has been the work of Melanie Yutzy of Plain City, OH, an MCC volunteer in Botswana, who has extensively researched the nature of the alcohol problem and the inner workings of the industry that profits from it. After intense all-day dialogue, they established a small working group to begin laying the ground work for such an effort. A second symposium was held in April to further guide this work. A proposal for an interim structure, which would allow the alliance to begin setting up a program, recruit staff and raise necessary funds, was expected to begin this summer."

"While not excluding cooperating with government, one delegate said, 'We do not want our action to be compromised. Faith is our point of departure. We're not going to give up that.' Already there have been warm messages of encouragement from various quarters in Botswana. Many are glad that the church is taking up leadership on a question that bears directly on development issues and the well-being of society." (3) Out of these initial gatherings there eventually was forged something called "A Church Coalition to Fight Alcohol Abuse" which at one point gathered over 1,000 signatures for a petition to the Botswana Parliament calling for legislative help in combating alcohol abuse in their country.

a first ever AIC youth fest

While AIMM personnel in Botswana were very gratified by the response and seeming impact of seminars focusing on serious social issues within the country, there was ever a concern that ways be found to use the same format to address issues of Christian faith both among AIC youth and adults. On one occasion, while traveling together, AIMM missionary Jonathan Larson and Otsile Ditsheko (pr. oh-TSEE-lay di-TSHEH-ko), a deeply committed young layman of the Eleven Apostles Healing Spirit Church, found themselves dreaming about a youth gathering which would bring together members from as many AICs as could be persuaded to cooperate. Could a meeting like this actually happen? Larson picks up the story as follows: "Ditsheko and I traveled many weary miles together and sat for endless hours with skeptical leaders who shook their heads in the flickering candle light wondering if such a thing could ever happen. With the help of a small steering committee we hatched an idea, laid out a program, raised some money and began to make arrangements. As the day approached, we had no idea how many people to expect at the gathering. This made meal and accommodations planning a little dicey. Would we be 25 or 100 or more?" (4)

As the announced weekend arrived, people began converging on the village of Mahalapye (pr. mah-hah-LAH-pyay), the headquarters, at the time, for the Spiritual Healing Church. A report sent later to the AIMM office described the event as follows: "What a weekend! Two hundred young people from twenty African Spiritual Church groups descended on Mahalapye for Bopaganang '85 (i.e., the Youth Fest of '85). . . . Choirs and music groups performed, pastors exhorted, we snake danced through and around the Spiritual Healing Church grounds, there were lively question and answer periods, a red-hot Bible knowledge quiz where the women soundly trounced the men, a late-night Saturday musical free-for-all which served also to raise money to cover some conference expenses, a Sunday morning procession through the village of Mahalapye demonstrating in dramatic fashion the unity of the young people who sang and marched in their colorful uniforms, a concert and a tree-planting ceremony at the public square, and a lively worship service under the brilliant Botswana sun."

"When it was all over, we were a bit breathless and even disbelieving that it had actually come off! I suspect that this is the start of something which will become a significant element in the Spiritual Church scene, a rare meeting ground for those who are going to lead these churches in the next decade. And I have no doubt that it will help to turn the tide of division and quarreling that have so often bedeviled the present generation of leaders."(5)

yet another "first"

If Mennonite Ministries personnel in Botswana were agreed that church planting, per se, was not part of their agenda, this did not mean that traditional Mennonite convictions were to be shelved. There were sad, daily reminders of the swirling racial conflict in the Republic just across the border. And within Botswana itself, there were many divisive issues which were creating friction. As MM personnel met in various settings in their work, the question continually surfaced: "What can/should we do as peace church representatives at this time in this part of the world?" Out of this concern was eventually born the idea of sponsoring a "Peacemaker Festival." Largely funded by MCC and planned by a mix of MM people, the eventual program and festivities gave a large place to the AICs. Events of the festival were described as follows by one of the participants: "In a first-of-its kind festival bringing together Botswana Christians from across the church spectrum, participants set out peacemaking priorities for this desert African country."

"The festival, organized with the help of Mennonite Ministries workers, unfolded under a large banner bearing the Biblical greeting "Peace Be With You." The light blue banner, sewn with the help of refugees from several neighboring countries, had been circulating among local churches for several weeks before the festival as an invitation to participate. Between 150 and 200 Christians did so. The three-day event took place at a community hall in Old Naledi (pr. nah-LAY-di), a squatter settlement on the fringe of Gaborone. Included were the showing of the 'Jesus' film, a choir festival highlighted by the participation of Black Dutch Reformed Church singers from Bushman communities in western Botswana, community drama groups, a Saturday morning procession led by a uniformed brass band from an African Independent Church, workshops dealing with peacemaking needs in such areas as gender violence, alcohol abuse, AIDS victims, refugees and human rights, as well as small group discussion."

"One of the speakers, a traditional chief, who is also a minister in one of the African Independent Churches, made a plea for elders to see the laying of a foundation for strong marriages as a critical peacemaking activity. The chief reflected on the breakdown of families as a cause of much of the conflict brought to his court. The theme of gender and family violence was also taken up powerfully by the community drama groups and by workshop leaders. This message was particularly apt when seen against the backdrop of the poverty and social stress of the surrounding squatter settlement. Youngsters from the community came to participate in special children's activities centered on the story of Jesus stilling the storm. They later formed a choir and processed into the main hall with a boisterous song, 'I will never lose my faith!'"

"Among participants from such nearby countries as Swaziland and Lesotho, was Graham Cyster of the Broken Wall Community in Cape Town, South Africa, who shared stories of the search for peace in Kayelitsha (pr. kah-yeh-LEE-tsha) and other troubled townships. Cyster also preached at the closing worship service that included foot-washing and the Lord's Supper. Africa Inter-Mennonite Mission worker, Jonathan Larson, explained that the festival approach was an attempt to make the peacemaking theme accessible to everyday Christians. Previous regional gatherings on peacemaking had been seminars and workshops for the top level of church leadership. Larson indicated the festival was to be Botswana specific: to focus on local needs and resources. The festival approach also recognizes the need to go beyond a crisis understanding of peacemaking and places it in the context of every day living."

"'As with any new idea, there is a need to overcome the reticence of Christians who have often been manipulated and exploited,' said Larson. 'There is a long term task here to encourage the full breadth of the Christian community to consider the Gospel call to peacemaking. The real significance of this gathering will be seen in time as we build with patience on this delightful beginning.'"

"Among the peacemaking activities that Mennonites in Botswana are considering is a Victim-Offender Reconciliation process that the government prison system wants to discuss. There will also be peacemaking festivals held in scattered locations to stimulate local congregations to engage in peacemaking work and witness." (6)

university openings

With passing time, Mennonites inevitably came to the attention of the small university communities of Lesotho and Botswana. Limited both in budget and staff, they were always alert to possibilities for overseas sources of grants and qualified personnel. Hearing good reports of the stance and abilities of Mennonite volunteers in their respective countries, inquiries began to come as to the possibility of securing academic help for their institutions.

AIMM's first placement was at Roma, the National University of Lesotho (NUL). Originally a Catholic enterprise, the school was nationalized as Lesotho acquired its political autonomy. In that process the government established a policy whereby chaplaincy ministries on campus would be provided by the three major Churches of the country, i.e., the Roman Catholics, the Anglicans and the Lesotho Evangelical Church. As for the LEC, the job description for their appointees took on a broad character. While the University expected pastoral care for Protestant students plus availability for teaching in their department of Religious Studies, the LEC also expected this person to provide pastoral leadership for a small LEC parish which met for worship in the campus chapel. And there was even more. In case of need, the LEC expected their university appointee to teach an occasional class at their Theological College at Morija, a short commute away.

In spite of AIMM's less than satisfactory involvement with the LEC in the early 1970's, the leadership of the Church had been repeatedly assured that AIMM remained open to examining new opportunities of collaboration at any time. During this era David Miller was in Lesotho working with the LEC. Sponsored by the American Southern Presbyterian Church, he had formerly worked many years in Zaire where he had become well acquainted with a number of AIMM missionaries. Knowing the Mennonite emphasis upon peace and reconciliation, he quietly suggested to LEC leaders that a Mennonite appointee to the Roma campus might well be a happy one given the tense partisan atmosphere and the frequent violent encounters among students. Thus it was that AIMM took seriously an invitation from the LEC to present a candidate for appointment to the Protestant chaplaincy in 1981.

The eventual appointment of Titus and Karen Loewen Guenther provided an intriguing glimpse of the far reaching inter-Mennonite nature of the AIMM team. Born and reared in the Menno Colony in Paraguay, Titus pursued his education first in the Canadian Mennonite Bible College (CMBC) in Winnipeg, Man. There then followed degrees in anthropology and theology at the University of Manitoba and St. Michael's College. It was in Manitoba that he met and married Karen, a fellow graduate of CMBC.

The assignment at Roma in the early 80's was not one to be undertaken lightly. Completely surrounded by the Republic of South Africa, the student body was highly politicized. There were many ardent student supporters of the African National Congress movement and its growing espousal of violence in its opposition to Shaka. Added to this was a second layer of tension due to the internal political division of the time which pitted the illegitimate government of Prime Minister Leabua Jonathan and his Basutoland National Party against the opposition and agitation of the Basutoland Congress Party. Feelings were intense. Police raids on the campus and in the dorms were not uncommon. What could be the contribution of a Mennonite chaplain/teacher in such a setting?

In the course of a three year term, Guenther shared a number of learnings and experiences in his reporting to the home office. "What does my missionary role consist of? In terms of the Great Commission the emphasis probably falls less on bringing the Christian witness here and 'making disciples of all nations' and more on 'teaching them to observe all the commands I gave you.' Perhaps because of the socio-political atmosphere in which we find ourselves, classroom and informal discussion quite naturally turn to questions like how a responsible Christian should respond to situations of racism, socio-economic oppression, and institutional or systemic injustice and violence. Questions of this nature come up both in the university and seminary classrooms. At the seminary we read in church history that perhaps there was not only one Reformation but many; that the pacifist wing of the Hussite reform movement called itself 'the First Reformation,' and in contrast to the imperial reformers, took the Sermon on the Mount seriously."

"But my students found this lesson unacceptable and disturbing. They rejected the validity of this lesson because if we took the Hussite pacifists seriously, we might have to accept the Sermon on the Mount as normative for our social ethics. In a practical theology course at NUL, we discovered that Jesus also encountered imperialist exploitation by the Romans but rejected the violent program of the Zealots, not because it changes too much but because it changes too little. The old tactics of violence cannot produce a truly new society. It is not easy to say how far the students accepted this finding. Several essays on related topics would indicate that they were convinced by the argument but at least one honest student was unable to adopt this position. While she congratulated those who take such a stand, she said she found it impossible to love her enemies and could therefore not pray all of the Lord's prayer."

"If church and chapel services are attended by only a fraction of the LEC students on campus, memorial services bring out just about the whole university population. The Student Council always invites the chaplains to attend and to lead in prayer and a short meditation. A student by the name of Abel had been stabbed to death. As chaplains, we decided each of us would pray for certain individuals involved in the tragedy. Several months later a member of the faculty recalled with admiration, 'They even prayed for the murderer!' Somebody had noticed and been touched."

"Thus my missionary activities consist of a combination of my formal assignment and informal interaction with people outside this assignment. Many things I had assumed I would do have not materialized.

Most come for help in getting scholarships. But many things which I had not expected have come as gifts to me in the form of fruitful communication. Failure and success tend to follow one another but I continue to draw strength from the closing words of the Great Commission: 'And know that I am with you always; yes, to the end of time.'" (7)

In Botswana, AIMM was at first introduced to the university scene in an indirect manner. It was in the spring of 1984 that AIMM staff received a phone call from John H. Yoder of Belleville, PA, explaining that he had just signed a contract with the University of Botswana. A Ph.D in educational psychology, he had already served a number of years as an administrator in public and private schools. Members of the Allenville Mennonite Church of the Allegheny Conference, he and his wife, Madonna Miller, had first made inquiry with the Eastern Mennonite Board of Missions and MCC but found no openings at the time. Desirous of serving overseas in some capacity or other, the job offer from the Botswana University had come and he and his family decided to accept it.

Learning that the AIMM had personnel in that country, they made inquiry both about the country and the Mennonite team there. Did AIMM have any sort of "Partners in Mission" category under which they might serve? Although there had been earlier AIMM board discussion of such a possibility, no action had yet been taken. The call from the Yoders precipitated action. A few weeks later, at its annual spring board meeting, a personnel category of "Partners in Mission" was approved. In the same sessions action was taken to accept the Yoder family under this newly established relationship. (8) While they much appreciated the opportunity to identify and collaborate with a Mennonite team, country program planning was much enriched by the academic experience and perspective they provided during their seven years of ministry on the University campus.

The Yoders arrival on the university campus in the fall of 1984 sparked immediate interest on the part of university personnel regarding the Mennonite team in the country. At the request of staff of the University Religious Studies Department, traveling AIMM delegations went to the campus for discussions of personnel needs in late 1984 and in early 1986. On the second occasion the meeting was with Dr. John Parratt, the newly-appointed head of the department. (9) He wasted no time in laying his request before the visitors. As the new department head he had discovered "a lot of South African liberation theology floating around" but a distinct lack of disciplined study of the Bible itself. He particularly sought someone who was competent to teach biblical languages - - especially Greek. All four salaried posts in the department were already filled but the need for additional staff was great. Could the Mennonites possibly second and support a qualified person for their department?

Once again the broad inter-Mennonite constituency of the AIMM was equal to the opportunity. This time it was Ivan and Rachel Hilty Friesen who responded to the news of the teaching opportunity in southern Africa. A Ph.D candidate in Old Testament studies with broad background in teaching, Ivan's file was quickly approved by the university staff in Botswana. Rachel's graduate studies also stood AIMM in good stead for she elected, for the purposes of her thesis, to research and write a history of the Spiritual Healing Church, this to the great delight of Archbishop Israel Motswasele.

Ivan's academic and administrative skills soon became apparent to the head of the department. Consequently he early came to Friesen with the request to stand in for him as department head on the rather frequent occasions he needed to be absent from the campus. Functioning at such times in an administrative role, Ivan soon found himself sitting with various committees. On one occasion, in a session with the faculty of the "Humanities Board," he heard a discussion regarding the place for and approach to Biblical studies within a secular university. A key question was whether such teaching should be "a value laden exercise" or "an exclusively empirically taught exercise." (10)

On this issue Friesen made his personal convictions clear. In a prepared statement he wrote, in part: "The case for teaching the Bible in a university setting may be summarized as follows: a) The teaching of the biblical languages (Hebrew and Greek) is appropriate to a university setting. Learning Hebrew and Greek is essential if the Bible is to be translated into the world's languages. b) The Bible is one of the great literary productions of the world and it has had an enormous impact on human life during the past three millennia. The study of this literature deserves a place in a university curriculum. c) The study of the history and composition and social setting of the Bible is important in the continuing mandate to make the Bible understandable in the modern world. Finally, d) the Bible's message, one which calls for faith and commitment, is inescapable no matter where it is taught . . . . "

"The challenge of teaching the Bible in a university setting is simply to present the Bible in such a way that its power will be evident to students, students who may or may not have any particular commitment to the Lord to whom the Bible witnesses. Stated this way Bible teaching is one dimension of mission in which Christians are called to express the Good News in their associations and relationships with others. To let the Bible speak with power means that it is handled with warmth and appreciation and reverence even when difficult literary or historical or theological questions and problems present themselves. These problems should not be 'whitewashed' but neither should the Bible be ridiculed when there are problems. The opposite of this - - a detached, skeptical, coldly objective, uncommitted approach - - looks for no direction in the Bible and finds none!" (11)

Curiously enough, during his stint in Botswana, the time came when he felt it appropriate to address himself to his fellow members of the Mennonite Ministries team. Under the MM umbrella, his appointment had been worked out by AIMM. In the meantime, some MCC appointees, under the same umbrella, had come to feel that Mennonite efforts in Botswana should focus in a very clear and even exclusive manner upon the disadvantaged and marginalized people of the country. Ministry among the AICs fit this vision perfectly. But the University? Were these students not a privileged minority?

Picking up on these occasional "vibrations," Friesen on one occasion wrote: "Apart from whether the labels 'elite' and 'marginalized' are accurate, is it a good thing to apply them? I have wondered about this especially when my university classes have been peopled with students from the Independent Churches. Now if there is anything I hate it is elitism. (It is worse than marginalism.) Having said this, I also know that people in the academic community are often elitist or even worse, to borrow a phrase from the former vice president of the United States, the honorable Spiro Agnew, 'effete snobs.' I may be hiding my head in the sand to think that I can be part of a university community and not be elitist. But I still think it is possible to seek knowledge as a servant of God and to do so not with arrogance but with humility."

"If you will excuse a small but important digression here, it is important to state that the cultural foundation of Botswana is its own languages, its world-view, its values, its traditions, its way of life. This is basic. The university through its teaching should be able to help Batswana students build on this foundation (and perhaps reshape it) by giving them tools to understand what the foundation is made of and the best way of erecting a building that will not collapse but will meet the needs of the people. A modern society needs a cadre of people who can produce this kind of leadership and vision. But if this cadre of people comes to think of itself as being the elite, elite in the sense of being the choice part, the best there is, it will no longer be in touch with the needs of the people but with its own ever-expanding needs as an elite. . . ."

"I am not making a big point in this paper. I only think that MM should think of itself as working with people in Botswana, not with classifications. I know that MM has to have priorities but people are people wherever you go. Among the 'marginalized' and among the 'elite' you meet the good and the bad, the ripe and the rotten, the humble and the arrogant, those who work for others and those who work only for themselves. The point of discernment should be seeking out those who are interested in the church and its mission in the world." (12)

even a place in government

One of the least expected openings for Mennonite personnel in Botswana was that afforded Mary Kay Larson. She arrived in Gaborone with a graduate degree in public health and previous experience as a consultant in the Minnesota State Department of Public Health. Upon arrival in Botswana in July 1981, her husband Jonathan's assignment among the AICs was clear enough. Her contribution to the team effort was yet to be determined. Through friends she was early introduced to a remarkable woman, Dr. Mashabala (pr. mah-shah-BAH-lah), who at the time was the principal medical officer of the Family Health Division of the government's Ministry of Health. Born in the Transkei, she grew up a barefoot girl in the home of poor rural parents. Blessed with a bright intelligence she pursued the education available to her and eventually was among the first blacks of the region to be admitted to a white medical school. There she met a fellow student from Botswana who, upon graduation, became Dr. Moeti (pr. moh-AY-ti), her husband, and in time the chief medical officer of the Ministry of Health of his country.

Learning of her credentials, Dr. Mashabala offered Mary Kay a position in the department which made her one of three expatriates on a staff of some twenty people. A relationship of mutual respect and trust soon formed between the two women which opened a variety of significant service opportunities. Among other things, Dr. Mashabala was greatly concerned about the growing problems of alcoholism and spreading venereal diseases both of which were having tragic impact upon Botswana society. Amidst these twin plagues she was also concerned about the health of mothers and infants and the increasingly important issue of rapid population growth in the country. It was not long that Mrs. Larson was asked to give leadership to a government effort to gather and collate precise data from across the country relative to these last two issues. Such was the confidence of the Doctor in Larson's ability that, upon her retirement, Mary Kay was asked to serve as interim director of the department until a Motswana replacement could be found.

from Thaba Khupa to Tabola

AIMM's openness to minister to both body and spirit was not limited, in southern Africa, to Botswana. From the time of the earliest investigative travels of AIMM personnel in Lesotho, the term "hiring halls" was one of common usage. Located strategically in downtown Maseru, on most any week day they were the scene of clusters of blanket-clad figures, their mountain ponies tethered nearby. Faces impassive, they awaited the arrival of hiring agents of the enormous mining enterprises of the neighboring Republic of South Africa.

On one occasion a traveling AIMM Secretary was invited to visit such a hall. He later wrote of that experience: "On long rows of backless benches worn to a glossy sheen by constant use, some 200 males varying in age from 18 to 50 sit hunched in their blankets against the chill of a winter's morning. At a table are seated some clerks armed with forms and rubber stamps. One by one the blanketed men move to the table to sign contracts to work in the mines of South Africa. The visitor viewing the scene is courteously allowed to pose a question: 'Why is it that you come down from the mountains and sign for months of work away from your families in the heat of the deep mines?' After a moment of uncertain silence there comes a reply: 'Up in the mountains, there is neither food nor money. Our wives, our children and our aged look to us for help. We must earn money somehow. We don't like the mines; we don't like the separation but we have no choice.'" (13)

Literally by the thousands, able bodied men continually left wives, children and aging dependents up in the mountains to commit themselves to contracts of varying lengths which took them into the harsh environment of the infamous "bachelor dorms" of the mining compounds and the withering heat of the gold mines. Pre-agreed portions of the their monthly pay checks were efficiently delivered to dependents back in Lesotho. But for months on end, as many as 75% of the men of the country, between the ages of 20 and 40, lived separated from their families.

The churches of Lesotho were all too aware of this festering social problem in their midst. Thus it was that, after several years of effort, an ecumenical vocational training program was established at a rural location known as Thaba Khupa (pr. TAH-bah KHOO-pah). The declared aims of the center were spelled out as follows: "To provide training in intensive agriculture and show that agriculture can be a satisfying and worthwhile way of life. To instill in the student a love of the land, a desire to develop it and the necessary skills to do it. To get together young people representing different churches, to teach them how to live together through common work and worship. To help alleviate unemployment and migration by showing young people

522

that agriculture can provide a viable commercial alternative to other more sought after sources of employment." (14)

AIMM had already been approached about possible recruitment of personnel for this project in the early 1970's but, at that time, response was noncommittal. But by the late 70's, AIMM had not only made a commitment to working among AICs in the country, AIMM personnel had also come to an understanding of the tragic impact of migrant labor upon thousands of Basotho families. AIMM's historic tradition of trying to minister to the needs of the whole man required some attempt in Lesotho to respond to the physical as well as the spiritual needs of the people there.

As AIMM began a recruitment process for this new African frontier of its ministry, an interested inquiry came from an improbable corner of the globe - - Papua New Guinea. John Bohn, with training in botany and horticulture, had done three years of voluntary service with MCC among refugees in Germany following WW II. When, upon his return to the States, he failed to find an opening for further service with Mennonite organizations, he eventually signed a contract with the Papua New Guinea government as an extension worker dealing with the production of coffee and rubber. Desiring to apply his training more directly to food production, he secured a transfer to a food crop station in the highlands. Along the way he had also reactivated an acquaintance made with Tina Warkentin. A fellow MCC volunteer in earlier years in Europe, she later served with the AIMM in Zaire. The AIMM appeal for a couple with training in agronomy found them married and enjoying the lush and verdant surroundings of their highland base. At last! An opportunity to use John's skills overseas under the appointment of a Mennonite organization.

From the earliest discussion of their envisioned service in Lesotho, it was proposed that a way be found to incorporate their efforts into an overall ministry among and with the AICs. While Sam Mohono and the Federal Council of Spiritual Churches immediately encouraged this approach, it soon became apparent that on AIMM's timetable the Bohns would arrive in Lesotho before necessary preparatory plans could be worked through with the Council.

It was at this point that an appeal came to AIMM from the Christian Council of the country requesting help for an emergency need at the Thaba Khupa Ecumenical Institute. The Mosotho acting principal had secured an overseas study grant. The Institute staff needed help both with administrative duties and teaching during this study leave. From an AIMM perspective, the request was well-timed. It would mean that the Bohns could be at work in the country without pressure to make hasty judgments regarding the eventual shape of AIMM's own efforts in a rural ministry.

For the next three years the AIC wheels turned slowly but surely. Ever the visionary, Sam Mohono dreamed of a rural AIC center under the wing of the AIC Council where there would be housing for both expatriate and African personnel which could minister to both the body and soul of people who needed help. He envisioned a resident agriculturist and a resident prophet/healer with quarters to receive and shelter those who came for counsel, prayer and healing. In the meantime Mohono was working quietly with the chief of his own home village Tabola, some forty-five miles north of Maseru. Would it not be a valuable enhancement of his village were such a center to take shape there? Eventually, under Mohono's knowledgeable guidance, approval was given, papers drawn up and signed. The Federal Council of AICs now had a terrain on which to pursue its dream.

As a first step toward the launching of the center, AIMM agreed to provide funds for driving a well on the premises and for a dwelling for the Bohns. They terminated their services at Thaba Khupa in the summer of 1981 and by Christmas time of that same year, they moved to Tabola into a typical Sotho rondavel secured for them by the Mohonos adjacent to their own courtyard. Roughly fifteen feet in diameter and without inner dividing walls, it afforded a thatch roof overhead and a slightly concave dirt floor under foot. That efficient and imaginative use had to be made of every square inch was obvious. It was equally obvious that a generous shot of grace and good humor was required to make it their interim home as they pioneered their rural ministry and the building of a residence on the terrain at the edge of the village.

That the Bohns were up to coping with their new arrangement was soon enough apparent to visitors who dropped in on them. Little wooden shims under legs of furniture effectively leveled them. They frequently offered to take visiting guests "on a tour of their home." Standing in the center of their tiny round shelter they would slowly turn on their heels while gesturing in different directions of the compass announcing: "We are now in the kitchen; now we are in the study; and now in the bedroom, etc.! On occasion, when things got a bit too snug, they always had temporary storage available in their "mobile closet" parked outside under a peach tree: their VW Bug!

first, a model highland home

Since the Bohns were to live among the people and had the opportunity for planning their home, John set out to make it a teaching model of what could be economically built in the foothills of Lesotho's mountains. Of modest size, the walls were laid up with locally-made, fired clay bricks. It had a gable roof covered with corrugated galvanized roofing. A striking feature of the house was something called a "Trombe wall" (so named for Felix Trombe, its French designer). After carefully establishing the course and positions of the sun in winter and summer, John oriented the house and the roof overhang in a manner that allowed the sunrays of winter to fall on the northern side of the house and its windows in the cold season while being shaded during the other times of the year. Just inside the northern windows was laid up a wall of solid cement block painted black. When in winter time the direct rays of the sun slanted through the windows and fell on the blocks, (because situated in the southern hemisphere) they absorbed heat. In the chill of the night they acted as "radiators" as they released the solar heat stored during the day.

A bicycle pedal arrangement powered an augur type pump which lifted water from the drilled well into an overhead tank on a stand behind the house from where it was gravity fed into the dwelling. A simple interior loft, accessible by a stairway, provided additional sleeping and storage space. Without electricity, lighting was provided by lamps readily available to the local people. A latrine was housed in an outside unit which provided a special venting device which served the dual functions of trapping insects and circulating air. Gradually the little yard around the house began to model other facets of self sustained life such as a compost pit, a vegetable garden and a cluster of young fruit trees.

With their own village operational base established, the Bohns gave more and more of their time to the rural people scattered all about them. This point in their service came at a time when there was an abundance of international aid organizations with offices and personnel in the country. Oriented toward large development schemes, there were trucks on the roads, motorized equipment working large plots of ground and frequent fanfare regarding the "progress" being made. Yet somehow, year in and year out, there seemed to be little direct benefit for the simple village folk. AIC leader Sam Mohono was once heard to comment: "We see the vehicles running around and, once a year, we see some agricultural produce on tables at the annual agricultural fairs but somehow none of this produce finds its way into our cooking pots in the villages."

Very aware of this, the Bohns looked for practical, low profile, inexpensive ways of improving the life of village folk. Using the format of weekend seminars from area to area, they covered a range of topics such as food preservation, basic sanitation, nutrition, the proper use of pesticides, simple bookkeeping and utilization of compost pits. The Bohns purchased vegetable seeds in large bulk lots thus making them available to village people at significantly lower cost. They also secured fruit tree seedlings in large quantities for distribution in the villages. They introduced a rope-making device secured from Tina's parental Warkentin home in Saskatchewan which became the "low tech equipment" for a number of rope making sessions in the surrounding area. Wherever they went, they carried with them a good supply of Bibles, hymnals and Christian literature which could be purchased on the spot. Whenever and wherever possible, such training and demonstration projects were incorporated into the already established Bible teaching ministry among the AIC people. In her work with women, Tina frequently organized sewing projects conducted on a bimonthly basis in a village setting. As projects were launched and fingers fell into automatic routines, conversation flowed easily on all manner of topics which reflected the concerns, pains, hopes, hardships and faith of these village women. A Biblical meditation and time of prayer were always part of such gatherings.

On one occasion Tina was able to secure a quantity of four-inch cloth squares from North America and a comforter project was launched. Furniture was pushed aside and the floor became the "arranging table". Enthusiasm grew as the women saw the artistic creations of their own hands taking form before their eyes. Such was the excitement that a special celebration was organized to bring the project to a festive conclusion. Regarding that occasion Tina later wrote: "Following village protocol, the village chief opened the program with a speech and the pastor followed with a prayer. Songs were sung, and then as the women's names were called out, each went into the church to choose her blanket. The women danced their way back to the gathering with the blankets around their shoulders amidst clapping and cheering. In the speeches that followed the pastor encouraged the women to continue to work together. I gave a history for the project, stressing the fact that this was a joint effort between the women of Ha Thuhloane [pr. hah-too-WHLAH-ni, the name of the village where the women met] and North American women."

"John compared the completed blankets to the church. The many patches that made up the tops are the people, the backing which is underneath everything is God's Word, the batting symbolizes prayer, and the thread that holds it all together is love. One of the women spoke on behalf of the sewing group. They would always remember these days spent sewing together. She expressed thanks and appreciation to the North American women for making this project possible and she extended an invitation for them to visit Lesotho and see for themselves what had been accomplished."

"On reflecting on the months of sewing together, I asked myself what had been the most important aspect of the project. Was it that each of the women can now proudly display a hand-stitched blanket in her home? Was it that women in North America were also a part of this project by providing hundreds of squares of material? Significant as these may be, I think there was something of even more value. In Lesotho, where there is much conflict and mistrust between churches, the fact that women representing five independent and mission denominations could work and fellowship together cannot be overlooked. To me the whole experience is a wonderful example of what can happen when people can set aside their differences and emphasize their oneness in Christ." (15)

the Maseru United Church experiences change

Under Bob and Joyce Gerhart's energetic and gifted leadership, the MUC experienced a prompt and sustained revitalization. There was not, however, unanimous support of AIMM's involvement with the MUC among the sons and daughters of Menno in southern Africa. It was particularly young MCC volunteers who tended to raise questions. Deeply committed to ministry among the poor, exploited and powerless people around them, they viewed the MUC as something of a sanctuary of privileged, elite power brokers. (16) For what reason would AIMM want to associate with and, much less, provide pastoral leadership for such a group? But if there really was some viable rationale for what was going on, it was insisted that at the very least the pastoral personnel provided should adopt a sharp, confrontational stance vis-à-vis the brutal socio-political realities which surrounded the Church and its people.

Such remonstrance did not fall on deaf AIMM ears in North America. When toward the end of their first pastoral term the MUC board invited the Gerharts to return following a year's furlough, the AIMM Board engaged in a careful review of its supportive role of this Church. In the course of reporting to the General Conference Commission on Missions in February 1978, the AIMM Executive Secretary reviewed this issue in the following terms:

"A question of priority. In view of various opportunities of service opening to us in Lesotho, are we justified in assigning personnel to minister to a comparatively small and elite group made up heavily of non-Basotho? While no one will deny that they too have spiritual needs which are now being met thanks to the Gerharts' ministry, a question still remains as to whether there may not be greater needs to which we should be addressing ourselves with the limited personnel and funds available to us."

"A question of strategy. For what has the Lord brought Mennonites to southern Africa at such a recent date and in such a maelstrom of human conflict? As a people who carry deep concern for a witness to a nonviolent way among men seemingly bent upon violence, where and in what manner may we seek to bring our resources and witness most effectively to bear? In a ministry which focuses primarily upon the African to the practical exclusion of the expatriate? or in a ministry which seeks to demonstrate that in Christ a multiracial fellowship of concern and compassion is possible - - even in southern Africa?"

"A question of image. What are the implications for us, as AIMM, in the South African setting of continually escalating black/white confrontation in a continuing relationship with and ministry to the United Church? Can this in any manner ally us, in the minds of the Africans, with the white minority government of South Africa? Or is it supportive of our claims that the Gospel of Christ is for all men everywhere? That the Maseru Church is heavily expatriate in composition is clear. It is, however, also heavily multinational and multiracial."

"It is in probing and evaluating the above issues that in the next months we must come to some conclusions with regard to our continuing role with that Church." (17)

It was the same year that the full AIMM Board reviewed this issue and, criticisms notwithstanding, reaffirmed its policy of providing pastoral leadership for the MUC. The reasoning remained the same as it had been at the outset: if it was, in fact, possible to pull together and nurture a broad interracial worshiping, confessing, praying and ministering congregation literally within the shadow of Shaka, this was surely worth doing.

With passing time a growing volume of testimony underscored the wisdom of this AIMM stance.

With passing time the Mennonite contingent in southern Africa steadily grew. By the fall of 1982, AIMM had missionaries in Lesotho, Botswana and the Transkei. Meanwhile the Eastern Mennonite Board of Missions (now known as Eastern Mennonite Missions, or EMM), maintained a presence and ministry in Swaziland. Furthermore, MCC was fielding a steady stream of volunteers in all four countries as well as in some adjacent areas. Geographical proximity, common interests and, often, shared administrative structures continually brought this mix of Mennonites together in one manner or another. Early on, a tradition of annual South African retreats was launched which gathered Mennonites from all across the southern tip of the continent. (In the mid-1980's these became biennial gatherings.) Much time was allocated for sharing country reports, experiences, problems and convictions. While some agenda items were primarily relevant to only those coming from a given country, others were much broader in scope and impacted all Mennonites regardless of their area of appointment or sponsoring agency.

the Organization of African Independent Churches

Beyond the growing circle of ministries in which AIMM was directly involved, there were yet some broader issues which eventually demanded an AIMM response. Among them was the emergence of the Organization of African Independent Churches (OAIC). The leadership of the Coptic Orthodox Church of Egypt had for some time been desirous of extending its presence and ministry into sub-Saharan Africa. This vision eventually took shape in the person of Bishop Antonious Markos. Originally a pediatrician by vocation, he had been drawn by the Church and eventually underwent training in a monastery setting. A man of obvious intelligence and charisma, he was in due time appointed as the Church's "Bishop for African Affairs with the special responsibility of initiating a spiritual ministry of teaching, reconciliation and evangelism among the AICs." (1)

Making Nairobi, Kenya, his base, he traveled widely during his first year visiting AIC leaders in central, eastern and southern Africa. Wherever he went, his message was clear and could be summarized by the following excerpts from his circulated materials: "The AIC movement has become increasingly influential in Africa, and is now recognized as basically a Christian movement by much of the Christian World. . . . Communication and mutual contact between AICs are sparse or nonexistent in many areas, and most bodies are ignorant of the existence of the rest of the 'movement.' . . ."

"There is a gradually increasing number of requests for African or foreign missionary help from individual AICs. To date the vast majority of such requests (over 99%) have been ignored or otherwise left unanswered. As a result, the AIC movement constitutes a new frontier in world mission, a challenge to the fraternal concerns of historical churches in Africa and beyond and, for the next 10 years or so, an opportunity of the first magnitude for joint action for mission in the name of Christ. Many churchmen and scholars are convinced that the evangelization of the African continent can only be brought about in cooperation with this dynamic movement. . . ."

"A handful of international Christian organizations outside Africa are now assisting the movement with limited aid. . . . A small number of foreign mission boards in Europe and America also have responded to specific calls for help by assigning at least one missionary each for limited periods. . . . In sum, help from both outside and inside Africa over the past ten years has been negligible. . . ."

"Despite this almost total lack of response, over the past ten years hundreds of letters from individual leaders of AICs have been sent almost at random to church organizations outside Africa. . . . As the enormous size of this call for assistance gradually becomes known, popular imagination in the churches outside Africa is likely to be fired to the point where responses can be expected to mushroom too, not necessarily always for the best motives. . . ."

"Indiscriminate or uncoordinated responses on such a scale by individuals or groups in the churches outside Africa are likely to introduce serious complications of which a few might be as follows: a) A resurgence of the older type of missionary control or paternalism . . . b) A similar stifling of this initiative might result from any large scale fund raising in Europe or North America, which could have the effect of reintroducing the past economic dependence of African Christians on the churches outside Africa. c) An increasing unedifying race and competition and rivalry might develop among AICs for such western aid as funds, scholarships, personnel, etc. . . ."

"There exists, therefore, an urgent need both to coordinate, and to inform all such potential aid from the entire Christian world, both within Africa and beyond, and also from such Asian and other third world churches as may later become interested in this opportunity for mission." (2)

During his first round of travel and consultation, both his emphases and proposals encountered a sympathetic hearing with AIC leaders. They wholeheartedly agreed that they generally had been both neglected and ostracized; they felt their need of help and they clearly were disorganized. If this energetic Bishop from Egypt could suddenly offer solutions, of course they were interested.

Building on this initial enthusiastic response, the Coptic Church in 1978 organized the first continent-wide meeting of AIC leaders. Once in Cairo, the AIC representatives soon discovered that the agenda had as much to do with a thorough exposure to Coptic Church history, traditions and beliefs as it did with their own immediate concerns. Among those invited to attend was Sam Mohono of Lesotho. Though he expressed great appreciation for the opportunity of meeting for the first time many of his AIC contemporaries from across Africa, he frankly expressed some reservations about the high profile of Coptic Church concerns and their claim to be the oldest "indigenous church in all of Africa."

Using the Cairo meeting as a springboard, Bishop Markos brought into being "The Organization of African Independent Churches." Carried along by his considerable skill and fervor, an administrative board and an executive committee were organized comprised of the heads of major AICs. A central office was opened in Nairobi and Sam Mohono was invited to come there to serve as the OAIC's first executive secretary. An information service was launched which began to publish an OAIC newsletter. An OAIC TEE department was opened under the direction of two expatriate consultants who were made available to interested member groups for counsel.

And there was more. Once the central Nairobi office was in place, regional structures were also envisioned. With OAIC encouragement from Nairobi, regional conferences were held, officers chosen and efforts made to secure regional office facilities. At the first regional meeting held in southern Africa, Otsile Ditsheko was chosen as the regional secretary. A respected AIC leader who for years had been a close collaborator with AIMM Bible teachers in Botswana, he was enthused with the idea of a regional organization and devoted much time and energy to promoting the project.

It was at this point that the OAIC, for the first time, became an issue in AIMM's and EMM's work in Botswana, Lesotho and Swaziland. Challenged by the Nairobi office to raise their own regional funds, local AIC leaders now began to approach AIMM and EMM personnel with requests for help with travel costs, operating expenses and accommodations for meetings.

By this time the OAIC was receiving mixed reviews among Mennonite personnel in southern Africa. They were quick to recognize the genuine contribution the OAIC had made in enabling key AIC leaders from across black Africa to meet and discuss common concerns. The consequent raised awareness and self-esteem was all to the good. But there were also serious reservations. There was, first of all, Bishop Markos himself, his assumptions and his manner of operation. While decrying the paternalism of an earlier era of mission work, he himself began to demonstrate some paternalistic traits of his own as he became the dominant force and voice in the new organization. While condemning the dependence of mission established churches upon overseas funds, he unabashedly turned to all overseas sources available to him with requests for subsidies for an OAIC operating budget which very quickly came to a sizeable figure. There was, furthermore, the claim of the Coptic Church to be the first "indigenous African church" and, by implication, the forerunner of the AICs on the continent. It is true enough that the Coptic Church can trace its origins back to apostolic days on the rim of the Mediterranean Sea. But it seemed to escape the Bishop that culturally and psychologically, North Africa stood worlds apart from sub-Saharan Africa. And, finally, for AIMM personnel, the whole issue of the real reason behind the sudden interest of the Coptic Church in the AICs of Africa remained an open question. Bishop Markos nonetheless clearly struck a responsive chord among the AIC folk. Suddenly they were no longer isolated and unaware of each other. Suddenly there was a continent wide organization with headquarters in Nairobi of which they could be a part. All of this was not easily dismissed.

Recognizing the AICs right to freely forge fraternal relations across country borders, Mennonites in southern Africa adopted an attitude of sympathetic interest. While declining to contribute financially to the OAIC regional operating budget needs, much appreciated logistical support was given as regional meetings were called in various places in succeeding years.

With passing time, Bishop Markos encountered increasing problems with the organization he had brought into being. Counting heavily on substantial overseas help for his ambitious program, he soon moved beyond his financial resources. Having called Sam Mohono to Nairobi to set up the OAIC central office, he faced the deep embarrassment of being unable to underwrite his promised salary. While Mohono eventually had to return to Lesotho, he never expressed personal bitterness but only disappointment that the dream he shared with the Bishop was not fully achieved. Mohono remained an enthusiastic supporter of the concept of OAIC regional organizations. As it turned out, southern Africa became the only region where local AICs organized and met on a regular basis on their own initiative. This was in large part due to the influential support of Sam Mohono in Lesotho and to Otsile Ditsheko in Botswana, the regional OAIC secretary who devoted much time and effort to the cause.

When the Bishop attempted to make his OAIC office the channel for forwarding requests overseas and the channel of distribution for such funds as might be sent in response, he found himself in conflict with some of the key AIC personalities of his administrative board. Ultimately internal pressures resulted in his being ousted from his position within the organization. He nonetheless left a precious legacy of a new continent-wide AIC sense of fraternity and a heightened confidence among many of them in their own capacities for shaping their own destinies in the future.

to plant or not to plant?

In the reporting and recommendations of the first two Mennonite Mission Board representatives to engage in investigative travel in southern Africa, the following statement is found:

"It is not enough to be in southern Africa simply as an expression of American or European Mennonite interest in a crucial area of the world. We are and ever will be interested in the development of fellowships of believers who will together seek God's way from within a situation." (3) (cf ch 47)

The thrust of this proposed strategy statement was clear. If Mennonites chose to seek involvement in southern Africa, it should be for the purpose of unabashed witness with a view to "the development of fellowships of believers." While the planting of Mennonite Churches was not specifically called for in the report, the language used pointed in that direction.

But as the early AIMM and EMM personnel arrived, they were soon confronted by what appeared to be opening doors of ministry among the AICs. A decision needed to be made. Could the Mennonites keep faith with the AICs and still try to keep their options open for possible church planting on their own? For the contingent of early Mennonite Mission workers, the answer was soon clear. It was "No." Winning the confidence and respect of the AICs would take both time and effort. In the emotionally-charged atmosphere which prevailed between the AICs and the mission established churches, it was clear that the Mennonites were before an either/or proposition. They could choose one or the other, but not both. The Mennonites chose the AICs.

a persistent question

But with passing time, this was a decision that was to be questioned and reviewed repeatedly. Interestingly enough, it was typically new MCC recruits who most frequently wanted to know why Mennonites were making no effort to plant Mennonite Churches in a part of the world where there were none. Most of the AIMM and EMM missionaries posted to that part of Africa were basically recruited for service among the Independent Churches. They came with the orientation that these churches were to be the exclusive focus of their ministry. MCC volunteers, however, came with a wide range of service assignments. They furthermore were highly inspired and motivated by their Anabaptist convictions and commitments. How could it be that they found Mennonite missionaries who were seemingly unconcerned about founding Mennonite Churches? It was a question that could not be laid to rest - - and rightly so. It had been, after all, a landmark decision which carried all manner of implications and one that it was wise to revisit now and again.

For those who most persistently questioned the decision, there were several personal dynamics at work. There was first the simple fact of deep allegiance to their Church, its history, its distinctives and its teachings. Mennonite Churches had been planted around the world; why not here? There was furthermore the dream that somehow Mennonites in southern Africa might, at least in some small ways, be agents of reconciliation. Would the realization of this dream be helped or hindered by the deliberate decision not to establish a formal Mennonite identity in that troubled landscape?

Still others raised questions of a personal nature having to do with their need for spiritual nurture. In the semi-isolation of their assignments amidst a non-Mennonite setting, where could they turn for personal spiritual enrichment and accountability for their work - - valid questions all.

By the year 1988 there seemed to be a general consensus, both in southern Africa and in North America, that it was time to review the stance adopted there. In preparation for the renewed round of discussion on this topic planned for that year, AIMM missionary Jonathan Larson sent a memo to several people who had been or were still involved in the shaping of policy. It read in part: "There is a diffused conversation underway in the Mennonite mission world about how to see our future in southern Africa. Though the discussion is wide-ranging, it has been occasioned, as you know, by the issue of whether or not to plant Mennonite Churches in the region. It may be that the rising level of interaction will lead in the future to some form of consultation by the interested parties. In anticipation of such an eventuality, and to help stimulate further probing of this frontier, several of us in Botswana have undertaken to write and to seek from others written expressions of such a vision. To that end I am approaching you as people close to the regional scene asking that you give some thought to this and commit your perspective to paper for circulation both on the field here and with interested groups in North America." (4)

In his reply, a former AIMM executive secretary suggested that as a background to the proposed discussion, there was a set of prior questions which needed to be examined first: "- Is there still need and opportunity for Mennonite ministry and witness among the AICs? - Are the presuppositions of 15 years ago which shaped our approach to our ministry among the AICs still valid? - Is there any reason to believe that after 15 years of presence and ministry we could in effect engage in church planting and still make ourselves effectively available to AICs in a given region? - Is there any reason to believe that our ministry among AICs has within it a cumulative dimension which will continue yet for some time to grow in effectiveness and value? Or have we made our contribution? - In the swiftly evolving southern Africa context, is the AIC community still a good arena within which to live out and teach our Anabaptist views and beliefs or would Mennonite Churches of our own planting offer greater flexibility and potential for sharing and instilling in others our convictions and faith? - What are some commitments, explicit and/or implicit, which have been made to the AICs which we must keep in mind in the event we shift in our focus and intent? - In the event we should at some point choose to disengage from our present partnership with the AICs, what would be the implications of such a move as regards our present image and integrity with the AICs themselves and in the broader Christian community? (5)

By this time, the position of an MCC South African coordinator had been established. In 1988 this was the shared role of Robert and Judy Zimmerman Herr. Based in Gaborone, they were intimately involved in this round of talks. That they had already reached some personal conclusions on the topic was clearly reflected in some of their writing which was published in mid-1988. Addressing themselves to the question "Are we accountable?" they wrote in part: "Except for those in Zimbabwe and Zambia, no established Anabaptist/Mennonite Church exists in southern Africa. During the past two and a half decades, Mennonite agencies have not undertaken to plant such churches. No doubt the lack of access to South Africa has contributed to this. But more than that, while discussions on this issue have taken place on many occasions, the consensus has generally been that starting a church-planting ministry would not be appropriate or needed."

"This understanding holds that the Anabaptist/Mennonite spiritual heritage is not housed exclusively within an Anabaptist/Mennonite institutional structure. That does not mean that an institutional base is negative; it is the way God's people communicate and work together, making it a basic component of the church's mission in the world. But in southern Africa Mennonites have felt that this is not the time or place to build yet another Western institutional base. Starting another denomination would not contribute to the current edge of Christian growth in southern Africa. The church is well established in South Africa and generates its own internal agenda; thus, an Anabaptist/Mennonite ministry should be at its base ecumenical or interdenominational in nature. We should work to feed our spiritual heritage into the structures that already exist in a kind of incarnational model of ministry. Although this model for ministry should not be used everywhere, it is appropriate to the South African context. . . ."

"A second theme important to an ecumenical ministry in South Africa relates to the centrality of the unity of the church. We simply must, as followers of Christ, take seriously other people who profess the same allegiance. Today we are more aware than ever that our definition of the Christian life is greatly influenced by personal and cultural assumptions. When we move to a context different from the one that nurtured us in the faith, we need to avoid creating divisions in the body of Christ that need not exist or that do not arise in that new context. . . ."

"Within southern Africa, Mennonite willingness to work in locally-established organizations and churches has opened more doors than we have been able to respond to. A significant example has been the work with African Independent Churches. These churches, though growing numerically at a rapid pace, do not automatically translate into stable institutions and organizations. Whether that will happen or how it will happen in the future is an open question. Whatever happens will surely be on their own terms and in ways that meet needs within their own context. Mennonites have been seen as safe, nonthreatening and perhaps controllable. We are in the midst of these churches at their request and hopefully have been able to assist them to become stronger . . . but on their terms. Other churches and church organizations have also invited us into their midst in ways that would perhaps not have happened if our goal was more centered on developing another denominational structure and base." (6)

In the course of discussions which took place in southern Africa in 1988, it was essentially this mix of stance and self-understanding which was again affirmed as that of the inter-Mennonite team on the scene.

state-side discussions, as well

In the late 1960's, as Mennonite interest in and concern for the southern tip of Africa grew, the Council of Mennonite Board Secretaries (COMBS) now known as the Council of International Ministries (CIM) took the initiative of creating a Southern Africa Task Force (SATF). This group played a very active role in organizing the investigative travel of early delegations and even in suggesting possible allocation of geographical areas of ministry for AIMM and the Eastern Board. As Mennonite personnel placements became more numerous and regional administrative structures took shape, the SATF became much less directive in its role and, in time, met only sporadically. Of particular importance was the emergence of a group known as the South Africa Coordinating Group (SACG). Comprised of country representatives and program directors on the African scene, the SACG began meeting annually to evaluate existing programs, assess new opportunities and to coordinate overall Mennonite presence and ministry in that part of Africa.

By the spring of 1989, however, there was a growing consensus among North American mission board and MCC administrators that it was perhaps time to again convene a group representing Mennonite agencies which had specific interest in southern Africa in order to review together their ongoing involvement there. A meeting convened on May 23, 1989, at Elkhart, IN, brought together representatives from AIMM, Brethren in Christ World Mission, EMM, and MCC. The stated purpose of the gathering was "to review our past and current work/presence in South Africa and examine our commitment to a continued common vision for mission and service in that area."

Reporting and dialogue were wide ranging in scope. Understandably, at one point, the non-church planting stance of Mennonites in southern Africa came under scrutiny. In a circulated summary of this particular discussion it was stated that there are a set of "commonalities we can agree on: - Christian fellowships do not have to carry the Mennonite name to be whole. - While there were differences in language it was agreed that being open about and sharing our Anabaptist distinctives is right and good. - The following statement received broad affirmation: 'There are groups of people in South Africa who are dedicated Christians, committed to Christian discipleship in community, to reconciliation, evangelism and to Christ's way of peace. Our calling is to encourage that Abrahamic minority in their pilgrimage. We can support them without encouraging them to carry a Mennonite logo.'" (7)

This servanthood stance among the existing churches of southern Africa, adopted by Mennonites upon their arrival, received yet further affirmation in the same year on the part of Nancy Heisey and Paul Longacre. Commissioned in 1987 by five Mennonite mission boards (8) plus MCC to undertake a two year period of travel, reflection and writing, their assignment was described as follows: "To arrange settings where we can listen to Christians in other countries and cultures communicate their vision for evangelism, outreach, and Christian service in order to discover what role North American Christians should play in the worldwide community of faith, and bring back suggestions of creative methods and models through which we can participate with them in extending God's rule in the world."

In their subsequent reporting there is found a major section entitled "On Mennonite Identity and Mission." They observed that often in their travels they had been told "that North American Mennonites have something to offer the church at large. Our gifts have been named: commitment to simplicity, commitment to the Bible, readiness to follow Christ in life, a history of suffering, commitment to witness for peace and justice, willingness to be servants and commitment to whatever expression of the local church we find where we are sent." (9)

Moving, then, to a discussion of what they termed "a new challenge for Mennonites," they said: "The writers do not believe that in the next decades the primary North American effort in other parts of the world should be to build more Mennonite Churches. There will continue to be places where groups will grow up around mission and service efforts in which we participate, especially together with Mennonite Churches from other parts of the world, and these groups will choose Mennonite identity. But in most cases as North Americans we should put our energy into supporting inter-church efforts to bring new churches into being. The efforts which we believe have greatest credibility for the overall Christian witness are those whose presence is clearly rooted locally but with an understanding of connections to the church around the world. They should be more defined by the need to meet the world of unfaith in positive confrontation and less defined by historical theological rigidities. They should be respectful of the richness of denominational pasts and even ready to draw on the strengths of these traditions but willing to call the new church to take shape in its own way and to shape those traditions to the realities of its own context." (10)

As the decade of the 1980's wound to a close, there was clear consensus among Mennonites, both in southern Africa and in North America, that we should continue to make ourselves available to the church groups we found for purposes of ministry and service - - and do so without ulterior motives.

but what about *apartheid*?

If there was broad consensus among Mennonite personnel in southern Africa as to approach and methodology in their ministry, this was not the case when it came to attitudes vis-à-vis the brooding evil of *apartheid*. Just as this horrendous socio-political reality evoked heated debate in the broader world, so it did also within the Mennonite camp. While there were some exceptions, this debate tended to range younger, shorter term activist inclined MCC personnel on one side of the issue and older, longer term Mennonite mission personnel on the other. While all shared the same outrage at the incredible injustice and inhuman treatment of the black population, there was sharp difference of opinion as to what the Mennonite stance and response should be.

Those who argued for aggressive action encouraged polemical statements in North American publications, letters to national leaders in the United States and Canada urging the use of all possible international political and financial leverage to weaken and/or overthrow the South African regime. Boycotting of South Africa was urged in all possible areas. Exercised spirits were not soothed when early in the game South African authorities began what appeared to be systematic denial of visitors visas to all Mennonite personnel. In this heated atmosphere, there was at one time serious discussion of the idea of trying to secure an audience at a South African ministerial level for a group of "blue ribbon" North American Mennonite leaders to challenge the lion in his lair.

Amidst the rising crescendo of crisis, AIMM struggled to spell out its own perspective. With time, AIMM personnel both in Africa and in North America came to the conviction that a frontal attack of vilification of the institution of *apartheid* and its Afrikaner creators was counterproductive. One reason for this view was a growing awareness of the haunting and unsettling similarities between the lengthy and often painful Afrikaner's history and that of many North American Mennonites. Hounded out of Europe, they had overcome the decimation of disease, the privation and isolation of rugged frontier life while clinging resolutely to the faith of their forefathers as they understood it.

There was, furthermore, the growing realization that unlike the Belgians, Portuguese and British citizens who at one point populated colonial Africa, the Afrikaners had no European homeland to which to return. Feeling that their very survival was at stake, their response to castigation and condemnation was simply to close ranks and to vow resistance to change at whatever price. If *apartheid* was a flawed system, they had come to see it as their only hope for survival. There was dogged determination to cling to what they had. The AIMM view came more and more to be that outright assault on the Afrikaner stronghold might well delay rather than hasten the desperately needed change which one day would inevitably come.

And, finally, there was the gnawing realization that, as North Americans, we were poorly qualified to engage in fiery condemnation of the Afrikaner race policies. Pioneering generations of American immigrants had also found a dark-skinned indigenous population. The result was a sordid history of brutal suppression and broken treaties.

Jim Juhnke, a former MCC country director in Botswana and a later AIMM Board member, sought to set a tone of moderation already as early as 1972. In a paper entitled "North American Businesses in South Africa," he wrote: "If Mennonites decide to involve themselves in expression of concern regarding North American investments in South Africa, a number of guidelines would be in order: 1) Mennonites are not in a position to bring meaningful economic pressure to bear upon companies with operations in South Africa. . . . We are not in a position to threaten withdrawal of investments, even if we were inclined to do so. Our approach would be to help business men see their moral and social responsibilities. Where we happen to be speaking to fellow Christians, we should not hesitate to remind them of their Christian responsibilities to the disadvantaged. 2) A moral witness easily loses all of its force if it can be shown to be based upon ignorance or misinformation. . . . 3) While our approach would need to be persistent and clearly focused, it should not be designed as a high pressure publicity stunt. We should be interested in genuine dialogue. . . . 4) A meaningful witness would involve work both in North America and in South Africa. . . . 5) Our most effective witness at this time would be in the direction of reforms within South Africa rather than in demanding withdrawal of North American investments. . . . " (11) While the focus of this particular writing was that of investment vs. disinvestment, his argument for engagement and exertion of whatever influence possible within the South African context obviously had much broader implications.

Perhaps most significantly for AIMM was the growing realization that within South Africa itself there were more and more people of immense integrity and courage, both white and black, who at high personal risk were voicing condemnation of *apartheid* and calling for change. As long as South Africa was pictured as a nameless, faceless, monolithic evil entity, global condemnation and calls for its overthrow came easily. But with time, awareness grew of people within the country and the system who were agonizing and struggling with their understandings of Scripture on the one hand and the inescapable dehumanization of black fellow South Africans around them. By the mid-1970's their number was growing.

There was, for example, Willie Cilliers, a descendent of Huguenot immigrants who had sought to escape persecution in Europe in flight to southern Africa. Credentialed by the Dutch Reformed Church, the financial support assured by that Church made possible a comfortable life in Germiston, a lovely suburb of Johannesburg. With a higher sensitivity toward and concern for his black fellow countrymen than that of many of his peers, he accepted an appointment as Secretary of Missions and Evangelism of the Black Dutch Reformed Church. In this setting he soon came to the conviction that the traditional supportive stance of his own white Church vis-à-vis *apartheid* was irreconcilable with Scripture.

It was in summer of 1976 that he briefly hosted the AIMM executive secretary in his home just outside Johannesburg. The visit coincided with the highly publicized June 1976 student riots in Soweto, the immense black township a short rail commute outside Johannesburg. Clearing immigration the AIMM Secretary joined Cilliers in his vehicle outside the building. Sitting behind the steering wheel, Cilliers stared straight ahead through the windshield of his vehicle for a long moment of silence, then began a painful recital of events. The secretary's trip journal contains the following notations: "The government has been insisting that teaching in the black schools be done 50% in English and 50% in Afrikaans. (12) In spite of growing unrest over the policy and various appeals made to government authorities to rescind it, the officials remained adamant. They were paying for their schooling; they would establish the curriculum."

"On June 16 students ranging in age from 12 to 20 began marching in Soweto with the intent of holding a peaceful protest rally in a park area. The number of students grew rapidly and soon they were confronted by police. Ordered to disperse, they refused. Tear gas and dogs were released and still they came. Finally police began firing at the massed students. A few were killed, many wounded. When in the evening parents returned from their jobs in the city and found dead and wounded children, 'all hell broke loose.' In the rampage which followed, government offices, libraries, dispensaries and schools were looted and burned. More police were rushed to the location; there were more dead and wounded. During the following two days sympathy demonstrations erupted in other townships all across the country. By the weekend, a tense calm had been restored." (13)

The South Africa Christian Council (SACC) had held an emergency session and issued some recommendations to the government. Cilliers himself had written an article for the Sunday issue of a leading Afrikaans paper pleading for understanding of the deep black frustration which had triggered the explosion.

Then it was Sunday evening. The Cilliers family, including a son home for the weekend from Stellenbosch University at the Cape, gathered around the table with the guest from America. Following the meal Pastor Cilliers called for his Bible and read from Isaiah chapter 61:1-2, a passage which speaks of bringing good news to the poor, ministering to the broken hearted, announcing relief for captives and freedom for those in prison. There followed a poignant moment as, in a time of family prayer, each adult and child around the table took their turn. To hear a troubled teen-aged son pray for "our dear land" and the father of the home pour out his distress of spirit was an unforgettable experience.

It was on the occasion of a second brief overnight with the Cilliers family on the secretary's return trip from Lesotho that Rev. Cillier shared his personal struggle amidst the traumatic events of those days. It went something like this: "What am I to do? I cannot deny my past. I am a part of it. How long do people need to live somewhere before they've earned the right to call it home? But I am a follower of Christ. What does it mean, in our situation, to speak as a Christian? What does it mean in our setting to be a confessing church? My son, now in university, is asking me: 'Who am I? What am I? Do the vows of my forefathers in this land have a claim on me? What direction should my life take as a Christian? Most of my friends are either agnostics or atheists. They are cynical regarding the South African churches they know because they see the glaring inconsistencies between what their government leaders preach and sing on Sunday and what they do and perpetrate on fellow black human beings the rest of the week.'"

Cilliers went on to observe that if he defied his own Church to the point of having his credentials canceled, it would mean losing his financial security. While he and his wife could adjust to life on the modest salary the Black Church could provide for them, it might well mean that the university training his children hoped to pursue would be put in jeopardy. But, on the other hand, if he remained in the good graces of his Church and enabled his children to pursue their education, was he not launching a new generation of his own family into the privileged social status with which he himself was at odds?

As departure time came, the sharing concluded with the same question with which it had begun - - "What am I to do?" The AIMM Secretary could only respond by expressing sincere thanks to his South African friend for having opened a very personal and private window upon the tormented world of people of conscience in his country. Other than expressing admiration for their courage and affirmation for them as fellow pilgrims of faith, the secretary made no pretense of having answers. He did, however, take his place on the departing plane with a growing conviction that whatever stance AIMM adopted with regard to the evil of *apartheid* and the brutal structures which enforced it, there had to be clear recognition of and sensitivity toward those who were enmeshed within the system and fought often lonely battles to oppose it with every means at their disposal.

There were also others of whom Mennonites became more and more aware. Father Desmond Tutu, a clergyman of the Anglican Church of South Africa, had steadily risen through the ranks of both the Church's hierarchy and the ecumenical structures of his land. Serving, for a time, as the Bishop of Lesotho, he was then sent to the Republic of South Africa and appointed as the first black Dean of Johannesburg. Deeply involved with the South African Council of Churches, he soon was named its General Secretary. A man of nimble wit and immense courage, in the decade of the 1980's he became a powerful, fearless, high-profile spokesman for many of his fellow black clergy in the Republic. Again and again he hurled challenge and defiance into the teeth of leading white government figures.

Excerpts from an address entitled "Where I Stand," once delivered in the Pretoria Press Club, will serve to illustrate the timber and determination of this man: "Yours is a high calling because you are searchers after truth and when you have found it, are obliged to disseminate it as far as is humanly possible without distortion or embellishment. It can be very costly and demanding as a vocation because the powerful are not loathe to use their power to crush those who may possess truth about them which could have embarrassing or even disastrous consequences for them. . . . My understanding of Jesus Christ is of the God-man who, when He encountered human suffering, said it was part of the Gospel of the Kingdom to alleviate it because He had come into the world so that we might have life and that we might have it in abundance."

"He could see no dichotomy between serving the physical and spiritual needs of human beings and serving and glorifying God. The horizontal and the vertical dimensions of human existence had to be held together, the secular and the sacred. . . . A God who does not care about the suffering of the poor, the oppressed, the exploited ones, the victims of injustice is a God I will not worship. . . ."

"We, the Church of God, betray our Lord and Master when we don't speak for the voiceless ones, those without power, when we curry favor with the powerful in the land and remain silent in the face of injustice, of exploitation, of oppression, when we cry 'Peace, where there is no peace' we compromise the Gospel of Jesus Christ so that the poor and the hungry and the downtrodden turn away from the Church of God which has abandoned God there in the gutter, there in the resettlement camp, when it lets its voice be drowned by the bulldozer demolishing homes so that people must now live in tents. . . ."

"This is a system which is not only unjust but it is totally immoral and totally unchristian. It claims that God created us human beings for separation, for apartness, for division, whereas the Bible and the whole tradition of undivided Christendom aver that God has created us for fellowship, for community, for friendship with God, with one another and so that we may live in harmony with the rest of creation as well. For my part, there will never come the day when *apartheid* or whatever else it gets called in our South African semantic pastime, will ever be acceptable. It is an evil system and is at variance with the Gospel of Jesus Christ. That is why I oppose it and will always oppose it and can never compromise with it - - not for political reasons but because I am a Christian. . . ."

"We shall be free, then will all be free, for whilst we blacks are unfree then nobody can be free. We shall be free because the God whom we worship is a God of liberation, of justice, of peace, of love, of reconciliation. We will lead the world in the matter of how people of different races, cultures and backgrounds can live together - - for we will stride into this glorious future, black and white together with our heads held high, hand in hand, black and white together, into this new South Africa, where everyone will count, black and white, because they are each created in the image of God to whom be praise, and glory and worship and adoration and honour forever and ever, Amen." (14)

Mennonites became aware of still more voices from within the land of *apartheid*, voices which did not originate with those in circles of power but rather from the rank-and-file. One such was the letter of the wife of an Afrikaner pastor which found its way to an American periodical in which it was published in the spring of 1986: "I am a minister's wife like many of your readers, middle-class, Afrikaans-speaking, white, mother to Danila (15) and Naomi (10). Our congregation consists primarily of retired people who have lived all their lives in this suburb of Bloemfontein. Tradition is held in high esteem here: 'Fiddler on the Roof' could well have been written in the capital of the Orange Free State. The elderly people dress up for church; pop music is out; so are novel ideas to improve the church fete, the annual barbecue dinner. We also have young families in the congregation. The kids come to Kinderkrans, which is the equivalent of your church youth club. Being kids, they succeed in setting the paper plates on fire during the Christmas carol service. We help them build models of the broad and narrow ways. We light the candles of heaven while some little pilgrim puts a nervous toad on the broad way - - to the delight of the rest of the little pilgrims."

"Sounds familiar, doesn't it? All this might as well take place in Raleigh, North Carolina, or in Whittier, California - - yet there is a vast and terrible difference. We live in the Republic of South Africa; the only country on the continent of Africa where Western values and a Western way of living prevail. We live in South Africa: a storm-tossed multi-racial, civilized, uncivilized, Christian, heathen, developing, complex, drought-stricken world. We are citizens of a struggling country."

"I have only to take my daughter to art class to be reminded of the great diversity. On Maitland Street I see them at a glance: the slow and obese Boerelannie (an old Dutch auntie), the young Englishman carrying his attache case, the fruiterer from the Portuguese fruit gardens. Right behind the pizzeria in the heart of town, there is a new hairdressing salon for black women, the Mahogany. In the streets and arcades the tongues of the world intermingle: Sotho, Tswana, German, English, Dutch, Afrikaans, Greek, Lebanese and the unique dialect of Afrikaans spoken by the colored people of this country. At the same intersection, a sprightly little black boy and an old, weather-beaten white pensioner are selling the same afternoon paper to motorists."

536

"This is our country, these are our people. None of us has any other place to go. This is where the white population came three centuries ago. With the white man came Christianity, technology, job opportunities, schools, universities, medical care - - but also the mistakes and errors common to man. Yes, we made mistakes. Now we live in a time of transition. Elderly people with decades of *apartheid* behind them have to adjust to intelligent, ambitious black faces behind counters, in offices, in uniform. Europe has to get used to Africa; Africa has to tolerate Europe. It is an exciting time, a time of reevaluation, of adjustment, of bewilderment, of hope and pain."

"Yes, there is pain. . . . We want peace for South Africa - - the kind of coexistence that is according to the will of God. All over the country Christians of all races are quietly praying together, organizing, trying to understand, to conquer ignorance and senseless prejudice. We are battling - - and, may I add, we are suffering. Somewhere, far away, you see us on your TV screens. Much of what you saw during the last few months, did indeed happen here. But often you saw only the dark side of the story. You did not see Christians who are talking, planning, negotiating, praying, confessing deliberate as well as unintended sins. . . ."

"May we appeal to you to pray for us without prejudice, without anger. We follow the same Shepherd; we listen to the same Voice. We need your support. We may never meet you personally, but we need your loving prayers. The fate of Christianity is at stake in this troubled country. . . . Because Africa has changed, we have to change. We have no choice. The Word of God leaves us no other option. We have but one homeland; we want peace; we want hope and life for every person living here. We want the Kingdom of God to come - - in South Africa. But we desperately need the prayer support of the Christians around the world." (15)

the forging of a Mennonite statement

It was with this growing access to and awareness of myriad voices from within South African society that Mennonites and Brethren in Christ continued their ministry in bordering areas. (16) Tensions were growing steadily as African opposition groups increasingly turned to sabotage and violence in their campaign to force political change. In retaliation, South African security forces were making wholesale arrests within the country while making "preemptive strikes" across the borders of neighboring countries on the pretext of wiping out staging bases for terrorist attacks.

In this increasingly tense atmosphere, more and more organizations and groups were issuing "statements" in which they sought to lay out their views and recommendations regarding the Republic of South Africa and its brutal regime. Given the significant Mennonite presence in that part of the world in the decade of the 80's, it was only a matter of time until the question was posed: "And you Mennonites, have you nothing to say?" After consultation between EMM, AIMM and MCC administrators, it was agreed to work at creating a joint statement. An original draft was written by MCC personnel in consultation with nearby EMM staff. This, in turn, was forwarded to AIMM for evaluation and suggestions.

While AIMM was in agreement with much of the original draft, it was nonetheless felt that it was a bit sharp edged and categoric in tone. There were, furthermore, a few AIMM perceptions and concerns which were not adequately reflected. AIMM's response was not to return an edited draft but rather to spell out some views that it hoped to see incorporated in a joint statement. Among the AIMM observations/convictions cited were the following: " - that exploitation and injustice is not limited to South Africa but is also present in vicious forms elsewhere in Africa and around the world; - that we need to express our concern for and abhorrence of all exploitation of people by people wherever it happens and in whatever form it appears; - that from the safety of our sanctuaries of privilege and comparative security, as North Americans, we are poorly placed/qualified to empathize adequately with those who struggle in the midst of conflict, whether those who are under the brutal impact of discrimination or those who are in power and struggle to salvage some future for themselves as a people; - that for us there may be greater wisdom in adopting a listening stance than in yielding to the temptation to editorialize; - that there are many people of integrity and tremendous courage of all colors within South Africa who are confronting evil at great personal risk, something which makes it impossible for us to make sweeping statements couched in broad generalities; - that all conflict stems basically from human selfishness and sin; - that the inevitable dismantling of *apartheid* will not in and of itself automatically usher in a new day of peace and prosperity for all; - that the efforts to achieve horizontal reconciliation which exclude or ignore vertical reconciliation will ultimately fail; - that the Church of Christ represents our only real hope for reconciliation and healing; - that prayer is a powerful oft neglected resource."

With all of this as background, it was in August, 1986, that four administrators from AIMM, EMM, and MCC met in Akron, PA, to work on a final draft. (17) It was over the date line of August 26, 1986, that a joint statement was released entitled "A Commentary on Mennonite Ministries and the Southern African Situation." It was comprised of ten paragraphs. Following are some salient points:

The South African *apartheid* system continues to be an inevitable frame of reference for all southern African Mennonite activity. All states in southern Africa are politically and economically linked to the power of the Republic of South Africa."

While the South African government has recently implemented some substantive changes within the *apartheid* system, it has not yet publicly repudiated its fundamental policy of separation for the races. We join the large majority of South African Christians in asserting that *apartheid* is sin and incompatible with the Christian Gospel.

The South African conflict is extremely complex. We as North American Mennonite/Brethren in Christ organizations do not have a long history there. . . . As a result we feel it is particularly important that Mennonite workers listen and relate to South Africans from a broad variety of backgrounds, for we recognize that the unfolding tragedy in Southern Africa spares no one.

As North American church organizations it is important for us to relate as partners to the churches in southern Africa. As a result Mennonite agencies in southern Africa engage in a variety of ministries under the auspices of national councils of churches as well as those of individual denominations and congregations, including African Independent Churches.

Mennonite workers in southern Africa long for a peaceful, non-violent end to *apartheid*. It is our belief that all human conflict, including *apartheid*, is ultimately rooted in selfishness and sin. Efforts to achieve reconciliation which exclude calls to repentance and submission to the power of Christ cannot but fall short of their objectives. . . . But in South Africa, as in every country where Mennonite/Brethren in Christ mission and service agencies are involved, Mennonite workers relate closely to, and come to love and respect Christians and others who are deeply concerned about injustice and oppression, but who do not share the Anabaptist commitment to non-violence. While we affirm our historic convictions regarding non-violence, we nonetheless encourage our workers to establish such relationships as a part of a listening and learning servanthood posture.

North American Mennonites ask the question of violence/non-violence in a particularly personal way; i.e., how will I or will I not participate in a violent act or activity. Black South Africans encounter the issue of violence/non-violence from another perspective - - namely that of being victims of violence on a daily basis. . . . Before Mennonites can with any credibility share something of our own convictions regarding non-violence in southern Africa, it is imperative that we understand as fully as possible how black South Africans experience the violence of *apartheid*. Again, that understanding comes through listening and participating in the life of the people.

Mennonites, if we are faithful to Christ, are likely to be misunderstood in South Africa. We believe that the example of Christ will lead us to be less concerned about how we are perceived by Pretoria or by the revolutionary movements and more concerned about whether we are standing with the hurt and suffering.

We resist the call from both 'right' and 'left' to take organizational policy positions on South Africa. Rather we encourage our workers to incarnate Christian love and a longing for justice in the diversity of situations in which they find themselves, and to share with North American sisters and brothers the insights and convictions on specific issues which they gain from such service.

Because we claim allegiance to the God of all history rather than to a national god, and because we believe that the church is the universal community of people of the Kingdom of God, the suffering of human beings in South Africa is a necessary focus of our love and concern. North Americans are called upon to inform themselves about the South African situation, to reject the simplistic interpretations of the conflict which try to put it primarily in the context of East/West struggles, and to identify and respond to ways in which North American governments and corporations may be participating in support for *apartheid*.

While the above comments reflect our understandings of the current situation, we look ahead to the equally critical time which will follow the dismantling of *apartheid*. We seek the guidance of the Spirit for understanding, wisdom and enablement to be God's people in that context as well as now. (18)

Someone once aptly observed that a ship at anchor in a sheltered harbor is safe, but it is not for this that ships are built!

Across the more than eight decades of its work in Africa, the Congo Inland Mission/Africa Inter-Mennonite Mission has been extremely fortunate in that it has experienced the death of only four missionaries while on active status in Africa; three by illness and one by drowning. (1) As of the writing of this history, CIM/AIMM has never lost anyone to violence.

In the explosive decades which followed political independence in the Congo, AIMM continued to send missionaries to that country fully aware that they could very quickly find themselves amidst violence with the danger of injury or death. As a matter of fact, the AIMM Board considered the potential for violence so real that a set of guidelines was drawn up for its personnel to consult in the event they found themselves in danger. In an introductory paragraph it was stated: "We live in a volatile world. The societies of many countries, including some in Africa, are in a state of ferment and flux. Viewed from a purely human perspective, many areas afford little reason for optimism. And yet it is the world of our day, the world in which we are called to be Christ's witnesses. We therefore go out into this world believing that He who calls us will also go before us. We do trust the Lord for guidance and protection. We do believe in the power of prayer. We nonetheless also realize that we need to be prudent and wise as we seek to be ambassadors of the Lord Jesus in our day." (2)

In the document which follows, AIMM missionaries were reminded "that we are at work in Africa at the invitation of various church groups in the countries where we serve" and that "any decision as to relocation . . . should be made in consultation with responsible national and church leaders; that embassies are usually quick to recommend and/or implement evacuation of their citizens in a time of unrest but that embassy personnel rarely understand or share missionary motivations or commitments and that missionary decisions in times of stress, therefore, are of necessity made on different grounds; that even though missionary personnel in times of uncertainty normally have options as to relocation, our fellow church leaders and national believers normally do not; that at other points in our experience in the past we have discovered that our reactions/decisions in times of uncertainty have had implications for the church and our witness to and influence among our fellow Africans; that while the claims of stewardship of mission/church physical resources amidst insecurity should be taken seriously, material assets of whatever nature should be considered as expendable and that lives and the best interests of the Christian community must have first priority." (3)

While this set of guidelines was originally drafted with Zaire primarily in mind, as AIMM began to place increasing numbers of people in southern Africa, it soon became evident that they had equal relevance for them as well. Though early AIMM missionaries were placed on the borders of the Republic of South Africa, its seething racial conflict in the 1970's and 80's kept splashing across these borders with increasing regularity.

the Gaborone Raid

In the early 1960's, Gaborone was a typical rural village of less than 4,000 inhabitants located in southeastern Botswana along the main north/south road and rail line. (Originating at the Cape in the south, the railroad terminates in Harare, Zimbabwe.) When in 1966 Botswana acquired its political independence, its political leaders chose this village as the site for the development of the country's capital. By 1985, its population had exploded to 70,000 and was rapidly growing as both government and private enterprise rushed to engage in construction on every hand.

The newly independent country of Botswana made a startling early decision. It would not waste its precious, limited resources on a military force. A lightly armed police force and the authority of traditional clan chiefs and their councils of elders were all they needed to maintain internal order. Resolute in their condemnation of *apartheid*, they let it be known that no legitimate political refugee would be turned away at their borders. As for their powerful and belligerent neighbor to the southeast, they would rely on moral force and the support of the international community to maintain the integrity of their frontiers. This remarkable stance was due in large part to the influence and vision of Botswana's first Prime Minister, Seretse Khama (pr. seh-REH-tsay KHA-mah).

Located as it is just minutes away from the South Africa border, Gaborone quickly began to attract people who were seeking political asylum. While some were members of or sympathetic toward the African National Congress (ANC), which by this time had launched a campaign of selective sabotage within the Republic, others fled because they had found their way onto the "wanted subversives" lists of the South African Security Forces. Frequently this was for no other reason than their criticism of *apartheid*. In Botswana, some pursued their education, some looked for work; all looked for shelter as they sought to establish temporary residence in that bustling new capital city.

The summer of 1985 found AIMM with three missionary couples living in the city - - Fremont and Sara Janzen Regier and their son; Henry and Naomi Zacharias Unrau and three daughters; and Jonathan and Mary Kay Burkhalter Larson also with three daughters. In addition there were John and Madonna Yoder and their children who were in the city due to John's contract with the University of Botswana. In this capacity they were welcomed as AIMM Partners in Mission. All lived in simple housing surrounded by Batswana residents. The Regiers and Unraus happened to be situated near each other on the same street. The Unraus shared a back fence with a residence which had been rented by Somalian-born Ahmed Mohammed de Geer and his Dutch wife Roelie. A refugee from his homeland, Ahmed failed to find either employment or acceptance for their mixed marriage in Holland. Hearing of Botswana's open, multiracial society, they had come to Gaborone hoping to start a new life together. Living in a small servant's quarters at the back of this same residential plot was Michael Hamlyn, a conscientious objector who refused to serve in the South Africa army and fled to Botswana. Continuing his education at the University of Botswana, mild mannered, red headed Mike received highest honors in his studies in science and physics. Upon receiving his diploma, there was a standing ovation.

In the Republic across the border, the government was becoming more and more ruthless in its efforts to stamp out political opposition. In addition to filling its detention centers and prisons with suspected ANC members, it was engaging in what it called "preemptive strikes" into neighboring countries to wipe out what they claimed to be terrorist bases on their borders. Though there had been such armed incursions into Lesotho, Swaziland and even Zambia, it was generally felt that Botswana's open, nonbelligerent stance toward its powerful neighbor and its high profile in the world community made it unlikely that the South African government would violate its borders.

Then came the night of June 14, 1985. Fremont and Sara Regier later described their experience in the following terms: "On June 13 we had a late night birthday party for Mrs. Ndupiwa [pr. NDOO-pi-wah]. She and her husband who is the pastor of a small independent church way out in the boonies far west of Francistown were spending the week with us as house guests. This was her birthday so we had invited a lot of people in. We hadn't been in bed very long that night, hardly long enough to be asleep, when we were awakened by machine gun fire at the neighbor's house."

"We heard orders being shouted in Afrikaans. Nathan [their son] came running into our room and he and Sara and I stood at our window and watched the blue flashes of fire with each shot as they were fired. For five minutes or so there was constant machine gun firing. Then there was a moment of silence as the get away van drove away, then a horrendous bomb blast blew the roof off our neighbors house and a piece of roofing fell just outside our bedroom window."

"Then there was silence - - deadly silence - - not even the dogs barked. There were no police sirens. We heard a few more grenades and bombs going off and then in the distance we heard cars rushing back to the South African border. We rushed to Rev. and Mrs. Ndupiwa's bedroom and asked them to pray with us. Together we huddled on the floor at the foot of their bed in the darkness as he implored God to have mercy on us, on the victims and their mourners at this time of peril. He prayed; 'God forgive them for they know not what they do.'"

"We knew that the blasts had gone off in the house just back to back with Henry and Naomi Unrau also living on our street. So though we were terribly afraid, Nathan and I went out in the darkness that night, over to Henry and Naomi's to see if they were all O.K. We found that they were. They'd also been standing at their kitchen window watching what was happening in their back yard. And then Henry and Nathan and I, driven by desire to know if maybe someone was still alive over there and also a strange curiosity that draws one at a time like that, climbed over the fence into our neighbor's yard. In the first house the lock had been riddled with machine gun fire and the door kicked in. We went in, and in the light of our flashlight we saw Mike's room, or Red as we called him."

"A young white South African university student, . . . he had come to Botswana about four years ago. In the light of our flashlight we saw that his bed was empty. His blankets had been folded back, there was a powder burn on the wall where a hand grenade had gone off in his bed. And we thought, 'Thank God, he was gone, he escaped.' But then we saw slumped at the foot of his bed, his body. It was a horrible sight, bones protruding from gaping wounds and a green pall settling over his face."

"We went back outside and the air was heavy with the smell of blood and gunpowder and gas from a leaking main which had been ruptured in the explosion. We didn't have stomach enough to shine our flashlight into the window of what was left of the other house and so terrified we went back home and waited for the dawn."

"When morning came the streets were full of police and security people and vehicles. . . . Stories began coming out of what had happened in other places in the city. And when the newspaper came out in the afternoon we began to realize the magnitude of what had happened. Let me just read a few descriptions from the Guardian newspaper. 'A six year old child was shot as he ran crying into the living room. In the village the tiny servants quarters where two teen age girls lived was blown apart. The two girls have not been identified. Police could not initially state the number or sex of the dead here. They said the bodies were disfigured beyond recognition.'"

"'Tom Nyele, a refugee artist (who used to live across from Henry and Naomi) was another one of the victims. As he slept, a tear gas canister was fired through a window of his home cum studio. When the choking smoke forced him out of the house South African defense force men waiting in a vehicle shot him in the back. The soldiers then embarked on a carnival of wanton destruction, a symbol of the philistinism of the regime which sent them. Paintings, paint, easel, furniture were flayed with automatic fire. About a hundred R-4 type bullets must have been expended on crude wrecking. Forty cartridge cases were found in the living room alone. In political terms it has been a failure for Pretoria. None of these killed were terrorists, most were working, some indeed, were public officers, but clearly for the South African defense force the pointless slaughter of innocent civilians has been an emotionally satisfying experience. An angry and indignant witness who had been standing outside the Beach Street Bar reported, 'When they passed here they were waving and grinning at the crowds.'"

In their reporting, the Regiers reflected on the surging mix of emotions which engulfed them in the aftermath of the attack. First there was "horror, shock; something like this couldn't happen so close to us! Then came fear." But above all, there was anger, "intense anger at the South African government that would do such a thing to defenseless Botswana" followed by the lies which were published in the South African press which reported attacks on "terrorists" when in fact many who died were innocent Batswana civilians and political refugees who had fled South Africa for reasons of conscience. But life had to go on."

"The next day I helped load up Mohammed Geer's furniture and haul it away and clean up around the house. We don't collect a lot of souvenirs, but one we brought was this spent machine gun bullet which I found in his chair from their living room."

543

The Regiers' report written after their end of term return to the States continued: "We're very happy that our story doesn't end there. Hope sometimes arises out of tragic situations and since we've been back here in this country we've gotten several marvelous letters from friends in Gaborone with beautiful news of hope. One is from a newly established group called 'The June 14th Rebuilding Fund.' Let me read you a little bit out of this letter: 'Quakers and Mennonites have initiated a project to rebuild one of the private homes destroyed in the attack. We have started a buy a brick campaign and established the June 14 Rebuilding Fund to raise funds, organize a voluntary work force and solicit material donations. We have selected the home of a Botswana citizen who is among many of the innocent victims of the attack. She is a widow who depends upon the rental income of that house to pay for the education of her three daughters. (This is the house on our street.) The purpose of this effort is to bring all parts of our community together in a common work effort to repair the destruction imposed upon us. By doing the hard physical construction work ourselves we believe relationships can be healed, trust restored, and faith in the future renewed. We seek to demonstrate how many people from many faiths, racial groups and national backgrounds can work together and overcome the suspicion and fear sown by the attack.'"

Quoting from yet another letter, they wrote: "'Our rebuilding effort is going great guns. We are rebuilding the house where Michael Hamlyn and Mohammed Geer died. Lots of volunteers are coming forward. On the first day, after a moving sunrise service in which we literally washed the blood off the walls, thirty to forty of us tore the remaining house down, cleared the yard, repaired the servants quarters and sorted material. Now, a month later, the walls are going up and our fund raising is very successful.'"

The letter then concluded with a little poem: "'With brick and love we build this home, to give the dove of peace a throne; With hearts and hands we strive to heal the wounds both friends and foes must feel.'" (4)

Though located in a different part of Gaborone, the Larsons were also jolted from their beds that traumatic night. They wrote of their experience in the following terms: "The echo of shooting came from nearly every quarter of the city. After about fifteen minutes, an eerie silence fell on the town. We lay awake for better than an hour in our bewilderment trying to piece together what had happened."

"Daylight brought the first news via radio that the South African military had sent a team of commandos on a cross-border raid into Gaborone with the object of attacking refugees who were suspected of sabotage and attempted assassination. The commandos struck 10 sites in the city, mainly in residential areas. Though the final toll is still being tallied it is known that at least fifteen were killed and numbers of others wounded. Among the dead are at least one 6 year-old child and several women. This normally bucolic country was suddenly brought face to face with the reality of regional violence: shattered windows, pulverized masonry, splintered furniture and blood-stained blankets. It is also apparent now that though South African exiles figured among the dead, some of them known to be politically active, others were innocent locals whose only crime was that they were neighbors to those who had found a haven there. One of the dead, a colleague of Mary Kay's, was a civil servant whose work was to oversee child day care centres in this nation. Another was an acquaintance who had recently completed his university studies with the highest marks of his graduating class. It is difficult to understand why such people would be seen as a threat to the system of *apartheid* except perhaps in this regard, that they were fundamentally good and decent people who worked selflessly and who had left their country because they loved it too much to stay."

"In the midst of all this depressing news, a most beautiful thing happened. The widow who has been helping us part-time was about to leave for the day when she asked if we would join her in prayer. She led us into a back bedroom and knelt down clasping her hands together. We knelt beside her, all five of us, as she began to pray. First she commended to God's care all those who had been ravaged by the day's startling events. Then she reminded him that there had once been three young men, Shadrach, Meshack and Abednego, who had been flung into a raging furnace there to find themselves in the company of the Faithful One. She asked that this presence be made known to us all in our own furnace. We echoed her fervent Amen and then she rose and dismissed herself. Even now as I think back to her prayer, I wonder if she realizes that for us, she was the fulfillment of her prayer. Her little pin identifies her as a member of the Full Gospel Apostolic Church, one of the many Independent Churches we have come to serve. Today, she came to us as the embodiment of the Gospel, inspiring in us the hope without which we cannot go on." (5)

Although the South African forces never engaged in another assault of these proportions upon Botswana's soil, there still were occasional isolated attacks on specific targets which, they always insisted, sheltered "terrorists" who posed a threat to their security. One such took place, roughly a year later, at Mogoditshane village on the outskirts of Gaborone. Hearing of the attack, Larson hurried to the scene and then wrote: "The dust still hangs in the shafts of sunlight and (is it just my imagination?) there is the faintest whiff of smoke left in the room. Scattered all about in confusion are the tatters of a one-room existence, shredded furniture, shards of glass and bits of plaster scattered by the slam of automatic rifle fire. Only hours before this was the scene of a South African Defence Force raid against supposed terrorist targets."

"The pool of blood on the floor is mute but wrenching testimony to the price paid by one person. He was Jabulani Masalela [pr. jah-boo-LAH-ni mah-sah-LEH-lah], a local citizen affectionately claimed as a native of the village though his real home was in the far northeast of the country. The reasons for this affection are not hard to uncover. In addition to his professional responsibilities he had taken on the task of running the village night school where older students came to complete their studies during evening hours. A local pastor described Jabulani's participation in the congregation of the Spiritual Healing Church where he held the office of Evangelist. He was often called on to lead worship and in the absence of the pastor gave able guidance to the believers of that group. And clearly, he had a love of life in its youthful goodness; he was known for his zealous play as a defender on a local soccer club."

"A final touch of irony is that his fiancee had herself been the victim of a car-bomb attack only late last year. She had been an innocent by-stander at a nearby hospital when a still unexplained explosion left her with fatal injuries. For us, this is only a small clue to the agony of this whole region, fraught with random violence, dreamless troubled sleep and so many unanswered questions."

"My thoughts go back again to the room where Jabulani used to live. Standing in a corner are three gas lamps which he used to take with him to lighten the classrooms of the night school. Somehow they had escaped any damage; their glass globes AND fragile mantles are still perfectly intact. An insistent question echoes in the aftermath of the gunfire, 'Who will light the lamps now?'" (6)

a knife at the throat

While AIMM missionaries of the mid-1980's in Botswana were living amidst the threat of violent raids across its borders, our missionaries in Lesotho lived not only with this same reality but, in addition, were surrounded by a local population that was deeply and bitterly divided along political lines. The struggle between the two groups striving for dominance (the incumbent Basutoland National Party and the Basutoland Congress Party) frequently erupted into conflict. Although the expatriate population in this little country was not directly involved, the erosion of public security plus the menace of cross-border violence on the part of South Africa Security Forces were nonetheless clearly felt.

It was at one o'clock, one morning in 1982, that a unit of the South Africa Defense Force attacked an apartment complex in the heart of Maseru. Their "intelligence" said that the family of an ANC leader was living in one of the apartments. Stan and Lorri Nussbaum and children, about one half mile away, were awakened by the sound of automatic gunfire. As it turned out, the wrong apartment was attacked. An innocent Mosotho woman was killed.

It was earlier that same year that Lorri and their son Adam walked passed a vehicle parked at curbside along their route to the business district. They were barely a block past the vehicle when a time bomb exploded ripping the vehicle to pieces.

Harris and Christine Duerksen Waltner arrived in the country in early July of 1984 where they followed Virgil and Mary Kay Ramseyer Gerig as the AIMM-recruited couple to provide ongoing pastoral leadership for the Maseru United Church. Barely settled into their new home, an African became a regular caller at their door. Stating that he had been a friend of the Gerigs, he explained that he now wanted to learn to know the Waltners, as well. Writing later to the home office, Waltner described the unfolding story as follows: "He returned a number of times, sometimes looking for help, sometimes simply cultivating my friendship. On several occasions I gave him a ride in my car. Always he seemed very appreciative and trusting. On Tuesday evening, August 14, he again stopped with a friend. They wanted a ride to the home of a grandmother. I had once before taken them there. This time, however, when I stopped to leave them off, they both turned on me . . . ordering me out of the vehicle, threatening me with a knife, and striking me in the face to persuade me that they were serious. They demanded some money. Fortunately I was able to keep my bill fold. Then they drove off and left me alone on a dark street. A Basotho couple drove by soon and were willing to take me to the police station. That was a restless night for us but our good neighbors and other friends really stood by and kept us in their prayers."

Four days later their vehicle was spotted, some 80 miles north of Maseru, and it was soon returned to them. The Waltners concluded their report with the comment: "We now have our car back in our possession and are driving it again. We are also extremely grateful to God for His protecting care and for some really good lessons that were gained through this unpleasant episode." (7)

fifteen days of detention

Once installed in the family courtyard of AIC Bishop Mpehla at Misty Mount, Transkei, Larry Hills plunged into a full schedule of Bible teaching among the AIC folk of the area. More and more doors were opening to him. Using Misty Mount as his base, his VW "Bug" was often seen on the rural roads of the area.

Gradually Hills became aware, however, that it was not only the AIC people who were interested in his presence and travels in the region. In the nearby village of Libode (pr. li-BOH-deh), there was an outpost of the Transkei Security Police. Though theoretically independent, the black homeland of the Transkei was under the dominating influence of the South African government. With informants everywhere, the local police fed constant information to Pretoria Security personnel who, in turn, sent continual directions to the Transkei regarding surveillance and particular individuals they wanted taken into custody for questioning or detention. Above all else, there was concern that the ANC be prevented from making inroads into the Transkei.

It all started in a low key manner. Occasionally a security vehicle was noted driving slowly past the gateway to Bishop Mpehla's courtyard. Then one day Hills was "invited" to come to the police post at the nearby village to provide some needed information. Going with his Bishop host, they were politely received but the questions which followed reflected a strong undercurrent of suspicion: "Who are you? Why are you, a white man, living in an African village? Why are you traveling about so much in our area? Where do you go? Whom do you see? What really is your business among us?" To all of these questions Hills and the Bishop gave open and honest responses and they were soon allowed to leave.

On a couple of further occasions similar encounters took place and the same routine was followed. Then, one day, came another summons to the same police post. Upon arrival they were informed: "This time your problem is in Umtata. You drive ahead; we will follow." Making their way to the city, they soon found themselves in the headquarters of the Security Police. At the outset, the routine was one of answering a set of questions which, by now, were familiar. But to those already asked several times in earlier encounters, others were now added: "What are your ties with the Transkei Christian Council? In what ways do you serve the Council? What are your ties with the ANC?"

Once again Hills responded openly to all questions presented and concluded by declaring that he had nothing to hide and that they were welcome to attend any of his meetings at any time to see for themselves what they were all about.

Then the interview took an ugly turn. The African in charge spoke with obvious hostility: "We do not believe what you are telling us. We believe that you have ties with the ANC and that you are using your Bible classes in various places as a 'front' behind which to carry on your activities which in the Transkei are illegal." The time of interrogation concluded on an unsettling note. "You are under suspicion and we want you to know that we will be watching you very closely from now on."

Following this session, Hills and his host Bishop discussed at length what course of action would be the best for all concerned. The interrogation had come at a time of great unrest in the Transkei homeland. In response to a student strike at the University, classes had been suspended for several weeks and six professors had been ordered out of the country on forty-eight hours notice. If the church leader was uneasy about his continued presence in his family courtyard, Hills was willing to move. Bishop Mpehla's response was quick and emphatic: "I know the laws of my country. You have broken none of them. If you were to move now, the police would take it as either an evidence of fear or an admission of guilt. We want you to stay."

In late 1985 Hills took a four month break in the States. Upon his return in early 1986, he soon became aware of a drama which was being played out in Umtata, the capital, around a well-known African named Ezra Sigwela (pr. si-GWAY-lah). One of a group of men from the Transkei area who had been sentenced to a prison term some ten years earlier on infamous Robben Island, he had very nearly died of starvation. Upon his release he evinced dramatic courage by returning directly to his home area and accepting a position with the Transkei Christian Council which made him a principal liaison person with the families of other men who were still on the Island or held in detention elsewhere in the South African prison system. Often without any means of livelihood, it was the simple rations distributed by the TCC which saved these families from constant hunger and abject poverty. Such a role, of course, quickly brought Sigwela under the suspicious scrutiny of Security Police. It was not long until he was once again taken into custody. After six months of imprisonment he was brought to trial on trumped-up charges of collaboration with the ANC. Declaring "evidence" submitted against him by the security agents to be suspect, the white judge threw the case out of court and Sigwela was again set free.

MCC-appointees Robert and Judy Zimmerman Herr were resident in Umtata during this time and provided crucial support to the Sigwela family during his incarceration and trial. It was late in 1986 that arrangements were made for Sigwela to spend a few months in Akron, PA, as "an international in residence." Concerned about the temporary loss of this able man, TCC personnel came to Larry Hills with an urgent request that he help with the administrative load at their office during Sigwela's absence. Reluctant to cut back on his work with AICs even for a short period of time, he nonetheless accepted to provide interim help.

This came at a time of growing dissent within the Transkei. More and more, common people were feeling that the agreement to turn their region into a "homeland" had taken place over their heads and without their consent. Many villagers were increasingly sympathetic with the exiled leadership of the banned ANC which absolutely insisted that they would never give up their battle to overthrow the regime of *apartheid*. It was in this context that pamphlets fell into the hands of the Transkei police which advocated violent opposition against the State. It was not long after that a raid was made on the TCC office and word was flashed to the States that a number of TCC people had been taken into custody including AIMM missionary Larry Hills.

This time, the accusations of the Security Police were true. The anti-government pamphlets had indeed been printed in the TCC office. Under interrogation, two young secretaries admitted to having produced the pamphlets on TCC equipment. No one else in the office had known about it, much less given approval. Long suspicious of the Council, its agenda and its staff, the Police were not easily convinced.

Days slipped by. Efforts made by friends of the church community to contact the detainees or to provide them food and clothing were unsuccessful. There was, furthermore, the growing apprehension regarding the possibility of brutal treatment at the hands of the jailers in their efforts to extract more information from the detainees. It was during these days of uncertainty that the North American penchant for trying to wield diplomatic pressure in international affairs came to the fore. A representative from the U.S.

Embassy in Durban flew into Umtata and tried hard to secure an appointment with the Prime Minister and/or the head of the Police Force. She was unable to do either and wisely followed the counsel of local leaders to cease and desist in her efforts. In other quarters, there was talk of making a direct appeal to a Senator from Hills' home state. Fortunately, wiser and more experienced people carried the day. Low-key inquiries were made daily about the detainees and their status. But most importantly of all, prayer vigils were mounted - - particularly on the part of the AIC people who had come to know and love Hills through his gentle ministry among them.

Then suddenly, on the morning of November 13, 1986, Hills and four fellow TCC staff people were released without fanfare or prior announcement. They had been spared barbarity. They were free to return to their work. Ripples of relief and joy spread across the church community of the Transkei and of North America as well.

In subsequent correspondence with Earl Roth, the AIMM Secretary in the home office, Hills wrote: "I want to express my appreciation for the way you handled it and especially for standing firm in the face of pressure to go for the big story. I have since discussed the matter with local people and they all agreed that it could have been disastrous had you given in to those pressures. That approach has been used with at least two other people and they are still in prison after many months."

Hills then went on to comment: "I also have questions of a biblical/theological nature regarding this matter. In times of crisis is it right for us to turn to the secular media for help? I think it is unlikely that the media will ever understand our motivation for being here or that they will portray it in a manner in keeping with a Mennonite perspective on the use of power. I say that realizing that there may be no such thing as one 'Mennonite perspective on power' but I am thinking of what I believe is the traditional Mennonite emphasis on prayer, quiet appeals, cross-bearing, and love of enemies. . . . As for inviting the United States government, when do we start relying on one of the super powers and all of the violence, implicit and explicit, which lie behind that power?"

Hills then concluded his letter by making three "modest proposals for action should we ever find ourselves in this situation again. 1) Use of the Mennonite and other appropriate publications for the purpose of communicating facts as they become known. . . . 2) Encourage congregations and other bodies to organize prayer for the person(s) detained. While in prison I was always aware of people praying for me. 3) Encourage carefully written appeals for proper treatment and speedy release of person(s) detained. Such appeals should be low key, non-demanding, courteous and non-threatening to the extreme, expressing concern for the detainees and their captors (love of enemies once again). Written appeals should be seen as an opportunity for Christian witness." (8)

ballots and bombs

The general elections that were set in South Africa in late April 1994 found Gary and Jean Kliewer Isaac living in Umtata, the capital of the Transkei. They had joined AIMM missionary Larry Hills in the fall of 1986. Having with them two school-aged sons, they had settled in the urban center and made this their base of outreach to the AICs of the area. Their home was modest by European standards. Their neighbors on all sides were Africans.

The long and tortuous route by which the black people of South Africa had come to the incredible opportunity of casting their first ballots in a general election resulted in immense excitement and expectation. As an ultraconservative fringe of Afrikaners became more and more vocal in their opposition to the approaching elections, feelings in Umtata ran high. Was it possible that, in spite of everything, these whites would still be able to sabotage the event so long dreamed of and hoped for? Fed by rumor, fear and anger, anti-white sentiments ran high in Umtata in the spring of 1994. For those who knew the Isaacs and other church-related expatriates, there was no problem. But for the many Africans who knew them only as white faces amidst a black sea, suspicion and animosity came easily and quickly. Knowing that authorities would deal harshly with any who sought to disrupt the peace during these highly emotional days, young discontents decided to signal their suspicion and ill will under cover of darkness.

The Isaacs themselves pick up the story at this point: "At 1:45 the morning of March 29 the unimaginable happened. Our house was firebombed! A loud crash against the house catapulted us from our bed. We could see flames shooting up outside our house. Cautiously we opened the back door, not knowing what awaited us. We poured water out the door to put out the fires and, seeing no one, we went out to investigate. Five half-liter Coke bottles filled with petrol [the British term for gasoline], rubber-tire pieces and sand, with dozens of matches taped to the outside, had been hurled over our back wall eight meters away, bursting and lighting on impact. Most burned harmlessly on the sidewalk or grass. In the outbuilding two meters from the back wall, one bottle had caused a curtain to melt where the window was open. No windows, the main targets, had been broken, so little damage had been done. We were grateful for that, but shaken, especially when we learned that Parkers, our Australian missionary friends two houses down, had been similarly attacked. We're the only white families in the area."

"We made the necessary police statement but had no idea who was responsible. Although hopeful that the attack wouldn't be repeated, we cut a few pieces of cardboard to fit into the windows for night-time use. Five days after the firebombing we were to leave for meetings in Zimbabwe well over 1000 miles away. Doubt overwhelmed us. With it being Easter weekend and election month, was it wise to travel on the roads? Was it advisable to leave our house unoccupied, just in case more fires broke out? In the end we flew, and a neighbor couple stayed in the house. All went well; all was quiet."

"So after a couple of weeks we slackened off covering our windows - - except one night, when feeling uneasy, I slipped a cardboard in Mitchell's window just before going to bed. That was the night of our second attack. At 1:15 April 15 we heard that all-too-familiar crash and once again bounded from bed. Two windows in the outbuilding had been broken in the room next to where Mitch still slept peacefully. By the time we arrived, flames had already consumed the fabric seat of the folding chair and were starting on the bed frame and bedding. The entire room, including Mitch's clothes on hangers, was thoroughly sooted. Simultaneously, Parkers' house had been attacked. They'd even had a tear-gas canister hurled at their house."

"More police, more statements and investigations, and more uncertainty filled those next days. Local people advised us to move to a more secure part of town. However, the more secure areas had no houses available, and all available houses were incredibly higher in rent, with much less space. We spent two depressing days house hunting, and eventually decided to increase the security of this house rather than move. The day of the second attack Gary cut Masonite pieces to cover all exposed windows. Even though we expected no more attacks, we barricaded our windows nightly until the back wall got heightened. . . ."

"On April 17 we went to our congregation at Misty Mount, this time to be ministered to, not to minister. During the service, Bishop Mpehla had us kneel in the center while the congregants surrounded us and prayed for us. Four of them accompanied us home where they again prayed." (9)

Amidst tension and great uncertainty the Isaacs pursued their schedule of Bible conferences among the AICs. One had been scheduled in mid-May, scarcely two weeks after the elections. This meeting was to trigger a memorable experience for them. They later explained: "Over the weekend we had conducted a Bible conference among thirty mostly Zionist church leaders on the timely topic of 'Democracy and the Bible.' On the opening evening Bishop Adonis, our program chair, informed the group of the two pre-election fire-bombings we had experienced. There was great concern expressed. Many had already heard; others hadn't. As a result of that information and their concern they decided the entire group should come to our house for prayers Sunday morning before they returned to their homes."

"They arrived by the van load as Gary was able to transport them. We had seating for twenty in the living room, but then the furniture was piled along the sides of the room to provide more space in the center. Bishop Benesh (pr. beh-NESH) took charge. The service began with Bible reading, singing and praying. We clapped and swayed in song, then knelt and cried out to God in prayer. The candles on the coffee table were lit. During the course of the service, we lit others on the table and the bookshelf. Bishop Benesh asked for a basin of water over which he prayed."

"When Gary returned with the last load, the four of us were called to kneel in the center. With their voices raised in petition for us, the group encircled us with their presence and their love and care. We then began a slow march to our back yard. Filling the space over which the fire bombs had been hurled a month earlier, we sang our praises of joy, thanking God for his protection. Our neighbors across the fence joined us, singing and dancing along with us. Bishop Benesh flicked the blessed water around the house both inside and out."

"In the closing minutes Gary was given opportunity to speak. He thanked them for coming and conducting this service. I had the closing prayer followed by the benediction by Bishop Koti (pr. KOH-ti). As the last of the group left our premises we remained feeling relieved of the heaviness the bombings had had on us." (10)

"My friend, you left too soon."

Brushes with violence have been all too common for AIMM personnel in Africa. Such experiences have often brought with them moments of real danger and anxiety. At other times, however, there has been anguish of a different kind as our missionaries have become deeply involved in the suffering and tragedy of Africans around them.

Tim and Laura Gilbertson Bertsche joined the Mennonite Ministries team in Botswana in 1989. Both the children of former missionaries to Africa, they had first served a term with the AIMM in Zaire. Approached by the AIMM Board about an opening for Bible teaching among the AICS of Botswana, they agreed to the new assignment. Based in Francistown along the northeastern border of the country, they made particular effort to include AIC youth within the scope of their ministry. In due time they were able to organize a special series of studies oriented specifically toward young people. While numbers were never large, there was a committed core group which came faithfully and followed the studies intently. None showed greater interest than a young man named Mpho. Slight of build and a bit shy, he walked with a limp but was always present for class when he was in town. When, at one point, he lost his job, he explained to the Bertsches that he would have to drop out of the class because he needed to return to his home village to help his family. The groundwork for the heart-wrenching experience which was to follow had been laid.

Bertsche later tried to put his struggle and pain into words in the following manner: "Mpho, my friend, you left too soon. When you returned to your village after losing your job, to help your Mom mind the family shop, I missed you in the evening Bible study - - your lively presence, your insightful questions, your ungainly gait as you walked down the evening path. Your handicap was so slight. Is that why you left?"

"'Thanks for calling me from your village. I really must come and visit you, see how you are doing. It's just that 80 kilometers seems a long way, and I am so busy. But I really do plan to come and visit you one day.' Funny, I never made it then, yet this week I'll manage the trip three times."

"I see your home, Mpho. It's a nice yard, a strong yard. The room where you stayed is clean and neat. The plaques on the wall read 'The Lord is my strength, in Him will I trust' and 'When I cry to the Lord, He will hear my voice.' Is that what you were doing on Tuesday, when your friend found you in the bush, on your knees in fervent prayer? What battle were you fighting? Was it really a matter of life and death? I see your Bible and songbooks, Mpho. I asked for them. Flipping through the pages, I find the verses we studied together, passages underlined, marked in ink. For nearly two years I 'taught' you. But did it really help? I mean after two years of classes, did you find anything, any comfort at all when it really mattered? I see the tree where you hung yourself early Friday morning. It's such an ordinary tree. The branch wasn't so high. They say you wrapped the nylon rope twice around your neck. You didn't want to fail, did you. What was it that drove you to this? I never guessed the battle you fought. But was it so simple? They say you died with your hands free at your sides. You could have stopped at the last minute. Did you not have second thoughts near the end?"

"Mpho, did you think of me? Did you try and call me Thursday night after the argument with your Mom? I'm sorry, Mpho, that I was gone . . . out of town. I would have come out if you had asked. I would have had the time this time. I see you Mpho, as you rest. Our youth group has gathered around you to show our care, to demonstrate to those who don't know, what 'the church' is. We are singing your favorite song. We weep in our sadness, but our spirits are strong. We are comforted by the testimonies of so many others . . . affirming your goodness, your kindness. Many speak of seeing you walk through the village, carrying your 'church books' off to the service. Your best friends affirm that you never kept a girlfriend, you never fathered children - - unusual at age 25. Others speak of you personally paying the difference at the shop when the children came up short. I know that you believed, that you desired to follow Him with all your heart."

"I don't understand but you have helped me to see more clearly. Spending time together doesn't mean knowing someone well. We met, we talked, we laughed, we prayed, we studied . . . but in all that I missed your deepest struggle. Knowing comes from trusting enough to share. Knowing someone well comes from caring enough to ask."

"Next time, Mpho, let's study less, and share much more." (11)

CHAPTER 58   A MIRACLE FEW DARED HOPE FOR

As the decade of the 1980's dawned, the Republic of South Africa was a beleaguered and maligned nation. Within, there was a steady escalation of racial friction and animosity. Without, there was a rising crescendo of condemnation on the part of the international community. Led by Prime Minister Pieter Willem Botha, (1) the Afrikaner-dominated government's response was dogged and clear. As far as the menace from within was concerned, raids, arrests, incarceration, lengthy jail sentences and bannings became more and more frequent. Regarding the vilification and boycotts of the exterior world, this was waved off as yet further evidence of a sinister, international communist-led plot to weaken and bring South Africa to its knees.

An excerpt from an address by Botha before the South Africa House of Assembly provides a case in point: "The onslaught is a result of the expansionist policy of Soviet Russia and the so-called liberation struggle in which it joins forces with Black Power organizations and actually exploits Black nationalism for its own purposes. The fact remains that Soviet Russia has identified the Republic of South Africa as a target area. It has done so, not only because it has got its eye on us, but also because it wants to use us in the struggle against the West. The rationale lies in the strategic position and the mineral wealth of RSA. Soviet Russia believes that if it can control the supply of oil from the Middle East and of minerals from South Africa to the West, it can dominate the West and force it to surrender. Therefore the struggle which Soviet Russia is helping to wage and is increasingly instigating in southern Africa is one which has a bearing on its total onslaught on the West as well." (2)

The basic thrust and ideology of *apartheid* had already been carefully spelled out. It was simply a matter of implementing what had been decided regardless of all opposition and condemnation they encountered. The creation of black "homelands" was continuing on schedule in spite of the massive disruption and impoverishment which it inflicted upon tens of thousands of Africans. In 1976, the Transkei was the first area to be declared a homeland. Others followed in rapid succession: Bophutatswana (pr. bo-POO-tah-tswah-nah) in 1977, Venda (pr. VEH-ndah) in 1979 and the Ciskei (pr.SIS-kayi) in 1981. In all of them there were Prime Ministers who had been installed because of their "friendly attitude" toward the Pretoria government. Furthermore, there were an additional six homelands on the drawing boards to be established as soon as "qualified African leaders" could be found within the different ethnic groups in question. (3)

the ANC story

This somber, dangerous situation had not taken shape over night. There were a number of critical strands which, by the 1980's, had already been woven into the flammable fabric which was South Africa. None was of more critical importance than that of the African National Congress (ANC).

Founded in 1912, the ANC for years maintained a strict stance of nonviolence. Led by educated Africans who, for the most part, were also sincere Christians, they consistently called for dialogue with the leaders of the white minority believing that, with good faith on both sides, it would be possible to establish a multiracial society which would safeguard the interests and meet the needs of all concerned. Probably no one better embodied this early ANC stance than its long serving President of earlier years, Chief Albert Luthuli (pr. loo-TOO-li), who at one point was accorded a Nobel Peace Prize.

But a bloody encounter in 1960 opened a new chapter of ANC history. Already in the late 50's voices within the ANC ranks were heard calling for greater militancy in opposing the white minority regime. It was in response to these voices that the ANC launched a country-wide campaign against the hated passbooks which Africans were required to carry. The strategy was to march on local police posts without the booklets and thus trigger mass arrests, something which obviously would have a very disruptive impact wherever it happened.

One such march took place at a police post in the township of Sharpeville. There are conflicting reports as to what exactly happened thereafter. Africans insist that the crowd of several thousand remained nonviolent as they encircled the fence around the police post. Government sources insist that rocks were thrown and guns fired. Whatever the case, the small police garrison panicked and began unauthorized point-blank rifle fire into the surrounding crowd. Before it was over, sixty-seven people lay dead with many more wounded.

This proved to be a watershed incident in the history of the ANC. Younger members began to challenge the older generation of leadership. Their position was clear. "We've followed your philosophy of nonviolence now for nearly fifty years. Where has it gotten us? We continue to be exploited, jailed and shot down. We have no more patience. We must meet force with force and violence with violence. This is the only language our white oppressors understand." Among this younger generation of ANC activists were two whose names were, in time, to acquire world-wide recognition. They were friends and law partners: Nelson Mandela and Oliver Tambo.

first, sabotage

Angry they were, but ANC leaders still shied away from any activity which could endanger human life. Thus there followed a period of carefully planned sabotage of government installations and public utilities. Electric pylons were dynamited, fuel depots were set ablaze. Police barracks were bombed, equipment destroyed.

Government retaliation was swift. In July, 1963, a police raid on a secluded farm in Rivonia, Sandton, uncovered a cache of explosives and considerable literature which outlined strategies for ongoing efforts to disrupt government. Nelson Mandela and several others were brought to trial in the Pretoria Supreme Court in what came to be known as the Rivonia Trial. Central to the case of the prosecution were two basic accusations: a proven campaign of sabotage directed against the government and the allegation that the ANC was, in fact, nothing other than a front for the South African Communist Party, which had formed an alliance with the ANC in 1955. As the trial unfolded, it was Mandela who soon emerged as the spokesman for not only the ten men on trial but for the ANC as a whole. Following are excerpts from a statement he made from the court dock: "The allegation made by the state is that the aims of the ANC and the Communist Party are the same. The allegation is false. The creed of the ANC is and always has been African nationalism. The ANC has never at any period of its history advocated a revolutionary change in the economic structure of the country. Nor has it, to the best of my recollection, ever condemned capitalist society. The ANC's chief goal was, and is, for the African people to win unity and full political rights. The Communist Party's main aim, on the other hand, is to remove the capitalists and to replace them with a working-class government. The Party sought to emphasize class distinctions whilst the ANC seeks to harmonize them. This is a vital distinction."

"It is true that there has often been close cooperation between the ANC and the Communists. But cooperation is merely proof of a common goal - - in this case the removal of white supremacy - - and is not proof of a complete community of interests. It is perhaps difficult for white South Africans to understand why experienced African politicians so readily accept Communists as their friends. But to us the reason is obvious. The theoretical differences amongst those fighting against oppression are a luxury we cannot afford at this state. What is more, for many decades Communists were the only political group in South Africa who were prepared to treat Africans as human beings and their equals; who were prepared to eat with us; talk with us, live with us and work with us. They were the only political group which was prepared to work with the Africans for the attainment of political rights and a stake in society."

"I turn now to my own position. I have always regarded myself, in the first place, as an African patriot. I have been influenced by Marxist thought but this is also true of many leaders of the new independent states. We all accept the need for some form of socialism to enable our people to catch up with the advanced countries and to overcome their legacy of extreme poverty. But this does not mean we are Marxists. From my reading of Marxist literature and from conversations with Marxists, I have gained the impression that Communists regard the parliamentary system of the West as undemocratic and reactionary. But, on the contrary, I am an admirer of such a system. I have great respect for British political institutions and for the country's system of justice. I regard the British Parliament as the most democratic institution in the world. The American Congress, that country's doctrine of separation of powers, as well as the independence of its judiciary, arouses in me similar sentiments."

"I have been influenced in my thinking by both West and East. All this has led me to feel that in my search for a political formula, I should be absolutely impartial and objective. I should tie myself to no particular system of society other than socialism. I must leave myself free to borrow the best from the West and the East." (4)

At the conclusion of the trial, two men were acquitted; eight were sentenced to life imprisonment. Among the eight was Nelson Mandela. It was shortly thereafter that the ANC was banned in South Africa and Oliver Tambo fled to Lusaka, Zambia, where he set up an ANC headquarters in exile. Meanwhile Mandela was taken to the infamous penal installation on Robben Island.

now it is war

There followed 25 years of rising tension. Whereas earlier ANC sabotage strikes were carefully planned so as to avoid loss of human life, with passing time it was reluctantly decided that strikes would need to be made in government offices and police stations which would inevitably result in injuries and death. Following this strategy, car bombs and explosives secreted in trash cans and rest rooms became increasingly common. Death tolls of both blacks and whites began to rise.

The response of government was always the same. Security sweeps through townships, mass arrests, brutal interrogations and lengthy detentions without trial. The black homeland scheme was pursued with dogged thoroughness as blacks continued to be rounded up and transported, against their will, to isolated, inhospitable rural areas.

A sinister dimension of the years of rising crisis was the increasingly bloody conflicts which began to erupt in the black townships adjacent to major urban centers. The Zulu people, whose presence and power in southern African predated the arrival of the first white settlers, followed these political developments with keen interest. While sharing ANC's determination to work toward fundamental political change, Zulu Chief Gatsha Buthelezi (pr. GAH-tshah boo-teh-LAY-zi) did not support the ANC's growing use of violence. There was the further reality that the ANC drew heavily on ethnic groups other than the Zulu, something which did nothing to allay tribal rivalries which always lay close to the surface. As bands of activist ANC youth became more aggressive in their efforts to secure recruits in the black townships, they increasingly came into violent conflict with other youth groups who were loyal to Chief Buthelezi. As a result of this growing conflict, the death toll steadily mounted. The situation in the townships became even more volatile and brutal as blacks suspicioned of collaborating with the government police as informers were hunted down and assassinated.

Before this growing carnage the South African government pretended great concern. With passing time, however, increasing evidence surfaced that the government was, in fact, not only sympathetic to the armed conflicts with ANC supporters but was surreptitiously providing weapons for their opponents while turning a blind eye to the spreading loss of life. Meanwhile, the official line of the *apartheid* regime remained always the same - - minority white rule was an unalterable fact of South African life. Any deviation from this political scheme would be to court disaster for everyone, both black and white.

cracks in the dam of *apartheid*

As long as voices of condemnation and calls for radical change came from the African community, the government found it easy to rally support for its political philosophy within the white minority. It was important for all whites to stand united in shoring up the system which protected them from a "black sea" which threatened to engulf them all. As for the strident attacks which came from the world outside its borders, it was standard policy to cast the issue in terms of "them against us" and to rouse national determination to reject the efforts of the international community to meddle in their internal affairs. To be sure, the growing boycotts in trade and the denial of credits by the international banking community were making a harsh impact on the South African economy. It was also true that the freezing of South African athletic teams out of international competition was a particularly galling experience for the hardy, athletic Afrikaners. But what else was new? Discrimination had been their experience throughout their history. They had always overcome; they would overcome again.

But as the decade of the 1970's wound its way to a close, there were all kinds of unsettling signs of a dangerous ferment quietly at work within the very heart of Afrikanerdom. At first, incidents were only occasional, isolated and, so thought the government, easily controllable by swift reprisal. There had been Rev. Beyers Naude who was described by one observer of the South African scene as a man "at the heart of the Afrikaner party, a member of the inner cabinet of the *Broederbond*, or 'Brotherhood,' the shadow government which approved all political appointments and policies. Appalled by the police brutality and the violence, he turned around like a great Jewish prophet and shook his fist at his own people." (5) In 1977 he founded what came to be known as the "Christian Institute" which opened dialogue with African church leaders and began to encourage the development of an indigenous liberation theology. Quickly seen as a subversive organization, the Institute was closed by government authorities and Naude himself was placed, for a while, under a ban. (People under ban were restricted to their home communities, were allowed few visitors, were not allowed to speak publicly or to be quoted.) What at the time appeared to be a lone, courageous Afrikaner voice, however, proved to be the forerunner of others to come.

It was also in the mid-1970's that a young student activist named Steve Biko rocketed onto the South African scene and into the international press. A young man of enormous courage, he rallied students around himself already in 1968 and founded the "South African Students' Organization" (SASO) of which he became the first president the following year. In 1972 he began to develop what were termed "Black Community Programs" (BCP). In 1973 he and six other SASO leaders were banned. Restricted to his home area, Biko promptly founded an Eastern Cape Branch of the BCP. In and out of detention for questioning he was arrested a final time in August of 1977 and died September 12 while in police detention.

It was undoubtedly the belief of police authorities that this would bring final closure to the troublesome history of yet another brash, black activist. His story, however, proved to be a different one thanks to a South African journalist named Donald Woods who was unwilling to allow the bland police version of Biko's death to go unchallenged. After a period of determined sleuthing he came up with a cluster of evidence which made it clear that Biko had been savagely beaten while in custody. Denied any medical care, he had, in fact, died of his injuries in their hands. For his trouble, reporter Woods was placed under house arrest with his family. With the help of friends and carefully orchestrated incognito travel, he and his family were able to escape to Britain where he made known the sordid details of the Biko tragedy. Though highly embarrassing for the South African authorities, this too was viewed as just another incident that had gotten unfortunate publicity but which would, with time, be forgotten.

a voice from a distant island prison cell

Nelson Mandela followed the harsh routine of life on Robben Island. There were long days in a limestone quarry where rock was broken by hand with sledge hammers. There was the harassment of hostile guards; food at times was of poor quality and insufficient quantity. But he used every spare moment to nurture his mind, to encourage his fellow political prisoners and to envision the change which he firmly believed would one day come to his homeland. Permitted books, he studied whenever he could, perfecting - - among other things - - his command of *Afrikaans*, the language of his tormentors. He also followed all news of events on the mainland with intense interest.

One day came the tragic reporting of the Soweto student riots and the subsequent death and imprisonment of children. In the aftermath of this wrenching news he began to craft, in secret, a message to his people. Upon completion he found a way to smuggle it off the island. It took over two years, but after passing through an unknown number of secretive hands it one day arrived at the ANC headquarters in exile in Lusaka, Zambia, some 1500 miles to the north. There it was released by Oliver Tambo with the following comment: "We believe the message remains fresh and valid and should be presented to our people. The ANC urges you to respond to this call and make 1980 a year of united mass struggle."

Following are brief excerpts from the Mandela statement: "In the midst of the present crisis, while our people count the dead and nurse the injured, they ask themselves: 'What lies ahead?' From our rulers we can expect nothing . . . for they are neither capable nor willing to heed the verdict of the masses of our people. The verdict of June 16 [the date of the Soweto student riots] is loud and clear: '*Apartheid* has failed.' Our people remain unequivocal in its rejection, the young, the old, parent and child, all reject it. . . . The measure of this truth is the recognition by our people that under *apartheid*, our lives individually and collectively count for nothing. We face an enemy that is deep rooted, an enemy entrenched and determined not to yield. Our march to freedom is long and difficult. But both within and beyond our borders the prospects of victory grow bright. . . . The revulsion of the world against *apartheid* is growing and the frontiers of white supremacy are shrinking. . . . The world is on our side. . . . At all levels of our struggle, within and outside the country, much has been achieved and much remains to be done. But victory is certain! We who are confined within the grey walls of the Pretoria regime's prisons reach out to our people. With you we count those who have perished by means of the gun and the hangman's rope. We salute all of you - - the living, the injured and the dead, for you have dared to rise up against the tyrant's might. . . . We face the future with confidence. . . . Between the anvil of united action and the hammer of armed struggle we shall crush *apartheid* and white minority racist rule." (6)

This was but an opening salvo of a man who was to exert an increasingly powerful force in subsequent South African history. He was isolated in body but his stature as a symbol of African opposition to *apartheid* was to grow to legendary proportions with passing time. While such statements from the universally acclaimed Mandela were reason for concern on the part of white government authorities, they were, after all, the sort of sentiments to be expected from the banned ANC and its leaders. There were, however, other voices from another quarter which by this time were also being heard and which were of far greater concern to the defenders of *apartheid*.

the Koinonia Declaration

It was issued in 1977 by a mixed group of Afrikaner and Anglo-Saxon Christians who represented a spread of church backgrounds and ecclesiastical traditions. What brought them together and became the focus of their declaration was their growing belief that *apartheid* was incompatible with their understandings of the Gospel of Christ. It was crafted around seven fundamental "convictions" which were, in essence: "1) We as Christian citizens are convinced we must continue to practice love towards those people in authority. . . . When there is a conflict between the law of God and the state's expectations of us, it is, however, our firm conviction that we should always obey God rather than men. . . . 2) The Bible gives us guidelines as to what the duties of the citizen as well as civil government are. . . . 3) We believe that freedom, sufficient to fulfill one's calling before God, is essential. 4) We believe that God is a God of justice, and that his justice is a principle implanted in the hearts and the lives of his children. We believe God should be obeyed by practicing his justice in all spheres of life and at this time especially in politics. . . . We believe that justice embraces, inter alia, equity. . . . 5) We believe that the Body of Christ is one, and this unity includes rich diversity. . . . On this basis we deem it necessary that particularly within the state, the legitimate interests of each group as well as the common interest of all, should be fully recognized within the framework of a just political dispensation. . . . 6) We believe that God who is Creator and Judge of all men has given his children the task of ordering life according to his Word alone. . . . We believe that it is our task to speak out according to God's Word against any distortion of and disobedience to the Word for society. . . . We believe we must pronounce God's judgment on all forms of dehumanization, oppression and discrimination and not be afraid of doing so. 7) We believe that God alone is the absolute Sovereign and that Christ was given all power in heaven and on earth. Both civil government and the people are to acknowledge this and are therefore obliged to keep the commandments of God. . . . Thus believing it is our conviction that . . . the government ought to enact and obey just laws for its own and for its citizens' good so that the blessing of God might rest on our society." (7)

While this statement was worrisome for the government, it nonetheless was a statement of individuals which had no official backing of the church community. As long as the hierarchy of the white Dutch Reformed Church remained quiet, their ideological base was still secure. But there soon followed other disquieting voices from other quarters.

There was the irritation caused by Nico Smith, a credentialed clergyman of the white Dutch Reformed Church and an instructor at the Stellenbosch Theological Seminary who, in 1981, took a group of "missionary science students" on a field trip to a squatters community of thousands of black homeless people. He was shocked by what he found. "In the desperate faces of mothers separated from their children during forced deportations [to black homelands] Smith saw the harsh reality of his government's policy of *apartheid*. The seminary professor began to view the scheme of *apartheid* as a political failure, a theological abomination, and a social blight on the nation his European ancestors had claimed as their own for seven generations." (8)

Shaken by what he and his students had witnessed, he prepared a statement in which he criticized his government and charged that his own church hierarchy needed to address its own responsibility to act on behalf of the homeless among them. "Migrant labor is inhuman and the church must emphasize that it is a cancer in our society," he wrote. "Wives see their husbands only a few weeks a year. For the rest of the time, there exists only an emptiness." (9)

It was not long that word came to him that his outspoken criticism of his government and his church was "an embarrassment" to the Seminary where he had taught for sixteen years. His response was to resign his post and to accept a call to minister to an all-black congregation in Mamelodi, a black township outside Pretoria. (10)

It was an annoying incident for both church and government authorities but was undoubtedly still viewed as an isolated voice of an eccentric clergyman. What seemed still to escape the authorities, even at this late date, was the fact that Pastor Nico Smith's actions reflected a realization which was gradually filtering through the consciousness and conscience of the white minority society, a realization that not only was *apartheid* untenable in the long term, but that it was also wrong.

an explosive open letter

The year 1982 marked two events which had powerful impact upon the structure of *apartheid*. The first took the form of a surprising and unexpected open letter crafted and signed by 123 credentialed clergymen of the powerful white *Nederduitse Gereformeerde Kerk*. (NGK) Written at a time when the Reformed Church was carefully divided into white, colored, Asiatic and black watertight compartments, it was clear in its language and far-reaching in its implications. An opening paragraph read as follows: "We ministers and ordained clergy of the *Nederduitse Gereformeerde Kerk* express our conviction that real conciliation in Christ between individuals and groups is the greatest single need in the church and therefore also in our country and society. We believe that the Church of Christ in South Africa has to make a particular contribution in this respect 1) by giving a clear form to conciliation and the unity of the church and 2) by expressing its prophetic calling in respect of society."

There then followed a wide range of statements among which the following excerpts are worthy of note: "We are convinced that the primary task of the church in our country is the preaching of the conciliation in Christ. This means in the first place that the propagation of the Gospel of conciliation between God and man is the inalienable privilege of the church. Without this aspect of conciliation the whole matter here concerned would lose its deepest sense and meaning. . . . Therefore it follows that the church will battle against factors threatening its unity. Such factors include errors in doctrine, lovelessness, self-righteousness, exclusivity, prejudice or the giving of priority to personal or group interests. The unity of the church leaves room for diversity within the church in respect of language and culture. Precisely because of conciliation this diversity serves as mutual enrichment and not division."

Having laid out a basic principle, the document went on to spell out some of the implications for the church in South Africa: that no single church (denomination) can be deprived of conversation and community with other churches, nor may they close doors against each other; that the church may not impose any other norm for membership than the profession of true faith in Christ; that the different churches within the family of the *Nederduitse Gereformeerde Kerk* which, in any case, share the same confession and originate historically from the same church, ought to do everything in their power to give visible form to the unity being confessed; that already now, while negotiations for a clearer structural unity are being held, all members of churches within the family of the *Nederduitse Gereformeerde Kerk* should be welcome at all times at any gathering of any of these churches; that the members of the one body of Christ accept each other as brothers and sisters, not doubt each other's Christianity, care for each other's interests, deem the other higher than him or herself, carry each other's burdens, show mutual love through word and deed and remember each other in prayer. "We are convinced that the church's calling goes farther than preaching of conciliation within the four walls of the church. We reject therefore the belief that the church should solely busy itself with so-called 'spiritual matters' and withdraw further from the other areas of society. Conciliation includes a prophetic testimony to society as a whole and therefore the church may not stay silent about phenomena like moral degeneration, disruption of family life and discrimination. The church will always give testimony that no arrangement of society may be based on the fundamental irreconcilability of people and base a communal arrangement on such a premise."

The open letter then became even more specific regarding the situation in South Africa. These foregoing truths, it was stated, clearly mean "that the church may render its prophetic testimony with great boldness in South African society; . . . that a dispensation which elevates irreconcilability to a communal principle and estranges the different parts of South Africa from each other, is unacceptable; that such a system makes it almost impossible for South Africa's inhabitants to really get to know each other, to trust and be loyal to each other; that the laws which have become symbols of this estrangement among them, those about mixed marriages, race classification and group areas, cannot be defended scripturally; that justice and not mere law and order, should be the directive premise in the ordering of society."

"We believe that the incidence of compulsory removals of people, disruption of marriage and family bonds as a result of migratory labor, under-spending on black education, insufficient and poor housing of black people and low wages cannot be reconciled with the biblical demands of equity and human worth; that all people who consider South Africa as their fatherland should be involved in the working out of a new dispensation for society; that this dispensation ought to be built on order and peace which are the fruits of justice, which means that all people should enjoy equal treatment and opportunities."

The letter was brought to a close with a confession of "our deep guilt before God because we ourselves do not sufficiently practice the unity of the church in Christ and that we are co-responsible for many of the social inequities which we have pointed out. . . . We confess that we believe in repentance, the forgiveness of sins and a new life in obedience to God." A concluding sentence pledges continuing prayers "for the church as well as for the authorities in their extremely difficult task." (11)

a meeting in Ottawa

On the heels of "the letter" came a second blow which originated in an unlikely and distant place - - the Canadian city of Ottawa. It was there that the World Alliance of Reformed Churches met that year representing some 70 million members worldwide. One of the delegates was Allan Boesak, a thirty-seven year old colored theologian from South Africa, who represented the "colored" branch of the Dutch Reformed Church of South Africa. Due largely to his impassioned urging, the Alliance took the startling decision to suspend the two white Dutch Reformed Churches of South Africa because of their support of the *apartheid* system of their country. But that was not all. Before closing their sessions, the delegates elected Boesak as their new president! Returning to South Africa with a sudden international stature, he made clear that the suspension applied only to the white churches and that the "daughter churches," i.e., colored, Asiatic and black, were to officially separate from the white church and to amalgamate into a single church.

South African CO's?

Theological arguments against *apartheid* advanced by a minority group of Dutch Reformed clergymen were disturbing enough to those in power. But the idea that there might be young white men who would refuse to bear arms in the South Africa Defense Forces was unimaginable. Nonetheless, in the mid-1980's, suddenly there they were. They were just a handful, to be sure, but that there could even be one was tremendously threatening to government officials.

But word was getting out. Young men who were being conscripted for "the defense of their fatherland" found themselves taking part, in the mid-80's, in preemptive strikes across the borders of neighboring countries. Homes were bombed and people were indiscriminately cut down with automatic rifle fire. There was also a large expeditionary force based in northern Namibia (earlier known as Southwest Africa) which was making raids into Angola against government forces of that land. Hated by the local Namibian population, the young troops at times found themselves witnessing inhumane interrogations of black prisoners. In a very real sense, South African troops were embroiled in their own controversial "Viet Nam."

Meanwhile, at home within their own country, things had taken a new and ugly turn for young troops of the Defense Force. As violence steadily increased within the seething black townships, local police more and more found themselves unable to maintain order. Thus Defense Force units began to be ordered into the townships with bloody, destructive results. For many young recruits, participation in these sorts of brutal forays both within and without their country resulted in profound soul-searching on their part. Suddenly the unthinkable happened. Here and there, young white South African males were daring to say: "This is wrong. We cannot be a part of it."

Official response was predictable and swift. They were treated with scorn, accused of being traitors of their fatherland, roughly handled in custody, brought into court and threatened with six year jail sentences. Through this process some young men became known to Mennonite personnel in southern Africa. There was Charles Bester, a member of a close-knit religious family who, in his student days, was active in a "Student's Christian Association." After finishing his secondary education he served as a volunteer for African Enterprise, a widely-known South African based Christian organization which regularly sponsored interracial evangelistic campaigns and seminars.

Upon being called up for duty with the SADF, Bester issued a statement. Though knowing he was menaced with a trial and possible imprisonment, he said: "I believe that as a Christian I must follow Christ and this precludes me from serving in the SADF. Fundamental to my Christian beliefs is that firstly I must love God with all my heart, soul and mind and secondly I must love my neighbor as myself. Loving one's neighbor entails loving one's immediate family and friends, but it also has a broader context, which embraces the human family, and therefore has social and political implications. Throughout the Bible runs the theme of God's desire for justice, freedom and peace on earth, as well as his concern for the poor and oppressed. '*Apartheid*' means separation and its application is a denial of Christ's exhortation to love one's neighbor as oneself."

"The role the SADF is playing in South Africa underpins the policies of division of the present government. Evil is manifesting itself in a political system and the government of the day is using the army and people of my age to uphold and defend that system. It would be arrogant for me as an eighteen year old to enter the townships on a military vehicle and impose 'law and order.' I am fully aware that I am breaking the law of the land. I cannot obey both this law and God. I believe that in order for me to follow a path that will best demonstrate my love for God, my country and my fellow South Africans, I must pursue the way of reconciliation and non-violence. I will therefore refuse to serve in the SADF." (12)

There was David Bruce. In the course of his student days in Johannesburg he had read about the experience of the Jews in Nazi Germany and came to feel that there were parallels to be drawn between the raw racism of that chapter of German history and that which he witnessed in his own country. As he approached the age of conscription, he struggled with his alternatives. He could go into exile, as some he knew had done, but he felt he would be miserable outside his own country and away from his family. He decided to stay and face likely incarceration.

Upon being called up, he declared his refusal to serve. After appearing in court several times he was brought to trial in the Johannesburg Magistrates Court where he made the following statement: "I am fundamentally opposed to racism. Because of their race the majority of South Africans are denied the status of full citizens in this country of their birth. The government would like us to believe that the SADF is a neutral force whose main task is to defend this country against an external threat."

"But all the evidence available to me shows very clearly that the SADF is directly involved in upholding and defending the racist political system against the aspirations of the majority of South Africans. In other words, the SADF is involved in defending the privileged position of a minority of South Africans in what is basically a civil war. I would be willing to serve in an army which is involved in fighting for and defending all the people of this country. I am not prepared to serve in the defense of a racist political system."

"I also feel that young men who are called on to serve in the army should have the right to be fully informed about what they are being asked to fight and possibly die for. Those in positions of power in this country are using their control over the education system, the press and television to provide us with a highly one-sided and distorted picture of the history of this country and of what is happening at present in South Africa. This adds to my determination not to serve in the SADF." (13)

And there was the case of Philip Wilkinson. Unlike the other two, he had initially accepted induction, received his training and over a two-year period had been assigned here and there. One day it fell his lot to be part of an SADF force sent into the Port Elizabeth townships. What he witnessed and was forced to be a part of convinced him that he could not continue. Refusing further duty he was at first jailed and then was called to a series of court appearances.

In his formal trial he made a lengthy and moving statement of which excerpts follow: "I am a Christian brought up in the beliefs of the Catholic Church. I am committed to peace and to working for a better future for all South Africans. I abhor violence and have consciously not used violence myself since my childhood. I have been brought up to respect all people, regardless of their color, sex, religion or status. I believe that all armies legitimize the use of violence and dehumanize the enemy. The SADF defends *Apartheid*, which in terms of my Christian understanding is a heresy. For me to participate in the SADF would therefore be a betrayal of all that I know to be good and just. . . . Shooting and detaining people willy-nilly is no solution for our country. It is brutally obvious that the SADF's main task is to prop up a political system that is based on the denial of full political rights to the majority of South Africans. . . ."

"For all of us there comes a point when we can no longer compromise. A situation becomes so difficult to live with that we have to stand up for what we believe in - - no matter what the cost to ourselves and our loved ones. I have reached that point with military service. . . . Your worship, I have stated my reasons for refusing to be conscripted into the SADF clearly and honestly. If this court should choose to punish me on account of them, so be it. . . . I stand before you, I stand for peace and I stand for justice. I stand here in the spirit of the South Africa we have yet to build." (14)

Statements continued to be issued by different groups within the white South African population. There was the "Kairos Document" originally signed by 111 women and men, black and white, theologians, clergy and lay people from Catholic, mainline Protestants, evangelical, charismatic and African Independent Churches. Eventually signed by others as well, it basically took the form of a critique of what it termed "state theology" and "church theology" which had been put in place to validate and support *apartheid*. It concluded with a call for "prophetic theology."

There was a joint statement issued by the Koinonia Group and the Youth Association of the Dutch Reformed Church of the Cape Peninsula which stated categorically: "The situation of our country is a direct result of political injustice that has denied human dignity to the majority of the people of our land for over 300 years." The declaration went on to "call on the church to take the steps necessary to ensure that the state of emergency be lifted immediately" and that "negotiation with the true leaders of our people take place . . . ."

And from the evangelical community of South Africa came a belated but amazingly candid self critique of what had been a very passive and, by implication, an accepting stance vis-à-vis *apartheid*. Published by a group identified as "Concerned Evangelicals" it stated among other things: "Having realized that there was something wrong with the practice and theology of evangelicals in this country we felt God's calling to us to rectify this situation for the sake of the Gospel of the Lord. . . . We have undertaken therefore to critique our own theology and practice, not to disparage our faith but to turn it into an effective evangelical witness in South Africa today."

Taking this initial statement as a point of departure, an article appeared in an evangelical periodical in 1987 which bluntly stated among other things: "We wish to confess that our evangelical family has a track record of supporting and legitimating oppressive regimes here and elsewhere. . . . We wish to confess that the people who regard themselves as evangelicals across all the churches in South Africa condemn and campaign against all efforts to change the racist *apartheid* system in South Africa. . . . Evangelicals go to great lengths claiming Jesus did not teach what he clearly did. . . . Like the Sadducees and Pharisees, we are claiming the authority of the written law but we refuse to let it address the real issues of our day."

"Faced with this trouble-torn country, faced with the war between the *apartheid* regime and the oppressed masses, faced with the ideological conflicts which are tearing our communities apart, and confronted with the possibility of a revolution, our response and choices will determine the future of our Christian faith in this country." (15)

And from outside the country came something called the "Harare Declaration." Convened in Harare, Zimbabwe, by the World Council of Churches, leaders from across the international church scene drafted a statement calling for continued prayer, increased financial pressures, comprehensive sanctions, support for liberation movements and trade union efforts within the country and immediate action on the part of the UN to force South Africa to free Namibia.

a ticking bomb

By the mid-1980's, *apartheid* was under siege both from without and within. Recognizing genuine crisis in the making, Prime Minister (after 1984, President) P. W. Botha took the offensive on two fronts. First he began to talk of dismantling *apartheid* and, indeed, some changes were made particularly in the urban centers. Some beaches were opened to blacks. In some theaters, parks and restaurants "for whites only" signs began to disappear. And there was vague talk of creating "a three chamber parliament with separate representatives for colored, Asians and whites." It soon became evident, however, that the government was only tinkering around the edges for cosmetic effect for in July 1985 the government declared a state of emergency which broadened even further its already incredible freedom for arbitrary arrest, lengthy detention without trial, demolition of black "squatter" camps and further forced deportation of helpless blacks.

Response from black leaders was not long in coming. While recognizing that the removal of "for whites only" signs around the country represented some change, they accurately pointed out that this was not reform and that the government was just as determined as always to maintain its minority rule. More than ever, this was unacceptable.

Interviewed in Lusaka, Zambia, ANC leader Oliver Tambo made their stance chillingly clear. Revealing that they had just held their first executive meeting since 1969, he said that they had resolved to intensify the struggle at any cost. We have declared war because *apartheid* has been waging war on our people anyway. . . . In the past we were saying that ANC will not deliberately take innocent life. But now, looking at what is happening in South Africa, it is difficult to say civilians are not going to die." (16)

And from the Christian black community, the view was just as somber. Interviewed in early 1988 by a journalist of the magazine Africa Report, Rev. Frank Chikane (pr. tshi-KAH-nay), the general secretary of the South Africa Council of Churches commented: "My assignment is to assist the church leadership in South Africa to look at ways and means of ministering to the victimizer, to actually stop the victimizer from continuing with *apartheid*. The big question is what do we do? . . . There has been the adoption of a new position with the Council of Churches, moving away from condemning those who resort to violence to saying we understand why you have resorted to violence. . . ."

"We are nevertheless still committed to finding ways and means of settling this problem so that it becomes unnecessary for the people to take up arms and fight the system. The churches are moving away from broad pronouncements to committing themselves to action. . . . The ANC is saying to us, 'Give us an alternative. We don't like fighting. We don't like killing people. We don't want anybody, black or white, to die, but give us an alternative.' . . . As it is now, there is no sign of hope, but I don't believe that we need to wait for them to change so that we can see some signs of hope. We need to force them"

As the interview drew to a close, Chikane was asked: "How do you see the next five years?" He responded: "I think there are two options." He expressed his belief that the international community had it within its power to bring all of the concerned parties to a conference table within five years. This was their hope and prayer. But if the international community left them to work out their problem on their own, it would take more than five years. It would also mean "a bloody war in South Africa - - a very violent war." (17)

an Afrikaner named Frederik Willem de Klerk

In every sense he was a son of his country, proud of his people, land and history. He believed in its future and was convinced that his Afrikaner dominated National Party and its policies were crucial to the ongoing security of the white minority population. While the scheme of *apartheid* admittedly had its imperfections, there simply were no workable alternatives. He therefore plunged into the service of his party while fiercely defending its policies. By 1985, he was a cabinet minister and a rising figure on the political scene.

But as the decade of the 1980's drew to a close, de Klerk began to experience troubling uncertainty about the political philosophy to which he had devoted his life. Though he was deeply loyal to his Party, he was also a pragmatic man. Evidence was mounting on every side of a society that was in mortal crisis. While his fellow political functionaries seemed to have no answer other than "more of the same," he acknowledged the bitter truth that *apartheid* held no hope for the future of the country he loved. On the contrary, it held the seeds of anarchy and destruction.

In 1989 when President Botha suffered a stroke, de Klerk quickly submitted his candidacy to replace him. In a spirited campaign he laid before the white electorate an amazing proposal: "If I'm elected, I will dismantle *apartheid* within five years." To the radical fringe of Afrikaner society, this was lunacy and all but treason. Under the leadership of Eugene Terre Blanche (a name which in French literally meant 'Eugene White Land'), a protest movement took shape which was named the Afrikaner Resistance Movement. Holding public meetings, loyalists appeared in brown uniforms reminiscent of Nazi storm-trooper garb complete with arm bands, side arms, salutes and roared slogans. To the surprise of many both inside and outside the country, de Klerk emerged triumphant from the elections. It was stunning proof that many white South Africans shared de Klerk's alarmed reading of the catastrophe which was steadily building around them. As risky as it was, they were ready to abandon *apartheid* and to seek new political formulae which would make place for all South Africans regardless of their color.

Sworn in as the new President in 1989, de Klerk plunged into an amazing five year period of transition and change. Coupling his political authority with endless hours of negotiation with National Party colleagues, he launched a deliberately-crafted series of moves. If he was to dismantle *apartheid* by 1994, as he had promised during his campaign, he had no time to lose. On October 15, 1989, he ordered the release of eight political prisoners from detention on Robben Island. Seven were members of the ANC; an eighth was a member of the Pan-Africanist Congress.

an African named Nelson Mandela

Even as the first political prisoners were being released, de Klerk was already engaged in secret conversations with the best known political prisoner of all. When in 1964 he and eight of his fellow prisoners were condemned to life imprisonment, the government mistakenly hoped that in thus isolating its key spokesman, the root of the ANC had been cut. They were soon to learn, as have many other tyrannical regimes, that the truth cannot be confined behind the bars of a penal institution.

Submitting to the harsh and often dehumanizing regime of Robben Island, Mandela from the first day maintained his dignity. While obeying his captors in the daily routine of hard labor, he successfully extracted from many of his guards the grudging recognition of a fellow human being. Turning all of his leisure hours to personal study, he expanded his knowledge of law, history, and economics. Young revolutionaries thrown into prison with him often sought him out for information, instruction and encouragement. Indeed, as one observer put it, he transformed the confines of that penal colony into "Mandela University." Frequent messages were smuggled off the island and into ANC hands. To the dismay of the government, Mandela's influence in southern Africa grew with each passing year.

De Klerk recognized all of this and instinctively knew that if he was to succeed in a five year campaign to change the face of South Africa, he had to somehow tap the moral and political power of the towering figure still imprisoned on an island off the tip of Cape Town. (18) It was in February of 1990 that de Klerk ordered Mandela released and unbanned 33 different organizations. It was also in 1990 that he rescinded the Population Registration Act and the Group Areas Act, the twin pillars which carried the roof of the structure of *apartheid*. In response to all of this, the ANC halted its campaign of sabotage.

As historic and revolutionary as these moves were, there was a sense in which they were only a preface to the hard work which lay ahead - - negotiating some sort of political agreement which would point the way toward the future and make place for all South African people on a common footing. It was a formidable assignment. Mandela immediately came under enormous pressure from his fellow Africans. Long the victims of abuse, discrimination and exploitation, they wanted to see a quick and dramatic end to their suffering. A second explosive factor for him was the determined insistence of Zulu Chief Gatsha Buthelezi that, whatever the shape of things to come, he and his people be assured a large degree of autonomy. De Klerk, on the other hand, faced the real possibility of a split in his white community and, worse yet, the possibility of outright armed resistance. There was, furthermore, the concern of the powerful industrial and financial figures of the country who were not about to accept or support a plan which would amount to economic suicide.

But an irreversible force had been unleashed. There was no turning back. By September, 1991, a "National Peace Accord" had been forged by Mandela, de Klerk and Buthelezi. An extensive document, it covered the South African socio-political landscape with thoroughness. The prologue to the body of the Peace Accord immediately set the tone and captured the essence of the incredible breakthrough that had been achieved in human relations. "To signify our common purpose to bring an end to political violence in our country and to set out the codes of conduct, procedures and mechanisms to achieve this goal, we, participants in the political process in South Africa, representing the political parties and organizations and governments indicated beneath our signatures, condemn the scourge of political violence which has afflicted our country and all such practices as have contributed to such violence in the past, and commit ourselves and the parties, organizations and governments we represent to this National Peace Accord. . . ."

"The signatories acknowledge that the provisions of this Peace Accord are subject to existing laws, rules, and procedures and budgetary constraints. We the signatories accordingly solemnly bind ourselves to this accord and shall insure as far as humanly possible that all our members and supporters will comply with the provisions of this accord and will respect its underlying rights and values and we, the government signatories, undertake to pursue the objectives of this accord and seek to give effect to its provisions by way of the legislative, executive and budgeting procedures to which we have access." (19)

Nothing in the entire document better captured the heart of the "accord" or its historic import than the following set of statements: "The establishment of multi-party democracy in South Africa is our common goal. Democracy is impossible in a climate of violence, intimidation and fear. In order to ensure democratic political activity, all political participants must recognize and uphold certain fundamental rights described below and the corresponding responsibilities underlying those rights. These fundamental rights include the right of every individual to freedom of conscience and belief; freedom of speech and expression; freedom of association with others; peaceful assembly; freedom of movement; [and to] participate freely in peaceful political activity." (20)

In March, 1992, President de Klerk called for a white referendum on the Accord. It received affirmation from a large majority. There was then put in place a timetable of events designed to lead up to the crowning event of de Klerk's five year plan: the first general elections in the history of South Africa.

"like the Second Coming"

The dates April 26-28, 1994, were finally set for the wondrous event. As the first day dawned, people came literally by the millions in all manners of garb, settings and racial mixes. Some rode in expensive vehicles to their polling places in urban centers. Some bounced in the rear of open pickup trucks to their designated areas. Some queued up in long lines snaking across grasslands to rural voting booths. And a few even bought tickets for jet flights to the land of their birth to take advantage of this once-in-a-lifetime opportunity.

In the ensuing days comments, observations and reflections were heard on all sides. Two quotes capture so very well the emotion and joy of those April days of 1994. The first reads: "What perversity drives one to travel 10,000 kilometers to cast a vote? I was wondering this during the long day of April 27, as I stood in a queue in pouring rain, for six hours, to enter the polling booth. The ranks of the waiting had been swollen by busloads of people from the black township of Khayelitshia (pr. kah-yeh-li-TSHEE-yah), where no ballot papers had arrived - - part of the confusion that characterized South Africa's first democratic elections. There were, indeed, moments when the whole enterprise seemed mad."

"On the morning of the 27th we woke up to the news of a bomb attack; it was followed by several more. Was this to be the outcome of all the years of waiting and hoping? Then came the six hour queue in the rain - - one of the most moving and exhilarating experiences of my life. There we were, thousands upon thousands of us, representing every race and group and section of South Africa; rich and poor, powerful and socially insignificant, galvanized by the knowledge that each one was of equal importance, every vote of equal weight in deciding our shared future. Everybody was talking to everybody else not about politics, but about our daily lives, our jobs, our friends, our children."

"It had all been worthwhile; that much one could read on the beaming faces of the people emerging from the hall after they had cast their votes - - exhausted, aching in every limb, but ecstatic that at last their human worth had been recognized. We were there, said the faces, and our being there together has made a difference. For six hours whole lifetimes of separateness had been suspended. We had discovered, in the simplest and most basic ways imaginable, and in the smallest of everyday actions - - a shared umbrella, a mug of coffee passed from hand to hand, communal laughter, hands touching in the throng - - the grounds of our common South African-ness and our common humanity. That brief experience has marked us for life. In achieving for a few hours, what had seemed for so long impossible, we had caught a glimpse of the possible." (21)

And a second participant wrote: "The jubilation of my soul knew no bounds. I cried, I danced, I rapturously sang 'Nkosi Sikeleli Afrika' (pr. NKOH-si si-keh-LEH-li AH-frikah), South Africa's new national anthem, as I witnessed the historic and unforgettable sight of millions of blacks voting for the first time in their homeland. It was a moment to be savored for a lifetime, to relate misty-eyed to one's grandchildren and great-grandchildren. It was like the Second Coming, the polling stations scattered across South Africa seemed like so many images of Jesus drawing to his side multitudes of the weak, the hungry, the poor, the infirm, the desperate, the illiterate, the disenfranchised: promising them hope, justice, peace, equality and plenty."

"Among the millions who voted was my beloved grandmother, now nearly 90 years old. She had to wait a lifetime to be recognized as a human being in the land of her birth. . . . As I thought of Granny voting I wondered if she had defied the odds and clung to life so long because . . . with her vote she was saying emphatically: 'Never again! Never again will we and our children and grandchildren be treated as sub-humans in the land of our birth." (22)

As expected, when the election results were tallied, Mandela's ANC won a majority of the seats (252 of 400) of the newly-constituted parliament. De Klerk and his National Party won the next largest block. In early May, just days later in Pretoria, at a ceremony attended by representatives of more than 200 governments and organizations, Nelson Mandela was sworn in as the first black President of South Africa. Thabo Mbeki became the First Vice President and F. W. de Klerk the Second Vice President. In his inaugural speech, Mandela vowed: "We shall build the society in which South Africans, both black and white, will be able to walk tall, without any fear in their hearts, assured of their inalienable right to human dignity - - a rainbow nation at peace with itself and the world." (23)

The government, newly elected in 1994, was to have a five year mandate during which, among other things, a final draft of a South African constitution was to be hammered out. The next general elections were set for 1999.

how was this possible?

Afro-American journalist William Raspberry put it as clearly as anyone: "Five years ago, it might have been said that, barring a miracle, South Africa was headed toward racial disaster. Today, it can be said that, barring unforeseen disaster, South Africa is headed toward a racial miracle." (24)

How, indeed, can this dramatic turn of events be explained? What really were the determining causes? There are those who are quick to attribute great significance to international pressures such as the boycotts, refusal of credit and the mounting storm of condemnation in the world press. These undoubtedly did have some bearing. Others suggest that the collapse of international communism and the UN-leveraged departure of South Africa from Namibia exerted significant psychological pressure upon the South African psyche. These too undoubtedly played some role. Still others insist that the growing ferment of courageous internal dissent and opposition on the part of both whites and blacks wielded incalculable influence for change. This also must be granted its full weight.

But there can be little doubt that at the very heart of the miracle that few dared to hope for stood two men who rose to the enormous challenge of their day. Coming respectively from twenty-seven years of harsh incarceration on Robben Island and from the privileged circles of Afrikanerdom, Mandela and de Klerk were caught up and thrust together by the powerful riptides of South African history. They stood together, for a brief moment, on the edge of an abyss and caught a glimpse of something which, to use the words of Bishop Desmond Tutu, was "too ghastly to contemplate." Men of uncommon integrity and decency and courage, they agreed that if they failed to find a solution to the racial conflagration that was about to break loose, the diplomatic, economic and human costs would simply be too high. Ever overshadowed by the very real potential for failure, they together became the driving force which eventually saw the adoption of The Peace Accord and South Africa's first national elections open to every citizen.

But in order for this to happen, Mandela first had to put behind him and forgive years of lost personal freedom as well as the brutalization of uncounted thousands of his fellow countrymen under the inhuman regime of *apartheid*. And, from his side, de Klerk had to confront his privileged white minority with the reality of the evil system of which they had become a part and to set in motion a process which would remove him as well as his party from power.

Columnist Raspberry sensed all of this well when he concluded his column, cited earlier: "As with Gorbachev, I think Mandela and de Klerk have come to see themselves not as politicians and factional leaders but as agents of destiny. I think they are right." (25) It was with abundant reason that these two men were honored in 1993 with the Nobel Peace Prize.

the impact of God's people

And, finally, there was one more dynamic force at work which certainly must be recognized, that being the powerful presence, influence and prayers of literally millions of deeply committed Christians across southern Africa.

One key figure of the South African Christian community during those historic days was Dr. David J. Bosch. An ordained minister of the Dutch Reformed Church, he had earned degrees in languages from the University of Pretoria and a doctorate in New Testament from the University of Basel, Switzerland. He served for nine years as a missionary of his Church in the Transkei during which time he also taught in a seminary of the Black Dutch Reformed Church of that region. He later took a position as professor of theology in the University of South Africa in Pretoria and served as the General Secretary of the South African Missiological Society.

Dr. Bosch was an early courageous voice of dissent regarding the evil of *apartheid* enforced by his government and supported by his Church. Hearing of the arrival of Mennonites on the South Africa scene, he made it a point to become acquainted with some of them and, in the process, became an invaluable source of information and counsel. When AIMM missionary Stan Nussbaum enrolled in the University at Pretoria in a doctoral program. Dr. Bosch became his faculty mentor.

Regarding Bosch, AIMM missionary Jonathan Larson observed: "He was a great encouragement to us as Mennonites and left his mark not only on us personally but had tremendous influence on the course of church events in South Africa and touched the entire missiological world with his astute and prophetic insights." (Dr. Bosch came to the particular attention of North American Mennonites when in 1978 he brought a series of lectures at a meeting of the Mennonite Missionary Study Fellowship at AMBS in Elkhart, IN, based on II Corinthians and entitled "A Spirituality of the Road.")

Even as little as ten days before the elections, Zulu Chief Gatsha Buthelezi was still threatening a boycott by his people. It was Michael Cassidy, the founder and leader of a South African organization called African Enterprise, who sought out the Chief and persuaded him to lead his large, powerful ethnic group in participation in the elections, something which surely contributed largely to its success while very likely avoiding a bloody confrontation.

Still another major contribution was made during those critical days, interestingly enough, by the largest African Independent Church in all of Africa - - the Zion Christian Church, or ZCC as it is known far and wide in its acronym form. In reference to this group Stan Nussbaum states: "Reliable numbers showed in 1992 that [this] single AIC had 11% of South Africa's [population] in its membership. ZCC had always on biblical grounds taken an open view of white leaders as authorities appointed by God. They even gave [Prime Minister] Botha "the key to Zion City" [their headquarters in rural northern Transvaal] one year when he came to address the Easter gathering of over a million people. The ZCC supported the transition to democracy but absolutely opposed violence. This stable, sizeable block of people, invisible to the western media in my opinion deserves some credit for the fact that the South Africa tinder box did not catch fire."(26)

For many years, as dark clouds gathered over South Africa, agonized prayers of intercession were offered across that troubled land and around the world. While paying tribute to the courage of political and church leaders, thousands of South African Christians were sure that God had heard their prayers and granted a peaceful transition from *apartheid* to political freedom, something many thought to be impossible. Bishop Tutu in addressing a largely white congregation of some 3,000 people in the National Cathedral in Washington, D.C., put it simply: "It is God's doing." Commenting that South Africa had been "on the verge of a ghastly civil war," it was spared by divine intervention and was reborn as one nation seeking healing, reconciliation and unity. (27)

but what of the future?

As general elections were held and the first black president was inaugurated, people were euphoric. The impossible had happened. Suddenly they were free. All of the hated, dehumanizing restraints of *apartheid* were gone. They were, at last, masters in their own house. But with this mood of elation came boundless expectations. *Apartheid* left a horrendous backlog of inadequate black education, black housing, black employment opportunity and salary scales. *Apartheid* left hundreds of thousands of people in "black homelands" where they had been transported against their will. *Apartheid* left a nation which was all but isolated from the international world of finance and trade. *Apartheid* also left a young generation of Africans with marginal education and few, if any, marketable skills. *Apartheid* also left a bitter legacy of murderous violence between warring black political factions in the black townships. There was, indeed, much to be done and, as far as the average people were concerned, everything needed to be done at once. They had waited a long time for their day of opportunity. They now wanted to see quick action, quick improvement. The situation could quickly become explosive.

No one understood this better than President Mandela. In his earliest speeches he urged restraint and discipline as his government went to work. Moving quickly to mend its international fences, his government rejoined such organizations as the United Nations, the Organization of African Unity and the British Commonwealth. On the home front the government unveiled a $11 billion national reconstruction and development plan designed to at least make a start on the construction of desperately needed new housing, water and sanitation projects, merging of segregated school systems and the return of land confiscated from blacks under *apartheid*. But everyone knew that drawing up such plans on paper was one thing; finding the resources to fund them was another. The road ahead was long and steep and strewn with difficulties. Thus it was that themes of restraint and discipline were constantly sounded in Mandela's early addresses to his people.

Above all, the government underscored the necessity of forging a single, multiracial nation to replace one that only recently had been engaged in a bitter civil war. Fortunately for all concerned, to this formidable task President Mandela brought enormous moral authority and he proceeded to lead by example. This was reflected in many small but significant ways. One observer of the scene wrote: "All of his activities bear the simple dignity he has made famous. Before signing one of his first official letters, he crossed out 'Mr.' before his name and 'President' after it, preferring plain 'Nelson Mandela'. . . . He urges all South Africans to learn the two national anthems of the post-*apartheid* era, *Die Stem* (The Voice), the Afrikaner anthem of the past, and *Nkose Sikelel iAfrika* (Lord Bless Africa), a traditional African hymn. Images of Mandela singing both with hand over heart symbolize the national spirit he wants to kindle." (28)

To hope that a new, peaceful, thriving, multiracial society will automatically rise out of the ashes of *apartheid* is a stretch. But the South African story of the past five years has been nothing short of miraculous and the major ingredients of that story are still in place: a power-sharing transition government led by two extraordinary men, black and white communities which have come to believe that ways for racial accommodation and partnership can be found. And the prophetic voice and fervent prayer of a Christian community continue. Out of its black night of suffering and hatred, may South Africa emerge as an example for our strife-torn world as we wind down this century and millennium.

In the meantime, AIMM and MCC are suddenly in South Africa! For years Mennonites had encountered varying degrees of hostility on the part of South African officials such as arbitrary refusal of visas and surly encounters at border crossings. For years it had been clear that there was no hope of securing clearance for the placement of Mennonite personnel within the Republic for whatever purpose. Mennonites had more or less adjusted to the stance of people on the outside looking in. But, all at once, as the *apartheid* relocation scheme was rescinded by the new government and the homelands were reincorporated into the Republic, AIMM and MCC personnel in the Transkei automatically became part of the reincorporation process. The door was suddenly open for others to follow.

Once again, Mennonite personnel ponder the question: "For what purpose has God placed us here in such a time as this?"

CHAPTER 59   LEARNING AS WE GO

AIMM missionaries originally approached their work with AICs with three broad assumptions - - that the basic TEE model which had proven so successful in other parts of the world could be applied, as such, with equal success among rural AIC folk; that there would be a level of literacy which would permit the liberal use of printed handouts, quick and frequent references to Biblical passages and the taking of lecture notes; and that class schedules, once agreed upon, could be counted on and kept. Very early in the game, AIMM personnel discovered that all three assumptions needed drastic revamping.

dealing with African logistics

In the early going AIMM missionaries assumed that in planning Bible studies, most any location available would do and most any mix of AIC people would be fine. The more the better. It was, however, soon discovered that locations could matter a great deal. If, as frequently happened, a Bishop would propose that classes be held in one of his chapels, there was sometimes a subdued but recognizable hesitation on the part of others to accept that arrangement. Over time it became apparent that sometimes it was best to schedule a study series in a neutral location where all could meet on an equal footing without concern that their gathering would somehow work to the advantage of one particular church.

Furthermore, it was soon learned that not just any mix of AIC people could be brought together in a class with everyone being comfortable. The ancient African dynamic of seniority rights quickly came into play. For a bishop to be in a class with young people from his own church left him very uneasy. To adopt the stance of a learner with fellow bishops was one thing. But to adopt such a stance with those young enough to be his grandchildren was too much to expect. AIMM personnel learned soon enough that it worked best all around if classes were organized keeping age groups and status in mind.

functioning in the African context

Another early lesson AIMM personnel had to learn was how Africans view time. It was a common experience to discuss a series of studies with a group of AIC leaders, to receive enthusiastic affirmation and promises of participation only to discover that the weekly classes agreed upon were not always promptly or well attended. There was even the occasional day when a missionary made a long trip to an isolated place to find no one at all!

It took a while for the white-skinned teachers to understand. While the commitments to attend the scheduled Bible studies were made in good faith, the church leaders continued to live and move within a context which made many demands upon them, their resources and, above all, upon their time. Perhaps it was someone gravely ill in the family or within the church group; perhaps there was a death; perhaps it was planting or harvest time in their little family plots; perhaps it was a serious rift between members of his church. Whatever the case, family and human needs around them on a given day clearly had priority. If such demands happened to fall on a day when Bible class was scheduled in his area, s/he was sorry, but it couldn't be helped. Other claims upon them that particular day simply had higher priority. It soon became apparent to AIMM personnel that different study formats needed to be explored.

getting acquainted with AIC students

But missionary learning had only begun. It was not long that AIMM teachers discovered that traditional western classroom approaches to teaching and learning were not working very well - - particularly in the rural areas where much of the Bible teaching was taking place. In fact, in some cases, they seemed not to be working at all.

Early in his experience with AIC students in Lesotho, Stan Nussbaum shared a series of "learnings" that he had accumulated in his work: "Symbols do not communicate. Punctuation marks, underlining and indentation are a foreign language to most people. . . . There is little idea of numerical sequence. . . . Students will not write while you talk unless you dictate. The idea of abstracting the main idea from a lecture and writing it down in your own words is not common. . . . Details are remembered better than main points. . . . Don't talk long without asking a review question. . . . Songs and poems can get off the track easily. . . . The certificate counts. . . . Factual information is fascinating, not boring. . . . Memory and creativity, not reading and logic, are the most productive methods." (1)

In his early years of teaching experience in Botswana, Jonathan Larson found that his experience was very similar to Nussbaum's in Lesotho. Larson's reflections also eventually found their way into writing: "It is late afternoon. A familiar circle of faces assembles for the monthly class. Before the sun sets on this small edge of the desert farming settlement eight to ten church leaders, men and women, young and old, meet together for a customary study. They come as select, acknowledged leaders in their community. Several hold prominent office in village institutions. All are significant members of the two Independent Churches of the community. They greet one another with sincere warmth, obviously eager to begin study and interaction. I open my briefcase to pass out prepared notes while Bibles are distributed to the group. We stand to sing a song. The door is closed as God's presence is invoked."

"By the time we are seated, ready to work, I cannot help but remark that a change has overtaken my friends and it is unmistakable even in the fading light. They begin to fidget and by the time the text has been announced and read, their air of self-confidence has visibly melted away. Most of them are still groping midst the maze of pages while one picks his way through the hopelessly unfamiliar orthography of Robert Moffat's 19th century translation of the Setswana Bible (the first in a black African tongue). All of them are clutching the prepared notes, peering at the bookish questions and wondering how they will ever muster a written response. Many struggle to form the letters of their name 'in the upper right hand corner.'"

"I know that each of these persons is mature emotionally. Many have been Christians for longer than I have been alive. I know that all are respected for seasoned judgement and for their grasp of Tswana culture and mores. Furthermore, they are heirs to a theology that reaffirms the gift of God's Spirit irrespective of station in life. Yet, when they meet with me to study the Bible, they seem helpless and diffident."

"I have mused about this familiar and disheartening pattern, wondering what prevented the participants from bringing their full selves, their maturity, experience, understanding and gifts to the study. Why were these assets shut off from the learning process, and further, why did these assets so seldom figure in the task of teaching and preaching in their congregations? Though there is much about this that still eludes me, I have come to believe that the answer is to be found in the nature of the encounter between literate and non-literate" (2)

In his writing, Larson goes on to observe that the literate/non-literate dichotomy was largely nurtured by governmental and societal attitudes in the country. And yet, in a village setting where traditional cultural values and traditions still pertained, social skills and tribal wisdom of immense value were to be found in abundance. In the village setting "it is plain that Tswana society prizes the skills of oral persuasion, the ability to engage in broad-gauged verbal communication. High value is given to deferential speech which is full of nuance, color, humor, wisdom and compelling turn of phrase. The proverbs and local village lore swirl in eddies and cross-currents in the repartee. No one is excluded from this rich and ultimately satisfying process which lies close to the heart of Tswana foundations. But this dynamic, so personal, so freeing, so basic for Batswana is rarely enticed into the setting of Bible study, mainly, I believe, because the focal point there is an alien exercise of reading and writing."

Larson went on to highlight the broad overlap between Biblical culture and that of primal societies like that of the Batswana and to suggest that "Bible teachers in such settings should not underestimate the affinity that traditional people have for its message and their ability to grasp its significance." He then concluded his discussion by a proposal to AIMM personnel to shift ground in their approach to their teaching: "I have been rethinking the TEE enterprise in light of this experience of the encounter between literate and non-literate. The premise of TEE is to take the stimulus and training to the people. In a geographical sense, this is a significant advance over earlier models. But beyond shifting the physical locus of the encounter we must ask if there is a second journey required to shift the inner ground of the encounter from our strength as literates to theirs as non-literates. Or at least to find ground where both can come with their strength." (3)

AIMM missionaries were echoing themes that Ed and Irene Weaver had sounded several decades earlier as AIMM was first contemplating work with the AIC's - - "We must begin with the churches where they are, not where we are institutionally. . . . The African understands religion not in terms of doctrine but as part of his daily life." (4)

making adjustments

An early shift came in the study formats used. Weekly classes scattered over two or three month periods worked quite well in urban centers where AIC leaders were clustered in close proximity to each other. But in more isolated rural areas where they needed to travel some distance to attend classes, it soon became evident that some other approach was needed. One alternative which proved successful was the weekend conference format. When well advertized ahead of time with study topics and speakers announced in advance, response was good. Time was scheduled not only for Biblical study but also for discussion, sharing and celebratory times of singing, dancing and praying together.

AIMM teachers also discovered that there were some built-in traditional occasions in the annual cycle of AIC life which brought crowds of people together which they were not only welcome to attend but at which they were given opportunity for speaking and teaching. Typical of such gatherings are the annual migrations at Easter time to church headquarters for protracted worship and celebration. (Among the AICs, greater emphasis is placed upon Easter than on any other religious holiday.) Special gatherings for baptism, commemoration of founding prophets, dedication of new chapels or the investiture of new leaders all afforded AIMM personnel excellent opportunities to meet, mingle with and teach/preach as opportunity afforded.

Another shift in approach was that of trying to tap some of the latent talent of rural AIC students which lay outside the traditional western approach to teaching. In Lesotho Stan Nussbaum early noted the deeply rooted cultural tradition of praise poems and praise songs. Seeing this as an excellent cultural device for actively involving his students in his study program, he required of each student, by course's end, an original praise poem which elaborated on a passage of Scripture or on some scriptural truth which had become particularly meaningful to them in the course of their study. These, then, were gathered, reproduced in booklet form and distributed to all who had attended the study series in question.

In the ongoing adjustment process there was still another "frontier" which challenged the AIMM teachers, that of coaxing the AIC students to bring to the fore the needs, issues, problems and questions which really preoccupied them in their churches. For this to happen, there were two preconditions: first they had to be brought to the place where they really believed that in their class sessions there was no such thing as a foolish or ignorant question.

Second, the missionary teachers had to be prepared to set aside the neatly packaged Bible College and Seminary notes they had brought with them and allow the focus of Bible study to stem from the student's questions rather than from their Western notebooks. Once this level of trust was established, questions were forthcoming in abundance. Following is a sampling of the sort of inquiries encountered: "Why baptize? What is the correct way of baptizing someone? Should shoes be removed before entering church? Should there be special clothing worn for church? Should we follow the Old Testament or the New Testament? Is it alright to accept money after laying on hands? Why are women allowed to preach and pray in some churches and not in others? Some people say when they do wrong, that it is just human nature. Does God accept this explanation? What about polygamy? Was it wrong for David to take Bathsheba? Is it alright for Christians to beat each other with sticks in church? Some say it is not on purpose but that 'the Holy Spirit came upon them'. Why can't we send away demon spirits today? What about ashes and drinking ashes in water for healing? Is it alright to drink beer? Jesus made it once. Where does the Bible come from? Who wrote it? Is it OK to write or pray to someone who is dead to ask them to prepare a place for us? What is the difference between believing in God and repentance? Is it OK to offer sacrifices as was done in the Old Testament? People see flames along the road at night and say they are ghosts. Where do they come from? Who baptized Abraham? Is it alright to ask for help from ancestors? Can we say that when a Christian dies, he or she has gone to be with God?" (5)

Such lists of seemingly haphazard questions might seem, at first flush, to be improbable material to use as a basis for organizing an AIC Bible Conference. But it was as AIMM personnel began to take such questions seriously and allowed them to become springboards for searching Scripture for guidance that Bible study became relevant and helpful for their students.

It was against this sort of background that Fremont and Sara Regier, co-directors of Mennonite Ministries, once observed: "I think we see a shift of moving away from classroom to new models. . . . Writing histories, stories, more dialogue with church leaders. . . . A shift away from lessons, mimeographing things, to more participant dialogue kind of teaching, where the AIC or church group sets the agenda, and this can vary within the hour." (6)

The shift in approach to AIMM Bible teaching efforts in Southern Africa was highlighted by Nussbaum when he once wrote in a report that the Africans "need to hear the voice of God, not just the words of the missionary. For them to hear His relevant and clear voice, we have to 1) study parts of the Bible that Americans don't emphasize, 2) meet spiritual needs that Americans don't feel deeply, 3) teach truths that Americans don't often realize clearly, and 4) use educational methods that Americans don't usually employ." (7)

dealing with tough issues

If, with passing time, clear progress was made in the methodology and format of AIMM Bible teaching among AICs, this is not to say that the ongoing ministry was problem free! From the very beginning there have been three major areas of concern which have generated much discussion and heart-searching on the part of Mennonite personnel. The first has to do with the necessity of recognizing those leaders within the AIC community who are self-serving schemers. Oriented and much counseled by AIMM Board and home staff to approach the AICs with an accepting, nonjudgmental attitude, missionaries have, at times, considered it a more redemptive stance to regard extreme groups as "not yet Christian" rather than as "irretrievably pagan." This, in turn, has on occasion led AIMM personnel to be more charitable in their evaluation of some AIC groups than the facts actually warranted. (8) AIMM missionaries nonetheless continue to carry in their hearts the belief that no one is beyond the reach of God's redemptive grace and therefore want to remain open to being channels of that grace as the Lord may see fit to use them.

A second continuing and troublesome area for those who work with the AICs is that of knowing how to react in the presence of procedures and practices which they do not fully understand. Warmly invited to not only attend their services but to fully enter into all that transpires, our missionaries not infrequently find themselves in the midst of activities the exact meaning of which are not clear to them. What then? What about the "blessed" water which is sprinkled or drunk? What about the ashes which are traced on the forehead or sprinkled and mixed into water which is sprinkled on the ground around the chapel? What about the thank offering placed in the fire on the little altar out behind the chapel? What about all of the clothing and sashes required for entrance into worship services? Is there a line at which symbolism stops and magic takes over?

Elinor Miller, an MCC volunteer member of the Mennonite Ministries team who took particular interest in the AIC community around her, put her personal quandary into sharp focus when she wrote in a study paper: "What am I doing being prayed for under this cloth? Should I drink holy water? What do I do at a sacrifice? Should I stop eating pork? Should I be immersed seven times for cleansing? Should we have our vehicle sprinkled and blessed by the prophet? Should I take a ritual bath for cleansing?" (9)

Over time, a rough rule of thumb emerged among the MM personnel: "When in genuine doubt, don't; otherwise reserve judgement, participate and learn all you can in the process." It was in this spirit that Miller was part of a moving, learning experience she later described as follows: "One of these moments occurred during my first participation at the Feast of Unleavened Bread. I was not at all sure whether the sacrifice of bread was made as a thank offering or as an offering for the forgiveness of sin. Yet I attended the all-night service. I knelt in the dark with the congregation as they formed a circle around the altar. The ministers placed a large circle of unleavened dough over the brightly burning fire. Smoke billowed up with a strangely sweet odor. The embers glowed brightly in the darkness as the sweet odor and the audible prayers of the people ascended. I had the strong sensation that I had moved back in time and was among the Children of Israel; God's people. Later that night I heard a sermon about sin as yeast that will work through a whole batch of dough (I Cor 5:6). Following the sermon were numerous testimonies and confessions with a New Testament ring to them. . . . It helped me to understand the role of Mennonites in Bible Teaching ministries with AICs, as those AICs continue to grow toward a fuller knowledge of Christ. We can walk with them in their journey and become New Testament Churches." (10)

Yet a third issue, and probably the stickiest of all, is the struggle of knowing when or if to confront AIC leaders who in the midst of Bible studies indulge in unwise practices or in personal sin or tolerate such activity within their churches. Is it best to simply trust the Bible teaching under which they sit to accomplish its own pruning effect under the guidance of the Holy Spirit or is it, at least sometimes, incumbent upon the white-skinned teacher to seek occasion to confront?

The thrust of a study paper on this issue, presented at a Bible teachers' conference in Botswana, clearly reflects this dilemma. "What if we see a real problem of malnutrition because of certain health procedures ordered by a prophet? What if we note a skin rash that would respond much better to a bit of cortisone ointment than the repeated washing in water 'blessed' by the prophet? What about morality? It is rare to hear good preaching against the sin of adultery. Is there not a time and place for us to bring direct teaching regarding that for which God will judge his people? We do have a unique position and opportunity among the AICs. If we become too direct and confrontational, might we forfeit that opportunity? Might we see doors, now open to us, swing shut? On the other hand, if we do not speak up clearly, what does this do to our own credibility among the people we seek to serve? And yet we must also realize that there are undoubtedly some aspects of our own practices and manners among them which they could justly criticize were they of a mind to do so." (11)

The struggle with this issue continues.

learning from the AICs

Across the first two decades of AIMM's involvement with the AICs of southern Africa, primary concerns have had to do with learning to know the AIC folk better and discovering more appropriate ways of working among them. In this process, however, AIMM personnel soon discovered that working with these people was a two-way street. More and more they realized that, as relationships of trust were established, they - - the missionaries themselves - - were learning a great deal from the AICS and, in the process, were being challenged and led along startlingly new paths of spiritual pilgrimage which they had never imagined possible.

Testimonies and accounts of experiences received in the home office from AIMM personnel have found their way into ever thicker files. Following are some excerpts typical of their sharing. Gary and Jean Kliewer Isaac first arrived in the Transkei in the fall of 1986. On a furlough in early 1991 they were interviewed by Beth Hege, a journalist of the General Conference Mennonite offices in Newton, KS. A subsequent article read, in part, as follows: "The Xhosa people of Transkei, South Africa, know how to dance. And sing. And pray. At least once a month their worship services last all night and into the next day. 'This is the uniqueness of Christianity, that it's adaptable to the culture of the people. That is the beauty of the African Independent Churches,' said Gary Isaac. 'People come directly out of tribal traditions because they are attracted to AIC belief and practice which is much closer to their own belief and style of worship. Most people actually become converted to Christ by coming to healers and prophets in the church.'"

"Gary's wife Jean described the worship experience: 'Often the service starts with someone beating the drum. People are singing and clapping. Some time into the service, someone will begin a circle of dancing and, toward the end, there will be time for healing.' . . ."

"'I remember the first Sunday in Montana [Jean's home community]. The preacher was preaching and really saying some good things,' said Gary, 'but people were so quiet! It seemed strange.'" (12)

Also from the Transkei came another perceptive comment made by Larry Hills at a point before the fall of the *apartheid* regime: "In discussing our work among Zion Churches in South Africa, at least passing reference must be made to *apartheid*. These churches are trying to live out their commitment to Christ under the dark cloud of racism, economic and political oppression, and police and military violence against black people. That they are often able to live lives of hope, joy and spiritual vitality in the midst of *apartheid* is an ongoing testimony to the presence of Christ among them. As we work among them, the reality of Zion Church life should elicit from us a response of humility, servanthood, and a quest for mutual learning. We have at least as much to learn from them as they have to learn from us." (13)

The learnings of another AIMM missionary were clearly reflected in an interview with a Mennonite journalist who wrote as follows: "Jonathan Larson describes himself as 'one of the few Mennonites who has to dance to work.' As a Bible teacher among the African Independent Churches, he experiences a style of worship that is distinctly different from most Mennonite Churches in North America. 'We tend to suppress the response of the body. They throw their voice, body and spirit into worship', says Larson. 'They are not inhibited about expressing joy or sadness. These people are pushing another frontier, . . . there is wholeness present in their churches.'"

"'One of the reasons I find my work so compelling is that it helps me understand Anabaptism. I am catapulted back to the 16th century. They practice a believer's church. They say God's Spirit has seized us.'"

"'The churches practice believer's baptism, usually by immersion, and view the Bible as their guide for everyday life. It is so refreshing to do Bible studies with them. They ask: What should we do?'"

"Larson believes Mennonites' work with AICs 'gives us an extraordinary chance to do mission in a new way. It is a selfless kind of mission where we are willing to work, without imposing our name.' He recalls a prayer session with two AIC leaders: 'We were in a circle holding hands, and they prayed, Thank you for the three great trees of Menno, Matitta and Motswasele. [The latter two are founders of Independent Churches in Lesotho and Botswana, respectively.] These three prophets stand at the head of history. I was moved by this experience. I thought to myself, we don't have to be twins to be brothers and sisters in Christ.'" (14)

It was also Larson who, in another context, reflected on further learnings from the AICs regarding the nature and function of the church as the body of Christ. "Yesterday we worshiped with Independent Church believers in the small edge-of-the-desert settlement of Pitseng, Botswana. It was a little awkward getting the service under way. Not everyone arrived at once. Though singing and prayers had already begun, the door kept creaking as latecomers crept in to take their places. Each influx derailed the order of service, since these Independent Churches insist that all entering and leaving be accompanied with song."

"Each arrival touched off confusion in the ranks as there ensued a great shuffling of chairs, rearrangement of people and lurching back and forth in an attempt to accommodate those 'who were being added to the church.' Whenever the congregation reached a provisional equilibrium, the door would creak open again, and the exercise would be repeated. This aroused in me a sense of discomfort, even irritation, which eased, thankfully, as the text was read, 'Now when Jesus was born in Bethlehem of Judea - - '"

"This slightly grating stir, this shuffling of chairs and rearrangement for inclusion goes back to the stable in Bethlehem, I see now. Just when the Jewish Christians thought the door could be closed for a final count, to get on with the Good News task, the door would creak open and someone new would creep in. First it was the Greek seekers. Then it was the Samaritans, and finally complete disorder erupted when the Gentiles barged in . . . ."

"I thought about the Independent Churches not only here in Botswana but across Africa and the global movement of traditional people seeking access to the community of faith. In a larger sense, they have stood at the threshold of the gathered faithful. They sought entrance though their welcome has been hesitant at best. Here we stand in a kind of anteroom trying to see the kingdom under way. Meanwhile there is abroad in the church a discomfort as newcomers come in and bring with them new questions. It is unsettling as we seek to make room for them not only in the pews but also in our theologies, in our liturgies and in our hearts. By nature this is a disturbing experience. And all equilibrium in the community is only provisional, awaiting that next inclusion."

"What should we do then in this anteroom experience as the family gathers? First, we must learn to sit lightly in our chairs. Soon others will come and my chair may be needed for someone else. Second, the order of service should have room. It must be susceptible to revision. And third, we need people of grace to be bold enough, even when the rest of us cast grim glances at the creaking door, to strike up a song of joyful welcome. The brothers and sisters in the hard scrabble of Pitseng have already mastered that ethic. Surely they are showing the way." (15)

AIMM files of missionaries who have worked with AIC people in southern Africa contain many references to meaningful discoveries made as they learned to look at Scripture and the church through African eyes. But even more significant are the references to times and places when missionaries themselves became the recipients of AIC ministry and love. On one occasion, a traveling AIMM executive secretary and his wife found themselves in Lesotho at Christmas time. A written report later contained the following observations: "The little stone chapel has sat on that knoll overlooking a broad valley for many years. Its walls are laid up in flat, thin slabs of rock. It had a metal roof until a recent high wind peeled it off. It now stands covered by a thatch roof of local grass. It is the place of worship of members of the Church of Moshoeshoe (pr. moh-SHWAY-shway, the name of the founding chief of the Basotho Kingdom) from three nearby villages. In that rural setting, there stands nearby a four wheeled farm wagon with makeshift harness lying where the last team of oxen had been unhitched. Adjacent to the chapel is a small plot of freshly worked ground which is soon to be seeded. There is a brilliant blue sky above us dappled here and there by white clouds. At 5,000 feet, the air is a bit nippy. Across the nearby border with the Republic of South Africa, the carefully tended fields of Afrikaner farmers are clearly to be seen."

"It is the Sunday before Christmas and the time for a special annual celebration planned and organized for all of the area church members by Samuel and Emily Mohono. We approach to the sound of singing and find them in process of carrying their benches outside since the crowd, by now, can no longer be accommodated in the little chapel. One row of benches is lined along the chapel wall; a table carrying a small lectern is situated near us. The people then congregate, some on benches, some seated on the grass, some standing, facing us. Samuel Mohono, tall, balding, gray bearded, the son of the original and founding pastor of this congregation, presides."

"First there is a round of introductions as all visitors are presented to the home folks. There are two visiting pastors from another Independent Church some distance away. There are two MCC couples, three AIMM couples and the visiting travelers from Elkhart. There then follows a program of singing interspersed with the reading of passages of Scripture and commentaries on the significance of this time of the year. Periodically Samuel leads in an impromptu song of joy and is immediately joined by the group as he signals the beat with his long arms."

"As the program moves along we become aware of a bustle of activity behind us in the recently vacated chapel. Unbeknown to us, a feast is being prepared. As the service outside comes to a close, a special prayer of thanksgiving is offered in which God is in a particular way praised for the gift of his Son, for the gift of his church and for the gifts of friendship and love. As we are ushered into the chapel, we find a long table laden with food. Emily Mohono has slaughtered a cow from her own herd for the occasion. There were also large bowls of rice, vegetables, greens and gravy. For a drink we were served a local variety of ginger tea. To top everything off, there was even a bowl of 'sweets.' Emily had not overlooked anything."

"Even as we were being served and seated as special guests, heaping plates of food were being carried to others as well, some in the chapel with us and others outside seated on the grass. Some of the older widows had known the pinch of hunger in previous months and likely would again in the days ahead, but not today. It was Christmas and the Mohonos were sharing lavishly of what they had with their friends, both black and white."

"As the afternoon drew to a close and guests began to express their appreciation and their farewells, we were yet to have one more surprise. Emily appeared from around the corner of the little chapel with a broad smile on her face and a bundle in her hands. Signaling Jenny [Bertsche] to come forward, she proceeded to drape a lovely Basotho blanket around her shoulders which had been tailored in the form of a cape. Then turning and looking out across the valley below our knoll which contained some of her green growing fields of 'mealies' or corn, she said quietly: 'This is where I belong. This is my home; these are my people; this is my life.' As we shook hands a last time with Sam, our gracious host, we tried to express our appreciation for the hospitality and fellowship of the day at their hands. 'It is rather we who thank you for having accepted our invitation,' he countered. 'This has been a very special Christmas for us.'"

"As we made our way slowly along the bumpy country lane to the main road, we reflected on the events of the day and realized how blessed, enriched and humbled we were by this encounter with the warmth and generosity of this extraordinary African couple." (16)

Another encounter between an AIMM missionary and spiritual instruction at AIC hands took place in a shanty town just outside Gaborone, Botswana. The subsequent account ran like this: "I'm still not sure just what to call it. The phrase 'ordeal by joy' comes to mind. It happened under shreds of plastic and tattered canvas in a squatter settlement called Old Naledi (pr. nah-LAY-di). Gathered there were the faithful of the Christ the Word of God congregation, radiant in their blue and white uniforms. Present were visitors from several other churches who had shared together in a Bible study for which this was a kind of graduation ceremony."

"Midway through the sermon a neighboring congregation, the Holy Apostolic Church of God in Zion, decided to throw their lot in with us. We could hear them forming up in the courtyard, breaking out into song as they processed in. And then the elements joined in. Overhead, claps of thunder rolled out from heavy clouds. As the rain came down, sieving through the makeshift roof, I hastily concluded the sermon with the suggestion that we run for cover."

"My instincts for convenience, propriety, comfort and safety were being checked by entirely different impulses. People were not prepared to bring to a close a spiritual gathering that had not yet run its course. What of the dancing? And what of the sacramental sharing of food? Were these to be given up in a demeaning scramble for shelter? And had we not, after all, pled for this rain in prayer? My shaky resolve on these points was quickly put right as several people stood to speak inspired messages. 'We have come together here to taste the oneness of God's people,' said one, 'and we are not going to run away in disarray.'"

"The inescapable truth is that while mission, as we are experiencing it, does indeed mean giving, it is just as much receiving and hearing the Gospel speaking to our own unredeemed instincts." (17)

One memorable encounter between AIC people and an AIMM missionary took place at Misty Mount in the Transkei. The reporting of it was as follows: "I celebrated Easter with the church at Misty Mount. I had also been with them for Easter a year ago. The celebration begins on Friday evening and continues until Sunday afternoon, virtually nonstop. For me the most moving part of the celebration comes at about 3:00 A.M. on Sunday morning with footwashing and the Lord's Supper. Last year was the first time a white had ever attended this church's Easter celebration. During the foot washing and communion I sat and observed, but I was not invited to participate. The following morning Bishop Mphehla came to me and apologized for excluding me. He said that he had been afraid to ask me to join in. This year things were different. Early Sunday morning the benches were brought forward and Bishop Mphehla told me to sit on the front bench. While another man read from John 13, Bishop Mphehla wrapped a towel around his waist, poured water into a basin and washed my feet. Then the words of institution were read and the Bishop served communion. When he had finished he sat on the bench. As the reading was repeated, I bent down and washed those feet which had descended into the mine shafts and worked the farms of white South Africans and which now work on a small plot of land from which Bishop Mphehla feeds his family and sends his children to school, the feet of a man whom I have come to love. I have never before experienced as powerfully the grace and presence of the Lord through the simple elements of water, bread and wine as I did that early Easter morning on a hillside in Misty Mount." (18)

On one occasion Gary and Jean Isaac were conducting a Bible Conference with fifty-eight AIC men and women in the Transkei. The conference theme: "The People of God as Witnesses in the World." It was pointed out that since God's people have very different values, they live differently. Against this background there was a review of the eight Beatitudes. In a succeeding session, as an illustration of the price African Christians of another era had paid for living Christ-like lives, the story of the martyrdom of early Ugandan Christians was told. It was explained that all were given opportunity to recant by the King. Among the young men was a son of the King and a son of the chief executioner. When they refused to deny their faith a final time, all were put to death, some by beating and some by fire.

Jean then picked up the account: "I sat down when I had finished the story. Next Gary would deal with the 'salt and light' passage. But before he could start, a woman in the front row spoke. 'Please,' she pleaded, 'after such a sad story, couldn't we pray?' I was astonished. These people have known oppression all their lives. For them to be moved by a story which happened so long ago and so far way amazed me. But we answered, 'Of course we can pray.'"

"But who will pray and what, I wondered. The Bishop leading the session took charge and indicated that we pray. We knelt beside our chairs, and our sixty voices rang out to God from the depths of hearts that God had touched. Now I was the one who was moved. I was moved by the compassion and the love of these people who face difficulty daily, but who do it with reliance upon God. Truly, 'Blessed are the merciful, for they will be shown mercy.'" (19)

On another occasion AIMM missionary Larry Hills had occasion to be the recipient of the spiritual undergirding of AIC folk in an outstandingly graphic manner. He had just submitted to major surgery in East London, South Africa. He picks up the account at that point as related by journalist Carla Reimer: "'I was staying in a 'whites only' hospital ward in East London,' he said. 'One evening I was lying on my bed with eyes closed, when I heard praying in Xhosa, the language of the people I work with in Transkei. Since it was unlikely that black people would be in the ward at that time of night, I assumed that the pain-killing drugs were causing hallucinations and I kept my eyes closed.'"

"'The Xhosa prayers continued. Finally I opened my eyes to find two African men kneeling at the foot of my bed. When they saw that I was awake, they came and stood by my bed. They spoke softly with me; they touched me; they prayed for me.' The two men, who were AIC members, had traveled four hours to visit Hills. They also had convinced the hospital workers that even though they were black, they had a right to visit their Christian friend."

"'The two men had come from a large meeting of Zionist Church leaders in Transkei, where they had gathered to pray for my recovery from surgery. But the leaders had not been satisfied to pray for me at a distance and decided to send two members to pray for me in person. This is the most powerful memory I have about that anxious period of my life,' said Hills."

"Hills found his initial contact with AICs confusing and disorienting. 'I was experiencing all night prayer services, drum beating and long prayers for healing. Their expression of faith was so different from what I had experienced in the United States,' he said. 'No matter how we talk about faith in North America, it tends to be rational. AIC members start with a spiritual premise. They operate on the assumption that it is possible to be in contact with God on a daily basis. For them, God is not locked in a particular church tradition or the Bible. God is a living reality.' ..."

"'If we are serious about working with overseas churches, we need to move beyond our posture of superiority. I think it would be healthy for North American Mennonites to meet with the Independent Church leaders and say, These are the areas where we are deficient, can you help us? They certainly evangelized me.'" (20)

Blessing and inspiration at the hands of AIC people were not limited to AIMM missionaries on the scene. More than once junketing AIMM Board and staff people experienced memorable moments as well. One such was described by an AIMM executive secretary in the following terms; "The setting was the small office of the Spiritual Healing Church in Gaborone. The occasion was the leave-taking of a small AIMM delegation. As the exchange of farewells and good wishes came to a close, Bishop Motswasele closed both office doors. A circle was then formed. We joined hands and he led in a heartfelt prayer in Setswana, his own tongue. As a conclusion to his prayer, he began to sing softly the familiar praise chorus 'Alleluia, Alleluia.' One by one the members of the hand-joined circle slipped into harmony parts of an impromptu male quartet. As the singing subsided, the Bishop looked up at us, eyes glistening with emotion, his face wreathed in a smile as he squeezed hands to either side of him. It was a moving, transcendent moment. Across the barriers of language and culture, hearts had touched hearts and spirits had been lifted as they had worshiped the Lord Jesus together. (21)

CHAPTER 60   HAVE WE MADE ANY DIFFERENCE THUS FAR?

Across generations of mission work around the world, criteria for measuring accomplishment and progress have been quite uniform - - ethnic groups reached, churches planted, converts and baptisms per year, statistics on educational programs, Christian marriages, distribution of Christian literature, health ministries and so on. In AIMM's work in southern Africa, however, few of these criteria are of help in attempting to assess the degree to which the cause of Christ has been served. We've not gone to southern Africa to plant churches but rather to reach out to and minister among churches we've found there. We therefore have no statistics of baptisms or new congregations founded or of church growth. We have not built any institutions and therefore have no reports on school attenders or medical services. Given these circumstances how then, after some twenty years of AIMM presence and ministry in that part of Africa, can we assess what we've accomplished for our Lord? Given the unstructured, non-directive approach we've adopted there, how can we determine if we've made any difference at all?

Although few of the usual measurements can be used in attempting to evaluate our work, there are nonetheless some indicators of a different sort which throw helpful light on this question. First of all, there are the comments and observations of a wide variety of people on the scene. There are, for instance, the representatives of mainline churches with long local histories that AIMM found upon arrival. When, after a few years, it became clear that the Mennonites had, in fact, not come to plant churches of their own denomination, there were expressions both of amazement and appreciation. Typical of such comments were those addressed to Nancy Heisey and Paul Longacre in the course of their travels during 1987-1989. In an interview with Catholic leaders in Botswana, one commented: "Initially I found your work with them [AICs] very questionable. I felt that we need to bring them to our understanding of the Gospel, to convert them. But now I value what you are doing. What you are doing is washing the feet of the disciples." (1)

reaching out across the border

Another source of commentary has come from people who were enmeshed within the power structures of *apartheid*. Early on Mennonites became aware of courageous, lonely people within the Republic of South Africa and made effort to reach out to them in affirmation and encouragement. One such was Axel Ivar Berglund, a Swedish missionary who in 1975 was serving as the director of the Department of Theological Education of the South Africa Council of Churches. He was one of the first people from the Republic to be sponsored for a fraternal visit to North America by the Southern Africa Task Force.

At one point in his itinerary, he met with representatives of this Task Force. In discussing the AICs of southern Africa he stated that "part of the dynamic of these movements is the drive to achieve dignity, worth, stature and competence which are denied the black man in so many other areas of life . . . ." Commenting on the Mennonite approach to AICs, he affirmed our stance of offering people and their gifts and skills rather than funds; our readiness to accept them as a part of the Body of Christ; our desire to encourage, affirm and enable them and our vision for inductive, non-formal, need-oriented Bible study."

Reflecting on the painful situation in southern Africa in the mid-1970's he said: "We are in an evil situation and the evil will still intensify. . . . We live in a certain isolation in which we tend to turn in on ourselves and 'just chew our cud.' . . . We need the exposure and stimulus of recognized theologians from outside our country."

Toward the end of the gathering he made the following poignant comment: "You cannot imagine what it has meant to me to be able to breath the air of freedom for these few weeks. I go back to my task refreshed and with new courage to stand for what is right." (2)

Not content to limit his expressions of gratitude to those verbally expressed along his North American path, he added a letter upon his return home. Speaking of his travels and the many people he had met along the way he wrote: "Many of you were not new acquaintances. Others were new discoveries. Whether we had met previously or not, did not matter. Because of a common faith, a united committal to Jesus Christ and His Church, and a similar mission to the world, I never experienced myself as a stranger. . . . Living with you, entering into your homes and sharing your lives with you, our discussions and very many meetings - - - all this and so much more is a richness that I wish so many others could have shared with me. . . . Please receive my thanks. . . . Would that God grant me grace to spend the new courage and enthusiasm brought about by the visit with you in renewed service and labors for and in His Kingdom!" (3)

equipping a Cabinet Minister unawares

Mennonite efforts to reach out to people under the grim shadow of *apartheid* at one point took an unexpected turn. Ezra Sigwela, of the Transkei, was imprisoned for 13 brutal years on Robben Island because of his opposition to the regime of the white minority government of his country. Eventually released, he returned directly to the Transkei and soon accepted a high-profile role with the Transkei Christian Council as a liaison person with the families of other men who were still political detainees on the Island or elsewhere. Greatly impressed by his courage and resolve in the face of personal suffering, MCC took the initiative to bring him to North America for a fraternal visit, rest and a time of reflection. When it came time for his return, he was intercepted in England with a message from TCC personnel in Umtata advising him not to return at that time because Transkei Security Police were once again searching for him. Thus delayed, it was arranged that he return to the States where Ezra enrolled at AMBS in Elkhart, IN, where his family was soon able to join him. He graduated in 1989 with a certificate in theology.

Upon returning to his homeland he found that powerful forces for change had been unleashed by the newly-elected President de Klerk. When in 1994 Nelson Mandela became the first black president of South Africa, Sigwela was soon swept up in the groundswell of change. By this time recognized as a man of integrity and education, he was named a cabinet member in South Africa's eastern Cape Province. In a newspaper article reporting on this startling turn of events, it was said: "Sigwela praised the support he received from Mennonites and their example of working among the poor. 'I almost became a Mennonite,' said Sigwela, who continues to serve his own Methodist Church as a lay preacher." (4)

MUC echoes

Though the focus of considerable Mennonite critique at the outset, AIMM made a commitment of collaboration to the Maseru United Church which was eventually to carry across a period of 16 years. (5) Subsequent developments bore out that it had been a good decision. Finding the Church in 1973 with less than a dozen dispirited expatriate members who were at the point of disbanding, the picture was dramatically different in 1990 when AIMM terminated formal relations with the Church. During this time a hall at the rear of the church plot had been repaired and enlarged. The chapel itself had been lengthened to increase seating capacity by 50%. The congregation had long since gone to a format of two morning services. Increased giving made possible a steady expansion of local ministries both within the capital city and the surrounding countryside.

Gratifying as such signs of growth were for AIMM, there was a different set of measurements of the spiritual health of this growing Church which were far more significant and rewarding. From the beginning AIMM was driven by the conviction that the MUC offered a truly unique opportunity for bringing into being and nurturing a multiracial worshiping and serving church family - - and this just across the border from the land of *apartheid*. The following glimpses of church life during those 16 years of partnership clearly illustrate that this conviction was well founded.

One short-term Mennonite pastor wrote: "We began to discover that God is sending his people from all around the world to teach what the good news of Jesus Christ is all about and what the meaning of Christian community is: - a builder from Korea; - a solar expert from Switzerland and the list goes on. . . . The cosmopolitan nature of this congregation is simply amazing. There are people from almost every race, theological background and political persuasion worshiping and fellowshiping together. Perhaps the greatest reward for anyone serving here comes through the mail when the Church receives letters from former participants who have gone home and are seeking to establish congregations where people are loved, accepted and helped to find new life in Christ Jesus." (6)

In one MUC newsletter, the following information was found: "New church members: Marguinad Silvia (France), Danny Kwagasana (Uganda), Honoria and Howard Bell (Sierra Leone), Lyagoba-David Mukasa (Uganda), Mrs. Gertrude Unamboowle (Sri Lanka), Eja Sisko Irmeli Pennanen (Finland). Visitors: Terry and Ludi Thompson (USA), Victor Banda (Zambia), Harry Lionis (Republic of South Africa), Jun Wook Yoon (Korea), Barbara Kolisang (RSA), Loraine Wescott (RSA), Dan and Ann Lee Thomas (South Korea), Alan Backhurst (UK), Liesbeth Rombouts (Netherlands), Ben Lenai (Uganda), L.C. Hlonguune (Swaziland), Bill and Eileen Page (RSA), Kai B. Flaa (Norway)"

And in the same newsletter there was this comment regarding a book entitled The Passing Summer. Speaking of the author it was said: " Michael Cassidy is hard and uncompromising about *apartheid* and the system that supports it. But he is passionately loving and concerned for all people as God's children. Wherever you are from and whatever your knowledge and opinions about South Africa, you'll find this book well worth reading." (7)

One day a letter found its way into the MUC postal box sent from South Korea and written in the language of that country. Addressed to Harris Waltner, the AIMM-appointed pastor of that time it read, in part: "I am writing this letter with my vivid memory of you in Maseru, warmly holding my hands in love and kindness on Sundays in spite of my English handicap. You may not remember a Mr. Lee, a Korean, rather thin and tall, but now I feel strongly that I should have left Maseru with a special good-by to you and I am writing this letter to apologize for not having done so. While in Maseru I attended your services and listened to your sermons even though I could not understand English. But it is amazing that I have found the Lord and became a Christian in your church, and the life of prayer which started in MUC and is still continuing has now become the only strength supporting my life today. Wonderful is the way our Lord works, calling me to such a remote country like Lesotho and making me a new man in Him. The 17 months I have been converted has been a wonderful and joyful life I never experienced before. . . ."

"I am now in good hands of my family and country and will do my best under the given circumstances for the glory of my Lord. Praying for your continued and successful ministry in Lesotho and blessings on you, Christine and the members of MUC." (8)

And from another source: "James is a South African refugee. He is in his mid-40's and seems nervous about meeting with me. I am not sure if it is because I am a journalist or because I am a white. Perhaps both. Since he is still waiting for his Lesotho citizenship papers, we decided not to use his real name. 'I felt uneasy about my life. I wanted to find peace,' says James, explaining why he made the 'hard' decision to leave his wife and three children in the black township of Soweto in 1979. 'Life in the townships was horrible,' he says. 'Oppression was a way of life. You would be on the train and the police would start to search you for no reason. You might have changed your clothes and forgotten to bring your pass. These kinds of things would build up to a certain fear. There was a time when I started protesting . . throwing away passes, pulling down a radio station . . . because I was so frustrated,' he says. 'As a result, I was arrested three times and put in prison for a total of 128 days.' After the last arrest in 1971, James says he 'started to not trust my friends. I stopped being politically active.'"

"It was while growing up in a mixed neighborhood outside of Johannesburg that James says he learned his first lesson about *apartheid*. He remembers how he often played with a white boy from the community. One day, when his friend didn't show up at their usual meeting place, James went to his friend's home to see why he hadn't come. The friend told James, 'I'm not going to play.' 'Why not?' 'I'm no longer supposed to play with you. My parents will beat me if I do.' James was shocked. He went home to ask his father for an explanation. His father told him that 'you have to learn that between you and the white person there is a barrier. Forget that you knew him.'"

"James persisted: 'What is the difference between us?' 'The color of your skin,' his father said. 'That day hate was born between me and the white person,' he told me. When he decided to leave his home in Soweto for Maseru, James says he hoped to escape his past. 'I wanted to forget everything.' But he found he couldn't. To help ease the pain he began drinking, often with other South African refugees. Last year, after a particularly heavy drinking bout, James decided to ask God what to do because he felt his life was going nowhere. His answer came in the form of a friend who came to visit him that day to invite James to come with him to the worship service at Maseru United Church. James agreed to attend."

"On the Sunday he visited the Church a man gave his testimony about how alcohol had almost ruined his life. 'I felt he was speaking only to me,' James recalls. The man told how the local chapter of Alcoholics Anonymous had helped him deal with his addiction. As a result of this man's testimony James decided to join AA and recommit himself to God. 'I prayed to God to give me the courage and power to forgive even the white man. This was difficult for me, since those roots were deep,' he says. 'But through prayer I relieved myself of the barrier of hatred. I no longer believed the white man was my enemy. . . . I used to believe that violence will bring about change. Now I believe that people must sit down and talk to each other. If there were more churches like Maseru United Church where people of mixed nationalities can come together and show love to each other, that could bring change to the character of people in South Africa. I am hopeful that one day blacks and whites will live together as friends.'" (9)

And yet other stories by the same visiting journalist: "Rose Ramorothole (pr. rah-moh-roh-TOH-leh) is a domestic worker for two missionary families in Maseru. When I arrive to interview her, Rose is sitting at the kitchen table studying her Bible. The Bible is in English, a language she's proud to have learned through correspondence courses. Rose is a Lesotho national who has already experienced much in her 37 years of life. In 1970 her parents were shot and killed by the Lesotho government because they were members of the opposition party. Soon after, Rose, at the age of 19, was put in prison because the government thought she was active in the opposition party too. Two years later she was kidnaped in order to be forced to marry a man she did not want as her husband. But she escaped and went to work in South Africa."

"The church has always been an important part of Rose's life. But in 1980 she decided to stop attending the Lesotho Evangelical Church." It was not long before she became interested "in the Maseru United Church after attending Bible study groups led by . . . Christine Waltner. 'I feel freer at Maseru United Church,' she says. 'It's not a church of man but a church of God. We're all brothers and sisters. It doesn't matter whether we're rich or poor.'" (10)

And yet one more. "One of the first things Nigel Widgery and his wife do when they move to a new country is look for a church. 'We aren't settled until we know that we will be with the Lord's people,' says Nigel, who is from England and is here to work as a civil engineer with the Lesotho Highlands Water Project."

"'Maseru United Church was the only church where we fit in,' he says. 'The people are friendly and the spiritual life is exciting and encouraging. It is international, interdenominational and above all evangelical.' Nigel says he's impressed by the 'great sense of unity amid the diversity. What brings us together is the Lord.' He is certain that when he and his wife return to England 'we will look back at the fellowship at Maseru United Church as a highlight of our experience here.'" (11)

As he prepared to leave the MUC upon the conclusion of a six-year stint of pastoral service there, Harris Waltner expressed not only his own sentiments but those of the AIMM when he wrote: "I have been heartened to realize that the teaching and preaching of basic Biblical truth speaks to the deepest needs of people, regardless of their background. It helps us face the pressures of life and cope with the dark forces of evil. Bible study has taken on deeper dimensions as we have been able to share insights and experiences in the setting of multi-cultural groups." (12)

Glen and Elizabeth Unger Koop were the last AIMM pastoral couple to serve with the MUC. Upon their return to Canada in 1992, the MUC called its own new pastor, a former missionary of South African nationality.

"you have untied tight knots"

As AIMM wound down its second decade of presence in southern Africa, it was not difficult to find supportive and appreciative comments on the part of expatriates or on the part of denominational and government leaders. But what of the AIC folks themselves and their leaders? They, after all, were the declared primary focus of AIMM concern in southern Africa. Here, too, there were a variety of appreciative commentaries to be heard. One Bishop of the Transkei put it thus: "He [Larry Hills] has untied knots which have been tight for a long time." (13)

A Botswana AIC leader commented: "Before the Mennonites came, we knew the white *baruti* [i.e., preachers or teachers] as bosses but not as people who had come to accept us, live among us and be friends with us. Before Mennonites came, we often were isolated from each other and suspicious of each other. We had a [AIC] federation but it was largely inactive. You are the first people to approach us openly, honestly and with love; we have accepted you now as our own. Have patience with us, we continue to need your help." (14)

Similar themes were heard by the Heisey/Longacre team as they traveled through southern Africa in the late 1980's: "Mennonites are not here to start a new work but are here to help strengthen the existing churches. They are not here to change and redirect us but to arm our leaders with skills." Another said simply, " What Mennonites have been doing is God-sent." (15)

a dream about a six pence

October 24, 1993, was a red letter day in Botswana since it marked a formal celebration commemorating 25 years of Mennonite ministry in that country. Attended by some 120 guests, representing a broad spectrum of the Botswana church community, there was no lack of celebration, song and speech-making. As regarded the sentiments of the AIC leaders who were present, a written report on the happenings of the day contained the following: "A number of speakers described past racial humiliations experienced at the hands of white church leaders and how the Mennonites are different. They pointed out how the Mennonites came to them in a very unobtrusive way and asked them where they needed help. . . . One church leader from the Eleven Apostles Church described how their prophet, just before he died in 1972, had a dream involving a six pence. In the dream a black man and a white man ate from this one coin together. For many years the church leaders tried to decipher the dream and the unlikely scenario where blacks and whites did something together in an intimate way. In 1976 it began to dawn on the Eleven Apostles Church that the white man in the Prophet's dream were the Mennonite Bible teachers who had come to teach and work together with them."

"Several church leaders addressed the theme of pacifism, a concept that had been foreign to them before meeting Mennonites. They related the strong impressions former Mennonite workers had left on them when watching them attempt to live out the ideals of Christian pacifism. The speakers strongly argued that it was not yet time for the Mennonites to leave Botswana. It was stressed that Mennonites still have an important role to play in many areas of development, including Bible teaching and in bringing a sense of unity to the over 200 different denominations in the country." (16)

After more than two decades of ministry in southern Africa, favorable AIC commentary is readily found. Given the African propensity for glowing and colorful tributes, AIMM has received its share of AIC praise.

But to get back to the question which heads this chapter, have we made any significant difference thus far? What, if anything, have we really accomplished in the course of our ministry among them? By way of response, the following observations can, for now, be made:

we've listened

Oriented at the outset in the mid-70's by the experience and wisdom of Ed and Irene Weaver, AIMM missionaries came to southern Africa with no prepackaged plans but rather with the vision of allowing agenda and focal points of teaching to emerge out of dialogue with the AIC people themselves. For this to happen, there had to be much more listening than talking.

Unforeseen at the outset of AIMM involvement with AICs was the impact this experience would have upon the spiritual pilgrimages of the missionary Bible teachers themselves. In this regard Stan Nussbaum comments: "None of us are the same people we were when we started relating to AICs. My opinion is that the best measure of a missionary's impact on others is the measure of impact which the context has on him/her. People who connect with the local situation are influenced by it **and** they influence it. These are two sides of a coin." (17)

The mix of study themes which have been pursued with the AIC folk across the years provides evidence that there has indeed been a listening stance. Interspersed with Bible studies have been such topics as church administration, handling church finances, marriage counseling, maintenance of church records, adolescent problems, alcoholism, sexuality and related diseases.

we've built some bridges

One of the first and more readily discernible results of our presence are numerous "bridges" which have been constructed over barriers that have isolated the AICs for so long. One bridge has carried traffic between the AICs and government. Upon our arrival in Botswana in the early 70's, we found that government attitudes frequently reflected suspicion while official policies posed various legal problems for the churches. Government attitudes were well stated by a Botswana government official at an interchurch gathering in Gaborone held in October, 1981. A journalist covering the event quoted him as saying: "There is growing concern and disappointment within the Government and particularly the Ministry of Home Affairs over some churches especially spiritual churches which register as true Christians and then act and behave 'in a manner not befitting Christians.' . . . Minister Mmusi [pr. MOO-si] told the congregation which numbered more than 800 that disputes within churches were becoming the order of the day and in a majority of cases, they were based on leadership. . . . The government had come to the conclusion that some people wanted to use religious congregations for their own personal benefits."

The Minister was further quoted as saying: "'People have resorted to what is tantamount to taking the law into their own hands. Such action has resulted in break-away groups which have existed as unlawful societies.' The Minister warned those concerned that this kind of action was not permissible and that the Government of Botswana was not going to tolerate it any more." (18)

While government criticism was well founded in some cases, the tendency was to view most AICs as being of similar nature. Thus all tended to be tarred with the same brush. A case in point were the government requirements for the accreditation of "marriage officers." The government assumption was that AIC leaders were all basically uneducated and thus unable to qualify. Approached by AIMM missionaries, the government proved to be remarkably conciliatory. As a result Mennonite personnel were able to conduct special training seminars for AIC church leaders which enabled them to qualify for government approval. Further bridges with government were also built as Mennonite Ministries personnel involved the AICs in the organization of seminars dealing with problems of alcoholism and AIDS, issues of major concern for the government.

Bridges have also been built with mainline churches in various places. AIMM personnel, upon first arriving, frequently found these church leaders in a defensive and negative posture in relation to the AICs. Viewed by many as schismatic at best and outright pagan at worst, it did not help that there was steady leakage of members from their churches to the growing AIC communities. A typical comment encountered was:

"AICs? If they really are interested in spiritual truth and growth, let them come to us. We are prepared to instruct them and to receive them into our fellowship if we feel they are sincere."

It therefore came as a shock to some mainline church leaders to learn that there was a Mennonite organization prepared to take these churches seriously and to work with them. Forced to take another more objective look at these "pagan" churches, a softening of attitude became more and more noticeable. Here and there the comment was heard: "It is true that they demonstrate an amazing vitality and have great attraction for the African. Since ostracism clearly is having no effect upon them, it is good that the Mennonites are willing to meet them on their own ground and work with them."

But the most significant bridges of all have been built between AICs themselves. The Bible classes and seminars launched by AIMM missionaries have created neutral settings within which many of the leaders have sat, studied and prayed together for the first time in their lives. Significant also have been the international conferences and consultations which have brought AIC leaders together from Swaziland, Lesotho, the Transkei and Botswana.

And there have been the occasional Mennonite-built bridges which have enabled a few AIC leaders to experience the world beyond the continent of Africa. (19)

we've won trust and affection

Over time, the growing trust and affection of many AIC people for Mennonite personnel has been shown in a variety ways. Perhaps one of the most dramatic was the official ordination of AIMM missionary Jonathan Larson to the Christian ministry by the Spiritual Healing Church of Botswana. Though licensed to preach before leaving the States, Larson had never taken the step of ordination. In 1994, as he and his wife Mary Kay were bringing their thirteen years of ministry in Botswana to a close, fellow missionary Don Rempel-Boschman and a cluster of AIC leaders felt it would be an appropriate act of affirmation and blessing to send him back to North America as a fully ordained minister.

Larson himself later described the event in the following terms: "No church surpasses the African church in exuberant celebration. When Don shared his feeling with a circle of church leaders, they seized upon this as a matter of urgent destiny and began to prepare for the occasion. There was a spate of letters exchanged with North America. A date was set in late May. A hall was rented. Letters were sent out and announcements made on Radio Botswana. Choirs began to practice. The outline of a progamme took precarious shape largely for the benefit of nervous North Americans who are still learning to abandon themselves to the extemporaneous leading of the Holy Spirit! . . ."

"On the afternoon of May 29, [1994] people began to gather from the many Christian communities we have come to know around Botswana. Present were a bevy of choirs, resplendent not only in melody but also in attire. Nearly a score of robed bishops and archbishops trooped in clutching their staves and other accoutrements of authority. Soon the hall was full of the faithful, many of whom were participating for the first time in such a shared event. At the front of the hall hung a light blue banner bearing Jesus' words of assurance after his resurrection: *Kagiso e nne le lona* (Peace be with you).

"As the choirs began to sing each in its turn, there was furious consultation and reconsideration as the programme melt down occurred. The one presiding struggled to contain the clamor of those who wanted a chance to speak. One elderly bishop, in his exuberance, pitched over backwards as his chair slipped off the edge of the dais but found himself safely in the arms of alert bystanders. The event which began with tea in the early afternoon lasted well into the evening. During the course of that afternoon, there were anthems, a traditional African praise poem, numerous and effusive speeches (in the Old Testament phrase, 'great is the company of the preachers!'), even the waving of sheaves of old course certificates as evidence of our shared narrative. And then came the steps of the ordination itself. It began with three bishops, two men and a woman, bringing a basin of water and washing my hands in the customary African manner before a meal is served.

Having prepared me in this way, two old bishops consecrated and laid a gift Setswana Scripture in my hands inscribed with a host of names and churches."

"With that I was solemnly charged to be disciplined and faithful in ministry by an old mentor, Archbishop Israel Motswasele of the Spiritual Healing Church, known to many North American Mennonites from his visit there in 1992, who then poured his vial of oil on my head and invited representatives of the congregation to lay hands on and encircle 'this child' in prayer. Kathy Fast (wife of MM director Eric Fast) had sewn a colorful preaching stole, bearing appropriate African Christian symbols, which the Mennonites draped over my shoulders as an emblem of the mission conferred. Following my halting words of response and reflection, the congregation, midst profuse words of thanks, singing and benedictions, dispersed in the gloaming having left me with a sense of wonder and even trembling at what had overtaken me. (20)

the gift of a horse's tail

Yet another colorful evidence of the acceptance and affection AIMM missionaries have encountered among AIC folk has to do with a horse's tail! Eugene Thiezsen of Henderson, NE, first arrived in Botswana in 1984 as a pilot to serve with an organization there known as The Flying Medical Mission. In this capacity he flew doctors about the flat, arid, Texas-sized country to distant clinics. With passing time he began to long for the opportunity to relate more directly to the Africans himself. This eventually led him to apply to AIMM and, in 1992, he was sent back to Botswana where he became the first AIMM missionary to be stationed in the northwest area of the country at the edge of the Okavango Swamps at a place called Maun (pr. mah-OON).

During his years in Botswana as a pilot, he had met many of the AIC church leaders including Archbishop Israel Motswasele. Their paths had again intersected unexpectedly in the summer of 1992 in North America when, during the Bishop's fraternal visit, Thieszen had been asked to accompany him during one segment of his itinerary. Casual acquaintance deepened into a relationship of friendship and trust. When Thieszen returned to Botswana as an AIMM missionary and was placed in an area where the Bishop had one of his churches, it was an occasion of joy for the church leader.

This friendship between the two men took an unexpected turn when one day the Bishop presented Thieszen with the gift of the tail of a horse. He explained that it had been a favorite animal of his and that its death represented for him a regretted loss. In their tradition the tail is sometimes cut and kept as a remembrance of a cherished animal. If given as a gift to a friend, it becomes a special cultural symbol of their relationship. As the tail passed from hand to hand, the Bishop said: "I give you the nation."

While not fully understanding at the time all of the implications either of the gift or of the statement which accompanied it, Thieszen attached it to his living room wall. One thing, however, was clear. Thieszen, and by extension the Mennonite team of which he was a part in Botswana, had been the recipient of an unusual symbol of the acceptance and esteem they were accorded in the Church of which the Bishop was the head.

but what about the Bible classes?

At the end of two decades of AIMM work with the AICs in southern Africa, it is clear that hearts and doors of opportunity have swung open in many places. Noteworthy accomplishments of various kinds comprise a lengthening list. But what about the Bible classes as such? What effect have they had thus far? What changes are observable to date as a result of our efforts to study the Scriptures together with them?

On an individual basis, first of all, there are many personal testimonies on the part of AIC members to new, clearer understanding of God's grace and salvation through faith in Jesus Christ. The resultant impact on their lives has been a source of joy and reward for the AIMM people who have known and observed them.

As for AIC leaders, there is also evidence of change on the part of some as a result of their Bible classes. There have been those who with intense interest have followed widely divergent studies such as The

People of God, a New Tribe; or the Holy Spirit and Ancestral Spirits. Other issues such as transitions in church leadership and the question of Old Testament sacrifices also generated a lot of interest. In response to frequent studies which underscored the death of Jesus Christ as the perfect, one-time sacrifice for all sin, there is an observable shift in emphasis in the preaching of some leaders.

And there are some who, in their leadership roles, give evidence of understanding that Biblical standards of morality do not allow for capricious rulings on an ad hoc basis in church life. There are also some who reflect a personal pilgrimage from Leviticus toward Hebrews in their preaching. One by-product of this journey have been smoke smudged altars behind some AIC chapels on which sin offerings are no longer offered. And there are AIC leaders who, after a careful study of the life of Christ, have told AIMM teachers that some changes had to be made in their own preaching and in the activities of their churches.

There are, furthermore, AIC leaders who, as a result of their interaction with AIMM personnel, have acquired a new sense of self-worth and have begun to dream about ways of asserting themselves more effectively vis-à-vis the society around them and the mainline churches who long have tended to hold them in disdain.

AICs in transition

The AICs are experiencing many pressures which are forcing changes of various kinds. Typically tracing their origins to charismatic prophets who often exercised powers of healing and prophetic utterance, they usually had little formal training and simply preached as they felt led by the Spirit. The followers of these first generation prophets tended to be marginally literate, rural people who lived their daily lives firmly embedded in their traditional world-views and who looked to their prophets for guidance and manifestations of spiritual power.

With passing time, many AIC leaders have experienced the pressure of higher expectations from members who with better education look to their Bishops for better sermonizing, for improved administrative skills and for upgraded places of worship, expectations which often are not easily met. Many AICs are experiencing real difficulty in holding their own youth within their churches. As founding prophets pass from the scene, fragmentation frequently occurs as rivals aspire to roles of leadership. Adequate and appropriate training of new leadership remains a constant challenge.

Nonetheless the AICs, even in the midst of change, represent a continuing spiritual vitality and demonstrate a variety of spiritual gifts which will remain attractive and of great value for Africans in the future even as they have in the past. Their search will continue for ways of being both genuine Africans and genuine Biblical Christians at the same time.

And what of AIMM in all of this? Our ministry in southern Africa is an ongoing learning process for AIMM and its missionaries even as it is for them. Efforts to broaden AIC understandings of Scripture and of salvation history will continue. There will be a continuing concern to affirm and nurture the many strengths they have without damaging the admirable self-reliance which has been such a remarkable feature of their history. There will also be continuing concern for some AICs who, thus far, have decided to keep their distance from ministries offered by AIMM. This reality calls for continual review and evaluation of our presence and approach among them.

Bishop Khuwe Masole (pr.KOO-way mah-SOH-lay) of the Memorial Apostolic Church of Botswana perhaps said it best. In an interview with Don Rempel-Boschman and Jonathan Larson, he was asked about his views and hopes regarding his own ongoing relationship with the Mennonites. Within the setting of Botswana's chronic shortage of moisture and its vast expanses of thornbush thickets, he said simply: "What we want to do is to plant a green tree with you, a tree that will be a legacy to the next generation." (21)

The story of AIMM in southern Africa has, at times, been one of uncertainty and struggle to find the way. But, thanks be to God, it has also been a story of God's marvelous grace at work in the lives of his followers, both black and white.

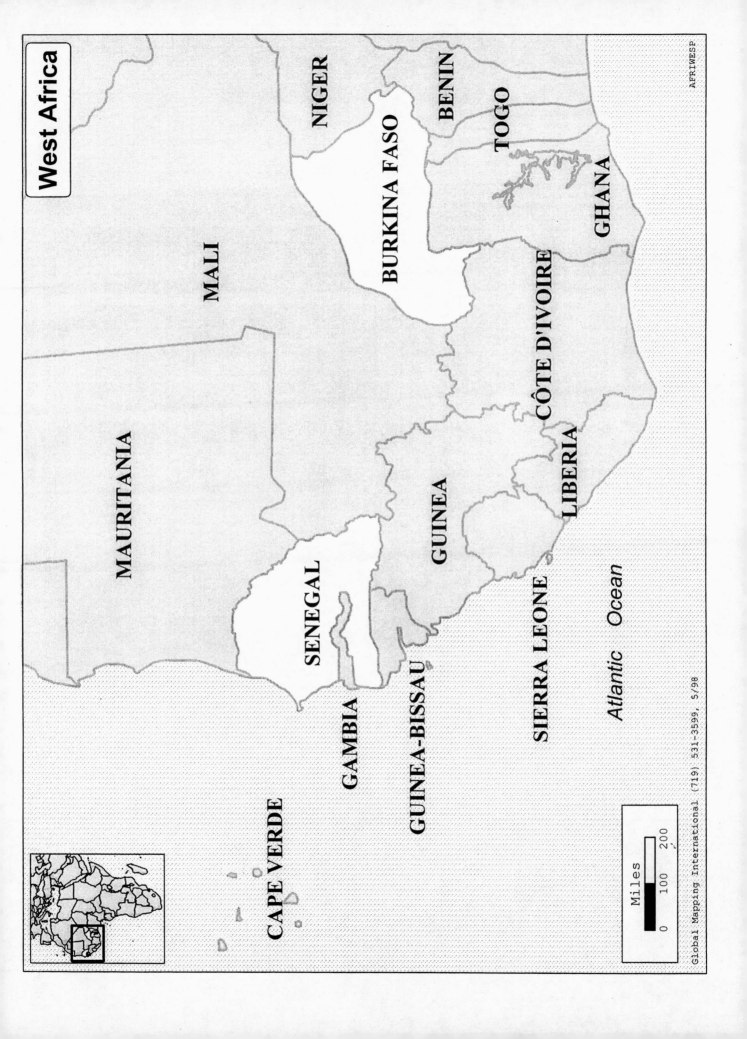

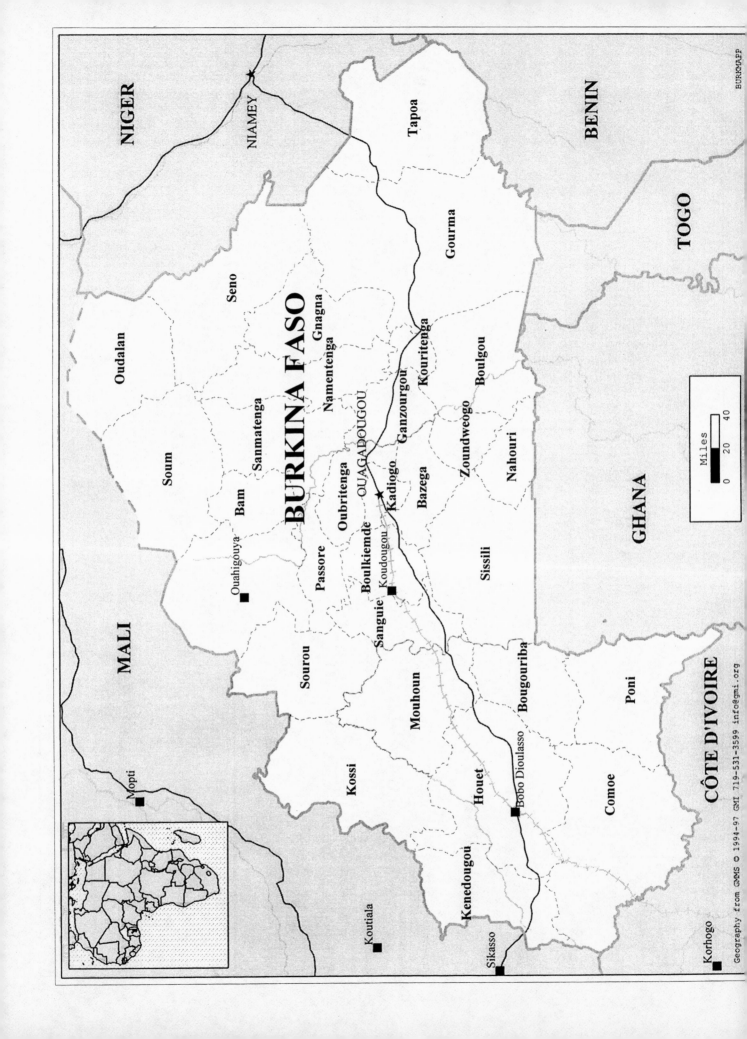

NIGER

NIAMEY

BENIN

TOGO

Tapoa

Gourma

Seno

Gnagna

BURKINA FASO

Namentenga

Kouritenga

Oudalan

Boulgou

Ganzourgou

Oubritenga

OUAGADOUGOU

Sanmatenga

Soum

Bam

Kadiogo

Bazega

Zoundweogo

Nahouri

Passore

Ouahigouya

Koudougou

Boulkiemde

Sissili

GHANA

Sanguie

Sourou

Mouhoun

Bougouriba

Poni

Kossi

Houet

Bobo Dioulasso

Mopti

Kenedougou

Comoe

Koutiala

Sikasso

Korhogo

MALI

CÔTE D'IVOIRE

Miles

0   20   40

Geography from GNMS © 1994-97 GMI 719-531-3599 info@gmi.org

BURKMAP

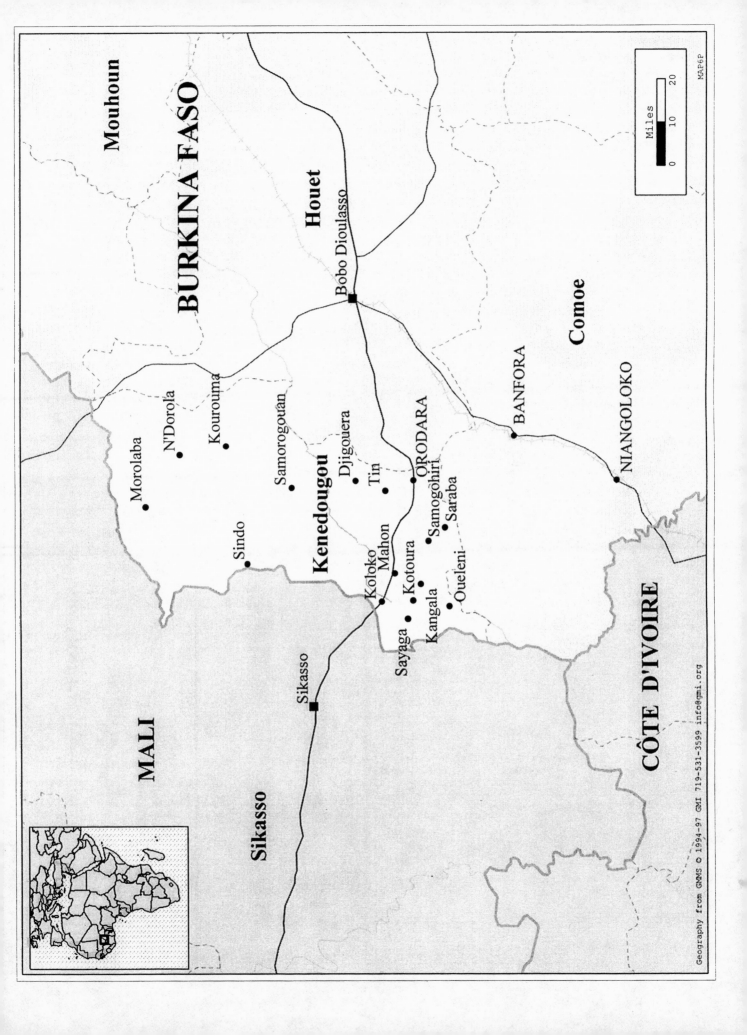

Mouhoun

BURKINA FASO

Houet

Bobo Dioulasso

Comoe

MALI

BANFORA

NIANGOLOKO

Morolaba

N'Dorola

Kourouma

Samorogouan

Kenedougou

Djigouera

Tin

ORODARA

Samogohiri

Saraba

Sindo

Koloko

Mahon

Kotoura

Sayaga

Kangala

Oueleni

Sikasso

Sikasso

CÔTE D'IVOIRE

Miles

0 10 20

MAP6P

Geography from GMMS © 1994-97 GMI 719-531-3599 info@gmi.org

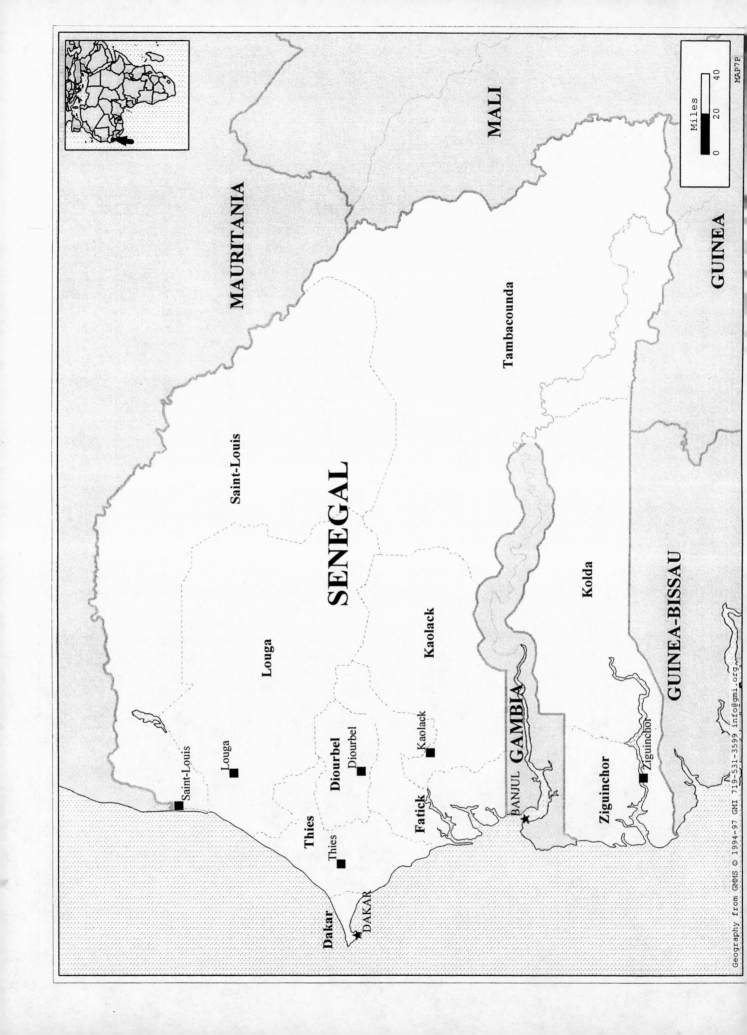

MAURITANIA

MALI

GUINEA

SENEGAL

Saint-Louis

Louga

Diourbel

Thies

Dakar

Kaolack

Fatick

Tambacounda

Kolda

GUINEA-BISSAU

GAMBIA

BANJUL

Ziguinchor

Saint-Louis

Louga

Diourbel

Thies

DAKAR

Kaolack

Ziguinchor

Miles

0   20   40

MAP7P

Geography from GMMS © 1994-97 GMI 719-531-3599 info@gmi.org

CHAPTER 61   A PLEA FOR HELP

The impact of the five-year drought of 1969-1974 along the southern fringes of the Sahara Desert was both stark and brutal. Known as the Sahel, it was the latitude along which the prolonged failure of rain cut a withering west-to-east swath across much of Africa resulting in horrendous devastation. In an area where moisture was, even in good years, marginally sufficient to raise food crops, the failure of seasonal rain quickly became a life and death matter for all living things. Planted seed simply lay in dusty soil without sufficient moisture to even germinate. Grazing vegetation for livestock gradually disappeared. Streams and lakes dried up leaving dusty beds with sun baked, cracked hulls of wooden boats dotting the banks.

At first, the afflicted tribal groups clung fiercely to their home areas hoping, each year, that the rains would at last return. Steadily, however, their animals died of hunger and thirst, their bleached bones littering the countryside. Their last resources exhausted, the drought sparked massive human migration as, in desperation, whole villages packed what few belongings they could carry and began a southward migration driving before them what few animals they had managed to keep alive. Most of them had no set destination. They were simply in search of somewhere, anywhere that would afford ground for fields, pasture for their remaining animals and a place to erect a simple shelter.

As the thousands of refugees slowly made their way from the north, they soon discovered that the drought was more general than they realized. While they found other tribes people still resident in their traditional areas, their water tables were also slowly dropping with the result that many of them had wells which were going dry as well necessitating for many - - residents and refugees alike - - long walks to wells which still contained precious, life-sustaining water. Human suffering was widespread and acute.

MCC investigates

Well aware of the worsening situation, in 1970 Vern Preheim, MCC's Africa Secretary of the time, visited a number of the worst effected areas. In a meeting of COMBS (i.e., Council of Mennonite Board Secretaries now known as Council of International Ministries, or CIM) and MCC administrators in the spring of 1971, he reported on his findings and impressions. He then shared an action taken by the MCC executive in December of 1970 "that staff be authorized to explore the possibility of opening an agricultural development program somewhere in French-speaking West Africa with the possibility of a combined approach with a Mennonite mission or church if there appears to be mutual interest but with another mission or church if there is no Mennonite mission or church interest." He then added, "My personal opinion is that Upper Volta would be first with a toss up between Togo and Dahomey for second and third to be considered for Mennonite development assistance."

Among the concluding comments of Preheim's report was a question: "Are there any of the Mennonite mission boards interested in working together with MCC in French-speaking West Africa?" (1)

Though there was no immediate mission board response to the proposal of opening a joint agricultural/water development program with MCC in the Sahel area, MCC continued its own investigations. Following through on Preheim's suggestion that Upper Volta be an initial concern, MCC staff made a second trip. Of the several mission organizations which were at work in Upper Volta, it was particularly the Christian and Missionary Alliance personnel who urged MCC to consider their area in the southwestern end of the country. A critical need was a water team equipped to deepen existing wells and/or dig new ones. Providing a mission vehicle and chauffeur, the MCC representative was driven throughout the area, a journey which convinced MCC that both a location and a focus for its proposed new development effort had been found.

It was a year or so later that MCC fielded its first water development team in the persons of Peter and Esther Hiebert. Settling in a mission house near the Mali border at a village called Djibasso (pr. djee-BAH-ssoh), Peter began the tedious and arduous task of boring test holes from one place to another trying to ascertain water levels and the feasibility of hand digging wells in areas strewn with boulders and frequently underlain by bedrock of granite. Gradually, as suitable locations for wells were found, the MCC philosophy of development quickly came to the fore. As well projects were begun, local villagers were required to provide labor and/or cement to ensure their own investment in the effort to restore a water supply. "This is the difference," it was explained, "between development and relief."

finding more than water

Joined by other MCC recruits, the water team began to circulate over an ever broader area along the Mali/Upper Volta frontier. In the process they gradually became aware that they were encountering a series of distinct ethnic groups, each with their own language. Furthermore, they noted little evidence of Christian presence or witness anywhere. When in conversations with area missionaries they were able to confirm that, in fact, there was a cluster of isolated tribal groups who had never been effectively touched with a witness to the Gospel, they reported their findings to the MCC office in Akron, PA.

It was in response to this information that William Snyder, the MCC executive secretary at the time, made a second contact with Mennonite board offices sharing this discovery and once again asking if there might be a board interested in making its own investigation in Upper Volta.

Drilling for water was one thing. Ethnic groups untouched by a witness to Christ was another. The Mennonite Brethren were the first to react to the Snyder memo. Rev. J. J. Toews was planning an administrative trip to Africa in the summer of 1974. He arranged to spend several days in Upper Volta with Zaire missionary Arnold Prieb (2) to become better informed on the needs and opportunities there.

While AIMM had by this time also expressed interest in the unfolding story of that drought-blighted country, the summer of 1974 marked a time of transition in leadership in its home office. (3) Any further Africa travel by AIMM personnel awaited this transition.

Aware of this, Vernon Wiebe, the General Secretary of the Mennonite Brethren mission office kept lines of communication with AIMM open and clear when he informed the Elkhart office that it was in no way his intent "to race AIMM to Upper Volta." (4) It was in this spirit that trip reports and findings were regularly shared with the AIMM office. It is intriguing to note that within two decades the Mennonite Brethren were to become full members of AIMM and would collaborate in recruiting and sponsoring missionary personnel in that country as part of that inter-Mennonite team.

CHAPTER 62   AIMM RESPONDS

The J. J. Toews and Arnold Prieb team did visit Upper Volta in the summer of 1974 as planned. The interest of MB BOMAS (i.e., Mennonite Brethren Board of Missions and Services, now MBMS International) at the time was not to seek an immediate opening for establishing a new work but rather to assess the need and feasibility of beginning a ministry in that country. It was hoped that this might be achieved by temporarily placing a missionary couple under the auspices of an existing mission on the scene. After dialogue with several mission leaders of the country, the men concluded that this was not a viable option.

seeking information

Meanwhile the transition in AIMM staff in Elkhart had been accomplished. As preparations were being made for the new secretary's first trip to Africa, he was instructed to include Upper Volta in his itinerary. His traveling companion in the summer of 1975 was board member and former Zaire colleague, Allan Wiebe.

Flying into the nation's capital Ouagadougou (pr.oo-wah-gah-DOO-goo), they were met and graciously hosted by personnel of the local Assemblies of God Mission and Church. For the purposes of a fact-finding trip, this proved to be an excellent arrangement since the local Assemblies pastor, Daniel Compaore (pr. koh-mpah-OR-ay), was both the president of his Church and the chairman of the country's Federation of Churches. Furthermore, the local Assemblies missionary, Rev. Jim Bryant, was the country director of his Mission. Preparing for our visit, they had arranged for time with Rev. Samuel Yameogo (pr. yah-may-OH-goh), an ordained Assemblies pastor who served also as the Projects Secretary for the Federation's Department of Development.

In this man the AIMM delegation soon discovered a kindred spirit. Schooled and trained in the Assemblies resolute focus on evangelism and church planting, he along the way began to believe that a full-orbed Gospel could not address only the spiritual needs of the African to the exclusion of his physical and social needs. When at first he began to gently raise this issue with his missionaries, he encountered not only disinterest but, in some cases, warnings as well. He was reminded that the missionary call was to win the lost. To seek to create a church affiliated office of development - - even in the context of a drought-stricken country - - was to risk entanglement with a "social gospel." It is an enduring tribute to his diplomacy and tenacity that, over time, he was able to bring into being a service arm of the Federation which became a channel for desperately needed material and technical help for thousands of his fellow countrymen.

The AIMM delegation had many questions for their hosts. But in an initial meeting, Rev. Yameogo asked if they might first make an inquiry of their own. By the summer of 1975 the church leaders in the capital city had had contact with three different Mennonite groups. The AIMM delegation was the fourth! (1) His question was simple and direct: "Would you tell us how many sorts of Mennonites there are and, especially, what kind are you!?"

The AIMM delegation took this unexpected opportunity to explain that the broad Mennonite family was composed of people who had their roots in the Reformation, who considered the Bible to be God's inspired Word, who believed Jesus to be God's Son whose life, teachings, death and resurrection were crucial to the life and salvation of all who placed their faith in Him. It was further explained that Mennonites believed the true church to be made up of people who had witnessed to saving faith in Christ via adult baptism and who believed that Christ's teachings regarding discipleship and sacrificial service were to be taken seriously by his professed followers of every generation. Indeed, it was a desire to investigate possible need and opportunity for Mennonite witness and service that had prompted their trip to Upper Volta.

Assured that they were talking with people of evangelical spirit and faith, a great deal of helpful information was quickly forthcoming. The country had known a Christian missionary presence since the arrival of the first Catholic personnel in 1899. With the arrival of American Assemblies of God missionaries in 1921, a succession of Protestant arrivals was begun with the Christian and Missionary Alliance in 1923, the World

Evangelical Crusade in 1931, the Sudan Interior Mission in 1932, the Canadian Pentecostal Church in 1945, the European Assemblies of God in 1948 and the Southern Baptists in 1972.

There existed a council of missions and churches known by its French acronym FEME (i.e., the Federation of Evangelical Missions and Churches). It had been officially established in 1945 and had crafted a country-wide comity agreement which allocated roughly the eastern fourth of the country to the Sudan Interior Mission, the great central plateau to the Assemblies and roughly the western third of the country to the Christian and Missionary Alliance. Two smaller areas in the southwest bordering the frontier with the Ivory Coast were allocated to a Canadian Pentecostal group and the World Evangelical Crusade Team. Across the years these ecumenical borders had been respected. But by the summer of 1975 it was clear that the severe drought of the previous five years had not only impacted agriculture, commerce and animal husbandry. The massive migration of various ethnic groups had also scrambled the comity borders which earlier had been carefully drawn by the Protestant Missions.

Furthermore, the influence of Islam was steadily growing in the country. While those professing faith in Allah were still in a minority, trends were clear. The freedom of Christian missions to carry on their work could not be assumed for an indefinite future. Professing Christians still comprised only a small percentage of the population. And, above all, there were in Upper Volta many ethnic groups who were still basically untouched by the Gospel. (2)

Would the Mennonites be welcome to begin a new work of witness and ministry somewhere in the country? Indeed they would. And as far as the Assemblies representatives were concerned, Mennonites needed to look no further than the capital city where they were. Since political independence it had been steadily growing. Although traditionally considered to be "their field," it was outstripping their resources. They needed and welcomed help.

But the AIMM men wanted to visit the area in which the MCC water team had settled and to visit the Mission which had aggressively sought their help. An early morning flight of one hour to the southwest put the men in Bobo Dioulasso (pr. BOH-boh dee-oo-LAH-soh, and locally referred to simply as Bobo), the second largest city of the country which was also the administrative center of the Christian and Missionary Alliance (C&MA) Mission.

Key contacts made here were with the Hieberts and with Rev. David Kennedy who was the field director of the C&MA Mission at the time. Both he and the MCC couple confirmed what had earlier been reported to visiting MCC administrators, i.e., that there were ethnic groups who basically remained outside any effective Christian witness or influence. Most of these people lay along the western fringes of the territory which had for years been designated as the C&MA region of responsibility.

What were the reasons for this? Kennedy suggested several factors such as deeply rooted traditional cultures, distinct tribal languages which differed from one group to the next, languages which none of their missionaries had ever learned. This, in turn, necessitated the use of translators whenever efforts of evangelism were undertaken among them. There were, furthermore, high rates of illiteracy among these groups and, in some cases, difficult access because of terrain. But above all else it was, Kennedy said, insufficient missionary personnel which posed the biggest problem. There simply were not enough missionaries to maintain sustained and systematic contact with these tribal groups on the fringes of their area.

Was there place for or need of a Mennonite effort among these unreached people? Kennedy stated that while the Mission could not speak for or commit their Church in any way, the Mission would encourage AIMM to give serious consideration to such a possibility.

another AIMM delegation

Their findings, when reported back to the AIMM Board, sparked animated discussion. It had been verified that there was both genuine need for an increased missionary effort in Upper Volta and that AIMM would be welcomed to join forces with other Missions already at work on the scene. As plans were laid for an annual administrative trip to Africa in 1976, it was decided that board member Elmer Neufeld accompany the AIMM Executive Secretary and that Upper Volta be revisited with a view to formulating some clear proposals for board action in the fall of 1976.

In the process, AIMM board members kept asking if the Mennonite Church of Zaire could not in some manner also be involved in this venture. Missionaries had often encouraged CMZa leaders to face their own responsibility, as an autonomous Church, for outreach beyond their own national borders. Might this not be an opportunity for a joint AIMM/CMZa effort in an area of Africa new to them both? When approached with an invitation, there was quick response. Chosen to join the AIMM delegation in Upper Volta was Reverend Ghymalu Kianza (pr. gi-MAH-loo KYAH-nzah). Having worked for over a year with Jim Bertsche on a revision of the Phende New Testament, they knew each other well. Perceptive, fluent in French and supportive of the idea of CMZa outreach elsewhere in Africa, Ghymalu was a good choice to round out the trio.

Their travel in Upper Volta was greatly facilitated by having access to an MCC vehicle and driver - - MCC volunteer Paul Kaufman. Once again there was contact and discussion with Assemblies of God personnel in Ouagadougou and with C&MA people in Bobo. Once again AIMM was encouraged to undertake a new work in Upper Volta. There were, however, two conditions: 1) that AIMM focus its effort upon unreached areas and people and 2) that formal approval be secured from the country's Federation of Missions and Churches. With regard to unreached people, the C&MA folk were this time more specific. To the west of Bobo, some fifty miles along the main road toward the neighboring country of Mali, was a large market town named Orodara (pr. or-oh-DAH-rah). To the north, west and south of this commercial center and government outpost was a collection of ethnic groups about which they had been talking. Although they were located in what was historically considered to be their mission area of responsibility, they had made little headway in reaching them, strung out as they were along the country's national frontiers with Mali and Ivory Coast.

One of the major groups was commonly referred to as the Senoufo (pr. seh-NOO-foh). Another group mentioned were the Siamou (pr. SEE-ah-moo). The first group was known for its resolute resistance to change of whatever kind it might be. The other was heavily Islamized. At one point the C&MA had stationed a missionary couple in Orodara. A chapel had been built and a nucleus of believers established. But due to a lack of personnel, they had been unable to maintain a missionary presence there. For a time there was an African pastor from Mali who gave leadership to the new group of believers. But when political tension erupted between the two countries, he returned to his homeland with his family and there had been no leadership available since. The small group of believers had partially scattered in the meantime. If the AIMM/CMZa delegation was looking for a needy area and a challenge, they needed to look no further!

the first trip to Orodara

That said, the delegation continued their travel westward accompanied by a C&MA pastor named Thomas who knew the area and the trade language, Dioula (pr. DJOO-lah). Approaching the outskirts of Orodara, they immediately had the impression of arriving at a frontier settlement. A police post and local government office at the roadside required a stop. After presenting their passports they continued along the wide, crowned, red dirt road into the center of the town. Here and there were small cement block shops with metal shutters and doors. One had a gas pump in front. The market area saw vendors under bits of shade; women sat under roadside mango trees with fruit displayed in large enamel pans. On the weekly market day, people converged upon the town from all directions on foot, bikes or vehicles bringing all manner of local food stuffs and handcraft. Not far from the market stood a grey, rectangular cement block mosque from whose square tower were heard the traditional daily calls to prayer. A small building off the main road sheltered the town's postal/telegraph/telephone service. At one end of town was a short dirt airstrip which accommodated small planes. The flowing gowns and fez headdress typical of Muslim garb was seen on every side.

After some inquiry someone was found with a key to the little chapel. Set off the main road in a clump of mango trees, it was whitewashed and swept. A low cement platform at one end, a chalk board, a lectern and a half dozen backless benches comprised its furnishings. The ten or so Protestant believers in Orodara attempted to maintain a weekly schedule of worship on their own. They deplored the departure of their former pastor and spoke freely of their need for a shepherd.

Since Pastor Thomas had a friend in Dieri (pr. DYEH-ri), the first village along the road beyond Orodara, it was decided to pay a visit there. Parking along the roadside, the men followed the pastor into the village in search of his friend. The AIMM Secretary's trip journal carried the following notations of that occasion: "Everything built with adobe brick and mortar with grass or straw mixed in to bind it; thatch, conical roofs for everything. Houses are built close to each other with winding paths between. . . . At the village entrance was a small mosque. Nearby was 'weavers row' with traditional, simple looms where one man was at work today. The long vari-colored strands are stretched out in the distance tied to a weight which is pulled along by the tension as the weaver gradually winds the woven material around a spindle. . . . Saw several hand-dug wells today and nearly all were 45 to 60 feet deep. . . . A striking feature of their culture is an elaborate exchange of greetings whenever they meet. It goes back and forth for several rounds and they seem, at times, to be talking over each other in the process. . . . As we were leaving the village, a distinguished looking man in a voluminous gown, fez and silver-rimmed glasses caught up with us. He turned out to be the friend the pastor was looking for. He invited us back to his house but we demurred because of time. He then insisted that at least his pastor friend return with him. He wanted to send a gift of a hat full of guinea eggs back with us. To these were also added a quantity of fresh mangos." (3)

Returning to Orodara, the group sought out an open air market "restaurant." Their pastor tour guide cautioned them that Orodara restaurants were not like those in Bobo, but they did offer hot food. Ushering us under a thatch lean-to, the proprietor explained that there was a choice of rice, salad and mutton or guinea. The delegation settled on an order of mutton, rice and cokes. From the vantage point under their thatch overhang, the waiting men had a clear view of the back yard kitchen facilities comprised of several no nonsense cast iron kettles over open fires. In no time at all they were served heaping portions of their ordered food.

As the sun began to dip toward the west, the delegation started their return trip to Bobo carefully guarding a hat full of guinea eggs and pondering the man who had presented them as a gift. Tall, well groomed, courteous, courtly and even cordial in his welcome of the visitors to his village, he nonetheless represented a leadership that had effectively blocked Christian influence in his village as had many others like him in other villages of the area.

a Sunday at Ouarkoy (pr. oo-wahr-KOY)

Before concluding their visit to Upper Volta, the delegation wanted to contact the president of the C&MA Church. He was Rev. Bonzi (pr. BOH-nzi) who pastored a church in the village of Ouarkoy. Following one of the dirt roads out of the city on a Sunday they arrived mid-morning to find the pastor presiding over a worship service. Following the service, the visitors were escorted to chairs under a nearby shade tree. The AIMM Secretary's journal later observed: "It was a lovely rural setting. Things greening up with the first rains. Livestock roaming around grazing, chickens and guinea fowl about; a sleek donkey tethered nearby. Apparently from here north, things dry out rapidly. It is said that many people moved into this area during the drought years and that some have stayed." (4)

As the last of the Sunday congregation left the chapel, pastor Bonzi came to join the visitors under the tree. The trend of conversation was similar to that of previous days with mission/church leaders elsewhere, i.e., explaining a bit about AIMM and how it was that opportunities for a work in their country were being investigated. They then explained that they had sought him out as the president of his Church, first to seek his counsel and, in the event of Mennonite entry into the area, his blessing.

Pastor Bonzi responded that while their missionaries seemed to know about Mennonites, he personally knew little about them. It was true that there were tribal groups in their area who continued to resist change. It was also true that, as a Mission and Church, they were not in a position to meet that challenge in their backyard. In the event that Mennonites did enter the area, it was his request that they not settle in areas where they had already planted churches. As for his blessing as the head of his Church, if FEME approved, they as a Church would be supportive and give every help they could.

decision time

Retracing their path to the C&MA guest house in Bobo, the delegation prepared an evening snack. Dishes done, they sat together to compare notes, observations and thoughts. The trip had been the easy part; now came the hard part. They were to return to their respective organizations not only with a report on their findings but also with clear recommendations as to what the future course of action should be. It did not help that it was a hot, humid night in Bobo at the end of a long tiring day. A small fan on a bureau top did little to improve things. And the responsibility of their assignment weighed upon them.

As conversation flowed around the little living room, parallel lists of pros and cons began to emerge. On the plus side, Upper Volta seemed to afford several opportunities that were attractive. For years the AIMM Board had talked about the idea of looking for a new area in French-speaking Africa as the Zaire churches assumed increasing responsibility for their life and future. There was also concern about the haunting reality of unreached peoples. And, more and more, AIMM was interested in some sort of ministry access to the Muslim world. In a remarkable way, Upper Volta brought all three of these strands of interest together. There was, furthermore, the advantage of an area of comparatively good soil and rainfall, the possibility of some initial help from C&MA pastors and Christians who knew the area. And, significantly, in spite of a high level of Muslim influence both within and without the country, the Upper Volta government was favorably disposed toward Christian missions.

But that was not the entire picture. Working in Upper Volta, they were warned, was financially costly. The dollar exchange rate for local currency plus high tariffs on most imported goods made things expensive. There was also the reality of the comparative isolation and spartan rural African lifestyle that any prospective AIMM/CMZa missionaries would have to cope with in the event of assignment there. But, above all else, there was the brooding reality of a cluster of tribes with a long history of great pride in their own traditions, languages and religious beliefs. They had by and large resolutely resisted outside influence from whatever source. Semi-isolated in their often arid surroundings, they were well known for their religious beliefs which revolved about a broad based system of animal sacrifice and elaborately carved ritual masks.

Indeed so resistant were they that a Catholic priest of the area, after years of effort to make converts among them, was one day heard to comment: "It is impossible to convert these people to the Christian faith."

Closer at hand, sympathetic C&MA missionary personnel had commented: "If you are serious about reaching this mix of people along the Mali border, we'll be of all the help we can. But don't expect too much."

And now, what about the Mennonites? The three men, after sharing their observations and impressions, had fallen silent, each deep in his own thoughts. Finally one of the men said: "The problems are great and real. There are many valid questions to be posed and some will certainly be asked by the Board. But I'm afraid to vote no. There is too clear a sense of God's leading. A series of events has brought us here which surely are more than coincidental. If doors continue to open before us, I do not find it in me to turn aside or to retreat."

Pastor Ghymalu then said: "My presence here indicates the interest of my Church in cooperating with AIMM in a new mission outreach. I cannot vote no for my church. If this is to be our vote, it will have to be cast by CMZa administrators back in Zaire. True, we have seen the area and we realize that it has been a difficult one in the past. But it still remains to be seen what would happen if some missionaries came who are willing to live and work hard among these resistant people demonstrating love and compassion even as they share the Gospel."

Board Chairman Neufeld then commented: "Orodara and its surrounding area is a primitive frontier and calls for another generation of pioneers like those who planted early AIMM mission stations in Zaire years ago. Can we still find such recruits in our North American constituency? How ready really is CMZa to provide some personnel and some support? Is this an idea held by the church in general or only by its executive committee? This will be a costly venture. Furthermore, there are some missiologists who would argue against this venture, i.e., why work among resistant people if there are more responsive ones elsewhere? And some would ask why we think of settling into the semi-isolation of a rural area rather than in an urban center?" Nonetheless Neufeld concluded: "I'm ready to recommend that we come and try. The great need is all too obvious. This area offers us the opportunity of involvement with Islam in somewhat more favorable circumstances than is the case in many parts of the Islamic world. It is also an opening into another Francophone area of Africa. It affords an opportunity for collaboration with CMZa in evangelism and a possible joint effort with MCC in agricultural and water development efforts." (5)

Consensus reached, the men worked into the night on drafting a formal proposal to the AIMM Board and the CMZa Executive Committee. After a general statement of findings, the document concluded with a series of eight specific recommendations: " 1) that the AIMM, in collaboration with the CMZa, open a field of missionary work in the Republic of Upper Volta; 2) that official request be made to the Federation of Evangelical Missions and Churches for admission of the AIMM as a member and for the Federation's support in our entry into the country; 3) that we immediately begin formalities for securing a legal charter from the Voltaic government; 4) that we envision the *sous-préfecture* [governmental administrative area] of Orodara as our first area of work; 5) that we also envision work in the urban centers of the country in the future as needs and possibilities arise; 6) that we envision close collaboration with MCC in the country in shared programs or in shared representation before the government; 7) that we issue an urgent call to the CMZa as well as to the churches in North America for workers who are ready to serve the Lord in this country; 8) that we ask AIMM and the CMZa to arrange a meeting of representatives of both groups to study and draw up administrative guidelines for our collaboration in Upper Volta. Signed in Bobo Dioulasso, June 7, 1976." (6)

It was not long after the men had turned off the lights and drifted off to sleep that the pre-dawn sounds of calls to the day's first prayers at the nearby mosque could be heard through the open windows of the guest house.

The findings and recommendations of the AIMM/CMZa investigative team drawn up in the summer of 1976 in Upper Volta were submitted to the full AIMM Board a few weeks later in its fall sessions. There was no lack of questions. There was much about the findings that was intimidating. If the ethnic groups in their semi-isolation along the Upper Volta/Mali boarder had so successfully rejected the mission efforts of others for so long, was it not presumptuous to think that Mennonites would have any better results? In the event AIMM decided to try, what would be the approach? the methodology? the strategy? Where would AIMM seek relevant orientation regarding Islam? And, most troubling of all, where would candidates be found among AIMM's partnering conferences who would be prepared to make at least open-ended commitments to an extremely simple life style in rural surroundings of sub-Saharan Africa? Where indeed!

As the discussion finally wound down, there were few answers to the questions which had been posed. And yet the stance of the board members was much like that of the three-man team a few weeks earlier in Upper Volta. There was the same keen sense of standing before an open door which led to great need and daunting challenge. No one found it in their heart to propose that AIMM turn aside. If this was of the Lord, there would be a way. God had often honored CIM/AIMM ventures of faith in the past. Why not trust divine guidance and provision yet once again? A board member simply moved "that we endorse the written report . . ." The motion was seconded by several and carried by a unanimous vote. (1)

the first candidates close at hand

In keeping with the AIMM Board tradition of the time, a number of prospective and furloughing missionaries were present at the October 1976 board sessions for purposes of reporting, fellowship and counsel. Among them were Loren and Donna Kampen Entz. Enrolled as students in the Overseas Mission Training Center (OMTC)at AMBS in Elkhart, IN that fall, they had already been in dialogue with GC/COM staff and AIMM office personnel about a possible assignment with AIMM somewhere in Africa. They had not come to that interest abruptly.

Loren was the son of Godly, wheat farmer parents near Elbing, KS. (2) His childhood had been powerfully shaped by his parents' love for their church and their land. Service in the name of Christ was an all-pervading concept in their home. Following high school, Loren studied for a couple of years at Bethel College at Newton, KS, after which he volunteered for PAX service with MCC in 1968. He was assigned to the joint AIMM/MCC agricultural development program of the time in Zaire and was placed at Mukedi Station where he worked for 2½ years. Returning home, he enrolled at Kansas State University where he graduated with a degree in agricultural economics in the spring of 1974. He returned to the family farm for two years but soon discovered what many others before him had experienced - - the sand of Africa is not easily dislodged from the sandals of those who have served there.

Along the way someone else had entered his life in a special way. Donna Kampen also spent her childhood in a Christian farm home (3) near Fiske, SK, where she spent much of her time outdoors helping her father with routine farm chores. Following her graduation from high school, she served with an MCC VS unit in Lancaster, PA, an experience which firmly oriented her toward a life of mission and service. In 1973, as a member of an MCC recruiting team, she made a stop on the campus of Kansas State University where Loren was a student. Their meeting there, though brief, triggered "good chemistry" which led to their marriage in the summer of 1976. Their wedding and reception sharply reflected their personal values. Married in a simple ceremony in the Fiske Mennonite Church, the church of her youth, they held a reception in a new machine shed on the Kampen farm which she had helped to build.

They soon approached John Sommer, the personnel secretary of the GC/COM office in Newton, KS, where they were counseled to give one year to general studies in the area of Christian mission at AMBS in Elkhart. It was there that they early sought out AIMM personnel for dialogue regarding their future. Thus it was that they found themselves at the October AIMM Board sessions in the fall of 1976 where they were given opportunity to give personal testimony to the Lord's leading in their lives.

Donna later reflected on this series of events as follows: "We came to seminary with a general commitment to missions, but no specific leading. In October of last year, we heard of the possibilities of a new mission venture among the Senoufo people of Upper Volta. . . . We knew the decision was not for us to make, so we simply asked AIMM to place us where we could best be used and believed God would lead through them. But we could not shake the Upper Volta challenge. . . . In January, when AIMM asked us to accept this West African assignment, we were not surprised." (4)

and a second couple, too

Even as the first candidates for a new work in Upper Volta were coming into focus, AIMM had become aware of a second couple who offered clear interest and potential. John Sommer, himself originally from the west coast, had been in contact with Dennis and Jeanne Sonke Rempel of Alta Loma, CA. After three years of pre-medical studies, Dennis had switched tracks to agricultural science. Married in the summer of 1975, the fall of 1976 found Dennis in the last year of a master's degree program in soil science. Jeannie was in her last year of a BS program in nursing. Actively involved with Inter-Varsity on the campus, they were making plans to attend the triennial IV mission conference scheduled that year at Urbana Champaigne, IL. Aware that the Entz's were also planning to make the trek from Elkhart, John Sommer suggested that the two couples plan to meet at the AIMM display table in the campus armory. In spite of the pressure of round-the-clock conference activity, they managed to spend some time together and to share their personal aspirations for overseas service. In the process, deep bonds of respect and friendship quickly formed. As they shared their backgrounds with each other, an intriguing facet of Dennis' study program came to light. For his master's thesis, he had chosen to zero in on agricultural problems in sub-Saharan Africa in a remote country called Upper Volta - - this prior to any knowledge of AIMM's decision to place a team of missionaries there!

Following the Urbana Conference, events gathered speed for both couples. The Entzes left North American in the fall of 1977 to begin a year of language study at *Le Chambon* in southern France. Fall of the same year saw the Rempels go to AMBS at Elkhart for a term of study at OMTC. In January, 1978, they also went to France for language study. Overlapping with the Entzes for six months, many hours were spent in thinking, brainstorming and praying about their joint assignment. Both couples brought a strong dose of excitement and idealism to their planning. For one thing, they were keenly aware of the unusual opportunity they were being offered of pioneering a new work with AIMM among unreached tribal people - - this after several decades of mission endeavor elsewhere in Africa under a colonial regime. What did it mean, now, that in the Africa of the late 1970's they were being offered the opportunity of first generation evangelism? What was to be learned from broad Mennonite experience of previous decades in other parts of Africa and the world? Was there even any need to envision a mission structure at all? Why not simply go as "the church" right from the start? Why not seek to model Christian community from the very beginning among the people they hoped to reach? Why not make a deliberate effort to witness by how they lived as much as by what they said - - especially in the early going when language would be a problem?

Mennonites arrive at Orodara

The Entzes concluded their year in France in the summer of 1978 and went directly to Upper Volta. Terry Stuckey, the MCC country representative of the time, had provided invaluable help in making initial arrangements for their arrival. He had found an African businessman in Orodara who owned a house, built of permanent materials, which he was willing to rent. Built on a modest scale, it afforded a small kitchen, three rooms that could serve as bedrooms, a living room and a cement veranda. The roof was of sheet metal; windows and doors were of steel. The house was set toward the back of a rectangular plot of ground surrounded by an eight foot cement block wall with a metal gate at the front entrance. Just inside the gate was a hand-dug, open well with a low cement collar around the top. Adjacent was an African "kitchen" with a clay "stove/oven." Behind the house was a pit latrine. The house had neither electricity nor plumbing. It was surrounded on all sides by African neighbors in their traditional small, adobe-walled, mud-floored, thatch-roofed dwellings. It was here that the Entzes settled in August of 1978. They were joined four months later by the Rempels and their little one year old daughter, Heidi. At least initially, they planned to share the house and courtyard secured for them by MCC personnel.

Furniture was simple and functional. (5) A dining room table was held together by bolts. Beds were foam sponge pads on the floor. Food was prepared on a small butane gas stove. They deliberately had come with little in the way of supplies determined to learn early how to draw upon the food resources of the large African market a few minutes walk from their yard gate - - some familiar, some strange. The missionaries soon learned that an early morning signal that fresh meat was available in the market were the large buzzards circling low over the place of slaughter.

as seen through western eyes

It was nearly a decade later that Marian B. Hostetler, a North American writer, had occasion to visit the AIMM team in Orodara. In spite of elapsed time, the setting had not changed all that much. After her visit she wrote: "To some people Orodara is a city. To me it barely qualified as a town. Most of the houses are mud brick or mud plastered huts with thatched roofs plus the occasional block and tin roofed buildings. Until recently there was no electricity or running water, no trash collection or paved streets. However, there is a post office where mail arrives and leaves once a week; a hospital, pharmacy, weekly market, gas station, school, and a few little shops. But Orodara is the largest population center of the province and the place where missionaries from the outlying villages come for supplies or a change of scene. If one really wants a change of scene and needs some 'exotic' supplies such as butter, meat, cheese, or flour, one can go two hours further on the dirt road to reach the city of Bobo Dioulasso. Bobo has hotels, an airport, electricity and water, C&MA and Catholic church centers, a large daily market, stores and restaurants. However, the large mosque, the throngs of motorbikes, goats and chickens in the streets, women with babies riding on their backs and all kinds of merchandise on their heads, quickly inform you that you're not in a North American city."

"In the village the 'thump, thump, thump' of the women pounding grain becomes a background noise to the day, the 'Muzak' of Africa. The ground seems to reverberate to the pounding of the great wood pestles. You almost feel it rather than hear it. Every day grain must be pounded. The pounded grain is cooked into a thick cereal which is the basis of their diet. They also pound peanuts into a kind of chunky peanut butter but not for sandwiches . . . . It is used in sauce or stew and eaten with the pounded cooked grain called 'tô.' They pound nuts from a tree to get an oil to use in cooking. The pounded nuts look like a giant batch of chocolate cake batter. The oil will separate when the gooey batter is beaten."

"Another sound is the squeak of the pulley as the women or girls are drawing water from the well. The rope has a rubber bucket at each end so that as you are pulling up the full one, the other is going down to be filled. One hears the splash of the water being dumped into a galvanized bucket, a large enamel basin or plastic tub. The full container is so heavy it is hard to get it onto your head but once there it is easily carried to the house." As her descriptive article drew toward its close, Hostetler posed the question: "How do missionaries learn to live here?" She promptly answered her own question: "Not always easily." (6)

Soon after his return to Zaire, Rev. Ghymalu was invited to a meeting of the CMZa Executive Committee at which time he submitted the recommendations which had been drawn up just days earlier in Bobo Dioulasso. There was lively discussion and a sense of excitement among the committee members as they plied Rev. Ghymalu with many questions regarding Upper Volta, its land, its customs and its people. It was not long, however, that questions began to turn around the implications of such a joint venture for them as a church. What would be the academic expectations for candidates that would need to be met? What sort of gifts and prior experience? What about language? Could Zairian missionaries use their French or would they be expected to learn a new African dialect? What about the education of their children? What sort of diet adjustments might a Zairian family need to make?

a key issue

But the topic which generated more questions and, ultimately, the greatest concern had to do with the financial implications of what they were discussing. There was quick consensus that CMZa could indeed find worthy candidates for such a new cooperative venture with AIMM. But what would be expected of CMZa in the way of support? How were housing, health care, travel expense and field budget monies to be provided? If their responsibility was simply to find qualified candidates, they were prepared to proceed immediately.

Since it was known that an AIMM delegation was planning to visit Zaire in the summer of 1977, the CMZa Executive recommended that any further formal discussion of the proposal await the opportunity for face-to-face dialogue with AIMM representatives.

administrative questions

Meanwhile in North America, there was also a buzz of conjecture as to how a new partnership in mission with the Zaire Church might work. There was genuine openness and interest on the part of AIMM. There was so much about the idea which was appealing. After decades of work in Zaire, it now seemed right to launch out in a new effort in a new place in partnership with Zairian Mennonite missionaries.

AIMM, however, also had some questions. While the CMZa was hesitant about possible financial obligations it might incur, the AIMM Board was wondering about something else, namely, how such a partnership might be envisioned administratively. If the Zaire Church became, in some sense, a partner in mission with AIMM, how could the CMZa be given a genuine role and voice in the organization and administration of this new venture? Did not genuine ownership in the new effort demand this?

Considerable time was given to all of this in the 1977 spring board sessions. Staff had prepared a rather detailed study guide in which effort was made to highlight some of the key issues which needed to be addressed. Referring to the set of recommendations made by the investigative team the previous summer, the paper read in part: "It is at the point of the first recommendation that much thought, discussion and prayer still needs to be invested. The recommendation simply states: 'That the AIMM, in collaboration with the CMZa, open a field of missionary work in the Republic of Upper Volta.' How is this collaboration to be envisioned? structured? implemented?"

"Many questions come quickly to mind. With regard to administrative structure: 1) What new ingredient would CMZa bring to the administrative picture? Do we envision CMZa as being simply another constituent group of AIMM with the privilege of voice and vote on the board as this becomes workable? Or do we see AIMM and CMZa creating some new administrative entity? 2) In applying for legal status in Upper Volta, will it be AIMM applying as AIMM, or as a broader entity of some kind?"

"With regard to recruitment and functioning of Zairian staff: 1) Who is to determine the spiritual, educational and experiential qualifications to be required? What group is to serve as a candidate committee?

2) Would a Zairian couple have any administrative link with CMZa as opposed to AIMM? 3) In case of differences of opinion or personality clashes, where would final authority lie? In case of necessity, where would disciplinary authority reside? 4) Who establishes the personal support package and benefits for Zairian members of the team? Is AIMM scale to be taken as a model?"

"With regard to overall support patterns: 1) Do we feel that CMZa should carry the total support of its missionaries as do our other constituent groups? What about their travel costs? housing? field budgets? 2) Or, given the tremendous imbalance of resources available to them and to us, ought we seek to arrive at some sort of support ratio in which AIMM would share? If so, what? 50/50? 60/40? 80/20? something else?"

"With regard to program development: 1) How can we implement meaningful CMZa input in the spelling out of priorities, goals and strategies for Upper Volta? 2) What precautions can be taken so as not to completely overshadow and dominate CMZa in such a relationship?"

"With regard to church planting: 1) As people respond to a Gospel witness and begin to form local fellowships, what will be the identity of these groups? In what sort of tradition will they stand? With what broader church fellowship should they be encouraged to identify?" (1)

Board minutes of that session noted that special attention was given "to questions about structure, recruitment and function of Zairian staff, support patterns, program development and church planting. Three different options for structure and relationships were presented for discussion: Option 1: Both AIMM and CMZa would have representation on an Upper Volta Board with its seat in Zaire. There would be a Field Council in Upper Volta. The conjoint board would handle such matters as salaries of missionary personnel, field budgets and the proportions for CMZa and AIMM. Option 2: An AIMM-operated and -administered Upper Volta work. CMZa would provide missionary personnel and funds as available, but they would be channeled and cleared by AIMM. Communication would continue open with CMZa regarding the Upper Volta work. Option 3: If CMZa is not prepared for or desirous of involvement in Upper Volta at the present time, then AIMM would go ahead entirely on its own."

"Some cautionary notes sounded were that any conjoint arrangements need to be clearly defined with guidelines adequately understood; dual systems are usually fraught with problems; projections about Upper Volta at this point should be thoroughly explored with CMZa leadership. Keep flexible in procedures and structure planning and get as broad involvement as possible from CMZa in the decision making process now." (2)

It was against this background that an AIMM delegation traveled to Zaire in the summer of 1977. (3) In sessions with the CMZa administration, the Upper Volta issue soon surfaced. Zairian interest was obvious on the part of all. Did AIMM have a proposal to make to them? The delegation responded that AIMM had come with no prepackaged plan to hand to them. The delegation had come for open dialogue but with the concern that whatever arrangement was worked out, CMZa make some contribution, however modest, to a joint venture beyond that of providing missionary candidates.

It was at this point that President Kabangy observed that "a new element" had been introduced into the discussion which would require further serious reflection on their part. Since he was scheduled to spend some time in North America the summer of that same year, it was decided that he was to carry on the discussion with AIMM when he visited Elkhart.

decision time once again

It was late in August that President Kabangy's itinerary brought him to AIMM headquarters in Indiana. While the agenda for discussion was lengthy, both he and the AIMM Secretary knew that the weightiest item, by far, was the need to come to some conclusion regarding the proposed joint AIMM/CMZa mission venture in Upper Volta. In preparation for this dialogue, AIMM staff had drawn up a working paper which once again reviewed possible models of collaboration in the new venture in Upper Volta. It was once again stated that AIMM was ready to consider almost any sort of plan which provided for a viable and credible collaboration on the part of CMZa.

Kabangy and Bertsche quickly became aware that their discussion was taking them into uncharted territory and that there were many more questions than answers. Nonetheless, the idea of an AIMM/CMZa shared venture im Christian mission in a new part of Africa challenged and excited them both. It was in trying to tackle the issue of support and program costs that Kabangy expressed his frustration and personal sadness. The idea stirred him and he wished so much that CMZa could be part of the envisioned pioneering effort. While he was sure that the CMZa could offer candidates with the training, experience and commitment required for such an undertaking, he was unable to promise that the CMZa would be prepared to commit itself to any sort of annual financial share in the undertaking - - even the most modest and token share. CMZa was already under financial stress because of the failing Zaire economy, on the one hand, and the gradual limitation of AIMM contributions to CMZa's annual operating budget needs, on the other.

As the day-long discussion drew toward its close, there was a growing sense of resignation on the part of both men. President Kabangy knew that he could not commit his Church to even symbolic financial support for the new venture at that point. As for the AIMM Secretary, he too shared the Board's concern that the Zaire Church not be swept along into a relationship which was unrealistically conceived and which would launch the Church into its first mission effort outside Zaire's borders without credible participation in its cost.

A document prepared to clarify understandings arrived at that day read, partially, as follows: "1) that AIMM should proceed with the recruitment and preparation of personnel which will eventually be members of the missionary team in Upper Volta; 2) that the first personnel of the AIMM be placed in Upper Volta during the year 1978; 3) that in the meantime missionary personnel needs which could be open to and met by CMZa candidates be studied and made known to the CMZa; 4) that all information having to do with missionary life in Upper Volta and support costs be regularly transmitted to the CMZa and 5) that these AIMM/CMZa discussions be continued further in July of 1978." (4)

It was with a mix of disappointment and sadness that the two men initialed an agreement which fell short of what they had both hoped for. While the door was not closed on possible collaboration at a later date, both knew that, for the immediate future, AIMM would be opening the new work on its own.

CHAPTER 65   DEFINING A CORE STRATEGY

With the Entzes and the Rempels established in Orodara and settled into language study, reporting to the home office began to fill in some of the finer details - - not only of their setting but also of the dimension of the task to which AIMM had committed itself.

a land of hardy, resistant people

The term, Upper Volta, was coined by French colonial administrators and referred to a Colorado-sized area of land along the fringes of the Sahara Desert. Cradled under the arching loop of the Niger River, which makes its way to the sea through Nigeria to the east, Upper Volta itself is intersected by three branches of the Volta River - - the Black, Red and White, all of which converge in the land of Ghana across its southern border.

A land of rich history, caravan routes had for generations wound across its area en route to and from the coastal region beyond its borders to the south. Its central section, a plateau oriented from north to south, is the homeland of a large ethnic group known as the Mossi (pr. MOH-see). An energetic, proud people, they are known for a former kingdom which predated the arrival of French explorers in the 19th century. Under a king with a highly organized army, so effective were they in defending their homeland that the tide of Islam, which swept across North Africa, by-passed it to the north and south leaving a non-Islamic island in an Islamic sea which today is North Africa.

As the French colonial era ran its course, frontiers were finally fixed and what was then known as Upper Volta was granted its political independence in August 1960. Incorporated within its borders were also a mix of other tribal groups to the east and west of the Mossi plateau who had profited from the presence of their powerful neighbors. They had also resisted Islamic pressure while clinging resolutely to their traditional animistic cultures and world views.

In early discussion with local missionaries and government officials, frequent reference was made to the Senoufo people (pr. seh-NOO-foh). A large group, they live along the southwest frontier of the country spilling across its borders into Mali to the west and Ivory Coast to the south. Clinging to the traditions of their ancestors, they are known for tightly organized village life which centers upon an extensive system of animal sacrifice. Significant events of many kinds in their rural village settings such as birth, death, illness, digging wells, building/occupying new houses, seed time and harvest are all preceded and/or followed by the killing of an animal accompanied by appropriate rituals on the part of elders designated for these roles. Any deviation from the routine of sacrifice is feared and resisted.

Government figures found by AIMM personnel upon their arrival in the late 1970's, listed 68.7% of the population as being animist, 27.5% Muslim and 3.8% Christian. Statistics notwithstanding, however, there was marked and growing Muslim influence readily observable everywhere in the country. The flowing white garments and fez headdresses were much in evidence. Muslim times of fasting and daily prayer schedules were common knowledge across the country. The prostrated forms of Muslims on their kneeling mats were a common sight along road sides and in market places at the appointed times of prayer. Even in small villages, simple adobe "mosques" were to be found.

Surrounded on all sides by influential and powerful Muslim countries, it was no secret that Upper Volta was the focus of an intense desire to bring this island of unbelievers into the fold of Allah. By the 1970's, practicing Muslims of means and influence had found their way into government posts and the commercial community. They were not hesitant to use their influence and resources to make converts when and as they could. Although the Islamic faith, as understood and practiced in Saharan Africa, is strongly diluted by traditional African beliefs and cultures, it nonetheless is a growing force to be reckoned with. What earlier generations of Islamic crusaders could not accomplish with their swords is slowly but steadily being accomplished by gentler means.

not only Senoufo

Although an early AIMM focus was on the Senoufo people, it soon was learned that there were still other ethnic groups in the area which had been designated as AIMM territory. Little by little, new names and places were sketched onto the AIMM map. First of all, it was discovered that the town of Orodara itself lay in a pocket of people known as Siamou (pr. SEE-ah-moo). Gradually the map came to carry more and more tribal identifications. To the south and north were a mix of names such as Turka (pr. TOOR-kah), Gouin (pr.GOO-weh), Karaboro (pr. kah-rah-BO-roh), Tyefo (pr. TYAY-foh), and Tussian (pr.TOOSEE-yah). And if that was not enough, it was learned that among the Senoufo were to be found pockets of other people identified as Samogho (pr. sah-MOH-goh), Sembla (pr. SEH-mblah), and Bolon (pr. boh-LOH). All of them had their own distinct dialects. All of them, like their Senoufo neighbors, also clung tenaciously to their own ancestral practices and beliefs. From a purely human standpoint, the more that was learned, the more reason there was to wonder if AIMM's decision to begin a new ministry in southwest Upper Volta had been a bit hasty, naive or both!

some underlying principles

Pioneering AIMM personnel had not gone to Orodara without orientation. Prior to their departure from North America, there had been lengthy sessions of discussion and brainstorming with staff. There was keen awareness that the opening in Upper Volta offered AIMM a second chance at first generation evangelism, another opportunity of contacting tribal people essentially for the first time with a witness to Jesus Christ. There was a high level of concern, both on the part of staff and missionaries alike, to learn everything possible from an earlier chapter of similar pioneering work in Zaire. Out of such discussions there finally came a set of "commitments." In a study/reference paper of the time, the following is found: "Looking forward to the pioneering of a new Mennonite work in Upper Volta, we affirm: - a commitment to a holistic ministry which views physical and social problems along with spiritual needs with genuine concern and compassion; - a commitment to study local culture sympathetically and to seek to understand the 'why' of cultural traits and traditions; - a commitment to seek for cultural bridges by means of which understanding and appropriation of Christian faith and truth can be illuminated, facilitated and communicated; - a commitment to allow freedom for the expression of Christian faith in African terms and idiom; - a commitment to allow the Holy Spirit to speak to missionary and Upper/Voltan believers alike through joint study of his Word; - a commitment to seek to lead and to walk with local believers into serious discipleship in their local socio-cultural setting; - a commitment to embrace a simple life style and a desire to identify as closely as possible with the people among whom our missionary personnel will be living; - a commitment to form a fellowship of Anabaptist believers with national Christians in which the missionary and the African together form the body of Christ; - a commitment to focus on quality of discipleship within the body rather than upon growth for growth's sake." (1)

the need for a core strategy

What AIMM envisioned for its new work in Upper Volta was made quite clear at the very outset. What was much less clear was how the AIMM goals were to be achieved in the face of what seemed to be unpromising circumstances. Until that point, whatever "seed" had been sown among the Senoufo and neighboring tribal groups appeared to have fallen upon exceedingly hard and stony soil. How did AIMM, now, propose to go about reaching these same people?

Early on, AIMM personnel had made some observations as to the previous efforts of evangelism in the area. Regarding the work of the C&MA, it was noted that they had been successful in planting a strong church among the Bobo people who surrounded Bobo Dioulasso, their historic base of operations. It was further noted that in doing this, some of the C&MA missionaries had learned the tribal dialect of the Bobo people well and had established residence among them in several places outside the center of Bobo. While considerable energy and resources had been devoted to evangelistic itineraries among the Senoufo and neighboring tribes, the preaching was largely done in Dioula, the widely known and used trade language of western Africa. With the exception of one brief period at Orodara, no C&MA missionary personnel had ever taken up residence among any of these other ethnic groups. This observation meshed well with AIMM's own previous experience in Zaire. By far the strongest church communities emerged in areas where AIMM personnel had taken up residence among tribal people and mastered their dialects. Results had consistently been marginal among tribes where sporadic evangelistic itinerating had taken place while using languages other than their own.

Roman Catholics had also been present and active in Orodara and the surrounding region for decades. Their methodology was to establish a center, take up residence there and to make evangelistic forays into the hinterland around them. Efforts to place personnel in rural village settings or to learn the languages of the people they were attempting to win to the Catholic faith were rare. For them, there seemed yet to be additional problems. In a society which was gradually coming under increasing Muslim influence, the Catholic tolerance of alcoholic beverages was viewed askance. There was, further, the celibacy required of their clergy which was both puzzling and amusing to the Africans around them.

In observing and reflecting on the experience of missionaries of the area who had preceded them, the AIMM team and Board decided to borrow a page from the book of the widely known Wycliffe Bible Translators. With a single-minded commitment to giving people God's Word in their own language wherever they may be, they locate trained linguists among the people whose language they seek to learn. This has resulted in the frequent placement of their personnel in isolated and primitive settings. As a result of this approach, Wycliffe personnel have been able to reduce many languages to writing and to begin the process of opening Scripture to people in their own languages.

Although not part of their basic assignment, Wycliffe translators also consistently accomplish something else. Invariably in the course of their residence among and intimate interaction with people in their own setting, they leave some believers behind when their assignments are accomplished. There clearly are some dynamics which come into play in such circumstances which open doors for presenting the Gospel story to minds and hearts newly opened by bonds of trust and friendship. If this methodology produced such results for Wycliffe personnel, for what reason, AIMM personnel asked, would it not also be a productive approach for them in their new venture in Upper Volta?

So, the decision was made. AIMM would seek to add to its team candidates who could combine linguistic training with a deep desire to use these skills within the context of a Mennonite evangelism and church planting team.

But even as the decision was made, there was a certain apprehension on the part of the AIMM Board and staff. The new work in Upper Volta was already intimidating enough just in terms of the frontier kind of lifestyle which it demanded. Would not the adding of linguistic competence to candidate requirements complicate the whole recruitment process still further? Once again the pesky question surfaced: "Do we really have such people available to us in our AIMM circle of support?"

The answer was not long in coming.

CHAPTER 66   WATCHING GOD ASSEMBLE A TEAM

the impact of a year of VS in Zaire

Even before the AIMM Board had reached a point of decision regarding the strategy it proposed to follow in its new work in Upper Volta, God was at work preparing a team. It was already in the summer of 1975 that Anne Garber offered herself to AIMM for a year of voluntary service. Her offer coincided with a need at Nyanga Station in Zaire where several families were requesting tutoring help for their young school age youngsters. Garber, at this point, was midway in her college education. She had done the studies of her sophomore year in French in Quebec, Canada. Her grasp of French made her doubly attractive for VS at Nyanga since it was the location of a secondary school for Zairian girls which also had need of teaching staff.

Regarding her experience in Zaire she later wrote: "My stay in Zaire was an experience which I will never regret. The people I met and learned to know, the experience I had teaching both the children and the girls, the exposure to a different culture; these were all much more valuable than any university year could ever be. This past year has helped to shape my plans for the future. Several months ago I decided with confidence to major in Linguistics. . . . After one year of working in Zaire under your mission I have come away with a better vision of what I want to do in the future. The Lord will show his will in time." (1)

Returning to North America, Garber enrolled in the University of Ottawa. During her studies, she followed AIMM reporting on the new venture in Upper Volta with keen interest. Particularly was she drawn toward the growing AIMM focus on language analysis and translation of Scripture as a strategy of evangelism. In the spring of 1978, she wrote in part: "The year is drawing to a close and pending successful completion of my courses I shall graduate this spring with a BA in Linguistics. . . . I am happy to say that I have been granted a fellowship by the Linguistic Society of America covering the tuition and fees for the 1978 Linguistic Institute. This will take place from June 12 to August 5 at the University of Illinois at Urbana. . . . A couple [of instructors] are professors from the University of Ibadan in Nigeria and from the University of Ghana. Hopefully this summer will give me a chance to think more effectively about my possible involvement with African Linguistic research."

"As you know, I would like to enter a graduate program specializing in African Linguistics. . . . The reason I am writing you all of this is that I believe you may be interested in my plans and dreams for next year and the following years. I do not know how much linguistic work needs to be done under the auspices of a mission, but I would like to offer my services particularly in the context of the Senoufo people of Upper Volta. Please let me know how you feel. I trust the Lord will let us know at the right time what is his will for me." (2)

Upon attending the Linguistic Institute referred to in her letter, she decided to stay on campus and enroll in a graduate program in her chosen field of study. By the spring of 1980, she had earned her MA in this discipline and in an additional year of study was able to meet course requirements for her Ph.D. The conferring of her degree would await later research and the writing of a thesis.

By this time, Garber had formally applied via GC/COM for service with AIMM in Upper Volta and had been accepted. After studying one year at AMBS in Elkhart, IN, she became the first recruit with graduate level training in linguistics.

the result of a suggestion

The spring of 1981 saw Loren and Donna Entz on a six month study break in North America at AMBS, in Elkhart, where they were taking courses in missions and doing guided independent study in Islamics. It was here that they had frequent contact with fellow-Kansan Gertrude Roten who was at the time the Greek instructor at the institution.

It was through such contacts that Roten became particularly aware of the AIMM's search for missionary candidates with linguistic training. On one occasion she reminded Loren of one of his cousins, Gail Wiebe, who Roten knew was seeking opportunity for service somewhere overseas which would allow her to use her linguistic training. And where was she then? Working as a secretary in a bank in Whitewater, KS - - just waiting!

Approached by the Entzes, she in turn made inquiry of GC/COM personnel in Newton, KS. By the summer of 1981, the inter-Mennonite administrative cogs were turning. A COM memo in early June 1981 carried the following information: A graduate of Bethel College in North Newton, KS, in 1976 with majors in English and education, she contacted the GC mission office about a possible overseas assignment. When no opening was forthcoming, she taught 5th and 6th grades for two years at the Hopi Mission School in Oraibi, AZ. Working with American Indian children on a day-to-day basis provided Wiebe with an intriguing opportunity for cross-cultural experience and exposure to a different language. Her interest thus whetted, she took three semesters of work at the Wycliffe Summer Institute of Linguistics which is their basic orientation and preparation for assignment under their organization. (3)

Though encouraged to accept an assignment with the Wycliffe organization, Wiebe decided against the proposal because of her growing hope that sometime, somewhere there would be opportunity to use her training within a Mennonite mission team. So, when she finished her third semester of work, she opted to wait for the Lord's timing and leading in her life. In the meantime, she took a position in a local bank where the news about AIMM eventually reached her from the Entzes.

Meanwhile in Orodara, Upper Volta, there was detailed discussion about the placement of the first missionary-linguists. By this time it had been discovered that while Orodara, a frontier government post and market town, made a good base for AIMM in the area, linguistically it was a mixed bag. A variety of ethnic groups were represented there. The language of communication and commerce was the trade language, Dioula. The language of government and the schools was French. Furthermore, Orodara was situated in a pocket of people known as the Siamou who spoke a still different language. Given AIMM's major concern for reaching the Senoufo people, it was clear that the first team of linguists would need to be placed somewhere away from Orodara in a Senoufo village where the language was spoken in its own cultural setting.

When it became apparent that the first two AIMM linguists would be two single women, several concerns quickly surfaced. Was it feasible, or even possible, to place two single women in a rural African setting where no white-skinned person had ever lived before? And even if they could cope with a camping style of life on a long term basis, how would they be viewed by local village folk in a cultural setting where adult unmarried women were basically unheard of? And what about the candidates themselves? What right did the AIMM have to simply expect that two women, who were total strangers, be compatible enough to share living quarters under the pressures of a radically different environment, on the one hand, and the responsibility of pioneering a new chapter of AIMM history on the other? Valid, serious questions all.

Plans were made for Garber and Wiebe to meet in late summer of 1981 in Elkhart where Garber was enrolled as a student at AMBS. Wiebe would live temporarily on campus while commuting to the nearby University of Notre Dame for an introductory course in French. This arrangement made possible frequent, long talks as the two candidates shared their spiritual pilgrimages with each other. Also shared were their respective interest and competence in linguistics and their longing to use their tools within the context of an overseas Mennonite mission effort. Above all, they discovered that theirs was a mutual sense of God's clear leading in their lives which had brought them each to apply for service with AIMM at approximately the same time. True, they were different personalities and their focus in linguistic study had been somewhat different. But as the time came for Wiebe to leave Elkhart, they both let it be known that they felt they could and would be a functioning, productive missionary team in Upper Volta.

The 1981-1982 school year was devoted to further study for both of them, Garber at AMBS in the OMTC program ,and Wiebe at *Le Chambon* in southern France in French study.

a suggestion from an altitude of 35,000 feet

Gail Wiebe was aboard an airline jet between Chicago and New York on the first leg of her flight to France. Pulling several sheets of paper from her briefcase, she addressed a letter to the AIMM executive secretary in Elkhart which read, in part, as follows: "This is just a note to introduce a couple of friends who are interested in a possible connection with Mennonite mission work in Africa. While I have some time here on the plane I'd like to tell you a bit about them and, hopefully, it will help if you do receive communication from them."

"I met Dan Petersen and Kathy Fluth my first semester at SIL [the acronym for the Wycliffe Summer Institute of Linguistics] Dallas. Dan lived next door and Kathy became my roommate the following semester. I was attracted to them mostly because of their very sincere desire to live what they believed, even if it meant the struggle to live simply in a place like Dallas. Dan and Kathy had come, through their own study, to belief positions very similar to our Mennonite positions, even though their backgrounds were not directly Mennonite. Their personal relationships with the Lord are very important to them, as is active participation in a church."

"They are both trained in linguistics; Kathy having received her BA with that major and Dan receiving his Masters in Linguistics this fall semester. I speak of them together because they have known each other for several years and were married this summer. I believe that Kathy and Dan's desire is to work with a group of believers. They are not people who could sit behind a desk analyzing language all day without seeing a close connection between their linguistic work and church building. However, they are very sharp linguists, both creative and hardworking. . . . I want to drop this in the mail in New York." (4)

Wiebe's letter, written aloft on her flight to New York, sparked a remarkable paragraph in the chapter of AIMM's fielding of a team of missionary linguists in Upper Volta.

where to begin?

The two women arrived in Orodara within 48 hours of each other in April, 1982. Initially they spent time studying the local trade language but, by August, it was agreed that it was time to make some contacts with Senoufo villages. But where? How could they go about testing the options? How could they ascertain the degree of openness from one Senoufo village to the next? Where was the most reliable dialect spoken? With the Entzes they planned a tour of some well known villages. Of this experience Wiebe later wrote: "In mid-August we made a quick, drive-through tour of Sifarasso, Koloko, Mahon, Kangala and Kotoura on our way home from Sikasso" [pr. si-fah-RAH-soh, Koh-LOH-koh, MAH-hawn, kah-NGAH-lah, koh-too-RAH, si-KAH-soh; Sikasso is an important center just across the border in Mali where a C&MA couple, Ralph and Ruth Herber, had for years worked among the Senoufo people on their side of the border. The AIMM missionaries went to hear of their experience and to seek their counsel].

"The first week in October the Secretary of the *Canton*, [a local civil servant] himself a Tagba [pr. TAHG-bah, a major Senoufo clan], took us on an official tour to the same five villages plus Oueleni [pr. oo-way-LAY-ni]. We introduced ourselves to the chiefs and responsible elders explaining that we were with the Protestant Church in Orodara and that we hoped to move into a village to learn Tagba; that we had the skills to put their language into writing."

"We had polite welcomes in all the villages but felt most warmly received in Kotoura and Oueleni. Oueleni is at the edge of the Tagba area and has some language variations, so we couldn't consider it. . . . Kotoura has a central location within the Tagba area though it is not on a main road. It is a completely Senoufo village . . . so 2 weeks ago we went out for a day, greeting and making arrangements for this weekend stay."

"In our conversation with the chief and elders, they've said it would be possible for us to live with a family for 3 months and that we will need more permanent housing after harvesting is completed in January or February. The decision has been made to help us in every way possible. So we plan to go out for the day of the 18th of November with Dennis and to move on the 24th. . . . I'm really thankful for the way he Lord has led us to choose Kotoura . . . and for the way He's prepared the people of Kotoura to welcome us." (5)

Little did anyone know, at that point, the mission/church history that would be spun around the name "Kotoura" in the years ahead.

Regarding their introductory weekend visit, Wiebe wrote: "We went by cycle on Friday, arriving in the early evening. After we had rested and eaten at the chief's concession, his son took us to the village center where balaphones and drums were playing and young men were dancing. After a few minutes he explained that this was the last evening of *la fête du diable*! [i.e., the celebration of the devil]. What a beginning! We were given a very warm welcome. Our housing was a 2-room rectangular hut, and food was abundant. Everyone seemed to know why we were there and to make it their personal responsibility to teach us their language; an exhausting but efficient language-learning method. Their tiny Sunday morning market consisted of 10 or 15 sellers, none of whom sold vegetables." (6)

It was just eight weeks after their move to Kotoura that an administrative trip was made by AIMM board member Andy Rupp and Secretary Jim Bertsche. A trip journal carried some observations regarding the village context into which the two missionary women were in process of settling. "The road toward Mali . . . is in good shape. After the turn south, [toward Kotoura] the road becomes a typical bush trail. No trouble in dry season but would have some bad water holes in rainy season. The women are temporarily housed in the back rooms of a cement block dispensary built for the village by one of the native sons now away in one of the urban centers. A front room facing the road houses a little private pharmacy."

"Sounds like there are only two or three wells in the whole village so the women have to carry their water like everyone else. Also sounds like the Senoufo have a 'central john' for the village! A large crowd quickly assembled, especially children, partially to see the little blond missionary [Rempel] children. Lots of confusion, odors and noise. African culture may vary significantly from area to area but some things in Africa are still everywhere the same, e.g., the appearance of a black skin in a dusty dry season, the curiosity of a rural people and corresponding lack of privacy, the importance of seniority and status of clan elders, striking friendliness and an animistic world -view."

"After initial greetings . . . we walked over to the acting chief's house where we were offered chairs under a shelter at his doorstep. There were some pleasantries exchanged; Andy and I were introduced. The chief Kunandi (pr. koo-NAH-ndi) sat with two of his elders. . . . He is a tall, spare, quiet, kindly, dignified sort of person and a praying Muslim. He wore a blue robe with a small safety pin holding the front slit opening at the throat together."

Invited to speak, the AIMM Secretary made the following points: "Appreciation was expressed for their kind welcome to their village and for the welcome extended the two missionary women. We've come because we are interested in you and your language. We could give you many things such as bicycles, clothing, houses but all of these will eventually 'die.' But if we can give you words of wisdom and truth, these will last forever. We want to learn your language so we can share with you God's Word in your own language. Take good care of our missionaries we are leaving with you. . . . I hope to come to see you again." (7)

As good as his word, Chief Kunandi came to the missionaries after their harvest season to discuss their permanent location in his village. A couple of available spots were visited but both would have somewhat isolated Garber and Wiebe from the daily flow of village life. Sensing their desire to really live among the people, Chief Kunandi invited them to visit yet another location - - a parcel of ground which he himself owned. Might this be satisfactory? It was an ideal location and they quickly accepted. One beautiful feature was an immense tree which provided a great patch of shade at all hours of the day. It furthermore was situated where it was readily visible and available to the villagers in their daily and weekly routines of life.

Over a period of several months, Dennis Rempel demonstrated his mix of abilities by directing the construction of a simple three-room cement block house. Adjacent to it was built an accompanying round adobe thatch-roofed kitchen and another two room thatch and stick set of "bedrooms" with a third "shower room." A pit latrine was dug at an edge of the yard. But the greatest challenge for Rempel would prove to be the women's need of a well of their own.

Finding water in this semiarid part of Africa can be and usually is a grueling task. At Kotoura, the few village wells had all been hand dug and went to depths of 60 feet and better. In the digging process, the deepening pits lacked adequate ventilation with the result that dangerous methane gas often accumulated which could quickly render the digger unconscious. Thus it was that a rope was always tied about the waist of those laboring below filling buckets with excavated dirt to be hand pulled to the surface. Whenever, as frequently happened, the man working below fell silent or inactive, he was unceremoniously hoisted to the surface where he was revived in the fresh air.

The time eventually came when the women would write about feeling "at home" in Kotoura. They had everything they could want; their own well, their own pit latrine, their own huge shade tree, their own ready access to the village and its people and the people's equal access to them. On one occasion, one of them wrote: "We're getting settled in our new home. It's beautiful and cool and more private. It seems luxurious after our pharmacy home." (8)

meanwhile in Texas

Back in North America, the letter written by Wiebe on a flight between Chicago and New York in the fall of 1981 had triggered a steady series of consequences. Upon receiving the letter, the AIMM executive secretary immediately called the Petersens at the University of Texas where their study program with the Wycliffe organization, based on that campus, was coming to a close. With that call, their story began to unfold.

In a responding letter they wrote: "We come from the Minnesota area, but are presently in Dallas where we have both taken the translation/literacy training offered by the Summer Institute of Linguistics/Wycliffe Bible Translators. Kathy's program completed her BA in sociology, and my studies should end this fall with an MA in linguistics from the U. of Texas. We first came here for this training with a clear desire to be used of the Lord in missions but with no certain direction in mind beyond SIL. . . . As our studies have progressed, we have often wished that opportunities existed for such work with a Mennonite mission; . . . we both have Mennonite family histories, and our personal beliefs are quite similar to traditional Anabaptist norms . . . but our few contacts with current Mennonite mission work informed us of little need for linguistic-trained workers. Gail and Anne have suggested, however, that you might be interested in knowing of our situation. We would certainly be interested in possibilities of your expanding linguistic work in Upper Volta. Unless some such unexpected opportunity arises, we plan to apply to WBT/SIL." (9)

In a second letter, written a few days later, Petersens shared further about their backgrounds. Regarding Kathy, "She grew up in the Cameroonian bush, at the North American Baptist Mission hospital where her father is a doctor. Her mother's family are Russian-German Mennonites from Mt. Lake, MN." In the same letter Dan went on to explain that he had a great aunt named Fanny Schmallenberger, who had been a long time missionary with the Congo Inland Mission. Concerning this family link he commented: "Our family has supported Aunt Fanny's work . . . since as early as my childhood memory can recall."

The Petersens continued: "Certainly the most significant component of our relationship with Mennonites is our spiritual affinity to distinctively Mennonite beliefs. . . . Our location has not, unfortunately, allowed us involvement in a Mennonite church." So we have "immersed ourselves in an inner-city black church near us in South Dallas. . . . And our interests/aptitudes? . . . We bake our bread, sew our clothes, fix our car, sing, run, climb mountains, read books, have tea with friends, fish of an evening, enjoy a Bach motet. We hope this has been helpful. Until we hear from you again . . ." (10)

Correspondence between Elkhart and Dallas continued. In a letter addressed to the AIMM office in November, they wrote: "You asked whether we are 'open to long-range involvement in overseas missions.' We are not only open, we have planned on little else for the past three years. Because of our involvement here at Dallas SIL, we have naturally looked most into the options available with them. The organization is interested in us. . . .We are presently just waiting, however, and have not made any decisions either way. . . The only other option left at this time is our contact with you. . . . We continue to wait prayerfully for your response." (11)

Even as AIMM office staff was in conversation with the Petersens in Texas, there was also dialogue with Rev. Milo Nussbaum, the founding pastor of the EMC Grace Church in Morton, IL. A long-time AIMM Board member, Nussbaum followed AIMM's ongoing story with keen interest. Learning of the Petersens and their family connections in his Illinois community, he invited them to visit the church. From that point events moved swiftly. The Grace Church pledged significant financial support. January 1982 found them at AMBS in Elkhart for courses in the OMTC program there. By the fall of 1982, they were in France for language study and in May of '83 they arrived in Orodara. Even as they studied Dioula, the trade language, they were part of animated team planning. Viewed as the next linguistic team, there was a question as to their long-term placement. It was clearly to be among the Senoufo, but where?

a place called N'Dorola (pr. ndo-roh-LAH)

By the summer of 1984, the Garber-Wiebe team was well settled to the southwest of Orodara among a people sometimes referred to as the Southern Senoufo. But, by then, it was known that there was another major grouping, referred to as the Northern Senoufo, which numbered in the tens of thousands and had their own distinct dialect. Located quite centrally among them, some 75 miles to the north of Orodara, was another government outpost called N'Dorola. A bush road between the two centers was well enough maintained to permit year-round travel. Any roads beyond, however, were only passable six months of the year and then only by four wheel drive vehicles. Hotter, drier and dustier than Orodara to the south, it was described by some as "the place where the real Sahel begins." Living and working there clearly would be more demanding than at Orodara. Undaunted by the climate or the setting, the Petersens began to make contacts with the village elders. Upon making a formal inquiry about settling in their village, the N'Dorola chief called his elders together. An official invitation quickly ensued with the assurance that they would be given any available plot in the village as a place to establish their home.

After cement floors and cement block walls were put in place by African artisans, a VS building team was pulled together and led by Orville Fricke, a building contractor from the EMC Church of Wauseon, OH. (He was joined by Rob Fricke, Dale Klopfenstein, Elmer Oyer Jr., Derald Seiler and Jim Yoder. All, like Fricke, paid their own way.) The structure was roofed and some interior finishing work added. A small kitchen and well were installed nearby. Strangely enough, amidst a bleak and often dusty landscape, the water level at this village was high due to its location near a low, marshy area. A shallow well and a hand pump sufficed to produce a good supply of water. A large black painted steel tank was placed atop a cement block base. Via solar heating there was a daily supply of warm water for showering. With the installation of a pit latrine in an opposite corner of the plot, the Petersens were able to settle into their new location among the Northern Senoufo before the rainy season of 1985.

an inquiry from Saskatchewan

Even as the first two linguistic teams were being processed and placed, a letter written the spring of 1980 lay in AIMM files in Elkhart. It read in part: "My wife and I [Paul and Lois Fast Thiessen] have been considering career missions as a future ministry for a number of years already. As we have studied these last three years here at the Briercrest Bible Institute, God has confirmed our interest in the area of linguistics and Bible translation. At this time we are considering the needs and opportunities of service in this field. Does your mission have any openings for linguists or Bible translators?" (12) In closing their letter they explained that they had become aware of AIMM and its involvement with Scripture translation through the work of fellow Canadians Ben and Helen Reimer Eidse and their revision of the Chokwe Bible in Zaire.

Although upon graduation the Thiessens opted to accept a two-year assignment of evangelism in northern Saskatchewan, correspondence with AIMM continued and packets of material were forwarded for their study and prayer. In the meantime, they were using their summers for study sessions with the Wycliffe Summer Institute of Linguistics.

By the fall of 1983, their applications for service with AIMM had been processed and they traveled to southern France for French study. By August, 1984, they were in Orodara.

the Siamou too

With two linguistic teams placed among the Senoufo, what was the next priority to be? By this time there was growing awareness of and concern for the Siamou (pr.SEE-ah-moo) people who completely encircled Orodara on all sides. As a matter of fact, they comprised a significant part of the population of Orodara itself. They too, like the Senoufo, remained basically untouched by the Gospel. Situated literally at the front door of AIMM personnel since their arrival at Orodara, their need could no longer be ignored. They, and their language, would become the primary assignment for the Thiessens.

Initially it was thought that, given the sizeable contingent of Siamou right in Orodara, the Thiessens could begin their study of the language right there. It was soon discovered, however, this would not be feasible. By the spring of 1985, they moved to a village some nine miles out of Orodara named Tin (pr. like the English word tan without sounding the letter "n"). Here they were situated in a Siamou village where much of their culture was intact and where the language of everyday life was that of their forefathers. They initially lived in the courtyard of a village family which took them in as their guests.

A fascinating insight into this early village "live in" experience was provided by Lois in a newsletter of that time. "A little African girl suddenly appears framed in the doorway of our thatch-roofed mud hut. *Tombelay*, she calls, *Bay mukal di*. She's calling me to come and eat. Ruthie and I wash our hands and pick up our low stool and tupperware cup of water, then make our way across the star-lit courtyard to the circle of women gathered for the evening meal. We slip our stool into the circle and sit down, our right sides toward the inside of the circle. On the ground in the middle are two bowls of food. One, a large bowl of *mukal*, which is a thick porridge of millet flour cooked in water. (It resembles gray cream-of-wheat cooked so thick that it holds its shape.) Beside the *mukal* is a small earthen bowl with *fra* or sauce. It's a thinnish sauce made with water, ground tomatoes, onions and hot peppers."

"I look around the circle of women and children, their faces dimly lit up by a small storm lantern on the ground. There are the three wives of the 'old man,' then there are two of his brothers' wives and three younger women who are the wives of older sons in the family. There are also some girls and little children. After the calabash with hand washing water has been passed around, one of the oldest women takes a piece of *mukal* from the bowl and we begin. With my right hand I pull off a lump from the mass in the bowl (often it's too hot for my sensitive fingers, and the women graciously find 'cool' parts for me). I casually work this lump in my hand until the moment is right for dipping it into the *fra*. I'm careful when dipping, not to let my fingers touch the sauce too much, then with a little twist of the wrist I lift out my lump and pop it into my mouth. After that I delicately lick my fingers before taking some more . . . . "

In her account, Thiessen describes the banter and story telling that often takes place around the circle of women as they eat. Then one of the older women says that she has finished eating. She then "calls for the hand washing calabash and moves her stool a little ways out of the circle. One by one the rest of us finish eating and the children finish anything still left in the bowls. There's rarely any food left in the bowls when they're carried back to the kitchen hut. Some women leave to make evening preparations for bed. Several children are already asleep on straw mats and their mothers wake them to lead them into the round sleeping huts. Others sit in the faint light shelling peanuts into a basket. Occasionally someone speaks to me. I try hard to remember all the Siamou I know, but usually I just can't get the message without a lot of gesturing and pantomime. We all laugh and have fun trying to get new sounds and their matching ideas into my head."

Lois then reflected on their new setting and life in the Siamou village of Tin. "There's so little, so very little we can say to each other . . . only a few, halting words in Siamou but we live together and we're daily getting to know each other. . . . My senses reel sometimes with all the new sights, sounds, smells, thoughts. In the past three weeks I have learned to wash my clothes at the river, eat with my hands, take my evening shower out under the stars, greet people . . . how could I ever write it all down?"

"Sometimes I think about Canada. What would these African friends think of my homeland? In the wildest stretches of imagination they could not imagine the luxury I've left behind. They'll never know. I think about Jesus. If I pushed my own imagination to its limits I couldn't even begin to picture the beautiful home He left behind when He came to live on earth for me. Some day, though, my African friends and I will be together in that home in Heaven and there will be no culture or language barriers between us. We will see only Jesus, the One we will worship together." (13)

In due time a cement block home was erected on a village plot given by the elders. The cement work was done by African masons. It was roofed by the same VS team from Wauseon, OH, which had helped the Petersens settle in at N'Dorola.

By the summer of 1985 three AIMM linguistic missionary teams had been installed in the African bush country in western Upper Volta.

More were to follow.

CHAPTER 67   OH WE OF LITTLE FAITH!

As new AIMM missionaries arrived, one after the other, and settled into their locations and assignments, their overall frame of mind was essentially the same. Given the somber warnings regarding the resistant people among whom they were proposing to work, it was assumed that the missionary team might well have to labor and witness for years on their own before they would see any response.

But one day in 1979, during the Entzes first year in Orodara, there was a knock at their door. Responding, they found a tall, slim, neatly dressed young man. A bicycle was leaning against a nearby mango tree. In a quiet, gracious manner he opened a conversation with the Entzes. He came from a village some 10 miles to the south of Orodara. He explained that he had met a mason from Orodara who was building a house in his village. He had asked the mason if perchance there were any Protestants living in Orodara. The mason responded: "Yes, there are some Protestant missionaries who have recently arrived there. I have met them."

The visitor at the Entzes' back door that morning had come to seek out the white newcomers and to make inquiry for himself.

Siaka Traore (pr. see-AH-kah trah-OR-ay)

Over the ensuing months and years, Orodara missionaries were to become intimately acquainted with this young man and his amazing story. He had been born twenty-four years earlier into the home of a prosperous Muslim plantation owner in south central Ivory Coast. As a child he was sent to a local Koranic school. Finishing primary school, he was sent by his father to enroll in a secondary school

A bright student, he easily moved through the first three-year cycle of the French secondary system. On vacations he rode the train home to visit family and friends. On one such trip he encountered a colporteur in a railway station. Out of curiosity he purchased a French New Testament which he began to read. Although he had no acquaintance with or understanding of the Christian faith, the New Testament fascinated him. Back at school he began to seek out other Christians. For a time he worshiped at a local Catholic Church. Later he attended a Baptist chapel - - all this while reading and pondering the New Testament bought in a railway station. While he sensed a strange power in the passages he was reading, there were many unanswered questions.

Upon finishing the lower three-year cycle of secondary schooling, he felt restless and decided to drop out and go to Upper Volta where an uncle was a shopkeeper in a village just south of Orodara among their fellow clansmen, the Turka people (pr. TOOR-kah). When it became clear that he had no interest in further study at the time, his uncle put him to work in his store. With considerable leisure, he not only continued reading his New Testament but also happened across French language broadcasts from ELWA, the Christian radio station based on the west coast of Africa in Liberia. Via these broadcasts he began to hear systematic teaching regarding the Scriptures he had been reading and thinking about so much. The Holy Spirit used this channel of instruction to bring convicting light to Siaka's mind and heart. Entirely alone in his village, he struggled his way to a conversion experience which was to transform his life.

Though he had, in his own way, reached out a hand of faith to the Lord and had experienced a profound encounter with his grace, there was yet much he wanted to know. He was also hungry for fellowship with other Christians. But in his rural context, there was no place to turn. There were no other Christians in his village. It was at this point in his life that the commuting mason told him about new white-skinned residents in Orodara ten miles to the north. It was shortly thereafter that the Entzes answered the knock at their door.

Once assured that they were indeed missionaries, he briefly told them his story and then asked: "If I come to your house a couple of times a week, would you teach me more about the Christian faith?" There was quick assurance and a schedule was agreed upon. It did not take many such study sessions for the AIMM missionaries to discover that behind the soft-spoken, appreciative demeanor of this young man was a sharp intelligence coupled with a profound commitment to Christ. Here was a potential church leader who needed to be encouraged and further trained.

An initial step was a school year in a Bible Institute operated by the C&MA in Bobo. Though not yet baptized, Siaka's abilities were quickly evident and he was admitted into the first year of study. In this setting his innate leadership qualities quickly surfaced among his fellow students. Though he had a better educational background than most of them, there was nothing of condescension in his manner among them. By year's end, it had become clear that his academic level was well beyond that of the training program in which he was enrolled.

Returning to Orodara at the end of the school year, he let it be known that he wanted to follow his Lord in a public act of baptism. Much sooner than they had originally dared to hope, the Orodara missionaries were called to lay plans for their first baptismal service.

When his Muslim father and family heard about this, there was swift reaction. The first response took the form of enticements to give up his idea which would bring shame upon them all in their village. If it was more schooling he was interested in, they would provide money for study in a choice Muslim school in the neighboring country of Niger. When Siaka politely declined this offer, the family attitude hardened. If he insisted on following through with this proposal of Christian baptism, he would be formally cut off from his family. Not only did this mean that he could no longer count on any material or financial help from them, they would also socially disown him. In discussing all of this with missionaries and the little circle of believers in Orodara, he simply said: "I've made my choice to follow Jesus. I cannot turn back."

Plans were laid for October 5, 1980. A little stream down the hill from Orodara was temporarily dammed to provide a small pool of waist deep water. Word was circulated in Orodara that a Christian believer was to be baptized in a service open to all. There was, by this time, a small handful of Christians in Orodara who had come in from other areas and who were worshiping with the missionaries on a regular basis. They entered enthusiastically into the planning for the baptism of the first believer under the sponsorship of the new AIMM ministry in town.

A missionary letter of the time clearly reflected the flavor and excitement of the occasion: "It happened, yes it really did. Yesterday was a big day, and it will be remembered for some time."

The letter went on to describe the festivities as having taken place in three stages. First there was a gathering of the believers at the chapel in Orodara at which time basic Christian beliefs were reviewed and Anabaptist understandings highlighted. It was then noted that a person had asked to join the group and that today, via baptism, he would be welcomed into their fellowship. After a prayer and a hymn, the group made its way through the town and down the hill to the little stream.

The baptismal service was brief. Some missionaries made some comments, as did Siaka himself, underscoring that his baptism in water signified God's cleansing and saving grace which he had experienced in his life. He wanted all to understand that his action was a public witness to his conversion experience and his commitment to be a follower of Jesus.

Returning back up the hill, they all went to the courtyard of the house where Siaka was living where the little group of believers organized a time of joyous celebration complete with music and generous servings of food for all who came.

The most memorable event of all, that day, was the formal establishment of the first Mennonite Congregation in Upper Volta. There were nine charter members, i.e. four local Christians, four missionaries (1) and Siaka Traore.

difficult, but possible

Even amidst the celebration of this first Christian baptism, there was an underlying question which needed to be addressed immediately. What about Siaka's ongoing training? His potential for university-level study was clear, but first there was the need to pursue his secondary education which had been earlier dropped in Ivory Coast. There were schools to which he could go but all would take him away from Orodara. This both he and the little circle of Christians there were reluctant to consider. His influence and witness as a convert out of a Muslim family were already making an impact in their community.

There was a further problem. Given the rupture his baptism had caused with his family, he could count on no help whatsoever from them. Not only was there a question of his further education. There were also pressing needs for food, shelter and clothing which needed to be met. As for these latter concerns, his earlier experience in his uncle's store in his home village came into play. In discussion with AIMM missionaries it was decided to help him secure a stock of books and paper supplies. Orodara, a busy market town, was accustomed to vendors displaying their wares under the shade of mango trees along the bustling main thoroughfare. From time to time Siaka also spread his mat and display his wares. Not only did this provide him with a modest margin of profit but it also afforded endless opportunities for conversation with those who passed by, conversations which frequently turned to questions of religious faith.

As for further study, in the fall of 1981 Siaka enrolled in a correspondence school in Paris, France, and began the upper three-year cycle of his secondary education via mail! Well aware of the rigors of this upper cycle in the French system, missionaries cautiously wondered if he really thought he could manage this successfully via correspondence? His response was simple: "It will be difficult, but it is possible."

Once decided, he settled into a weekly routine which saw him arise a couple of hours before daybreak, five and six mornings a week, to study in his little room by lamp light while the village around him was still cloaked in slumber. Week in and week out he made his way to the post office of that dusty frontier town to mail and to receive his written work. He had set a path for himself and he would follow it.

the son of a chief

Christmas of 1982 found Anne Garber and Gail Wiebe newly installed in Kotoura. Having arrived just the month before, they had their hands full with the multitudinous details of trying to adjust to and fit into life in a Senoufo village. But could they allow their first December in Kotoura to pass without some effort to witness to the birth and the person of Jesus? No, they could not, but what could possibly be done? Their own grasp of the local language was extremely limited. Furthermore, in a rural African society powerfully oriented toward male dominance, how much leadership could they or dared they attempt as female newcomers to the village?

They sought the counsel of the little cluster of believers and fellow missionaries in Orodara. It was consequently decided that Siaka would join them for a couple of days over Christmas at Kotoura and that they together would seek a way to explain the meaning of Christmas for the first time to the Tagba speaking Senoufo of that village.

First, the chief was approached with the request to hold a meeting in the village "square," an open area reserved for public gatherings. Their request granted, a time was set for the early evening of Christmas day. Siaka would speak in the trade language of the area. But this was not good enough. Though most of the men would understand quite a bit, few if any women and children would hear what was said. They needed someone who could translate what was said into the mother tongue of the Senoufo villagers. They wanted to make certain that everyone heard, in their own tongue, this first ever public witness to Jesus. This problem was quickly solved in the person of Cheba (pr. tshay-BAH), the son of the village chief.

It had been soon after their arrival in the village that Chief Kunandi had presented his son to them. Knowing that they would often have questions and would often need information, he designated one of his sons as the person of his family to whom they could turn whenever they needed help. Twenty-four years old and the husband of two wives, he was the father of three children. By nature an alert, friendly, outgoing person, he soon made it a practice to drop by the missionaries' house to greet them and to inquire if they needed anything. Eager to improve his reading skills, he started to come evenings for help in reading French and Bambara (pr. bah-MBAH-rah), an area language from which the Dioula trade language was derived.

Concerning those early evenings of tutoring, Garber on one occasion wrote: "One night he picked up a children's book account of Jesus' parable of the prodigal son. I told him a bit of the story. He was immediately interested and announced his desire to learn how to read it. After a few nights of laboriously working on words that he did not really understand, our language helper picked up the book and translated it into Tagba for Cheba. You should have seen how excited they were about that story. They couldn't really tell me why they liked it so much but they were obviously impressed." On one occasion he told the women he wished the stories could be translated into the language of his people. To this they replied: " That's why we have come." (2)

When, three weeks later, Garber and Wiebe were discussing whom they might ask to translate for Siaka in the public gathering on Christmas evening, Cheba was a ready and obvious solution. In a later written report, Anne Garber described that historic gathering : "Evening had come in Kotoura. The supper meal of guinea hen served in rich tomato sauce over rice was finished and we proceeded to the kitchen hut to congratulate the cooks, women of the chief's family. Then Cheba, the chief's son, led us to the social center of the village. The kerosene pressure lantern was lit, chairs appeared and the crowd began to gather. Once the children were quieted down and the elders were in their places, we were ready to begin."

"Cheba stood up and introduced Siaka, a Voltaic Christian from Orodara. The topic of the evening: 'What Christmas Means to Christians.' The people listened attentively as Siaka explained who Jesus was and why God sent him into the world. Everything that Siaka said was totally new for these partly Muslim, partly animist people. It provided a lot of food for thought. When Siaka sat down people stayed in their places and murmured quietly among themselves. Soon, an elder challenged Siaka with a question. Was he a little skeptical of this young man who claimed to possess the wisdom of an elder? A little later the chief first thanked Siaka for coming and then excused himself because of a funeral in the village. But the people continued to sit and reflect. Even the children were quiet. Finally Cheba stood up and told everybody they could go home. . . ."

"The day after Christmas, two elders of the village came by to thank Siaka for his talk, and to exchange a few words of wisdom with him. The elders and the chief invited him to come back again periodically to talk more about the same things. We were especially touched that these older men appreciated and welcomed words of wisdom from a man half their age." (3)

Among those present that Christmas evening in the village public square, no one had followed Siaka's presentation with greater interest than his translator, Cheba, the chief's son. He, like his fellow villagers, had heard a story entirely new to him. It was amazing news. In the evenings as he continued coming to the home of the missionaries for tutoring in reading, he frequently asked questions about "the story."

Meanwhile the missionaries in Orodara had for some time been discussing the idea of sponsoring open air meetings in that center with a converted ex-Muslim as the evangelist. Named Almamy (pr. ahl-MAH-mee), he was from Ivory Coast and the descendent of a long line of influential Muslim leaders. He had experienced a genuine conversion to Christ and was much in demand as a gifted voice of Christian witness. By October, 1983 prayers and plans finally came together. Almamy could come and would speak at meetings arranged and publicized by the Orodara Mennonite Christians.

In Kotoura, Garber and Wiebe followed these plans with great interest. How might all of this fit into their situation in their village? One day they told Cheba of what was being planned in Orodara and asked if he might be interested in attending one of the scheduled meetings. "Not one, but all of them" was his reply! Garber later picked up the story as follows: "As Cheba sat and listened to Almamy . . . he became convinced that he wanted to commit his life to Christ. On Saturday night, October 15, 1983, in the privacy and quietness of the Rempels' courtyard, Cheba told Almamy that he wanted to become a Christian. Almamy called Gail and I over and others gathered around us as he led Cheba in a prayer of confession and dedication to Jesus Christ. The next morning Cheba drank in every word of Siaka's message in Dioula before returning to Kotoura a new man."

"Of course, the first and natural act of a new and excited Christian is to spread the good news. The first night back, Cheba took us to a sick cousin of his to pray for him. Gail and I had done this for other family members in the past; this time it was Cheba who took the initiative. In the following days, he came morning and night to sing and pray with us, each time bringing along a few friends. Within a week, two younger cousins and a close friend of Cheba's decided to follow Christ. A week later, Cheba's younger brother made a decision . . . ."

"Since then, morning meetings have become less important, with the occasional person or persons coming by before taking off to the fields for the day. In contrast, the after supper hours have become prime time for new believers as well as their friends to come by and learn some more. During the study session of the evening, beginners work through the Dioula syllabary or labor away with the French primer, while Cheba and his friend Ousmane [pr. oos-MAH-nay] read Biblical materials in French or Bambara . . . . At 9:30 P.M. or later, we stop reading and sing a few songs before finishing in prayer. Lately, the sessions have been finished off with a few words of wisdom from the Bible or a Bible story to encourage the new believers on this new road that they have taken. They have also begun memorizing Bible verses which they thoroughly enjoy doing." (4)

Excitement was in the air. No one on the missionary team had ever imagined that there would so soon be a growing nucleus of believers in the Senoufo village of Kotoura. But attracted by the fervent witness of Cheba, the chief's son, new individuals kept coming to their times of Bible study, singing and prayer. Regular visits were made by Orodara personnel to meet with and instruct the little cluster of new believers. On one such occasion, the teaching session had to do with the topic of sacrifice, a dominant and powerful theme in the Senoufo culture. Effort was made to underscore the Scriptural teaching that there was no longer need for blood sacrifices since Jesus on the cross had become the one and final sacrifice for us all.

It was not long after that this issue became a crisis for Cheba. As his pregnant first wife approached full term, the village elders reminded him that their custom demanded that he, the husband, offer a chicken to assure the safety of both the woman and child during delivery. A missionary letter of the time comments: "Cheba was shaken. We prayed hard and he refused to do it. Six days after the meeting, his wife Mariam gave birth to a bawling baby boy. Both mother and son are doing just fine, thank-you! There was a proud and relieved Daddy that day." (5)

It was the tradition of the Muslim villagers to seek the counsel of the local Muslim leader in naming a newborn child. Thus it was that Cheba came to Garber and Wiebe for suggestions. Taken aback, their first reaction was to demur. After Cheba explained the reason for his request, they finally made two tentative suggestions - - Elijah or Daniel, two examples out of Old Testament history of men who defied the powers of false gods and had demonstrated that the true God is more powerful than the lesser gods of this world. Cheba quickly responded: "His name will be Daniel."

It was on May 19, 1984, that the first five Kotoura believers were baptized. Among them was Cheba. Amidst the joy of witnessing the dramatic spiritual growth of "the son of the chief," little did the missionaries and the newly-established, embryo church of Kotoura know that his invaluable leadership was to be cut short all too soon.

go find Bakary (pr. bah-kah-REE)

It was not long after Paul and Lois Thiessen's arrival in Orodara in the fall of 1984 that Paul and fellow missionary Dan Petersen traveled by motor bikes to the Siamou village of Tin, some nine miles to the north. With a population of upwards of 2,000 people, it was solidly Siamou in composition. Their language was constantly in use throughout the village by all age groups. Indeed, this was the primary reason which had brought the two men to pay the village a visit.

But not only was the village of Tin a place where the language of the Siamou people could be heard and their culture observed, it was also a village which reflected the near total conversion of that ethnic group to Islam a generation or two earlier. In the village there was no resident adult who did not profess at least nominal allegiance to the Islamic faith.

Riding slowly along the main road, the missionaries came to a stop before a courtyard where some older men were engaged in conversation. The visitors were greeted politely but conversation quickly became a problem. Not yet fluent in Dioula, the trade language, the missionaries were trying to use French, a language the village men did not understand at all well. Then one of elders gestured toward the courtyard just across the road and called out: "Go find Bakary." Little did anyone present that day imagine the long range impact that roadside encounter was to have on this young man's life.

Coulibally Bakary (pr. koo-li-bah-LEE bah-kah-REE) was one of the few young men of his village age group who had had the opportunity of attending primary school for any length of time. In the process he had learned to speak French. In village custom he was in due time given a wife by his clan elders from one of the village households. A bit later he himself chose a second wife. With marriage and the establishment of his own courtyard, he acquired status in the village which brought new influence and responsibilities.

With his brothers he worked hard in the fields with the short-handled, broad-bladed hoes of the region to produce millet and sorghum grain, corn, okra and peanuts. In addition he belonged to a village agricultural association of young men who joined forces each Wednesday to cultivate the fields of others. During lulls in the agricultural cycle of labor, Bakary busied himself with seasonal chores such as cutting thatch grass and making sun-dried adobe bricks for the maintenance of dwellings and granaries which were constructed of these materials.

Bakary soon appeared in response to the call of the village elder. There followed a conversation in which the men explained, with his help as translator, that they were missionaries from nearby Orodara and that they were interested in the Siamou people and their language. They had come to pay them a visit and to get acquainted with their village. During this initial contact with the people of Tin, Bakary proved to be a pleasant and valuable source of information. After some further conversation, the men thanked the villagers for their kind reception, said their farewells and promised to return before long.

A few weeks later, Thiessen returned to the village for a follow-up visit. This time he asked to see the village chief. Accompanied to his courtyard, there was the usual leisurely round of greetings and introductions. Eventually the chief asked what it was that had brought Thiessen to his village that day. He replied that, as he had explained during an earlier visit, he hoped for permission to move to his village with his family. He wanted to study their language so that one day the Siamou people could have the Bible in their own tongue so they could read God's Word for themselves. After discussing the matter with his village elders, the chief declared that if indeed it was possible for them to have God's Word in their own language, this was surely something which could benefit all their people. The missionary and his family were welcome to take up residence in their village.

Bakary quickly moved into the forefront of the events which followed. When, initially, the Thiessens were unable to find adequate lodging to rent, Bakary went to an uncle who accepted for the Thiessen family to move temporarily into an empty hut in his courtyard and to take meals with his own family. It was also

Bakary who approached another uncle, who was the land chief of the village, to ask for a parcel of ground upon which a home could be built for the missionary family. (6) (cf. ch. 66)

In his capacity as a semi-official link between the village elders and the new white-skinned residents in the village, Bakary had nearly daily contact with them. Thiessen early took advantage of his literacy and gave him a French copy of the Gospel of Matthew which he began to read. Out of this reading arose many questions which sparked numerous conversations in the months which followed. Bakary early expressed his support for the missionaries' dream of one day seeing the Scriptures written in the language of his people.

Once installed in the village, the Thiessens established other links with the people around them. Needing help with the work load of maintaining a household in the African bush for a growing family, a second young man named Solo was brought into their lives. Gently the Thiessens began to plant seeds of witness in his mind and heart, as well.

Yet another encouraging link with the close knit Muslim village took shape in the person of Abraham. A committed young Muslim, he had graduated from the University of Abidjan in the Ivory Coast in 1983. When he was unable to secure employment, he returned to Tin, his home village, where he joined his brothers in the labor-intensive routine of agricultural life. Upon meeting the Thiessens, he quickly became intrigued with their dream of reducing his maternal language to writing so the Scriptures could be made available to them. With his university background he demonstrated quick understanding of the problems of linguistic analysis with which the Thiessens were struggling. While he showed only casual interest in the Christian faith itself, he became an enthusiastic and valuable helper in the early stages of Thiessens language study.

one sows, another reaps

While the first AIMM missionaries to Orodara and Kotoura had experienced early and dramatic responses to the Gospel, things moved more slowly in Tin. Whether because of the closely-knit and powerful circle of Muslim elders in the village or for other factors, response to the new Christian witness among them was much more tentative. Several of the young men in the village had expressed interest and secured their own portions of Scripture whereupon the Thiessens sought opportunity for times of Bible study with them. But in the spring of 1991, as they were preparing for a furlough year in North America, no one had yet made a public confession of faith. It was therefore with joy that they shared some good news in their final quarterly report before leaving for home: Bakary had become a Christian! (7)

This news was all the more welcome and reason for rejoicing because of Siaka's role in bringing Bakary to his conversion experience. It was one day as Siaka sat with his roadside supply of books for sale that Bakary, during a bicycle trip to Orodara, stopped by. Always alert to people who were spiritual seekers, Siaka quickly sensed in Bakary someone who was near a decision. Sharing his joyous testimony of God's grace at work in his own life, he led Bakary to accept Christ as his Savior.

Paul and Lois Thiessen's departure for North America coincided with the return of fellow AIMM missionaries Elmer and Jeannette Dueck Thiessen to Africa. Assigned to the city of Bobo Dioulasso, they were in need of experienced house help. Having heard good reports about Solo from Paul and Lois, word was sent to the village of Tin inviting him to work for them for a year. It was not long till they sensed that the seed sown during his years in the missionary home in his village had fallen on good soil. Shortly thereafter, in conversation and prayer with Elmer and Jeannette, Solo also made a personal profession of faith.

Hearing of this in Canada, Paul and Lois Thiessen understandably made this news the focus of a special newsletter sent to family and friends: "Praise God and thank him for another Siamou man who has become a child of God. . . . Pray for Solo that he will remain faithful to Jesus Christ in the face of opposition, that he will grow strong in the Lord and that he will help his wife and two children to believe in Jesus as well . . . ." (8)

the Lord provides yet again

Even as the Thiessens were pursuing their installation among the Siamou people in the village of Tin, simultaneous pioneering was taking place on another front. By the summer of 1984, Dan and Kathy Petersen had installed themselves in N'Dorola, some seventy-five miles to the north of Orodara. This village was at the northern end of an all-weather road from Bobo. An active commercial center was located there as well as a government outpost and a Catholic Mission. It also was hotter and drier than Orodara. During the time of the harmattan winds, fine sifting sand filled the air which cut visibility to near zero and found its way through tiny cracks and key holes into every living quarter.

But this, too, was part of the area for which AIMM had accepted responsibility for Christian witness. Dan and Kathy had responded to the challenge of an assignment there. Though in early contacts with the village elders they had been received with courtesy and were invited to take up residence among them, the Petersens had no idea whom they would find - - if anyone - - who might be prepared to identify and collaborate with them. No more than installed in their temporary rented quarters, they received many people who came by their yard to greet them or simply watch the new white-skinned people who had come to live among them. Particularly were they fascinated by the baby daughter Joy who, they said, had hair the color of cotton!

It was not long that the Petersens particularly noticed one young man who returned frequently to greet them and to ask questions. His name was Jibiril (pr. dji-bi-RILL). One day he mentioned that he would be happy to help them with any odd jobs they might have. Among other things he had some experience as a mason's helper and knew how to make cement blocks. This was an important discovery for the Petersens since they intended to build their own quarters somewhere in the village as soon as such a project seemed appropriate. But first, there was a question of a parcel of ground and permission to build on it. For this Jibiril had a suggestion: "Come talk to my father."

About this visit the Petersens later wrote: "Last week we had an official talk with Jibiril's father about their family land. We knew their family as very friendly people, kind to Nyagali [pr. nyah-GAH-li, i.e., Joy, their little daughter] and patient with our language learning. So I told the old man that we weren't just asking for land, but that we were asking for a family - - we wanted to become part of their family, eat with them each week, learn to cook their food, and let our children grow up together. He said he would like that very much and gave us a plot right next to theirs, about 20 meters by 30." (9)

Once again, in a rural Muslim village community, AIMM missionaries were finding friends and experiencing acceptance as steps of venturesome faith were taken.

But as welcome as these developments were, a longer-range need still remained unresolved. The Petersens needed an African with both the abilities and the interest with whom to team in their ongoing struggle to analyze a complicated African dialect and reduce it to writing. They had prayed much about this problem but 1986 came and went without an apparent answer.

a solution found in "Elephant Town"

Intent on broadening their base of acquaintance and resource among the Senoufo beyond N'Dorola, the Petersens made contacts during dry season when the sub-Saharan sand trails were passable. It was one such foray which found Dan late one afternoon in early 1987 in a village some eighteen miles to the west in a village called Famberla (pr. fah-mbear-LAH). He arrived to discover that he had happened upon the scene in the midst of village-wide observance of certain rituals of a secret male society. He was quickly intercepted and told that, in keeping with their tradition, all women were confined to their houses and that any men in the village who were not members of their society needed also to be placed in a house by themselves until the ceremonies had been completed. Without further ado, Petersen was escorted to a village hut and told to enter. The door was shut behind him.

As his eyes became accustomed to the shadowy interior which was illuminated only by a single flickering oil lamp, he became aware of a second figure slouched against the wall on the opposite side of the room. Petersen soon learned two things about his fellow detainee: first, that he, too, was a non-member of the male society which held sway in the village outside, and second, that he was in a well-advanced stage of intoxication. His condition, however, made him no less curious about the white-skinned man who had just joined him in his quarters. Who was he? From whence and for what reason had he come? Without other options for passing the time, Petersen decided to respond fully to the questions of his tipsy but obviously curious hut-mate. After a bit of background regarding AIMM in general and himself in particular, Petersen concluded by explaining that he was intent on learning the language of that region so that he could, one day, help translate God's Word into their own tongue. But for this he needed someone from that region to help him.

After a long moment of silence, the dim figure across the room spoke up: "I know just the man for you. He's a very intelligent young man; he speaks French well and has been looking for work. He lives in Silorola [pr. see-loh-ROH-lah, which in the local language literally meant "elephant town!"]. In a few days I'll bring him to you in N'Dorola." Petersen thanked the man across the dimly lit room, but inwardly received the announcement with more than a little private amusement and skepticism.

It was not long after this exchange that there was the sound of footsteps outside their door. The rituals having been concluded, the two men were free to leave. Bidding his unsteady fellow detainee farewell, Petersen made his way home and gave the incident little further thought.

It was about two weeks later that one day a motorcycle made its way into their N'dorola courtyard. Driving was none other than his new acquaintance. Perched on the back was a young man. "See," announced the driver with a broad smile, "I told you I'd bring you someone to help you in your work. His name is Maliki Ouattara [pr. ma-LEE-kee wah-TAH-rah]. Like I told you, he is from Silorola" [i.e., elephant town!].

a gifted youth with a hungry heart

It did not take the Petersens long to discover that the Lord had brought them an exceptional young man. A secondary school graduate, he had applied for a scholarship to continue his studies in the university but was not fortunate enough to receive one. Even though he had taken an additional year of secondary studies and reapplied for a scholarship, he was again denied. At the time of Petersen's encounter with the inebriated man in a dimly lit hut in a remote Senoufo village, Maliki was at loose ends looking for something to do.

Petersens further discovered in Maliki an innate linguistic talent. After working with him for some time, Dan sent him to the capital city, Ouagadougou, for an intensive two-week session conducted by Wycliffe personnel there. He returned from these sessions with high marks. Petersens later wrote as follows: "What can beat the thrill of a new discovery? Some things can be newly rediscovered by anyone who puts their effort into it, like discovering for oneself the music of a great composer, or the high country of a distant mountain range. Other discoveries are made only once, like leaving the first dusty footprints on the moon, or creating a vaccine for an incurable disease. This year in Burkina has been for us a year of such discoveries, and the most rewarding have been the 'made-only-once' discoveries."

"We had hoped that by the end of the dry season we would be able to teach some Senoufo people to read and write in their own language using our trial alphabet. Our hopes have been realized in one young man - - Maliki - - who has not only become accomplished in using the alphabet, but who also enjoys working with us on the unknowns that need solving in the language. With his help, we have been able to make progress on even the toughest problems."

In the same newsletter the Petersens continued: "We have made some discoveries in that language, that's an important step. But let's pray for a still greater discovery. Pray that many of these people will recognize God's love for them as truly GOOD news. That will be the greatest discovery any of them - - or any of us - - will ever make." (10)

Silorola, "the elephant town," proved to be an ideal setting as an outpost of the Petersens ongoing work among the Senoufo of that region. It is a large, centrally-located village, with kinship ties throughout the surrounding villages. The Petersens were warmly accepted by Maliki's extended family. The villagers built a simple, two-room mud hut with a tin roof as their "guest house" for such times when they could come with Maliki from N'Dorola to pursue their linguistic research among them.

With passing time the Petersens learned that Maliki's father had converted to Islam. Before his death, however, he had called his children and told them: "Choose a religious faith which believes in God. Never return to the paganism of our forefathers."

On one occasion Petersen gave Maliki a copy of the widely-known book entitled "Peace Child" written by Don Richardson. Upon reading it he said: "Now I understand why you have come. Receiving the Scriptures in our own language is the most important thing that could happen to my tribe."

In the course of his work with the Petersens and his own personal study of Scripture, Maliki reached a point of belief in and personal commitment to Christ. One day, subsequent to that experience, he expressed a nagging concern: "My understandings of the Christian faith are couched in French terminology. My faith grows as I study my French Bible. But I'm concerned for my two wives and my children. They do not understand French. How am I to put these discoveries and truths into our maternal tongue so they too can understand and believe?"

In Maliki, the Lord had not only provided the Petersens with a gifted language consultant; he had also provided them with a fellow believer who shared fully in their longing to help the Senoufo people of that area to understand who Jesus is.

Siaka in Orodara, Cheba in Kotoura, Bakary in Tin, Maliki in N'Dorola. Each one, in each place, surprising early collaborators who became fellow believers with pioneering AIMM personnel - - and this in areas where we had not dared to expect much!

Oh we of little faith!

in the shadow of a third colonial power

AIMM missionaries arrived in Upper Volta in a time of political instability. AIMM missionaries were no strangers to the disruptive impact of crumbling colonial rule. In Congo/Zaire they had lived and served through the violent aftermath of the Belgian withdrawal. In southern Africa they had witnessed firsthand the struggle of black governments in former British territories and the agonizing process whereby the grip of *apartheid* had been broken in the Republic of South Africa. In northwest Africa they found themselves under the receding shadow of yet a third former colonial power, the country of France.

The French entry into this sprawling often parched area of Africa had not been an easy one. As early as the 12th century there had already been established what for hundreds of years was known as the Mossi Kingdom. Situated on the central plateau region of what was long referred to as Upper Volta, the Mossi (pr. MOH-see) had demonstrated a remarkable gift for organization and disciplined administration. With kings known as Naabas (pr. NAH-bahs), they utilized mounted cavalry to establish and defend their borders. So effective were they that they were able to resist the Islamic tide which had succeeded in inundating all else around them in its sweep to the Atlantic coast. By the 15th century, several other ethnic groups had been integrated into the Mossi Kingdom such as the Peul, Samo and Bissa (pr. PUHL, SAH-moh, BEE-ssah). (1)

The first French expeditions arrived in this area in 1894. There had been spirited resistance but, as was the story all across black Africa in that era, arrows and spears were no match for gunpowder. By 1904, the last pocket of resistance had been subdued and Upper Volta simply became part of an area which on European maps came to be referred to as French West Africa.

In 1947, however, the region situated under the great loop of the Niger River was given its own administrative identity and was called Upper Volta. Caught up in the political ferment that was everywhere present in Africa in the 1950's, a broad-based political party had taken shape in the region and, in 1956, was officially organized under the name "the Voltaic Democratic Union." Thereafter, the pace of events quickened. On December 11, 1958, Upper Volta was proclaimed a Republic. The president of the governmental council was Maurice Yameogo (pr. yah-may-OH-goh). A year later, on December 10, 1959, he became the first president of the Republic. And, on August 5, 1960, Upper Volta was granted its political independence. As did nearly all of the former French colonial areas, Upper Volta also opted to become part of the French economic and monetary community thus profiting from preferential trade agreements and a stable currency linked with the French *franc*.

turmoil erupts

As was the case in many other newly-independent African countries, the first years of political autonomy were a time of euphoric rejoicing and boundless expectations. Free to govern themselves as they saw best, there soon emerged a small elite group of privileged people who had access to circles of influence as well as public funds. When, by 1965, the government began experiencing financial problems, it was decided to cut back salary scales across the country. This was not how independence was supposed to work. Public protest took the form of several nation-wide strikes. This, in turn, triggered a period of political instability.

On January 3, 1966, the first of several military coups took place which brought Lt. Col. Sangoule Lamizana (pr. sah-NGOO-leh lah-mi-ZAH-nah) to power. During an eight year period he exercised rule largely via ordinances and decrees. In February of 1974 the army declared itself as the only authority in the country. The first AIMM missionaries arrived four years later to find that elections had been held and that Lamizana had been chosen to be the second president of Upper Volta.

He did not hold his office long, for on November 25, 1980, the military again staged a coup and installed a ruling military committee headed by one Saye Zerbo (pr. SAH-yeh ZER-boh). Two years later in

November, 1982, still another coup by military officers installed a military doctor named Jean-Baptiste Ouedraogo (pr. oo-way-DRAH-go) as head of state.

Captain Thomas Sankara arrives on the scene

Probably the most noteworthy action of the new doctor-president was to tap a rising military officer to serve on his cabinet as the Secretary of Information and, eventually, as the Secretary of State. Sankara (pr. sah-nkah-RAH) was not a man easily ignored. He was born in a simple village setting to mixed parentage - - his mother a Mossi, his father a Peul. Because of this parental ethnic mix, he grew up in a society in which he did not really fit anywhere. The proud Mossi majority would not accept him as truly one of them because of his non-Mossi father. The Peul, on the other hand, would not accept him because of his non-Peul mother. As one writer later observed: "Sankara was obliged, very early, to define himself in terms of his own acts and his own convictions." (2)

Bright, curious and energetic, Sankara took advantage of every educational opportunity which was available to him. After his primary and secondary education, he was able to secure a place at a military academy in Madagascar. His time there coincided with a time of political ferment which saw a young naval officer successfully challenge the political establishment of that country. Sankara was an attentive witness of all that transpired during his student days there.

Returning home, upon graduation, he was three years later sent with fellow countryman Blaise Compaore (pr. kah-mpah-OR-ay) to a military school in Rabat, Morocco. Here, as he studied, he observed the extreme gap which existed between the poverty-stricken peasantry of the country and the luxurious lifestyle of those who moved in circles of power. Upon completing their studies, he and his companion returned home determined to review the political scene of their own country with a critical eye.

It was at that point that President Ouedraogo tapped Sankara to serve as his Secretary of State. Soon thereafter he went to represent his country in New Delhi, India, at a gathering of nonaligned nations. There he fell under the spell of the oratory and views of Fidel Castro. Sankara himself also took the floor on a couple of occasions during plenary sessions to express his own views in colorful, emphatic terms.

All of this did not go unnoticed by French advisors back in Ouagadougou, the country's capital. They discreetly expressed their displeasure to President Ouedraogo. Concerned to maintain cordial relations with the former colonial power, he ordered Sankara arrested in May 1983. By this time Blaise Compaore, his friend of military school days, had been named commanding officer of an elite commando force in the country. When in June Compaore threatened to lead his troops in rebellion against the government in protest, Sankara was released. Less than three months later, President Ouedraogo was overthrown in yet another coup. Key instigators were Blaise Compaore and Thomas Sankara who was named President of a ruling body called "The National Council of the Revolution."

a slaughter of sacred cows

Jean Ziegler, one of Sankara's biographers, described him in the following terms: "A curious paradox impacts Sankara's personality: warm, extroverted, a passionate debater driven to convince others, laughs easily, loves music, loves parties, loves evening gatherings that last late into the night, a jovial guest, Sankara is at the same time a secret, solitary, nearly inscrutable man." (3)

Sankara came to his role of authority with some deep-seated, passionately-held convictions. As a student in the last days of the French colonial system, he had had some personal experiences of prejudice and discrimination simply on the basis of his color. In his study, reading and travel, he had come to view the colonial era as one of exploitation and injustice. He found the reading of literature extolling the cause of world communism to be exciting for it addressed issues of injustice about which he, by now, cared deeply. He had also come to see that, in the post-colonial era, there were black governments in various places which maintained friendly ties with their former colonizers often with great personal profit for the African leaders in power. In the meantime, given his own humble origins, he was closely in tune with the ongoing, unmet needs of the ordinary, illiterate, rural folk. Though political independence had come, the lot of the simple people was no better under black governments in his country than they had been under the former colonial regime. Sankara was determined to change that.

Seeking to rally broad support among the common people, Sankara traveled widely. Sitting with villagers and their elders, he drummed the themes of self-sufficiency. There was much they could do themselves to better their own lives. To involve rural people in the revolution he sought to lead, special committees were organized all across the country called "Committees for the Defense of the Revolution," or CDRs. Every village eventually had one. Every township of the cities also had one. Made up of ordinary local people, they were urged to be the advocates and enthusiasts of the movement and the organizers of local self-help initiatives.

A traveling journalist on one occasion described a village gathering he attended as follows: "For several hours they stood under the scorching sun, listening attentively to the speakers - - whether the more polished orators who had come from Ouagadougou or the villages's own representative of the Women's Union who, only recently literate, haltingly read out the text of her brief presentation. The crowd was not passive. The peasants applauded and laughed; they pumped their fists in the air and chanted in More [pr. MAW-ray], the local language."

"The villagers' enthusiasm was not so much for the words of the speakers but for the changes that had come to Pibaore [their village]; a recently formed peasants' union, a schoolhouse of brick and iron sheeting, a cereal bank to store surplus grain, literacy classes, several thousand newly planted trees to combat deforestation, improved harvests of millet and sorghum. When a speaker mentioned Thomas Sankara's name, there was applause. A number of the younger villagers wore tee-shorts bearing Sankara's portrait. As in other Burkinabe villages this reporter has visited, the inhabitants of Pibaore identified the revolution with their young president. 'He doesn't just make promises, like the old politicians,' one commented, 'He gets things done.' A moment's thought, and then he added, 'He's shown us that we can get things done.'" (4)

But Sankara was also forging ahead on other fronts. Since the accession of the country to political independence, government budgets were, in his view, being squandered without benefit to their desperately poor country. They were still suffering from the after-effects of a serious drought. There was genuine malnutrition in some of the rural areas. There was inadequate water supply in others. Medical services were minimal in many rural regions.

When he came to power, he discovered a bloated civil service which - - though representing only 0.3 percent of the population - - was consuming nearly 60 percent of the total annual budget! Determined to do something about this, Sankara ordered cuts in civil servants' salaries. He also established mandatory contributions on the part of these government employees to development and famine relief funds. This ruling applied to army officers as well. If government officials needed to travel outside the country, they were to travel economy class. As for transportation within the country, Sankara ordered the fleet of government limousines sold. The government officials were to travel by pickups or smaller vehicles which cost less to purchase and to maintain. And to reduce the need for travel, Sankara insisted that civil servants responsible for government services in more remote areas of the country move out of the capital to take up residence in the areas for which they were responsible. Those who refused to move were summarily sacked.

It was in August 1984, on the first year anniversary of Sankara's rise to power that the change of name for his country was announced. Known for years as Upper Volta, the term made geographic sense but also carried overtones of an earlier colonial era. A new name was needed which reflected the new day and new spirit of the "Revolution." The new name? Burkina Faso (pr. boor-KEE-nah Fah-soh). For some time there was uncertainty as to its actual meaning since it combined terms from two local dialects, More and Dioula. Eventually it was defined to mean "the land of incorruptible men" or "the land of men who stand upright." (5)

And there was still more. Sankara attacked corruption and dishonesty in high places. Dismissals from civil service for embezzlement and graft became commonplace. In sessions of the Council of Ministers, Sankara continually drummed the theme of honest service in the interests of the masses of their country who had for too long been neglected.

All of this was taking place against the background of Sankara's open courting of leftist support outside his country. French authorities had long since noted Sankara's biting commentary on their colonial legacy left in Africa and were not amused. Their displeasure was expressed in a sharp reduction in their financial aid for their former colony. Sankara openly expressed his admiration for such nonaligned country leaders as Cuba's Fidel Castro and Libya's head of state, Muammar al-Qaddafi. There was, furthermore, a steady drumbeat of leftist, revolutionary rhetoric in the country's press. Following is an example: "A people are not freed, people free themselves. Without this a people will never take charge of their own destiny but they will always permit themselves to be dominated. The Voltaic people must never hide this truth from themselves so that the revolution unleashed on August fourth may realize its fullest meaning and be the source of deliverance. . . ."

"Today it is the left which has triumphed in spite of its little armament because it was a victory won by the people. This victory, however, has not eliminated physically, politically or ideologically the reactionary right which is tied to international imperialism. In its own way it continues to fight in various ways and forms which are dangerous for us. It is especially a question of rumors. Before such maneuvers, our revolution which follows inexorably its route must redouble its vigilance and its determination to not yield the slightest ground to the political faction which works in the shadows. The victory belongs to the people." (6)

mixed feelings

AIMM personnel, located as they were in comparatively isolated parts of the country, were largely on the fringes of all of the political hubbub. They heard the news on government radio. They often heard the animated conversation of Burkinabe (pr. boor-kee-nah-BAY), the new term used to refer to citizens of the country. There was so much of Sankara's agenda with which the missionaries could whole-heartedly agree. They applauded the emphasis upon literacy campaigns, crash vaccination programs in the villages, the rallying of rural people in support of simple community development projects.

But the missionaries were also having rather frequent encounters with the village CDRs as they traveled from place to place. Frequently they established road blocks in their villages in order to stop and scrutinize the passengers and contents of each passing vehicle or truck. While on some occasions the missionaries were recognized and waved through, on other occasions they encountered belligerent, illiterate youth who demanded to see vehicle registration documents and drivers' licenses which they could not decipher. Occasionally missionaries were required to get out of their vehicles and submit to an inventory of all contents within. The loosely organized CDRs were impossible to monitor on a regular basis. In some cases they became the pretexts for self-important local officials to abuse their power and even to extort money or favors from the local population and those passing by. With time, missionaries found it expedient to allow for more travel time in the event they were held up and had to cajole their way through such road blocks. And, above all else, there was an uneasiness among AIMM folk with regard to the aggressive leftist rhetoric which they heard constantly from government sources. How seriously were they to take it? Was the Sankara government in process of becoming a genuine communist regime with all that might imply?

a revolution derailed

Unknown to the general population, political opposition had quietly been taking shape during the four years of Sankara's regime. Though the general public was overwhelmingly supportive of Sankara and his policies, there was a small group of people who were becoming increasingly angry with what was taking place. One writer explained the growing dissent as follows: "Opposition came from the right-wing business men and traders, some military officers and village chiefs, and supporters of the ousted politicians of earlier regimes whose positions were threatened. . . ."

"Sankara also confronted resistance and opposition from some of those who professed support for the revolution. There was hostility toward certain specific measures and fundamental political differences over the course of the revolution itself. . . . At one level, there was resentment and grumbling among a layer of senior civil servants and public functionaries who resented the sacrifices asked of them. . . . They resisted Sankara's efforts to reassign them to the provincial towns because unwilling to give up the relative comforts and pleasures of life in the capital. . . . Nor did the government's anti-corruption measures sit very well with some functionaries who continued to view government employment as a license for self-enrichment. . . . Still another major difficulty Sankara faced was mediating the bitter factionalism of the different left-wing organizations and tendencies represented within the National Council of the Revolution." (7)

But none of this was common knowledge. It was therefore a stunned populace, both black and white, that heard the announcement over government radio the evening of October 15, 1987, that "patriotic forces" had brought an end to "the autocratic power of Thomas Sankara." The end, they later learned, had come that same afternoon. A small group of unidentified assailants had simply walked into his office and shot him dead.

Captain Blaise Compaore, Sankara's comrade in arms and supposed friend, replaced him as president. A new ruling body was declared to be in place called "The Popular Front." Early propaganda vilified Sankara with terms such as "traitor, a messianist, a fascist who ran a one man show." In the face of massive protest and anger, the government quickly softened its language and spoke of "a revolutionary comrade who had gone astray" whose death was a tragic accident. He had made the unfortunate mistake of bypassing the "historic leaders" of the country while trying to consolidate personal power. There followed a period of transition which quickly reflected the stance and priorities of the new president. Policies which had been unpopular with an ousted group of elite were gradually rescinded. Familiar faces from other days began to reappear in the halls of power. The wealthy business community was assured that things would soon be back to "normal." As for its foreign relations, Burkina Faso soon let it be known that the country wanted to mend relations with France and other western powers.

But perhaps the most telling change of all was the new president's retreat behind armed security guards. Whereas his popular predecessor had moved about freely everywhere and without armed escort, the new president limited his public appearances and when he did venture out, it was only with maximum security.

Once again, AIMM missionaries had found themselves on the fringes of bloody violence, the observers of a society torn by internal dissension. And, once again, missionaries and home staff alike had occasion to ponder the question: "What is our role as followers of the Prince of Peace at this time, in this place?"

CHAPTER 69   EXPANDING FRONTIERS

time to organize

Upon arrival in Upper Volta in 1978, AIMM's pioneering team was in no hurry. They were planning to settle in for the long-haul and were prepared to take time for cultural orientation and language learning. There also was no sense of urgency regarding the detailing of formal and legal structures. Invited and even urged by Protestant Missions already on the scene to undertake a new work in the southwest corner of the country, AIMM had come in under the umbrella of the country's Federation of Evangelical Missions and Churches (FEME), an organization known and trusted by people in government. It was hoped that this arrangement would allow time for unhurried assessment and planning.

And there was still another factor which wielded early influences on the thinking and planning of the team. AIMM had just worked through a plan of mission/church fusion in Zaire in which AIMM was legally dissolved in that country. In starting a new work in Upper Volta, was it really necessary to enter as a mission? Might it not be possible, with a little time, to register right away as a Mennonite Church of which the mission personnel could be full and active members? It was an intriguing idea.

It was not long, however, that both the neighboring C&MA Mission and the FEME officers began to urge the AIMM to pursue its own registration with the government. Given the political instability of the country, they warned, delaying legal formalities was to risk serious problems in the future. Thus it was that, with some reluctance, work began on a set of statutes for the creation of a Mennonite Mission in Upper Volta. Idealism had to yield to reality. In 1981 there simply were not yet enough African believers to meet the government requirements for the establishment of a church.

By late 1981, a working draft of a constitution was being circulated for comment and feedback. There were two noteworthy features. The first was the requirement that Africans be incorporated into the Mission administrative committee and general assemblies. There was, furthermore, a stipulation that the Mission be dissolved no later than ten years after its founding. (1) If circumstances were obliging the establishment of a mission structure, the mood in 1981 was to spell out a clear time-frame in the statutes for its existence and dissolution.

a revolutionary regime invites a Mennonite doctor

As the AIMM team became better acquainted with the Kenedougou (pr. keh-neh-DOO-goo) Province of which Orodara was the administrative center, it quickly became apparent that urgent needs surrounded them on every side. None was more readily apparent than that of public health. There was a small government rural hospital and maternity ward in Orodara under the supervision of a Burkinabe doctor and a small staff. In conversations with him, AIMM personnel soon learned of semi-isolated medical outposts for which he was also responsible but, for lack of time and supplies, was unable to supervise adequately. What was more, the newly installed Sankara government was talking of unleashing a blitz program of immunizations in the villages coupled with public health education. If all of this was to happen in the Province for which he was responsible, the Orodara doctor clearly had to have more help. If the Mennonites were prepared to solicit personnel, he would be delighted.

But for AIMM there were two basic questions. First, could qualified candidates be found at home who would consider an assignment to this sort of an African outpost with minimal equipment and supplies with which to work? Furthermore, what would be the attitude of this newly installed, Marxist-oriented government toward possible Protestant missionary collaboration in its medical services? Both questions were soon answered.

The fall of 1984 found Dr. Steven and Judy Dickerson Harder examining options for service. Steve, a graduate of Eastern Mennonite College, had finished his medical studies at the University of Minnesota in

1980 and a three-year residency in family practice in 1983. Along the way he had twice served three-month stints in a rural hospital in Thailand.

Judy was the daughter of Baptist missionary parents who had served in Thailand. Meeting Steve at EMC, they were married after graduation in the summer of 1976. Trained as a dietician, this daughter of missionaries came easily to a consideration of overseas service with her husband. It was with these files in hand that AIMM personnel approached African medical staff in Orodara. Response was prompt. On government departmental letterhead stationary the government Secretary for Public Health stated his agreement. In a concluding paragraph he wrote: "I do not doubt that he [the missionary doctor] will be able to install a climate of good collaboration and that he will make his experience available for the health of the populations of Kenedougou." A final line reflected the militant tone of the times; "The homeland or death; we will overcome!" (2)

planting cashew nut trees

In terms of statistics based on gross national product, Burkina Faso found itself well toward the bottom of the international ladder in the early 1980's. Located along the southern fringes of the Sahara Desert, it had little in the way of natural resources. Rainfall was typically marginal. Overgrazing was a growing problem which steadily contributed to the deterioration of a fragile ecology. And yet, in terms of the distribution of its people, Burkina Faso had one of the highest concentrations of rural population of any country in Africa. Villages were numerous. The rural people worked hard plowing and planting each year in spite of frequent crop failures. They also bred and cared for a variety of livestock. Chickens and guinea fowl were much in evidence.

All of this was not lost on the first AIMM couples to arrive there. Loren Entz had grown up on a Kansas wheat farm. Dennis Rempel had done graduate studies on soil science with a special focus on agriculture under semiarid conditions. These men increasingly felt that a long-term Mennonite presence and witness in that part of Africa could not ignore the annual struggle of the rural people around them to provide for themselves amidst the often grim climatic conditions inflicted upon them.

After much discussion among themselves and with African friends, there was born the idea of seeking to create an agricultural demonstration plot. On it there could be experiments with different varieties of plants and trees. There could be special emphasis upon methods of water and soil conservation. As a preliminary step, Rempel prepared a study paper for presentation to local government officials. In the paper he insisted that if Burkina Faso had limited natural resources, it nonetheless had one very precious asset - - a rural population which was very attached to its soil and which was very willing to work hard in its cultivation. It was this resource which Mennonites wanted to affirm and encourage. (3)

Discussion and planning culminated in a meeting one December 1983 morning , on a twenty acre plot of land some three miles south of Orodara. Present were representatives of the local government as well as two local chiefs from a nearby village named Fon (pr. as "fawn" with a dropped "n"). Bordered by a bush road on one side, it sloped gently toward a small stream on the other. Other plots of ground already under cultivation by local villagers surrounded it. For purposes of experimentation and demonstration of new ideas, it was ideally located.

In typical African fashion, the assembled group was publicly asked if there was any objection to granting the missionaries permission to work this parcel of their land. After assent was given all around, an official document was drawn up in the government office in Orodara formalizing the transaction. To the thumb prints of the two local village chiefs were added the stamp and signature of the town mayor. The missionaries could go to work.

Eventually it was decided to first concentrate on three projects: circle the plot with a hedge of trees,; develop small earthen dams as catch basins to conserve soil moisture; and plant a grove of cashew nut trees.

Not only could the nuts provide a nutritious addition to the diet of the villagers but they also held the potential of becoming a cash crop. Perhaps mango and citrus trees could be added later. (4)

As the missionary team coordinator, Rempel's work had steadily grown making it difficult for him to give needed personal attention to the development of the Fon land. It was therefore a particularly welcome development when Russel Toevs married Gail Wiebe in the fall of 1986. With a graduate degree in agriculture he had already served two three-year terms under MCC in Bangladesh in agricultural development projects. Upon arrival in Burkina Faso, he brought broad experience to the AIMM team. Based in Kotoura with Gail, he not only made frequent trips to the Fon land south of Orodara but also spent a lot of time with the village farmers in and around the village where he lived. Word was circulating among the village folks that "the Mennonites are people who will pick up one of our hoes and go to our fields with us."

a book shop named "The Dove"

For some months Siaka spread his mats under a mango tree along the main thoroughfare of Orodara, just a short distance from the large market. A wide variety of people stopped to look over the material neatly displayed on the ground. Whether or not they purchased something, all were greeted courteously. Sometimes exchanges of greetings and questions about his booklets led to lengthy conversations about God and religious beliefs, this to Siaka's delight. It was true that he needed some source of financial support. His Muslim father had cut him off from his family in his home village some ten miles to the south. But even as he sought to make enough profit to pay for his meals and lodging in Orodara, his major motive for spreading his mat in the shade of the roadside tree was to spark conversations with those who passed by.

But Siaka had a larger vision for his Orodara wayside ministry. Mats on the ground greatly limited the amount of material he could display at any one time. There was also the problem of dust from the road traffic which continually sifted over his books. And storage was a problem as he had to gather up his materials at the close of each day of vending. Could he and the AIMM missionaries not think of securing a small building along that same road which could become a permanent book shop - - a symbol of Mennonite presence and witness in that bustling frontier town? Furthermore, with the added room, he reasoned, it would be possible to expand the inventory to include paper products and school supplies. Though available in other little outdoor shops in town, the vendors were making exaggerated profit. Such material could be offered at a reasonable price that would still generate a margin which he needed to help meet his personal needs

Not far from the tree under which he normally laid out his books there stood a small roadside shelter under which a tailor plied his trade. At some distance behind his work place was his home. Over time, water runoff from the road had cut a shallow drainage channel beside his shop. If the drainage problem could be solved, there was adequate space for both his work place and a book shop. In conversations between the tailor, Siaka and Dennis Rempel, it was agreed to install a culvert covered by a cement slab large enough to accommodate both his shop and a book store. Given this considerable improvement of the roadside frontage of his plot, it was agreed that the book store would occupy this new location rent-free until the year 2002. That settled, a rectangular cement block unit was built on the site with steel doors and shuttered windows. A storage area was walled off in the rear. A counter was built and rack space hung on a couple of walls. To finance a significant increase in inventory, a partnership of shares was worked out between Siaka, AIMM and one of the missionaries based upon the funds each provided for the enterprise. Siaka was to be the proprietor and manager. Ordering and pricing of merchandise would be worked out in consultation with some designated member of the missionary team. New inventory was to be purchased with proceeds from sales.

Early on Siaka stated that he planned to tithe profits realized from his new venture. And what about a name? "I think I'm going to name it *La Colombe* [the French term for a dove]. This best symbolizes for me," he explained, "what this book store is all about. I want it to become a place and source of peace for many who walk through the door in the years ahead."

Later, when Siaka left Orodara to continue his education, he left a friend, Paul Ouedraogo (pr. way-DRAH-goh), to manage the shop. On some days one missionary or another would also help. Eventually Paul was replaced by Abdias Coulibaly, a former classmate of Siaka's in the Bible School in Bobo. With passing time the little shop, with the sign *La Colombe* over the door, was to become a familiar symbol of Mennonite presence and witness in that setting.

a second wave of recruits

By the fall of 1983, AIMM had established a missionary presence in four different areas of Kenedougou Province, i.e., The Entzes and Rempels in the multi-ethnic town of Orodara; the Thiessens in the Siamou village of Tin; and among two different Senoufo clans, Garber/Wiebe in Kotoura and the Petersens in N'Dorola. It wasn't long that their reporting shared a common theme: "We've established some new beachheads but we need help." Qualifications especially sought were in linguistics and pastoral training. The languages they were tackling were complex and difficult. Furthermore, in some areas people were coming to faith in Christ. This was creating a bittersweet problem for missionaries working by themselves. If they concentrated on linguistic analysis, young Christians were neglected. If they focused on discipling new believers, the language data gathered dust. As the AIMM Board began to advertize these openings, once again it became apparent that the Lord was already at work.

Matthew Swora and Rebecca Jackson both graduated from Texas Christian University in the spring of 1979, Matthew with a degree in religious studies and Rebecca with a degree in nursing. By the spring of 1984, he had earned a degree in elementary education and she a master's degree in nursing with specialization in midwifery. Along the way they had also served two years with a Christian ministry in the National Parks system while based in Jackson Hole, WY. It was in the spring of 1984 that they became aware of AIMM's work in Burkina Faso. Members of the Faith Mennonite Church in St. Paul, MN, they had come in contact with GC/COM staff from Newton, KS. After a year at AMBS in Elkhart, IN, and a year in Belgium studying French, they were welcomed to Orodara in the summer of 1986. Matthew was assigned to a teaching and pastoral role with a steadily growing church in that town. Negotiations were under way with the local doctor regarding part-time service for Becky in the town's government-sponsored maternity ward.

At Kotoura among the Senoufo people, Anne Garber and Gail Wiebe had long expressed the hope that a couple could join them somewhere in their area for pastoral and teaching ministry. An answer to this hope appeared from Steinbach, MB, in the persons of John and Charity Eidse Schellenberg. A daughter of long-time AIMM missionaries Ben and Helen Reimer Eidse, Charity had spent her childhood on the rural station of Kamayala in southern Kwilu Province of Zaire. Both she and John were graduates of the Steinbach Bible College where she had majored in general Biblical studies and he in missions. Deeply involved in their home church, they carried a lively interest in missions wondering, the while, if there might be an opening somewhere which they could fill.

When their files were shared with the team in Burkina Faso, an invitation was soon extended. After two semesters of French study in Sherbrooke, PQ, they and their three children arrived in Orodara in the summer of 1987. During several months of study of Dioula, the trade language, they were asked by the team if they would consider a move to a village among the Southern Senoufo people. The Garber/Wiebe team was located to the southwest of Orodara. There was another large pocket of the same ethnic group to the northwest. Would they be willing to move there with their children in a team effort of church planting? They would.

Shortly after their installation in Kartasso (pr. kar-TAH-sso) village, Charity wrote: "Today our village had a ceremony adoring the fetish of the rainy season, for the purpose of calling the rains which have been slow in coming. I was caught in a downpour on the way from the river where I had been washing clothes. Now, changed into dry clothes and with a hot cup of tea beside me, I'm writing this letter and listening to the rain dripping through the thatch into the pail beside me. Rainy days in Burkina are never dreary, they're always welcome. I'm still pondering a question that an elder asked us this morning. He asked if we knew how to call the rain. How would you have answered that one?"

"Yes, we can finally say that Kartasso is our village. Located 60 kms [roughly 35 miles] west and slightly north of Orodara, this Senoufo village of about 400 people nestled in wooded hill country along a spring-fed river has become our home. Though it is Muslim, it is centrally located to other Senoufo villages north of the big road and already we have had contacts with some of them. 'Home' is three mud huts in the courtyard of our host who happens to also be the village government representative and respected son of the former chief. . . . The trick now is to stay motivated to learn as much as we can, as fast as we can, and to make the most use of these close living conditions to become insiders in this culture. For us, country living means constantly being watched, rather than having privacy. I sometimes need to be reminded that that's a privilege that may lead to these people being drawn to Christ. We just can't afford to be defensive about our time and space. People have sometimes asked how we can live like this. We respond that one learns to define privacy in a different way. To an African, if a person doesn't greet you, it's as if he isn't there . . . . It can be quite disruptive . . . but generally it's just a matter of accepting that people will always be around and, after all, they are the most valuable resource for our work and we need to encourage them to keep coming . . . ." (5)

None of the AIMM couples in Burkina Faso watched the expansion of the team with greater interest than Paul and Lois Thiessen. Some nine miles outside Orodara, they were the only ones who had a ministry focus on the Siamou people and their language. Their newsletters regularly reflected the weight of responsibility they carried in this assignment. Siamou was recognized as one of the toughest languages of the entire region to analyze. And there was their longing to see a church planted among that ethnic group. It was therefore particularly welcome news when they learned that fellow Manitobans Gerald and Beverly Dueck Neufeld had applied to AIMM for service in Burkina Faso. Both were graduates of the Winnipeg Bible College where they had earned degrees in Biblical studies. Gerald had also pursued Biblical studies at the Winnipeg Theological Seminary and a year of linguistic training at the University of South Dakota. Hearing of AIMM's venture in language analysis as a strategy of evangelism and church planting among unreached tribal groups in Burkina Faso, they sensed God's leading in that direction.

After spending a school year studying French in Sherbrooke, PQ, they arrived in Burkina Faso in the fall of 1988. Initial time was devoted to a study of Dioula, the area trade language. As it came time to integrate them into the AIMM field ministry, it was decided that they would team up with the Thiessens in a ministry among the Siamou people. Given that many of this group were resident in Orodara and used a somewhat different form of their dialect, it was agreed that Neufelds locate there. Given their proximity to the Thiessens, frequent consultation on matters of language would be easy. Together they could plan strategy for witness. Together they could work toward the day when a Mennonite Church would be planted among this heavily Islamized people.

Meanwhile the Petersens were reminding their fellow missionaries that they too were longing for missionary collaborators in the isolation of their work at N'Dorola. Once again it was discovered that the Lord was out ahead of the inter-Mennonite search process at home. After finishing their undergraduate studies in 1983, Phil and Carol Kliewer Bergen applied to MCC for a three-year term as teachers. Assigned to Zimbabwe, they had their first encounter with African languages. They discovered, as they later related, "a lot of Mennonite people doing work with other agencies because their churches weren't involved in translation." (6)

From Mennonite Brethren background, they raised this issue with their own mission board. They, in turn, were referred to the AIMM. At that point the Mennonite Brethren had not yet joined AIMM as a partner conference (7) and thus mission budget support was not available for the Bergens' proposed service in Burkina Faso. Their church leaders nonetheless encouraged them to share their vision of service among MB congregations. By the spring of 1990 they had taken linguistic training at the University of Oregon and had also raised their support. After a year of language study in France and Ouagadougou, they arrived at Orodara. Meanwhile it had already been decided they would partner with the Petersens in a linguistic/church planting venture among the Northern Senoufo at N'dorola and beyond.

a French Mennonite connection

It was in the summer of 1981 that the first official contact took place between AIMM and EMEK, (*Europaeische Mennonitische Evangelisation Komitee*) the European inter-Mennonite Mission Board of the time. The meeting took place at a Bible Institute in Nogent, a suburb of Paris. (8) Historical backgrounds of both organizations were traced and program involvements were shared. While there were some differences, the AIMM delegation made clear that these could all be dealt with and that AIMM would warmly welcome European Mennonite candidates for work, particularly in French-speaking Africa.

The next significant contact came approximately two years later in the person of Fritz Hege, a young French Mennonite conscientious objector who was doing alternate service in the North African country of Chad. On one occasion he traveled to Burkina Faso for the express purpose of getting acquainted with the inter-Mennonite team recently arrived in that country. Upon his return he submitted a report to his sponsoring body, the French Mission Committee, in which he shared his impressions. After describing the area, the AIMM team and its approach to Christian mission in some detail, he concluded: "I would like to encourage the French Mennonite Mission Committee to involve itself in this country in collaboration with the AIMM especially since these American Mennonites have well thought through their approach to mission. We would certainly benefit from working with them." (9)

It was a young French Mennonite woman who, just a year later, gave further impetus to the dialogue between the two inter-Mennonite mission organizations. Reared in a Mennonite home in the Alsace region of eastern France, Martine Ehrismann early was captivated by the vision and program of the Wycliffe Bible Translators. It was while taking some linguistic training under a European branch of this organization that she met fellow Frenchman Paul Solomiac who looked forward to similar service.

Approached by Rev. Raymond Eyer, a member of the French Committee, about serving on a Mennonite team in Africa under the appointment of the French Mennonite Mission Committee and EMEK, another meeting was set up in Nogent, Paris. Present this time were the Solomiacs and representatives from AIMM, EMEK and the Wycliffe organization. Details were worked out for their appointment to Burkina Faso where they would serve as members of the AIMM team while under the technical supervision of the country's SIL personnel. (SIL is the acronym for Summer Institute of Linguistics, as the organization is known internationally.) SIL and AIMM personnel in Burkina Faso would together determine where they were to be be placed. Once again, AIMM had established a link of collaboration with mission-minded Christians of Europe. This time it was especially meaningful because the candidates had Mennonite connections.

reaching out to the Samogho (pr. sah-MOH-goh)

Even as a concentrated effort was being made to strengthen the AIMM team ministry among the Southern/Northern Senoufo and the Siamou, missionary discussions kept coming back to other ethnic groups in their region among whom there still was no resident presence or witness. In such discussions, one group which kept cropping up was the Samogho tribe. A large pocket of people to the southwest of Orodara they, like all the others, had their own history, culture and dialect. They too, like the others, had a couple of generations earlier declared themselves converts to the Muslim faith. How could AIMM reach out to them also?

From the very outset, the Entzes let it be known that they considered their first calling to be evangelism and church planting. Though initially located at Orodara as one of the original two AIMM couples in the country, they declared their readiness to move beyond that market town and to take up residence in a village setting among one of the still unreached tribal groups. While they were prepared to work hard at acquiring a functional knowledge of whatever dialect they found, they insisted that a linguistic couple join them to tackle the exacting work of analysis and the reduction of the language to writing. With the arrival of the Solomiacs in Burkina Faso, that need was met. It remained to be decided where the new AIMM team was to be placed.

As AIMM and SIL field personnel began to compare notes, it was soon discovered that the Samogho people were not only of special concern to the AIMM but had also for some years been high on the SIL list of priorities for the area. Agreement came quickly. The new AIMM/SIL team would be placed among the Samogho.

After a few visits to several villages, the team settled on two which were centrally located among the people and were only a few miles apart. For the Solomiacs it would be Samoghoyiri (pr. sah-moh-goh-YEE-ree). The Entzes chose to locate a bit further south in a village named Saraba (pr. sah-rah-BAH). A cluster of some 400 people, it was small enough that the Entzes could, with time, learn to know all of the family groups well. Wanting to blend into the village and its life routine as much as possible, they had several mud brick houses built to form their own courtyard, each with its own use in the cultural pattern of the village.

In 1989, a visiting friend from Kansas put her observations and learnings on paper as follows: "Each day their family ate one African meal prepared by the chief's family. The main staple is a mush called *tô*, which is made from the corn, millet or sorghum that the villagers grow. The *tô* is served with a sauce containing okra, beans, peanuts or meat. '*Tô* has become our children's favorite food. They miss it when we go to North America to visit,' says Donna."

"'Our children are free to work and play anywhere in the village or surrounding fields without our having to worry about them. . . . We are so happy with this place God has given us to raise our children,' she says. 'Not only are they learning good values, such as respecting those who are older, but we also have quality time to read Bible stories and other books that tell of Christians in other times.'" (10)

but who has time for that?

The AIMM team in Burkina Faso was steadily growing. The borders of witness and service were gradually being pushed out to include more and more people. But all of this also resulted in steadily growing administrative detail, as well, which clamored for attention. A growing field budget meant more bookkeeping and more trips to the bank which was not in Orodara but in Bobo, the city some fifty miles to the east over dirt roads. There were calls to be made at various government offices most of which were also in Bobo. There were periodic shopping needs which could not be met in the local market in Orodara.

During the early years of AIMM presence in and around Orodara, frequent trips had been made by Dennis Rempel in his capacity as team coordinator. When in 1986 the Rempels took a leave of absence for family reasons, an immediate gap was created. More and more in missionary gatherings the comment was heard: "Someone really ought to go to Bobo to take care of this - - but who has time for that?" It was clear to all; someone needed to be placed in Bobo itself. Not only would this tremendously facilitate the conducting of AIMM mission and missionary business, it would also give AIMM a resident presence in that city which would be a first step in achieving the dream of planting a Mennonite church in that urban center as well.

And, finally, there was the need for an AIMM guest/rest house there. Missionaries traveling to Bobo for shopping and a break always had to request space in the guest facilities on the C&MA Mission grounds in the city. While the C&MA missionaries there were always considerate and gracious, there was common agreement that it was certainly time for Mennonites to make some provision in that city to take care of their own people.

It was against the background of this urgent need that two interesting files came to the hands of AIMM staff in Elkhart. Elmer and Jeannette Dueck Thiessen were making inquiry about possible service in Africa. He had training in civil engineering and had also earned a BA in Missions at the Winnipeg Bible College. As a single man, he had also served a term with MCC in the North African country of Chad. Jeannette had earned a diploma in Bible at the Steinbach Bible College and also had training in accounting. Active lay folk in their home church, they had experience in youth work, teaching Sunday School and counseling. After a school year of French study in Sherbrooke, PQ, they traveled to Burkina Faso where a rental home had been secured for them. In the fall of 1987, AIMM had its first resident missionaries in the city of Bobo Dioulasso.

I want to prepare myself

Siaka's first year of study via correspondence with the school in Paris, France had gone well. Admitted to the next level in the fall of 1982, he renewed his disciplined schedule of arising in the quiet of the predawn darkness to study his daily assignments by the flickering light of his kerosene lamp. Once again, as the school year drew to a close, his hard work paid off. He again passed his exams. There now remained a third and final year of secondary study in order to secure his secondary level diploma.

Then came a letter with disconcerting news. Before he could enter the sixth and final year of study, he would need to present himself in the French city of Nice in order to take a qualifying exam. He came with the letter to the Orodara missionaries. How could he possibly do that? The cost of travel, lodging and food for such an undertaking was clearly prohibitive. But there was, perhaps, a solution which lay closer at hand. There was a state school in Bobo. Might it be possible to enroll there even though his previous two years of study had been done by correspondence? If this were possible, there would be the further advantage of being able to take the final year in a class room setting - - not to mention access to a school library and the opportunity for direct dialogue with his instructors. But even so, there would still be a question of school fees to pay plus expenses for food and lodging.

After talking and praying with missionaries about all of this, Siaka went to Bobo to investigate the possibilities. Presenting himself to the school director, he explained his mission and submitted his papers. After reviewing the record of his studies and talking with him a while, the director agreed to admit him into the sixth and final year of study. But there was more. Unknown to Siaka, the director was looking for a candidate to serve as a house parent in a boy's dorm. Given Siaka's age, bearing and study record, the director asked him if he would be interested in such a position for the coming school year. If so, all fees including board and room would be covered!

As the school year moved along, Siaka occasionally went to Orodara to visit friends and fellow believers. On one such occasion he shared a prayer request. His studies were going well but he was concerned about the final exams which loomed ahead. Known in the French system as the *bac* exams, they were feared in Africa as well as in Europe. So rigid and demanding were they that students frequently failed them the first time they tried - - and even a second and third time. In conversation with missionaries Siaka repeatedly said: "I want to pass them the first time. I do not want to delay my training to serve my Church and my people."

An exchange of telegrams between Burkina Faso and the AIMM office in Elkhart in early July of 1983 was, therefore, the occasion for genuine rejoicing. They read as follows: "*SIAKA A REUSSI BAC*," i.e., Siaka has passed his bac exams. Within hours a response read: "FELICITATIONS. AIMM/ELKHART."

testing options

It was with heartfelt praise to the Lord that Siaka returned to Orodara. A high hurdle in the path of his continuing education had been cleared. So real had been the possibility of failure in his first attempt that no firm plans had been laid beyond the end of that school year. It was now soon agreed that he spend one year working with the young growing Church. There were widening contacts among professional people in Orodara itself that he wanted to pursue. He also much enjoyed traveling by motor bike to Kotoura and other villages where little clusters of believers were beginning to take shape. A year thus spent would also provide added opportunity for careful evaluation of his options for continued study.

It was on the occasion of a visit of the AIMM executive secretary that Siaka's future studies were discussed. It soon became clear that his hopes were basically two: to pursue Biblical and theological studies at the level of a *license* (a French term for a study program similar to that of an M.Div in North America), and to do so somewhere in Africa. While he was well aware that many young Africans were eager to go overseas for such study, he felt it better and wiser for him to do this somewhere in Africa closer to his own culture and his own people.

It was at this point that a theological school in the Central African Republic came into the discussion. Founded by a group of evangelical missions at work in Africa, it was known as the *Faculté de Théologie Evangélique de Bangui*, or FATEB. Having already founded a comparable school in Nairobi, Kenya, to serve English speaking Africa, this group of missions launched a second one in Bangui, a large urban center right on the border between the Central African Republic and Zaire with a view to serving francophone Africa. Though limited in physical facilities in its earlier years, excellent expatriate and African staff was found from the outset and a serious level of study was inaugurated.

Hearing of these discussions which were under way between Siaka and the Mission, Siaka's family made one last effort to deflect him from his course. Taking advantage of his newly-won *bac* diploma, the family offered Siaka an all-expenses-paid scholarship to a prestigious Islamic university in Niger. His response was appreciative but firm. While thanking them for the offer, he explained, yet once again, that his commitment to Christ was irrevocable. (11)

a Strasbourg interlude

The summer of 1984 proved to be a memorable one for Siaka for yet another reason, that being his opportunity to travel to Strasbourg, France to attend the Mennonite World Conference held there that year. It was in this connection that he was able to attend his first gathering of the Africa Mennonite and Brethren in Christ Fellowship which was convened just prior to the world gathering. This provided a golden opportunity to meet fellow Mennonites and Brethren in Christ people from across Africa and to hear reports of their work.

A high point came the very first evening at the formal opening of the Strasbourg Conference. In what has become a MWC tradition, representatives of each Mennonite and Brethren in Christ Church in the world were invited, country by country, to come to the platform before the assembled crowd. It was with excitement that Siaka, clothed in the colorful, flowing, brocaded garb typical of his sub-Saharan country, took his place as the representative of the newest Mennonite Church in the world that year. Just a few weeks later he bid farewell to his friends at Orodara and flew to Bangui to enroll as a first year student at FATEB.

a growing Mennonite community

As the AIMM work in Burkina Faso expanded its boundaries, the names of places such as Orodara, Kotoura, Tin and N'Dorola had become familiar in the reporting of AIMM personnel. But by the mid-1980's, the names of some new places and people were creeping into missionary correspondence. For example, there was Banzon (pr. bah-NZAW). A believer who had earlier worshiped with the missionaries at Orodara had moved some thirty miles north to this village and had found a few inactive Christians who had C&MA background. Taking the initiative to gather them together for weekly fellowship and worship, he requested help and encouragement from Orodara personnel. Efforts were made to schedule at least monthly visits.

About four miles beyond Banzon was another village called Kounseni (pr. coon-SEH-nee). A young couple lived there who were believers and who had been successful in bringing several others in their village to faith. In missionary reporting home at that time it was stated: "Yuhana and Therese want to be baptized there before leaving for Bible School. It will be their send-off, but more important to them it will be a testimony as a witness to both new Christians and those on the fringes as to what they have left and what they have given themselves to. It is to be an event where people from Kotoura, Banzon, Djigouera and Orodara take part as well." (12)

Djigouera? (pr. djee-GWEH-rah). Where was that? It was a small village twenty-one miles to the north of Orodara among the Northern Toussian (pr. too-SYAH) people, still another ethnic group which was of concern to the AIMM team. Located there was a remarkable couple named Phillipe Coulibale (pr. koo-li-bah-LAY) and Marte Tiera (pr. TYAY-rah). Born in the neighboring country of Mali across the northern border of Burkina Faso to parents of Bobo ethnic origin, they had migrated southward in search of land with sufficient rainfall to sustain themselves and their family. They had earlier come to faith through contact with the C&MA personnel of the area and arrived at Djigouera with a deep commitment to Christ.

No more than located in their new setting, they heard of the missionaries in Orodara and early sought opportunity to make contact with them. Viewed through Western eyes, they were yet another sad example of a family which had been uprooted by the brutal results of drought, a family which typified the grim struggle of tens of thousands to survive on the daily fringe of poverty and hunger. But in Philippe and Marte the missionaries quickly sensed an abiding commitment to Christ and a determination to make their new location a place of witness and the eventual site for a new church. Thus their village was also added to the itineration schedule of Orodara missionaries as yet another outpost of a growing network of believers in the region.

And at Orodara, the original handful of believers found by the first missionaries was steadily attracting new people. With Siaka's influence, a special effort was made to reach out to the students at the government secondary school in town. There was also regular contact with the professional people who had contracts of service with the government. Daily interaction with the Muslim commercial community was also gradually developing into friendships. Attendance at the little chapel in town was growing.

But it was Kotoura which was a particular focus of activity and growth. Cheba's conversion was generating all sorts of new excitement in the village. Under his enthusiastic leadership, the cluster of believers in the village was attracting new people. Regarding his role Gail Wiebe once commented: "Cheba has actual leadership abilities which must be due in part to the fact that he came from the chief's family and saw his father play the role of acting chief for years. Cheba has a lot of energy and is full of ideas. He is also sensitive to and aware of the needs of others in the group." (13)

To this, another missionary added the following observations about the group at Kotoura: "What a host of information people want to know: how to become Christians, how to get along with your husband, how to do the funeral rites? . . . The Christians are getting a good grasp on songs and singing and its importance in the Christian's life, as some songs are even translated into their dialect. The songs attract new people. They have no place to worship, they realize well that God can be worshiped everywhere. They are good at spreading their faith through open air meetings with lots of singing. People are interested in what is going on. . . ."

"It is so exciting to be in the midst of them, to see the Spirit moving. What a blessing to be with Cheba, to see him work and live. He is a man of prayer and knows that God answers him. Sometimes he seems burdened with all that is going on, realizing that he will be responsible for his example to others because everyone is following Cheba's example. It is one year since Cheba made the commitment to follow Christ. We wonder where the group will be a year from now?" (14)

a series of firsts

It was not surprising that the first Christian baptisms to take place outside Orodara were at Kotoura. After Cheba's own baptism, others began to follow. Among the early ones were Cheba's own younger brother Moussa Traore (pr. MOO-sah trah-OR-ay) and Cheba's two wives, an eloquent testimony to his quiet but persistent witness within his own family circle.

There then came the day when the Kotoura villagers witnessed their first Christian weddings. This event took place against a particularly dramatic background. Two years earlier, three brothers had made professions of faith and began worshiping with the growing nucleus of believers that was taking shape around Cheba. Alarmed by this development, the father and family elders had confronted the boys with an ultimatum: either they would abandon their Christian faith or they would be disowned and barred from any further family contact. When, in the face of this menace, they stood firm, the family elders were as good as their word. The boys were no longer given food or shelter at their father's courtyard.

Refusing to abandon their faith, they traveled southward into the neighboring country of Ivory Coast where they secured work on a plantation. As month followed month, the family elders had opportunity to ponder the action they had taken. About a year later the boys returned to visit their home village. They immediately sought out their Christian friends. Realizing that his harsh attitude toward his sons had not weakened their resolve, their father let it be known that he would again extend food and shelter to them. And now, two years after being driven away from their parental roof, the eldest of the three sons was one of the prospective bridegrooms!

When the Christians had become aware of the desire of two couples to seek a Christian marriage, Gail Wiebe and a church elder had set up a series of twenty sessions with them to study what the Bible had to say about Christian marriage and family. Since they would be the first Senoufo couples ever to take such a step, they were understandably concerned that a good example be set for others to follow.

Wiebe later wrote of the event: "The weddings themselves were an interesting mix of African and Western traditions, the mix determined by Africa Christians. One bride wore white; the other blue. Someone suggested at the last minute they needed witnesses, so some were hunted up. The couples exchanged vows and rings. Then they were danced home by the wedding guests. Later there was lots of rice and meat, then traditional music and dancing all night in our courtyard sponsored by one of the groom's friends."

"The best surprise came last. Maadou (pr. mah-DOO) is the oldest of the three young men who were kicked out of their family because of their faith almost two years ago, and then reunited a year ago. Maadou's extended family decided to sponsor music and dancing for Monday night to celebrate his wedding. And Maadou's uncle who two years earlier had gone out to find a stick to beat Maadou and his younger brothers, stood up in front of the crowd to announce that they had hired the musicians in order to help him and his bride celebrate their Christian wedding."

"The row of family elders that attended the wedding seemed to be impressed. One old man came by our house the next morning to say that the weddings had been very good. Several young people who were scared away from their faith two years ago are showing renewed interest. Two young fellows have recommitted themselves to the Lord. So the weddings were a long time in coming . . . but they've been an opportunity for the further spread of the Gospel among the Senoufo. We thank God." (15)

But there were other benchmark events which were also taking place within the young Burkina Faso Church. There was, for instance, the first intertribal gathering which interestingly enough was sparked by the women. Originally encouraged and organized by missionary women, the first gathering took place at Orodara with approximately fifteen women attending. It was a breakthrough for them. Imagine! Women meeting on their own without men to tell them what to do! Time was given to Bible study and discussions about child care, Christian marriage and hygiene in the home. For the first time, the Africans found themselves making friends with women from other tribal groups as they were drawn together by a common faith and their shared involvement in a new Church.

As the women returned to their home areas, positive spillover from the retreats was evident. On one occasion Anne Garber observed: "They returned . . . full of enthusiasm. This has motivated the two teenage girls to really dig in and learn how to read. Gail's been giving them daily one to two hour lessons. For the other women, this enthusiasm translated into boldness in sharing about their seminar during the church services. It is really a joy to see women more fully participating in worship. An interesting by-product; the men, who take turns conducting church services, have now decided that the women should take their turns too!" (16) As further women's retreats were held, interest and attendance grew. With passing time leadership for the periodic events passed to capable African hands.

Though the women were the first to initiate a retreat, the men were not far behind. Intrigued by the idea of a gathering with men from other areas, retreats were also soon organized for them. They too experienced the joy of making new friends in these cross-tribal gatherings as they shared in the study of Scripture and the discussion of common joys and problems as first generation believers in their areas. The groundwork for an intertribal Mennonite Church in Burkina Faso was being laid.

a visit with "the old man"

Though the bulk of the new converts in Kotoura in the mid-1980's were coming from younger people in their teens and 20's, there was one notable exception. His name was Babala (pr. bah-BAH-lah). It was in the course of an administrative trip to Burkina Faso that the AIMM executive secretary had occasion to meet him. He later described the encounter in his trip report in the following terms: "The time came for us to go home. I saw Gail look at Cheba, the first of the converts in Kotoura, and ask him, 'Do we have time to go see the old man?' Cheba's face lit up as he said, 'Yes, we'll take time.'"

"We followed him through those winding narrow alleyways of a traditional Senoufo village. We finally came to a little lean-to in front of an adobe house. Here on a bench sat the 'old man.' He had a little turban and a little wispy, white beard. Cheba pulled up a couple of stools and we sat down. The old man is blind now. When we met him he reached out an uncertain hand that often signifies somebody with defective sight. Milky white eyes turned in our general direction. His story began to unfold. It went something like this: 'I am an old man now. I've lived most of my life. Two years ago these missionaries came to our village. I've been a Muslim all my life. One evening in the public palaver square of our village we were told that there was going to be a meeting, so I asked my grandson to lead me out there with my chair and I sat down. I heard them talking about somebody called Jesus. I didn't understand much.'"

"'But I heard about this man Cheba. I know him, he's a son of our village. I called him. And for a while on a day-to-day basis Cheba came to sit with me under this lean-to here. I began to ask questions and he started to answer. The day came when I met this Jesus you were talking about that night in the public square. I am now old, and I am blind, but in my old age and in my blindness I have found what I was looking for all my life.'"

The secretary went on to comment: "In the corner of my folder I carry this little statement: 'In every human being there is a God-shaped emptiness that cries out to be filled.' That God-shaped emptiness in the 'old man' had been filled." (17)

walking untried paths

With a growing Christian community in the midst of deeply-rooted cultural traditions, the new Mennonite Christians increasingly found themselves confronted by decisions. Which of the traditional cultural practices could be retained in personal life and thus be incorporated in the life of the young church? What was there that was unacceptable by Biblical standards and thus needed to be discarded? It soon became evident that no feature of the culture would be more problematic than the extensive practice of animal sacrifice. Some sacrifices were associated with the cycle of the agricultural year to assure fertility and a successful harvest. Others had to do with the ebb and flow of life in the village: the digging of a new well, entry into a new house, birth of a child, placating of ancestral spirits and so on. In addition to a village chief and a land chief, there was also a chief who presided over all sacrifices required by their culture. Pressure to respect this tradition was enormous.

Wiebe and Garber and the nucleus of new believers encountered this issue in Kotoura as the construction of their new cement block, tin-roofed housing neared completion. Acting Chief Kunandi, who had welcomed them to the village and provided ground for their homes, was now gently reminding them that it was time "to provide a sheep." Though unexplained, it was perfectly clear why a sheep soon needed to be provided. There followed several times of intense discussion and prayer with Cheba and the Christians of the village. To

646

simply refuse to sacrifice a sheep before moving into the new living quarters would be to openly flaunt village customs. They knew all too well that they would stir strong reaction if not outright animosity. But if they did follow the custom, would not this imply that the Lord to whom they had so recently made commitments of faith and life was not powerful enough to care for them in all circumstances? Would this not be a denial of the faith they professed?

At last a plan of action was adopted. Going to Chief Kunandi with a sheep they said: "We have purchased a sheep as you suggested. But we do not believe we need to sacrifice it to assure our welfare and happiness in our new home. We love and seek to serve a God who one day gave his own Son to be the final sacrifice for us. God's Book that we have brought to you teaches us that beyond this sacrifice we have need of no other. Today we want to give this live sheep to you. Let it live and join your flock. Let it remind you of that great sacrifice many years ago when God gave his Son to die for you and for us."

The Chief did not refuse. The sheep was added to his flock. And there was appropriate celebration with Christians and villagers alike. Food was shared, prayer was offered, songs of praise were sung as the missionary women took up residence in their new village home.

On that occasion, a direct confrontation had been averted but the missionaries and the Kotoura Christians would continue to encounter the all-pervasive power of the cultural dynamics around them.

slicing the language cake

As new missionary recruits followed each other to Burkina Faso, the issue of language study was confronted again and again. English-speaking missionaries found themselves before a three layered linguistic cake. First, there was French, the language of government and the class room. Long-term residence in the country was not feasible without at least a conversational and reading knowledge of this language.

Then there was Dioula, the trade language which blankets a large region of western Africa. The language of trade, the road and the market place, it makes possible communication between the broad mix of tribal groups of the area. For missionaries to be conversant with rural people, most of whom do not know French, Dioula was a practical necessity.

Finally, there were the languages of the unreached tribal groups which were the focus of AIMM concern. Many hours were devoted to questions of language in early missionary business sessions. Should new arrivals study the trade language before starting their assigned tribal dialect? Or should the trade language be deferred until such time as there was a working knowledge of a local tribal dialect? Were both even really necessary for every AIMM missionary at the outset? Specific assignments also made a difference. For someone working with the inter-tribal Church in the market town of Orodara, Dioula the trade language was the obvious and, indeed, the only language possible to use with a fellowship of believers coming from different ethnic backgrounds. But for those assigned to language analysis and evangelism among the unreached groups, a third language, sooner or later, was inescapable.

There were no short cuts. AIMM goals in Burkina Faso required each missionary to slice his or her own way through the linguistic "cake" before them. It meant disciplined hard work for all. For none was this more true than for the linguists who set themselves to not only speak a language, but to reduce it to writing and, eventually, to produce passages of Scripture in those languages.

Some of the painstaking, time-consuming process is clearly reflected in an article submitted to the AIMM Messenger. Referring to the analysis/translation process in which Dan Petersen and his language consultant, Maliki Ouattara, were engaged in N'Dorola, twelve different steps were described as necessary to putting just a rough draft of a passage of Scripture on tape. Along the way there were such steps as translating from French into the local language; translating from the language back into French; putting a trial draft on cassette tape; playing the cassette for local villagers checking for comprehension or lack of comprehension; further refining, further testing with village people and once again recording the draft on tape. (1)

idealism encounters reality

The first contingent of AIMM missionaries arrived in Burkina Faso with an admirable mix of commitment and idealism. They had read widely. They had taken classes in cross-cultural communication. They were aware of some of the missiological issues with which AIMM missionaries had struggled in Zaire. They wanted very much to learn from this history and to blaze some new trails.

First there was the question of lifestyle. They were determined to identify with their African villagers around them as closely as possible. Against the background of the consumer, throw-away American culture out which they came, they proposed to share a common household, thus avoiding the expense of supplying two missionary homes in the same vicinity with duplicate equipment. Furthermore, diets were to be adjusted as broadly as possible to local food resources available around them. Water for drinking, cooking and bathing would come from the same sources upon which their village neighbors depended.

With passing time, experience gradually made it clear that if they were to maintain their emotional well-being, each family needed its own space. Resorting to boiling or filtering their water came to be seen not as a luxury but as a means of safeguarding their health and energy for the ministry they had come to undertake in the heat and dust of Orodara. The time also came when kerosene-burning refrigerators were no longer viewed as unnecessary luxuries, but as valuable means of safely preserving food and medications.

Then there was the thorny question of transportation. The idealism of some early AIMM personnel suggested that if the Africans around them could make do with public transport or motorbikes, so could they. Operating either personal or mission vehicles, it was felt, would instantly set them apart from the surrounding population as people of privilege, power and wealth. There was, furthermore, the desire to avoid the need for dealing with frequent requests to use the vehicle which would surely come from the African community were a vehicle to be secured. But the time soon came when public transport became less and less feasible. The public "taxis" kept largely to the main roads and ran on irregular schedules. Notoriously overloaded, they furthermore constituted a safety hazard for all those aboard. As the Mennonite community of believers began to grow, visits off the beaten path became more and more common. Public transportation was rarely available to such destinations. Motor bikes were only a partial solution.

Above all, there was a growing concern both on the field and at home for the welfare of isolated mission personnel in the event of an emergency. It was at this point that the AIMM Board provided a firm nudge. A mission vehicle would be purchased and based at Orodara to facilitate an expanding ministry and to assure transportation for missionary personnel as needed. (2)

Early idealism gradually gave way to reality on yet another front. Knowing well the pattern of immense building programs which had characterized Mennonite missions of an earlier era in various parts of the world, some of the early AIMM contingent in Burkina Faso frequently expressed their understandable concern that AIMM not get involved again with "bricks and mortar." African-style housing around them could be secured through rent or lease arrangements. A mission office? Business could be taken care of from the desk drawers of a missionary living room.

Orodara Kalanso is born

But missionaries have children who grow up and need education. It was not long that the Burkina Faso missionary family was wrestling with exactly the same needs and concerns that earlier generations of missionaries elsewhere had confronted. How can we assure an adequate education for our children? Where, how and to what level can this be provided on the scene? A family or two expressed strong interest in home schooling. For the majority of parents, however, this was not an option given heavy program responsibilities on the part of both spouses. A way needed to be found to bring children together so they could be taught and cared for by AIMM personnel recruited for that purpose. Classroom space and sleeping quarters could initially be arranged in one of the courtyards rented by AIMM in Orodara. But who could provide the teaching needed?

It was at this juncture that Judith Harder's name entered the discussions. She had earlier spent a year with the Burkina Faso missionary team as a volunteer. In this capacity she had endeared herself to all. Whatever support or held was needed by the team, Judy was always available. A trained teacher with a collegiate major in French, she had years of experience in Canadian public schools in the Provinces of Alberta and British Columbia. When in 1987 it became clear that some qualified educational personnel would have to be found, the missionary team sent inquiry to North America asking if Judy would accept to return for a two year tutoring assignment with their children.

Upon being approached by the AIMM Board, she promptly accepted. She herself later wrote of her return as follows: "In September, 1987, I arrived at Orodara with six boxes of books and materials, ready to start a school. September 21, the classes began in a make-shift classroom on the guest house compound. . ."

"The school facility was proving to be a real challenge. It was a guest house, a teacher's house, and a classroom at the same time, and these do not mix well. There was too much traffic and too many interruptions. Something had to be done about that situation." It was at this juncture that one of the missionary couples left for furlough and the decision was made to continue renting their house for the children's schooling needs. A temporary solution had been found. "At last we had real school! Even two classrooms, . . . real school desks, blackboards, bulletin boards, and a new teacher's desk. . . . In January, 1989, the name *Orodara Kalanso* [pr. kah-LAH-nsoh] was chosen." (3) The term *kalanso* was a combination of two words from the local dialect meaning literally "a study house." The name gave rise to the intriguing acronym "OK." A student news sheet eventually appeared entitled "The OK Reporter"!

Over time, a series of people with excellent qualifications were secured to serve as teachers in the *Kalanso* at Orodara. During Harder's last year it was Linda Cummings who saw this opening as an opportunity for service as well as for pushing out her own personal horizons. With a BS in music education, she had taught in public schools and served for a time on the secretarial staff of the EMC headquarters in Ft. Wayne, IN. After a year of language study in southern France, she arrived in Burkina Faso in time to overlap with Harder for six months before her return to Canada. It was during Cummings' three years of teaching that Elena Entz, a sister of Loren Entz, also came to Orodara as a teacher's assistant and a support person.

By the late 1980's the growing AIMM team was adding more school-age children with each new arrival. It was clear to all that the temporary arrangements in rented quarters for teaching and caring for the missionary children could not suffice long term. Adequate and permanent facilities had to be provided.

Once again an appeal was made in North America. Needed was a couple who could take charge of a building program and then serve as hostel parents for a growing resident student family. This time God's provision came in the persons of Gordon and Rebecca Balzer Klassen from Winnipeg, MB. Rebecca had training both in Christian Education and in nursing. Gordon's file revealed that he had experience in "carpentry, carpeting, maintenance, mechanics and youth work." An excellent fit! After a school year in Sherbrooke, PQ, studying French, they arrived in Orodara in the fall of 1990.

After some months of effort, a land-lease arrangement was worked out with the local authorities for a plot of ground on the western edge of Orodara. By the summer of 1991 the building project was under way. Two years later, a lovely L-shaped complex was ready for dedication and occupancy. Gordon himself told the story best: "The day of celebration had finally come. Three sheep were stewing in huge pots while about 80 pounds of rice were cooking to perfection nearby. The freezer was filled with Coke. All the benches from the Orodara Church were in our yard and our friends and neighbors were beginning to fill them up. . . ."

"When everyone was seated the program of dedication began with lots of singing accompanied by drums. Our goal in the celebration was to share with the people the reason behind the hostel building and at the same time to make it an evangelistic outreach. The church leaders led the service; our hostel family recited Psalm 103 and sang a song in French; a fellow missionary gave a challenge and then followed two prayers of dedication. . . ."

"I had started just over two years earlier with a piece of land, roughly 225 feet by 325 feet located on the outskirts of Orodara. Very quickly I realized that my background in carpentry hadn't given me much experience in the type of work that was ahead of me. The first job was to remove all the old mud huts of the squatters and to level the land. This, of course, was all done by hand. Next I was able to employ a number of the neighbor women to carry sand in from a nearby stream bed. They brought in the equivalent of thirty dump-truck loads of sand on their heads. I had some metal molds made and taught two of the church men how to make cement bricks. The cement had to be mixed by hand for the 12.000 plus cinder blocks which were needed to complete the three buildings. . . ."

"During the building process I was able to purchase an antiquated cement mixer which had been broken for over 30 years. With a lot of hope and prayer I ran literally all over the country to beg, borrow and 'acquire' the parts needed to make it turn again. It was a lot of work, but proved to be invaluable when it came time to mix the 900-plus bags of cement needed for foundations, floors, pillars and beams. The Lord led me to an excellent Burkinabe brick layer, a person very difficult to find. I was very thankful for this because it freed up time for me to work on plumbing, electrical, windows, doors, etc."

"The final months had us working against the calendar, since furlough dates were set and the building was advancing only slowly. Somehow roofs and ceilings, walls and gates, trees and landscaping, beds and sinks were all completed before our departure. This was truly a reason to give thanks to God and to celebrate!" (4)

With roomy facilities and grounds thus provided, the Klassens assumed the responsibility of house parents and maintenance. In the summer of 1993, they were joined by David and Elvera Dyck Stoez from Winnipeg, MB. Both graduates of the University of Manitoba with degrees in education and with teaching experience in the public schools, they brought great strength to the missionary children's school. When they concluded their term of service in the spring of 1995, they were followed by Bonnie Schmidt, a fellow Canadian. With a certificate in Biblical studies from Winnipeg Bible College and teacher's credentials earned at the University of Manitoba, she brought broad competence and training to the Orodara Kalanso.

A noteworthy dimension of this evolving educational program was the addition of an African to the teaching staff. Calixte Bananzaro (pr. kay-LIXTE bah-nah-NZAH-roh) had a position in the local government school in Orodara. He had a command of several languages including French and English. A Christian, he quickly came to the attention of Orodara missionaries. Schedules were worked out to allow him to teach French in the missionary children's school. When, in a government cut-back, Bananzaro lost his job at the town's secondary school, missionaries negotiated a contract with him to teach full-time in the children's school. His courses included math, French, language arts, physical education and music. Commenting on this arrangement, Stoez at one point wrote: "It has long been a goal of OK to bring a West African perspective to the curriculum, and our students are uniquely privileged to have a Burkinabe teacher to facilitate this. Bananzaro is able to lend his cultural perspective to subjects from music to French to language arts. He is a free and open teacher, and has been eager to assimilate Western educational models and practices, demonstrating much imagination and flexibility."

"Our students are not the only ones to benefit from Bananzaro and his family remaining in Orodara. He is a leader in the Mennonite Church, remains active in the local high school leading student Bible study, and has provided us with meaningful contacts with school administrators and teachers in Orodara." (5)

Reflecting on the organization and development of the AIMM school/hostel complex, Judy Harder observed: "Orodara Kalanso has opened a new era in the work of the Africa Inter-Mennonite Mission in Burkina Faso." (6)

Indeed it did.

a shift in missionary stance

After a decade of AIMM presence and ministry in Burkina Faso, "growing pains" were nowhere more evident than in the area of mission/church relations and, in some cases, missionary/African relations. The original set of statutes drawn up in early 1981 had resolutely envisioned a single legal entity. With insufficient African personnel at that point to register as a viable African church, it had been decided to register as a Mennonite Mission while specifying a ten year deadline for its formal dissolution. By that time it was envisioned that a Mennonite Church of Burkina Faso would have emerged with its own statutes of which missionaries would be members and within which missionaries would serve.

Upon submitting the original papers, they were returned for modification to meet government formats for such documents. They were again submitted in reworked form in February 1983. While a time limit for the existence of the Mission was dropped, the statutes still made it clear that missionaries and Africans were seen as a single body of colaborers engaged in a common effort to plant a Mennonite Church in Burkina Faso. A slate of officers was comprised of three missionaries and one Burkinabe. (7)

As to structure, a General Assembly was proposed comprised of the pastors and evangelists of the Mennonite Church, Burkinabe lay people as delegated by their local congregations and the missionaries sent to work in the country by AIMM. A *comité directeur* (French term for a guiding or oversight committee) was to be composed of four missionaries and two Africans designated by the Church's General Assembly.

Upon receiving the submitted statutes, the government's response was to request a set of bylaws before taking official action on the Mission's request for legal status in the country.

In May 1984, papers were again submitted to the government including, this time, a set of bylaws which named the six members of the oversight committee. (8) Across the top of document three words were written in block letters: SERVANTS PILGRIMS WITNESSES.

One article of the statutes was devoted to a definition of "Mennonite Communities" which could take shape under the administrative umbrella of the Mennonite Mission. (9) Although submitted as the bylaws of a mission, the language and concerns of the document were those of a church body. This language, and the concepts, had been threshed through in consultation with African church members who affirmed and supported them.

It was in the fall of 1984 that long-awaited word from the government was at last received. Signed by the Minister of the Interior and dated October 19, 1984, official recognition of the Mennonite Mission of Burkina Faso had been granted. This news was received with relief and joy on the part of all.

But within three years time, a noticeable change was in the wind. Dennis Rempel, who had played a major role in forging the documents eventually accepted by the government, had by 1986 decided with his family to take a leave of absence. Siaka, who had also been intimately involved in drafting the proposal, was studying at Bangui. Within the steadily growing missionary team, new views and voices were beginning to be heard. This was clearly reflected in a set of minutes of a strategy meeting held with missionaries in November, 1987, during a visit of the AIMM Executive Secretary Earl Roth. Early in the minutes it was stated: "We have considered various models of church/mission relationships and propose that we function as two separate organizations (church and mission) in partnership and accountable to each other." (10)

There were many strands of influence at work in bringing about this shift of missionary stance in such a comparatively short period of time. One had to do with missiology. In a paper written and circulated on the field for study and comment it was stated, in part: "Mennonite churches send us missionaries in order to do an evangelistic work in an unevangelized area. As missionaries we seek to establish churches in this area by evangelizing, forming new Christians into churches, teaching the leaders of the churches (including provision of the Scriptures) and leaving the churches independent and equal to our own churches, at which point we may be sent to another area."

"Our work as missionaries sent by our home churches is therefore essentially an itinerant and temporary work, while the work of the planted churches as the body of Christ in their locations is essentially permanent. . . . When the mission is understood as the evangelistic work of a sending church, it can be really seen that the sending church and planted church are two organizations. It follows then that the relationship between a mission (the evangelistic work of one church) and the mission-planted church is one of separate identities cooperating toward the independent equality of both churches so that both may in turn go to new places to do evangelistic work." (11)

In missionary meetings of the time it was asked, on one occasion, if AIMM had the right to create the structure of a single Mennonite Church in Burkina Faso without the emerging churches in the different tribal groups having opportunity to approve or disapprove. Given the often high walls of ethnic pride which existed between them, might the projected intertribal Mennonite Church, it was wondered, prove to be a bane rather than a blessing?

Another powerful strand of influence was the high level of awareness among the Burkina Faso missionaries of earlier chapters of Christian mission work in Africa which had left churches saddled with unmanageable institutions and a mind-set which assumed sizeable continuing subsidies from overseas for their ongoing institutional and administrative expenses. There clearly was a strong sentiment present among the Burkina missionaries which might have been summarized by the motto: "This time, let's get it right!"

And there was also a mix of practical issues which directly touched the lives of the missionaries. Some asked: "If we are to apply the letter of the present statutes, does this not mean that we need to consult our African church leaders in establishing and allocating mission budget monies? And what about such personal concerns as retreats, our children's education, scheduling of our furloughs and the nature of our assignments here?" Given this mix of growing reservations among the missionaries, it proved to be both tempting and easy to find unofficial ways of conducting some details of mission business - - especially in regard to the allocation and use of funds. As a result, the missionaries found themselves in the uncomfortable position of working under a constitution which called for a single organization but, in fact, functioning as though there were two.

One missionary put the issue succinctly, noting that: "New converts are in effect joining the mission. But the reality of the local church exists nonetheless!" In his study paper he went on to add: "Discussions of institutional patterns of relationship between Church and Mission are meaningless if interpersonal relationships between missionaries and local believers are found wanting." (12)

simmer comes to boil

Although meetings of the missionary/African oversight committee continued to be held as stipulated by the constitution, African church leaders early sensed the growing lack of missionary enthusiasm for the structure under which they were working. The Africans also soon discovered that some financial policy decisions were somehow being made, here and there, of which they were not a part. Once aware of this, they decided to express their displeasure by simply refusing to attend any more such meetings! There was clearly a festering resentment among the church leaders. It was the situation which AIMM Secretary Earl Roth found in the course of his administrative trip in the spring of 1988.

Missionaries and Africans alike wisely agreed that a special session of the General Assembly should be convened and an honest effort made to confront, together, a growing accumulation of misunderstandings and grievances. Present were six church leaders, ten missionaries and two AIMM Board representatives. (13)

Since Siaka was away in school in Bangui, Abdias Coulibaly, one of the local church leaders at Orodara, served as chairman of the sessions and as chief spokesman for the African Church. After opening preliminaries, he began the time of dialogue with a direct question addressed to the AIMM representatives: "We have in hand a set of statutes drawn up and approved by our government four years ago. Are you aware of them? We like them. What do you think about them?"

There followed a mix of observations and questions which laid bare a wide range of concerns shared by the African leaders. Among them were the following: "How do you view the Church in Burkina Faso? What do you mean when you speak of the Church? It seems more and more that missionaries are doing their own thing and leaving us work on our own. Does AIMM stop their missionaries from helping the Church even though they are members? When we needed to build a little bridge leading to our chapel, we were not allowed to use the mission truck because we couldn't afford to pay the mileage fee. We see the missionaries making decisions about missionary placement and program priorities without consulting with us. Why does AIMM not want to get involved in special projects for the Church? We would have several to suggest. What about leadership training? Siaka is in Bangui but we do not know where or how he will fit in when he returns. We need pastors now. Where are we to find them? How can we train our own? And when we do have pastors, how are they to be supported? Who decides when missionaries leave us? How are new missionaries chosen and sent to us? Cannot we have any say in this process?"

And there was the matter of language analysis of the various tribes. "We understand and appreciate the importance of this work. But we are eager to bring a witness about Jesus to these groups. Must we wait for this until we can use their own language or until some Scripture is available in their own tongue? Why not get started in whatever language they can understand?"

The Church leaders were not yet finished. There were still more questions: "How do you evaluate your first ten years of work in our country? How do you evaluate our Church at this point? Do you really intend for your missionaries to work side by side with us in our Church or independently and apart from us, leaving us to struggle? We are new, young, inexperienced and still a small Church. Still we hear you telling us to forge ahead on our own as a free and autonomous Church. We should and we want to, but are you missionaries not with us? A part of us? Is this not also your Church? Or is it only ours? We see how other Missions work in our country and the help they give to their Churches. Should they ever decide to plant congregations here in our province, the comparison between them and the AIMM may not be a good one for you and us." (14)

The Africans had not been unkind, but they had been totally honest in revealing their perplexity and their accumulated frustration. In the process, they also shared some personal hurts which they carried as a result of some specific incidents of interaction with some members of the missionary team.

This experience of intense probing and exchange left many of the missionaries in a subdued, chastened mood. Efforts to explain past actions and responses were mixed with appeals for understanding and forgiveness.

In later conversations with the AIMM delegation, various missionary comments were heard. While there was gratitude for the scope and honesty of their sharing sessions, there was sadness and regret for the deep rift in missionary/African relations which had become painfully clear. Some comments were: "We are probably much farther apart then we thought we were. Where do we go from here? There is a lot of misunderstanding still. Real communication is greatly needed." (15)

pointing a way out of the mission/church bramble patch

It was clear that the calling of the special session had been urgently needed and providentially timed. It was equally clear that some immediate follow-up on the discussions was also needed. For starters, some clarification of AIMM perspectives, goals and priorities was essential. Although a mission, AIMM did not plan to simply reproduce the programs of other older, established missions in Burkina Faso which, incidentally, reflected some of what AIMM had earlier done in Zaire. Since in Burkina Faso there was a functioning network of government schools, AIMM would not undertake anything in the area of formal public education. It was, however, sympathetic to literacy projects among new rural Christians. Since there was a network of government hospitals and clinics within the country, AIMM would not seek to establish a medical program, as such, but would consider supplementing government efforts in public health and child care in rural settings. AIMM would not provide salaries for pastors or evangelists but would provide scholarships for those who indicated a sense of God's call and who desired to seek Biblical training in schools available to them in Africa. AIMM would not subsidize church operating budgets but would help with special projects which were directly church related such as putting roofs on chapels built by local Christians or providing materials for TEE ministries or men's and women's seminars and retreats.

AIMM was committed to an ongoing strategy of evangelism via trained linguists resident in rural areas teamed with missionary church planters. But this did not mean that the Church needed to delay any evangelism initiatives it wanted to undertake among unreached people on its own. Indeed, AIMM encouraged this. AIMM was committed to ongoing recruitment of new missionary personnel to fill the places vacated by earlier personnel and to occupy new territories. But AIMM also wanted to seek the counsel of church leaders in the process.

As to structure, AIMM had earlier drawn up statutes at a time when an emerging church seemed yet some time in the future. AIMM's faith had proved to be too small. A church was taking shape more swiftly than had been foreseen. It was now AIMM's view that the Burkina Faso Church be encouraged to look seriously at its own structural needs and to pursue immediately its own legal registration with the government of the land. This did not mean that AIMM was isolating or distancing itself from the young Church. On the contrary, AIMM wanted to affirm, encourage and partner with the Church in every possible way that fell within the framework of its priorities and objectives.

AIMM now needed to review the statutes of 1984 and make amendments or changes in the light of the rapidly changing local mission/church scene. Such a review would focus clearly on the Mission, per se, while leaving full freedom for the Church to seek its own legal identity before its government. In the meantime, a new mission/church committee needed to be created which could be the medium of shared discussion, shared information and joint planning in all areas that were the mutual concern of both bodies. Every effort would be made to keep lines of communication open. Without this, misunderstandings and hurtful experiences would surely start to accumulate again and sap the joy and vitality of their ministry together.

A major logjam in communications had been broken loose. While the new structures proposed by AIMM were not the first choice of the Church leaders, they nonetheless expressed appreciation for the open dialogue that had taken place. They now understood the priorities and the principles that AIMM wanted to apply to its work in Burkina Faso. They furthermore could now immediately address themselves to spelling out priorities and structures which they felt best suited their needs and their Church.

CHAPTER 71   SIAKA RETURNS

The spring of 1985 found Siaka approaching the end of his first year of study at Bangui. It had been a challenging year for him. It was his first encounter with study at this academic level. A single man, he was housed with several other unmarried students in rather small quarters. Since meals were not provided by the school, the single students were obliged to fend for themselves. The cramped living situation had often made it difficult to find quiet study time. It had nonetheless soon become apparent both to teachers and fellow students alike that he was equal to the challenge and would give a good account of himself in the five-year theological study program in which he had enrolled.

But there was a problem. Siaka was nearly 30 years old. For him there was a growing concern about a life's companion who would share his desire to serve the Lord and his Church in their land. By this time most men of his age had long since been married. It was not that Siaka had no options. He had many. But on the question of his marriage, he was firm. Whoever he chose as his life's mate would have to be a committed Christian. He would marry no one who did not share his love for the Lord. He furthermore wanted a spouse with an educational level which would permit them to discuss and pray together knowledgeably about the many problems of leadership which he knew lay ahead of him. But, in the view of some of his friends, the conditions he had set for himself seemed impossibly high. Where was he to find such an educated Christian woman in a predominantly rural area under growing Muslim influence?

What if Siaka were to return to Orodara for the summer vacation to help with the work of the new, growing Church? Not only would this be of great help to the missionaries, but it would also give opportunity for him to keep in touch with his Church. And might it also be possible that a summer back in his home area would shed some helpful light on his quest for a life's partner?

wedding festivities in Orodara

Five years earlier, during his year of study at the C&MA Bible School in Bobo, he had met a fellow student named Claire Kienou (pr. KYAY-noo). The daughter of Christian parents and an apt student, she had encountered several proposals of marriage. But she too had set some high standards regarding a future husband. During their year in the Bobo school they had been only casual acquaintances. During the intervening years, however, she had kept hearing about Siaka. Upon returning to Orodara he soon made a trip to Bobo to see friends and acquaintances from an earlier school year there. It was not long that contacts were reestablished with Claire.

Respecting their culture, matrimonial discussions were initiated between clan elders on both sides. By fall, all the pieces had come together to their obvious delight. A civil wedding took place with three other couples in the office of the Mayor of Bobo on August 29, 1985. For them this was simply an exercise to meet the requirement of the law. All attention was focused on the religious ceremony which was set for September 7 at Orodara. Invitations went out to fellow Christians, both white and black. The ceremony and festivities were a blend of African culture and Christian tradition. The wedding was made an occasion for underscoring Biblical teaching regarding Christian marriage and the nature of a Christian home. There then followed festivities which gave place to the African gift for celebration. There was food in abundance for all. There was singing and dancing accompanied by the sound of the *balaphone*, a type of wooden marimba common to western Africa, which lasted far into the night.

Siaka had added another "first" to the history of the young Burkina Faso Church - - its first Christian wedding.

The summer passed swiftly. Siaka was respected and sought out by many. He often preached in worship services both in Orodara and in the villages where little groups of believers were taking shape. But it was in listening, counseling and teaching roles where his gifts came through most clearly.

Siaka and Claire returned to Bangui in the fall of 1985 where he plunged back into his studies. With the privacy of their own quarters as a married couple, Siaka found it easier to order a disciplined study schedule. But they were not only there to study. For instance, it was not long till they had their own vegetable garden to supplement the scholarship funds provided by AIMM. This venture was quickly noted by other students. A candidate for a *licence* in theology planting a vegetable garden? Indeed there were some among them who were writing letters to their sponsoring missions protesting that their scholarships were insufficient to meet their cost of living. Siaka and Claire did not need to verbalize their message to the students around them. There was more than one way in which they themselves could supplement a limited student budget.

There were also classmates who were actively seeking ways of making their time at Bangui a springboard for studies overseas. Was it not, after all, more prestigious to secure diplomas somewhere outside Africa? In conversations with them on this topic, Siaka quietly let it be known that he wanted to pursue his studies as near his homeland as possible. If their goal was to prepare to serve their people and the churches from which they had come, why would they want to subject themselves to the disorientation of a prolonged exposure to a western culture which, in so many ways, was contrary to their own?

an invitation to attend Normal '89

In North America the years 1988 and 1989 witnessed a buzz of activity in Mennonite circles as plans were laid for another joint GC/MC conference. It was staff of the GC/COM which took the initiative of extending an invitation via AIMM to Siaka and Claire to come as fraternal visitors from Burkina Faso on that occasion.

Advised of this invitation by the AIMM executive secretary, Siaka's response was swift and read in part: "It is with great joy that I received your letter . . . . I accept your invitation without reservation. In this invitation I see a desire on the part of the AIMM to collaborate with those to whom the Lord has sent it. This invitation affords me the privilege to meet my brothers and sisters in Christ in America." (1)

Aware of the plans under way, other member conferences of the AIMM also extended invitations to attend their annual conventions that summer as well. The end result was that the Traore couple followed a six week itinerary which took them from coast to coast in a loop across southern Canada and central United States concluding with a week in the Elkhart area. (2) An added facet of this inter-Mennonite project was the covering of Claire's travel costs by the AIMM Women's Auxiliary.

On their return to Africa, their travel was routed through Burkina Faso where they spent time renewing acquaintance with fellow believers there and hearing of the efforts to smooth relations between the mission and the church. They returned to Bangui in the fall of 1989 with personal horizons which had been greatly broadened and with growing convictions about the role of the Church of Christ in Africa.

Christian mission: a challenge to the African Church

As Siaka approached his fifth and final year at Bangui, he needed to declare a topic for a written thesis which was a requirement for graduation. By this time a theme had already taken shape in his thinking: the African Church's own responsibility for involvement in Christian mission. In finished form, an introductory section to the thesis carried the following observation: "One cannot approach a topic [of study] without genuine personal interest. Regarding this work [thesis] my interest was born following a course in missiology given at FATEB by Professor Goran Janzon. This course posed a personal challenge for me. I came to understand that the missionary task entrusted to the Church was the concern of every local church in every place and also the concern of every Christian who is a part of the body of Christ."

"This challenge led me to reflect on the understanding of the missionary task on the part of African churches. After some investigation I discovered that for most African Christians the missionary work of the church is reserved for those from the West. Lacking teaching, African Christians are unaware of their own missionary responsibility as was the case for me personally. It was this reality that impelled me to undertake this study with a view to arousing an interest in mission within the African Churches."

"Through this [written] work it is my objective to read again the missionary order given in Matthew 28:18-20 with its parallel texts and to lift out of them the message which is as relevant as ever and which addresses itself to every church and to every Christian. In the light of these Biblical texts I want to correct the erroneous conceptions which African Christians have concerning the missionary task and then to sensitize them so they may realize their missionary responsibility and, furthermore, show them that [Christian] mission is a challenge which is addressed to them today, a challenge which they must accept." (3)

This said, Siaka divided his thesis into three major chapters of material. The first was an exegetical study of Matthew 28:16-20. The second was an overview of the history of world mission. The final chapter was devoted to the general topic of Christian mission and the churches of Africa. Among many noteworthy sections, the following highlight sharply his personal convictions and his challenge to his fellow African Christians: "The mission to preach the Gospel to all the nations as the Lord Jesus Christ commanded it is a task which is incumbent upon every Christian as an individual, upon every local church as a community and upon the universal Church as the body of Christ (Mt 28:16-20; Mk 16:14-20; Lk 24:46-49). The mission of the Church is not entrusted to any particular category of people of any particular race or of any particular geographical area. It is the concern of everyone who accepts Jesus Christ as Savior and Lord. Mission is the reason for the existence of the Church." (4)

"The African continent, which at three different times in history was the object of mission, wants today to bring its contribution to the great cause. Some efforts are being made but much remains to be done. Along side the example of a minority of churches which are engaged in this task, the majority must fall in step." (5)

"The missionary imperative which remains valid until the return of the Lord allows no exceptions. Everyone, whether at the level of the individual or of the community, must be involved. It is from this perspective that I want to challenge the African Churches to assume their missionary responsibility." (6)

"Since this mission is not a human enterprise but a divine one, it would be better to search for the method which is revealed in the Scriptures. The original missionary method is that of Jesus and the apostles, one which is applicable for each church. Jesus and the apostles did not undertake the mission by using great material resources; they did it simply by the power of the Holy Spirit. This power continues to be available; Jesus himself promised to be with his own until the end of time, a presence which is manifested by the Holy Spirit. Thus we encourage the African Churches to re-read the New Testament in order to follow the Master of our mission and those who followed immediately after Him in this task which was entrusted to them." (7)

"Given its divine nature, its universal and unalterable character, the mission presents itself as a challenge to the Church with regard to a sinful world without Christ. This challenge is even further emphasized at the level of churches who do not assume their missionary responsibility. . . . Western missionaries responded to this challenge by bringing the Gospel to us. African churches must not continue to believe that this challenge addresses itself only to those from the West." (8)

In his concluding paragraph Siaka wrote: "Everything indicates that there is a challenge, that it is real and that it cannot be evaded. It must therefore be faced. The African Churches have great potential for taking up the mission. This mission is possible because the One who ordained it said: 'I am among you.' It is He who achieves the mission through His Church." (9)

facing a mixed agenda

Siaka returned to Orodara fully aware of the special meeting of missionaries and church leaders which had been convened in the spring of 1988 with AIMM representatives from North America. He knew very well the discontent on the part of the Burkinabe which had made this meeting necessary. He understood their irritation and shared some of their frustration. He had also been aware that missionaries were dissatisfied with some of the statutes of their own organization. On the other hand, against the background of his studies and his travel, he also understood that some of the expectations that his fellow Christians had regarding the AIMM were not in the best interest of the future well-being of their own Church.

Even before leaving Orodara for study at Bangui, Siaka had frequently found himself playing the role of a "go-between." A careful listener who had a gift for making gentle responses, he was uniquely gifted for engaging in "shuttle diplomacy" between a steadily growing, highly motivated missionary team, on the one hand, and an emerging and equally motivated intertribal church with its mix of cultural backgrounds, on the other.

Regarding Siaka's abilities, a missionary once described a typical scene as follows: "He arose from the circle of people beneath the mango tree for the third or fourth time. He had asked permission to check a matter with another church leader. 'It was like this,' he reflected, 'each time these types of meetings occurred. White skins trying to understand black skins, each with their own agenda.' It was the meeting of the missionary team and the fledgling national church. Both groups were trying to learn about the other. That was an accomplishment. While the mission agenda was carried out during the more official morning sessions, the church agenda was generally carried out during the schedule breaks and at lunch. Or, at times like this when, as liaison person, this young believer, Siaka, would ask to be excused to clarify a point, or raise a question with one of the church leaders in private." (10)

Now, newly returned from his studies at Bangui, his gifts were more needed than ever.

stiffening pagan resistance

For one thing, new village Christians in some areas were beginning to feel the pressure of opposition and menace from tribal leaders. At first village elders, though often being animist and/or praying Muslims, showed remarkable tolerance vis-à-vis the new white-skinned residents among them. They were intrigued and even pleased that there were people from other lands sufficiently interested in them and their languages that they would live among them to learn them. But as people began to make professions of Christian faith and, consequently, began to abandon some of the cherished cultural traditions, concern began to stir. The following entry was made in the journal of a traveling AIMM executive secretary already in 1984: "A sobering aside: there is some restlessness among the local fetishers. The 'Christian business' is moving too fast. The unofficial word in the village is that they want to test the strength of the Christians and their Jesus in some way or other. A reason for prayer." (11)

A case in point was that of Solo and Bakary, the two young men in the village of Tin who had made professions of faith in response to the teaching and influence of Paul and Lois Thiessen and Siaka. A comparatively small, closely-knit Muslim village of Siamou people, its response to the two new Christians was quick and resolute. Bible studies had been started in the homes of the men, and for a while a few other young people from the village joined them. When the elders expressed their disapproval, the studies were moved to the Thiessen home. Then only Solo and Bakary came.

At one point Thiessen wrote: "They are both facing opposition and alienation because of their break with the Muslim religion. They do not face blatant, open persecution, bur rather subtle, quiet rejection. This is not easy for them. Both of these men are married and have children. Both have had an addition to their family since they made a decision to follow Jesus Christ. Both men refused to have their newborn babies baptized according to the Muslim tradition. This has angered the elders of the village. Everyone in the village of Tin is Muslim and everyone always has their child baptized on the 8th day with the *Imam* giving the child a muslim name. Pray for Bakary and Solo that their faith in Jesus Christ will increase and that they will not give up!" (12)

At a later date Thiessen again wrote: "Among the Siamou people weddings are arranged by the parents. Recently Solo's father went to his friend's home to discuss wedding arrangements. Solo's younger brother, at the age of 29, needed to get married. He asked whether they could provide a daughter for his son. The answer was quite upsetting. No, they would not give a daughter to be married into that family. The reason given was that Solo was no longer a Muslim. Who knows, his younger brother might follow Solo's example and they could not have their daughter married to someone who was a Christian. . . . As a result of this, enormous pressure is being put on Solo to convince him to leave the Christian faith and turn back to Islam." (13)

As an African, Siaka understood these desperate struggles of faith all too well. He had had his own personal chapter of harsh conflict with his own family. He could reach out to new Christians around him sharing out of his own experience and witnessing to God's sustaining grace in his own life. His personal testimony and deep commitment to Christ was an invaluable, steadying influence for young Christians under fire.

working through uncertainties

But if Siaka's place as an intermediary between the mission and the church and an encourager of individual Christians was immediately clear, there were other areas of concern in which there was much less clarity. First and foremost, there was the issue of his household's own livelihood. They had been scrupulously honest in their use of AIMM scholarship monies at school. But now this chapter was coming to a close and there was no plan in place for meeting their ongoing financial needs.

It was not that they had had no other options. He had made his mark on the campus at Bangui. During his last year there, he had been approached about staying on and becoming a staff member. And among the steady stream of visiting professors and representatives of church organizations, more than one had offered him employment. But Siaka and Claire had made commitments to AIMM and to the young Mennonite Church of their homeland. They intended to honor those commitments. However, now that they had returned home, early discussions regarding their future with their Church had shed little light on their path. While the Church warmly welcomed them home, the leaders saw no possibility of supporting them financially in any way. Indeed, was it not the AIMM who had provided them a scholarship to study? For what reasons would AIMM not now simply continue to support them to carry on their work within the Church?

Indeed there had already been conversations with AIMM on this subject. Siaka and Claire were available and eager to serve. Was it possible that the AIMM Board would consider them as candidates for service under AIMM placement and assignment? (AIMM had already received similar proposals from some Zairian couples, but AIMM policies made no provision for such action.)

Along the way Siaka and Claire had listened with interest to descriptions of an earlier chapter of North American Mennonite history which had witnessed pastors basically earning their own livelihood among their fellow church members. Instinctively, they knew that even if some form of long-term AIMM support were open to them, it would clearly set them in a category apart from the young Church which they sought to serve. Furthermore, to allow the Church in its earliest formative years to assume that it had no responsibility for the livelihood of its own leaders and pastors would be a great disservice to it.

During this time of uncertainty AIMM took two actions. First, a one-time grant was made to help the young couple establish and furnish a home in Orodara. Financial support was also pledged for a six months period during which they were encouraged to make arrangements for a large measure of self-support.

Siaka early reviewed the status of the book shop he had opened years earlier. Accounts were reviewed and inventory upgraded. Using some of the funds generated by his bookshop, he also opened a small hardware shop in Orodara which offered the basic sorts of supplies and equipment which were always in demand among villagers in that frontier setting. Leaving both shops in the care of employees, he was largely free to devote his time and energy to his Church. After a period of uncertainty, Siaka and Claire were settling in.

CHAPTER 72   ENCOUNTERS WITH TRAUMA

Across the years of AIMM presence in central and southern Africa, its missionaries had on numerous occasions been surrounded by the violence of conflict. Arriving in northwestern Africa, it was thought that in the comparative isolation of this sub-Saharan part of the continent, the calm routine of rural life would not likely provide much disturbance. But here, too, AIMM missionaries were to experience the menace of conflict.

the sound of shot and shell

A special report prepared for the AIMM Board in early 1986, on what came to be known as "the border conflict," read in part as follows: "Both Burkina Faso and Mali were once part of an arid colonial expanse known as French West Africa. French rulers eventually reduced the region into smaller areas among which were Mali and Upper Volta. Both were accorded their political independence in 1960 with a common border of some 600 miles."

"Early in the era of independence, disagreement arose between the two countries as to the exact location of their shared border along a hundred mile stretch known as the Agacher (pr. ah-gah-SHAY) region. Situated along the last hundred miles of the eastern end of their joint frontier, it contains a significant deposit of manganese and presently lies in Burkina Faso territory. Rival claims to the area finally erupted in conflict in 1974 which sputtered on for some months before both countries accepted to submit their dispute to the International Court of Justice at the Hague."

"Late in 1985 the Burkinabe government undertook a census of its population in the Agacher region. Apparently in the process Burkinabe identification cards were issued to the villagers in the area whether they wanted them or not. When the Mali government became aware of what was happening, there was prompt retaliation in the form of air raids on some villages in Burkina plus troop clashes along the frontier which spread to the south. At one point, an air raid by Burkinabe planes was reported on Sikasso, a major Malian town just west across the border from Orodara. It was apparently in response to this action that Malian troops crossed the border and moved eastward along the Sikasso/Bobo road which passes directly through Orodara. At one point, we heard that Malian personnel had arrived at or near Kotoura and were advancing toward Orodara."

"Our AIMM team had planned for weeks to gather for a few days at Christmas time for a mixture of team discussion, festivity and the celebration of Christmas. Hostilities broke out on December 24 finding our team together at Orodara. For three nights in a row they joined the local population in a general evacuation of the town to bivouac in the surrounding bush. It was, therefore, a most welcome phone call which arrived at the AIMM office the morning of January 2, 1986. It was Dennis Rempel calling from Ouagadougou to inform us that hostilities had ceased; that all AIMMers were fine; that they were in process of returning to their villages of assignment." (1)

It was only a few days after the cessation of hostilities that Dennis Rempel accompanied Gail Wiebe to her village of Kotoura. Traveling by motor bikes, their journey along the main Orodara/Sikasso road was uneventful. But after they turned off the main road and began to travel in a southerly direction along a sandy track, they soon came across grisly evidence of the brief but violent clash which had taken place between the invading Mali military contingent and the defending Burkinabe forces. Alerted to the crossing of their border, Burkinabe troops took up hidden positions along the narrow, winding road. When the armored vehicles and troop carriers came abreast of their positions, they opened fire at point-blank range. Vehicles were quickly disabled. As troops dismounted and sought to scatter, they were cut down by automatic weapon fire.

En route to Kotoura, Rempel and Wiebe on several occasions had to thread their way past burned-out hulks of armored vehicles and the bloated, khaki clad figures of dead soldiers strewn about under the heat of the tropical sun. Yet once again AIMM personnel, in Africa and at home in North America, had occasion to ponder "what might have been" had not the protecting hand of God been extended. Once again there was much reason for thanksgiving.

a man named Abou Kabar Traore

But occasions of stress for Burkina missionaries were not limited to near encounters with physical harm. There were experiences of other kinds which also carried harsh emotional and spiritual impact. December 1984 found a three-man AIMM administrative team traveling in Africa. (2) Arriving in Burkina Faso they heard news of the recent dramatic profession of faith of a Muslim *karamogo* (pr. kah-rah-MOH-goh), i.e., a person of influence in the Muslim community who was considered to have special mysterious powers. His name: Abou Kabar Traore (pr. ah-BOO kah-BAR trah-OH-ray). He had only recently arrived in Orodara. A tailor by trade, he sometimes set up his table and hand-operated sewing machine in Orodara's marketplace.

The Orodara market day of November 19, 1984, had started out for him like any other but an event soon took place which had a revolutionary impact upon his life. As he himself described the morning, it all started when he noted Donna Entz making her way through the market pausing here and there for conversation with people and for purchases of food supplies from a variety of vendors. His account, as recorded later, went as follows: "As I saw her across the way in the market place, it was as if some supernatural force struck me - - a physical feeling like being hit with an object in the back of the neck. I did not understand what was happening but I suddenly realized that my life would never be the same again. I also knew I had to go talk with the missionaries." (3)

Of that encounter the Entzes themselves later wrote: "On November 19, 1984 Donna made a quick trip to the market to buy some okra to make the noon sauce when suddenly she was called by a fellow sewing in the market place. She answered to her African name Fatimata Gwe (pr. fah-ti-MAH-tah GWAY) . . . in astonishment because she did not know this market person. . . . But even more surprising were the words which came from his mouth . . . that he wanted to become a Christian. Never had she heard that before from someone she had not long known. She invited him to our house." (4)

Not seeing Abou the following day, the Entzes sought him out and gave him a cassette tape of a message by a Muslim leader of the area who had converted to the Christian faith. A day later Abou came to their home. He had listened to the tape. It had "broken his heart," he said. He couldn't go to work. He couldn't go to the mosque to pray as he had for the past 36 years of his life. He wanted to hear more. Another tape by the same converted Muslim leader was played for him and after some discussion the Entzes closed in prayer asking specifically that God would continue to reveal himself to Abou.

The following day the Entzes left Orodara to spend a week with Gail Wiebe and the young Christians in Kotoura. But Abou couldn't wait. In their absence he went to the Rempel courtyard where, one evening, Dennis explained in simple terms in Dioula, the trade language, the steps to faith and trust in Christ. With eagerness Abou followed the steps outlined for him and after reading some passages of Scripture and praying together, Abou returned through the night to his home.

an energetic witness

Upon the Entzes return to Orodara, Abou quickly sought them out to share his new experience with them. In their journal of events of those days they noted: "What a radiant face Abou had that morning. Again that evening he came over; we read a passage together and prayed as we did the next morning as well."

As he had already begun to seek out his Muslim friends to share his new experience with them, Entzes gave him a hand-crank cassette player which he carried and played wherever he could gather a group if people to listen. His testimony was starting to have an impact in Orodara. Some of his friends with whom he had formerly gone to Muslim prayers were now coming to his house to listen to the cassette player and to hear his story of the change which had occurred in his own life.

It was soon after he began circulating in Orodara with his player that he took violently ill. He spent days gagging and vomiting. These symptoms, plus the accompanying jaundice, gave missionaries reason to suspect hepatitis. But for Abou, he was sure that it was God's heavy hand upon him causing him to purge his inner being of all the sins of his past life. In his younger years he had dabbled in occult practices while employing a variety of fetishes which, he said, he had acquired at great cost. When he converted to Islam, he carried much of this occult baggage with him and continued practicing it in the name of Islam's god. He had much to confess; much of which to be purified.

Abou was a member of the Samogho tribe which was predominantly Muslim. He was the first person of this group to profess the Christian faith. News traveled fast and members of his immediate family in Sikasso, just across the nearby Mali border, soon heard this disconcerting news. Reaction was swift. Within the span of one week's time, three different family members came from Sikasso to attempt to deal with him. The first was his oldest brother who, after the death of their parents, was the head of their family. A man of means, he arrived in Orodara in a Mercedes Benz vehicle. "Why this folly? What had the new Protestants in town given him to persuade him to bring such shame upon their family and tribe?" Abou insisted that he had been given nothing but that "God himself had called him" and that he had responded to that call.

When his brother realized that Abou was not swayed by his presence or his questions, he asked to see his personal identification papers. Pocketing them he declared: "If you are determined to become a Christian, you no longer have need of these for you no longer are one of us."

Several days later his nephew arrived from Sikasso, Abou's confiscated personal papers in hand. The papers would be returned if he would renounce the foolishness of the Christian faith and return to the faith of his family, the faith of Islam. Again Abou described what had happened to him that day in the Orodara marketplace and talked about his new found faith and peace as a believer in Jesus Christ.

Before the week's end, a third family member arrived. This time it was another brother to whom he was particularly close. Going to the home of the local Muslim leader, Abou was called to join him there. After some friendly conversation he invited him to accompany him to the local mosque for prayers, an invitation which Abou declined. Immediately the atmosphere between them changed. Before an assembled group of onlookers, his brother openly vented his anger. A wealthy man, he had at that point already made eleven trips to Mecca and thus was known by the honorary term of *El Haji*. Lifting a sack, he opened it to reveal bundles of bills. Dangling the sack before Abou he let it be known that if he would turn his back on the Christian faith, he would be handsomely rewarded on the spot. Once again Abou told of his experience with God and the change it had made in his life. He could not give this up no matter what the financial enticement.

It was on the heels of these high-pressure encounters that the AIMM delegation arrived in town and had opportunity to meet and talk with him. In his written report presented later to the AIMM Board, the AIMM executive secretary wrote: "Abou is a well-built man of medium height in his late 40's. One of the first comments he made, after the round of introductions, was: 'This is the 18th day since I stopped praying.' What he meant was that it was now 18 days since he had quit going to the local mosque for daily prayers. He went on to say: 'I've finally found what I've been searching for all these years as a praying Muslim, and that is peace for my heart and people who love each other.'"

"In later conversation with the missionaries we learned of the marked change they observed in Abou. When he first came to them, he appeared to be tense and distraught with a 'wild' look in his eyes. But following his profession of faith, they found him to be at ease both with himself and with others. As this story unfolded for us, Abou sat quietly responding to our questions. At one point he said: 'I'm not afraid of what my family and former Muslim friends can do to me.' He often repeated what he'd said earlier: 'I have finally found what I've been searching for all of my life as a praying Muslim: I've found peace and this they cannot take away from me.'" (5)

economic pressure

Though his testimony spoke of peace of mind and heart, Abou was under very real pressure - - not only from his immediate family but also from the local Muslim community of Orodara. He had earlier negotiated a deal with a local Muslim business man for his sewing machine. A schedule of agreed-upon payments was to be met with the proceeds of his sewing jobs as a tailor in the market place. His break with the Muslim community, however, came with Abou carrying an unpaid debit balance on the machine. His creditor tradesman was demanding immediate liquidation of his outstanding debt or the return of the machine.

His profession of faith had also found him in the process of negotiating for a house in Orodara. Once again influential Muslim traders stepped in. Promises which had been made were canceled and he suddenly found himself with the real prospect of being without a shelter for himself and his wife.

Sharing all of his experiences with the missionaries, ways were found to meet these immediate material crises in his life. But even though he was able to pay the balance of his debt on his sewing machine, he discovered that requests for his services as a tailor dropped off sharply. Influential people were effectively diverting trade from his table in the market place.

dreams

With increasing frequency, Abou was having dreams which he believed to be God's way of revealing not only fresh insights into the Christian faith but also instructions for his life. Though he was basically illiterate, he began to talk of his sense of call to be the first African missionary to his people, the Samogho. In a taped testimony he said at one point: "My name is Abou Traore. I am the first Samogho to become a Christian but my problem is that my family is not happy that I have become a Christian. They are strong Muslims. I want you to pray that they will become Christians as well and that we can all walk the Jesus road together. I may be the first Christian but I am not going to be the last one. . . . I am very happy today. Don't say that there aren't any Samogho that are Christians; Abou is his name." (6)

Some of his dreams were arresting in their powerful simplicity. One morning he came to the Entz home to relate a dream of that previous night. "There was a judge who had a daughter who did not behave properly. One night she was caught. She was brought to court and it was her father who was the judge. The sentence of death was passed on to her by her own father. Then in the courtroom, the judge took off his white robe and folded it up, went and stood beside his daughter and told her to go free, that he would die in her place. And so it happened, he died in her place. This was to show that on judgment day God will judge in both justice and love." (7)

In relaying this incident Entz commented further: "Abou understands well the incarnation. Last night, as he was explaining the good news to a lady who is becoming a Christian, he suddenly said: 'Why bother about talking about God's Son, that just confuses; let's just call Him what He is - - God. It is God himself that became man and took the whole burden of sins upon himself with his death." (8)

incredulous stories

By April of 1985, Abou was coming to the Entz home with stories which they and the other missionaries found difficult to assimilate. He was speaking more and more of nighttime encounters with practitioners of the occult of the surrounding area. He would talk of being invited or challenged to meet for nocturnal power confrontations. He described how on one occasion he sat, in the night, across from six villagers in a desolate area separated by a deep open pit. At their command a large snake emerged which was to have swept him into the pit but, through God's protection and power, it only was able to brush his leg before falling back. The six opponents, said Abou, returned defeated to their village and the following day were all prostrated with illness.

On another occasion he was responding to a call for a duel of power with a woman renowned as a sorceress. Traveling by night on a borrowed bicycle, he suddenly was thrown to the ground as his bike was enveloped with flames of fire. Gathering up his cassette player and teaching materials he made his way back home, once again spared from death. Other stories of a similar nature were becoming more and more common. Unable to verify them, the missionaries were nonetheless hesitant to dismiss them as pure fabrication because of Abou's continuing declaration of faith and his often repeated desire to win his own people to Christ.

a disheartening turn of events

June of 1985 found the Entzes preparing for a furlough in North America. In conversations with other missionaries and with church leaders it was decided to grant Abou's request for baptism before their departure. This event took place on June 9, 1985. It was witnessed by a mix of Orodara people and followed by a time of celebration.

With the Entzes departure, Abou turned more and more to the Rempels for discussion, teaching and times of prayer. With the added administrative responsibilities which came to their hands as a result of a reduced missionary team at Orodara, there simply were not enough hours in the day for extended impromptu times of sharing to which Abou had been accustomed. A further factor was a missionary reticence to continue responding to his frequent requests for money for various personal needs.

Abou's visits became less and less frequent. Then, suddenly, he disappeared. This was soon noted and both missionaries and African Christians began to make inquiry. Then, one day, word came from Sikasso across the border in Mali. Abou had returned not only to his family but also to the Muslim faith. Furthermore, he had reverted to his former practices as a Muslim *karamogo*. It was even rumored that he was selling religious pictures, which he had formerly received from missionaries at Orodara, as potent sources of protection for householders who purchased them from him.

It obviously was a stunning reversal for missionaries and Burkinabe Christians alike. How could this all possibly be explained? Had Abou only been a clever, consummate actor who quickly sensed how to gain support and help from missionaries and the young Church at Orodara? Had his profession of faith been contrived? Had he really not been touched by God's grace as he claimed? Had nothing changed in his life after all? Was there nothing genuine in the testimonies he had so forcefully shared with fellow Muslims? In all of the reports of his experiences, had there been no truth?

Burkinabe Christians, it was later learned, had always been more guarded in their views of and response to Abou, especially as he began telling of spectacular but unverified nighttime encounters with the powers of evil. Siaka too, it was learned later, had had increasing reservations about him. Gradually consensus emerged among believers - - missionaries and Africans alike - - that Abou had truly had an encounter with the Lord and that his early testimonies were genuine. But somehow, as he attempted to engage the demonic powers with which he had been so well acquainted in the past, he had lost his way.

Needless to say, with passing time many missionary discussions have turned to "the Abou story." What was to be learned from the disheartening experience? What if he had been more carefully discipled before allowing him to engage in such high profile activity? Had his baptism been granted too hastily? What if more effort had been made to work carefully with him and the cluster of Muslim friends who for a time had also quit going to the mosque for prayers? Had local Burkinabe believers been sufficiently consulted? Had the young local Church been sufficiently challenged to offer counsel and support during those months? Should more have been done to verify the dramatic accounts he was bringing to the missionaries?

It was with a deep sense of sadness that, a few years later, the Christian community of Orodara received word of Abou's death. What had been the circumstances of his passing? In his last hours, had he once again turned in penitence to the Lord he had once professed to love and serve? In the end, this was the hope of all Christians who had known him.

Cheba is dead!

A missionary newsletter elaborated on the startling news: "The shock waves rippled out of Kotoura, to Orodara, then to Banfora, Bobo, Ouagadougou, and on across the ocean. Cheba Traore, the man with a ready warm smile is gone, no longer with us. A strong, energetic, and prosperous farmer, proud of being able to provide adequately for his family, a strong leader in the Church, he was well respected in the community in spite of the opposition he received because of his Christian faith. He was seen by Christians and non-Christians alike as an honorable and honest man. His home was practically the village bank as some people chose to entrust their money boxes to his care. He was known for his goodness toward others, helping people out in their need, lending a listening ear. His alcoholic brother who had been less and less able to provide for his family was especially appreciative of Cheba's decision to help supervise fieldwork on his farm and provide much needed food."

"Born in 1958 to a family that eventually had 13 children, he grew up with a Muslim father and a mother who held closely to the Senoufo traditions. When the first missionaries, Gail Wiebe and Anne Garber, arrived in his village Kotoura in 1982, Cheba was designated by his father Kunandi (then deputy chief) to look out for their new visitors. In October 1983 he committed his life to Christ with no solid assurance that anyone was going to follow his lead. He was the first known Christian in the entire region. But others did little by little, including his wives and several brothers. Some turned back for fear of witchcraft, ancestral spirits or because of family pressure, but Cheba refused to budge from his newfound faith. On May 19, 1984, Cheba and four others sealed their commitment to Christ through baptism. As Loren Entz had encouraged them, Cheba put his hand to the plow and never turned back. He became the pillar of the small church in Kotoura. Others looked to him for wisdom, guidance, encouragement. He was an innovator, a man of new ideas with the ability to rally people to his cause, both in the church and in the community where he took a lead role in the organization of several development projects. He was a member of the village pharmacy committee, active in Kotoura's equivalent of a parent-teacher association, president of a Sicite (pr. see-CHEE-tay, the name of the local Senoufo dialect) Bible translation administrative committee and a frequent delegate to the Burkina Faso Mennonite General Assembly meetings. During the past year Cheba took an active role in helping to evangelize and then to nurture new groups of believers that were springing up in neighboring villages at a phenomenal rate."

"Cheba was gravely ill for only two days before the Lord took him home at 12:20 AM, February 22, 1994. He is survived by his two wives, Mariam and Karidjah, eight children from ages one and a half to fifteen, and twelve brothers and sisters, including MoussaTraore, the Sicite Bible translator."

"Words cannot express how deeply he will be missed by the entire Mennonite Church and mission community here in Burkina Faso as well as by his friends, neighbors and family."(9)

Some years earlier, the story of Abou Kabar had created troubling questions and problems for the young Christian community in Orodara. But this was very different. While there always had been a bit of mystery which surrounded Abou, this was never the case with Cheba. With an innate love for people, an infectious optimism and his unshakable commitment to Jesus Christ, he had lived his life in the fish bowl openness of the African village of which he was a native son. Everyone knew him, what he believed and for what he stood. He resembled a sturdy, growing oak not only in the local Church at Kotoura, but also in the broader Mennonite community of his region, as well.

It was at an early stage of his inquiries about the Christian faith that the issue of the deeply-rooted practice of animal sacrifice of his people became a recurring issue of discussion. About this stage in his life, Gail Wiebe Toevs once reported: "A number of young men started joining Cheba and every evening he would have four or five of them sitting and struggling as they learned to read. We would sometimes just sit and converse and Cheba was especially curious about what we believed. He liked it when we read to him from the Bible. Often he wanted to talk about sacrifices and he wanted to know what the Bible said about them. He told us what the traditional village beliefs are and how he himself felt about traditional religion and Islam. He had been a practicing Muslim himself. He talked freely about spirits and sorcery and the fear people live under. As we talked and read together, numerous times he would say: 'I know this is the truth but I just can't quit making sacrifices.'" (10)

But the time came when he and his fellow Christians in Kotoura arrived at the conviction that they had to make a break with the practice if they were not to compromise their declared faith in Christ who, they had come to understand, had been the ultimate and final sacrifice for their salvation. He had been tested early and frequently on this issue. For instance, he had no more than returned from the evangelistic meetings in Orodara in October 1983 where he made his profession of faith, than he was requested by one of his brothers to kill a sacrificial animal for the family. He respectfully declined.

Then there was the story of Cheba and Babala, the elderly blind man in the village, who had come to faith through Cheba's faithful witness and teaching and with whom a visiting AIMM delegation had, on one occasion, had an interview. It was some time later that the old man fell ill. A missionary newsletter of the time described what happened: "In spite of his suffering, he maintained his good humor and faith. . . . Toward the end of 1993 . . . sensing that his time on earth was near its end, he showed no fear or anxiety. Rather he seemed to be continuously peaceful and . . . especially happy to be in the company of another Christian."

"The day after Christmas, December 26, 1993 he passed away. He was the first adult for whom the Christians in Kotoura had to conduct a funeral. But the question immediately arose, would they be able to bury their own? The chief elder of Babala's family, Meleke (pr. meh-LEH-keh), contacted Cheba informing him that Babala had communicated his wish to be buried the Christian way and that he, the elder, was willing to grant him that wish. And so the Christians contacted the Church in Orodara and they began to prepare the body for burial that was to take place the following day. The Christians from Orodara soon arrived to help in the preparations and in the negotiations with the elders of the village. Everything seemed to be going smoothly; the elders were very cooperative until the next morning when some out-of-town relatives and friends arrived. Immediately tension began to gather in the air."

"An elder began manifesting his discontent with the whole process. He, and others behind him, were bound and determined that no Christian funeral was going to replace the traditional way of doing things. Dissension arose among the elders. The elder went to Babala's home and found the Christians about ready to put the body into the casket. He started arguing and complaining there, accusing the Christians over certain details. He came back with his gun. Since Babala had been a famous hunter in his earlier years, he was to be honored, as is the custom here, with a few shots in the air. But instead of shooting off one, two or three shots, he shot off eleven rounds. When asked why he did that, he became furious and the scene threatened to erupt in chaos. Babala's eldest son was also a Christian, and pressure was put on him to have the funeral done the traditional way. His friends were angry when he did not agree."

"The Christians retreated to an area behind the house and began singing softly while the son talked with the dissenters. Miraculously, people calmed down, the air cleared, and the Christians were able to conduct the funeral as planned. Later, we were told that some young men in the village were on the verge of coming to beat up the Christians. We did not know if that was true or not but we do know that God did protect the believers at that critical time."

"A humongous funeral procession (many people were very curious) then moved on to the cemetery with the Christians singing all the way. A graveside service was then conducted and testimonies were given of Babala's life. Meleke, the consenting elder, was so impressed that he stated he would like to have a funeral like that too. His disapproving son cut him off. Surprisingly the elder who had created so much dissension got into the action too and helped to lower the body into the grave. When everything was finished and done, non-Christian members of the family and other village elders talked in admiration of how wonderful Babala's funeral was. As fellow missionary Loren Entz said, it was an excellent opportunity to share Christ with others."

"The funeral was truly a test case. If the Christians had failed to get their way the first time, it is highly unlikely that they would have been permitted to conduct Christian funerals later on. The traditional way of conducting a funeral is so incredibly important that any challenge to the norm is seen as a threat. Thankfully Babala's wishes were honored and the Lord was glorified on that day. This meant too that the Christians would likely be free to bury their own the way they choose from now on." (11)

Cheba had been in the foreground of this historic event. Commenting further on the occasion, a missionary later wrote: "Cheba was elated. Many village people were impressed. Babala's non-Christian family members had nothing but good to say about the way it all turned out. The village rumor that Christians did not bury their dead was gone forever. This event seemed to provide a potential opening for sharing Jesus with the elderly in Kotoura."

"Little did Cheba realize that he would be the next to be called home. February 1994 was full of activity for him. He had just completed a one-week course on teaching literacy in Dioula and he eagerly began his classes. In addition, another YWAM (Youth With A Mission) team came to Kotoura and helped the Christians evangelize there, in Kangala and Sayaga as well as a new village, Sarakanjala [pr. sah-rah-kah-NJAH-lah], that Cheba specifically wanted to reach. He eagerly accompanied the team, even walking all the way to Sayaga (about three miles) one night."

"Two days after their departure on Monday, February 20, he had to quit his literacy class and go home because he was not feeling well. He took a few malaria pills and rested. The next morning there was no improvement in his condition. So he was taken to the local dispensary for a malaria injection. At 3 P.M. his friends took him back to the dispensary for another injection, but instead of getting better he got worse. Shortly after midnight February 23, 1994, his family and friends tearfully acknowledged that he was gone."

"Cheba's death was a blow to both the non-Christians and Christians alike. His funeral was the second Christian adult funeral in the entire area. People came from far and wide to attend. This time the Christians faced no opposition to conduct the funeral as they wished." (12)

why?

The shock was brutal and was felt not only at Kotoura but all across the Mennonite Church landscape. In the villages, as at Orodara, the African culture immediately called for an explanation. A young man in the prime of life just dies after being sick for only forty-eight hours? The age-old African question always posed in times of crisis was posed once again: "Why?"

Inevitably murmurs began to circulate from hearth fire to hearth fire as villagers and their elders sat and shared news and opinions. Who didn't know that Cheba had led the Kotoura Christians in refusing to offer the sacrifices required by their traditions? Was this not a warning from the departed ancestors? Was this not proof that the power of Jesus that the Christians loved to talk about did, after all, have its limits beyond which they dared not go in challenging the ways of their forefathers?

In honesty it must be admitted that the "why question" was not voiced exclusively around village fires at night. It also surfaced in the hearts and conversations of missionaries and AIMM staff people at home. At this critical time in the history of the Burkina Faso Church, how could the Lord allow this death to take place? How could a sovereign, all-wise God allow the loss of this gifted and winsome African leader in a setting where he was needed so much? There was still so much that he eagerly wanted to do even as his testimony and influence became more effective day by day. It took extra faith and grace to affirm that, even in these circumstances, God was perfectly able to bring about that which pleased Him in the ongoing life and experience of the Kotoura Church.

Cheba's death did, in fact, have some somber repercussions. Over a year later the following news note appeared in a letter from Burkina Faso: "All of the churches of the area have suffered from reduced attendance because of Cheba's death last year. So we pray for courage and boldness to move ahead with joy." (13)

But amidst the trauma and uncertainty, a new courageous voice was heard in the village of Kotoura. It was the voice of Moussa Traore, Cheba's younger brother who had been one of the first people he had led to faith in Christ. He immediately let it be known that he was assuming the supportive responsibility for Cheba's widowed wives and orphaned children. In addition to these new responsibilities he declared that he would continue in his role as Anne Garber Kompaore's language consultant as they together pursued their dream of giving the people of Kotoura God's Word in Sicite, their own language. As for the future of their Church, he said simply: "Yes, those who counted on Cheba for their faith will fall away, but those who count on Jesus will remain firm." (14)

As Cheba was laid to rest in his village, another Christian stepped forward to fill the leadership vacuum in the grieving Church. His name: Traore Seydou (pr. trah-OR-ay SAY-doo). A quieter, less charismatic man than Cheba, he nonetheless was described by missionaries as a man of deep faith and commitment who is solidly grounded in the village life of Kotoura and carries great concern for their ongoing witness, as Christians, in their setting.

Meanwhile news of Cheba's home-going found another Kotoura Church member in the country of Mali finishing the third year of a five-year study program in a Bible Institute. His name: Madu Traore (pr. Mah-DOO trah-OH-ray). One of the three boys who years earlier had been shut out of their family courtyard because of their profession of faith in Christ and one of the two first grooms to celebrate a Christian wedding in their village, he was that year the top student in his class.

In spite of what seemed to be a shattering loss from a human standpoint, God continued to lay His hand upon people of his choice in the village of Kotoura.

CHAPTER 73   NEVERTHELESS

The years of the 1980's and early 90's in Burkina Faso brought a mix of encouragement and disappointment. There were occasions of elation and vindicated faith; there were also occasions of soul-searching and tested faith. But through all the experiences, AIMM missionaries never wavered in their commitment to their primary goal of evangelism and church planting among the unreached people in Kenedougou Province for which they had accepted responsibility. And by the mid-1990's, there was solid progress to report.

on the linguistic front

In Kotoura, where the Garber/Wiebe team had settled in early 1983 among the Sicite-speaking Senoufo people, a decade of effort had resulted in significant advance with a language that had never been reduced to writing.

Along the way Wiebe had married Russ Toevs of Whitewater, KS. After serving together at Kotoura for approximately four years, they terminated to permit them to take over a family farm in Kansas. During the same decade, Garber had also married but to someone closer at hand. In her work with the Sicite language, she had on several occasions traveled to Ouagadougou, the country's capital, to make contacts with government and university personnel who were involved with the country's literacy program and with Wycliffe personnel also based there. It was during these visits that she became aware of yet another organization known as "The National Association for the Translation of the Bible and Literacy of Burkina Faso," or ANTBA-BF in its French acronym form. It was in contacts with this latter group that she met its Executive Secretary, Daniel Kompaore (pr. koh-mpah-OR-ay).

He was a well-educated man. In addition to holding a responsible position with the Burkinabe government, he also devoted many hours of his personal time to his church as a layman and to the translation committee of which he was an officer. With his great desire to see Scriptures translated into as many of the languages of his country as possible, he took an immediate interest in the surprising linguistic approach to evangelism adopted by the recently-arrived Mennonites in the western tip of his country. In time, mutual professional interests broadened to make room for a growing personal friendship. A widower, he still had school-age children at home. In Anne he saw not only a potential mother for his children but an educated, deeply committed Christian who shared his love for his country, his people and the work of the national committee of which he was the head. When Daniel broached the idea of marriage, she accepted.

The wedding took place on January 2, 1993, in Daniel's church and was followed by a large reception attended by some 500 people including all fellow AIMM missionaries, MCC personnel and some of Anne's family members from North America. After some negotiation, her status and support as an AIMM missionary were reinstated and she continued her work with the Sicite language, a project which now came under the administration of ANTBA. It was in this capacity that she made periodic trips back to Kotoura for consultation and review of new materials in hand. On one such occasion she reported in a newsletter: "Most of this dry season, i.e., January to May, I'm in Kotoura helping Moussa and a new worker, Joel, test the translation drafts of I John, Mark and James to see if they accurately communicate the message intended."

"So now we are ready to do the final proofreading and within the next two months, I John will be published with help from the International Bible Society. After over ten years of analyzing, putting the language into writing, training, drafting, etc., we are finally beginning to reach our long term goal. For me, this is an immense joy, a time for gratitude to our Lord for bringing us this far, through all the ups and downs, joys and trials. It is truly a miracle when I contemplate that there were no Christians or written language in 1982, and through the power of His Holy Spirit people have come to the Lord and remain faithful to Him in spite of the fact that they face opposition." (1)

It was a special joy that Moussa Traore, the man mentioned in the report, was the younger brother of Cheba whose sudden death just a year earlier had rocked the young Church.

At N'Ddorola in the north, Dan Petersen and Maliki Ouattara, the gifted assistant that the Lord had providentially brought to his attention, were also registering progress with the Nanerige (pr. nah-neh-ri-GAY) dialect of the Northern Senoufo. Kathy Petersen shared an intriguing insight into the value of their work in late 1994: "'I like working at this! This is very good for me! I have never heard this before.' This is what Mawa, (pr. MAH-wah) my longtime friend here in N'Dorola, just said to me this afternoon as we finished another session of working together on her language. But she is more excited than usual because we have recently started working with the first chapters of Genesis."

"Mawa was born the same year I was, but she seems older than me. She has older children because she married very young. She has been widowed and then remarried. Two of her girls died of disease in 1990. I met her the first year we came to N'Dorola. She was the only Senoufo woman I could find that understood some French. Over these years she has patiently helped me learn hundreds of Senoufo words and corrected my sentences. All of this time she has known that we came here to translate God's words into her language, and in the last couple of years she has seen Dan and Maliki working hard in the office at Bible translation. Now she is hearing it for the first time."

"I play a few verses of Genesis that we have recorded on cassette tape. Then I stop and ask her to summarize what she heard and I ask several questions to find out if the verses were understood correctly. . . If people cannot answer a question about a verse correctly, then we know that something in the translation is confusing and not communicating well. . . .'"

"It is encouraging for me to see how interested Mawa is in hearing this for the first time. Pray with us that she will come to know Jesus through the translated Word of God. And not only her but many, many more." (2)

The language of the Siamou people is generally considered by linguists to be one of the most difficult in western Africa. By the summer of 1995, two AIMM couples were working with this group and its language: Paul and Lois Thiessen in the village of Tin, and Gerald and Beverly Neufeld in Orodara. A news note in the summer of 1995 reported: "Gerald has been putting some Siamou stories on cassette to continue to ensure that the Bible translation uses the same format and way of saying things that Siamou does. Simply translating the words into Siamou is not sufficient. Gerald has spent some time in analysis to work toward establishing a tentative alphabet. Our co-workers Paul and Lois Thiessen work in a different Siamou dialect in the village of Tin. Primarily Paul works on the alphabet while Gerald works on grammar, but we need to find out how different the two dialects are. Paul wants to have a tentative alphabet in place by June 1996. Siamou is a tonal language and the tone makes analysis slow and time consuming." (3)

And among the Samogho people to the southwest of Orodara, the Entz/Solomiac team was at work respectively in the villages of Saraba and Samogoyiri. The team had found two excellent language consultants in the persons of Traore Fabe, a young, educated Muslim, and Traore Ali (pr. trah-OR-ay fah-BEY, and trah-Or-ay ah-LEE). Members of the Samogho ethnic group, they both worked with the Solomiacs on dialect analysis while helping the Entzes in translating Old Testament stories into their own language. Recorded on cassette tapes, the stories were being used to acquaint the Samogho villagers with Biblical history as a prelude to the presentation of the message of the Gospel. On one occasion the Entzes wrote: "Perhaps you remember several years ago when we reported a discussion between Loren and Soundji (pr. SOO-ndjee) who reads the Koran. He read a verse to Loren in Arabic and then explained it as follows. 'It says here that the People of the Book have three books, the Torah, the Psalms and the Gospels, and that these books contain good counsel for us. How can we ever study all these books plus the Koran?' Loren's answer to him was, 'That is exactly why we have come here.' . . . Soundji was happy." (4)

By 1995, the Samogho team had grown to six adults with the arrival of two more Wycliffe appointees, Scottish-born Fiona Holburn and Mary Hendershott of Kansas, USA. Their specialized training in literacy meant that the Samogho team became the first with sufficient personnel to work simultaneously on three fronts: evangelism, language analysis and literacy.

Thus it was, in the summer of 1995, that of the seven language groups which had been identified in Kenedougou Province, AIMM missionaries were at work among four plus the multilingual population of Orodara. (5) Active recruitment was under way back in North America for candidates for assignment to the remaining three.

church planting: a variety of approaches

AIMM did not enter upon its new venture in Burkina Faso with a predetermined timetable of events it was going to try to meet. Language analysis, while living among the people, was adopted as a strategy for winning a hearing for the Gospel among traditionally resistant ethnic groups. But as to when and how churches were eventually to be planted, the AIMM team left its options open. There were too many unknowns. With passing time, however, different missionary teams in different settings soon discovered that no two situations were the same.

In Kotoura, for instance, the missionaries were practically overrun by a group of young people who initially came eagerly requesting help in their efforts to become literate. When Bible stories were used as reading material, there soon came probing questions about the Christian faith. And suddenly Cheba, the son of the village chief, made a profession of faith. Others of his age group soon followed. The missionaries had little time to ponder theories of church planting or fine points of missiology. New converts were enthusiastically sharing their faith discoveries with others - - and there was response. With a few exceptions, the older generation in Kotoura remained onlookers and, periodically, created problems for the younger believers.

In Tin, the AIMM team encountered its most resolute opposition to the Christian faith and its most determined harassment of early believers. To this point, AIMM methodology in that village might best be characterized as "presence evangelism," as missionaries continue to live and move among the people and quietly encourage the few who are receptive. Meanwhile, language analysis continues.

In Orodara, the approach has been to seek to gather a mix of believers who have come to that town from various ethnic backgrounds and to integrate them with new converts into a new church body.

It is at N'Dorola in the north and at Saraba and Samoghoyiri in the south that the most deliberate effort has been made to nurture a people's movement toward acceptance of the Gospel. It is for this reason that, initially, much time has been devoted to cultivating the interest and confidence of the opinion-setting, decision-making oldsters of these villages via the translation and telling, first, of Old Testament stories. Story telling is a powerful, traditional African way of communicating ideas and truth. In other heavily Islamized societies, it has been found by many missionaries that a Biblical bridge must be built from the Old Testament, with which many Muslims are familiar, to the Gospel account of the Word made flesh, a concept which is totally foreign and even troubling for Muslims.

Entzes themselves describe their experience as follows: "When our materials from the Torah were ready for teaching, we explained that we are the People of the Book, and that these are God's words given to the prophet Moses. In Saraba the old men were eager to listen to teaching from the Torah, because we had already been working with an older man in the checking process. The stories themselves already had credibility for him, so when we asked the old men for permission to teach, the two questions were when and where. There was great interest, but would they come? We went with our cassette to the men's meeting house. The men were there. Though they had invited the women, they hadn't come. . . so Donna began making a longer circuit through the village, which she continues to do each day, calling women as she goes. We meet every morning for about 30 minutes with a group of both men and women, about 15 people, all older than we are."

"Several nights ago, a story teller in town retold several of the Bible stories to a visitor with amazing recall. Though our language ability is not advanced enough to present the new materials tonally correct, we have acquired enough language skills to raise discussion questions at the end of each session so people get used to discussing, not just passively listening. Why do you think that a mixed group of men and women in Saraba are comfortable with each other to listen and discuss together? Our only explanation is that though Muslim religion and traditional customs have separated the sexes, traditional story telling happens in mixed groups. Teaching is in the form they appreciate. We are thankful that our reason for being here is now clearly understood."

"Almost all stories touch deeply the lives of these people in some way. In the story where Abraham begs God to save the good people in Sodom, the people were totally shocked that a human could ask God to change his mind and beg for mercy. When the story of Adam and Eve was retold, and a description of the garden was made, the story teller said that God came to visit with them every day and that there was no hunger. The woman's idea of shalom is adequate food because her courtyard often experiences food shortages. The midwife was delighted to deliver a baby the same day that we studied about the midwives who refused to obey Pharaoh's orders. Today a man referred to these stories as fables. He was corrected by another man who told him, 'These stories are not fables, they are true and this all happened.' Praise God with us as we experience God at work." (6)

on the church scene

The bombshell of Cheba's sudden death had not fallen into a vacuum. Even though the Church had scarcely a decade of history behind it, it had already acquired a certain image, a certain identity which stood it in good stead during those troubled months of rumor and conjecture which followed Cheba's death.

There was, for instance, the story of the church food banks. In the late 1970's and early 80's Burkina Faso was still suffering from erratic rain fall with resultant crop failures in some places. As the first cluster of Senoufo believers emerged at Kotoura, among the many topics of discussion which surfaced was one having to do with their responsibility as followers of Jesus among people who, at times, literally did not have enough to eat. Out of this discussion with their missionaries was born the idea of a food bank. The concept was that, as a group of Christians, they would build granaries and store any surplus grain they themselves produced or other grain which they could purchase at reasonable prices. When some months later there were villagers who ran out of food, they would open their granaries and sell grain to those in need at the same price it had cost them - - this at times when commercial people were typically gouging the hungry people with exaggerated prices.

This compassionate behavior became a powerful witness. Frequently they were asked: "But why do you do this?" The answer would always be: "Because we have experienced the love of the Lord Jesus for us and we want to share some of this love with others." As the rains gradually became more normal, the need for such emergency help diminished but the memory of their concern for others remained among the villagers.

A rural, agricultural people, the Christians found still other ways of demonstrating their compassion for those around them. Every year there were some in the village who, for reasons of accident or illness, were unable to plant, cultivate or harvest their crops. Sensing another opportunity for "practical Christianity," on several occasions Christians simply took their tools and volunteered much-needed physical labor in the fields of others. When questioned about the reason for such help, their answers were clear: "We are now followers of Jesus. In his Book He tells us to treat others the way we would like them to treat us."

Encouraged by Cheba's enthusiasm, the Kotoura believers had made frequent bicycle trips to neighboring Senoufo villages to simply share their new found faith. Over time names of new villages of the area began to find their way into reporting to the Elkhart AIMM office, such as Kangala, Sayaga and Sokouraba, as places where small groups of Christians could be found.

The popular interchurch and intertribal men's and women's retreats continued. Though at first not convened annually, attendance gradually grew as enthusiastic reports of the inspiration and joy of these gatherings were carried back to fellow believers at home.

In the troubled days following Cheba's death, there was nonetheless a negative whiplash of commentary and attitude among nonbelievers. Anne Kompaore, at one point, commented on that period as follows: 'Non-Christians predicted that the Church would fold now that Cheba was gone. Young people were told not to join or they would end up like Cheba. Weaker Christians made themselves scarce at church services. Another disappointing development was that the leader of the young group in Sokouraba had lapsed into alcoholism and the group was no longer meeting together. The core church members in Kotoura were shaken with grief over the death. But they remained firm in their faith. On Easter Sunday the Sayaga and Kangala Christians came to Kotoura with their first baptismal candidates. The procession to the nearby stream for the baptism was a witness to the Kotoura people that the Christians have not and will not disappear. . . . Cheba will be remembered as the one who had the courage to be the first believer in the entire Tagba Senoufo area, the zeal to spread the Good News to those around him, the initiative to try new ideas and the ability to convince others to join him in his walk with the Lord." (7)

a new Mennonite Church is officially born

The special consultation held in May of 1988 between church leaders and the AIMM delegation had made it clear that there would not be a single organization in Burkina Faso, but two: Mission and Church. While this was not what church leaders had envisioned or preferred, the decision was accepted and church business sessions, thereafter, were oriented toward the implications of this new reality. Upon Siaka's return from Bangui in the summer of 1990, church discussion and planning became more focused.

An immediate need was to formulate a constitution for the Church so that formal application could be made to the government for legal status. In the formulation of the statutes, two historic decisions were made. First, a name was chosen. It was: *Eglise Evangélique Mennonite du Burkina Faso* (i.e., The Evangelical Mennonite Church of Burkina Faso) with headquarters at Orodara in Kenedougou Province. The French acronym would be EEMBF. The second decision was the appointment of the Church's first set of officers. They were: Siaka Traore, President; Moussa Traore, Vice President (Cheba's brother from Kotoura); Namoana A. Amos, Secretary (a teacher in a government youth hostel in Orodara); and Da Oho Clarisse, Treasurer (a woman who held a position as bookkeeper in a office of the provincial government.).

Listed in the statutes were the following four principal objectives of the Church: 1) the announcement of the Good News of Jesus Christ; 2) the establishment of local churches; 3) the formation of servants of God; 4) involvement in social ministries such as education, health, agricultural and development projects.

The request for official recognition submitted early in 1993 took the usual time to make its way through the echelons of government. Then one day AIMM staff at Elkhart received a short, three-paragraph letter from Siaka. It read: "May the grace, peace and love of our Lord be with you."

"We have the joy to inform you that our Church has been officially recognized by the government of Burkina Faso since June 16, 1993."

"Let us praise God and let us pray that this Church may reach the objectives that it has set for itself, i.e., to be a witness to Jesus Christ in Burkina Faso." (8)

677

On the heels of this official recognition came a specially convened work session for which representatives of all the Churches were invited. The announced purpose of the meeting was to spell out "a work program" for the Church for the years 1994 and 1995. Meeting on December 11, 1993, the official record of the sessions highlighted four major areas of concern. The first had to do with teaching and nurture within the Church. It was decided to adapt the well-known TEE pattern and that Siaka Traore and Abdias Coulibaly would be responsible for the program. Given the distance to be covered, a request was presented to the AIMM for a Yamaha motor bike. Materials in Dioula were to be purchased in Bobo; French material was to be ordered from Abidjan in the Ivory Coast.

A second concern had to do with pastoral formation. This was to be studied further at the next General Assembly of the Church which was scheduled for February, 1994.

A third focus was that of evangelization. On this topic, the record of the meeting carried the following statement: "Until the return of the Lord of glory, evangelization remains one of our priorities. This activity is linked with the planting of new churches." In this regard a request was submitted to AIMM for some equipment such as a film projector, loud speaker and a means of transportation. Relative to such activity the Church would be responsible for associated expenses such as travel preparations and meals.

A final focus of discussion was that of development. It was observed that most of the leaders of new rural Churches which were being formed were receiving no support from those Churches. Thus the idea was proposed to help such leaders with a cash grant to start small hog raising projects. Once launched, it was envisioned each would be responsible, in turn, to make a donation of four young pigs to another church leader. (9)

a celebration twice delayed

The official recognition of the government had been the occasion of joy and excitement among the church members and missionaries alike. Now that legal papers were in hand, a celebration of praise was very much in order. The special event would have a double purpose - - to celebrate the birth of the EMMBF and to ordain the Church's first two pastors, Siaka Traore and Abdias Coulibaly, their newly-appointed President and Vice-President. This joyous occasion was to take place at some point during the first trimester of 1994. All of this was shared with former AIMM personnel in America with the expressed hope that some of them would find it possible share in the planned celebrations.

Eventually the date of February 26, 1994, was set for the historic occasion. Little did anyone imagine that the date set would rather become an occasion of shock and church-wide mourning due to the death of Cheba just three days earlier in his village of Kotoura.

But the Church was determined to move ahead. If the celebration of the official recognition of their Church in Burkina Faso was disrupted by their loss and sorrow, the ordination and installation of their first pastors was now more necessary than ever. Dates were set for October of the same year.

An AIMM news release described the occasion as follows: "On October 30th, 1994, the Orodara Mennonite Church gathered to ordain Siaka Traore and Abdias Coulibaly to the ministry, affirming that they were doing their work as pastors well. The council of the Orodara Church had selected these men for ordination and requested Africa Inter-Mennonite Mission missionaries Paul Thiessen . . . and Gerald Neufeld . . . to officiate at the ordination service. This service had originally been scheduled as part of the Evangelical Mennonite Church of Burkina Faso's recognition celebration at the end of February 1994 but both were postponed when Cheba Traore died suddenly. Cheba was a leader in the Kotoura Church, one of the five churches that comprise the EMMBF."

"Representatives from the five Churches joined in filling the backless benches of the Orodara Church on Sunday morning, October 30th. The service, chaired by Paul Ouedraogo, was conducted in French with translation into Dioula by Calixte Bananzaro. After much singing, Gerald Neufeld challenged the two men from I Timothy 3:1-7 with the qualifications necessary for church leaders . . . . Paul Thiessen and Gerald Neufeld then led in an ordination service."

"Members of the Church of Orodara were asked to stand to show their support for these two men. Then, since their ministry extended to the other four Churches as well, the representatives of the other four Churches also stood, signifying their support. Abdias and Siaka responded to several questions to indicate their willingness to undertake this ministry in the power and fear of God and with the support of their brothers and sisters in Christ. Siaka's wife Claire and Adias' wife Cecile stood beside their husbands to symbolize their support for them in their work. . . ."

"At the close of the service, Paul Ouedraogo announced that the council of the Orodara Church had decided that Abdias would now take on the pastoral duties of the Orodara Church while Siaka would be released to work with the other four Churches . . . ." (10)

An autonomous Mennonite Church was a reality in Burkina Faso.

Next, new dates were set for a church-wide celebration of the founding of their church, March 4, 1995. Once again there was preparation and mounting excitement when yet another unanticipated crisis disrupted everything. A missionary letter of the time explained as follows: "In the morning of March 4 the phone rang. A meningitis epidemic had broken out in Orodara and the medical authorities were refusing to allow the celebration to be held. We'd all been looking forward to this occasion for over a year - - Burkinabe and missionaries alike. Tears ran down our cheeks as we stopped to pray for the church leaders in charge of the celebration. We prayed for safety for our church people from the epidemic and for those who might die without having heard of Jesus. A special seminar had been planned in Orodara for all the EEMBF Churches for the following week. It too had to be canceled. . . ." (11) (12)

mission/church relations evolve

Following the mission/church consultation of May, 1988, a suggested set of guidelines for governing future relations between AIMM and the emerging Church were circulated for study. Prepared by Harry Hyde, an AIMM Board member who traveled there with AIMM Executive Secretary Earl Roth, the document reflected a high level of concern that AIMM create no institutions or programs for the Church in Burkina Faso which it later could not maintain on its own. There was also clear concern that the Church be expected to carry financial responsibility for its routine activities including support for its leaders so as to avoid creating a mind-set of dependency with which mission leaders had struggled in some other areas of the mission world. (13)

A need was also expressed for some sort of mission/church consultative body which would provide a setting for dialogue, for sharing of information and counsel between Mission and Church and for joint planning as this might be needed. All in all, the document tended to draw rather sharp structural and philosophical lines between Mission and Church.

By 1994, six years later, missionary discussions had begun to reflect a bit more flexibility in matters dealing with Mission/Church relations. In a March meeting of the AIMM field Administrative Committee (14) careful attention was given to the "work program" which had been traced and circulated four months earlier by the newly-founded Mennonite Church of the country. Minutes of the Mission meeting carried a number of warm commendations for some features of the document, e.g., its clarity and the careful thought it reflected, the high priority given to evangelism and church planting and the obvious ownership the Church was taking in spelling out its own priorities for the future.

Concerns about the EMMBF proposals had to do with the requested AIMM funding of equipment and supplies for the Church's envisioned efforts in evangelism. At one point, in the Committee minutes, it was observed that if AIMM were to respond to these requests, it would be "a major shift from past practice." (15)

And yet, the record of a meeting held just eight days later dealing with the same issue stated a variety of reasons why it might be time to reevaluate this policy of non-funding of Church program activities. Among those cited were: some missionaries who had earlier been designated for evangelism and church planting had terminated; the Church itself now had people very capable of undertaking such ministries; and the church leaders have seen other African Churches grow while using foreign funds and feel that due to their limited resources their own growth has been slower.

Two comments focused directly upon interpersonal relations: "Our past practice of providing very limited material assistance has not enhanced Church/Mission relations. We have come to realize that the way we missionaries have done things till now, independently of the Church, has not been good. We must begin to work in greater cooperation and harmony with our African brothers and sisters in Christ. We believe that the AIMM Board and Elkhart staff would be in favor of increasing financial contributions to church projects."

A concluding paragraph in this set of minutes was particularly significant: "Our relationship is not shallow. The Church has come of age, and we want to relate to the Church as adult to adult. We appreciate the project proposal. TEE is excellent; the plan to help the pastors is great. We have our differences about evangelism, but we are shifting our ideas about working together with the Church in evangelism. We want the Church to be patient with us; we want to talk to the Church about it." (16)

It was clear that Mission/Church relations in Burkina Faso were not in a static state. There was sensitivity, study, heart-searching and prayer going on among the missionaries in the summer of 1994 as they welcomed the emergence of the Mennonite Church of Burkina Faso. Without question, the issue of Mission/Church relations would be an ongoing story as Africans and missionaries continued to seek together, as fellow Mennonite believers in that land, God's purpose for them.

what it's all about

Across its long pilgrimage of witness and service on the African continent, AIMM has experienced its share of problems, setbacks and heartaches. But everywhere - - first in Congo/Zaire, then in southern Africa and in Burkina Faso, God has honored AIMM's efforts to witness in the name of Christ. God has frequently touched lives in spectacular ways and provided African brothers and sisters in Christ who became dedicated, effective collaborators in a common cause. Questions of structure, missiology, funding, missionary orientation, strategy and methodology in mission have always been debated and will continue to be subjects of assessment and change for as long as AIMM continues its cross-cultural witness in Africa.

What is not negotiable or subject to change, however, is the ultimate goal of Christian mission, that of seeing people touched by God's redemptive power and love with the end result of fundamentally changed, reoriented lives. An inspiring example of God's grace at work in African hearts is the story of Philippe Coulibale and Marte Tiera (pr. Philip koo-li-bah-LAY and Martha TYAY-rah), briefly referred to in chapter 69.

AIMM staff in the home office had early noted that the names of these two people kept appearing in missionary correspondence. Let some of the early reporting speak for itself: "Marte was embarrassed to say it but she shyly confessed to others attending the women's seminar, 'There is real love in our home.' In her Burkina Faso setting, that love is evident and people are learning to know Christ because of it."

"Marte Tiera and her husband, Philippe Coulibale, are faithfully sharing their love for Christ in the village of Djigouera, a bumpy hour's drive north of Orodara. Both were born in ethnic Bobo villages in Mali, just north of the Burkina Faso border. Philippe was raised as an orphan in the home of relatives. The family were fetish worshipers but Philippe somehow evaded such worship. The C&MA Church was strong in that area and Philippe became highly interested in Christianity. He studied diligently to learn the Bambara trade language in which the Bible was translated. He enjoyed the Bible stories so much. Philippe chose to follow Christ and was baptized as a young teenager. . . . "

"Marte enjoyed several years of formal French education during her childhood. When Marte and Philippe's marriage was being arranged by their families, she made her own commitment to Christ and was baptized. After the birth of their first child, relations with Philippe's family became strained. Philippe's brother wanted him to work on Sunday which Philippe thought was wrong to do. Finally he, Marte and their little baby set off to look for farmland in Burkina Faso. They lived in several areas, often isolated from other believers and remote from other people. This was a time of maturing in their faith in the Lord."

"Marte remembers how the other women ridiculed her [as a young bride] for not sneaking grain out of the family granary as they did. A woman could sell the pilfered grain for profit to buy clothes or dishes for herself. But Marte felt the Lord helped her to say no to such deeds which would have brought disharmony and food shortages to her own family. The Lord Himself was teaching her to be a Christian wife and mother. In her own tribe, field work was a man's work. She remembered how her mother would sit at home doing nothing while her father slaved in the field. So when she had time and the girls could help with housework, she went to the fields to help her husband, Philippe, especially with the big job of weeding. . . ."

"Several years ago they felt they needed to move on. (Drought conditions and poor crops contributed to this decision.) Their intended move to their present home was confirmed for Marte in a dream. . . . They moved onto new land about 21 miles north of Orodara. They settled much like homesteaders. But first they built a grass shelter as a church building. Then they constructed a house to sleep in."

"Philippe only had one bullock to use as a draft animal to help with the cultivating. Two were needed to pull a plow. They bought a second on credit but both animals died of sickness shortly thereafter. So there they were, back to cultivating with a short handled hoe, doubled over trying to grow enough crops for the year's supply of food and to pay off debts. The rains were not abundant. As a result food has been short. Yet they continue to welcome anyone and everyone to their home, sharing abundantly of their meager resources."

"Philippe and Marte have had a great impact on their little bush community. Their neighbors are also people who have left their previous homes for varied reasons to settle there. Several have now made commitments to Christ through their hospitality. Some come to join them around the fire after dark for food, singing and testimonies as the family shares its life together."

"During the days Marte's teenage daughters work beside their mother, learning to do all the hard tasks of living in the bush. They grind flour on a stone, pound grain in a mortar, extract oil from nuts, and collect baobab leaves from the trees to make a nutritious gravy. They must work very hard and yet are grateful for the good food they have. Marte has taught Mariam, the oldest girl, to read in the trade language so she can read the Bible herself."

"Philippe, with the help of a nephew and a young son, cultivates more land than most of the neighbors. It is all done by hand. Beside the lack of rain, agriculture is made difficult by chicken hawks which are a constant threat to baby chicks, monkeys that steal the corn, the squirrels that find the peanuts. But worst of all, the staple crop sorghum is always attacked by flocks of birds shortly before the grain is ripe." . . .

"Philippe and Marte are excited because they know that only Christ can build a church that brings together people of several ethnic groups and makes them one. Philippe says: 'When I first moved to this area I thought God would build his church with Bobo people (i.e., their own ethnic group) and we would worship in the Bobo language. But now we don't even sing Bobo songs in the church anymore. Our worship is in a common trade language because God is bringing people of various ethnic groups to us.' . . . Philippe knows there is better land elsewhere. He is often tempted to move on to an easier place but he feels God has called him to this specific area to be a witness to the many 'unreached tribes.'" (17)

AIMM Secretary Jim Bertsche was in the last year of his tenure when, in 1986, he was privileged to meet this family about which he had heard so much. He had just visited the Petersens at N'Dorola. They were en route to Orodara. Their route took them directly past Djigouera. It was hot. The extremely low humidity made it necessary to drink often from the water jug in the vehicle to avoid dehydration. The schedule for the day did not really allow much time for a roadside stop but there was no way the AIMM party could pass without greeting Philippe and Marte. Concerning this experience the secretary later wrote: "We pulled to the side of the road in the heat of the day. Nearby a couple of men were laying the first rows of sun-dried mud blocks of a small building. It was Philippe and another Christian. They came to meet us. We were led to Philippe's humble little home."

"He found a backless bench and set it in a strip of shade against the adobe wall of his home under the ragged overhang of roof thatch. Here obviously was a family living on the frazzled edge of poverty. Before we had said anything, he came quickly with a half-gourd of water and some smaller half-gourds. Dan Petersen leaned over and explained, 'This is tradition. The first thing they do in this parched land is offer a visitor water to drink.' Later I discovered their well had gone dry and the water they offered had come from a distant source. Every cup was precious. But what they had, they shared."

"I looked around that simple little courtyard. Yonder lay a short handled hoe; against a shrub lay a bush knife. Three or four bundles of thatch grass that had been clipped were standing against a wall of an unfinished hut. A few chickens were scratching around us and over there was a little pile of pods pulled from a baobab tree. As we were getting acquainted I asked, 'What are the baobab pods about?' 'Oh, it's one of our food sources we gather in the bush. Would you like to taste them?'"

"Out came Marte with another half gourd filled this time with a murky drink and again the little gourd cups were passed to us filled with a sort of baobab seed gruel, slightly astringent on our tongues. The seeds crunched like watermelon seeds. The conversation got around to the building project out near the road. 'What are you men doing out there?' 'Well, you see the little grass thatched shelter over here? That is where we have been worshiping, but it's only temporary. We are building a chapel out there, something that's fit for us to meet in, a place fit to worship God.'"

"At that point we were interrupted as Marte emerged again from her little kitchen. This time she was carrying a battered, smoke-smudged kettle that had spent many an hour over open cooking fires. It wasn't coffee. They couldn't afford that. It was chicory. The little half gourds were passed around again. I was amazed when I began to drink and discovered that it had been sweetened. Somewhere in her little mud and stick kitchen she had been hoarding a precious little packet of sugar for some very special occasion. The chicory had been sweetened for us."

"Then Philippe called one of his children: 'Go in the house and bring my Bible.' He opened it to Psalm 108 and began in a halting manner to read some of those verses which speak of triumph, of overcoming, of trusting in God and of conquering difficulties in his name. Even as the reading of the Psalm was coming to a close, there was a flurry of feathers and dust out behind the house. One of the sons came with a half-grown rooster. Philippe said: 'We are so sorry that you don't have time to spend here with us so we can have a meal together. But since you can't do that, we are sending meat with you for your cooking pot tonight.'"

"I desperately wanted a way to decline the half-grown rooster in a gracious manner knowing that most of the time there was no meat for their own cooking pot. But I caught a glimpse of Dan eyeing me across the shoulder of Philippe and I got the message: 'You dare not refuse the gift.'"

"We walked slowly back to the road, past the tiny 'house of God' they were building. This time I looked at it closely. I doubt that chapel will be much more than thirty feet square, but it will be a chapel, 'a place fit for the worship of God.' We arrived at the road, I with the rooster under my elbow. As we got into the truck, Philip took my hand and said: 'I have three words for you as you go. First of all, thank you, thank you for coming to visit us here at Djigouera. It has meant much to us.'"

"'Then, please carry our greetings to our brothers and sisters in Christ in North America. Tell them that Philippe and Marte greet them in the name of Jesus.'"

"'And then, as you return, if from time to time you think of us, please pray for us. We aren't many believers yet here at Djigouera but, with God's help, and the prayers of God's people, one day there will be more.'" (18)

It was a humbled and deeply moved mission secretary who made his way toward his evening's destination in Burkina Faso that hot, dry afternoon.

The story of AIMM in Africa has, on occasion, been one of heartache and struggle. But, thank God, it has always been a story of his marvelous, sustaining and transforming grace.

CHAPTER 74   RETROSPECT/PROSPECT

Christian Mission and single women

It was a cool December dry season morning in 1957 in a cemetery a short distance outside the Kahemba State Post in southern Kwilu Province in the Belgian Congo. Clustered around an open grave were a mix of Africans, missionaries and local Belgian government officials. In a simple wooden casket lay the body of CIM missionary Mary Miller.

She, with her sister Bertha, had first come to the Congo in 1928 under the sponsorship of the Unevangelized Tribes Mission. (1) Across the intervening years, the two sisters had carved out a mission post in the scrub bush country of southern Congo which came to be known as Kamayala. Sometimes they had other missionary personnel to help them; sometimes they worked alone. Hiring villagers to erect pole and thatch buildings, they gradually brought into being a multi-faceted ministry of service and witness among the Chokwe and Lunda tribal folk of the region. Bertha gave leadership to the organization of a primary school. Mary, a nurse, quickly opened a simple dispensary. Becoming aware that there were some villagers in the area who suffered from Hansen's disease, they were among the earliest Protestant missionaries in the whole of Congo to establish a place of residence for such folk where they could be seen regularly and treated. (2)

Since some of the couples in the camp brought children with them, the Miller sisters built a facility on the station where children of parents under treatment could be housed, fed and educated. In time, this home was expanded to make room for other needy children from the surrounding area. It is fascinating to note that the present General Secretary of CMCo (known as CMZa prior to the country's reversion to the name Congo under the new regime of Laurent Kabila) spent his childhood in this Kamayala shelter for children. His name: Mackunya Shalukombo (pr. mah-KUH-nyah shah-loo-KOH-mboh).

Early converts to Christ were pressed into service by the Miller sisters as the evangelists of their own people. It was not long that a church community took shape - - both on the station and in the surrounding villages.

All of this was well known to the people gathered about that open grave that morning. A missionary from a neighboring Mennonite Brethren Mission station brought a brief devotional message. Speaking in Kituba (pr. ki-TOO-bah), the trade language of the area, he at one point said: "Had the Miller sisters not come to this part of the Congo years ago, the history of Kahemba Territory would be very different than it is." In a striking fashion, these two sisters epitomized the enormous contribution that single women have made to the cause of Christian Mission, in general, and to the CIM/AIMM in particular.

The lot of single women missionaries has never been a simple or easy one. For many, their assignments have taken them to the isolation of bush stations. Though usually situated with missionary couples and families who have sought to be supportive and helpful, there inevitably come those times, at the end of the day, when in the solitude of their own living quarters, they are cast upon their own resources to hold loneliness at bay. Typically serving in support ministries in class rooms, dispensaries and among women and children, their service has often been low profile in nature and, consequently, has often not been recognized as it might have been.

And, there is the matter of housing. There likely is no other aspect of their missionary experience which more sharply highlights how much has been expected - - even required - - of them. Was there a new single lady coming to join the missionary staff at Station X? No problem. She can simply move in with the single missionary already installed on that station. (3) It has often been simply assumed that they would be happy to share a kitchen, work out menus and financial details of a shared household. As for compatibility, missionary couples on the station have often taken it for granted that all would be well. A good example of this flexibility was that of Anna V. Liechty who between 1946 and 1984 established African living quarters nine different times in six different places. That serious personality clashes have been infrequent is in and of itself eloquent testimony to the flexibility, commitment, grace and devotion which single missionaries have typically brought to their lives in Christian Mission.

But there has been more. Being single, it has been all too easy to feel that a move from mission post A to post B was uncomplicated for them: less things to pack and move; shared housing here, shared housing there; a classroom here, a classroom there. In spite of the disruption which such moves always entailed for them, the single missionaries who have served with the CIM/AIMM across the years have maintained a striking willingness to be moved and placed wherever the mission/church administrators felt they were most needed.

And for single missionaries, there is yet the issue of trying to find their way between two cultures, i.e., the one they leave back home and the one that surrounds them upon arrival at their new location. While all overseas workers soon become aware of the tension and friction engendered by trying to move between and function in two different worlds, married missionaries can at least work at this within a family unit with a spouse and children. Single workers are too often left largely to their own devices to find their way. Small wonder that one single worker once expressed herself as follows: "I feel like a perpetual visitor, always a transient, never wholly a part. 'Cultural relativism' is all very well, but sometimes I wish I could identify completely with something, some group, somewhere . . ." (4)

Stress factors notwithstanding, the CIM/AIMM has been blessed across the years of its ministry by a large staff of courageous, committed and extraordinarily gifted single women. Records reveal that they have comprised roughly twenty percent of the CIM/AIMM missionary force. They have come to us from across our inter-Mennonite supporting network of churches with a deep certainty of God's leading in their lives. They also have come at peace with themselves about their single state as they applied for service, believing that in God's purpose for them there was a place and ministry which they and they alone could fill.

No one has reflected those certainties any more clearly than Lois Slagle, a nurse who served seven terms, over a 32 year span, as a nurse and midwife in rural African settings - - usually with the barest equipment and supplies. On the occasion of the 70th anniversary celebration of the CIM/AIMM held at Carlock, IL., in May 1982, five years after her retirement, she was invited to reflect on her experiences as a single missionary. In her comments she said, in part: "I speak for a significant group within the AIMM family, a group who some people feel has been missed. As one from that group, I assure you that there is nothing amiss with us. We all have had those well meaning friends and associates who, with our best interest at heart, had the impression that the best way they could help us would be to find us a mate; that if we were really expecting to serve the Lord to the best of our potential, it would be advantageous to seek first the married life and then go for the business of establishing God's Kingdom in the hearts of men and women in Africa."

"As single missionaries we have gone forth assured that there is nothing in God's command to go into all the world to which we cannot respond as singles. . . . We have always been ready to serve where there have been needs. Our only desire is to share with our African brothers and sisters in Christ anything and everything that will make life more worth living for them."

"At this occasion of the Seventieth Anniversary of AIMM, I would like to express my appreciation for a mission that has always considered singles as full co-partners. We have never been assigned tasks that others did not wish to do because we were singles. We have never been left out of the planning and programming because we were singles. I have never felt that I had to swim against the tide of opinion because I was a single. Rather we have been encouraged to contribute what we have as single persons. The expression of our uniqueness has never been stifled in any way."

"Tonight I express for myself and for every one of my single colleagues sincere congratulations to a mission with a vision that has permitted and, I am sure, will continue to allow each one of us to serve wholeheartedly, to live richly, creatively, and joyfully as we pursue God's intentions for our individual lives." (5)

Christian Mission and missionary wives/mothers

The path to the station dispensary took the cluster of village women past a fenced-in missionary garden. What was transpiring in the enclosed area had brought the women to a halt. They stood staring in disbelief. The missionary mother had earlier planted peanuts along one end of the her garden. There had been good rains and the peanuts were thriving. But there was a workman, busy with his hoe, turning the green peanut plants under! The African women were excitedly gesturing and talking to one another. "We have always known that white people sometimes do stupid things, - - but this! Burying beautiful peanut plants!" Shaking their heads they continued on their path to the dispensary to secure medications for the children they carried astride their hips. (6)

Missionary wives, upon arrival in bush settings, soon learned that shopping trips to distant commercial centers came along every three months or so. They also soon learned that their shopping lists, on such occasions, needed to carry such items as 100 pound bags of flour and sugar, case lots of such tinned goods as oatmeal, powdered milk, sardines and margarine. Then there were items such as yeast, matches, fifty gallon drums of kerosene, twenty pound burlap bags of rock salt plus, perhaps, a tire and tube for a bicycle or a new kerosene lantern and a supply of candles. They also soon learned that a garden, during rainy seasons, could be a precious source of fresh vegetables.

But planting seed was one thing; growing anything was something else. Particularly on mission posts located in the rolling savanna areas of Africa, they found themselves dealing with light, sandy soil which was leached by heavy rains and baked by a tropical sun. Before tomatoes, beans and lettuce could find their way to her family table, some way had to be found to build up the nutrients in her sandy garden plot. Compost holes helped. Green peanut plants hoed under also helped - - this to the consternation of her African sisters from nearby villages.

Typically equipped with a wood-burning cook stove, her kitchen quickly took on the appearance of her grandmother's of an earlier era back in Kansas or Ohio or Manitoba. A sturdy wood box was located on one end and a hot water reservoir on the other. The stove served multiple purposes during the hours it was hot - - boiling water to make it safe for drinking, baking bread and rolls, heating flat irons on wash days and the cooking of food. A cupboard nearby often contained tropical fruits in various stages of ripeness and an entire stalk of bananas likely hung from the ceiling in a corner.

Any missionary mother who served in Africa for any period of time had the assignment of turning a series of simple houses into homes for her family. Typically they were basic shelters - - stone or cement block constructions with metal roofs, cement floors and screened windows with hinged wooden shutters. Missionary mothers quickly learned how to convert flour sacks into aprons or even curtains. To supplement basic furniture made at the station carpenter shop, she soon learned that wicker chairs could be secured from villagers nearby. Bamboo frames could be made to order to fit mattresses for children's beds. She soon discovered how to drape mosquito nets from the ceilings which could be tucked around sleeping children below at night.

But it was the care and education of small children which confronted missionary mothers on isolated mission posts with the greatest concern and challenge. Although the CIM/AIMM provided its missionary staff the best medical support it could under the circumstances, there were occasions when a missionary mother was alone with a feverish child in the middle of the night. And there were times of accident and injury which left her largely to her own devices and her little first aid kit.

As for the education of missionary children, CIM/AIMM policy across the years has been that parents in isolated areas arrange within their local missionary team to teach their own children through the first three years of primary schooling after which they are sent to a mission boarding school. (7) If there were several school age children on the station, the mothers arranged among themselves who would teach what. If not, the mother became the first and only teacher of her own children for the first years of their primary schooling.

But whatever the arrangement, the time always came when missionary children, one by one, reached the age of fourth grade and preparation needed to be made for their departure for boarding school. Time after time the scene would be repeated: bags packed into vans or planes, little packets of cookies to be hand-carried; last hugs, brave farewell waves and blown kisses. The parents would watch the departing vehicle or plane as long as it could be kept in view, then turn to pursue their work of the day with great lumps in their throats and with twisting pain in their hearts. (8)

Perhaps the greatest challenge of all for the missionary wife and mother was to find her own identity and role in the mission world of which she was a part. Across the years of mission history, placement of missionary couples has been largely determined by the training and gifts of the men. CIM/AIMM was no exception. Thus it was that, a high percentage of the time, missionary wives followed their husbands from one post to another and from one assignment to the next. To be sure, there were times when the training and experience of a missionary wife combined with those of her husband tipped the scales in the placement process for them. But, on the whole, missionary wives lived and served in a male oriented landscape. If, on occasion, a wife wanted to know what was planned for her at the new location, mission administrators found it all too easy to respond: "There is so much to be done there; we know you will quickly find more than enough to keep you busy."

To be sure, there truly was "much to be done." But this did not always mean that the waiting responsibilities meshed well with her interests, strengths or training. As has been the case with single missionaries, it must also be recognized that missionary wives too have often served willingly, graciously and with devotion as their moves were largely dictated by the assignments given their husbands. What has been crucial in all of this has been the attitude of the husband/wife missionary teams. Enduring, long term missionary couples have not allowed themselves to get caught up in a "my work/your work" mentality. Rather, their view and conviction has been that it is "our work." With the conviction that God called and led them to Africa as couples, the details of the assignment for either spouse were not of first importance. Their ongoing presence and ministry, together, in a land to which they believed God had led them, was their overarching concern.

Christian Mission and MKs

If parents live in some distant geographical and cultural setting by their own choice, missionary children do not. Their experience as MKs is thrust upon them by the circumstances into which they are born or taken.

This, in and of itself, is not necessarily a problem. Children, the world around, quickly accept and become part of the world which surrounds them. With the amazing adaptability and learning capacity of early childhood, they soon become fluent in the local language if exposed to it on a daily basis, something which confounds their missionary parents. Color-blind, they readily form friendships with other children around them. Introduced by friends to local diets, they often form lifelong affection for food items which, in an American context, prompt startled reaction. (9) While there is a dim awareness, on the part of young MKs, of cousins and grandparents in America, their lives are part and parcel of the overseas context of their daily routines. Other MKs become de facto "cousins;" adult missionaries around them quickly come to be regarded as "uncles and aunts."

vignettes of MK memories

"I loved the times when I ran wild with my Zairian friends. We would walk for miles into the savanna looking for *Mabombos* and *Ndulundulus* [i.e. wild fruit pr. mah-BOH-mboh and NDOO-loo-ndoo-loos]. Time was nonexistent and we were never aware of the dangers that lurked. The day would only end after someone would see a 'BIG snake' and we would all run as fast as we could until the grass cleared. We would return home, weary, dirty and sticky with *mabombo* juice around our mouths. It was always a chore to eat our suppers, faking an appetite so Mom wouldn't guess that we had stopped to eat on the way home. . . . Some of my favorite memories were of celebrations like Christmas, Easter and birthdays. Several times I was an angel in a Zairian Christmas pageant because of my blonde hair." (10)

Another MK writes: "There were adventures in the African hinterland, where we explored paths on the savanna, imagining we followed in Dr. Livingstone's footsteps. We trekked deep into the jungle with our naturally sagacious Zairian friends. We hunted field mice fleeing the seasonal fires, and returned home after dark, greedy for the first meal of the day - - roast rat." (11)

Another remembers: "We spent many happy hours wandering through the tall grass in search of the purple orchids and red lilies that grew wild. Or we picked wild fruit - - red plums called *ndulundulu*, [and] a hard-shelled fruit the size of a baseball called *mahole* [pr. mah-HO-lay], and a smaller red-shelled fruit called *tundulu* [pr. too-NDOO-loo]. Or we went swimming in the Bumbulu [pr. boo-MBOO-loo] River a mile below the station. In between was a small forest later dubbed *kishitu kia Yone* or John's forest after my brother John. We had a favorite vine that would swing us from one side of a gully to the other." (12)

And another: "I remember sitting on a barrel in the backyard, eating tangerines and spitting the seeds into the sand while the chickens chased around under my feet. Early on, I remember being hauled around by a *baba* [pr. BAH-bah, the Tshiluba term for a woman or mother] who I guess took care of me from infancy while my mother was working at the dispensary. I remember her shelling hard roasted corn off an ear and giving me one kernel at a time which took a long time to chew. I remember my mother telling of being horrified that my *baba* would wad up little balls of *bidia* [pr. BEE-dyah, the Tshiluba term for cassava mush] and stick them in my mouth with her thumb. Mother was sure I would choke to death. Later, I remember being cared for by my baby-sitter Ndaya [pr. NDAH-yah] who was probably about 6 years older than I. We would walk around Kalonda Station carrying my dolls or other toys. She was the one who taught me to sit over the flying ant holes and catch them as they flew out, pop them in my mouth and let the wings fly out the corner of my mouth. . . ."

"Kalonda was definitely home. I remember wandering up the hill to the village to visit the cooking fires of the various families that I knew. I never was afraid - - except of the occasional village dog - - and to my knowledge my parents never worried about me either. They knew that the Africans always looked after children and they knew that someone would bring me home. Often I would come home around dusk having already sampled someone's pot of *bidia* and so not hungry for my own supper." (13)

And still another MK says simply of his mission station childhood setting: "Having been born in the Congo, I was happy and secure there, it was my home." (14)

off to school

But if childhood memories of children of career missionary families are cherished by many of the MKs, a great majority of them carry the marks of the trauma of early separation from the warm security of their family homes for the purpose of their continued schooling.

Though missionary children typically accepted such times of separation with stoic resignation and little protest, for many, the honesty to admit the pain and loneliness of those years came only in later life. One delves into her memory as follows: "Fourth grade came, and with it the trip to the capital to begin living in the AIMM hostel and attending the American School of Kinshasa. . . . I don't remember the first day of school; I do remember the day our parents left. It was horrible! I cried hard and there was no stopping. . . . It was during these times that all of us children were forced to either turn to our inner selves or to go to each other for support. By thinking things through and finding ways to convince ourselves that we were OK, we were creating independent spirits that would serve us later in life. . . . My first two years in the hostel did not hold many pleasant memories but I did meet some friends for life. . . . During the third year I finally got used to leaving home and being away from my parents, so it wasn't so bad." (15)

Others shared memories as follows: "I did deal with homesickness for a time, and that unique grief which comes when you know it's not possible to have what you really want." (16)

There were times "when we locked ourselves in the bathroom so we could have a private place to cry those tears when homesickness overtook you and you were too proud to let other people know." (17)

On a brighter note, some commented: "The things that I feel are certainly pluses from my hostel experience include a sense of adaptability and some independence - - but most of all, it was the family of kids that continue to be extended family for me today. The kids I grew up with in those years have had and continue to have more impact on my life than my own cousins. There is a connection that I am confident will not break." (18)

"I usually enjoyed myself and got along well. I don't think I ever questioned the system of being sent away to boarding school . . even when I was older and in high school and knew that not everyone lived this way. That was just part of living in Congo and that was home." (19)

"It was not unknown to me as I had heard plenty from my two older sisters. The stories coming from the hostel aroused interest, expectation and excitement. . . . As I grew older I would not have wanted to remain by myself on the mission station. It did teach me valuable lessons of independence, self-confidence and learning how to get along with others." (20)

off to North America

But coming to terms with a boarding school experience in the country where missionary parents were stationed, with periodic trips back home to familiar bush settings, was one thing. Making the transition to the country of their parents' origin to enroll in college or to begin their lives on their own proved, for many, to be by far the most traumatic time of all.

Some poignant comments regarding MK efforts to fit into North American society, whether on college campuses or elsewhere, are as follows: "My first experience of being left behind in NA was my first year at college. That was one of the worst years of my life. I felt like a total misfit on campus, didn't make many friends and did not know what, where, or whom to turn to for personal security/comfort since parents and siblings returned overseas. Vacations from school were complicated because I wasn't sure where I could go where I was really wanted or wouldn't be in the way. The actual managing of schedules, studies, etc, was by that time not something new. I knew how to take care of myself. However, there were many times when the insecurity of not knowing how to act on the American college scene left me pretty scared. I did not know how to dress 'in style,' nor could I afford it for that matter. I did not know the correct things to talk about. I had never been to a football game and so could not relate to that experience. Most of the social things the college kids talked about and did were foreign to me. I found myself very lonely and out of touch with others around me. I did search out and eventually found a few kids who were also 'foreigners' - - many of them international kids who had come to study - - and found in them lots more in common." (21)

Another remembers: "I made an honest effort to settle into my parents' home town. . . . As I gained a North American perspective of my past, I envied stateside friends whose developmental experiences I did not share. . . . I found myself time-traveling in an effort to recapture a vital loss. Sometimes it seemed that I was nothing but a sealed memory capsule, bound by the past I couldn't relinquish." (22)

Missionary parents on trial?

In the face of such candid reflections of MKs, are missionary parents to be categorically condemned out of hand?

Long-term missionaries do not think of their service in terms of sacrifice. They rather think in terms of privilege. To serve in an area and among a people to which they believe God has led them and to witness the transforming impact of God's grace in the lives of people around them affords a profound sense of fulfillment.

But this is not to say that missionaries experience no pain. For many of them, across the years, there has been no anguish like that of being forced to decide whether or not they will provide an ongoing home for their children during their school years. Their dilemma is starkly clear. There are no painless alternatives. On the one hand there is their commitment to what they believe to be God's ongoing call upon their lives; on the other is their love and concern for the children the Lord has entrusted to their care.

Home schooling is one option, but this only postpones the time when adequate schooling can no longer be provided locally. Assignments of missionary families to urban centers where the needed schooling is available is sometimes an option but obviously cannot be arranged for all families

For families who have decided that their first responsibility lay with their children, there can be no criticism. No two families are alike. Everyone must be granted the freedom to make its own decisions. And for missionary families who endure the pain of separation in order to remain at their post of service, there ought be no criticism either.

Have there been cases of shipwrecked lives on the part of MKs early separated from their parents? Yes. Have there been MKs whose lives have fallen into disarray even though their parents suspended or terminated their missionary service to make a home for them in North America? Yes. Have there been children of Christian families who have never left their homelands, who have never experienced the stress of cross-cultural living and separation who repudiated their parents, their faith and their church? Of course.

It is clear that none of the above parental decisions automatically mitigate against or guarantee the realization of the parental dream of seeing their children come to maturity while adopting and affirming the Christian faith and its associated values which are so dear to them. Parental love and affirmation, like indifference and lack of understanding, can be conveyed across distance as well as at close proximity.

Mission boards, if belatedly, have come to a better understanding of the missionary experience and routinely provide reentry seminars for adults and special orientations for MKs. To this have been added reunions which, with increasing frequency, are organized by the MKs themselves bringing together fellow students of former overseas years.

In spite of heart-rending stories of MKs who have found the stress and disorientation of their experience too severe to overcome, there are many other stories of MKs who have found their way through their childhood and young adult years with growing appreciation for their experience and the commitment of their parents. Not only is there appreciation, but many have become second generation missionaries of their families often benefitting, in the process, from the acculturation they experienced in their earlier years.

MKs and their bi-cultural experience

On this issue as well, MK reflections are mixed. One respondent observed: "The experience of growing up away from parents and across several cultures and moving all the time was fragmenting. . . . Needing to compensate for changes all the time meant . . . having to work very hard mentally and emotionally all the time to meet the constantly new environment, parental figures, culture, whatever. . . . All this having been said, I still really value the kaleidoscope of experiences and memories. . . . I want to have had the opportunities for travel and adventure and living with other people and experiencing other ways that I've had. . . . I'm still trying to figure out what to do with all that and whether there is any way it fits together. . . . I've always realized, and still do, that there is more than one way to look at things, having grown up bi-culturally. That way of growing up has left me unable to be comfortable in any context which is too narrowly viewed, whether that be the

691

interpretation of custom, Christianity, the world, education, church, community, whatever. I am very impatient and very uncomfortable in situations where it appears people are interpreting whatever they are seeing with 'blinders' on." (23)

Another MK expressed himself: "My MK experience has shaped my faith, values, world view and my personality. I find that I am not really American nor Congolese in my thinking and attitudes. . . . Having attended many different schools, lived in many different places, I have no real roots anywhere. Home is here today and somewhere else tomorrow. . . . As a result of my experiences I think in a very different way than others around me. I plug different values into formulas when making decisions and evaluate results differently. As I learn to accept these differences, I find I can often make a meaningful contribution to those around me that can be rewarding and beneficial to both of us." (24)

Another observes: "Interacting with people of different religious backgrounds has made me more aware of other belief systems and has strengthened my own faith in God. Often, during discussions, my beliefs were challenged and I was forced to search further to back them up. My relationship with God is not stale and silent, but rather something I understand and enjoy discussing. It is difficult for me, sometimes, to relate to peers who've lived only on the North American continent. They cannot imagine - - and aren't interested - - in what we've grown up with. To know someone is also to understand the situations that shaped them. Conversely, it may be easy for me to make friends with Americans, but to understand them is difficult because I didn't grow up in a stifled environment. I hope to use my international experiences to better understand people of other races, to help others who are going through difficult cultural adjustments . . . ." (25)

And from yet one more: "Being a bi-cultural person has enriched me greatly. It is a privilege to be exposed in this way. It allows you a better sense of perspective on life and living, a healthier balance in world view and priorities, and teaches you much about yourself and your world. It promotes the values of people and places rather than things, and a more transient lifestyle, which for the believer is a needed sentiment. It has its consequences. One forfeits the ability to enter fully into either side, lacking either the roots or the desire to sink in deeply. One loses a 'home turf' to which you can return and be a part. But I believe the benefits gained from the 'large world view' outweigh the negative consequences. . . ."

"The overall impact this experience has had on me touches each area of life. My faith has been stretched and strengthened as I've learned to meet difficulties and make decisions on my own. . . . I think it's effected my personality - - made me more sensitive and compassionate toward others who struggle or are in difficult situations. It has tended to make me internalize things and sort them out for myself rather than by being vocal. It has made me independent to the point where I could work harder at expressing needs and concerns. In terms of values, it has taught me much about the good differences between people, the danger of ethnocentrism, the ability to examine my own culture more critically as it is enlightened by another. I really appreciate the love of travel, exploration and learning about new places and people that my MK experience spawned in me." (26)

CIM/AIMM's landmark decisions in review

As is the case with any organization, CIM/AIMM has, across the years, made some key decisions which have profoundly shaped its unfolding history. From the perspective of this writer, a list of such decisions must at least include those which follow.

Mennonite: to be or not to be?

Within the very first decade of its existence, the CIM's identity was challenged. Brought into being by the admirable vision and faith of a group of Mennonite farming pastors and laymen from Ohio, Indiana and Illinois who had only recently distanced themselves from their Amish roots and traditions, they were looking for missionary candidates. Among those who came forward was a visionary whirlwind of a woman named Alma Doering. After serving briefly under the Africa Inland Mission of East Africa, she volunteered for service with the fledgling inter-Mennonite CIM. Before her first term was up she, and other non-Mennonite candidates whom she had helped recruit, came to the conclusion that the CIM needed to cast itself in the mold of the large emerging "faith missions" of Africa, e.g., the Africa Inland Mission and the Sudan Interior Mission. Thus challenged, the new CIM board dug in its heels. It was Mennonites who had brought the CIM into being; Mennonite it would remain. It was their dream to one day plant a Mennonite Church in the heart of Africa.

Rebuffed by the CIM board, Doering and several other missionaries resigned. Under her dynamic leadership a new mission, the Unevangelized Tribes Mission (UTM) was launched. As long as she lived, she raised funds, recruited candidates and gave direction to a thriving mission enterprise just to the west of the CIM territory in the Congo. But with her death, the visionary heart of the organization disappeared. It is an interesting footnote of history that most of the mission posts she established eventually were taken over by Mennonite Missions - - the CIM and the American Mennonite Brethren Mission.

Bricks and mortar: would less have been enough?

In more recent years of CIM/AIMM history, new generations of board members have come on the scene and have had occasion to visit some of the historic stations developed by the Mission in the 1940's, 50's and 60's. After viewing the variety and size of the buildings on some of the older stations, more than one such board member has been heard to wonder out loud if the CIM/AIMM had not been guilty of over-building in the isolation of the African bush.

The question is certainly understandable since the stations visited had been typically located on roomy acres of land dotted with palm, mango and other trees. Paths were neatly laid out and lined with flowering bushes. And, there were the buildings - - schools, clinics, carpenter shops, chapels, offices, print shops, dormitories, guest houses, machine sheds, football fields and missionary dwellings. Typically constructed with stone, cement blocks or burnt bricks, they represented labor in herculean amounts and the expenditure of many tens of thousands of dollars provided by the offerings of a supporting Mennonite constituency of North America freely given across the years.

To put all of this in perspective, it must be remembered that pioneering missionaries sought out tribal groups wherever they were and thus settled in rural areas far from the few scattered urban centers of the land. Long-term survival required a high level of self sufficiency. Furthermore, the colonial government was clear. It was looking to the Christian Missions scattered across the country to assume primary responsibility for the education and health care of the African populations around them.

Viewing educational and medical services as excellent ways of demonstrating Christian compassion for an illiterate and often suffering population, early missionaries did all they could with the limited resources they had. What better way to open doors for witness to Christ than by ministering to the obvious needs at their doorsteps? When, following World War II, Protestant Missions were put on an equal basis with Catholic Missions, the CIM/AIMM opted to apply for generous government subsidies. Like other Missions across the land, with the help of these new funds the Mennonites too entered upon major program expansion.

A quick by-product of CIM's expanded educational system was the establishment of a growing network of rural school/church centers in all directions from the central mission stations. These, in turn, fed increasing numbers of African youth toward the upper levels of education in the station schools. With the lure of literacy, thousands of African youth sought admittance to CIM/AIMM schools. An overwhelming majority of them made professions of faith and sought baptism during their student years.

Such enlarged educational systems at the different stations required expanded teacher training programs which, in turn, required larger, better-equipped schools. Expanded medical services required nurses training programs which, in turn, required better equipment and buildings. A growing church required upgraded pastoral training programs which, in turn, required more adequate facilities. Concern for the education of girls required a training center with classrooms and dormitories set aside especially for them.

Situated, as several of them were, along main cross-country roads, CIM/AIMM mission stations became oases of lodging, food, refueling, repair and entertainment for travelers of all sorts - - fellow missionaries from other areas, Catholic priests and nuns with physical ailments, Portuguese business men and Belgian government officials en route to distant destinations. And it was not uncommon for such travelers to have heard, ahead of time, that they should plan their trip so as to seek accommodation at day's end at least once or twice in "Mennonite territory"! The welcome and amenities offered there were not to be exceeded by those found elsewhere along their path!

That was then; this is now.

What in the earlier years of the mission were called "stations" have now become regional centers of the Zaire Mennonite Church. Caught in the horrendous squeeze of inflation, great scarcity of supplies and gradually reduced AIMM subsidy for their annual operating budgets, the physical maintenance of these large stations has become immensely difficult. Consequently some of the earlier, older buildings, here and there, have begun to yield to the ravages of tropical weather. Here and there, patches of weeds have taken over what once were expanses of closely cropped grass. And there are the institutions of the missionary era. While the Mennonites of Zaire are insistent that they all be preserved for continued service to their Church, their staffing and maintenance remain a constant challenge.

So to pose the question again: Did CIM/AIMM over-build?

First, an observation. The major expansion of facilities and ministries of the Mission from the 40's through the 60's was not so much by design as it was the natural outgrowth of a mission strategy born of the socio-political dynamics of the Belgian Congo and the Republic of Congo during that era.

But were some of the CIM/AIMM station complexes larger than really necessary? Perhaps. Did early missionaries to some extent get caught up in a spirit of rivalry in developing their own stations? Yes. Were some of the missionary homes roomier than was really necessary? Probably. Might some of the buildings have been of more modest dimensions and thus more easily maintained long term? Yes.

But having conceded all of this, it is very difficult to imagine any other approach to Christian Mission in the rural isolation of the CIM/AIMM territory which could have resulted in the large and growing Zaire Mennonite community of today. Without these large mission/church centers which anchored and made possible multiple ministries of outreach in all directions, witness would at best have been sporadic and transient. It is very difficult to imagine the Mennonite Church of today in Congo without the hundreds of evangelists, pastors and officers who were trained in CIM/AIMM's own educational institutions across the years.

If the CIM/AIMM mission stations of Congo are viewed as monuments to be preserved for their own sake, then views of crumbling buildings, here and there, will be the cause of melancholy on the part of the graying generation of missionaries who created them. But they may also be viewed as a series of launching pads which, over several decades, enabled white-skinned Mennonite Christians to establish residence within reach of a wide spread of rural African tribal groups with a sustained witness to the Gospel. These centers are now finding their places in the African scheme of things as the Mennonite Church hammers out its own organizational structures and formulates its own visions of witness and ministry in the name of Christ.

And yet a comment about missionary "villas" which have frequently been the object of harsh commentary on the part of critics of an earlier era of Christian mission in Africa and elsewhere. Let it at least be recognized that missionary personnel of that day did not go with the notion of trying to fit Christian mission into a convenient two or three year parenthesis in their lives. Rather they were people who went, with their families, for the long haul. Isolated as many of them were by hundreds of kilometers of sandy bush trails from the nearest urban centers which they seldom visited, they sought to establish a home for themselves and a base of ministry where they were.

a consistent ecumenical stance

Only a few decades removed from their Amish identity and roots, it is truly remarkable that the founders of the Congo Inland Mission in 1912 found it important and proper to make it the joint mission enterprise of two Mennonite Conferences (cf. ch. 1). It is also significant that the ultimate selection of an area of ministry in the Belgian Congo was largely influenced by the reporting and counsel of personnel from the Southern Presbyterian Mission of the south central part of that country. Early ties of mutual respect emerged between the two neighbor Missions which were to culminate, over the years, in a wide variety of joint efforts. Though standing in two different streams of tradition and theology, the CIM early saw the value of coordinating efforts in the distribution of Scriptures and Christian literature in Tshiluba, the language of millions of people who had become the joint focus of concern for both Missions. In time, this partnership spread to medical services as well.

It was also in the first decade of CIM's presence in the Belgian Congo that the Mission joined with other Protestant groups of the country to launch the Congo Protestant Council, a consultative body which, in time, established an office in Kinshasa and became an effective counter-force to the massive Catholic influence and power of the colonial era in that country.

And, inter-Mennonite from its inception, the CIM also reached out to its Mennonite Brethren neighbors to the west who came into the picture after World War II. Soon faced by common needs and problems - - particularly in the area of education of missionary children, African youth and church leaders, informal discussions were soon taking place, here and there, as missionaries chanced upon each other. At first, discussions of possible joint educational programs were highly tentative. After all, personnel of both Missions came from North American backgrounds where relations between different Mennonite Conferences were often less than cordial. Histories, traditions and prejudice often comprised formidable barriers to inter-church projects - - and even to fellowship! How could what was impossible in North America be made to work in Congo? But the shared needs there were pressing and growing. Over time, a series of joint CIM/MB training programs were put in place which proved to be not only mutually beneficial but a blessing in the bargain.

In brief, CIM/AIMM has demonstrated across the years that Mennonites need not limit their cooperation to the distribution of tinned beef and blankets to suffering people of the world. Steadily broadening its base of participating Mennonite Conferences, CIM/AIMM has proven that Mennonites can also partner in efforts of Christian Mission and this to the immense benefit of all concerned.

the Djoko consultation of 1960

The era of the late 1950's in the Belgian Congo was one of building pressure for political change. By 1959 it had become obvious all across black Africa that dramatic change was in the making. It was no longer a question of "if" but rather a question of "how and when."

The Belgian colonial regime seemed somehow not to realize what was going on around it and was busily involved in the further spinning out of its colonial dreams for the future. As for the missionary community scattered across that immense land, there was more of an awareness of building tension and pressure. But also caught up in their long term plans and projects, they too found it easy to let their day to day schedules dominate their time and attention.

It remained for H.A. Driver, the CIM Executive Secretary of the time, to read the signals clearly and to push both the mission board and the large missionary staff to face squarely what was coming. Largely because of his insistence, a delegation was composed and sent to the Congo in early 1960. An extensive itinerary brought them in contact with other Congo mission leaders and many of the church leaders and missionaries on various CIM stations.

All of this travel culminated in a major consultation in late February (cf. ch. 6) with a cross-section of African church leaders. This meeting had long range impact on the CIM mission/church history which was to follow. First, the assembled leaders were invited, for the first time, to make a formal decision regarding their identity. For years the Africans had been both content and secure in being identified simply as *Bena CIM*, i.e., "people of the CIM." They were now being invited to identify themselves, independently of the CIM, as a church. With surprisingly little discussion the decision was made: "We will be known as the Evangelical Mennonite Church of the Congo."

The second significance of this gathering was the fact that the CIM had taken the initiative to confront the church leaders with the reality of impending political change in the country and declared CIM readiness to grant church leaders broad new roles of leadership and authority within their own church. This proved to be providential. A basic groundwork of trust had been laid which stood CIM in good stead in the supercharged atmosphere which soon burst upon the Congo mission/church scene. Some other Missions of the country which had not taken steps to prepare for what was coming soon found themselves in bitter wrangles with their church leaders which, in some cases, left permanent scars.

the fusion of Mission and Church in Zaire

The AIMM decision to accept fusion with the Zaire Church in 1971 was made at a time of immense excitement and pressure. President Mobutu was riding a crest of great popularity and power. The ECZ also was at a peak of influence in the country. While the government was requiring a single Protestant Church in the country, the ECZ was, in fact, the church the government was talking about. The ECZ, in turn, was demanding that mission organizations "fuse" with the churches they had planted. In the process, missions were to disband as legal entities in the country while ceding all property and assets to their churches. With some reluctance, a large majority of Protestant mission leaders across the country finally indicated their willingness to implement the plan urged upon them. CIM missionary leadership recommended to the home board that CIM do likewise. Given the climate of the time, to have refused would have invited immense suspicion and resentment on the part of CMZa leaders as well as the ECZ with the very real possibility of some sort of retaliatory action on the part of the government.

To implement the fusion plan was not only expedient at that point in Congo/Zaire history, it also opened a new dimension of missionary/Zairian partnership within the Church. One result was that missionaries were integrated into the life of the Church in a new way. They were frequently named to commissions, elected as officers, named as delegates of the Church to various inter-church functions in the country. It was an immensely rewarding experience for the writer of this history to share intimately in the ebb and flow of the life of the Zaire Church during that era. Many hours were spent in committee meetings debating issues and making decisions. Rarely did votes fall along black/white lines. Individual convictions regarding issues at hand were rather the determining factor. Mixes of black and white skins typically found themselves coming down together on both sides of debates. There was mutual respect and confidence which was rarely - - if ever - - attained while the Mission and Church stood side by side as dual organizations.

Having said that, it is also true that, over time, missionaries discovered a down side to the fusion plan. At a personal level, missionary personnel sometimes found that support commitments made by the CMZa under the fusion plan were not always kept - - this frequently due to financial pressures experienced by the Church. And, occasionally, missionary personnel felt they were assigned to roles and responsibilities which were not their first preference or for which they did not feel particularly well qualified.

But most troublesome of all for AIMM was the fact that under the fusion plan, the Mission was unable to explore possible new opportunities of service within Zaire independently of the CMZa. While this created a certain level of frustration for AIMM it, on the other hand, also provided some of the impetus which saw AIMM actively pursue other options for ministry and witness elsewhere in Africa.

an aborted joint AIMM/CMZa mission effort in West Africa

The investigative AIMM/CMZa team sent to Upper Volta in 1976 (cf. ch. 62) proposed not only that a ministry be undertaken in that country but that it be a joint effort of the AIMM and the Zaire Mennonite Church. This proposal sparked immediate interest and discussion both in North America and in Zaire. The AIMM Executive Secretary and CMZa President Kabangy discussed the proposal at length both in Zaire and in Elkhart.

From the CMZa side, there were valid candidates available and the hope that something could be worked out which would not require any sort of financial commitment from the Zaire Church. From the AIMM side, there was a readiness to move ahead with the proposed joint effort providing the Zaire Church would commit to some level of support, however modest, for its missionaries.

In the midst of all of the discussion, a letter arrived in Elkhart from a Zairian couple well known to the AIMM Secretary, sharing their sense of call and a readiness to volunteer for service in the envisioned new venture. And, if their own Church did not feel it possible to support them, they wanted to apply to AIMM itself, as did other candidates from elsewhere.

On the one hand, AIMM had no policy or structure permitting consideration of their application. There was, further, AIMM's conviction that it was unwise to incorporate Zairian personnel on the new pioneering team entirely devoid of any material support from their own Church. It was, consequently, with deep disappointment that CMZa and AIMM administrative personnel came to the conclusion that AIMM would proceed on its own in the new venture.

Was this a golden opportunity missed? Should AIMM have been more ready to experiment with some new formula of partnership which would have made it possible for Zairian candidates to partner with AIMM candidates in opening a new work in Upper Volta? In view of subsequent events in Zaire, it appears that the Lord had other things in mind for Mennonites in that country.

For one thing, efforts have been made to maintain contact and provide encouragement to Angolan refugees who have returned to their homeland after worshiping with Mennonites in Kinshasa. But above all, there is the exciting new development of a joint Mennonite mission outreach supported by all three Churches of Zaire (i.e., CMCo, CEFMC and CEM) in Bukavu in eastern Zaire on the shores of Lake Kivu. A Mennonite presence in this region first materialized in the aftermath of the atrocities of the ethnic conflicts of 1994-97 in Rwanda which resulted in the flight of hundreds of thousands of panic-stricken Rwandans across their border into nearby Zaire. Immense refugee camps took quick shape with immediate desperate need for food, shelter and medical care. The efforts of the UN to provide help and broker political solutions dominated the evening news in North America for weeks on end. It was during these dreadful days that Zaire Mennonites sought to be of help.

The first initiative came from MCC/Zaire which provided some funding and material supplies. An early couple sent to give leadership to the MCC response to the emergency were Fidel and Krista Lumeya (pr. loo-MAY-ah) who were soon joined by a second lay couple from Kinshasa, Dr. and Mrs. Kalumuna (pr. kah-loo-MOO-nah). They early determined that their work among the refugees could not be limited simply to the meeting of physical needs. Efforts also had to be made to address the psychological and emotional suffering of the refugees as well. The resultant blend of ministry to physical needs and calls for repentance, prayer and reconciliation did not go unnoticed by the churches of the area. So impressed were they that an official invitation was sent to Mennonite Churches by the regional ECZ personnel of the Great Lakes Area to undertake a church planting ministry of their own.

Seizing upon this opportunity, CONIM personnel began to lay plans to respond. Said Pakisa Tshimika (pr. pah-KEE-sah tshi-MEE-kah), the MB Board representative in Kinshasa: "This is not a window, but a door of opportunity." Two candidate couples were selected to serve as the first Mennonite missionaries to eastern aire - - Rev. Philemon and Pauline Beghela (pr. beh-GAY-lah) of the CMZa and Rev. and Mrs. Mayoto (pr. ah-YOH-toh) of the CEFMC. They, in turn, followed a nine week training program especially designed for them at the International Missiology Center founded and directed by Dr. Nzash Lumeya (pr. NZAHSH loo-MAY-ah), a Mennonite Brethren leader who returned home from his doctoral studies in France with a vision for establishing a missiological training program in his homeland. This, in and of itself, is a remarkable story. That he could play a significant role in the orientation and preparation of the first missionaries of an inter-Mennonite effort of church planting on the eastern frontier of his country was surely a vindication of his dream.

To give clear structure and guidance to this joint effort, CONIM brought into being an inter-Mennonite Mission Board called "The Zairian Council of the Anabaptist/Mennonite Mission for Central Africa," or COZMAMAC in its French acronym form.

In an explanatory article written by President Fimbo Ganvunze (pr. FIh-mboh gahn-VUH-nzeh) of the CMZa, (27) a variety of statements are found. Referring to the early Mennonite ministry in the area he observed that "the Mennonites brought the message of peace, justice and reconciliation which impacted the lives of the refugees." As a result, the refugees "requested the presence of Mennonite Churches in the countries of the Great Lakes" (i.e., Rwanda, Burundi and Eastern Zaire). President Fimbo continued: "It is a privilege for the CMZa to participate in this first transcultural missionary experience with other Mennonite Churches. . . . May Bukavu not be the point of arrival, but rather the point of departure to reach all the Great Lakes Region; and why not all of Africa and the world in general!" (28)

In an attached project proposal, the objectives of this pioneering inter-Mennonite mission effort in Zaire are simply stated: - to consolidate a ministry of peace and reconciliation; - to provide humanitarian assistance; - to plant local Mennonite congregations; - to start micro-development projects to help the disadvantaged.

Against all of this background, the following news release makes exhilarating reading: "As mist rose off Lake Kivu at 7 a.m., August 24, 1997, Pastor Philemon Begela baptized 10 new members into the Mennonite Church of the Great Lakes. One by one the new members 'died' and were reborn with Christ."

"While all baptisms are cause for joy, this baptism was special. The Mennonite Church in Bukavu, eastern Congo (formerly Zaire) was planted on March 7, 1996, by Congolese lay missionaries as an outreach program of the Congolese Mennonite Churches. The new Church attracted members from all ethnic groups and tribes, a rarity in this region torn by ethnic tension. Tired of war and drawn by Anabaptist teachings on peace, people from all backgrounds - - local people and Rwandan and Burundian refugees as well as several street children - - began praying together."

"The Beghelas, a Congolese missionary couple, were slated to come from Kinshasa, the country's capital, to Bukavu to assume the pastorate when war broke out in eastern Congo in October 1996. Rebels advanced and took ever increasing amounts of territory, separating the Church and its intended pastor. Though divided by war, both the pastor and the congregation continued to pray for an eventual uniting."

"Finally, one and a half years later, the Beghelas arrived in Bukavu. Against all odds, they found an alive, vibrant Church, one that not only survived a devastating war, but one that was growing and had 10 baptismal candidates to present. The Church, however, had lost some members during the war, including two young men caught in the cross fire and several Rwandan refugees whose whereabouts are still unknown."

"As the sun glistened off the lake, we thought of our brothers and sisters no longer with us, but were reminded of how gracious our Father is and how much we have ultimately gained." (29)

the AIMM pilgrimage with the AICs

Early Mennonite investigative reporting on the southern African mission/church scene came with a tacit assumption that, should Mennonites opt to place personnel in the region, it would be with a view to bringing new fellowships of believers into being - - Mennonite believers that is (cf. ch. 47).

But it was not long until it became clear to AIMM that southern Africa presented a mission/church scene which was already heavily populated. Not only was there a variety of Missions with long histories of ministry and churches they had long since planted, there were also many churches born of African initiative and vision - - African Independent Churches.

AIMM was early confronted by three options, i.e., 1) ignore the many denominational churches already on the scene and seek to erect still another denominational flagpole from which to fly a Mennonite pennant; 2) not send anyone to southern Africa and look elsewhere; 3) explore the possibilities of adopting a servant stance among the churches already there.

The decision to opt for the third alternative has taken AIMM on a fascinating journey with the AICs. It is an ongoing journey. Along the way there have been moments of perplexity, joy, disappointment, learning, discomfort, ministry, rich fellowship, stretching, broadened faith, fresh looks at familiar Scriptures and, withal, immense reward.

While AIMM has decided not to seek to plant Mennonite churches as such, AIMM has never said that no Mennonite Churches should ever appear as a result of its presence and ministry in that part of Africa. Should there be those who through their studies of Scripture with Mennonite personnel one day come to the conviction that they want to organize and identify themselves as Anabaptist believers, this will certainly be their privilege. In the meantime, AIMM is satisfied that it has adopted a correct and fruitful approach to witness and service in that unique part of Africa. It has proven beneficial in many ways, not only to the AIC folk but also to the AIMM personnel who have undertaken a teacher/learner pilgrimage of faith with their AIC brothers and sisters (cf. chs. 59-60).

something called Mennonite Ministries

It was in the post-war decade of the 1950's in Congo that CIM and MCC personnel first began to interact in joint projects of service. Traveling on one occasion with CIM Executive Secretary H.A. Driver, Orie Miller was introduced first hand to the need and opportunity of that immense land. There promptly followed a steady stream of MCC volunteers who were assigned to a wide variety of CIM programs. When AIMM ventured into southern Africa in the 70's, it found MCC folk already on the scene.

It must be admitted that relations between CIM/AIMM/MCC personnel have not always been friction-free. Representing different organizations, different agendas and, frequently, different orientations and perspectives, it should not be surprising that views and personalities sometimes clashed.

Upon arrival in Botswana, both AIMM and MCC needed to work out formalities with the government of that newly-independent country. In view of MCC's status as a service organization, most entry formalities were waived for its personnel. When the first AIMM folk arrived, they were simply viewed as more welcome Mennonites. But as the AIMM contingent gradually grew in size, the time came when AIMM's identity as a mission organization became clear to the government and official registration was consequently required. AIMM was faced with a decision. Would the Mission insist on its own identity in the country apart from MCC? Or would AIMM recognize the confusion that dual Mennonite organizations would soon create in the minds of government personnel and the general public alike?

While MCC had already worked through patterns of joint administration with the Eastern Mennonite Board of Missions in East Africa, AIMM had no such previous experience - - and tended not to be interested in such an arrangement. However, a decision about the Botswana situation could not be deferred. After much dialogue between AIMM and MCC personnel both in Botswana and North America, a joint constitution was drawn up, a joint filing for legal registration in the country was submitted to the government, a jointly-appointed country director was put in place and something called Mennonite Ministries was born (cf. ch. 52).

It was the right decision and has proven to be a mutually beneficial experience in Botswana. Once again, an inter-Mennonite approach to service, which was initially viewed askance by some in North America, resulted in an enriched ministry and witness overseas. In time, the inter-Mennonite venture came to be referred to as the "Botswana Model." Eventually a similar joint AIMM/MCC arrangement was established in Lesotho, as well.

approaching the unapproachable

When, in the late 1970's, AIMM decided to put missionaries along the western border of Upper Volta among a cluster of resistant ethnic groups, the first and crucial question was how to approach them. With deeply-rooted traditional world views overlaid by aspects of Islam, they were characterized by some long term missionaries of the area as "unreachable." Traditional strategies of itinerant evangelism using a trade language, sometimes coupled with translators, had clearly proven to be largely ineffective.

Taking a leaf from the book of the Wycliffe Bible Translators, it was decided to approach these resistant people as the Wycliffe people do, i.e., by asking missionaries to take up residence among them in their villages. Their first assignment was not to preach but rather to listen, observe and fit into their village cultural setting as gently as they could and, in the process, begin serious study of their language.

Hiding their initial skepticism, village elders in place after place offered shelter, food and acceptance to these strange white people. Comments and questions emerged soon enough. "This has never happened before. What brings you here to our village?" When thus questioned, the AIMM pioneering missionaries responded openly and honestly: "We've come to be your friends and to learn your language so that one day we can translate God's Book into the language you speak."

Among these so-called unapproachable groups of Upper Volta, this was startling news. Under the influence of Islam, they had come to view the Koran and its teachings with respect. This Koran made many favorable references to the Bible's Old Testament and even declared that Jesus was an important prophet. If, indeed, these new white people were prepared to live among them and honor their dialects enough to try to learn them, they were surely welcome. And if their goal was to share God's book with them in their own tongues, this was something indeed special.

During AIMM's first two decades of ministry in Upper Volta/Burkina Faso, there has been a mix of breakthroughs and disappointments; elation and sorrow; progress and setbacks. But "unapproachable" ethnic groups have been approached. There has been response. An autonomous Mennonite Church is already a reality in that land (cf. chs. 72-73). We look to the future with anticipation as the Lord continues to use our witness in that isolated region of Africa to the honor of his name.

the Mennonite Churches of Congo: how Anabaptist are they?

The conduct of Christian Mission by Mennonite missionaries has come under critical scrutiny during the past couple of decades or so on the part of some Mennonite scholars. In developing the critique, it is stated that earlier generations of Mennonite missionaries unthinkingly allowed their view and practice of mission to be unduly shaped by three basic streams of non-Mennonite influence: 1) a Reformed theology with its focus on the sin of a fallen mankind and the consequent need for salvation and release from guilt by faith in Christ; 2) a Pietist influence with its accent on intimacy with Jesus on the part of spiritually reborn people; and 3) American revivalism with its emphasis upon inner tranquility as a result of a conversion experience and acceptance of Jesus as Savior. (30)

Gospel v Gospel

Central to this critique of the Mennonite mission endeavor of the past is the impact of the landmark presidential address brought by Harold S. Bender in December 1943 to the American Society of Church History. Oft-quoted and much studied thereafter, it has come to be regarded as a concise and incisive statement of the Anabaptist view of Christianity as consisting of 1) the Christian life as discipleship, 2) the Church as community and 3) the practice of nonresistant love. (31)

Along the way, the Bender address has also come to be regarded by some as an Anabaptist formulation of the very heart of the Gospel itself. More and more it has been suggested that the essence of the Gospel has to do with themes of nonresistance, peace and justice as embodied in the Hebrew concept of *Shalom*.

It is, then, against this background that some have reviewed the conduct of Mennonite mission of the past and have found it largely wanting.

Other voices; other perspectives

There are, however, some corners of Mennonite academia which view this formulation of the heart of the Gospel as being too restrictive. One articulate spokesman with differing convictions and interpretations is Stephen F. Dintaman. In a variety of articles, he has made his position and perspective clear. First, regarding Bender's oft-quoted "vision statement," he points out that "it is too seldom noted that for Bender himself Christianity was never reducible to behavior. . . . In particular two unstated assumptions lie behind Bender's vision: 1) he held firmly to basic evangelical doctrines about the being and work of God in Christ. 2) He believed and repeatedly taught that the living out of the vision was only possible through the indwelling presence of Christ and the power of the Holy Spirit."

"The next generation of 'Anabaptist vision' theologians taught passionately about Christian behavior and greatly deepened and expanded the concept of discipleship. But they gave only passing, non-passionate attention to the work of Christ and the work of the Spirit in the inner transformation of the person. . . . The unfortunate consequence of this approach to teaching the Anabaptist vision was that it resulted in generations of students and church leaders learning some of the behavioral aspects of the Christian faith without learning equally well that discipleship is only meaningful and possible because it is an answer to who God is and what God is doing in the world. Nor did they necessarily experience what it means to have a vital and life-changing personal friendship with the crucified and risen Jesus."

In the same article Dintaman observes that decades of a near exclusive focus on the "vision statement" has resulted in a certain impoverishment of those pursuing it. He cites three key results: "1) The vision gave us little insight into human behavior. . . . We tend to think that changing basic behavior regarding wealth, violence and personal relationships is simply a matter of changing your mind and then exerting your will. . . . Change is simply a matter of seeing a better way and deciding to do it." This approach has "left us frustrated and impotent when we meet deeply troubled people who seem incapable of change."

Pressing his theme, Dintaman states further: "2) We were left an inadequate awareness of the liberating work of God through the death and resurrection of Jesus. First, foremost, and fundamentally, faith is not about us and our discipleship. Faith is about God and the work of redemption that only God can and has done for us. . . . I find that many people who are schooled in the vision find it difficult to give a clear expression to just what the good news is. And that is understandable, since nowhere does the Anabaptist vision state the gospel the Anabaptists believed and proclaimed! . . . Peace and justice social activism and engagement in conflict mediation can be authentic expressions of faith in Christ, but I believe that has become more of a *substitute* for faith. . . . This is not a call for us to forsake social awareness and active work for social change, but it is just a reminder that ALL THIS IS NOT THE GOSPEL!"

Dintaman cites yet a third area of concern: "3) We have also . . . been impoverished in our sense of the spiritual presence and power of the risen Christ." Referring to the early history of the Apostolic Church he observes: "It is only when Christ's redeeming death and resurrection has taken place and his empowering presence has been poured out through the Holy Spirit that fruitful apostolic ministry begins to happen." (32)

Along the same line, another observer of the Mennonite scene has commented as follows: "A focus on discipleship which does not begin with a call to personal conversion and new birth . . . is not sufficient to address the great inner needs of people in an age marked by hopelessness and despair. It offers no more motivation to follow Jesus than to pursue any other form of altruistic humanism." (33)

And yet another: "The question is often asked: 'Is peace or evangelism the heart of the gospel?' The answer is clear: Evangelism cannot be effective without promoting peace. Similarly, peace cannot be realized unless the redeeming power of God through faith in Jesus Christ is accepted. The Christian peace witness must take full recognition of this fact. Peace and evangelism are inseparable." (34)

One participant in this ongoing Mennonite dialogue in the States has observed: "Church history, after all, did not begin with a baptism of water in a house in Zurich in 1525. It began with a baptism of fire in an upper room in Jerusalem around 30 AD." (35)

Don Jacobs has perhaps put the issue as succinctly as anyone: ". . . shalom does not save; Jesus Christ does." (36)

so what about CIM/AIMM?

In response to the commentaries above, CIM/AIMM board members and personnel across the years would have sounded a hearty "Amen."

While CIM/AIMM personnel have not become directly involved in this North American theological dialogue, there have been observations and reflections which apply directly to it. A clear case in point was a letter written by AIMM missionary Larry Hills during his years of service in southern Africa. In early January of 1984 he joined other AIMM/MCC personnel of the region at a retreat. The adopted theme was "Peacemaking" and the invited speaker (37) addressed the topic against the background of the grim impact of *apartheid* which at that time was brutalizing the black population of the Republic. In a letter to the AIMM Executive Secretary at Elkhart, Hills shared the following observations: "Ultimately the message of the retreat speaker was that repressive governments should be toppled and the best way of doing that is through nonviolent action: strikes, boycotts, nonviolent confrontation. I believe the New Testament and the Mennonite tradition calls us to a higher standard of righteousness. As I read the Gospels I am confronted with a Jesus who lived and moved within one of the most brutally repressive regimes of history yet I never hear him calling on his disciples to overthrow that regime through either violent or nonviolent means. It seems his call was always a call to discipleship and to the formation of a redeemed community which would live out the values of the coming new age in the midst of the present evil age. That the new age community should have an impact on the surrounding world seems clear in Jesus' assertion that we are to be salt and light. But that this new community would make its presence felt by the toppling of government seems far less clear. . . . Peacemaking as discipleship presents us with a radically different picture. This form of peacemaking makes no promises of short term political success. The Prince of Peace experienced little if any worldly success and his activity got him nailed to a cross. It is only in the light of the resurrection that the way of Jesus can be said to be a success, a success which far surpasses the destruction of an earthly government. Why then should we be peacemakers? Because we claim allegiance to Jesus Christ the Prince of Peace and he calls us to walk in his way. . . ."

"A second concern deals with what I call commitment to abstract principles versus commitment to Jesus Christ. At retreat I heard much talk about commitment to certain principles: justice, freedom, human rights, nonviolence and a disturbing lack of talk about commitment to Jesus Christ as risen Lord and center of our lives. I personally find abstract principles curiously lacking in the power to move me to action but the concrete reality of Jesus does move me. I believe that this abstraction of biblical principles carries with it a subtle but destructive danger. When Jesus is removed as center and foundation of our life together, the circle

702

collapses upon itself and what remains are hollow statements about peace and justice which all too frequently degenerate into an unloving and intolerant arrogance. When Jesus stands at the center, not only do we have a firm foundation for our activity on behalf of the poor and oppressed but those efforts become tempered with warmth and humility and love for the sinner as well as the sinned against, the oppressor as well as the oppressed." (38)

An AIMM executive secretary expressed himself in similar terms in a paper presented in the opening session of a major self-study sponsored by the AIMM Board in the fall of 1979 at Miracle Camp near Lawton, MI. "It is my sincere hope that as we work during these days on our assignment of redefinition and restatement of AIMM stance, objectives and strategies for the decade ahead, we can make it abundantly clear that AIMM carries genuine concern for peace and justice in a world, and more particularly a continent, that is so cruelly torn by hatred, brutality, exploitation and greed. But I also hope that this statement will leave no uncertainty as to our ongoing and unswerving commitment to witness to the fact that God was in Christ, reconciling the world unto Himself, and to seek to be the agents and facilitators of that reconciliation which is a prior and enabling reconciliation for all others that we may seek to effect. For until men and women have made their personal peace with the Prince of Peace, our best intentioned efforts are but an exercise in futility." (39)

But to return to the original question posed: "The Mennonite Churches of Congo: how Anabaptist are they?"

The answer depends, obviously, upon the plumb line of assessment used. If the theological perspective which has grown around the Bender address is exclusively employed, the African churches are found with some shortcomings. But if it is allowed that the Gospel also has something to do with joyous faith in a risen Savior, the "reading" is considerably different.

It is true that early generations of CIM/AIMM missionaries did not particularly highlight themes of nonviolence, peace and justice per se. Neither, however, were these themes ignored. CIM/AIMM missionaries of the past would maintain that in their teaching in the Mission schools and in their preaching, Christ's Sermon on the Mount was examined along with all other passages studied. And, in the process, the relationship of such passages to Mennonite church history and conviction were clearly stated.

Are there Congolese Mennonite pastors and evangelists who can quote Menno Simon's writings or H.S. Bender's vision statement? Not many.

Have there been Mennonites in the past, who, when caught in a sweep of a village or a neighborhood of an urban area, reluctantly accepted induction into the military forces rather than risk incarceration in Mobutu's infamous prisons? Yes, some have. Have there been any who have volunteered for chaplaincy service in their government's armed forces? Yes, a few.

Are there instances of Mennonites taking each other to courts of law? Yes. Have there been Mennonites who, during President Mobutu's corrupt and brutal regime, took the personal risk of speaking out boldly against the injustice of his policies and his greed? Not many.

But there are still other dimensions of Congolese Church life which also need to be taken into account:

- if a lengthening roster of Congolese Mennonites martyred for their faith has Anabaptist overtones;
- if a resolute commitment to evangelism which reaches across ethnic borders to unbelievers has any Anabaptist ring to it;
- if a growing Church bringing together a multiplicity of tribes in a self-disciplining, nurturing, worshiping community has an Anabaptist flavor about it;
- if a resolute theme of joy and hope amidst abject poverty and oppressive governments has any Anabaptist aroma about it;

- if rallying around the bereaved in times of loss, illness or death as a supportive community has any Anabaptist scent about it;
- if a reverent approach to the translated Scriptures they hold in their hands in search of comfort, guidance and reassurance for daily life has anything Anabaptist about it;
- if a simple, trusting, uncluttered faith in God as a loving father and Jesus as a merciful Savior sufficient for whatever hardship life throws at them bears any resemblance to the stance of our Anabaptist forefathers;
- if weaving prayer into the fabric of daily life stirs any memory of things Anabaptist of the past;
- if readiness to share what little they have with those who have even less bears any resemblance to our Anabaptist history;
- if their joyful approach to adult baptism and their hushed entry into communion services resembles anything from bygone Anabaptist days,

then there may be some reason for pause on the part of those in North America who tend to view the African Mennonite Churches primarily in terms of what are considered to be their Anabaptist deficiencies.

a plea from overseas Mennonites

In a letter from an AIMM executive secretary once addressed to MCC/Akron, the following is found: "I recall so well our mission/church consultation in Hesston the week prior to the Wichita MWC of 1978. The basic thrust of those sessions was to give the overseas church leaders opportunity to state the needs and dreams of their churches as they felt and defined them. At one point, Charles Christano [the MWC President of the time] had the floor and, in an aside, shared how weary they as overseas Mennonite leaders become of having Western Mennonites sidle up to them and ask where their churches stand on the issues of nonresistance and nonviolence. He went on to comment that it seems to them sometimes that we from the West have no other interest, no other concern, no other agenda as regards the overseas Mennonite churches. In other conversations he and others let it be known that we in North America, with our assured right of political dissent and options for alternate service, are poorly placed to coach and critique young churches who must find their way under harsh governments and surrounded by bloodshed. Between the lines, furthermore, I thought I heard him saying: 'We've heard the message of your missionaries; we've responded in faith to Jesus Christ; we've formed ourselves into Mennonite Churches and seek to be faithful followers of Jesus in our context. With Scriptures in hand, we pray that God will lead us in faithful discipleship in our setting. Can you trust us? Can you pray for us rather than criticize us?'"

"It strikes me as curious that while, on the one hand, Mennonite missionaries have frequently been taken to task for being too authoritarian and paternalistic in trying to shape the contours and practices of the overseas churches, when it comes to issues of peace and justice, they are accused of having failed to plant churches whose views and statements are facsimiles of ours."

"Interestingly enough, it was just days later that Bishop Festo Kivengere of the Anglican Church of Uganda spoke to us at Wichita. I'll never forget his opening comments which were to the effect that he'd heard a great deal about 'the Kingdom' since his arrival there among us. He, however, was going to talk to us about 'the King.' His soft nudge to the assembled sons and daughters of Menno that day seemed to me to be clear, i.e., 'First the King, then the Kingdom.'" (40)

Is there need among Congo's Mennonite Churches for more growth and maturity in God's grace? Is there need for an ever deepening understanding of what obedient discipleship means in the context of their socio-cultural setting? Is there need of a fuller, more sacrificial response to Christ's sermon on the mount? Of course.

And of what Mennonite congregation in North America cannot the same be said?

In the meantime, there is a genuine spirit of quest noticeable on the part of African Mennonites. There are two key questions which we hear Mennonite leaders asking themselves. First: "What does it mean for us to be genuinely Christian and genuinely African at the same time?" And a second, surrounded by millions of fellow Christians in Africa: "In what ways should we as Mennonite Christians be distinctively different within our broad African Christian community? What of our heritage and our Scriptural understandings should we be exemplifying and teaching and preaching in our setting?"

A revealing reflection of this ongoing process is found in a summary statement issued in 1994 at the conclusion of a meeting of the Africa and Mennonite Brethren in Christ Fellowship (AMBCF), a gathering which brought together forty-one men and women from eight different African countries representing twelve Mennonite conferences.

1. We of the AMBCF affirm our spiritual connections to the Anabaptists of the 16th century. We want to live as they lived.
2. We believe the Bible is the sole Word of God for all time and situations.
3. We are in a social context of suffering and potential suffering but we will be faithful to God's principles.
4. The Gospel of Jesus Christ brings radical transformation strengthened by the discipling process in the minds, emotions, and volition.
5. We understand peace is not a technique but a style of life. "Christ is our Peace."
6. Mennonites must be people of grace and this must begin in our homes. We must put our own houses in order.
7. Reconciliation means walking together in a biblical way not understood by social science. This is a spiritual process which impacts all of life.
8. We as Mennonites in Africa recognize that we are bridge people, people who need to act as agents of reconciliation across cultural lines and at times in the midst of conflict.
9. The church's center is Jesus Christ our Lord and the community of faith is a global family of peace, mission, sharing and deeds of mercy.
10. Mission is the work of every believer. We as African Mennonites must focus on evangelization beyond (Mat. 28:19-20). Mission is presence, proclamation and participation.
11. Even if Africa seems hopeless now, we believe there is hope and the transformation we are presently experiencing will make Africa the hope of the world (Psa. 68:31). Emmanuel is with us still, "Those who walk in darkness will see a great light."
12. As we go back to our respective nations and conferences, we do so believing that we must [have] unity as people of peace in prayer for Africa. We propose that all members (315.000 plus) be called to prayer and fasting on the first weekend in each month. United in prayer we will see Africa saved. (41)

Africa and the future

The past 100 years have witnessed dramatic history in Africa - - particularly in the sub-Saharan part of the continent. Without question the key features of these hundred years have been the suppression of the slave trade, the near simultaneous arrival of European explorers and Christian missionaries, the dismantling of colonial empires and the era of tumult which has followed as black governments have struggled to shape their own destinies.

As this century and millennium in Africa draw to a close, the political picture, sadly, is not bright. While there are some areas of stability and a few shining examples of responsible government, the sad fact is that entirely too much of the continent witnesses turmoil, insecurity and suffering. Some of the major contributing factors are: ancient ethnic loyalties and rivalries which forever lie just below the surface ready to erupt violently with little provocation; a hodgepodge of national boundaries arbitrarily drawn on the African map by former colonial powers which often make no geo-political sense but which now are fiercely defended by black governments; the flow of raw products to the West at prices dictated by Western markets; the choking noose of ill-advised national debts; the frequent squandering of limited resources for the maintenance of military forces; rampant greed and corruption in high places; the brutal exploitation of poverty-stricken masses in order to maintain the status quo of privileged minorities.

Nowhere in all of Africa has this conglomerate of evil dynamics been more clearly showcased than in Zaire/Congo.

Commentaries on Africa are abundant. If, in the decades of the 1960's and 70's, there was a tendency on the part of journalists - - both black and white - - to excuse inept black governments on the basis of the colonial legacy with which they were saddled, attitudes now have sharply shifted. The new mood is well reflected by Keith Richburg, an Afro-American journalist who has spent time both in East Asia and Africa. In a hard-nosed article entitled "The Same Old Excuses," he argues that it is time that African governments be held to the same standards of accountability and responsibility that apply to other members of the international community. He maintains that the West has for too long trodden lightly in its dealings with black Africa for fear of being accused of having a "neo-colonialist" mentality and agenda. The result, in his view, is that African governments are allowed to continue in their irresponsible ways, this to the unending detriment and suffering of millions of underprivileged citizens of their countries.

He concludes by stating that if there is a conspiracy against Africa on the part of the West, as some African leaders like to suggest, it is a conspiracy of silence in the face of inexcusable irresponsibility. (42)

There are some observers of the current African scene who express their uncertainty that Africa can even survive in its present geo-political configuration. But others see the recent demise of Mobutu and the fall of his corruption ridden regime in the great heartland of Africa as a harbinger of better things to come. With major help from neighboring countries such as Rwanda, Uganda and Angola, Laurent Kabila (pr. kah-BEE-lah) and his "Alliance of Democratic Forces for the Liberation of Congo" (AFDL in its French acronym form) erupted out of the murky chaos surrounding the massive refugee camps along Zaire's eastern borders. When, in late 1996, the back of Mobutu's military force in eastern Zaire was broken, Kabila and his troops began a steady sweep across the country from east to west encountering only token armed resistance while being welcomed with wild acclaim by the rural populations en route. By mid-May 1997, he and his forces took control of Kinshasa without armed opposition by what was left of Mobutu's army. (43) There were a few immediate popular measures taken by Kabila. One was to restore order to Kinshasa's dangerous streets and to curb burglary and looting. Another was to clean up the incredible chaos which existed at Njili, the country's international airport, and to restore efficiency to its operation. He also renounced the country's name inaugurated by Mobutu and declared a return to it's original designation. Thus Zaire was replaced by the Democratic Republic of Congo.

At least one columnist saw this intervention of Zaire's neighbors in its internal affairs as a positive development which augurs for a brighter future in Africa. "It's becoming possible to talk of a benign conspiracy among 'second-generation' African regimes to rescue their neighbors from the depredations of 'first-generation' post-independence regimes like Mobutu's. They are doing it partly to protect their own borders . . . But they also have a higher mission: to rid Africa of monsters. It is a huge change for the better . . . and it is being accomplished by Africans themselves." (44)

Perhaps. But as of this writing in late 1997, there is again a spreading sense of impatience and resentment among the people of Congo - - a sense that in spite of Kabila's new regime and the glowing predictions of change for the better, there is little substantive improvement. Congo's external debts remain. The infrastructure continues in ruins. UN efforts to investigate persistent rumors of massacres in eastern Congo are hamstrung by the government. Public services, for all practical purposes, remain at a standstill. What national revenues remain still are controlled by an elite minority while the population in general continues its grim struggle, amidst unemployment and inflation, to keep body and soul together.

the perspective of Africa's people of faith

In some ways the most realistic commentary comes from Africa's Christian community. In an article entitled "Africa by the Year AD 2000," Dr. Tokunboh Adeyemo (pr. toh-KUHN-boh ah-day-YEH-moh), the General Secretary of the Association of Evangelicals of Africa and Madagascar (AEAM) based in Nairobi, Kenya, suggests there are three possible approaches to an evaluation of Africa as this millennium winds down to its conclusion. One can be that of naive optimism which wants to believe that everything will somehow work out for them. Another view is that of deep pessimism in the face of oft recounted problems which seem to have no solution.

Rejecting both of these extremes, he suggests what he calls a "realist view." He does not discount Africa's problems. He acknowledges that they are many and that they are all too real. But in his article he goes on to state: "As evangelicals we prayerfully look at Africa through the Bible. . . . Jesus is the only hope for Africa! The bottom line is fourfold: Proclamation of Jesus as Lord; Prayer that taps into the Supernatural; Participation that gets Christians involved as salt and light; and Power of the Holy Spirit in all wisdom and righteousness. It is our role as an AEAM family to rally all evangelicals together throughout Africa for the realization of the realist viewpoint. It is possible. It can be done. It shall be done. So help us Lord!" (45)

Africa and Christian Mission in the future

Viewed from the perspective of Christian Mission, the Africa of the closing years of this century affords a formidable landscape of obstacles linked with enormous opportunities. Colonial regimes have long since crumbled. *Apartheid* has been dismantled. Urban drift is noted all across black Africa resulting in steadily growing numbers of ragged shanty town dwellers on the fringes of the cities. Populations of some countries are under the severe stress of inflation, unemployment, poverty, inadequate public services and subject to the harsh treatment of violent governments. In a resultant atmosphere of insecurity and staggering need, cults flourish. Revival of ancient tribal customs is frequently noted.

And there is the looming reality of the surging influence of Islam across black Africa. Possessed of a new missionary zeal and often funded by large donations from sympathetic oil rich countries, impressive and costly mosques are under construction in more and more of the important urban centers of black Africa. In Congo, for example, where government-funded public education has practically ceased to exist, a growing Muslim community has taken a page from the book of historic Christian Missions. Capitalizing on the universal hunger of Congolese youth for an education, Muslim sponsored schools are cropping up all over, even in rural areas of what has been traditional Mennonite territory.

But overarching all other considerations is the reality of a rapidly growing Christian Church. It is by now common place to refer to a shift of the Christian Church's center of gravity from the North to South of the equator. The major reason for this shift is the sustained rapid growth of Christian communities in both Africa and South America. This new reality requires a careful self-scrutiny on the part of AIMM. As the year 2000 rushes upon us, it is crucial that AIMM review its conceptualization of mission, its objectives, its priorities and, above all else, how it plans to take into account and collaborate with the rapidly growing Christian community in Africa.

needed: a new mind-set

For generations of Christian North Americans, Christian Mission was a process of sending people from a "Christian" America to a non-Christian area elsewhere in the world. We were the guardians of the Gospel and the messengers of good news to those who "dwelt in darkness." The rapidly growing world church has made this view of things obsolete. Myron Augsburger has framed the issue well: "It is time for us to get beyond the feeling that [foreign] churches are an extension of North America. . . . We've got to quit thinking that we dominate the world scene." (46) Christian Mission must no longer be seen as something which basically takes place in a distant land surrounded by tropical forest or rolling savanna. Mission must rather be understood as needing to take place wherever and whenever belief meets unbelief. By that definition, incidentally, North America is an immense mission field.

Not only should our understanding of Christian Mission be recast but so also do we need to review our relations with fellow African Christians. We need to make a transition from gratefully viewing them as the result of God's blessing upon our efforts in mission to inviting them to become partners with us in ongoing mission. Granted; this is a concept more easily talked about than accomplished. It is, nonetheless, a challenge which remains before us. There are some mission boards which have found ways to integrate non-Americans into their overseas missionary teams. There are also some Mennonite boards which have incorporated non-Americans into their administrative staffs. (47) These people provide unique perspectives and insights in planning sessions and program projections. Questions of logistics and support are real, but long range benefits are enormous.

And, finally, genuine effort must be made to move beyond a relationship which has cast the African Churches in a role of dependence upon mission boards to one which is based on genuine interdependence. Across the years the axis of relationship has been African Mennonite Churches/Mennonite mission boards. For years, already, overseas church leaders have been requesting - - yes longing - - for opportunities to relate in a more direct manner to the church groups which comprise AIMM. To be sure, part of this desire stems from the hope that as fraternal relations are established, some material help may be forthcoming for the many needs and projects the African Churches confront. But at a deeper level, there is also the desire to experience the meaning and blessing of a world Mennonite family and to make their own unique contribution to it.

Viewed from a strictly organizational stance, this proposal conjures up an "administrative nightmare" for old time Mission administrators! But if this is an idea whose time has come, perhaps the role of Mennonite mission boards should be less one of administrative oversight and more one of facilitation.

There is, yet, the further fact that a new, young generation of North American Mennonite church members needs to be confronted with and challenged by their own opportunities and responsibilities for ongoing witness in today's world. Supporting and giving to impersonal "mission budgets" no longer stirs the response it once did. Precise, focused information needs to be provided. The cause of ongoing Christian Mission needs to be personalized. Acquaintance and direct supportive links with specific missionaries are helpful. Making possible personal encounters with overseas brothers and sisters in Christ is of great value.

Stan Nussbaum sees such contacts not only as a good idea but as a necessity for the ongoing spiritual welfare of the American church itself. Though his comments are focused specifically on the potential contribution the AICs of southern Africa can make to the North American Mennonite community, his comments are relevant to African Christians in general. In a paper presented at an AIMM/AIC consultation in Kuruman, South Africa, in May 1997, he wrote: "We have always given lip service to 'teaching/learning' but it takes on added significance now that we can see the huge myth which North America, including AIMM Board and constituency, has bought into without thinking. It is that 'mission' is largely cross-cultural and 'Christian growth' happens in mono-cultural isolation. In other words, international contacts are unnecessary for the N[orth] A[merican] church to mature in Christ at this stage of Christian history. On the basis of that myth, rooted in 19th century circumstances rather than in Scripture, AIMM was set up in the 'overseas mission' business but not in the 'Christian growth at home' business."

"I am arguing that Scripture has the power to pull us out of that cultural myth and help us recognize that we North American Mennonites NEED AICs to help us grow in Christ and to carry out his mission. . . ." In the area of theology, "their experience of God is bigger, broader, and nearer than the experience of most of us. They know God as the God of all history and all nations; their faith is not boiled down to 'Jesus and me.' God has more than 'spiritual' things on his agenda; he cares about physical healing, ethnic matters, extended families, societies. And God does not keep himself at a safe and comfortable distance; sometimes he is so close that he grabs you, shakes you up and turns you around."

"AIC's know how to make a house church work. A denominational structure they may not do so well at, but where the rubber meets the road they have traction. . . . Let's face it. North Americans are the infants of the world church when it comes to prayer. Absolutely anybody can outpray us."

And finally, "most AICs know the folly of trusting in possessions. [That] is easier to see when you don't have so many. They trust God, they have joy, they continue in faith - - one week at a time. If they could help us see that we don't really 'need' a lot of things we think we need, that would be a terrific help to our maturity in faith." (48)

In a presentation at the Mennonite World Conference held in Calcutta, India, in the summer of 1997, Myron Augsburger sounded the same theme: "I believe the vitality of the church has shifted from the West to the East. We need you to help keep us from losing our souls. . . . We are now a global community." (49)

A further positive dimension of such heightened interaction between overseas Mennonite Christians and local North American congregations is the likelihood of aroused interest to become directly involved with mission boards in some form of mission outreach. This is already happening.

A cluster of churches in Ohio have established a partnership in mission arrangement with the Mennonite Board of Missions in an outreach project in Mongolia. The Communion Fellowship of Goshen, IN, with dual MC/Church of the Brethren affiliation, has worked out a partnership arrangement with the AIMM Council for a new outreach in the West African country of Senegal. (50)

Regarding such new patterns of congregational collaboration with mission boards, MBM Vice President Ron Yoder says: "Partnership is and will be a central strategy for doing global mission and service in the future." (51)

amidst change, some unchanging anchor points

The scenes on the world stage are in constant flux. The world into which the pioneers of CIM went over eight decades ago was drastically different from the one confronting new AIMM recruits of the late 90's. CIM/AIMM Boards across the years have had to engage in periodic times of assessment and adjustment in order to meet the changing opportunities and challenges before them. Existing strategies and methodologies must always be susceptible to review and appraisal.

There are, however, some basic truths underlying Christian Mission which remain unchanged and which must ever underlie AIMM's ongoing ministry in the years ahead.

1) Our mandate for witness left us by our Lord stands and will stand until He himself returns.

2) Christian Mission, at its heart, has to do with introducing people, of whatever tribe or tongue, to Jesus Christ as Savior and Lord.

3) Discovering one another around a common Savior and Lord, believers are called to live lives in community as directed by Christ's teachings and as empowered by his Spirit.

4) Anything less than a holistic approach to Christian Mission is to preach a truncated Gospel. Much has been said and written about the relation of word to deed in the context of Christian Mission. One excellent summary goes as follows: "It is clear that deed and word are not the same. Reconciliation between humans is not reconciliation with God, social action is not evangelism, political liberation is not full salvation. But word also does not automatically save. Deed and word point to the one who saves. Deed and word are distinct but they must be inseparably bound together. We must not confuse them in definition or separate them in practice." (52)

5) When Scripture and culture come into conflict, it is culture which must yield and not vice versa. While AIMM personnel have increasingly been oriented across the years to approach the cultures surrounding them with sympathetic respect, AIMM understands that all cultures are of human origin and thus often contain traits and practices which simply cannot be reconciled with the teaching of Scripture.

how long AIMM?

In 1912 the Congo Inland Mission was truly something new under the Mennonite sun. Predating MCC by a decade, it was proposed that an inter-Mennonite effort in Christian Mission be launched in the heart of the African continent. In those early years, the odds against success were high. There were so many unknowns and so few resources. But not only did the CIM/AIMM survive; it thrived. Growing from an original missionary party of three pioneers, there have at times been over 100 adults on its active roster. After a long-time focus on a single country, presence and ministry have been extended into southern and northwestern Africa. Early converts were numbered by the tens. In time, figures moved into the hundreds and then into the thousands. (53) And, across the years, the CIM/AIMM has numbered a total of six different North American Mennonite Conferences within its circle of partnership in mission.

A former AIMM executive secretary once summarized the dynamics and experiences of this organization as follows: "From the very beginning, the AIMM (CIM as it was originally known) was conceived and launched as a cooperative and united effort of Christian witness and service on the part of two different Mennonite groups. There were undoubtedly early pragmatic reasons which contributed to this cooperative approach to a missionary venture half way around the world. Greatly limited in knowledge, experience, personnel and resources, these two small Mennonite church groups simply needed each other. But along the way, early discoveries have been reexperienced and early commitments have been reconfirmed by a growing circle of AIMM partners."

"Today the commitment to a continuing inter-Mennonite mission endeavor in Africa continues because *the partners believe that*

- an inter-Mennonite approach to mission endeavor on that continent, which has endured for over eight decades, is worth sustaining and nurturing;
- in spite of general tradition to the contrary, it is not only possible for Mennonites to engage in ministries of compassion together but also in evangelism and church planting as well;
- a common witness as a joint inter-Mennonite team lends credibility to our claims to be one in Christ;
- a united effort of mission avoids the introduction of multiple Mennonite churches in a given area, something which at this point in the history of world mission would seem to have uncertain value;
- together we can accomplish more than we can individually and independently of each other;
- a cooperative mission endeavor can result in significant savings as the costs of multiple administrative support structures in a given region are eliminated."

"In the course of our partnership in mission in Africa, *we have learned* that

- an inter-Mennonite mission effort does not happen automatically nor even easily;
- there must be readiness to allow for the diversity in the history, stance and internal patterns of operation which each partnering conference brings to the partnership;
- for a partnership in mission to function smoothly, there must be a high level of mutual respect and trust coupled with a flexibility which allows for adjustment and accommodation of viewpoints which may not always overlap completely."

"Through our collaboration *we have also discovered* that

- together the partnership becomes something more and different than the simple sum total of its parts;
- together we can provide a unique common ground of service, witness and fellowship upon which to stand;
- together we create a broadened pool of human and material resource upon which to draw for our common good and our common task;
- joint mission effort overseas has interesting positive impact in North America;
- with broad agreement on such fundamentals as the primacy of the biblical mandate for mission, the centrality and final authority of Scripture, the affirmation of salvation in Jesus Christ alone, the demands of discipleship and the nature and function of the Church, it is not only possible but immensely rewarding to engage in a cooperative Mennonite effort of Christian mission in today's world." (54)

But what of the future?

There clearly are trends abroad within our North American setting which are impacting the ongoing efforts of all churches to carry on their efforts in Christian Mission. Mennonite churches have not been spared. There is, first of all, the clear influence of what one writer has aptly termed "American affluenza." The constant clamor of the commercial community linked with the insidious ease with which credit cards permit the instant acquisition of an unending array of "new things" - - and consequent debt - - have without question invaded many Mennonite households of North America.

There is also the clear trend toward keeping more available church budget monies at home, something which easily translates into trimmed-back figures in the congregation's budget line for mission and outreach.

There is, further, a new, younger generation of church membership which, while well-read, educated and aware of the broader world around them, maintain a skeptical distance vis-à-vis the traditional mission efforts of their church. In this regard, one itinerating missionary on North American assignment observed: "There is a good deal of interest in mission in our churches, but not in the traditional sense of how people understand the word. It seems to me that both the 'traditionalists' and the 'critics' have a distorted view of mission (the first 'romantic' and the latter basically uninformed and stereotypical). I am impressed with two seemingly paradoxical things: there is a lot more interest in mission out there than what I had anticipated, and there is a lot more criticism of missions out there from the very people who really want to support it." (55)

Other "readings" of our Mennonite Church scene in the late 1990's are as follows: "Contemporary North American cultural perspectives sometimes characterized by isolationism, localism and a disinterest in the realities of the rest of the world. These perspectives are also found in our churches."

"Theologically, many in our churches are no longer convinced of the uniqueness and finality of Jesus Christ as the only Savior and Lord. There is an erosion of the biblical conviction of the validity of evangelism"

There are three attitudes evident: 1) great enthusiasm and good support; 2) apathy and poor support; 3) antagonism, anti-foreign and see no need to preach the gospel to anyone." (56)

And, for AIMM, there is yet another issue which has relevance for its future: the MC/GC merger which is in process in the late 90's. A major partner in CIM/AIMM for over fifty years of its history, the GC ongoing involvement with overseas mission from within the enlarged new Mennonite body is of particular interest to other AIMM partners. It is to be hoped that this new Mennonite entity will not only affirm AIMM's ongoing presence and ministry in Africa but seek to forge a partnering relationship with it. This would bring AIMM to a level of inter-Mennonite collaboration in mission in Africa that the founders of 1912 would never have imagined possible.

But to return to the original question: "As we wind down this millennium, how much longer AIMM?" The answer has to do with a trio of dynamics which originally gave birth to and carried CIM/AIMM across eighty-five years of its history - -vision, commitment and grace.

It was a *vision* of mission which gripped and inspired several dozen farming pastors and laymen in 1912 and drove them to create a fledgling inter-Mennonite organization and to send the first handful of pioneering missionaries to central Africa.

It was an unswerving *commitment* to the pursuit of this vision which saw successive generations of board members and missionary candidates follow each other across more than eight decades of service.

And it has been the *grace* of our Lord which has surrounded and undergirded CIM/AIMM's efforts across these years and has made fruit for its labors possible.

The two flames of *vision* and *commitment*, they are ours to keep burning and to transmit to those who follow us. As this is done, we may rest assured that God's *grace*, as it has ever been, will continue in abundant supply.

Leslie Newbigin, the widely-known and -read missiologist is quoted as having said: "Mission . . . is the overflowing of a great gift, not the carrying of a great burden."

May God grant that the story of the AIMM in the future will continue to be that of its past: a story of *vision*, a story of *commitment* and a story of His marvelous *grace*.

FOOTNOTES

CHAPTER 1

1   This village was located in Ilala District in what is now northern Zambia.

2   Located in central South Africa, it is known today as Botswana.

3   New Standard Encyclopedia, s.v. "David Livingstone" (Chicago: Standard Educational Corporation, 1989) vol.10, p.L334.

4   Buana Kabue, L'Expérience Zairoise: Du Casque Colonial à la Toque de Léopard (Paris: Afrique Biblio Club, 1975), p.28.

5   The (British) Baptist Missionary Society in 1878; The American Baptist Foreign Missionary Society also in 1878; The Swedish Baptists in 1881; The Christian and Missionary Alliance in 1885; The (American) Methodists in 1885; The Garaganze Mission in 1886; The Regions Beyond Mission in 1889; The Southern Presbyterians in 1889; The Swedish Free Church in 1892; The Church Missionary Society (British Anglican) in 1896; The Disciples of Christ in 1897; and the Westcott Mission of the North Kasai also in 1897.

Cecilia Irvine, comp., The Church of Christ in Zaire: A Handbook of Protestant Churches, Missions and Communities 1878-1978 (Indianapolis, IN: Department of Africa, Disciples of Christ, 1978), p.3ff.

6   After a furlough, Miss Kohm returned to the Congo in 1900 accompanied by Miss Alma Doering, a dynamic woman who came to wield large influence both within and outside Mennonite circles. During her second term in Congo, under the Swedish Baptist Society, Miss Kohm met and married Alvin Stevenson. He, in turn, eventually became one of the first three missionaries of the Congo Inland Mission.

William B. Weaver, Thirty Five Years in the Congo (Chicago: Congo Inland Mission, 1945), p.69ff.

7   Kabue, L'Expérience Zairoise, p.32.

8   Irvine, comp., The Church of Christ in Zaire, p.xv.

9   Kabue, L'Expérience Zairoise, p.33.

10   Stan Nussbaum, You Must Be Born Again: A History of the Evangelical Mennonite Church, rev. ed. (Fort Wayne, IN: Evangelical Mennonite Church, 1991), p.2-3, 23.

The name Egli Amish was officially adopted in 1893. In 1908 the name was changed to the Defenseless Mennonite Church. In 1948 the name was again changed to the Evangelical Mennonite Church.

The name Stucky Amish was adopted in 1872. This was changed to the Central Illinois Conference of Mennonites in 1899. As churches were planted elsewhere, the term "Illinois" was dropped. In 1946 this Conference merged with the General Conference Mennonite Church and became known as the Central District of that denomination.

11 <u>Manual of Faith, Practice and Organization</u> (Fort Wayne, IN: Evangelical Mennonite Church, 1991), p.3.

12 Nussbaum, <u>You Must Be Born Again</u>, p.19.

CHAPTER 2

1 Kabue, <u>L'Expérience Zairoise</u>, p.35

2 This early pattern of exclusive missionary gatherings reflected a certain paternalism which characterized the broad Protestant missionary community of the Congo of that era, a stance which changed drastically with passing time.

3 Field statistics of the 1933-34 era provided the following information: 16 missionaries on four stations; 3,577 church members with 5,012 awaiting baptism; two African assistant pastors, 189 outstation teachers and 13 overseers; 63,594 clinical treatments and sixteen African medical assistants; ten new buildings erected; 31 full time African workmen; 138 acres of land under cultivation primarily in corn, millet, manioc, sweet potatoes and peanuts.

4 Irvine, comp., <u>The Church of Christ in Zaire</u>, p.xviii.

5 After Ross came Wakelin Coxill (who was later transferred to Brussels to open a Protestant Mission office in the Belgian capital), Josef Ohrneman and V. de Carle Thompson. CIM missionary Vernon Sprunger also served in the Leopoldville CPC office as an interim secretary.

CHAPTER 3

1 Archie and Evelyn Graber, CIM missionaries stationed at Djoko Punda, reported the first baptisms and the first communion service off the station in Bashilele land at the village of Kanyinga Ibidi in May 1940. It was, however, several more years before it was possible to finally open a CIM station in that tribal area.

2 An interesting sidelight regarding these government funds channeled to a Mennonite Mission is the fact that they were largely raised in Belgium via a national lottery known by its French form as *le Fonds de Bien Etre Indigène*, i.e., The Fund of Well-Being of Indigenous People. It was conceived and put in place as a Belgian token of appreciation for Congo's great help to the allied cause during WW II.

3 These subsidies came from a special memorial fund created in Belgium called *le Fonds de la Reine Astride*, i.e., The Fund of Queen Astride, a woman who was loved by all Belgians who met an untimely death in a car accident.

CHAPTER 4

1 The African area over which the Belgians flew their flag was roughly equal in size to the United States east of the Mississippi River.

2 Pierre Wigny, <u>A Ten Year Plan for the Economic and Social Development of the Belgian Congo</u> (New York: The Belgian Government Information Center, 1950), p.6.

3 Ibid., p.19.

4 Ibid., pp.19-20.

5 Ibid., p.22.

6 Ibid., p.23.

7 Ibid., pp.23-24.

8 Ibid., p.28.

9 Ibid., pp.29-30.

10 Ibid., p.31.

11 Ibid., p.72.

12 Many a missionary candidate of the pioneering era of missions on Africa's malarial west coast packed and shipped their supplies in personal caskets. Such was the death rate among early recruits that expectations of returning home alive were basically nil.

13 Alvin Stevenson at Djoko Punda; an Andersson baby at Luebo.

14 Some of the implications for CIM missionaries were reduced field budgets, delayed salaries, extended terms without furlough, cement doled out to workmen by tin can measures rather than by the sack and used envelopes soaked over-night in bath tubs to be turned inside-out the next morning for recycling after drying under the tropical sun.

No less heroic measures were taken on the home end. Maurice Stahly, a long-time board member and supporter of CIM/AIMM tells the following story: His farmer father, Ali Stahly, a man of deep commitment to his church and to Christian mission, became aware in early 1933 that the departure of Russell and Helen Yoder Schnell, new CIM candidates, was being delayed for lack of a final $100 to pay their boat passage. In response to this need, his father hauled corn from his crib to the local grain elevator at the price of ten cents a bushel until the lacking $100 were raised!

15 Having lost his wife Evelyn Oyer to cancer on a furlough in 1948, he returned to Djoko Punda a widower. Long concerned for and about CIM believers in the employment of the *Forminière* Diamond Company at Tshikapa, he made the establishment of a new CIM station at that growing center something of a personal crusade.

16 A visionary woman with a deep commitment to Christian Mission and exceptional communication skills, her first appointment to Africa came via the Defenseless Mennonite Church in 1900 (now known as the Evangelical Mennonite Church). Mathilda Kohm had by that time already served a term under DMC sponsorship with the C&MA in lower Congo. Reappointed in 1900 to serve a second term, this time with the Swedish Baptist Mission, Doering was commissioned to serve with her. When in 1907 the DMC decided to send a contingent of missionaries to East Africa to work under the Africa Inland Mission, Doering was among those sent. The Central Mennonite Conference had in the meantime also sent some missionaries under a similar working arrangement with the same Mission. Both groups soon decided to terminate this relationship with the Africa Inland Mission and withdrew their missionary personnel. It was then in 1911 that the two Conferences decided to create a single inter-Mennonite Mission Board and to seek opportunity for opening a mission work on their own somewhere else in Africa. It was under this new board, the Congo Inland Mission, that Alma Doering again returned to Africa in February 1923.

Strongly influenced by her previous experience with the para-church structure of the Africa Inland Mission, she immediately began to urge that the CIM abandon its exclusive Mennonite identity and also become a "faith mission." When it became apparent that the founders of the CIM were determined to remain an inter-Mennonite organization, she submitted her resignation in December 1925 and turned her considerable talent to the goal of creating a new mission organization with a view to the installation of a series of mission posts to the west of CIM territory in a large region between the Kwilu River port of Kikwit to the north and the Angolan border to the south in which there was no Protestant presence or witness. Her vision and drive resulted in the creation of a new organization in the Congo known as the Unevangelized Tribes Mission, or the UTM as it came quickly to be known in its acronym form.

Weaver, Thirty Five Years in the Congo, p.70ff.

Alma E. Doering, Leopard Spots or God's Masterpiece - - which? (Cleveland, OH: Nalembe Publishers, 1916).

Stella C. Dunkleberger, Crossing Africa in a Missionary Way (Germantown, PA: The Mission Offices, 1935).

17 Coming from Mennonite Brethren in Christ background in Pennsylvania, they were a remarkable pair. They exemplified, in a striking manner, the dedicated ranks of single women who brought tremendous vitality and dedication to the pioneering era of Christian Mission in Africa.

18 An intriguing member of the UTM team which came under the CIM umbrella at that point was Victor Buck. An agriculturist by vocation, he was a brother-in-law of the renowned author Pearl S. Buck.

19 The agreement reached provided for a cash reimbursement of $8,000 while turning over responsibility for the medical, evangelistic and educational programs of the Kandala area. By this time Mrs. Near had returned to Canada. Rev. Near opted to stay on in his home on the station for another six years occupying himself with garden, poultry and a non-subsidized class for students who did not qualify for the upgraded school programs instituted by the CIM. Rev. Near left the Congo during the general missionary evacuation of the summer of 1960 and never returned.

20 Initially the government provided 80% of all subsidized teacher pay. But as the mission-sponsored school systems grew, even 10% of the cost became too heavy to carry. The time soon came when the government paid 100% of teacher salaries in approved schools.

21 The Belgian colonial school system at that time had a six year primary cycle after which a wide gamut of vocational training options were offered. In the early years there was little interest or intent to provide secondary education - - much less college-level training. Viewed from a colonial perspective, what was needed was a steady flow of literate youth who could be trained as clerks, mechanics, typists, masons, carpenters, chauffeurs and operators of industrial equipment.

22 This school was, in time, transformed into a full-blown secondary school which, in turn, became the springboard for university training for qualified Mennonite students of the CIM area.

23 The basic guideline of the new cooperative venture was that CIM would provide 2/3 of the teaching staff and student body while the AMBM would provide the remaining 1/3 of staff and students.

24 Growth projections which were in place in January, 1959, foresaw an eventual enrollment of over seventy children from the two Mennonite Missions.

Congo Missionary Messenger, January-March, 1959, p.21.

25 The first PAX contingent arrived in April, 1955, comprised of Larry Kauffman, David Claassen, Fremont Regier and Loyal Schmidt.

26 In October 1956 Max died suddenly of a heart attack. His wife Ruth and their three children returned to Switzerland. Klara Gut and Christine Schaeper also returned to Switzerland that year. Of the five, Berta Mangold served with CIM the longest, i.e., from 1954 to 1958.

27 Among CIM missionaries who later served at this large press were Larry/Alvera Klassen Rempel and Henry/Tina Weier Dirks. Both men served as managing directors at some point during their years of service.

28 Total church membership in 1950 was approximately 10,500. By 1959 the field figure stood at 23,000.

CHAPTER 5

1 Converts of other Protestant Missions at work in the Congo at that time identified themselves in a similar fashion with their missions.

2 Agnes died unexpectedly October 5, 1965, following surgery. Frank returned to the Congo alone in 1966 for a three year period of pastoral ministry among rural Mennonite churches. When fellow CIM missionary Aganetha Friesen retired in 1974, they were married on December 30 of that year.

3 Milo Rediger, "A Trinity of Central Themes," Congo Missionary Messenger, January-February 1952. pp.11 and 20.

4 Harve Driver, "Report of Promotional Secretary to CIM Board," April 10, 1951. Congo Missionary Messenger, May-June 1951. p.16.

5 Harve Driver, "Trip Report," Congo Missionary Messenger, January-February 1952. p.21.

6 Ibid.

7 Excerpts from letters to Jim and Jenny Bertsche in the mid-1950's.

8 "Report to CIM Board," Meadows, IL, October 12, 1954. Congo Missionary Messenger, January-February 1955, pp.5,22,23.

9 Congo Missionary Messenger, September-October 1955, p.5.

10 The three pastors involved were local Mukedi Pastor Falanga Elie, Banga Pastor Muadilu Philip and Mutena Pastor Kankonde Paul. The four missionary children were Judy and Bobby Schwartz, Laverna Dick and Evelyn Schnell.

11 Congo Missionary Messenger, July-September 1957, pp.3,17.

12 In the course of his itinerary he traveled in twenty-six states, participated in 225 services in 132 churches. When asked at the end of his travels what American food he liked best, he replied: "Cornflakes and pie"!

13 Congo Missionary Messenger, October-December 1957, pp.21-22.

14 Among many Congolese who visited the Fair was a young journalist named Joseph Mobutu who was sent by the Leopoldville newspaper <u>Actualités Africaines</u>. Unfortunately, the people of the Congo were to learn to know this obscure Congolese journalist all too well with passing time.

15 The seven Nyanga students were: Kakesa Leonard and Mbualungu Theodore from Mukedi, Mukanza Louis and Mbuya Zachee from Nyanga, Ngandu Leon and Ilunga Maurice from Djoko Punda and Mpoi George from Kalonda. The two from the Kalonda Bible School were Tshibola Eduard from Djoko and Pastor Kidinda David from Mukedi.

16 <u>Congo Missionary Messenger</u>, January-March 1957, p.17.

17 <u>Congo Missionary Messenger</u>, January-March 1958, p.6.

18 "Field committee" meant the missionary committee which met between the annual missionary conferences in order to conduct ongoing CIM business.

19 Enns document 1959, pp.1-2. 1959 Enns file, AIMM archives.

20 The committee was composed of Waldo Harder, John Zook, Peter Falk, Frank Enns and Pastors Kazadi Matthew and Falanga Elie.

21 By year's end church membership was to approach 25,000; listed places of regular worship would top 700; African pastors would number 27 assisted by nearly 45 African deacons and overseers plus another nearly 600 teacher evangelists. The number of teachers qualifying for government subsidized posts had grown to over 400 while a staff of 89 trained African medical personnel worked with missionary doctors and nurses. Enrollment in all mission schools would exceed 27,000 students in 1959.

22 <u>Congo Missionary Messenger</u>, July-September 1959, p.8.

23 Written by Annie Rempel Falk and Hulda Banman. <u>Congo Missionary Messenger</u>, July-September 1959, p.4.

CHAPTER 6

1 In 1952 Thomas Kanza became the first Congolese to be admitted as a student in a Belgian University. By 1956 there were thirty-plus including several who were studying for the priesthood. The *Centre Universitaire Louvanium* was opened in Leopoldville in 1954. The first graduates emerged in 1958.

2 Kabue, <u>L'Expérience Zairoise</u>, p.51.

3 Ibid.

4 Ibid., p.53.

5 Ibid., p.54.

6 Ibid., p.55.

7 Ibid., p.56.

8 <u>Africa Special Report</u>, September 1959, p.7.

9   A French term denoting Africans who were educated and who had acquired the technical and social skills necessary to work for Belgian employers. In other words, Africans who were upwardly mobile in the Belgian colonial setting of the time in Congo.

10 Thomas Kanza, The Rise and Fall of Patrice Lumumba: Conflict in the Congo (London: Rex Collings Ltd. 1977), p.29.

11 Ibid., p.50.

12 Ibid., p.54.

13 Elmer Dick, Congo Missionary Messenger, October-December 1959, p.3.

14 Harold Graber, Ibid., p.10.

15 Frank Enns, Ibid., p.21.

16 Vernon Sprunger, "Political Situation in Congo," Ibid., pp. 23,21.

17 Letter to Jim Bertsche, February 2, 1960.

18 "Why Delegates to Congo Now?" Congo Missionary Messenger, March 1960, p.4.

19 Congo Missionary Messenger, April-June 1960, p.11.

20 Ibid., p.8.

21 Ibid., p.9.

22 "The Political Situation and its Relevance to our Purpose," Ibid., pp.11,14.

23 Actually original plans had been to hold the integration conference at Mutena. But by the time the CIM delegation arrived, the tension and violence of the tribal conflict in the West Kasai had reached a level where it was deemed wise to convene the conference elsewhere.

24 The term "evangelical" was included to make perfectly clear that they were Protestant and not Catholic. This name was later amended in keeping with the changing circumstances within the broad mission/church community of the country.

25 This was done, properly signed by the Board delegation and presented at a later session as follows: "Be it hereby known that during a called conference of delegates of Congolese, missionaries and members of the Congo Inland Mission Home Board at Charlesville on February 25-27, 1960, it was unanimously agreed to approve and accept the plan of integration as outlined at the annual Field Conference at Tshikapa, July 28-August 2, 1959 and revised as per agreement contained in the official minutes of this present conference."

    "To this end we the undersigned members of the CIM Board on behalf of the home constituency pledge continued support with missionaries and funds as long as needed by the Congo Church and according to the capabilities of the home constituency to supply them as the Lord provides." Signed by Lotus E. Troyer, President; Reuben Short, Vice President; Orlando Wiebe, Secretary and R.L. Hartzler, Board Member.

    Congo Missionary Messenger, April-June 1960, p.10.

26 In response to this request the delegation offered to discuss the immediate transfer of one of the eight CIM stations to an African church staff. The response was: "We'll let you know when we feel we are ready."

27 Congo Missionary Messenger, April-June 1960, p. 10..

28 A constitution drafting committee was named consisting of Khanda Modial, a school teacher from Djoko Punda; Kapenda Jean, a pastor from Mukedi; F.J. Enns, J.E. Bertsche and V.J. Sprunger.

29 In later years, missionaries frequently encountered African pastors who asked: "How is that little short CIM board member who told us at Charlesville in 1960 that they were giving us a bride to be taken care of and loved?"

30 Congo Missionary Messenger, April-June 1960, p.11.

CHAPTER 7

1 Kanza, The Rise and Fall of Patrice Lumumba, p.155

2 Ibid., p.161.

3 Admirers of Gizenga Antoine, a fellow Muphende, who had been named a Minister of Lumumba's ill-fated government, Mukedi people listened to and circulated the contents of his speeches some of which had been made locally in their area. Tending to be critical of the white population in general, his comments were seized upon by some of the Mukedi people as good reason to grind any axe of personal grievance they had with individual missionaries in particular and the mission in general. A specially called meeting of the newly-integrated Field Committee was held at Mukedi on July 8-9 in an effort to come to terms with some of the grievances and accusations. Medical and educational personnel were particularly vocal in their complaints most of which had to do with salaries. The committee concluded its sessions by stating that the African personnel at Mukedi held it within their hands to determine whether or not missionary personnel would stay or be removed from their station. The committee would be watching and listening for further word from them.

4 Kanza, The Rise and Fall of Patrice Lumumba, p.187.

5 Ibid., p.193.

6 Selma Wiebe, report to CIM Board: "Our Evacuation from the Congo." AIMM archives.

7 Ibid., p.2.

8 Harold Graber,"I Told Kazadi Goodbye," Congo Missionary Messenger, July-September 1960, p.21.

9 Levi Keidel, "Congo Exodus," Congo Missionary Messenger, Ibid., p.7.

10 Ibid.

11 Dorothy Schwartz, report to CIM Board: "Evacuation Experiences," p.1. AIMM archives.

12 Lois Slagle, report to CIM Board: "Evacuation Experiences," p.1. AIMM archives.

13 Four people had just arrived at Lake Madimape (pr. mah-di-MAH-pay) some 35 miles to the north of Djoko Punda for what they hoped would be a 2-3 week vacation. (George and Justina Neufeld from Mutena; Lodema Short and Sue Schmidt from Nyanga). Bob and Mable Bontrager were in Leopoldville at LECO. Harold and Joyce Harms were on staff at the joint CIM/MB missionary children's school at Kajiji near the Angolan border.

14 Keidel, "Congo Exodus," p.9.

15 Slagle, "Evacuation Experience."

16 Keidel, "Congo Exodus," p.10.

17 Levi/Eudene Keidel from Banga Station and Peter/Gladys Buller from Nyanga. Both couples had small children.

18 Glenn and Ina Rocke were from Djoko Punda. The Kandala staff were: Peter and Annie Falk, Jim and Jenny Bertsche, Selma Unruh, and Kornelia Unrau. Both couples had small children.

19 Keidel, "Congo Exodus," p.12.

20 Edna Gerber, report to CIM Board: "Exodus Reflections," February 15, 1961. AIMM archives.

21 Jim and Jenny Bertsche newsletter, August 8, 1960, p.4. 1960. Bertsche file, AIMM archives.

22 Slagle, Ibid .

CHAPTER 8

1 The telegram was signed by Kandha Modial, a Djoko Punda school teacher and son-in-law of Pastor Kazadi Matthew. He had been sent all the way to Leopoldville by church leaders up-country for this purpose.

2 At an administrative level, Wiebe was field chairman and CIM legal representative. Bertsche was assistant legal representative. As regarded the home constituency, the three men respectively represented the Evangelical Mennonite Brethren (now known as FEBC), the General Conference Mennonite Church and the EMC/US. In terms of field experience, Wiebe and Dick were familiar with the Kasai and had command of the Tshiluba language. Bertsche had worked in the Kwilu and was conversant in Giphende.

3 Congo Missionary Messenger, April-June 1959, p.19.

4 The three men represented respectively the CIM, MCC and the American Baptist Mission.

5 The son of a committed Protestant layman, he was educated in Catholic schools. He was the first Congolese student not destined for a vocation in the Catholic clergy to be allowed to enroll in a Belgian University.

6 Kanza, The Rise and Fall of Patrice Lumumba, p.249.

7 Ibid., pp.250-51.

8 Bertsche report to CIM Board: September 4, 1960, p.1. AIMM archives.

9   The church delegation that traveled to Kikwit was comprised of Nyanga Pastor Ngongo David, Mukedi Pastor Falanga Elie, Katuku Robert, Nyanga teacher Mbuya Zachee, Djoko school teacher Kadima Paul. Pastor Kazadi was also a member of the delegation but was unable to come. He was replaced by Pastor Kindumba Jacques from Kandala.

10 Rev. Kazadi Matthew, president; Rev. Ngongo David, vice president; Rev. Falanga Elie, secretary; Rev. Wayindama Emmanuel, assistant secretary; Katuku Robert, legal representative; Kakesa Samuel, assistant legal representative.

11 People specifically suggested as possible staff for closed schools were Mel Loewen, Charles Sprunger, Loyal Schmidt, Art Janz, Archie Graber and Waldo Harder. It was also requested that "our CIM doctors return and that priority placement be made at abandoned government hospitals of CIM territory as requested by the government health service."

12 A classification used by US draft boards to indicate someone who was granted the option of alternate service.

13 Bertsche report to CIM Board: September 4, 1960, p.4a. AIMM archives.

14 Ibid., p.4.

15 Ibid.

16 Ibid., p.4a.

17   Ibid., p.5.

18 Gbenye would later play a key role in a rebel government which was formed in that city.

19 Kanza, The Rise and Fall of Patrice Lumumba, pp.273-274.

20 Ibid., p.282.

21 Ibid., pp.302-303.

22 Ibid.

23 Allan Wiebe, Elmer Dick, Jim Bertsche, Archie Graber, Merle Schwartz, Earl Roth, Henry Hildebrand, Glenn Rocke and Art Janz.

24 Present were seven Congolese: President Kazadi Matthew from Djoko, Vice President Ngongo David from Nyanga, Secretary Falanga Elie from Mukedi, Pastor Wayindama from Kamayala, Legal Representative designate Katuku Robert, Assistant Legal Representative-designate Kakesa Leonard, Pastor Mazemba Pierre from Nyanga. All seven missionaries resident at Nyanga at the time were also present, i.e., Wiebe, Dick, Roth, Rocke, Hildebrand, Janz and Bertsche.

25 Bertsche, "The Church in Congo's Crucible," December, 1960, unpublished. Personal files.

26 Glenn Rocke letter to Vernon Sprunger, November 27, 1960. 1960 Rocke file, AIMM archives.

27 Allan Wiebe letter to Vernon Sprunger, November 22, 1960, p.1. 1960 Wiebe field, AIMM archives.

28 Ibid., p.2.

29 Some missionaries specifically mentioned by the committee were Waldo Harder, Loyal Schmidt, Charles Sprunger and Mel Loewen.

30 Some Congolese suggested were Kakesa Leonard, Mapoko George, Ngolo Gilbert, Kadima Paul.

31 Pastor Mpanda Jean, chairman; Pastor Kuamba Charles, vice-chairman; Katuku André, secretary; Tshibuabua Antoine, assistant secretary; Tshingungu Jonas, legal representative; Bahatuila Jean, assistant legal representative and Tshilembu Nicodème, general treasurer.

32 Kanza, The Rise and Fall of Patrice Lumumba, p.306.

33 Ibid., p.319

34 Ibid., p.317.

35 Allan Wiebe letter to Vernon Sprunger, December 2, 1960. 1960 Wiebe file, AIMM archives.

36 Harve Driver letter to Allan Wiebe, December 9, 1960. 1960 executive secretary file, AIMM archives.

37 The executive committee was comprised of Kazadi Matthew, Ngongo David, Falanga Elie, Wayindama Emmanuel, Kakesa Léonard, Katuku Robert, Pumbu Fréderick, Art Janz and Jim Bertsche.

Members of the general council were Kakesa Samuel and Mbuyuyu Emmanuel from Kamayala; Mazemba Pièrre and Palanga Jean from Nyanga; Kindumba Jacques and Khelendende Pièrre from Kandala; Muadilu Philip and Mayamba Jean from Banga; Kabangu Tom, Kaleta Emile and Kikonge Isaac from Tshikapa; Kabate André, Fimbo Louis and Earl Roth from Mukedi; and Ntambue Paul and Tshibangu Isaac from Djoko Punda. In the absence of delegates from Mutena, Elmer Dick was asked to be their representative.

38 Bertsche letter to Harve Driver, February 23, 1961. 1961 Bertsche file, AIMM archives.

39 Ibid.

40 I.e., Vernon Sprunger, Art Janz and Jim Bertsche who were to work respectively with the Congolese legal representative, treasurer and recording secretary.

41 Bertsche, letter to Harve Driver, February 23, 1961, p.3.

42 Of the eight CIM stations in the summer of 1963, only Djoko and Banga did not have returned missionary personnel in residence. There was also CIM personnel at Kajiji assigned to the CIM/MB joint schools; at Kimpesi in a large intermission medical training center and hospital; in Léopoldville at the intermission press; at Luluabourg at the CIM/Presbyterian recording studio and at Bakwanga in the refugee rehabilitation program.

43 Ben and Helen Eidse newsletter, June 3, 1964. 1964 Eidse file, AIMM archives.

44 Sam Entz letter to CIM office, January 21, 1962. 1962 Entz file, AIMM archives.

45 Elmer Dick letter to CIM office, January 22, 1963. 1963 Dick file, AIMM archives.

46 Elmer Dick letter to CIM office, April 15, 1963. Ibid.

47 Vernon Sprunger report to CIM Board, October, 1964. 1964 Sprunger file, AIMM archives.

48 Glenn and Ina Rocke newsletter, April 13, 1963. 1963 Rocke file, AIMM archives.

49 Questions addressed to Jim Bertsche by Bible Institute students during an administrative trip at Nyanga in 1961.

50 CIM Board Minutes, February 28, 1961, p.3.

51 Vernon Sprunger letter to Congo missionary personnel, April 28, 1961, p.2. 1961 executive secretary file, AIMM archives.

52 I.e. Irma Birky, Agnes Sprunger, Bertha Miller, Frank and Agnes Enns, Russell and Helen Schnell and Vernon Sprunger.

53 Congo Missionary Messenger, July-September 1961, p.13.

54 Ibid., p.24.

55 Ibid.

56 In April, 1961, the CIM Board was composed as follows: EMC/US, six members; GC Central District, five members; General Conference Mennonite Church, four members and EMB, three members.

57 Tim Lind, MCC Africa Program: Historical Background, MCC Occasional Paper #10, August 1989, p.5.

58 A number of them were caught up in the July 1960 missionary evacuation from the rural posts where they were serving. A March 1960 roster of 1-W men on CIM stations read as follows: Banga: Larry Bartel; Charlesville, John Heese and James Peters; Kamayala: Robert Schmidt and Bernard Theissen; Kandala: Alfred Neufeld and Larry Unruh; Mukedi; Don Unruh; Mutena: Melvin Keim and Abe Suderman; Tshikapa: Paul Roth. A July roster added the names of Larry Graber, John Janzen, Wilmer Sprunger and Alan Siebert.

59 Mary Burkholder was the first TAP person to serve with CIM. She arrived at Nyanga in 1965.

60 In 1965 MCC had 88 people in Africa. By 1970 there were 238 of whom more than 50 were in Congo. Lind, MCC Africa Program, p.11.

61 This assignment fell initially to Jim Bertsche.

62 Loyal Schmidt was given this assignment. Practical work for the students consisted of helping with the completion of new dorms for the teacher training school, a project which had been interrupted by the missionary evacuation of July 1960.

63 Harold Graber joined Elmer Dick somewhat later in an effort to strengthen an EMC/CIM presence among the Lulua believers.

64 Three couples were chosen in the fall of 1960 representing three geographic areas and three tribal groups, i.e., Ilunga Maurice and Ana, Mbualungu Theodore and Jeanne, Ilunga Robert and Robertine. After an initial year of orientation together under the tutelage of Tina Quiring, Theodore enrolled at Taylor University in Upland, IN; Ilunga Robert at Bluffton (OH) College, and Ilunga Maurice at Freeman (SD) Junior College.

65 Glenn Rocke letter to George Neufeld, October 16, 1961. 1961 Rocke file, AIMM archives.

66 Congo Missionary Messenger, April-June 1962, p.4.

67 President Kazadi Matthew; Vice Presidents Ngongo David and Badibanga Apollo; Treasurer, Pumbu Frederick; Assistant Treasurer, Kahuku Andre; Secretary Falanga Elie; Assistant Secretary Wayindama Emmanuel; and Tshilembu Nicodème and Lamba Gérard inspectors of schools. Minutes of the General Council at Tshikapa, February 10, 1962.

68 The sixteen tribes as envisioned by the promoters of this scheme were: Bakuba, Bashilele, Bachokwe, Baphende, Banjembe, Basongo, Babindji, Basala, Bakete, Baluelue, Bakwa Mputu, Bayisambo, Baluba, Lulua, Basonge and Bena Konji.

69 Across the years there had been minimal response among the Bakuba people of the area to efforts of Djoko personnel to reach them. Consequently there were few local Christians among them and no leadership potential for the mission station adjacent to their area which they now coveted.

70 CIM's primary source of information was a letter from Harold Graber addressed to the home board dated August 17, 1961, in which he relayed the sparse information he was able to gather. 1961 Graber file, AIMM archives.

71 By this time CIM had been able to negotiate a very reasonable lease arrangement with the Formière Diamond Company for several residences which had been vacated by departing Belgian families as well as some office space.

72 At Tshikapa two rivers come together, i.e., the Kasai and the Tshikapa. The Lulua occupy the east bank of the Kasai, the Baphende the west banks of the two at their junction. The diamond company occupied and built on the terrain in the southern angle created by the two converging streams. It was here that the officials of the new province now wanted to establish their seat of government.

73 Elmer Dick report to the CIM office, November 9, 1962. 1962 Dick file, AIMM archives.

74 Glenn Rocke report to the CIM office September 16, 1962. 1962 Rocke file, AIMM archives.

75 Dick report to the CIM office, November 9, 1962.

76 Ibid.

77 Jim Bertsche letter to Harve Driver, March 2, 1961. 1961 Bertsche file, AIMM archives.

CHAPTER 9

1 CPRA News Sheet #8, January 10, 1961. AIMM archives.

2 MIBA, the South Kasai diamond consortium, estimated one million dollars of inventory and supplies lost to Lumumba's rampaging troops plus 360 of a fleet of 400 vehicles and trucks.

   Levi Keidel, War To Be One (Grand Rapids, MI: The Zondervan Corporation, 1977), p.143.

3 Archie Graber news letter, October 1960. 1960 Graber file, AIMM archives.

4 Keidel, War To Be One, pp.143-144.

5   Glenn Rocke letter to CIM office December 11, 1960. 1960 Rocke file, AIMM archives.

6   Other young MCC recruits who at different times joined Graber in the South Kasai were Ron Peters, Warren Yoder, Allen Horst and Henry Braun. The latter was based later in his term in Luluabourg on assignment with the Presbyterian Mission and in charge of their transport equipment which was frequently used to haul refugee supplies to the South Kasai. Later, Art and Frieda Banman served at Bakwanga for two years supervising a CPRA poultry project.

7   In addition to Day Carper, other Presbyterian missionaries who also worked with Graber were George Stewart and Glen Murray. At one point Carrol Stegell returned to Zaire for four months, out of retirement in the States, in order to give Graber a brief break from his responsibilities.

8   It was framed top and bottom by the bold black lettering *Eglise du Christ au Zaire*, i.e., Church of Christ of Zaire, which was the term used for the broad Protestant Church community of the country. In the center was a large colored circle carrying a white cross. In the four angles of the cross were inscribed the letters CPRA. In lettering around the outside edge of the circle were the words "Congo Protestant Relief Agency."

9   Glenn Rocke letter to CIM office, December 16, 1960. 1960 Rocke file, AIMM archives.

10 In the political chaos which followed political independence, a strong UN presence was established. After the collapse of the Lumumba regime, UN troops were dispatched to a number of trouble spots in the country. In the Bakwanga area they were seen as defenders of the central government in Kinshasa and, thus, an obstacle to achieving their own dream of regional political autonomy.

11 In the crush and pressure of his daily life, Graber found little time for formal reporting. Sometimes simple excerpts from his daily journal were forwarded to the CIM office to share not only information, but also the color and emotion of his day to day life there.

12 Keidel, War To Be One, p.172, citing The London Times, January 22, 1961, p.12.

13 Ibid., pp.170-171.

14 Ibid., p.171.

15 Ibid., p.172.

16 Records of distributed tonnage for that three month period were CPRA 526, UN 500, local government 209, and Red Cross 35.

17 Graber report, February 15, 1961. 1961 Graber file, AIMM archives.

18 Graber letter to Vernon Sprunger, February 22, 1961. Ibid.

19 Graber letter to Vernon Sprunger. March 1, 1961. Ibid.

20 Graber journal, June 27, 1961. 1961 Graber file, AIMM archives.

21 Graber report, May 23, 1961. Ibid.

22 Graber report, July 8, 1961. Ibid.

23 Graber report, July 15, 1961. Ibid.

24 Graber report, June 25, 1961. Ibid.

25 Graber report, March 26, 1961. Ibid.

26 Graber report, April 1, 1961. Ibid.

27 Graber report, August 17, 1961. Ibid.

28 Keidel, War To Be One, p.203

29 Graber report, April 15, 1962. 1962 Graber file, AIMM archives.

30 Ibid.

31 The eventual plan put into effect was a combination of rail and air. By rail the refugees were transported to Kamina, a large military base built by the Belgians some 270 miles to the northwest of Elizabethville. Due to a blown railway bridge, the refugees were air lifted the remaining 205 miles to Bakwanga.

32 Graber letter to CIM office, May 8, 1962. 1861 Graber file, AIMM archives.

33 Graber report, April 10, 1962. Ibid.

34 Letter from Robert Gardiner to Ernest Lehman dated August 27, 1962.

35 Graber news sheet #32, October 30, 1962, p.2. 1962 Graber file, AIMM archives.

36 Keidel, War To Be One, p.223.

37 Graber report, February 7, 1963. 1963 Graber file, AIMM archives.

38 Graber journal, March 15, 1963. Ibid.

CHAPTER 10

1 Glenn Rocke, "Nine Complete Church Leadership Training," Congo Missionary Messenger, April-June 1962, p.20.

2 Tshilembu Nicodème, March 8, 1962. Text of presentation in 1962 CMZa file, AIMM archives.

3 Peter Falk, letter to George Neufeld, October 16, 1963, p.2. 1963 Falk file, AIMM archives.

4 The initial vision for this historic task was largely her own. Having originally served in the Kasai, she had acquired a working knowledge of the Tshiluba language and had seen the immense value of the Bible available there in that language produced by Presbyterian pioneers. After being moved to Mukedi among the Baphende, she determined to make the Scriptures available to them in their own language as well. Working in her own home, a primary language consultant across the years was Khenda Isaac, a local Christian who also served as the cook for the household she shared with fellow Mukedi missionary Erma Birky.

5   The first people named to this revision committee were Djoko David from Mukedi, Kipoko David from Nyanga, Kimbadi Paul from Kandala and Mukedi missionary Jim Bertsche. This project experienced many interruptions and setbacks along the way. But by the late 1980's it was entirely in the hands of a Zairian team comprised of Rev. Ghymalu Kianza and Lamba Gérard who, based in Kinshasa, brought it to a final conclusion. The first samples of a Giphende Bible arrived in Kinshasa from England by air the summer of 1996. The bulk of this long-awaited printing followed by boat.

6   Geraldine Sprunger and two children were evacuated from Mukedi with other station personnel. Charles, at the time, was trapped at Kandala and was eventually evacuated from there with the missionaries of that station.

7   Charles Sprunger, "At Long Last, CERPROKA," Congo Missionary Messenger, April-June 1964, p.12.

8   Though Zaire encompasses hundreds of dialects, there are four major languages which blanket the country, i.e., Swahili in the east, Lingala in the north, Kikongo in the west and Tshiluba in the south central part of the country.

9   Charles Sprunger, "At Long Last, CERPROKA."

10 Other AIMM missionaries who served at the Studio were Bob/Joyce Williams Schmidt, Henry/Betty Schroeder Loewen, Delbert/Susan Mast Dick, Rick/Marilyn Carter Derksen and Dennis/Dianne Smith Schmidt.

11 With a sense of humor and more than a little local pride, the Africans of the Nyanga area where the plane was based and serviced came to refer to MAF as AIR NYANGA! Across the years missionaries periodically wondered out loud as to how or for how long such costly high tech services could be justified in a setting where it likely would always require some exterior subsidy to function. But in the day-to-day routine of life amidst the isolation of the African bush, its services were too precious to give up voluntarily. Such philosophical and missiological decisions were easy to postpone for some future and, hopefully, less complicated time.

12 Reuben Short, "A Word From the Secretary," Congo Missionary Messenger, October-December, 1963 p.11.

13 Reuben Short, Congo Missionary Messenger, January-March 1964, p.6.

14 It is ironic that Kasavubu and Mobutu, who had so bitterly opposed Lumumba, would by January 1963 bring about what Lumumba so desperately sought to achieve - - the union of all of Congo under one flag.

CHAPTER 11

1   At the exchange rate of that time, these figures translated into approximately $350 and $650 a month. If modest figures by American standards, they nonetheless were princely incomes in the economic and social setting of that time.

2   Kabue, L'Expérience Zairoise, pp.87-89.

3   Melvin Loewen, "Thirty Months of Independence," Congo Missionary Messenger, April-June 1963, pp.10-11.

4   Kabue, L'Expérience Zairoise, p.89.

5   Kanza, The Rise and Fall of Patrice Lumumba, pp.105-106.

6   Ibid., p.111.

7   The Congo Rebellion (Leopoldville: Press Service of the Democratic Republic of the Congo, 1964), p.15.

8   It was at Mukedi, in October 1960, that the first missionary men returning to the station heard a Sunday morning sermon based on the Biblical story of Jonah. To the obvious appreciation of the African audience, the speaker underscored Jonah's failures as a messenger of the Lord - - not the least of which was his effort to flee from his God-given assignment.

9   Put on the plane were Stanley, Bradley, Carolyn and Emily Graber; Sandra and Linda Bertsche.

10 Present at Kandala, that night, were Harold/Gladys Graber and daughter Jeannette, Selma Unruh and Jim/Jenny Bertsche and son Timothy.

11 Jim Bertsche, The Profile of a Communist Offensive (Elkhart, IN: Congo Inland Mission, 1964), pp. 4-5.

12 Ibid., p.5.

13 Ibid.

14 Ibid., pp.6-7.

15 Ibid., pp.9-11.

16 Ibid., p.18.

17 Loyal Schmidt report to CIM Board, "69 Hours in the Hands of Terrorists," p.2. 1964 Schmidt file, AIMM archives.

18 Ibid.

19 Bertsche, The Profile of a Communist Offensive, pp.12-13.

20 Ibid., p.15.

21 Ibid.

22 As the legal representative of CIM in the chaos of Zaire's early political independence, Sprunger had the unenviable task of supervising the distribution of government subsidies for teachers' pay, a task which had been greatly complicated by delayed deposits, conflicting claims and, in some cases, the opening of unauthorized - - and thus unsubsidizable - - new classes. By 1964 there were many disgruntled teachers who had joined the *Jeunesse* movement with personal axes to grind.

23 These were the results of labors of love on the part of women's groups of Mennonite Churches scattered across the US and Canada. Typically sheets which had been neatly cut into strips and rolled into tight little bundles, they found their way in barrels into scores of isolated mission bush dispensaries and maternities such as the one at Kandala.

24 Peter Buller, "Mukedi Evacuated," Congo Missionary Messenger, January-March 1964, p.6.

25 Peter Buller and his family were at Mukedi at the time because of his assignment as director of the station's secondary school which was opened following independence. Dr. Arnold Nickel and his family were there as volunteers in "Operation Doctor" launched by MCC in the troubled days following political independence.

26 Melvin Loewen, Three Score: The Story of an Emerging Mennonite Church in Central Africa (Elkhart, IN: Bethel Publishing Company, 1972), pp.26-27.

27 Peter Buller, "Mukedi Evacuated."

28 Ibid., p.7.

29 Ibid.

30 January 1964 found a sizeable missionary roster at Mukedi since efforts had been made at the request of the church to reopen area medical services as well as to launch a new secondary school. People on the station, during those crisis hours, were: Harvey/Avril Barkman and one child; Dr/Mrs. Arnold Nickel and two children; Gladys/Peter Buller and two children; Geraldine Sprunger and two children; Elda Hiebert, Betty Quiring and Faith Eidse, daughter of Kamayala missionaries Ben/Helen Eidse, who was being home-schooled with other station children.

31 Mrs. Nickel and two children; Geraldine Sprunger and two children and Betty Quiring.

32 Peter Buller, "Mukedi Evacuated," p.11.

33 Gladys Buller and two children; Avril Barkman and one child; Elda Hiebert and Faith Eidse.

34 Peter Buller, "Mukedi Evacuated."

35 Minutes of CIM Field Executive Committee held at Tshikapa, February, 11-15, 1964. 1964 field minute file, AIMM archives.

36 Though Kamayala Station never came under direct attack, such was the tension and uncertainty in the general area that AIMM personnel Ben/Helen Eidse had also been evacuated from there.

37 Minutes of CIM Field Executive Committee held at Tshikapa, February, 11-15, 1964.

38 Ibid.

CHAPTER 12

1 Jim Bertsche letter to Reuben Short, May 15, 1964, p.2. 1964 Bertsche file, AIMM archives.

2 David Reed, Save The Hostages (New York: Bantam Books, 1988), p.62.

3 Ibid., p.33.

4 Ibid., pp.70-71.

5 Melvin Loewen, "A Dramatic Answer To Prayer," Congo Missionary Messenger, January-March 1965, p.6.

6   Ibid.

7   Reed, <u>Save The Hostages</u>, p.12.

8   Loewen, "A Dramatic Answer To Prayer," pp.7-8.

9   Ibid., p.9.

10 Reed, <u>Save The Hostages</u>, p.96.

11 Levi Keidel letter to his mother Mrs. Anne Keidel, August 16, 1964. 1964 Keidel file, AIMM archives.

12 CIM staff evacuated from Nyanga were: Sam/Leona Entz; Earl/Ruth Roth; Ellis/Edna Gerber; Loyal/Donna Schmidt; Lodema Short and Mary Epp. Also evacuated were Martha Willems and Anna Goertzen, MB teachers assigned to the joint CIM/MB secondary school on the station. Some of the evacuees settled in temporary quarters in Tshikapa while others went to Leopoldville where they set up makeshift living arrangements wherever space was available.

13 Archie Graber letter to CIM office, June 17, 1964. 1964 Graber file, AIMM archives.

CHAPTER 13

1   Kabue, <u>L'Expérience Zairoise</u>, pp.90-92.

2   Reed, <u>Save The Hostages</u>, p.190.

3   Ibid., p.229.

4   Ibid., p.132.

5   Loewen, "A Dramatic Answer To Prayer," pp.9-10.

6   Ibid., p.10.

7   Reed, <u>Save The Hostages</u>, p.48.

8   Ibid.

9   Ibid., p.84.

10 Ibid., p.85.

11 Ibid., pp.164-165.

12 Loewen, "A Dramatic Answer To Prayer," p.10.

13 Reed, <u>Save The Hostages</u>, p.214.

14 Ibid., pp.225-226.

15 Loewen, "A Dramatic Answer To Prayer," p.11.

16 Reed, <u>Save The Hostages</u>, p.216.

17 Jim Bertsche letter to Reuben Short, November 23, 1964. 1964 Bertsche file, AIMM archives.

18 Reed, <u>Save The Hostages</u>, p.251.

19 Ibid., p.253.

20 Ibid., pp.256-257.

21 Ibid., p.275.

22 Ibid., p.277.

23 Al Larson was the field secretary of the Unevangelized Fields Mission and had his base at a center known as Kilometer Eight outside Stanleyville.

24 A missionary teacher with the Africa Inland Mission who had been seconded to the Theological School at Banjwadi north of Stanleyville, he had arrived with his wife and two children just two days before the *Simbas* took over the station.

25 Reed, <u>Save The Hostages</u>, p.281.

26 A missionary teacher of the Africa Christian Mission who worked with women and children and lived on the outskirts of Stanleyville.

27 Reed, <u>Save The Hostages</u>, p.284.

28 Loewen, "A Dramatic Answer To Prayer," pp.11-12.

29 Ibid.

30 Reed, <u>Save The Hostages</u>, p.196.

31 In all a total of 19 planes and 545 paratroopers were used in the rescue effort. Within a week they retraced their route to Kamina, Ascension Island and Belgium.

32 Reed, <u>Save The Hostages</u>, p.300.

33 Jim Bertsche, "Of Gorillas and Grace," <u>Congo Missionary Messenger</u>, October-December 1965, p.13.

34 Ibid., p.21.

35 Ibid., p.22.

36 Ibid.

CHAPTER 14

1 The revision committee at this point was composed of Mutshiabata Nestor from Mukedi, Kimbadi Paul from Kandala, Kipoko David from Nyanga and Jim Bertsche.

2   Jim Bertsche, "Sh'a Mulanga, A Contemporary Joshua," <u>Congo Missionary Messenger</u>, January-March 1965, p.14.

3   Ibid.

4   Ibid.

5   Anni Dyck, <u>*Ils N'Ont Pas Résisté*</u> (Belgium: Collection Le Phare, 5531 Flavion-Florennes), pp.148-154.

6   Ibid.

7   Katuku Robert, the first Congolese chosen for the post of legal representative, was caught up in the Baluba refugee migration to the South Kasai. Kakesa Léonard, the second one named for this post, eventually resigned when he felt he was not being adequately prepared for that role.

8   Levi Keidel, <u>Caught In the Crossfire</u> (Scottdale, PA: Herald Press, 1979), p.86.

9   Ibid., pp.99-100.

10   Ibid., p.120.

11   Ben Eidse, Kikwit, Kandala, Mukedi trip report, August 31-September 3, 1965. p.6b. 1965 Eidse file, AIMM archives.

12   Keidel, Keidel, <u>Caught In the Crossfire</u>, p.128.

13   The CIM/EMC delegation was composed of EMC President Ngongo David from Nyanga, Pastor Bomans Vincent, originally from the Kandala area and CIM missionaries Ben Eidse/Jim Bertsche.

14   Jim Bertsche, "Rebellion Within Rebellion," <u>Congo Missionary Messenger</u>, July-September, 1965, p.5.

15   Ibid., p.24.

16   Ibid., p.31.

17   Ibid.

18   Ibid., pp.32-33.

19   Ibid., p.33.

20   The Kimbanguists, named for their founder Simon Kimbangu, are the largest African Independent Church group in Zaire and one of the largest in all of Africa. Viewed with suspicion and disfavor by the Mukedi Church, in particular, and the Zaire Protestant community in general, these men like many others across the country sought to maintain their membership in their home church while attending and helping with activities of the new Independent Church of the area.

21   Jim and Jenny Bertsche

22   Eidse, Kikwit, Kandala, Mukedi trip report, August 31-September 3, 1965.

23 A mission post some 65 miles southwest of Kandala originally established by a Canadian Baptist Mission, it was offered to the CIM in the years following World War II. The center was relocated a few miles to the south and eventually became headquarters for a new district of the EMC.

24 Evangelist Mandala Solomon from Nyanga, Kakesa Samuel and CIM missionaries Ben Eidse and Dr. Merle Schwartz.

25 Eidse, Kikwit, Kandala, Mukedi trip report, August 31-September 3, 1965, p.6b.

26 Peter Falk, "Seeking Our Brethren in the Kwilu," Congo Missionary Messenger, October-December 1965, p.17.

27 Eidse, Kikwit, Kandala, Mukedi trip report, August 31-September 3, 1965.

28 Keidel, Keidel, Caught In the Crossfire, pp.227-228.

29 Wm. Snyder letter to Bob Miller in Akron, PA, October 25, 1965. 1965 CPRA file, AIMM archives.

30 Archie Graber CPRA report February 24, 1966. 1966 CPRA file, AIMM archives.

31 Graber CPRA report May 1965. Ibid.

32 Archie Graber, "The Danger of Becoming Used To It," June 1966. Unpublished. 1966 Graber file, AIMM archives.

33 Graber CPRA report, September 17, 1966. 1966 CPRA file, AIMM archives.

34 Ibid.

35 Graber CPRA report, November, 1966. Ibid.

36 In time, the administration of this cattle project came under an organization named The Protestant Agriculture Project (PAP). This organization was jointly sponsored by the local provincial government, the ECZ and the Mennonite Brethren Church. Small cooperatives were set up on the basis of purchased shares with each share eventually entitling the holder to a calf of his own. Over time, this venture in cattle ranching met with varying degrees of success depending on the care provided, grazing offered and cleanliness maintained in corrals.

37 Archie Graber letter to coworkers, January 14, 1968. 1968 Graber file, AIMM archives.

38 The CPRA Kwilu program continued one more year under the direction of three PAX men who had worked with Graber in the project.

39 The Raids were one of a number of such couples who across the years made tremendous contributions to the work and witness of CIM/AIMM in Africa. Typically asking only for plane tickets and housing, they met their living needs out of personal funds. Their example of servanthood was a constant inspiration to Africans and missionaries alike.

CHAPTER 15

1 Jim Bertsche letter to Reuben Short, December 16, 1964. 1964 Bertsche file, AIMM archives.

2 Kabue, <u>L'Expérience Zairoise</u>, p.98ff.

3 Ibid., p.113ff.

CHAPTER 16

1 Some key church leaders who had also fled to the South Kasai were Tshibangu Isaac, Ntambue Paul, Kaleta Emile, Kalala Paul, Kabangu Tom and Mutangilai Norbert.

2 Levi Keidel, <u>War To Be One</u> (Grand Rapids, MI: Zondervan Publishing House, 1977), p.224.

3 Archie Graber letter to coworkers, February 22, 1964. 1964 Graber file, AIMM archives.

4 <u>Congo Missionary Messenger</u>, July-September 1963, p.8.

5 Archie Graber letter to Reuben Short, December 14, 1963. 1963 Graber file, AIMM archives.

6 Keidel, <u>War To Be One</u>.

CHAPTER 17

1 Stations represented were Banga, Nyanga, Charlesville, Kamayala, Mutena and Kalonda. Missionaries present were V.J.Sprunger, Art Janz, Jim Bertsche, Earl Roth, Lodema Short, Ben Eidse, Elmer Dick, Glenn/Ina Rocke, Tina Quiring, Irena Liechty.

2 A graduate of the Nyanga EAP, a two-year post-primary teacher training program, he had been one of the earliest Congolese directors of a primary school in his area. His firm hand upon his school personnel and his excellent, detailed financial reporting as the Banga Church Treasurer early brought him to the attention of missionary staff. When asked at the Mutena Conference by church leaders if the missionaries had any suggestion for that important post, Mission Treasurer Art Janz simply pointed out Bukungu's excellent record. Although from a minority tribal group Bukungu was elected as EMC's first general treasurer by a large majority.

3 Members of that first board were Pastors Tshibola Ebelu, Mayele Isaac and Kasanda David; school director Mukanzo Louis, missionaries Elmer Dick and Jim Bertsche.

4 Mutena Conference Minutes, July 15-19, 1964. 1964 field minute file, AIMM archives.

5 Jim Bertsche letter to Reuben Short, February 16, 1965. 1965 Bertsche file, AIMM archives.

6 Lamba Gérard, "Report EMC/CIM Republic of the Congo, 1962-1965." 1965 CMZa file, AIMM archives.

7 Tshilembu Nicodème, "The Responsibility of Being Free," <u>Congo Missionary Messenger</u>, July-September 1965, pp.3,4,22

8 With his doctor wife Betty Bauman, they served at the time under AIMM appointment at a large inter-mission medical center at Kimpese in western Congo.

9 An open letter addressed to all active CIM personnel by field chairman James Bertsche, September 1964. 1964 field chairman file, AIMM archives.

CHAPTER 18

1   In all, nine EMC regions were represented: Banga, Charlesville, Kamayala, Kandala, Mbuji Mayi, Mukedi, Mutena, Nyanga and Tshikapa. A total of seventy-eight delegates were present of which fifteen were missionaries.

2   Some curiosity was stirred in North America at the time since EMC was also the acronym of two Mennonite groups there. This was simply coincidental.

3   He was one of the three young men who had been sent to the US in 1961 for a college education.

4   The composition of the executive committee of that time was President Ngongo David, Vice-President Badibanga Apollo and School Inspector Tshilembu Nicodème. CIM Missionary members were CIM Legal Representative V.J. Sprunger, CIM Treasurer Art Janz and CIM Field Chairman Jim Bertsche.

5   EMC Executive Committee Minutes, #18, Tshikapa, September 15, 1965. 1965 CMZa file, AIMM archives.

6   The missionary retreat held at Luluabourg in July 1965 had numbered some eighty adults, children and invited guests.

7   Jim Bertsche letter to V.J. Sprunger, Ben Eidse and Art Janz, December 17, 1965. 1965 field chairman file, AIMM archives.

8   There was, however, one fly in the EMC ointment at this point, i.e., there was no representation at this administrative level from the large Baluba tribal group. This was to become an increasingly volatile and divisive issue with passing time.

9   Committee members named were Mayambi Sosthène, Tshilembu Nicodème, Bukungu François, Kasanda David and Falanga Elie.

10 Committee members were Mayambi Sosthène, Pastor Mayele Isaac, Baba Eyeba, Ben Eidse and Jim Bertsche.

11 The Baphende people as well as a variety of other African tribes have the custom of naming parents in reference to their first-born child. The Enns' first born was a son whom they named John. Thereafter the parents were known as Sh'a Yone and Gin'a Yone, i.e., the father of John and the mother of John.

12 Jim Bertsche letter to Reuben Short, June 16, 1966, p.3. 1966 Bertsche file, AIMM archives.

13 Jim Bertsche letter to Reuben Short, August 23, 1966, pp.8-9. Ibid.

14 Jim Bertsche letter to Reuben Short, September 21, 1966, pp.3-5. Ibid.

15 Minutes of the Tshikapa CIM delegation/EMC Administrative Committee meeting in Tshikapa, February 9-14, 1967. 1967 delegation file, AIMM archives.

16 Reuben Short, "EMC Administrative Committee Headquarters Building," Congo Missionary Messenger, April-June 1967, pp.8-9.

17 Jim Bertsche, "Are We Understanding Each Other?" Congo Missionary Messenger, October-December 1967, p.3ff.

CHAPTER 19

1 Following their evacuation from Kandala in 1964, the Bertsches finished their term of service at Nyanga where the two men became well acquainted and spent considerable time together both as members of the local church council and in pastoral travel through the villages of Nyanga District.

2 Mutena Africans decided to give Fremont the name of an area chief - - Kasonga. To distinguish him from the village chief, the Tshiluba adjective "mule" (pr. MOO-lay) was added, thus "Tall Kasonga!"

3 Staff article on COMAS in Congo Missionary Messenger, April-June 1966, p.3.

4 Staff article on COMAS titled "Chickens in the Church," Congo Missionary Messenger, January-March 1967, p.15.

5 Among the earliest PAX men to work with Regiers at COMAS were Dean Linsenmeyer and Roger Busenitz.

6 Other missionary personnel who across the years served in administrative roles at the church farm were George/Shirley Klassen and Glenn/Phyllis Boese.

7 Three outstanding girls who with distinction braved the masculine world of secondary education of their time at Nyanga were Ntumba Louise, Leonie Khelendende and Yebera Astride respectively from Nyanga, Kandala and Banga areas.

8 Jenny Bertsche, "Girls We Are On The Way," Congo Missionary Messenger, July-September 1968, pp. 6-7.

9 Schwartz news letter, Congo Missionary Messenger, September-October 1942, p.4.

10 Across the years PAX men assigned to CIM/AIMM often worked on building projects. In this case it was John Janzen from Elbing, KS who played a major role in bringing the Mukedi hospital to completion.

11 Don Unruh had earlier done a VS assignment at Mukedi as a single man. During his term he acquired a good knowledge of the local dialect and of the Mukedi area. When opportunity later came for appointment under CIM to work at Mukedi, they quickly responded.

12 Peter Buller, "Will Be Constructed Here," Congo Missionary Messenger, October-December 1969, p.17.

13 Ibid.

14 Ben Eidse letter to Reuben Short, May 8, 1967. 1967 Eidse file, AIMM archives.

15 Jim Bertsche report to CIM Board, spring 1969. 1969 Bertsche file, AIMM archives.

16 School Bylaws, Article I, Section 2.

17 Peter Buller, "Will Be Constructed Here.".

18 As of 1996 there were eighteen CMZa congregations in the capital.

CHAPTER 20

1 Staff article, "Opportunities Unlimited," <u>Congo Missionary Messenger</u>, January-March 1962, p.4.

2 During those unstructured, uncontrolled days, CIM missionaries were often accosted by Congolese offering little vials of diamonds for purchase or barter. Had CIM missionaries been looking for that variety of diamonds, a few pieces of used clothing or a pair of shoes could have secured a thimbleful of these precious stones.

3 <u>Congo Missionary Messenger</u>, January-March 1962, p.5.

4 Ibid.

5 Ibid.

6 Jim Bertsche letter to Reuben Short, August 3, 1965. 1965 Bertsche file, AIMM archives.

7 It was particularly Drs. Ries and Hirschler who made a concerted effort to expand public health services with the Kalonda hospital as a supportive hub. Their interest coincided with a funding thrust in this same area mounted by USAID in Zaire in the early 1980's. On staff of this American government agency was a Mennonite, Franklin Baer. With a Ph.D. in public health, he gave leadership to an organization named SANRU (i.e., French acronym for rural health). During this period SANRU made a number of grants to the Kalonda medical program. Some funds were used for training seminars for African personnel. Some equipment was also purchased such as microscopes for bush dispensaries, motor bikes and a pickup truck for transport of visiting doctors and medical supplies.

8 The term *zaire* is an original local African term for the river. Europeans named it the Congo because of the Bakongo people they found along both banks of the lower course of the river.

9 Kabue, <u>L'Expérience Zairoise</u>, pp.199,203,206.

10 Ibid., p.178.

11 Other name changes of well known places: Elizabethville to Lubumbashi, Albertville to Kalamie, Stanleyville to Kisangani, Coquihatville to Mbandaka, Thysville to Basanza Ngungu.

12 Also effected by this government action was the Protestant University at Kisangani and the Free University at Lubumbashi.

13 A wide variety of interpretations/translations of this lengthy name have been offered. A literal translation of the terms is: Sese - earth; Seko - daring; Kuku Ngbandu - pepper; Wa Za Banga - powerful warrior.

14 In rural areas this anti-missionary agitation never resulted in more than rumor and surly attitudes. In Kinshasa, however, CIM teachers Peter Falk and Peter Buller experienced some threat of political reprisal for comments made in their classrooms at ISTK which were interpreted by JMPR members as being anti-MPR and critical of Mobutu.

15 Kabue, <u>L'Expérience Zairoise</u>, p.184.

16 The Kimbanguists, so named and known for their founding leader, Kimbangu Simon, form the largest African Independent Church in Zaire and is one of the largest in the whole of Africa.

17 Irvine, comp., <u>The Church of Christ in Zaire</u>, p.xvii.

18 Ibid., p.xviii.

19 It is not clear in available records when CIM became a member of the CPC. There is, however, record of CIM participation in a Congo Missionary Conference which was convened at the Presbyterian station Luebo February 21 to March 2, 1918. CIM missionaries who attended were Rev. J.P. Barkman, Rev. Lawrence and Rose Haigh, Rev. Henning Karlsson, Miss E. Lundberg, Miss Anna Meester and Rev. and Mrs. Emil Sommer. CIM Board secretary A.M. Eash and CIM missionary Erma Birky attended an All-Protestant Mission Conference in Leopoldville in September 1928. In 1935 the CIM Board authorized a contribution of $300 to the CPC. It is clear that from its earliest years, the CIM was involved with and supportive of inter-mission activity and collaboration in the Congo.

20 Other missionaries who succeeded Ross (1928-1933) in this post were H. Wakelin Coxill (British Baptist 1933-1946), Josef Ohrneman (Swedish Free Church 1947-1956), and R.V. de Carle Thompson (British Baptist 1956-1961). CIM missionary V.J. Sprunger served in that office during an interim six month period in 1959 to allow Secretary Thompson to take a brief furlough in England.

21 CIM/EMC delegates to the Kumbya gathering were Allan Wiebe, Jim Bertsche, Leon Ngandu, a teacher from Nyanga and Rev. Kapenda Jean, a pastor from Mukedi.

22 Jim Bertsche, "Observations at the 1960 CPC Meeting," <u>Congo Missionary Messenger</u>, January-March 1960, p.22.

23 Ibid., p.23.

24 Kakesa Samuel and Jim Bertsche.

25 Bertsche letter to Reuben Short, March 26, 1969. 1969 Bertsche file, AIMM archives.

26 Bertsche letter to Reuben Short, April 1, 1969. Ibid.

27 Bertsche Field Report to CIM Board Fall 1969, p.5. Ibid.

28 Bertsche Field Report to CIM Board Spring 1970, p.12. 1970 Bertsche file, AIMM archives.

29 Ibid., pp.11-12.

30 Ibid., p.12.

CHAPTER 21

1 The following composition of the administrative committee in January 1970, illustrates the broad mix of people who were incorporated into this body: Mulebo Samuel, a high ranking employee of the Company of the Kasai; Ngolo Gilbert, an EMC primary school director from the Kwilu; Mpoyi George, a primary school director and assistant legal representative from the South Kasai; Kombai Paul, a primary school director from Kananga; Funyi Remi, a business man from Mbuji Mayi; Kakesa Samuel, the EMC legal representative; Tshilembu Nicodème, the primary school inspector and assistant legal representative from the West Kasai; Bukungu François, the EMC general treasurer; Pastor Ngongo David, the EMC president; Pastor Kamba Jean, the committee recording secretary from the South Kasai; Pastor Muadilu Philip from Banga; Jim Bertsche, assistant to the president; and V. J. Sprunger, CIM legal representative.

2   Including VS personnel and children, there were 140 people at the missionary retreat held at Nyanga, July 17-24, 1970.

3   It was generally known that this "incident" had been the result of a discussion between representatives of the AEMSK and the local provincial government. Both viewed the Kabeya Kamuanga based EMC group with disfavor. Neither were favorable to their proposed meeting with the EMC delegation from Tshikapa.

4   EMC General Conference at Djoko Punda, December 23-29, 1967, Minute 12. 1967 EMC file, AIMM archives.

5   EMC Administrative Committee, January 13-15, 1969 at Kalonda, Minute 33. 1969 EMC file, AIMM archives.

6   Keidel, War To Be One, p.229.

7   Kazadi Matthew, Congo Missionary Messenger, July-September 1969, p.23.

8   Keidel, War To Be One, p.230.

9   Bertsche letter to Reuben Short, May 12, 1969, p.2. 1969 Bertsche file, AIMM archives.

10 Co-signers of the letter were Ghymalu Enos, Miteleji Philemon, Kabangy Moise, Muhaku Boniface, Mashimba Jean, Bomans Vincent and Lwoena Pierre.

11 EMC Administrative Committee, September 15, 1965 at Tshikapa, Minute 8. 1965 EMC file, AIMM archives.

12 The original concession of ground granted by the government for the establishing of Kalonda Station was less than 20 acres in size. By 1965 most of the concession was already occupied by station buildings. As a matter of fact, some construction already stood outside the concession lines.

13 EMC Executive Committee, December 2, 9-10, 1968 at Kalonda, Minute 4. 1968 EMC file, AIMM archives.

14 EMC Administrative Committee, January 13-15, 1969 at Kalonda, Minutes 15-16. 1969 EMC file, AIMM archives.

15 EMC General Conference, July 9-16, 1969, at Kabeya Kamuanga, Minute 15.

16 Ibid., 14.

17 By this time there were separate committees dealing with secondary education, literature, the Kalonda Bible Institute, Christian ed, evangelism and COMAS. The EMC was also sending representatives to meetings of boards of interchurch organizations such as LECO, ETEK and IMCK.

18 Luashoro Emory was at the time a student at the Free University in Elizabethville. His consultants were Mayembe Vernon and Mimburu Josue who were respectively the primary school director and instructor in the Bible Institute on the station.

19 EMC Administrative Committee, March 24, 1970 at Kalonda, Minute 45. 1970 EMC file, AIMM archives. The three men named were EMC legal representative Kakesa Samuel, primary school inspector Tshilembu Nicodème and CIM missionary Jim Bertsche.

20 Bertsche field report to CIM Board, Spring 1970. 1970 Bertsche file, AIMM archives.

21 Commission members named were: Muhaku Boniface, Mpoyi George, Kadima Isaac, Kakesa Samuel, Tshilembu Nicodème, Ilunga Robert, Lamba Gérard, Mrs. Mulebo Rebecca, V. J. Sprunger, Ben Eidse and Jim Bertsche.

22 Bertsche letter to Reuben Short, July 16, 1970, p.1. 1970 Bertsche file, AIMM archives.

23 Pastor Kadima Isaac had served first at Mutena station and was among those who were swept up in the massive flight of the Baluba refugees to the South Kasai in the early 1960's. His peppery personality equipped him well to serve as the spokesman for his frustrated colleagues.

CHAPTER 22

1 Bertsche letter to Reuben Short, July 16, 1970, p.3. 1970 Bertsche file, AIMM archives.

2 Ibid.

3 Nyanga meeting July 15, 1970, establishing "The Conference of the North Zone of the EMC," p.2. 1970 EMC file, AIMM archives.

4 Ibid.

5 Ibid.

6 Circular letter addressed to all the EMC districts, August 5, 1970, p.2. 1970 EMC file, AIMM archives.

7 Ibid.

8 It was reported at Kalonda later that representatives from the eastern EMC districts had in fact approached government officials testing the possibility of an outright break with the EMC with a view to attempting the creation of yet another autonomous Mennonite Church in the Congo. According to the report, this initiative was firmly rebuffed by officials. Whatever the case, the official record of the August meetings reflected a striking conciliatory tone.

9 Minutes of the Luluabourg consultation August 21-22, 1970, p.1. 1970 EMC file, AIMM archives.

10 Ibid., p.3.

11 Bertsche field report to CIM Board, Fall 1970, p.6. 1970 field chairman file, AIMM archives.

12 All MAF planes are given code names which are used for purposes of identification in short wave communication. As it happened, the Nyanga-based plane was given the code name Charlie Mike Zulu. The letters CMZ were emblazoned on the fuselage. When the name of the country was changed from Congo to Zaire and the national Protestant Church took shape, the term EMC (i.e., Evangelical Mennonite Church of Congo) also underwent change and became the CMZa or the Mennonite Community of Zaire. Thus, suddenly, the Mennonite Church acronym CMZ became identical to the code name on the plane, this to the delight of all CMZ members.

13 Bertsche field report to CIM Board, Fall 1970, p.1.

14 Ibid., p.6.

15 Ibid., p.9.

CHAPTER 23

1   Bertsche field report to CIM Board, Fall 1970, pp.9-10.

2   Ibid., p.17.

3   Ibid., p.20.

4   Reuben Short editorial, <u>Congo Missionary Messenger</u>, April-May 1970, p.4.

5   Milo Nussbaum, "Let's Clarify Our Approach To Unity," <u>Congo Missionary Messenger</u>, April-May 1970, pp.5-6.

6   Reuben Short editorial, <u>Congo Missionary Messenger</u>, October-December, 1970, p.16.

7   Peter Buller, "Confronting or Colliding?" <u>Congo Missionary Messenger</u>, July-September 1970, p.17.

8   Ibid., pp. 18-19.

9   Elmer Neufeld, "Reconciling The Exploited" <u>Congo Missionary Messenger</u>, April-May 1970, pp.16-20.

10 Bertsche letter to Reuben Short, November 17, 1970, p.6. 1970 Bertsche file, AIMM archives.

11 "The Charlesville Convention," <u>Congo Missionary Messenger</u>, Spring 1971, p.4.

12 Ibid., Article 6

13 Ibid., Article 1

14 Ibid., Articles 3,5,8,10,14-17.

15 Ibid., Articles 7-11,19. Shares acquired in intermission organizations specifically referred to LECO, UMH, COMAS, ETEK, STUDIPROKA, LIPROKA, IME and IMCK.

16 Ibid., Article 13.

17 Ibid., Article 18

18 Ibid., Articles 21-22.

19 Ilunga Robert, "The Fusion Meeting," <u>Congo Missionary Messenger</u>, Spring 1971, p.18.

20 Ibid., pp.18-19.

21 Kidinda Jean, "Fusion," <u>Congo Missionary Messenger</u>, Spring 1971, pp.8-9.

22 Kakesa Samuel, <u>Congo Missionary Messenger</u>, Spring 1971, p.11.

23 Milo Nussbaum, <u>Congo Missionary Messenger</u>, Spring 1971, p.3.

24 Reuben Short editorial, <u>Congo Missionary Messenger</u>, Spring 1971, p.7.

25 George Loewen, <u>Congo Missionary Messenger</u>, Spring 1971.

26 Ilunga Robert, <u>Congo Missionary Messenger</u>, Spring 1971, p.19.

27 Kakesa Samuel, <u>Congo Missionary Messenger</u>, Spring 1971, p.11.

28 Kidinda Jean, <u>Congo Missionary Messenger</u>, Spring 1971, pp.9-10.

29 Composed of EMC Treasurer Bukungu François, lay business man Kumbi Bartolomé and CIM missionary Herman Buller who, by this time, had been appointed the missionary associate in the Church Treasurer's office.

30 CIM missionaries named to this committee were Nyanga secondary school director Earl Roth and Djoko Punda professional school director Wilmer Sprunger. It is interesting to note that Roth's request to be replaced in the Nyanga school was tabled for later consideration by the full EMC educational commission.

31 The five CIM missionaries were Rudy Martens, Ben Eidse, Don Unruh, Elmer Dick and Tina Quiring.

32 CIM doctors present were Elvina Martens, Merle Schwartz and Ralph Ewert.

CHAPTER 24

1   Jenny Bertsche.

2   An interesting historical footnote: Rev. Andrew Shelly, the executive secretary of the GC/COM was touring the CIM area at the time and was present for this ordination service.

3   The visiting missionary was Jim Bertsche.

4   The three-man delegation was composed of Pastor Kabangy Moise, Pastor Kamba Jean from the South Kasai and school director Mapoko George from the Banga area. Thus the delegation was comprised of two pastors and a layman who represented the older and younger generations and three major tribal groups.

5   Minutes of the general conference at Nyanga, June 15-22, 1971, Article 4. 1971 CMZa file, AIMM archives.

6   The missionary was Earl Roth with whom he had worked closely in his role as chaplain in the Nyanga secondary school.

7   Waldo Harder, "Kabangy/Harder Dialogue Regarding Church Harvest," <u>Congo Missionary Messenger</u>, Fall 1972, p.8.

CHAPTER 25

1   Representing CMZa Tshikapa were President Ngongo David, Vice President Jim Bertsche, Legal Representative Kakesa Samuel and Primary School Inspector Tshilembu Nicodème. Representing CMZa Mbuji Mayi were Pastor Kadima Isaac, CMZa Secretary Kamba Jean, Rev. Kalala Joseph and South Kasai CMZa Primary School Inspector Mpoyi George. Representing the CEM were President Kazadi Matthew, Vice-President Ntambue Paul, Legal Representative Ntumba Andre, Assistant L.R. Mutangilayi Norbert, General Secretary Ilunga Maurice and Bookkeeper Nkumbi Zecharie.

2   Representing the CEM were Ntumba Andre, Kumbi Zecharie and Ilunga Maurice. Representing the CMZa were Kakesa Samuel, Mpoyi George, Tshilembu Nicodème and Charles Sprunger.

3   Keidel, War To Be One, p.231.

4   The three secretaries were: Tshilembu Nicodème for Tshiluba; Mukanza Simon for French; Ilunga Maurice for English.

5   Keidel, War To Be One, p.232.

6   Ibid.

7   Ibid., pp.233-234.

8   Ibid.

9   Ibid., pp.235-236.

10   Earl Roth letter to Reuben Short, January 21, 1972. 1972 Roth file, AIMM archives.

11   Present were MB representatives Lumeya Gedeon, Mukoso Matthew and missionary Willie Baerg. Pastor Kazadi Matthew represented the CEM. CMZa was represented by Pastor Kabangy Moise, Mukanza Simon and Levi Keidel.

12   By this time, there were three autonomous Mennonite Churches in Zaire: CMZa, the Mennonite Community of Zaire with offices in Tshikapa; CEM, the Evangelical Mennonite Community of Zaire with offices in Mbuji Mayi and the CEFMZ, the Mennonite Brethren Community of Zaire with offices in Kikwit.

13   Present were 45 pastors from CMZa, 23 from CEFMZ and 16 from CEM. In addition there were 18 African lay leaders and six missionaries.

14   A reference to Aaron and Ernestina Janzen who, after serving two terms with the CIM (1912-16 and 1919-21) pioneered a new work in the Kikwit area which eventually came under the sponsorship of the MB Board of Missions.

15   Levi Keidel, "All-Zaire Mennonite Pastors' Conference Convenes," 1973 Keidel file, AIMM archives.

16   By this time both CMZa and the Mennonite Brethren (CEFMZ) had active congregations in the rapidly growing city of Kikwit located on the Kwilu River roughly an hour's flight west of Tshikapa.

17   Jim Bertsche letter to Reuben Short, July 24, 1973, pp.6-7. 1973 Bertsche file, AIMM archives.

18 The delegation was composed of Board Chairman Elmer Neufeld, Secretary Howard Habegger, Treasurer Andrew Rupp and Art Janz, the AIMM home office accountant. Jim Bertsche, who was by then the new AIMM Executive Secretary designate, joined the delegation in its travel in Zaire and South Africa.

19 The CEM delegation: Pastor Kazadi, Pastor Tshibangu Isaac, Ntumba Kalala.

20 "The 1974 Delegation report to the AIMM Board." 1974 delegation file, AIMM archives.

21 Ibid.

22 Ibid.

23 Ibid.

CHAPTER 26

1 Kabue, L'Expérience Zairoise, p.157.

2 Ibid., p.156.

3 So enormous was the envisioned voltage load that transformers had to be specially designed and built in Europe.

4 Kabue, L'Expérience Zairoise, p.208.

5 Ibid., p.210.

6 Jim Bertsche, "Zaire Gleanings." 1972 Bertsche file, AIMM archives.

7 Kabue, L'Expérience Zairoise, p.226.

8 Among the agreements signed with the Chinese government were the opening of sea and air links, establishment of official diplomatic relations, a multimillion dollar 20 year interest-free loan, a supply of medical doctors and rice experts and the eventual building of an immense auditorium in Kinshasa which was called "The Palace of the People."

9 Kabue, L'Expérience Zairoise, pp.203,221.

10 Ibid., pp.223,230.

11 Ibid., pp.231-232.

12 Ibid.

13 Ibid., p.240.

14 Ibid., p.247.

15 Ibid., p.241.

16 Ibid., pp.167,250.

17 Bertsche memo to AIMM Board, January 24, 1975, p.3. 1975 executive secretary file, AIMM archives.

18 Ibid., p.4

19 Ibid.

20 Ibid., p.5.

21 Ibid., p.6

22 Kabue, L'Expérience Zaïroise., pp.211-212.

23 Arthur Swana, "The Church of Zaire on the Threshold of the Year 1979," *Le Courrier d'Afrique*, January 1, 1972.

24 Rev. Bokeleale had by this time been granted the honorary degree of Doctor of Divinity by a church related college in the States.

25 Jean Bokeleale, "From Missions to Mission," International Review of Mission, October 1973, p.433ff.

26 By this time it was generally known that less than 10% of the expanding ECZ operating budget, plus the major building project in Kinshasa, was being funded by Zairian sources. The balance was being generated outside the country by General Secretary Bokeleale who, by then, was making trips not only to Europe but also to North America as well. This exterior support at one point was of such scope that the ECZ was able to provide new vehicles for provincial secretaries across the country.

27 Bertsche report to Reuben Short, 1971. 1971 field chairman file, AIMM archives.

28 Jean Bokeleale interview with a journalist of *Le Courrier d'Afrique*, January 1, 1972.

29 Two Missions, the Dearmore Mission and the Baptist Mid-Missions, found the trend of events to be so threatening to their views of mission autonomy that they formally closed down their programs in Zaire. A few Baptist missionaries stayed on independently to work with their Zairian Church.

30 Bertsche, "Aspects of a Swiftly Changing Scene," report to the AIMM Board, February 1973, p.12. 1973 field chairman file, AIMM archives.

31 Jean Bokeleale interview with a journalist of *Le Courrier d'Afrique*, January 1, 1972.

32 Bertsche, "Aspects of a Swiftly Changing Scene," p.13.

CHAPTER 27

1 Vernon Sprunger letter to James Bertsche, February 23, 1972. Bertsche personal files.

2 Copies of French documents in AIMM archives.

3 AIMM Board Meeting Minutes, September 23, 1971, p.3.

4 Composed of Reuben Short, Allan Wiebe, Howard Habegger and Jim Bertsche.

5   Draft of a revised constitution submitted to the full AIMM Board October 12-13, 1972. Article I. The proposed name change prompted a lively discussion in an ensuing Board session in the course of which other intriguing possible options were bounced around such as Mennafrica, Mennica and Afromen!

6   Ibid., Article III-3. The original two stated purposes were "to engage in a united effort in carrying out the last command of our blessed Lord and Savior Jesus Christ (Mt 28:19-20; Lk 16:15) and to build his church in accordance with his purpose. (Mt 16:16-18; I Cor 3:11)."

7   Ibid., Article IV.

8   Originally launched in 1911 by two groups, i.e. the Central Conference of Mennonites and the Defenseless Mennonite Church, this new inter-Mennonite Board soon began to attract candidates from the Evangelical Mennonite Brethren Church. Eventually the CIM Board was composed of members named by these three groups. In 1946, the Central Conference became the Central District of the General Conference Mennonite Church and, in 1953, the GC/COM assumed responsibility for the former Central District Conference commitments to the CIM. GC appointments to the CIM Board gradually reflected its broader constituency. In 1948, the Defenseless Mennonite Church changed its name to the Evangelical Mennonite Church.

9   Revised constitution, Article VI a-b. The new alignment of board members: six from the GC, four from the EMC/US, two from the EMB with one member appointed by the AIMM Women's Auxiliary.

10   Jim Bertsche, "Four Observations," Zaire Missionary Messenger, Spring 1972, pp.7-8.

11   After eleven years of able and wise leadership, Reuben and Kathryn Short moved to Ft. Wayne, IN. A career churchman, Reuben served yet in a variety of roles with the EMC/US, his home conference, before his retirement in the early 1980's.

12   COMBS Meeting May 23, 1968, Minute #17, p.4. 1968 COMBS file, AIMM archives.

13   Reference here is to an Africa-wide fellowship of Mennonite and Brethren in Christ Churches. As this organization eventually acquired structure and officers, it came to be known as the Africa Mennonite and Brethren in Christ Fellowship or AMBCF in its acronym form.

14   COMBS Meeting October 5, 1968, Minute #5, p.2. 1968 COMBS file, AIMM archives.

15   The two men erroneously fixed the Zambezi River as the southern perimeter of the long-time BIC mission endeavors in that part of Africa. The report should have read "south of the Limpopo."

16   Jacobs and Bertsche, Southern Africa Study, 1970. AIMM archives.

17   Preheim, Jacobs, Stauffer, Kraybill, Southern Africa Study II, November 17-20, 1970. AIMM archives.

18   "New Field in South Africa," CIM Board Minutes, December 12, 1970.

CHAPTER 28

1   Kabangy Sh'a Pasa, "What CMZa Thinks About Autonomy," December 15, 1975. 1975 CMZa file, AIMM archives.

2   The President of Zambia, at the time, known formerly as Northern Rhodesia.

3   Howard Habegger, "Mission Personnel in the Congo: The Changing Role and Relationship Under Mission/ Church Fusion." Report to the AIMM Board January 1971, pp.1,3-4. 1971 delegation file, AIMM archives.

4   Jim Bertsche, "Zaire Gleanings," May 1972, p.11. 1972 Bertsche file, AIMM archives.

5   "Miracle Camp Retreat Statement," AIMM Board Minutes, April 9, 1973, Appendix A.

6   Unruh had earlier served two years at Mukedi as a PAX volunteer. Returning home he finished college as a Bible and religion major while serving as a student pastor. Married in 1963, the Unruhs again returned to Zaire under MCC sponsorship for a two year term in Kinshasa at the UMH. After graduate work in anthropology and missions, they arrived at Mukedi in 1969.

7   In the reorganization of CMZa approved in the General Assembly in June 1971, Bertsche was voted vice president of the Church.

8   A local Mukedi pastor and member of the conference pastoral credentials committee.

9   Howard Habegger, "Ordination and Celebration at Mukedi," January 1971. 1971 delegation file, AIMM archives.

10 Composed at the time of Legal Representative Kakesa Samuel, Education Secretary Tshilembu Nicodème, Treasurer Bukungu François and President Ngongo David.

11 In fact, they were to return one more time to the land of their life-long love and service. Erie Sauder, a widely-known Mennonite businessman of Archbold, OH., had long known and helped support Archie in his African ministry. Upon Graber's retirement in the Archbold area, Sauder invited him to oversee a lot of the work done on the old wooden structures that he was transporting onto the site of a museum complex he was developing just to the north of his home town. Determined to see some of the Africa about which he had heard so much from the Grabers, in 1978 he invited them to accompany him on an all-expenses-paid excursion to Zaire, Kenya and Lesotho. This, finally, was the Graber's last time to walk on African soil.

12 In a political setting where graft and embezzlement of funds was swiftly becoming routine, Bukungu eventually resigned his position as the CMZa General Treasurer over the protests of church leaders who urged him to stay on in this sensitive post. His last audit, like his first, revealed total honesty in his handling of CMZa funds. Upon his resignation, Buller was asked to stay on in his role of associate treasurer of the Church, a position he held until the Bullers retired in 1986.

13 Manuscript Committee Minutes, September 10, 1975, Minute #3. 1975 CMZa file, AIMM archives.

14 Kangu Sualala (pr. KAH-ngoo swah-LAH-lah) was the first Zairian director of the Nyanga Secondary School. Having first been a student there himself, he later became an understudy of missionary director Earl Roth when he joined the teaching staff. Roth had the distinction of being the last missionary director of three different AIMM schools, i.e. the Nyanga Secondary School, the Djoko Punda Artisinal School and the Kalonda Bible Institute. In each case he was involved in the transition to and orientation of first time Zairian directors who followed him.

15 Minutes of the meeting of the Nyanga Secondary School "Cut and Sew" Section, March 12-13, 1973. 1973 CMZa file, AIMM archives.

16 Fremont Regier, "Congo: Hunger and Hope," Mission News, June 1967.

17 Fremont Regier, "Development: a Unique Challenge For SEDA," <u>AIMM Messenger</u>, Fall 1976, pp. 3-5.

18 Ngulubi Mazemba, an interview with Fremont Regier, <u>AIMM Messenger</u>, Ibid., pp.8-9.

19 The six stations were Kamayala, Mukedi, Banga, Nyanga, Kalonda, Mutena; the medical centers were IME at the Baptist station Kimpese in lower Congo and IMCK, the Mennonite/Presbyterian complex at Tshikaji just outside Kananga.

20 CMZa Executive Committee, July 25-26, 1975, Article 14. 1975 CMZa file, AIMM archives.

CHAPTER 29

1 CMZa Administrative Committee, January 9-10, 1973, Article 2. 1973 CMZa file, AIMM archives.

2 Lulua, Baluba, Baphende, Bashilele, Bawongo, Banjembe, Bachokwe, Balunda, Bakete, Basonde, Bambala, Bambunda and Babindi.

3 Jim Bertsche, "Tribal Groups Represented Within the Zaire Mennonite Church," <u>AIMM Messenger</u>, Winter 1974, pp.4-7.

4 Levi Keidel, "On the Road With the General Secretary," <u>AIMM Messenger</u>, Summer 1973, pp.3-4.

5 Ibid., p.4.

6 Ibid., pp.4-5.

7 CMZa statistics the summer of 1973 listed a total of 36,493 members in the sixteen districts visited.

8 Levi Keidel, "Report of the Second Annual Visit to Church District Centers," <u>AIMM Messenger</u>, Summer 1974, p.18.

9 Ibid., pp.19-21.

10 Ibid., p.21.

11 Kabangy Moise, "Pastoral Objectives," n.d.

12 Kabangy Moise, "A Return to the Bible for an Authentic Christianity", an open letter to all CMZa church communities, April 29, 1975. <u>AIMM Messenger</u> No.1, 1975, p.7.

13 CMZa Administrative Committee Minutes, August 25-28, 1972, Article 6e. 1972 CMZa file, AIMM archives.

14 CMZa Administrative Committee Minutes, January 9-10, 1973, Article 5 a b. 1973 CMZa file, AIMM archives.

15 Jim Bertsche. The topic: "The Church, Our Responsibility."

16 Kabangy Moise, "Annual Report of the General Secretary of the CMZa: 1972-1973," Banga General Assembly Minutes, July 2-6, 1973, pp.2-3. 1973 CMZa file, AIMM archives.

17 Ilunga Robert and his wife were one of the three young couples who were sent to the States for study in the early 1960's. He graduated from Bluffton College, Bluffton, OH.

18 "Record of the First Session of the Annual Assembly of the CMZa Held at Banga," July 2-6, 1973, p.8. 1973 CMZa file, AIMM archives.

19 Jim Bertsche letter to Reuben Short, July 24, 1973, p.4. 1973 Bertsche file, AIMM archives.

20 Ibid.

21 Banga Assembly Record, Ibid., Article 1.

22 Ibid., Article 20.

23 AIMM Board Meeting Minutes, April 9, 1973, Motion 8-1. This issue offered an interesting window into the internal dynamics of the AIMM at that point. The General Conference, a major AIMM partner, had traditionally adopted a stance of "nonalignment" vis-à-vis the NAE and the NACC, the two ecumenical camps in North America. Other AIMM related conferences, however, were clearly NAE/EFMA-oriented. But when the proposal for NAE affiliation was raised again, it was supported by a strong vote, a good example of the spirit of accommodation and mutual respect which has prevailed within this inter-Mennonite Board across the years.

24 Reuben Short letter to Jim Bertsche, December 11, 1973. 1973 Zaire field chairman file, AIMM archives.

25 "CMZa Admission to the WCC," an open missionary letter addressed to the members of the CMZa General Council, n.d. 1973 Roth file, AIMM archives.

26 Jim Bertsche letter to Reuben Short, January 15, 1974, p.2. 1974 Bertsche file, AIMM archives.

27 CMZa Administrative Committee Meeting, December 6-7, 1973, Article 18. 1973 CMZa file, AIMM archives. The five man committee appointed to seek dialogue with the missionary team: Pastor Kabangy, Pastor Muhaku Boniface, Mpoyi Mukula, Kakesa Samuel and Ilunga Robert.

28 Curiously, the WCC listed CMZa as a member church for some time. At the WCC gathering in Vancouver, BC, in 1983, this was noted by some North American Mennonites who had gone as observers. This, in turn, sparked a flurry of correspondence with the AIMM office. One individual in particular suggested that AIMM was engaged in a "cover up" of the supposed affiliation of the CMZa with the WCC. In 1993 the WCC sent Rev. Sakayimbo Chibulenu, the then-president of the CMZa, a complimentary air ticket to Australia, the venue of the WCC gathering of that year. The ticket was accepted and President Chibulenu attended as an observer.

29 Minutes of the joint meeting of the AIMM delegation and the CMZa Executive Committee at Tshikapa, July 25-26, 1975. 1975 CMZa file, AIMM archives.

CHAPTER 30

1 When the government decided to declare that all Zairians were automatically members of the MPR, church leaders suddenly found themselves enmeshed in politics regardless of their personal preferences or convictions. Mennonite church leaders were not exempt and, at times, yielded to pressures to conform. Already in 1971 Howard Habegger, an AIMM Board delegation member, expressed some uneasiness in his reporting. Reflecting on a visit to the Mutena church center he recalled that

"Mennonite school children marched and sang to welcome the delegation. They sang Christian hymns and almost in the same breath shouted political slogans such as 'Mobutu, he is strong and he is good!' Several of our pastors wore MPR buttons. . . . Our top church leaders are very grateful that Mobutu has brought peace and stability to Congo. . . .However, I am concerned (equally concerned about our Mennonite Church in the U.S.) that the EMC of Congo does not forget that her first loyalty is to God, not Mobutu."

Howard Habegger, "A Personal Observation and Concern," Report to the AIMM Board, 1971. 1971 delegation file, AIMM archives.

2   Mennonite Pastor Mazemba Pierre of the Nyanga District was a case in point. As a young man he recognized that his church would not be able to provide adequate support for him and his large, growing family. Thus he early carved out a modest-sized coffee and citrus fruit plantation near his home village along the banks of the Kasai River east of Nyanga Station. They had just started producing well in the last years of the Belgian colonial regime and found a ready sale with local Portuguese and Belgian commercial enterprises of the area. But as his fields finally reached the level of productivity toward which he had so long striven, the upheaval of political independence struck the west Kasai and his access to outside markets was suddenly cut leaving him with both coffee beans and citrus fruit for which there were no commercial buyers.

3   The FLNA led by Holden Roberto drew its support largely from the Bakongo tribal people of whom many are found in Zaire and Congo Brazzaville. The MPLA, originally led by Agosthino Neto, appealed largely to leftist intellectuals and the urban poor. UNITA, led by Jonas Savimbi, was composed primarily of the large Ovimbundu ethnic group.

4   Methodist Bishop Ralph Dodge was an early deportee because of his clear affirmation of the right of the Angolan people to political freedom. This incident early cast the Protestant community as supporters of the Angolan people in their struggle for independence.

5   *Documentation et Informations Protestantes*, March 15, 1977, p.54.

6   Kabue, L'Expérience Zairoise, p.168.

7   William D. Hartley, U.S. News and World Report, April 16, 1979, p.52.

CHAPTER 31

1   Missionaries present were Rudy/Elvina Martens, Elmer Dick and Earl Roth.

2   Minutes of the CMZa General Council Meeting held April 22-25, 1976 at Kandala, Article 42. 1976 CMZa file, AIMM archives.

3   President Kabangy's report on activities of the CMZa presented to the delegates to the Third General Assembly at Ilebo, July 15-17, 1976. Assembly minutes, p.1. 1976 CMZa file, AIMM archives.

4   Ibid.

5   Ibid., Article 10

6   Ben Eidse news letter, February 28, 1978, p.2. 1978 Eidse file, AIMM archives.

7   Kabangy Moise, "Regulations of Engagement of the CMZa," 1978, Article 5b. 1978 CMZa file, AIMM archives.

8   Kabangy circular letter to all directors of the CMZa primary and secondary schools, January 30, 1978. Ibid.

9   "Convention of the Administration of National Schools", March 15, 1977. Article IV-1. 1977 CMZa file, AIMM archives.

10 Eidse news letter, October 23, 1977, p.1. 1977 Eidse file, AIMM archives.

11 Levi Keidel, Black Samson (Carol Stream, IL: Creation House, 1975).
           War To Be One (Grand Rapids, MI: Zondervan Publishing House, 1977).
           Caught In the Crossfire (Scottdale, PA: Herald Press, 1979).
    Two previously published titles were:
           Footsteps To Freedom (Chicago: Moody Press, 1969).
           Stop Treating Me Like God (Carol Stream, IL: Creation House, 1971).

12 CMZa Administrative Committee Minutes, January 21-22, 1977, Article 2. 1977 CMZa file, AIMM archives.

13 CMZa Administrative Committee Minutes, January 23-24, 1978, Articles 2 and 3. 1978 CMZa file, AIMM archives.

14 Jim Bertsche, Africa Trip Report to the AIMM Board, November 6-7, 1978, p.7. AIMM archives. With passing time missionaries still assigned to rural areas observed with sadness the gradual deterioration of buildings and stations which had been so painstakingly built and maintained in an earlier era. Under financial stress, district church leaders simply had other needs which were of higher priority than expensive cement and paint for buildings acquired from the Mission. Missionaries had to remind themselves that the stations had been but a means to the end of planting a church and were never intended to be brick-and-mortar monuments to a passing chapter of missionary endeavor in the African bush.

15 The writer of this history carries an abiding memory of the first Annual Church Conference he attended in 1949. When the mix of tribes represented by the assembled African delegates became clear, he expressed his surprise and pleasure to a gray-haired pastor who replied: "There is only one power that makes a gathering like this possible; it is the power of Jesus."

16 He did his work at George Peabody College of Vanderbilt University. His dissertation title: "Higher Institutes of Pedagogy and Universities in Zaire: The Development of the Relationships After the Reorganization of Higher Education in 1971." He returned to Zaire in 1981 with a Ph.D. in Educational Policy Studies.

17 Kidinda Shandungo, "The Mennonite Church in Zaire: The Problem of Active Participation of its Members," n.d. p.14. AIMM archives.

18 Ibid., p.15.

19 MCC representatives: Carrol Yoder, Newton Gingerich and Ray Brubacher. AIMM representative, Jim Bertsche.

20 CMZa Administrative Committee Meeting, October 13-14, 1978, Article 1. 1978 CMZa file, AIMM archives.

21 Ibid., Article 3.

22 Kakesa Samuel, upon terminating his services with the CMZa, was immediately offered the position of director of a large community development project based at Kikwit in Bandundu Province. Known as the Protestant Agricultural Program (PAP), it was jointly sponsored by MCC, the CEFMZ (MB Church) and the regional ECZ. Oriented to this position by MB missionary Peter Kroeker, Kakesa became the administrator of a sprawling program which involved a cattle project, a peanut oil press, a supply store for farmers and a portable saw mill operation. In spite of his gifts and experience, he also became embroiled in controversy. Part of the problem had to do with program philosophy and priorities. But there were also questions of appropriate use of program funds and resources. Surrounded by increasing criticism concerning his administration, Kakesa resigned in protest.

23 Jim Bertsche letter to Ben Eidse, December 6, 1977. 1977 Eidse file, AIMM archives.

24 Jim Bertsche report to the AIMM Board, November 6-7, 1978, p.5. AIMM archives.

25 Kabangy's report to the CMZa Fourth General Assembly, August 14-20, 1978, at Kikwit, Annex 2 to the Assembly Minutes. 1978 CMZa file, AIMM archives.

CHAPTER 32

1 Minutes of the CMZa Fourth General Assembly at Kikwit August 14-20, 1978, Articles 12, 13, 18, 20, 25, 32 and 15. Ibid.

2 Jim Bertsche, "Rev. Kabangy Shapasa Succumbs," AIMM Messenger, Summer 1979, p.15.

3 AIMM Contact, Vol. 21, No.5, November 15, 1979, p.2.

4 Ben Eidse letter to Jim Bertsche, March 8, 1979. 1979 Eidse file, AIMM archives.

5 Ben Eidse open letter to fellow AIMM missionaries, April 12, 1979. 1979 Eidse file, AIMM archives.

6 Ben Eidse letter to Jim Bertsche, Ibid.

CHAPTER 33

1 i.e. "AIMM's View of Christian Mission in Today's World" by board member Allan Wiebe; "AIMM's Stance in Southern Africa" by board member Jim Juhnke; "AIMM's Stance vis-à-vis the African Independent Churches" by AIMM missionary Stan Nussbaum; "AIMM's Stance vis-à-vis Zaire's Autonomous Mennonite Churches" by AIMM missionary Ben Eidse; and "AIMM's Stance in North America" by former AIMM Board Chairman Elmer Neufeld.

2 The AIMM Board composition at this meeting: six GC, four EMC/US, two EMB, two members-at-large and one each from EMC/CAN, MB and AIMM Women's Auxiliary.

3 The camp was purchased from the University of Notre Dame in 1965. Receding water levels of the time had depressed lakeside real estate prices and EMC/US decided to buy the site believing that eventually the trend would be reversed. The camp had been used at one time as a hideaway pre-season training area for their football teams under the fabled coach Knute Rockne. In due time the water level did indeed again rise. This plus an early generous donation toward the fund drive by Viola Zurlinden of the Salem EMC Church of Gridley, Illinois combined to make this name seem appropriate.

4   Jim Bertsche, "AIMM and the 1980's," pp.2-4. 1979 Miracle Camp Consultation file, AIMM archives.

5   Ibid., pp.4-6.

6   Ibid., p.9.

7   AIMM Consultation Findings Statement mailed to all participants. May 25, 1979, pp.14-16. 1979 Miracle Camp Consultation file, AIMM archives.

8   AIMM Board Minutes, April 24, 1979, Action 11.

9   Jim Bertsche, "Now What?" AIMM Messenger, Fall 1979, p.20.

CHAPTER 34

1   Mbonza Kikunga letter to President Kabangy, November 21, 1973. 1973 CMZa file, AIMM archives.

2   Ibid.

3   He frequently came late to Sunday morning services in the station chapel in full view of the assembled audience, at times with a furled umbrella on his arm, and whisked the wooden bench before seating himself. On one occasion, when invited to bring the Sunday morning message, he chose as his subject *Le Verbe* (the French term for verb). While it provided him an opportunity to demonstrate his university level theological studies, his message was largely incomprehensible for many of the simple rural folk who were in his audience that morning. The secondary school students in his audience fared better.

4   Jim Bertsche letter to Reuben Short, September 13, 1973. 1973 Bertsche file, AIMM archives.

5   CMZa Administrative Committee Meeting at Tshikapa, March 12, 1979, Article 1. 1979 CMZa file, AIMM archives.

6   Kabongo letter to Jim Bertsche, April 2, 1979. 1979 CMZa file, AIMM archives.

7   The CMZa administration kept the Kabangy family on salary through the end of the year. AIMM also opened a special fund through which contributors in North America were able to help relocate Mrs. Kabangy and her family in Gungu, a growing center some thirty-five miles from their home area at Kandala. Both the CMZa and the CEFMZ had organized churches at this center.

8   CMZa Administrative Committee Meeting, June 18-19, 1979, Articles 3, 5, 9-10. 1979 CMZa file, AIMM archives.

9   CMZa Administrative Committee Meeting, October 5-7, 1979, Articles 4-8, 10, 18, 20-21, 24-25, 29, 33, 35-36. 1979 CMZa file, AIMM archives.

10   The Council of that time included four doctors, i.e., AIMM missionaries Elvina Martens and John Byler and Zairians Makina and Mukandila.

11   Among the sixty-six voting delegates there were four missionaries, i.e., Herman Buller, the associate general treasurer of the Church; Levi Keidel, co-director of the Department of Evangelism and Church Life; Earl Roth, missionary counselor and Dr. Elvina Martens, the medical department representative on the administrative committee.

12 Jim Bertsche report to the GC/COM, March 6, 1983, pp.1-2. AIMM archives.

CHAPTER 35

1   Philip M. Steyne, Gods of Power (London: Touch Publications, Inc. 1989), p.38.

2   E. Bolaji Idowu, African Traditional Religion (London: SIM Press Ltd., 1973), p.174.

3   John S. Mbiti, African Religions and Philosophy (London: Heinemann, 1969), p.16.

4   Stephen N. Ezeanya, "*Dieu, les Esprits et le Monde,*" in *Pour Une Théologie Africaine* (Ibadan, Nigeria: Editions CCE Yaounde, 1969), p.53., the published findings of a gathering of African theologians in Ibadan, Nigeria, January 1966.

5   Steyne, Gods of Power, p.72.

6   Ibid., p.78.

7   Ibid., p.39.

8   Ezeanya, "*Dieu, les Esprits et le Monde,*" p.54

9   Any missionary who has worked for any length of time in Africa has encountered repeated examples of this view of life. Jim Bertsche was once riding with some African pastors on a winding road in Lesotho. Rounding a curve they came upon a bus tilted at a sharp angle in the roadside ditch. Several passengers had been severely injured and evacuated by ambulance. As they stopped to investigate, the missionary's western eyes noted a right front blown tire. Back in the car as they continued their travel the missionary observed that a likely reason for the accident was a blowout as the heavily loaded bus veered around the curve. After a moment of silence one of the pastors responded: "Yes, we too noted the tire. But the people who were injured on the bus will want to know *why* the tire blew out while they were riding in it this morning."

    On another occasion Bertsche was discussing CMZa's medical program with Dr. Makina, an excellent Zairian doctor. In reflecting on the interaction of Western medicine with traditional African views of illness, he shared that Africans long viewed with skepticism the insistence of missionary nurses that malaria was caused by mosquito bites. When a younger generation of Africans finally accepted that there was some linkage between this insect and the debilitating fevers with which they were all so well acquainted, there still remained the unanswered question as to *why* the mosquito chooses the victims it does!

10 Personal conversation with Jim Bertsche in Pastor Mazemba's home.

11 At a later date Dr. Makina shared his ongoing personal struggle as a Christian doctor to come to grips with this phenomenon. Was Manesa to be rejected out of hand as a fake and manipulator of crowds for his own profit? Or was there a genuine cultural role for such people that the rural African population needed, from time to time, to vent explosive societal tensions? Dr. Makina was an excellent example of educated Africans who stand at a collision point between Western and traditional African world views and who seek to evaluate and integrate the two.

12 Delegation members: Board Chairman Jim Juhnke, Board member Peter Sawatzky; AIMM staff members Art Janz and Jim Bertsche.

13 Jim Bertsche report to AIMM Board, Fall 1980. AIMM archives.

14 Mbiti, <u>African Religions and Philosophy</u>, pp.78,91.

CHAPTER 36

1 Delegation members: Board Chairman Jim Juhnke, Board member Peter Sawatzky; AIMM staff members Art Janz and Jim Bertsche.

2 The missionaries were associate general treasurer Herman Buller and Dr. Dennis Ries as head of the CMZa medical department.

3 The French verb *lancer* used in the committee minute is a forceful one, i.e., to throw or hurl implying resolute action.

4 CMZa Administrative Committee meeting October 11-13, 1980, Article 38. 1980 CMZa file, AIMM archives.

5 CMZa Executive Committee Minutes, April 21-22, 1983. 1983 CMZa file, AIMM archives.

6 <u>AIMM Messenger</u>, Spring 1980, p.14.

7 CMZa Administrative Committee meeting, July 27-28, 1980, Article 3. 1980 CMZa file, AIMM archives.

8 Minutes of the CMZa General Assembly, February 23-28, 1983, Article 28. 1983 CMZa file, AIMM archives.

9 CMZa Administrative Committee meeting, January 23-24, 1978, Article 13. 1978 CMZa file, AIMM archives.

10 The study commission was composed of Mukanza Ilunga as chairman, Rev. Kabongo Bukasa, school director Mutango James and missionaries Richard Derksen and Levi Keidel.

11 Report of the study commission dated February 28, 1978, recommending the creation of an *Institut Supérieur Théologique Mennonite* (ISTM). 1978 CMZa file, AIMM archives.

12 Letter from Mukanza Ilunga to President Kabangy, June 27, 1978. 1978 CMZa file, AIMM archives.

13 Six groups and two schools were represented as follows: CMZa by President Mbonza and Vice President Mukanza; CEFMZ by President Kilabi Bilulu and Legal Representative Fumana Watunyina; CEM by President Kazadi and Legal Representative Mundeke Kalawu; BOMAS by Peter Hamm, Frank Buschman and Mr. Thiessen; MCC by country representative Ren Amell; AIMM by Board member Peter Sawatzky, missionaries Peter Buller, Earl Roth, Ben Eidse and Secretary Jim Bertsche; ISTK by director Kikweta Mawa; Kalonda Bible Institute by Director Malembe Tshingudi.

14 Representation this time was as follows: CMZa by Vice President Mukanza Ilunga, CMZa Treasurer Tshimowa Bisosa; CEFMZ by Administrative Secretary Kusangila Kitondo, Regional Legal Representative Masolo Mununga, Legal Representative Fumana Watunyina and Kilabi Bululu; CEM by Kapiamba Lunkelu; ISTK by Kikueta Mawa; Kalonda Bible Institute by Malembe Tshingudi; BOMAS by missionary Alf Schmidt; MCC by Tim Lind and Ren Amell; AIMM by missionary Peter Falk, Board member Andy Rupp and Secretary Jim Bertsche.

15 Representation on the continuing study commission was as follows: CMZa by Mukanza Ilunga; CEM by Mundeke Kalawu; CEFMZ by Kikweta Mawa; BOMAS by Alf Schmidt; MCC by Renton Amell and AIMM by Peter Falk.

16 Report on the first meeting of the International Mennonite Peace Committee held June 8-17, 1980, p.2, by CMZa Vice President Mukanza Ilunga. 1980 CMZa file, AIMM archives.

17 As assembled by Vice President Mukanza Ilunga and missionary Levi Keidel, the CMZa statistics for the fall of 1981 were as follows: 640 local congregations, 33 church districts, approximately 35,000 members, 50,000 students in primary and secondary schools and 120 ordained pastors. CMZa-wide offerings gathered and utilized for district level church activities totaled 333,000 zaires. Calculated at the exchange rate of that era, this represented $115,000.

18 AIMM Board Meeting, April 25-26, 1981, Minute 4-1, p.2.

19 President Mbonza's open letter to North American Mennonites, July 14, 1981. 1981 CMZa file, AIMM archives.

CHAPTER 37

1 Jim Bertsche letter to President Mbonza, November 5, 1980, pp.3-4. 1980 CMZa file, AIMM archives.

2 Jim Bertsche, AIMM Executive Secretary of the time, would later comment that in his twelve years in the home office he had found no letters more painful to write than those addressed to these Zairian candidate couples. In spite of what could only be accepted as sincere testimonies to the leading of the Lord in their lives to seek service in Upper Volta, Bertsche had to explain that, much to his regret, there was no CMZa/AIMM structure in place to permit him to process their applications.

3 Jim Juhnke's presentation at the AIMM Missionary Retreat of August 1-7, 1980 in Kinshasa. Bertsche trip journal 1980 II, pp. 176-177.

4 Jim Christensen letter to Jim Bertsche, April 16, 1983. 1983 Christensen file, AIMM archives.

5 Chuck Fennig, "Patience, Patience!" AIMM Messenger, Winter 1982, p.6.

6 Jim Christensen, AIMM Messenger, Winter 1983, p.12.

7 The delegation was composed of George Loewen and Peter Barkman of Steinbach, MB; Maurice Stahly of Morton, IL; Rev. Gary Franz EMB pastor from Nebraska and Art Janz, associate executive secretary of the AIMM.

8 AIMM missionaries recognized that evening were: Elmer/Esther Quiring Dick (67 years); Aggie Friesen Enns (33) ; Sam/Leona Enns Entz (54); Archie Graber (40); Frieda Guengerich (20) Betty Quiring (25); Tina Quiring (26); Fanny Schmallenberger (34); Russell/Helen Yoder Schnell (62); Merle and Dorothy Bowman Schwartz (63); Irena Liechty Sprunger (20) and Larry Alvera Klassen Rempel (44).

9 Jim Juhnke, "Out Of Our Quarry," AIMM Messenger, Winter 1983, p.5.

CHAPTER 38

1 The proposal was that Donna Colbert, at the time in charge of the central pharmacy across the Kasai River at Kalonda Station, serve at least part time in such a capacity. This never materialized since her responsibilities with the CMZa medical department already represented more than a full time position.

2 An intriguing dimension of Derksen's background was the fact that he was the son of Peter and Mary Derksen, career GC/COM missionaries to Japan where Rick spent his youthful years. He had the unique experience of receiving part of his missionary support from the Oita Japanese Mennonite Church where he carried his membership.

3 Rick's personal testimony of his spiritual pilgrimage which brought him to this moment in his life is found in the AIMM Messenger, Spring 1984, p.13.

4 I.e., either be graduates of the Kalonda Bible Institute, ISTK, or the Theological *Faculté* of Kinshasa. CMZa Administrative Committee meeting, October 11-13, 1980, Article 27. 1980 CMZa file, AIMM archives.

5 Ibid., Articles 2-3.

6 CMZa Administrative Committee meeting, October 29-31, 1981, Article 54. 1981 CMZa file, AIMM archives.

7 President Mbonza's report to the CMZa General Assembly at Mbuji Mayi, February 23-28, 1983, p.22. Assembly minutes, 1983 CMZa file, AIMM archives.

8 CMZa Administrative Committee meeting, July 27-28, 1980, Article 1. 1980 CMZa file, AIMM archives.

9 Ibid., Article 8.

10 CMZa Administrative Committee meeting, October 29-31, 1981, Article 9. 1981 CMZa file, AIMM archives.

11 Rev. Bokeleale was consecrated a Bishop in Kinshasa during special festivities May 15-16, 1977, by Rev. H. H. Harms, a Bishop of the German Evangelical Lutheran Church. Two other Zairians, both ECZ regional secretaries, were also consecrated by Bishop Harms during this Zairian visit. This, at the time, made a total of eight Protestant Bishops in the country. Four others already stood in the episcopal traditions of their own churches, i.e., two Methodists and two Episcopalians. (There was a fifth church leader also with this title but was a member of a separatist group.) Though there was considerable ECZ agitation for all ECZ member communities to follow suit, there was broad spread resistance to the idea.

12 He was the third to serve in this capacity in the West Kasai, the first having been a Presbyterian pastor and the second a Methodist bishop.

13 For many years the Presbyterian Mission had operated its mission press at Luebo, one of their rural stations. In the confusion and disruption of post-independence days, the press had declined. Both Presbyterians and Mennonites were eager to relaunch the production and distribution of Tshiluba literature, their shared language. It was consequently decided to install a press in Kananga. Basic funding for the project came from Presbyterian sources while AIMM provided qualified personnel.

14 One was entitled "The Anabaptists and the Gifts of the Holy Spirit" by Herbert Minich of Goshen, IN, and one by former AIMM missionary Frank Enns entitled "Three Teachings Regarding the Holy

Spirit" originally written in 1967. This choice of material for circulation among CMZa leaders was not without significance for it came at a moment when CMZa was struggling to combat anti-witchcraft movements, on the one hand, and to incorporate diverse renewal movements into the Church, on the other.

15 President Mbonza's report to the Sixth CMZa General Assembly, February 23-28, 1983 at Mbuji Mayi, p.5 . Assembly minutes, 1983 CMZa file, AIMM archives.

16 Ibid., pp.36-37.

17 Ibid., pp.12-13.

18 I.e. Herman Buller, Rick Derksen and Dr. Dennis Ries as members of the CMZa Administrative Committee.

19 Minutes of the Sixth CMZa General Assembly, February 23-28, 1983 at Mbuji Mayi. Articles 49, 66, 9, 16, 18, 24 and 27.

20 President Mbonza's report to the Sixth CMZa General Assembly, pp.14 and 35.

21 Minutes of the Sixth CMZa General Assembly, February 23-28, 1983, pp. 13, 11-12.

22 President Mbonza's report to the Sixth CMZa General Assembly, p.2.

23 Ibid., p.35.

24 Ibid., p.1.

25 Ibid., p.35.

26 Ibid., pp.1-2.

27 Ibid., p.31.

CHAPTER 39

1 Delegates named for the Amsterdam gathering were Vice-President Mukanza Ilunga; Kamayala District President Chibulenu Sakayimbo, and Kingambo Kihunji, a pastor of a CMZa congregation in Kikwit.

Delegates to the MWC were President Mbonza; Luingo Mudinda, regional representative from Bandundu Province, and layman Tshilembu Nicodème from Kananga. Treasurer Tshimowa Bisosa was named as an alternate delegate.

2 CMZa Executive Committee meeting, May 18, 1983. Article 1. 1983 CMZa file, AIMM archives.

3 CMZa Administrative Committee meeting, August 24-27, 1983, Articles 34, 36, 40, 41a-b. 1983 CMZa file, AIMM archives.

4 This conversation took place between Pastor Khelendende and Jim Bertsche. The men had been partners in ministry for two brief periods of time at Kandala Station and had together experienced the onslaught of the *Jeunesse* Rebellion in January 1964.

5   Jenny Bertsche, "Khelendende Graduates," AIMM Messenger, No. 1, 1985, pp.10-11.

6   When later her husband again secured a scholarship for further theological study, she eventually joined him in Kinshasa where she was named to the ISTK staff as director of the women's section of study.

7   Gladys Buller, "Zaire Joy!" AIMM Messenger, No. 2 1985, p.12.

8   The delegation was composed of AIMM Board members Henry Klassen and Erwin Rempel, AIMM staff members Art Janz and Jim Bertsche plus former Board member Elmer Neufeld.

9   Jim Bertsche trip journal, 1984 II, pp. 157-158.

10 Ibid., pp.160-161.

11 Ibid., p.117.

12 At the time, the State was attempting to operate a two year training program with three different study tracks. Eighteen people were on government pay. The agreement signed stipulated that this personnel would remain on government pay with the understanding that if, in the future, the hospital was taken over definitively by the CMZa, the State would terminate all responsibility for payment of salaries.

13 Other members were Kakesa Samuel, Kamba Lubadi and missionaries Leona Schrag and Rick Derksen.

14 Special Commission Minutes, September 20, 1984, Articles 04 a b e, 05 and 07. 1984 CMZa file, AIMM archives.

15 Notes of Jim Bertsche interview with President Mbonza, August 12-13, 1985, p.6.

16 CMZa General Assembly, April 10-14, 1985 at Nyanga, Articles 08 a,b,c. 1985 CMZa file, AIMM archives.

17 Ibid., Article 09.

18 Ibid., Article 20a.

19 Ibid., Preamble p.1.

CHAPTER 40

1   CMZa Executive Committee meeting, May 27-28, 1985, Article 12 a b c. 1985 CMZa file, AIMM archives.

2   CMZa Administrative Committee meeting, August 20-24, 1985, Article 25. 1985 CMZa file, AIMM archives.

3   Ibid., Article 14 a-b.

4   Letter from the CMZa Banga District to the CMZa Administrative Committee, February 27, 1984. 1984 CMZa file, AIMM archives.

5   Letter from Rev. Tshilembu Nicodème to Vice President Mukanza Ilunga, March 11, 1985. 1985 CMZa file, AIMM archives.

6   A letter sent to the CMZa offices at Tshikapa in the name of the believers of CMZa Kahemba, Kamayala District, May 10, 1985. Signed by Kamizelo Kalau and Kusanika Tendoshakabembe. 1985 CMZa file, AIMM archives.

7   Bukungu François letter to President Mbonza, October 2, 1985. 1985 CMZa file, AIMM archives.

8   Mupemba Mulenda letter to Jim Bertsche, May 4, 1985. Personal Bertsche files.

9   Leona Schrag letter to Jim Bertsche, April 27, 1985, in response to questions asked. 1985 Schrag file, AIMM archives.

10 Peter Falk letter to Jim Bertsche, May 4, 1985, in response to questions asked. 1985 Falk file, AIMM archives.

11 On one occasion, after underscoring CMZa's financial problems in a committee session, he approached the French delegate to the committee requesting that she exchange a sizeable sum of French *francs* for American dollars which, he explained, were personal funds and not church money.

12 The seven men were: Shakatanga Kipuka and Kutana Khenda from Shamuana; Matalatala Mulua from Mukoso; Kamonya Kibongo from Kahemba; Kikenda Khatshia, Kawashe Mukuta and Chibulenu Sakayimbo from Kamayala.

13 Jim Bertsche trip journal, 1986.

14 Jim Bertsche letter to President Monza, February 14, 1986. 1986 CMZa file, AIMM archives.

15 Kamayala District Conference Minutes, December 5-8, 1985, Article 5 a-b. 1985 CMZa file, AIMM archives.

16 Ibid., Article 18.

17 "Declaration by the Autonomous Districts of South Bandundu," January 2, 1986. 1986 CMZa file, AIMM archives.

18 Minutes of the Kinshasa Regional Assembly in special session, January 26, 1986, Article 4. 1986 CMZa file, AIMM archives.

19 Both documents were dated April 9, 1986. Both groups declared their autonomy from the CMZa central administration and their intention to remain Mennonites worshiping in their own manner in their own districts.

20 Other commission members were Regional President Luingo Mudinda and AIMM missionaries Rick Derksen and Don Unruh.

21 This action (cf.#3) had been seen by some of the more isolated CMZa districts as a political move by the central administration to block recognition of new districts which might bring dissenting views to CMZa general assemblies.

"Report of the Commission of Inquiry on the Declaration of Autonomy of the Districts of Tshitambi, Kamayala, Mukoso and Shamwana," March 13, 1986. 1986 CMZa file, AIMM archives.

22 Minutes of the Special Administrative Committee Meeting, June 10-14, 1986, Articles 14-15. 1986 CMZa file, AIMM archives.

23 Report of the Bandundu Regional Staff Meeting, Kikwit, December 18, 1986. 1986 CMZa file, AIMM archives.

24 Missionary letter addressed to President and Legal Representative Mbonza Kikunga, January 22, 1987. 1987 CMZa file, AIMM archives.

25 Leona Schrag letter addressed to fellow missionaries sharing the gist of the meeting, February 22, 1987. 1987 Schrag file, AIMM archives.

26 CMZa Executive Committee Minutes, February 21, 1987, Article 5. 1987 CMZa file, AIMM archives.

27 The four regional representatives were: Luingo Mudinda, Bandundu; Kakesa Mulume, Kinshasa; Lupaya Mushombi, West Kasai and Mpoyi Tshienda, South Kasai.

CHAPTER 41

1 AIMM Messenger, 1987, No. 2, p.3.

2 There were five from Sweden and one each from England and Holland who served under the CIM during the first decade of its history.

3 AIMM secretary Jim Bertsche and Board member Peter Sawatzky met with EMEK representatives Raymond Eyer, Jacques Baumann and Mr/Mrs.Eric Hege at a Bible School in Nogent, a suburb of Paris.

4 In the early 1990's, the supporting Mennonite organizations began to experience budget pressures. This plus the fact that Mennonite Mission Boards had not used this center for orientation of missionary candidates as frequently as had been anticipated, the Nussbaum appointment was terminated in the spring of 1993.

5 Erwin Rempel memo addressed, as Board chairman, to the AIMM missionary family April 17, 1986. AIMM archives.

6 Jim Bertsche, AIMM Messenger, Fall, 1986, p.18.

7 Kasdorf was at the time a professor at Mennonite Brethren Biblical Seminary, Fresno, CA.

8 AIMM staff discovered that the text could easily be used with the melody of the familiar hymn, "Lead On Oh King Eternal."

9 AIMM Search Committee Minutes, January 15-16, 1986, Minute 2.

10 AIMM Executive Committee Minutes, April 2-3, 1986, Minute 10 1 c.

11 AIMM Executive Committee Minutes, August 22-23, 1986, Minute 10 1 a.

12 Jim Bertsche, "Some Personal Reflections Upon Retirement," Addendum 1 of AIMM Board Minutes April 4-5, 1986.

CHAPTER 42

1   Archbishop Bokeleale letter to President Mbonza, March 18, 1987. 1987 CMZa file, AIMM archives.

2   CMZa Executive Committee Minutes, March 27, 1987, p.2. 1987 CMZa file, AIMM archives.

3   Ibid., Article 01 d e.

4   CMZa Administrative Committee Minutes, April 9-11, 1987, Article 04 b. 1987 CMZa file, AIMM archives.

5   Ibid., Article 18.

6   Derksen letter to President Mbonza, March 30, 1987 with copies to Administrative Committee members. 1987 CMZa file, AIMM archives.

7   CMZa Administrative Committee Minutes, Ibid., Article 17.

8   Ibid., Article 20 a b.

9   "Communication from the President," Ibid., p.2.

10 Ibid., Article 16 a b c e.

11 Ibid., Article 10 b.

12 President Mbonza letter to the Urban Commissaire of Kikwit, May 18, 1987. 1987 CMZa file, AIMM archives.

13 Following the gathering, AIMM eventually made a contribution to help cover part of the travel expenses incurred by the CMZa delegates.

14 CMZa Special General Assembly Report, Kikwit May 28-31, 1987, p.1. 1987 CMZa file, AIMM archives.

15 Ibid., Article 05 b c.

16 Ibid., Article 15.

17 Ibid., Article 09 a b.

18 Chibulenu Sakayimbo, "Why Am I a Mennonite?" AIMM Messenger, 1990, p.3.

19 Ben Eidse letter to Jim Bertsche, August 3, 1993. 1993 Eidse file, AIMM archives.

20 Peter Buller letter to Earl Roth, June 1, 1987, p.2. 1987 Buller file, AIMM archives.

21 President Mbonza's opening address to the CMZa General Assembly at Tshikapa, June 23-29, 1987. Assembly Minutes, p.19. 1987 CMZa file, AIMM archives.

22 Tshikapa General Assembly Minutes, Articles 03 b, 04, 06, 10-11. Ibid.

23 Ibid., excerpts from the minutes.

24 I.e., Mukanza Ilunga, Luingo Mudindu and Lupaya Mushambu.

25 Mbonza letter to Kraybill, July 10, 1987. 1987 CMZa file, AIMM archives.

26 Archbishop Bokeleale letter to the four Regional CMZa Presidents, August 22, 1987. 1987 CMZa file, AIMM archives.

27 Chairman Kadima Tshimbidi, Vice Chairman Tshilembu Nicodème, Secretary Kumakamba Mimboro, and Assistant Secretary Mackunya Shalukombo.

28 I.e., Educational Secretary Kamba Lukadi, Coordinator of Social Services Lovua Mujito, Hospital Administrator Kanda Nzamba and Secretary of Evangelism and Life of the Church Kasay Batshinyi.

29 People named were a representative from the National ECZ office in Kinshasa, the regional ECZ President from Kananga, a local Tshikapa state government official, the four CMZa Regional Presidents, Kadima Tshimbidi chairman of the Kinshasa Assembly and Pastor Bukungu François, the widely-respected former CMZa General Treasurer.

30 Report of the Transition Commission of the CMZa, February 20, 1988, p.13. 1988 CMZa file, AIMM archives.

31 Ibid., p.24.

32 Ibid.

33 Maurice Briggs letter to Earl Roth, February 1988. 1988 Briggs file, AIMM archives.

CHAPTER 43

1   Chibulenu Sakayimbo letter to Earl Roth, February 29, 1988. 1988 CMZa file, AIMM archives.

2   Letter presented to Roth/Giesbrecht in the name of the Mutena District, May 9, 1988. 1988 delegation file, AIMM archives.

3   Giesbrecht trip report to AIMM Board, p.20. 1988 delegation file, AIMM archives.

4   Ibid., pp.20-22.

5   "Word of Welcome of the Djoko District," May 11, 1988. Ibid.

6   "Word of Welcome in the Name of the Mennonites of Kananga," May 6, 1988. Ibid.

7   CMZa Administrative Committee Minutes, August 22-27, 1988, Article 01. 1988 CMZa file, AIMM archives.

8   Ibid., Articles 05 a, 12, 13, 18, 23, 27-28.

9   Ibid., Articles 09, 10, 14, 25, 41.

10 Chibulenu letter to Earl Roth, September 14, 1988. 1988 CMZa file, AIMM archives.

11 The delegation members were: Board Chairman Henry Klassen, Vice-Chairman Harry Hyde, Recording Secretary Jeanne Zook and AIMM Executive Secretary Earl Roth.

12 Erwin Rempel, "AIMM Ministry in Zaire: Perspectives and Suggestions for the Future." Addendum to the AIMM Board Minutes of October 20-22, 1988, p.1.

13 At the time of the consultation, AIMM had a total of twenty-seven adults in Zaire or on active status for that country. Sixteen of them were in urban centers. The rest were located or assigned to two of the traditional bush stations, i.e., Kalonda and Nyanga. AIMM Messenger, 1990, p.15.

14 Earl Roth report to the AIMM Board, January 1990, pp.6-7. AIMM archives.

15 Their original executive committee was comprised of President Kazadi Lukuna, Vice-President Ntambua Tshilumbayi, Treasurer Tshibangu Mulangu, Legal Representative Ntumba Kalala, Assistant Legal Representative Mutangilayi Nsumpi, Secretary Ilunga Kayembe and Accountant Nkumbi Mudiayi.

16 I.e., Ntumba Musenge.

17 Pastor Kazadi resolutely maintained that although his name allegedly appeared on the documents submitted to the government by the Nkumbi group, he never saw nor signed the documents himself.

18 The new slate of CEM officers: President Mukengeshayi Lukasu, Legal Representative Nkumbi Mudiayi, Assistant Legal Representative Mbuyi Nkashama, Accountant Nsumbu Mulunda, and General Secretary Tshiosha Kambemba.

19 Delegation members were: AIMM Board Chairman Elmer Neufeld, Board member Erwin Rempel, and staff members Art Janz and Jim Bertsche.

20 Bertsche interview notes taken December 13, 1984. 1984 trip journal.

21 Bertsche letter to Rev. Nkumbi Mudiayi, September 7, 1984. 1984 CEM file, AIMM archives.

22 Bertsche letter to Rev. Nkumbi Mudiayi, August 22, 1985. 1985 CEM file, AIMM archives.

23 Bertsche letter to Rev. Nkumbi Mudiayi, October 15, 1985. 1985 CEM file, AIMM archives.

24 Bertsche letter to Rev. Nkumbi Mudiayi, August 15, 1986. 1986 CEM file, AIMM archives.

25 The Center was largely the result of the vision and drive of Willys and Thelma Braun, former Zaire missionaries with the C&MA. Through a remarkable series of gifts of material resources from both overseas and Zairian donors, they were able to develop a large training center for evangelists. Confined to a single year of study, the focus was resolutely placed on equipping Africans to move into areas which were without a resident witness - - whether in isolated rural regions or in the teeming shanty towns of the sprawling cities - - for the purpose of reaching the unreached. At first viewed with great suspicion by the ECZ, the Brauns were later given full support and encouragement as the spirit and impact of graduates came to be known.

26 Earl Roth report to AIMM Board, January 1990, p.7. AIMM archives.

27 This included a refurbished Landrover, an all-terrain vehicle which was jointly provided by AIMM and MCC. AIMM also gave a grant of $4,000 to fund a number of priority projects which were on the list submitted by the CEM administration.

28 Jeanne Zook, "Perceptions," p.5. 1989 delegation file, AIMM archives.

29 Earl Roth report to the AIMM Board, January 1990. "Memo of Understanding of the Basic Principles of Partnership Between the AIMM and the CEM," Annex 2. 1989 delegation file, AIMM archives.

30 Ibid., p.8.

31 I.e,. CEFMZ, the Mennonite Brethren of Zaire; CMZa, the Community of Mennonites of Zaire and CEM, the Community of Evangelical Mennonites of Zaire.

32 Other staff people named were: Pastor Kumadisa sha Jetout, Director of Research and Documentation; Khakhenda Lukak, Director of Pastoral Formation and Inspiration; and Kumbi-Kumbi Kamwenyi, Secretary. An initial budget was set for $21,400 of which $14,500 was to be provided by RURCON. The three churches pledged to raise $3,000. Requests for additional help were to be addressed to the AIMM and MBM/S.

CHAPTER 44

1 Steve Askrin and Carole Collins, "Greed Trickles Down," Africa News, February 8, 1988.

2 Ibid, p.9.

3 Hesh Kestin, "God, Man and Zaire," Forbes, November 18, 1985, p.100.

4 Ibid.

5 Ibid., pp. 105-106.

6 Ibid., pp. 100,103.

7 Jeffrey M. Elliot and Mervyn M. Dymally, "I Have a Clear Conscience." Africa News, March 7, 1988, p.4.

8 Erwin Rempel, Zaire Trip Report, February 4-15, 1991. AIMM archives.

9 CMZa leadership for this initiative was provided by the CMZa Vice President due to the fact that President Chibulenu was in Canberra, Australia at the time having been offered an air ticket by the WCC to attend their General Assembly that year.

10 Other assembly officers elected were: Kumakamba Mimboro, vice moderator; Kadima Tshimbidi, secretary; and Ipola Mukanzo Ipo, assistant secretary.

11 Minutes of the Extraordinary CMZa General Assembly held in Kinshasa, March 18-19, 1993, Article 02. 1993 CMZa file, AIMM archives.

12 Members of the CMZa delegation were: President Chibulenu Sakayimbo, Mukanza Ilunga, Lupaya Mushambu, Kumakamba Mimboro and AIMM missionary Arnold Harder.

13 "Mobutu Holds on to Power as Zaire Crumbles," Washington Post, May 14, 1991.

14 Ibid.

15 "Mobutu Readies New Ploy," Africa News, February 11, 1991.

16 "Mass Rioting Spreads in Zaire as Military Mutinies," New York Times, September 25, 1991.

17 Henry Dirks fax to Earl Roth, September 23, 1991. 1991 Dirks file, AIMM archives.

18 Mobutu's choice was Nguza Karl-i-bond from the Shaba Province.

19 Memo from R. Hunter Farrell, Associate for East/West Africa of the Presbyterian Church U.S., February 14, 1992. AIMM archives.

20 Mbonza letter to the Chief Justice of the Supreme Court of Zaire, April 5, 1993. 1993 CMZa file, AIMM archives.

CHAPTER 45

1 AIMM missionary Dick Steiner was the only member of the 1991 team who had experienced the upheaval of 1960. He and his wife Gladys Cleveland (deceased in 1979) arrived at Kalonda in the fall of 1959 and were caught up in the general missionary evacuation of July 1960.

2 Arnold Harder and Maurice Briggs decided to send their families home and to stay on in Kinshasa to be of whatever help they could to the Mennonite Churches in the city and the Christian community in general. Rick Derksen sent his family to Europe and returned to Kananga to be with the Mennonite and student communities among whom he had been ministering in that city. At year's end all three men rejoined their families.

3 Tina Dirks, "Our Zaire Evacuation," p.2. 1991 Dirks file, AIMM archives.

4 Other AIMM Board and Staff members present were Henry Klassen, Jeanne Zook, Erwin Rempel, Harry/Lynette Hyde and Earl/Ruth Roth.

5 Maurice Briggs, "Zaire Evacuation, 1991," p.2. 1991 Briggs file, AIMM archives.

6 Tina Dirks, "Our Zaire Evacuation," pp.1-2.

7 Susan Dick, "A Personal Report," p.6. 1991 Dick file, AIMM archives.

8 Grace Harder, "Personal Report," p.1. 1991 Harder file, AIMM archives.

9 Phyllis Boese, "Experiences and Story of My Evacuation from Zaire," pp.1-2. 1991 Boese file, AIMM archives.

10 Tina Dirks, "Our Zaire Evacuation," p.2.

11 Henry Dirks, "Our Zaire Evacuation", p.5. 1991 Dirks file, AIMM archives.

12 Susan Dick, "A Personal Report," p.3.

13 Grace Harder, "Personal Report," pp.3-4.

14 Joyce Briggs, "Evacuation Report," pp.8-9. 1991 Briggs file, AIMM archives.

15 Maurice Briggs, "Zaire Evacuation, 1991," pp.1-2.

16 Grace Harder, "Personal Report," p.2.

17 Delbert Dick, "Evacuation Report," p.4. 1991 Dick file, AIMM archives.

18 "Criteria for Missionaries Returning to Zaire," points 2 and 5. AIMM 1992 Executive Committee Minutes. AIMM archives.

19 Glen Boese, "Experience and Story of My Evacuation from Zaire," p.2. 1991 Boese file, AIMM archives.

20 Delbert Dick, "Evacuation Report," p.6.

21 Dick Steiner, "Evacuation report," p.2. 1991 Steiner file, AIMM archives.

22 Maurice Briggs, "Zaire Evacuation, 1991," p.3.

CHAPTER 46

1   "The Message of Inkima John, the Captain of the Oregon," World Call, Vol XX (5) 1938.

2   Levi Keidel, Black Samson (Carol Stream, IL: Creation House, 1975).

3   Jim Bertsche, "A Shaft of Light in Clouded Skies," AIMM Messenger, April-June 1964, p.8ff

4   Henry Dirks, "Our Zaire Evacuation," p.3.

5   Arnold Harder/Maurice Briggs phone conversation with AIMM staff, September 30, 1991. 1991 Harder/Briggs files, AIMM archives.

6   "Nsongamadi Joseph," Mennonite Encyclopedia, vol. 5, (Scottdale, PA, Herald Press, 1990), p.640.

7   Lupera David, "He Did Not Run Off," AIMM Messenger, Fall 1986, pp.10-11.

8   Biographical details provided by Ina Rocke.

9   Information provided by Baptist missionary Maurice Entwistle via letter sent to CIM missionaries in Congo. July 8, 1960. Jim Bertsche personal files.

10 Annex to the Entwistle letter.

11 "Kibuza Joseph," Mennonite Encyclopedia, vol. 5, p.489.

12 Mary Hiebert, "How the Maternity of Mutena Continued Without a Missionary Nurse," Congo Missionary Messenger, October-December 1964, pp.12-14.

13 The missionary was Jim Bertsche.

14 Biographical details provided by Elmer Dick.

15 Biographical details provided by Archie Graber.

16 Grace Harder, "Nyanga Ordains First CMZa Deaconess," AIMM Messenger, Spring 1989, pp.8-9.

17 Rev. Shamuimba Mbombo letter to Earl/Ruth Roth, April 4, 1988. 1988 CMZa file, AIMM archives.

18 Biographical information provided by Glenn Rocke.

CHAPTER 47

1   Tim Lind, "MCC Africa Program: Historical Background," MCC Occasional Paper #10, 1989, p.8

2   Ibid., pp.8-9.

3   COMBS Minutes, May 23, 1968, excerpts from Minute 17, p.4. 1968 COMBS file, AIMM archives.

4   COMBS Minutes, October 5, 1968, p.2. 1968 COMBS file, AIMM archives.

5   Jacobs/Bertsche, "Southern Africa Study," May 1970, pp.1-2. AIMM archives.

6   November 17-21, 1970, Jacobs returned to Lesotho, Swaziland and South Africa with Vern Preheim, the MCC Africa Secretary of the time, and Harold Stauffer and Paul Kraybill who represented the Eastern Mennonite Board. In April 1971, Jacobs returned yet again with Harold Miller. In addition to a return to Swaziland they also traveled in the Transkei and Namaqualand.

7   As quoted in "A Report of Proceedings of the South Africa Consultation in Maseru, Lesotho," held April 30- May 1, 1972. p.1. AIMM archives.

8   Ibid., pp.4-5.

9   Ibid., pp.11-12, numbers 2-4,7.

10 Ibid., pp.5-6.

CHAPTER 48

1   Don Jacobs and Jim Bertsche who were in the process of their April 1970 investigative trip.

2   Peter Webb, "On a Collision Course," Newsweek April 27, 1970. p.23.

3   A derogatory term used to refer to an indigenous local population, also known as Khoi-Khoi, found by the early European immigrants. Short of stature and light skinned, it is thought that they had biological links with both the diminutive Bushmen of southern Africa and with larger, darker skinned Bantu groups. The Khoi-Khoi were a herding people who depended on their flocks of sheep and cattle for their livelihood.

4   History of South Africa (Pretoria, W. J. de Kock, 1971). Over time, the Afrikaner people were to come in contact with four major Bantu groups - - the Nguni (with the sub-groups Swazi, Xhosa and Zulu), the Sotho (with the sub-groups Southern Sotho, Pedi and Tswana), Venda and Shangana-Tsonga. Nineteen seventy-three statistics list the Xhosa at four million, the Zulu also at four million, the Pedi at 1.6 million and the Southern Sotho at 1.5 million.

6   It was during this period of menace and flight that two of today's southern African countries found their origins, i.e., Lesotho and Swaziland. In both cases there were chiefs of wisdom who gathered fellow clan folk about them and retreated into the comparative safety of rugged, mountainous areas where they could elude their pursuers. In both cases little kingdoms emerged. In Lesotho it was under King Moshoeshoe I; in Swaziland under King Sobhuza I. In the case of the Tswana speaking people of Botswana (originally known as Bechuanaland), their oral history tells of the arrival of their forebears on the eastern fringes of the Kalahari Desert already in the mid-17th century. But they also had to resist the forays of the rampaging Zulu warriors in the 1800's.

7   History of South Africa, pp.43-44.

8   Ibid., p.43.

9   Ibid., p.48.

10   Charles Villa-Vicencio, "South Africa's Theological Nationalism," Ecumenical Review, 29:4, (October 1977), pp.373-74.

11   John W. de Gruchy, The Church Struggle in South Africa (Grand Rapids, MI, Wm. Eerdmans Publishing Co., 1979) quoting from a DRC document "Human Relations and the South Africa Scene" adopted by the DRC General Synod in 1966.

12   Ibid., p.72.

13   Ibid., p.73.

14   Villa-Vicencio, "South Africa's Theological Nationalism,"quoting A. N. Pelser, ed., Verwoerd Speaks (Johannesburg, Perskor, 1966), p.21.

15   "The Defiant White Tribe," Time, November 21, 1977. p.54.

16   Jim Juhnke, "Mennonites and Afrikaners," Study Paper SAW 17, 1972. pp.1-2.

17   Ibid., p.3.

18   Ibid., p.4.

19   Villa-Vicencio, "South Africa's Theological Nationalism," p.380 quoting Allan Boesak, Farewell to Innocence (J. H. Kok, 1976), p.49.

20   Villa-Vicencio, "South Africa's Theological Nationalism," quoting H.M. Hugo, "South Africa's Theologized Nationalism."

CHAPTER 49

1   Jacobs and Bertsche, "Southern Africa Study," p.13.

2   I.e., Secretary A.A. Kikine, a layman, and Council President Bishop F. Makhatha of the Anglican Church.

3   Jim Bertsche, Lesotho Report to the AIMM Board, June 5, 1972, pp.9-10. 1972 Lesotho file, AIMM archives.

4   Ibid., p.11.

5   An illustration of this effort of adaptation is an outdoor semicircular enclosure with seating facing a central spot, this in the image of the rural tradition among the Basotho people of gathering village elders around the village chief for purposes of deliberation, instruction and decision making.

6   Stan Nussbaum reported having once had conversation with an American Presbyterian instructor who had been made available to the Morija Theological Institute for a period of time. It was his impression that the LEC placed little emphasis upon the doctrine of the Holy Spirit. It is interesting to conjecture as to how this apparent doctrinal oversight may have contributed to the defensive stance of the LEC at this point in its history.

7   The Lesotho Evangelical Church, the Anglican Church, the Wesleyan Methodist Church, the African Methodist Episcopal Church, the Assemblies of God Church and the Roman Catholic Church.

8   S.A. Mohono, "Walter Matitta Phakao," n.d. AIMM archives.

9   Tutu eventually acquired world-wide stature as he was named the Canon of the Anglican Cathedral in Johannesburg. From this prestigious setting he led a courageous movement of opposition against *apartheid* in his land in the name of Christ and his Church.

CHAPTER 50

1   Early researchers in this field who have been widely read are:
    Bengt Sundkler, Bantu Prophets in South Africa (London, Oxford University Press, 1961).

    Bengt Sundkler, Zulu Zion (London, Oxford University Press, 1976).

    Harold Turner, New Religious Movements in Black Africa (Garland Publishing, Inc., 1978).

    David Barrett, Schism and Renewal in Africa (London, Oxford University Press, 1968).

2   Sundkler, Bantu Prophets in South Africa, pp.53-55.

3   Sundkler, Zulu Zion, pp.28-29.

4   Ibid., p.30.

5   Stan Nussbaum: comments made in margins of a draft copy of this chapter.

6   John W. de Gruchy, Ibid., p.41.

7   Sipo E. Nzimela: quotation from a paper he presented at a symposium convened by Dr. Bruce Beaver. n.d. pp.6-9. Jim Bertsche files.

8   Jim Bertsche, "Watershed Issues for COM/AIMM Mission Activity in Africa in the Coming Decade," August 1, 1985. AIMM archives.

9   Nzimela: quotation from a paper he presented at a symposium convened by Dr. Bruce Beaver, p.23.

10 Ibid., pp.19-20.

11 Ibid., p.21.

12 Peter M. Mokamba, "The Contribution of Fambidzano to Independent Churches in Zimbabwe," in Ministry Partnership with African Independent Churches (Elkhart, IN, Mennonite Board of Missions, 1991), p.264

13 Minutes of the AIMM Semi-Annual Board Meeting, October 21, 1974, Appendix #1.

14 Ibid., Minute 21, p.6.

CHAPTER 51

1 Rachel Hilty Friesen, "A History of the Spiritual Healing Church in Botswana", a thesis submitted to the History of Christianity Department of Knox College and the Toronto School of Theology for her degree of Master of Theology, June 1990. p.35. AIMM archives.

2 Ibid., p.41.

3 Ibid., p.42.

4 Ibid., pp.43-44.

5 Ibid.,

6 Ibid., p.45.

7 David Shank, "A Survey of American Mennonite Ministries to African Independent Churches," Mission Focus, March 1985. p.1.

8 Edwin and Irene Weaver, The Uyo Story (Elkhart, IN, Mennonite Board of Missions, 1970).

9 Edwin and Irene Weaver, From Kuku Hill (Elkhart, IN, Mennonite Board of Missions, 1975).

10 In working out its own rationale for working with AICs, AIMM drew on a variety of helpful MBM materials. A case in point was a memo dated January 15, 1979 addressed to the MBM by David and Wilma Shank.

11 Weaver report to AIMM office, March 1975, pp.1-2. 1975 Weaver file, AIMM archives.

12 Irene Weaver, "A Prophet's Vision," July 13, 1975. 1975 Weaver file, AIMM archives.

13 The delegation was composed of Board Chairman Elmer Neufeld, Board members Howard Habegger/Andrew Rupp and staff members Art Janz/Jim Bertsche.

14 Nussbaum's undergraduate work was done at Taylor University at Upland, IN; his seminary work at the Trinity Evangelical Divinity School at Deerfield, IL.

15 Irene Weaver, "The Miracle at Palapye." 1975 Weaver file, AIMM archives.

16 Ed Weaver letter to Jim Bertsche, April 22, 1975. 1975 Weaver File, AIMM archives.

17 The delegation was comprised of Board Vice-Chairman Allan Wiebe and AIMM Secretary Jim Bertsche.

18 Bertsche/Wiebe trip report to the AIMM Board, 1975. pp.29-33. 1975 delegation file, AIMM archives.

CHAPTER 52

1 Those already present in the country were Ed/Irene Weaver, Harry/Lois Dyck, Irvin/Lydia Friesen, Norman/Virginia Derstine.

2 Ray Brubacher, Nancy Heisey and Tim Lind in the MCC office in Akron; Jim Bertsche in the AIMM office in Elkhart.

3 AIMM Executive Committee Minutes, January 21-22, 1977. Addendum #7.

4 AIMM Executive Committee Minutes, October 16-17, 1980. Minute 8-1, pp.2-3. AIMM Board Minutes, October 17-18, 1980. Article 8-2, p.4.

5 John W. Eby, "AIMM-MCC Relationships," February 19, 1980. p.2. 1980 Botswana file, AIMM archives.

6 Ibid., p.2.

7 Ibid., p.5.

8 AIMM Board Minutes, Ibid. Action 5. The action carried by the following vote: 9 yes, 1 no, 4 abstentions.

9 "Constitution of Mennonite Ministries in Botswana," Article II. 1980 Botswana file, AIMM archives.

10 Jim Bertsche letter to Tim Lind, May 13, 1985, pp.1,3. 1985 MCC file, AIMM archives.

11 Eric Fast letter to Arli Klassen in Lesotho, March 7, 1994. It is interesting to note that some time later an MM arrangement was also put in place in Lesotho.

12 Time, December 1982, cover story. pp. 50-56.

13 I.e., GC/COM 50%, MBM 30%, EMC/US 20%.

14 Norman Derstine, excerpts from "Reflections," November 4, 1976. 1976 Derstine file, AIMM archives.

15 Jim Bertsche trip journal, August 8, 1984. p.93.

CHAPTER 53

1 Don Boschman, "Counting Chickens and Doing Theology," The Mennonite, December 26, 1989. p.584.

2 Stan Nussbaum, "What Do I Do Now?" AIMM Messenger, Summer 1983, p.7.

3 I.e., Ed/Irene Lehman Weaver, Harry/Lois Riehl Dyck, Irvin/Lydia Gunther Friesen, John/Ruth Fast Kliewer, Gary/Dianne Falk Janzen, Jonathan/Mary Kay Burkhalter Larson, Tim/Laura Gilbertson Bertsche, Peter/Marge Penner Sawatzky, Don Boschman, Erica Thiessen, Gene Thieszen.

4   I.e., Stan/Lorri Berends Nussbaum, Jim/Vicki Birkey Egli, John/Tina Warkentin Bohn, Harlan/Claire Becker de Brun, Troy/Cathy Schmitze Couillard, Brian/Patricia Penner Reimer.

5   I.e., Larry Hills, Gary/Jean Kliewer Isaac.

6   AIC leaders Archbishop Monyatsi, Otsile Ditsheko, Archbishop Motswasele and J.C. Tshwene from Botswana; Isaac Dlamini from Swaziland; Samuel and Emily Mohono and Sanaka Ntlaloe from Lesotho; Anglican Father Patrick Kotta from the Transkei; Joshua Seithleko and Johan Smuts from the Xanagas Basarwa Resettlement project in western Botswana; MCC personnel John/Joyce Eby, Luke Maiyers, Randy/Roxie Ewert, Margreet/Maartin Van der Werf from Botswana; MCC personnel Neil Reimer and Peter Penner from Swaziland; AIMM personnel Harry/Lois Dyck, John/Ruth Kliewer, Fremont/Sara Regier, Irvin/Lydia Friesen, Jonathan/Mary Kay Larson from Botswana; AIMM personnel Stan/Lorri Nussbaum and Jim/Vicki Egli from Lesotho; Eastern Board missionaries Carl/Julia Sensenig from Swaziland; Eastern Board representatives Hershey/Leona Leaman; MB Board representative Peter Hamm; AIMM board representative Peter Sawatzky and AIMM secretary Jim Bertsche.

7   All quotations taken from the Report and Findings Statement of the AIC Consultation July 27-31, 1981 held at Gaborone, Botswana. 1981 Botswana file, AIMM archives.

8   Stan Nussbaum addendum, Ibid.

9   Paul Hiebert letter to the Schowalter Foundation, October 6, 1981. 1981 Botswana file, AIMM archives.

10   It is worth noting that the same sort of broad interaction was later carried on at a continental level by the Network on AICs and Missions formed at Abidjan in 1986 with subsequent gatherings at Kinshasa in 1989 and Johannesburg in 1993. Dave and Wilma Shank provided key organizational leadership for the Abidjan meeting as MBM personnel based there at the time. Stan Nussbaum gave leadership for the Kinshasa gathering from his base at Selly Oak Colleges in Birminghan, England with what is now known as the INTERACT Research Center. He also helped with planning the Johannesburg meeting from his new base at Colorado Springs, CO, with Global Mapping International. These gatherings have resulted in three volumes of conference papers, two published by MBM and the third by the OAIC.

CHAPTER 54

1   Gary and Jean Isaac, "A Bus-Rank Encounter," Isaac newsletter April, 1988. 1988 Isaac file, AIMM archives.

2   Ray Brubacher, "A Case Study of Southern Africa," a paper presented at a Peace Theology Colloquium in May, 1978. p.3. AIMM archives.

3   Ibid., p.4.

4   Ibid., p.5. Brubacher cited a letter received from Yoder regarding the issue.

5   Carla Penner, "Working Under Harassment," The Mennonite, December 26, 1989. p.582.

6   The founding pastor of the Grace EMC Church in Morton, IL, he had earlier served both as AIMM Board member and Board chairman. With his wife Violet he happened to be visiting their son and family at Maseru at the time and welcomed the opportunity to observe this probing of a possible new field of ministry for the AIMM.

7   Stan Nussbaum letter to Jim Bertsche, January 28, 1981. 1981 Nussbaum file, AIMM archives.

8   The original committee was comprised of Hennie Pretorius, Rev. Ngxoxo, two AIC Bishops Gwetyana and Dikwa, Judy Herr and an AIMM representative.

9   An intriguing dimension of this story is that the pastor Harlan de Brun and his wife Claire eventually also served with AIMM in a Bible teaching ministry among AICs in Lesotho.

10 It was during Larry Hills' first year of study at Gordon-Conwell that the school was looking for a new president. One name on their list was Myron Augsburger. When the school board learned of his stance on pacifism, his name was dropped.

11 It was shortly after that this small rural congregation decided to sell their place of worship and relocate on the south side of Goshen. The church is now known as the Silverwood Mennonite Church.

12 Larry Hills, "Sharing In Hope," AIMM Messenger, Spring 1984. p.9.

13 Hills letter to Jim Bertsche, April 8, 1984. p.1. 1984 Hills file, AIMM archives.

14 Hills, "Sharing In Hope."

CHAPTER 55

1   As of 1997, AIMM missionaries Harry/Lois Dyck, Gary/Diane Janzen, Ron Sawatzky and Tim/Laura Bertsche have served in this city.

2   Tim Bertsche, unpublished article. 1990 Bertsche file, AIMM archives.

3   Jonathan Larson, "Africans Oppose Alcohol Abuse," Mennonite Weekly Review, September 1988.

4   Larson letter to Jim Bertsche, October 17, 1985. 1985 Larson file, AIMM archives.

5   Ibid.

6   Jonathan Larson, "Botswana Christians Meet For First Peacemaker Festival," AIMM Messenger, 1993. p.9.

7   Titus/Karen Guenther, "Special Assignment," AIMM Messenger, No.1, Winter 1984. pp.4-7.

8   AIMM Board Minutes, March 23-25, 1984, Actions 2,17.

9   AIMM delegation members were GC/COM personnel secretary Bruno Bergen and AIMM Secretary Jim Bertsche.

10 Ivan Friesen, "Report to the AIMM/COM," March 5, 1987. p.3. 1987 Friesen file, AIMM archives.

11 Ivan Friesen, "Teaching the Bible in a University Setting," December 5, 1987. Ibid.

12 Ivan Friesen, "The University and its 'Elitist' Image," March 14, 1991. 1991 Friesen file, AIMM archives.

13 Jim Bertsche editorial, "Both Soil and Soul," AIMM Messenger, Fall 1976. p.16.

14 Tina Bohn, "*Thaba Khupa*," <u>AIMM Messenger</u>, Spring 1979. p.6.

15 Tina Bohn, "Blankets Are International Bonds," <u>Mennonite Weekly Review</u>, March 3, 1989.

16 While initially there was some truth to this characterization of the MUC, this situation rapidly changed after the arrival of AIMM pastoral personnel.

17 Jim Bertsche AIMM report to the GC/COM February 1978. pp.4-5. 1978 executive secretary file, AIMM archives.

CHAPTER 56

1   Bishop Antonious Markos, "A Project in World Mission," African Independent Churches Service, Coptic Orthodox Church, Nairobi, March 1977. p.2. 1977 OAIC file, AIMM archives.

2   Ibid., pp.1-2.

3   Jacobs and Bertsche, "Southern Africa Study," 1970, p.2. AIMM archives.

4   Jonathan Larson memo to Jim Bertsche, Darrel Hostetter, Garry Isaac and Stan Nussbaum. August 17, 1988. 1988 Larson file, AIMM archives.

5   Jim Bertsche letter to Jonathan Larson, September 6, 1988. 1988 Larson file, AIMM archives.

6   Robert and Judy Zimmerman Herr, "Listening to the Church: Mennonite Ministry in South Africa." MCC Occasional Paper #3, June 1988. pp.36-38.

7   Jim W. Shenk, "Summary Report CIM Southern Africa Discussion, May 23, 1989." Attachment 9. 1989 CIM file, AIMM archives.

8   The sponsoring boards were Eastern Mennonite Board of Missions, Franconia Conference Mission Commission, Mennonite Board of Missions, Virginia Mennonite Mission Board.

9   Nancy Heisey/Paul Longacre, "Mennonite International Study Project," Final Report, July 25, 1989, p.74. AIMM archives.

10 Ibid., pp.75-76.

11 Jim Juhnke, "North American Businesses in South Africa," Study Paper, SAW #15, March 1972. AIMM archives.

12 This arbitrary effort to impose an unwanted language upon Africans was reminiscent of the short-lived effort made by Belgian colonial authorities in the 1950's when they made the study of German a language requirement in the Congo.

13 Jim Bertsche trip journal, June 1976, pp.48-49.

14 Bishop Desmond Tutu, "Where I Stand," August 4, 1980, <u>EcuNews Bulletin</u>, 18/1980, August 12, 1980. pp.8ff.

15 Moretha Maartens, "An Appeal for South Africa," <u>Partnership</u>, March/April 1986, pp.33-34.

16 I.e., Botswana, Lesotho, Transkei, Swaziland and Zimbabwe.

17 I.e., Hershey Leaman, Nancy Heisey, Tim Lind and Jim Bertsche.

18 "A Commentary on Mennonite Ministries and the Southern Africa Situation," August 26, 1986. AIMM archives.

CHAPTER 57

1 Alvin J. Stevenson died at Djoko Punda, Congo in 1913; Max Grutter in 1956 and Mary Miller in 1957 both at Kamayala, Zaire; Paxman Larry Kaufman lost his life by drowning during an outing on the Kasai River in 1956.

2 AIMM Handbook, revised in October 1986, p.68.

3 Ibid., pp.68-69.

4 Fremont and Sara Regier report on the Gaborone raid. 1984 Regier file, AIMM archives.

5 Jonathan Larson letter to family and friends, June 14, 1985. AIMM archives.

6 Jonathan Larson, "A Story of Three Lamps," May 26, 1986. 1986 Larson file, AIMM archives.

7 Harris Waltner letter to family and friends, August 27, 1984. 1984 Waltner file, AIMM archives.

8 Larry Hills' report on his imprisonment, February 25, 1987, pp.2-3. 1987 Hills file, AIMM archives.

9 Gary and Jean Isaac, "Our Experience of South Africa's First Democratic Elections," Isaac newsletter, July 1994. 1994 Isaac file, AIMM archives.

10 Jean Isaac, "Home Blessing Follows Home Fire Bombing," AIMM News Service, May 19, 1994. AIMM archives.

11 Tim Bertsche, "Reflections on the Death of One of My Students by Suicide," November 1993. 1993 Bertsche file, AIMM archives.

CHAPTER 58

1 Botha was the fifth of an unbroken series of National Party figures who served as head of state. The preceding four were Daniel F. Malan 1948-54; J.G. Strijdom 1954-58; Hendrick Verwoerd 1958-66, who was assassinated while in office, and B.J. Vorster 1966-78. Botha served from 1978 to 1989.

2 P. W. Botha's speech before the House of Assembly, Cape Town, February 2, 1982, South Africa Report, September 10, 1982, p.15.

3 Other homelands which were intended at the time were Kazangulu, Lebowa, Qwaqwa, Kua Zulu, Kwa Nguane and Kwa Ndebele.

4 "Mandela On Communism," New York Times, July 19, 1986.

5   "Christians Lead Redemption of South Africa," <u>The Elkhart Truth</u>, March 22, 1991, p.B-2. Reporter Lin McGill quoting Peter Walshe, Director of African Studies at the University of Notre Dame, South Bend, IN.

6   "The ANC Releases Mandela Statement," <u>Southern Africa</u>, July-August, 1980, p.13.

7   "The Koinonia Declaration," <u>Christianity Today</u>, January 27, 1978, pp.24-25.

8   "A White South African Pastor Challenges His Country's Policy of Racial Separation," <u>Christianity Today</u>, August 9, 1985, p.41.

9   Ibid.

10   Four years later he requested and eventually secured permission to take up residence in this township among his parishioners and thus became, at the time, the only white person living among 250,000 blacks.

11   An open letter signed by 123 credentialed clergymen of the DRC which appeared in the South African newspaper <u>STAR</u>, June 10, 1982.

12   Brochure issued by the Charles Bester Support Group, n.d. Box 786136, Sandton, 2146, South Africa.

13   Brochure issued by four support groups, n.d. Box 591, Kengray, 2100, South Africa.

14   A brochure issued by the ECC Khotso House, Johannesburg, n.d.

15   A statement issued by a group of "concerned evangelicals" in <u>Evangelical Ministries</u>, May-August 1987, pp.18-22.

16   <u>Los Angeles Times</u> wire service, June 26, 1985.

17   Rev. Frank Chikane interview with a reporter of <u>Africa Report</u>, March-April 1988, pp.13-16.

18   Government figures had already carried on secret talks with Mandela on Robben Island as early as 1986. But when they proposed his release in exchange for his commitment that the ANC would renounce all further use of violence with no comparable promise on the part of the government, Mandela refused and remained in prison.

19   National Peace Accord, <u>Newslink Africa</u>, September 20, 1991. pp.12-13.

20   Ibid., p.12.

21   Andre Brink, "The End of Separateness," <u>Newsweek</u>, May 9, 1994, p.39.

22   Mark Mathabane, "Like the Second Coming," Ibid., p.38.

23   Tina Susman, "Mandela: Let Freedom Ring," <u>The Elkhart Truth</u>, May 10, 1994.

24   William Raspberry, "South Africa Near Miracle," <u>The Elkhart Truth</u>, December 27, 1991.

25   Ibid.

26   Stan Nussbaum comments after reading a first draft of this chapter.

27 "A Divine Intervention Saved South Africa: Tutu," <u>The Elkhart Truth</u>, October 10, 1994

28 Sahm Venter, "Mandela's Style Defines South African Presidency," <u>The Elkhart Truth</u>, September 18, 1994.

CHAPTER 59

1 Stan Nussbaum, "Some things We are Learning About Basotho Students," n.d. Nussbaum personal files, AIMM archives.

2 "The Encounter of Literate and Non-Literate in Independent Churches of Rural Botswana," July 1986, pp.1-2. Unpublished. 1986 Larson file, AIMM archives.

3 Ibid., pp.3-4.

4 Ed Weaver, COMBS News Release, December 13, 1973. 1973 COMBS file, AIMM archives.

5 Jonathan Larson, "Questions posed by representatives of AIC Church communities in Kobojango, Botswana in anticipation of a Bible Conference which was held May 22-24, 1987." 1987 Larson file, AIMM archives.

6 Fremont and Sara Regier. Botswana field report, Oct. 1985, p.12. 1985 Regier file, AIMM archives.

7 Stan Nussbaum, furlough report to the EMC/US COM, November 9, 1981. 1981 Nussbaum file, AIMM archives.

8 A good case in point was AIMM's early encounter in Botswana with Willie Gulubane, the head of what was then known as the St. Philip's Faith healing Church.

9 Elinor Miller, "The HOW of Working with the AICs," a study paper submitted for discussion at a Mennonite Ministries workshop in Botswana, n.d. AIMM archives.

10 Ibid.

11 Tim Bertsche, "When the Learner/Listener Meets Reality." A discussion paper presented at an AIC Bible Teachers' Conference March 15-16, 1991, Gaborone, Botswana. 1991 Bertsche file, AIMM archives.

12 Beth Hege, "Africans Find Christianity Adaptable to Their Culture," <u>Mennonite Weekly Review</u>, March 7, 1991.

13 Larry Hills letter to Jim Bertsche, April 21, 1988. 1988 Hills file, AIMM archives.

14 Carla Reimer, "Missionary Dances to Work; God's Spirit 'Seizes' Africans," <u>Mennonite Weekly Review</u>, February 22, 1990.

15 Jonathan Larson, "Jostling to Make Room," <u>The Mennonite</u>, September 8, 1987, p.388.

16 Jim and Jenny Bertsche, "Christmas Time at Peka," <u>AIMM Missionary Messenger</u>, Spring 1980, pp.6-7.

17 Jonathan Larson, "Signs of Glory," <u>The Mennonite</u>, March 8, 1988, p.105.

18 Larry Hills letter to Jim Bertsche, April 28, 1984. 1984 Hills file, AIMM archives.

19 Gary and Jean Isaac newsletter, December, 1987. 1987 Isaac file, AIMM archives.

20 Carla Reimer, "Africa Church Changed My Life," Mennonite Weekly Review, April 26, 1990.

21 I.e., Jim Bertsche.

CHAPTER 60

1 Heisey and Longacre "Africa Trip Report," Mennonite International Study Project, p.29. AIMM archives.

2 Jim Bertsche memo to South Africa Task Force members, December 19, 1975, p.2. 1975 SATF file, AIMM archives.

3 Berglund letter to Jim Bertsche, November 25, 1975. AIMM archives.

4 Tom Price, "Seminary Graduate Serves in South African Cabinet," The Elkhart Truth, June 17, 1994.

5 Bob/Joyce Stradinger Gerhart 1974-1978, 1979-1981; Ron/Cynthia Kirchofer Krehbiel 1978-1979; Virgil/Mary Kay Ramseyer Gerig 1982-1984; Harris/Christine Duerksen Waltner 1984-1990; and Glen/Elizabeth Unger Koop 1990-1992.

6 Ron Krehbiel, "The Little Church With a World-Wide Ministry," AIMM Messenger, Spring 1979, p.10.

7 Maseru United Church newsletter, October 1989. 1989 MUC file, AIMM archives.

8 Sang Bin Lee letter to Harris Waltner, June 22, 1989. Ibid.

9 Carla Reimer, "Three New Church Members in Maseru," The Mennonite, December 16, 1989, pp.582-83.

10 Ibid.

11 Ibid.

12 Harris Waltner, "Some Reflections on Pastoring an International Church," June 1989. 1989 Waltner file, AIMM archives.

13 Statement made during a meeting with AIC leaders in Umtata, Transkei, August 14, 1984.

14 Statement made during a 24-hour consultation with AIC leaders in Botswana at the Kanamo Catholic Retreat Center, December 27, 1986. 1986 Botswana file, AIMM archives.

15 Heisey and Longacre, "Africa Trip Report," pp.29, 27.

16 Kathy Fast fax to Paul Sensening regarding the October 24 Anniversary Celebration, November 2, 1993, p.2. 1993 Botswana file, AIMM archives.

17 Nussbaum comments in the margin of a draft manuscript.

18 Minister of Home Affairs Peter Mmusi, "Government Concerned About the Manners of Some Christians," as reported by Rudolph Majalemotho, The Daily News, October 29, 1981.

19 Overseas travel arranged for AIC leaders by Mennonites included the following: Sam and Emily Mohono to North America in 1978 representing the Moshoeshoe Berean Bible Readers Church of Lesotho; Otsile Ditseko to Selly Oak, Birmingham, England in 1989 representing the Eleven Apostles Healing Spirit Church; Israel Motswasele to North America in 1992 representing the Spiritual Healing Church; Paul and Betsie Mogomela to North America in 1995 representing the Diphapho Apostolic Church; and Isaac and Rebecca Moshoeshoe to North America in 1995 representing the African Apostolic Brethren Church.

20 Jonathan Larson, "A Sacred Surprise Party in Botswana: The African Church Ordains a Mennonite," September 19, 1994. 1994 Larson file, AIMM archives.

21 Don Rempel-Boschman letter to Carla Reimer, GC news services editor, February 8, 1994, p.2.

CHAPTER 61

1 Vern Preheim memo to COMBS/MCC meeting in Chicago, May 17-18, 1971. 1971 COMBS file, AIMM archives.

2 An interesting historical footnote: Arnold Prieb had a son named Garry who in 1994 would be installed as the Executive Secretary of AIMM.

3 Reuben Short was retiring from AIMM service and was to be replaced by Jim Bertsche in early fall.

4 Vernon Wiebe letter to Reuben Short and MCC staff member Ray Brubacher, February 18, 1974. 1974 BOMAS file, AIMM archives.

CHAPTER 62

1 Their first contact had been with MCC administrators and a water team. Then there had been the Mennonite Brethren delegation. But there was more. Within the previous year two Holdeman Church of God in Christ families had appeared on the scene and without dialogue with either the Federation or local mission/church personnel had taken up residence in Kaya, a village to the northeast of the capital and were seeking registration with the government. They also were understood to be Mennonites.

2 Statistics available in 1974 listed the population as being 68.7% animist, 27.5% Muslim and 3.8% Christian.

3 Jim Bertsche trip journal, May/June 1976, p.21ff.

4 Ibid., p.26

5 Ibid., p.43ff.

6 Report of the investigative trip of Rev. Ghymalu Kianza, Dr. Elmer Neufeld and Jim Bertsche from May 31 to June 8, 1976 in the Republic of Upper Volta drawn up and signed June 7, 1976 at Bobo Dioulasso, UV.

CHAPTER 63

1   AIMM Board Minutes, October 25, 1976, no. 25, p.13.

2   I.e., Albert and Frieda Busenitz Entz.

3   I.e., Peter and Hertha Klaassen Kampen.

4   Donna Entz, "Your Missionaries On The Way," AIMM Messenger, Fall 1977, p.7.

5   Most of the first furniture had been purchased by MCC from the two Holdeman couples who, after two years in the country, had decided that Upper Volta did not offer a promising setting for their ministry.

6   Marian Hostetler, "Glimpses of Burkina Faso," n.d., pp,2,7-8. 1988 Upper Volta file, AIMM archives.

CHAPTER 64

1   "Upper Volta Guideline Study," Spring 1977. 1977 Upper Volta file, AIMM archives.

2   Annual AIMM Board Meeting Minutes, April 29-30, 1977, pp.10-11.

3   Composed of John Sommer the GC/COM personnel secretary and AIMM secretary Jim Bertsche.

4   Statement of Agreement, August 27, 1977. 1977 CMZa file, AIMM archives.

CHAPTER 65

1   Jim Bertsche, "Some Seminar Issues Reviewed," Spring 1977, p.3. 1977 Upper Volta file, AIMM archives.

CHAPTER 66

1   Anne Garber, "My Experience in Zaire," October 1976. 1976 Garber file, AIMM archives.

2   Anne Garber letter to GC/COM personnel secretary John Sommer, April 24, 1978. 1978 Garber file, AIMM archives.

3   John Sommer memo to the GC/COM candidate committee plus Roelf Kuitse and Jim Bertsche, June 2, 1981. 1981 Garber file, AIMM archives.

4   Gail Wiebe letter to Jim Bertsche, September 11, 1981. 1981 Wiebe file, AIMM archives.

5   Wiebe letter to Jim Bertsche, November 11, 1982. 1982 Wiebe file, AIMM archives.

6   Ibid.

7   Jim Bertsche trip journal, 1983, pp.24-25.

8   Wiebe letter to Jim Bertsche, July 24, 1983. 1983 Wiebe file, AIMM archives.

9 Petersen letter to Jim Bertsche, September 11, 1981. 1981 Petersen file, AIMM archives.

10 Petersen letter to Jim Bertsche, September 22, 1981. Ibid.

11 Petersen letter to Jim Bertsche, November 12, 1981. Ibid.

12 Paul Thiessen letter to AIMM Elkhart, April 29, 1980. 1980 Thiessen file, AIMM archives.

13 "The Thiessen Tabloid," Vol.3. No.3. May 1985. 1985 Thiessen file, AIMM archives.

CHAPTER 67

1 The four local Christians were Musa, Bartholome, Paulette and Norbert. The missionaries: Loren/Donna Entz and Dennis/Jeanne Rempel.

2 Garber newsletter, January 4, 1983. 1983 Garber file, AIMM archives.

3 Ibid.

4 Garber newsletter, November 30, 1983. Ibid.

5 Ibid.

6 Among some of the West African tribal groups, there is frequently more than one chief in a village reflecting the cultural division of authority and responsibility. There typically is a chief who functions as the political head of the village; another who has jurisdiction over the allotment and use of land. There is still another who presides over the rituals of blood sacrifice at important times and occasions of village life.

7 Thiessen's quarterly report to the AIMM and EMMC, April-June, 1991. 1991 Thiessen file, AIMM archives.

8 Paul Thiessen, "Prayer Requests for Burkina Faso," January 28, 1992. 1992 Thiessen file, AIMM archives.

9 Petersen newsletter, March 11, 1985. 1985 Petersen file, AIMM archives. It was on this plot of ground that the VS work crew from Wauseon, OH, was soon to put the finishing touches to their new home. Among the Africans hired for cement work was Jibiril.

10 Ibid.

CHAPTER 68

1 Jean Ziegler, *Sankara: Un Nouveau Pouvoir Africain* (Lausanne CH 1012, Editions Pierre-Marcel Favre, 1986), p.111.

2 Ibid., p.17.

3 Ibid.

4 Ernest Horsch, "A Revolution Derailed," Africa Report, January-February 1988, p.33.

783

5   Laura Bohor editorial, "What's In A Name?" <u>Midland (MI) Daily News</u>, November 17, 1984.

6   Journalist Paulin Bamouni of the <u>*Carrefour Africain*</u> quoted in Jim Bertsche's report to the AIMM Board, March 24, 1984 in Waterloo, ON.

7   Ernest Horsch, "A Revolution Derailed," p.36.

CHAPTER 69

1   Draft of Official Statutes of the Mennonite Mission of Upper Volta, Fall of 1981. Article II 8a and 11; Article V 14. 1981 Upper Volta file, AIMM archives.

2   Letter from the General Secretary of Public Health to Dennis Rempel, August 28, 1984. 1984 Burkina Faso file, AIMM archives.

3   Dennis Rempel, "A Project of Rural Aid." 1983 Burkina Faso file, AIMM archives.

4   Burkina Faso Field Minutes, January 3, 1984, Article 12. 1984 Burkina Faso file, AIMM archives.

5   Schellenberg newsletter, June 30, 1989. 1989 Schellenberg file, AIMM archives.

6   "Bergens Delve Into Burkina Languages," <u>AIMM Messenger</u>, 1990, p.7.

7   The Mennonite Brethren Church became an associate member of AIMM in 1975 and shared in the ministry among African Independent Churches in southern Africa. The step of full membership was taken in 1993.

8   Present were AIMM board member Peter Sawatzky, AIMM secretary Jim Bertsche and EMEK representatives Raymond Eyer, Jacques Baumann and Rev. and Mrs. Eric Hege.

9   Fritz Hege, "AIMM Orodara," March-April Report, 1983. 1983 Burkina Faso file, AIMM archives.

10   Carla Reimer, "With a Spiritual People," <u>The Mennonite</u>, December 26, 1989, pp.579-580.

11   In the face of such resolute devotion to his faith, relations between Siaka and his family remained strained for several years. However he remained open and gentle toward his next of kin no matter what rebuffs he experienced. His loving manner eventually won out. Before his father's death, Siaka achieved genuine reconciliation with him and his family.

12   Loren Entz, "Burkina Update," <u>AIMM Messenger</u>, No. 1 1985, p.12.

13   Gail Wiebe, "The Beginnings of the Church in Kotoura," unpublished manuscript dated 1985, p.29. AIMM archives.

14   Loren Entz, "Burkina Update, p.13.

15   Gail Wiebe as quoted by Anne Garber in Garber newsletter, March 12, 1988. 1988 Garber file, AIMM archives.

16   Ibid.

17   Jim Bertsche trip journal, November 1986, p.4.

CHAPTER 70

1   Dan Petersen, "Twelve Steps to a Rough Draft!?" AIMM Messenger, 1993, p.11.

2   With the growth of the AIMM missionary team, the policy soon shifted to personal transportation. Single people frequently found motorbikes to be adequate for their needs whereas couples with children needed vehicles.

3   Judy Harder, "Orodara Kalanso: A New School for Missionary Kids," AIMM Messenger, No. 2, Fall 1989, pp.6,7,10.

4   Gordon Klassen, "Time to Celebrate," AIMM Messenger, 1993, p.3.

5   David Stoez, "Missionary Children Taught by a Burkinabe," AIMM Messenger, 1994, p.10.

6   Judy Harder, "Orodara Kalanso," p.10.

7   They were: Dennis Rempel, president; Siaka Traore, vice president; Donna Entz, secretary, and Loren Entz, treasurer.

8   They were: Dennis Rempel, president; Siaka Traore, vice president; Anne Garber, secretary; Loren Entz, treasurer and members Drabo Philippe and Dan Petersen.

9   "Bylaws of the Mennonite Mission of Upper Volta," Article 9: Affiliation, p.5. 1984 Burkina Faso file, AIMM archives.

10 Minutes of Mission Strategy Planning Meeting/AIMM Burkina Faso, November 17-18, 1987. 1987 BF file, AIMM archives.

11 Dan Petersen, "A Statement of Mission and Church Autonomy Under Christ: A Pattern of Mutuality and Equality," n.d., p.1. 1987 Petersen file, AIMM archives.

12 Mathew Swora, "Mission and Mission/Church Relationships," September 1, 1989, p.9. 1989 Swora file, AIMM archives.

13 The participants were: Orodara: Juhana Drabo, Paul Ouadreogo, Abdias Coulibaly; Kotoura: Cheba Traore; Banzon: Philippe Drabo; Djiguera: Philippe Coulibaly; missionaries: Loren/Donna Entz, Anne Garber, Judy Harder, Elmer/Jeannette Thiessen, Mathew/Rebecca Swora, Paul/Lois Thiessen; AIMM: Earl Roth, executive secretary and Lawrence Giesbrecht, AIMM board member.

14 Comments gleaned from a Burkina Faso trip report by Lawrence Giesbrecht, May 18-25, 1988. 1988 delegation file, AIMM archives.

15 Ibid.

CHAPTER 71

1   Siaka letter to Earl Roth, November 24, 1988. 1988 Siaka file, AIMM archives.

2   Contacts made were with the EMMC Convention in Morden, MB; the EMC/C Convention in Regina, SK; the FEBC Convention in Dallas, OR; two weeks with Dennis/Jeanne Rempel in California and travel to Normal, IL.

3 Siaka Traore, *"La Mission: un Défi aux Eglises Africaines,"* a thesis submitted for the degree of *Maîtrise en Théologie* in July, 1990, pp.x and xi. AIMM archives.

4 Ibid., p.28.

5 Ibid., p.65.

6 Ibid., p.66.

7 Ibid., p.87.

8 Ibid., p.99.

9 Ibid., p.104.

10 Dennis and Jean Rempel, "The Go-Between," <u>AIMM Messenger</u>, Fall 1984, p.12.

11 Jim Bertsche trip journal, 1984 II, p.201.

12 Paul Thiessen, "Prayer Requests From BF," March 5, 1993. 1993 Thiessen file, AIMM archives.

13 Paul Thiessen, "Prayer Requests from BF," October 20, 1993. Ibid.

CHAPTER 72

1 Jim Bertsche, "A Summary of the Recent Border Conflict Between Burkina Faso and Mali," January 6, 1986. 1986 executive secretary file, AIMM archives.

2 Composed of board member Elmer Neufeld, AIMM Secretary Jim Bertsche and Associate Secretary Art Janz.

3 Jim Bertsche, "Abou Kabar." Part of a written report to the AIMM Board, January 1985. 1985 executive secretary file, AIMM archives.

4 Loren Entz, "Journal of Events," November 19, 1984. 1984 Entz file, AIMM archives.

5 Jim Bertsche report to AIMM board, Ibid.

6 Loren Entz translation of Abou's testimony as recorded on cassette tape.

7 Loren Entz, "Update on Traore Abou," January 20, 1985, p.2. 1985 Entz file, AIMM archives.

8 Ibid.

9 Entz/Garber newsletter compiled jointly, November 4, 1994. 1994 Entz/Garber files, AIMM archives.

10 Gail Wiebe, "The Beginning of the Church in Kotoura," 1985, p.14. AIMM archives.

11 Anne Garber Kompaore newsletter, December 28, 1994. 1994 Kompaore file, AIMM archives.

12 Anne Garber Kompaore, "I Want To Pass It On," <u>AIMM Messenger</u>, 1994, p.6.

13 Kompaore, <u>The COMmunicator</u>, No. 125, June 1995. 1995 COM file, AIMM archives.

14 Kompaore, <u>AIMM To Inform</u>, July-September 1994, p.2. AIMM archives.

CHAPTER 73

1 Kompaore, <u>The COMmunicator</u>, No. 125, June 1995. AIMM archives.

2 Petersen newsletter, October, 1994. 1994 Petersen file, AIMM archives.

3 Bev and Gerald Neufeld, <u>AIMM to Inform</u>, April-June, 1995, p.3. AIMM archives.

4 Entz newsletter, March 27, 1995, p.2. 1995 Entz file, AIMM archives.

5 The seven language groups as identified and listed by AIMM missionaries were: Siamou, Northern Toussian, Northern Senoufo, Samogho, Southern Senoufo, Bolon and Sembla.

6 Entz newsletter, March 27, 1995.

7 Anne Garber Kompaore, "I Want To Pass It On," p.5.

8 Siaka letter to Leona Schrag, AIMM office, October 10, 1993. Siaka 1993 file, AIMM archives.

9 "A Program of Work of the EMMBF in Collaboration with the Mission AIMM in BF in the Years 1994-1995," December 11, 1993. 1993 BF file, AIMM archives.

10 Gerald Neufeld, "Pastors Ordained by the Evangelical Mennonite Church of Burkina Faso." 1994 Neufeld file, AIMM archives. Issued as an AIMM news release.

11 Jeannette and Elmer Thiessen newsletter in <u>AIMM to Inform</u>, April-June 1995, p.3. 1995 Thiessen file, AIMM archives.

12 After two attempts, the church leadership decided to put the twice-aborted celebrations on hold until some later date.

13 Harry Hyde, "Burkina Faso: Recommendations," September 15, 1988. 1988 BF file, AIMM archives.

14 A committee comprised of Elmer Thiessen, Loren Entz and Paul Thiessen.

15 BF Administrative Committee Minutes, March 15, 1994. 1994 BF file, AIMM archives.

16 BF Administrative Committee Minutes, March 23-24, 1994. Ibid. In these sessions Gerald Neufeld joined the three men who had met eight days earlier.

17 Donna Kampen Entz, "Faithful As A Family," <u>AIMM Messenger</u>, Winter 1986, pp.8-9.

18 Excerpts from Jim Bertsche trip journal, 1986, <u>AIMM Messenger</u>, Fall 1986, pp.5-6.

CHAPTER 74

1   The UTM was brought into being by Alma Doering just three years after her resignation from the CIM in late 1925. The Miller sisters, of Mennonite Brethren in Christ background, were among the earliest missionaries recruited and sent to staff a new mission venture in a large area to the southwest of CIM territory which was without an evangelical witness.

2   For this pioneering effort, Mary eventually received a special citation from the Belgian colonial government.

3   It was not at all uncommon for three single ladies to share a single dwelling on a bush mission post.

4   Ruth Goring Stewart quoted by Sarah Burkholder in "Support Needs of Bi-cultural Single Anabaptist Women," an article published in Mission Focus, March 1991, Vol.19, no.1 and submitted by Erica Thiessen for inclusion in the AIMM Board Handbook for its April 7-9, 1994 meeting in Des Plaines, IL.

5   Lois Slagle, "On Behalf of Singles," AIMM Messenger, Winter 1983, pp 6-7.

6   Jenny Bertsche's garden at Mukedi Station in the mid-1950's.

7   In the early pioneering days of CIM before there was any possibility of providing schooling, the parents had no choice but to leave their small children at home in North America. Later, CIM parents were able to enroll their children in a boarding school operated by the Southern Presbyterian Mission at their post Lubondai, a long drive to the southeast of CIM territory. Still later the CIM and AMBM opened a joint boarding school at the MB post of Kajiji far to the south of the Kwilu Province. Eventually AIMM built its own hostel in Kinshasa, a ten-minute drive from the American School of that city.

8   In the unfolding history of the CIM/AIMM, the time came when some missionary couples found themselves placed in urban centers with educational opportunities for their children close by. But with the launching of a new pioneering venture in Burkina Faso, missionary families there found themselves confronting many of the same circumstances and decisions that their predecessors of an earlier era did in Congo/Zaire.

9   In our home to this day, a favorite dish at a family gathering is a pot of chicken cooked in peppery palm oil served with a ball of slightly sour cornmeal/cassava flour mush.

10   Christy Harder, "African Living, Loneliness Enriched Me," AIMM Messenger, Spring 1989, p.4.

11   Faith Eidse Kuhns, "I Was a Grieving Third-Culture Kid," AIMM Messenger, Spring 1989, p.6.

12   Katharine Enns in response to a questionnaire, October 1997. Jim Bertsche files.

13   Nancy Graber Roth in response to a questionnaire, October 1997. Jim Bertsche files.

14   Delbert Dick in response to a questionnaire, October 1997. Jim Bertsche files.

15   Christy Harder, "African Living," p. 4.

16   Tim Bertsche in response to a questionnaire, October, 1997. Jim Bertsche files.

17   Nancy Graber Roth, response to a questionnaire.

18 Ibid.

19 Delbert Dick, response to a questionnaire.

20 Tim Bertsche, response to a questionnaire.

21 Sandra Bertsche King in response to a questionnaire, October 1997. Jim Bertsche files.

22 Faith Eidse Kuhns, response to a questionnaire.

23 Sandra Bertsche King, response to a questionnaire.

24 Tim Bertsche, response to a questionnaire.

25 Christy Harder, "Africa Living," p. 4.

26 Tim Bertsche, response to a questionnaire.

27 Fimbo Ganvunze was elected CMZa President at the Church's General Assembly held at Kikwit April 27 - May 01, 1995. The transition with outgoing President Chibulenu was smooth and cordial. Elected with President Fimbo were Vice President Shamuimba Mbombo and General Secretary Mackunya Shalukombo.

28 Fimbo Ganvunze, "Great Lakes Project," Addendum to a fax from Leona Schrag to Carla Reimer October 1, 1996. AIMM archives.

29 Krista Rigalo, "Mennonite Church in Eastern Congo Baptizes Ten New Members" in a joint news release of AIMM, MCC and MBM/S, October 13, 1997. AIMM archives.

30 Theron F. Schlabach, Gospel Versus Gospel: Mission and the Mennonite Church, 1863-1944 (Scottdale: Herald Press, 1980) p.181. While Schlabach's research was on the history of Mennonite Board of Missions, his critique is viewed by some as relevant to Mennonite missions in general.

31 Stephen F. Dintaman, "The Spiritual Poverty of the Anabaptist Vision," Gospel Herald, February 23, 1993, p.1.

32 Ibid., pp.2-3.

33 Eric A. Kouns, Evangelical Anabaptist Newsletter, Vol.2, No.3, Summer 1995, p.2.

34 Carl Kreider, "Viewpoint," Mennonite Weekly Review, August 3, 1995.

35 Eric A. Kouns, Evangelical Anabaptist Newsletter, Vol.3, No.3. Summer 1996, p.3.

36 Don Jacobs, Pilgrimage in Missions (Scottdale: Herald Press, 1983), p.133.

37 Hildegard Goss-Mayr from the Republic of South Africa.

38 Larry Hills letter to the AIMM Executive Secretary, January 5, 1984. 1984 Hills file, AIMM archives.

39 Jim Bertsche, AIMM archives.

40 Jim Bertsche letter to John Lapp, July 26, 1988. Bertsche personal files.

41 Paul Gingrich, MWC News Release, Limuru, Kenya, October 28, 1994. AIMM files.

42 Keith B. Richburg, "The Same Old Excuses," U.S. News and World Report, February 3, 1997. pp.36-38.

43 Mobutu meanwhile, a dying man, was helped onto a plane by his aides and sought refuge in Morocco where his cancer shortly took its ultimate toll on September 7, 1997. He died surrounded by the opulence of his own villa in that country. He was buried, a pariah in the international community, in a cemetery outside the capital city of Rabat.

44 Gwynne Dyer, "Africa Turning The Corner," The Fort Wayne Journal Gazette, March 30, 1997, 3C.

45 Tokunboh Adeyemo, "Africa By The Year AD 2000," Afroscope, September/October 1991, pp.9-11.

46 Myron Augsburger in a presentation made at the MC General Assembly at "Wichita '95," Mennonite Weekly Review, August 3, 1995, p.11.

47 Hector Valencia, a Colombian national, served as the Secretary for Latin America with the GC/COM in the decade of the 1970s. The MBM/S has named a Congolese, Tshimika Pakisa, as their official representative to their Congo Church. Stanley Greene from South Africa currently serves as the President of MBM.

48 Stan Nussbaum, "Paradigm Shifts in AIMM Relations with AICs in the Next Decade," a paper presented at an AIMM/AIC consultation at Kuruman, South Africa, May 9-12, 1997, p.4.

49 Myron Augsburger, The Mennonite, February 25, 1997, p.10.

50 Charles Buller, the son of long-time AIMM missionaries Peter and Gladys Buller, is the lead elder of this church group and was one of a delegation of four people who traveled with AIMM Executive Secretary Garry Prieb on an investigative trip to that country in November 1997.

51 Ron Yoder, in a statement made at the annual meeting of the Council of International Ministries, January 14-17, 1996 at Techny, IL.

52 Calvin E. Shank, A Relevant Anabaptist Missiology in the 1990s (Elkhart, IN: Council of International Minstries, 1990), pp.75-81.

53 In the "Mennonite and Brethren in Christ World Directory, 1994," the following membership figures are found: US 298,781; Zaire 136,200; Canada 117,932; India 84,195; Indonesia 60,709; Ethiopia 50,018. The Zaire figure is broken down as follows: Mennonite Brethren (CEFMZ) 53,700; Evangelical Mennonite (CEM) 21,000; Mennonite Church of Zaire (CMZa) 61,500. To these figures are yet added those of the newly-formed Mennonite Church of Burkina Faso which, in 1994, counted 63 members.

54 Jim Bertsche, "The AIMM Perspective on the Advantages and Strengths of a Partnership Approach to Mennonite Mission in Africa," May 1985. AIMM archives.

55 Jack Suderman, Overseas Prayergram, GC/COM, Jan/Feb 1995, Newton, KS.

56 GC/COM staff responses to the question: "What is your perception of the constituency attitude toward missions?" COMmunicator, No.108, Nov 1993.

GLOSSARY OF ACRONYMS

ABAKO	French acronym for The Association for the Protection of the Culture and Interests of the Bakongo
AC	Administrative Committee (CMZa)
AEAM	The Evangelical Alliance of Africa and Madagascar
AEMSK	French acronym for The Association of Mennonite Churches of the South Kasai, later known as CEM
AFCC	Africa Federal Church Council (Lesotho: one grouping of AICs)
AFDC	French acronym for The Alliance of Democratic Forces for the Liberation of Congo led by Kabila Laurent
AICs	African Independent Churches
AIM	Africa Inland Mission
AIMM	Africa Inter-Mennonite Mission earlier known as CIM
AIMM-BF	Africa Inter-Mennonite Mission/Burkina Faso
AMBCF	Africa Mennonite and Brethren in Christ Fellowship
AMBM	American Mennonite Brethren Mission
AMBS	Associated Mennonite Biblical Seminary, earlier Associated Mennonite Biblical Seminaries
ANC	African National Congress
ANC	French acronym for Congolese National Army, later known as ANZ
ANTBA	French acronym for The National Association for the Translation and Alphabetization of the Bible of Burkina Faso
ANZ	French acronym for the Zairian National Army, earlier known as the ANC
APCM	American Presbyterian Congo Mission
BCC	Botswana Christian Council
BCP	Basutoland Congress Party
BCP	Black Community Programs
BIC	Brethren in Christ
BNP	Basutoland National Party

BOMAS	Mennonite Brethren Board of Missions and Services, later known as MBM/S and MBMS International
BSCC	Botswana Spiritual Christian Churches (one grouping of AICs)
CAP	French acronym for an Inter-Protestant Guest Center in Kinshasa originally known as UMH
CCL	Christian Council of Lesotho (mainline churches)
CEDI	French acronym for an Inter-Protestant Press and Literature Distribution Center in Kinshasa, earlier known as LECO
CEFMC	French acronym for the Mennonite Brethren Church of Congo, earlier known as CEFMZ
CEFMZ	French acronym for the Mennonite Brethren Church of Congo, later known as CEFMC
CEM	French acronym for the Evangelical Mennonite Church of Zaire\Congo, earlier known as AEMSK
CENERM	Center for Study of Renewal Movements Among Primal Societies, later known as INTERACT based at Selly Oak Colleges in Birmingham, England
CERPROKA	French acronym for the Protestant Radio Center of the Kasai, later known as STUDIPROKA
CEPZA	French acronym for the short-lived Council of Protestant Churches of Zaire
CIM	Congo Inland Mission, later known as AIMM.
CIM	Council of International Ministries, earlier known as COMBS
CK	French acronym for a commercial enterprise known as the Company of the Kasai
C&MA	Christian and Missionary Alliance
CMBC	Canadian Mennonite Bible College
CMCo	French acronym for the Mennonite Church of Congo, earlier known as EMC and CMZa
CMZa	French acronym for the Mennonite Church of Zaire, earlier known as EMC and later as CMCo
COMAS	French acronym for The Congo Mennonite Agricultural Services, later known as SEDA
COMBS	Council of Mennonite Board Secretaries, later known as CIM
CONIM	French acronym for the National Inter-Mennonite Committee of Zaire and later of Congo
COZMANAC	French acronym for the Congo Council of the Anabaptist/Mennonite Mission for Central Africa
CPC	The Congo Protestant Council, later known as the ECZ
CPRA	Congo Protestant Relief Agency, later known as ZPRA

DMC	Defenseless Mennonite Church, later known as EMC/US
DRC	Democratic Republic of the Congo
DRC	Dutch Reformed Church also known by Dutch acronym NGK
EAP	French acronym for a two year teacher training school
EC	Executive Committee (CMZa)
ECC	French acronym for the Church of Christ of Congo, earlier known as the ECZ
ECZ	French acronym for The Church of Christ of Zaire, an outgrowth of an earlier Congo Protestant Council and later known as ECC
EE	French acronym for a two year Bible School
EEMBF	French acronym for the Mennonite Church of Burkina Faso
EFMA	Evangelical Fellowship of Mission Agencies
EMB	Evangelical Mennonite Brethren, later known as the FEBC
EMBMC	Eastern Mennonite Board of Mission and Charities, later known as EMM
EMC	French acronym for The Mennonite Church of Congo, later known as CMZa and CMCo
EMC/C	The Evangelical Mennonite Conference of Canada, earlier known as the *Kleine Gemeinde*
EMC/US	The Evangelical Mennonite Church of the US, earlier known as the DMC
EMEK	German acronym for a European Inter-Mennonite Mission Board (*Europaeische Mennonitische Evangelisation Komitee*), later restructured under the name EMMK (*Europaeische Mennonitische Missions-Konferenz*)
EMM	Eastern Mennonite Missions, earlier known as EMBMC
EMMC	Evangelical Mennonite Missions Conference
ETE	French acronym for Theological Education by Extension, also known by its English acronym, TEE
ETEK	French acronym for The Evangelical Theological School of Kinshasa, later known as ISTK and UCKin
FATEB	French acronym for the Evangelical Theology School of Bangui in the Central African Republic
FEBC	Fellowship of Evangelical Bible Churches, earlier known as EMB
FEM	French acronym for a Mennonite Student Association in the Congo
FEME	French acronym for the Federation of Evangelical Missions and Churches in Burkina Faso

FNLA	Portuguese acronym for the National Front for the Liberation of Angola
FTK	French acronym for the Theological Faculty of Kinshasa
GAM	French acronym for a Mennonite Business Men's Group in Congo
GC	General Conference Mennonite Church
GC/COM	GC Commission on Overseas Mission
IB	French acronym for the Mennonite Bible Institute at Kalonda in the Congo
ICE	The International Center for Evangelism launched in Kinshasa, Congo by C&MA missionaries Willys and Thelma Braun
IMC	The International Missionary Council
IMCK	French acronym for the Christian Medical Institute of the Kasai in Congo
IME	French acronym for the Evangelical Medical Institute at Kimpese in Congo
IMF	The International Monetary Fund
INTERACT	An AIC research center based at Selly Oak Colleges in Birmingham England, earlier known as CENERM
ISTK	French acronym for the inter-Protestant Superior Institute of Theology of Kinshasa, earlier known as ETEK and later as UCKin
JMPR	French acronym for The Youth of the Popular Movement of the Revolution (MPR), a youth organization of the former Mobutu regime in Congo/Zaire
LEC	Lesotho Evangelical Church
LECO	French acronym for the inter-Protestant Press and Distribution Center of Kinshasa, later known as CEDI
LIMZA	French acronym for the Mennonite Book Store and distribution center at Tshikapa, Congo
LIPROKA	French acronym for the Mennonite/Presbyterian book store and literature distribution center in Kananga
MAF	Mission Aviation Fellowship
MB	Mennonite Brethren Church of North America
MBM	Mennonite Board of Missions
MBM/S	Mennonite Brethren Board of Missions and Services, earlier known as BOMAS and later as MBMS International
MBMS Intl	Mennonite Brethren Board of Missions and Services, earlier known as BOMAS and MBM/S

MCA	Missionary Church Association
MCC	Mennonite Central Committee
MEDA	Mennonite Economic Development Association
MIBA	French acronym for the diamond mining consortium based at Mbuji Mayi, Congo
MM	Mennonite Ministries in Botswana and later in Lesotho
MNC	French acronym for The National Movement of the Congo, political movement of the early 1960's led by Patrice Lumumba in the Belgian Congo
MPLA	Portuguese acronym for the National Front for the Liberation of Angola
MPR	French acronym for the Popular Revolutionary Movement launched by Mobutu in the Congo
MTC	Mission Training Center based at AMBS, earlier known as OMTC
MUC	Maseru United Church in Lesotho
MWC	Mennonite World Conference
NGK	Dutch acronym for The Dutch Reformed Church, also known by English acronym DRC
NLC	National Liberation Committee
NUL	National University of Lesotho
OAIC	The Organization of African Independent Churches
OAIC/SR	The Organization of African Independent Churches, southern region
OK	Orodara *Kalanso*, AIMM school for missionary children in Burkina Faso
OMSC	Overseas Ministries Study Center
OMTC	Overseas Mission Training Center based at AMBS, later known as MTC
OPEC	Organization of Petroleum Exporting Countries
PAX	Latin term meaning "peace" used as the MCC program logo under which many young men volunteered for alternate service overseas in lieu of military service
PEMS	Paris Evangelical Missionary Society
RSA	Republic of South Africa
RURCON	Rural Development Consultancy for Christian Churches in Africa
SACC	South Africa Council of Churches
SACG	Southern Africa Coordinating Group

SADF	South African Defense Force
SANRU	French acronym for a USAID funded public health program in Congo/Zaire
SASO	South African Students Organization
SATF	Southern Africa Task Force, a sub-committee of COMBS
SEDA	French acronym for The Agricultural Development Service based at Nyanga in Congo/Zaire earlier known as COMAS
SHC	The Spiritual Healing Church based in Botswana
SIL	Summer Institute of Linguistics, the overseas arm of Wycliffe Bible Translators known by the acronym WBT
SPD	French acronym for a Special Presidential Division of Paracommandos organized by President Mobutu for his personal protection
STUDIPROKA	French acronym for the Mennonite/Presbyterian sponsored Protestant Studio of the Kasai earlier known as CERPROKA
TAP	The MCC sponsored Teachers Abroad Program via which many young people found their way into overseas school rooms
TASOK	The American School of Kinshasa
TEE	Theological Education by Extension, also known by its French acronym ETE
TCC	Transkei Council of Churches
TTC	A Teacher Training College in Botswana
UB	University of Botswana
UCKin	French acronym for The Christian University of Kinshasa, earlier known as ETEK and ISTK
UDPS	French acronym for The Union for Democracy and Social Progress, a political movement in Zaire/Congo led by Tshisekedi Etienne
UMH	Union Mission House, an inter-Protestant guest house in Kinshasa later known as CAP
UN	United Nations
UNITA	Portuguese acronym for The National Union for the Total Independence of Angola led by Jonas Savimbi
USAID	The United States Agency for International Development
UTM	Unevangelized Tribes Mission
WBT	Wycliffe Bible Translators, known overseas by the acronym SIL

WCC	World Council of Churches
WHO	World Health Organization
WMC	World Mennonite Conference
WRC	World Relief Commission
WWII	World War II
ZPRA	Zaire Protestant Relief Agency, known both earlier and later as CPRA

CHRONOLOGY OF DATES AND EVENTS

1482   First Portuguese sailors enter Congo River estuary.

1488   First Portuguese sailors round the southern cape of the African continent.

1652   The Dutch establish a supply post at the Cape for the Dutch East Indies Company.

1795   The Cape is occupied by British forces.

1824   King Moshoeshoe I establishes a kingdom of Sotho speaking people.

1833   The first missionaries of the Paris Evangelical Missionary Society arrive Moshoeshoe's kingdom.

1835-38   The Great Dutch Trek inland from the Cape is undertaken.

1838   (December 16) The Battle of Blood River.

1867   The discovery of the Kimberly diamond deposits.

1873   (May 1) David Livingstone dies in the isolation of the African interior at Chitambo village in present day northern Zambia.

1878   H. Morton Stanley leads expedition up the Congo River in the name of King Leopold II of Belgium.

1878   Arrival of the first Protestant missionaries in the Congo.

1885   Berlin Conference held; various European countries agree on division of African continent for purposes of colonization.

1885   Creation of the Congo Free State under the control of King Leopold II.

1886   Discovery of Witwatersrand gold reefs.

1896   Arrival of first Mennonite missionary in the Congo.

1898   Arrival of first BIC missionary party at Capetown to open a mission endeavor somewhere in southern Africa.

1899-1902 The Boer War

1902   The first inter-Protestant consultation in Congo.

1908   The Belgian government assumes control of the Congo Free State and renames it the Belgian Congo.

1911   (March 22) The United Mennonite Board of Missions created by the Stucky Amish and Egly Amish.

1912   (January 23) The new inter-Mennonite Mission Board renamed the Congo Inland Mission.

1912	The first CIM missionaries (Lawrence/Rose Haigh and Alvin Stevenson) arrive in the Congo. The first two mission posts established along the Kasai River at Djoko Punda and Kalamba.
1913	Alvin Stevenson dies and is buried at Djoko Punda.
1914	Alma Doering recruits CIM missionaries in Europe.
1915	Lawrence Haigh baptizes first two Christians at Djoko Punda.
1917	Rev. and Mrs. Emil Sommer aboard boat torpedoed by German sub. Are taken to Capetown, South Africa and eventually make their way north to the Congo.
1917	Twelve Christians, including three women, baptized at Djoko Punda.
1921	Nyanga Station founded among the Baphende people between the Kasai and Loange Rivers.
1923	Mukedi Station founded among the Baphende people to the west of the Loange River.
1924	Seventeen CIM missionaries meet for a conference at Kalamba Station.
1925	Ratification of the constitution of the Congo Protestant Council.
1925	The CIM Board resists pressure of Alma Doering and some of her fellow missionaries; votes to remain a Mennonite organization.
1926	Alma Doering resigns and founds the Unevangelized Tribes Mission (UTM).
1928	The Congo Protestant Council establishes its first permanent office in Leopoldville, Congo's capital.
1928	A. M. Eash becomes first CIM board member to visit the Congo.
1929	U.S. stock market crash triggers era of financial stress for CIM; sacrificial budgetary measures taken in U.S. and Congo to assure survival of CIM.
1929	(August) CIM starts publishing a monthly magazine entitled The Congo Missionary Messenger.
1934	Eastern Mennonite Board of Missions places first missionaries in Tanganyika, East Africa (now Tanzania).
1935	Agnes Sprunger's translation of the Giphende New Testament published by the British and Foreign Bible Society.
1935	CIM Women's Auxiliary created to encourage and coordinate sewing projects for the work in Congo among the constituent churches in North America.
1936	Christian E. Rediger appointed CIM corresponding secretary/treasurer.
1938	CIM published Twenty Five Years of Mission Work in the Belgian Congo by Harry Bertsche and William B. Weaver.
1938	The Evangelical Mennonite Brethren Church officially becomes a participating CIM partner.

1940	Onset of World War II disrupts CIM efforts. Dr. Merle and Dorothy Schwartz's boat, the *Zam Zam*, torpedoed by a German sub. They are eventually repatriated to the U.S. Roy/Bessie Yoder and Fanny Schmallenberger's boat is captured; they also are repatriated.
1941	CIM celebrates its 30th anniversary. Congo church membership reaches 5,000.
1942	First Congo Church pastors' manual adopted and printed.
1943	The General Conference Mennonite Church officially becomes a participating CIM partner. (The original Central Conference soon becomes part of the G.C. Central District.)
1946	CIM relocates Kalamba Station and names it Mutena.
1946	CIM Board requires French study in Belgium particularly for candidates looking toward medical and educational services in Congo.
1947	CIM adopts a death benefit and retirement plan for its missionaries.
1948	CIM decides to accept subsidies from the Congo Colonial Government for its educational and medical ministries; major expansion of both services ensues.
1949	CIM office moved to Mennonite Biblical Seminary building on the south side of Chicago.
1949	Three two-year training schools, called EAP's, started in Congo.
1950	Congo Colonial government lays out an extensive "Ten Year Plan" for the Congo.
1950	CIM starts new stations at Banga, among the Bashilele people, and at Tshikapa, the government post and administrative center of the *Forminière* Diamond Mining Company.
1951	Harvey A. Driver appointed to replace C.E. Rediger as corresponding secretary/treasurer.
1952	Harvey Driver travels to Congo with Orie O. Miller and Dr. C. B. Bowman who makes a film for CIM publicity purposes.
1953	Kamayala Station and resident missionaries acquired by CIM from the UTM.
1953	CIM opens a Bible Institute at Kalonda and enrolls its first pastoral students.
1954	Raymond and Susy Eyer become the first French Mennonites to serve in Africa (under the Sudan United Mission).
1954	Kandala Station is acquired from Canadian Baptist missionaries Percival and Rosalind Near.
1954	CIM's first vocational training school is opened at Mutena Station.
1954	Dr. Milo Rediger appointed CIM Board Chairman and travels to Africa.
1954	CIM approved as an organization for placement of young men with 1-W draft board classification for alternative service.
1956	New Bible Institute building dedicated at Kalonda.

1957	Mennonite Board of Missions places four missionaries in Ghana, West Africa.
1957	CIM headquarters moved from Chicago to Elkhart, IN.
1957	Pastor Kazadi Matthew becomes the first Congo Church leader to make a fraternal visit to North America.
1959	The last all-CIM missionary conference held in Congo.
1959	Rioting erupts in Leopoldville.
1960	Major CIM Board delegation meets with Congo Church leaders to discuss the future of their church. Africans adopt their first formal name: The Evangelical Mennonite Church of Congo (EMC). Groundwork for integration of mission and church is laid.
1960	(February) The last pre-independence meeting of the Congo Protestant Council.
1960	(June 30) Congo receives its political independence.
1960	(July 10) CIM missionaries begin evacuation from Congo as Congolese troops mutiny against their Belgian officers.
1960	(July 11) Moise Tshombe declares independence of Katanga Province from Congo's central government.
1960	(August) Upper Volta is granted its independence by France.
1960	(August) Tribal conflict flares along the Kasai River in Congo sparking massive flight of Baluba refugees toward the South Kasai.
1960	First post-independence church conference at Nyanga.
1960	Orie Miller establishes a cooperative MCC/Congo Protestant Council organization named the Congo Protestant Relief Agency (CPRA).
1960	(September) Three missionary men return to Congo alone to reestablish contact with the Congo Church and its leaders.
1960	(October) Archie Graber recruited by CIM/MCC to direct an emergency relief effort among thousands of Baluba refugees in the South Kasai.
1961	(April) Harvey Driver resigns as CIM Secretary; Vernon S. Sprunger appointed interim Secretary.
1961	(April) Africa Mennonite and Brethren in Christ Fellowship (AMBCF) is founded at Limuru, Kenya.
1961	(July) Three Congolese couples chosen to go to North America for college educations.
1961	Missionary Aviation Fellowship (MAF) begins occasional flights into Mennonite territory in Congo.
1962	(March) Archie Graber assesses crisis situation in a UN refugee camp in Elizabethville in Katanga Province, Congo.

1962	CIM negotiates with the *Forminière* Diamond Company for the leasing of a large hospital complex plus some housing and office space at Tshikapa at very nominal cost.
1962	(August) The last trainload of Baluba refugees is evacuated from the UN camp in Elizabethville under Archie Graber's supervision.
1963	Reuben Short is appointed CIM Executive Secretary.
1963	MCC TAP program is initiated in Congo.
1963	The Free University is opened in Stanleyville, Congo, with CIM missionary Melvin Loewen as its first academic dean.
1963	CIM Bible Institute moved from Kalonda to Kandala because of the tribal conflict in the West Kasai.
1963	A joint CIM/MB pastoral training school is opened at the MB Station Kajiji near the Angolan border.
1964	(January) The *Jeunesse* Rebellion explodes in the east of Kwilu Province in Congo; Kandala missionaries evacuated by UN; Mukedi missionaries by MAF.
1964	*Studiproka* establishes and airs first religious programming in the Tshiluba language over government radio stations of West and South Kasais.
1964	(September) The *Simba* Rebellion erupts in eastern Congo. Paxmen Gene Bergman/Jon Snyder, Mel/Elfrieda Loewen and children are trapped in Stanleyville; eventually evacuated by Belgian paratroopers.
1964	(November) EMC is officially recognized as a church by the Congo government.
1965	The Congo Mennonite Agricultural Service (COMAS) is founded at Nyanga.
1965	The relief program in the South Kasai is officially closed.
1965	CIM buys a Cessna 185, leases it to MAF and contracts for location of plane and pilot in the EMC/CIM area (initially at Tshikapa, then Nyanga).
1965	(November) Joseph Mobutu takes power in the Congo with backing of the army.
1966	(July) The Evangelical Mennonite Church of the South Kasai (AEMSK) recognized by the Congo government.
1966	CIM Board works out a mission/church integration plan with Congo church leaders.
1967	(March) A new inter-mission theological training school founded in Congo and temporarily located at the Baptist Station Kimpese.
1967	(May) Mobutu convenes a political consultation at N'Sele and the Popular Movement of the Revolution (MPR) is launched.
1967	CIM leases land in Kinshasa for construction of a hostel for missionary children.

1967	Pastor Ngongo David and Tshilembu Nicodème make a fraternal visit to North America and represent EMC at the World Mennonite Conference at Amsterdam.
1968	Rev. Jean Bokeleale is elected General Secretary of the Church of Christ of the Congo (ECC).
1968	The first TAP teachers arrive in Botswana, Southern Africa.
1969	The new inter-mission theological training school at Kinshasa enrolls its first students on its new campus and is named the Evangelical School of Theology of Kinshasa (ETEK).
1969	Under pressure CIM cedes the Tshikapa Hospital and some other buildings to the local government.
1969	CIM/EMC join the Presbyterian Mission/Church in the creation of a new hospital and training center at Tshikaji just outside Luluabourg. It is named *Institut Médical Chrétien du Kasai* (IMCK). Dr. John and Jeanne Zook become first CIM personnel assigned there.
1970	(1970) ETEK is officially dedicated.
1970	(April) Don Jacobs and Jim Bertsche investigative trip to southern Africa.
1970	The Congo Protestant Council is transformed into the Church of Christ of Congo (ECC).
1970	The AEMSK is accepted into full ECC membership.
1970	Sweeping name changes are introduced in the Congo including the name Zaire for the country itself. Thus the EMC becomes the CMZa, i.e., Mennonite Community of Zaire, and the AEMSK became the CEM, i.e., the Evangelical Mennonite Community.
1971	(January) A Mission/Church fusion agreement is signed with Zairian Church leaders at Djoko Punda.
1971	CMZa ordains CIM missionary Don Unruh.
1971	CMZa elects Rev. Kabangy Moise as its new General Secretary.
1971	Kabangy Moise, Kamba Jean and Mapoko George make a fraternal visit to North America.
1972	(January) A consultation at Lake Munkamba in the South Kasai witnesses a large degree of reconciliation between CEM and CMZa.
1972	An inter-Mennonite consultation at Maseru, Lesotho, regarding possible Mennonite ministry in southern Africa.
1972	(March) The name of the Congo Inland Mission is changed to Africa Inter-Mennonite Mission.
1972	CMZa launches a girls school at Nyanga which eventually is known as *Lycée Miodi*.
1972	Kakesa Samuel and Kafutshi Françoise make a fraternal visit to North America and represent their Church (CMZa) at the World Mennonite Conference at Curitiba, Brazil.
1972	(November) The first phase of the Inga Shaba Hydro Project is inaugurated in Zaire.

1973	AIMM places first missionaries in southern Africa: Allen and Marabeth Busenitz in Lesotho.
1974	(June) Remaining differences between CMZa and CEM reach final resolution.
1974	Zairian government takes over all schools of Protestant and Catholic mission/church groups.
1974	(September) Jim Bertsche follows Reuben Short as AIMM Executive Secretary.
1975	Mobutu at high water mark of his power and popularity.
1975	AIMM places first missionaries in Botswana: Ed and Irene Weaver.
1975	Mennonite Brethren Church becomes an associate member of AIMM.
1975	Egyptian Coptic Church sponsors first pan-African meeting of AIC leaders at Cairo.
1975	First AIMM delegation travels to Upper Volta.
1976	The Transkei declared to be a "black homeland" by the South African government.
1977	(March) Ex-Katangese troops invade Shaba Province from bases in Angola.
1977	Zaire Government returns schools to mission/church groups in total disarray.
1978	AIMM places first missionaries in Upper Volta: Loren/Donna Entz and Dennis/Jeanne Rempel.
1979	(February) President Kabangy dies of cancer.
1979	(April) AIMM Board engages in a major process of self-evaluation and definition of priorities with a broad mix of inter-Mennonite leadership from both North America and Africa.
1980	(March) CMZa elects Rev. Mbonza Kikunga as its next president and Rev. Mukanza Ilunga as Vice-President.
1980	(October) Baptism of the first convert in Upper Volta (Traoré Siaka).
1981	AIMM sponsors a major consultation in Gaborone, Botswana regarding Mennonite ministry among African Independent Churches.
1981	A joint AIMM-MCC work is officially recognized by the Botswana government under the name "Mennonite Ministries."
1982	The AIMM places its first missionary in the Transkei (Larry Hills).
1982	AIMM celebrates its 70th anniversary.
1983	Captain Thomas Sankara takes power in Upper Volta.
1983	CMZa ordains a second AIMM missionary (Richard Derksen).
1983	CMZa applies for membership in the Evangelical Alliance of Africa and Madagascar.
1984	Upper Volta is renamed Burkina Faso.

1984	Baptism of first converts in Kotoura Village in Burkina Faso.
1984	(October) AIMM is officially recognized by the government of Burkina Faso.
1985	Controversial CMZa general assembly at Nyanga.
1985	First Christian marriage in the Burkina Faso Mennonite community.
1986	AIMM, Eastern Board and MCC issue a joint statement regarding South Africa.
1986	The Evangelical Mennonite Mission Conference (EMMC) of Canada becomes a full partner of AIMM.
1986	(September) Earl Roth follows Jim Bertsche as AIMM Executive Secretary.
1987	(March) Four CMZa regional secretaries issue an ultimatum to President Mbonza regarding delayed CMZa General Assembly.
1987	(May) Emergency CMZa General Assembly convened by regional secretaries at Kikwit over President Mbonza's opposition.
1987	(June) President Mbonza convenes counter General Assembly at Tshikapa.
1987	AIMM celebrates its 75th anniversary.
1987	Captain Sankara is assassinated in Burkina Faso.
1987	Creation of CONIM in Zaire bringing together the three autonomous Mennonite Conferences of Zaire plus MCC.
1988	The Mbonza administrative team evicted from CMZa headquarters in Tshikapa. Newly-elected President Chibulenu Sakayimbo and his staff instated.
1990	AIMM Secretary Earl Roth makes investigative trip to Senegal and Guinea Bissau.
1993	Leona Schrag is named Interim Executive Secretary of AIMM.
1993	The Mennonite Church of Burkina Faso is officially recognized by the government.
1994	Garry Prieb is appointed AIMM Executive Secretary.
1994	The first free elections for all citizens in the history of South Africa.
1994	AIMM Canada is recognized by the provincial government of Manitoba.
1994	Church leader Cheba dies suddenly in Kotoura, Burkina Faso.
1995	Rev. Fimbo Ganvunze is elected President of the CMZa.
1995	An AIMM, CMZa and CEM joint delegation engages in a consultation in Senegal with local mission/church representatives regarding possible ministry among the Wolof people of that country.

1995   EMEK is restructured; continued European Inter-Mennonite collaboration in Christian Mission is affirmed.

1996   AIMM US and AIMM Canada create AIMM International (AIMM Intl).

1997   Exploratory discussions between AIMM, MBM and Communion Fellowship of Goshen, IN regarding possible joint ministry among the Wolof people of Senegal.

1997   Investigative trip to Wolof region of Senegal by a joint AIMM/Communion Fellowship delegation.

1997   Kabila Laurent and his "Alliance of Democratic Forces for the Liberation of Congo" overthrow the Mobutu regime in Zaire and rename the country "The Democratic Republic of Congo."

CIM/AIMM ADMINISTRATION

OFFICE LOCATIONS

1911 - 1926	Gridley, IL
1926 - 1930	Goshen, IN
1930 - 1954	Chicago, IL
1954 -	Elkhart, IN

EXECUTIVE SECRETARIES

1911 - 1926	Claudon, D. N.	EMC/US
1926 - 1930	Detweiler, Irvin R.	Central
1930 - 1936	Eash, A. M.	Central
1936 - 1950	Rediger, Christian E.	EMC/US
1951 - 1960	Driver, Harvey A.	EMC/US
1960 - 1963	Sprunger, Vernon J.	GC
1963 - 1974	Short, Reuben	EMC/US
1974 - 1986	Bertsche, James E.	EMC/US
1986 - 1993	Roth, Earl W.	GC
1993 - 1994	Schrag, Leona M. (interim)	GC
1994 -	Prieb, Garry L.	MB

CIM/AIMM BOARD CHAIRMEN

1911 - 1925	Struhbar, Valetine	Central
1925 - 1934	Slagle, Emmanuel M.	EMC/US
1934 - 1954	Neuenschwander, Albert	EMC/US
1954 - 1959	Rediger, Milo	EMC/US
1959 - 1963	Troyer, Lotus E.	Central
1963 - 1964	Short, Reuben	EMC/US
1964 - 1969	Hartzler, R. L.	Central
1969 - 1971	Nussbaum, Milo	EMC/US
1971 - 1975	Neufeld, Elmer	GC
1975 - 1979	Wiebe, Allan	EMB
1979 - 1984	Juhnke, James C.	GC
1984 - 1985	Rupp, Andrew M.	EMC/US
1985 - 1987	Rempel, Erwin	GC
1987 - 1989	Gates, Gary L.	EMC/US
1989 - 1993	Klassen, Henry	EMC/C
1993 - 1996	Hyde, Harry L.	EMC/US
1996 -	Klassen, Henry	EMC/C

CIM/AIMM BOARD MEMBERS

NAME	CONFERENCE		TERMS
Adrian, Victor	MB		1984-1987
Augspurger, Aaron	Central		1911-1917
			1922-1928
		(honorary)	1929-1950
Barkman, J. P.	EMC/US		1934-1935
Barkman, Peter	EMB		1978-1984
Beachy, Alvin J.	Central		1944-1948
Bertsche, Harry E.	EMC/US		1928-1971
Block, Tina	GC		1972-1975
Brooks, Reuben	EMC/US		1984
Brucks, Henry	MB		1978-1981
Carlson, Flo	EMC/US		1993-
Cecil, Earl	EMC/US		1990-1996
Claudon, D. N.	EMC/US		1911-1926
Classen, Milton	GC		1973-1978
Detweiler, Irvin R.	Central		1926-1943
Dick, H. H.	EMB		1941-1962
Diemer, Richard	EMC/US		1956-1959
Diller, Clarence	EMC/US		1956-1968
Driver, Harvey A.	EMC/US		1950-1956
			1964-1970
Dyck, David	MB		1990-
Dyck, Peter	GC		1977-1979
Dyck, Reuben	EMB		1963-1966
Eash, A. M.	Central		1928-1936
Ehresman, Judi	EMC/US		1990-1993
Eicher, P. L.	MCA		1929-1931
Eisenbraun, Max	EMB		1957-1958
Egle, Christian R.	EMC/US		1911-1926
Enns, Arthur	EMC/US		1959-1965
Ens, Anna	GC		1987-1992
Esch, Benjamin	Central		1950-1960
Falk, Anne	GC		1980-1983
Fast, George	EMB		1933-1935
Fast, H.P.	EMB		1939-1941
Fast, Henry J.	EMB		1964-1967
Flaming, Elsie	GC		1985-1987
Friesen, Ben	EMC/C		1975-1977
Friesen, David K.	EMB/FEBC		1985-1995
Funk, Henry H.	GC		1964-1969
Gates, Gary L.	EMC/US		1985-1988
Gerhart, Joyce	GC		1993-1996
Gerig, Joseph K.	EMC/US		1911-1929

Gering, Walter	GC	1969-1970
Giesbrecht, Lawrence	EMMC	1986-1993
Goldsmith, Noah O.	EMC/US	1925-1928
Graber, Archie	EMC/US	1969-1972
Graber. Irma	EMC/US	1981-1987
Gundy, George	Central	1942-1951
Guth, Rae V.	GC	1960-1967
Habegger, Howard	GC	1971-1982
Hamm, Peter	MB	1987-1989
Harder, David	EMC/US	1986-1992
Harder, Waldo	GC	1969-1971
Hartzler, R. L.	Central/GC	1937-1972
Hoover, Noble O.	Central	1933-1950
Hyde, Harry L.	EMC/US	1985-
Janz, B. B.	EMB	1957-1958
Janzen, Heinz	GC	1967-1973
Janzen, William	GC	1970-1973
Juhnke, James C.	GC	1974-1983
King, J. H.	Central	1911-1926
Klassen, Henry	EMC/C	1977-
Kliewer, John	MB	1976-1977
Kreider, A. E.	GC	1945-1963
Langereis, H. H. D.	Central	1921-1933
Lehman, John	EMC/US	1963-1964
Lehman, Naomi	GC	1976-1978
Leightner, B. F.	MCA	1928-1929
Link, Joy Phyllis	EMC/US	1976-1979
Loewen, George	EMB	1958-1964
		1967-1978
Loewen, William	EMB	1952-1953
Lugbill, Charles	EMC/US	1967-1972
Martens, Elmer	MB	1994-1997
Maurer, S. E.	Central	1925-1933
Miller, Milo	Central	1956-1968
Miller, Stanley	Central	1952-1956
Neuenschwander, Albert	EMC/US	1931-1956
Neufeld, Elmer	GC	1968-1977
Nickel, H. P.	EMB	1952-1954
Nussbaum, Milo	EMC/US	1964-1976
Nussbaum, Stan	EMC/US	1985-1986
Nyce, Howard G.	GC	1947-1953
Oyer, Amos	EMC/US	1928-1931
Oyer, Eli	EMC/US	1925-1934
Oyer, Lora	GC	1982-1983

Pannebecker, Samuel F.	GC	1952-1967
Peters, Frank C.	MB	1982-1984
Ramseyer, Alice Ruth	GC	1973-1978
		1985
Rediger, Ben	EMC/US	1925-1928
Rediger, Christian E.	EMC/US	1928-1933
		1936-1952
Rediger, Milo	EMC/US	1951-1960
Regehr, William	EMB	1962-1974
Regier, Sara	GC	1985-1990
Rempel, Dennis	GC	1988-
Rempel, Erwin	GC	1982-1994
Rempel, Peter	GC	1993-
Rocke, Emmanuel	EMC/US	1933-1966
Rupp, Andrew M.	EMC/US	1968-1985
Rupp, Benjamin	EMC/US	1911-1925
Rupp, Charles	EMC/US	1975-1981
Sawatzky, Leonard	EMMC	1993-
Sawatzky, Peter G.	GC	1975-1987
Schantz, Peter	Central	1911-1922
Schertz, A. H.	Central	1948-1955
Schmucker, Jacob	EMC/US	1925-1928
	(honorary)	1929-1942
Schmucker, Noah	EMC/US	1929-1931
		1935-1951
Schultz, George P.	EMB	1928-1933
		1937-1940
Shelly, Andrew R.	GC	1956-1971
Shelly, Wilmer	Central	1943-1946
Short, Dean	EMC/US	1982-1984
Short, Reuben	EMC/US	1943-1963
Slagle, Emmanuel M.	EMC/US	1917-1943
	(honorary)	1943-1945
Slagle, Lois	EMC/US	1979-1984
Sommer, E. A.	Central	1951-1952
Sprunger, Charles	GC	1986-
Stahly, Maurice	GC	1956-1975
Steiner, Eli G.	EMC/US	1957-1966
Steiner, Richard L.	EMC/US	1980-1985
Stoesz, Geneva	GC	1983-1987
Struhbar, Valentine	Central	1911-1926
Stucky, Elmer	EMC/US	1931-1936
Stutzman, Robert	GC	1967-1973
Suderman, John P.	GC	1953-1966
Thiessen, John	GC	1951-1952
Toews, A. P.	EMB	1952-1958
Troyer, Emmanuel	Central	1917-1942
Troyer, Lotus E.	GC	1951-1974

Wall, John	MB		1994-1995
Waltner, Christine	GC		1993-
Waltner, Orlando	GC		1960-1962
Weaver, Edwin	MC	(consultant)	1982-1983
Weaver, William B.	Central		1926-1952
Wiebe, Allan	EMB		1967-1992
Wiebe, Orlando	EMB		1954-1963
Wiebe, Willard	GC		1968-1969
Wiens, A. F.	EMB		1933-1935
Winteregg, Bryce	EMC/US		1979-1982
			1987-1994
Zehr, Robert	EMC/US		1970-1979
Zimmerman, Merlo	EMC/US		1967-1969
			1971-1974
Zook, Jeanne	GC		1978-1991

CIM/AIMM PERSONNEL
PAST AND PRESENT
(AS OF JUNE 1998)

(* = deceased)

NAME	COUNTRY	CONFERENCE	TERMS
ALBRECHT, Wayne & Annette (Jost)	Zaire	MC	5/72-12/74
AMIE, *Milton & *Beulah (MACMILLEN) (m.1927)	Congo	Michigan	8/28-4/32
ANDERSON, *Oscar & *Sarah (KROEKER) (m.1914)	Congo	Sweden/EMB	7/14-11/16
BANMAN THIESSEN, Hulda	Congo/Zaire	GC	5/56-6/60 8/61-6/64 6/67-7/71
BARKMAN, Harvey & Avril (Reimer)	Congo/Zaire	EMC/C	6/58-7/60 10/61-2/64 8/70-6/72
BARKMAN, *John P. & *Mathilda (Stucky)	Congo	EMC/US	3/16-8/18 8/20-6/24 10/26-4/31 10/36-9/45
BARKMAN, Sue	US	EMC/C	73-76
BECKER, *Alvin & *Martha (Foster)	Congo	EMC/US	11/23-9/27 10/28-2/35
BEITLER, Irma (m.4/51; see GRABER, Archie & Irma)	Congo	EMC/US	8/48-4/51
BERGEN, David	Zaire	GC	6/83-7/85
BERGEN, Phil & Carol (Kliewer)	Burkina Faso	MB	9/90-7/93 8/94-6/97 11/97-
BERGEN, Richard & Adela (Sawatzky)	Zaire Senegal	GC	1/85-5/88 8/96-
BERTSCHE, *Amelia	Congo	EMC/US	8/20-12/23 10/26-9/31
BERTSCHE, James & Genevieve (Shuppert)	Congo/Zaire	EMC/US	7/48-5/52 4/53-6/58 8/59-7/60

BERTSCHE, James & Genevieve (cont.) (Jim only)			9/60-7/61 8/63-8/67 9/68-8/71 11/72-8/74
(home office)			8/74-8/86
BERTSCHE, Sandra	Zaire	EMC/US	8/75-7/77 11/77-7/78
BERTSCHE, Timothy & Laura (Gilbertson)	Zaire Botswana	EMC/US	1/85-12/87 1/89-7/92 1/93-7/96 5/97-
BIRKY, *Erma (Cape Town 1/47)	Congo	Central/GC	4/23-1/27 8/28-2/35 4/36-11/49 7/50-8/55 4/56-6/60
BIXEL, *Lester (m.1924)	Congo	Central	11/21-6/24
BIXEL, *Lester & *Alma (DILLER)	Congo	Central/EMC/US	4/26-2/30
BOESE, Glen & Phyllis (Thomas)	Zaire	GC	1/84-9/87 4/88-4/90 8/90-9/91 2/92-7/92
BOHN, John & Tina (WARKENTIN) (m.4/75)	Lesotho	GC	8/78-4/81 8/81-7/84 11/84-7/87 11/87-3/90 10/91-6/93
BONTRAGER, Robert D. & Mable (Busch)	Congo	EMC/US	5/50-5/55 9/56-2/61 1/62-3/65
BORN, Bryan & Teresa (Toews)	Botswana	MB	6/92-8/95 1/96-
BOSCHMAN, Donald	Botswana	GC	9/85-8/88 6/89-6/91
(m.12/91, see REMPEL-BOSCHMAN, Donald & Kathleen)			
BRAUN, Henry & Sara Jo (Lehman)	Zaire	GC	12/70-3/72
BRAUN, Lois	Zaire	GC	1/86-7/86 8/86-9/91
BRIGGS, *Clio	Congo	Michigan	11/23-3/27

BRIGGS, Maurice & Joyce (Suran)	Zaire	GC	9/84-5/85 5/85-6/88 8/89-12/91
(Maurice only)			2/92-5/92
BROWN, Loyd & Marie (DILLER) (m.8/52)	Congo	EMC/US	8/52-4/57 8/58-7/60
BUCK, *Victor (formerly with UTM)	Congo	Independent	53-58
BULLER, Charles	Zaire	GC	8/81-10/83
BULLER, Herman & Ruth (Lehman)	Zaire	GC	2/66-8/69 8/70-8/74 8/75-7/78 12/78-9/81 1/82-11/83 1/84-3/88
BULLER, Peter & Gladys (Klassen)	Congo/Zaire	EMB/GC	8/51-3/56 6/57-7/60 7/61-6/64 8/66-7/71 8/73-8/77 8/78-7/82 8/83-6/85 9/85-8/87 10/92-3/93
BUSENITZ, Allen & Marabeth (Loewens)	Lesotho	GC	1/73-3/76
BYLER, John & Martha (Beiler)	Zaire	MC	8/63-5/64 4/68-11/70 8/74-8/75 7/79-8/80
(John only)			10/97-11/97
CAMPBELL, James & Cheryl (LeRoy)	Zaire	GC/MC	9/81-7/82 7/82-3/84
CECIL, Cheryl	US	EMC/US	94-
CHRISTENSEN, James & Jeanette (Myers)	Zaire	OM	6/78-7/81 1/83-8/84
CLAASSEN, Gordon (m.2/81)	Zaire	GC	2/76-2/79
CLAASSEN, Gordon and Jarna (Rautakoski)	Zaire	GC	9/83-6/86 1/88-8/91 2/92-12/93

CLAASSEN, Melvin & Martha (Buhler)	Congo/Zaire	EMB	3/58-7/60
			8/61-8/65
			8/66-8/70
			9/71-6/74
COLBERT, Donna	Zaire	EMC/US	8/79-7/80
			7/80-6/82
			6/83-7/85
			1/86-3/87
COUILLARD, Troy & Cathy (Schmitz)	Lesotho	GC	9/90-7/91
COUNTRYMAN, *Doris	Congo	EMC/US	2/36-4/37
CUMMINGS, Linda	Burkina Faso	EMC/US	1/88-8/90
			8/91-9/93
deBRUN, Harlan & Claire (Becker)	Lesotho	GC	8/83-4/86
DERKSEN, Rick & Marilyn (Carter)	Zaire/Congo	GC	6/76-5/80
			7/82-5/85
			9/85-6/87
			8/87-10/91
			1/92-7/93
			8/94-6/96
			8/96-7/98
DERSTINE, Norman & Virginia (Martin)	Botswana	MC	6/76-7/78
DICK, Delbert & Susan (Mast)	Zaire	GC	7/75-6/78
			8/90-9/91
(Delbert only)			11/91-5/92
			8/93-1/94
DICK, *Elmer & Esther (Quiring)	Congo/Zaire	GC	1/46-2/51
			5/52-8/57
			8/58-7/60
(Elmer only)			9/60-7/61
			4/62-5/66
			8/67-6/71
			8/72-5/76
			12/76-5/80
(special assignment)			2/89-5/90
DICK, La Verna	Zaire	GC	8/72-7/76
DILLER. Alma	Congo	EMC/US	8/20-6/24
(m.1924; see BIXEL, Lester & Alma)			
DILLER, Marie	Congo	EMC/US	8/51-8/52
(m.8/52; see BROWN, Loyd & Marie)			
DILLER, James & Jeanne (Miller)	Congo	EMC/US	9/56-6/60

DIRKS, Henry & Tina (Weier)	Congo/Zaire	GC	8/63-9/65
			12/65-6/68
			7/69-6/72
			10/72-8/76
			8/82-6/84
			8/84-6/85
			9/86-6/88
			8/88-5/90
			8/90-9/91
			11/91-5/92
(Henry, part-time CEDI/NA rep)			6/92-5/98
DIRKS, Rudy & Sharon (Andres)	Botswana	GC	7/96-
DOERING, *Alma	Congo	Independent	2/23-12/25
DYCK, B. Harry & Lois (Riehl)	Botswana	GC	8/75-9/79
			7/80-5/85
			6/96-1/97
DYCK, Sarah	Congo	GC	5/56-2/58
EDGHART, *Mr.	Congo	Sweden	1/16-10/16
EDIGER, Sam & Honora (Fast)	Congo	EMB	11/52-8/57
EGLI, James & Vicki (Birkey)	Lesotho	MC	9/80-10/83
EIDSE, Ben & Helen (Reimer)	Congo/Zaire	EMC/C	10/53-3/57
			4/61-9/61
			3/63-6/67
			5/69-6/73
			9/75-4/79
			6/80-12/82
ENNS, Bill & Betty (Giesbrecht)	Lesotho	GC	6/95-6/97
			7/98-
ENNS, *Frank J. & *Agnes (Neufeld)	Congo	GC	10/26-2/30
			9/31-2/37
			6/38-10/47
(Frank only)			8/48-8/50
			8/50-7/53
			8/54-6/60
(Frank after Agnes' death)			8/66-7/69
ENSZ, Lorin & Sandra (Barkman)	Zaire	EMC/C	8/75-8/77
ENTZ, Loren & Donna (Kampen)	Burkina Faso	GC	9/77-10/80
			6/81-6/85
			8/86-12/88
			1/89-7/90

ENTZ, Loren & Donna (cont.)			7/91-6/95 7/96-
ENTZ, Sam & Leona (Enns)	Congo/Zaire	GC	11/49-9/54 9/55-7/60 12/61-10/65 9/66-12/70 1/72-11/75
EPP, Mary	Congo/Zaire	GC	6/58-7/60 9/61-7/65 10/68-7/70 9/70-7/72 9/73-6/77 7/78-7/80 9/80-7/82 8/83-6/85 9/85-8/87
EWERT, Ralph & Fern (Bartsch)	Congo/Zaire	GC	8/61-6/67 8/68-6/72
(Ralph only)			3/78-8/78
FALK, *Peter & Annie (Rempel)	Congo/Zaire	GC	8/52-7/57 8/58-7/60 9/63-6/67 8/68-7/74 10/82-7/84 9/84-7/86 9/86-7/87
FAST, Eric & Kathleen (Harms) (AIMM/MCC)	Botswana	GC	7/87-8/94
FENNIG, Charles	Zaire	GC	3/81-8/83
FLUTH, Jerome & Ramona	Burkina Faso	N.A. Baptist	7/95-8/96
FRANZ, John & Betty (Rempel)	Zaire	MB	6/73-7/75
FRIESEN, *Aganetha K.	Congo/Zaire	EMB	9/38-2/47 6/48-12/53 1/55-12/58 12/6-7/65 8/70-10/74
FRIESEN, Donald & Norma (Klassen)	Zaire	GC	1/82-12/84
FRIESEN, Irvin & Lydia (Gunther)	Botswana	MB	11/76-11/79 6/80-11/82 3/83-4/86

FRIESEN, Ivan & Rachel (Hilty)	Botswana	GC	12/86-4/90 8/90-6/92
FRIESEN, Lena K.	Congo	EMB	7/51-7/56 7/57-7/60
FRIESEN, Margaret	Congo	EMB	7/57-6/60
FRIESEN, Rick & June (Ashton)	Zaire	GC	9/86-7/90
FRIESEN, Sandra	Zaire	EMB	9/83-6/86 8/87-6/89
FRIESEN, Sara K.	Congo	EMB	7/51-3/57 4/58-7/60
GARBER, Anne	Zaire Burkina Faso	GC	9/75-7/76 4/82-6/85 6/87-4/90 8/90-1/93
(m.1/93; see KOMPAORE, Anne)			
GERBER, Ellis & Edna (Buller) (Ellis only) (Ellis only)	Congo/Zaire	EMB	9/53-7/57 9/58-7/60 62-63 9/63-7/66 11/67-7/68 8/71-7/73
GERHART, Robert & Joyce (Stradinger) (home office)	Lesotho	GC	10/74-9/78 9/79-1/81 1/81-8/88
GERIG, Virgil & *Mary Kay (Ramseyer)	Lesotho	GC	3/82-7/84
GRABER, *Archie & *Evelyn (Oyer) (Archie only)	Congo	MC/Central	5/30-3/35 7/36-1/39 4/40-6/46 5/48-4/51
GRABER, *Archie & *Irma (BEITLER) (m.4/51) (Archie only) (AIMM/MCC) (AIMM/MCC)	Congo/Zaire	EMC/US	4/51-8/53 7/54-8/59 9/60-9/61 12/61-7/65 2/66-6/69 2/72-4/73
GRABER ROTH, Nancy	Zaire	EMC/US	8/83-10/85
GRABER, Harold & Gladys (Gjerdevig)	Congo	GC	1/51-6/55 5/56-7/60 8/63-6/64

GRASSE, John & Betty (Stover)	Zaire	GC	4/86-8/87 1/89-11/90
GROOT, Gary & Maureen (Penner)	Zaire	GC	9/83-5/86
GRUTTER, *Max & Ruth (Germann) (formerly with UTM)	Congo	Switzerland	55-56
GUENGERICH, Frieda	Congo/Zaire	Central	1/46-9/51 5/52-7/57 8/58-7/60 8/68-7/72 8/73-11/74
GUENTHER, Titus & Karen (Loewen)	Lesotho	GC	9/81-6/84
GUSTAFSON, *Theresa	Congo	Michigan	2/23-5/25 6/27-4/31
GUT, Klara (formerly with UTM)	Congo	Landlai Sisters, Switzerland	10/55-10/56
HABEGGER, Marlene	US	GC	91-97
HAIGH, *Lawrence & *Rose (Boehning)	Congo	Central	4/11-5/15 3/16-6/20
HALLER, *Archie & *Ella	Congo	MCA	9/25-8/27
HAMM, Elvira	Burkina Faso	EMC\C	7/96-
HANDRICH, Wade	US	MC	10/95-
HARDER, Arnold & Grace (Hiebner) (Arnold only)	Congo/Zaire	GC	10/68-7/72 8/73-6/77 8/78-5/81 8/81-5/84 8/84-6/88 8/89-6/91 8/91-9/91 9/91-12/91 1/92-4/92
HARDER, Judith	Burkina Faso	GC	9/85-6/86 8/87-6/89
HARDER, Steven & Judith (Dickerson)	Burkina Faso	GC	1/85-5/87
HARDER, *Waldo E. & *Abbie (Claassen) (Waldo only)	Congo/Zaire	GC	7/51-8/56 6/57-10/59 11/60-4/1 8/71-6/73

HARMS, Harold & Joyce (Ediger)	Congo	EMB	8/59-7/60 6/62-6/66 8/66-6/68
HENDERSHOTT, Mary (AIMM/SIL)	Burkina Faso	Kansas	95-
HERR, *Walter Scott	Congo	EMC	11/12-6/17
HERSHBERGER, Steve	US	MC\GC	90-95
HIEBERT, Elda	Congo/Zaire	GC	8/63-8/67 8/68-7/72 8/75-7/78 8/83-7/87 11/88-7/91
HIEBERT, Mary	Congo	EMB	4/57-7/60 7/62-3/66
HILDEBRAND, Henry & Hilda (Klassen) (Henry only)	Congo	MB	8/58-7/60 11/60-7/61
HILLS, Laurence	Transkei	GC	9/82-9/85 1/86-9/88 10/88-5/89
HIRSCHLER, Richard & Jean (Simpson) (Richard only)	Zaire	GC	4/71-3/75 8/81-7/84 9/84-12/84
HOLBURN, Fiona (AIMM/SIL)	Burkina Faso	Scotland	95-
ISAAC, Gary & Jean (Kliewer)	Transkei/ South Africa	GC	10/86-11/88 1/89-12/90 2/91-12/92 2/93-12/94 2/95-9/97 1/98-
ISAAC, Marvin & Edna (Mays)	Zaire	Independent	8/67-7/71
JANTZEN, John B. & Ann (Dick)	Congo	GC	8/49-12/53 5/55-8/59
JANZ, Arthur & Martini (Reimer) (Art only)	Congo/Zaire	EMB	12/51-7/56 9/57-7/60 10/60-4/61 8/63-6/66

JANZ, Arthur & Martini (cont.)			12/67-7/69
(Art, home office)			7/69-6/91
(Art, development coord.)			7/91-12/94
(Martini, home office)			3/77-12/94
JANZEN, *Aaron & *Ernestine	Congo	MB	11/12-7/16
			1/19-11/21
JANZEN, Anita	Congo/Zaire	GC	8/67-8/70
			9/76-6/78
			8/78-6/80
JANZEN, Garry & Diane (Janzen)	Botswana	GC	9/85-8/88
JOHNSTONE, *Frederick	Congo	England	7/14-4/17
KARLSON, Henning	Congo	Sweden	3/15-6/16
(m.6/16)			
KARLSON, *Henning & *Elsie (Lundberg)			6/16-6/18
KARLSON, *Sofi	Congo	Sweden	1/16-7/16
KEEFER, Cheri	Zaire	MC/US	9/71-8/73
KEIDEL, Levi & Eudene (King)	Congo/Zaire	GC	3/51-5/55
			10/56-7/60
			8/62-7/66
			6/71-10/74
			12/77-5/81
KEIDEL, Ruth	Zaire	GC	7/78-6/80
KENSINGER, *William. & *Edna (Moser)	Congo	EMC/US	1/19-4/22
			11/23-9/25
KLAASSEN, John E. &*Olga (Unruh)	Congo/Zaire	GC	8/64-8/67
			10/67-7/70
			8/72-9/76
KLASSEN, Gordon & Rebecca (Balzer)	Burkina Faso	EMMC	9/90-8/93
			7/94-6/98
KLIEWER, John B. & Ruth (Fast)	Botswana	MB	5/78-9/81
KLOPFENSTEIN, *Henry & *Phyllis	Congo	EMC/US	3/23-5/26
KOMPAORE, Anne (GARBER)	Burkina Faso	GC	8/93-4/96
(m.1/93; Daniel Kompaoré)			7/96-
KOOP, Glen & Elizabeth (Unger)	Lesotho	EMC/C	9/90-7/92
KRAUSE, John G. & Leona (Bergen)	Zaire	GC	11/78-6/81
			8/81-8/83

KREHBIEL, Ronald & Cynthia (Kirchofer)	Lesotho	GC	8/78-7/79
KROEKER, *Sarah (m.1914; see ANDERSON, Oscar & Sarah)	Congo	EMB	5/12-7/14
LANGDON, *Mr. & *Mrs. B. F.	Congo	Michigan	10/23-9/25
LARSON, Jonathan & Mary Kay (Burkhalter)	Botswana	GC	7/81-8/84 1/85-11/86 2/87-4/89 9/91-11/94
LEHMAN, Vernon J. & Phyllis (Lehman)	Zaire	GC	2/77-8/79
LIECHTY, Anna V.	Congo/Zaire	GC	4/46-11/51 6/55-8/60 9/62-7/65 8/65-7/67 10/68-8/72 8/73-6/77 8/77-7/79 9/79-8/81 5/82-7/84
LIECHTY, Irena (m.6/62; see SPRUNGER, Vernon & Irena)	Congo	GC	7/52-11/56 2/58-7/60 10/60-5/62
LOEWEN, Henry W. & Betty (Schroeder)	Zaire	GC	8/72-8/75 10/78-7/80
LOEWEN, Melvin & Elfrieda (Regier)	Congo	EMB	8/55-7/59 1/61-6/63 8/63-12/64 8/65-6/67
LOWENBERG, Lorraine	US	GC	64-69
LUTKE, Agnes	Congo	EMB	4/46-1/51 5/52-7/57 7/59-6/60
MACMILLEN, *Beulah (m.1927, see AMIE, Milton & Beulah)	Congo	Michigan	11/23-3/27
MANGOLD, *Berta (formerly with UTM)	Congo	Landlai Sisters, Switzerland	54-58
MANN, Darrell & Diana (Crane)	Congo	GC	8/67-1/69

MARTENS, Rudolph C. & Elvina (Neufeld)	Congo/Zaire	GC	8/52-4/57 8/58-7/60 7/70-7/74 8/75-3/78 9/78-5/80
MEESTER, *Anna	Congo	Holland	3/15-4/18
MERKEY, Anne	US	MC/GC	78-79
MILLER, *Bertha Mae (formerly with UTM)	Congo	MBC	2/29-8/32 7/34-3/45 6/47-7/53 6/55-7/59 2/63-12/69
MILLER, *Mary (formerly with UTM)	Congo	MBC	2/29-8/32 7/34-3/45 6/47-7/53 6/55-7/57
MOSCHEL, Tracy	US	EMC/US	89-90
MOSER, *Henry & *Emma (Bixler)	Congo	EMC/US	2/23-7/26 6/27-3/32 8/33-4/37 1/38-7/46
MYERS, Gordon L. & Kathryn (Graber)	Zaire	GC	9/85-6/88
NELSON, Stephen R. & Patricia (Wicke)	Zaire	EMC/US	8/84-5/87 8/88-12/91 8/92-8/93
NEUENSCHWANDER, Cindy	US	GC	93-98
NEUENSCHWANDER, Marjorie	Zaire	EMC/US	8/72-8/76 7/82-6/84 9/84-7/85
NEUENSCHWANDER, Wilbert &Ruby (Moser)	Congo/Zaire	EMC/US	7/64-6/68 8/69-8/73
NEUFELD, *George B. & *Justina (Wiens) (home office)	Congo	GC	11/44-5/50 7/51-3/56 6/57-7/60 7/61-7/69
NEUFELD, Gerald & Beverly (Dueck)	Burkina Faso	GC	9/87-8/88 9/88-7/90 10/91-6/93 10/93-7/95

NEUFELD, Gerald & Beverly (cont.)			10/95-8/97 10/97-
NOLT, Rachel	US	MC	97-
NUSSBAUM, Stan & Lorri (Berends)	Lesotho	EMC/US	3/77-4/79 8/79-8/81 10/81-9/83 6/86-7/93 7/93-
(Stan, Selly Oak CIM appt.) (Stan, Global Mapping)			
PAULS, John C. & Mary (Schrag)	Zaire	GC	8/80-6/83
PENNER, Mary	Congo/Zaire	GC	12/68-4/70
PETERSEN, Daniel R. & Kathy (Fluth)	Burkina Faso	EMC/US	9/82-1/84 7/84-10/87 10/88-5/93 6/94-
PLENERT, Stephen W. & Janet (Sinclair) (Stephen only)	Zaire Congo Brazzaville	GC	9/86-4/90 6/91-9/91 12/91-1/92 2/92-8/92
QUIRING, *Anna	Congo	GC	4/36-7/40 6/43-8/46 7/48-11/52 5/54-12/58
QUIRING, Betty	Congo/Zaire	GC	7/54-5/59 10/60-6/64 8/65-8/67 9/67-7/71 7/72-7/76 7/77-7/79 9/79-10/79
QUIRING, Tina	Congo	GC	10/49-6/54 7/55-6/60 4/62-5/66 3/67-10/71 10/72-7/76
RATZLAFF, Doreen	US	EMB	79-88
REDIGER, Glenn & Pauline (Gima)	Zaire	EMC/US	7/88-6/90 9/91-9/91
REGIER, Arnold & Elaine (Waltner)	Congo	GC	8/57-7/60
REGIER, Elmer & Gloria (Bridson)	Congo	EMB	7/56-5/60

REGIER, Fremont & Sara (Janzen)	Congo/Zaire	GC	1/64-2/67
			1/68-6/71
			6/72-6/76
	Botswana	GC	7/81-8/83
(AIMM/MCC)			10/83-7/85
REIMER, Amanda	Congo	EMB	8/53-8/57
			8/58-7/60
REIMER, Brian & Patricia (Penner)	Lesotho	EMC/C	8/92-7/95
			3/96-6/97
REMPEL, Dennis & Jeanne (Sonke)	Burkina Faso	GC	1/78-8/81
			9/82-8/84
			10/84-7/86
REMPEL, Eldora	US	EMB	52-58
REMPEL, Erwin & Angela (Albrecht)	Botswana	GC	6/94-11/96
(AIMM/MCC)			1/97-
REMPEL, Lawrence & Alvera (Klassen)	Congo/Zaire	EMB	8/48-12/52
			1/53-5/59
			10/60-7/63
			6/64-5/68
			7/70-8/71
REMPEL-BOSCHMAN, Don & Kathleen (m.12/91; see BOSCHMAN, Don)	Botswana	GC	9/92-2/96
(Don only)			3/97-5/97
RICKERT, *Emma	Congo	Central	2/23-9/26
			12/27-6/28
RIEDIGER, Evelyn	Burkina Faso	GC	1/85-11/85
RIES, Dennis D. & Shirley (Epp)	Zaire	GC	11/75-6/79
			7/80-5/82
			7/82-7/84
ROCKE, *Glenn & Ina (Rowell)	Congo/Zaire	EMC/US	6/46-9/51
			5/52-7/57
			7/58-7/60
(Glenn only)			11/60-5/61
			9/61-6/65
			7/66-6/70
			6/71-6/74
			1/75-8/77
			1/78-5/80
			11/82-10/84
ROCKE, David G. & Catherine (Bear)	Zaire	EMC/US	3/77-6/80

ROTH, Earl & Ruth (Jantzen)	Congo/Zaire	GC	7/54-7/59
(Earl only)			10/60-8/61
			1/62-8/66
			8/68-7/72
			8/73-7/76
			7/78-7/82
			1/84-7/86
(Earl in home office)			8/86-8/93
ROTH, Lynn & Kathleen (Brandt)	Botswana	MB	8/85-1/88
(AIMM/MCC)			1/88-5/89
RUPP, Jeanette	US	EMC/US	49-51
SAUDER, *Mabel	Congo	EMC/US	1/38-7/46
			10/47-6/52
SAWATZKY, Peter & Marge	Botswana	GC	9/79-7/80
SAWATZKY, Ronald D.	Botswana	GC	8/77-8/80
			12/80-12/82
			1/83-6/84
			9/84-12/86
			1/87-6/88
(home office)			6/88-7/89
SCHAEPER, Christine	Congo	Landlai Sisters, Switzerland	10/55-10/56
(formerly with UTM)			
SCHELLENBERG, John H. &Charity (Eidse)	Burkina Faso	EMC/C	8/86-12/89
SCHMALLENBERGER, Fanny	Congo/Zaire	EMC/US	2/35-4/39
			5/40-5/49
			6/50-6/55
			8/56-7/60
			8/63-8/67
			5/68-7/72
SCHMIDT, Bonnie	Burkina Faso	EMMC	7/95-7/97
SCHMIDT, Dennis & Dianne (Smith)	Zaire	GC	8/80-4/83
			7/84-7/87
SCHMIDT, Loyal	Congo	EMB	3/55-3/57
(m.3/57)			
SCHMIDT, Loyal & Donna (WILLIAMS)	Congo	EMB	3/57-3/58
			1/59-7/60
(Loyal only)			11/60-6/61
			3/63-7/64
SCHMIDT, Robert J. & Joyce (Williams)	Congo/Zaire	GC	8/69-12/72

SCHNELL, Russell & Helen (Yoder)	Congo	Central/GC	11/32-2/37
			9/38-6/47
			8/48-6/53
	11/54-5/60		
			9/61-5/64
SCHRAG, Leona	Congo/Zaire	GC	8/68-7/72
			8/73-8/77
			7/78-7/82
			1/84-7/87
			1/88-12/89
(home office)			6/90-
SCHRAM, Grace	Congo	Independent	9/25-8/27
SCHWARTZ, Merle & *Dorothy (Bowman)	Congo/Zaire	Central/GC	3/41-6/41
			8/42-11/47
			8/48-6/54
			12/54-6/58
			8/59-7/60
(Merle only)			10/60-8/61
			10/64-9/68
			9/69-10/74
			3/76-3/77
SHARPING, Kay Frances	US	GC	70-73
SHELLY, *Walter M. & Elizabeth (Bauman)	Congo/Zaire	GC	6/68-5/69
			5/69-7/72
			8/73-7/77
SHORT, Linda	US	EMC/US	76-78
SHORT, *Lodema	Congo/Zaire	EMC/US	4/47-9/53
			8/54-6/57
			9/58-7/60
			8/62-6/65
			10/67-5/69
			9/69-5/71
			9/71-7/72
			8/74-8/78
			7/79-4/81
SHORT, Rhoda	US	EMC/US	69-70
SLAGLE, Lois V.	Congo/Zaire	EMC/US	4/45-3/50
			7/51-3/56
			5/57-7/60
			7/62-7/66
			10/67-7/71
			8/72-7/75
			11/75-8/77

SOLOMIAC, Paul & Martine (Ehrismann) (AIMM/French Mennonite/SIL)	Burkina Faso	France	84-
SOMMER, *Mr. & *Mrs. Emil (Emil only) (Emil only)	Congo	Central	7/17-11/20 11/21-7/22 7/22-3/26 5/30-3/32
SPRUNGER, *Agnes	Congo	MCA	3/16-7/19 2/22-5/26 6/27-7/33 3/35-2/42 9/42-1/46 7/46-8/53
SPRUNGER, Charles & Geraldine (Reiff) (Charles only)	Congo/Zaire	GC	7/57-7/60 1/61-9/61 9/62-8/66 8/68-6/72
SPRUNGER, Jeanette	US	GC	61
SPRUNGER, *Vernon J. & *Lilly (Bachman) (Vernon in home office) (Vernon only) (m.6/62)	Congo	Central/GC	9/31-3/36 5/38-8/47 7/48-12/53 7/55-3/59 6/59-9/61 9/61-5/62
SPRUNGER, *Vernon and Irena (LIECHTY)	Congo/Zaire	GC	6/62-9/63 9/63-4/67 7/67-7/68 7/69-11/72
SPRUNGER, Wilmer & Kenlyn (Augsburger)	Congo/Zaire	GC	7/65-7/68 12/69-7/73
STEINER, *James & Mary Ellen (Wolber)	Congo/Zaire	MC	9/68-8/70
STEINER, Richard & *Gladys (Cleveland) (m.6/80)	Congo/Zaire	EMC/US	8/58-7/60 7/67-7/70 8/71-6/74
STEINER, Richard & Marilyn (Dissinger)	Zaire/Congo	EMC/US	8/85-7/88 8/89-9/91 1/92-7/93 7/94-6/98
STEVENSON, *Alvin J.	Congo	EMC/US	2/12-2/13
STIEGLITZ, Bill & Sally (Cadwallader)	Ivory Coast	EMC/US	9/97-
STOESZ, David M. & Elvera (Dyck)	Burkina Faso	EMMC	7/93-6/95

STOESZ, Helen C.	Congo	Independent	10/26-2/30 8/30-3/36
STORRER, Marvin & Dorothy (Leu)	Congo	EMC/US	8/66-6/69
SUTTON, Omar (m.9/22)	Congo	EMC/US	1/19-4/22
SUTTON, *Omar & *Laura (Becker)	Congo	EMC/US	5/23-1/27 12/27-2/34 2/35-11/42
SWORA, Mathew & Rebecca (Jackson)	Burkina Faso	GC	8/85-7/88
THIESSEN, Elmer & Jeannette (Dueck)	Burkina Faso	EMMC	8/86-6/90 8/91-6/95 7/96-
THIESSEN, Erica	Botswana	GC	2/91-2/94 10/94-8/95 9/95-6/97
THIESSEN, Paul & Lois (Fast)	Burkina Faso	EMC/C	9/83-8/84 6/87-5/91 7/92-7/96 7/97-
THIESZEN, Eugene	Botswana	GC	8/92-7/95 2/96-
THIESZEN, Helen	Congo	Independent	11/30-9/33
TOEVS, Russell & Gail (WIEBE)	Burkina Faso	GC	12/86-2/91
TOEWS, *Henry & *Mary (Wiens)	Congo	GC	2/36-8/40 5/45-6/51
TOLEFSON, *G.	Congo	Scotland	1/16-10/16
UNRAU, Henry & Naomi (Zacharius)	Botswana	GC	7/78-6/81 1/82-11/83 1/84-6/86
UNRAU, *Kornelia	Congo	EMB	3/26-7/29 4/32-7/37 3/38-10/47 12/48-12/54 12/55-6/60
UNRUH, Donovan & Naomi (Reimer)	Congo/Zaire	GC	10/68-7/72 8/73-5/76 9/77-8/81 8/82-6/85 9/85-8/87

UNRUH, Rudolph	Congo	Central	9/31-3/36
UNRUH, Selma	Congo	GC	4/46-1/51 7/51-7/57 7/58-6/60 8/63-1/64
VALENTINE, *Mr. & *Mrs. Raphael	Congo	Michigan	2/23-9/25
WAGLER, Susan	Zaire	EMC/US	9/82-4/84
WALTNER, Harris & Christine (Duerksen)	Lesotho	GC	7/84-3/87 7/87-7/90
WARKENTIN, Tina	Congo/Zaire	GC	64-67 67-70 73-75
(m.4/75; see BOHN, John & Tina)			
WEAVER, *Edwin & Irene (Lehman)	Botswana Lesotho, Burkina Faso	MC	1/75-4/77 5/79-8/79
WEITH, Meta	Congo	Michigan	2/23-7/26
WIEBE, Allan & Selma (Schmidt)	Congo	EMB	8/50-1/55 8/56-7/60
(Allan only)			9/60-2/61
WIEBE, Gail	Burkina Faso	GC	9/81-8/84 9/85-9/86
(m.9/86; see TOEVS, Russell & Gail)			
WILLIAMS, Donna (m.3/57; see SCHMIDT, Loyal & Donna)	Congo	EMB	7/54-3/57
YODER, Donna	US	MC	58-61
YODER, James & Linda (Bertsche)	Zaire	GC/MC/EMC/US	9/82-7/85
YODER, John H. & Madonna (Miller) (Partners in Mission)	Botswana	MC	7/84-7/86 8/86-7/91
YODER, *Roy & *Bessie (Burns)	Congo	Central/GC	4/35-5/39 10/41-11/47 5/48-1/50
ZOOK, John E. & Jeanne (Pierson)	Congo/Zaire	GC	8/55-2/60 4/61-12/61 4/62-7/65 8/69-7/73 8/74-7/77 6/81-8/81 10/97-11/97

VOLUNTARY SERVICE PERSONNEL ROSTER
(AS OF JUNE 1998)

CIM/AIMM has been tremendously enriched across the years hy the steady flow of voluntary service people who have offered their energy, skill and experience for varying periods of time under its umbrella in Africa. Some have been processed directly by the Mission; many others have come via MCC.

Among the latter have been some who opted to serve in Africa as an alternative to military service. As the US draft became less of a factor, others continued to come simply because they wanted to devote a period of their lives to overseas Christian service. In the process, two MCC programs were highlighted. Those with teaching credentials came under the Teachers Abroad Program (TAP) and found their way into many mission-sponsored classrooms in Congo/Zaire and elsewhere across Africa. Many others provided invaluable help in construction, mechanics, transport, medical services, public health and agricultural development projects. These volunteers quickly gave meaning to the term "PAX Service" in Africa. Still other people took early retirement to come or packed bags amidst retirement. To one and all, the CIM/AIMM and the African churches are immensely indebted.

In spite of the efforts of staff personnel both in Akron, PA and Elkhart, IN, we know this list may be incomplete and perhaps, at times, even inaccurate. Working with the records available to us, we have done the very best we could. For any names which may have been inadvertently omitted, we offer our apologies.

NAME	SPONSOR	COUNTRY	DATES
AUGSBURGER, Art/Clara	MCC	Congo	62-63
BANMAN, Art/Frieda	MCC	Congo	62-63
BARTEL, Harlan	MCC	Congo/Zaire	68-71
BARTEL. Larry	MCC	Congo	58-60
BEACHY, Elmer	MCC	Zaire	65-68
BERGEN, Gertrude	GC/AIMM	Zaire	86-87
BERGEN, Peter/Anne	GC/AIMM	Zaire	1/91-5/91
BOESE, Steven	GC/AIMM	Zaire	11/85-3/86
BONTRAGER, Wilbur	MCC	Congo	64-66
BULLOCK, Kris/Jill	EMC/US/AIMM	Burkina Faso	6/91-8/91
BUNDY KREHBIEL, Jean	MCC	Zaire	76-78
BURKHOLDER, Mary	MCC	Congo	64-67
BUSENITZ, Roger	MCC	Congo	66-69
CAMP, Ronald/Gloria	GC/AIMM	Burkina Faso	6/93-5/94 8/97-6/98

CHARLES, Edward/Rosemary	MCC	Zaire	75-81
CLAASSEN, David	MCC	Congo	55-56
CLIFTON, Susan	EMC/US/AIMM	Zaire	74-75
DAHL, Alvin	MCC	Zaire	65-67
DRUDGE, Albert/Annie	MCC	Zaire	70-73 74-77
EDIGER, Anna	EMB/AIMM	Congo	64-66 66-68
EDIGER, Sam/Betty	GC/AIMM	Zaire	72-74
EDIGER, Solomon/Lavina	GC/AIMM	Zaire	71-72
ENTZ, Elena	GC/AIMM	Burkina Faso	89-92 92-93
ENTZ, Loren	MCC	Congo/Zaire	68-/71
ENTZ, Russell	GC/AIMM	Burkina Faso	92-93
EPP, Dale	MCC	Congo	67-69
FINK, Maureen	MCC	Zaire	79-82
FOUNTAIN, Katherine	Baptist/AIMM	Zaire	83-85
FREEMAN, Mildred	MCC	Zaire	82-83
FREY, Aden/Sheryl	MCC	Zaire	73-76
GARBER, Anne	GC/AIMM	Zaire	75-76
GATES, Amber	EMC/US/AIMM	Burkina Faso	97-98
GEISINGER, Larry	MCC	Zaire	70-72
GETZ, Ann	EMC/US/AIMM	Burkina Faso	9/94-11/94
GERBRANDT, Henry	EMMC/AIMM	Burkina Faso	1/92-3/92
GOERTZ, Henry	MCC	Congo/Zaire	68-70
GRABER, Larry	MCC	Congo	57-59
HEESE, John	MCC	Congo	59-60
HEISEY, Nancy	MCC	Zaire	73-76

HERTZLER, Leslie	MCC	Zaire	70-72
HERSHBERGER, Wilbur/Elizabeth	MCC	Zaire	70-72
HIEB, Charles	MCC	Zaire	72-74
HODEL, Paul	MCC	Congo	62-64
HOLSOPPLE, Dennis	MCC	Congo/Zaire	69-72
HORST, Allen	MCC	Congo	60-62
JANZEN, John	MCC	Congo	57-59
KAUFFMAN, Larry	MCC	Congo	55-56
KAUFFMAN, Merle	MCC	Congo	57-59
KEIM, Melvin	MCC	Congo	58-60
KELLERSTRASS, Andrea	EMC/US/AIMM	Burkina Faso	10/95-12/95
KLASSEN, Brenda	EMMC/AIMM	Burkina Faso	7/92-8/92
LEHMAN, Angela	MC/AIMM	Burkina Faso	8/92-1/93
LEHMAN, David	MCC	Congo/Zaire	68-71
LEHRMAN, Verney	MCC	Zaire	71-73
LIECHTY, Ed/Ada	EMC/US/AIMM	Congo	55-57
LIECHTY, Gordon/Minda	MCC	Congo	62-63
LINSENMEYER, Dean	MCC	Congo	66-68
LLOYD, Don/Mary	MCC	Zaire	72-75
MAUGHAN, Karen	EMC/US/AIMM	Burkina Faso	5/85-8/85
MARTIN, Darrell	MCC	Zaire	76-79
MILHOUS, Raymond/Ruth	MCC	Congo	62-64
MININGER, Ron	MCC	Zaire	75-77
NEUENSCHWANDER, Willie	MCC	Congo	56-59
NEUFELDT, Alfred	MCC	Congo	4/60-7/60
NICKEL, Arnold/Lorene	MCC	Congo	63-65
PETERS, James	MCC	Congo	59-60

RAID, Arlo/Leontina	GC/AIMM	Congo/Zaire	66-67 68-69 70-71
REGIER, Fremont	MCC	Congo	55-57
REMPEL, Paul	MCC	Zaire	70-73
RICH, Phil/Gwen	MCC	Congo/Zaire	69-72
RITTER, David	MCC	Congo/Zaire	67-70
ROTH, Paul	MCC	Congo	58-60
ROUNDS, Bob	EMC/US/AIMM	Burkina Faso	6/92-7/92
SAWATZKY MARTENS, Beverly	GC/AIMM	Zaire	86-87
SCHELLENBERG, Charis	EMC/C/AIMM	Burkina Faso	8/95-12/95
SCHELLENBERG, Lisa	EMC/C/AIMM	Burkina Faso	8/97-3/98
SCHLEGEL, Les	MCC	Congo/Zaire	68-70
SCHMIDT, Loyal	MCC	Congo/Zaire	68-70
SCHMIDT, Olin/Tillie	GC/AIMM	Zaire	72-73 74-75
SCHMIDT, Robert	MCC	Congo	59-60
SHEAR, Jeffrey/Nancy	MCC	Zaire	71-74
SHETLER, Joe	MCC	Congo/Zaire	68-70
SIEBERT, Alan	MCC	Congo	58-60
SPRUNGER, Wilmer	MCC	Congo	57-59
STRAHM, Sonja	EMC/US/AIMM	Zaire	75
STUCKEY, Terry	MCC	Zaire	70-73
SUDERMAN, Abe	MCC	Congo	60-61
SUTER, Fred	MCC	Congo/Zaire	68-70
SWEEBE, Margaret	EMC/US/AIMM	Burkina Faso	6/92-7/92
THIESSEN, Bernard	MCC	Congo	59-60
THIESSEN NEUFELD, Rose	EMMC/AIMM	Burkina Faso	89-90

TRETHEWAY, Mary	UM/AIMM	Congo	66-67
UNRAU, Henry	MCC	Zaire	70-72
UNRUH, Donovan	MCC	Congo	59-60
UNRUH, Janinne	GC/AIMM	Zaire	90-91
UNRUH, Larry	MCC	Congo	58-60
VORAN, Adrian	MCC	Zaire	73-75
WEAVER, Mark	MCC	Congo	64-66
WIEBE, Lloyd	MCC	Zaire	72-75
YODER, Ernest	GC/AIMM	Congo	50-52
YODER, Galen	MCC	Zaire	70-73
YODER, Stan	MCC	Zaire	70-73
YODER MAUST, Martha	MC/AIMM	Zaire	1/81-4/81
ZACHARIAS, James/Leanne	GC/AIMM	Botswana	85-86
ZIMMERMAN, Greg	MCC	Zaire	70-72

INDEX

ABAKO 38 ff.

Abdias Coulibaly 638, 654, 678 f.

Abou Kabar Traore 664 ff.

Adeyemo, Tokunboh 707

Adoula, Cyrille 76, 105, 107, 133

AEAM 357, 707

AEMSK 177 ff., 185, 190, 219, 221 f., 242, 407 (also see CEM)

Africa Inland Mission (AIM) 443, 692

Africa Inter-Mennonite Mission (AIMM) 251 ff., 270 ff., 286 ff., 297, 311 ff., 331, 338, 340, 343 ff., 374, 379 f., 383 ff., 405 ff., 415, 423 ff., 441, 444 ff., 462 f., 465, 469, 476, 480, 483, 491 ff., 497, 502 ff., 510 ff., 527 ff., 537, 541, 569, 571 ff., 581 f., 590, 593 ff., 599 ff., 603 ff, 629, 635 ff., 643 ff., 652 ff., 674, 683, 685 f, 692 ff., 707 ff. (also see Congo Inland Mission)

Africa Mennonite and Brethren in Christ Fellowship (AMBCF) 75, 184 f., 273, 288, 339, 444, 643, 705

African Federal Church Council (AFCC) 465, 484 f.

African Independent Churches (AICs) 311, 314, 384, 470 ff., 479 ff., 501 ff., 515 ff., 527 ff., 544, 546 ff., 567, 571 ff., 585 ff., 699, 708 f

African National Congress Party (ANC) 508, 519, 542, 546, 553 ff., 563 f, 566

Afrikaans language 449 f, 454, 456, 536, 542

Afrikaner people 449 ff., 533, 548, 553, 556 f., 563

Agacher region 663

AIDS 515 f., 586

AIMM; see Africa Inter-Mennonite Mission

AIMM Auxiliary; see chapter 11, footnote 23, 658

AIMM hostel 171, 423

Albrecht, Wayne and Annette 201

alcoholism 498 f., 515 f., 586

Alliance of Democratic Forces for the Liberation of Congo (AFDC) 706

Almamy 622 f.

Ambunda people 161 f.

Amish 5 f., 692

Anabaptist themes 75 f., 164 f., 185, 222, 249 ff., 270, 278, 299, 337 f., 411, 422, 434 ff., 439 ff., 498 f., 502, 517 ff., 531, 538, 560 f., 567, 585, 692 f., 700 ff.

ANC (Congo National Army) 63 f., 127, 418

Anglican Church 499, 511, 518, 535, 704

Angola 1, 20, 53 f., 64, 293, 302, 706

animism 325

ANTBA-BF 673

apartheid 449 ff., 509, 533, 538 f., 542, 553 ff., 576, 583, 629, 702, 707

Ascension Island 142

Assemblies of God 593 ff.

Associated Mennonite Biblical Seminary (AMBS) 40, 298, 301, 322, 411, 483, 512, 567, 582, 599 f., 611 f., 638

Association of Evangelicals of Africa and Madagascar (AEAM) 189, 357

Augsburger, Arthur and Clara, 210

Augsburger, Myron 707, 709

authenticity, theme of 213 ff., 294

Baba Mimbembe and Toma 433 f.

Baba Naomi 432

Babala 646, 669 f.

Babindi people 20, 321

Badibanga Apollo 50, 185

Badibanga Valentin 434 f.

Badinga people 438

Bakary, Coulibaly 624 f., 628, 660

Bakatushipa, Rev. 354

Bakwanga 58, 77, 81 f., 168, 185, 214 (also see Mbuji Mayi)

Baluba people 9, 20, 24, 40 f., 45, 62, 64, 70, 75 f., 89 ff., 93, 168, 180, 201, 222, 224, 249, 355, 365, 407, 419, 432, 438, 441

Bambara language 622

Bananzaro, Calixte 652, 679

Banga Station 20, 50 f., 184, 277, 285, 373

Bangui 339, 658

Banjembe people 362

Banjwadi Station 127, 146 ff.

Banman, Hulda 212 f.

bantustans; see black homelands

Banzon village 643

Bapatuila Jean 127, 146 f.

Baphende people 9, 40, 64, 76, 78, 136, 161, 165, 191, 224, 245, 311, 326, 333, 379, 437

Baptist Mission/Church 4, 5, 12, 21, 24, 204, 245, 298, 511 f., 594, 615

Barkman, Avril 98

Barkman, Harvey 98, 123

Barkman, J. P. 9

Basarwa (Bushmen) people 495, 498

Bashilele people 14, 20, 40, 184, 191, 226, 432 f.

Basotho people 461

Basutoland Congress Party (BCP) 465, 519, 545

Basutoland National Party (BNP) 464, 519, 545

FATEB 643, 657 ff.
Faul, George 60
Federal Council of Spiritual Churches (Lesotho) 523
Federation of Evangelical Missions and Churches (FEME/Burkina Faso) 593 f., 635
Fennig, Chuck 346
Fimbo Ganvunze 698
Fish River, the 450
Fisher, Larry 488
FNLA 292 ff.
fon 636 f.
Force Publique, la 7, 48, 109, 131
Forminière, la 14, 20, 49, 78, 198, 209 ff., 277, 364
France 38, 293 f., 335, 417 f., 421, 449, 607, 629
Francistown 483, 487, 515
Free University, the (Kisangani, Zaire) 100, 127, 322, 351
French Mennonites 383, 640
Fricke, Orville 616
Friesen, Aggie 22, 78, 210
Friesen, Irvin and Lydia 488
Friesen, Ivan 520 f.
Friesen, June 210
Friesen, Lena 22
Friesen, Rachel 520
Friesen, Sara 22
fusion 218 ff., 229, 232, 235 ff., 275, 304, 696

Gaborone 446, 469, 478, 480, 493, 502 ff., 511, 521, 541 ff., 578
Gaeddart, John 168
Garber, Anne 611 f., 616, 621 f., 638, 645 ff., 668, 671, 673 (also see Kompaore, Anne)
Gbadolite village 414, 417
Gbenye, Christophe 46, 62, 67, 110, 131, 135, 146
General Conference Mennonite Church 383 f., 599, 611 f., 638, 658, 711
Gerber, Edna 56
Gerber, Ellis 57
Gerhart, Robert and Joyce 389, 484, 525 f.
Gerig, Virgil and Mary Kay 546
Ghymalu Kianza 595, 597, 603
Giesbrecht, Lawrence 403
Giphende language 16, 27, 75, 101, 169, 190, 317, 327, 361, 440
Givengere, Festo 704
Gizenga Antoine 46, 67, 85, 109, 111, 128
gold 452
Gordon, Bob and Edie 103
Gouin people 608

Graber, Archie 20, 57, 59, 64, 66, 81 ff., 90 ff., 133, 168 ff., 177 f., 203, 205, 222 f., 225, 249, 252, 277, 355
Graber, Gladys 100, 113, 131
Graber, Harold 50, 75, 100, 113, 131, 246
Graber, Irma Beitler 90, 98, 222, 277
Graber, J.D. 479
Graham, Billy 361
Grasse, John 212
Great Trek, the 450 f.
Grenfell, George 4
Groot, Gary 212
Grove, Erma 443
Grütter, Max and Ruth 23
Guengerich, Frieda 279
Guenther, Titus 519 f.
Gulubane, Willie 485 f.
Gungu 66, 75, 112, 117, 135, 163, 168

Habegger, Howard 236, 256, 313
Habitat for Humanity 363
Haigh, Lawrence and Rose Boehning 6, 24, 31, 443
Hammarskjold, Dag 60
Harare, the Declaration of 562
Harder, Arnold 200, 415, 423
Harder, Grace 200, 423
Harder, Judith 650 ff.
Harder, Steven and Judy 635 f.
Harder, Waldo 57, 82, 248
Harms, Harold and Joyce 171
Harriman, Averell W. 142
Hartzler, R. L. 42 ff., 203, 348
Hege, Beth 575
Hege, Fritz 640
Heisey, Nancy 532, 581, 585
Hendershott, Mary 675
Herber, Ralph and Ruth 613
Herr, Robert and Judy 509, 531, 547
Hershberger, Wilbur and Elizabeth 201
Hershey, Eusebius 443
Hertzog, James 452
Hiebert, Elda 210
Hiebert, Mary 78, 435
Hiebert, Paul 473, 502, 504
Hiebert, Peter and Esther 591, 594
Hildebrand, Henry 22, 57, 66, 75
Hills, Larry 349, 511 ff., 546 ff., 576, 578 ff., 585, 702
Hirschler, Jeanne 300
Hirschler, Richard 212, 300
Hoare, Michael 137

509, 516, 523, 527, 530, 532, 537, 569, 574, 577, 582, 591 f., 594 f., 599 f., 639, 699 f.
McVeigh, Malcom 169 f.
Meadows, IL 6, 73
MEDA 299, 314
medal chiefs 7
medical services 22, 78, 116, 203, 210, 212 f., 300, 320, 336, 352, 362, 364 f., 635 f.
Mengi, Dr. 432
Mennonite Board of Missions 384, 443, 479 f., 709
Mennonite Brethren Mission/Church 21 f., 52, 60, 64, 75, 98, 100, 132, 163, 168 f., 205, 254, 311 f., 318, 335, 338, 383, 412, 488, 492, 502, 592 f., 639, 685, 695, 697 f.
Mennonite Brethren in Christ 443
Mennonite Ministries (MM) 491 ff., 515 ff., 521, 574 f., 586, 699 f.
Mennonite World Conference (MWC) 192, 271, 288, 305, 307, 338, 358, 374, 398, 410 f., 643, 704, 709
Mercedes Benz 414, 418
Meserete Kristos 339
Methodist Mission/Church 54 f., 62, 91, 100, 177, 217, 265, 361, 467
Metzler, Roland 59
MIBA 81, 213
Miller, Bertha 20, 685
Miller, David 519
Miller, Elinor 574
Miller, Harold F. 273
Miller, Mary 20, 685
Miller, Orie 58 f., 81, 168
Million Belete 339
Miracle Camp 276, 311 ff., 703
mission/church relations 27 f., 30, 33 ff., 61 f., 65 f., 68, 71 f., 97 f., 163 ff., 184, 190 f., 193 ff., 210, 221, 235 ff., 243, 254, 275 f., 278, 297, 314, 343 ff., 358, 363 f., 379 f., 405, 595, 597 f., 603 ff., 652 ff., 677 ff., 695 ff., 708
missionaries and colonial powers 9 f., 13 ff.
missionary children (MKs) 687 ff.
missionary complicity? 10
missionary parents 687 f., 690 f.
missionary "villas" 693 f.
missionary wives/mothers 687 f.
Misty Mount 512 f., 578 f.
Miteleji Kibatshi 334 f.
Mobutu Joseph 39, 46, 48, 64, 66 f., 76, 109, 173 ff., 205, 213 ff., 257 ff., 266, 289, 291 ff., 302, 413 f., 430, 706
Moffat, Robert and Mary 1
Mohono, Emily 462, 577 f.

Mohono, R. M. 466
Mohono, Sam 461 f., 465 f., 484 f., 502, 504, 523 f., 528, 577 f.
Monyatsi, Bishop 487, 504
Mophato Youth Camp 462, 464
Morija Station 462 ff., 478, 518
Morocco 630
Morolong, Harry 477 f.
Mosemann, John and Ruth 443
Moshoeshoe I, King 461
Moshoeshoe, the Church of 577
Mossi people 607, 629 f.
Motswasele, Israel 469, 476 ff., 520, 580, 588
Motswasele, Jacob Mokaleng 477 ff., 482
Moussa Traore 644, 668, 671, 674, 677
Mpanda John 185
Mpande, Chief 451
Mphehla, Bishop 512 f., 546 f. 579
MPLA 292 f.
Mpoi Tshienda 297, 307, 365, 404
MPR 174, 213 ff., 257 ff., 266, 291 ff.
Muadilu Philip 192
Muamba Mukengeshayi 102
Muatende Pierre 370, 438
Muene Ditu village 82
Mufuta Ana 435 ff.
Muhaku Boniface 303, 309
Muizu Kabadi 318 f.
Mukanza Ilunga 286, 298, 301 f., 311, 322, 333, 336 f., 340 f., 343, 348, 351, 361, 363, 367 ff., 404, 410 ff., 416, 422
Mukedi Station 9, 15, 20, 42, 48, 51 f., 98, 101, 107, 111, 121, 123, 131, 136, 155, 159, 183, 200, 202 f., 245, 276, 333 ff., 338, 369, 376, 403, 432, 599
Mukoso village 378
Mulamba Leonard 127, 136, 174
Mulebo Samuel 154
Mulele Pierre 46, 67, 109 f., 119, 121, 136, 153 f., 167, 190
Mundeke Kalawu 407 f.
Mupemba Mulenda 321
Mushimbele, Ikutu and Mayindama Kasay 351
Muslim; see Islam
Mutangilayi Norbert 222
Mutena Station 15, 51 f., 54, 61, 127, 183, 185, 198 f., 351, 366, 370, 403
Mutombo Simon 321, 378
Mutshimba Philip 165

Naabas 629
Namaqualanda 273

Namibia 452, 560, 566 (also see Southwest Africa)
Namoana A. Amos 677
Nanerige language 674
National Conference, the 419 ff.
National Party, the 453, 563
National Peace Accord 564 f.
National University of Lesotho, the (Roma) 464, 518 f.
Naude, Beyers 556
N'Dorola village 616, 618, 626, 638 f. 643, 674, 682
Ndundu 54
Near, Percival and Rosalind 21, 245
Nelson, Steve and Pat 423
Neuenschwander, Albert 28
Neuenschwander, Margie 213
Neufeld, Beverly 639, 674
Neufeld, Dave 509
Neufeld, Elmer 74, 93, 168, 184, 194, 236, 238, 313, 469, 476, 598
Neufeld, George and Justina 104, 271
Neufeld, Gerald 639, 674, 678 f.
Neufeldt, Alfred 100
"New Life For All" 280, 300
Ngaba 417
Ngalula, Prime Minister 81, 89, 94, 180
Nganda Conference Center 406, 416
Nganga Paul 75
Ngbandi people 414
Ngongo David 31, 51, 61, 150, 166 f., 184, 189, 191, 197, 221, 224, 227, 231, 247, 322, 439
Ngongo Muteba 379
Ngulubi Mazemba 200, 280
Ngulungu Benjamin 103
Nickel, Arnold 121 f.
Nickel, Jake 205
Niger River 607, 629
Njili airport (Kinshasa) 58, 257, 417 f., 706
Nkongolo, Bishop 85
Nkose Sikelel 566, 568
Nkrumah, Nkwame 39, 59, 60, 63
Nku, Christina Mma 477
Nkumbi Mudiayi 407 ff., 419
N'Sele Manifesto 174 f., 214, 257
N'Sele village 174 f., 213, 261, 413
Nsongamadi Joseph 432
Ntambue Paul 223, 438
Ntombentle Zungula 510
Ntumba Batubenga 391, 396
Ntumba Kalala 181, 407
Nussbaum, Lorri 485, 545
Nussbaum, Milo 194, 236, 241, 511, 616

Nussbaum, Stan 384, 485, 511, 545, 567, 571 f., 586, 708
Nyanga Station 9, 20, 29, 44, 51, 65, 77, 103, 127, 132, 143, 151, 154, 169, 193, 199, 202, 246, 286, 329 ff., 333, 335, 367 ff., 437, 439, 611
Nzamba, Chief 123 f., 162 f., 166
Nzambi 325
Nzash Lumeya 335
Nzimela, Sipo E. 472 f., 475

Okavango swamps 483, 588
Olenga, Nicolas 128 ff., 136, 138 f., 140, 143, 146
OPEC countries 291
Opepe, Colonel 131, 144 f.
Operation Desert Storm 417
Orange Free State 452, 536
Organization of African Independent Churches (OAIC) 527 ff., 600
Orodara 595 f., 600 f., 607 f., 612 f., 617, 619 ff., 625, 628, 635 f., 638, 640, 642 ff., 659, 663, 669, 674, 677 ff.
Orodara Kalanso 650 ff.
Ouagadougou 593, 595, 630, 673
Ouedraogo, Paul 638, 679
Overseas Mission Training Center (OMTC) 599, 612
Oyer, Amos and Julia 443

Pakisa Tshimika 697
Palapye village 485
Paraguay 398, 519
Paris Evangelical Missionary Society 461 f., 466
Parratt, John 520
Partners in Mission 520
passbooks 456
PAX 23, 73 f., 100, 127, 131, 144, 170, 199, 498, 599
Peace Corps 444
Petersen, Dan 349, 613, 615, 618, 626 f., 638 f., 649, 674, 682
Petersen, Kathy 349, 613, 615, 618, 626, 638 f., 674, 682
Peul people 629 f.
Plenert, Steve and Janet 423
Pletcher, William 307
Portuguese 1, 8, 52, 54, 112, 292, 449, 533
Preheim, Vern 272 f., 311, 446, 591
Presbyterian Mission/Church 5, 24, 81 ff., 93, 101, 103, 113, 132, 177, 179, 190, 212, 319, 354 f., 361, 431, 467, 519, 695
Pretorius, Andries 451

Pretorius, Hennie 511
Prieb, Arnold 592 f.
Probst, L. S. 443
Protestant/Catholic rivalry 10, 19, 122
Protestant Missions 9, 11 ff., 19, 216, 262 ff., 295, 420, 464 f., 519, 594
"push-push" 9

Quessua 54 f.
Quiring, Betty 98, 300
Quiring, Tina 100, 211, 278, 298

Radio Botswana 496 f., 587
Raid, Arlo and Leontine 171, 204
Raynor, Jesse 443
Red Cross 136
Rediger, Christian E. 28, 58
Rediger, Glenn and Pauline 212, 423
Rediger, Milo 28 ff.
Reed, David 146
Regier, Arnold and Elaine 198
Regier, Fremont and Sara 199 f., 231, 279, 493, 542 ff., 574
Reimer, Amanda 22
Reimer, Carla 579
Rempel, Larry and Alvera 98
Rempel, Dennis 600, 607, 614 f., 636 ff., 641, 653, 663, 667
Rempel, Eric 495
Rempel, Erwin 415
Rempel, Jeanne 600, 607, 614, 638, 641, 667
renouveau 335
Republic of South Africa (RSA); see South Africa
Rhodes, Cecil 443
Richburg, Keith 706
Ries, Dennis 212, 300
Riviona, Sandton 554
Robben Island 457, 507, 555 ff., 564, 582
Rocke, Glenn 53, 57, 66, 75, 78, 82, 201
Rocke, Ina 78, 201
Roma see National University of Lesotho (NUL)
RURCON 411
Ross, Emory 12
Roten, Gertrude 611 f.
Roth, Earl W. 57, 246, 251, 278, 299, 385 f., 397, 403, 410, 415, 440, 548, 653, 654, 679
Roth, Ruth 98, 385
Rule, William 59
rump sessions 229 f.
Rupp, Andrew 192, 356, 358, 485, 614
Russia 59 f., 62 f., 112, 293, 417, 457, 553

Rwanda 706

Sacred Union 419
Sahara Desert 311, 591, 607
Sahel 591, 616
Sambi, Mr.and Mrs. 363
Samo people 629
Samogho people 608, 640 f., 665, 674 f.
Samogoyiri village 641, 674 f.
Sanga Mamba congregation 429 f.
Sankara, Thomas 630 ff.
Saraba village 641, 674 f.
Savimbi, Jonas 293
Sayaga village 677
saw mill 299, 337, 401
Sawatsky, Ron 492
Schellenberg, John and Charity 638 f.
Schmallenberger, Fanny 615
Schmidt, Alfred and Viola 100
Schmidt. Donna 100
Schmidt, Loyal 57, 100, 113, 117, 120, 201
Schneider, Marie 443
Schnell, Russell and Helen 77, 98, 210
Schoenheit, Miss 443
Schowalter Foundation 253, 273, 444, 502, 505
Schrag, Leona M. 242, 278, 298, 304, 320, 368, 379 f., 391
Schwartz, Dorothy 22, 29, 51, 166, 203 f. 210
Schwartz, Merle 22, 52, 57, 66, 75, 166, 203 f., 210
SEDA 199 f., 280, 298, 300, 304, 308. 336, 423, 425 (also see COMAS)
Selly Oak Colleges 384
Sembla people 608
Senegal 259, 709
Senoufo people 595, 600, 607, 612 ff., 616 f., 621, 638, 640, 645, 668, 674
Seretse Khama 498, 542
Shaba Province 258 (also see Katanga Province)
Chief Shaka 451, 461
Shakenge Station 166, 298
Shamuimba Mbombo 366 f., 440
Shamwana village 378
Sharpeville 553
Shaumba Pierre 217
Sheppard, William 24
Sherbrooke 638 f.
Short, Lodema 15, 33, 242
Short, Reuben 42, 44, 104, 184, 194, 241, 249 ff., 271, 287, 311, 348
Shungu, John Wesley 265

BIOGRAPHICAL SKETCH OF AUTHOR

Jim Bertsche was born in the farm home of Pastor Harry and Emma Steiner Bertsche just outside Bluffton, OH on June 20, 1921. Called to serve as pastor of the Salem EMC Church in central Illinois the fall of 1933, Pastor Bertsche moved his family to Gridley, IL where Jim entered school as a seventh grader.

Upon graduation from high school, he clerked for a year in a local grocery store after which he enrolled at Taylor University, Upland, IN the fall of 1940. During college days he met Genevieve Shuppert, a farm girl from near South Bend, IN. The relationship blossomed and led to marriage on June 9, 1946. (This marriage was blessed with three children, Sandra Sue, Linda Lou and Timothy Edwin. All three children have gone to Zaire as adults for a term of service under AIMM - - Linda with her husband Jim Yoder and Timothy with his wife Laura Gilbertson. Tim and Laura presently continue their service under AIMM sponsorship in Botswana.)

After college, Jim continued his studies at Northern Baptist Seminary in Chicago. Upon graduating in 1947, the Bertsches applied to the Congo Inland Mission for service in Africa. They were first sent to the Kennedy School of Missions in Hartford, CT for a year of study after which they went to Brussels, Belgium for a year to work on the French language and to take some courses required by the Belgian government for non-Belgian missionaries who hoped to serve in educational or medical services in the Congo. In 1963 Jim graduated with a degree in cultural anthropology from Northwestern University in Evanston, IL. In 1968 he was awarded an honorary doctorate by his alma mater, Taylor University.

The Bertsches' period of service in Congo/Zaire covered a period of 25 years. Their ministry typically found Jenny teaching in station schools and working with women and girls. Jim's assignments involved him at various times with evangelistic village itineration, teaching in Bible and Teacher Training Schools, translation and revision of Scripture in the Giphende language, legal representation of the Mission and serving in several administrative positions in the African Church at the request and appointment of the Church officers.

The Bertsches were resident at Kandala Station when it was sacked and burned by the *Jeunesse* rebels in January 1964. Evacuated after three days by UN helicopters, they were restationed at Nyanga where they continued their ministry, Jenny in a new girls school and Jim with the African Giphende Scripture revision committee.

Called by the AIMM Board to come to Elkhart, IN in the fall of 1974, they served in the home office, Jim as the executive secretary and Jenny as coordinator of the AIMM Women's Auxiliary. Both reached retirement age in 1986 and continue their residence in Elkhart.